Child Law

Child Law

H K Bevan, JP, LLM
of the Middle Temple and North Eastern Circuit, Barrister
Professor of Law at the University of Hull

Butterworths
London
1989

United Kingdom	Butterworth & Co (Publishers) Ltd, 88 Kingsway, LONDON WC2B 6AB and 4 Hill Street EDINBURGH EH2 3JZ
Australia	Butterworths Pty Ltd, SYDNEY, MELBOURNE, BRISBANE, ADELAIDE, PERTH, CANBERRA and HOBART
Canada	Butterworths Canada Ltd, TORONTO and VANCOUVER
Ireland	Butterworth (Ireland) Ltd, DUBLIN
Malaysia	Malayan Law Journal Sdn Bhd, KUALA LUMPUR
New Zealand	Butterworths of New Zealand Ltd, WELLINGTON and AUCKLAND
Singapore	Butterworth & Co (Asia) Pte Ltd, SINGAPORE
USA	Butterworths Legal Publishers, ST PAUL, Minnesota, SEATTLE, Washington, BOSTON, Massachusetts, AUSTIN, Texas and D & S Publishers, CLEARWATER, Florida

A CIP Catalogue record for this book is available from the British Library.

ISBN 0 406 117039

Typeset by Kerrypress, Luton

Printed and bound in Great Britain by
Biddles Ltd, Guildford and King's Lynn

Preface

In the preface of my book *The Law Relating to Children*, published in 1973, I referred to the 'growing and sustained attention which the last decade or so [had] given to the protection of the interests and welfare of children'. In so doing I neither expected, nor tried, to anticipate many of the profound changes in child law which have occurred over the past 15 years. I do not attempt here to rehearse the list of them: they will be self-evident throughout the succeeding pages. Suffice it to say that they have led me to attempt a wider and deeper treatment of the subject, though I have retained historical material which appeared in the earlier publication because, it seems to me, in a rapidly changing area of law it is desirable to retain a sense of historical continuity. The detailed format of some of the chapters has also been retained, but I have sought to emphasise the enormous increase in the intervention by government agencies in child law by a principal division of the subject into 'The Child and the Individual' and 'The Child and the State'. However, this is a line which can only be drawn with a broad brush, as the subject of wardship, in particular, amply demonstrates.

I owe an immense debt to two colleagues: my son, Mr Vaughan Bevan of the Faculty of Law of the University of Sheffield and Mr Martin Parry of the Law School of the University of Hull. I am indebted to both for reading almost all the chapters in draft, for drawing my attention to omissions and infelicities and for offering many other helpful suggestions for improvement of the text. Additionally, to the former I am particularly grateful for his enormous assistance over the preparation of Chapters 2, 11, 14, 15 and, most especially, Chapter 16; and to the latter for allowing me to use freely materials which appeared in our joint authorship of the Children Act 1975 and for suffering innumerable incursions into his office for consultation. I also wish to thank Mr Ken Lidstone, also of the Sheffield Law Faculty, for his close scrutiny of Chapters 12 and 13, and Mr Donald Blakey for reading most of the proofs. Convention requires me to record formally their total exculpation from any errors which may appear in the final product.

For the preparation in typewritten form of that product I thank my former secretary, Mrs Joan Wilson, who was assisted by Miss Helen Forrester. I am grateful to the President and Governing Body of Wolfson College, Cambridge, for a Visiting Fellowship which enabled me to make the delay in completion of the book less unconscionable than it might otherwise have been, and to my publishers for their continued, unfailing courtesy and assistance. My heaviest debt, however, is to my wife for her inestimable patience and support in what has certainly been a protracted period.

I have tried to state the law as at 1 October 1988, but the indefinite postponement of Part II of the Family Law Reform Act 1987 meant last minute amendments at proof stage, especially of Chapter 2. Reference is also made to a few decisions reported since that date, and I have been able to incorporate those relevant provisions of the Criminal Justice Act 1988 which subsequently came into force.

H K Bevan

October 1988

Contents

PART II   THE CHILD AND THE STATE

Table of statutes

Table of cases

C

D

H

S

PART I
The child and the individual

CHAPTER 1
Concepts

I   THE *GILLICK* CASE

1.01   Thanks to the persistence of Mrs Victoria Gillick child law will never be quite what it was, whatever may be the precise effects and implications of the majority decision of the House of Lords in *Gillick v West Norfolk and Wisbech Area Health Authority*.[1] It is as well, therefore to examine at the outset a case which concerned 'the independence of a teenager, the powers of a parent and the duties of a doctor'.[2] The facts are so well known that they require only a brief reminder.

1   [1986] AC 112, [1985] 3 All ER 402, HL.
2   Per Lord Templeman at 199 and 431 respectively.

1.02   Mrs Gillick, the mother of five daughters under the age of 16, challenged the lawfulness of a memorandum of guidance in a Circular issued by the Department of Health and Social Security to area health authorities.[1] The substance of the relevant part of the memorandum advised that any doctor consulted at a family planning clinic by a girl under 16 would not be acting unlawfully if he prescribed contraceptives for the girl, provided that in doing so he was acting in good faith to protect her against the harmful effects of sexual intercourse. The memorandum referred to the need for 'special care . . . not to undermine parental responsibility and family stability', and stated that a doctor should always seek to persuade the child to involve the parent or guardian or other person in loco parentis in the matter. It was pointed out, however, that the principle of confidentiality between doctor and patient applied to a girl under 16 seeking contraceptives, and therefore, in exceptional cases, the doctor could prescribe contraceptives without consulting the parents or obtaining their consent if in his clinical judgment it was desirable to prescribe them. Her local area health authority refused to give Mrs Gillick an assurance that they would not give advice and treatment on contraception to her daughters while they were under 16 without her prior knowledge and consent.

1   Quaere the legal effect of the Circular, which was not endorsed by statute; see R Baldwin and J Houghton, *Circular Arguments: The Status and Legitimacy of Administrative Rules* [1986] Public Law 239. *Gillick* also raises interesting procedural questions; for example, whether judicial review was not a more appropriate remedy; the *locus standi* of Mrs Gillick, since none of her daughters was directly affected by the Circular; and the defects in procedural rules which do not provide for separate representation of children where their interests are the central issue. See J A Jolowicz [1986] CLJ 1; Carol Harlow 49 MLR 768.

1.03   Consequently Mrs Gillick sought two declarations: (i) against the

Department and her health authority that the advice contained in the
Circular was unlawful and adversely affected the welfare of her children
and her own rights and duties as parent and custodian of them; (ii) against
the health authority that, in the terms of the above assurance, they would
not give her daughters contraceptive and/or abortion advice and/or
treatment. The plaintiff's action was dismissed by Woolf J,[1] but the Court
of Appeal unanimously allowed her appeal and granted the declarations
sought.[2] The Department appealed against the grant of the first declaration,
but the health authority did not against the second. By a majority,[3] the
House of Lords reversed the Court of Appeal.[4] In those proceedings Mrs
Gillick relied on three propositions of law.

1 [1984] QB 581, [1984] 1 All ER 365.
2 [1985] 1 All ER 533, [1985] 2 WLR 413. The consequent withdrawal of the Circular
   caused considerable concern not only to the medical profession but also to local education
   authorities who were uncertain as to the effect the withdrawal would have on the teaching
   of sex education in schools.
3 Lords Fraser, Scarman and Bridge, with Lords Brandon and Templeman dissenting.
4 For admirably succinct and critical analyses of the litigation see Glanville Williams, *The
   Gillick Saga*, (1985) 135 NLJ 1156 and 1179; S M Cretney, *The All England Law Reports
   Annual Review* 1985, 171–175; Andrew Grubb and David Pearl, *Medicine, Health, the Family
   and the Law*, [1986] Fam Law 227 at pp 235–240; John Eekelaar, *The Eclipse of Parental
   Rights* (1986) 102 LQR 4. For a wider examination of the implications of the case see
   Andrew Bainham, *The Balance of Power in Family Decisions* [1986] CLJ 262; and S P
   de Cruz, *Parents, Doctors and Children: the Gillick Case and Beyond*, [1987] JSWL 93.

1 The criminal law proposition

1.04 The essence of the proposition was that a doctor who gave
contraceptive advice and treatment to a girl under 16 without the parent's
consent was likely to commit a crime even though he honestly intended
to act in the best interests of the girl. The proposition was based on two
closely related grounds. First, that the Departmental advice was unlawful
because it amounted to advice to doctors to commit the offence of causing
or encouraging unlawful sexual intercourse with a girl under 16.[1] That
offence may be committed by, inter alios, any person who has 'the custody,
charge or care'. Capable though those words are of a wide application
in child law, Woolf J, rightly it is submitted, declined an artificial extension
to cover the doctor treating a girl at a clinic or in his surgery. Second,
that the advice was unlawful because it amounted to advice to doctors
to commit the offence of being an accessory to unlawful sexual intercourse.[2]
In his dissent Lord Brandon[3] gave these statutory provisions wide meaning.
For him the matter was not merely one of criminal law. Sexual intercourse
between a man and a girl under 16 was an unlawful act. The giving of
contraceptive advice, any consequent medical examination and the
prescribing of contraceptive treatment to the girl necessarily promoted,
encouraged or facilitated that unlawful act because they largely removed
the 'inhibition, arising from the risk of an unwanted pregnancy', against
committing the act. Consequently,[4] whether or not the advice, examination
and treatment amounted in the particular case to a crime they 'must, in
any event, be contrary to public policy'. This conclusion did not commend
itself to the majority of their Lordships, who very largely relied in this
regard on the judgment of Woolf J. It was recognised that there might
be the individual doctor who provided a girl with contraceptives intending

thereby to encourage or aid and abet her having sexual intercourse with a particular man, but in the vast majority of cases doctors in making their clinical judgment would be against unlawful sexual intercourse and would only prescribe contraceptives to a girl under 16 to protect her from unwanted pregnancy and sexually transmitted disease in circumstances where intercourse with her would take place whether or not the doctor prescribed contraceptives. As Woolf J put it,[5] the contraceptive pill prescribed to the girl is 'not so much "the instrument for a crime or anything essential to its commission" but a palliative against the consequences of the crime'. This narrower construction of the criminal law emphasises the protection of the girl and the interests of her health and well-being, as well as protecting the doctor from liability.

1 Contrary to s 28 of the Sexual Offences Act 1956; see further thereon post, para 10.25.
2 Contrary to s 6(1) of the 1956 Act, post, para 10.21.
3 [1986] AC 112 at 195–199, [1985] 3 All ER 402 at 428–431.
4 See Williams, op cit, p 1157, for a criticism of this reasoning.
5 [1984] QB 581 at 595, [1984] 1 All ER 365 at 372. For a closely reasoned and critical analysis of the judgment, see Grubb and Pearl, op cit, pp 236–237.

2 The age of consent proposition

1.05 Section 8(1) of the Family Law Reform Act 1969 enables a minor who is 16 or over to give a valid consent to surgical, medical and dental treatment without any need for the consent of his parent or guardian.[1] It was argued on behalf of Mrs Gillick that a minor under that age could not, therefore, lawfully consent to medical treatment in general and a girl under 16 could not so consent to contraceptive advice and treatment in particular. The majority of the House of Lords rejected the argument on the ground that it misunderstood section 8(3), which provides that 'nothing in this section shall be construed as making ineffective any consent which would have been effective if this section had not been enacted'. Its effect was to leave open the question whether consent under the age of 16 could be effective. Lord Fraser pointed to certain statutory provisions which indicated that there was capacity;[2] but the answer was closely related to the third proposition.

1 Similarly, he may decide for himself to enter hospital on an informal basis for treatment under the Mental Health Act 1983; see s 131(2).
2 A child under 16 could apply to register with a doctor as his patient, and could avail himself of medical and dental treatment provided at school by a local education authority (referring respectively to the National Health Service (General Medical and Pharmaceutical) Services Regulations 1974, SI 1974/160, as amended; National Health Service Act 1977, s 5(1)(a); and Education Act 1944, s 48(4)).

3 The parental rights proposition

1.06 The third, and most fundamental, argument advanced was that the provision of contraceptive advice and treatment without parental consent was an instance of unlawful invasion of parental rights, except where it is authorised by a competent court or is given in an emergency. To assess the validity of that argument and the response of the House of Lords necessitates a brief historical survey of the influence of parental rights.

History of parental rights[1]

1.07 As a learned commentator has demonstrated, the term 'parental rights' has not been used with juristic consistency and legislation has used a variety of other terms to describe the legal relationships it encompasses.[2] But significantly and hearteningly there has in recent years been an increasing tendency to adopt the language of 'powers and responsibilities' instead of 'rights and duties',[3] and the former is the collective term subsequently used throughout this book wherever possible. Use of 'parental rights' is eschewed, unless contained in statutory provisions to which reference has to be made. However, for the immediate purpose of setting the scene for *Gillick* the traditional term is employed. That is certainly the term consistently used historically to describe the relationship between parent and legitimate child, from the time of the omnipotence of the father through to modern legislation which recognises the parity of the parents — with the emphasis very much on rights and with duties seen as fulfilling a subsidiary purpose.[4]

1   As in so many aspects of child law, the literature on parental rights is voluminous. The articles by Hall, *The Waning of Parental Rights* [1972B] CLJ 248; Eekelaar, *What are Parental Rights?* (1973) 89 LQR 210; and Maidment, *The Fragmentation of Parental Rights* [1981] CLJ 135 remain seminal on the subject.
   Other major references are Stone, *Parental Custody and Matrimonial Maintenance*, [1966] BIICL; Craffe, *La Puissance Paternelle en Droit Anglais* (1971); Dickens *The Modern Function and Limits of Parental Rights* (1981) 97 LQR 462; and, on parental rights and children's rights, Freeman's challenging critique, *The Rights and Wrongs of Children* (1983). For the history see especially Pettit, *Parental Control and Guardianship (A Century of Family Law* (1957) Chapter 4); James, *Child Law* (1962).
2   Eekelaar, op cit, who analyses and relates the term to the parent-child relationship by reference to Hohfeld's *Fundamental Legal Conceptions* (1919, reprinted in 1964).
3   See, for example, Woolf J in *Gillick*, [1984] QB 581 at 596, [1984] 1 All ER 365 at 373; Law Commission Paper on *Illegitimacy*, No 118, para 4.19; Law Com Working Paper No 91 on *Review of Child Law: Guardianship*, para 1.11; Law Com Working Paper No 96, on *Custody*, Part VII; and Law Com No 172, *Family Law, Review of Child Law, Guardianship and Custody*.
4   In *Gillick*, Lords Fraser and Scarman took a different view of the history; see post, para 1.13.

1.08 At common law the parental rights in respect of the legitimate child, collectively described in the right to custody,[1] were vested in the father and were almost absolute.[2] So strong was his right to custody that he could even enforce it while in prison by insisting on the child being brought to visit him,[3] and could even claim from the mother custody of a child at the breast.[4] It was only in exceptional cases, where there was a risk of serious physical or moral harm to the child due to the father's cruelty or to gross corruption of the child resulting from his profligacy,[5] that his right was liable to be forfeited.[6] A further exception at common law was admitted in the so-called age of discretion cases in habeas corpus proceedings where it came to be accepted[7] that the court would not order a child who had reached that age to return to the father if he or she did not wish to do so. That age was fixed at 14 for boys[8] and, apparently in line with the offence of abduction of girls,[9] at 16 for girls.[10]

1   On the concept of custody see post, paras 1.57, et seq.
2   For the earlier history of parental rights see Lord Esher MR in *R v Gyngall* [1893] 2 QB 232, CA; and for the topic as a whole the speeches of the House of Lords in *J v C*

[1970] AC 668, [1969] 1 All ER 788 and those of Lords Fraser and Scarman in *Gillick*, together with the judgments of Parker and Fox LJJ in the Court of Appeal.
3 *Ex p Skinner* (1824) 9 Moore CP 278.
4 *R v De Manneville* (1804) 5 East 221.
5 *R v Greenhill* (1836) 4 Ad & El 624 at 640; *R v Clarke, Re Race* (1857) 7 E & B 186 at 198.
6 Proceedings were by way of habeas corpus, but could be brought in the Court of Chancery as well as in the Common Law Courts.
7 See *R v Howes, ex p Barford* (1860) 3 E & E 332.
8 Dicta state this age; see *Re Agar-Ellis* (1883) 24 Ch D 317 at 326, CA; *Thomasset v Thomasset* [1894] P 295 at 298, CA.
9 Abduction Act of 1557, 4 & 5 Phil and Mar, c 8.
10 *R v Howes*, supra; but cf Tindal CJ in *Re Lloyd* (1841) 3 Man & G 547 at 548, who seems to have regarded 14 as also the age for girls. See generally Craffe, op cit, pp 220–224.

1.09 Although increasingly during the nineteenth century litigants turned from the common law to the jurisdiction of the Court of Chancery, which was exercised on behalf of the Crown as parens patriae, it was only gradually that any appreciable change in judicial attitude becomes apparent. In the earlier part of the century the interests of the child tended to play a large part in cases where the father had surrendered custody and sought to recover it.[1] In *Wellesley v Duke of Beaufort*,[2] Lord Eldon LC refused to remove children from the care of their aunts and hand them over to the father, mainly on the ground that he encouraged them in habits of swearing and keeping low company; but it is arguable that this conduct would equally have justified forfeiture of custody at common law.[3] In 1848, in *Re Fynn*,[4] there is no more than a marginal relaxation of the common law rule when it was held that the equitable jurisdiction could only be invoked when it was 'essential to [the children's] safety or to their welfare in some very serious and important respect' and 'if the word "essential" is too strong an expression, it is not much too strong'.[5] Indeed, the most extreme application of the common law rule had still to come. That was in the 'horrendous *Agar-Ellis* decisions',[6] where the Court of Appeal[7] still spoke in strong terms of the father's rights and his being deprived of them only if he had by his conduct shown himself unfit to exercise them. Hence, it was unwilling to interfere with a father who unreasonably refused to allow free access and free correspondence between his 17-year-old daughter and her mother from whom he was separated because he was afraid the mother woud alienate the daughter's affections from him. It may well be, however, that even by Victorian standards the decision was extreme, so much so as to excite legislative action.[8]

1 See *Lyons v Blenkin* (1821) Jac 245.
2 (1827) 2 Russ 1, (affd by HL sub nom *Wellesley v Wellesley* (1828) 2 Bli NS 124).
3 In *Gillick* [1986] 1 AC 112 at 184, [1985] 3 All ER 402 at 420, Lord Scarman cited the case to support the proposition that the Chancery courts 'had long followed' the rule that in cases concerning the care and upbringing of a child, the child's welfare was treated as paramount in deciding upon the order to be made; sed quaere.
4 (1848) 2 De G & Sm 457.
5 Per Sir James Knight Bruce, V-C at 474–475.
6 Per Lord Scarman in *Gillick* [1986] AC at 183, [1985] 3 All ER at 419. Similarly in *J v C* [1970] AC 668 at 721, [1969] 1 All ER 788 at 829, Lord Upjohn described the case as 'dreadful'.
7 (1883) 24 Ch D 317.
8 See Fox LJ in *Gillick* [1985] 1 All ER 533 at 554, [1985] 2 WLR 413 at 439.

1.10 It was under the influence of statutory changes, which conferred on the mother rights to claim custody, that greater attention began to be paid to the child's welfare. Where a father was deprived of custody, whether proceedings had been instituted by way of habeas corpus or by petition to the Court of Chancery, the effect of the court's decision might be to allow the mother custody, but neither common law nor equity conferred on her a positive right to seek it. That was first done by the Custody of Infants Act 1839 (Talfourd's Act), which empowered the Court of Chancery to give the mother custody until the child reached the age of seven, provided she had not committed adultery. The Custody of Infants Act 1873, repealing the earlier Act without re-enacting the proviso concerning adultery, extended the right to the age of 16. Meanwhile, the Divorce Court, under the Matrimonial Causes Act 1857,[1] could make custody orders up to the age of 21 on such terms as to it seemed just, thus enabling it to give either parent custody, and, when magistrates' courts were first given matrimonial jurisdiction by the Matrimonial Causes Act 1878,[2] their powers included that of awarding the wife custody of those of her children under the age of ten. Much more significant was the Guardianship of Infants Act 1886, because, apart from giving the mother rights concerning guardianship, it not only widened her rights so as to claim custody of a child up to the age of 21, but also directed that in hearing her claim the court was to have regard to, inter alia, the welfare of the child.[3] Similarly, the Custody of Children Act 1891 referred the court to the child's welfare when it had to decide whether a parent who had abandoned or deserted his child or allowed him to be brought up by another person was now a fit person to have custody.[4] Meanwhile the court when dealing with the custody of orphans was committing itself to the principle that the dominant consideration should be the child's welfare.[5]

1 Section 35.
2 Section 4.
3 Section 5. The first statutory reference to the child's welfare was in the Custody of Infants Act 1873.
4 Section 3. The Act was passed as a result of a number of cases in which undeserving parents had successfully recovered from Dr Barnardo's Homes, by way of habeas corpus proceedings, children whom they had earlier abandoned. The Act is still on the Statute Book but is a dead letter. The Law Commission (Law Com No 172 paras 7.12–7.16) recommends its repeal.
5 See *Johnstone v Beattie* (1843) 10 Cl & Fin 42, [1843–60] All ER Rep 576, HL; *Stuart v Bute* (1861) 9 HL Cas 440, [1843–60] All ER Rep 595, HL; *Re McGrath (infants)* [1893] 1 Ch 143, CA.

1.11 As the judgments of the Court of Appeal in *R v Gyngall*[1] show, the cumulative effect was to weaken the father's rights, to strengthen those of the mother, but, above all, to lay greater emphasis on the child's welfare at the expense of both. During the earlier part of the present century this emphasis persisted 'behind the closed doors of the Chancery Division',[2] until section 1 of the Guardianship of Infants Act 1925 expressly affirmed the paramountcy of the child's welfare. Whether in so doing it took the law further or merely restated it is open to argument,[3] but at least it put the matter beyond doubt. In re-enacting the paramountcy principle, the Guardianship of Minors Act 1971[4] also reaffirmed the rule stated in the 1925 Act that the claim of the one parent in respect of the custody, upbringing and administration of the property of the child was not superior to that of the other. The Guardianship Act 1973[5] went further in this regard by enacting that the 'rights and authority' of the mother and father shall be equal and not merely that their respective claims concerning the above matters should be so. Two years later in the Children Act 1975 Parliament unhelpfully recognised the existence of parental rights and duties simply by describing them as 'all the rights and duties which by law the mother and father have in relation to a legitimate child and his property'.[6]

1 [1893] 2 QB 232, CA. See also Lopes LJ in *Re A and B (infants)* [1897] 1 Ch 786 at 792, CA.
2 *Per* Lord Upjohn in *J v C* [1970] AC 668 at 723, [1969] 1 All ER 788 at 831, HL.
3 See, for example, the differing views held in *J v C, supra.* Significantly, immediately after its enactment the Court of Appeal in *Re Thain, Thain v Taylor* [1926] Ch 676, [1926] All ER Rep 384 stated that the section was declaratory of the existing law.
4 Section 1.
5 Section 1(1).
6 Section 85(1); see post, para 1.17.

1.12 These statutory changes were therefore concerned with the dual purpose of ultimately establishing parity between the parents but more importantly of subordinating their respective rights to the welfare of the child. They did not, however, provide any further guidance on the consequent scope and strength of those rights. That was left for the courts to determine. The basic answers were provided in 1969 in two cases, in both of which there was unqualified disapproval of *Agar-Ellis*. In *J v C*,[1] the House of Lords rejected the proposition that prima facie parents had the right to custody of their minor child and, therefore, would only be deprived of it or of the care and control if they were unfitted 'by character, conduct or position in life'[2] to have control. It was held that even, in those terms, the 'unimpeachable' parent might be so deprived if the child's welfare so demanded. In *Hewer v Bryant* Lord Denning MR gave firmer guidance.[3] Having in a much cited passage rejected *Agar-Ellis* and its Victorian associations, he continued:

> 'The common law can, and should, keep pace with the times. It should declare, in conformity with the recent report on the Age of Majority . . . (Cmnd 3342), . . . that the legal right of a parent to the custody of a child ends at the eighteenth birthday; and even up till then, it is a dwindling right which the courts will hesitate to enforce against the wishes of the child, the older he is. It starts with a right of control and ends with little more than advice.'

No suggestion here that the age of 16 is the dividing line.

1 [1970] AC 668, [1969] 1 All ER 788, HL. See the speeches of Lords Guest and MacDermott. It was not until *J v C* that it was clearly established that the principle of the paramountcy of the child's welfare applied as much to a dispute between a parent and a stranger as between parent and parent.
2 *Per* Lord Guest at 692 and 805 respectively.
3 [1970] 1 QB 357 at 369, [1969] 3 All ER 578 at 582, CA.

The response of the House of Lords

1.13 The majority of the House of Lords in *Gillick* unequivocally accepted this essentially pragmatic guidance,[1] and were able to derive further support from *R v D*[2] where, also approving of Lord Denning's dictum, the House of Lords in holding that a father could be guilty of the common law offence of kidnapping his own child under 14, recognised that it would be a defence if the child, though under that age, had in fact understanding and intelligence to give and did give, his or her consent.[3] On these two authorities, supported by *J v C*,[4] there was sufficient support for the House of Lords to reach the conclusions it did in answer to the third proposition[5] advanced on behalf of Mrs Gillick, namely, (1) that there was no rule of absolute parental authority until a fixed age but the right to custody was a dwindling right, since (2) a child had the right to make his or her own decisions when he or she reached a sufficient understanding and intelligence to be capable of making up his or her own mind and, therefore, (3) that a girl under 16 did not, merely because of her age, lack legal capacity to consent to contraceptive advice and treatment.[6] But the majority were not content to rely on those authorities. Instead they preferred[7] to go beyond them and reach their conclusions on 'principle' — a principle, as their Lordships found it, of authoritative antiquity propounded by Blackstone,[8] namely that 'the power of parents over their children is derived from their duty',[9] the duty being to maintain, protect and educate. It was a duty lost in the mists of the nineteenth century, not only in the civil law where, as has been suggested,[10] the emphasis throughout was on parental rights, which were not then seen as derivatives of parental duties,[11] but also in the criminal law, where the duty to protect was often ignored[12] or at best reluctantly enforced.[13] Lord Scarman has given the principle modern form in these words:[14]

> 'It is that parental right yields to the child's right to make his own decisions when he reaches a sufficient understanding and intelligence to be capable of making up his own mind on the matter requiring decision.'

Throughout this book it is referred to as the '*Gillick* principle'. Its scope and application to the central issue in the *Gillick* case relating to contraception is considered within the broader question of medical treatment of the child, which itself forms part of the subject of parental powers and responsibilities.[15] First, its potential impact is considered in relation to the emergence of children's rights.

1   So, too, did Woolf J at first instance.
2   [1984] AC 778, [1984] 2 All ER 449, HL. See further post, para 3.89.
3   In *R v Howard* [1965] 3 All ER 684 at 685, [1966] 1 WLR 13 at 15, Lord Parker CJ recognised that a girl under 16, alleged to be the victim of rape, could give her consent; 'there are many girls who know fully well what it is all about and can properly consent'.
4   Supra.
5   Ante, para 1.06.
6   But see Lord Templeman's powerful rejection of this conclusion; [1986] AC 112 at 199–207, [1985] 3 All ER 402 at 431–437.
7   Lord Scarman enthusiastically, Lord Fraser 'if necessary' and Lord Bridge, who merely agreed with Lord Fraser and Lord Scarman, by implication.
8   *Commentaries;* 1 Bl Com (17th edn 1830) p 452, and generally Chapters 16 and 17.
9   Note the use of 'power' and not 'right'.
10 Ante, para 1.08.
11 Obviously the common law did not think much of the Blackstone duty to maintain, because it imposed no direct civil liability on the father; see post, para 16.02.
12 The statutory controls over the employment of children in factories and mines 'operated

only with regard to the severest depredations' (J M Eekelaar, *The Emergence of Children's Rights* (1986) 6 Oxford Journal of Legal Studies 161 at p 167).
13 See post, para 9.03.
14 In *Gillick* [1986] AC 112 at 186, [1985] 3 All ER 402 at 422.
15 Post, paras 1.17 et seq.

II CHILDREN'S RIGHTS

1.14 The same general comment may be made about the term 'children's rights' as about parental powers and responsibilities, namely, that it has not been used with juristic consistency.[1] Indeed, the comment applies even more to children's rights, where the notion of childhood and the different ages at which children acquire legal capacity to engage in various activities[2] add to the inherent difficulty of defining rights.[3] Nevertheless, viewed functionally, they fall into two broad categories, the protective and the self-assertive.[4] Examples of the former are rights designed to protect the child from ill-treatment;[5] the rights of the child as a dependant under the Fatal Accidents legislation. Examples of the latter are the right of the child to consent to medical treatment or, if aged at least 16, to acquire an independent domicile,[6] or from that age to work full-time if he has left school.[7]

1 Ante, para 1.07.
2 They are listed by MDA Freeman, *Coming of Age?*, [1977] LAG Bull 137. See also *At what age can I?*, *Childright*, Sept 1984 at p 11; Bainham, op cit, pp 272–273.
3 See MDA Freeman, *The Rights of Children When They Do Wrong* (1981) 21 Brit J Criminol 210; J M Eekelaar, R Dingwall and T Murray, *Victims or Threats? Children in Care Proceedings* [1982] JSWL 67 at pp 71–78.
4 See *The Rights of Children* (1967), published by the National Secular Society as its contribution to Human Rights Year. Compare J M Eekelaar, *The Emergence of Children's Rights* (1986) 6 Oxford Journal of Legal Studies 161, where the subject is traced historically by reference to the child's interests, these being classified into 'basic', 'developmental' and 'autonomy' interests.
5 See post, Chapter 9.
6 Domicile and Matrimonial Proceedings Act 1973, s 3(1).
7 Education Act 1944, s 58.

1.15 The former category reflects the policy of the law to protect children from harm or exploitation or to provide for their needs, and Children's Rights movements, which have been traced to the middle of the 19th century,[1] were for long concerned only with protective rights. Thus, the 1924 Declaration of the League of Nations on the Rights of the Child emphasised his material needs, and the same basic aim underlies the United Nations Declaration of 1959 that 'mankind owes the child the best it has to give'. Self-assertive rights are of more recent origin and reflect the gradual recognition which is being accorded to the child as an individual able to make his own decisions under the law. Some of the pressures of the early seventies to grant him wider rights of self-determination[2] may be seen as a 'propagandist exercise',[3] but there were other factors during that period which suggested that attempts at formulation of a legal concept of children's rights would not be indefinitely postponed. For example, the Children's Legal Centre, established in 1979 as a product of the International Year of the Child, has increasingly focused closer attention on the child as an individual under the law and on the need to provide him with new legal remedies. References to the European Commission on Human Rights and the European Court of Human Rights of such matters as illegitimacy, rights of education and corporal punishment in schools have produced similar effects,[4] and impetus has been given to this development by the creation of INTERIGHTS, The International Centre for the Legal Protection of Human Rights and Defence for Children. Nevertheless, the task of formulation remains formidable.[5] The nature and functions of family law do not lend themselves to precise concepts. Changing sociological patterns, especially in the relationship between the parent and the State over the upbringing of children, at best produce imperfect rights and obligations, imperfect both in formulation and in enforcement,[6] especially enforcement by the child against his own parents. There is, therefore, much to be said for a robust pragmatism which emphasises the needs of children and the responsibilities of adults, a sentiment long ago expressed in the following dictum:[7]

> 'The basic right of a juvenile is not to liberty but to custody. He has the right to have someone to take care of him, and if his parents do not afford him this custodial privilege the law must do so'

As a modern author has put it,[8] 'ensuring through education that society carries out . . . duties to children may ultimately prove of greater benefit than pretending we are conferring rights upon them.' Certainly the last two decades have seen a shift towards parental responsibility — not, however, merely in the sense of providing such physical needs as shelter, food and clothing but also in the larger sense of providing reasonably secure parent/child relationships,[9] with the law much readier to intervene if that relationship is not fulfilled.

1   Freeman, *The Rights of Children in the International Year of the Child* (1980) 33 Current Legal Problems 1, at p 12.
2   See, for example, the discussion paper of the National Council for Civil Liberties, especially No 5, *Children Have Rights* and *Rights of Children*, and the Draft Charter of Children's Rights prepared by the Advisory Centre for Education (1971) *Where* 56; and for general comment thereon Gavin Drewry (1971) 1 Fam Law 185 and (1972) 2 Fam Law 6.
    For similar pressures in USA see H Foster and D Freed, *A Bill of Rights for Children* (1974); J Holt, *Escape from Childhood* (1975) and R Farson, *Birthrights* (1978). There is an abundance of references provided by Freeman, op cit, pp 26–31.
3   J M Eekelaar, *What are Parental Rights?* (1973) 89 LQR 210 at p 211.
4   See *Marckx Case* (1979) 22 Yearbook of the European Convention on Human Rights 410 (adverse consequences of illegitimacy in Belgian law constituting breach of the Convention); *Inze v Austria* (1987) (on the same subject); *Kjeldsen, Busk, Madsen and Pedersen Case* (1976) 19 Year Book 502 (compulsory sex education in Danish state schools not a breach of Convention); *Tyrer's Case* (1978) 21 Yearbook 612 (birching in Isle of Man a breach of Convention); and see *Campbell and Cosans Cases* (1982) 4 EHRR 293 (insistence by Scottish schools on corporal punishment leading to breach of Convention). In 1979 the Parliamentary Assembly of the Council of Europe considered a draft European Charter of Children's Rights, but has not taken the matter further. For references of child care cases to the Commission and the Court see post, paras 15.130–15.132.
5   See DN MacCormick, *Children's Rights: A Test Case for Theories of Rights* (1976) 62 Archiv für Rechts-und-Sozialphilosophie 305; the references supra, para 1.14, note 2; and Beck et al, *The Rights of Children: A Trust Model*, (1978) 46 Fordham Law Review 669. Doubts continue to be expressed since the Gillick decision: ' . . . it remains the case that there exists no recognisable legal concept of children's rights. One of the principal challenges facing English law in the coming years will be to give meaning to the rhetoric of children's rights by constructing a legal theory of general application which gives proper weight to the child's role in family decisions'. — Bainham, op cit, at p 284.
6   See OM Stone, *The Child's Voice in the Court of Law* (1982).

7 *Ex p Crouse* 4 Whart 9 at 11 (1838) (Supreme Ct Pa).
8 Freeman, (1980) 33 Current Legal Problems 1 at p 23. But see his *The Rights and Wrongs of Children*, Chapters 1 and 2 where a theory based upon liberal paternalism is outlined.
9 See K Brill, *Parents' Rights and Responsibilities: Problems in Practice — The Social Services Angle* (1978) No 56–57, Law and Justice 13 at p 16. As Professor A H Halsey pertinently pointed out in the fifth of his Reith lectures (1978): 'Parents must also answer more than ever for the mental and moral character of their sons and daughters, despite influences from the strict, the so-called peer-group, the mass media and youth culture which they may fear but cannot escape. They are increasingly made to feel amateurs in a difficult professional world.'

1.16 This emphasis on needs will hardly commend itself to those who wish to see the main emphasis on self-assertive rights, and the fundamental question which the *Gillick* principle raises is the extent to which future law will shift from needs to rights. Lord Scarman's dictum[1] is clear in its terms. Once the child has the requisite understanding and intelligence he has the legal capacity and the right to enter into legal relationships, and the parental right is terminated. But will the courts apply the principle without clipping its wings? In *Gillick* Lord Fraser seems to have qualified the child's independent capacity, at least in relation to consent to medical treatment, by suggesting that a doctor would only be justified in treating the child without parental consent if this was in the child's best interests.[2] If this is the correct interpretation,[3] then is it to be inferred that parental consent is still required in relation to any other matter unless otherwise justified in the child's best interests? It is suggested that the courts are more likely to accept the full import of Lord Scarman's dictum *so far as terminating the parental power*, but will not allow a child independently to exercise a right if they consider that it is not in his best interests,[4] thus substituting the court's paternal jurisdiction for the parental power. In so considering they will have carefully to assess his understanding, intelligence and emotional maturity. That task, it is suggested, is likely to mean heavier reliance on welfare reports and, it is to be hoped, a greater willingness on the part of judges to interview children.

1 Supra, para 1.13.
2 See further post, paras 1.26 and 1.27.
3 But see J M Eekelaar, op cit, (1986) 6 Oxford Journal of Legal Studies 161 at pp 180–181, who also offers an alternative interpretation of Lord Fraser's speech, which 'would permit anyone to deal lawfully with a minor child who had acquired capacity, and restrict the requirements to consult parents (outside exceptional situations) to a rule of good practice applicable only in medical matters and enforceable only through professional discipline'.
4 Where the validity of the child's right is tested in wardship proceedings GMA 1971, s 1 will not apply, unless the right and its exercise relate to the 'upbringing' of the child. Instead, the test of best interests will rest on the protective nature of the court's inherent jurisdiction; see the Court of Appeal in *Re B (a minor) (Sterilisation)* [1987] 2 All ER 206 at 210, and see post, para 8.49.

III PARENTAL POWERS AND RESPONSIBILITIES[1]

1.17 Whatever may be the merits of emphasising child law from the point of view of the child's needs and/or (according to taste) his rights, the fact remains that much of it is still based on, and expressed in the form of, concepts which are themselves related to the concepts of parental powers and responsibilities or, as the legislature would still have it, parental rights and duties. Although we may hope for better things,[2] the most recent legislative pronouncement on the subject generally has done nothing to clarify it.[3] Section 85(1) of the Children Act 1975 enacts:[4]

> 'In this Act, unless the context otherwise requires, "the parental rights and duties" means as respects a particular child (whether legitimate or not) all the rights and duties which by law the mother and father have in relation to a legitimate child and his property; and references to a parental right or duty shall be construed accordingly and shall include a right of access and any other element included in a right or duty.'

No further guidance is given,[5] but those rights and duties which are commonly included by commentators[6] are set out hereunder. Many of them are examined in greater detail in other parts of the book; others are more conveniently analysed in the present section. They are here listed collectively for the purpose of determining the scope of other basic concepts.

1 In addition to the references set out ante, para 1.07, note 1, see generally Bromley, *Family Law*, 7th edn (1987), Chapter 8; Cretney, *Principles of Family Law*, 4th edn (1984) Chapter 11; Hoggett, *Parents and Children*, 3rd edn (1987), Part I.
2 See the Review of Child Law being undertaken by the Law Commission: Working Paper No 91 on Guardianship and Working Paper No 96 on Custody, together with its earlier Paper on Illegitimacy (Law Com No 118) and most recently Law Com No 172 on Guardianship and Custody, Part II.
3 For criticism see Cretney (1981) 44 MLR at pp 17–19.
4 The definition is now of general application; see Interpretation Act 1978, s 5 and Sch 1.
5 There is similar judicial reluctance: 'If one were asked to define what are the rights of a parent apropos his child, I for one would find it very difficult' — Ormrod J in *Re N (Minors) (Parental Rights)* [1974] Fam 40 at 46, [1974] 1 All ER 126 at 130.
6 See especially, J M Eekelaar, *What Are Parental Rights?* (1973) 89 LQR 210; Hoggett, op cit, p 7; Justice Report on *Parental Rights and Duties and Custody Suits* (1975). But compare the view of the Law Commission, Law Com No 172, para 2.6.

1 Care and control

1.18 This has been described as the personal power of physical control,[1] and includes the power to determine how and where the child spends his time. In accordance with the *Gillick* principle it 'starts with a right of control and ends with little more than advice'.[2] Confusingly the power is also referred to as 'possession',[3] or 'custody' or, since the Children Act 1975, 'actual custody'.[4] Notwithstanding this power, the parent can be guilty of the common law offences of kidnapping his own child, if, without the child's consent, he takes and carries him away by force or fraud, and of unlawful imprisonment if the child is forcibly detained against his will.[5] Kidnapping extends to any of his children who are minors and unmarried.[6] The Child Abduction Act 1984 goes further and makes it an offence for, inter alios, a parent to take or send his child, if under 16, out of the United Kingdom without the appropriate consent, for example, without the consent of the other parent or a guardian or without the leave of the court.[7]

1 Per Sachs LJ in *Hewer v Bryant* [1970] 1 QB 357 at 373, [1969] 3 All ER 578 at 585, post, para 1.58.
2 *Ibid*, per Lord Denning MR at 369 and 582 respectively.
3 The present writer finds this term offensive in the present context, but it has its eminent defenders; see Cretney, op cit, p 300; Eekelaar, op cit at p 214, note 27, who prefers

it to the 'euphemism of "care and control", which relates to distinguishable matters'. That, it is submitted, is one of its advantages, since it indicates the two main facets of the day to day upbringing of a child.

4 It has been suggested that 'care and control' is wider than 'actual custody', because it 'seems to allow a parent to exercise responsibility over all save the most serious and long-term decisions in the child's upbringing' (Law Com Working Paper No 96, para 2.47).

5 *R v Rahman* (1985) 81 Cr App Rep 349, CA; for comments see AN Khan [1986] Fam Law 69.

6 *R v D* [1984] AC 778, [1984] 2 All ER 449, HL.

7 Section 1. On kidnapping see further paras 3.89–3.90 and for the Child Abduction Act, paras 3.92 et seq.

2 Access (visits)

1.19 In *M v M*[1] the right to access was described as a right of the child rather than of the parent. It is difficult to determine why section 85(1) of the Children Act 1975 should single it out for special mention. Does the express reference impliedly reject the view expressed in *M v M* and reassert that the right is 'the basic right of any parent'[2]? The better view, it is suggested,[3] is to treat access as a mutual right of the parent and child to the other's companionship, of which each can only be deprived when the paramountcy of the child's welfare exceptionally so warrants.[4]

1 [1973] 2 All ER 81 at 85 per Wrangham J.
2 *Per* Willmer LJ in *S v S and P* [1962] 2 All ER 1 at 3, [1962] 1 WLR 445 at 448.
3 Bevan and Parry, *Children Act 1975*, para [211].
4 See post, paras 3.84 et seq.

3 Protection and maintenance

1.20 Consistent with the power to control are the responsibilities of protecting and maintaining the child. Indeed, the power is to be seen as facilitating the discharge of the responsibilities.[1] The common law responsibility or duty to protect, which does not depend on the child's age but on the necessity for protection, has very largely been replaced by statutory duties.[2] These are mainly to be found in Part I of the Children and Young Persons Act 1933 and relate to various forms of neglect and ill-treatment of children and other aspects of protection from physical and moral harm. Similarly the responsibility of maintaining the child is almost wholly a statutory one.[3] Over and above these responsibilities there is, at least for the purpose of adoption law, 'the natural and moral duty of a parent to show affection, care and interest towards his child'.[4]

1 See Lord Scarman in *Gillick v West Norfolk and Wisbech Area Health Authority* [1986] AC 112 at 185, [1985] 3 All ER 402 at 421.
2 See post, Chapter 9.
3 Post, Chapter 16.
4 Per Pennycuick J in *Re P* [1962] 3 All ER 789 at 794, [1962] 1 WLR 1296 at 1302; see similarly *M v Wigan Metropolitan Borough Council* [1980] Fam 36, [1979] 2 All ER 958, DC.

4 Discipline

1.21 This power emanates from that of care and control and is a facet of the wider parental power to determine the child's upbringing. It has a long history. Even the crude Anglo-Saxon laws did not give the head of the family powers of life and death over his children, but that was about the limit to the control which he exercised over them. Gradually, but by a process that has not been traced, his powers were attenuated and the common law came to accept the principle that the father was entitled, as an incident of his power to discipline, to administer reasonable corporal chastisement over his legitimate children. This power to punish is shared by the mother, but it is equally uncertain when this came to be so. So long as the parents lived together the question would not, in practice, arise, since correction was a matter for the father. On his death, however, the mother was entitled to the custody of her infant children for nurture[1] — unless, after 1660, the father appointed a testamentary guardian[2] — and therefore the power to discipline and punish them apparently became exercisable by her. Exceptionally, too, where the marriage broke up and the father had grossly ill-treated the children, she might acquire custody. Whatever the origin of her power it is clear that, since the mother's claim to custody began to be recognised by equity and then by legislation[3] the recognition of the incidental power to punish would necessarily follow. As for the unmarried mother, the recognition of her power to punish her child has, it seems, in a similar way depended on the gradual but later recognition of her claim to custody.[4]

1   *R v Clarke* (1857) 7 E & B 186 at 200.
2   By virtue of the Tenures Abolition Act 1660.
3   See ante, paras 1.09 and 1.10.
4   See post, para 2.19.

1.22   A person in loco parentis also has the power to discipline and punish.[1] The test for determining whether anyone stands in that relationship to a child may vary in emphasis for different legal purposes. In the present context the test seems to be whether the care and control[2] of the child has been entrusted to the person by the parent or, where the parent is absent or there is no parent, is assumed by that person.[3] But anyone living with the parent cannot assume his power without his authority, even though the parent may temporarily be absent. Thus, in *R v Woods*,[4] an elder brother was held not to be entitled to punish a younger, since the father had not placed him in loco parentis. With that case may be compared that of the step-parent who, with the natural parent's consent, assumes care and control. In addition to delegation or assumption, the power to punish will arise wherever custody in its wide sense[5] and/or care and control are entrusted by an order of the court to any person. Accordingly, the power may, for example, be exercised by an adoptive parent, a guardian, a custodian or a local authority.[6]

1   As did the master over his apprentice, but his right is obsolete.
2   The law reports usually refer to the 'charge' of the child. In relation to raising the presumptions of satisfaction and ademption in equity the emphasis is on whether the donor has taken upon himself the duty of a parent to make provision for the child; see Jessel MR in *Bennet v Bennet* (1879) 10 Ch D 474 at 477, citing with approval Lord Eldon in *Ex p Pye* (1811) 18 Ves 140 and Lord Cottenham in *Powys v Mansfield* (1837) 3 My & Cr 359 at 367. The same test seems to be used in deciding whether a presumption of advancement has displaced a presumption of resulting trust where property is purchased in the name of the child.
3   As, for example, in the case of a foster parent; cf *R v Cheeseman* (1836) 7 C & P 455 (assumption of care and control by an aunt).

4 (1921) 85 JP 272.
5 See post, para 1.58.
6 For the powers of discipline of a school authority see post, paras 11.56 et seq.

1.23 The power to discipline must be exercised reasonably.[1] Any corporal punishment which exceeds that standard renders the parent or other person in loco parentis criminally liable and subject to the possibility of care proceedings being instituted.[2] Reasonableness is to be assessed in the light of all the circumstances, with particular reference to the age, physical condition, intellectual understanding and emotional maturity of the child and the reason for administering the punishment.[3] Immigrants must conform to the standard of behaviour acceptable in England, and it is thus not a defence to a charge of assault to show that the standard of parental correction permitted in the foreign native country is harsher.[4] The significance of the power diminishes as the child grows older, and this is especially true with regard to the incidental powers to inflict corporal punishment and restrict liberty. However, it is highly unlikely that, in accordance with the *Gillick* principle, the courts would ever allow the parental power wholly to 'yield' to the child's right to control his own behaviour so as to countenance an action by him against the parent for assault or false imprisonment.

1 *R v Hopley* (1860) 2 F & F 202; *R v Woods* supra. The power is also recognised by statute; see Children and Young Persons Act 1933, s 1(7).
2 See post, Chapter 14.
3 See Bromley, p 274; Hoggett, pp 9–10.
4 *R v Derriviere* (1969) 53 Cr App Rep 637, CA. In *Re H (minors)* [1987] 2 FLR 12, [1987] Fam Law 196, a wardship case involving neglect, ill-treatment and bizarre cruelty on the part of a North Vietnamese mother towards her children, the court held that it should consider their welfare against the reasonable objective standards of the culture in which they had earlier been brought up so long as it did not conflict with minimal acceptable standards of child care in England. In the event the mother's conduct in England towards her children was so disgraceful that it offended both standards. Had it only offended the English, that, it is submitted, would have justified intervention by the court.

5 Secular education[1]

1.24 The emphasis here is on responsibility. The parent must ensure that his child, being of compulsory school age (ie five to 16), receives full-time education as prescribed by section 36 of the Education Act 1944 and must secure his regular attendance at school. Parental powers are strictly limited. There is that (rarely exercised) which enables him to secure his child's education otherwise than by sending him regularly to school, and that of choosing private education. With regard to State education, the local education authority must have regard to parental wishes, must make sufficient schools available,[2] and must consult parents before deciding whether or not to close or amalgamate any of them;[3] but this does not preclude them from taking into account other matters, the effect of which may be to defeat the parent's wishes.[4]

1 See post, Chapter 11.
2 Education Act 1944, ss 76 and 8 respectively.
3 *R v Brent London Borough Council, ex p Gunning* 84 LGR 168.
4 On the other hand, the parent may be able to exert some influence and control through parental representation on the Board of School Governors; see post, Chapter 11.

6   Religious upbringing[1]

1.25   There is no responsibility imposed on a parent to see that his child receives religious instruction, although the courts may take the view that some form of religion is better than none.[2] The parental power to choose the child's religious education is frequently tied to issues over his custody and sometimes to his secular education. Its relevance in those kinds of cases is variable, but as a generalisation it can be stated that today it does not carry great weight and, where the child is sufficiently mature to hold his own views, then, in accordance with the *Gillick* principle, his views will prevail over those of the parent. Different considerations apply in other spheres of the law. On the one hand insistence by the parent on a particular religious upbringing will not be tolerated if it causes harm to the child, and the parent may even be criminally liable and/or care proceedings may be the consequence. On the other hand state agencies which assume the care of the child are generally obliged to respect his religion. However, a parent can no longer impose conditions when agreeing to the adoption of his child.[3]

1   See post, Chapter 11; Hoggett, op cit, p 14.
2   It cannot be put any higher; see *Haleem v Haleem* (1975) 5 Fam Law 184, CA.
3   See post, para 5.91.

7   Medical matters[1]

(a)   Child under sixteen

1.26   The parent has the power and responsibility of determining whether or not to seek medical advice for his child who is under 16 and, having received it, of deciding whether to give or withhold consent to medical treatment. Three qualifications to this principle have long been firmly recognised. First, as part of his statutory duty to protect, the parent renders himself criminally liable if he fails to provide, or take proper steps to procure, essential medical aid for his child.[2] Second, an order of a court may override the principle by applying the test of the child's best interest. Third, an emergency may warrant the giving of medical treatment without the knowledge or consent of the parent.[3] Orders and emergency treatment are subsequently illustrated. The *Gillick* case has raised the question of the extent to which there is a further restriction on the principle. Since the case has already been examined generally, it is convenient to deal firstly with its implications in relation to contraceptive advice and treatment, although there are other matters relating to medical treatment for which the case might have more important consequences.

1   See especially Freeman, *The Rights and Wrongs of Children*(1983), pp 259–271; Skegg, *Consent to Medical Procedures on Minors*, (1973) 36 MLR 370, and *Justification for Medical Procedures performed without Consent* (1974) 90 LQR 512; Dickens, *Medico-Legal Aspects of Family Law* (1979) Chapter 6, and *The Modern Function and Limits of Parental Rights* (1981) 97 LQR 462; Hoggett, op cit, pp 10–11; Bromley, op cit, pp 274–277; Cretney op cit, pp 305–307; Grumet, *Just What the Doctor Ordered: Unconventional Therapy in the Treatment of Cancer in Minors*, (1980) 14 FLQ 63; Baron, *Medicine and Human Rights*, (1983) FLQ 1.
2   CYPA 1933, s 1(1) and (2)(a). See post, paras 9.33 et seq.
3   See the advice given to practitioners by Ministry of Health Circular F/PG/IB 1967.

(i) Contraceptive advice and treatment

1.27 The scope of the parental power/responsibility turns on whether the wider principle, the *Gillick* principle,[1] enunciated by Lord Scarman is, in relation to contraceptive advice and treatment, to be followed as applied by him or as qualified in the terms formulated by Lord Fraser.[2] Applying the principle to medical treatment, Lord Scarman held that[3]

> 'as a matter of law the parental right to determine whether or not their minor child below the age of 16 will have medical treatment terminates if and when the child achieves a sufficient understanding and intelligence to enable him or her to understand fully what is proposed. It will be a question of fact whether a child seeking advice has sufficient understanding of what is involved to give a consent valid in law'

Applying it then specifically to contraceptive advice and treatment His Lordship qualified it in these terms:[4]

> '. . . it has to be borne in mind that there is much that has to be understood by a girl under the age of 16 if she is to have legal capacity to consent to such treatment. It is not enough that she should understand the nature of the advice which is being given: she must also have a sufficient maturity to understand what is involved. There are moral and family questions, especially her relationship with her parents; long-term problems associated with the emotional impact of pregnancy and its termination; and there are the risks to health of sexual intercourse at her age, risks which contraception may diminish but cannot eliminate. It follows that a doctor will have to satisfy himself that she is able to appraise these factors before he can safely proceed on the basis that she has at law capacity to consent to contraceptive treatment. And it further follows that ordinarily the proper course will be for him, as the guidance lays down, first to seek to persuade the girl to bring her parents into consultation, and, if she refuses, not to prescribe contraceptive treatment unless he is satisfied that her circumstances are such that he ought to proceed without parental knowledge and consent.'

In his application of the principle Lord Fraser[5] began from the premiss that a doctor would only be justified in medically treating the child without parental consent if this was in the child's best interests:

> 'Once the rule of the parents' absolute authority over minor children is abandoned, the solution to the problem in this appeal can no longer be found by referring to rigid parental rights at any particular age. The solution depends on what is best for the welfare of the particular child. Nobody doubts, certainly I do not doubt, that in the overwhelming majority of cases the best judges of a child's welfare are his or her parents. Nor do I doubt that any important medical treatment of a child under 16 would normally only be carried out with the parents' approval. That is why it would and should be "most unusual" for a doctor to advise a child without the knowledge and consent of the parents on contraceptive matters.'

In deciding whether to exercise his discretion to give the girl contraceptive advice and treatment without that consent or even knowledge the doctor must, His Lordship held, be satisfied on five matters: (1) that the girl, although under 16, will understand his advice; (2) that he cannot persuade her to inform her parents or to allow him to inform the parents that she is seeking contraceptive advice; (3) that she is very likely to begin or to continue having sexual intercourse with or without contraceptive treatment; (4) that unless she receives contraceptive advice or treatment her physical or mental health or both are likely to suffer; (5) that her best interests require him to give her contraceptive advice, treatment or both without the parental consent. Those interests would especially include protection from risks of pregnancy and sexually-transmitted diseases. The first of these conditions is inherently wide and leaves the doctor with a wide discretion when assessing the girl's maturity of understanding. If he is not satisfied that she has sufficient maturity, he can, as the General Medical Council has professionally ruled, elect to tell the parents.[6]

1   See ante, para 1.13.
2   By expressly agreeing with the reasons expressed by both their Lordships on the matter the speech of Lord Bridge does not assist. See generally Parkinson, *The Gillick Case—Just What Has It Decided?*, [1986] Fam Law 11.
3   [1986] AC 112 at 188–189, [1985] 3 All ER 402 at 423.
4   At 189 and 424 respectively.
5   At 173–174 and 412–413 respectively.
6   Surprisingly, neither Lord Fraser nor the GMC has insisted that in giving the girl advice and, indeed, in testing her understanding of it, the doctor should inform her of the potential criminal liability of the girl's paramour, if he should have sexual intercourse with her.

1.28   Although there is intrinsically much that is concurrent in the views expressed by Lords Fraser and Scarman, a most significant difference is the positive emphasis put by the former on the child's interests.[1] It is respectfully submitted that with its precise formulation of the factors to be taken into account, Lord Fraser's approach is to be preferred.[2] It is noteworthy that the formulation has commended itself to the Department of Health and Social Security which has incorporated it into the advice it has given to health authorities and others, following a Departmental review of the *Gillick* case.[3] Nevertheless, it is suggested that additionally, in deciding whether the girl has sufficient maturity to understand, the doctor should put to her the matters specifically mentioned by Lord Scarman in the passage cited, though because of their complexity it may be a tall order to expect her to understand them.[4]

1   Cretney (The All England Law Reports Annual Review 1985 at p 173) crystallises the difference: 'For Lord Scarman the patient is the final arbiter, provided she has sufficient capacity (a matter to be assessed, it is true, by the doctor); but for Lord Fraser the final arbiter is the doctor. Mental capacity is a necessary but not a sufficient condition.'
2   It is arguable that, as Lord Scarman as well as Lord Bridge agreed with Lord Fraser, the formulation is part of the ratio decidendi.
3   See HC (86) 1; HC (FP) (86) 1; LAC (86) 3.
4   See Cretney, op cit; Bromley, pp 275–276.

(ii)   Abortion
1.29   Where a girl under 16 is pregnant and wants an abortion without her parents knowing about it, the doctor should follow the same basic lines in advising her as when advising on contraception, but in regard to abortion he has the additional obligations which the criminal law imposes.

It is suggested, therefore, that he should be satisfied on the following matters: (1) that the girl understands his advice and especially the risks attendant on abortion; (2) that he cannot persuade her to inform her parents or to allow him to inform them that she wishes to have an abortion–and, because of the risks involved, he should do his utmost so to persuade; (3) that she consents to abortion; (4) that abortion would be lawful in accordance with the Abortion Act 1967;[1] and (5) that it would be in her best interests. However, usually it will be difficult to conceal the proposed abortion from the parents, since the operation will entail a short absence from home. Where the parents know the facts and do not consent to the abortion it will, nevertheless, be permissible for the doctor, in accordance with *Gillick*, to rely on the girl's consent, provided he is satisfied about her understanding and maturity and, *pace* Lord Fraser, that abortion is in her best interests. In such circumstances it is, however, preferable to seek an order of the court by way of wardship proceedings authorising abortion, though obviously it will be essential to expedite the hearing. Indeed, it is highly arguable that, as the law now stands,[2] an order of the court must be obtained in all cases, even where the above conditions are satisfied. Certainly a doctor would now be unwise to proceed without it.

An order authorising a doctor to give contraceptive treatment will in most cases not be practicable, since it would involve disclosing to the parents the doctor's advice to the girl and would destroy its confidentiality,[3] but a striking illustration of a case where an order authorised both abortion and contraception was *Re P (a minor)*,[4] decided before the *Gillick* case. There a girl aged 15, who was in the care of a local authority, was pregnant for the second time. Both she and the authority were in favour of abortion, but this was strongly opposed by her parents on religious grounds. In wardship proceedings instituted by the local authority, Butler-Sloss J ordered not only that abortion should take place but also that the girl be fitted with an internal contraceptive device, since it was assumed that it was 'impossible for this local authority to monitor her sexual activities, and, therefore, contraception appears to be the only alternative'.

1 See post, paras 9.11 et seq. It seems that it would be sufficient for one doctor to advise and obtain the girl's consent, but, since two must certify that the conditions for lawful abortion exist (s 1), it is desirable that both advise.
2 See post, para 1.35.
3 See Lord Fraser in *Gillick* [1986] AC 112 at 165, [1985] 3 All ER 402 at 406.
4 [1986] 1 FLR 272, (1981) 80 LGR 301.

1.30 Where the girl does not have the requisite understanding and maturity to consent to abortion and the parents do not consent to it, the operation may still be performed without an order of a court where it is urgently needed because her life is in danger. That action would equally be justified where she did understand what abortion involved, but both she and her parents did not consent.[1] In both circumstances action is protected by the defence of necessity.[2]

1 See post, para 9.20. But there is the practical difficulty. How could the doctor operate if the girl refuses consent? Only, it seems, if the circumstances were such that he was in a position to administer a drug.
2 For a learned and speculative examination of the defence see Skegg, *Justification for Medical Procedures Performed Without Consent*, (1974) 90 LQR 512.

(iii)   Sterilisation[1]
1.31   Supposing a 15-year-old sexually experienced boy were to consult his doctor and request a vasectomy on the ground that there is a hereditary illness in his family, the risks of which he does not wish to perpetuate, and supposing further that he insists after full discussion with the doctor of its implications that he wants the operation but without his parents knowing about it. Will the doctor lawfully be entitled to perform it? The answer must be considered in the light of the court's attitude to sterilisation of children who do not have the intellectual understanding to enable them to give their consent.

1   See Grubb and Pearl, *Sterilisation and the Courts* [1987] CLJ 439.

1.32   In *Re D (a minor) (wardship: sterilisation)*,[1] a girl D, aged 11, was born with the condition of Sotos Syndrome and suffered from the symptoms associated with that condition, including certain aggressive tendencies, some impairment of mental function resulting in dull intelligence and some mental retardation. Impairment and retardation were not, however, excessive. She had an intelligence quotient of about 80 and the understanding of a child about nine or nine and a half years of age. Following her transfer to a school specialising in children with learning difficulties and behaviour problems, she showed marked improvement in her behaviour, social competence and academic skills. Worried that D might be seduced and possibly give birth to an abnormal child and having been so advised by a paediatrician and gynaecologist, the mother gave her consent for D to be sterilised; but the performance of the operation was anticipated by an alert educational psychologist, who was involved in the case, instituting wardship proceedings. Heilbron J refused to allow an operation. To do so would mean depriving the girl of a basic human right, that of a woman to reproduce, and to perform it for non-therapeutic reasons would be a violation of that right. On the evidence there was no real risk of unwanted pregnancy; D's mental condition already showed improvement and it was likely that in later years she would be able to make her own choice in the matter. The decision was, therefore, an affirmation of the general principle that, in cases where the *Gillick* principle is not relevant, the child's best interests prevail over the wishes of the parent, however well intentioned those may be, and were in *Re D*.

1   [1976] Fam 185, [1976] 1 All ER 326, CA.

1.33   But the intrinsically difficult question—what is in the child's best interests?—is nowhere more difficult to answer than in relation to medical matters, as the controversial decision of the House of Lords in *Re B (a minor) (sterilisation)*[1] demonstrates. The case raised the same question as in *Re D*, namely, whether the court in wardship proceedings should consent to a mentally retarded girl, 'Jeanette', being sterilised, but the facts compare sharply with those in *Re D* and need to be set out at length to indicate the exceptional circumstances with which the court was dealing. The girl was 17 years old.[2] She did not need protection under the Mental Health Act 1983, but she was of low intelligence with a mental age of five or six. She was an epileptic, but the fits were controlled by drugs. She could dress herself, look after herself during menstruation and perform simple domestic tasks, but her power of communication was limited to one or two words at a time. She could not be let out on her own, because she did not understand traffic or the use of money. She suffered from extremes of mood, could become very aggressive and violent and had a history of reacting badly to medication. She had all the physical sexual drive and inclinations of a physically mature woman of 17 and had already shown she was vulnerable to sexual approaches, having already once been found in a compromising situation in a bathroom. The local authority, in whose care the girl had been under a care order since she was four years of age, and her mother, with whom she spent weekends and part of the school holidays, having been advised by the social worker who knew her, a gynaecologist and a paediatrician, considered it vital that she should not become pregnant. The local authority, with the approval of the mother, therefore instituted wardship proceedings seeking leave for an operation for sterilisation (by occlusion of the fallopian tubes) to be carried out. In dismissing an appeal by the Official Solicitor, acting as guardian ad litem of the ward, from the order of the Court of Appeal upholding the decision of Bush J to grant leave, the House of Lords was at pains to emphasise that the case was concerned solely with the girl's welfare and best interests, and had nothing whatever to do with eugenics, did not involve any general principle of public policy and was not about the convenience of those caring for the ward or the anxieties of her family.[3] As for the basic right of a woman to reproduce, that right was relevant only when reproduction was the result of informed choice.[4] In the present case no such choice was available. The right to reproduce meant and would mean nothing to her. She did not understand and could not learn the causal connection between intercourse and pregnancy and the birth of a baby. She was and would remain incapable of giving an informed consent to sterilisation, abortion or marriage. On this reasoning of the House of Lords, *Re D* can be distinguished. There the mental condition of the girl was capable of such improvement that it was likely[5] that she would be able eventually to make an informed choice. It is submitted that the reasoning in *Re B* is subject to the proviso that where such likelihood exists a court is not justified in authorising immediate sterilisation, unless the operation is necessary for therapeutic purposes, for example, where there is carcinoma of the uterus.[6] Indeed, the proviso accords with the ruling of the Court of Appeal in *Re B* which the House of Lords approved, namely, that jurisdiction to authorise sterilisation should be exercised only in the last resort. The House rejected the distinction, drawn by Heilbron J in *Re D* and by the Supreme Court of Canada in *Re Eve*,[7] between therapeutic and non-therapeutic purposes of sterilisation. In the latter case it was held that the operation should never be authorised for non-therapeutic. That conclusion, in their Lordships' view, contradicted the principle that the court's duty is to exercise its wardship in such a way as to promote and ensure the best interests of the child. In *Re B*, it was held, there were several cumulative reasons why those interests would be best served by sterilisation. Were 'Jeanette' to become pregnant, that would create immense problems for her. She would not understand what was happening to her, and, were she to carry her child to full term, she would suffer 'uncomprehending fear and pain and risk of physical injury'.[8] There were also difficulties over potential abortion. Since the girl menstruated irregularly, pregnancy would be difficult to detect or diagnose in time to terminate it early. As for contraception, the difficulties were held to be much greater. The girl's limited intelligence effectively ruled out mechanical methods, and the likely adverse reaction between certain contraceptive drugs and the anti-convulsant drugs administered to her for her epileptic condition limited the choice to progesterone taken daily in pill form. However, the long-term side effects of that drug were not yet known as its effectiveness for her was 'entirely speculative'.[9] It would have to be taken for the rest of her life while fertile, and it would have only a 40% chance of establishing an effective régime.

1   [1988] AC 199, [1987] 2 All ER 206; for comment see Hinchcliffe, [1987] Fam Law 271.
2   The present section of this Chapter is concerned with medical treatment of children under 16 and their consent to it, but it is appropriate to deal with *Re B* at this point rather than post, para 1.43, because no issue of consent arose since there was no mental capacity to give it.
3   See Lord Oliver [1988] AC 199 at 212, [1987] 2 All ER 206 at 219.
4   See Lord Hailsham of St Marylebone, LC at 204 and 213 respectively.
5   The evidence was stronger. It made clear 'that she would almost certainly understand the implications of such an operation by the time she reached 18'—per Heilbron J [1976] Fam 185 at 193, [1976] 1 All ER 326 at 333.
6   If this statement of the law is correct, it will mean that eventually the courts will have to lay down a degree of likelihood for the proviso to operate.
7   (1986) 31 DLR (4th) 1.
8   Lord Templeman [1987] 2 All ER 206 at 215. Lord Hailsham (at 212) indicated the kinds of problems: ' . . . she would not understand what was happening to her, she would be likely to panic, and would probably have to be delivered by Caesarian section, but owing to her emotional state, and the fact that she has a high pain threshold she would be quite likely to pick at the operational wound and tear it open. In any event, she would be terrified, distressed and extremely violent during normal labour . . .'.
9   Per Lord Oliver [1987] 2 All ER 206 at 217.

1.34   Few decisions in family law have aroused such sharp conflict of medical, legal and popular opinions and, in some quarters, such emotive reaction as has *Re B*.[1] On the narrower front, namely, that potential abortion or contraception were not practicable alternatives, the decision is open to possible challenge. As for the former, the fact that there might be some delay in detecting pregnancy in the particular girl's case underestimates the permitted period for legal abortion, although against that may be set the risk of increasing harm in delaying the operation. As for contraception, it is arguable that the House of Lords exaggerated the practical difficulties of fitting the girl with some form of intra-uterine device or at least failed to clarify why the device would be unsatisfactory:[2] but against that argument may be set the risks of pelvic inflammatory diseases or infection associated with such devices. On the same front, it is arguable that the court failed to take, or take sufficiently, into account that there are long-term physical *sequelae* to a sterilisation operation, particularly of a person at such a young age as 17.[3] On the wider front, if it is accepted that sterilisation was the only realistic option, the decision is difficult to challenge. The current policy of trying to assimilate, wholly or partly, the mentally handicapped into the community instead of strictly institutionalising them is warmly to be welcomed, but it carries with it the consequent increase in opportunity for sexual relations. Who is to gainsay that the interests of a girl like 'Jeanette' are better promoted by protecting her from the consequences of pregnancy through sterilisation than by protecting her right to procreate? Those who defend that right tend to ignore the consequences of its exercise.[4] The right is not to be considered *in abstracto*. The House of Lords did not in any way base its decision on the need to protect any potential child of 'Jeanette'.[5] Indeed, if the law is not prepared to confer rights on an unborn fetus,[6] a fortiori it will not do so on a potential fetus.[7] But it does not follow that the responsibility of motherhood resulting from the exercise of the right to procreate should be totally ignored. Arguably, the emphasis should be on responsibility.[8] The decision in *Re B* is a realistic recognition that a girl with mental skills of a five or six year old would never on the medical evidence be in a position to discharge any responsibility as a parent and, even if the matter is considered from the point of view of a right to bring up one's child having exercised one's right to procreate, for 'Jeanette' tragically the exercise is meaningless.

1   But with the increasing medico-legal problems affecting the family more can be expected. See the problems over surrogacy, post, paras 2.10 et seq.
2   Because of the girl's moody, aggressive behaviour, there is little doubt that it would have had to be inserted under a general anaesthetic.
3   See a letter by Dr Patrick W Gill in The Times, 1 May 1987.
4   But a different view is that the right to procreate and the right to bear children are to be kept distinct.
    'One argument is that there is a fundamental right to procreate which no law can interfere with, except where medically necessary for the sake of the girl's present health. This argument does not assert that each woman has a right to bear children. That would fly in the face of reality. It asserts only that the state through its law may not deprive a woman of the opportunity of procreating.' See Kennedy and Lee, *This Rush to Judgment*, The Times, 1 April 1987.
5   Although Lord Hailsham LC expressly recognised that if the girl bore a child she would be unable to look after him; see [1987] 2 All ER 206 at 212.
6   See post, Chapter 9.
7   But would the court order sterilisation of a mentally handicapped girl suffering from a disease that could be passed on to any child she might have?
8   Compare the provisional proposals of the Law Commission which recognise that emphasis in its review of custody and guardianship, ante, para 1.17, note 2.

1.35   Whatever the arguments and merits in relation to *Re B*, one important change it apparently introduces is that it is no longer possible for parents or guardians or custodians or, where it has the parental rights and duties, a local authority to give consent for sterilisation of a child. Leave of the High Court in wardship proceedings is required. Although in the House of Lords only Lord Templeman dealt with the point,[1] it seems clear that it is to be taken now to be the law, as are the further guidelines given by His Lordship. The girl must be represented by the Official Solicitor or other appropriate guardian, and the parents must be made parties, if they wish to appear, as where appropriate must the local authority.[2] Expert evidence must be adduced setting out the reasons for the application, the history, conditions, circumstances and foreseeable future of the girl, the risks and consequences of pregnancy, the risks and consequences of sterilisation, the practicability of alternative precautions against pregnancy and any other relevant information, so that the court may be satisfied that the operation is really a 'remedy' of last resort. The judge may order additional evidence to be obtained.

The standard of proof should, it is submitted, be commensurate with the seriousness of the matter.[3] Lord Templeman accepted that principle by referring to the need for a 'sufficiently overwhelming case' to be established. It is a matter to which the courts need to return and give closer guidance, at least until the whole question of sterilisation receives Parliamentary attention.[4]

1 [1987] 2 All ER 206 at 214–215. It was the view taken by the Court of Appeal, the judgments of which were approved by Lord Hailsham (at 211), with whom Lord Brandon agreed (at 214).
2 But the pertinent questions have been asked (Maidment, 137 NLJ 468): who is to ward the child and will legal aid be available?
3 See *Serio v Serio* (1983) 4 FLR 756, and post, para 2.23.
4 Such attention needs to be given to a wide range of medico-legal problems affecting the family. See especially post, and for the proposal that there should in the first instance be a standing commission to review the problems and prepare for legislation see Kennedy and Lee, supra, para 1.34, note 4.

1.36 To return to the *Gillick* principle. Where does *Re B* leave the 15-year-old boy wishing to undergo a vasectomy in the circumstances outlined above?[1] Before that decision it could be argued that, provided the doctor is satisfied of the boy's intellectual understanding and maturity, he could, in accordance with the *Gillick* principle, lawfully perform the operation or, if Lord Fraser's view in *Gillick* is to be preferred, he could do so if additionally he was satisfied that the operation was in the boy's best interests. However, the nature of the request is such that he is likely to take the view that a 15-year-old does not have sufficient maturity to give consent, and, with regard to the additional requirement, that it is not in the boy's long term interests to be sterilised.[2] Even if satisfied on maturity and interests, the doctor would be best advised not to agree to operate without an order of the court. If these matters were to go to court, which would mean disclosure to the parents, it is submitted that these same factors would weigh with it in refusing to allow the operation. It may now be the law that those matters will have to go to court. Admittedly, Lord Templeman's remarks in *Re B* were directed to sterilisation of a girl under 18 and were made within the context of a case where the child did not have the mental capacity to give consent, but sterilisation of a child is such a 'drastic step'[3] that in all cases leave of the court should be regarded as a prerequisite. If that be so, the effect is to impose a significant restriction on the *Gillick* principle.

1 See ante, para 1.31.
2 His patient, when he becomes an adult, may well be grateful to him for not complying with his request.
3 [1987] 2 All ER 206 at 214.

1.37 If sterilisation is a drastic step, a fortiori is an operation which may or may not prolong the life of a child. The question will have to be put to the court. In *Re B (a minor) (wardship: medical treatment)*,[1] contrary to the considered decision of the parents that it would be kinder to allow her to die, the court gave consent for an operation on a Down's Syndrome baby on the ground that the effect of the operation might be that she would have the normal life span of a mongol child (some 20 to 30 years) and it was not demonstrated that the life of such a child was such that she be condemned to die.

1 [1981] 1 WLR 1421, CA (popularly known as the 'Baby Alexandra case'). For a critical analysis see Freeman, op cit, pp 259–263.

(iv)   Organ and tissue transplants

1.38   One area in which the *Gillick* principle is bound eventually to be
tested is that relating to the non-therapeutic procedures of organ and tissue
transplants. Supposing, for example, that a 15-year-old boy wants to donate
one of his kidneys to save the life of his brother, but after careful
consideration his parents do not agree. If he fully understands the
implications, then strictly on the authority of *Gillick* he will be able to
give a valid consent and the surgeon will be entitled to act on that decision
provided he considers that it is in the boy's best interests to do so. However,
in view of the present absence of statutory or direct judicial authority,
it would at least be much wiser for an order of the court to be sought
authorising the operation, and, if Lord Templeman's view in *Re B* prevails,
an order will be a prerequisite to such a 'drastic step' as organ (and some
tissue) transplants. Even if it were intended to proceed without an order,
it is very likely that an objector, for example, the parents, would take
out wardship proceedings to prevent it. If proceedings were instituted, then,
as has already been suggested,[1] the court is likely to hold that the child's
consent is subject to the court's overriding power that it must act in the
child's best interests and that may mean not allowing the operation to
take place. What factors is the court likely to take into account? Although
there is a substantial body of case law in the legal systems in the United
States, much of it must be treated with circumspection, since the systems
vary in the use of three basic tests.[2] These are: (1) that effect will be given
to the decision of the parents, provided it is fair and reasonable; (2) that
the issue is to be determined according to the best interests of the child
donor; (3) that, if the child donor is capable of consenting, effect will be
given to his consent. It is submitted that English law, being firmly committed
to the paramountcy of the child's welfare, will adopt the second test, except
where the *Gillick* principle applies. Where it does apply, the question then
is whether the court will give effect to the child's wishes or whether, as
has already been submitted, those wishes are subject to the court's deciding
that, if effect is given to them, that will accord with his best interests.
This leads inevitably to the question what are his best interests? In applying
the 'fair and reasonable' test courts have taken account of the interests
both of the donor and of the donee, with, possibly, emphasis on the latter.
Thus, in *Hart v Brown*,[3] the question was whether the parents could justifiably
consent to the transplant of a kidney of their seven-year-old daughter to
save the life of her twin sister. It was held that, since the life of the sister
was at stake, the risks to the donor were slight and, being identical twins,
the chances of success for the donee were high, to ban the parents' decision
would be unfair, and their decision was reasonable. If in a case like *Hart
v Brown*, the test of the best interests of the donor is to be applied, those
interests are not readily apparent. The question which has been asked in
the American cases is whether the staying alive of the intended donee is
emotionally and psychologically in the interests of the donor. The younger
the donor the more speculative, it is submitted, the question must be,[4]
but, if the donor is old enough and intellectually and emotionally mature
enough to give his consent in accordance with the *Gillick* principle, the
more difficult it may be for the court to find that it is not in his interests
to allow the operation to be performed, though clearly medical evidence
both of the psychological and emotional harm to the donor if the operation

is not performed and of the risks of physical harm to him if it is will be crucial.[5]

1 See paras 1.16 and 1.27.
2 The relevant literature is so extensive that choice of references is difficult, but the following are particularly helpful.
   Curran, *A Problem of Consent: Kidney Transplantation in Minors*, (1959) 34 NYUL Rev 891; Sharpe, *The Minor Transplant Donor* (1975) 7 Ottawa L Rev 88; Baron, Batsford and Cole, *Live Organ and Tissue Transplant of Minor Donors in Massachusetts* (1975) 55 BUL Rev 159; *Report of the Manitoba Law Commission on the Human Tissue Act 1968* (1986). On consent generally to medical treatment in USA see Bainham, [1986] CLJ at pp 275–277.
3 289 A 2d 386 (1972).
4 See, for example, *Nathan v Farinelli* Eq No 74–87 (Mass, July 3, 1974) transplantation of bone marrow from six-year-old to ten-year-old brother not allowed.
5 The difficulties confronting the court are illustrated by *Strunk v Strunk* 445 SW 2d 145 (1969) and *Richardson v Richardson* 284 So 2d 185 (1973), both concerned with prospective donors who were mentally ill. In the former case the prospective donee was the 28-year-old brother of a mentally subnormal man, who was a year younger. Held, that the latter's best interests would be served by a transplant of his kidney, since he identified with his dying brother. But in *Richardson*, where the prospective donor was a 17-year-old, it was held that a kidney transplant was not essential for his sister's life and that benefit to him was speculative.

1.39 One lesson especially to be learned from the United States experience is the procedural difficulties to which cases of this kind may give rise.[1] Proceedings are in practice lengthy, costly and traumatic to the family. Clearly they are of such serious implications for the child that appointment of a guardian ad litem and separate legal representation must be regarded as essential. One of the criticisms of the American proceedings has been the lack of vigorous representation of the donor's interests in some of the cases, especially where the child is younger and his wishes cannot be, or are not, consulted, and/or where the life of the prospective donee is not in danger, for example, where a parent and doctor of a seven-year-old boy agree that a skin graft will cosmetically help his five-year-old sister who has been badly burned and the operation will cause some discomfort to him. Where, however, there is not a transplant for the cosmetic benefit of another person, but an operation for the child's own cosmetic benefit, for example, acne or to remove warts or birth marks or to straighten one's nose,[2] the court may well be ready to authorise it, provided there is not a substantial risk of attendant harm.

1 See 55 Boston ULR 159 at p 162.
2 See *Lacey v Laird* 139 NE 2d 25 (1956) where the consent of a female minor aged 18 to such an operation was held to be effective, notwithstanding parental opposition.

1.40 Given the 'awesome power'[1] conferred on the court, it seems unlikely that it will often allow a transplant where the donor is to be a child, and it may well be persuaded that, so long as the law does not require adults to donate organs or tissue, children are to be protected from potentially harmful non-therapeutic procedures. The matter is of such deep consequence that it ought to be a matter for Parliamentary decision, one way or the other.

1 Per Justice Steinfeld in his dissenting judgment in *Strunk v Strunk* 445 SW 2d 145 (1969) at 149.

(v) Treatment of premature and young babies

1.41 Reports on medical experimentation on premature and young babies make this another grey area calling for urgent Parliamentary scrutiny. A Report published by the Institute of Medical Ethics has revealed that about 2,000 sick or premature babies are, with parental consent, used annually in medical experiments which are not of direct benefit to them but, on the contrary, are potentially harmful. There can be no doubt that such experiments are illegal, and, although they are conducted in the interests of scientific research and arguably for the public good, it is submitted that any parental consent does not legalise them.[1] On the contrary, it seems clear that if the parent were to consent he could be liable for an offence under section 1 of the Children and Young Persons Act 1933[2] for causing or procuring his child to be assaulted, (probably) ill-treated or neglected or exposed in a manner likely to cause the child unnecessary suffering or injury to health.

1 This conclusion is supported by the Parliamentary Social Services Committee in its Report ('The Short Report') on perinatal and neonatal mortality (1980), and is the view adopted by the Department of Health and Social Security and the Medical Research Council.
2 See post, paras 9.33 et seq.

1.42 Distinct from such invasive procedures are those which are conducted directly for the child's benefit. These, nevertheless, require the parent's consent. The most common are the blood test performed for diagnostic purposes,[1] and vaccination. The latter particularly highlights the importance of obtaining the parent's consent, because the risk of harm to the child, albeit small, does exist. That, indeed, is recognised by the Vaccine Damage Payments Act 1979, which provides for compensation for persons severely disabled as a result of vaccination against a range of diseases, namely, diphtheria, tetanus, whooping cough, polio, measles, rubella and tuberculosis.[2]

1 A blood test performed, with parental consent, for the purpose of establishing the paternity of the child is lawful, unless it is shown that the test would be against the child's interests; see Lord Reid in *S v S* [1972] AC 24 at 43–45, [1970] 3 All ER 107 at 111–113.
2 For the background to the Act and an evaluation of its provisions see Dworkin, *Compensation and Payments for Vaccine Damage* [1979] JSWL 330. The National Children's Bureau has recommended that parents should be required to show proof of their children's immunisation record when they start school, and that if immunisation levels have not reached 95% by 1990 legal measures should be considered, since immunisation should be seen as a child's legal right; see *Investing in the Future: Child Health ten years after the Court Report* (1987), which provides a ten point plan aimed at improving the declining health of the nation's 9.5 million under 15 year olds.

(b) Child aged sixteen or over

1.43 Section 8(1) of the Family Law Reform Act 1969 provides that once the child has attained the age of 16 he may give his consent to surgical, medical or dental treatment without the parent's consent, and it 'shall be as effective as it would be if he were of full age'. It seems clear, therefore, that, if a 16-year-old boy were to request a vasectomy or to consent to donating an organ or tissue, the doctor would be entitled to rely on the section. However, it is not clear whether the doctor's power is now to be regarded as restricted by the view taken by Lord Templeman in *Re*

B (a minor) (sterilisation),[1] that leave of the High Court in wardship proceedings is necessary before the operation could be performed. Even if *Re B* does extend to a child under 16 who falls within the *Gillick* principle and has the requisite intellectual understanding,[2] it is submitted that the terms of section 8 exclude that restriction,[3] where the child has reached that age, though until the doubt is judicially resolved, a doctor would be unwise to proceed without an order.

1   [1987] 2 All ER 206 at 214; see ante, para 1.35.
2   Ante, para 1.36.
3   For the contrary view see Lowe and White, *Wards of Court*, 2nd edn, para 6.55.

8   Child's services

1.44   The common law recognises a right of the parent, not as parent but as head of the domestic household, to the domestic services of those of his children who, being minors and unmarried but old enough to be capable of rendering services, are living with him as members of his family. In those circumstances a master-servant relationship is presumed. For practical purposes the right is now a matter of historical interest. It was never directly enforceable against the child, but it did give the parent a remedy against a person who wrongfully interfered with the right by committing a tort against the child with the result that the parent was deprived of his child's services. Persistent criticism of this anachronistic remedy[1] finally resulted in its abolition by the Administration of Justice Act 1982,[2] a legislative process begun with the Law Reform (Miscellaneous Provisions) Act 1970[3] which abolished the action where the loss of services was due to rape, seduction, enticement or harbouring.

1   See the 11th Report of the Law Reform Committee (1963), Cmnd 2017; the Law Commission: Report on Personal Injury Litigation—Assessment of Damages (Law Com No 56, para 157); Report of the Royal Commission on Civil Liability and Compensation for Personal Injury (1978) Cmnd 7054, para 447.
2   Section 2(b).
3   Section 5. Following the recommendations in Law Com No 25, paras 101–102.

9   Child's surname[1]

1.45   Change of surname is a matter primarily of custom not of law,[2] and by custom the child whose parents were married to each other at his birth[3] takes his father's surname[4] and the child whose parents were not so married takes his mother's, although where she is living with the father she may well choose to adopt his name for herself and the child.[5] It is, on the other hand, a matter of law that in the case of a child who comes into the former category one of his parents is not entitled to change the child's surname unless the other parent consents or a court authorises the change. This rule is not, it seems,[6] affected by that in the Guardianship Act 1973 which normally enables one parent to exercise a parental right independently of the other.[7] It seems, however, that on the death of one of them the survivor does have power to change it, but again this would, in the absence of a court order, be subject to the consent of any duly appointed guardian.

1 See generally the Law Commission's Report on Illegitimacy (1982) (Law Com No 118); Bromley, op cit, pp 277–278 and 337–338.
2 *Du Boulay v Du Boulay* (1869) LR 2 PC 430 at 442.
3 For the meaning of this term see the Family Law Reform Act 1987, s 1(2) and (4), post, para 2.20.
4 But see infra, para 1.47.
5 See post, para 2.32.
6 See Bromley, at p 337.
7 Section 1(1), ante, para 1.11.

1.46 A dispute between the parents over the surname usually arises after the break-up of their marriage and especially, though not entirely, where the parties are divorced and the mother marries again and wishes her child to take the step-father's name. Indeed, until the restrictions imposed by the Children Act 1975,[1] one of the main purposes of adoption of a child by a step-father was to enable the name to be changed. In such cases of re-marriage the change to the step-father's surname may be with the express or implied consent of the natural father or he may be indifferent to opposing it.[2] Where he does oppose, then the above principle that, in the absence of consent, an order of the court is necessary is given express statutory effect so far as concerns matrimonial proceedings in a divorce court.[3] Cases in the seventies reflected a sharp difference of emphasis to be attached to a change of name. One view was that it was an important matter and was only to be allowed if it was in the child's best interests.[4] The other regarded it as relatively unimportant in giving effect to those interests.[5] In *W v A*,[6] the Court of Appeal came down firmly in favour of the former view, and the effect would seem to be to raise a presumption against change. The difficulty that the mother may have in rebutting it is forcibly illustrated by *W v A* itself, where the fact that she, her two children and the step-father were emigrating to Australia to start a new life was not enough to justify the change. Nevertheless, emigration will always be a relevant factor. So will the stability of the mother's marriage to the step-father, the likely embarrassment which retention of the natural father's name may cause the child, for example among school friends, and any notoriety which that name has acquired. Also relevant should be the extent to which the father has maintained contact with the child. Where he has disappeared or abandoned all interest in the child the court is likely to allow a change, but the importance it attaches to maintaining a link with the father's family through his name may cause it to give insufficient weight to the fact that his contact has only been limited.

However, the risk when taking conduct into account is that the court may be led to see the issue as primarily a conflict between competing parental claims at the expense of the child's interests.[7] Even where the reason for the father's delay in challenging the change is his having been unaware of it, it may no longer be in the child's interests to revert to his former name. As for the views of the child, the *Gillick* principle should at least lead courts to giving greater weight to them,[8] and arguably they should be ready to recognise that a mature child has the power to change his name, but they are likely to make it subject to the overriding control of the court to be satisfied that the change accords with his welfare. Indeed, once a child reaches the age of 16 it may be difficult for a court to refuse to recognise a power to change. If a person of that age has capacity to acquire his own domicile,[9] it is illogical to deny him a similar capacity to acquire a name of his choice.

1　See post, para 5.58.
2　The mother may apply the new name to her child by usage without any formal act or she may choose to do so by deed and enrol it in the Central Office of the Supreme Court in accordance with the Enrolment of Deeds (Change of Name) Regulations 1983, SI 1983/680. A deed poll is of evidential value, but gives the change of name no greater legal significance. Outside the present topic, it can be particularly useful to strengthen the conclusion that the change was not made with any fraudulent intent.
3　MCR 1977, r 92(8).
4　See *Y v Y* [1973] Fam 147, [1973] 2 All ER 574; *Re WG* (1976) 6 Fam Law 210, CA; *L v F* (1978) Times, 1 August.
5　*R v R* [1978] 2 All ER 33, [1977] 1 WLR 1256, CA; *D v B* [1979] Fam 38, [1979] 1 All ER 92, CA.
6　[1981] Fam 14, [1981] 1 All ER 100, CA.
7　Compare the relevance of parental conduct in custody disputes; see post, para 3.10.
8　In *W v A supra*, the children were aged 12 and 10, but their wishes for a change of name did not prevail. That, however, was a decision before *Gillick*.
9　See the Domicile and Matrimonial Proceedings Act 1973, s 3. Cf Bromley, p 277 note 1, where it is doubted whether any minor has power to change his name.

1.47　In *D v B*[1] the question was not whether a change of name should be allowed after the break-up of the parents' marriage, but whether the mother of a child had the power to register her child in a surname other than that of the father, to whom she was married.[2] As already noted,[3] it is customary to choose his surname, but there is nothing in the Registration of Births, Deaths and Marriages Regulations 1968[4] which requires his name to be given priority. All that they require[5] is that the child shall be registered in the surname by which 'at the date of the registration of the birth it is intended that the child shall be known'. In *D v B* by the time of the child's birth the mother had left the child's father, and she registered the child in the surname of her lover, a surname which she herself had assumed.[6] The Court of Appeal held that she was entitled to do so, without any need for the father's consent or an order of the court. The decision might, therefore, be justified as the exercise of a parental power unilaterally in accordance with section 1(1) of the Guardianship Act 1973 without reference to the other parent, and the proviso that it is not to be exercised if the latter has signified disapproval did not apply, since the mother registered before the father objected. However, in the light of *W v A*,[7] it would seem that the same approach must be followed as in a case of a change of surname, namely, that the choice is to be determined in accordance with the paramountcy of the child's welfare, with a presumption in favour of the father's name. On this approach a case like *D v B* would be differently decided. To justify registration in a different name from that of the father, the mother would have to satisfy the court on the kinds of matters that would justify a change of name, for example, that the father had already made it clear before the birth that he wanted nothing to do with his child.

1　[1979] Fam 38, [1979] 1 All ER 92, CA.
2　See Fortin, *The Nature of the Right to Select a Child's Surname* (1980) 10 Fam Law 40; and a note (JMT) in 97 LQR 197.
3　Supra, para 1.45.
4　SI 1968/2049.
5　Reg 18(3).

6   There was no concealment of her husband's paternity, and he was named as the father in the Register of Births.
7   [1981] Fam 14, [1981] 1 All ER 100, CA.

10   Passports and emigration

1.48   The power of a parent to veto the issue of a passport to his child, if he is under 18, is a particular incident of the power to determine the place and manner in which the child spends his time. The Passport Department of the Home Office impliedly recognises the power. Provided that no objection has been lodged at the Department by a parent or other objector, standard passport facilities are normally granted with the written consent of either parent or, where the parents were not married to each other at the time of the child's birth, that of the mother.[1] Consent is required whether the child's name is to be added to a relative's passport or he is to be issued with his own passport. Since parental consent to the issue of a passport is required, it follows a fortiori that consent to the child's emigration is essential.

1   For details of the Department's revised leaflet on passport facilities for minors see [1986] Fam Law 50; and see further, post, para 3.106. No consent is required if the minor is married or a member of HM Forces.

11   Consent to marriage

1.49   Both parents of a child who was born when they were married to each other must normally consent to the marriage of their child if, not being a widow or widower, he or she is between 16 and 18 years of age. The detailed provisions are set out in section 3(1) and Schedule 2 to the Marriage Act 1949.[1] The following are relevant to the present topic. If one parent is dead, the consent of the survivor is necessary, either alone or, where he or she is acting jointly with a guardian, with the consent also of the guardian. Where the parents are divorced or separated by a court order or agreement, only the parent to whom custody has been granted must consent,[2] and, where one has deserted the other, the latter's consent alone is needed.[3] Should both parents have been deprived of custody by an order of a court, the person to whom it has been granted must consent.

1   As amended by the Children Act 1975, Sch 3, paras 7 and 9, and by the Family Law Reform Act 1987, Sch 2, paras 9–11.
2   Semble both must consent if there is no order or agreement.
3   How desertion is to be determined without prior legal enquiry is not made clear by the Act.

1.50   The need for this parental power has excited sharp differences of opinion,[1] but its importance has markedly declined, first through the reduction of the age of majority from 21 to 18 and more recently through the fact that more people are marrying for the first time later in life.[2] In the few applications[3] to magistrates' courts for consent to marry where parents refuse consent, refusal by the court is uncommon and likely reliance on the *Gillick* principle will further reduce the number.

1   Compare the reasons given by the Latey Committee on the Age of Majority, (1967) Cmnd

3342 paras 95 et seq, for retention of the power with those advanced by the Law Commission in PWP No 35 for its abolition.
2   In 1984 one in six spinsters marrying was a teenager; a decade earlier it was just over one in three; see Social Trends 1986 (HMSO) p 37.
3   See Cretney, op cit, p 17, note 43.

12   Agreement to adoption

1.51   Subject to the power of the court to dispense with it on specified grounds, a parent's agreement is a prerequisite to the making of an order for the adoption of his child.[1]

1   Adoption Act 1976, s 16(1) and (2). See post, paras 5.20 et seq.

13   Appointment of guardians

1.52   A parent may by deed or will appoint a guardian of the child after his or her death.[1]

1   Guardianship of Minors Act 1971, s 4(1) and (2). See post, paras 4.03 et seq.

14   Succession on death

1.53   Parents have rights of intestate succession on the death of their child in accordance with the Administration of Estates Act 1925, Part IV, as amended.

15   Administration of property

1.54   The extent of the power and duty of a parent to administer his child's property is uncertain.[1] The reason is historical. The father's natural guardianship extended only to the person of the child—to his custody and education, but not to his property. If the child should have landed property, the father might be guardian of it, but this could only be by virtue of the rules governing the feudal forms of guardianship and not because he was a parent. Both during and since the existence of the feudal rules the extent to which he has powers and duties has remained unresolved.[2] As already noted,[3] section 1 of the Guardianship Act 1973 recognises that the parity of 'rights and authority' between the father and the mother extends to 'the administration of any property *belonging to* or held in trust for a minor or the application of income of any such property',[4] but it does not define the scope of the right and authority. It is silent on any duty, though there seems to be no doubt that a duty is also attributable, which for the majority of parents will be limited at most to arranging and administering such minor matters as keeping a savings account on behalf of the child into which gifts to him may be paid. It has been suggested[5] that 'the father's power of control over the child's person would include the power to direct the child in the management of property in the child's possession', which, if valid, would apply equally to the mother in accordance with section 1 of the 1973 Act. But, if so, would that power be affected by the *Gillick* principle, so that if the child is old enough and mature enough the parent's power would no longer operate? The dearth of authority on the proprietary relationship between parent and child acquires some significance when the child starts to earn his own living. The questions have been asked[6] whether the parents can insist on the wages being paid over to them or whether they can at least insist on receiving some contribution to the child's upkeep. We start with the premiss that, notwithstanding the *Gillick* principle, an English court is highly unlikely to tolerate an action on behalf of the child against the parent or the parent against the child, since such litigation would be divisive of the family. That is a ground of public policy which has long been recognised. As already mentioned,[7] even when the parent's right to the services of his child had some practical significance it was never directly enforceable against the child, and the child has never been able directly to enforce the parental common law or statutory duty to maintain him during his minority.[8] The questions posed above may be tested against the 16-year-old who is in full-time employment. It is clear that for some purposes at least his wages are his property. For example, if fined for an offence, he can be ordered himself to pay the fine and not his parent.[9] If he is in the care of a local authority, he is liable to make contributions towards his own maintenance,[10] which are directly enforceable against him by a contribution order made by a magistrates' court.[11] Supposing the 16-year-old is not in care but living with his parents, has not paid them a penny out of his wages, refuses to do so and leaves home. It is scarcely conceivable that the court would 'find' a common law duty analogous to that of the duty under the Child Care Act 1980, so as to entitle the parent to claim reimbursement for maintaining his child during the period he was working and living at home. But to take a different example. Supposing the child continues to live with his parents until the age of 18 and during the previous two years when he has been working he has given all his wages to them except for keeping a small percentage of it as 'pocket money', with the result that the amount handed over substantially exceeds that required to maintain him. Would he after attaining majority be entitled to recover, if not all, the excess over maintenance? Arguably, he could, on the ground that the parent as natural guardian has a fiduciary duty to account at the end of the guardianship for all property of the child which passed into his hands. If this argument is valid only to the extent of excess over maintenance, then viewed from the point that the parent is a guardian, there is an implied right to set off expenses reasonably incurred in discharging his duties as guardian.

1   See Law Com Working Paper No 91 on Guardianship, paras 2.32–2.34; Law Com No 172, para 2.8.
2   There is also apparently still the anomaly that, whereas a guardian can give a valid receipt on the child's behalf (*M'Reight v M'Reight* (1849) 13 I Eq R 314), a parent cannot; see Law Com Working Paper No 118 on Illegitimacy, para 7.3, note 9, citing *Dagley v Tolferry* (1715) 1 P Wms 285; *Re Somech* [1957] Ch 165, [1956] 3 All ER 523; *Vestey v IRC* [1979] Ch 177 at 196. However, it has justifiably been pointed out that, in view of the rule that a guardian under the GA 1973 has all the rights, powers and duties of a guardian of the minor's estate'—which would include a power to give a valid receipt—'parents cannot be worse placed and must also have these "rights, powers and duties" '; see Freeman, *Law and Practice of Custodianship*, p 49.
3   Ante, para 1.11.
4   Italics supplied. See especially in relation to a child's earnings, infra.
5   Law Com Working Paper No 91, para 2.32.
6   Cretney, op cit, p 305.
7   Ante, para 1.44.
8   The Law Commission has recommended that a child over 18 whose parents are no longer living together should be eligible to apply for financial provision by them. The recommendation would not be contrary to public policy, since the family no longer exists

as a unit. So far the principle has been limited to allowing a child over 18 to intervene in existing legal proceedings between his parents so as to obtain financial provision; see *Downing v Downing* [1976] Fam 288, [1976] 3 All ER 474.
9 See post, para 13.20.
10 CCA 1980, s 45(1).
11 Section 47. He is also liable to pay tax on his earnings.

16   Representation in legal proceedings

1.55   Apparently a parent has the right to act as 'next friend', and a duty to act as a guardian ad litem, of a child in legal proceedings. Certainly the court gives preference to a parent to act in those capacities,[1] and will only substitute another person if the parent has acted improperly and against the child's interests.[2] In relation to proceedings in the juvenile court he occupies a special position. His right to conduct the case on behalf of the juvenile is subject to a number of exclusions or limitations.[3]

1 *Woolf v Pemberton* (1877) 6 Ch D 19.
2 *Re Birchall, Wilson v Birchall* (1880) 16 Ch D 41, CA; *Re Taylor's Application* [1972] 2 QB 369, [1972] 2 All ER 873, CA.
3 See post, paras 14.56 et seq.

17   Complaints relating to the Child Care Act 1980, section 3

1.56   A parent has the right to object to a resolution passed under section 3 vesting the parental rights and duties in a local authority or a voluntary organisation.[1]

1 See post, paras 15.38–15.42 and para 15.114.

IV   GUARDIANSHIP AND CUSTODY

1.57   A major reason for the complexity of child law is the confusing and overlapping terminology which is used to describe different legal relationships betwen a child and an adult or between a child and an institution. 'Guardianship', 'custody', 'care', 'charge', 'control', 'authority', 'possession' are used, often with bewildering variety, and the law is further complicated by the fact that some of them bear more than one meaning.[1] The Children Act 1975 added to the complexity by introducing the concepts of 'legal custody' and 'actual custody'.

1 See Hall, *The Waning of Parental Rights* [1972B] CLJ 248; Parry, *The Conundrum of Custody* (1981) 12 Fam Law 213.

1.58   The complexity of the relationship between custody and guardianship, 'two key concepts in any discussion of parent child law',[1] received the particular attention of Sachs LJ in *Hewer v Bryant*,[2] in which guardianship, custody in its wider meaning and custody in the narrower sense of the power of physical care and control are distinguished:

'In its wider meaning the word "custody" is used as if it were almost the equivalent of "guardianship" in the fullest sense—whether the guardianship is by nature, by nurture, by testamentary disposition or by order of a court (I use the words "fullest sense" because guardianship may be limited to give control over the person or only over the administration of the assets of an infant) . . . such guardianship embraces a "bundle of rights", or to be more exact a "bundle of powers", . . . These include . . . both the personal power physically to control the infant until the years of discretion and the right (originally only if some property was concerned) to apply to the courts to exercise the powers of the Crown as *parens patriae*. It is thus clear that somewhat confusingly one of the powers conferred by custody in its wide meaning is custody in its limited meaning, ie such personal power of physical control as a parent or guardian may have . . . The trouble is that, whilst the legislature has distinguished between guardianship and custody, the courts have tended often to use the latter word as if it were substantially the equivalent of the former thus leading to some confusion of thought . . . It would be a happier situation if by future legislation the courts were enabled to use the word "guardianship" [instead of custody in its wide meaning] in orders in appropriate cases.'

If some of the recent proposals of the Law Commission are supported and implemented, that judicial expression of hope may be realised. One major reform would be to isolate the powers and responsibilities of the parent from their historical association with guardianship, or more specifically guardianship by nature and nurture,[3] and to embody them within the concept of parenthood, thereby distinguishing guardianship as a concept embodying some or all of the parental powers and responsibilities which are entrusted to certain categories of persons who stand in loco parentis.[4] As will be seen,[5] a concomitant of this proposal is an extension of guardianship beyond the present limited class of persons who fall within it. It is earnestly hoped that proposals along these exciting lines are not relegated to the archives. As matters stand, custody in the wide sense of a 'bundle of powers' continues to be relevant for the purpose of the matrimonial jurisdiction of the divorce court[6] and for that of wardship.[7]

1 Cretney, op cit, p 296.
2 [1970] 1 QB 357 at 373, [1969] 3 All ER 578 at 585–586.
3 Originally guardianship by nature was limited to guardianship of an heir apparent, with the father having first claim to it and then the mother or remoter ancestor. Guardianship by nurture was guardianship by the father (and on his death by the mother) of their legitimate children under 14, but after 1557 under 16 in the case of girls; see Law Com Working Paper No 91, para 2.6.
4 See Law Com Working Paper No 91, paras 3.1–3.6; Law Com No 172, paras 2.2–2.3.
5 Post, paras 4.47–4.48.
6 See post. paras 3.47 et seq.
7 See post, Chapter 8.

1 Legal custody

1.59 This form of custody is a product of the Children Act 1975 which defines it, in section 86, as:

'so much of the parental rights and duties as relate to the person of the child (including the place and manner in which his time is spent)'

It was introduced in order to create the concept of custodianship which, as will be seen,[1] is designed to establish a legal relationship between a child and his relatives or step-parent or foster parents short of both adoption and guardianship; but the concept also extends to the jurisdiction of the magistrates' courts under the Domestic Proceedings and Magistrates' Courts Act 1978,[2] and by that Act[3] to courts exercising jurisdiction under the Guardianship of Minors Acts 1971 and 1973.[4] Consequently, the powers of courts granting legal custody under those Acts are narrower than those of a divorce court granting custody under the Matrimonial Causes Act 1973. A custody order carries with it the power to administer the child's assets: a legal custody order, being related only to the person of the child, clearly does not.[5] This distinction may be relatively unimportant in the case of the child who is earning his own living. Whatever may be the uncertainty surrounding the power of the parent to control his child's wages and even to claim any share of them,[6] it is clear that the legal custodian is entitled neither to control nor to share. That question apart, few children have their own assets (and if they have they are subject to a trust), so that the distinction between the divorce and other jurisdictions might be thought to be of very limited practical significance. However, the matter is not so straightforward, since there are other parental rights which do not fall within the category of those relating to the person of the child.

1   Post, Chapter 6.
2   Section 8(2), post, para 3.35.
3   Section 36.
4   See post, para 3.19.
5   But this difference must be qualified to the extent that, if in matrimonial proceedings under the Domestic Proceedings and Magistrates' Courts Act 1978 or in proceedings under s 9 of the Guardianship of Minors Act 1971 the mother is given legal custody and the father is ordered to make payments to her in respect of the child, the mother has the duty to administer the payments in the child's interests. However, if she does not, it is difficult to see what effective sanction the court has, except where her failure is so serious (for example, she is spending the money on drink) as to justify variation of the legal custody order in the father's favour or possibly to make the present order in her favour subject to a supervision order or, as a last resort, to make an order committing the child to the care of a local authority. For these orders see post, Chapter 3.
6   See para 1.54 ante.

1.60   Regrettably, the Children Act itself provides minimal information. There is one specified restriction. Section 86 itself precludes anyone who has legal custody, other than a parent or guardian, from effecting or arranging for the child's emigration from the United Kingdom. The Act (or amended legislation) also refers to three parental rights which do fall within legal custody. These are the right to determine the place and manner in which the child's time is spent[1] (subject to the restriction concerning emigration), the right to give or withhold consent to the marriage of the child[2] and the right to object to a section 3 resolution made under the CCA 1980[3] and vesting parental rights and duties in a local authority.

1   CA 1975, s 86.
2   MA 1949, s 3(1) as amended by the CA 1975, Sch 3, para 7 and the FLRA 1987, Sch 2, para 9.
3   CCA 1980, s 5(4).

1.61   Those apart, the 1975 Act offers no guidance for determining whether or not a parental right or duty lies within the scope of legal custody. On the one hand, it can safely be said that those listed earlier and numbered (1)–(7), together with the rights to veto the issue of a passport and to represent the child in legal proceedings, do come within its scope, since they all relate to the person of the child.[1] On the other hand, it is obvious that the rights of succession to, and (as already noted) the administration of, the child's property are outside legal custody. The remainder listed, namely, agreement to adoption, appointment of a testamentary guardian and changing the child's surname call for closer comment.

1 It has been pointed out (Cretney, op cit, p 311) that the right to change the child's religion 'would seem to relate to the child's soul rather than his person'. The logic is unassailable, but it is questionable whether the parliamentary draftsman intended such sophistication.
  While recognising that 'at first sight a child's religion might seem to relate to his person (including the place and manner in which his time is spent)' the Law Commission considers that 'it would be surprising if a custodian could change a child's religion when a local authority having parental rights (or powers) and duties is expressly prohibited from doing so'; see Law Com Working Paper No 96, p 40, note 120.

1.62   An adoption order cannot normally be made unless the child's parent or guardian agrees to the making of an order. The fact that the relevant provision[1] refers specifically only to the parent or guardian in itself might be regarded as conclusive that it is not within the power of anyone else, who has legal custody, to grant or withold agreement to adoption,[2] whether or not a parent or guardian exists. Supposing, however, that neither parent is alive, that no guardian has been appointed but that there is a person in whom legal custody has been vested. Is it to be inferred, notwithstanding the statutory silence, that his parental rights include that of agreeing to adoption? There is something to be said for the view that, being the only person with parental rights over an orphan, he should be able to determine whether or not the child should be the subject of adoption, especially in view of the fact that in such circumstances there is apparently no effective power to appoint a guardian who could then give the requisite agreement. Certainly there is no such power under the Guardianship of Minors Act 1971, since that Act only allows appointment where there is no parent, guardian or other person having parental rights with respect to the child.[3] There is the inherent jurisdiction of the High Court to appoint a guardian, whether with or without making the child a ward of court,[4] but in either case a guardian could, it is submitted, only be empowered to give agreement to adoption if the court expressly delegated the power to him, and it is questionable whether it would allow its inherent jurisdiction to be invoked for the purpose of so delegating.

However, logical reasons point to the conclusion that a person with legal custody does not have the right to agree to adoption. Otherwise it would mean that he could agree to adoption by himself.[5] Any other conclusion would also lead to the absurdity that, while an order granting a person legal custody cannot vest all the parental rights and duties in him, he could agree to some third person's acquiring them. These objections must be qualified in one respect. Hitherto the adoption legislation[6] has treated as a guardian for its purposes the father who has been granted legal custody of his illegitimate child by an order under section 9 of the Guardianship of Minors Act 1971.[7] This has produced the anomalous consequence that he can agree to the prospective adopters acquiring the power to administer the child's assets, even though he himself has not had that power.[8] The

Family Law Reform Act 1987 produces the strange consequence that on
the one hand it enlarges the anomaly, on the other hand it removes it.
This is due to the alternative circumstances in which the father may become
a guardian,[9] namely, (a) where he has a right to custody, legal custody
or actual custody or care and control by virtue of an order made under
any enactment, or (b) where an order is in force under section 4 of the
1987 Act giving him all the parental rights and duties with respect to the
child.

1   AA 1976, s 16(1).
2   Compare the specific reference to the 'custodian' in the CCA 1980, s 3(1)(a) and (10)
    in relation to the making of resolutions under that section.
3   GMA 1971, s 5(1).
4   For the power to appoint without wardship see post, para 4.13. Where a child is made
    a ward of court, it is the practice today to grant a person care and control of the child
    but not to make him a guardian.
5   See Lowe and White, *Wards of Court* 1st edn (1979) p 239 note 12a.
6   AA 1976, s 72(1).
7   As amended by the DPMCA 1978, s 36, which substitutes 'legal custody' for custody.
8   But he did and does have rights of intestate succession to the child's property, which
    on adoption would pass to the adopters; see formerly FLRA 1969, s 14, and now FLRA
    1987, s 18.
9   See FLRA 1987, s 7(2), substituting a new definition of guardian in AA 1976, s 72(1).
    This change is not yet operative.

1.63   As with agreement to allow adoption, it is arguable that a person
with legal custody does not have the power to appoint a testamentary
guardian, firstly, because the relevant provision[1] refers only to the mother
and father as having the power and, secondly, because a person with legal
custody has only rights and duties relating to the person of the child and
cannot additionally confer and impose proprietary ones. Moreover, a
guardian under the Guardianship of Minors Act 1971 not only is guardian
of the person, but also has all the rights, powers and duties of a guardian
of a child's estate.[2] Therefore, it is arguable that the right of appointment
does not relate to the person of the child. These arguments do not, however,
have the same cogency as their counterparts have in relation to adoption.
Section 86 of the Children Act 1975 defines legal custody as 'so much
of the parental rights and duties as relate to the person'—not 'such' or
'those' rights and duties as so relate. Accordingly, the definition is open
to the construction that a person with legal custody has so much of the
right to appoint as enables him to appoint a testamentary guardian of
the person, and so the rule in the Guardianship of Minors Act must to
that extent be qualified. Viewed more widely the arguments are evenly
balanced. On the one hand, it can be said that the conferment of such
a wide right as will enable the person with legal custody, in the event
of his death, to provide for the regulation of the child's future would scarcely
accord with the denial of the rights to agree to adoption and to consent
to emigration. On the other hand, a right of appointment seems consistent
with the custodian's right to consent to marriage. The effect of marriage
of a daughter or, apparently, a son under 18 is to emancipate the child
from natural guardianship.[3] If, then, the custodian has the right to withhold
the termination of that guardianship, should he not be able to provide
a substitute for it? These conflicting arguments, which can be advanced

both with regard to appointing a guardian and agreeing to adoption, demonstrate the unsatisfactory nature of the concept of legal custody.

1 GMA 1971, s 4(1) and (2).
2 GA 1973, s 7.
3 See post, para 1.71.

1.64 If the classification of parental rights relating to the person of the child turns on whether their subject matter can be said to relate to the care and control and upbringing of the child, it is doubtful whether the right to change the child's surname is a 'personal' right. The bearing of a name can have wider possible implications involving status and reputation. Moreover, if the person with legal custody were given that right, it could create difficulties should there be revocation of the order granting him legal custody. In the event of the parent then resuming legal custody, it would be incongruous if the child's name did not revert to that of the parent. It cannot be in the child's interests that his name should be subject to the risk of changes in this way. As already pointed out, the question of changing the surname has particular relevance for the step-father who often wants the name of the child of his spouse by a former marriage to be changed to his own. At one time that desire accounted for many step-parent applications to adopt.[1] It is unlikely that custodianship will be allowed to achieve the same result.[2]

1 See ante, para 1.46.
2 Compare Freeman, *Law and Practice of Custodianship*, p 53, who inclines to the view that a custodian does have power to change the child's name.

2 Actual custody

1.65 The Children Act 1975 has also produced 'actual custody', but this essentially corresponds to the traditional, narrow meaning of custody, namely, the personal power of physical care and control of the child. Section 87(1) states that a person has actual custody of a child if he has actual possession of his person. The possession may be shared with others; for example, spouses who act as foster parents. This definition is supplemented by sub-section (3), which provides that 'unless the context otherwise requires, references to the person with whom a child has his home refer to the person who, disregarding absence of the child at a hospital or boarding school and any other temporary absence, has actual custody of the child'. The supplementary rule creates uncertainty in that it may be difficult to decide whether or not any other absence is temporary. It would seem that the words are not to be construed *eiusdem generis* so as to limit temporary absences to those cases where the child is in an institution, and not in a place usually associated with home. The correct approach, it is submitted, is to emphasise the nature and quality of the child's residence rather than the reason for his absence. A child who spends a year living at the home of relatives and being brought up by them while his parents are working abroad is in the actual custody of his relatives. The same conclusion should be reached if for the same reason he has to spend the whole of his summer school holidays with relatives. Should it make any difference if his parents are not abroad but he is staying with relatives for that period because he is holidaying at their home? It is submitted, not. However, even with this emphasis on the quality of residence, the point must be reached, albeit arbitrarily, where the duration is such that his absence from the parents is only temporary, and there is no transfer from their actual custody, for example, a week-end visit.

Prima facie the answer to marginal cases is important, because anyone who has actual custody but not legal custody nevertheless has 'the like duties in relation to the child as a custodian would have by virtue of his legal custody.'[1] Closer scrutiny shows that this provision is likely to have no practical significance, since there are already other statutory provisions which impose the like duties. Thus, the duty to see that a child receives education extends not only to a parent and guardian but to everyone who has the actual custody of the child.[2] The duty to protect the child from harm is mainly imposed by legislation which binds not only those who have 'custody' but also those who have the 'charge or care' of a child.[3] Under that legislation the duty to maintain is inextricably linked to the duty to protect. Anyone who assumes the custody, charge or care of a child will be criminally liable if he wilfully neglects to provide the child with adequate food, clothing, medical aid and lodging. Thus, while a resident pupil at a boarding school clearly does not have his home at the school, it matters not whether the governing body or a teacher is to be treated as having actual custody within the meaning of section 87(2) of the Children Act 1975: the body and the teacher have the charge (and probably the care) of him for the purpose of the protective legislation.

1   CA 1975, s 87(2).
2   Education Act 1944, ss 36 and 114(1).
3   See CYPA 1933, ss 1(1) and 17.

V   THE EXERCISE AND DISCHARGE OF PARENTAL POWERS AND RESPONSIBILITIES

1   The power of independent action

1.66   Section 1(1) of the Guardianship Act 1973 finally established the principle that in respect of any legitimate child who is a minor the mother has the same 'rights and authority' as the father with regard to the legal custody[1] or upbringing of the child and the administration of his property or the application of the income thereof. As will be seen,[2] in the absence of any enactment or any court order to the contrary, parental rights and duties in relation to the child whose mother and father were not married to each other at the time of his birth reside exclusively in the mother.[3] In establishing the principle of parity the enactment proceeds to undermine it by allowing either parent to exercise his or her rights and authority without any need for the agreement of, consultation with or notification to the other parent. Section 85(3) of the Children Act 1975 has extended this power of independent action by providing that where two or more persons have a parental right or duty jointly either may exercise or perform it in any manner without the other, if the other has not signified disapproval of its exercise or performance in that manner. Thus, the extension will apply to, inter alios, any persons having joint legal custody, whether parents or not. With regard to parents, however, the effect of sub-section (3) is to modify the provisions in the Guardianship Act 1973 by imposing the restriction where there is disapproval;[4] but the scope of the restriction may be limited. The primary object of sub-section (3) is to enable one person to act alone in day to day affairs affecting the child or in any emergency, for example, in consenting to urgent medical treatment, but it does not attempt so to limit its scope. As it stands, the onus appears to be on the other person to signify disapproval. There is no express duty on the one exercising the right or performing the duty to consult or notify, or having regard to the circumstances to take reasonable steps to consult or notify, the other. It is still an open question how far, if at all, the court will imply that duty. Again, the enactment offers no guidance on the question whether a third person must inquire about possible disapproval before he decides to act. The better opinion, it is submitted, is that on practical grounds he should be able to rely on the consent given by the other parent (or other person having the parental right), for 'any other solution would create impossible difficulties for him'.[5]

Section 1 of the Guardianship Act 1973 and section 85(3) of the Children Act 1975 are both subject to the overriding rule that a particular enactment may normally require the consent of both persons.[6] The rule applies to agreement to adoption and consent to marriage.

1   GA 1973, s 1(1) is amended by the DPMCA 1978, s 36, which substitutes 'legal custody' for 'custody'.
2   Post, para 2.46.
3   GA 1973, s 1(7) as prospectively amended by FLRA 1987, s 2(2); CA 1975, s 85(7).
4   It has been argued by Maidment (126 NLJ 1024 and [1981] CLJ 135 at 140–141 and 142) that, in the absence of any court order granting joint custody to parents, s 85(3) does not restrict or qualify the equal and separate rights of either parent which the GA 1973 confers.
5   See *Bromley*, p 261, note 19.
6   GA 1973 s 1(7) expressly recognises this; for s 85(3) this is the necessary implication.

2   Disputes over the exercise and discharge of specific powers and responsibilities

1.67   Where there is disapproval or dispute over the exercise and performance of parental powers and responsibilities one or other of the parents (or other person having those powers and responsibilities) is likely to resort to the court. Usually litigation concerns the whole issue of legal custody (or custody in the divorce court) and/or access to the child. This subject is considered in Chapter 3. The dispute may, however, occasionally relate only to a specific question affecting the child's welfare; for example, in connection with religious upbringing or medical treatment or the vetoing of the issue of a passport. One way in which the matter may be challenged is wardship proceedings.[1] Alternatively, if the dispute is between the mother and father, application can be made to a court under the Guardianship Act 1973[2] for its direction.[3] The objects of the enactment are to enable the court to decide a specific question without any need, as there formerly was, to put in issue the whole question of the child's legal custody and to do so even where the parents are living together. These aims are facilitated by the rule which expressly prevents the court from making an order regarding legal custody or access.[4] Subject to that, the court may make any order it thinks proper and in so doing it is clear that it might apply the principle that the child's welfare is the first and paramount consideration.[5] So far there is no evidence of parents invoking the jurisdiction. Two reasons for this have been advanced.[6] First, if they are not separated, they have no occasion to go to court: if they are separated, the dispute will be over custody and access. Second, the court has no associated powers to make financial provision, and that might be essential to resolving the dispute, for example, over education.

Either parent or, after the death of either, a guardian or, before or after the death of either parent, anyone else having legal custody may apply for the order to be varied or discharged.[7] For example, an order may have been made relating to the upbringing of the child in a particular faith. Later the parents' marriage is dissolved and the divorce court grants custody to neither but instead to relatives. If the relatives only later find out that the religion is proving disturbing to the child, they can apply for variation or discharge of the earlier order made under the Guardianship Act 1973.

Orders under the Act may be made by the High Court or by any county court or magistrates' court which has jurisdiction to hear legal custody disputes under section 9 of the Guardianship of Minors Act 1971.[8]

1   For wardship see post, Chapter 8.
2   GA 1973, s 1(3). Where the mother and father were not married to each other at their child's birth, the rule will, when brought into force, only apply to them if there is in force an order under FLRA 1987, s 4 giving the father all the parental rights and duties or if he has a right to custody, legal or actual custody or care and control of the child by virtue of an order under any other enactment; see GA 1973, s 1(3A), as inserted by FLRA 1987, s 5.
3   A magistrates' court has a similar power under the DPMCA 1978, s 13(1) to settle a dispute between two persons over a parental right or duty which has been given to them jointly by an order made under that Act. Similarly, if joint guardians or joint custodians are in dispute they can refer the matter to the court; see respectively GMA 1971, s 7 and CA 1975, s 38.
4   GA 1973, s 1(4).
5   Although the paramountcy principle is to be applied under GMA 1971, s 1 to matters relating to the legal custody or upbringing or to proprietary matters, whereas GA 1973, s 1(3) speaks of 'any question affecting [the child's] welfare', any such question clearly falls within both the language and spirit of the provision in the 1971 Act.
6   See Law Com, No 96, para 2.3.
7   GA 1973, s 1(5).
8   For that jurisdiction, procedure and appeals see post, Chapter 3.

3   Agreements to surrender or transfer parental powers and responsibilities

1.68   At common law an agreement to surrender parental rights was void.[1] Section 85(2) of the Children Act 1975[2] is wider in its effect. Subject to one exception, it prevents anyone from surrendering or transferring any parental right or *duty* he has 'as respects a child', who, therefore, may not be his own. Thus, the rule will apply where the person who is purporting to transfer a parental right has that right as the result of an order of the court, for example, where he has been granted legal custody by an order. In those circumstances not only is the transfer void but also it will be a good ground for variation or revocation of the legal custody order. The rule also has special significance in relation to surrogacy. A woman who conceives a child as the result of artificial insemination of the sperm of a married man, who is not her husband, cannot be bound by any prenatal agreement made with him and his consenting wife that she will hand over the child to them.[3] The surrender will have to be effected by way of wardship proceedings instituted by the commissioning couple.[4]

The exception permitted by section 85(2) is an agreement between a mother and father (whether or not they are or have been married to each other) which is to operate only during a period when they are not living with each other in the same household. If it provides for the exercise by either of them of any of the parental rights and duties, it is enforceable, unless it is not for their child's benefit—a proviso to be applied in accordance with the general principle that the child's welfare is the paramount consideration.[5]

1   *Vansittart v Vansittart* (1858) 2 De G & J 249; *Walrond v Walrond* (1858) John 18.
2   As prospectively amended by FLRA 1987, s 33(4) and Sch 4.
3   *A v C (1978)* [1985] FLR 445, [1984] Fam Law 241, CA; *Re P (minors) (surrogacy)* [1987] 2 FLR 421, [1987] Fam Law 414. For surrogate parentage see post, paras 2.10 et seq.
4   *Re C (a minor) (wardship: surrogacy)* [1985] FLR 846, [1985] Fam Law 191. For consideration of other possibilities see post, paras 2.16–2.17.
5   GA 1973, s 1(2) as prospectively substituted by FLRA 1987, s 3. Currently the rule is restricted to payments between husbands and wives in respect of their children.
    Apart from this statutory exception, the principle contained in s 85(2) of the Children Act 1975 is also qualified to the extent that the rights and duties of a parent are transmissible on his death in that he is able to appoint a testamentary guardian (GMA 1971, s 4); See Cretney, op cit, p 310.

VI   THE TERMINATION OR SUSPENSION OF PARENTAL POWERS AND RESPONSIBILITIES

1.69   Custody or legal custody or any specific parental power or responsibility may be terminated in any of the following circumstances.

1   Attainment of majority

1.70   The custody (in the wide sense) which a parent has of his or her child automatically ends on the child's eighteenth birthday.[1] Similarly the powers of the Crown as parens patriae, exercised through wardship of court terminate on that date, as does any order of the divorce court vesting custody, or of other courts vesting legal custody, in a person, whether a parent or not.[2]

1   FLRA 1969, ss 1(1) and 9. Even before the attainment of majority, specific parental power or responsibility may, in accordance with the *Gillick* principle, have yielded to the child's right to make his own decisions.
2   See post, Chapters 8 and 3 respectively.

2   Marriage

1.71   Although the matter is far from certain,[1] dicta support the view that marriage, at least of a minor girl[2] and probably so also of a minor boy,[3] terminates custody.

1   See Hall *The Waning of Parental Rights* [1972B] CLJ 248 at 264–265; see also post, para 4.45.
2   See Lord Hardwicke LC in *Mendes v Mendes* (1748) 1 Ves Sen 89 at 91; Sachs LJ in *Hewer v Bryant* [1970] 1 QB 357 at 373, [1969] 3 All ER 578 at 585.
3   See in support Abbott CJ in *R v Wilmington Inhabitants* (1822) 5 B & Ald 525 at 526 and Cassels J in *Lough v Ward* [1945] 2 All ER 338 at 348; contra, *Eyre v Countess of Shaftsbury* (1722) 2 P Wms 102 and Sachs LJ in *Hewer v Bryant*. The uncertainty

is compounded by the fact that some of the dicta refer to natural guardianship and some to testamentary.

3   Military service

1.72   Custody of a minor is suspended so long as he serves in the armed forces.[1]

1   *R v Rotherfield Greys Inhabitants* (1832) 1 B & C 345 at 349–350. Bromley p 270 suggests the rule will apply to a minor engaged in a similar service such as the merchant navy.

4   Death

1.73   On the death of the mother or father, who were married to each other at the date of their child's birth,[1] the surviving parent becomes guardian either alone or jointly with any testamentary guardian appointed by the deceased parent.[2]

Where two or more persons jointly have a parental right or duty and one of them dies, it vests in the survivor(s), either alone or with any testamentary guardian appointed by the deceased parent. If the deceased had the sole right or duty it lapses on his death until someone else lawfully acquires it, for example, under guardianship proceedings.[3]

1   For the position in relation to the child whose parents were not married to each other when their child was born see post, para 2.39.
2   GMA 1971, s 3. The court itself has power to appoint a guardian to act jointly with the survivor either where there is no testamentary guardian or where such a guardian refuses to act, but the power is rarely invoked.
3   CA 1975, s 85(4) and (5). The rules apply in relation to the dissolution of a body corporate as they apply in relation to the death of an individual (sub-s (6)). This point may well have practical relevance where parental rights and duties are vested in a voluntary organisation in accordance with CCA 1980, s 64 and are shared jointly with some person, eg one of the parents.

5   Order of a court

1.74   A person having custody, legal custody or specific parental powers and responsibilities may lose them as a result of an order of the court. This forms the main subject matter of Chapter 3, which deals with disputes over custody. The other main orders which terminate or suspend parental authority are adoption orders, custodianship orders, wardship and care orders.[1] To them must be added the resolution passed by a local authority vesting in itself the parental 'rights and duties'.[2]

1   See respectively Chapters 5, 6, 8, 13 and 14.
2   See Chapter 15, paras 15.14 et seq.

CHAPTER 2
Parentage and parenthood

I INTRODUCTION

2.01 A major, albeit tentative, proposal of the Law Commission in its Review of Child Law is that parenthood should 'become the primary legal concept in the allocation of the responsibility for bringing up a child'.[1] The kinds of responsibility and the complementary and concomitant powers embodied within that concept have already been examined in relation to parents who were married at the time of the birth of their child.[2] Their application to parents not so married is considered later in this chapter.[3] Related to the particular child, this concept and status of parenthood presupposes identification of the parents. Identification, described here as parentage, has until recently given rise very largely to problems relating to the paternity of the child, rarely to maternity.[4] Such are the rapid changes in scientific knowledge and reproductive technology that for the lawyer there can now be problems as difficult over maternity as over paternity. It is as well, therefore, firstly to examine the exceptional methods of procreation.

1 Law Com No 96, para 7.15; Law Com No 172, para 2.3.
2 See ante, paras 1.17 et seq.
3 Post, paras 2.39, et seq.
4 Maternity and paternity are respectively to motherhood and fatherhood as parentage is to parenthood.

II HUMAN ASSISTED REPRODUCTION[1]

1 Introduction

2.02 This advance of science and technology in the field of human fertilisation over the past decade has aroused concern about the social, ethical and legal implications, all of which were the subject of examination by the Warnock Committee. Those affecting legal questions of parentage are our present concern.[2] Artificial insemination, in vitro fertilisation, embryo transfer and surrogacy all raise legal questions of maternity and paternity. Warnock saw 'real dangers in the law intervening too fast and too extensively in areas where there is no clear public consensus'.[3] The enactment of the Family Law Reform Act 1987 will remove some of the legal disabilities so far as they concern the status of the child, but problems of establishing who in law is the mother and/or who is the father also call for urgent legislative action.

1 See generally *Human Fertilisation and Embryology: A Framework for Legislation* (Cm 259);

the Law Com No 118 on Illegitimacy; the Report of the Committee of Inquiry into Human Fertilisation and Embryology (1984) Cmnd 9314 (the 'Warnock Report'); Warnock, *A Question of Life* (1985) (which republishes the Report but with extended comments); Priest (1985) 48 MLR 73 for an appraisal of that Report; Parker, *Legal Aspects of Artificial Insemination and Embryo Transfer* (1982) 12 Fam Law 103; Davies, *Close Encounters in a Test Tube* (1983) 133 NLJ 107; Brahams, *Legal and Social Problems of In Vitro Fertilisation – Why Parliament Must Legislate* (1983) 133 NLJ 859 and 881; Brahams, *Human Embryo Research and the Law* (1987) 137 NLJ 290; Bromley, *Aided conception: the alternative to adoption* in *Adoption, Essays in Social Policy, Law and Sociology* (1984) (Ed Bean). For comparative material see post, para 2.10 note 2, and for an early legislative attempt to tackle the area see the Infertility (Medical Procedures) Act 1984 (State of Victoria).

2 For the wider legal implications, especially those relating to the use of human embryos for scientific research see Chapters 9 to 13 of the Warnock Report, and for jurisprudential comments thereon see Jones, *Research on Human Embryos. The Ethics of Pragmatism* (1985) Professional Negligence 19; Parkin, *Research on Human Embryos: A Search for Principle* ibid at p 164; and Baroness Warnock, *The Enforcement of Morals in the Light of New Developments in Embryology* (1986) 39 Current Legal Problems 17 (who describes research on embryos as 'the most philosophically interesting of the issues raised' by her Committee). The Department of Health and Social Security issued a Consultative Paper inviting comments on the proposals for legislation of the Warnock Committee relating inter alia to the need for a statutory licensing authority, counselling of infertile couples, the legal status of children born as a result of artificial insemination and egg or embryo donation, anonymity of donors and information to children about their genetic origin, surrogacy and, the most controversial topic, research involving embryos. For a comparative examination of the difficulties surrounding that research see Kasimba (1986) 60 ALJ 675. In reply to a Parliamentary question (HC Debs 24 February 1987, col 153) it was reported that the Medical Research Council and the Royal College of Obstetricians and Gynaecologists have approved a research project into genetic handicap which necessitates the use of the human embryo. About the same time (March 1987) the Vatican issued a Paper uncompromisingly rejecting inter alia all experiments with fertilised embryos and any medical techniques which treat such embryos as being less than human. A month later the Voluntary Licensing Authority for Human In Vitro Fertilisation (an Authority sponsored by the Medical Research Council and the Royal College of Obstetricians and Gynaecologists) was reporting that human assisted reproduction offered 'the only hope of children of their own' for some 275,000 infertile couples aged between 24 and 35 in the United Kingdom.

In its White Paper (Cm 259), para 30, the Government has offered Parliament a choice between one of two options. The one would make it a criminal offence to do anything to a human embryo except with the intention of preparing it for transfer to a woman's uterus or of ascertaining its suitability for transfer. The other would allow embryo research but strictly licensed by the Statutory Licensing Authority which it is proposed should be set up.

3 Paragraph 1.9.

2   Artificial insemination

2.03 This method has been practised for many years,[1] with a marked increase in demand for it in the seventies and eighties.[2] It has also from time to time been the subject of various inquiries.[3] Yet, it still remains largely unregulated by the law.[4] Artificial insemination of a married woman with her husband's semen (AIH) has for some time been recognised as an acceptable form of treatment, at least for some married couples,[5] for example, where the husband is severely physically disabled and thus unable to achieve intercourse. It poses few legal problems. Conceived of both spouses, the child is a child of the marriage[6] and parenthood automatically attaches to both of them. Difficulties could arise, however, especially over rights of succession, if the husband's semen were frozen and insemination postponed until after his death. A child conceived naturally but born posthumously is entitled to succeed to his father's estate. But would the posthumous insemination and therefore conception deprive him of those rights, or would the conception be allowed to operate in law retrospectively to a moment immediately before his father's death? And is there any time limit to be imposed on posthumous insemination? It may be that, in the absence of statutory regulation, the court would be inclined to treat the child in those circumstances as being fatherless for purposes of rights of succession. Such is the possible abuse of posthumous insemination in order to defeat or modify rights of succession already vested in other members of the family that it seems wisest as a general principle to adopt the recommendation of the Warnock Committee that any child born by AIH who was not *in utero* at the date of the father's death should be disregarded for the purposes of succession to and inheritance from the father.[7] However, in order to give effect to a couple's bona fide wishes for posthumous insemination, an exception to that general principle might be allowed where the husband or male cohabitee stated those wishes in a will.[8] If those wishes were carried out the law should allow the child rights of succession.[9] After all in such circumstances what greater possession can a person transmit than his own line of succession?

1   For a neat summary of its history see Parker, op cit.
2   It is provided both privately and by the National Health Service. See Warnock, para 4.8.
3   See the Report of a Commission appointed by the Archbishop of Canterbury (Society for the Propagation of Christian Knowledge, 1948); the Report of a Departmental Committee (under the Chairmanship of the Earl of Feversham), HMSO, 1960 (Cmnd 1105); the Report of a Panel of the British Medical Association (under the Chairmanship of Sir John Peel), British Medical Journal Supplement, 1973, 7 April, Vol II.
4   But see infra the Family Law Reform Act 1987, s 27.
5   The Feversham Committee so regarded it.
6   If the marriage has not been consummated because there has not been an act of natural intercourse, AIH does not consummate it; *REL v EL* [1949] P 211, [1949] 1 All ER 141. But any reliance on impotence as a ground for nullity would almost certainly be met by the defence of 'approbation' of the marriage; see MCA 1973, s 13(1).
7   See Warnock Report, para 10.9. See also Bromley, op cit, at pp 175–176.
8   For example, made after he was injured in an accident and was terminally ill.
9   Compare to similar effect the recommendation of the First Report of the New South Wales Law Reform Commission, *Human Artificial Insemination* (1986); and note the *Parpalaix Case*, discussed at (1984) 58 ALJ 627. For the problems of succession by posthumous children in the New South Wales context see Atherton (1986) 60 ALJ 374.

2.04   These are exceptional possibilities. The problems relating to AID are more direct and immediate. By this method the wife is inseminated with semen from a donor other than her husband. There is no doubt that English law will follow Scots law in holding that AID is not an act of adultery,[1] although, if it were to take place without her husband's consent, that is highly likely to be behaviour justifying divorce proceedings.[2] However, in most cases AID is with his consent and has been arranged because of his sterility or, less frequently, because of the risk of his carrying an inheritable disorder such as Huntington's disease. Hitherto the worst consequences of illegitimacy have in practice been avoided, because the husband has treated the child as a child of the family, indeed as his own child. Usually, too, the donor is anonymous. So, the possibility of his being subject to affiliation proceedings has been avoided. Even if his identity was known, for example, in the rare case of a relative, that possibility was excluded by the fact that the mother could not qualify as a 'single woman', since she, as a married woman, would scarcely be likely to be living apart from her consenting husband, either at the time of the child's birth or when she was considering commencing the proceedings.[3] Section 27(1) of the Family Law Reform Act 1987[4] removes such difficulties by providing that a child born in England and Wales, after the new provision comes into force,[4a] to a married woman as the result of AID will be treated as a child of the parties to the marriage and of no-one else, unless it is proved 'to the satisfaction of any court' that the husband did not consent to the insemination.[5] The parties must be validly married at the date of the insemination, except that the rule also extends to a void marriage, provided that at that date both or either of the parties reasonably believed that the marriage was valid.[5a] There is a presumption that one of the parties so believed.[6] Although the 1987 Act does not spell it out, the consequence of section 27 is that, if the husband can prove that he did not consent, the child must be treated as fatherless since, but for a rare case, the donor will not be known. But where he is known he must, it is submitted, be treated as the father.[7] Surprisingly, the Act fails to impose any obligation to explain to the parties to the marriage the full consequences of giving consent.[8] Nor does it expressly state that the consent has to be freely given and with full understanding of the consequences of doing so. These omissions compare sharply with the statutory provisions relating to parental agreement to adoption.[9]

1   *MacLennan v MacLennan* 1958 SC 105, 1958 SLT 12.
2   See MCA 1973, s 1(2)(b).
3   To qualify as a single woman she had to be living apart from her husband and lost the right to be maintained by him because of her adultery or desertion. See *Jones v Evans* [1944] KB 582, [1945] 1 All ER 189; *Mooney v Mooney* [1953] 1 QB 38, [1952] 2 All ER 812.
4   The Act gives effect to a proposal of the Law Commission (Law Com No 118, para 12.9) which the Warnock Committee (para 4.17) supported.
4a Ie 4 April 1988.
5   *Semble*, the presumption that the child is the child of both parties is rebuttable on a balance of probabilities. The subsection refers to "the other party" to the marriage. This takes account of the possibility of the marriage being void. A rule similar to s 27(1) has a longer history in the USA. First introduced into the State of Georgia in 1964, it has been copied by many other States (see Wadlington, (1983) 69 Virginia L Rev 465 at p 483). But it differs from s 27(1) in that it imposes a positive duty on the spouses to give their written consent to AID. If they do so, the child is irrebuttably treated as their own.
5a Whether there is a valid marriage or not, the child is barred from succeeding to, or transmitting a right to, any dignity or title of honour (s 27(3)).
6   Section 27(2). Compare the Legitimacy Act 1976, s 1, post, para 2.26, which has been amended by FLRA 1987, s 28(2) so as to provide for a corresponding presumption.
7   So, too, if the woman is unmarried and the donor's identity is known. Apparently, some practitioners are willing to inseminate an unmarried woman living in a stable heterosexual relationship (Bromley, op cit, p 177). In those circumstances the donor will be able to seek an order under FLRA 1987, s 4 vesting in him all the parental rights and duties jointly with the mother. Alternatively, if they should separate he might seek custody or access; and the mother could seek maintenance from him. See further post, para 2.46. These possibilities will arise when Part II of the Act is brought into force.
8   Instead of patients at clinics are given an advisory booklet on *Artificial Insemination*, produced by the Royal College of Obstetricians and Gynaecologists.
9   See post, para 5.21. Another difference from adoption is that, unlike the adopted child (see ibid, para 5.99), the child born as the result of AID is not entitled on attaining the age of majority to have access to basic information about his origin, for example, about the donor's ethnic origin. The Warnock Committee (para 4.21) recommended that he should be so entitled.
    During the passage of the Family Law Reform Bill 1986–87 amendments to the effect that a birth certificate have the words 'By donation' endorsed on it or that the father

be named when possible were moved unsuccessfully; see HL Debs, 11 December 1986, col 1281; 10 February, col 544.

AID and AIDS

2.05 In the longer term what is more significant about the 1987 Act is its silence on some of the wider implications of AID for the child, the parents, the doctor and the donor. The omission is to be explained on the ground that the Act was only concerned with removing the disadvantages of illegitimacy so far as they affect the child, and is consistent with Parliamentary reluctance to intervene in this area, notwithstanding the recommendation of the Warnock Committee that 'AID should no longer be left in a legal vacuum but should be subject to certain conditions and safeguards and receive the protection of the law'.[1] However, the spread of the disease of AIDS and its fatal consequences may compel Parliamentary intervention sooner than many have wished or expected.[2] The risks of semen being infected with the disease will impose on those providing AID services, whether as recipient of semen donation or as the doctor performing the operation of artificial insemination, a high standard of safeguards if liability for negligence to the mother, the consenting husband and the child is to be avoided. That standard is more likely to be achieved if there is a statutory body licensing clinics or agencies that provide AID services, and the missed opportunity of including in the 1987 Act a provision therefor may be regretted.[3] Given the system of anonymity of donation, a remedy against the donor will not be available to the mother and husband, unless a system of 'discovery' is permitted.[4] If it is not permitted, it will be left to those providing the service to seek a remedy against him. That will depend upon the terms of the contract between them and the donor and its validity. It should provide for comprehensive screening of the donor. But that raises questions about not only his health but also his personal record and sexual associations, together with the need to provide counselling service for him in case it should be discovered that he is suffering from AIDS. If those providing the service are to protect themselves from liability for negligence, they should, it is submitted, insist on maximum disclosure by the donor. The contract should, in effect, be *uberrimae fidei*. Answers to these speculative questions[5] should, it is suggested, no longer be left to the occasional accidents of litigation: they require firm legislative guidance.

1 Paragraph 4.16. The Law Commission is rather more cautious and would prefer some delay until a comprehensive scheme can be legislated; see Law Com on Illegitimacy (Second Report) No 157, para 3.20.
2 Apparently, the immediate effect of discovery of AIDS has been the curtailment of the use of AID.
3 A clause so providing was unsuccessfully introduced by Lord Denning during the Third Reading of the Bill in the House of Lords; see HL Debs, 10 February 1987, col 560. The British Pregnancy Advisory Service has warned that all donors should be screened for the possibility of suffering from AIDS. Yet, as the law stands, there is nothing, for example, to prevent a childless woman from advertising in a newspaper for a sperm donor.
4 Bromley, op cit, p 181, states that in any action by the mother against the doctor she could force him to disclose the identity of the donor and produce the notes of any history he took; the donor himself could be called as a witness; or, indeed, the doctor could bring the donor in as a third party. Arguably the court has a discretion as to the extent to which it will allow such matters. It is suggested that, since the anonymity of the donor is essential in AID, statutory provision should be made for separate proceedings by parent against doctor and doctor against donor.

5   For others see Parker, op cit, p 104; and for discussion generally of the possible liability of the medical practitioner and the donor to the mother and her husband see Bromley op cit, pp 179–182.

3   In vitro fertilisation

2.06   Although it is almost ten years since the first child was born as a result of the reproductive technique known as in vitro fertilisation (IVF),[1] there is still no legislation on it, and the opportunity to provide it was turned down when enacting the Family Law Reform Act 1987.[2] The technique may take different forms.[3]

1   Literally 'in glass'; hence the popular description 'test tube baby'. Louise Brown was the first in July 1978.
2   In spite of efforts by members of the House of Lords to introduce it. But the government has apparently changed its mind and in the Parliamentary Session 1988–89 or, as seems more likely, 1989–90 intends to introduce legislation to implement Warnock. See the White Paper (Cm 259).
3   For a wide ranging discussion see P Singer and D Wells, *The Reproduction Revolution* (1984).

(a)   Without the donation of ova

2.07   Warnock describes the technique:[1]

'The concept of IVF is simple. A ripe human egg is extracted from the ovary, shortly before it would have been released naturally. Next, the egg is mixed with the semen of the husband or partner, so that fertilisation can occur. The fertilised egg, once it has started to divide, is then transferred back to the mother's uterus.

Often more than one embryo is transferred to the potential mother, thereby giving a better chance of achieving a pregnancy.[2] Where the semen is provided by the husband, the process may be seen, like AIH, as an extension of the process of reproduction by spouses and the child is thus a child of the marriage.[3]

1   Paragraph 5.2; and see 5.3–5.4.
2   For legal difficulties concerning abortion which may arise from the multiple transfer of embryos see post, para 9.20.
3   See ante, para 2.03. For the effect if the marriage is void see Legitimacy Act 1976, s 1, as amended by FLRA 1987, s 28(2) post, para 2.25.

(b)   With the donation of ova

2.08   This form of IVF involves two 'mothers' – the genetic and the mother who gives birth to the child. A mature egg from a fertile donor is fertilised in vitro using the semen of the husband of the infertile woman. The resulting embryo is transferred to the wife's uterus and if it implants she may then carry the pregnancy to term. In practice the donor is anonymous, as in AID. The Family Law Reform Act 1987 does not regulate the parentage. The answer seems obvious. The statutory principle now governing AID should correspondingly apply. Assuming that the mother who gives birth and her husband who provides the semen jointly consent to the IVF, the child should be treated as a child of both of them and of no-one else. It is submitted that, if the parentage were to be tested in court, the court would apply the analogy to be drawn from AID,[1] but it is to be regretted that the Act does not expressly cover the point.

1 This conclusion was supported by Warnock; see para 6.6.

(c) Embryo donation

2.09 This process involves donation both of ova and semen, and is intended for the case where both spouses are infertile. A donated egg is fertilised in vitro with donated semen and the resulting embryo transferred to the infertile wife. Here, too, Warnock recommends that the child should be treated as a child of the infertile spouses, subject, as with AID and other forms of IVF, to safeguards such as anonymity and a system of licensing and regulation.[1] It would, it is suggested, be open to the courts to reach this conclusion, and strong persuasive analogy can now be drawn from section 27(1) of the Family Law Reform Act 1987, with its recognition of the parentage of the spouses where the child is born as the result of AID.[2] A contrary view would mean that the child is in law parentless and the de facto 'parents' would be obliged to rely on the cumbersome artificiality of adoption.

1 See paras 7.6 and 7.7.
2 See ante, para 2.04. This point, too, should have been covered by the Act.

Embryo storage

2.10 When dealing with AID an indication was given of the kinds of legal problems relating to succession on death which could occur where the husband's semen was frozen and there was posthumous insemination of his widow. Similar problems could arise where there is a transfer of embryos to the woman after her husband's death. But the storage of embryos raises much wider issues. It has been pointed out[1] that there are an estimated 10,000 embryos stored around the world, of which some 3,000 are kept in Britain and a similar number in France. Practice may vary in the use of embryos. Should there be a maximum permitted period of storage? What should happen to the embryos if, for example, the parents show no further interest in the embryos after the first occasion of IVF treatment? What kinds of restrictions, if any, should be imposed on the contract made between patient and clinic.[2] And what measures, if any, should be taken to prevent international trading in embryos?[3] Such issues illustrate the need to expedite legislation on IVF.

1 See the Guardian (1987) 5 October.
2 Apparently at the Bourn Hall Clinic, Cambridge, patients sign a two year contract for their frozen embryos. At the end of that period they can renegotiate to keep them on ice, donate them to women unable to produce eggs of their own, or allow them to be used for research.
3 In this context see the Surrogacy Arrangements Act 1985, post, para 2.13. The *Independent* newspaper has produced a useful survey on IVF clinics (1987).

4 Surrogacy

2.11 Factual problems rarely arise over identifying the mother of a child, but occasionally in hospital births mothers may be handed over the wrong babies, and, if that should happen, maternity would, if possible, have to be determined by blood or other scientific tests of the babies and the persons who could be the mother and father of each.[1] Legal questions, on the other hand, arise where the identity of the woman who gave birth to the child is not in doubt, but her role is intended to be surrogate. The availability of AID, IVF and embryo transfer (ET) has increased[2] the practice of surrogacy whereby one woman, the 'surrogate mother', carries a child for another, the 'commissioning woman', with the intention that the child should be handed over after birth. The complexities of the subject have excited international concern, especially in the Commonwealth and the USA,[3] but there is a significant reluctance to reach firm conclusions on the extent of legal recognition.[4]

1 There is also the possibility of persons passing off a supposititious child as their own; see Bromley, op cit, p 246, citing *Slingsby v A-G* (1916) 33 TLR 120, HL.
2 Though surrogacy as a result of intercourse has apparently a long history; see Genesis, Chapter 16 (for the activities of Abram) and Chapter 30 (Jacob).
3 For England and Wales see Parker, *Surrogate Mothering: An Overview* [1984] Fam Law 140; Morgan, *Who to Be or Not to Be: The Surrogacy Story* (1986) 49 MLR 358 (and the copious references therein); Morgan, *Surrogacy: Giving it an Understood Name,* [1988] JSWL 216; Dickens, *Surrogate Motherhood: Legal and Legislative Issues in Genetics and the Law III* (edited by Milunsky and Annas) (1985); Freeman, *After Warnock – Whither the Law?* (1986) 39 Current Legal Problems 33; Montgomery, *Surrogacy and the Best Interests of the Child* [1986] Fam Law 59; Wright *Surrogacy and Adoption: Problems and Possibilities,* [1986] Fam Law 109; Payne, *The Regulation of Surrogate Motherhood* [1987] Fam Law 178; Harding, *The Debate on Surrogate Motherhood* [1987] JSWL 37. Considerable attention has been given to the subject in Australia. See, for example, in Victoria the Waller Report on the *Disposition of Embryos Produced by In Vitro Fertilisation* (1984); the Queensland Special Committee on the *Laws Relating to Artificial Insemination, In Vitro Fertilisation and Other Related Matters* (1984); the South Australian Working Party on *In Vitro Fertilisation and Artificial Insemination by Donor* (1984); the First Report of the New South Wales Law Reform Commission on *Issues for Reform with respect to Human Artificial Insemination* (1984) and Sappideen, *The Surrogate Mother – A Growing Problem* (1983) 6 UNSW Law Jo 79; in Tasmania the Report of a Committee on *Artificial Conception and Related Matters* (1985); and for a review of developments in Australia and USA see Waller (1984), 10 Monash ULR 113; Krause, (1985) 19 FLQ 185. In New Zealand the Department of Justice produced a Paper on *New Birth Techniques; an Issues Paper on AID, IVF and Surrogate Motherhood* (1985); and in Canada the Ontario Law Reform Commission produced a Report on *Human Artificial Reproduction and Related Matters* (1985).
    The literature on the subject in the USA is prolific. The following serve as a small sample: Terry, *'Alas! Poor Yorick,' I knew him ex utero: the regulation of embryo and fetal experimentation and disposal in England and the United States* (1986) 39 Vanderbilt L Rev 419; Brown *et al, Legal Rights and Issues Surrounding Conception, Pregnancy and Birth* (1986) 39 Vanderbilt L Rev 597-850; and for a wide-ranging review of the constitutional issues raised by new developments in the subject see Robertson, *Procreative Liberty and the Control of Conception, Pregnancy and Childbirth* (1983) 69 Virginia L Rev 405.
4 Hence the wide interest shown in 1986 and 1987 in the case (*Stern v Whitehead*) before a New Jersey Court, where enforcement of a commercial agreement against the surrogate mother was ordered at first instance, but reversed on appeal; see (1988) NJ LEXIS, 3 February. Although the agreement was held to be void, an order was made giving custody to the commissioning couple because that was in the child's best interests.

2.12 The surrogacy may be the result of several possibilities,[1] but the form most frequently used is that in which the surrogate mother's egg is fertilised through artificial insemination of the semen of the commissioning woman's husband.[2] The main alternative to this 'partial surrogacy' is probably the process of 'total surrogacy' whereby the commissioning woman's own egg is fertilised in vitro by the sperm of her husband and the resultant embryo is transferred and implants in the surrogate mother.[3] In the case of partial surrogacy there can be no doubt as to maternity. As the genetic and the carrying mother, the surrogate is in law the mother. Prior to the Family Law Reform Act 1987 there was also no doubt that the commissioning woman's husband, as the genetic father, was in law the father. That remains the position where the surrogate mother is unmarried, but where she is married the child is, by virtue of section 27 of that Act,[4] a child of the surrogate mother and her husband, unless it is shown that he did not consent to her artificial insemination. However, uncertainty surrounds the question of maternity where there is a total surrogacy, with the commissioning woman as the genetic mother and the surrogate the carrying mother. Warnock recommended that in all cases of egg donation the woman giving birth should for all purposes be regarded in law as the mother.[5] On that basis the question of recognition and enforceability of the surrogacy arrangement arises if the surrogate mother refuses to hand over the baby to the commissioning couple.[6]

1 See Warnock Report, para 8.1; Brahams, 133 NLJ at p 860. Some of the techniques are so simple that medical supervision can be avoided (see Independent (1987), 26 February). This facility frustrates legislative attempts to outlaw the practice.
2 It has been reported that some 500 babies have been born in the USA through this process over the past ten years; see Times (1987), 28 January.
3 There are no detailed statistics, but pregnancy of a surrogate by this method was announced by doctors in Los Angeles in November 1986; and for a case in South Africa in 1987 see post, para 2.15, note 3.
4 See ante, para 2.04.
5 Paragraph 6.8. The Surrogacy Arrangements (Amendment) Bill 1985–86, would have so enacted. Brahams, 133 NLJ at p 881 argues that the presumption that the carrying mother is the legal mother should be rebuttable on evidence of intention before implantation. The surrogate is 'in the position of a wet-nurse suckling another's offspring'.
6 Post, para 2.13.

2.13 It is clear that English law has set itself firmly against the commercial exploitation of surrogate maternity. The much publicised 'Baby Cotton' case[1] aroused such deep moral indignation[2] that the Surrogacy Arrangements Act 1985 reached the statute book unimpeded and unamended during its Parliamentary process. It makes it an offence for a person to be involved in negotiating or making a surrogacy arrangement on a commercial basis.[3] The Act is aimed at commercial surrogacy agencies,[4] and it also prohibits the advertising of surrogacy services.[5] To be caught by the Act the arrangement must be made before the surrogate mother begins to carry the child, and it must be made with a view to the child being handed over to, and the parental rights being exercised (so far as practicable) by, another person or persons. It applies to a partial and total surrogacy.[6] The payment will usually be in money, but may be in money's worth (for example, provision of free luxury accommodation during the pregnancy), and it may be paid either direct to the surrogate or for her benefit (for example, payment to trustees). The penalties for involvement in a surrogacy arrangement are imprisonment for up to three months or a fine not exceeding level 5 (currently £2,000) or both, and for unlawful advertising a fine not exceeding that level.[7] The consent of the Director of Public Prosecutions is necessary for prosecution. An information can be laid up to two years after the commission of the offence and not restricted to the usual period of six months.

1   Reported as *Re C (a minor) (wardship: surrogacy)* [1985] FLR 846, [1985] Fam Law 191.
    For the background to the case see Cotton and Winn, *Baby Cotton: For Love or Money*
    (1985).
2   The fact that the surrogacy arrangement had been made through a foreign commercial
    agency (based in the United States) appears to have exacerbated the indignation.
3   See ss 1 and 2. The Act gives effect to a recommendation of the Warnock Committee
    (para 8.18). See generally Sloman, 135 NLJ 978.
4   It follows that a charitable agency would not be caught by the Act. The Act has been
    criticised on the ground that it will drive surrogacy underground and so benefit no-one
    except illegal profiteers; see Freeman, *Children's Rights in Surrogacy,* Childright (1985)
    April No 16, p 8.
5   Section 3. The prohibition extends to all forms of advertisement, whether for example,
    in a newspaper or a journal or in a shop window or by telecommunication.
6   Section 1(6).
7   Section 4.

2.14   Although the prohibition on advertising extends to the surrogate
mother and to the commissioning couple, as it does to anyone else, those
persons are excluded from liability for their participation in a commercial
surrogacy arrangement.[1] But the 1985 Act offers no guidance on the legal
relationship between them and the possible validity of a surrogacy
arrangement. On the contrary, the Act is ambiguous in its provision[2] that
it 'applies to arrangements whether or not they are lawful and whether
or not they are enforceable by or against any of the persons making them'.
That can mean either that the liability imposed by the Act applies whether
or not such arrangements can ever be lawful and enforceable, a matter
for which the Act does not legislate, or it applies even though the Act
impliedly recognises that in some circumstances, whatever they be, an
arrangement would be valid and enforceable, whereas in others it would
not. The answer must, therefore, be found outside the Act.[3]

1   See s 2(2). Section 2 (2)(b) excludes the person who commissions the surrogate mother
    to carry the child 'for him'. Presumably this is intended to be construed in accordance
    with the Interpretation Act 1978 and applies as much to the commissioning woman as
    her husband.
2   Section 1(9).
3   The Surrogacy Arrangements (Amendment) Bill 1985–86 (which passed through all stages
    in the House of Lords) would have rendered unlawful all surrogacy arrangements whether
    made with a view to payment or not. That view has already been adopted in the State
    of Victoria; see the Infertility (Medical Procedures) Act 1984.

2.15   The first reported case to consider the possible validity of a surrogacy
agreement was *A v C*[1] There a man and his prospective wife, a divorced
woman who was unable to have any further children of her own, arranged
with C, a 19-year-old woman, that she would, for a fee, be artificially
inseminated with the man's semen and would hand over the baby to them.
However, when the baby was born she refused to do so, having at no
time accepted any payment from them. In subsequent wardship proceedings
the man applied for care and control, but on advice withdrew the application
at the hearing and applied for access. Although Comyn J found the
agreement to be contrary to public policy which the parties could not rely
upon or enforce in any way, he granted the father access. However, so
strong was its disapproval of the arrangement that the Court of Appeal
refused access on the ground that in the interests of the child the
circumstances warranted a clean break from the father. Nevertheless, it
is to be noted that the judicial strictures were directed at the essentially

commercial nature of the arrangement.[2] It is arguable, therefore, that *A v C* is not a binding authority for the proposition that an arrangement which does not involve a monetary payment is also unenforceable; for example, a family arrangement in which the surrogate mother may be a close relative of the commissioning couple.[3] With regard to a non-commercial arrangement the answer depends on whether or not the surrogate, carrying mother is married. If she is, then, as already noted,[4] the child is a child of her and her husband, unless it is shown that he did not consent to the insemination. Consequently, she has no power to surrender any 'parental right or duty'[5] and any agreement with the commissioning father which purports to do so would be void. Where, however, she is not married, the restriction on her power to surrender is prospectively modified by section 1(2) of the Guardianship Act 1973, as amended by the Family Law Reform Act 1987.[6] The agreement between her and the commissioning father for the transfer of her parental rights and duties will be enforceable unless the court considers that it will not be for the benefit of the child. For reasons which subsequently appear[7] it is more likely than not that the court will not see it as beneficial for the child to be removed from the surrogate mother. However, the operation of section 1(2) presupposes that the agreement is intrinsically valid, but it seems more likely that all surrogacy agreements will be held by the courts to be contrary to public policy.[8] Clearly the matter ought to be covered by legislation.

1   Although decided in 1978, it was not reported until 1985, see [1985] FLR 445; [1984] Fam Law 241, CA. Earlier comments (eg see Morgan, op cit, pp 363 and 365) based on a note of the decision in (1978) 8 Fam Law 170 and on transcripts of the judgments must therefore be treated with caution.
2   'A purported contract for the sale and purchase of a child' (Comyn J); 'a bizarre and unnatural agreement' (Ormrod LJ); 'a baby farming operation of a wholly distasteful and lamentable kind' (Cumming-Bruce LJ).
3   As in the *Crozier* case in France, reported in Times (1983) 29 April, where the surrogate was the twin sister of the commissioning woman. For a remarkable case of surrogacy by way of embryo donation where the surrogate was the mother of the commissioning woman, see Mail on Sunday 5 and 12 April 1987.
4   Ante, paras 2.04 and 2.12.
5   See CA 1975, s 85(2), prospectively amended by FLRA 1987, Sch 4.
6   See s 3, substituting a new s 1(2) in the 1973 Act.
7   Infra, para 2.16.
8   The Warnock Committee, para 8.19, so recommended.

2.16   Accordingly, where the surrogate mother is unwilling to hand over the child, the remedy of the commissioning couple must be found outside any enforceability of the arrangement. If it lies anywhere, it lies in wardship proceedings, with the commissioning couple seeking care and control; and, as in other disputed wardship and custody cases, the decision will be governed by the principle that the child's welfare is paramount.[1] As will be seen,[2] the commissioning couple start at an immense disadvantage, given the heavy insistence the courts place on the desirability of a very young child normally being brought up by his mother.[3] However, in deciding what is best for the child, it seems clear from *Re C*[4] that the matter is not to be approached from the point that the child was produced as a result of a surrogacy arrangement. Its commercial aspects and its ethical, moral and social implications are not relevant to the decision what is now best for the child. Certainly, on the authority of *Re C*, that is so where the commissioning couple are seeking care and control and the mother is willing to hand over the child.[5] There is no justification for approaching the problem differently where she is not. But, where she is willing, the advantages are very much on the side of the couple. Provided they can show that they are loving, caring and responsible and have the means to bring up the child, they are very likely to be granted care and control, especially as the court not only retains the residual powers and responsibilities but also may make a supervision order placing the child under the supervision of a welfare officer or of a local authority, where exceptionally it considers that appropriate.[6]

Where, however, the mother is unwilling to hand over the child, it would be exceptional for a court to compel her to do so. The point was forcefully illustrated by the decision of the President of the Family Division in wardship proceedings[7] to allow twins to remain with their surrogate mother, Mrs P, who had changed her mind and with whom the children had become bonded in the six months after their birth. Exceptional circumstances where the court, in accordance with the principle of the paramountcy of the child's welfare, might order the mother to hand over the child include cases where her motive for refusal is revenge or financial extortion *and* her record or capacity for parenthood is contrary to the child's best interests. But the lesson is clear – the position of the commissioning couple is precarious.

1   Guardianship of Minors Act 1971, s 1.
2   Post, paras 3.06 et seq.
3   See ibid.
4   [1985] FLR 846, ante, para 2.13.
5   Thus, the questionable motives of the commissioning couple (for example, where the surrogacy was arranged because the wife was unwilling to give up time for the pregnancy) will only be relevant in so far as they are likely to affect the child's welfare.
6   Family Law Reform Act 1969, s 7(4).
7   Reported in the national press on 13 March 1987. The President delivered his judgment in open court following a three day hearing in chambers. The case which may be referred to as 'the twin babies P Case' is a neat illustration of the privacy and confidentiality of wardship proceedings, and compares strikingly with the undesirable publicity which attended the hearing at first instance of the Baby M Case in the USA (ante, para 2.11, note 4) but of which, happily, the appellate process seems to have been free.

2.17   Is wardship the only possibility open to the commissioning couple where the mother refuses to hand over the child? The husband of the commissioning woman could, as the genetic and thus the legal father, seek legal custody under section 9 of the Guardianship of Minors Act 1971,[1] but his application would encounter the same difficulties as an application for wardship.[2] If he were successful and the child was handed over under the order, it would then be possible for his commissioning wife to apply, with his consent, for a custodianship order under the Children Act 1975.[3] But would they then both have legal custody, even though under different orders?[4] The answer depends on section 44 of that Act, which reads:

'(1) While a custodianship order has effect in relation to a child the right of any person other than the custodian to legal custody of the child is suspended, but, subject to any further order made by any court, revives on the revocation of the custodianship order.

(2) Subsection (1) does not apply where the person already having custody is a parent of the child and the person who becomes custodian

under the order is the husband or wife of the parent; and in such a case the spouses have the legal custody jointly.'

Prior to the Family Law Reform Act 1987 the father of an illegitimate child was not a parent,[5] since the powers and responsibilities of a parent did not vest in him on the child's birth. Notwithstanding the 'general principle' laid down by section 1,[6] the Act makes no change in this regard, and, if the father is to exercise those powers and responsibilities, he still has to obtain an appropriate order of the court.[7] It follows, therefore, that, since he is not a parent, subsection (2) of section 44 of the 1975 Act is excluded, and joint legal custody in the above circumstances is not possible.

1 See post, para 3.15.
2 Supra, para 2.16.
3 See s 33(3), post, para 6.02.
4 The possibility that this question can even arise speaks volumes for the complexity of child law.
5 Re M (an infant) [1955] 2 QB 479, [1955] 2 All ER 911.
6 Post, para 2.46.
7 Ie an order for custody or (when the section is brought into force) an order under s 4 of FLRA 1987.

2.18 Where the surrogate mother hands over the child, the best solution is adoption of the child by the commissioning couple, if the mother is agreeable.[1] That would be available where the surrogacy was a family or other non-profit making arrangement; but a commercial arrangement would offend section 57 of the Adoption Act 1976,[2] which makes payments in consideration of adoption unlawful,[3] and would bar the making of an adoption order.[4] The emphasis here lies on the commercial aspects, as is illustrated by *Re Adoption Application*[5] *(Payment for Adoption)*. There applicants for adoption had earlier entered into a surrogacy arrangement under which £10,000 was to be paid to the surrogate mother. The court found that there was no written contract, lawyers were not consulted and only £5,000 was in fact paid. It was held that the arrangement was one of trust and lacked the commercial or profit-making evils at which section 50 of the Adoption Act 1958 was aimed. It is submitted that this interpretation is difficult to justify in the face of the wording of the section which speaks of 'any payment or reward'.[6] Nevertheless, the decision is a welcome lifeline for the future of private, especially family, surrogacy arrangements. In any event the bona fide motives of the parties were such that Latey J was willing to authorise the payments retroactively by the exercise of his discretion under section 50(3) of the 1958 Act.[7]

1 If she is not, the commissioning couple might proceed with an adoption application and seek to persuade the court to dispense with the mother's agreement. Alternatively and possibly preferably they might initially seek care and control under wardship and later apply for adoption.
2 Formerly s 50 of the Adoption Act 1958.
3 See post, para 5.96.
4 AA 1976, s 24(2).
5 [1987] Fam 81, [1987] 2 All ER 826.
6 See now AA 1976, s 57(1).
7 See now AA 1976, s 57(3).

2.19   The availability of wardship, with its governing principle of the paramountcy of the child's welfare, and of adoption within the limits already noted, may prove an inducement to the Legislature, and meantime to the courts, not to hurry to countenance surrogacy arrangements and directly enforce them. It has been firmly suggested[1], that, like adoption, surrogacy should be the subject of regulation, but the Legislature may be reluctant to construct a legal labyrinth. Regulations which would assess the commissioning couple as prospective parents along the lines of the present Regulations which are designed to assess prospective adopters[2] are certainly feasible. They could also provide for surrogacy to be supervised and medically certified by registered clinics.[2a] They could impose the restriction that the mother receive only expenses incurred during and incidental to her pregnancy. But other Regulations to control her may be difficult to frame and enforce. It is difficult to see, for example, how they could prescribe, at least on the request of the commissioning couple, that she does not during her pregnancy smoke or take alcohol or drugs or otherwise so act as potentially to harm the child; and how the conditions could effectively be enforced; and what the consequences would be of any breach. Obviously answers will partly depend on the efficacy of screening and supervision by the registered clinics, assuming that they were compulsorily made part of any scheme. This much is already clear. Until Parliament intervenes by prohibiting or regulating the practice,[3] the eyes of a commissioning couple should be fully opened to the pitfalls. As Latey J has observed, the path of surrogacy is 'no primrose path'.[4]

1   Freeman, Childright (1985) April No 16, p 8; and further in 39 Current Legal Problems 39 at pp 46–49.
2   See post, paras 5.16 et seq.
2a Most of the IVF clinics have an unofficial system of vetting for parenthood. Those provided by the National Health Service have stringent rules of selection. However, it has been held that where a hospital's ethical committee has been set up as an essentially advisory body and a forum for discussion the court will not compel the committee to give advice or investigate as to whether treatment should be given or refused in a particular case; see *R v Ethical Committee of St Mary's Hospital (Manchester) ex p H* [1988] 1 FLR 512, [1988] Fam Law 165.
3   After its earlier support for surrogacy within some controlled circumstances the British Medical Association has now come down against it on social and ethical objections, even where there is no payment.
4   *Re Adoption Application (Payment for Adoption) supra.*

III   PARENTHOOD OUTSIDE MARRIAGE

1   Introduction

2.20   Like most systems of jurisprudence, English law has based the legal relationship between the parent and the child not simply upon the fact of parentage but upon the concept of legitimacy, to be determined by reference to the existence of a valid marriage of the parents. The feudal doctrine which insisted that the parents of a child must be lawfully married at the time of his birth or conception in order to entitle him to inherit an estate in land led to the principle that it was only in respect of such a child that legal powers and responsibilities attached to parents.[1] Otherwise, he was legally *filius nullius* and his exclusion seems to have been complete,[2] until the Poor Law began to impose a duty on the parent to maintain him.[3] Even thereafter parental 'rights' were still denied, until finally, late in the nineteenth century, the mother's legal right to custody was acknowledged.[4] The twentieth century has witnessed at first a gradual and then a quickening process of reform in respect of the legal position of illegitimate children, culminating in the Family Law Reform Act 1987. Thus, the illegitimate child was placed on an equal footing with his legitimate brother in a variety of areas (for example, the protection of the criminal law, the provision of social security, in respect of claims under the Fatal Accidents' legislation, and very largely for purposes of succession to property). His mother came to hold the same legal powers and responsibilities and rights as those of either parent of the legitimate child[5] and his father acquired some (viz in relation to custody, guardianship and succession).[6] Reform was achieved not only by extending rights to the illegitimate child and powers and responsibilities to the mother and father, but also by cautiously broadening the concept of legitimacy. Thus, the Legitimacy Act 1926 permitted legitimation of a child by the subsequent valid marriage of his parents and the Legitimacy Act 1959 conferred the status of legitimacy on some children born of a void marriage. Finally, the Family Law Reform Act 1987 has sought to remove 'illegitimacy' from the legal vocabulary and to abolish virtually all of the illegitimate child's legal disabilities. This latest reform recognises the changed social conditions, the decreasing stigma attached to illegitimate children and the reality that in 1985 approximately one child out of five (126,000) was born outside wedlock,[7] the large majority of whom are the issue of stable relationships, as the number of births jointly registered by the mother and father indicate.[8] It is, moreover, in keeping with the United Kingdom's international obligations[9] and with development in other jurisdictions.[10]

1 See Graveson, *Status in the Common Law*, pp 91–92; and the judgments in *Birtwhistle v Vardill* (1840) 7 Cl & Fin 895, 4 Jur 1076, HL.
2 See Lord Herschell in *Barnardo v McHugh* [1891] AC 388 at 399, HL. But for the earlier view that exclusion was limited to rights of inheritance see Bacon's *Abridgement*, vol I, p 758.
3 See post, Chapter 16. The duty to maintain may have existed in the ecclesiastical courts before the first enactment of the Poor Law in 1576; see Helmholz, *Support Orders, Church Courts and the Rule of Filius Nullius: A Re-assessment of the Common Law* (1977) 63 Va L Rev 431 (cited by Cretney, op cit, p 594, note 65).
4 See post, para 2.40.
5 See ibid.
6 See post, paras 2.40 et seq.
7 Out of 656,000 live births for that year; (source – Office of Population Censuses and Surveys).
8 In 1985, 65% of all illegitimate births were registered jointly; see further, Cretney, *Elements of Family Law*, para 19.05.
9 The United Kingdom is a signatory to the European Convention on the Legal Status of Children Born out of Wedlock (1975); and in *Johnston v Ireland*, Judgment, Series A, vol 112, (1987) 9 EHRR 203 the European Court of Human Rights ruled that an illegitimate child should be placed, legally and socially, in the same position as that of a legitimate child, so as to satisfy the requirements of the European Convention for the protection of Human Rights. See also *Marckx v Belgium*, Judgment 13 June 1979, Series A no 31; 22 YECHR 410, and for a commentary on the impact of the decision see Salzberg (1985) 13 Denv J Int LP 283.
10 For example, in New Zealand the Status of Children Act 1969; in Australia the Status of Children Act 1974 (Victoria); see further Finlay, *Family Law in Australia*, 3rd edn, paras 961–7.

2.21 Five general points need to be made about the 1987 Act. First, its
policy is not to abolish the status of illegitimacy. That would involve 'an
automatic extension of parental rights to fathers of non-marital children'[1],
many of whom would not want those rights or who would pose a threat
to the children if they had them.[2] The unmarried father who is keen to
assume parental powers and responsibilities must still, therefore, come to
court and ask for an order granting him the powers and responsibilities
of parenthood. Moreover, the Act does not prevent the law from attaching
disabilities to cohabitees (and indirectly to their offspring)[3] in deference
to the married couple. Instead, the Act concentrates on removing the legal
disadvantages of illegitimacy and on removing the terminology of
'legitimacy'. The passage of time and other factors will determine whether
the words disappear from everyday social use. Secondly and consequentially,
it is still relevant to consider much of the pre-1987 law. Thus, before the
Act, the following categories of children were recognised:

    (i) the legitimate;[4]
    (ii) the legitimated; and
    (iii) the illegitimate.

After the Act there is either:

    (a) the child of a married couple, or
    (b) the child of an unmarried couple.

Some legal differences remain between (a) and (b) and, in order to determine
into which category a child falls, reference may need to be made to (i)
and (ii). Moreover, since the Act generally applies prospectively there will
be a lengthy transitional period during which pre-1987 provisions are still
relevant. Consequently, under those provisions there will still be some
disabilities attaching to children born out of marriage. These are dealt with
later.[5] Thirdly, the Act is modelled closely on the approach taken by the
Law Reform (Parent and Child) (Scotland) Act 1986,[6] for the latter prompted
the Law Commission to publish a second report in October 1986 which
modified some of its earlier recommendations.[7] Fourthly, and an example
of the foregoing, concerns the terminology. In its First Report the Law
Commission opted for 'marital' and 'non-marital' to replace legitimate and
illegitimate.[8] The Scottish Law Commission objected because that would
still discriminate between children.[9] This view prevailed, because 'it is better
to label the parents than to label the children'.[10] This laudable aim does,
however, mean that for the purposes of exposition of the law clumsy phrasing
has to be employed. In future, as indicated above, a distinction will be
drawn between (a) a child whose father and mother were married to each
other at the time of his birth and (b) a child whose father and mother
were not so married at that time.[11] To take account of the various possible
methods of conception, the time of a person's birth includes any time during
the period beginning with (1) the insemination resulting in his birth, or
(2) where there was no such insemination, his conception and (in either
case) ending with his birth.[12] Category (a) includes[13] a child who is legitimate
by virtue of section 1 of the Legitimacy Act 1976;[14] a legitimated child
as defined by section 10 of that Act;[15] an adopted child; and a child who
is otherwise treated in law as legitimate, which in effect means is legitimate
in accordance with the conflict of laws rules.[16] Finally, it should be noted
that in pursuit of this policy section 30 empowers the Lord Chancellor,
by statutory instrument, to remove references to 'legitimate' and 'illegitimate'
in earlier legislation.[17]

1 Law Com No 118, *Illegitimacy*, para 4.49.
2 See Law Com Working Paper No 74 for the options for reform.
3 For example, in relation to property rights which can have devastating effects on the child's accommodation needs; see *Burns v Burns* [1984] Ch 317, [1984] 1 All ER 244, CA for a statement of the law.
4 This includes an adopted child, except for the purpose of succession to any peerage, dignity or title of honour; Adoption Act 1976, s 44.
5 Post, paras 2.39 et seq.
6 The full background is as follows: Law Commission Working Paper No 74 (1979); Law Commission Report No 118 (1982); Scottish Law Commission Consultative Memorandum No 53 (1982); Scottish Law Commission Report No 82 (1984); Law Commission Second Report No 157 (1986).
7 The Bill to implement the recommendations followed with remarkable speed in November.
8 Para 4.51.
9 Para 9.2.
10 Lord Hailsham, HL Debs 27 November 1986, col 684. There is a similar legislative history in the Republic of Ireland. Originally, the Status of Children Bill 1986 distinguished between 'marital' and 'non-marital' children, but it was revised and now the distinction relies on whether the father and mother were or were not married at the time of the child's birth.
11 FLRA, s 1(2). Subsequent references in the text will usually be to 'the unmarried mother' and 'the unmarried father'.
12 Section 1(4).
13 Section 1(3).
14 Post, paras 2.25 – 2.28.
15 Post, paras 2.30 – 2.31.
16 As to which see Cheshire and North, *Private International Law*, 10th edn, pp 441–451.
17 For example, this could be done in relation to the Registered Homes Act 1984, s 19(2)(b), or the Housing Act 1985, s 113(2)(d).

2   Who is a child of a married couple?

To answer this question resort must be had to the common law on legitimacy and to various statutory additions.

(a)   Common law

2.22   A child conceived before the marriage of his parents but born after his father's death would undoubtedly be treated as legitimate, but otherwise the common law admits no exception to its rule of legitimacy that the parents must be married when the child is born or conceived.[1] However, within those limits it went to great lengths to ensure the legitimacy of children by an unduly generous application of a presumption in favour of that status.[2] This was achieved by giving the presumption a wide scope and then by imposing a heavy burden of rebuttal. The presumption is that a child born of a married woman[3] during the subsistence of her marriage is presumed to be also the child of her husband. It arises even though the child must have been conceived before the marriage, because by marrying the mother the husband is prima facie taken to have acknowledged the child as his own. In such a case the strength of the presumption has depended on, inter alia, whether at the date of the marriage he knew of her pregnancy.[4] The presumption equally applies where the child is born within the possible period of gestation after the marriage has been terminated by the husband's death[5] or by a final decree of divorce.[6] If after the termination but before the birth, the mother remarried, the better opinion is that the child is presumed to be a legitimate child of the first marriage and not of the second, on the ground that the mother should be presumed not to have committed adultery.[7] The scope of the presumption is demonstrated in those cases where the spouses are living apart. If they do so under a decree of judicial separation or under a matrimonial order containing a non-cohabitation clause the presumption is reversed and the child is prima facie illegitimate, on the ground that the spouses are presumed to have strictly obeyed the order.[8] Otherwise, the presumption of legitimacy operates. So, it has been held to apply notwithstanding that at the date of conception (1) the parties were living apart under a deed or agreement[9] or (2) a state of desertion existed or (3) a matrimonial order without a non-cohabitation clause was in force[10] or (4) a petition for divorce or nullity had been filed or (5) a decree nisi of divorce or nullity had already been granted.[11] In each of these circumstances the presumption has, however, been readily rebuttable, and, in so far as a presumption is now needed,[12] there is much to be said for the view that in all cases where the spouses are not cohabiting at the relevant date a presumption of illegitimacy should operate.

1 Historically, it seems that the exception stated in the text would not have been regarded as an exception, because in the case where the conception, but not the birth, preceded the marriage, the marriage was deemed to have taken place before the conception; see Lord Brougham in *Doe d Birtwhistle v Vardill* (1835) 2 Cl & Fin 571 at p 591. For the modern meaning of conception, see s 1(4) of FLRA 1987 and post, para 2.26. It includes artificial insemination and in vitro fertilisation.

2 A secondary factor which contributed to the same result was the old rule, reaffirmed in *Russell v Russell and Mayer* [1924] AC 687, HL, which excluded evidence by a spouse at a time when the child was likely to have been conceived. The rule was abolished by the Law Reform (Miscellaneous Provisions) Act 1949, s 7. A spouse is now a competent and compellable witness in any civil proceedings; Matrimonial Causes Act 1973, s 48(1).

3 Disputes over factual matters as to maternity are rare, ante, para 2.11; but see also *Slingsby v A-G* (1916) 33 TLR 120, HL, and note possible disputes in the context of immigration, where a woman may have difficulty in satisfying the authorities that a child, for whom she seeks entry into the United Kingdom, is her own child.

4 *Gardner v Gardner* (1877) 2 App Cas 723, HL (Sc); cf the *Poulett Peerage Case* [1903] AC 395, HL.

5 This rule has a long history; *Alsop v Bowtrell* (1619) Cro Jac 541: Co Litt 123b: Bl Comm 456. For modern authorities see Romer J in *Re Leman's Will Trusts* (1945) 115 LJ Ch 89; and Wrangham J in *Knowles v Knowles* [1962] P 161, [1962] 1 All ER 659. Although *Re Heath, Stacey v Bird* [1945] Ch 417 is also frequently cited in support, Cohen J, surprisingly declined to decide firmly whether the presumption applied to the posthumous child.

6 *Re Leman's Will Trusts*, supra. There is no reason why the presumption should not similarly operate in the rare case where the decree is one annulling a voidable marriage and possibly, within certain limits, even if the marriage were void; see post, para 2.25.

7 Bromley, op cit, pp 241–242. Cf *Re Overbury* [1955] Ch 122, [1954] 3 All ER 308, where the court was able to decide on the facts, without relying on a presumption, that the child was conceived of the first marriage. In some continental systems a conflict of presumptions has been avoided by imposing a 'waiting period' (eg of 300 days) during which the mother is not allowed to remarry unless meantime the child is born; see Kahn-Freund, 18 MLR 71.

8 *Parishes of St George's v St Margaret's, Westminster* (1706) 1 Salk 123.

9 *Morris v Davies* (1837) 5 Cl & Fin 163, HL; *Ettenfield v Ettenfield* [1940] P 96, [1940] 1 All ER 293, CA.

10 *Bowen v Norman* [1938] 1 KB 689, [1938] 2 All ER 776.

11 *Knowles v Knowles* [1962] P 161, [1962] 1 All ER 659.

12 See infra, standard of proof.

2.23 In the *Banbury Peerage Case*,[1] the House of Lords laid down the limits within which the presumption of legitimacy could be rebutted. It must be proved that no sexual intercourse took place between the spouses during the possible period within which the child must have been conceived, and this burden of proof might be discharged by showing that during that period either (1) sexual intercourse was impossible because (a) the parties were physically absent from one another, or (b) one at least of them was impotent; or (2) the circumstances were such as to render it highly improbable that sexual intercourse took place. It is this second main alternative which has produced most litigation.[2] Much of it shows that, where sexual intercourse between the spouses at the time in question was not impossible, all the circumstances surrounding the particular case must be considered including (1) the kind of opportunities which existed for such intercourse to take place,[3] (2) the disposition of the spouses to have intercourse with each other,[4] (3) their conduct towards each other before and during the wife's pregnancy and after the child's birth[5] and (4) the respective attitudes of the wife, her husband and her paramour towards the child.[6] Where reliance is placed on the husband's impotence for the purpose of rebutting the presumption of legitimacy it might still be possible to establish his paternity, viz, by proving that the birth was the result of fecundation *ab extra*[7] or of artificial insemination with his seed.[8] The length to which the courts were prepared to go in upholding the presumption is demonstrated by the rule that once sexual intercourse between the spouses was proved to have taken place at the material time the child must be held to be the issue of that intercourse, even though it was shown that at that time the wife was committing adultery[9] and even though the spouses always practised contraception.[10] But there had to be some eugenic limits even to this extreme conclusion.[11] Thus, it has been widely accepted that dissimilarities in colour (as, for example, where the child is a half-caste and the mother and her husband are both white) or the husband's sterility would rebut the presumption. The principles laid down in the *Banbury Peerage Case* were at one time a realistic recognition of the difficulty which proof or disproof of paternity could cause, but the appearance of new serological techniques and the change in the standard of proof needed to rebut the presumption called into question their inflexibility.[12]

1 (1811) 1 Sim & St 153.
2 See *Phipson on Evidence* (13th edn) paras 41.08–09.
3 Compare, for example, *Cotton v Cotton* [1954] P 305, [1954] 2 All ER 105, CA, with *Sibbet v Ainsley* (1860) 3 LT 583.
4 Cf the *Aylesford Peerage Case* (1885) 11 App Cas 1, HL.
5 *Aylesford Peerage Case*, supra; *Burnaby v Baillie* (1889) 42 Ch D 282.
6 *Aylesford Peerage Case*, supra; *Bosvile v A-G* (1887) 12 PD 177, DC.
7 Cf *Clarke (otherwise Talbot) v Clarke* [1943] 2 All ER 540.
8 Cf *REL (otherwise R) v EL* [1949] P 211, sub nom, *L v L* [1949] 1 All ER 141.
9 *R v Hemmings* [1939] 1 All ER 417, CCA.
10 *Francis v Francis* [1960] P 17, [1959] 3 All ER 206, DC.
11 As Scots law recognised see *Slingsby v A-G* (1916) 33 TLR 120, HL.
12 The changing attitude towards the presumption was also reflected in *Blackwell v A-G* (1967) 111 Sol Jo 332 and in *Smith v May* (1969) 113 Sol Jo 1000, DC. In the former it was held that the bare fact that the petitioner in a legitimacy suit is the child of a person lawfully married at the date of conception is insufficient of itself to establish legitimacy. There must be some evidence that the husband of the mother had access to her at the relevant time. In *Smith v May* the Divisional Court held that the magistrates were entitled to 'take a very strong view' that the spouses had not had sexual intercourse, although they shared the same bed, and that, therefore, the presumption was rebutted.

Standard of proof
2.24 Since any attempted rebuttal of the presumption necessarily involves

the allegation that the mother was guilty of adultery (except for the possibility of the child having been conceived by way of artificial insemination), it would have been illogical to have allowed a standard of proof less than that required to establish adultery, ie, proof beyond reasonable doubt, but dicta in *Blyth v Blyth and Pugh*[1] that adultery could be proved on a preponderance of probabilities left judicial opinion divided as to whether the lesser standard was applicable to rebuttal of the presumption.[2] The uncertainty was supposedly removed by the Family Law Reform Act 1969, which laid down the test of balance of probabilities for the latter purpose.[3]

> 'Any presumption of law as to the legitimacy or illegitimacy of any person may in any civil proceedings be rebutted by evidence which shows that it is more probable than not that that person is illegitimate or legitimate, as the case may be, and it shall not be necessary to prove that fact beyond reasonable doubt in order to rebut the presumption.'

On one view this rule has far-reaching effects.

> '[It] means that the presumption of legitimacy now merely determines the onus of proof. Once evidence has been led it must be weighed without using the presumption as a make-weight in the scale for legitimacy. So even weak evidence against legitimacy must prevail if there is not other evidence to counterbalance it. The presumption will only come in at that stage in the very rare case of the evidence being so evenly balanced that the court is unable to reach a decision on it. I cannot recollect ever having seen or heard of a case of any kind where the court could not reach a decision on the evidence before it.'[4]

The competing view is that the civil standard of proof can vary according to the gravity of the particular issue to be resolved. Thus, a high degree of probability is required if a person's liberty[5] or livelihood[6] is at stake. It was this view which the Court of Appeal adopted in *Re JS (a minor)*[7] and then in *Serio v Serio*.[8] In the latter it decided that section 26 merely abolished any requirement of the criminal standard. This did not mean that the serious issue of paternity should be decided on a mere balance of probabilities, but instead on a suitably high degree of proof. It is difficult to justify this conclusion in the face of the plain words of section 26, but it must now be regarded as authoritative. Where does this leave the presumption of legitimacy? In *W v K (Proof of Paternity)*[9] it was held that this high standard of proof is required to rebut the presumption.[10]

However, as the case also illustrates, with the current use of blood and other scientific tests[11] of proving paternity, it may not be difficult to discharge that burden of proof.[12] But there can still be cases where such tests are not practicable, for example, when issues over rights of succession are raised, and the presumption could be crucial.

---

1 Per Lord Denning and Lord Pearce [1966] AC 643, [1966] 1 All ER 524, HL.
2 *Re L* [1968] P 119, [1968] 1 All ER 20, CA.
3 Section 26.
4 Per Lord Reid in *S v S; W v Official Solicitor* [1972] AC 24 at 41, [1970] 3 All ER 107 at 109, HL. See Lord Morris of Borth-y-Gest, ibid, at 54 and 120 respectively. The

dictum of Lord Reid applied in *T(H) v T(E)* [1971] 1 All ER 590, where the court was able to find enough evidence, without relying on the presumption, to hold that the husband of the mother was the father of her child.

5 *Khawaja v Secretary of State for the Home Department* [1984] AC 74, [1983] 1 All ER 765, HL.

6 *R v Milk Marketing Board, ex p Austin* (1983) Times, 21 March.

7 [1981] Fam 22, [1980] 1 All ER 1061, CA.

8 (1983) 4 FLR 756, 13 Fam Law 255, CA.

9 (1987) 151 JP 589, [1988] 1 FLR 86.

10 The decision runs counter to the view expressed by the Law Commission (Law Com No 157, paras 3.17–3.19) that a higher standard of proof should only be imposed in proceedings for a Declaration of parentage, legitimacy or legitimation (post, para 2.32) but not in other proceedings where paternity is in issue. The Commission thought 'that it would be unsatisfactory if some special standard of proof were automatically to prevent a child being granted access to or financial support from a man who after fully fought proceedings, was shown on a balance of probabilities to be the father'.

11 For these tests see post, paras 2.34–2.38.

12 In *W v K (Proof of Paternity)* during the relevant period when her child was conceived the mother was having sexual intercourse with both her husband and their friend, W, but with no one else. Blood tests indicated that the 'paternity index' for W being the father was 97.4%. There was also medical evidence that the husband was virtually infertile and was extremely unlikely to be the father. Latey J held that on the evidence the presumption was rebutted and W was the father.

(b) Statutory legitimacy

(i) Children of void marriages

2.25 Section 2 of the Legitimacy Act 1959 re-introduced into English law the doctrine of the putative marriage which, while popular in many other legal systems, had been obsolete in England since the Reformation.[1] The current law[2] provides for the legitimacy of the child of a void marriage if:

    (i) at the time of the insemination resulting in the birth, or

    (ii) where there was no such insemination, at the time of the child's conception, or

    (iii) at the time of the celebration of the marriage if later,

both or either of the parties reasonably believed that the marriage was valid. Situation (i) covers both normal intercourse and artificial insemination.[3] As for (ii), this is intended to deal with in vitro fertilisation. Conception takes place when the ovum is fertilised in the glass dish and not when the resulting zygote or (after 14–16 days) embryo is inserted in the uterus.[4] This raises the possibility that if, at the time of in vitro fertilisation, both or either of the parties reasonably believe that the marriage is valid, but the fertilised egg is then frozen and later inserted into the woman, even some years later (perhaps after the man has died), the child will be legitimate.

1 The doctrine was an established part of mediaeval ecclesiastical law, see Tucker (1960) 9 ICLQ 319–320.

2 Legitimacy Act 1976, s 1(1), as amended by Family Law Reform Act 1987, s 28(1).

3 For which see ante, para 2.03.

4 For a discussion of the point see HL Debs 10 February 1987, cols 519–22.

2.26 The reference to 'either' of the parties in the provision means that, for example, a child is still legitimate if his father deliberately marries polygamously but his mother genuinely believes that the marriage is monogamous. The father must have been domiciled in England and Wales at the time of the birth, or, if he died before that date, he must have been so domiciled immediately before his death.[2] The first part of this limitation accords with the rules of English conflict of laws, which refer the question of legitimacy exclusively to the law of the father's domicile at the date of the child's birth,[1] but it also has the advantage of avoiding any reference to the domicile of origin of the child. Similar accordance is not, however, to be found in the second part, since the better view is that the law governing legitimacy of a posthumous child is that of the mother's domicile at the date of birth and not of the father at his death.[3]

1   Subject to (1) the rule that, if a question of heirship is involved, the common law test of birth in lawful wedlock prevails and (2) the controversial decision of the House of Lords in *Shaw v Gould* (1868) LR 3 HL 55 which may be explained as an illustration of the first proviso or is open to other interpretations. See textbooks on the Conflict of Laws.
2   LA 1976, s 1(2).
3   See Cheshire and North, op cit, p 449.

2.27   In *Hawkins v A-G*[1] it was held that the reasonableness of the belief in the validity of the marriage must be determined objectively. The wording of the legislation may support the decision but its *raison d'être* scarcely does. This lies in the moral innocence of at least one of the parties, so that the appropriate test ought to be subjective honesty, not objective reasonableness. Did the party at the relevant date honestly believe that his or her marriage was valid? Some amelioration lies in the further statutory provision[2] whereby a reasonable belief can extend to a mistake as to the law (for example, as to the effectiveness of an earlier decree of divorce). However, the time factor may still give rise to problems, since the burden of proof seems to lie on those asserting legitimacy. It may be very difficult to prove that a party believed the marriage was valid at the relevant date, especially if that party is dead, or where that date is the date of conception (and not of marriage). For children born after section 28 of FLRA 1987 came into force,[3] considerable assistance lies in the provision that one of the parties to the marriage is presumed to have held a reasonable belief, unless the contrary is shown.[4] For those born before that date, the principles relating to the possible period of gestation which are followed in applying the presumption of common law legitimacy could, it is submitted, be adopted. If, for example, the child was born 310 days after the party found out that the marriage was void, it ought to be presumed that the child was already conceived before the discovery, assuming that the parties then had access to each other. There is also room, in marginal cases, for importing into the section a presumption of legitimacy analogous to that at common law. Supposing, for example, that F went through a ceremony of marriage with M, who at the time did not know that F was already a married person. M, having lived with F for some time, eventually discovered that her marriage was bigamous. On the same day she ceased to live with F, the last act of sexual intercourse between the parties having occurred on the previous day. A month later M began to have regular sexual intercourse with X. M gave birth to C 300 days after leaving F. It is submitted that if medical and other evidence fails to show whether F or X was the father, it should be presumed that F is and that C is therefore legitimate.

1   [1966] 1 All ER 392, [1966] 1 WLR 978. For criticism, see Samuels (1966) 29 MLR 559.

2   Legitimacy Act 1976, s 1(3), inserted by Family Law Reform Act 1987, s 28(2).
3   Ie 4 April 1988.
4   Legitimacy Act 1976, s 1(4), as so inserted.

2.28   The definition of a void marriage for present purposes is perplexing.[1]

'[It] means a marriage, not being voidable only, in respect of which the High Court has or had jurisdiction to grant a decree of nullity, or would have or would have had such jurisdiction if the parties were domiciled in England.'

'Marriage' includes not only a voluntary, exclusive union potentially for life of one man and one woman[2] but also a polygamous marriage.[3] But, unless the union is governed by English law, a marriage ceremony ought not to be a prerequisite, if the foreign law does not require it. However, concubinage or a union for a prescribed period is excluded. The reference to past jurisdiction is probably intended to cover the case of the posthumous child, but the inclusion of the words 'or had' seem odd, since the death of the father would not deprive the English court of jurisdiction: a decree of nullity in respect of a void marriage can be granted even though one of the parties is dead.

A person who is legitimate by virtue of section 1 of the Legitimacy Act 1976 enjoys the same legal rights as a legitimate-born child, including the right to succeed to a dignity or title of honour.[4]

1   Legitimacy Act 1976, s 10. See Jones 8 ICLQ 722, 725; Tucker, 9 ICLQ 319, 321; Kahn-Freund, 23 MLR 56, 58, in relation to the previous, identical provision.
2   *Hyde v Hyde and Woodmansee*, (1866) LR 1 P&D 130 at 133.
3   Matrimonial Causes Act 1973, s 47.
4   Legitimacy Act 1976, Sch 1, para 4, provided that he was born after 28 October 1959 when the original provision came into force; but succession to the throne is not covered, ibid, para 5.

(ii)   Children of voidable marriages
2.29   Any nullity decree granted after 31 July 1971 in respect of a voidable marriage does not operate retrospectively,[1] so that the children of such a marriage remain legitimate.[2] They enjoy the same rights as children born of a valid marriage.

1   Matrimonial Causes Act 1973, s 16.
2   Prior to this date relief was offered by the Matrimonial Causes Act 1937, s 7(2), the Law Reform (Miscellaneous Provisions) Act 1949, s 4(1) and the Matrimonial Causes Act 1965, s 11.

(iii)   Legitimated children
2.30   The policy of English domestic law before 1926 to refuse to extend legitimacy beyond cases of birth or conception in lawful wedlock was not pursued in the conflict of laws rules. Provided that no question of heirship was involved, the legitimation of a child by the subsequent marriage of his parents was recognised by the common law if the father was domiciled both at the time of the child's birth and at the time of the subsequent marriage in a country whose law recognised the legitimation.[1] The Legitimacy Act 1926 supplemented the common law by providing an alternative rule of recognition which excluded the illogical reference to the father's domicile at the time of the child's birth[2] but it also introduced

legitimation by subsequent marriage into the domestic law,[3] save for the adulterine child who remained unprotected until the Legitimacy Act 1959 removed the injustice.

A question of legitimation may, of course, raise a preliminary issue as to paternity. The fact that the husband married the mother is of limited evidential value in proving his paternity, but evidence of recognition by the husband that the child is his is much more cogent.[4] So, too, is the fact that the mother has already obtained a maintenance order against him. The existence of the order may be adduced in later civil proceedings whether or not the husband defended the proceedings for maintenance.[5]

1   The rule was finally established in *In re Grove* (1888) 40 Ch D 216.
2   Now Legitimacy Act 1976, s 3. For the conflict of laws aspects of legitimation see textbooks thereon, eg Dicey and Morris, 11th edn, pp 846–860; Cheshire and North, op cit, pp 451–455.
3   Ibid, s 2. Consistently with the conflict of laws rule, recognition depends on the father being domiciled in England or Wales at the time of the marriage; ie, the child's status is determined solely by the personal law of the father at that date, without reference to that of the mother.
4   See *Battle v A-G* [1949] P 358.
5   Civil Evidence Act 1968, s 12. Strong evidence of paternity would be the fact that the husband had, in accordance with the Births and Deaths Registration Act 1953, s 10, (prospectively substituted by the Family Law Reform Act 1987, s 24), signed the register of births, even though at that date he and the mother were not married. Where a person has been found to be the father in any relevant proceedings before any court in England and Wales or has been adjudged to be the father in affiliation proceedings before any court in the United Kingdom, that constitutes prima facie evidence of paternity in any subsequent proceedings; see CEA 1968, s 12, as amended by FLRA 1987, s 29.

2.31   A child who is legitimated by the subsequent marriage of his parents is, from the date of his legitimation,[1] largely in the same legal position as if he had been born legitimate. In particular he has the same rights and is under the same obligations in respect of the maintenance and support of himself or of any other person as if he had been born legitimate, and any claims for damages, compensation and the like apply in respect of him as they would in the case of a legitimate person.[2] This general legal effect, created by the Legitimacy Acts, is specifically supplemented by certain statutory provisions, eg those relating to nationality[3] and to social insurance.[4] As regards property rights, the legitimated person is in the same position as if born legitimate, save that he cannot succeed to a dignity or title of honour;[5] and, as regards his domicile, he probably acquires his domicile of origin from his mother.[6]

1   Ie the date of the marriage or the date of commencement of the particular Legitimacy Act which applies to him, whichever be the later. Thus, an adulterine child whose parents married in 1956 was legitimated from 29 October 1959 when the 1959 Act came into operation.
    The parents must arrange for re-registration of their legitimated child by providing the Registrar-General with the requisite information. See Legitimacy Act 1976, s 9, and for re-registration see the Births and Deaths Registration Act 1953, s 14 (as extended by the Legitimation (Re-registration of Births) Act 1957).
2   Legitimacy Act 1976, s 8.
3   British Nationality Act 1981, s 47(1).
4   See post, Chapter 16.
5   Legitimacy Act 1976, s 5(3) and Sch 1, para 4. For special rules where a disposition depends on the date of the child's birth see ss 5(4) and 6.
6   See Dicey and Morris, p 155.

(c) Establishing parentage

(i) Declarations of parentage etc

2.32 The need to ascertain the identity of a child's parent and his consequent legal status can arise in a wide variety of contexts (for example, in a dispute over entitlement to property, a claim for maintenance from the child's alleged father, the immigration status of a child) and either as a collateral or direct issue in the proceedings. Part III of the Family Law Act 1986 offers methods of determining a person's status, and in particular section 56[1] enables a court[2] to grant declarations of parentage, legitimacy or legitimation.

(1) Declaration of Parentage. This is a new kind of declaration introduced by FLRA 1987, which enables a person to apply for a declaration that a person named in the application is or was his parent.

(2) Declaration of Legitimacy. A person may apply for a declaration that he is the legitimate child of his parents. However, no court, whether in proceedings under FLA 1986 or not, can declare that a person is or was illegitimate.[3]

(3) Declaration of legitimation. A person may apply for a declaration that he has or has not become a legitimated person, ie legitimated under the Legitimacy Acts 1926 or 1976 (ante para 2.30) or by a foreign law which is recognised by English law.[4] To qualify as an applicant for any of those declarations a person must either be domiciled in England and Wales at the date of the application or have been habitually resident there for one year immediately prior to the application.[5]

Section 56 can only be used by the person whose status is in issue. Thus, a person whose claim to intestate succession depends on establishing the illegitimacy of another cannot use it.[6] The Law Commission was concerned at 'the scope for disturbance'[7] which a wider jurisdiction might offer at the hands of interfering third parties. Whilst this attitude is consistent with the previous law,[8] it is objectionable in principle and expressed fears of abuse are unsubstantiated.[9] Why should a person, who claims to be a parent, not be able to ask a court to endorse the claim?[10] Moreover, the court cannot grant declarations in respect of other matters, for example, that a person other than the applicant is legitimate. It can only make orders for parties to the proceedings.[11] Although FLRA 1987 abolishes the legal concept of legitimacy, it does so prospectively. Consequently, for many years it may be necessary to refer back to laws which relied on that concept and to inquire whether a child is or was legitimate, legitimated or illegitimate.[12]

With regard to the standard of proof, the truth of the proposition to be declared must be proved 'to the satisfaction of the court'.[13] Given that a declaration is binding in rem,[14] it is suggested that the courts will require a high degree of probability in accordance with the principle established in *Serio v Serio*[15] The court does, however, have a discretion to refuse a declaration if it would be manifestly contrary to public policy.[16] As to procedure,[17] the Attorney-General may be invited to appear or may intervene of his own motion.[18] Where a declaration of parentage or a declaration of legitimacy is made the court must notify the Registrar General of that fact.[19]

---

1 As substituted by FLRA 1987, s 22. More limited types of declaration existed formerly

under MCA 1973, s 45. For background to the reform of the law see Law Com No 132 (1984).

2 Ie the High Court or a county court (FLA 1986 s 63).

3 FLA 1986, s 58(5)(b).

4 Ibid 1986, s 56(5).

5 Ibid 1986, s 56(3). Cf Law Com No 118, paras 10.21 and 10.24, which proposed confining jurisdiction to those born in England and Wales.

6 He could, however, use s 55 (declaration of status), whereby a person with 'sufficient interest' can apply to determine the validity of a marriage; see sub-s (3).

7 Law Com No 118, para 10.17.

8 *Re JS (a minor)(declaration of paternity)* [1981] Fam 22, [1980] 1 All ER 1061, CA, where it was held that the court had no inherent jurisdiction to grant a declaration of paternity to a man who claimed to be father of a child.

9 It is hard to believe that there are many meddlesome individuals waiting to disrupt.

10 A declaration of parentage, supra, does not cover such a case.

11 Thus, if a second husband is abroad and the former husband is examined by the court and excluded as father, the court cannot declare the second to be the father.

12 It may also be necessary to refer to the concept if legitimacy under a foreign law is relevant.

13 FLA 1986, s 58(1).

14 Section 58(2).

15 (1983) 4 FLR 756, 13 Fam Law 255, CA; and see ante, para 2.24.

16 FLA 1986, s 58(1).

17 Rules of Court will be prepared (s 60(1)).

18 Section 59.

19 Section 56(4), as inserted by FLRA 1987, s 22. The procedure for notification is to be prescribed by Rules of Court.

(ii) Registration of births

2.33 Inclusion of the father's name in the register of births can be crucial evidence of his paternity of the child. Under the Births and Deaths Registration Act 1953 the parents of every child born in the country must register particulars of the birth.[1] But the opportunities for the father of an illegitimate child to register his name as father are limited.[2] Under the FLRA 1987[3] the opportunities for the unmarried father will be enlarged. Registration of his name can take place:

(i) at the joint request of the mother and father, in which case both must sign the register; or

(ii) at the request of the mother and on production of declarations by her and the father to the effect that he is the father; or

(iii) at the request of the father and on production of declarations by him and the mother to the effect that he is the father; or

(iv) at the written request of either the mother or father and on production of a copy of a court order which gives the father parental rights (under FLRA 1987, s 4 (when it comes into force) or GMA 1971, s 9) or which requires him to maintain the child (under GMA 1971, s 11B). If the child has reached the age of 16 his written consent to this type of registration is also required.

It should be noted that these provisions are exclusive and are exceptions to the general rule that the unmarried father of a child is under no duty to register himself as father; nor does he have a general right to do so. Where the father's name was not originally entered in the register, re-registration is permissible, on identical grounds to (i)–(iv) above, so that his name can be added.[4] Finally, where a declaration of parentage[5] has been obtained, the Registrar General of Births and Deaths will be informed and the register will be amended accordingly.[6]

1 Section 2. For discussion of this topic, see Law Com No 118, paras 10.55–10.75.
2 Under s 10, viz, (a) at the joint request of the mother and father, (b) at the request of the mother and on production of a declaration of acknowledgement by the father, (c) at the request of the mother and on production of a copy of an affiliation order.
3 Section 24, substituting a new s 10 in the 1953 Act. S 24 is not yet in force.
4 FLRA 1987, s 25, substituting a new s 10A in the 1953 Act for that originally inserted by the Children Act 1975, s 93(2). S 25 is not yet in force.
5 See ante, para 2.32.
6 FLRA 1987, s 26, adding s 14A to the 1953 Act. This provision is now operative.

(iii) Scientific tests

2.34 Blood tests are a particularly valuable means of proving parentage and can be used in a variety of legal proceedings. For example, a husband may want to show in proceedings under the GMA 1971 that a child is not his but the result of his wife's extra-marital affair. A woman may need to prove her maternity of a child for the purpose of qualifying for entry into the country under the immigration rules. The most frequent use is in affiliation proceedings since a blood test can amount to corroborative evidence,[1] a specific requirement under the Affiliation Proceedings Act 1957.[2] They will retain their usefulness when, following the abolition of affiliation proceedings,[3] a maintenance order is sought in the magistrates' court from an alleged parent. The law is contained in the Family Law Reform Act 1969, Part III, as prospectively amended by section 23 of the Family Law Reform Act 1987.

The conventional type of blood test does not seek to prove directly that a particular person is the parent, but does so indirectly by excluding other candidates. Thus, if only A, B or C could be the father and tests exclude A and B, C emerges by a process of elimination. Over the years more sophisticated techniques have brought increased accuracy to blood tests. For example, in *Turner v Blunden*[4] it was reported to the court that 998 out of 1000 randomly chosen men would be excluded from paternity by use of the test, but that the respondent had not been so excluded. 'Such a high statistical probability'[5] could amount to corroboration that he was in fact the father. Much greater accuracy is now offered by the test known as DNA fingerprinting.[6] This technique examines the deoxyribonucleic acid in chromosomes. This DNA contains the individual's genetic characteristics as transmitted by his parents. The unique quality of these characteristics means that the test can positively identify a person's parents.[7] It is still in its earlier stages of development and, like other scientific and technological changes affecting the family, its full social and legal implications have yet to be explored.[8] But it is becoming increasingly available at a comparatively modest cost,[9] and the indications are that Legal Aid Committees are favourably disposed to the testing.[10] Nevertheless, the alternative conventional techniques of blood testing will continue to be used for some time and the provisions discussed below allow of either test.[11]

1 *Turner v Blunden* [1986] Fam 120, [1986] 2 All ER 75.
2 Section 4(1).
3 Prospectively by FLRA 1987, s 17; see post, para 16.67.
4 Supra.
5 Per Hollins J, at pp 78 and 495 respectively; cf *Serio v Serio* (1983) 4 FLR 756, 13 Fam Law 255, CA, where the degree of probability was 88.5%. See Dodd (1980) 20 Med Sci Law 231 for Tables as to the degrees of probability.
6 For a layman's guide, see Kelly, Rankin and Wink [1987] Crim LR 105.

7 Samples can be taken of blood, semen, body tissue and even hair, provided that the root is still attached.
8 See Bradney, *Blood Tests, Paternity and the Double Helix* [1986] Fam Law 378. For one problem, namely, whether there should be a duty on the mother to disclose the identity of the man alleged to be the father see post, para 2.38.
9 £105 per person (ie child, mother and alleged father). The test is available from Cellmark Diagnostics, Abingdon, Oxfordshire; telephone 0235–28609.
10 See Maidment (1987) 137 NLJ 469. See also Gold, ibid, at 1104.
11 Viz, FLRA 1969, s 20(1)(a), refers to tests establishing whether a person 'is' (DNA tests) 'or is not' (conventional techniques) the father or mother. Until the amendments of the 1969 Act are implemented DNA testing may only be ordered in wardship proceedings.

2.35   *Availability.*[1] In any civil proceedings where the parentage[2] of a person is in issue, the court may direct first that scientific tests be employed and second that samples be taken from specified persons. It can do this of its own motion or on the application of a party to the proceedings. However, the only persons who can be tested under these provisions are the person whose parentage is in dispute and a party to the proceedings. Consequently it may often be necessary to join a person as a party.[3] A direction is revocable or variable. No test may be carried out on a person aged 16 or over without his consent and, if he is under that age or is so mentally disordered as not to be able to understand the nature and purpose of the tests, the consent of the person having care and control is necessary.[4] Where a guardian ad litem has been appointed his consent is not necessary (since he does not have care and control of the child),[5] but he has the right to make submissions against the child being tested. If the court decides in favour of a scientific test, it should be taken promptly.[6]

1 The FLRA 1969 is supplemented by the Blood Tests (Evidence of Paternity) Regulations 1971 and procedure in the High Court is governed by RSC Ord 112, in the county court by CCR Ord 47, r 5 and in the magistrates' court by the Magistrates' Court (Blood Test) Rules 1971. For a full discussion of the procedural aspects, see Parry, Butterworths Family Law Service, E[228]–[250].
2 The reference to parentage is an addition of FLRA 1987, present law being confined to paternity; see FLRA 1969, s 20(1), as prospectively substituted by FLRA 1987, s 23. An example of maternity being in issue is a woman who abandons her child, later returns and claims custody under GMA 1971.
3 Butterworths Family Law Service, para E[228].
4 FLRA 1969, s 21(3) and (4). For the mentally disordered, his medical adviser must also certify that the taking of a sample will not prejudice his proper care and treatment. For the question of the child's consent, see infra, para 2.38.
5 See *Re L (an infant)* [1968] P 119, [1968] 1 All ER 20.
6 *P v P* (1969) 113 Sol Jo 343, CA.

2.36   A direction is not compulsory in its effect so as to empower the court to impose a sanction, but a refusal to comply with it will entitle the court to draw such inferences as the circumstances may properly warrant,[1] which usually but not necessarily[2] will be adverse to the refusing party. For example, if a mother for no justifiable reason, such as medical or religious grounds, will not allow herself or her child, whose care and control she has, to be blood tested, the court may conclude that the alleged father is not the father. Moreover, the 1969 Act specifically provides[3] that a person, who without reasonable cause fails to comply with a direction after the court has adjourned a hearing in order to enable him to do so, may not be able to rely on the presumption of legitimacy although there is no evidence to rebut it. The main object of this provision is to prevent a refusing wife from relying on the presumption in a claim against her husband for maintenance of the child. As a result of her refusal the court may well draw the inference that she has committed adultery, but her husband may also have had access to her at the relevant time and, as we have seen, the presumption of legitimacy, but for the present statutory rule, would operate.

1   FLRA 1969, s 23(1).
2   See *B v B and E* [1969] 3 All ER 1106, [1969] 1 WLR 1800, CA. See generally Hayes, *The Use of Blood Tests in the Pursuit of Truth* (1971) 87 LQR 86; Hall, [1979] CLJ 34.
3   Section 23(2) and (3), as prospectively amended by FLRA 1987, Sch 2, para 24.

2.37   The FLRA 1969 is concerned with conferring a power to direct the taking of scientific tests, but it does not indicate how the court is to exercise its discretion. Before the Act's provisions came into force,[1] there was a conflict between the view that the child's best interests should determine whether a test should be ordered[2] and the view that the need to do justice was the overwhelming consideration.[3] In *S v S* and *W v Official Solicitor*[4] the House of Lords preferred the latter approach and formulated the principle that a court should allow a test of a child to be taken unless it is satisfied that such a course would be actively against the interests of the child: it is not necessary that it should positively be satisfied that the outcome of the test will be for the child's benefit. Save in exceptional cases, as, for example, where a test would be harmful to his health, it will be in the child's interests to resolve parentage doubts on the best available evidence. Better that he should know the truth than that he should be sheltered behind the presumption of legitimacy, especially now that most of the former legal disabilities attaching to illegitimacy have been removed. His interests are not likely to be furthered by holding, on a presumption of legitimacy, that his mother's husband is his father when the latter is firmly convinced that he is not.

1   1 March 1971.
2   *W v W* [1970] 1 All ER 1157, [1970] 1 WLR 682, CA.
3   Ibid, per Lord Denning, and again in *S v McC* [1970] 1 All ER 1162, [1970] 1 WLR 672.
4   [1972] AC 24, [1970] 3 All ER 107. These were the appeals from the Court of Appeal, *sub nom W v W* and *S v McC, supra.*

2.38   Beyond venturing the opinion that the discretion to order tests under the 1969 Act was not unfettered, the House of Lords declined to offer guidance on the principles which should govern its exercise. However, its general approach in favour of testing and ascertaining the truth has been adopted, at least in regard to young children. There are two important provisos. First, a test should not be ordered unless the child's parentage genuinely falls to be determined. Thus, a test merely to satisfy a husband's curiosity, but which would make no difference to the outcome of the proceedings is inappropriate.[1] Second, as Lord Reid remarked in *S v S, supra,* 'as soon as a child is able to understand [the purpose and implications of a blood test] it would generally be unwise to subject it to this operation against its will'.[2] This sentiment is of particular relevance in the light of the *Gillick* principle.[3]

Because of the accuracy of DNA testing and its positive determination of parentage, the question is likely to arise whether the mother should be obliged to disclose the identity of the man she believes to be the father, instead of her present entitlement to refuse to do so, with the possible evidential effects where she does refuse.[4] A warning shot has already been fired. In *Re I (a minor)*,[5] a mother placed her three day old baby in the care of the local authority, who seriously doubted her ability to care for the baby. The putative father was willing to assume the care but only if satisfied that he was the father. Sheldon J held that in the child's interests and with consideration for those of the putative father an injunction would be granted restraining the mother from going to South Africa until completion of DNA tests.

1   *Hodgkiss v Hodgkiss and Walker* (1984) 148 JP 417, [1984] FLR 563, CA; and see *Re JS (a minor)* [1981] Fam 22, [1980] 1 All ER 1061, CA.
2   [1972] AC 24 at 45, [1970] 3 All ER 107 at 113; and see *Re JS (a minor)* [1981] Fam 22 at 30, [1980] 1 All ER 1061 at 1067.
3   See ante, para 1.13.
4   Supra, para 2.36.
5   (1987) Times, 22 May [1987] NLJ 613.

3   Effects of birth outside marriage

(a)   Effects prior to FLRA 1987

2.39   Those children who are illegitimate according to the rules described above[1] suffer the following legal disadvantages or discriminations.

1   Paras 2.22 et seq.

(i)   The relationship with the father

2.40   Prima facie the mother alone had the parental powers and responsibilities in respect of her illegitimate child, but it took English law an unconscionably long time to accord this recognition. In 1841 it was still being asked on what legal ground she had powers and responsibilities,[1] and as late as 1883 the Court of Appeal was denying any legal relationship between her and her child,[2] except that the rule had already been recognised that the child took his domicile origin from his mother.[3] But in *Barnardo v McHugh*[4] the House of Lords eventually recognised that, in view of her duty[5] to maintain her illegitimate child up to the age of 16, it was impossible to deny her a legal 'right' in relation to custody. Once this had been done the way was open for further legal recognition both by the courts and by the Legislature, with the eventual implied acceptance that there was vested solely in the mother the powers and responsibilities which both parents enjoy in respect of their legitimate child.[6] The Children Act 1975 expressly adopted this principle in its provision[7] that 'except as otherwise provided by or under any enactment, while the mother of an illegitimate child is living she has the parental rights and duties exclusively'.

Although the father is liable, once his paternity is established, to maintain his child under the system of social security or under an affiliation order, the law offers him no inducement to assume that or other responsibilities by conferring powers upon him. Of course, in many cases a putative father is anxious to evade responsibilities and is not interested in securing powers, especially where his child is the consequence of a casual sexual relationship with the mother; but he is equally denied recognition where he, the mother and their child are living in a stable relationship, and even though in those circumstances, because he has actual custody (albeit jointly with the mother), he acquires the responsibilities of seeing that his child receives full-time secular education[8] and of protecting him from harm.[9] Nor does the substantive 'right' to custody (in the wide sense)[10] vest in him on the mother's death;[11] and his paternity does not entitle him to appoint a testamentary guardian, even where the mother predeceases him.[12] Apart from the expensive possibility of obtaining an order giving him care and control of his child in wardship proceedings, the only ways in which he can acquire parental powers and responsibilities are by the mother appointing him a testamentary guardian or by his being appointed a guardian by the court[13] or by his obtaining an order for legal custody under the Guardianship of Minors Act 1971.[14] Obtaining guardianship or legal custody has specific additional consequences for the father. It means that his agreement to his child's adoption is required unless the court dispenses with it.[15] His consent to the child's marriage (if under the age of 18) is needed where the mother has been deprived of legal custody and he has been granted it or where she is dead and has appointed him testamentary guardian.[16] His consent is also necessary to a change of the child's name if he is a guardian, whether testamentary or appointed by the court.[17] Moreover, if he is a guardian (but not otherwise), he has the rights of removing his child who has been received into care by a local authority under section 2 of the Child Care Act 1980 and of objecting to a resolution of the authority vesting in itself parental rights and duties under section 3.[18] If he has legal custody by virtue of an order under section 9 of the Guardianship of Minors Act 1971, he also has power to appoint a person to be guardian after his death, provided that at that date he is still entitled to legal custody.[19] However, such an order does not give him, any more than it does the mother, the right to claim maintenance under the 1971 Act.[20]

---

1 *Re Lloyd* (1841) 3 Man & G 547, where Maule J doubted whether she was 'anything but a stranger' to her child. The earlier decision in *Ex p Knee* (1804) 1 Bos & PNR 148, that she was entitled to custody, does not seem to have been treated as authoritative.

2 See Lindley LJ in *R v Nash, Re Carey* (1883) 10 QBD 454 at 456, CA.

3 *Re Wright's Trusts* (1856) 2 K & J 595; *Urquhart v Butterfield* (1887) 37 Ch D 357, CA.

4 [1891] AC 388, [1891–4] All ER Rep 825.

5 At that time under the Poor Law Amendment Act 1834, s 71.

6 That was the inference to be drawn from the GMA 1971; see Hall, *The Waning of Parental Rights* [1972B] CLJ 248, at p 263, note 19.

7 Section 85(7).

8 Education Act 1944, ss 36 and 114(1). For s 36 see post, para 11.18.

9 See post, Chapter 9. But see para 9.52 for the limits of his liability under s 1 of CYPA 1933 where he does not have actual custody. Liability has depended on whether there is an affiliation order against him.

10 See ante, para 1.58, for its meaning.

11 *Ex p St Mary Abbotts Guardians* (1887) 4 TLR 63.

12 *Horner v Horner* (1799) 1 Hag Con 337 at 355.

13 Under GMA 1971, s 5(1); see post, para 4.13.

14 Section s 9 and 14. This right of the mother or father to seek custody or access was first conferred by the Legitimacy Act 1959, s 3. For orders under s 9 of the 1971 Act and the factors to be considered in making them see post, Chapter 3.

15 For agreement to adoption see post, paras 5.20–531.

16 See the Marriage Act 1949, Sch II. For the changes when the relevant provisions of the FLRA 1987 are brought into force see post, para 4.32.

17 Whether he can change the name where he has legal custody is doubtful. It turns on

whether the power to change a name falls within the scope of the concept of legal custody; see ante, para 1.64.

18 Where he has neither guardianship nor legal custody and the local authority assumes the rights and duties of the mother under a s 3 resolution, this would preclude the father from applying for legal custody under s 9 of GMA 1971 (*R v Oxford City Justices, ex p H* [1975] QB 1, [1974] 2 All ER 356; *R v Oxford Justices, ex p D* [1987] QB 199, [1986] 3 All ER 129); but the effect of the decision of the Court of Appeal in *Re M and H (minors) (local authority: parental rights)* [1987] 3 WLR 759, [1987] FLR 97, CA; affd [1988] 3 WLR 485, HL has been to make his application no more than a paper application, since it was there held that the court which deals with it must refuse to go on and hear its merits; see further para 15.37.

19 GMA 1971, s 14(3).

20 Section 9(2), as originally enacted.

(ii)   Maintenance

2.41   The mother does at least have the right to seek maintenance for her child from the father, even if it is by the anachronistic mechanism of affiliation proceedings in a magistrates' court.[1] These proceedings are to be abolished by FLRA 1987,[2] but for some time there will be the question of variation of earlier orders after the new provisions of the 1987 Act come into force.[3]

1   For discussion of the many special rules see Law Com Working Paper on Illegitimacy and Report No 118, Part VI.

2   Section 17.

3   On this see post, para 16.67.

(iii)   Citizenship

2.42   Although the British Nationality Act 1981 made the major change of allowing transmission of citizenship through mothers as well as fathers, it continues the earlier discrimination of not allowing a child of unmarried parents to acquire citizenship through his father. This disadvantage was, however, only of practical consequence under the former law (British Nationality Act 1948) if the child was born abroad, because of the rule that a child born in the United Kingdom thereby acquired British citizenship. This rule has disappeared and been replaced by the principle that the child's citizenship very largely depends on the citizenship status of his parents.[1] The rules under the 1981 Act are complicated,[2] but the general consequence for the child of unmarried parents who is born in the United Kingdom is that, unlike the child of married parents, he does not acquire British citizenship if his mother is neither a British citizen[3] nor 'settled'[4] in this country, even though his father is a British citizen.[5]

1   But see BNA 1981, s 1(4) which enables a child aged at least ten to register as a British citizen if he complies with certain residential requirements.

2   For a clear summary in relation to the present topic see Law Com Working Paper No 118, paras 11.2–11.5.

3   If she herself is a British citizen only by descent she cannot transmit citizenship unless she falls into one of the specified categories (ss 2(1)(b), 3(3) or 3(5) and 14).

4   See s 50(2)–(4) for the meaning of 'settled'.

5   See ss 1(1) and 50(9).

(iv)   Property rights

2.43   One of the consequences of the common law treatment of the bastard as *filius nullius*[1] was the rule of construction that prima facie any reference in an instrument to 'children', 'issue' and the like was exclusively to those who were legitimate, and, although it was a presumptive and not an absolute rule, it was not easily disturbed.[2] Contrary to the recommendation of the Russell Committee on the Law of Succession in Relation to Illegitimate Persons,[3] section 15(1) of the Family Law Reform Act 1969[4] introduced the contrary rule so that prima-facie references to children and other relatives included references to, and to persons related through, illegitimate persons. The presumption extended not only to illegitimate children but also to legitimated, and it applied to any disposition (including an oral disposition) whether inter vivos or by will or codicil, which was made on or after 1st January 1970.[5] However, it did not affect the construction of the word 'heir' or 'heirs' or of any expression used to create an entailed interest; and it did not sever property which would (apart from s 15) have devolved along with a dignity or title of honour. Trustees and personal representatives who had distributed property without having ascertained whether there was a person who could have benefited by reason of the section were protected from personal liability.

1   Ante, para 2.20.
2   See *Hill v Crook* (1873) LR 6 HL 265 HL; *Dorin v Dorin* (1875) LR 7 HL 568, HL; *Sydall v Castings Ltd* [1967] 1 QB 302, [1966] 3 All ER 770, CA.
3   Cmnd 3051, paras 57–58.
4   See Morris, *The Family Law Reform Act 1969, ss 14 and 15* 19 ICLQ 328; Samuels, *Succession and the Family Law Reform Act 1969* 34 Conv 247, at p 249; Ryder, *Property Law Aspects of the Family Law Reform Act 1969* [1971] CLP 157 at pp 166–167.
5   The Act (s 15(7)) also abolished the rule that a child conceived after the making of a disposition could not benefit under it, however clear the intention was that he should.

2.44   As for intestacy, prior to the FLRA 1969 the limits of recognition accorded to the illegitimate child by the law of intestate succession were that he and his issue were entitled to succeed on the intestacy of his mother provided that she left no legitimate issue, and she was entitled to succeed on his intestacy as if she were the only surviving parent.[1]   The Act of 1969 was a significant event in the legal emancipation of the illegitimate child because section 14 enabled him or, if he was dead, his issue to succeed on the intestacy of either of his parents as if he were their legitimate child.[2] Correspondingly, each of them had a right of succession on his intestacy, if they survived him. Nevertheless, there were a number of limits to the section. It applied to persons dying intestate on or after 1 January 1970, but not to earlier intestacies. It did not affect the right to take an entailed interest. Nor did it entitle the illegitimate child to succeed to a title or dignity of honour. But its most serious defect was that it did not confer on him a right to inherit on the intestacy of any relative other than a parent.

For the purposes of intestate succession by the child's father, there was a presumption that he had not survived his child unless the contrary was shown,[3] a presumption which reflected the reality that in the vast majority of cases the father was unknown. On the other hand, English law did not provide a procedure for formal acknowledgement of paternity, so that there could be practical difficulties of establishing the relationship between the claimant and the deceased. Therefore trustees and personal representatives who distributed without ascertaining whether there was a person entitled under section 14 were protected, but this did not prevent the beneficiary from following the property.[4] The rule equally applied to distribution under a will or other disposition of property.

1   Legitimacy Act 1926, s 9.
2   For the rights of succession see Administration of Estates Act 1925, s 47 as amended by Family Law Reform Act 1969, s 3(2).
3   FLRA 1969, s 14(4).
4   FLRA 1969, s 17.

2.45   Another significant improvement made by the FLRA 1969[1] was to extend the provisions of the Inheritance (Family Provision) Act 1938 to cover illegitimate children as dependants. The principle was re-enacted in the Inheritance (Provision for Family and Dependants) Act 1975 and the effect is that for the purpose of the Act illegitimate children are to be treated equally with legitimate.[2]

1   Section 18(1).
2   Section 25(1); *Re McC's Estate* (1978) 9 Fam Law 26.

(b)   Effects since FLRA 1987

The general principle
2.46   Section 1(1) of the Act, which is now operative, reads:

'In this Act and enactments passed and instruments made after the coming into force of this section, references (however expressed) to any relationship between two persons shall, unless the contrary intention appears, be construed without regard to whether or not the father and mother of either of them, or the father and mother of any person through whom the relationship is deduced, have or had been married to each other at any time'

Apart from being restricted by its own terms in that it applies only to future legislation,[1] prima facie the effect of this general principle is to abolish illegitimacy and place all children on an equal footing whether or not their parents have been married to each other. As the following analysis shows, that is not the complete picture.

1   But see also s 2(1) (not yet in force). Moreover, the Lord Chancellor is (prospectively) empowered (by s 30(1)) to extend it by order to legislation passed before s 1 came into operation, but the practical efficacy of the power is virtually removed by the proviso (in sub-s (2)) that 'an order under [s 30] shall so amend the enactments to which it relates as to secure that (so far as practicable) they continue to have the same effect notwithstanding the making of the order'. This seems to be no more than a power to remove references to the term illegitimacy in relation to the enactments which are the subject of the order; see ante, para 2.21, note 17.

(i)   The relationship with the father
2.47   The Act does not automatically confer parental powers and responsibilities on the father whose child is born outside marriage.[1] As under the present law,[2] he will still have to rely on being appointed a testamentary guardian or on taking the initiative of asserting his relationship by applying to the High Court, a county court or a magistrates' court for an order in his favour. He will still be able to apply for legal custody under section 9 of the Guardianship of Minors Act 1971, but the 1987

Act alternatively will enable him to seek a wider order under section 4 of that Act, namely, an order giving him 'all the parental rights and duties' which *subject to any order made by the court otherwise than under this section* he will have jointly with the child's mother or, if she is dead, with a guardian appointed under the GMA 1971.[3] The main use of the order will, it is suggested, be to regularise the relationship between the child and the father where the father and mother are living together in a stable relationship. If they should later break up, the court could, on the application of either of them (most likely the mother) discharge the order,[4] the effect of which would be to re-vest the rights and duties exclusively in the mother except in so far as any statutory rule otherwise provides. If a section 4 order has been made and the mother dies, those rights and duties will vest solely in the surviving father, except that he will share them with any testamentary guardian appointed by the mother.[5] Where there has been no section 4 order made during the lifetime of the mother, there seems to be no reason why the father should not apply for an order after her death.[6] Alternatively he could apply under section 5(1) of the GMA 1971 to be appointed a guardian. The position is not, however, so clear where the deceased mother has appointed a testamentary guardian. Arguably, the father could still seek a section 4 order the effect of which would be that he would share the rights and duties with the guardian. Alternatively he might try to obtain an order under section 6 of the GMA 1971 for the removal of the testamentary guardian and his own appointment in place of that guardian.

Even less clear is the effect of the above italicised proviso, particularly with its reference to 'the court' and not 'a court'. No objection can be taken if its effect will be that the parental powers and responsibilities will vest jointly by virtue of the section 4 order except in so far as the court otherwise directs. For example, where the mother and father have ceased to live together but he remains deeply interested in and involved with his child, a section 4 order might well be appropriate, subject to the mother being given actual custody and the father access. But by virtue of what statutory authority 'otherwise than under [section 4]' would the court be empowered so to order actual custody and access in proceedings brought under section 4?

1 For the convincing reasons which led the Law Commission to change its views and recommend this rule and for the various possible degrees of recognition of the child's father see Law Com No 118, paras 4.24–4.51; and for criticism see Eekelaar, *Second Thoughts on Illegitimacy Reform* [1985] Fam Law 261.
2 Ante, para 2.40.
3 Subsections (1) and (2). Italics supplied. There is no legal objection to the father applying in the alternative for a s 4 order and an order under s 9 of the 1971 Act.
4 The power to discharge is conferred by FLRA 1987, s 4(3). Where the mother is dead application can be made by any guardian appointed under GMA 1971.
5 Section 4 refers to a guardian 'appointed under the 1971 Act'. Bromley, p 263, note 18 questions whether this extends to a testamentary guardian. It is submitted that it does. The power of a mother or father to appoint such a guardian arises under the 1971 Act, s 4, and under no other common law or statutory authority.
6 Bromley, p 268, reaches the same conclusion.

(ii) Maintenance
2.48 Affiliation proceedings are to be abolished by the 1987 Act,[1] although existing orders made under the Affiliation Proceedings Act 1957[2] will survive

and remain governed by that Act.[3] In their place either parent, but usually the mother, will be able to seek in a magistrates' court, a county court or the High Court orders for financial provision in favour of the child.[4] In a county court or the High Court wider orders, including provisions dealing with capital, may be made, and for that reason where an application is made to those courts and an affiliation order is already in force, the court will be able to direct that it is to cease to have effect.[5]

1   Section 17.
2   Or by virtue of the National Assistance Act 1948, s 44, the Supplementary Benefits Act 1976, s 19, the Child Care Act 1980, s 49 or s 50, or the Social Security Act 1986, s 25.
3   FLRA 1987, Sch 3, para 6.
4   Under GMA 1971, s 11B, to be inserted by FLRA 1987, s 12. See further, post, para 16.67.
5   FLRA 1987, Sch 3, para 7.

(iii)   Citizenship

2.49   The 1987 Act does not alter the law, so that citizenship can still not be transmitted to the child via the father, if the latter and the mother were not married to each other at the time of the child's birth. The Government argued[1] that any change in this rule was inappropriate for inclusion in a family law provision and that further consultation was needed. In the meantime applicants for citizenship must rely on the Home Secretary exercising his discretion benevolently in applying the criteria for naturalisation.[2]

It is convenient briefly to note here that there is also no change in the rule that the child acquires his domicile of origin from his mother. This necessarily follows from the fact that the 1987 Act does not confer on the father parental powers and responsibilities when the child is born.

1   See, for example, HL Debs, 27 November 1986, cols 684–5; 11 December 1986, col 1262.
2   HL Debs 11 December 1986, col 1267. The criteria are contained in the British Nationality Act 1981, Sch 1.

(iv)   Property rights

2.50   In relation to property rights, the position for children born to unmarried parents is improved as follows:

(i) On intestacy[1] the relationship of a child with any other person is to be construed without reference to the marital status of the child's parents. In other words the limited reform of section 14 of FLRA 1969, which equated an illegitimate child with a legitimate child vis à vis his parents, is carried further so that he can inherit on the intestacy of any other relative, such as grandparent, uncle or aunt.[2]

As for succession to the child, the effect is to extend rights not only to the mother and father but also to other relatives in accordance with the rules of succession, but the 1987 Act retains the presumption that the father does not survive the child unless the contrary is shown and extends it to a person who is related to the child only through the father.[3]

(ii) Section 19 of the 1987 Act provides that as regards dispositions inter vivos made on or after the date on which the section comes into force (ie 4 April 1988) or dispositions by will or codicil where the will or codicil is made on or after that date, all relationships are to be construed in accordance with the principle of equality set out in section 1 of the Act.[4] Moreover, the words 'heir' and 'heirs' and any expression used to create an entailed interest are similarly to be construed unless a specific contrary intention is shown.[5] However, the bar against succession to property carrying a dignity or title of honour survives.[6]

(iii) The protection formerly given to trustees,[7] who had distributed the assets of an estate without ascertaining whether there was a claimant who could rely on a link with an illegitimate person, is abolished.[8] The conventional method of discharging their duty is for the trustees to place an advertisement.[9] On the other hand, for the purpose of a grant of probate or administration, it is presumed that the deceased is not survived by a person who could claim a grant through a relationship of unmarried parents.[10]

1 See s 18.
2 The extension does not affect any rights under the intestacy of a person dying before the coming into force of s 18 (4 April 1988); see sub-s (4).
3 Section 18(2).
4 Subsection (1). By FLRA 1969, s 15, there was a presumption to this effect, but it only applied to the illegitimate child in his capacity as a beneficiary, or if a beneficiary's entitlement depended on it.
5 Section 19(2).
6 Section 19(4).
7 FLRA 1969, s 17.
8 FLRA 1987, s 20. The reasons for doing so and the implications for trustees are set out in the Law Commission's First Report (No 118), paras 8.34–39. The Commission changed its mind in its Second Report (No 157, at paras 3.8–13) and recommended abolition.
9 See Trustee Act 1925, s 27. The cost of doing so is £80; HL Debs, 11 December 1986, col 1272.
10 FLRA 1987, s 21. See Law Com No 118, paras 8.40–42. The rule does not apply in relation to the estate of a person dying before the rule comes into force (ie before 4 April 1988)..

CHAPTER 3
Issues of custody and access[1]

I THE WELFARE OF THE CHILD

1 The meaning of the paramountcy of the child's welfare

3.01 The determination by a court of any issue relating to custody or access is governed by the principle contained in the well known section 1 of the Guardianship of Minors Act 1971 (as amended[2]), which provides:

'Where in any proceedings before any court . . .
(a) the legal custody or upbringing of a minor; or
(b) the administration of any property belonging to or held on trust for a minor, or the application of the income thereof,
is in question, the court, in deciding that question, shall regard the welfare of the minor as the first and paramount consideration, and shall not take into consideration whether from any other point of view the claim of the father, in respect of such legal custody, upbringing, administration or application, is superior to that of the mother, or the claim of the mother is superior to that of the father.'

The operation of this principle, which makes the child's welfare the paramount consideration, is in some respects wider, in others narrower than the wording of the section might suggest.

1 For general references to various aspects of this topic see Law Commission Working Paper No 96 on *Custody* and, as a Supplementary Paper, (by Priest and Whybrow) *Custody Law in Practice in the Divorce and Domestic Courts* (1986); Working Paper No 100 on *Care, Supervision and Interim Orders in Custody Proceedings*; Law Com No 172 on *Family Law Review of Child Law Guardianship and Custody;* Bromley, Chapter 9; Cretney, Chapter 12; Freeman, *The Rights and Wrongs of Children,* Chapter 6; Hoggett and Pearl, Chapters 12 and 13; Eekelaar, *Family Law and Social Policy* (2nd edn) 1984, Chapter 4; Eekelaar and Clive with Clarke and Raikes, *Custody after Divorce* (1977); Maidment, *Child Custody and Divorce* (1984); Mnookin, *Child Custody Adjudication: Judicial Functions in the Face of Indeterminacy* (1975) 39 Law and Contemporary Problems 226, and *Bargaining in the Shadow of the Law: The Case of Divorce* [1979] CLP 65; Murch, *Justice and Welfare in Divorce* (1979); Booth, *Child Legislation: Custody: Its Judicial Interpretation* (1982) Statute Law Review 71.
Among the extensive literature of psychologists and child development specialists the following are especially helpful: Bowlby, *Child Care and the Growth of Love* (2nd edn); Goldstein, Freud and Solnit, *Beyond the Best Interests of the Child,* and *Before the Best Interests of the Child*; Richards and Dyson, *Separation, Divorce and the Development of Children: A Review* (1982); Richards, *Behind the Best Interests of the Child: An Examination of the Arguments of Goldstein, Freud and Solnit Concerning Custody and Access at Divorce* [1986] JSWL 77; Rutter, *Maternal Deprivation Re-assessed* (2nd edn) 1981; Wallerstein and Kelly, *Surviving the Break Up: How Children and Parents Cope with Divorce* (1980).
2 By GA 1973, ss 9(1) and 15(3) and Sch 3; DPMCA 1978, s 36; and prospectively by FLRA 1987, s 33(1) and Sch 2, para 28.

3.02 Thus, although the section refers only to legal custody, it extends equally to questions of custody in the widest sense[1] or, on the other hand, to those involving only care and control or actual custody[2] or only some specific parental power or responsibility which is part of, or incidental to, one of those concepts (for example, the power/responsibility relating to religious education of the child),[3] while the reference in the section to 'upbringing' is wide enough to embrace questions relating to access.[4] Although, too, the section refers to the legal custody or upbringing or the property matter being 'in question', this does not necessarily mean in dispute. The parties may have in mind a consent order, but the court must still be satisfied that the proposed order accords with the paramountcy principle. In proceedings for divorce, nullity or judicial separation, before being able to grant a final decree the divorce court must act in accordance with that principle in determining whether proper arrangements have been made for the child, whether or not a custody order is sought.[5] A similar provision operates in matrimonial proceedings under the Domestic Proceedings Magistrates' Courts Act 1978.[6] Nevertheless, the principle is most frequently invoked where the custody or upbringing is in dispute.[7] It may be between the mother and father or between a parent and non-parent or between persons neither of whom is the parent.[8] It usually arises in matrimonial proceedings or under the Guardianship of Minors Act 1971 or in custodianship proceedings[9] or wardship proceedings. It has been held that in wardship proceedings the principle enables the court to look beyond the issues raised by the parties and exceptionally to adopt a course of action not advocated by them.[10] There can be no doubt that the same power exists in custody disputes so that, for example, the court may grant legal custody to a person not contemplated by the parties.

1 See ante, para 1.58.
2 Ibid, para 1.65.
3 For disputes between the child's father and mother over a specific power/responsibility see GA 1973, s 1(3), ante, para 1.67, and for such a dispute between persons holding a power/responsibility jointly under DPMCA see ss 13(1) and 15 of that Act.
4 Where the proceedings relate to access to a child who is in the care of a local authority, it is expressly provided that the paramountcy principle applies; see CCA 1980, s 12F(1) (as inserted by HASSASSAA 1983, s 6 and Sch I) post, para 15.92.
5 MCA 1973, s 41, post para 3.48.
6 Section 8; see post, para 3.35.
7 But the fact that most custody cases are uncontested (see Priest and Whybrow, op cit) makes it all the more important that the court should be alert to the need to apply the principle.
8 *J v C* [1970] AC 668, [1969] 1 All ER 788, HL per Lord Guest (at 697, 809); per Lord MacDermott (at 715, 724); per Lord Upjohn (at 724, 832).
9 So far as concerns matrimonial proceedings under DPMCA 1978 and custodianship proceedings the paramountcy principle is expressly adopted; see respectively DPMCA 1978, s 15 and CA 1975, s 33(9). See also supra note 4.
10 *Re E (SA) (a minor) (wardship)* [1984] 1 All ER 289, [1984] 1 WLR 156, HL.

3.03 Notwithstanding the variety of proceedings in which section 1 is invoked, it does not cover, as it states, 'any proceedings in any court' in which the legal custody or upbringing of the child is in question. Its paramountcy principle is excluded from adoption proceedings where 'the need to safeguard and promote the welfare of the child throughout his childhood' is accorded only 'first consideration',[1] although, as will be seen, in practice the court in the vast majority of adoption applications determines what is in the child's best interests. For care proceedings in the juvenile court there is also a different standard imposed,[2] but here, too, once the case is proved the choice of order to be made is in practice governed by the child's best interests, and there is strong judicial support for that approach.[3] Where a resolution vesting 'parental rights and duties' in a local authority is challenged by the parent and the authority seeks the approval of the resolution the court must be satisfied that, inter alia, 'it is in the interests of the child' that the resolution shall not lapse, a requirement which apparently is similarly construed to mean the best interests of the child.[4]

1   AA 1976, s 6; see post, para 5.12.
2   By CYPA 1933, s 44(1).
3   See post, para 14.106.
4   CCA 1980, s 3(6), post, para 15.39.

3.04   Well known though the paramountcy principle is, its scope is not free from uncertainty and the likely result of its application in a particular case is sometimes difficult to predict. Its meaning was explained by Lord McDermott in the leading case of *J v C* in the following dictum:[1]

'Reading those words in their ordinary significance and relating them to the various classes of proceedings which the section has already mentioned, it seems to me that they must mean more than that the child's welfare is to be treated as the top item in a list of items relevant to the matter in question. I think they connote a process whereby, when all the relevant facts, relationships, claims and wishes of parents, risks, choices and other circumstances are taken into account and weighed, the course to be followed will be that which is most in the interests of the child's welfare as that term has now to be understood. That is the first consideration because it is of first importance and the paramount consideration because it rules on or determines the course to be followed.'

The essence of this paramountcy principle is that the child's welfare must prevail over any other consideration; but its operation is subject to the limitation that the child's legal custody or upbringing must be directly in issue. So it was held by the majority of the House of Lords in *Richards v Richards*,[2] where in an application for an ouster injunction in pending matrimonial proceedings section 1(3) of the Matrimonial Homes Act 1967 was so construed that the needs of the child were treated as only one factor, albeit an important one, in deciding whether it was 'just and reasonable' to grant an injunction. Section 1 of the Guardianship of Minors Act 1971 was held not to override section 1 of the 1967 Act, even though, as Lord Scarman emphasised in his dissenting opinion, the ouster jurisdiction has a great impact on the welfare and upbringing of children. The paramountcy principle may also be excluded in order to protect wider interests, such as freedom of publication[3] or control of immigration of children,[4] and, as will be seen,[5] the protection of such interests cannot be circumvented by relying on wardship proceedings and the argument that in those proceedings section 1 of the 1971 Act must prevail. Nor can wardship be so used to supervise the statutory powers conferred on local authorities to deal with children in their care.[6]

1   [1970] AC 668 at 710, [1969] 1 All ER 788 at 820–821, HL respectively.
2   [1984] AC 174, [1983] 2 All ER 807, HL.
3   *Re X* [1975] Fam 47, [1975] 1 All ER 697. CA.
4   *Re Mohamed Arif* [1968] Ch 643, sub nom *Re A* [1968] 2 All ER 145, CA.
5   Post, para 8.49.
6   *A v Liverpool City Council* [1982] AC 363, [1981] 2 All ER 385, HL; see post, para 15.124.

3.05   Subject to those limitations, Lord MacDermott's dictum has been so interpreted judicially as to make welfare the sole consideration.[1] Every factor (other than those mentioned in the previous paragraph) is relevant only in so far as it helps to answer the question, 'What is most in the interests of the child's welfare?' But that is a large question, because welfare is to be understood in the widest sense so as to include not only the physical and mental but also the moral, spiritual and (increasingly) the emotional well-being of the child.[2] Moreover, it is wholly within the court's discretion whether to award custody by reference only to what is best for the child in the immediate future or to base it on his long term interests,[3] and the older he is the easier it may be to take account of the latter. However, it is not possible to list definitively all the circumstances which will have certain results in custody proceedings.[4] The circumstances of each case and their possible impact are so variable that earlier decisions should be treated circumspectly, and the older they are the less reliable they may eventually become through changing social attitudes towards parental responsibility in bringing up children. Nevertheless, all facts that may be of any relevance should be investigated, and, while the weight to be accorded to each must depend on judicial discretion and is not determinable by any formula or 'points system',[5] there are some which tend to carry greater weight than others. The following are the ones which most commonly are relevant, but it cannot be stressed too strongly that, since some or all of them are closely inter-related in any particular case, any separate examination of them must be artificial,[6] especially as 'it is surprisingly difficult to find judicial articulation of what is thought to be meant by the term 'welfare'.[7]

1   The Law Commission recommends removing any reference to 'first' consideration; see Working Paper No 96, para 6.9; Law Com No 172, paras 3.13–3.16.
2   See Lindley LJ in *Re McGrath* [1893] 1 Ch 143 at 148.
3   *T v T* [1987] 1 FLR 374, CA. In the context of adoption proceedings (Adoption Act 1976, s 6) and in the treatment of children in local authority care (CCA 1980, s 18(1)) regard must be had to the need to safeguard and promote the child's welfare throughout his childhood.
4   *Thariyan v Thariyan* (1974) 5 Fam Law 123, CA. For the special difficulties in decision making which those proceedings create see Mnookin, op cit, pp 249–262.
5   Per Megarry J in *Re F (an infant), F v F* [1969] 2 Ch 238 at 241, [1969] 2 All ER 766 at 768. See also Dunn LJ in *Pountney v Morris* [1984] FLR 381 at 384, [1984] Fam Law 176, CA.
6   For a comprehensive examination see Poulter, *Child Custody – Recent Developments* (1982) 12 Fam Law 5; but see Bradney, *Developments in Child Custody Law,* [1987] Fam Law 246 for a timely warning that 'the importance of previous decisions and the manner of that importance, may vary depending upon the area of custody law under consideration'.
7   Bromley, p 317. But see Law Com No 172, post, para 3.12 note 11, for a statutory checklist of relevant factors.

2   Principal factors

(a)   Age and sex of the child

3.06   Although it is not strictly a rule, in practice the courts accept as a firm and realistic guide that where children are young their mother is normally the appropriate person to have the care and control (actual custody) of them.[1] The younger the child is the stronger the position of the mother,[2] and the more so if she is not out at work.[3] In the case of older children she is also at an advantage if the child is a daughter approaching puberty,[4] and, although the courts have more recently shown a slight inclination towards allowing a father to bring up an older son,[5] it is much more likely, where there are daughter and son, that both will be entrusted to their mother rather than separate them, especially if there is not a wide difference in their ages.[6] Occasionally there may be special circumstances justifying the separation of children,[7] particularly if staying access can be arranged so that they can spend their school holidays together.[8] Generally, however, the court will not allow separation, especially if the children are close together in age and fond of each other,[9] and this attitude invariably works in the mother's favour.[10] The court may also be ready to overlook her material disadvantages (eg concerning the provision of accommodation[11]) compared with the father's more favourable circumstances or her own shortcomings (eg laziness) if she is a caring mother, since she is still seen as primarily 'the secure and loving figure around which things should revolve'.[12] This emphasis runs the risk of underestimating in the particular case the psychological attachment which the child has to the father or, indeed, to some other adult.[13] However, if the mother has for a long period jettisoned her responsibilities and shown no interest in her child, the court may look unfavourably on any claim by her to custody and grant it to the father.[14] So, too, where he is able to provide a stable life for the child and the mother is not.[15]

1 *Re B (an infant)* [1962] 1 All ER 872, [1962] 1 WLR 550, CA; *Re C(A) (an infant), C v C* [1970] 1 All ER 309, [1970] 1 WLR 288, CA; *Faulkner v Faulkner* (1979) 2 FLR 115, 10 Fam Law 88; *H v H* [1984] Fam Law 112, CA; *Townson v Mahon* [1984] FLR 690, [1984] Fam Law 204, CA; *Bowley v Bowley* [1984] FLR 791, CA; *Allington v Allington* [1985] FLR 586, [1985] Fam Law 157, CA.

2 *Re S (an infant)* [1958] 1 All ER 783, [1958] 1 WLR 391; *Re F (an infant) F v F* [1969] 2 Ch 238, [1969] 2 All ER 766; *Ellard v Ellard* (1974) 5 Fam Law 29, DC; *Re K (minors) (children: care and control)* [1977] Fam 179, [1977] 1 All ER 647, CA; *Southgate v Southgate* (1978) 8 Fam Law 246 CA; *M v M* (1978) 1 FLR 77, 9 Fam Law 92, CA.

3 *Re O (infants)* [1971] Ch 748 at 752, [1971] 2 All ER 744 at 746.

4 *Pinch v Pinch* (1973) 3 Fam Law 171, CA; *Riley v Riley* (1986) 150 JP 439, [1986] 2 FLR 429, CA.

5 But there is no rule about this; see *Re C(A) (an infant), C v C,* supra, note 1.

6 See eg *Dorschler v Dorschler* (1973) 3 Fam Law 183, CA; *Pinch v Pinch* (1973) 3 Fam Law 171, CA; *Baldrian v Baldrian* (1974) 4 Fam Law 12, CA; *Reynolds v Reynolds* (1974) 4 Fam Law 193, CA; *Re C (minors)* (1978) 8 Fam Law 202, CA; *C v C* (1981) 11 Fam Law 147, CA; *Guery v Guery* (1982) 12 Fam Law 184, CA; *C v C (Custody)* [1988] Fam Law 338, CA.

7 See eg *Re O (infants)* [1962] 2 All ER 10, [1962] 1 WLR 724, CA.

8 *Re P (infants)* [1967] 2 All ER 229, [1967] 1 WLR 818; *Re B (an infant)* (1966) Times, 5 April, CA.

9 *Adams v Adams* [1984] FLR 768, [1984] Fam Law 249, CA.

10 *Doncheff v Doncheff* (1978) 8 Fam Law 208, CA; *C v C* (1981) 11 Fam Law 147, CA; *H v H (child custody)* [1984] Fam Law 112, CA; *Cossey v Cossey* (1980) 11 Fam Law 56, where the Court of Appeal refused to affirm the decision of the lower court which gave custody of one daughter (aged 8½) to the father and of the other daughter (aged

10) to the mother and the parents were living on opposite sides of the same road, but instead granted the mother custody of both children. See similarly *Guery v Guery* note 6 and *C v C* (1988) ibid.
11 *Barham v Salter* (1974) 5 Fam Law 19, CA.
12 *Greer v Greer* (1974) 4 Fam Law 187, CA.
13 See King, *Maternal Love – Fact or Myth* (1974) 4 Fam Law 61.
14 *H v H and C* [1969] 1 All ER 262, [1969] 1 WLR 208, CA; *Aldous v Aldous* (1974) 5 Fam Law 152, CA; *Stephenson v Stephenson* [1985] FLR 1140, [1985] Fam Law 253, CA.
15 *Stovold v Stovold* (1973) 4 Fam Law 14, CA; *Hilton v Wilson-Jones* (1975) 5 Fam Law 149, CA; *Hutchinson v Hutchinson* (1978) 8 Fam Law 140, DC; *Re G (a minor)* (1980) 10 Fam Law 190, CA; *Hutchinson v Hutchinson* (1980) 2 FLR 167, 11 Fam Law 24.

(b)   Continuity of care: the status quo

3.07   The father's position may be strengthened where the child has already been with him for a lengthy period before the commencement of custody proceedings,[1] for continuity of care is another cogent factor.[2] The court is very reluctant to uproot a child from a parent, unless there are powerful reasons for doing so.[3] Indeed, it may be willing in the interests of the child exceptionally to countenance the father's remaining unemployed so that he can devote all his time to bringing up the child.[4] There is strong empirical evidence to show that only in a very small number of custody cases arising from divorce will the transfer of care and control be ordered,[5] and there is no reason to doubt a similar pattern in other proceedings concerned with issues over custody.[6] Nevertheless, there is a sufficient number of reported decisions to show that the strength of the guideline that young children should normally be with their mother may sometimes override the status quo factor and lead to care and control being transferred to her, even where she has not looked after her children for a long time.[7] In this regard her claim is stronger if there has previously been substantial and satisfactory access by her to the children[8] or if the father has done everything to frustrate opportunities for access[9] or has taken the children from her against her will.[10] Another relevant consideration is the reason for her not having taken the children with her when she left the father. The court is more likely to be kindly disposed towards her if the only reason was that she had nowhere to take them.[11] So, too, she is likely to be given care and control if the transfer is likely to produce minimal harm to the children, for example, because they are well balanced and happy children[12] or if there will be limited disruption to their lives in that they will keep the same school and friends.[13] These matters are, of course, equally relevant where the dispute is not between the mother and father but between her and some other person from whom she seeks care and control, but in such a case her claim is much stronger and there must be powerful reasons to deprive her of her child.[14] Even where the dispute is between mother and step father, the fact that the latter is not a natural parent is a matter to be borne in mind.[15]

1 Cf *Allington v Allington* [1985] FLR 586, [1985] Fam Law 157, CA, where the separation of a two-year-old daughter from her mother had only been for a few weeks and during that period there had been regular contact between them. Not surprisingly the court granted the mother custody.
2 In *H v H and C* [1969] 1 All ER 262, [1969] 1 WLR 208, CA; and *Aldous v Aldous* (1974) 5 Fam Law 152, CA the respective mothers had not seen their children for over 18 months; in *Stovold v Stovold* (1973) 4 Fam Law 14, CA the period was two years. For striking illustration of the importance attached to the status quo factor see *P v P*

(1975) 6 Fam Law 75, CA where custody of four girls (aged between three and ten) was given to the father even though he had been convicted of sexual offences, one of them involving a girl of eight.

3 See especially Ormrod LJ in *Re C (a minor) (wardship and adoption)* (1979) 2 FLR 177 at 194; *D v M (minor: custody appeal)* [1983] Fam 33, [1982] 3 All ER 897, CA. See *May v May* [1986] 1 FLR 325, [1986] Fam Law 105, CA, for an exceptional case of the father upsetting the status quo and being granted care and control. See Michaels, *The Dangers of a Change of Parentage in Custody and Adoption Cases* (1967) 83 LQR 547.

4 *B v B (custody of children)* [1985] FLR 166, [1985] Fam Law 29, CA. His case will be strengthened where he has already cared for the child before he becomes unemployed; *B v B (custody of child)* [1985] FLR 462, [1985] Fam Law 119, CA. In refusing to allow the father to continue to have care and control the judge in the first of these cases relied heavily on the notion that it was 'plainly wrong and silly if the father were to remain unemployed in order to look after one four and a half-year-old boy. The father's primary role must be by his work to generate resources which provide for the support and maintenance of this child and himself, rather than remain at home performing what traditionally is regarded as the mother's role, that being made possible by support of the tax-payer's money' ([1985] FLR at 177–178). While the Court of Appeal expressed general approval of that notion (see Oliver LJ at 179, and Cumming-Bruce LJ at 183–184), it recognised that 'the prospect of an able-bodied man being permanently unemployed' could only be one and not a conclusive consideration in applying the principle of the paramountcy of the child's welfare. In view of the current high level of unemployment some of the dicta in *B v B* may be found to be controversial. Indeed, where a father has remarried it has regrettably to be said that it is often easier for his second wife or, where he is not married, girl friend to obtain a part-time job than for him to gain full employment. That additional financial support is likely to be more in the interests of the child than total reliance on Social Security payments.

5 Eekelaar and Clive *Custody and Divorce* (1977) paras 13.14 and 13.29. See also Maidment *A Study in Child Custody* (1976) 6 Fam Law 195 and 236; and *Child Custody and Divorce*.

6 In the vast majority of cases the parents agree that their young children should remain with the mother.

7 The following examples of transfer to the mother indicate the period of separation from the child: *Re W (a minor) (custody)* (1982) 4 FLR 492, 13 Fam Law 47, CA (one-and-a-half years); *Townsend v Townsend* (1973) 4 Fam Law 127, CA (three years); *Pinch v Pinch* (1973) 3 Fam Law 171, CA (three-and-a-half years); *P v McK (formerly P)* (1973) 4 Fam Law 128, CA (three-and-a-half years); *Ives v Ives* (1973) 4 Fam Law 16, CA (almost four years); *Thariyan v Thariyan* (1974) 5 Fam Law 123, CA (almost five years); *D v D* (1979) 2 FLR 74, 10 Fam Law 53, CA (four years); *S v W* (1980) 11 Fam Law 81, CA (five years); *Re B and G (minors) (custody)* [1985] FLR 134, [1985] Fam Law 58; affd [1985] FLR 493, [1985] Fam Law 127 (five-and-a-half years); *B v Y* (1980) 11 Fam Law 82, CA (six years); *Re DW (a minor) (custody)* [1984] Fam Law 17, CA (eight years). In the converse case, where the father is seeking transfer from the mother, his chances are much slimmer, *Re C (minors)* (1978) 8 Fam Law 202, CA; *M v M* (1978) 1 FLR 77, 9 Fam Law 92, CA.

8 *Greer v Greer* (1974) 4 Fam Law 187, CA. See also *Stephenson v Stephenson* [1985] FLR 1140, [1985] Fam Law 253, CA (access by mother on six occasions in two-and-a-half years).

9 *Cutts v Cutts* (1977) 7 Fam Law 209, CA.

10 *G v G* (1975) 6 Fam Law 43, CA; *Witter v Drummond* (1979) 10 Fam Law 149, CA.

11 *Thariyan v Thariyan; Cutts v Cutts*. See also *Stephenson v Stephenson* (where mother abandoned child when seven months old).

12 *Greer v Greer*.

13 *Pinch v Pinch; P v McK (formerly P)*, supra, note 7.

14 *Barham v Salter* (1974) 5 Fam Law 19, CA; cf *Re DW (a minor) (custody)*, supra, note 7.

15 *Bowley v Bowley* [1984] FLR 791, CA.

(c)   Claims, wishes, conduct and character of the parent or other claimant

3.08   Where there is an application for legal custody or access under section 9 of the Guardianship of Minors Act 1971 by either parent, the section expressly directs the court that, when deciding upon the appropriate order, it is to have regard to the welfare of the child and to the conduct and wishes of the mother and father. It was reasonably clear following *J v C*[1] that in proceedings under that section, as much as in any other proceedings relating to custody (in whatever form) or access, the claims, wishes, conduct and character of a parent or other claimant could no longer be treated as separate, independent factors. The Family Law Reform Act 1987[2] will put the matter beyond doubt by removing from section 9 of the 1971 Act any reference to the child's welfare and to the conduct and wishes of a parent, leaving section 1 of that Act to apply its paramountcy principle.

1   [1970] AC 668, [1969] 1 All ER 788, HL; see the dictum of Lord MacDermott, supra, para 3.04.
2   Section 10.

(i)   Claims and wishes

3.09   Moreover, so far as concerns claims, where the dispute over custody (in whatever form) is between the mother and the father the court is expressly directed by section 1 not to take into consideration from any point of view other than the paramountcy of the child's welfare whether the claim of the father is superior to that of the mother or vice versa. Where, on the other hand, the dispute is between the natural parents and a non-parent the former 'have themselves a strong claim to have their wishes considered as normally the proper persons to have the upbringing of the child they have brought into the world'.[1] The courts do not ignore the fact that normally it will be in the child's interests to live with his parents and therefore their wishes will 'preponderate in many cases'.[2] Nevertheless, parental wishes are no more than one of the factors in applying the principle that the child's welfare is paramount, and it is probably wise to go no further than to say that 'if therefore there is no clear advantage to the welfare of the child in one of several courses of action, the wishes of the parents will no doubt be followed'.[3] The fact that the child's welfare must prevail over the parent's claim to access does not make the paramountcy principle inconsistent with the fundamental notions of family life and ties which Article 8 of the European Convention for the Protection of Human Rights and Fundamental Freedoms is designed to protect, because both the principle and Article 8 express the same common concept that the natural bond and relationship between parent and child ought not to be gratuitously interfered with but can be interfered with if the child's welfare dictates such a course.[4]

1   Per Lord Upjohn in *J v C* [1970] AC 668, [1969] 1 All ER 788 at 724 and 832 respectively.
2   Per Lord MacDermott, ibid, at 715 and 824 respectively.
3   Cretney, p 331. As the learned author points out (at note 53) none of the relevant dicta in *J v C* provides a precise formula for assessing the weight to be given to parental wishes.
4   *Re KD (a minor) (ward: termination of access)* [1988] 1 All ER 577, [1988] 2 WLR 398, HL.

(ii)   Conduct and character

3.10   The weight to be attached to a party's conduct and character is variable. A parent's past ill-treatment of the child or another child of the household[1] may, for example, be so serious as to influence the court against granting him or her custody. His or her mode of living and social practices, such as heavy drinking or past criminal activities,[2] may lead to the same conclusion. In *S v S (custody of children)*[3], for example, the Court of Appeal denied custody to a lesbian mother not because there was any possibility of the children being led into deviant sexual ways by her lesbian relationship (although that could be a possibility in another case) but because, on the evidence, there was a risk of their suffering social harm if her relationship became known in the locality and they were living with her. An essential question is whether a person is likely to act as a responsible caring parent, notwithstanding his or her defects in conduct and character. The question has received special attention in the case of the so-called unimpeachable parent.

Usually the case is that of the father who sees it as unjust that custody[4] should be entrusted to the mother and not to him when it is her adulterous conduct that has caused the break-up of the family, while his own has been blameless. It is now firmly established[5] that the child's welfare is not to be balanced against the father's wishes or against the justice of the case as between him and the mother. Indeed, the notion of impeccability and justice between the parents in this context has been questioned.[6] Rarely is any parent's conduct blameless and evaluating justice between parents may lead to unhelpful attempts to make moral judgments. This reasoning ought logically to apply where the dispute is between a 'blameless' parent and a non-parent, but it has been suggested[7] that the concept of unimpeachability may still have some relevance in that kind of case. The relevance seems to be associated with the strong claim which the natural parent has vis-a-vis strangers to have his or her wishes considered as normally the person to bring up the child.[8] In any event it counted for nought in *J v C*,[9] where the House of Lords refused to alter in favour of 'unimpeachable' Spanish parents an order in wardship proceedings which granted care and control of their son to English foster parents who had brought him up for many years.

Because of the mother's natural advantages in custody disputes the father may sometimes seek to attach greater significance to her adultery than he might otherwise do,[10] but adultery in itself is not today a weighty factor in applying the paramountcy principle. As already emphasised, the need is to consider the parent's conduct (whether adulterous or not) and character from the point of view of his or her suitability to look after the children. Thus, an adulterous mother may be deprived of custody not because of her adultery but because of the uncaring attitude shown to her children by putting her paramour's interests before theirs,[11] especially if his antecedents are such as to put their welfare at risk were they and he to share the same home.[12] Similarly, there may be a defect in the mother's character of such gravity as to put the child's welfare in jeopardy if she were given custody.[13]

It is highly desirable that the court should see the parties to the proceedings and everyone else concerned, for example, a substitute parent with whom the child is living,[14] and should not rely only on affidavits or welfare reports.[15] Otherwise it cannot properly decide whether or not a person is a fit and proper person to look after the child. Indeed, with regard to custody disputes arising in matrimonial proceedings in the High Court or a county court neither the applicant nor the respondent is entitled to be heard unless he is available at the hearing to give oral evidence or the judge otherwise directs.[16] As for any other person, who is, or is proposed to be, responsible for the child's care and upbringing or with whom the child is living or is proposed to live, the judge may refuse to admit any affidavit by that person unless he is available to give oral evidence.[17]

1 *I v Barnsley Metropolitan Borough Council* [1986] 1 FLR 109, [1986] Fam Law 21, CA.
2 *Re R (minors) (custody)* [1986] 1 FLR 6, [1986] Fam Law 15, CA.
3 (1978) 1 FLR 143. Contrast *Re P (a minor) (custody)* (1983) 4 FLR 401, where the Court of Appeal preferred the risk of granting custody to the mother rather than the only alternative of committing to the care of the local authority.
4 The real issue is over the actual custody (care and control).
5 *S(BD) v S(DJ) (children: care and control)* [1977] Fam 109, [1977] 1 All ER 656, CA; *Re K (minors) (children: care and control)* [1977] Fam 179, [1977] 1 All ER 647, CA. See also *D v D* (1976) 6 Fam Law 149, CA. For criticism see Hall [1977] CLJ 252; Berkovits (1980) 10 Fam Law 164.
6 By Ormrod LJ in *S(BD) v S(DJ)* at 115–116 and 660–661 respectively and in *Re K* at 190 and 654.
7 By Ormrod LJ in *S(BD) v S(DJ)* at 116 and 661.
8 Supra, para 3.09.
9 [1970] AC 668, [1969] 1 All ER 788, HL.
10 See Hoggett, *Custody and Justice* (1977) 121 Sol Jo 469; Bates, *The Changing Position of the Mother in Custody Cases* (1976) 6 Fam Law 125.
11 *P v P* (1975) 6 Fam Law 75, CA.
12 *Hilton v Wilson-Jones* (1975) 5 Fam Law 149, CA; *Hutchinson v Hutchinson* (1978) 8 Fam Law 140, DC; *Hutchinson v Hutchinson* (1980) 2 FLR 167, 11 Fam Law 24, DC.
13 *Stovold v Stovold* (1973) 4 Fam Law 14, CA (mother's dominant personality and excitable temperament); *Re PA and MA (minors), Arensman v Pulman and Liverpool City Council* (1975) 5 Fam Law 183, CA (mother's alcoholism). Cf *L v L* (1980) 2 FLR 48, CA, where the mother was granted care and control of her three-year-old daughter even though she was unstable and suffered depression; but some protection was given to the child through the making of an accompanying supervision order.
14 *S v S* (1972) 117 Sol Jo 34, DC. It is wholly improper for the judge to interview a party on his or her own in the judge's private room; *C v C* (1981) 11 Fam Law 147, CA. The restriction does not apply to interviewing the child.
15 *H v H and C* [1969] 1 All ER 262, [1969] 1 WLR 208, CA; *E v E* (1969) 113 Sol Jo 721; *P v P* (1969) 113 Sol Jo 999, CA; *W v W* (1971) 115 Sol Jo 367, CA; *Ives v Ives* (1973) 4 Fam Law 16, CA.
16 MCR 1977 r 92(4)(a).
17 MCR 1977 r 92(4)(b).

(d) Wishes and feelings of the child

3.11 In adoption proceedings the court is expressly directed so far as is practicable to ascertain the wishes and feelings of the child concerning the proposed adoption and to give due consideration to them, having regard to his age and understanding.[1] Section 1 of the GMA 1971 does not similarly so direct, but the child's wishes and feelings, especially the latter, are relevant in applying the principle of the paramountcy of his welfare in accordance with that section. However, it may be difficult both to find out what are a child's real wishes and then to assess the weight properly to be given to them. They may be expressed for the most unreliable or fickle motives.[2] They may be no more than the wishes which have been instilled into him by the mother or father – in practice by the one with whom he is currently living. Even if they are found to be genuinely his own, they may be clearly contrary to his long-term interests and therefore not to be carried out.[3] On the other hand, they may sometimes be based on sensible reasons which accord with those interests.[4] Occasionally they may disclose such firm opposition to the idea of living with a particular parent that a court may be willing to give effect to them.[5] Indeed, in the light of *Gillick v West*

Norfolk and Wisbech Area Health Authority and Department of Health and Social Security[6] arguably the court should prima facie do so, if they are the result of informed opinion,[7] but it seems likely that it will refuse to do so if it finds that the child's wishes conflict with what it sees as his best interests. However, in all cases it is important not to allow children to feel that they had to make the decision between their father and mother.[8]

The child may have expressed his wishes at various times and in various ways, for example, to a parent, to a schoolteacher,[9] in letters he has written;[10] but usually they are best ascertained through an independent court welfare officer, who may in talking to the child also more readily be able to assess the child's feelings, for example, the extent of his affection for a parent. It is important that the child's views are presented in this way. It is certainly undesirable that it should be done through persons who are parties to the proceedings. Thus, where a local authority is a party, reliance should not be placed on the report and evidence of one of its own social workers.[11] It is equally undesirable for a parent or lawyers to get a child to swear an affidavit, save in rare circumstances.[12]

As for the judge's seeing the child in private, practice varies widely. It is entirely a personal and sensitive matter within his discretion.[13] The Court of Appeal has held that reliance ought not to be placed on an interview unless the child is more than eight years old,[14] and the younger he is the less the weight likely to be given to his views. If he is interviewed, the judge should take every step to encourage him to express his feelings freely. In this way, for example, the judge's suspicions about a parent's conduct may be strengthened by what the child tells him.[15] However, the judge should not, save possibly in rare circumstances, say anything to the child which could be understood as a promise that what the child tells him will not be communicated to anyone else.[16] Such a promise may inhibit the judge's own actions and also prevent advocates from making submissions to him on the matters disclosed. The child may reveal something which would, in the child's interests, justify the judge's calling for further investigation of the matter, for example, by the court welfare officer, but it might not be possible to take this step without the judge's disclosing what he has been told. His promise will certainly put a court exercising appellate jurisdiction and those advising on the possibility of appeal in an impossible position if they are prevented from knowing of a matter which affected the judgment at first instance.

It has been held[17] that magistrates should not interview children in private. No valid explanation can be found for this discrimination. Interviewing lies as much within the discretion of county court judges as High Court judges. It is not therefore possible to justify the discrimination on the basis of the High Court's prerogative jurisdiction over children and the fact that that of the magistrates' court is entirely statutory.[18]

1 AA 1976, s 6.
2 *Re C (minors)* (1978) 8 Fam Law 202, CA,
3 See Cross J in *Re S (infants)* [1967] 1 All ER 202 at 210, [1967] 1 WLR 396 at 408; *Guery v Guery* (1982) 12 Fam Law 184, CA.
4 *Re S; Marsh v Marsh* (1977) 8 Fam Law 103, CA. In *Re S* the learned judge talked to a thirteen-year-old boy and accepted his statement that he would like to stay with his friends at a boarding school in England where he was settled rather than go to live with his mother in California and attend there the same school as a step-brother of the

same age. The boy's wishes were the major factor in leading to an order that the existing arrangements for his education were not to be changed.

5 See *Peters v Peters* (1974) 4 Fam Law 165, CA; *M v M (Minor: Custody Appeal)* [1987] 1 WLR 404, [1987] 2 FLR 146, CA. But cf *Re DW (a minor)(custody)* [1984] Fam Law 17, CA, where the court ignored the 'unusually mature stance' of a ten year old.

6 [1986] AC 112, [1985] 3 All ER 402, HL.

7 See Eekelaar, *Gillick in the Divorce Court,* (1986) 136 NLJ 184; and *The Eclipse of Parental Rights* 102 LQR 4. But see also Bainham, *The Balance of Power in Family Decisions* [1986] CLJ 262, 275, for a more cautious view.

8 *Adams v Adams* [1984] FLR 768, [1984] Fam Law 249, CA.

9 *M v M* (1976) 7 Fam Law 17.

10 The phraseology of letters should be carefully scrutinised. It may strongly indicate that the child's wishes have been much influenced by the parent; *Doncheff v Doncheff* (1978) 8 Fam Law 208, CA.

11 *Re A (minors)(wardship: children in care)* (1979) 1 FLR 100.

12 *W v W and Hampshire County Council* (1979) 2 FLR 68, CA.

13 See Ormrod LJ in *D v D (custody of child)* (1979) 2 FLR 74, 10 Fam Law 53, CA.

14 *Ingham v Ingham* [1976] LS Gaz R 486. But welfare officers frequently speak to children aged seven and sometimes to those as young as five; see Eekelaar, (1982) Ox JLS 63 at p 84.

15 *S v S* (1971) Times, 15 July, CA.

16 *H v H (child: judicial interview)* [1974] 1 All ER 1145, [1974] 1 WLR 595, CA; *Dickinson v Dickinson* (1982) 13 Fam Law 174, CA; *Elder v Elder* [1986] 1 FLR 610, [1986] Fam Law 190, CA.

17 *Re T (a minor)* (1974) 4 Fam Law 48.

18 Even if the magistrates were to interview, it would not follow that their decision would be invalidated (per Sir John Arnold P in *W v Sunderland Borough Council* (1981) 2 FLR 153 at 156 B).

(e) Material advantages

3.12 It is particularly difficult to assess the weight that the court is likely to give to the material advantages which the parties are able respectively to provide for the child. Unless there is a very wide disparity, their financial circumstances will be of peripheral significance, since the court is concerned with trying to provide for the child's happiness, and material benefits have a limited role in fulfilling that purpose. Accommodation is a matter which tends to be more important, particularly where the children are of different sexes, but even here the fact that the mother may be at a marked disadvantage is not likely to outweigh the factor that young children should be with her.[1] Moreover, the provision of a home is not to be considered merely in material terms but also in the light of the time and care the parent will devote to the child.[2] In this regard the mother who is not out at work obviously holds an advantage over the father who is so occupied.[3] Even where she is working the courts tend to be more willing to accept as satisfactory the arrangements which she makes for the child during her absence than they are in the corresponding circumstances of the absent father.[4] Indeed, for the working father the arrangements for daily care of his young children by relatives or neighbours will often be crucial to his chances of securing care and control (actual custody).[5] The provision of material comforts may help in providing a stable life for the child, but the question of stability may also turn on satisfying his academic, emotional, moral and spiritual needs.[6] These may sometimes involve questions of parental values and standards,[7] sometimes questions of cultural and ethnic advantages,[8] sometimes questions of schooling[9] and/or religious upbringing, but most importantly questions of loving care.[10] The Law Commission includes the child's emotional needs in its proposed statutory checklist of factors which the court should take into account when applying the paramountcy principle,[11] but regrettably does not give those needs and the child's emotional ties the marked prominence it gave them in the earlier tentative proposals contained in its Working Paper on Custody.

1 See, for example, *Barham v Salter* (1975) 5 Fam Law 19, CA.
2 See Bromley, p 331.
3 *Re O (infants)* [1971] Ch 748 at 752, [1971] 2 All ER 744 at 746; *Plant v Plant* (1982) 4 FLR 305, CA.
4 *Townsend v Townsend* (1973) 4 Fam Law 127, CA.
5 In *D v M (minor: custody appeal)* [1983] Fam 83, [1982] 3 All ER 897, CA the fact that the child would spend most working hours with a child minder and not with the father was one factor in persuading the Court of Appeal that the mother should have custody.
6 'Instability is now one of the fashionable words round which custody cases tend to rotate' per Ormrod LJ in *S(BD) v S(DJ) (children: care and control)* [1977] Fam 109 at 113, [1977] 1 All ER 656 at 659. For cases illustrating the point see ante, para 3.06 note 15.
7 *May v May* [1986] 1 FLR 325, [1986] Fam Law 105, CA.
8 See *Re O (infants)* [1962] 2 All ER 10, [1962] 1 WLR 724, where the Court of Appeal allowed the father, a Sudanese, to remove his seven-year-old son to the Sudan, leaving his daughter, aged six, with her mother, an English woman in England.
9 As in *Re B (an infant)* (1966) Times, 5 April, CA.
10 'However, while material considerations have their place, they are secondary matters. More important are the stability and the security, the loving and understanding care and guidance, the warm and compassionate relationships, that are essential for the full development of the child's own character, personality and talents.' Per Hardie Boys J in *Walker v Walker and Harrison* noted in [1981] N Z Recent Laws 257 and cited in Law Com Working Paper No 96, para 6.10.
11 The proposed checklist is:
   (a) the ascertainable wishes and feelings of the child considered in the light of his age and understanding;
   (b) the child's physical, emotional and, where relevant, educational needs;
   (c) the effect upon the child of any change in his circumstances, having regard to their duration and to his separation from any person with whom he has been living;
   (d) the child's age, sex, background and other relevant characteristics;
   (e) any harm which the child has suffered or is at risk of suffering;
   (f) how capable each parent and any other relevant person is of meeting the child's needs.
   See Law Com No 172, paras 3.17–3.21.

(f)   Education and religion

3.13   Where education is an issue it is normally the child's religious upbringing which is involved. That factor is examined in Chapter 11.[1] If there is a dispute over secular education, it is likely to be associated with a dispute over religion,[2] since a parent will want the child to attend a school where he will receive instruction in a particular faith. Occasionally, however, the issue may relate only to secular matters.[3] The question of a child's schooling can prove a significant factor in those cases where a parent is seeking to take the child out of the jurisdiction. In such cases his welfare may best be served by his continuing to be educated in England,[4] especially if removal to a foreign country would create immediate language problems for him.[5]

1 See paras 11.04 to 11.09.
2 For example, as in *J v C* [1970] AC 668, [1969] 1 All ER 788, HL.
3 *Re S (infants)* [1967] 1 All ER 202, [1967] 1 WLR 396; *B v B (parental rights: dispute)* (1978) 1 FLR 87, CA; *May v May* [1986] 1 FLR 325, [1986] Fam Law 105, CA.
4 See, for example, *Re S; J v C; Bevan v Bevan* (1973) 4 Fam Law 126, CA.

5   For example, as in *Dyter (now Kandler) v Dyter* (1973) 4 Fam Law 52, CA. Note this
    authority must be treated with caution in so far as the decision turned upon the need
    to take account of the wishes of a 'blameless' parent; see ante, para 3.10.

II   MEANS OF RESOLVING DISPUTES OVER CUSTODY

3.14   A parent or anyone else who can show a proper interest in the
upbringing of a child may invoke the inherent jurisdiction of the Family
Division by way of wardship proceedings,[1] which, if the court so orders,
will enable him or her to be given care and control of the ward while
the custody (in the wide sense)[2] and, therefore, the supervision of the exercise
of the parental powers and responsibilities remains with the court.[3] Wardship
is examined later.[4] Otherwise, disputes over custody are usually determined
as the result of an application under the Guardianship of Minors Act 1971
or as part of matrimonial proceedings.[5]

1   The writ of habeas corpus is regarded as no longer an appropriate procedure in the Family
    Division; *Re K (a minor)* (1978) 122 Sol Jo 626.
2   See ante, para 1.58
3   Independently of wardship the court has power to grant an injunction to restrain a person
    from interfering with a parent or another person's right to custody of a child; *Lough
    v Ward* [1945] 2 All ER 338.
4   Chapter 8.
5   The significance of these jurisdictions is indicated by the fact that some 170,000 children
    are annually affected. See the figures for 1984 listed by the Law Commission (Working
    Paper No 96, para 1.4, note 6.) and for most informative data and comments on orders
    made in the divorce and domestic courts see *passim* Priest and Whybrow in the Supplement
    to Working Paper No 96. In its Working Paper the Law Commission has highlighted
    the lack of clarity and consistency 'on such important matters as the meaning of custody,
    who may apply, which children are concerned, how their own point of view may be put
    before the court, what kinds of orders may be made and what test the court should
    apply. The different powers are classic examples of ad hoc legislation designed for particular
    situations without full regard to how they fit into the wider picture'; see ibid, para 1.04.

1   Jurisdiction to make a custody order under the Family Law Act 1986

3.15   The Family Law Act 1986, which aims at avoiding conflicts of
jurisdiction within the United Kingdom, prescribes the circumstances in
which there is jurisdiction to make a custody order, as defined by the Act.
In the case of jurisdiction of a court in England and Wales the definition
cover the following:[2]
(i)   orders for legal custody or access made on the application of the mother
      or father, or made where it is ordered that a person shall be sole guardian
      to the exclusion of a parent or where joint guardians disagree, or certain
      access orders in favour of grandparents; ie orders made respectively
      under the Guardianship of Minors Act 1971, sections 9(1), 10(1)(a),
      11(a) or 14A(2);
(ii) interim custody or access orders made in any of the above proceedings,
      under the Guardianship Act 1973, section 2(4)(b) or 2(5);
(iii) orders for custody or access made under the Matrimonial Causes Act
      1973, section 42(1) in proceedings for divorce, nullity or judicial
      separation;
(iv) orders for custody or access made under the Matrimonial Causes Act

1973, section 42(2) in proceedings brought because of the failure of a spouse to maintain the other spouse and/or the children of the family;

(v) custodianship orders made under the Children Act 1975, section 33(1) or interim custodianship orders under the Guardianship Act 1973, section 2(4)(b) as applied by the Children Act 1975, section 34(5);

(vi) orders for legal custody or access including interim orders made under the Domestic Proceedings and Magistrates' Courts Act 1978, sections 8(2) or 19(1)(ii); and also

(vii) certain orders in wardship.[3]

Special jurisdictional rules apply to categories (iii) and (vii) and these will be considered when dealing respectively with custody orders in the divorce court and with wardship. In all the other categories the court has jurisdiction if the child[4] concerned is either habitually resident in England and Wales[5] or is present in England and Wales[6] and is not habitually resident in any part of the United Kingdom on the relevant date[7] and in either case the jurisdiction is not excluded. Jurisdiction is excluded if on the relevant date proceedings for divorce, nullity or judicial separation are continuing in Scotland or Northern Ireland in respect of the child's parents,[8] except if that court has made an order either waiving jurisdiction[9] or sisting or staying custody proceedings so as to enable proceedings with respect to the custody of the child to be taken in England and Wales.[10]

A court which has jurisdiction to make a custody order has a discretion under section 5 of the 1986 Act to refuse an application or to stay proceedings.[11]

1 Sections 2–7. Part I of the Act implements the recommendations of the English and Scottish Law Commissions in the Report, *Custody of Children – Jurisdiction and Enforcement within the United Kingdom* (Law Com No 138; Scot Law Com No 91).

2 Section 1(1)(a).

3 See s 1(1)(d).

4 Ie a person who has not attained the age of 18; see FLA 1986, s 7.

5 FLA 1986, s 3(1)(a). Habitual residence is not defined in the Act, but is a concept now common in legislation. For habitual residence after removal without consent, see s 41.

6 Ibid, s 3(1)(b).

7 In the case of an application for a custody order under GMA 1971, ss 9(1) or 14A(2) or CA 1975, s 33(1) the relevant date is the date of the application, or first application if two or more are determined together, for example, if there are cross applications; see FLA 1986, s 3(5). Otherwise the relevant date is the date of the commencement of the proceedings in which the order is made (FLA 1986, s 3(4)), for example where there is no application for custodianship but a court exercising its powers under the CA 1975, s 37 or the DPMCA 1978, s 8(3) directs some other application be treated as if it were an application for custodianship.

8 FLA 1986, s 3(2); see also s 42(2)–(4).

9 Under FLA 1986, s 13(6) (except ss 13(6)(a)(i)), 21(5), 14(2) or 22(2).

10 Provided that any such order is in force (ibid, s 3(3)).

11 Section 5 is discussed in the context of wardship, post, Chapter 8.

Where a magistrates' court stays proceedings or removes such a stay, it must notify the parties accordingly and in the case of removal proceed to deal with the application accordingly; see the Magistrates' Court (Family Law Act 1986) Rules 1988, SI 1988/329 (L4), r 7.

A party to proceedings for or relating to a custody order in a magistrates' court who knows of other proceedings (including proceedings out of the jurisdiction and concluded proceedings) relating to the child must give particulars of other proceedings in accordance with FLA 1986, s 39 and the MC (FLA 1986) Rules 1988, r 6 and Form 2. For the corresponding provisions in the High Court and county court, see RSC Ord 90, r 55, as inserted by SI 1988/298 (L 3); CCR Ord 47, r 11(9), as inserted by SI 1988/278 (L 1).

2 Jurisdiction to make an order other than a custody order under the Family Law Act 1986

3.15A A custody order does not include (a) an order which varies or revokes a previous order made under the same Act; (b) an order under section 14A(2) of the Guardianship of Minors Act 1971 which varies a previous custody order.[1] Thus, the jurisdictional rules in paragraph 3.14A do not apply to variations or revocations. Once a court has made a custody order its powers of variation remain exercisable notwithstanding that the original basis of jurisdiction has ceased.[2]

1 FLA 1986, s 1(2)(a) and (b).
2 See Law Com No 138, para 4.30.
   Additionally, a custody order does not include (a) any order made before the commencement of Part I of the FLA 1986 on 4 April 1988 (b) any order which was made under GMA 1971, ss 9(1) and 14A(2), CA 1975, s 33(1), or (a remote possibility) the Guardianship of Infants Act 1886, s 5 on or after that date on an application made before that date; see FLA 1986, s 1(3) and (4).

3 The Guardianship of Minors Act 1971

(a) Jurisdiction

3.16 The mother or father of a child, whether or not they are or ever have been married to each other may apply for an order under section 9 of the Guardianship of Minors Act 1971. The courts authorised to hear applications are:
(a) the High Court;
(b) the county court
    (1) for the district in which the minor to whom the application relates has his habitual residence, or
    (2) where the minor has no habitual residence in any district, the county court for the district in which he is present at the time when the proceedings are commenced, or
    (3) where the minor, having been habitually resident in a district, leaves or remains outside, or is removed from or retained outside that district either without the agreement of the person or of all the persons having the right to determine where he is to reside or in contravention of an order made by a court in any part of the United Kingdom, the county court for that district, for the period of one year beginning with the date of leaving, remaining, removal or retention;[2]
(c) a magistrates' court for the commission area in which a child has his habitual residence or, where the child has no habitual residence, for the commission area in which the child is present when proceedings are commenced.[3]

1 GMA 1971, s 15(1). Most cases are heard by the magistrates' courts and very few in the High Court. Priest and Whybrow, op cit, para 8.2, note 5, record that in 1984 only

ten orders were made in the High Court, 1,757 in the county courts and 8,500 in the magistrates' courts.
2   CCR Ord 47, r 6(1) as inserted by the County Court (Amendment) Rules 1988, SI 1988/278 (L 1), r 22.
3   Magistrates' Courts (Family Law Act 1986) Rules 1988, SI 1988/329 (L 4), r 5(1).
      Where a child, having been habitually resident in a commission area, leaves or is removed from or retained outside that area, either without the agreement of the person or of all the persons having the right to determine where he is to reside or in contravention of an order made by a court in any part of the United Kingdom, he is to be regarded for the purposes of r 5(1) as continuing to be habitually resident in that commission area for the period of one year beginning with the date on which he was left or was removed therefrom (r 5(2)); see above for a similar rule relating to county court jurisdiction.

3.17   Where proceedings have been instituted in the High Court, the court may, either of its own motion or on the application of any party to the proceedings, order the transfer of the whole or any part of the proceedings to such county court as the High Court directs.[1] The High Court must not order transfer unless the parties have either had an opportunity of being heard on the issue or consented to the order.[2] Conversely, a county court may, either of its own motion or on the application of any party, order the transfer to the High Court of the whole proceedings which have been commenced in the county court or which under the above rules were transferred to it by the High Court.[3] However, these powers to order transfer between the courts are subject to the following restrictions:[4]

(a)   Proceedings must be dealt with in the High Court where it appears to the court seised of the case that, because of the complexity difficulty or gravity of the issues, they ought to be tried in the High Court.

(b)   Without prejudice to the generality of that rule, the following proceedings, inter alia, must be dealt with in the High Court unless the nature of the issues of fact or law raised in the case makes them more suitable for trial in a county court than in the High Court: proceedings concerning children in divorce and under the Guardianship Acts where (i) an application is opposed on the grounds of want of jurisdiction, or (ii) there is a substantial foreign element, or (iii) there is an opposed application for leave to take a child permanently out of the jurisdiction or where there is an application for temporary removal of a child from the jurisdiction and it is opposed on the ground that the child may not be duly returned.

(c)   Subject to the above, proceedings concerning children in divorce and under the Guardianship Acts may be dealt with in a county court.

(d)   Proceedings in the High Court which under the foregoing criteria fall to be dealt with in a county court or a divorce county court, as the case may be, and proceedings in a county court which likewise fall to be dealt with in the High Court must be transferred accordingly, unless to do so would cause undue delay or hardship to any part or other person involved.

1   MFPA 1984, ss 32 and 38. The transfer does not affect any right of appeal from the order directing transfer or the right to enforce in the High Court any judgment signed, or order made, in that Court before the transfer; see s 38(4).

2 RSC Ord 90, r 2B(1), as inserted by Rules of the Supreme Court (Amendment) 1986, r 27, SI 1986/632.
3 MFPA 1984, s 39.
4 See *Practice Direction* [1988] 2 All ER 103, [1988] 1 WLR 558.

3.18 There is no power of transfer in relation to a magistrates' court and the parties themselves have no right to have their case transferred,[1] for example, on the ground of its complexity. Appeal[2] from a magistrates' court lies to a judge of the Family Division,[3] with a further appeal to the Court of Appeal, apparently without leave.[4] In exercise of its appellate jurisdiction the High Court may make such orders as may be necessary to give effect to its determination of the appeal (for example, ordering repayment of payments already made in accordance with the magistrates' court decision on that matter), and any order of the High Court is to be treated for the purposes of enforcement, variation, revival and discharge as if it were a magistrates' court order.[5]

1 *Beaumont v Beaumont* [1938] Ch 551, [1938] 2 All ER 226.
2 On appeals generally see post, paras 3.75 et seq.
3 GMA 1971, s 16(3). There is no appeal against a refusal by the magistrates to make an order on the ground that the matter could more conveniently be dealt with by the High Court (s 16(4) as amended by CA 1975, Sch 3, para 75(3)(b)). However, where the custody or maintenance of children is involved, a magistrates' court should carefully consider assuming rather than declining jurisdiction. See *Cooper v Cooper* [1953] P 26, [1952] 2 All ER 857; *Kaye v Kaye* [1965] P 100, [1964] 1 All ER 620; *Lanitis v Lanitis* [1970] 1 All ER 466, [1970] 1 WLR 503; and *Jones v Jones* [1974] 3 All ER 702, [1974] 1 WLR 1471, CA.
4 *Re W (an infant)* [1953] 2 All ER 1337, [1953] 1 WLR 1405, CA.
5 GMA 1971, s 16(6)–(8) as added by DPMCA 1978, s 48.

(b) Orders

(i) Legal custody and access

3.19 The main orders that can be made under the 1971 Act are orders relating to legal custody and access.[1] The parent does not have to establish any specific ground in order to justify the making of an order. The duty of the court is to have regard to all the circumstances presented to it by the parties, to determine the application in accordance with the principle of the paramountcy of the child's welfare and in so doing then to make such orders as it thinks fit. This discretion in the choice of orders enables the court to attach conditions to the order. These are more common with regard to access, but may be attached to an order for legal custody, provided they do not impose unduly onerous burdens on the person granted it or are not impracticable to enforce.[2]

1 No order may be made when the minor is free for adoption; GMA 1971, s 9(2)(b), as prospectively substituted by FLRA 1987, s 10. For freeing for adoption see post, Chapter 5.
2 *B v B (custody: conditions)* (1979) 1 FLR 385; sub nom *Bell v Bell* (1979) 10 Fam Law 117, CA.

3.20 Under section 9 of the 1971 Act only one or other of the parents can be an applicant and in practice the proceedings are between them. Strictly the terms of the section are such that they do not exclude the possibility of either parent bringing proceedings against any other person for an order for legal custody or access,[1] but in practice the appropriate remedy is wardship proceedings in which the parent seeks care and control. In the converse case, a person who is not a parent cannot invoke section 9. He must either rely on wardship proceedings or apply for a custodianship order under section 33 of the Children Act 1975.[2] Moreover, the court can, on a parent's application under section 9, grant legal custody, including actual custody, to a third person by directing that the parental application be treated as if it had been a custodianship application by that person under section 33 of the 1975 Act, even though that person could not have qualified as an applicant under that section.[3] Where the court so directs, Part II of the 1975 Act then operates, just as if there had been an application under section 33. Thus, the court could, for example, make accompanying orders relating to access and maintenance.[4] The only exception is that section 40 does not apply. For obvious reasons the 'notional' applicant is relieved of the duty imposed by that section to notify the local authority of the application and the authority of any duty to present a report to the court.[5] If the court so wishes, it may call for a welfare report.[6]

1　For a rare instance see *Re K (an infant), Re M (an infant), Hertfordshire County Council v H* [1972] 3 All ER 769, DC.
2　For custodianship orders see post, Chapter 6.
3　CA 1975, s 37(3) and (4). Subsection (3) is prospectively amended by FLRA 1987, s 33(1) and Sch 2, para 64. Section 9(2) of the GMA 1971, as prospectively substituted by FLRA 1987, s 10 expressly forbids granting legal custody under that section to anyone other than a parent of the child.
4　See post, Chapter 6, paras 6.02 et seq.
5　Post, para 6.23.
6　For welfare reports see post, paras 3.70 – 3.74.

3.21　Section 11A(1) of the Guardianship of Minors Act 1971 reads:[1]

> 'An order shall not be made under section 9 or 10 of this Act, giving the legal custody of a child to more than one *person*; but where the court makes an order under one of those sections giving the legal custody of a child to any *person*, it may order that a *parent* of the child who is not given the legal custody of the child shall *retain* all or such as the court may specify of the parental rights and duties comprised in legal custody (other than the right to the actual custody of the child) and shall have those rights and duties jointly with the *person* who is given the legal custody of the child.'

A number of points arise with regard to this provision, whose scope and consequences will be further complicated by the Family Law Reform Act 1987.
(1) In view of the fact that an order under section 9 can grant legal custody only to a parent the reference to a person may seem surprising, but the reason is that section 11A(1) also applies to orders made under section 10. The latter section deals with granting legal custody where there is a guardian, and he may be the appropriate person to be granted it rather than the parent.[2]
(2) Although the provision is not entirely free from ambiguity, its effect is to enable the court to grant one parent, say the mother, legal custody including actual custody but to allow the father to be involved in the upbringing of the child by expressly allowing him to retain jointly with

the mother such rights and duties as fall within the meaning of legal custody and are specified by the court, for example, those relating to secular education or religious upbringing. Since the court can specify all rights and duties other than actual custody, an order to that effect is equivalent in practical terms to a joint legal custody order; but there is no firm evidence of extensive use of such an order.

(3)   Section 11A(1) refers to the power of the court to order that the non-custodial parent 'retain' specific rights. If this provision is to be construed literally, no such order can be made in respect of an unmarried father, since he has no rights and duties that can be retained.[3] It has, however, been suggested that the word 'retain' 'probably . . . means the retention *for* a party of rights and duties comprised in legal custody which the court is to distribute'.[4] It is to be hoped that the courts will so interpret it. Otherwise the child of unmarried parents is placed at a disadvantage, a consequence which militates against the philosophy of the Family Law Reform Act 1987.

(4)   Legal custody and actual custody have the same meaning here as they have in the Children Act 1975.[5] So, in whom do those rights and duties vest which do not relate to the person of the child? When the relevant amendments made by the Family Law Reform Act 1987 come into force, a distinction will still have to be drawn between those parents who are married to each other when their child is born and those who are not. In the case of the former the 'non-personal' rights and duties remain vested in the mother and father equally in accordance with section 1(1) of the Guardianship Act 1973.[6] But that principle of equality does not apply where the parents were not so married.[7] In those circumstances the residual non-personal rights and duties will continue to vest in the mother alone in accordance with the common law, unless the father has obtained an order under section 4 of the Family Law Reform Act 1987 giving him all the parental rights and duties. If he has, he will have the non-personal rights and duties jointly with the mother. Supposing, for example, that M, the mother, and F, the father, live together unmarried and a child, C, is born to them. F obtains an order under section 4. Later the relationship breaks up and M seeks an order for legal custody under section 9 of the 1971 Act. The above rule will then operate with regard to the non-personal rights and duties, unless the order under section 4 is discharged.[8]

(5)   Where, as in the illustration given in sub-paragraph (2) above, legal and actual custody are given to the mother but subject to specific rights jointly to her and the father and there is disagreement over the way in which the mother is exercising one of those rights, for example, is allegedly being uncooperative over the religious upbringing of the child, the father can apply to the court for its direction on the matter.[9] On the other hand, if it is the father who is proving unco-operative, the mother, as the parent having legal custody, may prefer to seek variation of the section 9 order by deleting the provision relating to the jointly held right, rather than a direction with regard to how the right is exercised.[10] There seems to be no reason why she should not seek those remedies in the alternative.

(6)   In relation to the case just instanced there appears to be a gap in the law if the mother and father were not married to each other at the child's birth. The father in those circumstances is excluded from invoking section 1(3) of the 1973 Act, unless (when the amendment takes effect) an order under section 4 of the Family Law Reform Act 1987 giving him all parental rights and duties has been made or he has 'a right to custody,

legal or actual custody or care and control of the child by virtue of an order made under any other enactment'.[11] In the above illustration it is the mother who has the legal and actual custody. The only remedy of such an unmarried father in respect of a joint right 'given' to him when making the legal custody order lies therefore in variation of the legal custody order and not in a direction under the 1973 Act.[12]

(7)   The reference in the previous sub-paragraph to a right to legal *or* actual custody by virtue of an order marks a new departure. At present there appears to be no enactment authorising a court to make an order for actual custody alone,[13] whereas an order for care and control has long been known to the divorce court.

(8)   If in section 9 proceedings the court decides to grant legal custody to a person other than a parent (for example, to young grandparents) and thus treats the parental application as an application for custodianship by the grandparents, the order granting legal custody is made under the Children Act 1975 and not under section 9 of the 1971 Act. The effect is that there is then no power to order that the parent retain specific rights and duties jointly with the custodian.[14] Yet, in cases where relatives are the custodians such retention may well be particularly appropriate.

1   As inserted by DPMCA 1978, s 37 and prospectively amended by FLRA 1987, s 33(1) and Sch 2, para 30.
2   For orders under s 10 see post, paras 4.20 and 4.21. Until s 10, as substituted by FLRA 1987, s 11, comes into force, reference must be to orders made under ss 10(1)(a) and 11(a) of GMA 1971.
3   Unless an order giving him rights and duties is already in force; see infra.
4   See Law Com Working Paper No 96, para 2.46.
5   See GMA 1971, s 20(2), as prospectively amended by FLRA 1987, s 33(1) and Sch 2, para 43.
6   For the principle of equality of parental rights see ante, para 1.66, and for an examination of those rights and duties which, *semble*, do not fall within the scope of legal custody see paras 1.61 to 1.64.
7   GA 1973, s 1(7), as prospectively amended by FLRA 1987, s 2(2).
8   See FLRA 1987, s 4(3). The applicant for discharge may be the mother or the father. In the illustration it is likely to be M.
9   GA 1973, s 1(3). An order under s 1(3) can be varied or discharged, s 1(5).
10 Given the very limited reliance on s 1(3), the alternative of variation is likely to be preferred.
11 GA 1973, s 1(3A), as prospectively inserted by FLRA 1987, s 5.
12 This argument assumes that he can be 'given' a right; see supra, for the meaning of 'retain'.
13 But see further Law Com Working Paper No 96, para 2.48; Law Com No 172, para 4.2.
14 See ibid para 2.49.

(ii)   Other orders

3.22   (i) *Supervision order.*   If by virtue of the making of, or refusal to make, an order on the application under section 9 the actual custody of the child is given to, or retained by, a parent, but it appears to the court that there are exceptional circumstances making it desirable to do so, it may order that the child be placed under the supervision of a specified local authority or a probation officer.[1]

(ii) *Order committing care of the child to a local authority.*   Instead of making an order for legal custody, the court can commit the care of the child to the local authority in whose area the child is resident, but this power, too, can only be invoked in exceptional circumstances which make it impracticable or undesirable to entrust the child to either parent.[2] If an order is made, there is no power to grant access to a parent or other individual under GA 1973.[3]

Both kinds of orders may also be made in matrimonial and wardship proceedings and their scope is examined under the divorce jurisdiction.[4]

(iii) *Orders for financial relief.*   The court may require a parent to provide various forms of financial relief for the benefit of his child.[5] These are examined in Chapter 16.

(iv) *Order restricting removal out of jurisdiction.*   On making an order, or an interim order, regarding legal custody or at any subsequent time while it is in force, the court *may*[6] on application direct that no one is to take the child out of the United Kingdom or out of any part of the United Kingdom specified in the order, except with the court's leave.[7] Any party to the original proceedings may apply for the direction, which means in effect either parent, save for the rare case where a non-parent was a party.[8] Additionally, any other person to whom the court granted the legal custody can apply.[9] Where an application for leave to take a child permanently out of the jurisdiction is opposed or an application for temporary removal from the jurisdiction is opposed on the ground that the child may not be duly returned, the application must normally be heard in the High Court.[10]

As a result of the Family Law Act 1986, section 36, an order restricting removal of a child out of the United Kingdom or any specified part thereof has effect in other parts of the United Kingdom as if it had been made by the appropriate court[11] in that other part.[12] Also, if the order prohibits removal from England and Wales without leave of the court but the child has, for example, been taken to Scotland, it automatically has effect in Scotland as if including a provision prohibiting further removal except back to England.

For the purpose of section 36 a child is a person under 16 and the section ceases to apply to an order relating to a child who attains that age.[14]

Where an order prohibiting removal of a child is in force, the court which made the order, or by which it is treated under section 36 as having been made may require any person to surrender any United Kingdom passport which has been issued to the child or contains particulars of the child.[15]

---

1 GA 1973, s 2(2)(a), as prospectively substituted by FLRA 1987, s 33(1) and Sch 2, para 54. The prospective amendment takes account of the fact (which the present law does not) that the court may refuse to make an order for custody. If the court should decide to grant legal (and therefore actual) custody to a third person by treating the application as if it were one for a custodianship order under s 33 of CA 1975, but it felt that a supervision order should be made, it could do so by virtue of its powers under that Act (s 34(5), as substituted by DPMCA 1978, s 64, and prospectively amended by FLRA 1987, s 33(1) and Sch 2, para 61(3)). If the supervision order under GA 1973 is made by the High Court the officer responsible will be such probation officer as may be selected under arrangements by the Secretary of State (ibid, s 3(1)(a)). Otherwise it will be a probation officer appointed for or assigned to the petty sessions area in which the minor is or will be resident (s 3(1)(b)).

2 GA 1973, s 2(2)(b), as substituted by FLRA 1987, s 33(1) and Sch 2, para 54. See *Cooke v Cooke and Sutton London Borough* (1981) 3 FLR 396, 12 Fam Law 61.

3 *Re L (child in care: access)*, [1985] FLR 95, [1984] Fam Law 281, CA. But once the child is in care the parent has the right to apply under the Child Care Act 1980, Part IA (as inserted by HASSASSAA 1983, s 6 and Sch I); see post, paras 15.86 et seq.

4 See post, paras 3.55 and 3.57; Law Commission Working Paper No 100, *Care, Supervision*

and Interim Orders in Custody Proceedings; and for orders committing to local authority care see also para 15.56.

5 Payments can also be ordered where the child is committed to the care of the local authority: GA 1973, s 2(3), (3A) and (3B) as substituted by DPMCA 1978 s 44(1).

6 Compare the *duty* of a divorce court to include in a custody order a prohibition on removal 'unless otherwise directed'; see post, para 3.60.

7 GMA 1971, s 13A, as inserted by DPMCA 1978, s 39 and as amended by FLA 1986, s 35(1) and prospectively amended by FLRA 1987, s 33(1) and Sch 2, para 37. Where wrongful removal of the child out of the jurisdiction is threatened the assistance of the Police, by way of a port alert, and the Passport Office may be sought; see post, paras 3.103–3.104 and 3.106.

8 See ante, para 3.20, note 1.

9 See DPMCA 1978 (Commencement No 4) Order 1980, SI 1980/1478, Sch 2, para 10.

10 See the restrictions imposed by the *Practice Direction* [1988] 2 All ER 103, [1988] 1 WLR 558, ante, para 3.17.

11 Ie in England and Wales or Northern Ireland the High Court and in Scotland the Court of Session; see FLA 1986, ss 40 and 32.

12 FLA 1986, s 36(1) and (2)(a).

13 Ibid, s 36(2)(b); see Law Com No 138, para 6.17.

14 See sub-s (4).

15 FLA 1986, s 37.

(iii)   Duration of orders (other than for financial provision)[1]

3.23   Any of the above orders may be made in respect of a child who is under 18,[2] except that one committing him to the care of a local authority cannot be made after he has attained the age of 17.[3] An order remains in force until he reaches 18,[4] unless it is earlier discharged or varied or ceases to have effect where an order is made for the child's return under Part I of the Child Abduction and Custody Act 1985 or a decision, other than one relating to rights of access, is registered under section 16 of that Act.[5] Normally it takes effect from its date, but the court is empowered to direct that the operation of an order for legal custody or any specified provision of it shall be postponed until the occurrence of a specified event or the expiration of a specified period.[6] For example, the order may provide for transfer of the actual custody from father to mother but this is to be postponed until she returns home from hospital.

The Family Law Act 1986[7] provides that if a custody order (or a variation of a custody order) made in Scotland or Northern Ireland comes into force at a time when a custody order (including an interim order)[8] made under section 9 of the Guardianship of Minors Act 1971 is in effect, the Scottish or Northern Ireland order will prevail over the English order in so far as they overlap. Thereafter the English court does not have power to vary its own order so as to make provision for the matters covered by the later order.[9] Any supervision order which is dependent upon the section 9 custody order ceases to have effect.[10] The English court also does not have power to vary its own order made under section 9, if at the relevant date[11] proceedings for divorce, nullity or judicial separation are continuing[12] in Scotland or Northern Ireland in respect of the marriage of the child's parents,[13] unless the court in Scotland or Northern Ireland waives its jurisdiction to make an order or decides to sist or stay proceedings before it in favour of the English court.[14]

1 For duration of orders for financial provision see post, paras 16.09.

2 GMA 1971, ss 9(1) and 20(2), as prospectively amended and substituted respectively by FLRA 1987, s 10 and s 33(1) and Sch 2, para 43.

3 GA 1973, s 4(2A), as inserted by DPMCA 1978, s 38(4).

4 GMA 1971, s 11A(3), as inserted by DPMCA 1978, s 37 (legal custody and access); GA 1973, s 3(2), as amended by DPMCA 1978, s 38(3) (supervision); GA 1973, s 4(1) (committal to care).
5 See ss 25(1) and (2), 27(1) and Sch 3, para 1(1), and for the Act generally see post, paras 3.108 et seq.
6 GMA 1971, s 11A(2), as inserted by DPMCA 1978, s 37. The court may further extend a period of postponement.
7 S 6(1).
8 See FLA 1986, s 1(1)(a)(i).
9 Ibid, s 6(2).
10 Ibid, s 6(6)(c).
11 As defined in FLA 1986, s 6(7).
12 See ibid, s 42(2) and (3).
13 Ibid, s 6(3); and see also s 42(4).
14 Ibid, s 6(4).

3.24 An order for legal custody may be varied or discharged on the application of either parent or, after the death of either parent, on the application of any guardian.[1] Any of them may apply for variation or discharge of a supervision order, but additionally the supervisor is entitled to do so.[2] An order committing to the care of the local authority may be varied or discharged on the application of that authority as well as that of either parent or, after the death of a parent, of a guardian.[3] Any person who can apply for an order restricting the removal of the child out of the jurisdiction can equally apply for its variation or discharge.[4]

1 GMA 1971, s 9(1), as prospectively substituted by FLRA 1987, s 10. These rules are currently contained in s 9(1) and (4) of the 1971 Act. 'Guardian' means a testamentary guardian or one appointed under the GMA 1971; see post, paras 4.03 to 4.15.
2 GA 1973, s 3(3).
3 Ibid s 4(3A), as inserted by CA 1975, Sch 3, para 80(2).
4 GMA 1971, s 13A(2) and (3), as inserted by DPMCA 1978; see ante, para 3.22.

3.25 An order under section 9 of the 1971 Act, or an interim order,[1] which grants actual custody to one of the parents is enforceable even if the parents are living with each other in the same household when it is made or if they should subsequently live with each other;[2] but the order ceases to have effect if after that date the parents marry each other or live with each other for more than six months.[3] The rationale of the six-month rule is that, if parents, whether married to each other or not, continue to cohabit for such a period, that is firm evidence of their reconciliation and an order is no longer appropriate. In the case of unmarried cohabitees, their subsequent marriage is seen as similarly evidential.[4] Similarly, unless the court otherwise directs, a supervision order or one committing the child to the local authority's care is, and remains, enforceable even though the parents are living, or will live, together.[5] In respect of these orders there is no express restriction that the order ceases to have effect if the parents marry each other or live with each other for more than six months after the date of the order. Thus, if either event should occur where an order committing to the care of the child to the local authority is in force, the child will remain in care.

1 For interim orders see infra, para 3.26.
2 Usually by resuming living together; but the rule would also cover the case where they first start living together after the date of the order. The latter possibility will in practice arise where they are not already married to each other.

3   GA 1973, s 5A(1), (as prospectively substituted by FLRA 1987, s 33(1) and Sch 2 para 57) and (3).
4   See Law Com No 118 on Illegitimacy, para 6.41.
5   GA 1973, s 5A(2), (as prospectively substituted by FLRA 1987, s 33(1) and Sch 2, para 57) and (3).

(iv) Interim orders
3.26   At any time before it makes a final order or dismisses the application under section 9 the court may make an interim order requiring a parent to make to the other parent or to the child periodical payments towards the child's maintenance. An interim order may also make 'provision regarding the legal custody of and right of access to the child', but only if special circumstances so require.[1] Although the point is not made explicitly, it seems clear that, just as an interim order for care and control may be made in a divorce court, so an interim order dealing only with actual custody may be made, that being a provision regarding the legal custody. Indeed, an interim order for actual custody is preferable to one for legal custody, since the latter may lead to psychological complications in that one party may think he has 'won' the substantive hearing.[2] Courts tend to be diffident about making an interim order (whether for actual or legal custody), but it can be useful to meet an emergency, for example, where the court has it in mind that ultimately the mother should have legal and actual custody but circumstances, such as her illness, temporarily preclude that possibility.[3] Moreover, the fact that divorce proceedings are imminent or in their initial stages should not deter a magistrates' court from assuming jurisdiction and making an interim order.[4] A magistrates' court can also make an interim order if it refuses to make an order on a section 9 application because it considers that the matter would more conveniently be dealt with by the High Court[5] – a rare occurrence.

1   GA 1973, s 2(4) and (4A) as prospectively substituted by FLRA 1987, s 33(1) and Sch 2, para 54. For a general review of interim orders see Law Com Working Paper No 100.
2   *Re B (a minor) (interim custody)* (1983) 4 FLR 683, 13 Fam Law 176, CA. That case was concerned with an application for an interim order under GMA 1971 and 1973. Surprisingly, the Court of Appeal made an interim order for 'care and control'. It is submitted that the appropriate order should have been one for actual custody.
3   An alternative would be to make a final order but postpone its operation. For an illustration of the use of an interim order in an emergency, see *Beard v Beard* [1981] 1 All ER 783, [1981] 1 WLR 369, CA.
4   *F v F* (1976) 6 Fam Law 208, CA.
5   GMA 1971, s 16(4), as amended by CA 1975, Sch 3, para 75(3)(b); GA 1973, s 2(5) as prospectively substituted by FLRA 1987, s 33(1) and Sch 2, para 54.

3.27   Where the interim order provides for legal custody its commencement of operation may be postponed in the same way as a final order.[1] Unless it is earlier varied or discharged,[2] the maximum period of an interim order is three months, but there is power to extend the period provided that the total period(s) for which it is extended must not exceed a further three months.[3] There is, however, no power to make a second interim order,[4] even if the first was for a period for less than three months.[5] The restriction is designed to make the court come to a firm decision as soon as possible, since uncertainty about his future is unlikely to be in the child's best interests. It is apparently for the same reason that interim orders can only be made

in special circumstances. Whatever the period fixed the order automatically·
ends when a final order is made or the section 9 application is dismissed.[6]
Where an existing order granting legal custody to one parent has been
violated by the other parent wrongfully removing or detaining the child,
a judge making an interim order, pending the hearing of an application
by the other parent to vary the original order, should restore the status
quo in the absence of particular reasons to the contrary. If there are such
reasons, it is important that they be recorded.[7]

1   GA 1973, s 2(5A), as inserted by DPMCA 1978, s 45(4); see supra, para 3.23.
2   GA 1973, s 5(2), as prospectively substituted by FLRA 1987, s 33(1) and Sch 2, para
    56.
3   GA 1973, s 2(5C) and (5D), as inserted by DPMCA 1978, Sch 2, para 44.
4   Section 2(5E), as prospectively substituted by FLRA 1987, s 33(1) and Sch 2, para 54.
5   *Edwards v Edwards* [1986] 1 FLR 187, [1986] Fam Law 99, affd [1986] 1 FLR 205, CA.
6   Section 2(5C) and (5D).
7   *Townson v Mahon* [1984] FLR 690, [1984] Fam Law 204, CA.

(v)   Enforcement of orders
3.28   Failure to obey an order for legal custody or access made by the
High Court or a county court is punishable with committal or sequestration
until the child is handed over to the person granted the legal custody or
access.[1] If the order is made in a magistrates' court, the penalty is either
the payment of a sum not exceeding £2,000 or up to £50 for every day
in default but not exceeding a maximum of £2,000 or committal to custody
until compliance with the order or for a period of two months, whichever
be the shorter.[2] Where there is an alleged breach of an order for access
it must be shown that the breach was deliberate, and every other course
should be attempted before issuing proceedings for contempt, since they
are likely to aggravate the hostility between the parents.[3] The court should
try to find out why the custodial parent has prevented access and then
endeavour to vary the order so as to make the terms of access acceptable
to both parents.[4] The summons should give clear details of the alleged
breach of the order,[5] and it is essential that notes of evidence be taken
by the clerk to the justices and that the justices give reasons for their decision.[6]
    Where a person is required by a custody order, as defined by the Family
Law Act 1986,[7] or an order for the enforcement of a custody order, to
give up a child to another person, and the court which made the order
is satisfied that the child has not been given up, it may make an order
authorising an officer of the court or a constable to take charge of the
child and deliver the child to that other person.[8] The authorisation includes
authority to enter and search any premises and to use such force as may
be necessary.[9]

1   RSC Ord 45, r 5; CCR 1981 Ord 29, r 1. For a comprehensive review of committals
    see Judge Nigel Fricker QC, *Committals for Contempt in the County Court,* [1988] Fam
    Law 232.
2   GMA 1971, s 13(1); Magistrates' Courts Act 1980, s 63; *Re K (a minor) (access order:
    breach)* [1977] 2 All ER 737, [1977] 1 WLR 533n.
3   *Thomason v Thomason* [1985] FLR 214, [1985] Fam Law 91, DC; cf *I v D (Access Order:
    Enforcement)* [1988] Fam Law 338, CA.
4   *T v T* (1984) Times, 19 July, CA.
5   *P v W* [1984] Fam 32, [1984] 1 All ER 866. Quaere whether a magistrates' court has
    power to punish a person who has acted in breach of its order but who has remedied
    the breach before a summons has been issued.

6   *Tilmouth v Tilmouth* [1985] FLR 239, [1985] Fam Law 92, DC.
7   See ante, para 3.15.
8   FLA 1986, s 34(1).
9   Ibid, s 34(2).

(c)   Procedure

3.29   Proceedings under section 9 of the Guardianship of Minors Act 1971 are commenced in the High Court by originating summons;[1] in a county court by originating application;[2] and in a magistrates' court by way of complaint.[3] Applications to the High Court may be (and in practice usually are) disposed of in Chambers;[4] those in the county court must be heard in Chambers unless the court otherwise directs;[5] and those in a magistrates' court must be dealt with by a domestic court sitting in accordance with the restrictions regulating domestic proceedings.[6] The domestic court may go further and decide to hear the application in camera.[7]

1   RSC Ord 90, r 5, as amended. Where, however, wardship proceedings are pending, an application with respect to the child may be made by summons in those proceedings.
2   CCR 1981 Ord 3, r 4 and Form N393.
3   For the procedure in magistrates' courts see Magistrates' Courts (Guardianship of Minors) Rules 1974–80.
4   RSC Ord 90, r 7.
5   CCR 1981 Ord 47, r 6.
6   See Magistrates' Courts Act 1980, ss 65, 66, 69 and 71.
7   MC (G of M) Rules 1974, r 6.

3.30   In the vast majority of section 9 applications the only parties to the proceedings are the parents. The High Court procedure expressly, and the county court procedure by implication, allow a child to be made a defendant but only if the court so directs,[1] and this should be done only in special circumstances.[2] The child is represented by a guardian ad litem who must act through a solicitor.[3] Both in High Court and county court proceedings any other person appearing to be interested in or affected by the application is to be made a defendant or respondent respectively, except that the High Court has power to dispense with service of the summons.[4] There is no corresponding provision for an application in a magistrates' court, but there are a number of persons who are required to be made defendants to an application for variation or discharge of orders made by those courts.[5] However, regrettably, there is no provision for the child to be made a party or to be represented separately in a magistrates' court, even in special circumstances. The reason for the omission is apparently the 'unacceptably heavy burden' it would place on the welfare services,[6] especially since the great majority of section 9 applications are heard by magistrates' courts. Resort to a welfare report is always available to the court, if it so chooses.

1   RSC Ord 90, r 6(1); CCR 1981 Ord 15, r 1, read with RSC Ord 15, r 6.
2   See *Practice Direction* issued by the Family Division [1982] 1 All ER 319, [1982] 1 WLR 118.
3   RSC Ord 80, r 2(1) and (3); CCR 1981 Ord 10, r 1(2). Compare proceedings under MCA 1973. There the court may appoint a guardian ad litem without making the child a party; see Matrimonial Causes Rules 1977, r 115(1) and (2).
4   RSC Ord 90, r 6(1) and (2); CCR 1981 Ord 47, r 6.
5   See MC (G of M) Rules 1974, r 9.

6   See Law Com No 77 paras 10.15–10.36 (*Matrimonial Proceedings in Magistrates' Courts*);
    and Law Com Working Paper No 96, para 2.81 note 253, (*Custody*).

3.30A   Where in proceedings for or relating to a custody order under the
Family Law Act 1986[1] the court does not have available to it adequate
information about the child's whereabouts, it may order any person who
it has reason to believe may have relevant information to disclose it to
the court.[2] A person is not excused from supplying information on the
ground that to do so might incriminate him or his spouse of an offence;
but any statement or admission made in compliance with an order for
disclosure is not admissible in evidence against either of them in proceedings
for an offence other than perjury.[3]

1   See ante, para 3.15.
2   See FLA 1986, s 33(1). The section does not indicate the consequences of non compliance.
3   Ibid, s 33(2).

3.31   In the High Court and county court issues relating to legal custody
and actual custody are reserved to a judge, but, in High Court cases
proceeding in the Principal Registry, an application relating to legal custody
and access in which the parties are agreed on the terms (save for the extent
of access to be given) may be made to the Registrar and should be so
made, unless there are exceptional circumstances making it desirable for
the matter to be brought before a judge for decision.[1]

1   See *Practice Direction* [1977] 3 All ER 944, [1977] 1 WLR 1226; and *Practice Direction*
    [1980] 1 All ER 813, [1980] 1 WLR 321. For custody and access applications during
    the Long Vacation see *Practice Direction* [1984] 2 All ER 320, [1984] FLR 501.

4   Matrimonial proceedings in magistrates' courts

3.32   The Domestic Proceedings and Magistrates' Courts Act 1978
introduced a number of changes concerning the powers of magistrates'
courts to make orders affecting children when exercising their matrimonial
jurisdiction.[1] As the numerous references to the Act in the preceding
paragraphs indicate, it also amended the Guardianship of Minors Act 1971
and the Guardianship Act 1973 so as to bring some of their provisions
into line with its own. Consequently, many of the statements of law already
set out in those paragraphs will need little elaboration in the examination
of the Act of 1978. However, by the very nature of the respective proceedings
there are significant differences.

1   The Act is largely based on the Law Commission's *Report on Matrimonial Proceedings
    in Magistrates' Courts* (Law Com No 77).

(a)   Jurisdiction

3.33   A magistrates' court has jurisdiction if at the date of the application
either the applicant or the respondent ordinarily resides within the
commission area for which the court is appointed.[1] The rule applies even
(1) where the respondent resides in Scotland or Northern Ireland and the
applicant in England and Wales, provided the parties last ordinarily resided
together as man and wife in England and Wales, and (2) where the applicant
resides in Scotland or Northern Ireland, provided the respondent resides

in England and Wales.[2] Jurisdiction may be exercised notwithstanding that a party is domiciled outside England and Wales.[3] So far as concerns orders for legal custody and access, all the above provisions have to be read subject to the new jurisdictional rule of the Family Law Act 1986, that the child is habitually resident in England and Wales or present within that jurisdiction and not habitually resident in any part of the United Kingdom.[4] It is, however, to be noted that, unlike the jurisdiction to make custody orders under section 9 of the Guardianship of Minors Act 1971 and custodianship orders under the Children Act 1975, the child does not have to be either habitually resident or present within the commission area of the magistrates' court in order to confer jurisdiction.

1   DPMCA 1978, s 30(1). There are special rules relating to courts in the Inner London Area. Subject to the overriding restriction that a court for that area may not hear any domestic proceedings if the committee of the magistrates so determines, a domestic court for one area may hear proceedings which could be heard by a domestic court for another area – but only in such cases or classes of cases as may be determined by the committee; see s 70.
2   Section 30(3). Where the application is to vary or revoke an order there is jurisdiction even though the applicant or respondent is residing anywhere outside England and Wales (s 24(1)).
3   Section 30(5).
4   See FLA 1986, ss 2 and 3, and DPMCA 1978, s 30(1), as amended by FLA 1986, s 68(1) and Sch 1, para 24. See ante, para 3.16.

(b)   Children of the family

3.34   Whereas section 9 of the Guardianship of Minors Act 1971 is limited to a child of the mother and father, the Domestic Proceedings and Magistrates' Courts Act 1978 applies to a child of the family. He may be either (a) a child of both parties to the marriage, or (b) any other child who has been treated by *both* parties as a child of their family, other than one who *is being* boarded-out with them by a local authority or voluntary organisation.[1] So, a child may come within the second category though he is a natural or adopted child of only one of the parties or of neither.

The question whether a child has been treated as a child of the family is a broad question to be answered by applying an objective test to the facts and drawing therefrom a reasonable conclusion.[2]

> 'It is [therefore] impossible and undesirable to define circumstances in which a step-daughter may be held to have been treated by a step-father as a child of his family. Amongst the factors the court bears in mind (and there may be many others) there must be the question of where the child lives, who pays for the child, who exercises discipline and whether the step-father had in fact exercised or claimed any of the responsibilities of a parent.'[3]

Thus, on the one hand, a child who is living with his grandparents only while his mother and step-father are temporarily abroad does not cease to be a child of the latter family. On the other hand, if he lives with his grandparents for most of each year, spending but the small remainder with his mother and step-father, it is highly unlikely that he will be held to be a child of the family of mother and step-father.[4] Indeed, in a case of that kind, if it were to be held that by consenting to generous staying visits by the child with his mother the step-father was treating the child as a child of the family, there would be a serious risk that he would restrict access in order to prevent that conclusion being drawn.[5]

Obviously a child cannot be treated as a member of the family until the family comes into being. The earliest possible date is that of the marriage,[6] but for present purposes it may be later. Thus, there is no family if the spouses cease to live together before the wife gives birth to a child, of whom the husband is not the father, and their subsequent relationship bears no relation to that of a husband and wife.[7] It follows also that, where the wife and her child have been living with the husband before their marriage, the question is how they both treated the child after that date; but the way in which they jointly behaved towards the child before the marriage may, it is suggested, be adduced as presumptive evidence to show that the same attitude continued thereafter and amounted to their treating the child as a child of the family.[8] It has also been held that an unborn child cannot be a child of the family because 'treatment' involves behaviour towards a living person.[9]

It is not necessary that a husband should know the facts relating to the paternity of his wife's child and his mistaken belief, whether or not induced by his wife's deception, that he is the father does not preclude the conclusion that he treated the child as a child of the family.[10] Nevertheless, knowledge that the child is not one's own is relevant in determining what is the appropriate financial provision to be ordered.[11]

1 DPMCA 1978, s 88(1). Cf the definition in MCA 1973, s 52(1), post, para 3.47, note 3.
2 *Teeling v Teeling* [1984] FLR 808, CA; See also Ormrod LJ in *D v D (child of the family)* (1980) 2 FLR 93 at 96; and, to similar effect, in *M v M (child of the family)* (1980) 2 FLR 39 at 43 and 47.
3 Per Templeman LJ in *D v D* at 98.
4 *D v D*.
5 Ibid, per Orr LJ at 96.
6 *W v W (child of the family)* [1984] FLR 796, CA.
7 *M v M* (1980) 2 FLR 39, CA.
8 Cf *C v G* [1975] CLY 2158. Cf also *Re Leach, Leach v Lindeman* [1986] Ch 226, [1985] 2 All ER 754, CA.
9 *A v A (family: unborn child)* [1974] Fam 6, [1974] 1 All ER 755. For criticism see *Bromley* p 293, but the decision has received judicial approval from Sheldon J in *W v W (child of the family)* [1984] FLR at 802; Slade LJ in *Re Leach, Leach v Lindeman,* supra n 8, [1986] Ch at 233, [1985] 2 All ER at 758.
10 *W(RJ) v W(SJ)* [1972] Fam 152, [1971] 3 All ER 303.
11 DPMCA 1978, s 3(4)(b). Cf MCA 1973 s 25(4)(b).

(c) Orders

(i) Legal custody and access

3.35 Under section 8 of DPMCA 1978 the court can make an order for legal custody and access[1] where a spouse has applied for an order for financial provision under sections 2, 6 or 7 of the Act. The interests of the child take precedence over those of the spouse in that the court cannot make its final decision on the spouse's application until it has decided whether or not, and if so how, to exercise its powers with regard to the child.[2] Moreover, these powers can be exercised even if it does not make the order for which the spouse applies.[3] If, on the other hand, it does make such an order (ie under section 2, 6 or 7) but does not make one with respect to the child, either spouse is free to apply subsequently for an order relating to the child, so long as the original order remains in force.[4]

1   For orders relating to access see post, paras 3.84–3.88.
2   Section 8(1).
3   Section 8(2).
4   Section 21(2).

3.36   The court may grant the legal custody (including the actual custody)[1] to either spouse, or, if the child is not the child of both of them, to a parent. It may instead grant legal custody of any child of the family to some other person by directing that that person be treated as if he had applied for a custodianship order under section 33 of the Children Act 1975.[2] Moreover, its discretion to make such order as it thinks fit enables it to attach conditions to the order.[3]

1   For the meanings of these terms see ante, para 1.59 and 1.65.
2   DPMCA 1978, s 8(3). Compare the similar provision in custody proceedings under s 9 of GMA 1971, ante, para 3.20.
3   See ante, para 3.19.

3.37   As with orders under the Guardianship of Minors Acts 1971 and 1973, legal custody (including actual custody) cannot be granted to more than one person, but the court may also order that a party to the marriage who is not given the legal and actual custody is to retain specified parental rights and duties which are to be held jointly with the person who has been given the legal custody.[1] Should there be any dispute between them over the exercise of a right or discharge of a duty either may apply to the court for its direction on the matter.[2] It is submitted that alternatively application may be made to vary the original order, for example, by deleting the provision which retained the right for the non-custodial parent. This second alternative would be more appropriate where the dispute between the spouses relates to whether the right should continue to be exercised by the non-custodial parent rather than to the manner in, and extent to which, it is being exercised.

1   DPMCA 1978, s 8(4).
2   Section 13(1). An order may be varied or discharged; s 13(2).

3.37A   Where the court does not have available to it adequate information as to the child's whereabouts, the court may order any person who it has reason to believe may have relevant information to disclose it to the court.[1] He is not excused from supplying information by reason that to do so might incriminate him or his spouse of an offence; but any statement or admission made in compliance with an order for disclosure is not admissible in evidence against either of them in proceedings for an offence other than perjury.[2]

1   FLA 1986, s 33(1).
2   Ibid, s 33(2).

(ii)   Other orders
3.38   (i) *Supervision order.*   Where the court makes an order regarding legal custody it may, if there are exceptional circumstances making it desirable, order that the child be placed under the supervision of a specified local authority or a probation officer.[1]

(ii) *Order committing care of the child to a local authority*. Instead of making an order for legal custody, the court can commit the care of the child to the local authority in whose area the child is resident, but may only do so where exceptional circumstances make it impracticable or undesirable to entrust the child to either of the spouses or to any other individual.[2]
The scope of these two orders is examined under the divorce jurisdiction.[3]
(iii) *Orders for financial provision*. The court may require a spouse to provide maintenance for the benefit of a child of the family or to the child by way of periodical payments or a lump sum or both.[4] These orders are examined in Chapter 16.
(iv) *Orders restricting removal out of jurisdiction*. On making an order, or an interim order, regarding legal custody or at any subsequent time while it is in force[5] the court may on application direct that no one is entitled to take the child out of the United Kingdom or out of any part of the United Kingdom specified in the order except with the court's leave.[6] The persons qualified to apply for an order are those eligible to seek variation or revocation of an order for legal custody.[7]

1 DPMCA 1978, s 9(1).
2 Ibid, s 10(1) and (2).
3 See post, paras 3.55 and 3.57; Law Com Working Paper No 100; Law Com No 172, Part V.
4 DPMCA 1978, ss 2, 6, 7 and 11. Payments can also be ordered where the child is committed to the care of a local authority (s 11(4)).
5 The court may make orders concerning legal custody even though the child is out of the jurisdiction (*Philips v Philips* (1944) 60 TLR 395, CA), but should do so only in exceptional circumstances (*R v Sandbach Justices ex p Smith* [1951] 1 KB 62, [1950] 2 All ER 781). Moreover, under ss 2 and 3 of FLA 1986 it is a prerequisite that the child is habitually resident within the jurisdiction even though not currently present within it.
6 DPMCA 1978, s 34(1), as amended by FLA 1986, s 35(1), and compare the *duty* of a divorce court to include in a custody order a prohibition on removal, 'unless otherwise directed'; see post, para 3.60. Where wrongful removal is threatened, the assistance of the Police, by way of a port alert, and the Passport Office may be sought; see post, paras 3.103–3.104 and 3.106.
7 See DPMCA 1978, s 34(3) and DPMCA 1978 (Commencement No 4) Order 1980, SI 1980/1478, Sch 2, para 9.

(iii) Duration of orders (other than for financial provision)[1]
3.39 Here, again, the rules run parallel to those in the Guardianship of Minors Acts 1971 and 1973. Any of the above orders may be made in respect of a child of the family under the age of 18,[2] except that one committing him to the care of a local authority cannot be made after he has reached 17.[3] An order remains in force until he is 18,[4] unless it is earlier revoked or varied or ceases to have effect where an order is made for the child's return under Part I of the Child Abduction and Custody Act 1985 or a decision, other than one relating to rights of access, is registered under section 16 of that Act.[5] As under the Guardianship of Minors Acts, there is power to postpone the operation of an order for legal custody or any specified provision of it.[6]
The Family Law Act 1986[7] provides that if a custody order (or a variation of a custody order) made in Scotland or Northern Ireland comes into force at a time when a custody order (including an interim order)[8] made under section 8(2) of the Domestic Proceedings and Magistrates' Courts Act 1978 is in effect, the Scottish or Northern Ireland order will prevail over the English order in so far as they overlap. Thereafter the English court does

not have power to vary its own order so as to make provision for the matters covered by the later order.[9] Any supervision order which is dependent upon the section 8(2) custody order ceases to have effect.[10] The English court also does not have power to vary its own order made under section 8(2) if at the relevant date[11] proceedings for divorce, nullity or judicial separation are continuing[12] in Scotland or Northern Ireland in respect of the marriage of the child's parents,[13] unless the court in Scotland or Northern Ireland waives its jurisdiction to make an order or decides to sist or stay proceedings before it in favour of the English court.[14]

1 For duration of orders for financial provision see post, paras 16.15–16.16.
2 DPMCA 1978, ss 8(1), 9(1) and 34(1).
3 Ibid, s 10(7).
4 Ibid, ss 8(5), 9(3), 10(6) and 34(1).
5 CACA 1985, ss 25(1) and (2), 27(1) and Sch 3, para 1(1) and for the Act generally see post paras 3.108 et seq.
6 DPMCA 1978, s 8(6).
7 S 6(1).
8 See FLA 1986, s 1(1)(a)(v).
9 Ibid, s 6(2).
10 FLA 1986, s 6(6)(e).
11 As defined in FLA 1986, s 6(7).
12 See ibid, s 42(2) and (3).
13 Ibid, s 6(3).
14 Ibid, s 6(4).

3.40   Any of the above orders[1] may be varied or revoked on the application[2] of either spouse[3] and, if the child is not a child of both of them, on the application of a parent of the child or any other person having the legal custody.[4] Additionally the supervising local authority or probation officer may apply for variation or revocation of a supervision order[5] and the local authority may do so for revocation of an order committing the child to its care.[6] On hearing the application[7] the court may exercise any of its powers relating to legal custody, access, supervision or committal to care;[8] for example, in revoking an order committing to care, it may substitute an order granting legal custody to one of the spouses if changed circumstances justify it.

1   For the variation and revocation of orders for financial provision see post, paras 16.09. For the person or persons to be made respondents see Magistrates' Courts (Matrimonial Proceedings) Rules 1980, SI 1980/1582, r 6.
2   An application to vary or revoke an order may be brought by or against a person residing outside England and Wales (DPMCA 1978, s 24).
3   DPMCA 1978, ss 21(1) and 34(2) and (3).
4   Ibid, s 21(7)(a), as amended by DPMCA 1978 (Commencement No 4) Order 1980, SI 1980/1478, Sch 2, para 7; s 34(2) and (3) as amended by DPMCA 1978 (Commencement No 4) Order 1980, s 1 1980/1478, Sch 2, para 9.
5   DPMCA 1978, s 21(7)(b).
6   Section 21(7)(c).
7   Other than an application to vary or revoke an order restricting removal of the child out of the jurisdiction.
8   DPMCA 1978, s 21(1).

3.41   An order under section 8, or an interim order,[1] granting actual custody to one of the spouses is enforceable even if the spouses are living with each other in the same household when it is made or remains enforceable if they should subsequently resume living together, but it will cease to have effect if they continue to live together for a period exceeding six months.[2] This automatic termination rests on the assumption that after that length of time there has been an effective reconciliation. However, if the legal custody is given to another person, whether a parent of the child who is not one of the spouses or someone else, or if a supervision order or an order committing to local authority care is made, the continued 'cohabitation' of the spouses, even beyond six months, will not terminate the order unless the court otherwise directs.[3]

1 For interim orders see infra, para 3.43.
2 DPMCA 1978, ss 25(1) and 88(2). There may be uncertainty about the date when the spouses ceased to live together. Either of them may therefore apply to the court to fix the date when the order ceased to operate; see s 25(4).
3 Section 25(2), as amended by SI 1980/1478 Sch 2, para 8; s 25(4).

(iv) Restrictions on the making of orders
3.42 Although the court has power to make such orders with respect to legal custody as it thinks fit, this discretion and all its powers in relation to children are expressly governed by the principle in section 1 of the Guardianship of Minors Act 1971 that the child's welfare is the first and paramount consideration.[1] There are other specific restrictions. If the court commits the child to the care of a local authority, it cannot make an order for access.[2] If the child is already in a local authority's care, it cannot make an order for access, a supervision order or an order committing to care;[3] but in those circumstances it is not precluded from making an order as regards legal custody.[4] There is also the wider restriction that the court cannot make any of the above orders if there is already in force an order made by a court in England and Wales in respect of the child's custody.[5]

1 DPMCA 1978, s 15.
2 Ibid, ss 10(9) and 14(2).
3 Ibid, ss 8(7)(b), 9(4), 10(8) and 14(2).
4 See *M v Humberside County Council* [1979] Fam 114 at 119, [1979] 2 All ER 744 at 748.
5 DPMCA 1978, s 8(7)(a). Note the reference therein to 'custody' and not 'legal custody'. The restriction will therefore extend, for example, to the case where an order for custody has been made by the divorce court in proceedings relating to a former marriage of one of the parties to the present proceedings.

(v) Interim orders
3.43 The court's power to make an interim order which contains provisions regarding legal custody, or only actual custody, and access closely corresponds to that which it has under the GMA 1971 and 1973.[1] Thus, it can make that order at any time before it makes a final order or before it dismisses the application.[2] It can do so in the rare case where it refuses to make an order on an application by a spouse under section 2 of the DPMCA 1978 because it considers that the case would be more conveniently dealt with by the High Court.[3] If the High Court thinks otherwise and orders the application to be reheard by the magistrates' court, it, too, can make an interim order.[4] All these powers to make an interim order are, however, only exercisable where special circumstances make such an order desirable.[5]

1   See ante, paras 3.26–3.27, and Law Com Working Paper No 100.
2   Ie, an application by a spouse under DPMCA 1978, ss 2, 6 or 7.
3   DPMCA 1978, ss 19(1) and 27.
4   Ibid, s 19(1). It may also do so where there has been an appeal from the magistrates' court and it orders a rehearing. For the purposes of enforcement and variation or revocation, the High Court order is to be treated as if it were an order of the magistrates' court; see s 19(9).
5   DPMCA 1978, s 19(1).

3.44   The commencement of operation of an interim custody order may be postponed in the same way as a final order.[1] Unless it is earlier varied or revoked,[2] the maximum period of an interim order is three months.[3] The court may, however, make one or more orders extending the period of an interim order, provided that the total period(s) for which it is extended must not exceed three months from the date when the original order would have ceased to have effect.[4] Whatever the period fixed the order automatically ends when a final order is made or the spouse's application is dismissed. There is no power to make a second interim order, even if the first was for a period for less than three months.[5]

1   DPMCA 1978, s 19(4).
2   Ibid, s 21(3).
3   Ibid, s 19(5).
4   Ibid, s 19(6).
5   Ibid, s 19(7).

(vi)   Enforcement of orders
3.45   Orders may be enforced in the same way as orders made in a magistrates' court under the Guardianship of Minors Acts 1971 and 1973.[1]

1   See ante, para 3.28; DPMCA 1978, s 33, and Magistrates' Courts Act 1980, s 63(3).

(d)   Procedure
3.46   Where the child is not a child of both parties to the marriage any parent who is not one of the parties must be present or legally represented at the hearing or adequate steps must have been taken to give him or her an opportunity of attending the hearing. Unless one of these conditions is fulfilled the court 'shall not exercise' its powers to make orders for legal custody and access or to commit the child to the care of a local authority.[1] Any order made in breach of those conditions would, it is submitted, therefore be void. Additionally, before exercising its powers the court must give each party to the marriage and any other person who, as a parent of the child, is present or legally represented an opportunity of making representations.[2] If there is compliance with this additional requirement, the order would, it seems clear, be binding on the parties to the marriage and the parent; but the effect of non-compliance is not clear. It is arguable that the order would be void;[3] but it could certainly be the subject of judicial review.

It has already been pointed out[4] that there is no provision for the child to be made a party or to be separately represented in a magistrates' court.

1   DPMCA 1978, s 12(2). No notice needs to be given to 'the father of an illegitimate child'

unless he has judicially been found to be the father, and it seems that this rule has not
been affected by the FLRA 1987.
2   Section 12(1).
3   Cf *M v M (divorce: care order)* (1980) 1 FLR 327, CA, post, para 3.57 note 3, where
    it was held in divorce proceedings that a care order made without hearing representations
    was void.
4   Ante, para 3.30.

5   Matrimonial Causes Act 1973

3.47   In proceedings for divorce, nullity or judicial separation or in those
brought on the ground of failure to provide reasonable maintenance[1] the
High Court or a county court having jurisdiction over matrimonial causes[2]
has powers to make orders relating to children of the family, a term which
has the same meaning as it has for the purposes of the Domestic Proceedings
and Magistrates' Courts Act 1978.[3] As with proceedings under the latter
Act or under the Guardianship of Minors Act 1971, the jurisdiction to
make custody orders is subject to the provisions of Part I of the Family
Law Act 1986.[4]

1   Under s 27 of MCA 1973.
2   For the transfer of proceedings between the High Court and a divorce county court see
    the Matrimonial and Family Proceedings Act 1984, ss 38 and 39 and for the restrictions
    thereon see the *Practice Direction* [1988] 2 All ER 103, [1988] 1 WLR 558, ante, para
    3.17.
3   S 88(1) of DPMCA 1978 excludes from the term a child, not being a child of both parties,
    who 'is being' boarded-out with them by a local authority or voluntary organisation.
    S 52 of MCA 1973 excludes a child who 'has been' so boarded-out. There seems no doubt
    that the words 'and is being' are to be interpolated and this construction has Law
    Commission support (WP No 96, para 2.14). Otherwise it would mean that spouses who
    have custodianship of a child by virtue of a custodianship order could not treat him
    as a child of their family if, prior to that order, he had been boarded-out with them
    by the local authority. The relevant consideration is, and certainly ought to be, the child's
    status at the time of the matrimonial proceedings.
4   See post, para 3.51.

(a)   Proper arrangements for the children

3.48   The powers to make orders are subject to the overriding principle
that the interests of the children are to be protected before the spouse
is granted his or her matrimonial remedy. Section 41 of the MCA 1973
provides that the court must not make absolute a decree of divorce or
nullity or pronounce a decree of judicial separation unless it has by an
order declared that it is satisfied on one of the following matters:[1]

(a)   That there are no children of the family to whom s 41 applies. It
      applies[2] to any child of the family who is: (i) under 16; or (ii) under
      18 and receiving instruction at an educational establishment or
      undergoing training for a trade, profession or vocation, whether or
      not he is also in gainful employment; or (iii) any other child of the
      family if the court so directs because it considers that there are special
      circumstances which make the application desirable in the interest
      of the child. Thus, for example, a direction might so be given in
      respect of a child over 18 who is continuing education or training
      or a severely handicapped child who is over 16 but whose earning
      capacity is impaired; or

(b)   that the only children who are or may be[3] children of the family
to whom s 41 applies are those named in the order and that:
 (i)   arrangements for the welfare of every child so named have been
made and are satisfactory or are the best that can be devised in the
circumstances,
(ii)   it is impracticable for the party or parties appearing before the
court to make such arrangements;

(c)   that there are circumstances making it desirable that the decree should
be made absolute or should be made, as the case may be, without
delay, notwithstanding that there are or may be children to whom
s 41 applies and that the court is unable to make a declaration in
accordance with paragraph (b) above. But the court may only make
an order in these circumstances if it obtains a satisfactory undertaking
from either or both of the parties to bring the question of arrangements
for the children before it within a specified time.[4] A declaration in
accordance with paragraph (c) may be appropriate where neither
spouse is able to make long-term arrangements for the children until
after their divorce, eg, where those arrangements depend on remarriage
or the allocation of housing.[5]

For the purpose of paragraph (b)(i) 'welfare' is defined to include the custody,
access, education and training of the child and financial provision for him.[6]
If the child is at school it is generally desirable that the court should have
before it a school report on his educational progress and prospects,[7]
particularly in the case of older children or where there has been a recent
change of schools following the separation of the spouses. Nevertheless,
as with so much of section 41, practice varies considerably and some judges
are less insistent on the production of school reports than others. With
regard to the factor of financial provision for the child, the fact that the
family (ie the child and the spouse with whom he is living) is being supported
by social security payments is not in itself a ground for the judge's refusing
a declaration of satisfaction under the section[8] even though the other spouse
may be financially able to make some contribution. The question is whether
in the particular case the money available for the family is such as to
provide adequately for the child's needs or, failing that, is the most that
may reasonably be expected to be obtainable. However, a declaration may
be refused in any of the following circumstances:[9]

(a)   if the judge has reasonable grounds for supposing that a maintenance
order could be obtained, or an existing order varied, so as to make
provision for the child and the family significantly in excess of that
they obtain from social security; or
(b)   if the judge has insufficient evidence to enable him to form any realistic
opinion on that question;[10] or
(c)   if there is some particular circumstance to arouse his suspicion; eg,
where a husband puts pressure on his wife to agree that his payments
for the maintenance of the child should be at an unreasonably low
rate and not to be increased at any time.[11]

The court should not certify its satisfaction with the arrangements unless
they are going to be reasonably permanent,[12] but the issue of a certificate
should not be postponed until all the information necessary for a registrar's
order for financial provision or property transfer is available.[13] Difficulties

quite frequently arise where custody of the child is contested. In A v A[14] the Court of Appeal laid down the following guidelines.

(a)   Where there is no issue over custody a declaration under the section ought to be made, unless there is any specific matter on which the judge still requires to be satisfied (eg the health of the spouse with whom the child is to live) or for some other reason the sanction of withholding a decree absolute would be useful. If a declaration is withheld, the judge can issue directions on any further steps to be taken, eg the provision of a welfare report, and, if possible, fix the date of the further hearing.

(b)   Where, however, custody is in issue, a declaration can be deferred until that issue is decided, provided there will not be a lengthy delay. Where considerable delay is likely, the judge should make a declaration in accordance with paragraph (b)(i) or, if necessary, paragraph (c). In such a case it might be appropriate to grant interim custody to one spouse and order the other to file an application for custody and evidence in support within a time limit, with liberty to the first spouse to apply for a full order if no such application is made within that limit.[15] If no order under s 41 is made, any decree of divorce or nullity made absolute or decree of judicial separation pronounced is void,[16] but once an order is made the validity of the subsequent final decree cannot be challenged on the ground that the declaration did not fulfil the prescribed conditions,[17] e g because the court did not know all the facts.[18]

---

1   See sub-s (1). If the court is not satisfied, either party can require it to make an order to that effect (sub-s (4)). The power to grant or refuse a certificate of satisfaction must be exercised by the judge himself and cannot be delegated, for example, to a registrar; *Hughes v Hughes* [1984] FLR 70, [1984] Fam Law 23, CA.
2   See sub-s (5).
3   Thus an order can be made without having first to determine any dispute between the spouses over the status of the child. That can be decided at a later stage in the proceedings.
4   MCA 1973, s 41(2).
5   See Ormrod LJ in *A v A (children: arrangements)* [1979] 2 All ER 493 at 494, [1979] 1 WLR 533 at 535.
6   MCA 1973, ss 41(6) and 52(1).
7   *Leech v Leech and Dolleman* (1972) 116 Sol Jo 274.
8   *Cook v Cook* [1978] 3 All ER 1009, [1978] 1 WLR 994, CA. See also *England v England* (1979) 10 Fam Law 86, CA.
9   See Goff LJ in *Cook v Cook* [1978] 3 All ER 1009 at 1015, [1978] 1 WLR 994 at 1001.
10   As in *McDermott v McDermott* (1979) 10 Fam Law 145, CA.
11   As in *Dennett v Dennett* (1977) 7 Fam Law 173, CA.
12   *McKernan v McKernan* (1970) 114 Sol Jo 284.
13   *Yeend v Yeend* [1984] FLR 937, [1984] Fam Law 314, CA.
14   [1979] 2 All ER 493, [1979] 1 WLR 533.
15   As in *A v A*, supra, note 5.
16   *Scott v Scott* (1977) 7 Fam Law 142.
17   MCA 1973, s 41(3).
18   See *P v P and J* [1971] P 217, [1971] 1 All ER 616, CA (child born after decree nisi); *Healey v Healey* [1984] Fam 111, [1984] 3 All ER 1040 (child born between date of petition and of decree nisi). The fact that a s 41 order does not cover a particular child of the family does not, however, prevent a subsequent order being made for financial provision for him.

(i)   Procedure

3.49   The petitioner must file with his petition a statement as to the arrangements proposed for the children. It must be signed personally by him and it must contain the information required by Form 4 of the MCR 1977.[1] Full details should be set out. Form 4 is defective in that, while it expressly relates to a child under 16 or over 16 but under 18 and receiving education or training, it does not refer to any other child of the family whose special circumstances may make it desirable for the court to direct that s 41 should apply to him. Nevertheless, the appropriate way of dealing with his exceptional case is, it is suggested, to draw the court's attention to the matter by inclusion of details in the petitioner's statement.

The respondent may file a written statement of his views on the arrangements proposed by the petitioner.[2] This should accompany his acknowledgement of service, but in any event must be filed before the judge makes an order under section 41. The vast majority of cases are dealt with under the special procedure. Where this is so and the registrar has filed his certificate that the petitioner is entitled to a decree,[3] he may then fix an appointment for a judge in chambers to consider the arrangements, unless the registrar thinks it inappropriate in the particular circumstances. In practice the date of appointment is fixed for that on which the judge is to pronounce the decree nisi. This procedure, it must be stressed, is only permissible if the respondent has not filed a statement proposing materially different arrangements from those of the petitioner, is not objecting to the petitioner's claim for custody and is not himself applying for custody or access.[4] In the vast majority of special procedure cases judges are satisfied with the existing and proposed arrangements, but may occasionally issue further directions, eg for the provision of a welfare report. Such steps are, however, more likely in contested cases.[5] The petitioner's personal attendance is required at an appointment, but, if for good cause this is impracticable (eg because of illness), leave to give evidence on affidavit should be sought, preferably from the registrar prior to the hearing or, if time does not permit, from the judge at the hearing.

---

1   See MCR 1977, r 8(2).
2   Ibid, r 50.
3   See ibid, r 48(1).
4   Ibid, r 48(4).
5   For the guidelines to be followed where custody is contested see ante, paras 3.06 to 3.13. In contested applications in matrimonial proceedings for custody, access and variation thereof the Principal Registry of the Family Division is running an in-court conciliation scheme. The scheme has been extended to include (1) applications under s 41 of MCA 1973 referred by a judge to a registrar for further inquiry, and (2) contested applications for custody and access in certain wardship proceedings, other than those in which a local authority is involved. For the detailed procedure to be followed see *Practice Direction* [1982] 3 All ER 988 [1982] 1 WLR 1420 and *Practice Direction (child: custody: conciliation guardianship and wardship)* [1984] 3 All ER 800, [1984] 1 WLR 1326. To assist in reducing delays in obtaining hearing dates for, inter alia, custody summonses proceeding in the Principal Registry, arrangements have been made for hearings to take place by duly authorised circuit judges, sitting as Deputy High Court judges where appropriate, either in specified London county courts or in the provinces. The arrangements do not, however, extend to custody cases which involve local authorities, or the Official Solicitor, or where there is an issue of jurisdiction or a foreign element or where leave is sought to remove a child permanently from the jurisdiction or where the case involves a novel point of law or is of exceptional complexity. See *Practice Direction* [1985] FLR 536.

(ii)   Reform
3.50   The requirement relating to approval of arrangements was inspired by the Royal Commission on Marriage and Divorce,[1] was first enacted in 1958,[2] and, with minor amendments, appears in its present form in section 41. Throughout its comparatively short history it has excited much empirical research and constant review and assessment.[3] The most recent examination has been undertaken by the Law Commission.[4] Drawing upon the earlier sources, the Commission has admirably and succinctly pinpointed the strengths and weaknesses of the procedure. Although there have been significant improvements in it since the introduction of the 'special procedure' in divorce cases, especially by way of reducing formality, easing communication between parents and judge and relying more readily on the court welfare service, one of the most recent surveys has again emphasised the persistent variations in practice.[5] The Booth Committee has made a number of proposals to strengthen the present procedures,[6] particularly with regard to the parties providing more detailed information in their statements about the present and proposed arrangements for the children and for those details to be judicially considered at an earlier stage in the proceedings. The proposals have received the qualified approval of the Law Commission, but the Commission provisionally goes further, with a preference for a rule in divorce proceedings similar to that in section 8(1) of the DPMCA 1978, 'whereby the court's duty is to decide whether there are circumstances requiring an order to be made'.[7] The improved procedures proposed by the Booth Committee would help decide that question.

1   See (1956) Cmnd 9678, para 379.
2   Matrimonial Proceedings (Children) Act 1958, ss 5 and 6.
3   Many of the sources have already been listed at the beginning of this chapter (ante, para 3.01, note 1). The following are also of direct relevance to s 41 and to the making of custody orders: Hall, *Arrangements for the Care and Upbringing of Children (Section 33 of the Matrimonial Causes Act 1965)* (1968) Law Com Working Paper No 15; Elston, Fuller and Murch, *Judicial Hearings of Undefended Divorce Petitions* (1975) 38 MLR 609; Maidment, *A Study in Child Custody* (1976) 6 Fam Law 195 and 236; Eekelaar, *Children in Divorce: Some further Data* [1982] OJLS 63; Davis, McLeod and Murch, *Undefended Divorce: Should Section 41 of the Matrimonial Causes Act 1973 be Repealed?* (1983) 46 MLR 121; Dodds, *Children and Divorce* [1983] JSWL 228; Maidment, *The Matrimonial Causes Act, s 41 and the Children of Divorce: Theoretical and Empirical Considerations* in *State, Law and the Family, Critical Perspectives*, ed by Freeman (1984); Report of the Matrimonial Causes Procedure Committee (1985) (Chairman: The Honourable Mrs Justice Booth – the 'Booth Committee').
4   Law Com Working Paper No 96, paras 4.4–4.16.
5   Dodds, op cit.
6   See particularly paras 4.35, 4.37, 4.51 and 4.69.
7   Law Com Working Paper No 96, para 4.15.

(b)   Orders

(i)   Custody and access
3.51   The court may make such order as it thinks fit, but subject to the overriding principle of the paramountcy of the child's welfare,[1] for the custody[2] (including access) and education (including training) of any child of the family under 18.[3] Alternatively, it may direct that proceedings be taken to make the child a ward of court, but it rarely exercises this power.[4] An order for custody may be made before, by or after the decree absolute of divorce or nullity or, in the case of judicial separation, the decree. The

power is similar to that of a magistrates' court under the DPMCA 1978 in that it may be exercised even if the petition is dismissed,[5] provided that this is done forthwith or (if an application for the custody order is made on or before the dismissal) after the dismissal.[6] The power to make an order after granting a decree of judicial separation is, however, excluded by the Family Law Act 1986 if on the relevant date[7] proceedings for divorce or nullity in respect of the child's parents are continuing in Scotland or Northern Ireland;[8] but this exclusion does not operate if the court in Scotland or Northern Ireland has made an order either waiving jurisdiction or sisting or staying proceedings so as to enable proceedings with respect to the custody of the child to be taken in England and Wales, provided that order is still in force.[9]

The court is also empowered[10] to make an order for custody[11] (including access) for any child of the family under 18 in proceedings for failure to provide reasonable maintenance under section 27 of the MCA 1973, but subject to the restrictions that an order for financial provision must first be made under that section[12] and that any order for custody can remain operative only so long as the other order is in force and the child is still under 18. An order under section 27 is a custody order within the meaning of FLA 1986,[13] and the provisions of that Act apply to such an order as they do to a custody order made under section 9 of GMA 1971.[14]

1 In accordance with the GMA 1971, s 1.
2 Custody here bears its widest meaning.
3 MCA 1973, s 42(1). Orders for custody in respect of children over 16 are only made in exceptional circumstances; *Hall v Hall* (1945) 175 LT 355, 62 TLR 151.
4 See post, para 8.12.
5 See ante, para 3.35. The reason for the dismissal is immaterial; *P(LE) v P(JM)* [1971] P 318, [1971] 2 All ER 728.
6 MCA 1973, s 42(1)(b), as amended by FLA 1986, s 4(2).
7 This means, where an application is made for a custody order under s 42(1)(a), the date of the application or first application if two or more are determined together, for example, if there are cross applications. Where no such application is made the relevant date is the date of the custody order. See FLA 1986, s 4(6).
8 FLA 1986, s 4(3).
9 Ibid, s 4(4).
    Correspondingly, where the English court has jurisdiction under s 4 of MCA 1973 to make a custody order, it may waive its jurisdiction in favour of a court outside England and Wales (FLA 1986, s 4(5)), or it may refuse an application for custody (s 5(1)), or it may stay proceedings relating to custody (s 5(2)).
10 By s 42(2).
11 See above, note 2. S 42(2), unlike s 42(1) does not also refer to education, but, in view of the wide meaning of custody, the omission will not, it is submitted, preclude a custody order from dealing with that matter. See however, *Dipper v Dipper* [1981] Fam 31, [1980] 2 All ER 722, CA, infra, para 3.53.
12 It is, however, permissible for the judge to make a formal order relating to financial provision, leaving the registrar to determine the rate of periodical payments. See *Practice Direction*, 3 February 1959.
13 See s 1(1)(a)(iii).
14 See ante, para 3.15.

3.52 Custody may be granted to either party or to a parent (if the child is not the child of both parties) or a relative[1] or any other person.[2] Moreover, applications for custody are not limited to the petitioner or the respondent. Certain categories of person may apply without obtaining leave to intervene.[3] These are a guardian[4] or a step-parent or any other person who has custody or control of the child by virtue of an order of a court. Oddly, a parent of the child (not being a party to the proceedings) is not specifically mentioned. Probably he is to be treated as a guardian or possibly as 'any other person entitled to apply',[5] but it is surprising that there is neither an express rule nor an authority on the point.[6] The position of the father who was not married to the mother at the date of the child's birth will, it seems, depend, when the section is brought into force, on whether or not he has been given all the parental rights and duties by an order under section 4 of the Family Law Reform Act 1987.[7] If he has not, he will have to obtain leave, as will a relative or any other person. In practice the registrar will need to be satisfied that the applicant has a sufficient interest in the child before granting leave. Custody may be granted to a third party even after one of the parties to the marriage has died.[8]

1 See, for example, *Cahill v Cahill* (1974) 5 Fam Law 16, CA (grandparents); *Morgan v Morgan* (1974) 4 Fam Law 189, CA (aunt and uncle).
2 Cf DPMCA 1978, s 8(3), where there has to be a notional application for a custodianship order in order to enable the court to grant legal custody to a person other than a spouse or parent; see ante, para 3.36.
3 See MCR 1977, r 92(3).
4 Ie a testamentary guardian or a guardian appointed by the court. For guardianship see post, Chapter 4.
5 Rule 92(3).
6 Even if he has to apply for leave, it is highly unlikely that he will be refused it.
7 If an order were made, he would have the rights of surviving parent as to guardianship; see GMA 1971, s 3(3) and (4), as prospectively added by FLRA 1987, s 6(1).
8 *Pryor v Pryor* [1947] P 64, [1947] 1 All ER 381; *B v B and H (L intervening)* [1962] 1 All ER 29, [1961] 1 WLR 1467.

3.53 As with an order granting legal custody under the GMA 1971 and 1973 and under the DPMCA 1978 conditions may be attached to a custody order,[1] but, apart from a provision restricting removal of the child out of the jurisdiction,[2] the only other condition which is fairly common in practice is that relating to changing the child's surname.[3] The discretion of a divorce court is, however, wider than that of the other two jurisdictions in that, in principle at least, it has a wider choice in the kinds of orders that it can make. Thus, it is possible to make an order granting care and control to one party, say the wife, and custody to the husband, thereby leaving to him the decision on such major questions as the child's education.[4] Such an order is rare and in general 'undesirable'.[5] Equally rare is an order merely granting care and control to one parent without providing for custody, the effect being that all parental rights and duties other than care and control remain vested equally and separately in both parents in accordance with the GA 1973.[6] A third possibility is to grant care and control to one parent and joint custody to both. Such an order has been commended in those cases where both parents have the welfare of their child at heart, it is reasonably likely that they will co-operate for his well-being and they are qualified to give wise guidance to him.[7] Even where co-operation is not immediately likely, that kind of order may also occasionally be appropriate where the party who is not given care and control has shown responsibility and concern for the child, especially if the granting of joint custody might eventually ease any bitterness between the parties.[8] There are now signs of increasing use being made of joint custody orders,[9] but the courts are still taking the view that an order granting joint custody, care and control, whose effect is that the child spends alternate short periods with each of the parties, is prima facie wrong and should be avoided on the ground that it deprives the child of a settled home.[10] The argument should not, it is suggested, prevail where the child is happy when spending his time, albeit separately, with two concerned and cooperative parents. After all the courts are willing to grant a parent staying access, entitling the child to stay for example with the non-custodial parent regularly for week-ends, which effectively means that the parents are sharing care and control. It is heartening to find that the Law Commission is favourably disposed to a notion of 'time sharing' in the form of an order allocating care and control[11] which could be the subject of agreement between the parties or specific allocation by the court. The usual order is one granting custody, including care and control, to one parent. Notwithstanding the wide meaning of custody in this context, the effect of such an order is not to deprive the other parent of all rights. Subject to any order a court may make, he still retains some as natural guardian, in particular the following: the rights to reasonable access,[12] to apply for variation of a custody order,[13] not to have the child's surname changed without his consent,[14] to appoint a testamentary guardian, to veto adoption and to object to a resolution vesting parental rights and duties in a local authority under s 3 of the CCA 1980. However, the Court of Appeal controversially went further in *Dipper v Dipper*,[15] and stated that a custody order does not entitle the parent to whom it is granted to take all the decisions about broader questions, such as education and religion, without consulting the other parent. Consultation will then enable the latter to bring the matter before the court, if he disagrees with the action proposed by the custodial parent. These effects of a custody order on a non-custodial parent who is a party to the marriage will equally apply in the exceptional case where custody is granted to someone other than a parent, for example a step-parent. Not only will the non-custodial parent retain rights as natural guardian but also the step-parent will be obliged to consult him on such matters as education. As for a non-custodial parent who is not a party to the marriage, not only will the above effects equally apply to him but his rights as a parent will in no way be affected by a custody order, unless he was a party to the application for the order and the other parent was one of the parties to the marriage.[16]

The wider implications of *Dipper* are that it will apply whatever order is made in divorce proceedings, whether it is a custody order in favour of one party or a joint custody order or an order dealing only with care and control. What has yet to be decided is whether it also operates in proceedings under GMA 1971 and 1973 and DPMCA 1978 in favour of a parent to whom the legal and actual custody is not given, so that he is entitled to be consulted. Logically it should, but in any event the court can directly give effect to the decision by expressly conferring on the non-custodial parent joint rights relating to such 'broader questions' provided they fall within the definition of legal custody.

1 See ante, para 3.19.
2 See post, para 3.60.
3 See ante, para 1.46.
4 *Wakeham v Wakeham* [1954] 1 All ER 434, [1954] 1 WLR 366, CA. But see infra, *Dipper v Dipper* [1981] Fam 31, [1980] 2 All ER 722.

5 *Dipper v Dipper* at 45 and 731 respectively; *Williamson v Williamson* [1986] 2 FLR 146, [1986] Fam Law 217, CA. Exceptionally, a split order may be appropriate; see *Jane v Jane* (1983) 4 FLR 712, 13 Fam Law 209, CA, where care and control was given to the mother but custody to the father on the ground that he should have sole responsibility for the child's medical treatment because of the mother's religious views on that matter.

6 GA 1973, s 1. Such an order was apparently made in *Allington v Allington* [1985] FLR 586, [1985] Fam Law 157, CA.

7 *Jussa v Jussa* [1972] 2 All ER 600, [1972] 1 WLR 881; *Owen v Owen* (1973) 4 Fam Law 13, CA; *Hoey v Hoey* [1984] FLR 334, [1984] 1 All ER 177n, CA.

8 *Caffell v Caffell* [1984] FLR 169, [1984] Fam Law 83, CA; *Hurst v Hurst* [1984] FLR 867, CA.

9 See Maidment, *Child Custody and Divorce,* Chapter 11; Booth Committee Report, para 4.130–4.131; Priest and Whybrow, Supplement to Law Com Working Paper No 96 (13%) of cases). Cf an earlier report in (1981) NLJ 543 (2% of cases).

10 *Riley v Riley* [1986] 2 FLR 429, CA, where the order was varied so as to grant care and control to the mother, even though the arrangements under the original joint order had lasted for five years with no apparent detriment to the child.

11 See Law Com Working Paper No 96, paras 4.51 – 4.59; and for data and judicial attitudes see the Supplement (Priest and Whybrow), paras 5.33 – 5.37, and [1987] Fam Law 57.

12 See post, para 3.84.

13 See post, para 3.63.

14 See ante, para 1.45.

15 [1981] Fam 31, [1980] 2 All ER 722. See Maidment (1981) 44 MLR 341.

16 MCA 1973, s 42(5).

(ii) Procedure

3.54 A petitioner who seeks custody must include a prayer for it in the petition.[1] A respondent who does so must include a prayer in the answer.[2] If he does not file an answer but seeks custody, he should point out in the acknowledgment of service that he wishes to be heard on that matter.[3] An application by any other person is by summons in the High Court or by notice if the cause is proceeding in a divorce county court.[4] Subject to applications for agreed orders, every application for custody (including access) or education or for an order committing the child to the care of a local authority[5] or for a supervision order[6] must be made to a judge.[7] An application relating to custody or supervision or education or access which is unopposed or in which the parties are agreed on the terms (save for the extent of access to be given) may be made to the registrar[8] and should be so made unless there are exceptional circumstances making it desirable for the matter to be brought before a judge for decision.[9] A court should have good reasons for not giving effect to an agreement made by the parties.[10] In the High Court it is practice automatically to reserve matters relating to children to the judge who first deals with the case, unless he indicates to the contrary, whereas in a county court a matter is reserved to a particular judge only if he so directs.[11]

In proceedings under section 27 of the MCA 1973 a claim for custody must be included under that section.[12]

1 MCR 1977, r 9 and App 2.

2 Ibid, r 21(3).

3 Ibid, r 15(1) and Form 6.

4 Ie notice under CCR 1981, Ord 13, r 1 (applications in the course of proceedings).

5 See infra, para 3.57.

6 See infra, para 3.55.

7 MCR 1977, r 92(1).

8 Ibid, r 92(2) as amended.

9 *Practice Direction* [1977] 3 All ER 944, [1977] 1 WLR 1226. Applications for agreed orders

for custody or, as the case may be, for care and control in guardianship and wardship cases proceeding in the Principal Registry should be dealt with in the same manner; *Practice Direction* [1980] 1 All ER 813, [1980] 1 WLR 321. See also *Practice Direction* [1980] 1 All ER 784, [1980] 1 WLR 301 on the need to adjourn the hearing so as to give each party the opportunity to be heard if the court is unwilling to make an agreed order.
10 *C v C* (1981) Times, 21 January, CA.
11 *Practice Direction* [1972] 1 All ER 1056, [1972] 1 WLR 392.
12 MCR 1977 r 98(1) and Form 19. The application is by originating application.
   For the power to order disclosure of the child's whereabouts see ante, paras 3.28 and 3.37A.

(c)   Other orders

(i)   Supervision order[1]

3.55   Where the court grants a person care of the child it may, if there are exceptional circumstances making it desirable, order that the child be placed under the supervision of a welfare officer or a specified local authority.[2] There is no judicial authority on the meaning of exceptional circumstances, but the making of an order is certainly exceptional and the number made in divorce and other matrimonial cases is declining.[3] An order is usually the result of a recommendation in a welfare officer's report. It may be desirable or essential where there is a serious risk of harm to the child whether because of the past behaviour, state of health or emotional condition of the child or of the parent[4] or because of some extrinsic cause such as poor housing of the family or where the parent is being given care after a lengthy separation from the child.[5] Any of these factors may be reflected in the fact that the probation service or the local authority has already been involved with the family, and this will strengthen the case for ordering supervision.

1 See Law Com Working Paper No 100, Part III; Law Com No 172, paras 5.10–5.18. Lavery, *Care, Supervision and Interim Orders in Custody Proceedings* [1987] Fam Law 261; Rutherford, *Care and Supervision in Custody Proceedings* (1987) Law Soc Gaz 1030; James and Wilson, *Matrimonial Supervision Orders: The Case for Change,* [1988] Fam Law 343; and James and Wilson, *When the Bough Breaks . . . Matrimonial Supervision Orders* [1988] JSWL 240.
2 MCA 1973, s 44(1), as amended by CA 1975, Sch 3, para 78. It is a condition of making a supervision order that an order by the court granting care is in existence; *Baczowski v Baczowski* (1980) 10 Fam Law 218, CA.
3 See Priest and Whybrow, op cit, para 7.12 et seq and Table 14.
4 Eg see *L v L* (1980) 2 FLR 48, CA.
5 *Ellard v Ellard* (1974) 5 Fam Law 29, CA.

3.56   Where a supervision order is made under the GMA 1971 and under the DPMCA 1978, it is expressly provided[1] that it must cease when the child reaches the age of 18, unless it has already been revoked. There is no corresponding provision in the MCA 1973, but it is submitted that the court will imply the same limitation. In none of those Acts is there provision that an order can be for a limited period. Surprisingly, the practice of some courts to make orders for finite periods[2] has not been challenged, although it is questionable whether the power is conferred. None of the Acts empowers the court to make such order 'as it thinks fit'. This is in marked contrast to the powers to make custody or legal custody orders.[3] Certainly the matter ought to be clarified. There is now influential support for a rule expressly enabling orders to be made for a definite period,[4] subject to review either by way of revocation of the order or variation for a longer or shorter period.

1 See GA 1973, s 3(2); DPMCA 1978, s 9(3).
2 See (1981) 145 JPN 137; Priest and Whybrow, op cit, para 7.23.
3 GMA 1971, s 9(1), as prospectively substituted by FLRA 1987, s 10; MCA 1973, s 42(1); DPMCA 1978, s 8(2).
4 See Booth Committee Report, para 4.139; Review of Child Care Law (1985), para 18.26. Both the Committee and the Review recommend that the court should be able to impose the same requirements upon the child in supervision orders made in custody proceedings as they can include in such orders made in care proceedings (see post, para 14.110); and further that in both kinds of proceedings there should be power to impose requirements upon the parent; see Law Com Working Paper No 96, para 2.64. Indeed, the latter requirements may be particularly desirable where there has been marital breakdown.

(ii)   Order committing care of the child to a local authority
3.57 Where the court considers that there are exceptional circumstances making it impracticable or undesirable for the child to be entrusted to either of the parties to the marriage or to any other individual, it may commit the child to the care of the local authority in whose area he is resident.[1] The meaning of 'entrusted' must be given very wide scope. It denotes a state of affairs in which the parent or other individual has total responsibility for the child. If, therefore, a parent is unwilling or unable to arrange access to the other parent, it may be impracticable or undesirable to entrust the child to him, and an order committing to care may be appropriate.[2] Before an order can be made the court must hear representations from the local authority, including any as to the making of a financial provision order in favour of the child.[3] The care order is even less frequently made in matrimonial proceedings than the supervision order,[4] and it, too, is unlikely unless a welfare officer's report has recommended it.[5] It may, however, as a last resort be the only effective order available to the court, for example, if the living conditions which the parent is able to offer are so inadequate or deplorable as to put the child's welfare at serious risk.[6] Moreover, where the divorce proceedings are already active and the local authority have taken the child into their care, application for an order committing to care should be sought in the divorce court rather than by way of care proceedings in the juvenile court.[18] The effect of the order is that the child is to be treated as if he had been received into care under section 2 of the Child Care Act 1980,[7] but the powers of the local authority relating to the welfare and accommodation of the child under that Act are subject to any directions given by the divorce court,[8] including directions as to access.[9] A care order made by the High Court in wardship proceedings or by that court under the GMA 1971 and 1973 can similarly be made subject to directions,[10] but, anomalously, not a care order made by any other court under the GMA or by a magistrates court under the DPMCA 1978.[11] The court's jurisdiction is original and not merely a review of the local authority's decision. It can, therefore, give any proper direction which is for the child's benefit, although if the local authority has acted bona fide in reaching its decision (for example, refusing a parent access), the court should take that fact into account in reaching its own decision.[12] Moreover, the local authority cannot arrange for the child's emigration.[13] So long as the care order is in force neither a parent nor anyone else may claim the child,[14] except by means of an

application to discharge the order.[15] Since the order is subject to the supervision of the court and subject to the right of the parties to apply to it for the matter to be reviewed, the local authority should not make any immediate arrangements for long-term fostering but seek to rehabilitate the child with the parent or other person claiming the child.[16] Indeed, because of the desirability of attempting rehabilitation, it may exceptionally be appropriate to make a care order even though it is the intention of the local authority, if an order is made, to leave the child in the actual care of one of the parents. In those circumstances, if the experiment should fail, the local authority will be able to remove the child promptly from the parent without the expense and delay of further recourse to the court.[17] If the parent objects, his remedy lies in seeking revocation of the care order.[18]

1   MCA 1973, s 43(1) and (2), as amended by HASSASSAA 1983, s 9 and Sch 20, para 20. See generally Law Com Working Paper No 100, Part III; Law Com No 172, paras 5.2–5.9. Lavery, op cit; Rutherford op cit (supra, para 3.55 n 1).
2   See Sir John Arnold P in *R v G (Surrey County Council intervening)* [1984] Fam 100, [1984] 3 All ER 460, CA.
3   MCA 1973, s 43(2); MCR 1977, r 93(1)–(3) and Form 18. A care order made without first hearing representations is void; *M v M (divorce: care order)* (1980) 1 FLR 327, CA.
4   For statistical details see Priest and Whybrow, op cit, paras 7.6 – 7.11 and Table 13.
5   Cf *Cooke v Cooke and Sutton London Borough* (1981) 3 FLR 396, 12 Fam Law 61.
6   *F v F* [1959] 3 All ER 180n, [1959] 1 WLR 863; *W v W and Hampshire County Council* (1979) 2 FLR 68, CA.
7   MCA 1973, s 43(1).
8   Ibid, s 43(5)(a).
9   *Re Y (a minor) (child in care: access)* [1976] Fam 125, [1975] 3 All ER 348, CA. See also *Lewisham London Borough v M* [1981] 3 All ER 307, [1981] 1 WLR 1248.
10 See respectively FLRA 1969, s 7(3) and GA 1973, s 4(4)(a).
11 But that is not the only anomaly; see Law Com Working Paper No 96, para 2.68 note 204. Where there is power to give directions, the rules differ. Under MCA 1973, s 43(5)(a) directions may be given in respect of the duties imposed on the local authority by ss 18, 21 and 22 of CCA 1980 (which deal with respectively (1) general duties, (2) duty to provide accommodation and maintenance, and (3) boarding-out of children). Under the GA 1973, s 4(4) (c) directions may relate to the duties under ss 18 and 21 but not to those under s 22. A care order made in wardship adopts the rules of MCA 1973 (FLRA 1969, s 7(3)): an order made in custodianship proceedings follows those of GA 1973 (CA 1975, ss 34(5) and 36(6)).
12 *Re R (a minor)* [1983] 2 All ER 929, [1983] 1 WLR 991, CA.
13 MCA 1973, s 43 (5)(b).
14 Ibid, s 43(3).
15 For discharge of an order see post, para 3.63. Any parent or guardian of the child must keep the local authority informed of his address; see s 43(6).
16 *Turney v Turney and Devon County Council* (1981) 4 FLR 199, CA.
17 *R v G (Surrey County Council intervening)* [1984] Fam 100, [1984] 3 All ER 460, CA. Cf *Cooke v Cooke and Sutton London Borough Council,* supra, note 5.
18 See *M v M* (October 1986) unreported but noted at [1988] NLJ 311.

3.58   A child who is committed to the care of a local authority by a divorce court cannot be made the subject of a supervision order.[1] Moreover, if he should later be the subject of criminal proceedings while the care order is in existence, the juvenile court should not make a concurrent care order under the CYPA 1969. The proper and practical course is for that court to adjourn the case and, with the co-operation of the local authority, have the matrimonial care order revoked, and then make a care order under the 1969 Act.[2]

1   MCA 1973, s 44(3).
2   *W v Heywood* [1985] FLR 1064, [1985] Fam Law 282, DC, and contrast *Re C (a minor) (wardship: care order)* [1983] 1 All ER 219, [1982] 1 WLR 1462.

(iii)   Orders for financial relief

3.59   The court may require a spouse to provide financial relief for a child of the family in the form of financial provision orders and property adjustment orders. These orders are examined in Chapter 16.[1]

1   See paras 16.19 – 16.66.

(iv)   Order restricting removal out of jurisdiction

3.60   Unless otherwise directed, any order relating to the custody or care and control of the child must provide for the child not to be removed out of England and Wales without the leave of the court except on specified terms.[1] In accordance with section 36 of the Family Law Act 1986 an order restricting removal is effective in any other part of the United Kingdom. Where the child is being temporarily removed but there is a real danger that he may not be returned to the jurisdiction, the court may exceptionally impose one or more of the following safeguards: (i) an undertaking by the removing parent to enter into a bond with the registrar of the court in an appropriate sum to secure compliance with the order; (ii) an undertaking to procure a surety (or sureties) to be similarly bound; (iii) the provision of further security for due performance of the bond by way of a deposit of money or a charge on some property, for example, the shares or the home of the removing parent.[2] At any time the petitioner or the respondent may apply for an order prohibiting removal except on terms.[3] An application for leave to remove must be made to a judge, except where it is unopposed or is for the temporary removal of the child and is opposed only with regard to the arrangements for care of the child during the removal, when it may be made to a registrar.[4] Where an application for leave to take a child permanently out of the jurisdiction is opposed or an application for temporary removal from the jurisdiction is opposed on the ground that the child may not be duly returned, the application must normally be heard in the High Court.[5] In deciding whether or not to allow permanent removal the court is governed by the principle of the paramountcy of the child's interests, so that if, for example, the disappointment felt by the custodial parent in not being able to go abroad would have serious adverse effects on the child, the court may well allow removal,[6] although it may be more difficult to reach this conclusion if there is a close relationship with the non-custodial parent. Any incompatibility between the interests of the child and those of the custodial parent is to be assessed in the light of the paramountcy principle.[7] Where the child is already resident abroad, the court has jurisdiction to make an order for custody, but the general rule is that it will require the party to whom custody is granted to give an undertaking to return the child to the jurisdiction. Any application for custody by a party should be accompanied by such an undertaking by way of an affidavit.[8]

1   MCR 1977, r 94(2). To anticipate and prevent removal the assistance of the police, by way of a port-alert, and the Passport Office may be sought; see post, paras 3.103 and 3.106. For the assistance of the Consular Department of the Foreign and Commonwealth

Office where a child is removed from the jurisdiction without leave of the court or in contravention of a court order, see post, para 3.123.
2 See the guidance given to practitioners by the Family Division Sub-Committee of the Supreme Court Procedure Committee (1987) 84 Law Soc Gaz 661.

Moreover, while the order restricting removal is operative the court may require a person to surrender any United Kingdom passport which has been issued to, or contained particulars of, the child (FLA 1986, s 37).
3 MCR 1977, r 94(1). In cases of emergency, where there is imminent danger of the child being removed from the jurisdiction, an order may be sought before the matrimonial proceedings are issued; see *L v L* [1969] P 25, [1969] 1 All ER 852.
4 Ibid, r 94(3).
5 See the restrictions imposed by the *Practice Direction* [1988] 2 All ER 103, [1988] 1 WLR 558, ante, para 3.17.
6 *L v H* [1986] LS Gaz R 1554, CA.
7 *Poel v Poel* [1970] 1 WLR 1469; *A v A (child: removal from jurisdiction)* (1979) 1 FLR 380, 10 Fam Law 116, CA; *Chamberlain v de la Mare* (1982) 4 FLR 434, 13 Fam Law 15, CA; *Lonslow v Hennig (formerly Lonslow)* [1986] 2 FLR 378, [1986] Fam Law 303, CA.
8 *Armstrong v Armstrong, Huff v Huff* [1986] 1 FLR 95, [1986] Fam Law 21, CA.

(v)   Declaration of unfitness

3.61   Very occasionally the court may include in a decree absolute of divorce or a decree of judicial separation a declaration that either party to the marriage is unfit to have custody of the children of the family. If the party to whom the declaration relates is a parent of any child, that party will not, on the death of the other party, be entitled as of right to the custody or guardianship of the child.[1] Because of these serious consequences of a declaration and the stigma attaching to it a court will want clear evidence of very serious conduct before it will make it. The object of a declaration is to protect the child, not to punish the party to the marriage,[2] but courts have other wide powers for protecting children, and the Law Commission has recommended that the power should be repealed.[3]

1 MCA 1973, s 42(3) and (4).
2 *B v B (declaration of unfitness)* (1979) 3 FLR 187, CA. Declarations against husbands were made in *Webley v Webley* (1891) 64 LT 839 (ill treatment of his children); *S v S* [1949] P 269, [1949] 1 All ER 285n (his gross sexual practices committed against his wife); *B v B,* supra (his sexual misbehaviour with daughter). Cf *Woolnoth v Woolnoth* (1902) 86 LT 598 , 18 TLR 453 (his adultery and failure for ten years to maintain his children were held not to justify a declaration).
3 Law Com No 172, paras 7.2–7.3.

(d)   Duration of orders (other than those for financial provision)

3.62   Any of the above orders may be made in respect of a child under 18,[1] except that one committing him to the care of a local authority cannot be made once he reaches the age of 17.[2] In practice no order is made once the child has become 16 unless there are special circumstances[3] and, whatever his age, any order made will cease to operate when he attains 18,[4] unless it is earlier varied or discharged or ceases to have effect where an order is made for the child's return under Part I of the Child Abduction and Custody Act 1985 or a decision, other than one relating to rights of access, is registered under s 16 of that Act.[5] Moreover, the Family Law Act 1986[6] provided that, if a custody order (or a variation of a custody order) made in Scotland or Northern Ireland comes into force at a time when a custody order made in an English divorce court in divorce, nullity or judicial separation proceedings is in effect, the Scottish or Northern

Ireland order will prevail over the English order in so far as they overlap. This possibility can arise where the child's habitual residence has changed to Scotland or Northern Ireland after the English proceedings. Thereafter, the English court does not have power to vary its own order so as to make provision for the matters covered by the later order.[7] Any supervision order which is dependent upon the English custody order ceases to have effect.[8] The English divorce court may vary its own order made in divorce or nullity proceedings, but cannot vary any custody order made under section 42 of MCA 1973 after granting a decree of judicial separation if at the relevant date[9] proceedings for divorce or nullity are continuing in Scotland or Northern Ireland in respect of the child's parents,[10] unless the court in Scotland or Northern Ireland waives its jurisdiction to make an order or decides to sist or stay proceedings before it in favour of the English court.[11] A supervision order automatically ceases to operate if the order relating to care and control ends before the child reaches 18.[12] Similarly, an order for custody made in proceedings for failure to maintain terminates if the order for financial provision ceases to operate before attainment of that age.[13]

1 MCA 1973, s 42(1) and (2).
2 Ibid, s 43(4).
3 *Thomasset v Thomasset* [1894] P 295.
4 MCA 1973, ss 42(6) and 43(4); but for supervision orders see ante, para 3.56.
5 See ss 25(1) and (2), 27(1) and Sch 3, para 1(1), and for the Act generally see post, paras 3.108 et seq.
6 S 6(1).
7 Ibid, s 6(2).
8 Ibid, s 6(6)(b).
9 As defined in FLA 1986, s 6(7).
10 Ibid, s 6(3). The subsection also refers to proceedings for judicial separation in Scotland or Northern Ireland, but this possibility would not be likely to arise where the English court had already granted a decree of judicial separation since, in accordance with s 44(2) of the Act, that decree would normally be recognised in Scotland or Northern Ireland.
11 S 6(4).
12 MCA 1973, s 44(1).
13 Ibid, s 42(2).

3.63 The court has a general power to vary and discharge orders relating to custody, committal to care and supervision.[1] Although the MCA and MCR do not explicitly set out who may be applicants for variation or discharge, it seems clear that anyone eligible to apply for an order is equally eligible to apply for variation or discharge. Additionally the supervising welfare officer or local authority may apply for variation or discharge of a supervision order and the local authority may do so in relation to an order committing the child to its care.[2]

1 MCA 1973, ss 42(6), 43(7) and 44(5). It has been pointed out that the power to vary a committal to care order 'seems to be a limited one, since the committal to care has the effect of applying the statutory provisions of the Child Care Act 1980. Possibly the power is linked to the separate power to give directions' – see Law Com Working Paper No 96, para 266, note 198 and for the power to give directions see ante, para 3.57.
2 MCR 1977, r 93(4).

(e)   Interim orders and injunctions

3.64   Unlike the GMA 1971 and 1973 and the DPMCA 1978, the MCA 1973 does not expressly provide for the making of interim orders, but it has been judicially accepted that a power to do so falls within the general power of the court to make custody orders,[1] including proceedings under section 27 of that Act.[2] An incidental consequence of this absence of express statutory provision is that, also unlike the other Acts, there is no limit on the number or duration of interim orders,[3] an omission which, it has been observed,[4] might encourage unreasonable delay in reaching a final decision on custody of the child. An order may be sought before the hearing of the cause and should accompany the filing of the petition. An order may be necessary where the hearing of the application for custody is adjourned for a welfare officer's report[5] and one of the parties is not content with the status quo pending the full hearing.[6] Such opposition is more likely where the child has been 'snatched' by one parent from the other. In deciding whether to order the return of the child to the other the paramountcy of the child's welfare governs.[7] The question of granting interim custody or care and control to one parent may be closely connected to exclusion of the other from the matrimonial home and the court may be required to grant an injunction for that purpose.[8] An exclusion order should not be made unless it is just and equitable to do so, but any injustice to a spouse may be outweighed by taking into consideration the interests of the children.[9]

1   See *Spratt v Spratt* (1858) 1 Sw & Tr 215 and *Re B (a minor)* (1983) 13 Fam Law 176, CA. Exceptionally, the court may split the care and control between the parties; *Re H (a minor)* (1982) 12 Fam Law 218, CA.
2   See ante, para 3.51.
3   Cf ante, paras 3.23 and 3.39.
4   See Law Com Working Paper No 96, para 2.71. and generally Working Paper No 100.
5   But, where there are serious allegations against a party who is claiming interim care and control, it is necessary to obtain evidence or a report from a welfare officer before an interim order can be made in favour of that party; *Re W; Re L (minors: interim custody)* [1987] 2 FLR 67, [1987] Fam Law 130, CA.
6   *Boyt v Boyt* [1948] 2 All ER 436, CA. The order must not, however, empower the welfare officer to remove the child from the care of either parent; *Kirkham – Woodcraft v Kirkham – Woodcraft* [1984] Fam Law 57, CA.
7   Compare *W v D (interim custody order)* (1979) 1 FLR 393, CA with *Re R (minors)* (1981) 2 FLR 416, 11 Fam Law 57. The same principle applies in wardship proceedings; *Re B (minors) (wardship: interim care and control)* (1982) 4 FLR 472, CA; *Re W; Re L (minors) (interim custody)* [1987] Fam Law 130.
8   *Boyt v Boyt*, supra; *Beard v Beard* [1981] 1 All ER 783, [1981] 1 WLR 369, CA.
9   See *Re W and W (interim custody)* (1983) 4 FLR 686, 13 Fam Law 209, CA.

(f)   Enforcement of orders

3.65   Failure of a party to obey an order relating to custody or access is punishable with committal until the child is handed over to the person granted custody or access.[1] An order cannot be enforced against a child.

1   RSC Ord 45, r 5; CCR 1981 Ord 29, r 1; MCR 1977, r 90. See also the power under FLA 1986, s 34, ante, para 3.28, to order the recovery of the child.

6   Evidence and reports in custody cases[1]

3.66   In proceedings in a magistrates' court the parties and their witnesses can only give evidence orally, but, as has already been pointed out,[2] even where the procedure in other courts allows them to file affidavit evidence their availability at the hearing to give oral evidence will be necessary unless the court otherwise directs. Where an affidavit is filed it should not be so voluminous as to impede the proceedings, and no affidavit should be sworn without exhibiting the documents on which the party swearing it intends to rely.[3] If the cause or matter is proceeding in the Principal Registry of the Family Division and a date has been fixed for the hearing, any affidavit or other document must normally be lodged in the Principal Registry not less than 14 clear days before that date.[4]

1   Since the rules relating to the form and admissibility of evidence and welfare reports apply to wardship as well as to custody proceedings it is convenient to deal with these matters here in relation to both kinds of proceedings, but for wardship generally see post, Chapter 8.
2   See ante, para 3.10. As for the court's seeing the child, see para 3.11.
3   See *T v T* (1976) Times, 10 June, See also Practice Note [1983] 3 All ER 33, [1983] 1 WLR 992 for detailed requirements relating to affidavits, exhibits and bundles of documents which must be observed in order to comply with RSC Ord 41 in proceedings in the Court of Appeal and the High Court. Any document that does not comply with the Order and with the Practice Directions may be rejected by the court or made the subject of an order for costs.
4   See *Practice Direction* [1984] 1 All ER 684, [1984] 1 WLR 306.
   It is also important that all documents such as medical notes should be copied, agreed and paged before the hearing. If problems arise over the production of such documents, application should be made to the court for an order for production, and the application should be made a week or so before the hearing; see *Re P (minors)(child abuse: medical evidence)* [1988] 1 FLR 328 or 343.

3.67   The paramountcy of the child's welfare requires the court to have regard to all the evidence available,[1] even if the only evidence is hearsay,[2] provided that proper notice is given so that it may be challenged.[3] However, solicitors must always be mindful of their duty to public funds and the legal aid fund in particular, and thus should avoid adducing overlapping evidence. For example, where members of the same psychiatric team have been concerned with the child, it will, save in rare circumstances, be sufficient to call only one of them.[4] In an application for variation or discharge of an order evidence may be adduced even though it was available at the date of the order,[5] and an appellate court concerned with custody may look at material which was not before the court below.[6] The paramountcy principle also accounts for the power to call for confidential reports.[7] Notwithstanding this power, the court ought not to withhold other important evidence on which its decision is based, unless disclosure would be harmful to the child.[8] The case records which a local authority must keep in respect of children in care who are boarded out must not be disclosed, unless the court overrules the privilege.[9] It is a question in each case of whether the public interest dictates disclosure or not.[10] The privilege will certainly not operate where there is no discernible public interest.[11] These rules equally apply to information obtained by the probation service or by an adoption agency.[12] Moreover, the legal practitioner has special responsibilities with regard to non-disclosure. In wardship cases proceeding in private he must obtain leave to disclose evidential documents to persons who are not parties, eg psychiatrists, psychologists and medical experts or any other person. Disclosure without leave may be a contempt of court, even where the purpose of disclosure is only to obtain advice from the expert concerned whether relevant expert evidence would be forthcoming or would be helpful to the court.[13]

It is essential that all courts of first instance make findings of fact. Failure to do so makes it impossible for the appellate court to determine whether the judge's conclusion was right or wrong.[14]

1 Magistrates when hearing a domestic matter, particularly if it concerns children, have the power to admit further evidence at any time up to the final determination of the case; *R v Leeds Justices, ex p Thompson* (1983) 4 FLR 773, [1984] Fam Law 20, DC.
2 See for example Lord Devlin in *Official Solicitor to the Supreme Court v K* [1965] AC 201 at 242, [1963] 3 All ER 191 at 211. In cases concerned with the lives of children the court should not approve of technical objections to admissibility of evidence; *Hurwitt v Hurwitt* (1978) 3 FLR 194, 10 Fam Law 183, CA. But there are limits to relaxation of the rules. Thus, a distinction should be drawn between hearsay evidence which relates to purely historical matters or peripheral allegations which are not likely to be challenged and that which relates to a component part of the allegations against a parent and there is a serious issue raised by the parent. In the latter circumstance the original source of the information should depose to an affidavit so that he might be tendered for cross-examination; *Re N (minors) (wardship: evidence)* [1987] 1 FLR 65, [1987] Fam Law 87. See also *Re D (a minor) (wardship: evidence)* [1986] 2 FLR 189, [1986] Fam Law 263, where notes of an interview taken by a solicitor with the mother (since deceased) and making allegations against the father were held not to be admissible either as a 'statement' made orally or in a document by the mother or alternatively as a 'record' under s 2(1) and (4) of the Civil Evidence Act 1968.
3 Cf *Jackson (formerly Roberts) v Jackson* (1980) Fam Law 17, CA.
4 *Re Yeomans (minors)* [1985] Fam Law 121.
5 See *B (BPM) v B(MM)* [1969] P 103 at 114, [1969] 1 All ER 891 at 900.
6 *B v W (wardship: appeal)* [1979] 3 All ER 83, [1979] 1 WLR 1041, HL.
7 See post, para 3.70.
8 *B v W* supra, note 6.
9 *Re D (infants)* [1970] 1 All ER 1088, [1979] 1 WLR 599; *Re S and W (minors) (Confidential Reports)* (1982) 4 FLR 290, CA. The principle is of wider application; see *Gaskin v Liverpool City Council* [1980] 1 WLR 1549. Where there has been a long history of involvement with a family by social services, it may be convenient for the past history to be given from the local authority records in the form of hearsay evidence in the affidavit of the main witness; see *Re P (minors)(child abuse: medical evidence)* [1988] 1 FLR 328 at 344.
10 See Booth J in *Re M (minors)* [1986] Fam Law 336.
11 *R v Bournemouth Justices, ex p Grey and ex p Rodd* [1986] Fam Law 337.
12 See respectively *Re M (minors)* and *R v Bournemouth Justices, ex p Grey and ex p Rodd,* supra.
13 See *Practice Direction* [1987] 3 All ER 640, [1987] 1 WLR 1421. For the procedure to be followed where it is sought to issue a writ of subpoena duces tecum in respect of documents which are protected by privilege from disclosure, see *Re SL (a minor) (wardship: medical evidence)* [1987] 2 FLR 412n.
14 See *M v M* [1988] 1 FLR 225, [1988] Fam Law 52, CA; *Gray v Gray* (1986) 150 JP 587 [1987] 1 FLR 16.

3.68 The courts have not been ready to accept as evidence diagnostic interviews recorded on videotape in cases of alleged sexual abuse of children. The questioning technique, applied in child abuse clinics and designed to help the diagnostic process, involves the use of anatomically explicit dolls. Hitherto it has been open to the legal objections that the interview includes leading and hypothetical questions and has built into it the preconception that sexual abuse is likely to have taken place. Considerable doubt and reservations have therefore been expressed about its evidential value.[1]

1   See the collection of cases on the subject reported in [1987] 1 FLR 269–346, and see further on this topic post, para 10.53.
    Although the civil standard of proof on a balance of probabilities normally applies in custody and wardship proceedings, a more stringent degree of probability is required to satisfy a court that a parent has sexually abused his child than is necessary to justify the conclusion that the child has been the victim of sexual abuse by some other person; *Re G (a minor)* [1987] 1 WLR 1461. See also Radevsky, *The Standard of Proof on Wardship Proceedings* (1988) 138 NLJ 125.

3.69   In cases where it is sought to remove the child from one parent to the other (usually the mother) or to some other person, medical evidence on the likely effects on the child of the change of home may be highly relevant.[1] Nevertheless, such evidence is still exceptional, both in custody and wardship proceedings. Any psychiatric or psychological examination of the child with a view to a report being submitted in evidence is subject to leave of the court,[2] but leave is not necessary for a purely physical examination. In accordance with a Practice Direction,[3] leave should normally be granted only if (a) the child is separately represented and his representative supports the application or if the application is supported by a local authority having the care or supervision of the child and (b) there is or is suspected to be a specific and identifiable problem or potential problem on which the court needs assistance which can only or most conveniently be provided by a qualified psychiatrist or psychologist. This Direction accords with repeated statements of the Court of Appeal that in neither custody proceedings nor wardship proceedings should a party unilaterally refer the child to a doctor with a view to a medical report being prepared.[4] Indeed, in the case of wardship since proceedings have been instituted the child is under the court's protection and no steps can be taken without its consent. Hence, such unilateral conduct might constitute contempt.[5] Where consent is given, the costs of the examination and report will normally be allowed on taxation, but where consent has not been obtained it is highly likely, in the light of the Direction, that the court will refuse to admit the report in evidence and will direct that the costs of obtaining the examination and report be disallowed.[6]

1   See *S v S (custody of children)* (1978) 1 FLR 143, noted ante, para 3.10, where surprisingly the court relied on the evidence of a psychiatrist even though he had not seen the parties and even though his evidence conflicted with that of a psychiatrist who had at least seen one of them.
2   See *Re S (infants)* [1967] 1 All ER 202, [1967] 1 WLR 396; *Re R (PM) (an infant)* [1968] 1 All ER 691n, [1968] 1 WLR 385; *B(M) v B(R)* [1968] 3 All ER 170, [1968] 1 WLR 1182, CA; *Re A-W (minors)* (1974) 5 Fam Law 95.
3   [1985] 3 All ER 576, [1985] 1 WLR 1289.
4   See Ormrod LJ in *W v W and Hampshire County Council* (1979) 2 FLR 68 at 70. As an example of the undesirable consequences which may result from unilateral reference see *Gunn v Gunn* (1982) 12 Fam Law 177, CA.
5   *Barnes v Tyrrell* (1981) 3 FLR 240, CA.
6   *Practice Direction* [1985] 1 All ER 832, [1985] 1 WLR 360.

Welfare reports

3.70   The court may call for a welfare officer's report either at its own request or at the request of a party. In wardship proceedings, in custody proceedings in the High Court or a county court under the GMA 1971 and 1973 and in custody proceedings in a divorce court[1] a report may be called for by either the judge or the registrar. A request for a report may be made before the hearing or at any stage of the proceedings and, in wardship cases, even after the hearing if the court wishes to be informed on how its order is working out in practice. A report should always be sought by the High Court, a county court or a divorce court from the court's own welfare service,[2] but, whether it be any of these courts or a magistrates' court, a person who has already been involved in conciliation should not subsequently act as a welfare officer in the case.[3] It is very doubtful whether in custody cases there is jurisdiction to appoint an independent social worker,[4] but the High Court in matrimonial, wardship or guardianship proceedings or a divorce county court in matrimonial proceedings may entertain the evidence of an independent reporter who has been instructed by one of the parties. His role is, however, strictly limited.[5] In custody proceedings in a magistrates' court, whether under the GMA 1971 or the DPMCA 1978, the court at any stage of the proceedings may call for a report either from an officer of a local authority or a probation officer, and a single justice may request one before the hearing of the application.[6]

1   See MCR 1977, r 95.
2   In the provinces probation officers serve as welfare officers, but the Royal Courts of Justice have their own full-time welfare officers. Only reports prepared by a court welfare officer should be described as 'welfare' reports; *Re El-G (minors) (wardship and adoptions)* (1982) 4 FLR 421 at 428–429, 12 Fam Law 251 at 252. See generally Murch, *Justice and Welfare in Divorce Part 2;* James and Wilson, *Reports for the Court: The Work of the Divorce Court Welfare Officer* [1984] JSWL 89.
3   *Re H (a minor)* [1986] 1 FLR 476, [1986] Fam Law 193.
4   *Cadman v Cadman* (1981) 3 FLR 275, 12 Fam Law 82, CA.
5   See *Practice Direction* [1983] 1 All ER 1097, [1983] 1 WLR 416, and *Re C (a minor) (wardship proceedings)* [1984] FLR 419, [1984] Fam Law 273, CA. See also *Re C (wardship: independent social worker)* [1985] FLR 56, [1985] Fam Law 56. If in legally aided proceedings it is proposed to seek the service of an independent reporter, the proper course is to apply in advance to the legal aid committee, because, if prior leave is not obtained, the parties may have to justify that it is an unusual case; *Bishop v Wiltshire County Council* [1984] Fam Law 118.
6   GA 1973, s 6(1) (as amended by CA 1975, Sch 3, para 81) and s 6(6) (as added by CA 1975, s 90(2)); DPMCA 1978, s 12(3) and (9). Section 6(1) of the GA 1973 also extends to the High Court and a county court, but in practice those courts rely on their welfare services and not on local authority officers.

3.71   Reference to a welfare officer is entirely within the discretion of the court. Comparatively little reliance is placed on reports in uncontested cases, and in contested cases practice varies considerably.[1] A report is more likely than not to be of assistance to the court,[2] but to be so it must involve detailed investigation.[3] The welfare officer should see the parents, the children and other people involved in the family and perhaps also doctors and teachers, but especially important is the opportunity of observing the child and the grown-ups in both homes.[4] The practitioner should always be alert to the desirability of pressing for a report. For example, it may be essential where an interim order has already been made and the case is obviously fraught with difficulties.[5] However, the circumstances may be such that no real advantage is to be derived from calling for one; for example, where on divorce each party is proposing to move to a new home a welfare officer is not likely to be able to report on the rival merits of two non-existing and competing homes.[6] Normally, there should be only one report by one welfare officer and not two separate reports by two officers each of whom has seen only one of the homes in which the child might live;[7] but circumstances may exceptionally make it impossible to have a single report; for example because of unacceptable expense or delay.[8] The risk of several months' delay may, indeed, lead the court to proceed without calling for a report;[9] and where there is already one report it may be reluctant to postpone a decision in order to obtain a further report.[10]

1 See Maidment, *Child Custody and Divorce* pp 73–74; Priest and Whybrow, op cit, para 4.18.
2 See Davies LJ in *Re O (infants)* [1971] Ch 748, [1971] 2 All ER 744; Stamp LJ in *Southgate v Southgate* (1978) 8 Fam Law 246. Before ordering an inquiry and report a judge or registrar should, where local conciliation facilities exist, consider whether the case is suitable for attempts to be made to settle any of the issues by the conciliation process, and, if so, a direction to this effect should be included in the order. If conciliation fails, the court is very likely to order a report. Any report which is consequently offered must be made by an officer who did not act as a conciliator. See *Practice Direction* [1986] 2 FLR 171, [1986] Fam Law 286. The function of conciliation should not be confused with that of preparation of a welfare report; *Clarkson v Winkley* (1987) 151 JPJo 526; *Merriman v Hardy,* infra, note 3.
3 Cf *Merriman v Hardy* (1987) 151 JPJo 526, where, after two conciliation meetings with the parents, the welfare officers submitted a report merely stating that the parents could not agree. But, where an interim custody order is appropriate and there is no time for a full report to be obtained, a short adjournment might be necessary so that a welfare officer can give oral evidence; *Re W and L (minors) (interim custody)* [1987] 2 FLR 67, [1987] Fam Law 130, CA.
4 *Re W (a minor) (custody)* (1982) 4 FLR 492, 13 Fam Law 47, CA; *H v H (child: custody)* [1984] Fam Law 112, 127 Sol Jo 578, CA; *Re H (a minor)* [1986] 1 FLR 476, [1986] Fam Law 193; *Edwards v Edwards* [1986] 1 FLR 187, [1986] Fam Law 99, affd [1986] 1 FLR 205, CA.
5 *R v R (interim custody)* (1978) 8 Fam Law 169, CA.
6 *Ashbridge v Ashbridge* (1974) 4 Fam Law 192, CA.
7 *C v C* (1972) Times, 6 November; *B v B* (1973) Times, 24 January.
8 See *Practice Note* (1973) 117 Sol Jo 88 of Family Division.
9 *Re G (a minor)* (1980) 10 Fam Law 190, CA. For the need to avoid delay in the preparation of reports see Ormrod LJ in *Plant v Plant* (1982) 4 FLR 305, 12 Fam Law 179, CA and *Caffell v Caffell* [1984] FLR 169, [1984] Fam Law 83, CA. See also *H v H (child: custody),* supra, note 4; *Scott v Scott* [1986] 2 FLR 320, [1986] Fam Law 301, CA; cf *Re H (conciliation: welfare reports)* [1986] 1 FLR 476, [1986] Fam Law 193.
10 *Corbet v Corbet* (1978) 9 Fam Law 119, CA. Delay should also be avoided by the solicitor of the party, who is applying for a hearing, obtaining from the welfare officer an estimate of the likely date when the report will be available. In the light of that information he should then apply for a date of hearing to be fixed. See *Practice Direction* [1972] 2 All ER 352, [1972] 1 WLR 598, which applies to any application in which the duration of the hearing is estimated to exceed one half hour.

3.72 Some hearsay evidence may be unavoidable in a welfare officer's report, and, if it relates to uncontroversial matters, objection to it is unlikely,[1] but the report should not contain allegations based on secondhand information, which are serious and which either or both parties have had no opportunity to consider or meet.[2] It is not, however, open to the judge to expunge from the report matters based on hearsay.[3] If there are controversial matters the officer should give sworn evidence on his observations and assessments,[4] and the evidence may be tested in the ordinary way and within the normal rules.[5]

1 But the report should not include a recital of all conversations with the parties; *Malsom v Malsom* (1982) 12 Fam Law 91, CA.

2　*Edwards v Edwards* [1986] 1 FLR 187, [1986] Fam Law 99, affd [1986] 1 FLR 205, CA.
3　*Webb v Webb* [1986] 1 FLR 462, [1986] Fam Law 155, CA.
4　*Thompson v Thompson* [1986] 1 FLR 212n, CA. Certainly there must be no private conversation about the case between the judge and the welfare officer; *H v H (irregularity: effect on order)* (1982) 4 FLR 119, 12 Fam Law 178, CA.
5　*Edwards v Edwards*, supra, note 2.

3.73　It is expressly provided by the relevant legislation[1] that in proceedings in a magistrates' court the court may, and, if so requested at the hearing by a party or his legal representative, must require the welfare officer to give evidence on any matter referred to in his report. If he does, then a party may give or call evidences with respect to any matter referred to in the report or in the officer's evidence. The court may take account of any statement contained in the report and any evidence given by the officer in so far as it is relevant to the application, notwithstanding any enactment or rule of law to the contrary. There are no such express statutory provisions governing welfare reports in the High Court or a county court, but the same rules should be followed.[2] Where it is likely that the hearing will be lengthy, the parties should agree a convenient date and time for the attendance of the reporting officer where his attendance is required, so that valuable time is not wasted.[3]

1　GA 1973, ss 6(3) and (3A) (as substituted by CA 1975, s 90(1)); DPMCA 1978, s 12(5) and (6).
2　See *Practice Direction* [1981] 2 All ER 1056, [1981] 1 WLR 1162, which directs that, if a party considers it desirable that the reporting officer should attend the hearing, the proper course is to ask the registrar so to direct or, if time does not permit, to inform the reporting officer that it is proposed at the hearing to ask the judge to direct that he attends.
3　See ibid. This practice should equally be followed in a magistrates' court.

3.74　The court should make available to the welfare officer all the relevant papers,[1] but, because of the heavy demands on the court welfare service, the court should specify the matters on which the report is to be made. This, however, should not prevent the reporting officer from bringing to the notice of the court any other matters which he considers the court should have in mind,[2] and certainly the court does not have power to give instructions to a welfare officer on how to conduct his investigations;[3] but it may have to remind him that his duty is to investigate and assist the court to resolve disputes that the parties cannot solve and not to exercise his other function of acting as conciliator in helping the parties themselves to a resolution,[4] although he may encourage the parties to settle their differences if the likelihood of a settlement arises during the course of his enquiries.[5] By the same token the court is not bound by any recommendation which the officer may decide to make,[6] though it should give it proper consideration and give reasons for not following it.[7] In practice recommendations carry great weight and in most cases are adopted by the court.[8] In preparing his report the reporting officer may request from the police details of any convictions of the parties to the proceedings, their cohabitees or future marriage partners, and it seems that details of spent convictions may, by virtue of the Rehabilitation of Offenders Act 1974, section 7(2)(c), be included in the report.[9] The parties to the proceedings are entitled to copies of a report in proceedings in a magistrates' court[10] or divorce court[11] and it is normal practice for the report to be made available to them in wardship[12] and in custody cases in the High Court or a county court. In proceedings in a magistrates' court a copy of the report must be given to each party or to his legal representative 'either before or during a hearing of the application',[13] but in *Edwards v Edwards*[14] it was emphasised that reports should be disclosed to the parties in advance of the hearing so that they may have adequate opportunity to consider controversial assessments of their character and behaviour, especially those based upon hearsay.[15] For these reasons the practice should equally be followed in custody proceedings in other courts.

All court welfare officers' reports filed in Family Division proceedings and all copies supplied to the parties or their solicitors must be endorsed with the following statement:

> 'This report has been prepared for the court and should be treated as confidential. It must not be shown nor its contents revealed to any person other than a party or a legal adviser to such a party. Such legal adviser may make use of the report in connection with an application for legal aid'.[16]

1 In proceedings in a divorce court it is expressly provided that he may inspect the court file; MCR 1977, r 95(3)(a).
2 See *Practice Direction* [1981] 2 All ER 1056, [1981] 1 WLR 1162.
3 *Re A (a minor)* (1979) 10 Fam Law 114, CA.
4 *Re H (conciliation welfare reports)* [1986] 1 FLR 476, [1986] Fam Law 193; see also *Scott v Scott* [1986] 2 FLR 320, [1986] Fam Law 301, CA. See also on this point the Booth Committee Report, paras, 4.61 and 4.62; Latham, *Welfare Reports and Conciliation* [1986] Fam Law 1951; Davis and Bader, *In Court Mediation: The Consumer View* [1985] Fam Law 42 and 82; Maidment, *Divorce Court Welfare Service* 136 NLJ 438; and the letters of Sir John Arnold and Pugsey in [1986] Fam Law at 197 and 338 respectively.
5 See *Practice Direction* [1986] 2 FLR 171, [1986] Fam Law 286.
6 *J v J* (1978) 9 Fam Law 91, CA; *S v W* (1980) 11 Fam Law 81, CA; *Plant v Plant* (1982) 4 FLR 305, 12 Fam Law 179, CA; *Leete v Leete and Stevens* [1984] Fam Law 21, CA.
7 *Hutchinson v Hutchinson* (1980) 2 FLR 167, 11 Fam Law 24, DC; *Foxon v Foxon* [1981] CLY 1778; *Dickinson v Dickinson* (1982) 13 Fam Law 174, CA; *Stephenson v Stephenson* [1985] FLR 1140, [1985] Fam Law 253, CA.
8 For the influence of welfare reports see Murch, *Justice and Welfare in Divorce,* Chapter 8.
9 Home Office Circular No 88/1982.
10 GA 1973, s 6(2)(a) (as substituted by CA 1975 s 90(1)); DPMCA 1978, s 12(4)(a).
11 MCR 1977, r 95(3)(b) as amended by MC (Amendment No 2) Rules 1986, r 2 (SI 1986/1096). See *Clode v Clode* (1982) 3 FLR 360, 12 Fam Law 175, CA.
12 *Re F (otherwise A) (a minor) (publication of information)* [1977] Fam 58, [1977] 1 All ER 114, CA.
13 See note 9, supra.
14 [1986] 1 FLR 187, [1986] Fam Law 99.
15 Presumably the sanctions for refusal by a person to cooperate with a court welfare officer are (a) contempt, since he is an officer of the court, and (b) a possible adverse finding in his report, which will harm the refusing person's chances on the merits.
16 *Practice Direction* [1984] 1 All ER 827, [1984] 1 WLR 446.

7 Appeals

(a) Procedure

(i) From the High Court or a county court[1]

3.75 Appeal from a decision of the High Court or a county court in respect of custody or access under GMA 1971 or MCA 1973 lies to the Court of Appeal. No leave is required.[2] Appeal is on notice of motion, called a 'notice of appeal', which must be served within four weeks from the date of judgment or order on all parties directly affected by the appeal,[3] subject to power to extend the time limit. The notice of appeal must specify the grounds and the precise form of order which is sought.[4] Within seven days after service of the notice (or such further time as may be allowed) the appellant must have the appeal set down in the proper list. To do this he must lodge with the Registrar of Civil Appeals two copies of the notice, a copy of the judgment or order and an office copy of any list of exhibits.[5] Within 21 days after the notice of appeal has been served on him the respondent, if he wishes to contend any of the following matters, must serve a notice on the appellant and on all parties directly affected by the contentions, specifying the grounds of his contention. Within two days after service, two copies of that notice must be furnished to the Registrar.[6] The matters are that the judge's order should be varied or that it should be affirmed on grounds other than those relied on by the court or, by way of cross-appeal, that the order was wrong in whole or in part.

1 For details of the procedure see RSC Ord 59; and Butterworths Family Law Service, Vol I, Division C, paras 179–191 (KW Wills).
2 Supreme Court Act 1981, s 18(1)(b). The rule extends to an order relating to education (including training and religious instruction), but not to one dealing with payment of fees for education; see *Beale v Governors of Edgehill College* [1984] LS Gaz R 516, CA.
3 RSC Ord 59, rr 3(5) and 4(1).
4 Ibid, r 3(2).
5 Ibid, r 5.
6 Ibid, r 6. There is power to extend the time.

3.76 Not more than 14 days after the appeal first appears in the 'List of Forthcoming Appeals' the appellant must lodge with the Registrar three copies (or two, if only two judges are to hear the appeal) of each of the following:[1]

(a) the notice of appeal;
(b) the respondent's notice;
(c) any supplementary notice served by the appellant or respondent;
(d) the judgment or order;
(e) the originating process by which the proceedings in the court below were begun and the pleadings (including particulars);
(f) the transcript of the official shorthand note or record, if any, of the judge's reasons for his judgment or order or, in the absence of such a note or record, the judge's note of his reasons or, if that note is not available, counsel's note of the judge's reasons approved wherever possible by the judge;
(g) the notes of evidence relevant to any question at issue on the appeal;[2]
(h) any list of exhibits;
(i) such affidavits or exhibits or parts of exhibits as were in evidence before the judge and which are relevant to any question at issue.

The importance of strict compliance with Rule 9 cannot be emphasised too strongly. The Court of Appeal has issued several Practice Directions, Notes and Statements[3] relating to the lodging of documents. Failure to comply can result in solicitors being ordered personally to pay the costs wasted through non-compliance, and the Court of Appeal may report a defaulting solicitor to the Law Society.

1   RSC Ord 59, r 9.
2   For the importance of there being a full note of the judge's reasons and of the evidence
    see post, para 3.79.
3   See *Practice Direction* (1983) Times, 20 May; *Practice Direction* [1985] 1 WLR 739; *Practice
    Note* [1983] 2 All ER 34, [1983] 1 WLR 1055; *Practice Note* [1983] 3 All ER 33; sub
    nom *Practice Direction* [1983] 1 WLR 922; *Practice Note* [1985] 1 All ER 841; *Practice
    Note* (1986) Times, 13 June; *Practice Note (court of appeal: chronologies of events)* [1985]
    3 All ER 384, [1985] 1 WLR 1156, CA.

3.77   Appeal from the Court of Appeal lies to the House of Lords[1] with
leave of the former or the latter, and must be lodged within three months
from the date of the order of the Court of Appeal. A petition for leave
of the House of Lords must be lodged within one month of that order,
but there is power to extend these time limits.[2]

1   Administration of Justice (Appeals) Act 1934, s 1. For the exceptional procedure allowing
    appeal direct from the High Court to the House of Lords see the Administration of Justice
    Act 1969, s 12.
2   See *Practice Direction* [1966] 2 All ER 928, [1966] 1 WLR 1084; and *Procedure Direction*
    [1983] 1 All ER 524, [1983] 1 WLR 404, HL.

(ii)   From a magistrates' court[1]
3.78   Appeal from a decision of a magistrates' court in respect of custody
or access under GMA 1971 or DPMCA 1978 may be made to the Family
Division of the High Court,[2] and is heard by a single judge, unless the
President otherwise directs.[3] Further appeal lies to the Court of Appeal
and thence to the House of Lords, in accordance with the procedures already
noted. Appeal to the Divisional Court is by notice of motion[4] and a special
form of notice must be used.[5] Three copies[6] of the notice and the following
documents must be lodged in the Principal Registry of the Family Division
within six weeks of the court's decision:

(a) the summons and the order appealed against;
(b) the clerk's notes of the evidence;
(c) the justices' reasons for their decision;
(d) any document put in as an exhibit in the magistrates' court.

Certificates must also be lodged stating that the notice of motion has
been served on the clerk and every other person affected by the appeal.
When the documents have been lodged the appeal will be listed for hearing
as soon as possible after the expiration of the time given in the notice
of motion. If it is not heard within six months of being listed it will be
struck out.

1   For details of the procedure see Butterworths Family Law Service Vol I, Division C,
    paras 192—193 and 195.
2   GMA 1971, s 16(3); DPMCA 1978, s 29(1). Where the magistrates' court refuses to make
    an order because it considers that the matter is one which would more conveniently be
    dealt with by the High Court, there is no appeal against its refusal; see respectively s 16(4)
    and s 27 of those Acts.
3   RSC (Amendment No 2) 1983, r 34.
4   The procedure is governed by RSC Ord 90, r 16.
5   See Appendix to *Practice Direction* [1977] 2 All ER 543, [1977] 1 WLR 609.
6   Only one copy needs to be lodged if the appeal is to be heard by a single judge.

3.79   In order that an appellate court may properly fulfil its functions, it is essential that it be fully informed of the reasons on which the lower court based its decisions.[1] The point has needed particularly emphasising in relation to magistrates' courts,

Under the Magistrates Courts Rules 1981[2] justices must, before announcing their decision, cause the reasons for their decision to be recorded in writing, the terms of the record being drawn up in consultation with the clerk of the court or his assistant; and the clerk must supply a copy of the record to anyone on application, if satisfied that it is required in connection with an appeal or possible appeal. In so doing it is unnecessary to include inessential information relating to the background of the case and the contentions. It is sufficient for the justices to set out clearly their findings of fact, and then to give an account of the reasoning which led them to their conclusion.[3] In formulating their reasons they should not be influenced by the contents of the notice of appeal.[4] Where they have not adopted a plain recommendation of a welfare officer, they should spell out their reasons for not doing so.[5] A full note of evidence in the proceedings before the justices should be placed before the Divisional Court. This is particularly important where there is an appeal from enforcement procedures, for example, relating to an order for access.[6] Where a note is not produced, the Divisional Court may admit any other evidence or statement of what occurred in the proceedings before the magistrates' court and that may be sufficient to determine the appeal;[7] but in the absence of a note of evidence the court may have no option other than to allow the appeal and remit the matter to a fresh panel of justices.[8]

The account of the reasons which led the justices to their conclusion must be sufficiently detailed to enable the appellate court to examine the reasons.[9] The principle should be observed by all courts of first instance, not only because there may be an appeal, but also because the parties should know of those findings and reasons in subsequently considering the possibility of applying for variation of the order.[10]

1 In a case where detailed chronology has to be grasped by the court, it is helpful if, on opening the appeal, counsel tenders a document setting out the detailed chronology: *Goodbody (formerly Jupp) v Jupp* (1983) 13 Fam Law 150, CA.
2 See rr 36 and 37.
3 See Sir John Arnold P in *Hutchinson v Hutchinson* (1980) 2 FLR 167, 11 Fam Law 24.
4 *Faulkner v Faulkner* (1979) 2 FLR 115, 10 Fam Law 88.
5 *Re T (a minor) (welfare report recommendation)* (1977) 1 FLR 59, DC. The same principle applies to a recommendation made by a guardian ad litem; see *Devon County Council v Clancy* [1985] FLR 1159, [1986] Fam Law 20, CA.
6 *Tilmouth v Tilmouth* [1985] FLR 239, [1985] Fam Law 92, DC.
7 RSC Ord 90, r 29(5).
8 *Gray v Gray* [1987] 1 FLR 16, [1986] Fam Law 267 (no record made of oral evidence in a hearing of a custody case lasting four hours).
9 *Re M (a minor)* (1980) 11 Fam Law 58. But once notice of appeal is served the justices should not amplify the reasons which they gave when making their decisions; *W v P* [1988] 1 FLR 508.
10 *Hoey v Hoey* [1984] 1 All ER 177n [1984] 1 WLR 464n, CA.

3.80 The following procedure is to be observed in an appeal to the Divisional Court of the Family Division where a child was a party to the proceedings in the court below and is affected by the appeal. The notice of motion should be served on the guardian ad litem of the child appointed in the court below and no order is required appointing him guardian at litem in the Divisional Court proceedings, provided his consent to act and his solicitor's certificate, referred to in RSC Ord 80, r 3(8), are filed in the Principal Registry. The heading of the notice of motion should show the child as a party to, and represented by his guardian ad litem in, the proceedings in the court below and the address at which the guardian ad litem was served with the notice should be shown in the certificate required by Ord 90, r 29(4)(d). The written consent of the person to act as guardian ad litem in the appeal proceedings and the certificate by the solicitor for the child, referred to in Ord 80, r 3(8), should be filed in the Principal Registry by that solicitor as soon as practicable after service of the notice of motion. If there was a legal aid certificate in respect of the child in the proceedings in the court below, an application for a separate certificate is required if legal aid is sought in respect of the appeal, in accordance with reg 47 of the Legal Aid (General) Regulations 1980.[1]

1 *Practice Direction* [1986] 1 All ER 896, [1986] 1 WLR 384.

(b) Powers of the appellate court

3.81 After several years of uncertainty, inconsistent decisions and conflicting dicta in the Court of Appeal, the House of Lords in *G v G*[1] clarified the role of the Court of Appeal when reviewing a judge's exercise of discretion in cases involving the welfare of children. Having regard to the fact that in such cases there are often no right answers, that the judge at first instance is faced with choosing the best of two or more imperfect solutions and that he has had the advantage over the Court of Appeal of seeing the parties, the Court of Appeal should normally intervene only when it considers that the judge has exceeded the generous ambit within which judicial disagreement is reasonably possible. The court must be satisfied that he was in fact plainly wrong and not merely that it itself, had it carried out the balancing exercise of weighing the various factors for and against each party, would have preferred a solution which the judge did not choose. However, it may also intervene even where the judge has not exceeded the generous ambit, if it appears from events subsequent to the judge's decision that his decision was ill-founded. In such circumstances the court will remit the case to him for a rehearing.[2] The principle laid down in *G v G* applies equally to the appellate duties and powers of the Divisional Court of the Family Division, since they are to be exercised in the same way as those of the Court of Appeal.[3] It will be interesting to see the extent to which the House of Lords ruling will stem the flood of appeals (so readily apparent from the law reports over several years) and thus encourage an end to litigation, which can be particularly important where the welfare of children may be jeopardised by protracted uncertainty.[4] Already the Court of Appeal has criticised the legal aid authorities for granting legal aid for an ill-founded appeal,[5] and has warned[6] that the appellant may incur the risk of an order for costs against him or her if the appeal is considered by the court to be unjustifiable in accordance with the principles of *G v G*. Nevertheless, there is the risk of over-reaction to those principles.[7] Given the inherent indeterminacy of many child custody cases and the undoubted difficulties they create for a judge, determination by two or three heads is likely to be more in the child's interests than *G v G* is ready to concede.

1   [1985] 2 All ER 225, [1985] 1 WLR 647, HL.
2   *A v A* [1988] FCR 205, [1988] 1 FLR 193, CA.
3   *P v P* [1984] FLR 99, sub nom *Peebles v Peebles* (1983) 13 Fam Law 213. In the light
    of *G v G* supra, intervention by an appellate court where the order at first instance is
    only an interim order is particularly unlikely; see *G v G (interim custody: appeal)* (1982)
    4 FLR 327, 12 Fam Law 185, CA.
4   See Lord Fraser [1985] 2 All ER 225 at p 228; [1985] 1 WLR 647 at 652. There is another
    factor which the practitioner should remember when giving legal advice to his client on
    the possibility of a custody appeal. If any matrimonial property is involved, its market
    value on a sale would be diminished by the costs of the custody litigation because of
    the Law Society charge; per Dunn LJ in *M v M* (1983) Times, 20 April, CA.
5   *Re T (a minor)* [1986] Fam Law 189.
6   *Re G (a minor) (role of the Appellate Court)* [1987] 1 FLR 164, [1987] Fam Law 52,
    CA; *R v R and H (Harrow London Borough Council Intervening)* [1988] Fam Law 171,
    CA.
7   For a valuable appraisal of *G v G* see Eekelaar (1985) 48 MLR 704.

3.82   If circumstances exist for the appellate court to exercise its powers
it has three courses open to it.[1] Firstly, if it is satisfied that the order
was wrong, it may substitute its own order. Thus if, for example, the court
below applied the wrong principle of law but all the relevant facts appear
to be before the appellate court, the latter will re-exercise the discretion,
paying close attention to the views expressed by the judge at first instance.[2]
The advantage of adopting this course is that it is likely to be in the child's
best interests that the dispute over custody or access be resolved at the
earliest opportunity, especially as that may help reduce prolonged bitterness
between the parties.[3] Secondly, if it is satisfied that the order was wrong
but is unsure on the evidence what order ought to be made, the appellate
court can remit the case with such directions for the custody, care and
control of the child in the meantime as it thinks best in the child's interests.
Thirdly, and exceptionally, it may hear evidence to resolve the matter. But
there may be difficulties where it is sought to admit fresh evidence. In
M v M[4] the Court of Apeal has given the following guidance. Where the
decision below was an exercise of a discretion, admissibility is subject to
the restrictions imposed by *G v G*. The proper approach is firstly to consider
that decision on the basis of the evidence before the judge, ignoring the
fresh evidence at that stage. If, observing the principles in *G v G*, it is
apparent that the judge was plainly wrong or misdirected himself in a relevant
respect, the appellate court should allow the appeal, and then it may exercise
its own discretion as indicated above.[5] If, on the other hand, applying
G v G the court is minded to dismiss the appeal on the basis of the evidence
which had been before the judge, it should then consider the fresh evidence
available to it, but always bearing in mind the disadvantage in which the
court is placed by reason of its not having seen the witnesses.

1   See Lord Scarman in *B v W (Wardship: appeal)* [1979] 3 All ER 83 at 95, [1979] 1 WLR
    1041 at 1055.
2   See *S(BD) v S(DJ) (Children: care and control)* [1977] Fam 109, [1977] 1 All ER 656,
    CA.
3   *B v B* [1985] FLR 166, CA.
4   [1987] 1 WLR 404, [1987] 2 FLR 146, CA. See also *Re G (a minor) (wardship: access)*
    [1988] 1 FLR 305, [1988] Fam Law 170, CA.
5   As it did in *M v M*, after finding that the judge's decision was plainly wrong because
    it had failed to take into account the child's adamant view that she was not willing to
    live with her mother.

3.83 If a custody order directs that the child be transferred from one person to another but there is no urgency to do so, the court should order a stay pending appeal, since it is not in the child's interests to be bandied about from the one person to the other.[1] Such a measure is also essential where there is to be an appeal and there is a likelihood of the child mean time being removed from the jurisdiction.[2] However, a stay of an order should only be made on the application of the person intending to appeal and not by the court of its own volition,[3] and should only be for a short period to enable notice of appeal to be filed.[4] If it is, the appellant can then apply to the appellate court for an extension, and arrangements can be and should be made for the appeal to be heard speedily.[5] In an appeal from an order transferring a child from one parent to another or from a local authority to a parent the maximum acceptable period before the hearing of the appeal is 28 days[6] and a stay of execution should therefore seldom exceed 14 days.[7] Counsel's convenience is not an acceptable reason for delaying the hearing of an appeal involving the transfer of a child. If counsel accepts a retainer to appear in such a case he must make it plain to his instructing solicitor that he will follow the case to appeal, if there is one, in spite of other commitments. If he cannot give that assurance, his clerk should tell the solicitor so that the client will know that in the event of an appeal it will not be conducted by the counsel who conducted the case at the trial.[8]

1 *Re S (an infant)* [1958] 1 All ER 783, [1958] 1 WLR 391.
2 *Smith v Smith* (1971) 115 Sol Jo 444, CA.
3 *S v S (custody order: stay or execution)* [1986] 1 FLR 492, [1986] Fam Law 67.
4 *Townson v Mahon* [1984] FLR 690, [1984] Fam Law 204, CA. Up to a week is likely to be allowed.
5 *H v H* (1976) Times, 13 November; *Wyatt v Wyatt* (1976) 6 Fam Law 106, CA; *P v H* (1976) 120 Sol Jo 199. The legal aid authorities should also be mindful of the need to deal promptly with appeals when deciding whether to grant legal aid; see *Ridgway v Ridgway* [1986] Fam Law 363, CA.
6 *Re W (minors)* [1984] 3 All ER 58n; sub nom *Practice Note* [1984] 1 WLR 1125, CA.
7 *Hereford and Worcester County Council v EH* [1985] FLR 975, [1985] Fam Law 229.
8 *Re W (minors)*, supra, note 6.

III ACCESS

3.84 As already indicated,[1] courts having jurisdiction to make orders relating to custody may also grant a person access to the child. Whatever the conceptual nature of access may be,[2] the important practical consideration is that in deciding whether to make an order for access the child's interests are paramount, in accordance with section 1 of the GMA 1971.[3] Basically the courts have not departed from the view judicially expressed over 100 years ago by Lord Cairns in *Symington v Symington:*[4]

'On both sides there ought to be a careful opportunity of access, so that none of the children may grow up without as full knowledge and as full intercourse as the case will admit of with both parents.'

Courts usually take the view that the child's interests are best served by granting access to the parent who is not given the care and control (or actual custody) of the child,[5] even though that parent has failed to carry out his parental duties adequately.[6] Access may even be granted to a father who has never lived with the child, (because he and the mother have never been married to each other or cohabited), provided the court is satisfied that he genuinely wants to get to know his child and promote his welfare.[7] There must, then, be cogent reasons for refusing access. Most of them relate to the conduct or condition of the parent; for example, his past cruelty to the child,[8] his bad criminal record,[9] his past irresponsible attitude to access,[10] his mental illness[11] or unstable condition.[12] Sometimes, however, the parent's conduct or condition is not in question and the reason for refusal is directly related to the child; for example, where access seriously affects his health[13] or would otherwise be harmful to him,[14] or where his opposition to it is so marked that to allow it would similarly harm him,[15] even if that opposition was the result of indoctrination by the parent having care and control of him.[16] Where such reasons exist, the parent's claim to access must yield to the paramountcy principle.[16a]

In *Corkett v Corkett*,[17] the Court of Appeal held that, where there is more than one child, the question of access must be considered in relation to each of them independently and not collectively. On that basis a court may refuse a parent access to one of his children (for example, because of past ill-treatment) but grant it in respect of his other(s). However, in *S v S*,[18] the court has held that, where there are very young children who have to continue to live together as a single family unit under the daily control of one parent, it would be undesirable to grant access only to some of them. There would be problems of satisfactorily explaining the situation to them and it would be likely to lead to tensions in their family relationship. It remains to be seen how far *S v S* has eroded the basis of the ruling in *Corkett*. It is submitted that each case should be considered on its own merits in accordance with the principle of the paramountcy of the particular child's welfare. So regarded, the decision in *S v S* is justified, for in that case all three children were girls and the father had already sexually abused the eldest of them over a substantial period. Clearly it was in the interests of the other two to protect them from the risk of similar abuse.

If the court refuses access, the order should normally be in terms of no access until further order, leaving the parent denied access to apply at such time as he is advised;[19] but there seems to be power to exclude a right to reapply for a specified period.[20] Where it is not in a child's best interests to grant access immediately, the court may consider the possibility of access starting in the future. If that is the case, the matter can be reviewed after a specified period and the submission to the court of a report.[21]

1 See ante, paras 3.19, 3.35 and 3.51.
2 See ante, para 1.19.
3 See Wilkinson, *Children and Divorce*, Chapter 4; and for data Law Com Working Paper No 96 Supplement, Part VI. In 1985 access orders were made by the divorce courts in 80% of the cases in which custody orders were made.
4 (1875) LR 2 Scot Div 415 at 423, HL.
5 See Templeman LJ in *Williams v Williams* (1980) 11 Fam Law 23, CA; Ormrod LJ in *D v M (minor; custody appeal)* [1983] Fam 33 at 37, [1982] 3 All ER 897 at 900. See also Richards [1986] JSWL 73 for criticism of the contrasting views of Goldstein, Freud and Solnit, op cit, who argue for the finality of a custody order, with access only being allowed if it is likely to be successful.
6 See Willmer LJ in *S v S and P* [1962] 2 All ER 1 at 3, [1962] 1 WLR 445 at 448. A court may even allow visits by a child to a parent who is in prison; *Re N (minors)* (1975) 119 Sol Jo 423.

7 *S v O (illegitimate child: access)* (1977) 3 FLR 15, 8 Fam Law 11. Cf *M v J* (1977) ibid, at 12, and 3 FLR 19, where the parents, though unmarried, cohabited for some 18 months after the child's birth, but access was refused to the father, who was unstable and, by the time of the proceedings, 'rootless'.

8 See Willmer LJ in *S v S and P*, supra note 6.

9 *Anon* (1963) Times, 24 October.

10 *Rashid v Rashid* (1978) 9 Fam Law 118, CA (breach of access orders, including taking child out of jurisdiction without consent); *Starling v Starling* (1979) 4 FLR 135, (failure to seek access for three and a half years); *Re C (minors) (access)* [1985] FLR 804, CA, (initial access unsuccessful followed by period of three years when no access).

11 *G v G* (1963) Times, 3 May, DC; *C v C* (1971) 115 Sol Jo 467, CA. Cf *Re R (an infant)* (1963) Times, 8 October, CA, where the father's epilepsy did not justify refusing him access.

12 *M v J* supra, note 7; *Re BC (a minor) (access)* [1985] FLR 639, [1985] Fam Law 223, CA.
Bromley, op cit, p 334, citing as an example *G v G* (1981) 11 Fam Law 148, CA, where access was granted to a transsexual father, points out that 'when considering access the court is less concerned with a person's overall ability to look after the child' and so it 'might be less inhibited about granting access rather than custody to a homosexual parent, provided, of course, such an order is in the child's interests'. It is submitted that in such cases, however, staying access, as opposed to visiting access, should not be granted unless there is overwhelming evidence that the child will not be at risk. Even where there is visiting access, it may well have to be on the basis of constant supervision; see Fox LJ in *S v S (child abuse: access)* [1988] 1 FLR 213 at 217. See also *C v C (child abuse: access)* [1988] 1 FLR 462, [1988] Fam Law 254.

13 *Geapin v Geapin* (1974) 4 Fam Law 188, CA; (child's asthmatic condition).

14 *Wright v Wright* (1980) 2 FLR 276, 11 Fam Law 78, CA, (harmful religious indoctrination); *A v C* [1985] FLR 445, [1984] Fam Law 241, CA, (adverse effects of access by father to child conceived *by AID*); *Re C (minors) (access)* [1985] FLR 804, CA (access would undermine child's security).

15 *B v B* [1971] 3 All ER 682, [1971] 1 WLR 1486, CA; *M(P) v M(C)* (1971) 115 Sol Jo 444, CA; *Churchard v Churchard* [1984] FLR 635, CA.

16 *Williams v Williams* [1985] FLR 509, [1985] Fam Law 129, CA.

16aSee *Re KD (a minor) (ward termination of access)* [1988] 1 All ER 577, [1988] 2 WLR 398, HL, ante, para 3.09.

17 [1985] FLR 708, [1985] Fam Law 258, CA.

18 [1988] 1 FLR 213, [1988] Fam Law 128, CA. See also *Re R (a minor) (child abuse: access)* [1988] 1 FLR 206, [1988] Fam Law 129, CA.

19 *Re N (wardship)* (1982) 4 FLR 150, CA.

20 See Lowe and White, op cit, pp 116–117.

21 *Re BA (Wardship and adoption)* [1985] FLR 1008, [1985] Fam Law 306.

3.85 There is no statutory definition of access. In practice it takes the form either of short visits, usually by child to parent rather than parent to child since the parents are likely to be at arms' length, or of a continuous period, usually weekends or school holidays, during which the child stays with the parent.[1] But there seems to be no reason why it should not take other forms;[2] for example, if the father is living abroad, the court might expressly allow him to make regular telephone calls to his child in a case where the mother has been obstructive in that regard. In the vast majority of cases[3] the order is for reasonable access. Courts prefer to leave it to the parties to fix details. One advantage of that kind of order is that it allows for flexibility where for unexpected reasons, such as the child's illness, access is temporarily impracticable.[4] If there are difficulties over an order for reasonable access, either party can seek variation so that the order prescribes specific conditions. Sometimes an order of that kind may be necessary at the outset. In either event the terms specified should still, as far as possible, avoid annoyance to the child and inconvenience to the parent.[5] In a minority of cases the court may allow visiting access but not staying access,[6] or it may be obliged by the circumstances to impose carefully controlled conditions covering, inter alia, time, place and duration of access.[7] Save possibly for very unusual circumstances, an order will not be made refusing access for all time.[8] The appropriate order is refusal until further order, leaving the disappointed party to apply if and when circumstances change.[9] If there is to be any regulation of access—or a fortiori total refusal—a proper application should be made with a full hearing, so as to give a party an opportunity to present his submission.[10]

1 Staying access is unlikely to be granted where the child is very young; *Williams v Williams* (1980) 11 Fam Law 23, CA (11 months old).
2 See Hayes and Bevan, *Child-Care Law*, para 5.3. But in *Allette v Allette* [1986] 2 FLR 427, [1986] Fam Law 333 the Court of Appeal held that for the purpose of having to obtain leave to appeal in accordance with the Supreme Court Act 1981, s 18(1)(h) access means physical access. It is, with respect, to be hoped that the decision relates only to that statutory provision and that otherwise access may take other forms.
3 Close on 90%. See Maidment (1976) 6 Fam Law 195 and 236; Eekelaar and Clive, *Custody after Divorce*, para 5.7.
4 See Balcombe LJ in *L v L (interim custody; access)* (1980) 1 FLR 396 at 398.
5 See the Report of Justice on *Parental Rights and Duties and Custody Suits* (1975). The guidance there offered may also usefully be followed where the parties are conciliating, whether in or out of court, over arrangements for the child.
6 Eg *Williams v Williams* (1980) 11 Fam Law 23, CA, supra note 1.
7 *Re R (an infant)* [1968] 1 All ER 691n, [1968] 1 WLR 385; *G v G* (1981) 11 Fam Law 148, CA; *D v D (infants: access)* (1974) 4 Fam Law 195, CA; *T v T* (1974) 4 Fam Law 190, CA. The court may allow access abroad if satisfied that there is no serious risk that the non-custodial parent will not return the child to this country; see eg *Peters v Peters* (1974) 5 Fam Law 23, CA. Conversely, when allowing the custodial parent leave to remove the ward permanently from the jurisdiction it may grant the non-custodial parent access, so that he may visit the ward abroad (*Re S infants*) (1964) Times, 6 August) or the child may visit him in this country (*Bates v Morley* (1981) 3 FLR 244, CA).
8 *Murdoch v Murdoch* (1978) 8 Fam Law 247, CA.
9 See *Re N (wardship) (care and control: access)* (1982) 4 FLR 150, CA.
10 *Cox v Cox* [1984] Fam Law 58, CA.

3.86 By its nature access under the supervision of a third party is not likely to be very successful. It has a better chance if a person can be found who is likely to be agreeable to both parties. If he is, his consent to supervise should be sought before the matter comes before the court. Mutual friends, unprejudiced relatives and godparents are the kinds of person who should be approached.[1] Only when every effort has been made to obtain the help of such persons and has failed should welfare officers and similar persons be involved, subject to first obtaining their consent. Supervision by a welfare officer should be confined to a very few specified occasions and should not involve the officer in undue travelling.[2] Nor should the court delegate to the welfare officer a discretion to regulate the access,[3] or call upon him to decide whether or not access should take place.[4] However, a welfare officer or, where he has been appointed, the Official Solicitor may be asked to assist in making arrangements for access.[5]

1 See *Practice Direction* [1980] 1 All ER 1040, [1980] 1 WLR 334.
2 See ibid.
3 *Mguni v Mguni* (1979) Times, 30 November, CA. The Practice Direction, supra, seems impliedly to support the Court of Appeal ruling, which is to be preferred to its earlier decision in *V-P v V-P* (1978) 1 FLR 336, 10 Fam Law 20, where access was ordered 'as and when the supervising officer thought right'.
4 *Orford v Orford* (1979) 1 FLR 260, 10 Fam Law 114, CA.

5 *Re R(PM) (an infant)* [1968] 1 All ER 691n, [1968] 1 WLR 385.

Enforcement of access orders[1]

3.87 Difficulties can arise where the parent who has custody refuses to allow the other parent access.[2] Normally, this should not deter the court from granting it, because, as already pointed out,[3] it is of very real importance in the interests of the child's emotional well-being that normally there should be contact with the non-custodial parent. However, exceptionally the custodial parent's hostility may be so strong that to impose access would have harmful effects on the child. Nevertheless, in refusing in those circumstances to make an order, it may be desirable for the court to direct that a welfare report be prepared at a later date (for example, a year later), and delivered to the solicitors of each parent with a view either to a further application to the court or to agreed access.[4] A similar problem arises where the custodial parent resolutely refuses to comply with the terms of an existing access order. He or she should be warned of the court's powers of enforcement.[5] If there is no co-operation, one solution may be to vary the order so as to grant custody to the other parent, if the best interests of the child are thereby served. However, that solution may not be practicable. For example, the non-custodial parent (more likely the father) may not be in a position to provide day to day care of the child, or the child may be implacably opposed to seeing him. In such circumstances it is futile and contrary to the child's interests to commit the custodial parent for disobedience of the access order,[6] although the circumstances and his interests may require such drastic action as entrusting the child to the care of a local authority by substituting a care order for the custody order.[7] Initially, the threat of such action may be sufficient to induce co-operation on the part of the custodial parent.

1 Booth Committee Report, paras 4.142–4.143; *Saturday Parent* (1980) 144 JPN 353; Samuels (1981) 11 Fam Law 156; Poulter (1982) 126 Sol Jo 283.
2 *Williams v Williams* [1985] FLR 509, [1985] Fam Law 129, CA.
3 Ante, para 3.84.
4 *Re B (a minor) (access)* [1984] FLR 648, CA.
5 *Re E (a minor: access)* [1987] 1 FLR 368, [1987] Fam Law 90, CA. For the court's powers see ante, para 3.28.
6 *Churchward v Churchward* [1984] FLR 635, CA. See also *V-P v V-P* (1978) 1 FLR 336, 10 Fam Law 20, CA; *P v W* [1984] Fam 32, [1984] 1 All ER 866.
7 As in *R v G (Surrey County Council Intervening)* [1984] Fam 100, [1984] 3 All ER 460, CA. In view of the court's understandable reluctance to order access under supervision, ante, para 3.86, and given the recalcitrance of the custodial parent, the possible alternative of allowing the custody order in his or her favour to continue but adding a supervision order is very unlikely.

Jurisdiction

3.88 The power to order access is expressly given by the GMA 1971, the DPMCA 1978 and the MCA 1973. Access may also be granted in wardship proceedings in exercise of the prerogative jurisdiction. However, the scope of the powers under the relevant provisions is not precisely or uniformly formulated. The power of the divorce court is wide. It may make such order for access as it thinks fit,[1] thus enabling a spouse, parent or anyone else, including a grandparent, to be given access. Equally the court may do so in wardship proceedings. Moreover, the divorce court can order access whether or not it makes an order for custody or care and control. Under the GMA 1971 the court may grant access to either parent whether or not it also makes an order for legal custody,[2] but may grant it to a grandparent if there is in force such an order for legal custody.[3] If either or both parents of the child are dead, access may be granted to a parent of a deceased parent.[4] Similarly, under the DPMCA 1978, it may grant access to either party to the marriage or to a parent who is not a party, whether or not it also orders legal custody,[5] but to a grandparent only if there is such an order.[6] Under neither Act can the court grant access to any other person, even though there may be persons, for example, an uncle and aunt, with whom the child has had close contact. Nor under either Act can it order access if the child is in the care of a local authority.[7] As already noted, [8] where under either Act the court decides to grant legal custody to some person other than, as the case may be, a parent or a party to the marriage, namely, by treating the case as if that other person had applied for a custodianship order under section 33 of the Children Act 1975,[9] then the power to order access arises by virtue of that Act and no longer under the GMA 1971 or DPMCA 1978. Under the 1975 Act the court can grant access to a parent or, if he or she has treated the child as a child of the family, to a party to the marriage or to a grandparent.[10]

As for the classes of person eligible to apply, anyone showing sufficient interest may do so in wardship proceedings; and in the divorce court, in addition to the spouses, any other person may apply with leave of the court or without leave if he is a guardian or a step-parent or has custody (without care and control) by an order of the court.[11] In proceedings under the GMA 1971 or the DPMCA 1978, apart respectively from the parents[12] or the parties to the marriage, the only other persons eligible to apply are grandparents.[13]

The powers to vary or revoke access orders have already been examined when dealing with custody orders.[14]

1 MCA 1973, ss 42(1), (2) and 52(1).
2 Section 9(1), as prospectively substituted by FLRA 1987, s 10. Although the subsection refers to the power 'to make such order regarding (a) the legal custody of the child; and (b) access to the child by either parent as the court thinks fit', (a) and (b) are to be read disjunctively in the sense that the court may order legal custody and access or only the one or the other. There is similar power to make orders for legal custody and access in guardianship cases. See GMA 1971, s 10, as prospectively substituted for ss 10 and 11 of that Act by FLRA 1987, s 11. The proposed substitutions of ss 9 and 10 do not alter the substance of the present law.
3 GMA 1971, s 14A(1). The grandparent must apply for access.
4 Ibid, s 14A(2). The grandparent must apply for access.
5 DPMCA 1978, s 8(2)(b).
6 Ibid, s 14(1).
7 GMA 1971, s 14A(4); DPMCA 1978, s 8(7)(b). Compare the power of the court to do so in wardship proceedings, for example, with a view to the possible return of the ward to the parent; see *Re C (child in care: access)* (1982) 4 FLR 396.
8 Ante, paras 3.20 and 3.36.
9 See post, Chapter 6 for s 33 applications.
10 See post, para 6.60.
11 MCR 1977, r 92(1) and (3), read with MCA 1973, s 52(1) which defines custody to include access.
12 Where paternity is in issue that issue must be determined before the person claiming to be the father can apply for access; *Re O (a minor; access)* [1985] FLR 716, [1985] Fam Law 135, CA.

13 GMA 1971, s 14A, as added by DPMCA 1978, s 40; DPMCA 1978, s 14
14 See ante, para 3.24.

IV CHILD ABDUCTION

1 The criminal law

(a) Kidnapping

3.89 The general lack of concern for children shown by the early, pre-nineteenth century law is reflected in the apparent unwillingness to rely on the common law offence of kidnapping, defined as 'the stealing and carrying away or secreting of some person'.[1] Indeed, it was that unwillingness that eventually prompted statutory intervention, in the form of the offence of child-stealing,[2] to meet an increasing social evil. Once the statutory offence had been introduced and extended to children under 14 it seems to have led to the assumption that kidnapping could not apply to those under that age, and it is only recently that the assumption was held, by the House of Lords in the leading case, *R v D*,[3] to have been misconceived. The offence has, in fact, received something of a modern judicial revival. Its broad scope was emphasised in *R v Reid*,[4] where it was held that a husband could kidnap his wife; but, more significantly in the present context, it was held in *R v D* that a father could kidnap his own child who was still under 18 and unmarried. Such a conclusion would have been inconceivable in the nineteenth century[5] when the father was regarded as having virtually absolute and paramount authority over his legitimate child, but 'in the face of the radically changed social and legal attitudes of today'[6]—and now the more so in the light of the *Gillick* principle—the father can no longer rely on that omnipotence as a lawful excuse for taking away his child. However, to constitute kidnapping the 'stealing and carrying away' must be without the victim's consent. That should pose problems where he is a very young child, but *R v D* rules that, since he would not have the understanding or intelligence to give consent, absence of consent is a necessary inference. But, if he does not have the requisite understanding or intelligence, it is equally a 'necessary' inference that he cannot withhold consent. The ruling is clearly a policy decision. Where he is older it is a question of fact whether the jury considers he has sufficient understanding or intelligence. If it finds he has, it must then be satisfied that he did not give his consent.[7] As for the consent of the person with custody or care or control of the child, it is not material to the question of the child's consent, but it may be relevant in supporting a defence of lawful excuse.[8]

1 East 1 PC 430.
2 See infra, para 3.91. The earliest Act was 'An Act for the more effectual Prevention of Child Stealing'; see the Preamble.
3 [1984] AC 778, [1984] 2 All ER 449, HL.
4 [1973] QB 299, [1972] 2 All ER 1350, CA. The case also decided that the offence is complete when the victim is seized and carried away against his will. Kidnapping is not a continuing offence involving concealment of the person seized. Nor is concealing an alternative form of kidnapping. It is submitted that if a person conceals someone without removing him that is false imprisonment.
5 To the Court of Appeal in *R v D* it was still inconceivable.
6 Per Lord Brandon [1984] AC 778 at 805, [1984] 2 All ER 449 at 457.
7 Lord Brandon (ibid) expressed the view that he would 'not expect a jury to find at all frequently that a child under 14 had sufficient understanding and intelligence to give its consent'.

8   *R v D*[1984] AC 778 [1984] 2 All ER 449.

3.90   Where a child is already the subject of an order relating to custody and a parent unlawfully removes him in defiance of the order, he should normally be dealt with as a contemnor: a criminal prosecution should only be used in exceptional circumstances and rarely, if ever, against a parent by way of a private prosecution.[1] That suggests that prosecutions for kidnapping may more frequently be adopted against a parent where there is no court order, but, in creating the new offence of child abduction by a parent (or other persons connected with the child), the Child Abduction Act 1984 expressly provides[2] that the prosecution of a parent or such person for kidnapping requires the consent of the Director of Public Prosecutions, if the child is under 16, thus emphasising that normal family obligations are to be enforced by civil and not criminal remedies.

1   *R v D* supra.
2   Section 5.

(b)   Child-stealing

3.91   The statutory offence of child-stealing was created by an Act of 1814,[1] re-enacted in substance but with some changes in 1828 and given its final form in section 56 of the Offences against the Person Act 1861,[2] which increased the age of the child in respect of whom it could be committed from 10 to 14. The offence consisted in unlawfully by force or fraud taking or enticing away or detaining the child with intent to deprive the parent, guardian, or other person having lawful care or charge of it, of its possession. It was therefore seen primarily as an offence against a right of possession rather than against the child.[3] The original enactment exempted from prosecution the father of the illegitimate child and section 56 expressly extended the exemption to the mother and to any person 'who shall have claimed any right to the possession of the child'. Surprisingly, it did not explicitly refer to the father of the legitimate child, and it was not until *R v Austin*[4] that his exemption, as a person claiming a right to possession, was finally established. With the passing of the Child Abduction Act 1984 the significance of the decision proved short lived.

1   54 Geo 3, c 101.
2   9 Geo 4, c 31.
3   A view reaffirmed by the House of Lords and the Court of Appeal in *R v D* supra.
    For a different view see Eekelaar, *What are Parental Rights?* (1973) 89 LQR 210 at pp 214–
    215, where the offence is seen not as protecting a *parental* right but as being primarily
    directed at keeping the peace.
4   [1981] 1 All ER 374, CA.

(c)   The Child Abduction Act 1984[1]

3.92   This Act[2] repealed section 56, and largely gave effect to the recommendations of the Criminal Law Revision Committee in their 14th Report, *Offences against the person*.[3] The Act distinguishes between abduction by persons who have a 'connection with a child', including especially parents, (section 1) and abduction by persons not so connected (section 2). To understand the Committee's recommendations the better, it is more convenient to deal firstly with abduction under section 2.

1   See generally Lowe (1984) 134 NLJ 960.
2   Section 11(5)(a).
3   (1980) Cmnd 7844. The Home Office has provided guidance on the Act; see HOC Circular No 75/1984.

(i)   Abduction by a person not connected with a child

3.93   It is an offence for such a person without lawful authority or reasonable excuse to take or detain a child under 16 so as to remove, or, as the case may be, keep him from the lawful control of any person having, or entitled to, that control.[1] One of the defects of section 56 was that it required the use of force or fraud. So, if the child was induced to go voluntarily with the abductor, with no fraud being used against either parent or child, no offence was committed.[2] The 1984 Act plugs this gap by expressly providing[3] that a person is regarded as taking a child, if (apart from other means of doing so) he induces the child to accompany him or some other person. Similarly, he can induce a child to remain with him or someone else.[4]

1   CAA 1984, s 2(1).
2   *R v Mears* [1975] Crim LR 155.
3   CAA 1984, s 3(a).
4   CAA 1984, s 3(b).

3.94   The essence of child-stealing was that it was a wrong against possession, which the 'parent, guardian or other person having lawful care or charge' had of the child.[1] The essence of child abduction under section 2 is that it is a wrong against lawful control. In the absence of a statutory definition that latter term has a wide meaning and is capable of implementing the recommendations of the Criminal Law Revision Committee.[2] It does not require a permanent or long-standing relationship between the person having control and the child. Thus, it includes not only a parent or guardian or custodian or other person having a legal right to custody of the child but also, for example, a schoolteacher, child-minder or person to whom the parent or other person having the right to custody has temporarily entrusted his authority, for example, a relative who is looking after the child while the parent is abroad or in hospital. Nor does section 2 state that the degree of interference with the lawful control has to be substantial.[3] If it has not,[4] it means for example, that if X, a keen fisherman, knowing that a thirteen-year-old boy is expected by his parent to come straight home from school, nevertheless persuades the boy to meet him and, with no sexual motive, takes him for a few hours' fishing, he will be guilty of abducting him.[5] There would, it is submitted, be no reasonable excuse for his action, although the lack of seriousness of the offence would clearly go to mitigation of sentence.

1   See similarly s 20 of the Sexual Offences Act 1956 for the offence of abduction of a girl under 16—'taking out of the possession' of the parent or guardian (the latter term meaning anyone having the lawful care or charge of the girl).
2   See paras 240–243.
3   Cf *R v Jones* [1973] Crim LR 621, a decision under s 20 of the Sexual Offences Act 1956, where it was held that there had to be a substantial interference with the possessory relationship.
4   As the Criminal Law Revision Committee recommended (para 242).
5   The Criminal Law Revision Committee recognised the liability in such a case (para 244).

3.95   One major difference between the Committee's recommendations and the Act is that both sections 1 and 2 apply to children under 16 and not, as the Committee recommended,[1] to those under 14. The lower age was proposed because 'parental control after that age may be difficult or non-existent'.[2] That view may now accord more with the *Gillick* principle, but the Act has erred on the side of caution; some 14 and 15-year olds are impressionable and may too readily consent to being taken away from their parents.[3] Whether the lower age would have been enacted had the House of Lords decided *Gillick v West Norfolk and Wisbech Area Health Authority*[4] before the legislation was introduced must remain conjectural.[5]

1   Paragraph 242.
2   Paragraph 239.
3   Even on the Committee's recommendation there would still be liability if the taking away of the child was for an unlawful sexual purpose. In *R v Mousir* [1987] Crim LR 561 the Court of Appeal held that the question of a child's maturity and understanding was not a question for consideration by the jury in considering whether he was or might have been removed from the lawful control of his parent.
4   [1986] 1 AC 112, [1985] 3 All ER 402.
5   See further on this, para 10.36, (abduction of girls).

3.96   There is no offence where the removal or detention of the child has been with lawful authority (for example, lawful arrest) or with reasonable excuse. But there are also two special defences,[1] the onus being on the defendant to establish that one or other of them existed at the time of the alleged offence.

(a)   He may show that he believed that the child was 16 or over.
(b)   If the child is illegitimate,[2] he may show that he had reasonable grounds for believing that he was the child's father. This defence is in line with the former exemption of the father from prosecution for child-stealing under section 56. It recognises that, since he does not have lawful control of the child, his taking the child away from the mother or, indeed, anyone else with lawful control would otherwise constitute child abduction. The law is not prepared to go to this length in its non-recognition of the father. The defence will be particularly relevant where he and the mother have at one time been cohabiting, and there should be little difficulty in establishing the requisite reasonable grounds for belief in his paternity.

1   CAA 1984, s 2(2).
2   *Sic* CAA 1984 has not been amended by FLRA 1987.

(ii)   Abduction by a person connected with a child
3.97   It matters not for the purpose of satisfying section 2 whether the child is being removed to another part of the country or is being taken abroad; but removal abroad is clearly a more serious step and once it has happened may lead to practical difficulties in securing the child's return.[1] Since section 2 does not apply to a parent or other person connected with the child,[2] section 1 is concerned with filling the gap to prevent removal abroad by the parent or other such person.

1   The Criminal Law Revision Committee proposed that it should be one of the forms of a new offence of aggravated abduction which it recommended (para 247).

2   The reason why removal by a parent within the country was not made an offence of
child abduction was that in nearly all cases of conflict between the parents there would
be a custody order in being or one would be obtained quickly, and breach of it could
be dealt with by a court having family jurisdiction, so long as the intention was not
to take the child abroad.

3.98   *Persons connected with a child*   An offence is committed under section
1 when a person connected with a child takes or sends the child out of
the United Kingdom[1] without the appropriate consent. Three categories
of persons are connected with a child.[2]

(a)   His parent or guardian, the latter having its usual meaning of a person
appointed by deed or will or by a court.[3]

(b)   A person to whom by an order of a court in the United Kingdom
custody has been awarded, whether solely or jointly with another. The
category extends also to a person granted legal custody or care and
control.[4] It thus admits of various possibilities, as the following examples
illustrate.

It includes a relative to whom a divorce court has granted custody
or care and control; a step-father who has obtained in his favour a
variation of a custody order that was made in earlier divorce proceedings
between his wife and her former husband, whether the order is varied
solely in his favour or jointly with his wife; a person granted care
and control in wardship proceedings;[5] and a custodian or joint custodian
appointed by a custodianship order under the Children Act 1975. A
point which the section does not clearly meet is the case of a person
who is not given custody, legal custody or care and control but to
whom the court awards specific powers and responsibilities to be shared
with another. The point is particularly relevant to an order for legal
custody, since legal and actual custody must be given to the same person,
allowing specific powers and responsibilities to be granted jointly.[6]
Supposing, for example, that in proceedings under the Domestic
Proceedings and Magistrates' Courts Act 1978 the mother is given legal
custody, but her husband, the step-father of her child, is given joint
powers relating to the child's education. If he takes the child abroad
without the mother's consent, does he fall within section 1 or section
2? The point could be important because the defences to a section
1 offence are wider than those to a section 2. As already indicated,
where there is only a removal within the country but there is a custody
order already in being resort to the family jurisdiction is available and
section 2 is not necessary. On that criterion the step-father should come
within section 1.[7]

(c)   In the case of an illegitimate child,[8] the person for whom there are
reasonable grounds for believing that he is the father of the child.
The tortuous extent to which the Legislature has sometimes to go to
limit its recognition of the unmarried father of a child is fully
demonstrated in the 1984 Act. As already noted, he is in principle
liable to be an abductor under section 2, but may exempt himself from
liability by showing that he had reasonable grounds for believing his
paternity. In order, therefore, to 'catch' him for abduction abroad he
is classified as a person concerned with the child.

1 Ie Great Britain (England, Wales, Scotland) and Northern Ireland but not the Isle of Man or Channel Islands (Interpretation Act 1978, s 5 and Sch 1).
2 CAA 1984, s 1(2), as amended by FLA 1986, s 65.
3 CAA 1984, s 1(7)(a).
4 CAA 1984, s 1(7)(b).
5 For this illustration see infra.
6 See ante paras 3.21 and 3.37.
7 This construction is, it is submitted, indirectly supported by the rule relating to the giving of leave to take abroad, given by a court when making specific directions about the child's welfare under the Guardianship of Minors Acts 1971 and 1973; see the next paragraph dealing with consent.
8 See ante, para 3.96, note 2.

3.99 *Consent*   There is no offence committed if the 'appropriate consent' is obtained. This means:[1]

(a) (i) the consent of each parent or guardian; or
     (ii) the consent of each person to whom custody (whether sole or joint) or legal custody or care and control has been awarded by an order of a court in the United Kingdom; or
(b) if the child is the subject of an order for custody, legal custody or care and control, the leave of the court which made it; for example, a parent who removes a ward of court from the person to whom the court granted care and control and takes him abroad without the leave of the court commits not only contempt but also an offence under section 1, for there is no indication that wardship is outside the scope and effects of the section, given that the section extends to an order awarding care and control;[2] or
(c) the leave of the court granted on an application for a direction under section 7 of the Guardianship of Minors Act 1971 or section 1(3) of the Guardianship Act 1973.

These respective provisions enable the court when there is a dispute between joint guardians or between the mother and father over any question affecting the child's welfare to 'make such order regarding the matters in difference as it may think proper'. What is not entirely clear is whether the court can grant leave to take the child out of the United Kingdom only when the matter in difference is the taking of the child abroad or whether it can also exercise that power when dealing with some other matter, for example education of the child, which is in dispute. The above wording of those provisions tends to support the fomer conclusion. It does seem clear, however, that sub-paragraphs (a), (b) and (c) are to be read disjunctively, so that where the child is the subject of a custody order the consent to remove may be obtained either from the person having custody, legal custody or care and control or from the court. Doubts have been expressed on whether the rules within sub-paragraph (a) are also to be read disjunctively. It is submitted that they are.[4] Admittedly, a person who has been granted legal custody cannot arrange for the child to emigrate,[5] but he can consent to the child being taken abroad temporarily. It is therefore difficult to see how an offence can be committed under the Child Abduction Act 1984. If the consent of the parent or guardian was also needed, one would have expected the Act to provide rules for those cases where, for example, the parent or guardian was unable or unavailable to give his consent, even though the Act does provide in section 1(5) that no offence is committed if all reasonable steps have been taken to communicate with the person whose consent is required. Consistent with this disjunctive construction of the rules is the conclusion that, where the child is a ward of court, no offence is committed if the person with care and control gives consent and, in spite of its general overriding jurisdiction, leave of the court is not additionally required to exclude liability under the Act, though failure to obtain leave would constitute contempt.

1 CAA 1984, s 1(3) (as amended by the Family Law Act 1986, s 65).
2 Contra, Clarke Hall and Morrison, para C [951].
3 See Lowe and White, *Wards of Court*, 2nd edn, p 326, para17–17.
4 For an apparently contrary view see the Local Authority Circular LAC (85) 13 on Custodianship Orders, para 104.
5 CA 1975, s 86.

3.100 Even where the requisite consent has not in fact been obtained, an offence is not committed if any of the following conditions is satisfied:[1]

(a) the alleged abductor believes that a person whose consent is required has consented or would consent if he was aware of all the relevant circumstances; or

(b) he has taken all reasonable steps to communicate with that person but has been unable to do so; or

(c) that person has unreasonably refused to consent, except that this defence does not apply in a case where the child is the subject of a custody order or where the alleged abductor acts in breach of any direction made under the Guardianship of Minors Acts 1971 and 1973, as noted above.

Whether consent is unreasonably refused is obviously a question of fact, but whether the courts will eventually formulate any test, as they have in cases of unreasonable refusal to agree to adoption, remains to be seen. They may be inclined to adopt a test of the attitude of the reasonable parent in the circumstances. Once there is 'sufficient' evidence to raise one of these defences relating to consent, the onus is on the prosecution to prove that it does not apply.[2]

1 CAA 1984, s 1(5).
2 CAA 1984, s 1(6). Compare the onus on the defendant to prove one of the defences in section 2 proceedings.

3.101 Special rules relating to consent apply where the child is in the care of a local authority or voluntary organisation or is in a place of safety or the subject of an order relating to adoption or of custodianship proceedings,[1] and in none of those circumstances do the above rules relating to appropriate consent apply. A defendant cannot, therefore, raise the issue that he believed that consent was given or was unreasonably refused. The appropriate consents in those circumstances are as follows:

(1) *Child in care*—the consent of the local authority or voluntary organisation, as the case may be.

(2) *Child in place of safety*—the consent of a magistrates' court for the area in which the place of safety is.

(3) *Adoption and custodianship*—
(i)   when the child has been freed for adoption, the consent of the adoption agency in whom the parental rights and duties have been vested;
(ii)   where an application for a freeing order, or for an adoption order or for a custodianship order is pending, the leave of the court to which the application was made;
(iii)   where there is an order, or a pending application for an order relating to adoption abroad, the leave of the court that made the order or to which the application was made.

In the event of a child falling within paragraphs (1) and (3) the rules under the latter apply.

1   CAA 1984, s 1(8) and Schedule.

3.102   *Prosecution and penalties*   Prosecution for an offence under section 1 requires the consent of the Director of Public Prosecutions,[1] but not for proceedings under section 2. The maximum penalties for an offence under section 1 and an offence under section 2 are the same, namely, on conviction on indictment seven years' imprisonment and on summary conviction six months' imprisonment or a sum not exceeding the statutory maximum[2] or both.[3]

1   CAA 1984, s 4(2).
2   Currently £2,000.
3   CAA 1984, s 4(1).

(iii)   Preventing removal out of the jurisdiction
3.103   *Port Alerts*   For some parents and other persons the sanctions of the Child Abduction Act 1984, if known to them, may be a sufficient deterrent against wrongful removal of the child to a foreign country, but, clearly, effective practical measures to forestall such removal are preferable. The 'All Ports Warning System' is currently the main attempt to reduce the incidence of international child abduction.[1] Introduced[2] to replace the 'Stop List' procedure, which was run through the Home Office, the System provides a 24-hour service, involving direct liaison between the Police and port immigration officers. The procedure is detailed in a *Practice Direction*[3] and amplified by guidelines in a Home Office Circular.[4]

Where the child, whose removal is threatened, is under 16, it is not necessary first to obtain a court order before seeking police assistance, but, if he is between 16 and 18, it is a prerequisite that an order is obtained which restricts or restrains removal or confers custody. The distinction recognises the creation of the offence under section 2 of the 1984 Act in respect of those under 16. However, where the child is a ward of court, whatever his age (under 18), evidence will have to be produced to the police that he is a ward. This may be an order confirming wardship, an injunction or, if no such order has been made, in cases of urgency, a sealed copy of the originating summons. In all cases the application for police assistance must be made by the applicant himself or his legal representative to a police station, usually the applicant's local police station, but in urgent cases, or where the wardship originating summons has just issued or where the court has just made the order relied on, contact may be made with any police station.

The decision whether to institute the port-alert system rests with the police, and they will have to be satisfied that the danger of removal is 'real and imminent', which means 'within 24–48 hours and . . . that the parent is not just seeking a port alert by way of insurance'. The Home Office Circular[5] advises that in assessing whether these conditions are met police officers may wish to consider:

(a) whether threats of removal have recently been made;
(b) whether the person considered likely to abduct the child has unsupervised access; and, if so,
(c) whether the child is with the 'abducting' person at present; and
(d) whether the 'abducting' person has previously returned the child on time after periods of access.

In assessing the likelihood of removal abroad it will also be relevant to establish:

(e) whether the 'abducting' person has ties abroad, ie a home, relatives, money and/or a job.

It has been pointed out[6] that 'because the police have to be satisfied that the complaint is bona fide, a prior court order will be an advantage in all cases', but it has also been recognised[7] that in some cases by seeking to obtain an order before contacting the police the child has been abducted before the police have known about it. It is suggested that at this comparatively early stage of implementing the Scheme any doubt should be resolved in favour of application to the police without an order[8] and referral by them to the port authorities. In the longer term careful monitoring of applications and of police practice may enable useful lessons to be drawn.

The request for assistance should be accompanied by as much of the following information as possible:[9]

The child: names, sex, date of birth, description, nationality, passport number (if known).
The person likely to remove: names, age, description, nationality, passport number (if known), relationship to child and whether child likely to assist him or her.
Person applying for a port-alert: names, relationship to child, nationality, telephone number (and solicitor's name and number if appropriate).
Likely destination.
Likely time of travel and port of embarkation.
Grounds for port alert (as appropriate);
    (1) suspected offence under section 1 of Child Abduction Act 1984;
    (2) child subject to court order.
Details of person to whom the child should be returned if intercepted.

If the police decide on a port-stop, the particulars of the child are circulated to all ports[10] through the Police National Computer broadcast facility. Receiving forces are asked to make local arrangements with the immigration service, where necessary.[11] If the immigration service is alerted and an immigration officer makes an identification, he will hand the matter over to the police for action. He has no general power to detain a child or the person seeking to remove him,[12] but, since an offence under the 1984 Act is an arrestable offence, an officer could where appropriate lawfully effect a citizen's arrest.[13] Where a child's name is put on the stop-list it will remain on it for four weeks and will then be removed unless a further application for a port-stop is made. The purpose of this limited period is to keep the list as short as possible and so assist the immigration service to identify children, but it runs the risk of underestimating the determination and persistence of some parents to try to remove their children. The applicant for a port-alert should not, therefore, be diffident about re-applying, nor the police about re-alerting.

1 There are no firm annual statistics, covering a reasonably lengthy period, about the number of actual or threatened removals, and figures vary over the number of port alerts; see Lowe and White, op cit, para 17.10.
2 In May 1986.
3 [1986] 1 All ER 983, [1986] 1 WLR 475.
4 No 21/1986.
5 Paragraph 9.
6 See Lowe and White, para 17.21.
7 Ibid.
8 Unless the child is a ward of court or is at least 16, see supra.
9 See the *Practice Direction*, supra, note 3.
10 The efficacy of the system is enhanced by the fact that it extends to Scotland and Northern Ireland so as to enable the police to alert ports in those countries; for details see Lowe and White, para 17.20.
11 See para 5 of the 1986 Circular.
12 Ibid, para 6.
13 See Lowe and White, para 17.22.

3.104   *Powers of arrest*   If at the port the police are not able to dissuade the 'abducting person' from trying to embark with the child, they may be able to invoke various powers of arresting him. If they have been obliged to use force, they may arrest for breach of the peace. If there is a court order prohibiting removal, there is the power to arrest for contempt. If neither power is available, they may be able to rely on the power to arrest on reasonable suspicion that there has been an attempt to commit an offence under the 1984 Act.[1] Given the imminence of threatened removal, there should be no difficulty about having the requisite suspicion. But they may also be able to invoke this power in respect of an attempted offence at an earlier stage—exceptionally, it may not even be necessary to institute a port alert—but at such a stage there are likely to be difficulties about having sufficient information to found a reasonable suspicion, although they may, it is suggested, be able to derive assistance from those guidelines which they have been recommended to consider in deciding whether, for the purpose of a port alert, the threatened removal is 'real and imminent'.[2] Intervention at an early stage is, it is suggested, unlikely: ' . . . whether or not arrest should be resorted to will depend on the urgency of the situation (for example, if a suspect is about to embark) and will have to have regard to the highly charged emotions which may surround the case'.[3]

1 This power is available since offences under ss 1 and 2 are arrestable offences.
2 See supra, para 3.103.
3 Home Office Circular No 75/1984, para 6. As the Circular points out (para 5), the nature of an offence under s 1 is such that 'it will require sensitivity in its enforcement'.

2 The civil law

3.105 The Child Abduction Act 1984 is a partial response to the increasing incidence of 'child-snatching', but, as already mentioned,[1] it recognises that normally family obligations are to be enforced by civil and not criminal remedies. In nearly all cases where there is a conflict between the parents (or guardians or custodians) there will either already be a custody or similar order in force or one which can be relatively quickly obtained, especially by way of wardship proceedings,[2] and breach of the order can be dealt with by a court having family jurisdiction, which can in particular invoke its powers of contempt.[3]

1 Ante, para 3.90.
2 See post, especially paras 8.32, 8.51 and 8.53, and particularly the powers to trace a ward.
3 It has already been pointed out (ante paras 3.22 note 7, 3.38 note 6 and 3.60) that, whereas there is a duty on a divorce court to include in a custody order a prohibition on removal of a child out of the jurisdiction, 'unless otherwise directed', a court exercising jurisdiction under GMA 1971 or DPMCA 1978 has a discretion whether or not to include a prohibition. It is suggested that there should be a uniform rule along the lines of the divorce court jurisdiction. Even then, it would not have the automatic prohibition which attaches to wardship from the moment proceedings are instituted.

(a) Preventing removal out of the jurisdiction

Passports
3.106 As with the criminal sanctions of the CAA 1984, the prohibition on removal imposed in wardship cases or by a provision in a custody order may not be sufficient to deter attempted removal to a foreign country. Apart from the port warning system, the non-issue or the surrender of passports is a further measure aimed against international abduction.
(i) Non-issue
The need for parental consent to the issue of passport facilities to their minor child has already been mentioned.[1] Where it is known that the child is a ward of court, passport facilities are not granted by the Passport Office unless the court's permission is obtained.

In its revised leaflet[2] the Home Office makes it clear that objections to the issue of passports for minors can be considered only in the following circumstances:[3]

either (a) there is a court order made in the UK: (i) confirming that the minor's removal from the jurisdiction is contrary to the wishes of the court; or (ii) awarding the objector custody of the minor; or (iii) awarding the objector care and control over the minor; or (iv) specifying that the objector's consent to the child leaving the jurisdiction is necessary; or (v) upholding the objector's objections to the child having a passport or leaving the country.
or (b) in the absence of a court order, that: (i) the objection comes from the mother of a child and she and the father were not married at the time of his birth; or (ii) the police have notified the Passport Department of an intention to exercise their power of arrest under the Child Abduction Act 1984.

(ii) Surrender
Should the minor already have a passport or should he already be included in a relative's, the Passport Department is not empowered to order the

surrender of the passport, but it notes the child's name for 12 months so that, if the passport comes into the Department's possession or if another application for passport facilities for the child is made, the Department can then act on the objection.

However, in matrimonial, wardship and guardianship cases in which the child already holds a British passport or the threat of removing the child comes from the holder of such a passport, the court has power to order the surrender of any passport issued to, or which contains particulars of, the child. If it so orders, it will notify the Passport Office in order to prevent the issue of a replacement.[4]

Where the threat of removal comes from the holder of a foreign passport, the court may grant an injunction restraining the removal of the child from the jurisdiction.[5]

1   See ante para 1.48.
2   See [1986] Fam Law 50.
3   The restrictions are reinforced by *Practice Direction (Minor: Preventing Removal Abroad)* [1986] 1 All ER 983, [1986] 1 WLR 475.
4   See *Practice Direction* [1983] 2 All ER 253, [1983] 1 WLR 558.
    It should be noted that s 37 of the Family Law Act 1986 provides that, where there is in force an order prohibiting or restricting the removal of a child from the UK or from any specified part of it, the court by which the order was made or by which it is treated under s 36 of that Act as having been made may order surrender of a passport.
5   See *Practice Direction*, supra.

(b)   Recovery of child from another jurisdiction

(i)   Child removed from England and Wales to another part of the United Kingdom

3.107   If a child has been removed from England and Wales to another part of the United Kingdom, ie to Scotland or Northern Ireland, one option available at common law to the aggrieved parent who seeks to recover his child is to institute proceedings in the Scottish or Northern Ireland court.[1] However, the Family Law Act 1986 now provides a more convenient remedy.[2] It enables a 'custody order', as defined by the Act,[3] which is granted in one part of the United Kingdom to be recognised and enforced in another part.[4] Since the definition includes an order for care and control granted in wardship, a parent who does not already have a 'custody order' (for example an order granting him care and control in divorce proceedings or legal custody in proceedings under GMA 1971 or DPMCA 1978) can first institute wardship proceedings, obtain care and control and then rely on the 1986 Act. A prerequisite of enforcement in another part of the United Kingdom is registration of the order in that part. The person on whom rights have been conferred by the 'custody order' must apply to the court which made the order and that court arranges for a certified copy of the order and the relevant documentation to be sent to the 'appropriate court'[5] in that other part of the United Kingdom.[6] Once registered the latter court has the same powers of enforcement as it would have if it had itself made the order,[7] but an application for enforcement, distinct from that for registration, must be made.[8] Any person who appears to the court to have an interest in the matter may then apply for the proceedings to be stayed (or in Scotland sisted) on the ground that he is taking other proceedings (in the United Kingdom or elsewhere) which may result in the 'custody order' ceasing to have effect, or having a different effect, in the part of the United Kingdom in which it is registered.[9] A person appearing to the court to have an interest may apply for the enforcement proceedings to be dismissed on the ground that the original 'custody order' has (in whole or in part) ceased to have effect in the part of the United Kingdom in which it was made.[10] Should such an application itself be dismissed, the registering court will proceed to enforce the order.

The 1986 Act provides a potentially effective remedy for enforcement, but there are circumstances where it is still necessary to rely on the common law and institute 'original' proceedings in Scotland or Northern Ireland. That will be so where the child has reached the age of 16, since registration is restricted to those under that age.[11] The same applies to a child who is in local authority care when abducted, since he is not the subject of a 'custody order', as defined by the Act.

1 If there is already an order in force restricting removal out of England and Wales, the parent may seek to rely on the court's powers of contempt, but with the 'abducting' person out of the jurisdiction those powers are not likely to assist in enforcement.
2 See ss 25–32. The Act is the result of the proposals of the Law Commissions; see Law Com No 138 and Scot Law Com No 91, 1985.
3 See FLA 1986, s 1, ante, para 3.15.
4 FLA 1986, s 43 enables the Act to be extended to the Isle of Man, any of the Channel Islands and any colony.
5 This means the High Court in England and Wales or Northern Ireland and the Court of Session in Scotland.
6 See FLA 1986, s 27. For cancellation and variation of registration see s 28.
7 FLA 1986, s 29(1).
8 The court may give interim directions in order to secure the child's welfare or prevent changes in the circumstances (ibid, s 29(2)).
9 FLA 1986, s 30(1).
10 FLA 1986, s 31(1).
11 See FLA 1986, ss 25(1) and 27(5).

(ii) *Child removed out of England and Wales to a foreign contracting state*
3.108 Part I of the Child Abduction and Custody Act 1985 ratifies and implements the Hague Convention of 1980 on the civil aspects of child abduction,[1] to which the United Kingdom is a signatory.[2] The provisions of the Convention are set out in Schedule 1 of the Act and have the force of law in the United Kingdom, but are here examined specifically in relation to their operation within England and Wales[3] and primarily in regard to the case of the child who is abducted out of England and Wales and removed to a foreign Contracting State.

1 (1981) Cmnd 8281; and see Anton (1981) 30 ICLQ 357.
  For a detailed examination of the 1985 Act see Lowe and White, op cit, paras 17.32 et seq.
2 The other Contracting States to the Convention who to date have ratified it are Australia, Canada, France, Hungary, Luxembourg, Portugal, Spain, Switzerland and the United States of America; see the Child Abduction and Custody (Parties to Conventions) Order 1986 SI 1986/1159 and the Child Abduction and Custody (Parties to Conventions) (Amendment) (No 2) Order 1988, SI 1988/1083.
3 See Art 31 of the Convention.

3.109 The Convention applies to the wrongful removal or retention of a child under 16 who immediately before the removal or retention was habitually resident in England and Wales.[1] A removal or retention is wrongful where it is in breach of rights of custody 'attributed to a person, an institution or any other body'[2] under the law of the habitual residence. The rights may arise by operation of law or by reason of judicial or administrative decision or by reason of an agreement having legal effect.[3] Normally it will be the person in whom the rights are so vested, whether jointly or alone, who will invoke the Act and seek the return of the child. Applied to the law of England and Wales, the following therefore, for example, are eligible to apply: a married parent, an unmarried mother, a person granted legal custody by an order of a court, an unmarried father who has been given all the rights and duties by virtue of an order under section 4 of the Family Law Reform Act 1987 (when that section is brought into force),[4] a local authority in whom parental rights and duties are vested under a care order or by a resolution passed under section 3 of the Child Care Act 1980,[5] or a spouse who has custody by virtue of a provision in a separation agreement between a husband and wife. But the term 'rights of custody' includes 'rights relating to the care of the person of the child and, in particular, the right to determine the child's place of residence',[6] and neither the Convention nor the 1985 Act states that *all* rights of custody have to be vested in a person in order to entitle him to rely on the Convention and the Act. Arguably, therefore, the definition would entitle a local authority in whose care a child is under section 2 of the Child Care Act 1980 to invoke the 1985 Act, even though a section 3 resolution has not been made.

Although the applicant will usually be the person whose rights of custody are breached, anyone is entitled to apply if there has been a wrongful removal.[7] For example, the mother may have been granted custody in divorce proceedings but has allowed her child to live with grandparents. If the father were to remove the child without the mother's consent, the grandparents could apply.

1   Art 4 of the Convention.
2   Art 3.
3   Ibid.
4   See ante, para 2.47.
5   See post, paras 15.48 and 15.33 respectively.
6   See Art 5.
7   See Art 8. But see infra, para 3.112, note 10.

3.110   Organisationally, the key body is the Central Authority of each Contracting State. For the purpose of operating the Convention in England and Wales the Central Authority of the United Kingdom is the Lord Chancellor.[1] A Central Authority may discharge its functions through judicial or administrative authorities of the State. For England and Wales the judicial authority is the High Court.[2] However, neither the Convention nor the Act gives specific guidance on how a Central Authority is to make use of its authorities. Nor have any Rules of Court been made (as the Act empowers[3]) or any Practice Direction or any advice been issued by the Lord Chancellor. In this mist of uncertainty solicitors and counsel who are involved in a case under the Act are therefore best advised to seek further information from the Lord Chancellor's Department before making an application for the return of a child; especially as one of the functions of the Lord Chancellor, as the Central Authority, is 'to indicate or facilitate the institution of judicial or administrative proceedings with a view to obtaining the return of the child and in a proper case to make arrangements for organising or securing the effective exercise of rights of access'.[4]

1   CACA 1985, s 3(1)(a).
2   CACA 1985, s 4(a).
3   CACA 1985, s 10.
4   Art 7(f).

3.111   A parent[1] seeking the return of his child who has been removed to a foreign Contracting State may apply either to the Lord Chancellor or to the Central Authority of that State,[2] the 'requested' State. Obviously, since he will be unfamiliar with the latter's procedures, he should apply to the Lord Chancellor. The Lord Chancellor will direct that the application be made through the High Court.[3] The application must contain the following matters:[4]

(a) information concerning the identity of the applicant, of the child and of the person alleged to have removed or retained the child;
(b) where available, the date of birth of the child;
(c) the grounds on which the applicant's claim for return of the child is based;
(d) all available information relating to the whereabouts of the child and the identity of the person with whom the child is presumed to be.

It *may* be accompanied or supplemented by:

(e) an authenticated copy of any decision or agreement, for example, a certified copy of an order granting the applicant legal custody;
(f) a certificate or affidavit concerning the relevant law of England and Wales. The certificate or affidavit may 'emanate' from the Lord Chancellor or other competent authority or from a qualified person, but apparently the onus is on the applicant to obtain it. It remains to be seen whether the Lord Chancellor's Department has it in mind to produce standard forms of certificate stating the relevant law.[5] It is suggested that a certificate or affidavit should always be included, since this will help avoid delay if the Central Authority or any court of the requested State should want the information;
(g) any other relevant document.

The application and any accompanying documents must be in English as the 'original language', but must be accompanied by a translation into the official language of the requested State or, where that is not feasible,[6] apparently a translation into French.[7]

1   For present purposes the term is used to include any person whose rights of custody have been breached.
2   Art 8.
3   If the Central Authority which receives the application—be it the Lord Chancellor or the foreign Central Authority—has reason to believe that the child is in another Contracting State, it must without delay transmit the application to the Central Authority of that Contracting State and inform the Lord Chancellor, or the applicant, as the case may be; see Art 9.
4   Art 8.
5   See also Art 7(e) for the duty of the Lord Chancellor to 'take all appropriate measures . . . to provide information of a general character as to the law of [the United Kingdom] in connection with the application of the Convention'.

6   It is difficult to visualise a case where it is not feasible.
7   Art 24. The Article states that, where translation into the official language of the requested
    State is not feasible, there must be a translation into French or English, but it does not
    make it clear whether this alternative translation is necessary if the 'original' language
    is English. On balance it seems that the documentation must always be in two languages.

3.112   The Central Authority of the Contracting State where the child
is, on receiving the application, must take all appropriate steps to obtain
the voluntary return of the child.[1] If proceedings have to be taken, the
judicial or administrative authority must act expeditiously, and, if a decision
has not been reached within 6 weeks from the commencement of the
proceedings, the applicant or the Central Authority of the requested State[2]
has the right to request a statement of the reasons for the delay.[3] If the
child has wrongfully been removed for less than a year, the authority, which
is likely to be a court [and is subsequently assumed to be so], must order
the return of the child forthwith. So, too, if the period is more than one
year, unless the child is settled in his new environment. However, if the
court has reason to believe that the child has been taken to another State,
it may stay the proceedings or dismiss the application for the return of
the child.[4] Moreover, the foreign court is 'not bound to order' the return
of the child if the person who opposes the return establishes (a) that the
person having the care of the child was not actually exercising the custody
rights at the time of removal or retention or had consented to or acquiesced
in the removal or retention, or (b) that there is a grave risk that his or
her return would expose the child to physical or psychological harm or
otherwise place the child in an intolerable situation[5] or if the child objects
to being returned and has attained an age and degree of maturity at which
it is appropriate to take account of his or her views.[6] In considering any
of these matters the foreign court must take into account the information
relating to the social background of the child provided by the Lord
Chancellor or, on his behalf, by the High Court.[7] That information may
be obtained by him or the High Court from a local authority or probation
officer's written report or from any court to which a written report relating
to the child has been made, for example, a welfare report submitted to
the court which made the order granting legal custody to the parent who
is applying for the return of the child.[8] Before making an order for the
return of the child the foreign court may request the applicant to obtain
in England and Wales a decision 'or other determination' that the removal
of the child was wrongful.[9] The applicant may apply to the High Court
for this and obtain a 'declaration' to that effect,[10] but it would, it is suggested,
be preferable to anticipate this possible request by the foreign court by
seeking the declaration when the applicant submits his application for the
return of the child to the High Court for transmission to the foreign
Contracting State. A decision concerning the return of the child is not
to be taken to be a determination on the merits of any custody issue,[11]
and the foreign court must not decide on the merits of rights of custody
until it has been decided that the child is not to be returned or unless
the application for return of the child is not lodged within a reasonable
time following receipt of the notice that there has been a wrongful removal.[12]
If, on the other hand, that court or any other court or administrative
authority within the requested Contracting State made a decision relating

to custody before the application for return, that in itself does not justify refusing to return the child to England, but the court, in deciding whether to order return, may take account of the reasons for the earlier decision.[13]

1 Art 10.
2 Either on its own initiative or if asked by the Lord Chancellor.
3 Art 11.
4 Art 12. Cf Art 9, ante, para 3.111, note 3.
5 For example, if the applicant was committed to keeping the child away from school without providing suitable alternative education. The psychological harm must be substantial and not trivial. The court will therefore require a high standard of proof before it will refuse to return a child to a foreign Contracting State. See *Re A (a minor) (abduction)* [1988] 1 FLR 365, [1988] Fam Law 54, CA, where an order was granted for the return to British Columbia of a child whose mother in breach of a custody order made in that Province was wrongfully detaining her child in England. It was held that, since the mother had indicated that, if the child was ordered to be returned to Canada, she would go with him, there was not the requisite grave risk of substantial psychological harm.
6 Lowe and White point out (op cit, para 17.36) that, whereas the burden of proving grounds (a) and (b) lies on the person opposing the return, the court itself can find that the child objects to return etc.
7 Art 13.
8 CACA 1985, s 6; Arts 7(d) and 13.
9 Art 15.
10 CACA 1985, s 8. Section 8 requires the applicant 'to have an interest in the matter'. Art 15 does not impose that restriction. But the point is academic. The applicant seeking return of the child will obviously have the requisite interest.
11 Art 19.
12 Art 16.
13 Art 17.

Access

3.113 An application to make arrangements for organising or securing the effective exercise of rights of access may be made in the same way as an application for the return of a child.[1] The Convention also expressly provides that those rights include that of taking a child for a limited period of time to a place other than the child's habitual residence.[2] So, if, for example, under an order made in divorce proceedings the mother was granted custody, care and control with leave to take the child permanently out of the jurisdiction to a Contracting State and the father was given reasonable access including provision for staying access in England during school holidays, he will be able to invoke the 1985 Act if there are difficulties over access. The objects of the Convention in relation to access are laudable. The Central Authorities are bound to 'promote the peaceful enjoyment of access rights and the fulfilment of any conditions to which the exercise of those rights may be subject'. They must 'take steps to remove, as far as possible, all obstacles to the exercise of such rights', and they 'may initiate or assist in the institution of proceedings with a view to organising or protecting these rights and securing respect for the conditions to which the exercise of these rights may be subject'.[3] But, at the end of the day, the foreign court may find it even more difficult to enforce right of access than the English court does in enforcing its own orders within the jurisdiction.

1 Art 21.
2 Art 5.
3 Art 21.

3.114   A distinctive feature of the Convention is the way in which it provides free legal and other aid for the applicant. A Central Authority and other public services of a Contracting State cannot impose any charges in relation to an application. In particular they may not require an applicant to pay towards the costs and expenses of the proceedings or, where applicable, those arising from the participation of legal counsel or advisers, whatever the means of the applicant may be.[1] As for counsel and their advisers, a Contracting State may, as the United Kingdom has done,[2] restrict payment of their fees to the rates allowed under its system of legal aid and advice. However, the person who removed the child or prevented the exercise of rights of access may be ordered to pay necessary expenses incurred by or on behalf of the applicant, including travel expenses, any costs incurred or payments made for locating the child, the costs of legal representation of the child and those of returning the child. The applicant, too, may have to meet some or all of the expenses incurred in implementing the child's return.[3]

1   Art 26.
2   CACA 1985, s 11.
3   Art 26.

(c)   The European Convention–recognition and enforcement of custody decisions

3.115   Part II of the Child Abduction and Custody Act 1985 ratifies and implements the European Convention of 1980 on the recognition and enforcement of decisions concerning custody of children,[1] to which the United Kingdom is a signatory.[2] The provisions of this Convention are set out in Schedule 2 of the Act and have the force of law in the United Kingdom, but, as with the Hague Convention, are here examined specifically in relation to their operation within England and Wales.[3] The European Convention is also administered by the Central Authorities of Contracting States and their judicial or administrative authorities, and here too in relation to its application to England and Wales the Central Authority is the Lord Chancellor.[4] The Convention applies to the 'improper removal' of a child of any nationality so long as he is under 16 and has not the right to decide on his own place of residence under the law of his habitual residence, the law of his nationality or the internal law of the State addressed.[5] It remains to be seen what effect, if any, the decision of the House of Lords in *Gillick v West Norfolk and Wisbech Area Health Authority*[6] has on this definition. It is doubtful but arguable that now under English law an intellectually mature 15-year-old has the right to choose his own place of residence. Supposing that he is living with his mother in England by virtue of a custody order made in her favour, but on an access visit to his father in a Contracting State he decides that he wants to remain there. Arguably the Central Authority is no longer entitled to recognise and enforce the custody order.[7] Even if this is not a valid conclusion, the Authority may refuse to recognise and enforce it on the separate ground that that would not be in the child's interests.[8]

1   (1981) Cmnd 8155; and see Jones (1981) 30 ICLQ 467; Lowe and White, op cit paras 17.38 et seq.

2   The other Contracting States to the Convention who to date have ratified it are Austria,
    Belgium, Cyprus, France, Luxembourg, Portugal, Spain and Switzerland.
3   See Art 26 of the Convention.
4   CACA 1985, s 14.
5   Art 1. For the meaning of 'the State addressed' see infra, para 3.116.
6   [1986] AC 112, [1985] 3 All ER 402.
7   'Improper removal' covers not only the removal of a child across an international frontier
    in breach of a custody decision given and enforceable in a Contracting State but also
    the failure to return a child across an international frontier at the end of the exercise
    of the right of access to the child or at the end of any other temporary stay in a territory
    other than that where the custody is exercised. (Art 1(d)). See also post, para 3.119.
8   See Art 10(1)(b), infra, para 3.118.

(i)   The application

3.116   Any person who has obtained in England and Wales a decision
relating to the custody of a child may apply for it to be recognised and
enforced in a foreign Contracting State, the 'State addressed'. He may apply
either through the Lord Chancellor or direct to the Central Authority of
that State.[1] As already noted,[2] the former alternative is very likely to be
adopted, because the applicant will be unfamiliar with the procedures of
the foreign State. A decision relating to custody is widely defined to mean
'a decision of an authority in so far as it relates to the care of the person
of the child, including the right to decide on the place of his residence,
or to the right of access to him'.[3] The decision need not, therefore, be
one made by a judicial authority, and thus it could, it is submitted, include
a resolution of a local authority under section 3 of the Child Care Act
1980 vesting the parental rights and duties in the authority. The application
for recognition or enforcement must be accompanied by the following
documents:[4]

(a) a document authorising the Central Authority of the State addressed
     to act on behalf of the applicant or to designate another representative
     for that purpose;
(b) an authenticated copy of the decision; usually this would be a certified
     copy of a court order;
(c) where the decision was given in the absence of the defendant or his
     legal representative, a document which establishes that the defendant
     was duly served with the document which instituted the proceedings;
(d) if applicable, any document which establishes that, in accordance with
     the law of the State of origin, the decision is enforceable;
(e) if possible, a statement indicating the whereabouts or likely whereabouts
     of the child in the State addressed; this may well be the most difficult
     document to complete;
(f) proposals as to how the custody of the child should be restored.

1   Art 4(1). If the application is to the Lord Chancellor he must send the documents without
    delay to the foreign Central Authority (Art 4(3)).
2   Ante, para 3.111.
3   Art 1(c).
4   Arts 4(2) and 13. A certified copy of any such document is sufficient evidence of anything
    stated in it (CACA 1985, s 22(3)). Where the application is made to the Lord Chancellor
    and not direct to the foreign Central Authority, the Lord Chancellor may require the
    court which made the decision to furnish him with all or any of the documents mentioned
    in paras (b), (c) and (d) above; see CACA 1985, s 23(1).

(ii)   Enforcement
3.117   Unless it is manifestly clear that the conditions laid down by the Convention are not satisfied,[1] on receipt of the application the Central Authority of the State addressed must without delay take all appropriate steps to intervene and in particular:[2]

(a) to discover the child's whereabouts;
(b) to avoid, in particular by any necessary provisional measures, prejudice to the interests of the child or the applicant;
(c) to secure the recognition or enforcement of the decision;
(d) to secure the delivery of the child to the applicant where enforcement is granted;
(e) to inform the Lord Chancellor, as the requesting authority, of the measures taken and their results.

Intervention may well require the Central Authority having to institute proceedings 'before its competent authorities'. The most likely step is judicial proceedings, but it may also mean alerting administrative authorities such as the police and port authorities.[3]

---

1   Art 4(4). If the application has been directed to the Lord Chancellor, that conclusion may already have been reached and the application therefore not transmitted to the foreign Central Authority.
2   Art 5(1).
3   Where the Central Authority of the State addressed has reason to believe that the child is in the territory of another Contracting State, it must without delay send the application and documents to the Central Authority of that State, (Art 5(2)).

(iii)   Refusal of recognition and enforcement
3.118   Although the decision on custody made in England may not be reviewed as to its substance,[1] there are several grounds on which recognition and enforcement of it may be refused. They are as follows:[2]

(1) In the case of the custody decision being given in the absence of the defendant or his legal representative, the fact that he was not duly served with the document instituting proceedings in sufficient time to enable him to arrange his defence, the failure to serve not having been due to the defendant's own concealment of his whereabouts.
(2) In the same kind of case, the competence of the court or other authority giving the decision was not founded on the habitual residence of the defendant or of the child or on the last common habitual residence of the child's parents, at least one parent being still habitually resident there.
(3) The decision is incompatible with a decision relating to custody which became enforceable in the State addressed before the removal of the child, unless the child has had his habitual residence in the territory of the requesting State for one year before his removal. This very exceptional ground might arise, for example, where the mother obtained a custody order in England, but the father, having obtained a similar order in his favour in the foreign Contracting State, removed the child to that State before the child had lived in England with his mother for at least one year.
(4) The effects of the custody decision are manifestly incompatible with the fundamental principles of the law relating to the family and children

in the State addressed. At the risk of chauvinistic arrogance it must be said that it is difficult to conceive of circumstances in which a custody order of an English court would be refused recognition on this ground, especially as the paramountcy of the child's welfare is the basis of such an order *and* the order has to be *manifestly* incompatible with the foreign principles.

(5) Because of a change in the circumstances, including the passage of time but not including a mere change in the residence of the child after an improper removal (ie from England to the Contracting State), the effects of the original custody decision are manifestly no longer in accordance with the welfare of the child. Before reaching a decision on this ground, the Central Authority or a court or other authority of the Contracting State must ascertain the child's view unless this is impracticable having regard in particular to his age and understanding, and it may request that appropriate enquiries be carried out, at the expense of the regulating authority.[3]

(6) At the time when the proceedings were instituted in the State of origin:
  (i) the child was a national of the State addressed or was habitually resident there and no such connection existed with the State of origin;
  (ii) the child was a national both of the State of origin and of the State addressed and was habitually resident in the State addressed.

(7) The decision is incompatible with a decision given in the State addressed or enforceable in that State after being given in a third State, pursuant to proceedings begun before the submission of the request for recognition or enforcement, and if the refusal is in accordance with the welfare of the child. This ground should be compared with ground (3). The circumstances may overlap both grounds, but the present ground will be particularly relevant where the removal of the child to the foreign Contracting State precedes the making of the custody decision in that or a third State.

1 Art 9(3). But see ground (5) below.
2 See Arts 9 and 10.
3 Arts 10(1)(b) and 15. Where a request for inquiries is made to the Lord Chancellor, he in turn may request a written report from a local authority or a probation officer on any matter relating to the child, and he may also request any court to which a written report relating to the child has been made to send him a copy of the report; see CACA 1985, s 21.

3.119 As this last illustration implies, the provisions of the Convention can apply to a custody decision following removal, and when making the decision the English court can declare the removal to be unlawful,[1] if it is satisfied that the applicant has an interest in the matter and that the child has been removed out of England without the consent of the person(s) having the right to determine the child's place of residence under English law.[2] Usually, the person with an interest will be the person, for example, a parent or guardian, whose consent to removal has not been obtained.

1 Art 12.
2 Art 12 and CACA 1985, s 23(2), as applied specifically to England and Wales. An application in custody proceedings for a declaration under s 23(2) must be made by summons if those

proceedings are in the High Court (RSC Ord 90 r 33(2)), by notice if they are in a county court (Ord 47 r 10(5)) and either orally or in writing if the proceedings are in a Magistrates' Court (Magistrates' Courts (Child Abduction and Custody) Rules 1986, r 9.

3.120 If recognition or enforcement is refused, the Central Authority of the State addressed may nevertheless comply with a request of the disappointed applicant to bring in that State proceedings concerning the substance of the case. If it does, it must do its best to secure the representation of the applicant in those proceedings under conditions no less favourable than those available to a person who is resident in and a national of that State.[1]

1   Art 5(4).

(iv) Access
3.121 Decisions on rights of access and provisions dealing with rights of access contained in decisions relating to custody are to be recognised and enforced subject to the same conditions as other decisions relating to custody. But the Central Authority or a court or other authority of the State addressed may fix the conditions for the implementation and exercise of the right of access. In so doing they must take into account, in particular, undertakings given by the parties on the matter. Where there has been no decision about access or where recognition or enforcement of the decision relating to custody is refused, the Central Authority of the State addressed may apply to its competent authorities, most likely a court, for a decision on the right of access if the person claiming it so requests.[1]

1   Art 11.

(v) The inter-relationship of the two Conventions
3.122 Where there is a custody order in force and the child has been removed to a foreign Contracting State which has implemented both Conventions, the person seeking return of the child will be able to rely on either. The respective advantages and disadvantages of each have been admirably pinpointed.[1] They can be briefly particularised as follows:
(i)   If the foreign State to which the child has been removed has implemented Article 8 of the European Convention[2] and the removal was within the last six months, the applicant should rely on that Convention, provided he applies within that six-month period for the return of the child. The reason is that in those circumstances the return of the child is 'virtually mandatory',[3] whereas under the Hague Convention its requirement in Article 12 that the foreign Central Authority must order the return forthwith of a child who has been wrongfully removed for less than a year is subject to the grounds of the refusal allowed by Article 13.[4]
(ii)   If the circumstances do not fall within (i), the applicant must carefully weigh comparatively the grounds on which under the respective Conventions the foreign Central Authority might refuse an order to return the child.[5] This is likely to prove a demanding and uncertain exercise. For example, it may mean a comparative assessment of the ground in the Hague Convention that there is a grave risk that the return of the child would expose him to physical or psychological harm or otherwise place him in

an intolerable situation with the ground in the European Convention that the effects of the original custody decision are no longer in accordance with the welfare of the child. If, for example, it is thought that the approach of the foreign Authority to the Hague Convention ground were to follow that of the English Court in *A v A*[6] and require a high standard of proof to warrant refusal to return the child, the applicant might be better advised to proceed under that Convention.

(iii)   The European Convention has the advantage that the costs of the application must be borne by the Central Authority of the State addressed, whereas costs under the Hague Convention might be limited to those permitted by any domestic legal aid scheme.

1   See Lowe and White, paras 17.44–17.46
2   Some States, including the United Kingdom and apparently France, Italy, Spain and Switzerland have not done so.
3   Lowe and White, para 17.44.
4   See ante, para 3.112.
5   See respectively Art 13 of the Hague Convention, ante, para 3.112 and Arts 9 and 10 of the European Convention, ante, para 3.118.
6   Ante, para 3.112, note 5.

(d)   Child removed from England and Wales to a foreign Non-Contracting State

3.123   Because of the availability of free legal aid[1] a person who claims that there has been a breach of custody or access rights within the meaning of the Hague Convention is likely to rely on the Convention and the 1985 Act,[2] even though he is not precluded from applying directly to the judicial or administrative authorities of a Contracting State without relying on the provisions of the Convention.[3] For the person seeking return of a child to England and Wales from a Non-Contracting State direct resort to the foreign court is likely to be the most effectual method. Even though a wardship or custody order prohibiting removal abroad may be in force, it may well not be enough to ensure the child's return. Such orders are not enforceable in a Non-Contracting State. Although the removal will constitute contempt of court and sequestration will be appropriate if the contemnor has property in England and Wales,[4] that may not be sufficient sanction to influence him to return the child. The same comment applies to the forfeiture of any bond which, as a term of the original order, he was made to lodge in court.[5] So, too, his extradition from the foreign country[6] on the ground of having committed an offence under the Child Abduction Act 1984 or the common law offence of kidnapping will not extend to extradition of the child, although if the alleged offender is extradited he might be readier to surrender the child and allow his return. Consequently, the 'aggrieved' person may find that the only other possibility open to him is to commence proceedings in the foreign court. Where a child is wrongfully removed the Foreign and Commonwealth Office Consular Department can offer practical, but not legal, advice on the recovery of custody. Such advice is intended to supplement that given by the claimant's legal representative.[7]

1   Ante, para 3.114.
2   The fact that the claimant will not be means tested or required to make a contribution should prove persuasive.

3 See Art 29.
4 For sequestration see post, para 8.67.
5 For bonds see ante, para 3.60.
6 For the list of countries with which the United Kingdom has extradition treaties see Lowe and White, op cit, p 378.
7 Enquiries should be referred to the FCO Consular Department, Clive House, Petty France, London, SW1H 9HD; see *Practice Direction* [1984] 3 All ER 640; sub nom *Practice Note* [1984] 1 WLR 1216. An organisation entitled 'Children Abroad', c/o 33 Barlow Road, Keighley also offers advice and help.

3.124 Where a person seeks an order for the return of a child about to arrive in England by air and wishes to have information to enable him to meet the aeroplane, the judge should be asked to include in his order a direction that the airline operating the flight and, if he has the information, the immigration officer at the appropriate airport should supply such information to that person. To obtain such information where a person already has an order for the return of a child, that person should apply to a judge ex parte for such direction.[1]

1　*Practice Direction* [1980] 1 All ER 288, [1980] 1 WLR 73.

(e)　Recovery of child from England and Wales

(i)　Child removed to England and Wales from another part of the United Kingdom

3.125 It has already been pointed out[1] that in future the Family Law Act 1986 enables a 'custody order', as defined by the Act, which is made in Scotland or Northern Ireland[2] to be recognised and enforced in England and Wales, but there are still circumstances where it will be necessary to rely on the common law rules for dealing with children who have been brought to England and Wales from another jurisdiction; ie the English court will have to decide whether, in accordance with the paramountcy of the child's welfare, it should immediately order the child's return to Scotland or Northern Ireland or fully investigate the circumstances.[3] The circumstances where the 1986 Act does not operate are (i) where the Scottish or North Ireland custody order has not been registered in accordance with the Act, (ii) where the child has reached the age of 16, or (iii) where he is under that age but he has been removed to England and Wales without the consent of all the persons having the right to determine where he is to reside or in contravention of a court order and is therefore deemed by virtue of section 41 of the Act to continue for one year to be habitually resident in Scotland or Northern Ireland, as the case may be.[4] In these last mentioned circumstances the English court would not be able during that year to make a custody order as defined by s 1(1)(a) of the Act, for example an order under section 9 of the Guardianship of Minors Act 1971, since it will not have jurisdiction.[5] However, the High Court will be able to invoke its wardship jurisdiction if the child is present in England and Wales and the court considers the immediate exercise of its powers is necessary for his protection.[6] In those circumstances it is not likely to make a summary order for the child's return but rather to investigate all the circumstances. Havng done so, it may still reach the conclusion that the child should be returned and not allowed to remain in England and Wales.

1 Ante, para 3.107.
2 Or in any other part of the United Kingdom when the Act is extended to it; see para 3.107 note 4.
3 For the common law rules see post, paras 3.130–3.131.
4 This notional habitual residence ceases if the child becomes 16 or becomes habitually resident in England and Wales with the agreement of all those having the right to determine where the child is to reside and not in contravention of a court order (s 41(3)).
5 For jurisdiction to make custody orders as defined by s 1(1)(a), see ss 2 and 3 of the 1986 Act.
6 See ss 2(2)(b) and 3(6).

(ii)   Child removed to England and Wales from a foreign Contracting State
3.126 *Hague Convention*   Where a child is wrongfully removed to England and Wales in breach of the Hague Convention the functions which, as already explained,[1] are discharged by a foreign Central Authority and foreign court in the converse case of wrongful removal to a foreign Contracting State, will be discharged by the Lord Chancellor and the High Court, assisted by such administrative authorities as the police and port authorities. Any application to secure the return of the child may be addressed to the Lord Chancellor.[2] It must contain the requisite information and be accompanied by the appropriate documents.[3] The Lord Chancellor's Department will then refer the matter to one of the specialist firms of solicitors which deal with applications under the Child Abduction and Custody Act 1985.[4] It becomes the solicitor's responsibility to take all appropriate measures[5] to discover the whereabouts of the child, to prevent harm to him and to secure his voluntary return. Where voluntary return is not likely it may be necessary to institute judicial proceedings in the High Court[6] to secure his return. The defendants to the application shall be (a) the person alleged to have brought the child to the United Kingdom; (b) the person with whom the child is alleged to be; (c) any parent or guardian within the United Kingdom who is not otherwise a party; (d) the person in whose favour a decision relating to custody has been made, if not otherwise a party; (e) any other person appearing to the court to have a sufficient interest in the child's welfare, for example, grandparents.[7] Before final determination of the application[8] the court may give such interim directions[9] as it thinks fit for securing the child's welfare or preventing changes in the circumstances; for example, it may direct that the child is to reside with a specified person or at a specified place pending the hearing of the application. If there are custody proceedings[10] in a county court or a magistrates' court and the court is notified by the High Court that an application has been made under the Hague Convention, the court must order that its proceedings be stayed.[11]

In exercising its jurisdiction to deal with applications under the Hague Convention the High Court has power to order any person who it has reason to believe may have relevant information about the child's whereabouts to disclose it to the court, and he is not excused from complying with the order on the ground that he may incriminate himself or his spouse, though any statement made is not admissible in proceedings against either of them for an offence, other than perjury.[12] However, the court has no power to compel a defendant to the summons to give evidence after the child has been found and surrendered, an omission which deprives the foreign government of welcome information about how the defendant was able to leave the foreign jurisdiction and about what has been happening to the child in the intervening period.[12a]

Apart from this special power, the court's powers, under Articles 12 and 13 of the Convention, apply as they correspondingly do where a foreign court is dealing with an application in respect of a child removed from England and Wales. These and their limits have already been examined,[13] and it was noted that so far as refusing to return a child on the ground that there is a grave risk that his return would expose him to psychological harm the Court of Appeal has held[14] that a high standard of proof is needed before it will so refuse. It remains to be seen whether a standard has been imposed which is heavier than that which English courts have applied at common law when deciding whether or not to order return.[15]

1 See ante, paras 3.110 et seq.
2 CACA 1985, s 3(2).
3 See Art 8 of the Convention, ante, para 3.111.
4 The firms were selected by the Department after consultation with the Law Society. For criticism of this delegation to private practitioners instead of to the Official Solicitor see Lowe and White, para 17.74.
5 See the list of duties set out in Art 7.
6 See CACA 1985, s 6. Proceedings are by way of originating summons; see RSC Ord 90, rr 34 and 35(1).
7 RSC Ord 90, r 36. R 38 provides for evidence of the plaintiff and a defendant by way of affidavit to be lodged in the principal registry.
8 The application is heard by a judge in chambers, unless the court otherwise directs (r 39).
9 An application for such directions may in a case of urgency be made ex parte on affidavit, but otherwise must be made by summons (r 44).
10 For the meaning of 'custody' see CACA 1985, s 9.
11 County Court Rules 1981, Ord 47, r 10(2) (as inserted by the County Court (Amendment No 2) Rules 1986); the Magistrates' Courts (Child Abduction and Custody) Rules 1986, rr 3–6.
12 CACA 1985, s 24A, as inserted by FLA 1986, s 67(4).
12aSee *Re D (a minor)* [1988] Fam Law 336.
13 Ante, para 3.112.
14 *Re A (a minor) (abduction)* [1988] 1 FLR 365, [1988] Fam Law 54, CA.
15 See post, para 3.131.

3.127   *The European Convention*   Where it is sought to register and enforce, in accordance with the European Convention and section 16 of the Child Abduction and Custody Act 1985, a decision relating to custody made in a foreign Contracting State in respect of a child who has been improperly removed to England and Wales, the main procedural rules governing applications under the Hague Convention correspondingly apply. The functions of the Lord Chancellor as the Central Authority are delegated to specialist firms of solicitors[1] and any application to register and enforce the foreign decision is made to the High Court by way of originating summons, which is dealt with by a judge in chambers unless the court otherwise directs.[2] As with applications under the Hague Convention there is a power to order a person to disclose information about the child's whereabouts.[3] So, too, before final determination of the application for registration the court may give interim directions for securing the child's welfare or preventing changes in the circumstances.[4]

1   Under Art 5(3) of the European Convention the Lord Chancellor as the Central Authority bears the applicant's costs, except those of repatriation.

2 See RSC Ord 90, rr 34, 35(2), 38 and 39, and for the appropriate defendants see r 36, and see supra, para 3.126.
3 FLA 1986, s 24A.
4 CACA 1985, s 19; and see RSC Ord 90, r 44, ante, para 3.126, note 9.

3.128 The High Court must refuse to register the foreign decision in the following circumstances:[1]

(1) If it is of the opinion that one of the grounds of refusal specified in Articles 9 or 10 of the European Convention applies. These have already been examined[2] in relation to a foreign Contracting State refusing to register an English custody decision. One in particular calls for present comment, namely, where the effects of the foreign custody decision are manifestly incompatible with the fundamental principles of English law relating to the family and children.[3] But what are the fundamental principles? In the absence of a Bill of Rights, they may not wholly be discernible. An obvious answer is that in this context there is only one fundamental principle, namely, the paramountcy of the child's welfare. But, in the light of the *Gillick* decision, is there also another such principle, namely, the right of the intellectually mature child to assert his own choice?[4] Suppose, for example, that the foreign decision gave the custody of a 14-year-old daughter to her mother because it found that to be in the girl's best interests, even though it was known to be against her wishes, that her father has improperly removed her to England and that she is adamant that she wants to continue to live with him. Assuming that the High Court sees the girl's self-assertive right as a fundamental principle, can it refuse to register on the ground of manifest incompatibility? And how far is it bound by the rule that the foreign custody decision can 'in no circumstances . . . be reviewed as to its substance'?[5] If, however, the only fundamental principle is that of the paramountcy of the child's welfare, it is arguable[6] that it should not be applied with 'the same latitude as under the common law' and the onus should be on the person opposing registration to show that the child will not be harmed by a return to the foreign State.[7] On that basis it would be difficult in the above illustration to justify refusal to register the decision and enforce the return of the girl to her mother.

(2) If the High Court is of the opinion that the decision is not enforceable in the Contracting State where it was made. This ground is not likely to be invoked unless a defendant who is opposing the registration adduces evidence of non-enforceability, though, it is submitted, there appears nothing to prevent the court of its own motion taking cognisance of the matter.

(3) If an application in respect of the child is pending.

1 See CACA 1985, s 16(4).
2 Ante, para 3.118.
3 See Art 10(1)(a).
4 But compare ante, para 1.16 for the alternative view that the child's right to choose is subject to the court's being satisfied that the choice is in her interests.
5 Art 9(3).
6 See Lowe and White, paras 17.71–17.72.
7 The same point is also made by Lowe and White, ibid, in respect of the ground of refusal that because of the change of circumstances the foreign decision has become manifestly no longer in accordance with the child's welfare (Art 10(1)(b)).

3.129 If the High Court does register the foreign decision, it then has the same powers for the purpose of enforcing the decision as if it had made the decision itself.[1] An order which is registered may be varied or revoked if the foreign decision has been varied or revoked in the State of origin.[2] Once an order is registered any custody order[3] ceases to have effect,[4] and once an application for registration is made the powers of a court in which custody or similar proceedings[5] are pending are suspended, unless the application is refused.[6]

1   CACA 1985, s 18.
2   CACA 1985, s 17 and RSC Ord 90, r 46.
3   As defined by CACA 1985, s 27(1) and Sch 3.
4   CACA 1985, s 25(1).
5   As defined by CACA 1985, s 20(2), (amended by FLA 1986, s 67(1)).
6   See CACA 1985, s 20.

(iii)   Child removed to England and Wales from a foreign non-Contracting State

3.130   Where a child has been removed from a State which is not a party to either the Hague Convention or the European Convention, the question whether the English court should order his return to the foreign country must be answered by applying the principle that his welfare is the first and paramount consideration. However, case law reveals some change of emphasis in the application. In most cases the question has arisen where the child is already the subject of a custody order made by the foreign court. Because of the paramountcy principle the foreign order does not have the effect of a foreign judgment binding on the English court. As the Judicial Committee of the Privy Council put it in *McKee v McKee*, 'comity demands not its enforcement but its grave consideration'.[1] The English court has to decide, in the light of the parmountcy principle, whether to make a summary order for the return of the child in compliance with the foreign order or to inquire into the merits of the case and then decide whether to order return or itself make a concurrent order. The English jurisdiction has usually been invoked by way of wardship proceedings,[2] and thus, if a concurrent order is made, it is one granting the applicant care and control of the child.

1   Per Lord Simonds, [1951] AC 352 at 365; [1951] 1 All ER 942 at 948.
2   The child's physical presence or ordinary residence in England and Wales normally confers jurisdiction, see *post,* paras 8.02–8.05.
    If the party seeking removal of the child out of England applies for habeas corpus, the High Court may stand over that application until the party opposing it is given the opportunity to make the child a ward of court; *Re JET (an infant)* (1966) Times, 18 October, CA.

3.131   Re *B's Settlement, B v B*,[1] the first case to apply the paramountcy principle,[2] suggested a readiness on the part of the English court not to order the child's return, especially if he had lived for some time in this country with the kidnapping parent. However, a number of decisions in the 1960s, beginning with that of the Court of Appeal in *Re H (infants)*,[3] showed some hardening of attitude by the English court in favour of the parent from whom the child had been kidnapped.[4] There had to be compelling reasons for not ordering the return of the child, since it was the court's duty to see that the kidnapper did not gain advantage by his wrongdoing. It therefore had to be shown that the child would be harmed if he returned. The decision of the Court of Appeal in *Re L (minors)*[5] marked a departure from this approach with a new positive emphasis being placed on the child's best interests, with the consequence that it was a matter for the parent from whom the child had been kidnapped to show that it was in those best interests for his child to be returned to the foreign country. This change of emphasis was a reaffirmation of the paramountcy principle as applied in *Re B's Settlement, B v B*,[6] and accords with the decision of the House of Lords in *J v C*[7] and with subsequent decisions[8] that that principle is not to be qualified by a need to recognise an injustice to a parent. Subsequent decisions have confirmed that the approach adopted in *Re L* is the correct one.[9] In deciding whether it is in the child's best interests to make a summary order for his return without investigating the merits of the case, the court should be guided by the following considerations.[10]

> 'To take a child from his native land, to remove him to another country where maybe his native tongue is not spoken, to divorce him from the social customs and contacts to which he has been accustomed, to interrupt his education in his native land and subject him to a foreign system of education are all acts (offered here as examples and, of course, not a complete catalogue of possible relevant factors) which are likely to be psychologically disturbing to the child, particularly at a time when his family life is also disrupted. If such a case is promptly brought to the attention of a court in this country, the judge may feel that it is in the best interests of the infant that these disturbing factors should be eliminated from his life as speedily as possible. A full investigation of the merits of the case in an English court may be incompatible with achieving this . . .. An order that the child should be returned forthwith to the country from which he has been removed in the expectation that any dispute about his custody will be satisfactorily resolved in the courts of that country may well be regarded as being in the best interests of the child.'

If the English court does decide to investigate the merits of the case, it must as in all other cases where it applies the paramountcy principle consider all the circumstances. These will include the matters to which Buckley LJ referred, such as the child's links with the country from which he has been taken and any differences in education, language and social customs. Also particularly relevant will be the length of time since the order was made and the time spent in England or Wales.[11] The conduct of the parties is also relevant, but the court is not concerned with penalising a party for his conduct.[12] Where there is no foreign order in force the court may be readier to investigate and hear all the evidence. At least, if there are allegations that the parent who wishes to take the child back to the foreign country is unfit to act as a parent, an order must not be made allowing this until the answers to those allegations have been considered.[13] Any other course would contravene the paramountcy principle.

1 [1940] Ch 54, [1951] 1 All ER 949n.
2 Nineteenth century cases decided before that principle was established show greater respect for the foreign order; see *Nugent v Vetzera* (1866) LR 2 Eq 704; *Re Savini, Savini v Lousada* (1870) 22 LT 61, 18 WR 425. But there were already indications to emphasise the child's interests; see Lord Cranworth in *Stuart v Marquis of Bute* (1861) 9 HL Cas 440 at 469, ('There is but one object which ought to be kept strictly in view and that is the interest of the infant.').

3 [1966] 1 All ER 886, [1966] 1 WLR 381, CA.
4 See also *Re E(D) (an infant)* [1967] Ch 761, [1967] 2 All ER 881; *Re T (infants)* [1968] Ch 704, [1968] 3 All ER 441, CA; *Re A (infants)* [1970] Ch 665, [1970] 3 All ER 184, CA; *Re G (an infant)* [1969] 2 All ER 1135, [1969] 1 WLR 1001.
5 [1974] 1 All ER 913, [1974] 1 WLR 250, CA.
6 Supra.
7 [1970] AC 668, [1969] 1 All ER 788, HL.
8 See for example, *S(BD) v S(DJ) (children: care and control)* [1977] Fam 109, [1977] 1 All ER 656, CA; *Re K (minors) (children: care and control)* [1977] Fam 179, [1977] 1 All ER 647, CA; and see ante, para 3.10.
9 *Re K (infants)* (1976) 6 Fam Law 150, CA; *Re NC, JC and AC (minors)* (1977) 7 Fam Law 240, CA; *Re R (minors) (wardship: jurisdiction)* (1981) 2 FLR 416, 11 Fam Law 57, CA; *Re B (minors) (wardship: interim care and control)* (1982) 4 FLR 472, CA.
10 See Buckley LJ in *Re L* [1974] 1 All ER 913 at 926, [1974] 1 WLR 250 at 265. See also *Re G (a minor) (wardship: jurisdiction)* [1984] FLR 268, [1984] Fam Law 244, CA.
11 *Re T (an infant)* [1969] 3 All ER 998, [1969] 1 WLR 1608; *Re W (an infant)* (1974) 4 Fam Law 186, CA; *T v T* (1975) 6 Fam Law 78, CA; *Re A (a minor)* (1978) 1 FLR 140, 9 Fam Law 151, CA.
12 See, for example, *Re C (minors) (wardship: jurisdiction)* [1978] Fam 105 at 115, [1978] 2 All ER 230 at 236, CA; *Re G (a minor) (wardship: jurisdiction)*, supra note 10.
13 *Re M (an infant)* (1968) 112 Sol Jo 94, CA; *Re C(S) (an infant)* (1971) Times, 26 June.

CHAPTER 4
Guardianship

I INTRODUCTION

4.01 Mediaeval law, as Pollock and Maitland noted,[1] 'never laid down any . . . rule that there [was] or ought to be a guardian for every infant'. Had it done so, it might have led to the formulation of a comprehensive definition of guardianship, which, even allowing for the strength of feudal land law, might have checked the proliferation of different kinds of guardianship. As it was, even with the disappearance of the incidents of feudal tenure, different kinds continued to emerge, whether the product of custom, the common law, equity or statute.[2] Many of them have, however, long been obsolete, especially those limited to the estate of the minor, since they were absorbed into the law of trusts, and most of the customary guardianships.[3] Other kinds are of minimal significance, for example, guardianship created in exercise of the High Court's inherent jurisdiction[4] and guardianship which the child himself may create.[5]

1 *The History of English Law*, 2nd edn (1968) Vol II p 444; and see generally ibid pp 436-447 and Vol I pp 318-329.
2 In the nineteenth century there were as many as 13. See Simpson, *Infants* 3rd edn (1909), p 183 for the list and see generally 4th edn (1926), pp 149 et seq and Holdsworth, *History of English Law* 7th edn (1966) Vol III, pp 511-513. See also Jessel MR in *Rimington v Hartley* (1880) 14 Ch D 630 at 632.
3 But not all; for example, the customary rights of guardianship exercised by the Lord Mayor and Aldermen of the City of London, through the Court of Orphans, over the orphans of deceased freemen of the City.
4 See post, para 4.11.
5 A remote possibility, even with the fillip of the *Gillick* principle. The powers of a guardian appointed by a child remain uncertain; *Re Brown's Will Trusts* (1881) 18 Ch D 61, at 65, 67 and 72.

4.02 It has already been mentioned[1] that two of the traditional categories of guardianship were those of guardianship by nature and guardianship by nurture, which expressed the relationship between the parent and his legitimate child, but today the term 'guardian' most commonly means a person who has been appointed either by a parent under a deed or will, or by a court, to stand in loco parentis to a child, a meaning sometimes expressly adopted by statute.[2] It is so used in this chapter.

1 Ante, Chapter 1, para 1.58.
2 For example, as in Adoption Act 1976, s 16(1)(b) (adoption); Marriage Act 1949, s 3(1) and Second Schedule (consent to marriage).

II APPOINTMENT OF GUARDIANS

1   Testamentary guardians

(a)   Introduction

4.03   As part of the 'reorganisation' following the abolition of knight service
and the incident of wardship, the Tenures Abolition Act 1660 gave the
father of the legitimate child the power, operative from the date of his
death, to 'dispose of the custody and tuition' of his child.[1] The mother
had to wait until the Guardianship of Infants Act 1886, and then her power
was restricted. Whereas a guardian appointed by the father acted alone,
without interference by the surviving mother, one appointed by a mother
could only act jointly with the surviving father, and even then the
appointment needed the court's confirmation, which could only be granted
if the father was considered unfit to be sole guardian. The Guardianship
of Infants Act 1925 extended to the power of appointment, as it did to
claims for custody, the principle of parity. The powers are now contained
in the Guardianship of Minors Acts 1971 and 1973, subject to substantial
amendment by the Domestic Proceedings and Magistrates' Courts Act 1978
and prospectively the Family Law Reform Act 1987.

1   Apparently, he had had a similar power for at least a century earlier. See Law Com
Working Paper No 91 p 37, note 33, citing an Act of 1557 dealing with the abduction
of girls under 16 (post, para 10.27), wherein a guardian is described as a person to whom
the father by his will or 'by any other act in his lifetime hath or shall appoint . . . the
order, keeping, education or governance of such maid or womanchild . . .' (s 3).

(b)   Scope of the power to appoint

4.04   The father or mother[1] may by deed or will appoint a guardian or
guardians[2] for any of his or her children who are under 18 at the date
of his or her death.[3] However, in the case of the child of unmarried parents,
the father's (but not the mother's) power of appointment is restricted in
that an appointment by him is only effective if at the time of his death
he had legal custody by virtue of an order under section 9 of the Guardianship
of Minors Act 1971.[4] When the relevant provisions of the Family Law
Reform Act 1987 come into force, the scope of his power of appointment
will be wider. He will be able to exercise it if at the time of his death
either (a) he had all the parental rights and duties with respect to the child
by virtue of an order under section 4 of the Family Law Reform Act 1987
or (b) he had a right to custody, legal or actual custody or care and control
of the child by virtue of an order made under any other enactment.[5] Even
where he falls only within condition (b), it seems that his power to appoint
will extend both to guardianship of the person and to guardianship of the
estate of the child, as it does to other parents. Given that he will need
only to have actual custody or care and control, whereas under the present
law he has to have legal custody (including actual custody) under the
Guardianship of Minors Act 1971 condition (b) confers a generous power.

1   Including an adoptive parent; *Re W (a minor)* (1980) 2 FLR 161, 10 Fam Law 190.
2   See GMA 1971, s 3(1)(b) and (2)(b).
3   GMA 1971, s 4(1) and (2); FLRA 1969, s 1.
4   GMA 1971, s 14(3).
5   GMA 1971, ss 3(3) and (4) and 4(7), as inserted by FLRA 1987, s 6(1) and (2). A father

who is granted care and control by an order in wardship proceedings does not therefore have a power to appoint, since the order is not made under an enactment.

4.05 This last point is but one illustration of the uncertainty that surrounds the scope of the power to appoint. This is due partly to the general terms in which section 4 of the 1971 Act is enacted[1] and partly to uncertainty about the extent to which authorities under the former provisions of the Tenures Abolition Act 1660 are still binding. The following rules apparently apply.

1 As prospectively amended by FLRA 1987, Sch 2, para 28, it simply states: 'The father of a child may by deed or will appoint any person to be guardian of the child after his death'. There is a corresponding provision in respect of the mother's power.

4.06 (1) The power extends to the appointment for any child alive at the parent's death, including one *en ventre sa mere*, but some doubt still exists as to whether the child must be unmarried at that date. Section 8 of the Tenures Abolition Act so required, but the Guardianship of Minors Act 1971 does not expressly do so.[1] The point is very largely academic, because, as has been pointed out, even if appointment is permitted, a court might well remove a guardian who attempted to control a married ward.[2]

1 As to the effect of marriage after guardianship has come into being see post, para 4.45.
2 Bromley, op cit, p 352. Rarely, if ever, does a court appoint a guardian for a married minor.

4.07 (2) A guardian may be appointed conditionally[1] or until the child reaches a specified age less than the attainment of majority or until some other event happens. Provision may also be made for successive appointments, and, although the office of guardian is not assignable,[2] a parent may, in an instrument appointing two or more guardians, authorise the survivor(s) to nominate a replacement for one who dies.[3] There are, however, no modern authorities and no evidence of practice to suggest that these conditions, restrictions or extensions are included in appointments.

1 *Selby v Selby* (1731) 2 Eq Cas Abr 488.
2 *Bedell v Constable* (1668) Vaugh 177; *Mellish v De Costa* (1737) 2 Atk 14.
3 *Parnell's Goods* (1872) LR 2 P & D 379.

4.08 (3) The general law relating to wills applies to appointments, with some modifications. Thus, no particular form of words need be used in the deed or will, but there must be a clear intention to create guardianship.[1] In the very unlikely case of a minor who is a parent wishing to appoint a guardian for his child, he would have to do so by way of deed, since he cannot make a valid will,[2] unless – and that possibility is, perhaps, not so remote – he is a soldier or airman on active service or a seaman at sea, in which event he can appoint by will.[3] An appointment is not invalid if the guardian was a witness to the will or deed,[4] but where made by will it is revoked by the testator's subsequent marriage unless when the will was made he intended that it, or at least the provision in it appointing a guardian, should not be revoked by a particular marriage he had in mind when he made the will.[5] It was held in *Earl Shaftsbury v Hannam*[6] that an appointment by deed is revoked by a later appointment by will on the ground that the deed in these circumstances is no more than a testamentary instrument in the form of a deed.[7] Logically on this ground an appointment by will should be revoked by a subsequent appointment by deed and the rule of revocation by subsequent marriage should apply where the instrument is a deed as it would if there were a will, but it seems that the wording of the Wills Act 1837 precludes both conclusions.[8] However, this statutory objection does not, it is submitted, prevent an appointment by deed being revoked by a later appointment by deed.

The complexity of these rules justifies the availability of a simpler form of appointment, at least as a substitute for the present methods.[9]

1   Compare *Miller v Harris* (1845) 14 Sim 540 with *Bedell v Constable* (1688) Vaugh 177; *Edwards v Wise* (1740) Barn Ch 139; and *Re Lord Norbury* (1875) IR 9 Eq 134.
2   Wills Act 1837, s 7.
3   Wills Act 1837, s 11; Wills (Soldiers and Sailors) Act 1918, ss 4 and 5(2); FLRA 1969, s 3(1).
4   *Morgan v Hatchell* (1854) 19 Beav 86.
5   Wills Act 1837, s 18, as substituted by the Administration of Justice Act 1982, s 18. *Semble*, for this purpose the appointment of a guardian is 'a disposition in the will'; see sub-s (4).
6   (1677) Cas *temp* Finch 323.
7   See also Lord Eldon in *Ex p Ilchester* (1803) 7 Ves 348 at 367.
8   Sections 20 and 18 respectively. See Bromley, op cit, p 351.
9   See Law Com Working Paper No 91, paras 3.41 – 3.45; Law Com No 172, para 2.29.

(c)   The surviving parent and the testamentary guardian

(i)   Where the parents were married to each other at the time of the child's birth
4.09   Usually, when one of the parents dies, the other becomes sole guardian; but, if the deceased has appointed a testamentary guardian, he and the surviving parent will normally act jointly.[1] However, the latter may object to this or the former may consider the parent to be unfit to have the legal custody of the child. In either event (which may occur at the outset or at any time during the guardianship), the *guardian* may apply to the court,[2] which has the following options.[3]
(a)   It may refuse to make an order, in which case the parent remains sole guardian. Presumably, the implied effect is revocation of the testamentary guardianship,[4] so that there is no question of the testamentary guardian assuming office on the death of the surviving parent.
(b)   It may make an order that they act jointly. Such an order is very unlikely. If they are not in accord, the order would not be in the child's interests.
(c)   It may make an order that the testamentary guardian be the sole guardian. But here, as in paragraph (a), the precise effect is not explained. It has been stated that 'the parent is, in effect, deprived of his guardianship of the child'.[5] But for how long? Presumably only during the continuance of the testamentary guardianship, so that if the guardian dies during the child's minority the parent's natural guardianship revives. Otherwise there would be no one having parental rights and yet the court would not be able to appoint a guardian to fill the vacuum since its power to do so depends, inter alia, on there being no parent.[6]

Because of the potentially divisive effect of these rules the Law Commission, while supporting retention of the power to appoint a testamentary guardian, recommends that appointments should generally take legal effect only after the death of the surviving parent (paras 2.26–2.27). However, if there is a court order that the child should live with the parent who later dies and he has appointed a testamentary guardian, the appointment should have immediate effect (para 2.28).

1 GMA 1971, s 3.
2 For the courts with jurisdiction see infra, para 4.12.
3 GMA 1971, s 4(3) and (4).
4 See Law Com Working Paper No 91, p 41.
5 Law Com Working Paper, ibid.
6 See s 5, infra, para 4.13. Further support for the view that the natural guardianship is only suspended may be derived from the wording of s 4(4). That enables the testamentary guardian to apply for an order if the parent is 'unfit to have the custody', not unfit to be the guardian of his child.

(ii) Where the parents were not married to each other at the time of the child's birth
4.10 In those circumstances it depends on whether or not at the time of the mother's death the father is entitled to legal custody by virtue of an order under section 9 of the Guardianship of Minors Act 1971. If he is, he becomes entitled to guardianship either alone or jointly with any testamentary guardian the mother has appointed.[1] Those rules correspondingly apply where the mother survives, if at the date of the father's death a section 9 order in his favour is in force. If there is no such order, the mother's guardianship to which she was entitled as sole natural guardian during his lifetime remains unaffected.

When the relevant changes made by the Family Law Reform Act 1987 come into force, the father's entitlement to guardianship, within the scope of the above rules, will depend on whether or not at the time of the mother's death he either (a) had all the parental rights and duties by virtue of an order under section 4 of the Family Law Reform Act 1987 or (b) had a right to custody, legal or actual custody or care and control of the child by virtue of an order made under any other enactment.[2]

1 See GMA, ss 3 and 4 and 14(3).
2 GMA 1971, s 4(3) and (7)(a), as inserted by FLRA 1987, s 6(1) and (2).

2 Guardians appointed by the court

(a) The court

(i) Inherent jurisdiction
4.11 The Family Division of the High Court has an inherent jurisdiction to appoint guardians, which has been confirmed[1] as being distinct from its inherent jurisdiction in wardship and exercisable without the child being made a ward of court. At one time, especially before the Guardianship of Infants Act 1886, it could serve a variety of purposes,[2] and, although today it has virtually been superseded by wardship, it may occasionally be useful, namely, to provide immediate protection to a child before a summons in wardship can be issued.

1 See *Re N (infant)* [1967] Ch 512, [1967] 1 All ER 161; *L v L* [1969] P 25 [1969] 1 All ER 852; *Re F* [1973] Fam 198; [1973] 3 All ER 493, confirming nineteenth century dicta in *Brown v Collins* (1883) 25 Ch D 56 at 60–61; *Re McGrath* [1892] 2 Ch 496 at 511.

The contrary view expressed in *Re E (an infant)* [1956] Ch 23, [1955] 3 All ER 174 no longer holds.
2   See *Rayden on Divorce,* 15th edn, p 1441 for case law.

(ii)   Statutory jurisdiction

4.12   This rests on the Guardianship of Minors Act 1971 (as amended), and is conferred on the Family Division, county courts and magistrates' courts,[1] with power to transfer proceedings between the High Court and a county court, the details of which have already been examined.[2] As part of the changes made by the Family Law Act 1986, rules of court have prescribed which county courts and which magistrates' courts are authorised to hear prescribed applications,[3] but no magistrates' court can entertain an application involving the child's property or its income.[4]

1   GMA 1971, s 15(1), as amended by FLA 1986, Sch 1, para 10 (1) and (2). Additionally, the High Court has a separate power to appoint a guardian only of a minor's estate (GA 1973, s 7(2)), but such a possibility is remote. Jurisdiction is assigned to the Chancery Division and not the Family Division (Administration of Justice Act 1970, Sch 1).
2   See *ante,* para 3.17.
3   See CCR Ord 47, r 6(1), as inserted by the County Court (Amendment) Rules 1988, SI 1988/278; Magistrates' Courts (Family Law Act 1986) Rules 1988, SI 1988/329 (L 4) r 5(1) and for the details *ante,* para 3.16.
4   GMA 1971, s 15(2)(b).

(b)   The appointment

4.13   The courts may appoint a guardian in the following circumstances:

(i) Where one parent dies without having appointed a testamentary guardian.[1]

(ii) Where one parent dies having appointed a testamentary guardian, but the guardian dies or refuses to act.[2]

In both cases the guardian appointed by the court will act jointly with the surviving parent, and will continue on the death of that parent to act as sole guardian or, as the case may be, jointly with any testamentary guardian whom that parent has appointed,[3] just as where, if both parents appoint testamentary guardians, those guardians act jointly after the death of the surviving parent.[4]

(iii) Where the child has no parent, no guardian of the person and no-one else (for example, a custodian) having parental rights with respect to him.[5]

An appointment may be made even though a local authority or voluntary organisation has parental rights by virtue of a resolution under sections 3 or 64 of the Child Care Act 1980,[6] but once it is made the resolution ceases to have effect.[7] The scope of this provision has not been fully tested,[8] probably because persons, most likely relatives, who have de facto control in circumstances which would entitle them to apply for guardianship, see little practical point in doing so, especially as the court has no power under the section to make orders for legal custody;[9] and/or they may be reluctant to assume the additional responsibilities which guardianship might entail. Whether the availability of custodianship in some cases will prove a further inhibiting factor remains to be seen. Nevertheless, a step-parent in particular may find the section useful, whether or not as an alternative to custodianship, where both the natural parents of the step-child, are dead. In those circumstances the conditions of the section are satisfied, because, though he has obligations by virtue of caring for his step-child, he does not have parental rights. Indeed, a person can only have those rights for the purpose of section 5 if he has been granted them by a formal legal process.[10]

    (iv) Where the High Court removes a guardian it may appoint another in his place.[11]

The Law Commission (Law Com No 172, para 2.30) recommends that the courts' powers to appoint should continue to mirror those of the parent. They should therefore be able to appoint when there is no parent with parental responsibility or when there is an order that the child should live with a parent or guardian who has died but not with the other parent.

1 GMA 1971, s 3(1)(a) and (2)(a).
2 GMA 1971, s 3(1)(b) and (2)(b). Presumably under (1) and (2) the parent or anyone interested in being appointed may apply.
3 GMA 1971, s 4(6).
4 GMA 1971, s 4(5).
5 GMA 1971, s 5(1). Only the applicant can be appointed guardian, whereas, *semble,* there is no such restriction on appointments under heads (1) and (2) above; and see n 2, supra. In the case of a child whose mother and father were not married when he was born, the father is to be treated as a parent only if there is an order under s 9 of GMA 1971 giving him legal custody (see s 14(3)). When the changes made by FLRA 1987 come into force he will instead be so treated if there is an order under s 4 of the latter Act giving him all the parental rights and duties or an order giving him custody, legal or actual custody or care and control (see GMA 1971, s 5(3) as added by FLRA 1987, s 6(3)).
6 GMA 1971, s 5(2), as prospectively amended by FLRA 1987, Sch 2, para 29. *Semble* the local authority could appear to contest the application.
7 CCA 1980, s 5(2)(c). But an appointment of a testamentary guardian does not so affect a resolution. The appointment of any guardian, testamentary or one appointed by the court, does not affect the existence of a care order.
8 The only reported case on it is *Re N (minors) (parental rights)* [1974] Fam 40; [1974] 1 All ER 126.
9 See Arnold J in *Re N* at 44, 45 and 129 respectively. Cretney, op cit, p 318, points out that consequently a guardian would have to rely on wardship or habeas corpus to enforce his rights of guardianship.
10 *Re N*, supra.
11 GMA 1971, s 6; for removal see post, para 4.43.

Choice of guardian
4.14 In deciding whom to choose as a guardian the court must apply the principle of the paramountcy of the child's welfare in accordance with section 1 of the Guardianship of Minors Act 1971. As with disputes over custody, it should be ready to cover a variety of factors. It is likely to lean in favour of the appointment of a blood relative of the child,[1] but the child's welfare may demand a complete severance from relatives, for example, where the father has killed the mother.[2] The court should be ready to consider the wishes of the parent (including a deceased parent),[3] of the child's nearest relatives[4] and, if he is sufficiently mature, of the child, which since *Gillick* are likely to carry greater weight than they might hitherto have done. It must seek to avoid the creation of religious difficulties between an appointee and the child, and it must try to appoint persons who are likely to get on with each other as joint guardians. When exercising the statutory jurisdiction to appoint a joint guardian with the surviving parent, the sole question is whether the appointment is per se desirable for the

child and not whether it can achieve some collateral purpose. In *Re H (an infant)*[5] a magistrates' court appointed the child's elder sister to act as joint guardian with her father. At the time of the mother's death the child was in the care and control of the sister and the father was estranged from the family. What the sister wanted was custody, but, since the (then) Guardianship of Infants Act 1925 did not enable her to claim this directly, she first sought appointment as a joint guardian which would then entitle her to apply for custody. The magistrates' order was discharged. The court indicated that the appropriate method of achieving this would have been an application by the sister to make the minor a ward of court. A possible alternative today would be custodianship proceedings.[6]

1　But this is a factor which may not carry the weight it once did; see *Ord v Blackett* (1725) 9 Mod Rep 116; *Johnstone v Beattie* (1843) 10 Cl & Fin 42, HL; *Re Nevin* [1891] 2 Ch 299 at 303, CA.
2　*Re F* [1970] 1 All ER 344, [1970] 1 WLR 192, CA.
3　*Re Kaye* (1866) 1 Ch App 387 at 390, CA in Ch; cf *Hartley v Smith* (1862) 6 LT 734.
4　*Johnstone v Beattie*, supra, note 1.
5　[1959] 3 All ER 746; [1959] 1 WLR 1163.
6　See post, Chapter 6.

4.15　A major defect in the present procedures for appointment is the absence of any provisions, corresponding to those in adoption or custodianship, which enable the court to assess the suitability of an applicant for guardianship.[1] Given that in principle a guardianship order has wider effects than a custodianship order, the anomaly is pronounced. Nor do the procedures allow for the appointment of a guardian ad litem as they do in adoption proceedings. A further matter for consideration is whether the child should have a right in all cases to be made a party to the proceedings,[2] instead of being denied it in the magistrates' court and only permitted it in the High Court or county court at its discretion.

1　See Law Com Working Paper No 91, para 3.52.
2　Ibid, para 3.53.

III　POWERS AND DUTIES OF GUARDIANS

1　Introduction

4.16　Until the Guardianship Act 1973 repealed it, the powers and duties of a guardian were construed by reference to the Tenures Abolition Act 1660,[1] which entrusted to him the 'custody and tuition' of the child and enabled him to 'take into [his] . . . custody to the use of such child . . . the profits of all lands, tenements and hereditaments of such child . . . and also the custody, tuition, management of the goods, chattels and personal estate of such child . . . and [to] bring such action in relation thereunto as by law a guardian in common socage might do'. The effect of this provision was that his powers and duties had still to be found in the common law. Section 7(1) of the 1973 Act substituted a provision in general terms, namely, that 'a guardian under the Guardianship of Minors Act 1971, besides being guardian of the person of the minor, shall have all the rights, powers and duties of a guardian of the minor's estate'. Thus, under this reformulation, which is singularly uninformative, the two concepts of guardianship of the person and guardianship of the estate are still at the centre of the law, and the problem of determining their scope and the extent to which reliance can be placed on cases decided in a bygone age remains. This continued uncertainty has been reflected in the approaches of the Law Commission to the subject. In its Report on Illegitimacy,[2] it saw the guardian as having for practical purposes all the powers of a parent, except where statute specifically requires an act by the child's parent, as, for example, in agreeing to the child's adoption.[3] Guardianship in general terms is thus equated with custody in its wide meaning.[4] A later examination[5] emphasised the distinction between guardianship of the person and guardianship of the estate, but the most recent[6] has recommended considerable simplification of the law by abolishing the distinction and substituting the general principle that, subject to certain modifications,[7] all guardians be given the same responsibility as parents.

1 Section 9(1) and Sch 3 of the 1973 Act repealed s 9 of the 1660 Act, together with s 8 of GMA 1971 which provided that 'every guardian under this Act shall have all such powers over the estate and person or over the estate (as the case may be) of a minor as any guardian appointed by will or otherwise has under the Tenures Abolition Act 1660 or otherwise'.
2 Law Com No 118, paras 7.2–7.3.
3 See post, para 5.21.
4 See ante, para 1.58.
5 Working Paper No 91.
6 Law Com No 172, paras 2.24–2.25.
7 See *post,* paras 4.25 and 4.33.

2 Guardianship of the person

4.17 In its Working Paper[1] the Law Commission, while recognising that 'the distinction between the two concepts is not clear', saw that of legal custody as 'the nearest equivalent' to that of guardianship of the person. The parental 'rights and duties' embodied in the former[2] are here examined in relation to guardianship mainly in the order in which they were considered in chapter one and subject to any modification which the fiduciary nature of guardianship requires. It will be seen that the respective powers and duties of parents and guardians are not identical, with some of the guardian's duties being more onerous and his powers less extensive.

1 No 91 at p 52.
2 See CA 1975, s 86, ante, para 1.59.

(a) Actual custody

4.18 In considering this parental right it is necessary to take account of the substitution of legal custody for custody (in its wide sense) in the Guardianship of Minors Act 1971. The implications of the changes in relation to guardianship seem to have been overlooked by the Legislature. The crucial change is to be found in section 11A(1) of the Act, the terms of which, already noted elsewhere,[1] are such that in making an order for legal custody the court cannot separate actual custody from it. A person who is given legal custody must be given actual custody.

1 Ante, para 3.21. The change was made by DPMCA 1978, s 37.

4.19   A person who is sole guardian will prima facie be entitled to the actual custody of the child and will be able to enforce his right to it by habeas corpus proceedings[1] or by wardship or, *semble,* by invoking the court's inherent jurisdiction without making the child a ward of court.[2] But he is not automatically entitled. Thus, if he is a testamentary guardian and the testator directs that some other person is to have actual custody, he must comply with the direction, unless he satisfies the court that it would not be in the child's interests to do so.[3] If it does grant actual custody to someone else, the guardian retains all other powers and duties and thus remains responsible for the general supervision of the child and his interests.

1   *R v Isley* (1836) 5 Ad & El 441.
2   See ante, para 4.11.
3   *Knott v Cottee* (1847) 2 Ph 192. The appropriate proceedings would, it is submitted, be for a mandatory injunction, brought by the person claiming actual custody, if the guardian is unwilling to surrender it. There is, it is submitted, no remedy under the GMA 1971.

4.20   Where, on the other hand, a testamentary guardian has been appointed and there is a surviving parent, he is likely to consent to the latter having actual custody, but, consent apart, the parent will prima facie be entitled to the actual custody. That consequence is, it is submitted, implicit in section 4(4) of the 1971 Act because, as already noted,[1] if the testamentary guardian considers that the parent is unfit to have the 'custody' of the child, he may apply to the court and if it upholds his claim it will almost certainly make him sole guardian rather than jointly with the parent.[2] If it does, then, under section 10(1)(a), it may make such order regarding the 'legal custody' as it thinks fit having regard to the child's welfare.[3] But this provision is to be read with section 11A(1), so that whoever is given legal custody must also be given actual custody, and, if the testamentary guardian is made sole guardian, it is inconceivable that anyone else be given the legal custody if guardianship of the person and legal custody are to be treated as virtually statutory equivalents. What would be permissible, in accordance with section 11A(1), would be an order that, while the sole guardian had legal and actual custody, the surviving parent be allowed to share specific rights (for example, relating to the child's religious upbringing) jointly with the guardian.[4] Where an order for legal custody is made, it may be varied or discharged. Such an order is a custody order for the purposes of the Family Law Act 1986.[5]

1   Ante, para 4.09.
2   See ibid.
3   The same restrictions apply to orders for legal custody made under s 10(1)(a) as apply to orders under s 11(a); see infra, para 4.21, note 4 and 6. S 11 of FLRA 1987 prospectively substitutes a new s 10(1) in GMA 1971 which does not expressly refer to the child's welfare. The exclusion takes account of the fact that welfare is covered by the paramountcy principle expressed in s 1 of the 1971 Act.
4   For the possibility of the parent being given access and/or having to make financial provision see infra, para 4.23 and para 4.26.
5   See *ante,* para 3.15.

4.21   The above rules will apply where the surviving parent is excluded from being a guardian. What if a parent and a guardian (whether testamentary or one appointed by the court[1]) are acting as joint guardians with the parent having actual custody, but they later disagree over it and the guardian wishes to have it? When there is a dispute between joint guardians (whether between parent and guardian or between two guardians) over any question affecting the welfare of the child,[2] either of them may apply to the court for its direction and the court may make any order it thinks proper.[3] Consequently, if there is a dispute over actual custody, the court may grant it to the one or other guardian or even to a third person. But where the dispute is between a parent and a guardian, whether over actual custody or any other matter, the court has additional powers.[4] Apart from orders relating to access and financial provision,[5] it may make an order regarding legal custody.[6] If it grants this, and thus actual custody, to the guardian, it may, as indicated above, confer on the parent specific rights jointly with the guardian. If, on the other hand, it grants legal and actual custody to the parent, the result is effectively to deprive the guardian of his guardianship of the person, leaving him only with guardianship of the estate. Where an order for legal custody is made it may be varied or discharged. Such an order is a custody order for the purposes of the Family Law Act 1986.

1 In accordance with s 3 of GMA 1971, ante, para 4.13.
2 Apart from actual custody the other matter on which they are most likely to disagree is education, both religious and, less commonly, secular.
3 GMA 1971, s 7.
4 GMA 1971, s 11(a). There is no power under s 11(a) to make either an order committing the child to local authority care or a supervision order. Section 11 of FLRA 1987 prospectively substitutes a new s 10(2) for s 11(a) in GMA 1971 and adds s 10(3) to the latter Act which, when operative, will preclude an order for legal custody and access being made if the child is already the subject of a freeing for adoption order made under s 18 of the Adoption Act 1976.
5 Infra, paras 4.23 and 4.26.
6 The court may direct that the child is not to be taken out of the United Kingdom without its leave; see GMA 1971, s 13A(1), as amended by FLA 1986, s 35(1).

4.22 It has already been pointed out[1] that, where a guardian is appointed for a minor who has no parent, guardian of the person and no other person having parental rights, the court has no power to make an order for legal (and actual) custody. If the guardian wants the child to live with him, he has to enforce his guardianship by making the child a ward of court and seeking care and control or, which is less likely, by way of habeas corpus proceedings. If, however, the child is already living with him, the guardian is prima facie entitled to actual custody, and the onus is on any other person seeking it to proceed by way of wardship.

1 Ante, para 4.13.

(b) Access

4.23 If guardianship of the person is equivalent to legal custody, the logical conclusion from the definition of that concept and the meaning of parental rights and duties[1] is that a guardian has a right of access to the child. There is, however, no direct authority to support a right of access. Indeed, its existence has been denied,[2] on the ground that section 11(a)[3] of the Guardianship of Minors Act 1971, which can be invoked when there is a dispute between joint guardians, one of whom is a parent, refers only to a right of access of the parent and the power of the court to make an order with regard to it. There is no mention of a guardian having any right of access. The practical effect is not, however, serious because, if a guardian is denied access by a joint guardian, whether by a parent or other guardian, he can rely on section 7 of that Act which empowers the court to make such an order 'regarding the matters in difference' as it thinks proper.

In the case of a sole guardian who does not have actual custody and the person having it denies him access, the guardian's remedy lies in wardship and an order granting him access and that person care and control, unless the guardian himself seeks care and control.

A grandparent may apply for access where one or both of the child's parents are dead,[4] and his right to do so is not affected by the fact that a guardian has been appointed. It is anomalous that the 1971 Act directly gives a grandparent a right to apply but denies it to a sole guardian.

1 See respectively ss 86 and 85(1) of CA 1975; and see Law Com Working Paper No 91, para 2.28.
2 See Eekelaar, *What are Parental Rights?* (1973) 89 LQR 210 at 233.
3 Prospectively substituted by FLRA 1987 s 11 as s 10(2)(a) of GMA 1971.
4 GMA, s 14A(2).

(c) Protection

4.24 A guardian is under the same common law and statutory duties to protect the child from physical and moral harm as the parent. These duties are examined in Chapters 9 and 10. Under the Children and Young Persons Act 1933 various offences may be committed by a person having the 'custody, charge or care' of a juvenile under 16, and for that purpose a legal guardian (ie a guardian appointed by deed or will or by the court), like a parent, is presumed to have the custody of the juvenile.[1] One of those offences relates to various forms of cruelty, including wilful neglect of the juvenile in a manner likely to cause him unnecessary suffering or injury to health,[2] but the provision[3] that a parent or other person legally liable to maintain a juvenile is deemed to have neglected him if he fails to provide adequate food, clothing, medical aid or lodging for him does not apply to a guardian, since he is not legally liable to maintain the child.

1 CYPA 1933, s 17.
2 CYPA 1933, s 1(1).
3 CYPA 1933, s 1(2)(a). See further para 9.53.

(d) Maintenance

4.25 A guardian is under a duty to maintain the child out of the income of the latter's property,[1] but he is not obliged personally to do so. So, in the absence of a contract or an authority to incur a debt on his behalf, he is not liable to a third person for a debt incurred by the child. Unlike the mother or father, he is not liable for the child for the purposes of the Social Security Act 1986,[2] so that if benefit is given for the child it cannot be recovered from the guardian. Nor, unlike the mother or father, is he liable to contribute to the child's maintenance, should the child be in the care of a local authority.[3] The only possible personal liability is in proceedings based on his marriage having broken down and the child has become a child of the family.[4]

1   See post, para 4.38.
2   See s 26, as prospectively amended by FLRA 1987, s 2(1). The Law Commission (Law Com No 172, para 2.25) recommends retention of the rule excluding liability.
3   See CCA 1980, s 45, as amended by HASSASSAA 1983, ss 9, 19 (1) and (2) and Sch 2, para 54.
4   See Law Com, Working Paper No 91, para 2.29; Law Com No 172, para 2.25.

4.26   Where a person is a sole guardian to the exclusion of a surviving parent or where there is a dispute between joint guardians, one of whom is a parent, the court may order the parent to pay to the sole or joint guardian for the benefit of the child or to the child himself periodical payments and or a lump sum, which, if the court is a magistrates' court, must not exceed £1,000.[1] If the court is the High Court or a county court, any one or more of the following orders will also be available when the relevant provisions of the Family Law Reform Act 1987 come into force, namely, an order that the parent make secured periodical payments; an order transferring specified property of the parent to the guardian for the child's benefit or to the child himself; and an order settling specified property of the parent for the benefit of the child.[2]

If both parents are dead or one of them is dead but the other cannot be traced or is serving a prison sentence, a guardian may be entitled to claim a social security guardian's allowance.[3]

1   GMA 1971, ss 10(1)(b) and 11(b). Orders may be varied or discharged. The maximum for a lump sum payment was raised to £1,000 by the Capital Magistrate's Courts (Incorporation of Lump Sums) Order 1988, SI 1988/1069.
2   GMA 1971, s 11C as inserted by FLRA 1987, s 13.
3   Social Security Act 1975, s 38.

(e)   Discipline

4.27   A power incidental to actual custody is that which enables a guardian, like a parent, to exercise disciplinary control over the child. When the child reaches the age of mature discretion the power is almost as tenuous as that of the parent; for example, subject to his duty to see that the ward is protected from physical and moral harm, he cannot prevent the child from living where he chooses.[1] If he considers the child is at risk, he should seek the aid of the court by way of wardship. However, because of the fiduciary relationship he may, notwithstanding the *Gillick* principle, still exceptionally be under a *duty* to chastise and control in circumstances where a similar obligation would not be legally demanded of a parent; for example, where the child, in spite of his maturity, is dissipating his personal income.[2]

1   *Anon* (1751) 2 Ves Sen 374. A possible exception arises where the guardian has sent the child away to school; *Tremain's Case* (1719) 1 Stra 167.
2   *Kay v Johnston* (1856) 21 Beav 536.

(f)   Education

4.28   A guardian's obligations concerning the child's religious upbringing and his secular education are examined in Chapter 11.[1] In certain respects, because of the fiduciary relationship, they differ significantly from the corresponding parental obligations.

1   At paras 11.13 and 11.20 respectively.

(g)   Medical treatment

4.29   There is no common law or statutory rule to suggest that the powers of the guardian with regard to giving or withholding consent to medical treatment for the child are different from those of the parent, which have already been considered.[1]

1   Ante, para 1.26.

(h)   Change of surname

4.30   As already indicated,[1] it would seem that on the death of one parent the survivor, being the only person in whom the right then vests, may change the child's surname; but, where there is a guardian acting jointly with the surviving parent, his consent would seem in principle to be required by analogy with the rule that where both natural guardians are alive both must consent. Whether a sole guardian or joint guardians can ever change the child's name is an open question. It is submitted that where both parents are dead a guardian or guardians have the right to do so. Supposing, for example, that both parents of a very young child are killed in an accident and the maternal grandparents are appointed testamentary guardians. It is more likely than not that the child's best interests would be served by being brought up in the grandparent's name.[2] Unfortunately, the Guardianship of Minors Act 1971 does not provide a procedure to enable a testamentary guardian or one appointed by the court to apply to the court under that Act for a direction on the matter without having to involve the inherent jurisdiction and (probably) make the child a ward of court. Only where there are joint guardians and they are in dispute over the name can an application be made under that Act[3] for an order.

1   Ante, para 1.45.
2   Quaere whether it would make any difference if the parents in their wills had expressly directed that the child should be brought up in that name.
3   Ie, under s 7, ante, para 4.21.

(i)   Emigration

4.31   Section 86 of the Children Act 1975 makes clear the position of the guardian. It provides that 'a person shall not by virtue of having legal custody be entitled to effect or arrange for [the child's] emigration from the United Kingdom unless he is a parent or guardian'.[1]

1   Guardian means a testamentary guardian or one appointed by a court; CA 1975, s 107(1).

(j)   Consent to marriage

4.32   A guardian's consent is a prerequisite to the marriage of his ward who is under 18, and, in accordance with his fiduciary obligations, he is under a duty to prevent the child from entering into a marriage which is unsuitable on the ground of age, fortune or rank, although in practice fortune and rank will rarely be relevant factors. If he gives consent, the court may intervene and prevent the marriage on the application of anyone opposed to it.[1] This may be done without making the minor a ward of court, but it is desirable to take that further step because, if the marriage does take place, the court is able to invoke its powers of contempt against those involved in bringing it about.

1   *Lord Gordon v Lady Irwin* (1781) 4 Bro Parl Cas 355, HL; *Wellesley v Duke of Beaufort* (1827) 2 Russ 1 at 28–29.

4.33   The rules governing consent are complicated. They turn mainly upon whether one or both parents are dead and whether or not they were married to each other at the time of the child's birth. They are set out in Schedule 2 to the Marriage Act 1949.[1]

(a) Where the parents were married to each other at the time of the child's birth. If one parent is dead but has appointed a testamentary guardian, the consents of the surviving parent and of the guardian are both necessary if they are acting jointly; if one of them is acting as sole guardian, only his consent is required. Where both parents are dead, the guardians or guardian, whether they are testamentary or appointed by the court under section 3 or section 5 of GMA 1971, must give their (or his) consent. A notable but apparently unintended omission is the guardian appointed in place of a guardian removed under section 6 of the 1971 Act.[2]

(b) Where the parents were not married to each other at the time of the child's birth. Here an additional factor is whether or not the father qualifies as a guardian. As already noted (ante, para 4.10) under the present law he does if he has legal custody by virtue of an order made under section 9 of GMA 1971. When the amendments by the Family Law Reform Act 1987 come into force, he will qualify if he has either all the parental rights and duties by virtue of an order under section 4 of the Family Law Reform Act 1987 or has a right to custody, legal or actual custody or care and control by virtue of an order under any other enactment.[3] If he is a guardian, the above rules will correspondingly operate.[4] Where, however, he does not qualify as a guardian and the mother predeceases him he has no locus standi, and the person whose consent will be required is any testamentary guardian appointed by her or any guardian appointed by the court.

1   As amended by GMA 1971, s 18(1) and Sch 1, and FLRA 1987, Sch 2, para 11 and, prospectively s 9.
2   Nor does the Schedule cover the very rare case of a guardian appointed under the inherent jurisdiction.
3   See ante, para 4.10.
4   But the rules prospectively introduced by FLRA 1987 have created an anomaly. They are wider in the case of parents not married to each other at the time of the child's birth, because they refer to appointments made 'under the Guardianship of Minors Act 1971' and not only to appointments made 'under section 3 or 5' of that Act. Thus, they extend to a guardian who replaces one removed under s 6 of the 1971 Act (cf supra). Moreover, unlike the rules governing parents who were married to each other at the time of the child's birth, the 1987 amendments make it clear that they extend to a guardian whom the *court* appoints to act jointly with the surviving parent (under s 3(2) of the 1971 Act) and not only to a testamentary guardian. The precise terms of the Schedule to the Marriage Act 1949, as amended, call for careful scrutiny.
    See generally on consent Law Com No 172, paras 7.5–7.11.

(k)   Agreement to adoption

4.34   Like a parent a guardian must agree to the adoption of his ward unless the court dispenses with it on one of the statutory grounds.[1]

1   AA 1976, s 16; see post, para 5.21.

(l)   Appointment of testamentary guardian

4.35   Although there are cogent arguments for allowing a guardian power to appoint a testamentary guardian,[1] the widely accepted conclusion is that the Guardianship of Minors Act 1971[2] does not confer the power, since it refers only to the mother and father of the child; but, as already noted,[3] there is authority for the view that a parent in appointing joint testamentary guardians may empower the surviving parent to nominate a successor to the one who dies.[4]

1   Ante, para 1.63, and see Law Com Working Paper No 91, para 3.74.
2   Section 4.
3   Ante, para 4.07.
4   *Re Parnell's Goods* (1872) LR 2 P & D 379.

(m)   Right to represent child in legal proceedings

4.36   Although a parent is prima facie entitled to act as 'next friend' or 'guardian ad litem' of a child in legal proceedings,[1] a court will, it is submitted, readily accept a guardian as a suitable person, especially where both parents are dead or incapable or unsuitable. The position of a person who is a 'guardian' for the purposes of the Children and Young Persons legislation will be considered later,[2] as will the special use of the guardian ad litem.

1   RSC Ord 80, r 2(1). *Woolf v Pemberton* (1877) 6 Ch D 19, ante, para 1.55.
2   See Chapters 9 and 14.

(n)   Complaints relating to section 3 of the Child Care Act 1980

4.37   Like a parent, a guardian has the right to object to a resolution passed in respect of him which vests the parental rights and duties in a local authority.[1]

1   CCA 1980, s 5(4), post, para 15.45.

3   Guardianship of the estate

4.38   Mention has already been made of the assimilation of the old forms of guardianship into the law of trusts.[1] The property of a ward will be vested in trustees with the usual powers of applying income for maintenance, and capital for the advancement, of the child.[2] Unless the High Court has appointed a person to be guardian of the minor's estate alone,[3] a guardian of the person has all the rights, powers and duties of a guardian of the estate, including in particular the right to receive and recover in his own name for the benefit of the ward any property to which the ward is entitled.[4] Thus, subject to the rights and powers of statutory owners, personal representatives and trustees for sale, the guardian has the right to recover rents and profits from the ward's land; receive the income from the ward's estate; receive a legacy due to the ward;[5] recover any payments due from a parent where an order against the parent has been made under sections 10(b)1 or 11(b) of the Guardianship of Minors Act 1971.[6] Any property he receives must be administered in accordance with his duties as one in the position of a trustee. The fiduciary relationship between him and the ward is important in two respects.

1   Ante, para 4.01.
2   Either under express powers conferred by the settlement or powers under the Trustee Act 1925, ss 31 and 32. The High Court may also order income and capital.
3   GA 1973, s 7(2). For example, the Official Solicitor is sometimes appointed guardian where the child has received money from a particular source, such as an award of compensation for criminal injuries or from an insurance policy. See Law Com Working Paper No 91, para 2.23 note 95. Another circumstance where guardianship of the estate might be appropriate is where the child has an interest in property administered abroad.
4   Section 7(1).
5   Apparently he may validly give a receipt for it *M'Creight v M'Creight* (1849) 13 I Eq R 314, whereas a parent can not *Dalgley v Tolferry* (1715), P Wms 285; *Re Somech* [1957] Ch 165, [1956] 3 All ER 523; *Vestey v IRC* [1979] Ch 177 at 196.
6   These provisions are prospectively replaced by s 11C of GMA 1971, as inserted by FLRA 1987, s 13. See ante, para 4.26.

4.39   Firstly, any transaction between them which benefits the guardian comes under the closest scrutiny.[1] Indeed, the presumption is that the transaction was the result of his having improperly influenced the ward into entering into it and the onus on him to rebut is heavy. If he fails to do so, he must restore any property received (for example, by gift) to the ward who, if necessary, can recover it from any third person other than a bona fide purchaser for value without notice of the original transaction. The presumption of undue influence continues to apply even if the transaction is entered into some time after the ward comes of age, because there is the obvious risk of his still being under the guardian's influence.[2] The likelihood of continued influence and the period for which it lasts will largely depend on the nature of the past relationship between them[3] and on whether 'the reduction of the age of majority to 18 implies greater maturity and judgment on the part of a person over that age' so that the court will 'give correspondingly less weight to the presumption'.[4] As a general proposition the answer, it is submitted, must be 'yes', but the reduction makes it all the more essential that the court thoroughly investigates the particular relationship and carefully assesses the maturity of the particular ward.

1   See especially Lord Brougham LC in *Hunter v Atkins* (1834) 3 My & K 113 at 135.
2   *Hylton v Hylton* (1754) 2 Ves Sen 547 (attempt by guardian to obtain annuity out of the ward's estate at the time when he was rendering an account). For other illustrations see *Maitland v Irving* (1846) 15 Sim 437 and *Maitland v Backhouse* (1848) 16 Sim 58. Compare the operation of the presumption in the parent-child relationship after the child attains majority; *Bainbrigge v Browne* (1881) 18 Ch D 188; *Lancashire Loans Ltd v Black* [1934] 1 KB 380, CA.
3   *Hatch v Hatch* (1804) 9 Ves 292.
4   Bromley, op cit, p 581, note 18.

4.40   Secondly, when the guardianship comes to an end, the guardian must account to the ward for all the property that has come into his hands and lapse of time does not in itself bar the ward from demanding an account.[1] If, at the ward's request, the guardian continues to manage the ward's property after the latter has come of age and before the accounts for the period of the ward's minority have been settled, he must account on the same principle as if the later transactions had taken place during the minority.[2] An account may always be re-opened on the ground that it contains errors, whether fraudulent or not,[3] or that the ward was not independently advised.[4]

1   *Mathew v Brise* (1851) 14 Beav 341.
2   *Mellish v Mellish* (1823) 1 Sim & St 138.
3   *Allfrey v Allfrey* (1849) 1 Mac & G 87.
4   *Revett v Harvey* (1823) 1 Sim & St 502.

IV   TERMINATION OF GUARDIANSHIP

4.41   Unless the appointment is expressly limited to a shorter period or until the happening of some earlier event, a guardianship must come to an end when the ward attains majority. But apart from these temporal or conditional limitations it will be terminated in any of the following circumstances.

1   Resignation of the guardian

4.42   A testamentary guardian is entitled to refuse the appointment,[1] but neither he nor a guardian appointed by the court can resign the office once he has accepted it,[2] except with the leave of the court. That is likely to be granted, because it is not in the ward's interests to have an unwilling guardian.[3]

1   *Ex p Champney* (1762) 1 Dick 350; GMA 1971, s 3; *O'Keefe v Casey* (1803) 1 Sch & Lef 106.
2   *Spencer v Earl of Chesterfield* (1752) Amb 146.
3   Bromley, op cit, p 361.

2   Removal of the guardian by the court

4.43   Apart from its inherent jurisdiction to remove (as to appoint) guardians,[1] which is rarely invoked, the High Court has statutory power to remove a guardian and may, but need not, appoint another in his place, if it considers that the child's welfare demands this action.[2] The sole criterion, it is submitted, is his welfare,[3] and on this basis there should be no difference between a testamentary guardian and one appointed by the court. Thus, the rule that a testamentary guardian should not be removed solely on the ground that he is resident abroad[4] should also apply to a court appointed guardian.[5] The most likely ground for removal is misconduct or the likelihood of misconduct,[6] which is prejudicial to the child's interests. This may take a variety of forms, including a breach of an undertaking, for example, to see that the child continues to be brought up in his religion.[7] But the court's jurisdiction is not limited to cases of misconduct. It may also act where the guardian is otherwise unfit to hold office, for example, because of mental ill-health or even where there is neither misconduct nor unfitness but the circumstances warrant removal so as to ensure the child's welfare, as in *F v F*[8] where by changing her own religion the guardian deprived an eleven-year-old child of the guidance and advice of the religious faith in which the latter had always been brought up.[9]

1 See further Law Com Working Paper No 91, para 2.19.
2 GMA 1971, s 6. See also s 17(1) and CA 1975, s 104. There is no power to transfer proceedings to a county court under the Matrimonial and Family Proceedings Act 1984, since transfer is only permitted in respect of family proceedings which are within the jurisdiction of both that court and the High Court (s 38(2)(a)).
3 For the wide meaning to be given to welfare see *Re McGrath* [1893] 1 Ch 143 at 148.
4 *Re Two Infant Children, ex p Nickells* (1891) 7 TLR 498.
5 That might happen where the guardian has gone abroad after appointment; but a court is unlikely to appoint one already resident abroad.
6 *Re X, X v Y* [1899] 1 Ch 526 at 531.
7 *Re Savini, Savini v Lousada* (1870) 22 LT 61, 18 WR 425.
8 [1902] 1 Ch 688.
9 But the fact that the religions of guardian and child are different does not in itself justify removal, although the court may choose to appoint a joint guardian; see *Re Read (an infant)* (1889) 5 TLR 615.

4.44 One of the powers of a court where there is disagreement between joint guardians[1] is to remove one of them if the child's interests so require.[2] There are also powers to remove outside the Guardianship of Minors Act 1971. Note has already been made of the power of a court to remove a male guardian whom it has convicted of incest with the ward[3] and of the power of a divorce court to declare a parent unfit to have the custody of the children of the family with the consequence that on the death of the other parent, the survivor is not entitled as of right to the custody or guardianship of the children.[4]

1 Ante, para 4.43.
2 *Duke of Beaufort v Berty* (1721) 1 P Wms 703.
3 See further post, para 10.18.
4 Ante, para 3.61.

3 Marriage of the ward

4.45 The effect of the ward's marriage on the guardianship is wholly uncertain. The answer depends upon how much reliance is placed on old cases dealing with guardianship and with the parental right to custody. There are three main views.

The first is that a distinction is to be drawn between a male ward and a female ward. The marriage of the former does not affect the guardianship whereas in the corresponding case the guardianship is brought to an end. Reliance for this conclusion is placed upon dicta of Lord Hardwicke, LC, in *Mendes v Mendes*.[1]

Both the other views reject the distinction, but they lead to diametrically opposed conclusions. There is judicial support for the argument that marriage terminates the guardianship of a male as it does that of a female ward. Thus, there is the following observation of Abbott CJ in *R v Wilmington Inhabitants*[2] which by its terms deals with the effect of a son's marriage:

'during the minority of a child there can be no emancipation unless he marries and so becomes himself the head of a family, or contracts some other relation so as wholly and permanently to exclude the parental control.'

Admittedly, that case was concerned with the question whether a child was still a member of a family for the purpose of a poor law settlement and did not directly deal with parental right to custody or guardianship.

That comment, however, equally applies to *R v Rotherfield Greys Inhabitants*,[3] at least so far as concerns custody, yet, the latter is often cited in favour of the proposition that parental right to custody is suspended so long as a minor is serving with the armed forces of the Crown. Apart from these dicta, strong persuasive support that the marriage of a minor terminates the right to custody is to be derived from the Marriage Act 1949 in that its rules requiring the consent of a parent or guardian or custodian to the marriage do not apply to one who, being a widower or widow, wishes to remarry during minority. There is, therefore, much to be said for the opinion that marriage ends the right to custody and, given that custody is the source of all other parental rights,[4] it can be argued that marriage equally ends the parent's guardianship. On that basis it might further be contended that no distinction is to be drawn between the natural guardian and a testamentary guardian or one appointed by the court.

On the other hand, it has been pointed out[5] that there is nothing in the Guardianship of Minors Act 1971, anymore than there was in the Tenures Abolition Act 1660, stating that guardianship is to end on the marriage of a ward. Nor, significantly, does wardship of court cease on that event.

1   (1748) 1 Ves Sen 89 at 91.
2   (1822) 5 B & Ald 525 at 526; see also *Lough v Ward* [1945] 2 All ER 338 at 348.
3   (1823) 1 B & C 345.
4   See ante, para 1.58.
5   Bromley, op cit, p 360.

4   Death

4.46   Obviously, the death of the ward terminates the guardianship. So does the death of a sole guardian, but where there are joint guardians the rights and duties vest in the survivor(s).[1]

1   See CA 1975, s 85(4). Under the former law the doctrine of survivorship applied to testamentary guardians (*Eyre v Shaftesbury* (1725) 2 P Wms 103) but not to joint guardians appointed by the court (*Bradshaw v Bradshaw* (1826) 1 Russ 528), where the death of one ended the guardianship of all of them.

CHAPTER 5
Adoption[1]

I INTRODUCTION—NATURE AND USES

5.01 In its first report, which led to adoption being introduced into English law in 1926, the Tomlin Committee defined it as 'a legal method of creating between a child and one who is not the natural parent[2] of the child an artificial family relationship analogous to that of parent and child'.[3] The legal method is a court order, and its effect is to sever irrevocably[4] and for almost all purposes[5] the legal relationship between the natural parents and the child and to transfer all the parental powers and responsibilities to the adopters.

1 For general reference see Bromley, Chapter 12; Cretney, Chapter 18; Hoggett, Chapter 11; Hoggett and Pearl, Chapter 15; Josling and Levy, *Adoption of Children* (10th edn); the Report of the Houghton Committee (1972) Cmnd 5701.
   See also *Child Adoption* (Association of British Adoption and Fostering Agencies (ABAFA) 1979); *Adoption: Essays in Social Policy, Law and Sociology* (ed Bean). The reader is also referred to the Adoption and Fostering Journal published by ABAFA.
2 The term 'birth parent' seems to be currently in vogue.
3 (1925) Cmnd 2401, p 3.
4 But see post, para 5.113.
5 See post, para 5.112.

5.02 A distinctive feature of its comparatively short history is the continuing change of emphasis in the social purposes which legal adoption has been made to serve;[1] but throughout that period one of the principal beneficiaries has been the illegitimate child. At first, in mediaeval England his needs were largely met by a society which, reacting against contemporary notions of marriage, showed a kindly tolerance towards illegitimacy.[2] Since marriage was so often a family arrangement and not the result of affection between the parties, breakdown was frequent, and, with no remedy of divorce available,[3] the stable illicit union was widely accepted. Moreover, even when the parents of the adulterine child did not cohabit, there was a marked readiness of members of the mother's family to assume responsibility. However, a change in moral and social attitudes by the time of the Puritan era, with a consequent stigma now attaching to illegitimacy, led to parental rejection of the child. Stable unions were less common, and the mother, finding herself abandoned by the father and her own family, was often driven to submitting to the severity of the Poor Law. A similar hardship was usually suffered by the orphan and the abandoned legitimate child. Deprived of the care which the mediaeval church had shown for the needy, they too, were compelled to put themselves upon the parish, unless they were one of the few more fortunate who became wards of court or found sympathetic foster parents. During the second half of the nineteenth century fostering became more common, being sometimes arranged by the voluntary

societies then coming into being. It is remarkable that these de facto
adoptions were so popular as they were. However much affection and
material benefit the foster parents bestowed upon the child, the arrangement
was liable at any time to be upset by the natural parent asserting his common
law rights[4] and claiming back the child, without any regard for the child's
welfare or the interests of the foster parents.[5] The readiness of persons
to come forward as de facto adopters of many orphans and illegitimate
children both before and after World War I, notwithstanding the legal
risks involved, stirred the public conscience[6] into setting up Committees
in 1921 and 1925 whose Reports[7] culminated in the Adoption of Children
Act 1926. The object of the Act was, therefore, to provide for the child
and the adopters the security of a permanent relationship.[8]

1 The recognition of de facto adoptions for certain purposes must also not be overlooked;
   for example, so as to allow entry into the UK under the Immigration Rules (*R v Immigration
   Appeal Tribunal, ex p Tohur Ali* (1987) Times, 9 January, CA) or to enable a person
   to claim succession to a statutory tenancy under the Rent Acts (*Brock v Wollams* [1949]
   2 KB 388, [1949] 1 All ER 715, CA; cf *Sefton Holdings Ltd v Cairns* [1988] Fam Law
   164, [1988] 14 EG 58, CA).
2 See Ellison, *Adoption and the Deprived Child in History*, p 13 et seq.
3 But the use of the nullity decree must not be ignored.
4 The common law did not allow either parent of the legitimate child (*Brooks v Blount*
   [1923] 1 KB 257) or the mother of the illegitimate child (*Humphrys v Polak* [1901] 2
   KB 385) permanently to divest himself or herself of parental powers and responsibilities
   by voluntary agreement.
5 But, if the parent was forced to take proceedings to recover the child, the High Court
   had to refuse his application if he had abandoned or deserted the child or allowed him
   to be brought up by another person at that other's expense for such a length of time
   and under such circumstances that the parent was unmindful of his parental duties, unless
   the parent satisfied the court that, having regard to the child's welfare, he was a fit person
   to have custody; see s 3 of the Custody of Children Act 1891.
6 There are other factors which contributed to this pressure for reform; see Cretney, p 420.
7 Cmnd 1254, 2401 and 2469. The first of these (the 'Hopkinson Report') is the most instructive
   and positive in recommending reform.
8 Its immediate impact is seen in the fact that there were almost 3,000 entries in the Adopted
   Children Register for 1927.

5.03   With that purpose fulfilled, the shift of emphasis was towards the
dual function of providing a stable home for the unwanted child, especially
the illegitimate child, of the 'depression' years of the late 1920s and 1930s
and of meeting the needs of the childless couple. The resultant emergence
of adoption societies led to their compulsory registration and regulation.[1]
At the outbreak of World War II adoption was, therefore, still very largely
as the Tomlin Committee had seen it in 1925, namely, as an artificial transfer
of legal parentage.

Important changes were made by the Adoption of Children Act 1949,
particularly with regard to citizenship and to rights of succession,[2] and,
although the law was consolidated in 1950, within a few years a further
Departmental Committee was set up[3] to review the whole field of legal
adoption and to recommend any changes of policy and procedure thought
desirable *in the interest and welfare of children*. Many of its proposals found
their way into the consolidating Adoption Act 1958, much of which, together
with amending legislation,[4] survived for 30 years. It was this period of
the 1950s that marked the beginning of the use of adoption by the natural
parent.[5] Initially, this new feature related to the mother of the illegitimate
child who saw adoption of her own child as a means of escaping the social

stigma of illegitimacy and of improving the legal relationship between them.[6] However, it was the high incidence of divorce in the 1950s and 1960s, of remarriage and subsequent adoption by the natural parent and step-parent that largely explained the substantial increase in natural parent adoptions. Indeed, by the time of the Children Act 1975 over half of the total number of annual adoptions were joint adoptions by parent and step-parent.

1 Through the Adoption of Children (Regulation) Act 1939. The enactment was the result of an adverse report by the Horsburgh Committee (Cmnd 5499) which drew attention to the number of bad placements due to lack of skilled inquiries undertaken by some societies. The Act also dealt with the supervision by welfare authorities of certain adopted children, prohibited payments and advertisements in respect of adoptions and restricted the sending of children abroad. All these matters were incorporated into later changes in the law.
2 This delay in recognising the proprietary effects of adoption contrasts sharply with the emphasis placed on them by civil law systems.
3 For its Report in 1954 see Cmnd 9248.
4 By Acts of 1960, 1964 and 1968.
5 The right of the natural parent to seek adoption of his or her own child was first unequivocally affirmed by the Adoption of Children Act 1949, s 1(1) in a declaration that the power to make an adoption order under the Adoption of Children Act 1926 'includes and has always included power to make an adoption order authorising the adoption of an infant by the mother or father of the infant, either alone or jontly with her or his spouse'. There is, however, no evidence that it was so used under the earlier Act.
6 See Lord Denning in *Re D (an infant)* [1959] 1 QB 229, [1958] 3 All ER 716, CA.

5.04 The legislative response, through that Act, though to some extent obscure and clouded by varying judicial interpretation,[1] has resulted in a sharp decline in the number of those adoptions.[2] The other major factor which has caused a dramatic reduction in the total number of annual adoptions[3] has been the steep drop in the number of adoptions of children under one year old. This factor relates particularly to the reduced number of babies of unmarried parents available for adoption,[4] a reduction partly explained by increased use of contraception and abortion, but also, as has been pointed out,[5] because more unmarried mothers are keeping their babies, especially where mother and father are living together in a stable union. On the other hand, in 1980 there was a sudden rise in the number of adoptions of children aged five or over and, though the number of children in the total population who are adopted will continue, mainly for demographic reasons, to fall, the number adopted at older ages is likely to show a modest growth.[6] This proportionate increase is largely explained by an increase in the number of children in local authority care who are placed for adoption, including handicapped and coloured children,[7] and by a greater willingness for local authorities to proceed with adoption even where there is parental opposition to it.[8] The introduction of custodianship as an alternative to adoption[9] has not had any appreciable effect on this sustained and publicised[10] policy of local authorities to rely on adoption.

1 See post, para 5.59.
2 From a figure of 10,256 for 1970 to 4,409 for 1984.
3 From a peak figure of 24,831 in 1968 to 7,892 in 1986.
4 Of the total number of adoptions in 1968 60% were non-parent adoptions of illegitimate children. By 1977 the percentage of such adoptions was down to 32; see Leete, *Adoption Trends and Illegitimate Births 1951–1977* in *Population Trends*, Vol 14 (OPCS 1978).
5 Bromley, p 381; see also the 'Warnock' Report (1984) Cmnd 9314, para 2.1.

6 See Howe, *Adoption Trends and Counter Trends* 11 Adoption and Fostering, No 1, 44. Of the total number adopted in 1986 27% were aged 10–17 compared with 21% in 1976.
7 There is a growing body of literature on the difficult problems relating to the fostering and adoption of coloured children. See, for example, Gill and Jackson, *Adoption and Race: Black, Asian and Mixed Race Children in White Families* (Batsford/BAAF 1983); Rowe, Cain, Hundleby and Keane, *Long Term Foster Care* (Batsford/BAAF 1984); Prescod, *The Task for White Professionals* 11 Adoption and Fostering, No 3 p 7; Richards, *Family, Race and Identity*, ibid at p 10; Hayes, *Placing Black Children*, ibid at p 14; *Placed in a White Family–Views of Young Black Children*, Childright No 22 pp 7–10.
8 See House of Commons' Second Report on the Children Act 1975 (HMSO, 1984).
9 For custodianship see post, Chapter 6.
10 See Bromley, p 382, referring particularly to the scheme 'Be My Parent' organised by the British Agencies of Adoption and Fostering.

5.05   The question of step-parent adoptions was but one of several matters for which, as a direct result of the Houghton Committee's review of adoption,[1] Part I of the Children Act 1975 provided major changes. The Adoption Act 1976 consolidated Part I and the provisions in the Adoption Acts 1958, 1960, 1964 and 1968. Yet, the implementation of the 1976 Act was postponed for some 12 years until 1 January 1988, an unenviable record for consolidating legislation, explained but hardly justified on the ground that all the provisions of the Children Act were first to be brought into force.[2] In the event postponement inevitably meant numerous amendments to the 1976 Act, so that by the time of its commencement its value as a consolidating measure had already been undermined.

1   For comments generally on the Committee's Report ((1972) Cmnd 5107) see Davies 36 MLR 245 and Samuels, ibid, at p 278.
2   For organisational and financial reasons there was delay in implementing much of the Children Act, notably its freeing for adoption and its custodianship provisions.

II   THE ADOPTION SERVICE

5.06   Section 1 of the Adoption Act 1976 requires every local authority[1] to maintain a service to meet the needs of children who have been or may be adopted, their parents and guardians[2] and prospective or actual adopters. To discharge this general duty the authority must either themselves provide the requisite facilities or ensure that they are provided by adoption societies approved in accordance with the Act.[3] Collectively, these local adoption services provide a national service, known as the Adoption Service.[4]
The Act does not explicitly define the scope of a local adoption service, but potentially it can be very wide, since it must not only be available for those who may adopt, for example foster parents, but also remain available after an adoption order has been made. Indeed, it is expressly enacted[5] that one of the facilities to be provided as part of the service is counselling for persons with problems relating to adoption. This will include those refused an adoption order. An adoptive parent may also wish to avail himself of this facility in the immediate post-adoption period, if problems over the upbringing of the child should arise. However, apart from counselling,[6] the only other facilities expressly mentioned which must be provided as part of the service are:

(a) temporary board and lodging where needed by pregnant women, mothers or children;[7]

(b) arrangements for assessing children and prospective adopters and placing children for adoption.[8]

The Act gives no indication of other facilities which are to be regarded as requisite for a service. Nor does it enable the Secretary of State to make regulations which will ensure fulfilment of the general duty and the fixing of a minimum national standard. Much depends on the influence which may be exerted by Departmental Circulars and guidance offered to local authorities.[9] With the severe financial restrictions imposed on local authority spending, financing the adoption service is not likely to secure high priority.

1   The appropriate local authorities are the council of a county (other than a metropolitan county), a metropolitan district, a London borough or the Common Council of the City of London (AA 1976, s 72(1)).
2   For the meaning of 'guardian' see post, para 5.22.
3   See infra, paras 5.08–5.11.
4   AA 1976, s 1(4).
5   Ibid, s 1(2).
6   For counselling where an adopted person seeks a copy of his birth certificate see post, para 5.99.
7   This provision is obviously discriminatory in that it ignores the plight of a motherless family.
8   AA 1976, s 1(2).
9   A helpful draft DHSS Circular was published for discussion during 1987, but an approved Circular has yet to appear.

5.07 A keynote of s 1 is the importance it attaches to co-operation.[1] It is essential for an effective adoption service not only that there should develop a partnership between local authorities and approved adoption societies but also that close links are maintained with departments of local and central government. Section 1 requires that the facilities of the service be provided in conjunction with the local authority's other social services and with the adoption societies in its area, so that help may be given in a co-ordinated manner, without duplication, omission or avoidable delay. Section 2 defines 'other social services' as those functions which are referred to the local authority's social services committee. These include, for example, support for homeless persons, but the section spells out particularly those relating to:

(a) the promotion of the welfare of children by diminishing the need to receive children into care or keep them in care, including (in exceptional circumstances) the giving of assistance in cash;
(b) the welfare of children in the care of a local authority;
(c) the welfare of children who are privately fostered within the meaning of the Foster Children Act 1980;
(d) children who are subject to supervision orders made in matrimonial proceedings;
(e) the provision of residential accommodation for expectant mothers and young children and of day-care facilities;
(f) the regulation and inspection of nurseries and childminders;
(g) care and other treatment of children through court proceedings.

By particularising in this way the AA 1976 stresses that adoption should be seen in the context of a comprehensive child care service which itself should ensure that wherever possible children do not come into the care of local authorities unless it is in their interests to do so.

1 A point also emphasised in the First Report to Parliament on the Children Act 1975 (HC 268, 1979), paras 11–13, and particularly relevant to the placement for adoption of children with special needs.

Approval of adoption societies

5.08 Approval of adoption societies resides in the Secretary of State,[1] who, in deciding whether or not to approve a particular body,[2] has to take into account a number of specified matters in addition to any other relevant consideration. These are:

(a) the society's adoption programme, including in particular its ability to make provision for children who are free for adoption;[3]
(b) the number and qualifications of its staff;
(c) its financial resources; and
(d) the organisation and control of its operations.[4]

All these matters will be equally relevant whenever an approved society seeks further approval, and the Secretary of State will also have to pay regard, in first application and on renewal, to the society's record and reputation in the adoption field and the areas within which it is operating or has operated.[5] Moreover, where the society is likely to operate extensively within the area of a particular local authority, that authority must be asked by the Secretary of State whether or not it supports the application.[6] This requirement recognises that the authority will have a far clearer appreciation of the needs and resources of its own area than will the Secretary of State.

1 AA 1976, s 3(1).
2 The body must be a voluntary organisation; see HASSASSAA 1983, Sch 2, para 22. An unincorporated body is not eligible to apply under s 3; Adoption Agencies Regulations 1983, SI 1983/1964 reg 2(2). An application for approval must be in writing on a form supplied by the Secretary of State; see reg 2(1).
3 On freeing for adoption see post paras 5.32 et seq.
4 AA 1976, s 3(3).
5 Ibid, s 3(5).
6 Ibid, s 3(4).

5.09 If the application is approved, written notice to that effect will be served on the society;[1] but, if the Secretary of State is not satisfied that the society is making, or is likely to make, an effective contribution to the Adoption Service, he must give it written notice that he intends to refuse approval, setting out his reasons therefor and informing it of its right to make written representations to him within 28 days. He must then take into account any such representations before reaching his final decision.[2]

1 AA 1976, s 3(2). Approval is effective from the date specified in the notice or, in the case of a renewal, from the date of the notice.
2 Ibid, ss 3(6), 5(1), (2).

5.10 Continuing central control is ensured by the rule that, unless withdrawn earlier, approval is for a period of three years, when fresh approval has to be sought.[1] Approval can be withdrawn at any time if it appears to the Secretary of State that the society is not making an effective contribution to the Adoption Service, or if it fails to provide him with, or to verify, the information necessary to determine whether or not it is making the requisite contribution.[2] The rules governing the giving of notice of refusal of approval apply *mutatis mutandis* to notices of withdrawal of approval.[3] The most important practical problem created by withdrawal will be the question of the welfare of the children who are in the society's care. The Sectretary of State may, but is not obliged to, direct the society to make such arrangements concerning the children and such other transitional matters as seem to him expedient.[4]

1 AA 1976 s 3(7). See also the duty of every approved society to provide the Secretary of State with information in accordance with AA 1976, s 58A.
2 AA 1976, s 4(1) and (2). There is also a general duty imposed on every approved adoption society to provide the Secretary of State with two copies of its annual report and also with such information as he may from time to time require; see Adoption Agencies Regulations 1983, reg 3(a).
3 AA 1976, ss 4(1) and 5(3)–(5).
4 Ibid, s 4(3).

5.11 Section 8 of the AA 1976 gives powers to the Secretary of State in respect of any child in the care of an adoption society which appears to be inactive or defunct, and the powers are available whether or not approval has been withdrawn from the society. He may direct the appropriate local authority to take any action which the society could have taken, whether it had been acting alone or with the local authority.[1] Thus, the authority could apply to a court for an order freeing the child for adoption, thereby vesting the parental rights and duties in the authority, or, where the rights and duties were already vested in the society by virtue of a 'freeing' order, the authority could apply to the court for them to be transferred to it.[2] Before directing the local authority the Secretary of State must consult both it and the society.[3] He is under a duty to do no more than consult and, unlike a case of refusal to approve or a withdrawal of approval, the society does not have the right to make representations to him. The justification for this rule is that the power under s 8 is for emergency situations where the need to make new arrangements for the children's care is urgent. If the need is so urgent that, even to consult the society and authority would be prejudicial to the children's welfare, the Secretary of State, on the ground of impracticability, need not do so.

When is a society inactive or defunct? A defunct society is presumably one which has ceased to exist and an inactive society one which still exists but ceases to operate. The Adoption Agencies Regulations 1983 help to answer the question by the requirement that a society which proposes or expects to cease to act as an adoption society must give the Secretary of State notice to that effect and must inform him when it has ceased so to act.[4]

There is no right of appeal against a refusal to approve or a withdrawal of approval under sections 4 to 6 or against a direction under section 7. The only means of redress will be to seek judicial review by way of mandamus or certiorari.

1 AA 1976, s 8(1).
2 On freeing for adoption see post, paras 5.32 et seq.

3   AA 1976, s 8(2).
4   Adoption Agencies Regulations 1983, reg 3(c) and (d).

III   THE WELFARE OF THE CHILD

5.12   One of the inadequacies of the law prior to the Children Act 1975 was its failure to provide clear guidance on the weight to be given to the child's welfare when reaching decisions which might ultimately lead to his adoption.[1] Section 6 of the AA 1976, which re-enacts section 3 of the 1975 Act, provides:

> 'In reaching any decision relating to the adoption of a child a court or adoption agency shall have regard to all the circumstances, first consideration being given to the need to safeguard and promote the welfare of the child throughout his childhood; and shall so far as practicable ascertain the wishes and feelings of the child regarding the decision and give due consideration to them, having regard to his age and understanding.'

So, the child's welfare is not paramount, as it is in custody, custodianship, guardianship and wardship proceedings. The essential reason for rejection of the paramountcy test is that an adoption order means the irrevocable severance of the tie between the child and the natural parent, and its finality therefore justifies special weight being given to the interests of the natural parent.[2] It has been argued[3] that the rejection of the paramountcy test 'was based upon misconceived Parliamentary reasoning [when the present rule was being enacted in the Children Bill] and upon an excessive significance attributed to the case law governing the dispensation of parental consent where it is being unreasonably withheld'. As will be seen,[4] the irony is that Parliament, having relied on that case law for enacting the present rule, the courts have held that the rule does not govern the question whether a parent has unreasonably withheld his or her agreement.

In *Re W (a minor) (adoption)*[5] Cumming Bruce LJ saw the distinction between 'first' and 'first and paramount' as 'manifestly an extremely fine distinction'. There can hardly be a sounder reason advanced for rejecting the rule in section 6. If the distinction is to have some reality of meaning, the approach must be in the terms of Lord MacDermott's analysis in *J v C*,[6] as elaborated by the statement of Lord Simon in *Re D (an infant) (adoption: parent's consent)*[7] that—'In adoption proceedings the welfare of the child is not the paramount consideration (ie outweighing all others) as with custody or guardianship, but it is the first consideration (ie outweighing any other)'.

A distinctive feature of section 6 is that it lays down a directive not only for the courts but also for adoption agencies, but, as has been pointed out[8] 'this extension pinpoints the inherent weakness of a formula which makes the child's welfare the first consideration at all stages of decision making in the process leading to adoption'. The formula does not take account of the fact that there are different kinds of circumstances that may lead to the adoption process.[9] For example, where the parent is considering whether or not to place the child with an adoption agency with a view to adoption or freeing for adoption, the whole emphasis should be on ensuring that the powers and responsibilities of the parent are safeguarded in that he should be fully informed of the effects of adoption, of the statutory provisions relating to parental agreement and of the process which culminates in the making of an adoption order.

On the other hand, once the parent's provisional agreement to adoption or agreement to freeing for adoption has been given, then in caring for the child until placement, in choosing the placement and in the exercise of its subsequent functions the agency should be concerned solely with doing what is best for the child. During these stages in the process it is not concerned with any possible conflict between the welfare of the child and the interests of the parent. Indeed, the Adoption Agencies Regulations 1983 recognise that an adoption agency panel should in making a recommendation decide whether adoption is in the best interests of the child.[10] In examining those Regulations and the Adoption Rules the question should be asked whether they reflect the spirit of section 6 or whether they impliedly support a paramountcy test. Whichever the theoretical answer, in practice, it is suggested, agencies are governed by the latter.

1 The Adoption Act 1958, s 7(1)(b) merely stated that, when deciding whether or not to make an adoption order, the court had to be satisfied that the adoption would be for the welfare of the child.
2 For criticism see Bevan and Parry, *Children Act 1975,* Chapter 3, and for the difficulties facing the Parliamentary draftsman in drafting s 3 of the 1975 Act see Bennion, *First Consideration–A Cautionary Tale* (1976) 126 NLJ 1237.
3 Bevan and Parry, ibid, para [33].
4 Post, para 5.25.
5 [1984] FLR 402 at 404.
6 [1970] AC 688 at 710, [1969] 1 All ER 788 at 820–821. See ante, para 3.04.
7 [1977] AC 602 at 638, [1977] 1 All ER 145 at 160, 161.
8 Bevan and Parry, op cit, para [38].
9 See infra, para 5.13.
10 See post, para 5.18.

IV   THE PROCESS PRECEDING THE APPLICATION FOR ADOPTION

1   Placement for adoption

5.13   The circumstances which may lead to a child's being adopted fall broadly into five categories. Firstly, the prospective adopter may be the child's natural parent. Although adoption by the natural parent alone is legally possible, there are severe restrictions,[1] and such adoptions are now rare. This category nearly always relates to a joint adoption by the natural parent and the step-parent.[2] Secondly, the prospective adopter may be a relative of the child, for example, where the latter is an orphan; but, in principle at least, the availability of custodianship[3] ought to discourage this kind of adoption. Thirdly, the child may already have been entrusted by the natural parents to private foster parents who wish to adopt him. The Adoption Act 1976 largely, but not entirely, prevents such adoptions.[4] Fourthly, the child may already be in the care of somebody other than the natural parents or private foster parents, for example in the care of a local authority, which is looking for a permanent substitute family for him by way of adoption. Finally, the natural parent may offer his or her child for adoption through an adoption agency; for example the unmarried mother of a child may do so. A number of statutory provisions are designed to deal with these several categories, particularly the last two listed.

1 See post, para 5.56.
2 See post, para 5.58.
3 See post, Chapter 6.
4 See post, paras 5.63–5.64.

Placement by an adoption agency[1]

5.14 When an adoption agency is considering adoption for a child it has at the outset specific responsibilities to him (if he is old enough to understand) and to his parent or guardian.[2] It has similar responsibilities when it is considering whether a person may be suitable to be an adoptive parent.[3] Thus, so far as is reasonably practicable, the agency must provide a counselling service for all of them, explain to them the legal implications and procedures in relation to adoption and provide them with written information about these matters. In addition, the parents and, where appropriate, the child must also be informed about what the process of freeing for adoption involves. Given the immense consequences of adoption for all parties, these responsibilities are crucial.[4]

1 Ie by a local authority or an approved adoption society; see AA 1976, s 1(4). A list of all the adoption agencies appears annually in *Adopting a Child*, published by BAAF.
2 Adoption Agencies Regulations 1983, reg 7(1).
3 Reg 8(1),
4 For the subsequent responsibilities of a reporting officer see post, para 5.39.

5.15 Since the first consideration in adoption must be the need to safeguard and promote the welfare of the child throughout his childhood,[1] the investigations by an adoption agency before and during the placement of a child for adoption should be thorough and wide-ranging. The Adoption Agencies Regulations 1983 are aimed at fulfilling this purpose. The agency must compile a case record for every child for whom it is considering adoption and obtain particulars on matters, prescribed by the Regulations, which relate to him and to each of his parents or his guardian.[2] The matters prescribed are varied and extensive.[3] They cover the personal and social history of the child and each parent. The information on the parent must also deal with his or her health, past and present, and there must be a separate written medical report on the child. In the light of the medical information and report, the adoption agency's medical adviser may recommend other examinations, screening procedure and tests on the child and his parents. As part of its investigation the agency must inquire into the wishes and feelings of the parent in relation to adoption and freeing for adoption and his wishes, if any, in respect of the child's religious and cultural upbringing. Where the child's father is not married and his identity is known, the agency must, so far as it considers reasonably practicable and in the child's interests, comply with all the above requirements as for other natural parents together with the requirements described in the preceding paragraph.[4] It must also ascertain so far as possible whether he intends to apply for custody of his child.[5]

1 AA 1976, s 6.

2 Adoption Agencies Regulations 1983, reg 7(2).
3 See ibid, Schedule, Parts I-IV. The information required about a guardian is more restricted; see Part V.
4 Reg 7(3).
5 For the significance of this information see post, para 5.43. If the father already has legal custody by virtue of an order under GMA 1971, s 9, he is for the purpose of adoption law a guardian (AA 1976, s 72(1)). Nevertheless in such a case it seems clear that for the purpose of adoption agency inquiries all the requirements relating to a natural parent, and not those concerning a guardian, will apply to him. This conclusion, it is submitted, will still be correct when the amendment by FLRA 1987, s 7(2), of the definition of guardian comes into force and covers the unmarried father who either jointly has all the parental rights and duties or has a right to custody, legal or actual custody or care and control by a court order.

5.16 The agency must similarly compile a case record for any person who it considers may be suitable to be an adoptive parent. There are similar but even more extensive requirements in relation to him.[1] In addition to prescribed particulars and a medical report on him there must be the agency's reports on the premises he intends to use as his home if he adopts a child and on interviews with his nominated referees, and a report from his local authority in relation to him. As part of its investigation the agency must inquire into his reasons for wishing to adopt, his previous experience of caring for children and an assessment of his ability to do so, especially the ability to bring up an adopted child throughout his childhood.

1 See Adoption Agencies Regulations 1983, reg 8(2) and Schedule, Parts VI and VIII. Clearly there will be no separate local authority report where the adoption agency is itself the local authority.

5.17 All the information obtained by the agency in preparing its case records on a child and a prospective adopter, supported by its own comments thereon, will then be passed to its adoption panel.[1] In the light of the information it has gathered the agency may feel that placement of the child for adoption with a prospective adopter is appropriate. Any proposed placement must similarly be referred to the panel.[2] If, however, the child is in the care of a local authority or voluntary organisation or if either body has parental rights and duties in respect of the child as the result of an order under section 18 or section 21 of the AA 1976,[3] the agency proposing the placement must first consult that authority or organisation and obtain its agreement to the proposal.[4] Moreover, any other adoption agency which has already decided that adoption is in the child's best interests or that the prospective adopter is suitable to be an adoptive parent must first be consulted about the proposal.[5]

1 Adoption Agencies Regulations 1983, regs 7(2)(e) and 8(2)(g). For the establishment of a panel and appointment of its members see ibid reg 5.
2 Ibid reg 9(1).
3 Ie an order freeing the child for adoption (s 18) or an order (under s 21) transferring parental rights and duties to an adoption agency from another adoption agency in which they have been vested by an order under s 18; see respectively post, para 5.32 and para 5.70.
4 Reg 9(2)(b).
5 Reg 9(2)(a).

5.18 The basic function of an adoption panel is to make recommendations to the agency: it is for the latter to reach decisions. In the light of the information presented to it and subject to legal advice (eg on difficult questions relating to parental agreement or freeing for adoption) the panel can make recommendations on any one or more of the following matters:

(a) whether adoption is in the best interests of a child and, if the panel recommends that it is, whether an application should be made to free the child for adoption;
(b) whether a prospective adopter is suitable to be an adoptive parent; and
(c) whether a prospective adopter would be a suitable adoptive parent for a particular child.[1]

In considering what recommendation to make it must have regard to all the circumstances, but give first consideration to the need to promote the child's welfare,[2] and it must take account of any wishes of the parent or guardian as to the religious upbringing of the child.[3] It is submitted that the duty to give only first and not first and paramount consideration to the child's welfare is inconsistent with the panel's duty to consider whether adoption is in the child's best interests. When the agency has been informed of the panel's recommendations it then decides on the matters to which the recommendations refer and accordingly informs the parents, including an unmarried father where the agency considers this to be in the child's interests, any guardian and the prospective adopter of its respective decisions.[4] In practice these decisions will be taken by the agency's management committee, if the agency is an approved adoption society, by its social services committee, if it is a local authority.

1   Adoption Agencies Regulations 1983, reg 10(1)–(3)
2   See AA 1976, s 6.
3   AA 1976, s 7.
4   Reg 11(1) and (2).

5.19   Where the agency decides that a prospective adopter would be a suitable adoptive parent for a particular child, it must provide him with written information about the child, his history and background, and notify him of its proposal to place the child with him.[1] If he accepts the proposals, it must inform the child and alert certain other persons to the proposed placement, namely, the prospective adopter's doctor (sending him a medical report on the child), the local authority, the district health authority and, if the child is of compulsory school age or the agency's medical adviser considers him to be handicapped, the local education authority. The agency will then arrange to place the child with the prospective adopter. However, in those cases where the child already has his home with the prospective adopter, eg where the latter has been a long-term foster parent, the agency will notify the prospective adopter of the date from which the placement is to begin. Once the child has been placed his parents[2] or guardian must be so notified in writing.[3] Following the placement the agency has a number of duties to discharge. The child must be visited within one week after placement and on such other occasions as the agency considers necessary to supervise the child's well being. Reports must be made of each visit. The agency must provide advice and assistance to the prospective adopter and must monitor the child's health. If the prospective adopter has not applied for adoption within three months of the placement, the agency must review the placement and clearly will want to know the reason for the failure to do so. If there has been an application, it should review whenever it considers it necessary.[4]

1   Adoption Agencies Regulations, reg 12(1).
2   Including the unmarried father where the agency considers this to be in the child's interests.
3   Reg 12(2)(*f*). No notification is to be given to a parent or guardian who has made a declaration that he prefers not to be involved in future questions concerning the adoption of the child; see AA 1976, s 18(7) post, para 5.44. Written notification must also have earlier been given to the parent or guardian of the agency's decision to place for adoption (reg 11(2)(*a*)). Failure to give written notice does not necessarily vitiate the adoption procedure, since the Regulations are intended to be directory and not mandatory. However, the nature and degree of any breach of the regulations is a factor to be taken into account in deciding whether to make an adoption order and dispense with parental agreement, and, if it is substantial, may justify refusing both: see *Re T (a minor)* [1986] Fam 160, [1986] 1 All ER 817, CA.
4   For the details of an adoption agency's duties once a prospective adopter has accepted a proposed placement see reg 12(2).

2   Agreement to adoption

(a)   Introduction

5.20   Since the effect of an adoption order is to remove the parental powers and responsibilities from the parent or guardian, his agreement to it is a prerequisite, unless dispensed with on one of the permitted statutory grounds.[1] However, the Adoption Act 1976 provides alternative procedures for granting or dispensing with agreement. Under the one, although the agreement is usually given in written form at an early stage in the adoption process,[2] it is provisional and must still be operative at the moment when the application for an adoption order is heard,[3] unless the court exercises its powers of dispensation. Under the other, the freeing for adoption procedure, the agreement, once given or dispensed with at an early stage, is final and not open to withdrawal when later the adoption application is heard.

1   AA 1976, s 16.
2   See Adoption Rules 1984, SI 1984/265, Form 7; Adoption (Magistrates' Courts) Rules 1984.
3   *Re Hollyman* [1945] 1 All ER 290, CA; *Re K (an infant)* [1953] 1 QB 117, [1952] 2 All ER 877, CA; *Re F (an infant)* [1957] 1 All ER 819.

(b)   Agreement of the parent or guardian

5.21   The court must be satisfied that each parent or guardian freely and with full understanding of what is involved agree unconditionally to the making of an adoption order.[1] The positive terms in which the rule is stated suggest that the burden of so satisfying the court falls on the applicant for adoption and not on the parent or guardian to prove otherwise. Any agreement given by a mother less than six weeks after her child's birth is ineffective,[2] the purpose of the rule being to avoid the risk of her succumbing to pressure (eg from her parents) to allow adoption before she has recovered from the birth. Where there is no freeing for adoption procedure, the agreement must be in relation to a specific application for adoption,[3] even though the identity of the applicant can be, and more often than not is, withheld.[4]

1   AA 1976, s 16(1)(b)(i).
2   Section 16(4).
3   The forms of agreement prescribed by the Adoption Rules 1984 intend a specific applicant; and see Scrutton LJ in *Re Carroll* [1931] 1 KB 317 at 329, CA.
4   AA 1976, s 16(1)(b)(i).

5.22   For the purpose of adoption law the term 'parent' is not expressly defined, but by the normal rules of construction it means the mother and father if they were married at the child's birth but only the mother if they were not. In the latter circumstance the father is not a parent,[1] but is included in adoption law as a guardian if he has legal custody of the child by virtue of an order under section 9 of the Guardianship of Minors Act 1971. When the relevant provisions of the Family Law Reform Act 1987 come into force, he will qualify as a 'guardian' if either he has the parental rights and duties by virtue of an order under section 4 of that Act or by virtue of an order has a right to custody, legal or actual custody or care and control of the child.[2] Apart from that special inclusion, a guardian has its commonest meaning, namely, a person who has been appointed guardian by deed or will under the Guardianship of Minors Act 1971 or by a court of competent jurisdiction.[3]

By statutory implication the term 'parent' includes the adopter of an adopted child,[4] but the 'powers and duties'[2] of a parent which are vested in a local authority by virtue of a care order or the 'parental rights and duties' so vested by virtue of a resolution passed by the authority under section 3 of the Child Care Act 1980 do not confer on the authority the right to agree or refuse to agree to the making of an adoption order.[5] The same restriction applies to a voluntary organisation in which the parental rights and duties are vested by a resolution of the local authority in accordance with section 64 of that Act.[6]

1   *Re M (an infant)* [1955] 2 All ER 911, CA.
2   AA 1976, s 72(1) and (1A) as amended by FLRA 1987, s7(2) and Sch 2, para 68.
3   AA 1976, s 72(1).
4   AA 1976, s 12(1).
5   For these rules in relation to care orders see CCA 1980, s 10(5), as added by HASSASSAA 1983, Sch 2, para 47 and qualified by CCA 1980, Sch 4, para 8; and in relation to local authority resolutions see CCA 1980, s 3(10) as qualified by Sch 4, para 8.
6   See sub-s (6), as qualified by Sch 4, para 8.

(c)   *Dispensing with agreement*[1]

5.23   The agreement of a parent or guardian to the making of an adoption order may be dispensed with on one of several grounds.[2]

1   See Hayes and Williams, *Adoption of Babies, Agreeing and Freeing* (1982) 12 Fam Law 233; Sachs, *Agreement to Adoption* [1985] Fam Law 203, and *Adoption* and *Dispensing with Parental Agreement* (1983) 13 Fam Law 26.
2   AA 1976, s 16(1)(b)(ii) and (2). It is clear that, even if a ground is proved, the court still has a discretion whether or not to dispense. Section 16 states that an adoption order *shall* not be made unless the agreement *should* be dispensed with.

(i) *Parent or guardian cannot be found or is incapable of giving agreement*
5.24   It is clear that incapacity to give agreement because of mental ill health falls within this ground, but only if the parent has attempted to give his agreement. If he has refused to do so, the appropriate ground

is section 16(2)(b) below, and then his mental state may be relevant in applying the test whether his refusal is unreasonable.[1] That apart, agreement may be dispensed with if the court is satisfied either that every reasonable step by reasonable means has been taken to trace the parent or guardian[2] or that there are no practical means of communicating with him, because, for example, for political reasons it would be dangerous to him to try to do so.[3] If an adoption order is made without all reasonable steps having been taken and the parent or guardian later comes forward, he may be given leave to appeal out of time,[4] but the longer the delay in the application the less likely is it to be granted, since it may not be in the child's interest to set aside the order.

1   Re L (a minor) (adoption: parental agreement) [1987] 1 FLR 400, [1987] Fam Law 156.
2   Reasonable steps include writing to the last known address of the parent (see Re B [1958] 1 QB 12, [1957] 3 All ER 193, CA) and, where there is no response, making enquiries of the Post Office and of any known relatives, friends or neighbours and possibly advertising in the local press; see Re F (R) (an infant) [1970] 1 QB 385, [1969] 3 All ER 1101, CA.
3   Re R (adoption) [1966] 3 All ER 613, [1967] 1 WLR 34.
4   Re F (R) (an infant), supra.

(ii)   The parent or guardian is withholding his agreement unreasonably
5.25   This ground accounts for most of the contested applications.[1] The key authoritative decisions on this ground are those of the House of Lords in *Re W (an infant)*[2] and *O'Connor v A and B.*[3] The former approved, and defined the scope of, the principle formulated by the Court of Appeal in *Re L (an infant)*[4] that the question whether or not a parent is withholding agreement unreasonably is to be answered by applying an objective test, namely, whether or not a reasonable parent, taking into account all the circumstances of the case, would refuse his or her agreement. The latter held that in applying that test 'a reasonable parent would have in mind the interests or claims of all three parties concerned – the child, the parents and the adopting family'.[5] In practice the conflict is likely to be over the relative weight to be given to the interests of the child and the claims of the parent. Elsewhere, when deciding any matter relating to adoption the court must, in accordance with section 6 of the 1976 Act, give first consideration to the child's welfare.[6] It was argued in *Re B (an infant) (adoption: parental consent)*[7] that the predecessor of section 6, section 3 of the Children Act 1975, had not changed the law laid down by the House of Lords because it did not impose any new duty on the parent, who had only to be reasonable. That argument was rejected on the ground that, in making an objective appraisal of the reasonableness of the parent, the section had changed the law since the court had now to regard the child's welfare as the first consideration when weighing the conflicting factors to be taken into account. However, in *Re P (an infant) (adoption: parental consent)*[8] the majority of the Court of Appeal accepted the argument. Section 3 had not changed the relevant law because the section bore no relevance to it. The section related to decisions of courts and adoption agencies and not to a decision whether a parent was withholding agreement unreasonably. The requirements governing agreement or dispensing with it were not factors in the exercise of the court's discretion to make or refuse an adoption order, but conditions precedent to the exercise of the discretion. This conclusion has been seriously doubted.[9] It is difficult to reconcile it with, now, section 6, which refers to *any* decision relating to adoption by a court

or agency. It is the court which has to decide whether the parental agreement can be dispensed with on the ground of its being unreasonably withheld, and therefore in applying the objective test it should decide whether the parent as a reasonable parent has given first consideration to his or her child's welfare. In the event, the majority view in *Re P* has proved to be of little, if any, practical significance, because it is clear since the rulings of the House of Lords that the courts have been placing considerable emphasis on the child's welfare. This is to be expected, because a reasonable parent in deciding whether or not to withhold agreement would give great weight to what is best for the child. As Lord Hailsham put it:[10]

> 'Although welfare *per se* is not the test, the fact that a reasonable parent does pay regard to the welfare of his child must enter into the question of reasonableness as a relevant factor. It is relevant in all cases if and to the extent that a reasonable parent would take it into account. It is decisive in those cases where a reasonable parent would so regard it.'

Nevertheless, it has to be accepted that the test has a certain unreality about it:

> '. . . it is very difficult to have to decide what a reasonable mother would do; and it is very difficult for a mother . . . where ties of blood and emotional matters are involved to be reasonable at all.'[11]

1   The Second Report to Parliament on the Children Act 1975 (HMSO 1984) recorded (in Table B) that in 1983 11% of all adoption orders were made without parental agreement. In practice most of them are based on the present ground or on that of the parent not being found or being incapable of giving agreement.
2   [1971] AC 682, [1971] 2 All ER 49.
3   [1971] 2 All ER 1230, [1971] 1 WLR 1227, HL.
4   (1962) 106 Sol Jo 611, CA.
5   Per Lord Reid [1971] 2 All ER 1230 at 1232, [1971] 1 WLR 1227 at 1229.
6   See ante, para 5.12.
7   [1976] Fam 161, [1976] 3 All ER 124.
8   [1977] Fam 25, [1977] 1 All ER 182, CA.
9   In *Re P* Ormrod LJ concluded [1977] Fam at 36, [1977] 1 All ER 182 at 191 that s 3 did 'apply to the decision to dispense with consent, but I do not think it materially alters the law as it stood before it came into force'. In *Re D (an infant) (adoption: parental agreement)* [1977] AC 602 at 638, [1977] 1 All ER 145 at 161 Lord Simon expressed the view, obiter, that the section was 'no more than elucidatory and confirmatory of the pre-existing law'. Regrettably the House of Lords refused leave to appeal in *Re M (a minor)* [1980] CLYB 801, when the point could have been settled.
10 In *Re W (an infant)* [1971] AC 682 at 699, [1977] 2 All ER 49 at 55.
11 Per Davies LJ in *Re S (an infant)* [1973] 3 All ER 88 at 91.

5.26   Applying the objective test means taking into account all the circumstances of the case.[1] Each case, of course, depends on its own facts,[2] but the answer may partly turn on whether it concerns a baby adoption placement or a long-term foster parent placement. The kinds of questions most likely to be relevant are these. Is there a serious risk of harm to the child if he is returned to his parent.[2] What is the likelihood of a recurrence of any earlier harmful conduct on the parent's part.[3] Is there a serious defect in the mental condition, stability of character and temperament[4] or the health[5] or the mode of living of the parent[6] which could be harmful to the child? Is there a reasonable prospect of the parent being able to provide a home for the child.[7] Will reuniting the child with his brothers and sisters be conducive to his welfare,[8] and is the parent's refusal to agree due to a wish to bring up all her children together?[9] The mother, for example, who on her own admission is not in a position so to provide but who withholds her agreement to adoption because to give it would break the natural bond and give the impression that she had abandoned her child, withholds unreasonably.[10] Another cogent factor is the length of the period of separation of the child from the parent. The longer the period the more difficult it is for the parent to show that refusal of agreement is reasonable, especially if the child is well settled with the applicants for adoption,[11] and the more so if he has been the subject of earlier, unsettling, short-term placements.[12] Moreover, the fact that a mother has vacillated over whether or not to agree to adoption, while not conclusive evidence of unreasonableness, is evidence that she may not possess the insight to enable her to make the judgment of a reasonable parent.[13] The mere fact that the parent is prepared to agree to the making of a custodianship order does not necessarily mean that it is reasonable for him to refuse to agree to adoption.[14]

1 The issue of reasonableness must be decided on the facts as they exist at the date of the hearing of the adoption application or, as the case may be, of the appeal; see *Re S (an infant)* [1973] 3 All ER 88, 4 Fam Law 74, CA; and *Re W (adoption: parental agreement)* (1981) 3 FLR 75, CA.

2 For a close analysis of several cases which are illustrative of the guidelines which the courts follow see Bromley, pp 394-401 and Cretney, pp 448-454.

3 *Re S,* supra, note 1.

4 As in *O'Connor v A and B* [1971] 2 All ER 1230, [1971] 1 WLR 1227, HL.

5 *Re El-G (minors) (wardship and adoption)* (1983) 4 FLR 589, CA.

6 *Re D (an infant) (Parent's consent)* [1977] AC 602, [1977] 1 All ER 145, HL (father's homosexuality); *Re H (adoption: Parental agreement)* (1981) 3 FLR 386, 12 Fam Law 142, CA (mother's addiction to alcohol).

7 *Re W,* supra, note 1 (mother already living in overcrowded accommodation); *Re F (a minor) (adoption: parental consent)* [1982] 1 All ER 321, [1982] 1 WLR 102, CA (where mother conceded that child should be brought up by foster parents); *Re V (adoption: parental agreement)* [1985] FLR 45, [1985] Fam Law 55, CA (mother unable to formulate any plan as to future care of her child). But the material benefit which the prospective adopters will be able to give the child whose parents live in poor circumstances must not be given too much weight, since affluence and happiness are not necessarily synonymous; *Re P (an infant)* (1984) Times, 19 May, CA.

8 Cf *Re C (a minor) (adoption: conditions)* [1988] 1 All ER 705, HL, where it was held that a mother's refusal to agree to the adoption of her daughter on the ground that it would interfere with the relationship between the daughter and her son was unreasonable: contact between the children could be maintained by including a provision for access in the adoption order; see *post,* para 5.94.

9 *Re V (a minor) (adoption: consent)* [1987] Fam 57, [1986] 1 All ER 752, CA.

10 *Re H (adoption: parental agreement)* (1981) 3 FLR 386, 12 Fam Law 142.

11 As in *Re W* [1971] AC 682, [1971] 2 All ER 49, HL; *O'Connor v A and B,* supra, note 4; *Re El-G (minors),* supra note 5; *Re H* Adoption and Fostering, Vol 5 No 3 (1981) p 62, CA; *Re F,* supra, note 7; *Re M (adoption: parental agreement)* [1985] FLR 664, [1985] Fam Law 223; *Re R (a minor) (adoption: parental agreement)* [1987] 1 FLR 391, [1987] Fam Law 95, CA. Cf *Re Application No 41 of 1974* (1975) 5 Fam Law 181, CA; *Re J (wardship: adoption: custodianship)* [1987] 1 FLR 455, [1987] Fam Law 88 (where a West Indian mother was held entitled to rely on the fact that the applicants were white and Jehovah's Witnesses).

12 *Re W (adoption: parental agreement)* [1984] FLR 880, [1984] Fam Law 89, CA.

13 *Re P (adoption: parental agreement)* [1985] FLR 635, [1985] Fam 254, CA.

14 *Re A (a minor) (adoption: parental consent)* [1987] 2 All ER 81, [1987] 1 WLR 153, CA.

5.27 The answers which have been given by the courts to the kinds of questions posed above in cases decided since *Re W* and *O'Connor v A and B* accord with the House of Lords rulings. It was therefore surprising to find the Court of Appeal in *Re H (a minor)* and *Re W (adoption: parental agreement)*[1] calling for a limit on this shift of emphasis in favour of the child's welfare. Its criticisms of the trend seem to stem primarily from the court's own readiness to look too subjectively at the attitude of the natural parent to refusing agreement and to minimise the significance of his past conduct towards the child. Fortunately, *Re H* and *Re W* have proved to be no more than a judicial hiccup.[2] In *Re V (adoption: parental agreement)*[3] the court appears to have reverted to the trend of placing predominant emphasis on the welfare of the child by firmly applying the objective test of the reasonable parent, a test which it further reaffirmed in *Re R (a minor) (adoption: parental agreement)*.[4]

1   (1982) 4 FLR 614, 13 Fam Law 144; and see thereon Bromley, pp 399-400, who, in observing that 'there seem to be more reported instances of adoption being refused because parents were withholding agreement reasonably', points out that in most of them the parent is or has been exercising access.
2   They are, however, significant in another respect. They show the need in cases involving the present ground for the most careful investigation and preparation of the evidence by those representing the parties to the adoption application, a feature noticeably deficient in both those cases.
3   [1985] FLR 45, [1985] Fam Law 55, CA.
4   [1987] 1 FLR 391 [1987] Fam Law 95, CA.

(iii)   Parent or guardian has persistently failed without reasonable cause to discharge the parental duties in relation to the child

5.28 In *Re P (infants)*[1] it was held that 'parental duties' in this context must include:

> 'first the natural and moral duty of a parent to show affection, care and interest towards the child; and, secondly, as well, the common law or statutory duty of a parent to maintain his child in the financial or economic sense.'

But the expression also covers any other legal duty of a parent towards his child, for example, the duty to protect from harm and the duty not to harm. Indeed, the most likely instances of this ground being successfully invoked are those where the child is in the care of a local authority either by virtue of a care order[2] or by a resolution of the authority[3] made because of parental failure in bringing up the child. However, whether the child is the subject of adoption proceedings as a result either of those consequences or of having been placed by the parent for adoption, to justify dispensing with the parent's agreement his failure has to be culpable to a high degree and so grave and complete that the child would derive no advantage from maintaining contact with him.[4] Moreover, 'persistently' is to be construed in the sense of permanently, so that the ground is not established unless it is shown that the parent (or guardian) has washed his hands of the child.[5] Thus, failure to visit one's child after deliberately placing him for adoption does not per se constitute persistent failure. Indeed, not visiting him may well be best for him in the circumstances.[6] On the other hand, continued inactivity on the parent's part over a lengthy period can eventually amount to such failure.[7]

1   [1962] 3 All ER 789, [1962] 1 WLR 1296.
2   Under CYPA 1969, s 1.
3   Under CCA 1980, s 3.
4   *Re D (minors) (adoption by parent)* [1973] Fam 209, [1973] 3 All ER 1001.
5   Ibid. In that case the husband, after separating from his wife and two children then aged
    four and five years, saw the children at irregular intervals. He sent them Christmas and
    Easter presents and some clothes, but did not provide maintenance for them. Held that
    there was not persistent failure.
6   *Re M (an infant)* (1965) 109 Sol Jo 574, CA.
7   See, eg, *Re P (infants)* note l; *Re B (S) (an infant)* [1968] Ch 204, [1967] 3 All ER 629.

(iv)   Parent or guardian has abandoned or neglected the child

5.29   The conduct must be such as to give rise to criminal liability, for
example, for the offence of abandonment or neglect under section 1 of the
CYPA 1933.[1] It is doubtful whether emotional rejection of the child
constitutes neglect for this purpose. It would be safer to rely on ground
(c).

1   See *Watson v Nikolaisen* [1955] 2 QB 286, [1955] 2 All ER 427; *Re W* unreported cited
    in *Re P* [1962] 3 All ER 789 at 793.

(v)   Parent or guardian has persistently ill-treated the child

5.30   It seems that here, too, the conduct must be of a kind and degree
that would render the parent or guardian criminally liable. The use of
the word 'persistently' implies a need to prove a series of acts, but they
could be over a short period.[1]

1   As in *Re A (a minor)* (1979) 2 FLR 173, 10 Fam Law 49, CA, where most, if not all,
    of the acts were committed within three weeks.

(vi)   Parent or guardian has seriously ill-treated the child

5.31   It seems clear that this ground also requires conduct of a criminal
nature, especially since the ill-treatment has to be serious. If it is sufficiently
serious, then one act may be enough. However, the ground does not apply
unless the rehabilitation of the child within the household of the parent
or guardian is unlikely, whether that is because of the ill-treatment or for
some other reason,[1] for example, because of the parent's mental condition
or the fact that he is serving a long term of imprisonment for the ill-treatment
of his child or because of poor housing accommodation and its attendant
pressures on the parent.

1   AA 1976, s 16(2).

3   Freeing for adoption

(a)   Nature and effect

5.32   A child will be free for adoption if he is the subject of an order
made under section 18 of the Adoption Act 1976. This procedure enables
the parent or guardian to give his agreement to adoption at an early stage
in the adoption process. By so doing it seeks to avoid the disadvantages
and uncertainties of the alternative procedure already examined. The rule
thereunder, which requires the agreement to be operative at the hearing
of the adoption application (notwithstanding the fact that written agreement

usually has already been given), may place a strain on the parent and even encourage indecisiveness on his or her part. Correspondingly, it may create in the applicants the anxiety that agreement may be withdrawn, so that they may hesitate to give total commitment to the child. In turn the child's welfare is at risk since his future remains in doubt.

5.33   Section 18 provides for a preliminary hearing at which the court can make an order declaring the child free for adoption. Application for it is made by an adoption agency and, if it is granted, the parental rights and duties vest in the agency[1] until either the order is revoked or an adoption order is made. Consequently, any parental right or duty which immediately before the date of the section 18 order was vested in a parent or guardian or, by virtue of an order of the court, in any other person will be extinguished. So, too, will any duty under an agreement or the order of a court to provide maintenance for the child (eg by the putative father), except a duty arising by virtue of an agreement which constitutes a trust or which expressly provides that the duty is not to be extinguished by the making of section 18 order.[2] A section 18 order does not, however, affect the parental rights and duties so far as they relate to any period before the making of an order.[3]

1   AA 1976, s 18(5).
2   Ibid, ss 18(5) and 12(3), (4).
3   Ibid, ss 18(5) and 12(2).

(b)   Making a section 18 order

5.34   The freeing process involves two distinct acts: agreeing to the making of an adoption order and consenting to the application by the adoption agency for a section 18 order. The general principle is that each parent or guardian must give his agreement to the former, unless it is dispensed with on one of the specified statutory grounds,[1] and one of them at least must, apart from one exception, consent to the application. Section 18(1) and (2) cover three possibilities where a freeing order can be made. They are illustrated by taking the case of two parents.

(a)   Both parents agree to adoption and both consent to the section 18 application (although it is sufficient for one of them to consent).[2]

(b)   One of them agrees to adoption, the other does not. A section 18 application can be made with the consent of the former. The court, if satisfied, can dispense with the other's agreement to adoption, his consent to the application not being necessary.[3]

(c)   Neither parent agrees to adoption and therefore neither will consent to a section 18 application. An application can only be made if the child is in the care of the adoption agency and the court will have to dispense with the agreement of each parent to an adoption order before it can make a section 18 order.[4] Although there is no minimum period for which the child must have been in the agency's care before it makes a section 18 application, this third possibility is intended primarily for children in long-term care.

1   AA 1976, s 16(2), ante, paras 5.23-5.31.
2   Ibid, s 18(1)(a) and (2)(a).

3 Ibid, s 18(1)(a) and (b) and 2(a).
4 Ibid, s 18(1)(b) and (2)(b).

5.35 The parental agreement cannot be dispensed with in section 18 proceedings unless the child is already placed for adoption or the court is satisfied that it is likely that the child will be placed for adoption.[1] This rule is readily understandable in those cases where the parents deliberately entrust the child to the adoption agency for him to be placed for adoption or where the child is already in the care of the agency who have placed or are intending to place him for adoption. But, in the case where the child is in the care of an agency, eg a local authority, and is living with foster parents and they decide that they want to adopt him, it cannot be said that he is already placed for adoption. Nor literally will there be a placement, since he is already with them. It therefore seems necessary to hold for the purpose of subsection (3) that there is a notional placement for adoption when the agency notifies the foster parents that it will support them in an adoption application. However, in a case of that kind it may well be more appropriate for the foster parents, with the concurrence of the agency, to rely on the alternative procedure and proceed with an application for adoption instead of the freeing procedure.

1 AA 1976, s 18(3).

5.36 In section 18 proceedings the parent's agreement is given generally for his child to be adopted and not, as under the alternative procedure, with a specific adoption in mind.[1] Otherwise the same general rules apply, namely, that agreement is given freely, with full understanding and unconditionally, and that in the case of the mother her agreement is ineffective if given less than six weeks after the child's birth.[2]

1 Cf AA 1976, s 18(1) and s 16(1)(b).
2 Ibid, s 18(4).

5.37 Once the adoption agency has decided that rehabilitation of the child with his parents is not possible and that adoption is the proper alternative all further steps in the section 18 process should be taken as expeditiously as possible, and it is not necessary that the agency should have particular prospective adopters in mind. The court will only have to be satisfied that it is likely that the child will be placed for adoption. There should be no delay by the agency in making the section 18 application, and, once this is done and the prescribed documents filed at court, a reporting officer and/or a guardian ad litem[1] should be immediately appointed and a hearing date fixed at a reasonable time ahead, which should never be more than three months. Failure on the part of the agency or the court to proceed promptly is likely to raise difficult and unnecessary problems over the upbringing of, and access to, the child in the meantime.[2]

1 See post, paras 5.38 and 5.41.
2 *Re PB (a minor) (application to free for adoption)* [1985] FLR 394.

(i) Reporting officer

5.38 Reference has already been made to the obligation of an adoption agency, which is considering adoption for a child, to ensure that the parents or guardians are fully informed about, inter alia, the implications of adoption and the process of freeing for adoption.[1] The Adoption Rules recognise the need for the parents or guardians to continue to be fully informed of the consequences of their possible actions after the agency has made a section 18 application. So, as soon as practicable after the commencement of proceedings, or at any subsequent stage, a reporting officer must be appointed in respect of a parent or guardian who appears to be willing to agree to adoption.[2] In High Court and county court proceedings the 'proper officer' appoints: in a magistrates' court either the court itself appoints or, at any time before the hearing of the application, a single justice or the justices' clerk may do so.[3] Appointment is made from a panel established under the Guardians ad Litem and Reporting Officers (Panels) Regulations 1983,[4] but the officer appointed must not be a member or employee of the applicant agency or of any body which is a respondent nor have been involved in making arrangements for the adoption of the child.[5]

1 See ante, para 5.14.
2 Adoption Rules 1984, r 5(1); Magistrates' Courts (Adoption) Rules 1984, r 5(1) and (9).
3 The 'proper officer' means, in the High Court, a registrar of the Principal Registry of the Family Division and, in the county court, the registrar, except that in relation to a formal or administrative act it includes also the chief clerk or other officer of the court. Appointing a reporting officer would not, it is submitted, be such an act. See AR 1984, r 2; CCR 1981 Ord 1, r 3. In proceedings in a magistrates' court the justices' clerk is the person most likely to appoint.
4 See further, post, paras 5.74.
5 See AA 1976, s 65(2) and AR 1984, r 5(3); MC(A)R 1984, r 3.

5.39 A reporting officer has a number of specific duties:[1]

(a) He must ensure that an agreement to adoption is given freely, unconditionally and with full understanding. It is, it is suggested, implied in this obligation that he informs and advises the parent or guardian of the nature and consequences of adoption.

(b) He must witness the signature by the parent or guardian to his agreement. The written agreement must be in a form prescribed by the Adoption Rules.[2] The form also states that the parent or guardian consents to the section 18 application.

(c) He must confirm that the parent or guardian has been given due opportunity of making a declaration that he prefers not to be involved in future questions concerning the child's adoption.[3] Here, too, the implication seems to be that he informs and advises on the nature and consequences of freeing for adoption and of the declaration.

(d) He must investigate all the circumstances relevant to the agreement or any declaration (if made).[4]

(e) On completing his investigations he must make a written report to the court, drawing attention to any matters which he thinks may assist the court in considering the application.

(f) He may find it necessary to make an interim report with a view to obtaining the court's directions. He must report the fact that a parent or guardian is unwilling to agree to adoption. The court will then notify the adoption agency, so that it can decide whether or not it has grounds on which to rely for the agreement to be dispensed with. Any final or interim report by the reporting officer is confidential.

(g) The court has a residual power to require the officer to perform such other duties as it considers necessary, and it may require him to attend any hearing of the application.

1 AR 1984, r 5(4)-(8); MC(A)R 1984, r 5(4)-(8).
2 See AR 1984, Form 2; MC(A)R 1984, Form 2.
3 For a declaration and its effect see post, para 5.44.
4 For investigation where the child's mother and father were not married to each other at the time of his birth see infra, para 5.43.

5.40 An adoption agency which is requesting the court to dispense with the agreement of the parent or guardian must provide the court with a statement of the facts on which it intends to rely.[1] If the child has already been placed with a person for adoption and the latter wishes his identity to remain confidential, the statement must be so framed as not to disclose his identity. The court must inform the parent or guardian of the agency's request and provide him with a copy of its statement. A copy must also be sent to the reporting officer and to the guardian ad litem (if different persons).

1 AR 1984, r 7; MC(A)R 1984, r 7. The statement may accompany the agency's application or be sent later.

(ii) Guardian ad litem

5.41 A reporting officer is appointed where it appears that a parent or guardian is willing to agree to adoption.[1] A guardian ad litem is appointed where it appears he is unwilling.[2] It follows, therefore, that each officer is necessary where one parent or guardian is apparently willing to agree and the other apparently is not. However, the same person may be appointed to fulfil both roles.[3] If the proceedings are in the High Court, the Official Solicitor may be the guardian ad litem, if he consents.[4] Otherwise, in that court and any other court, appointment is from a panel established under the Guardians Ad Litem and Reporting Officers (Panels) Regulations 1983,[5] but, as with a reporting officer, the guardian ad litem must not be a member or employee of the applicant agency or of any respondent body nor have been involved in making arrangements for the adoption of the child.[6]

1 See ante, para 5.38.
2 AR 1984, r 6(1); MC(A)R 1984, r 6(1). For the persons empowered to appoint see ante, para 5.38. There is also power to appoint where there are special circumstances and the child's welfare appears to require it; see r 6(2) of each of the above set of Rules.
3 AR 1984, r 6(3); MC(A)R 1984, r 6(3).
4 But see *Practice Direction* [1986] 2 All ER 832, [1986] 1 WLR 933. Subject to certain exceptions there listed, the Official Solicitor will not so consent if the adoption or freeing for adoption application is proceeding in the High Court with the consent of the natural parent. Should the proceedings later become opposed, the Official Solicitor will, if the court considers it appropriate, be prepared to accept appointment as the child's guardian ad litem.
5 AR 1984, r 6(5); MC(A)R 1984, r 6(4). For the 1983 Regulations see further post, paras 5.72-5.74.
6 AA 1976, s 65; AR 1984, r 6(5); MC(A)R 1984, r 6(4).

5.42 The basic duty of a guardian ad litem is to safeguard the interests of the child before the court. To discharge this duty he is required to investigate the matters alleged by the adoption agency in its application, the report which it has to supply to the court and any statement of facts on which it bases its case for having the parental agreement dispensed with. This does not preclude him from investigating any other matter which appears relevant to the making of a section 18 order. The report which the agency has to provide relates to the child and his parents and covers very largely the same matters as the agency covers when preparing its case record on a child for proposed adoption.[1] It means, therefore, that the guardian ad litem has extensive duties of investigation. On completing them he must submit a written confidential report to the court, but may find it necessary to make an interim report in order to obtain the court's directions on any matter. As with the reporting officer, the court may require him to perform such other duties it considers necessary, and may require him to attend any hearing of the application. A particularly important function of the guardian ad litem is to consider whether the child should be present at the hearing. The reason for this is that he must attend, unless there are special circumstances which,having regard to the report of the guardian ad litem, enables the court to direct otherwise.[2]

The parties to freeing for adoption proceedings or to proceedings for an adoption order[3] are not entitled to see the report of the guardian ad litem, but the judge has a discretion to allow them to do so. If, however, any matter in the report is adverse to a party and would influence the judge's mind, that party must be given an opportunity to know about it. It is then for the judge to decide how to proceed in order to give the party an opportunity to answer any criticism in the witness box.[4]

1   See ante, paras 5.15-5.16. The matters to be covered in the report are set out in AR 1984, Sch 2 and MC(A)R 1984, Sch 2.
2   AR 1984, r 10(4) and (5); MC(A)R 1984, r 10(4) and (5).
3   See post, para 5.70.
4   *Re B (a minor)* (1983) Times, 21 October, CA.

(iii)   The unmarried father

5.43 The unmarried father who is guardian of his child[1] can oppose the section 18 application by withholding his agreement to the making of an adoption order. The father who is not a guardian can frustrate the application, temporarily or sometimes permanently by applying for an order for legal custody under section 9 of the Guardianship of Minors Act 1971[2] or, when the relevant provisions of the Family Law Reform Act 1987 come into operation, by applying for either an order under section 4 of that Act giving him all the parental rights and duties or an order under any other enactment giving him a right to custody, legal or actual custody or care and control of his child.[3] It is therefore highly desirable, if possible, that his intentions be ascertained at the earliest opportunity. Hence the obligation on an adoption agency, when it is considering adoption for a child whose father and mother were not married to each other at the time of his birth, to try to ascertain those intentions.[4] After a section 18 application has been made that inquiry must be pursued by the reporting officer, who must interview the person claiming to be the father.[5] In the light of the officer's advice the court can then decide how to discharge its duty under section 18(7) of the Adoption Act 1976. This provides that before a freeing order is made the court must satisfy itself that the putative father does not intend to apply for legal custody or, when the provisions of the 1987 Act operate,[6] for a section 4 order or an order giving him custody, legal or actual custody or care and control, or that, if he did, his application would be likely to be refused. This requirement is a wise precaution in view of the need to ensure that the result of freeing the child for adoption will be an unchallengeable transfer of parental rights and duties. If it is found that the father does wish to apply for one of the above orders, and it cannot be said that refusal would be likely, then it is desirable that the section 18 application be adjourned so that it and the application for one of those orders may be heard together by the same court.[7] But these are the limits of the father's rights. He is not entitled to resist the section 18 application by the use of wardship proceedings against the adoption agency.[8]

1 See ante, para 5.22.
2 For s 9 see ante, para 3.15.
3 See ante, para 2.46.
4 Adoption Agencies Regulations 1983, reg 7(3).
5 AR 1984, r 5(4)(e); MC(A)R 1984, r 5(4)(e).
6 See AA 1976, s 18(7), as substituted by FLRA 1987, s 7(1); see also AA 1976, s 18(8) as inserted by FLRA 1987, Sch 2, para 67.
7 There may be a preliminary issue of paternity to determine.
8 *Re TD (a minor) (wardship: jurisdiction)* [1985] FLR 1150, [1986] Fam Law 18.

(iv) The declaration

5.44 Before making an order freeing a child for adoption the court must be satisfied that each parent or guardian who can be found has been given an opportunity of making, if he so wishes, a declaration that he prefers not to be involved in future questions concerning the child's adoption. The court must record any declaration made.[1] The reporting officer must confirm that the parent or guardian has been given the opportunity to make the declaration,[2] and it is to be hoped that he will advise and inform the parent or guardian on its effects. If the latter chooses to make the declaration, he will do so in the form of written agreement to adoption which he signs.[3]

1 AA 1976 s 18(6).
2 AR 1984, r 5(4)(b); MC(A)R 1984, r 5(4)(b).
3 AR 1984, Form 2; MC(A)R 1984, Form 2.

5.45 A parent or guardian who was required to be given an opportunity of making a declaration but did not do so (whether or not the opportunity was in fact given to him) is entitled to progress reports on the child and eventually will have the right, within limits, to apply for revocation of the freeing for adoption order.[1] A progress report must be made to 'the former parent', as the AA 1976 describes him, by the adoption agency within 14 days following the first anniversary date of the making of the section 18 order, unless it has already notified him that an adoption order has been made. This first report must tell him whether an adoption order has been made and, if not, whether the child has his home with a person with whom he has been placed for adoption.[2] Therefore he must be notified

of any adoption order (if not already made) or any placement for adoption
or cessation of a placement, as the case may be.[3] It is open to the former
parent at any time to make a declaration to the agency that he no longer
wishes to be involved in future questions concerning the adoption of his
child.[4]

1   AA 1976, s 19(1).
2   Ibid, s 19(2).
3   Ibid, s 19(3).
4   Ibid, s 19(4). The agency must see that the declaration is recorded by the court which
    made the s 18 order. The agency is released from making further progress reports once
    the declaration has been made.

(c)   Revocation of an order freeing for adoption

5.46   The duty of the adoption agency to make progress reports is linked
with the right of the former parent to apply, on the ground that he wishes
to resume the parental rights and duties, to the court for the revocation
of the section 18 order which it made. Application is not allowed within
the first 12 months after the date of the order. The period is to give the
agency an adequate opportunity to place the child for adoption. If a
placement has not been made within that period, it is likely that difficulties
have been encountered and placement may be a lengthy, perhaps impossible
process, eg in the case of a handicapped child.[1]

1   AA 1976, s 20(1). For process of application see AR 1984, Form 4; MC(A)R 1984, Form
    4.

5.47   It is too late to make an application once an adoption order has
been made, since the parental rights and duties have already been irrevocably
transferred to the adopters. Nor can application be made while the child
has his home with a person with whom he has been placed for adoption.[1]
On the other hand, if the child is not currently placed when the application
for revocation is made, the agency must not place him without leave of
the court.[2] Leave is unlikely to be granted. The court will want first to
hear why the former parent is seeking revocation. In deciding on the
application the court is governed by section 6 of the AA 1976,[3] so that
in giving first but not paramount consideration to the child's welfare it
will have to give due weight to the claims and wishes of the parent. One
cogent factor will be any delay in seeking revocation after the minimum
12-month period. The longer the former parent and child have been apart
the less inclined will the court be to revoke, especially if there is a likelihood
of immediate placement for adoption. If the former parent agreed to
adoption and consented to the section 18 application, much will depend
on the reason for doing so. Was it, for example, inspired by a selfish disregard
of his child or was it the consequence of explicable pressures such as poverty
or inadequate accommodation or, in the case of the unmarried mother,
pressure from her parents to agree to adoption? If the section 18 order
had been made after dispensing with the former parent's agreement to
adoption, are there now fresh circumstances which, if the section 18
application were being heard de novo, would not justify such dispensation.
These are the kinds of matters which courts are likely to have to consider
when applying section 6 on an application for revocation. They are therefore

matters which the guardian ad litem should be considering when preparing his report.[4]

1   AA 1976, s 20(1).
2   Ibid, s 20(2).
3   For s 6 see ante, para 5.12.
4   A guardian ad litem must be appointed for revocation proceedings; AR 1984, r 12(4); MC(A)R 1984, r 12(3).

5.48   If the application is dismissed 'on the ground that to allow it would contravene the principle embodied in section 6' the applicant will normally be barred from making any further application for revocation and the adoption agency is released from the duty of giving to him any further progress reports.[1] However, the court which dismissed the application may later give the former parent leave to make a further application where, because of a change in circumstances or for any other reason, it is proper to allow it.[2]

1   AA 1976, s 20(4).
2   Ibid, s 20(5).

5.49   If revocation is allowed, the parental rights and duties will normally revest in the person or persons in whom they were vested immediately before the section 18 order was made.[1] In practice this is most likely to be the applicant himself, but there are various possibilities. For example, the effect may be that there will be revesting in him and the other parent. However, supposing that they are now living apart or that the other parent had made a declaration that he no longer wished to be involved in future questions concerning the child's adoption; will the fact of separation in the one case and the lack of interest of the parent in the other influence the court against revocation or will it grant it and leave either parent to seek a custody order? It is suggested that in cases of this kind the court revoking the section 18 order should be ready concurrently to entertain an application for custody. In those cases where the parental rights and duties, or any of them, vested in a local authority[2] or a voluntary organisation[3] immediately before the section 18 order was made, they will revest in the person or persons in whom they were vested immediately before they were vested in the authority or organisation.[4] It is suggested that where the vesting in either of those bodies was due to the misconduct or inadequacies of the parent the court is not likely to grant revocation.

Revocation of a section 18 order revives any duty relating to payment towards the child's maintenance, eg by an unmarried father, which was extinguished when the section 18 order was made.[5]

Revocation does not affect any right or duty so far as it relates to any period before the date of the revocation.[6]

1   AA 1976, s 20(3)(a).
2   By virtue of a care order (under CYPA 1969) or a resolution of a local authority (under CCA 1980, s 3).
3   Under CCA 1980, s 64.
4   AA 1976, s 20(3)(b).
5   Ibid, s 20(3)(c).
6   Ibid, s 20(3).

V THE ADOPTION APPLICATION

1 Jurisdiction

5.50 The High Court, county courts and magistrates' courts are all authorised to hear applications relating to adoption.[1] Their jurisdiction very largely depends upon the presence of the child in England or Wales[2] when the application is made. So far as concerns the jurisdiction of a county court or magistrates' court, he must further be in the district or area respectively of those courts at the date of the application. Where there is a section 18 application to free a child for adoption, any county court or magistrates' court within whose district or area a parent or guardian of the child is, also has jurisdiction.[3] This extension aims to provide for maximum convenience.[4] A court also has jurisdiction if the proceedings are transferred to it from another court.[5] These general rules are subject to the following special provisions:

(a)   If the application is for an adoption order or a section 18 order and the child is not in Great Britain when the application is made, only the High Court has jurisdiction.[6]

(b)   Similarly, where there is an application for a Convention adoption order[7] and the child is in England and Wales the High Court alone has jurisdiction.[8]

(c)   Magistrates' courts cannot hear applications under section 55 of the AA 1976 relating to children in England and Wales whom it is intended to adopt abroad.[9]

(d)   In the case of an application under section 29[10] of that Act for a child who has been wrongfully removed to be returned to the applicant, the High Court, the county court within whose district the applicant lives and the magistrates' court within whose area he lives are the authorised courts, except that, where there is already pending an application for an adoption order or a section 18 order, the court in which that application is pending is the authorised court.[11]

There are also powers to order transfer of proceedings from one court to another.[12]

1 AA 1976, s 62.
2 For the further requirement concerning the domicile of the applicant for an adoption order see post, para 5.53.
3 AA 1976, s 62(2).
4 But a magistrates' court is the least suitable forum for hearing an opposed application for a freeing for adoption order, because the hearing could last several days and it would be difficult to arrange for the same panel of justices to sit without a break; *Re Adoption Application No 118/1984* (1985) Times, 15 February.
5 AA 1976, s 62(7).
6 Ibid, s 62(3).
7 Under ibid, s 17.
8 Ibid. s 62(4).
9 Ibid, s 62(6).
10 See post, paras 5.84-5.86.
11 AA 1976, s 62(5).
12 See post, para 5.102.

5.51 Proceedings in a county court must be heard in camera,[1] while those in the High Court may be,[2] and usually are, disposed of in chambers, except when there is some point of law of significance for the future. Proceedings in a magistrates' court are domestic proceedings, and privacy of those proceedings is ensured by excluding the normal rule that representatives of newspapers and newsagencies may be present.[3]

1 AA 1976, s 64(b).
2 Ibid, s 64(a).
3 See Magistrates' Courts Act 1980, s 69.

2 Preliminary considerations

(a) Eligibility of the applicants

5.52 Domicile, age and marital status are the main legal conditions governing eligibility to adopt. On the basis that a child should normally be brought up by two parents, the vast majority of adoptions are joint adoptions by a married couple.[1] Otherwise, only one person is allowed to adopt, for example, the unmarried mother or a relative of the child. However, certain restrictions are imposed on adoption by married persons, natural parents, relatives and step-parents. Their effect has been to reduce overall the number of adoption orders but especially those in favour of sole applicants.

1 An adoption order granted to joint adopters whose marriage turns out to be void is itself voidable and not void; *Re F* [1977] Fam 165, [1977] 2 All ER 777, CA.

(i) Domicile

5.53 The applicant must be domiciled in a part of the United Kingdom, the Channel Islands or the Isle of Man.[1] In the case of a joint application both spouses will invariably have the requisite domicile, but it is enough if only one of them has.[2] In that event, however, any adoption order made might not be recognised by the foreign *lex domicilii* of the other spouse.

A 'limping adoption' might also arise where the child has a foreign domicile. Such does not prevent an adoption order being made, but, if the order were not to be recognised by the foreign *lex domicilii,* that is a matter which the court should take into account when discharging its duty under section 6 of the AA 1976 to have regard to all the circumstances in deciding whether or not to make an order.[3]

1 AA 1976, s 15(2).
2 Ibid, s 14(2). The domiciliary rule does not apply where there is an application for a Convention adoption order. Then s 17 will have to be complied with. For Convention adoption orders see post, paras 5.104 et seq.
3 See *Re B(S) (an infant)* [1968] Ch 204, [1967] 3 All ER 629.

(ii) Age

5.54 In all cases the applicant or joint applicants must be at least 21 years of age.[1] The minimum age, instead of attainment of majority, takes account of the high incidence of breakdown of marriages entered into by persons under 21.[2] No maximum age is imposed, but in applying the 'welfare' principle in accordance with section 6 of the 1976 the court should take age into account where, for example, the applicants are grandparents. Where there is an adoption agency placement applicants are not in practice considered suitable for baby adoptions if they are over 40, but they may well be able to cope with adopting an older child.[3]

1   AA 1976, ss 14(1) and 15(1).
2   On proposals for a uniform age see the Houghton Committee Report, Cmnd 5107, paras 70-78.
3   See Bromley, p 287.

(iii)   Status
5.55   *The married person as sole applicant.*   It is obviously undesirable to allow one of two spouses, who are living together, to adopt a child when the other is unwilling to do so. Accordingly, only in the following circumstances may the court make an adoption order in favour of a sole applicant who is married:[1]

(a)   That the other spouse cannot be found. It seems clear that the words 'cannot be found' have the same meaning as they have for the purpose of dispensing with a parent's agreement to the making of an adoption order.[2]

(b)   That the spouses have separated and are living apart and the separation is likely to be permanent. The concept of living apart is well known in matrimonial causes and decisions thereon are relevant by analogy.

(c)   That the other spouse is by reason of ill-health, whether physical or mental, incapable of making an application for an adoption order. This restriction is understandable where that spouse is mentally ill, but it is difficult to see how physical ill-health can render a person incapable of making an application for adoption. It may, however, make him unsuitable to be an adopter. Indeed, in each of the above circumstances the court is likely to be wary about making an order, since adoption may well not be for the child's benefit. However, if an order is made and the other spouse should reappear or his health improve or the spouses resume living together, the spouses could apply for a joint adoption order.

1   AA 1976, s 15(1)(b).
2   See ante, para 5.24.

5.56   *Mother or father as sole applicant.*   An adoption order cannot be made on the sole application of the mother or father of the child unless:

(a)   the other natural parent is dead or cannot be found;[1] or
(b)   there is some other reason justifying the exclusion of the other natural parent.[2]

Although the precise scope of these restrictions is uncertain, it is clear that adoption even within the permitted circumstances will be exceptional. Indeed it is highly unlikely that the natural parent alone will want to adopt his or her legitimate child. Take the case of the mother as sole applicant. If the father is dead, she will be able to rely on her rights of guardianship as surviving parent[3] as well as any existing order granting her custody. It seems that this rule of survivorship applies even if at the date of death the father had custody by an order.[4] In circumstances other than his death there will, in addition to the present provisions, be those concerning the father's agreement to an adoption order. They will be closely interwoven.

Thus, if the mother is relying for the purpose of her sole application on the fact that he cannot be found, that fact will enable the court to dispense with the agreement.[5] It would seem that 'some other reason' justifying the exclusion of the father must be a reason relating to the child's welfare,[6] and the restriction would seem primarily to contemplate such serious circumstances as would justify not only dispensing with the father's agreement[7] but also severing the links between him and his child, eg such persistent or serious ill-treatment of his child as led to his conviction of serious criminal offences. There is a faint possibility of the mother's wishing to adopt alone where she is no longer married to the father, but just as the AA 1976 encourages relatives and others to seek custodianship rather than adoption, so the court will expect the mother to rely on her right to claim custody under the MCA 1973.[8] It will be even more reluctant to grant adoption where the parents are still married to each other, and there will in such a case be the further restriction imposed by s 15(1)(b) of the AA 1976.[9]

For all these reasons the chances of adoption of a legitimate child by a natural parent alone are minimal. But if an order is made the court must record its reason for excluding the other parent.[10]

1 For the meaning of these words see ante, para 5.24.
2 AA 1976, s 15(3).
3 GMA 1971, s 3(1).
4 Surprisingly the relevant statutes enabling the making of custody orders (MCA 1973; GMA 1971 and 1973 and DPMCA 1978) are silent on this basic point. There are three possible qualifications to the survivorship rule. A divorce court can on the death of the parent to whom it had granted custody give the custody to a person other than the surviving parent; see *Pryor v Pryor* [1947] P 64, [1947] 1 All ER 381; *B v B and H (L intervening)* [1962] 1 All ER 29, [1961] 1 WLR 1467. Similarly the GMA 1971, s 9(4) allows for variation after the death of a parent. It also seems that the survivorship rule is qualified by any declaration made earlier by a divorce court, under MCA 1973, s 42(3) that the parent who survived, was unfit to have custody.
5 AA 1976, s 16(2)(a).
6 That view seems to be confirmed by the first reported case on s 11(3); see *Re C (a minor) (adoption by parent)* [1986] Fam Law 360.
7 AA 1976, s 16(2)(c)-(f).
8 See ante, para 3.51.
9 See ante, para 5.55.
10 AA 1976, s 15(3).

5.57 Doubt exists as to whether section 15(3) extends to the unmarried father. While it is clear that generally in adoption law he is not a parent but a relative,[1] he is still the natural father and subsection (3) refers to 'the other natural parent' and not merely to the other parent. It may well be, therefore, that the presumption that the term 'parent' does not include the unmarried father[2] is excluded by the context. Certainly, one circumstance where section 15(3) could be particularly relevant for him would be where the mother is dead and he wishes to adopt. If, for example, she has no surviving near relatives, adoption would not, from the child's point of view, distort natural relationships. Save for exceptional circumstances of this kind, the father should be expected to turn to his right to claim custody under the GMA 1971 or alternatively, when the relevant provision comes into force, an order under section 4 of FLRA 1987 granting him all the parental rights and duties.[3]

1   AA 1976, s 72(1).
2   *Re M (an infant)* [1955] 2 QB 479, [1955] 2 All ER 911, CA.
3   The terms of s 4 are such that they do not exclude the possibility of an order being made after the mother has died.

5.58   *Step-parent as applicant.*[1]   As the Houghton Committee emphasised,[2] a joint adoption by a parent and step-parent has the artificial effect of changing the legal relationship between the parent and the child from a natural to an adoptive one and at the same time of severing the child's links with the other natural parent and thus with the other half of his family with whom he will usually have spent part of his life. An adoption order granted to a step-parent alone will not only have this latter effect, but will also sever the child's links with the natural parent who is or was the spouse of the step-parent. To avoid, where desirable, these consequences and to reduce step-parent adoptions, the Adoption Act 1976 expects the step-parent in certain circumstances to turn to the divorce court for relief by way of a custody order. Where a step-parent applies, whether jointly with his spouse or alone, for an adoption order, the court must dismiss the application if it considers that the matter would be better dealt with under section 42 of the Matrimonial Causes Act 1973.[3]

1   See generally Maidment, *Step-Parents and Step-Children: Legal Relationships in Serial Unions* in Eekelaar and Katz (eds), *Marriage and Cohabitation in Contemporary Societies* (1980); Masson, Norbury and Chatterton, *Mine, Yours or Ours* (1983); Priest, *Step-Parent Adoptions: What is the Law?* [1982] JSWL 285; Rawlings, *Law Reform with Tears* (1982) 45 MLR 637.
2   Cmnd 5107, paras 103-110.
3   AA 1976, ss 14(3) and 15(4), re-enacting ss 10(3) and 11(4) of CA 1975. For early reactions to the 1975 provisions see Bissett-Johnson, *Step-Parent Adoptions in English and Canadian Law;* Bromley, *The New English Law of Adoption* (both in Baxter and Eberts, *The Child and the Courts* (1978). For MCA 1973, s 42 see ante, paras 3.51 *et seq.*

5.59   This duty usually arises on a joint application, for example, where the mother marries the step-father after divorce or annulment of her earlier marriage. In *Re S (infants) (adoption by parent),*[1] the Court of Appeal stated that the effect of what was formerly section 10(3), construed with section 3,[2] of the Children Act 1975 was to ask, 'Will adoption safeguard and promote the welfare of the child better than either the existing arrangements or a joint custody order under section 42?' Since in cases of this kind the child will already have acquired all the material advantages that adoption could provide 'the advantages of adoption will have to be found, if at all, in the intangible results which might flow from it'. On this test, in the majority of cases, the emphasis would be firmly against making adoption orders.[3] However, the Court of Appeal in *Re D (minors) (adoption by step-parent)*[4] appears to have shifted from its position in *Re S* and no longer requires the court to find that adoption would itself be better than a custody order. The proper question is: can the matter be dealt with better by a custody order? Only if there is an affirmative answer will it be necessary to dismiss the adoption application.[5] In *Re D* joint custody in favour of the mother and step-father would not have been the better solution. They were about to emigrate with the children; the natural father had dropped out of the children's lives and he agreed to the adoption; and the children themselves (aged 13 and 10) wished to be adopted.[6] In spite of the apparent shift of emphasis in *Re D,* it cannot be denied the present law makes it difficult for the practitioner to advise his client on the chances of a successful step-parent adoption, especially with the knowledge that dismissal of the adoption application means a fresh application to the divorce court under section 42 of the MCA 1973.[7]

1 [1977] Fam 173, [1977] 3 All ER 671, CA. See also *Re W* (1976) 120 Sol Jo 857.
2 See now s 6 of AA 1976.
3 In the first year of operation of the rule the number of joint parent/step-parent adoptions fell by 42%; see Bromley, p 389.
4 (1980) 2 FLR 102, 10 Fam Law 246, CA.
5 Bromley, p 389, comments that 'this seems the more natural interpretation of the actual provision'; and support for it may also be derived from the argument (Cretney, p 435) that 'a joint custody order made by the divorce court in favour of the step-parent and his spouse almost inevitably entails the risk that there will be further unsettling litigation'; and this risk has been exacerbated by the decision in *Dipper v Dipper* [1981] Fam 31, [1980] 2 All ER 722, CA, ante, para 3.53, to the effect that 'a non-custodial parent nevertheless remains entitled to know and be consulted about decisions affecting the child's upbringing'. Nevertheless, the approach in *Re D* does not accord with the Parliamentary history of the Children Bill. That emphasis was intended on resort to the divorce court is strengthened by the complementary provision (in s 33(5) of CA 1975) which normally prevents a step-parent applying for a custodianship order where there have been earlier divorce proceedings, leaving him instead to seek an order under s 42 of MCA 1973. See also Local Authority Circular LAC (76), para 10 for support for this view.
6 Earlier in *Re S* (1978) 9 Fam Law 88, CA, the natural father had only seen his son once when he was three weeks old. Adoption was ordered, since it was 'really a case of . . . bringing the legal situation into direct relationship with the human situation' (per Ormrod LJ).
7 The practical difficulties to which ss 10(3) and 11(4) of CA 1975 (now ss 14(3) and 15(4) of AA 1976) have given rise and the wide regional variations in applying them have been forcibly demonstrated in the study by Masson, Norbury and Chatterton, op cit.

(b) Age and status of the child

5.60   To be adopted a child must be under the age of 18[1] and never have been married.[2] An adopted child may be further adopted or even re-adopted by the natural parents, whether the earlier adoption was made by an English court or another court or otherwise.[3]

1   AA 1976, ss 12(1), 72(1).
2   Ibid, s 12(5).
3   Ibid, s 12(7).

(c) Living together

5.61   Before an adoption order can be made there must be sufficient opportunity to see whether the child is likely to settle in the home of the applicants and that they are likely to be suitable parents to bring him up. Where the applicant, or one of them, is a parent, step-parent or relative of the child or the child has been placed with the applicants by an adoption agency or in pursuance of an order of the High Court,[1] an order cannot be made unless the child is at least 19 weeks old and at all times during the preceding 13 weeks had his home with the applicants or one of them.[2] In the case of any other application, the child must have had his home with one or both of them for the whole of the preceding 12 months.[3] This longer period is considered necessary for assessing the suitability of adoption, since there will not have been the thorough inquiry into the circumstances of the child and the applicants which precedes a placement by an adoption agency.[4] This will be the case, for example, where the placement of the child was not with a view to adoption, as where a local authority places a child who is in its care with persons for fostering and they later apply to adopt.[5] The relevance of this 12-month rule to independent (ie not adoption agency) placements for adoption has to be seen against the rule which seeks to ban such placements.[6]

1 Presumably this means in pursuance of either its prerogative jurisdiction or its statutory jurisdiction under GMA 1971 or MCA 1973. If its statutory jurisdiction is included, it creates anomalies. For example, a person who is granted care and control by a divorce county court under MCA 1973 could not bring himself within the present rule (assuming he is not a parent, step-parent or relative) whereas he could if the order was made by the High Court.
2 AA 1976, s 13(1).
3 Ibid, s 13(2).
4 See ante, paras 5.14–5.19.
5 In practice the child is very likely to have been with the foster parents much longer than 12 months before they apply.
6 See post, para 5.64.

5.62 A child has his home with the person who, disregarding absence of the child at a hospital or boarding school and any other temporary absence, has actual custody of him.[1] In any case of a joint application it will be sufficient if the child has had his home with only one of the applicants during the relevant period, thus facilitating adoptions where, for example, the husband's job requires him to be away for periods at a time. The child's interests are, nevertheless, substantially protected by the requirement[2] that the court must be satisfied that sufficient opportunities to see the child with both applicants together in the home environment have been afforded to the adoption agency which placed the child or, in non-agency cases, to the local authority within whose area the applicants have their home.[3] The same opportunities must be given in the case of adoption by one person. No time limit is imposed, but the rule envisages a number of opportunities and their actually being taken up. The effect of this requirement where the child is temporarily absent, eg at a boarding school, will mean that the actual period before adoption is permitted will have to be extended. 'Home environment' is not defined, but apparently is intended to signify the household of which the applicants and the child form part: its location, its size and the interrelationship of its members.

It is not unknown for applicants to allow the child to visit or spend short periods with his parent during the period preceding the hearing of the adoption application. Such absences, being temporary, would not break the continuity of actual custody.[4] Nevertheless, they ought to be considered by the court when deciding whether or not to make an adoption order. In those cases where the child has been placed with the applicants with a view to adoption, as opposed to those where he has had his home with relatives or long-term foster-parents who later seek adoption, such absences could be a cogent factor in refusing an order.

1 CA 1975, s 87(3); see further ante, para 1.65.
2 AA 1976, s 13(3).
3 Cf *Re Adoption Application AA 121/1984* (1985) Times, 5 July where the applicants lived in Hong Kong, the children were in boarding school in England and only spent short holidays with them.

4   It was held under the law prior to the CA 1975 that continuity was broken where the
    applicants allowed the parent to take the child away to her own home on one occasion
    for two consecutive nights and on the other for a night and a day; see *Re CSC (an infant)*
    [1960] 1 All ER 711, [1960] 1 WLR 304. Bromley, p 405, raises the question whether
    continuity could still be broken in such circumstances. It is submitted that the express
    statutory reference now in s 87(3) to allowing for temporary absences covers those
    circumstances.

(d)   Independent placements

5.63   It is an offence for a person (eg a doctor) other than an adoption
agency[1] to make arrangements for the adoption of a child or place him
for adoption, unless the proposed adopter is a relative of the child or he
is acting in pursuance of a High Court order.[2] Equally it is an offence
for a person to receive a child who has been placed with him in breach
of that rule.[3] The two offences are therefore inextricably linked, but there
cannot be conviction for the offence of receiving unless it is first established
that there was an illegal placement.[4] Where, therefore, the person placed
the child genuinely with fostering and not adoption in mind, the person
receiving him cannot be convicted even if he at the time he intended after
a period of 12 months to apply for adoption. On the other hand, if there
were an illegal placement, it seems[5] that equally there could be no conviction
for receiving if the real purpose of the person receiving the child had at
the time been fostering or custodianship. Nevertheless, in most cases it
is likely that there will be mutual intention to evade the rule. Neither of
the exceptions to the rule is likely to have a marked impact. High Court
orders are rarely made for this purpose and, now that the relevant provisions
are in force, relatives may be encouraged to seek custodianship rather than
adoption.

1   Where the agency is an approved adoption society as respects England and Wales, it
    cannot act as such in Scotland except as far as the society considers it necessary in the
    interests of a child who has been or may be adopted, his parents and guardians or those
    who have adopted or may adopt him. The restriction applies *mutatis mutandis* to a society
    approved for Scotland; AA 1976, s 11(2).
2   See *Re K (a minor) (adoption and wardship)* (1983) 13 Fam Law 146; *Re S (arrangements
    for adoption)* [1985] FLR 579, [1985] Fam Law 132, CA; *Re Adoption Application AA
    113/67* (1987) Times, 29 November.
3   AA 1976 s 11(1) and (3). The penalties are a maximum term of three months' imprisonment
    or a maximum fine of £2,000 or both. The same penalties attach to the offence of taking
    part in the management or control of a body which exists to arrange adoptions but is
    not an adoption agency.
4   *Gatehouse v R* [1986] 1 WLR 18.
5   See Watkins LJ, ibid at 27.

5.64   Apart from the two recognised exceptions, the general prohibition
will not totally prevent the independent placement, because it is possible
for a child to be placed with private foster parents ostensibly on a temporary
basis but after 12 months for them to rely on the 12 month rule[1] and
seek an adoption order. However, in a case of that kind the court is highly
likely to be put on its inquiry and it would be advisable for the foster
parents to delay their application beyond the 12 months, especially in view
of the duty to investigate imposed upon the local authority.[2] The authority's
report to the court hearing the adoption application must state whether
the child was placed with the applicants in contravention of the rule

forbidding private placements. If there has been contravention but criminal proceedings have not yet been instituted,[3] the court should, it is suggested, adjourn the hearing pending the outcome of those proceedings. The law is far from clear about what may happen to the child if criminal proceedings are taken before the hearing of the adoption application and the applicant is convicted of receiving the child in contravention of section 11 of the AA 1976. It is expressly provided that where a person is so convicted, section 26 of the AA 1976 is to apply as it applies where an application for an adoption order is refused.[4] This means that the convicting court can invoke the powers of that section. The section enables a court either:

(a)   to make an order placing the child under the supervision of a local authority or probation officer if it considers that exceptional circumstances make it desirable; or

(b)   to commit the child to the care of a local authority if exceptional circumstances make it impracticable or undesirable for the child to be entrusted to either of the parents or to any other individual.

Is it implicit in the conferment of these powers that, if there are no such exceptional circumstances, the convicting court has the power to return the child to the parent[5] or to allow him to continue to live with the intending adopter, even though both parent and recipient may have been convicted, or to place him with some other individual? If so, what is the precise order to be made? If, on the other hand, it is not implicit that the court has these powers when it does not make an order under section 26, it seems to follow that the court hearing the adoption application would have to determine the child's future. Although it is not prevented from making an adoption order, notwithstanding the conviction,[6] there would have to be strong reasons, based on the child's welfare before it would do so. Instead, it would be likely to rely on the powers it has when refusing adoption.[7]

---

1   See ante, para 5.61.
2   AA 1976, s 22(2), especially sub-s (3)(b), see post, para 5.66.
3   The illegality of the original placement may not have been discovered until shortly before the date of the hearing of the adoption application.
4   AA 1976, s 11(5).
5   Compare the power of a court convicting for an offence relating to unlawful payments to remove the child to a place of safety until he can be restored to the parent or guardian or until other arrangements can be made; see AA 1976, s 57(2), post, para 5.95.
6   Compare the express prohibition on making an order where the applicant has contravened the rules relating to payments in relation to adoption: see AA 1976, s 24(2), post, para 5.95.
7   See post, para 5.101.

5.65 Two other provisions in the AA 1976 are also designed to discourage independent placements. Section 57 makes it an offence to make or receive payments in consideration of an adoption,[1] and section 58 prohibits any advertisement indicating that a parent or guardian wishes to have a child adopted, that a person desires to adopt a child or that anyone except an adoption agency is willing to make arrangements for adoption.

---

1   See post, para 5.95.

(e) Notification to local authority

5.66 Section 22(1) of the Adoption Act 1976 provides that no adoption order can be made in respect of a child who was not placed by an adoption agency unless the applicant has given at least three months' written notice to the local authority within whose area he has his home that he intends to apply for the order. This provision is closely related to section 13 of the Act,[1] which requires the applicant to have a home in the area of the local authority and thereby to afford the authority the opportunity to see the child with the applicant in the home environment. Their effect is to create difficulties for the applicant who is domiciled in England and Wales but resident abroad. The term 'home' is incapable of precise definition, but the test to be applied in deciding whether he has a home here is whether or not there is a regular occupation, with some degree of permanency and based on some right of occupation whenever it is required.[2] It is, therefore, essentially a question of fact. However, for the purpose of section 22(1) it is not necessary that the child and the applicant should be actually living in the home at any particular time or for any particular length of time. What is required is merely that they should spend sufficient time there to enable the local authority to see them together in a home environment.[3] On giving of the notice to the local authority the child becomes a protected child,[4] and the authority must then investigate and submit a report to the court.[5] It must deal with the suitability of the applicant and any other matters relevant to the operation of section 6 of the AA 1976. Since that section requires the court to consider all the circumstances, the report must be wide ranging. As already noted,[6] the local authority must investigate whether an illegal placement or reception of the child has taken place.

The reason why the local authority does not submit a report in the case of an adoption agency placement is that the agency itself must do so and assist the court in any manner it may direct.[7]

1   See ante, para 5.61.
2   *Re Y (minors) (adoption: jurisdiction)* [1985] Fam 136, [1985] 3 All ER 33.
3   *Re Y*, supra.
4   See infra, para 5.67.
5   AA 1976, ss 22(2). In practice this will be a written report, but the Act does not exclude an oral report at the hearing of the adoption application.
6   See ante, para 5.64.
7   AA 1976, s 22(3).

(f) Protected child

5.67 A child is a protected child while he has his home with the applicant for adoption who has given the local authority notice of his intention to apply.[1] The child is subject to the supervision of the local authority during the period of 'protection' which continues until:

(a)   the appointment of a guardian for him under the GMA 1971;
(b)   the notification to the local authority that the application for an adoption order has been withdrawn;
(c)   the making of an adoption order, an order under s 26 of the AA 1976,[2] a custodianship order, an order under sections 42, 43 or 44 of the MCA 1973;[3] or
(d)   he attains 18, whichever first occurs.[4]

The local authority must see that the child is visited from time to time, be satisfied about his well being and give advice about his care and maintenance.[5] It can authorise its officers to inspect any premises in its area where the child is being kept.[6] The Secretary of State may also authorise inspection.[7]

1   AA 1976, s 32(1).
2   See post, para 5.101.
3   See ante, paras 3.51, 3.55 and 3.57.
4   AA 1976, s 32(4).
5   Ibid, s 33(1).
6   Ibid, s 33(2). Refusal to allow the visiting of a protected child is an offence punishable by imprisonment for up to three months and/or a fine of up to £2,000 (AA 1976 s 36(1)(b) and (2)). It also justifies the issue of a warrant to search for and remove the child (s 37(1)). If the prospective adopter moves he must notify the local authority at least two weeks in advance, or, in the case of an emergency, within one week of the change. The notified authority will in turn notify any new authority into whose area he has moved giving details of the child's birth, name and sex and the name and address of any parent or guardian (s 35(1)). Non-compliance is an offence carrying the same penalties as above (s 36(1)(a) and (2)).
7   CCA 1980, ss 74, 75 and Sch 4, para 8.

5.68   A local authority may complain to a juvenile court that the child is being kept, or is about to be received by, a person who is unfit to have his care or in premises or an environment detrimental to him.[1] The court[2] may order the child to be removed to a place of safety until he can be restored to a parent, relative or guardian or until other arrangements can be made, including the possibility of the local authority receiving him into their care under section 2 of the CCA 1980, even if he appears to be over 17.[3] In a case of imminent danger to the health or well-being of the child, a justice of the peace may make an order for removal on the application of an officer of the local authority. Where a child is removed the local authority must, if practicable, inform the child's parent or guardian.[4] The person who maintains the protected child is deemed to have no interest in the child's life for the purposes of the Life Assurance Act 1774.[5]

1   AA 1976, s 34(1).
2   The usual restrictions on the sittings of juvenile courts do not apply here and proceedings are held in open court. Appeal lies to the Crown Court (AA 1976, ss 37(4) and (3) respectively).
3   AA 1976, s 34(3). Failure to comply with an order is an offence (s 36(1)(c) and (2)). An order may be executed by any person authorised to visit protected children or by any constable (s 34(2)).
4   Ibid, s 34(4).
5   Ibid, s 37(2).

3   The application for adoption[1]

(a)   Procedure

5.69   An application for an adoption order is made by originating summons in the High Court, by originating application in a county court and by application in a magistrates' court in accordance with the appropriate form prescribed by the relevant Adoption Rules.[2] Applications for a section 18 order are by similar process.[3] If the child is a ward of court, leave of the court is required to commence adoption proceedings or, as the case may be, freeing for adoption proceedings, but application for leave may be made before the foster parents are known.[4] Where leave is sought to commence proceedings in the High Court or in a county court, application may be made ex parte to a registrar.[5] However, where a local authority has already been granted leave to place a ward of court with foster parents with a view to adoption, application for leave to commence adoption proceedings[6] is not necessary unless the court otherwise directs.[7]

An applicant for adoption who wishes to keep his identity confidential can apply to the proper officer of the court or, in a magistrates' court, to the justices' clerk for a serial number to be assigned to him for the purpose of the proceedings.[8] Moreover, where, in accordance with the above rules, leave is given to commence adoption proceedings in respect of a ward of court, the registrar may direct that any subsequent proceedings are conducted with a view to securing that the proposed adopter is not seen by, or made known to, any respondent or prospective respondent who is not already aware of his identity, except with his consent.[9]

1   Where appropriate, note will be made of similar provisions governing s 18 applications.
2   See AR 1984, Form 6 and MC(A)R 1984, Form 6. The great majority of adoption orders are made by county courts. Figures for 1985 and 1986 (6,410 and 6,477) show a slight fall from 85% in 1984 to 82% and 84% with a corresponding slight increase in magistrates' court orders from 13% in 1984 and 1985 to 15% in 1986. High court orders remained at less than 4% of all orders in 1986. See OPCS Monitor FM3 87/1 and for comment thereon 11 Adoption and Fostering No 4 p 48.
3   See AR 1984, Form 1 and MC(A)R 1984, Form 1.
4   *F v S (adoption: ward)* [1973] Fam 203, [1973] 1 All ER 722, CA; *Practice Direction* [1985] 1 All ER 832, [1985] 1 WLR 310, as amended by *Practice Direction* [1986] 1 All ER 652, [1986] 1 WLR 286.
5   RSC Ord 90, r 4A(1)(a) and (c), as substituted by RSC (Amendment) 1988, r 8.
6   Or custodianship proceedings.
7   RSC Ord 90, r 4A(2). But it has been pointed out (see White, 138 NLJ 222) that, where the adoption application is contested and it is sought to dispense with parental agreement, it may well be necessary, notwithstanding r 4A(2), to apply for leave for disclosure of the wardship papers.
8   AR 1984, r 14; MC(A)R 1984, r 14.
9   Ord 90, r 4A(3). A similar direction may be given where a local authority has applied for leave to place a ward of court with foster parents or the foster parents request such a direction.

(b)   Notification of hearing

5.70   Unless the child has already been freed for adoption, each parent or guardian must be made a respondent to the proceedings,[1] but, depending on the circumstances, so must a number of other persons or bodies.[2] The most frequent will be adoption agencies and local authorities. An adoption agency will be a respondent if it has placed the child for adoption or taken part in the arrangements for the adoption or, where there has been a section 18 order, because the parental rights and duties were vested in it by that order or transferred to it[3] following a section 18 order. A local authority may be a respondent for a variety of reasons, viz:

(a)   as the authority to whom notice of intention to adopt has been given in a non-adoption agency placement;[4]

(b)   as the authority in whom the parental rights and duties are vested as the result of a resolution passed under section 3 of the CCA 1980 or of a care order;[5]

(c)   as the authority in whose care a child is by virtue of an enactment.[6]

Similarly a voluntary organisation which has the care of the child or in whom the parental rights and duties are vested[7] must be made a respondent, as must any person liable by virtue of any order or agreement to contribute to the maintenance of the child, for example, the father who is subject to an affiliation order in respect of the child. In the exceptional case of a sole applicant who intends to rely on the fact that he is living apart from his spouse and the separation is likely to be permanent he must make that spouse a party. The court also has a residual power to direct that anyone else (other than the child) may be made a respondent.

1   In a s 18 application each parent or guardian must be a respondent; AR 1984, r 4(2); MC(A)R 1984, r 4(2).
2   AR 1984, r 15(2); MC(A)R 1984, r 15(2). For the possible respondents to s 18 applications see r 4(2) of each set of rules. It will be seen that the list closely follows that for adoption applications.
3   Under AA 1976, s 21.
4   In accordance with ibid, s 22 see ante, para 5.66.
5   See CCA 1980, s 10.
6   Eg under ibid s 2 or where an order is made committing the child to the care of the local authority in matrimonial or guardianship proceedings.
7   By virtue of ibid, s 64.

5.71   Notice of the hearing must be served on all the parties and on the reporting officer and the guardian ad litem (if appointed).[1] Where the proceedings are in the High Court and notice has been given to a natural parent by the court asking if he wishes to be heard in the proceedings and he has not acknowledged receipt of it within 21 days, the Principal Registry will inform the applicants' solicitor, who must then serve the parent at the latest address known to the Registry with a notice informing him of the earlier notice and of his right within ten days to give his views to the judge on whether or not an adoption order or a freeing for adoption order should be made.[2] Where it has been necessary for the applicant to give notice to the local authority of his intention to apply,[3] a copy of the originating process must be given to the local authority. The adoption agency or the local authority, as the case may be,[4] must submit its report to the court within six weeks of receipt of the notice, with a copy being sent to the reporting officer and the guardian ad litem.[5]

1   AR 1984, r 21; MC(A)R 1984, r 21. The notice must be in a Form 8. For notice of a s 18 application see r 9 with Form 3.
2   For further details and form of notice see *Practice Direction* [1986] 1 All ER 1024, [1986] 1 WLR 443.
3   In accordance with AA 1976, s 22.
4   See ante, para 5.66.
5   AR 1984, r 22; MC(A)R, r 22.

(c)   Reporting officer

5.72   As in section 18 proceedings,[1] the court must appoint a reporting officer in respect of a parent or guardian who appears to be willing to agree to adoption.[2] His duties are almost identical with those in respect of a section 18 application, and have already been set out.[3]

1   See ante, para 5.38.

2   AR 1984, r 17; MC(A)R 1984, r 17.
3   See ante, para 5.39. The one duty which does not apply to an application for adoption
    is that of confirming a declaration by a parent or guardian that he prefers not to be
    involved in future questions concerning the child's adoption.

(d)   Guardian ad litem

5.73   A guardian ad litem must be appointed where the child is not free
for adoption and it appears that a parent or guardian is unwilling to agree
to adoption. Where the child is free, the proper officer[1] of the court has
a discretion to appoint,[2] but the Adoption Rules do not give him guidance
on the kinds of circumstances where appointment would be desirable.
Otherwise the rules relating to appointment are the same as in section
18 proceedings.[3] His duties, too, are very largely the same as they are in
respect of a section 18 application and have already been noted.[4]

1   For the meaning of 'proper officer' see ante, para 5.38.
2   AR 1984, r 18; MC(A)R 1984, r 18.
3   See ante, para 5.41.
4   See ante, para 5.42.

(e)   Panels

5.74   The Guardians ad Litem and Reporting Officers (Panels) Regulations
1983 provide for the establishment in each local authority area of a panel
from whom guardians ad litem and reporting officers may be appointed
by the court in, inter alia, adoption proceedings. The local authority appoints
the members of a panel after inviting nominations from:

(a)   any probation committee in its area;
(b)   the clerk of each magistrates' court in its area;
(c)   any local authority of an adjoining area; and
(d)   any other person as it considers appropriate.[1]

The authority is not restricted to appointing members so nominated, but
it must ensure that an adequate number are appointed.[2] The Rules do
not lay down any criteria for selecting members. It is a matter for the
authority to decide whether the qualifications and experience of a person
are suitable, but the Department of Health and Social Security have issued
a handbook giving local authorities guidance on the matter. Subject to
ability and fitness to act, appointment is for three years. The Rules are
silent on the question of eligibility for re-appointment. The local authority
must pay the expenses, fees and allowances of all panel members except
those who are employed by local authorities or probation committees for
more than 30 hours a week.[3]

In adoption proceedings any member of a panel who is employed by
an adoption agency is ineligible for appointment as a guardian ad litem
or reporting officer in any application for an adoption order or for a freeing
for adoption order in which the agency is or has been involved.[4]

1   Reg 3.
2   Ibid, reg 2(2).
3   Reg 4 as amended by the Guardians ad litem and Reporting Officers (Panels) (Amendment)
    Regulations 1986, SI 1986/3.
4   AA 1976, s 65(2).

(f) Preliminary examination of adoption application

(i) Where there has been a previous unsuccessful application

5.75 Once applicants have been refused a British adoption order[1] no further application by them can be heard in respect of the same child, unless the court directed otherwise when refusing the previous application or it appears to the court hearing the later application that there has been a change in circumstances or some other reason making it proper to proceed with the application.[2] If it appears to the proper officer of the court on receipt of the originating process for an adoption order that the application may be precluded from proceeding because of the above restriction, he must refer the process to the judge for directions.[3] The Adoption Rules do not indicate how either the officer or the judge is to exercise his discretion. It is suggested that, once it appears from the originating process that there has been an earlier application,[4] the officer should refer it to the judge, leaving the latter on a preliminary examination to decide whether or not one of the permitted conditions is satisfied. A similar duty is imposed on a justices' clerk to refer an adoption application in a magistrates' court to the justices for preliminary examination.[5]

1 A British adoption order means an adoption order made by a court in England and Wales or Scotland authorised to make an adoption order or any provision for the adoption of a child effected under the law of Northern Ireland or any British territory outside the United Kingdom (AA 1976, s 72(1)).
2 AA 1976, s 24(1). See *Re V (a minor) (adoption: consent)* [1987] Fam 57, [1986] 1 All ER 752, CA.
3 AR 1984, r 16.
4 See ibid, Form 6, para 19, where any earlier proceedings have to be indicated.
5 MC(A)R 1984, r 16 and Form 6, para 19.

(ii) Where there is any other reason

5.76 The proper officer must also refer the process to the judge where it appears to him that for some other reason appearing in the process there is no jurisdiction to make an adoption order. Under the former adoption rules it was expressly provided that the officer had to refer to the judge for preliminary examination any step-parent application for adoption if it appeared that the court might be required to dismiss the application pursuant to what was then section 10(3) or 11(4) of the CA 1975.[1] The Adoption Rules 1984 do not so provide, but it would seem that such a case falls within the meaning of 'any other reason'. Because of the continued uncertainty surrounding those sections it is highly desirable that the procedure for preliminary examination should be available. Where there is to be a preliminary examination the officer will fix a hearing date and should give notice to the applicant, the guardian ad litem (if appointed) and any parent who is not an applicant.[2]

1 See ante, para 5.58 and see now AA 1976, s 14(3) and s 15(4).
2 See *Practice Direction* [1981] 2 All ER 1115, [1981] 1 WLR 1212, relating to the former adoption rules.

(g) The hearing[1]

5.77 The child must attend the hearing, unless the court directs that because of special circumstances his attendance is unnecessary,[2] for example, where he is ill and it is not in his interests to postpone the decision on adoption, or where it is clear from the evidence of the guardian ad litem that the child understands the nature of the application and wants it to succeed.[3] So, too, the personal attendance of the applicant is necessary, but where there is a joint application the judge may make an adoption order or interim order after attendance of only one of the applicants, provided the other has verified by affidavit the originating process or, if he is outside the United Kingdom, by a declaration.[4] Any other person on whom notice of the hearing has to be served[5] may attend and be heard on the question whether an adoption order should be made,[6] but the court may direct the attendance of a party if it considers that there are special circumstances making that necessary.[7] Any member or employee of a party which is a local authority, adoption agency or other body may address the court if duly authorised to do so on its behalf.[8]

1 For the same or similar rules relating to the hearing of a s 18 application see AR 1984, r 10; MC(A)R 1984, r 10.
2 AR 1984, r 23(4) and (5); MC(A)R 1984, r 23(4) and (5).
3 *Re P (minors)* (1987) Times, 1 August, (1988) Adoption and Fostering Vol 12 No 1, p 57, CA.
4 AR 1984, r 23(4) and (7); MC(A)R 1984, r 23(4) and (7). Verification by affidavit is not available in proceedings in a magistrates' court.
5 See ante, paras 5.70, 5.71.
6 AR 1984, r 23(1); MC(A)R 1984, r 23(1).
7 AR 1984, r 23(6); MC(A)R 1984, r 23(6).
8 AR 1984, r 23(2); MC(A)R 1984, r 23(2).

5.78 Where the identity of the applicant is to be kept confidential, the hearing must be conducted so as to protect the confidentiality, for example, by ensuring that, unless he otherwise consents, he is not seen by or made known to any respondent who is not already aware of his identity.[1] For this reason the judge may consider it necessary to hear separately matters relevant to dispensing with parental agreement before hearing the adoption application, but this is permitted only as an exceptional procedure and normally both should be heard together.[2]

1 AR 1984, r 23(3); MC(A)R 1984, r 23(3). An applicant who wishes his identity to be kept confidential should, before commencing adoption proceedings apply to the court for a serial number to be assigned to him (see ibid, r 14).
2 *Re LS (a minor) (adoption procedure)* [1986] 1 FLR 302, CA; *Re K (a minor) (adoption: procedure)* [1986] 1 FLR 295, [1985] Fam Law 314, CA; *Re R (a minor) (adoption: parental agreement)* [1987] 1 FLR 391, [1987] Fam Law 95, CA.

(h) Restrictions on removal of child

5.79 There are a number of provisions in the Adoption Act 1976 which are designed to prevent the sudden removal of a child from a stable environment, while adoption is pending.

(i) Restrictions where adoption agreed or application made for freeing for adoption (AA 1976, s 27)

5.80 These are imposed upon the parent or guardian:

(a) While an application for an adoption order is pending and the parent or guardian has agreed[1] to an adoption order being made in favour of a specific applicant, whether or not he knows his identity, he cannot remove the child from the custody of the person with whom the child has his home against that person's will, unless the court[2] gives him permission,[3] as, for example, could occur where for reasons of ill health the applicant is unable satisfactorily to look after the child. It seems clear that, if the person with custody is willing, the parent or guardian will be entitled to remove the child without recourse to the court. It is questionable whether this is desirable, since there must be some risk that return to the parent or guardian will not be in the child's interests.

(b) The second restriction relates to certain applications under section 18 of the Adoption Act 1976 affecting children who are in the care of adoption agencies. Where the child is in the care of the adoption agency which has applied for a freeing for adoption order and the application was not made with the consent of each parent or guardian, then, so long as the application is pending, no parent or guardian who did not so consent is entitled to remove the child against the will of the person with whom the child has his home, unless the court grants leave.[4] This restriction similarly does not operate if the person having custody consents to removal.[5] Although the child is in the care of the agency, it is not its consent but that of the person having actual custody which has to be obtained. That person may only have temporary actual custody and may not be the eventual applicant for the adoption order; for example, he may be a short-term foster parent or a house-parent in a local authority community home or in a voluntary home. He is not statutorily required to consult the agency before giving his consent, but failure to do so would be a breach of any undertaking to the agency.

1 Oral agreement is enough to prevent lawful removal by the parent or guardian; *Re T (a minor)* [1986] Fam 160, [1986] 1 All ER 817, CA.
2 Ie actual custody; see CA 1975, s 87(3).
3 For the appropriate court see ante, para 5.50.
4 AA 1976, s 27(1).
5 Ibid, s 27(2). For the appropriate court see ante, para 5.50

(ii) Restrictions where applicant has provided home for five years (AA 1976, s 28)

5.81 These restrictions very largely affect the foster parent with whom the child has had his home for at least five years. Under section 28(1) once the foster parent applies for an adoption order, then, subject to certain qualifications,[1] the position is frozen until the application is heard, as it is in cases under section 27 of the Act, but the protection under section 28 is wider since no one, and not just the parent or guardian, is entitled to remove the child. Under subsection (2) he can secure further protection at an earlier date. As a 'prospective adopter' he can notify the local authority[2] of his intention to apply for an order whereupon there cannot (subject to the same qualifications) be a lawful removal before either an application for such an order is made or three months have expired since receipt of the notice by the authority, whichever first occurs. Effectively, therefore, this means that, if the application is first made, the protection afforded by subsection (1) then operates. Otherwise the foster parent cannot shelter behind subsection (2) indefinitely. Nor can he evade the time limit by issuing successive notices to the authority before the previous one expires. There must be a gap of 28 days before a new notice can be served, thus enabling the child meantime to be removed by the natural parents or the local authority or a voluntary organisation, if his interests so warrant.[3]

1   See infra, para 5.82.
2   Ie the local authority within whose area he has his home. If the authority knows that the child is in the care of another local authority or voluntary organisation it must, within 7 days, inform that other authority or organisation that it has received the prospective adopter's notice (AA 1976, s 28(5)).
3   Ibid, s 28(6).

5.82   The parent or guardian or anyone else will not commit an offence if the five-year applicant or prospective adopter changes his mind and allows him to remove the child,[1] but the chances of this happening are unlikely. The court,[2] however, has power to grant leave for removal. An order may be made not only because removal would be in the child's interests but also on a technical ground, for example, that the continuity of actual custody for five years has been broken. Additionally removal is lawful on the arrest of the child or under authority conferred by any enactment. The kind of enactments intended are those which enable removal to a place of safety where there is actual, or immediate risk of, harm to the child.[3]

1   If the child is in the care of a local authority or voluntary organisation and boarded out with the applicant or prospective adopter, his consent to removal is a breach of his undertaking to the authority or organisation not to hand over the child to anyone without their approval.
2   See AA 1976, s 28(1) and (4).
3   The main examples are removal on the strength of a warrant issued by a justice of the peace under CYPA 1933, s 40 or under the Sexual Offences Act 1956, s 43 or on his authorisation in accordance with CYPA 1969, s 28 or, in the case of a foster child who is being kept in unsuitable surroundings, by an order of the juvenile court under the Foster Children Act 1980, s 12.

5.83   Wrongful removal of a child in contravention of sections 27 and 28 is an offence punishable with imprisonment for not more than three months or a fine of up to £2,000 or both.[1]

1   Sections 27(3) and 28(7).

(i)   Return of the child who is unlawfully removed

5.84   The person from whose custody[1] a child has been removed in breach of section 27 or section 28 can apply to the court[2] for an order that the person who has wrongfully removed the child return him to the applicant.[3] An application can also be made where the applicant has reasonable grounds for believing that another person is intending to remove the child in breach of either of those sections: the court may then forbid removal.[4]

1   Ie actual custody; see ante, para 5.80, note 2.
2   For the appropriate court see ante, para 5.50.
3   AA 1976, s 29(1).
4   Ibid, s 29(2).

5.85   When the High Court or a county court has made an order for the child to be returned and it has not been complied with, the court has additional enforcement powers[1] to order one of its officers to search specified premises and, if the child is found, to return him to the applicant. If the order to return was made by a magistrates' court, and also as an alternative to the above procedure where the order was made by the High Court or a county court, search and return can be authorised by a justice of the peace if he is satisfied by information on oath that there are reasonable grounds for believing the child is in specified premises. These additional powers will therefore enable the child to be recovered from any third party to whom the person committing a breach of section 27 or section 28 has entrusted actual custody of the child.

1   AA 1976, s 29(3) and (4).

(j)   Jurisdiction and procedure relating to applications to remove child

5.86   Jurisdiction and procedure are governed by the Adoption Rules 1984.[1] The appropriate court to hear:

(a)   an application under section 27 or 28 of the Adoption Act 1976 for leave to remove a child from the actual custody of the person with whom the child has his home; or

(b)   an application under section 29 of the Adoption Act 1976 for an order to return a child or to forbid removal

depends on whether an application for an adoption order or, where applicable, for a freeing for adoption order is pending.

If it is, then the application to remove etc must be by process on notice, or in a magistrates' court by complaint, in the adoption or section 18 proceedings. If there is no adoption or section 18 application pending, the application to remove etc is by way of originating process, or in a magistrates' court by way of complaint, to the 'appropriate court'. That means the High Court, the county court within whose district the applicant lives or the magistrates' court in whose area he lives, but where the application is under section 28(2) the county court within whose district, or the magistrates' court within whose area, the child is also has jurisdiction. Where proceedings for an adoption order or freeing for adoption order are pending in the High Court or a county court the proper officer of the court must serve a copy of the process and a notice of the date of the hearing of the application to remove etc on all the parties to those proceedings and on the reporting officer and guardian ad litem. In any other case the copy and notice is served on any person against whom an order is sought in the application etc to remove and on the local authority to whom the prospective adopter has given notice of his intention to apply for adoption. Unless otherwise directed, any prospective adopter who wishes to oppose the application to remove etc must himself file his process for an adoption order. If process is so filed, but the application to remove is granted, the court may thereupon refuse the adoption order.[2] Similar rules apply to proceedings in magistrates' courts.[3]

1   AR 1984, r 47; MC(A)R 1984, r 27.
2   For the details of procedure see AR 1984, r 47(4)–(11).

3   MC(A)R 1984, r 27(3)–(11).

4   The adoption order

(a)   Making an adoption order

(i)   The welfare of the child

5.87   The weight to be given to the child's welfare has already been examined.[1] The court must take into account the interests and attitude of all parties concerned, namely, the child, the natural parents and the adopting family,[2] and, where the adoption application is contested, (usually over the issue of dispensing with parental agreement) there must be a proper hearing, with witnesses giving evidence on oath, with opportunities for cross-examination and with a note being made of the court's reasons.[3] Although the unmarried father's agreement to the adoption of his child is not normally required,[4] regard will be had to his interests if he opposes the adoption.[5] Where, however, there is no issue over the agreement or interests of the natural parent, the court does in practice ask itself what is best for the child. Even where some other factor, such as public policy, has to be considered, the court may be ready to allow the child's welfare to prevail. Thus, in a proper case an adoption order will be made overriding an immigration decision.[6] On the other hand, adoption will not be ordered where its purpose is primarily to confer British nationality on the child and a right of abode in the UK rather than to promote his welfare during the remainder of his childhood, especially if only a short period of that remains.[7]

1   Ante, para 5.12.
2   See *Re S (a minor) (adoption by step-parents)* [1988] FCR 343, [1988] 1 FLR 418, CA, where it was held that the adamant refusal of a foster mother to disclose to the 13-year-old girl, whom she sought to adopt, the fact that she was not her natural mother was an attitude she was entitled to take, and was to be taken into account in applying s 6 of the 1976 Act.
3   See *Re C (adoption application: hearing)* (1981) 3 FLR 95, CA. The parents or guardians should normally be legally represented and legal aid should normally be granted; see Sachs LJ in *Re M (an infant)* [1973] QB 108 at 120; *Re C (adoption application: legal aid)* [1985] FLR 441n, [1985] Fam Law 197n.
4   See ante, para 5.22.
5   *Re W (a minor) (adoption)* [1984] FLR 402, [1984] Fam Law 179, CA.
6   *Re H (a minor) (adoption: non patrial)* [1982] Fam 121, [1982] 3 All ER 84; *Re Adoption Application 58/80* (1982) Times, 12 March.
7   *Re W (a minor) (adoption: non patrial)* [1986] Fam 54, [1985] 3 All ER 449, CA. On adoption and immigration see Khan 130 Sol Jo 213.

5.88   The kinds of matters that may be relevant may be as varied as they are in custody cases.[1] Essentially they relate to 'material and financial prospects, education, general surrounding, happiness, stability of home and the like'.[2] Specifically they include the following.

1   See ante, para 3.06 et seq.
2   Per Davies LJ in *Re B* [1971] 1 QB 437 at 443, [1970] 3 All ER 1008 at 1012.

5.89   *The comparative character and conduct of the parent and the prospective adopter.*   This includes past conduct towards other children as well as the

child to be adopted. Conduct has special relevance when considering whether
to dispense with parental agreement to adoption.

5.90   *The strength of the natural tie between the father and mother and
the child.*   Regard should be given to this 'not on the basis that the person
concerned has a claim which he has a right to have satisfied, but only
if, and to the extent that, the conclusion can be drawn that the child will
benefit from the recognition of this tie'.[1] Problems over the natural tie
have tended to be more frequent since the putative father's right to claim
custody was strengthened,[2] and the tie may lead to a custody order in
his favour[3] and the refusal of an adoption order. Prima facie, however,
since an adoption order legitimises an illegitimate child,[4] an adoption order
should be made if the natural father has nothing to offer the child in
comparison,[5] even if it should mean depriving him of a present right of
access,[6] and that would be the very likely consequence.[7]

1   Per Wilberforce J in *Re Adoption Application (No 2) 41/61* [1964] Ch 48 at 53, [1963]
    2 All ER 1082 at 1085.
2   See GMA 1971, s 9.
3   Or, when s 4 of FLRA 1987 comes into force, an order under that section granting him
    all the parental rights and duties.
4   It is expressly enacted that an adopted child is not illegitimate; see AA 1976, s 39(4),
    which has not been repealed by FLRA 1987.
5   *Re C (an infant)* (1969) 113 Sol Jo 721, CA. The natural father of a legitimate child
    may similarly have little or nothing to offer; *Re B (a minor), S v B* (1973) 4 Fam Law
    75, CA.
6   *Re E (P) (an infant)* [1969] 1 All ER 323, [1968] 1 WLR 1913, CA.
7   For the granting of access to the natural parent when an adoption order is made see
    post, para 5.94.

5.91   *Cultural, racial and religious factors.*   The weight to be given to the
respective cultural, racial and religious backgrounds of the natural parents
and the applicants for adoption is very variable. Applications for adoption
of coloured children are today more common, and in such cases the adoption
agency and the court should be particularly careful in satisfying themselves
that the applicants appreciate the additional responsibilities and difficulties
which absorption into a different cultural environment may create.[1] As
for religious upbringing of the child, an adoption agency is required when
placing a child to have regard to the wishes of the parent on the subject,[2]
but the parent cannot impose conditions concerning it when agreeing to
adoption.

1   See also ante, para 5.04, note 7.
2   AA 1976, s 7.

5.92   *Health of applicant and child.*   The Adoption Rules 1984 provide
for the health of the applicant and the child to be brought to the attention
of the court.[1] Medical evidence to show the risks arising from a change
of parentage can be important but rarely decisive. Acceptance of such
evidence as a general rule has not gained judicial support.[2]

1   See AR 1984, rr 4(4) and 15(4) and Schs 2, 3; MC(A)R 1984, rr 4(4) and 15(4) and Schs
    2, 3.

2 See Lord Reid in *O'Connor v A and B* [1971] 2 All ER 1230 at 1232, [1971] 1 WLR 1227 at 1230.

5.93 *The wishes and feelings of the child.* The adoption agency or the court 'shall so far as practicable ascertain the wishes and feelings of the child, and give due consideration to them, having regard to his age and understanding.'[1] It does not necessarily mean that effect will be given to them, since the child's welfare may require otherwise, but the court may well be strongly influenced by them.[2]

1 AA 1976, s 6. Cf *Re S (a minor) (adoption by step-parents)* [1988] FCR 343 [1988] 1 FLR 418, CA, where there was a failure to ascertain.
2 *Re D (minors) (adoption by step-parent)* (1980) 2 FLR 102, 10 Fam Law 246, CA; *Re B (a minor) (adoption)* [1988] Fam Law 172.

(ii) Conditions which may be imposed in the order
5.94 The court may impose such terms and conditions as it thinks fit in the adoption order.[1] The exercise of this power is likely to arise over granting access[2] to the natural parent or to another close member of the child's family, such as a brother or sister.[3] The scope of the power, both generally and specifically in relation to access has recently been analysed by the House of Lords in *Re C (a minor) (adoption: conditions)*.[4] It is a wide power and may extend to conditions which would involve the future intervention or supervision of the court, provided the particular condition is not contrary to the basic concept of adoption – and an access condition is not repugnant to that concept.[5] Normally, it is desirable that there should be a complete break with the child's natural family, especially where a baby is placed for adoption and there has been no contact between the parents and the adopters; but in exceptional circumstances access may be granted if it is clearly in the child's best interest. Even then it will not, save in very rare cases, be granted unless the adopters agree. In considering the child's welfare,[6] cogent factors will be his age and the extent of past access. The older he is and the more frequent the contact with the parent or other member of the family the stronger the chances of access being allowed.[7] On the other hand, the parental access may have been so successful as to justify refusing an adoption order.[8] Where access or any other condition is included in an adoption order, failure by the adopters to comply with the order renders them liable to committal proceedings.[9]

1 AA 1976, s 12(6).
2 Another possible condition is the religious upbringing of the child. Although the parent can no longer impose conditions concerning that matter when agreeing to adoption (supra, para 5.91), the court may include a condition, but it is unlikely to do so without the agreement of the adopters.
3 On access conditions see Maidment, *Access and Family Adoptions*, (1977) 40 MLR 293; Triseliotis, *Adoption with Contact*, Adoption and Fostering Vol 9, No 4, p 19; White, *Adoption and Access*, Adoption and Fostering Vol 11, No 4, p 47.
4 [1988] 1 All ER 705.
5 The possibility that it was was canvassed by Sir John Arnold P in the Court of Appeal in *Re C*; see [1987] 2 FLR at 387–388. Compare *Re C (a minor) (adoption order: condition)* [1986] 1 FLR 315, CA, where a condition that the adopters inform the natural father of the child's progress was held to be inconsistent with an adoption order.
6 In accordance with s 6 of AA 1976, ante, para 5.12.
7 In *Re C* [1988] 1 All ER 705 the child was almost 13 years old and was very attached to her brother, who was six years older. For other illustrations of access being allowed

see *Re J (a minor) (adoption order: conditions)* [1973] Fam 106, [1973] 2 All ER 410; *Re S (a minor) (adoption order: access)* [1976] Fam 1, [1975] 1 All ER 109, CA; *Re C (a minor) (wardship and adoption)* (1979) 2 FLR 177, CA; *Re GR (adoption: access)* [1985] FLR 643, [1985] Fam Law 255, CA. As illustrations of the point that an access condition will not (with rare exception) be included against the wishes of the adopters see *Re H (a minor) (adoption)* [1985] FLR 519, [1985] Fam Law 133, CA; *Re M (a minor) (adoption order: access)* [1986] 1 FLR 51, [1985] Fam Law 321, CA; *Re V (a minor) (adoption: consent)* [1987] Fam 57, [1986] 1 All ER 752, CA. *Re W (a minor) (adoption: custodianship: access)* [1988] 1 FLR 175, [1988] Fam Law 92, CA.

8   *Re M (minors) (adoption: parent's agreement)* [1985] FLR 921, CA; *Southwark London Borough Council v H* [1985] 2 All ER 657, [1985] 1 WLR 861; *Re M (a minor)* [1986] 1 FLR 51, [1985] Fam Law 321, CA.

9   *Re C* [1988] 1 All ER 705, [1988] 2 WLR 474 HL. In *Re J* [1973] Fam 106, [1973] 2 All ER 410 Rees J took the view that an alternative method of enforcement would be to make the child a ward of court and to request the court to enforce the terms of the adoption order. In *Re C* the House of Lords did not directly express an opinion on that possible alternative but did regard the order made in *Re J* as being 'of a somewhat complicated kind, the implementation of the access being at the discretion of and under the supervision of the Official Solicitor' (per Lord Ackner, [1988] 1 All ER 705 at 711).

(iii)   Payments by or to applicants

5.95   The court hearing the adoption application must be satisfied that no unlawful payments, in contravention of section 57 of the AA 1976, have been given or received by the applicants in consideration of adoption. If they have, no adoption order can be made.[1] Where an offence has been committed the convicting court may order the child to be removed to a place of safety until he can be restored to his parents or guardian or until other arrangements can be made for him.[2]

1   AA 1976, s 24(2). Cf *Re M* (1986) 10 No 4 Adoption and Fostering 58.
2   AA 1976, s 57(2). Penalties for an offence are a maximum of three months' imprisonment or a maximum fine of £2,000 or both.

5.96   A payment *to* an adoption agency by the parent or guardian or by the applicant for adoption which is made to meet expenses reasonably incurred in connection with adoption is exempt from the general prohibition. So are payments sanctioned by the court, although these are not frequent.[1] Where the court is satisfied that the payment is not the result of any commercial arrangement, it may in its discretion not only approve it but also authorise it to operate retroactively.[2] Payments are also allowed to be made by an adoption agency to actual or intended adopters, provided that the Secretary of State has approved a scheme for such payments being made by the agency.[3] The Department of Health and Social Security has issued a circular setting out the basis for approval of schemes.[4] Payments by agencies are intended for a minority of children whose chances of being adopted need special encouragement; for example, the child in long-term institutional care whose links with his natural family have long been tenuous or the handicapped child whose particular needs will impose additional financial burdens on his adopters.

1   AA 1976, s 57(3); see also sub-s (3A).
2   *Re Adoption Application* [1987] Fam 81, [1987] 2 All ER 826. It is submitted that this interpretation is difficult to justify in view of the wording of s 57(3), which speaks of 'any payment or reward'. Nevertheless, the decision is a welcome lifeline for the future of private, especially family, surrogacy arrangements.
3   AA 1976, s 57(4)–(10).

4   (1982) LAC (82) 1.

(b)   Interim orders

5.97   Instead of making an adoption order the court may postpone the determination of the application and make an interim order vesting the legal custody of the child in the applicants for a probationary period of not more than two years, with power to extend to that maximum if, in the first instance, the order is made for a lesser period.[1] This probationary period is not simply designed to provide a further opportunity of assessing the characters and suitability of the applicants. It should be used for investigating all the circumstances which bear on the welfare of the child. Thus, the court may, for the interim period, impose such terms for the maintenance of the child and otherwise, as it thinks fit. It may, for example, prescribe conditions about his education and religious upbringing. It may even allow the natural parent access, especially where it is uncertain whether the child should live with him or be adopted by the applicants.[2]

1   AA 1976, s 25.
2   *S v Huddersfield Borough Council* [1975] Fam 113, [1974] 3 All ER 296, CA.

(c)   Registration and amendment of adoption orders

5.98   Every adoption must be registered by the Registrar General in the Adopted Children Register in accordance with the particulars given by the adoption order.[1] The court which made the order may, on the application of the adopter or adopted person, amend it by correcting any error in the particulars,[2] for example, the date of the child's birth.[3] It may also substitute or add any new name which was given to the adopted person within the first year of the order. There is also the power to revoke the order if it was made in favour of the mother or father alone and the child is subsequently legitimated by the marriage of his parents.

1   AA 1976, s 50 and Sch 1.
2   Ibid, Sch 1, para 4.
3   *R v Chelsea Juvenile Court Justices (Re an infant)* [1955] 1 All ER 38, [1955] 1 WLR 52.

5.99   The record kept by the Registrar General enables the connections between the entry in the Adopted Register and the Register of Births to be traced. Until the CA 1975 the only possibility of tracing an adopted person's origin was through an order of a court directing the Registrar General to provide the necessary information.[1] The order, which is rarely sought, is intended as a means of tracing parentage where it is relevant to claims of succession on death. The applicant may be the adopted person or someone else, eg personal representatives. The AA 1976 in effect confers on an adopted person a right, fettered only by the restrictions of counselling, to obtain a copy of his birth certificate once he is 18 years old.[2] Counselling is only compulsory in those cases where the new right operates retrospectively ie where the child was adopted before 12 November 1975, the date on which the CA 1975 was passed.[3] The responsibility for providing counselling services falls upon the Registar General, each local authority and each approved adoption society.[4] An adopted person who wishes to have access to his birth record must apply to the Registrar General for the necessary 'linking' information using the appropriate form prescribed by the Adopted Persons (Birth Records) Regulations 1976. The role of the counsellor has been left to extra-legal guidance, but the Department of Health and Social Security has issued a very helpful pamphlet, Notes for Counsellors.[5]

1   AA 1958, s 20(5) as amended by CA 1975, s 26(1). The High Court, the Westminster County Court and the court which made the adoption order are the courts with jurisdiction; see now AA 1976, s 50(5).
2   AA 1976, s 51. The Registrar General must provide the applicant with such information as is necessary to enable him to obtain the copy. This 'linking' information includes the appellant's original name, that of his natural mother and possibly the natural father, together with the name of the court where the adoption order was made.
3   AA 1976, s 51(6).
4   Ibid, s 51(3).
5   See also Day and Leeding, *Access to birth records: the impact of section 26 of the Children Act 1975,* ABAFA Research Series No 1; Haimes and Timms, *Adoption, Identity and Social Policy: the search for distant relatives;* Triseliotis, *Obtaining Birth Certificates* in *Adoption: essays in social policy, law and sociology* (ed Bean).

5.100   An adopted person who is under 18 but intending to marry in England or Wales has the right to require the Registrar General to inform him whether or not it appears from the records that he and the person whom he intends to marry may be within the degrees of relationship prohibited by Schedule 1 to the Marriage Act 1949.[1] Clearly, an application is only going to be made where the applicant has been put on his inquiry. The Adoption Act 1976 does not specify the amount of information to which he is entitled. A mere declaration that the parties are within the prohibited degrees will therefore strictly satisfy the subsection, but it is likely that the applicant will be told the nature of the relationship.

1   AA 1976 s 51(2).

(d)   Refusal of an adoption order

5.101   Where the court refuses to make an adoption order or interim order it has a number of courses open to it. If the child was placed for adoption by an approved adoption society or a local authority, it must be returned to that body within seven days of the court's refusal.[1] The particular adoption agency may then try to find another suitable placement. In a non-agency case, if the court takes no further action, the child will remain with the unsuccessful applicant for adoption unless and until the natural parent takes proceedings to reclaim him. However, both in agency and non-agency cases, the court is empowered[2] in exceptional circumstances and if the child is under 16 to make an order placing him under the supervision of a specified local authority or probation officer or to commit him to the care of a specified local authority.[3] In the latter event the court may order either parent to pay to the authority (in the form of weekly or other periodical payments but not a lump sum) reasonable maintenance for the child.[4] An order committing the child to the care of a local authority ceases to have effect where an order is made for the child's return under Part I of the Child Abduction and Custody Act 1985 or a decision, other than one relating to rights of access, is registered under section 16 of that Act.[5]

1   AA 1976, s 30(3).
2   Section 26(1).
3   The effect of these exceptional orders is the same as that of similar orders made under the GMA 1971 and 1973. The supplementary provisions of the GA 1973, ss 3, 4 apply *mutatis mutandis* to orders made under AA 1976, s 26; see s 26(3).
4   Section 26(2).
5   See ss 25(1) and (2), 27(1) and Sch 3, para 1(1), and for the Act generally see ante, paras 3.108 et seq.

(e)   Appeals and transfer of cases

5.102   Where proceedings have been instituted in the High court, the Court may, either of its own motion or on the application of any party to the proceedings, order the transfer of the whole or any part of the proceedings to such county court as the High Court directs.[1] Conversely, a county court may, either of its own motion or on the application of any party, order the transfer of the whole of the proceedings which have been commenced in the county court or which under the above rules were transferred to it by the High Court.[2] However, these powers to order transfer between the courts are subject to the following restrictions:[3]

(a)   Proceedings must be dealt with in the High Court where it appears to the court seised of the case that, because of the complexity, difficulty or gravity of the issues, they ought to be tried in the High Court.

(b)   Without prejudice to the generality of that rule the following adoption proceedings must be dealt with in the High Court unless the nature of the issues of fact or law raised in the case makes them more suitable for trial in a county court.

Applications for adoption and freeing for adoption (i) which are opposed on the grounds of want of jurisdiction, (ii) which would result in the acquisition by a child of British citizenship.[4]

(c)   Subject to the above, proceedings concerning children in adoption may be dealt with in a county court.

(d)   Proceedings in the High Court which under the foregoing criteria fall to be dealt with in a county court, and proceedings in a county court which likewise fall to be dealt with in the High Court must be transferred accordingly, unless to do so would cause undue delay or hardship to any party or other person involved.

1   MFPA 1984, ss 32 and 38.
2   Section 39.
3   See *Practice Direction* [1988] 2 All ER 103, [1988] 1 WLR 558.
4   See *Re N and L (minors)* [1987] 2 All ER 732, [1987] 1 WLR 829, CA.

5.103   Section 101 of the CA 1975[1] lays down two general rules concerning appeals and transfer of cases heard under the Act:

(a)   where there is an application to a magistrates' court appeal from its decision lies to the High Court;

(b)   where an application is made to a magistrates' court but the court considers that the matter would more conveniently be dealt with by the High Court, the magistrates' court must refuse to make an order. In that case no appeal lies to the High Court. This provision corresponds to similar ones in other enactments.[2] They are rarely invoked.

1 As amended by MFPA 1984, Sch 3.
2 See GMA 1971, s 16(4); DPMCA 1978, s 27.

VI CONVENTION ADOPTION ORDERS

5.104 Additional jurisdiction to make adoption orders was conferred by the Adoption Act 1968, which implemented the Hague Convention on Adoption[1] by empowering the High Court (or, in Scotland, the Court of Session) to make 'inter-country' adoption orders, ie adoption orders in which the applicant does not have the same nationality as, or resides in a different country from, that of the child. These orders are known as Convention adoption orders, and the law is now to be found in section 17 of the Adoption Act 1976.[2]

1 See Cmnd 2613 and for a comment on the Tenth Hague Conference which led to the Convention see Graveson (1965) 14 ICLQ 528.
2 The 1968 Act was amended by CA 1975, s 24. See generally McClean and Patchett, *English Jurisdiction in Adoption*, 19 ICLQ 1; Blom, *The Adoption Act 1968 and the Conflict of Laws*, 22 ICLQ 109.

1 Qualifications of the parties

(a) The applicants

5.105 Jurisdiction is based on nationality and habitual residence. The rules are complicated.

A sole applicant is 'qualified' to apply if either (a) he habitually resides in Great Britain and is a national of the United Kingdom or a Convention country, or (b) he habitually resides in British territory or a Convention country and is a United Kingdom national. A Convention country is any country outside British territory designated by the Secretary of State as a country in which the Convention is in force.[1] British territory means the United Kingdom, the Channel Islands, the Isle of Man and a colony, being a country designated for this purpose, or, if no country is designated, any of those countries.

A husband and wife are qualified to make a joint application if either (a) each is a national of the United Kingdom or of a Convention country and both habitually reside in Great Britain, or (b) both are United Kingdom nationals and each habitually resides in British territory or a Convention country. There must, therefore, be either common United Kingdom nationality or common residence in Great Britain.

1 So far only Austria and Switzerland have been so designated; SI 1978/1431.

(b) The child

5.106 Under section 17(2) a child is qualified to be adopted if (a) he is a national of the United Kingdom or of a Convention country, and (b) he habitually resides in British territory or a Convention country. As with other children who are adopted under the 1976 Act he must be under 18 and not been married.[1]

1 See respectively s 72(1) and s 12(5).

2   Restrictions on the making of orders

5.107   There are three restrictions on the making of orders:
(1) Where joint applicants are nationals of the same Convention country or a sole applicant is a national of a Convention country, an adoption order cannot be made if the proposed adoption is prohibited by a provision of the internal law of that country and, in pursuance of the Hague Convention, that provision is notified to the United Kingdom government and then specified in a statutory instrument.[1]
(2) The applicants or applicant must not all be United Kingdom nationals living in a British territory.[2] But it has been pointed out[3] that the effect of this restriction is to leave a gap in the law. If all parties are United Kingdom nationals and living in a British territory, but neither of the applicants is domiciled in a part of the United Kingdom or in the Channel Islands or the Isle of Man,[4] there is no jurisdiction at all to make an adoption order.
(3) Section 17 requires the conditions which it imposes to be satisfied both at the time of the application and when the order is made.[5] Thus, the requirements concerning the nationality and habitual residence of the applicant(s) and of the child must be referred to both dates. It follows also that, in the exceptional case where a prohibition under the foreign law is notified and then specified in a statutory instrument which is made after the application has been presented but before the order is due to be made, the notified provision cannot prevent such an order.

1   Section 17(4), (5) and (8).
2   Section 17(3).
3   Bromley, op cit, p 414.
4   See s 14(2), ante, para 5.53.
5   Section 17(1).

3   Consents and consultations

5.108   The provisions in section 16 of the Adoption Act 1976 relating to freeing for adoption and to parental agreement to the making of an adoption order do not apply to an application for a Convention adoption order where the child is not a United Kingdom national.[1] The Hague Convention accepts the principle that consents and consultations are matters to be governed by the *lex patriae*, ie by the internal law[2] of the Convention country of which the child is a national.[3] The court must be satisfied that each person who consents to the order in accordance with that law does so with full understanding of what is involved. This rule is not, however, directed at any requirement which the foreign law may impose concerning consent by or consultation with the applicant and members of his family.

1   Section 16(3).
2   Where the country of nationality contains more than one legal system, the court will apply the rules of selection operating in that country to determine the relevant legal system. If there are no rules, the system is that which appears to the High Court to be the one most closely connected with the case; see AA 1976, s 71(2).
3   See s 17(6) and (7).

VII   GENERAL EFFECTS OF AN ADOPTION ORDER

5.109   The general effect of an adoption order is to create between the adopter and the child a legal relationship almost wholly the same as that between a parent and his natural, legitimate child. In the case of adoption by a married couple the child is treated in law as if he had been born a child of their marriage: where there is a sole adopter, as if born in wedlock but not as a child of any actual marriage.[1] It means, therefore, that he is included within the terms 'a legitimate child' and 'a child born in lawful wedlock'.[1] Indeed, it is expressly declared that he is prevented from being illegitimate. This general effect of an adoption order is reinforced by the rule that an adopted child is to be treated as if he were not the child of any person other than the adopters or adopter, unless any enactment or instrument (whether passed or made before the adoption or later) indicates to the contrary.[2]

1   AA 1976, s 39(1).
2   Ibid, s 39(2) and (6). See, for example, *Secretary of State for Social Services v S* [1983] 3 All ER 173, [1983] 1 WLR 1110, CA.

5.110   The consequence of this status is that the parental rights and duties relating to a child vest in the adopters,[1] but the adoption order does not affect the rights and duties so far as they relate to any period preceding the date of the order.[2] Vesting operates prospectively and every right or duty which was vested in a parent or guardian immediately before that date is extinguished, except where the parent or guardian is one of the adopters.[3] In the vast majority of cases all the rights and duties will have been vested in one or both of the parents. However, any right or duty which has been vested in someone else by a court order is similarly extinguished.[4] Although extinguishment is automatic once the adoption order is made, procedural steps should be taken by the court making the order to ensure that the court which made the earlier order[5] is notified of the adoption.[6] Similarly, adoption discharges a care order made under the CYPA 1969[7] and a resolution under section 3 of the CCA 1980 vesting parental rights and duties in a local authority.[8]

1   AA 1976, s 12(1).
2   Ibid, s 12(2).
3   Ibid, s 12(3)(a)(i).
4   Ibid, s 12(a)(ii).
5   Eg an order under GMA 1971 granting legal custody to a relative.
6   Where the earlier order had been made in wardship proceedings leave would have been necessary to start the adoption proceedings; *F v S (adoption: award)* [1973] Fam 203, [1973] 1 All ER 722, CA.
7   CYPA 1969, s 21A, added by CA 1975, Sch 3, para 70.
8   CCA 1980, s 5(2)(a).

5.111   Where there was at the date of the adoption order a duty to make payments in respect of the child's maintenance, whether the duty arose from an agreement or an order of a court, adoption will not affect continued liability for arrears existing at the date of the adoption order. But subsequent liability for maintenance and for payments relating to any other matter comprised in the parental duties, such as payments of school fees is extinguished, except where the duty arises under an agreement which constitutes a trust or which expressly provides against extinguishment.[1] These rules have special significance in relation to an affiliation order. Such an order will cease to operate from the date of adoption, but it also means that if no order exists at that date it will be too late to seek one. The rule of extinguishment will operate even in the exceptional case where the adoption order is made in favour of the mother. Moreover, she cannot apply for affiliation after adopting, a restriction which accords with the principle that prevents an adopted child from being illegitimate.[2] These rules will correspondingly apply to orders, and applications for orders, for financial relief by an unmarried mother under section 11B of the Guardianship of Minors Act 1971 when affiliation proceedings are abolished.[3]

1   AA 1976, s 12(3)(b), (4).
2   Ibid, s 39(4).
3   By FLRA 1987, s 17.

5.112   Notwithstanding the acquisition of the status of adoption, the child's original relationship as a child of his natural family remains relevant for certain purposes. For example, adoption does not affect the prohibited degrees of relationship in which the child stood to other persons before the date of adoption,[1] although additionally intermarriage between the child and the adoptive parent is prohibited and continues even if the child is later adopted into another family.[2] Again, incest continues to relate to the natural relationship, but adoptive parent and child are not within the prohibited degrees for the purpose of that offence.[3] Adoption does not prejudice any rights which the child acquired prior to adoption with regard to such matters as entitlement to pensions[4] or citizenship of the United Kingdom.[5]

1   AA 1976, s 47(1).
2   CA 1975, Sch 3, para 8, amending Pt I of Sch 1 of the Marriage Act 1949. The prohibition does not, however, extend to intermarriage between the child and other adoptive relatives.
3   AA 1976, s 47(1).
4   Ibid, s 48.
5   Ibid, s 47(2).

Revocation of an adoption order

5.113   There is power to revoke an adoption order if it was made in favour of an unmarried mother or unmarried father alone and the child is subsequently legitimated by the marriage of his parents.[1] This rule equally applies to a Convention adoption order, but in respect of such an order the High Court may also annul it on the ground that the adoption was prohibited by the internal law of which the adopters were nationals or that it contravened provisions relating to consents of the internal law of the country of which the child was a national.[2]

1   AA 1976, s 52.
2   Ibid 53(1).

CHAPTER 6
Custodianship

I INTRODUCTION

6.01 Although the Houghton Committee was primarily directed to consider 'the law, policy and procedure on adoption',[1] its inquiry inevitably involved examination of matters closely connected with the adoption process, especially long-term fostering and the needs of children in long-term residential care. One of the consequences of the Committee's recommendations was the creation, in Part II of the Children Act 1975,[2] of the new status of custodianship. The legalistic way in which that was achieved, namely, by the creation of the concept of legal custody, has already been examined.[3] This chapter is concerned with the acquisition of that status and its consequences. Its basic purpose is to provide, as the Houghton Committee recommended, a legal relationship between the child and those who care for him which provides effective security but without the permanent and irrevocable consequences of adoption,[4] although wider than the care and control which would be the normal consequences of wardship proceedings. It has special significance for the foster parents of the child in local authority care, because it releases them from the threat of unilateral removal of the child without reference to the court and more immediately from the control given to the social worker by the fostering regulations, especially in the form of what are often seen as intrusive visits to the foster home. Whether that latter consequence is in the child's best interests[5] is one of the primary matters the court will have to consider when hearing an application for a custodianship order, because, if an order is made, legal custody vests in the custodian.

1 See Cmnd 5107.
2 Sections 33-46. These have been amended by the Domestic Proceedings Magistrates' Courts Act 1978, ss 64-70 and Sch 2, paras 46-48; the Magistrates' Courts Act 1980, Sch 7, para 138; the Criminal Justice Act 1982, s 46; the Health and Social Services and Social Security Adjudications Act 1983, Sch 2, paras 23, 24 and 60(b); and prospectively the Family Law Reform Act 1987, Sch 2, paras 60-66, and Sch 4.
3 See ante, paras 1.59 et seq.
4 See Sir R Ormrod, *Child Care Law: A Personal Perspective* (1983) 7 Adoption and Fostering, 10 at pp 14–15. But the efficacy of that security has been questioned; see M Adcock, *Alternatives to Adoption* (1984) 8 Adoption and Fostering, 12 and post, para 6.94.
5 For a spirited attack on custodianship on this and other grounds see R Holman, *In Defence of Parents*, [1975] New Society 268-269.

II THE APPLICANT

6.02 Eligibility to apply for a custodianship order depends partly on the status of the applicant, partly on the length of the period for which he has had actual custody of the child and partly on whether or not the application has the consent of a person who has the legal custody. The following are qualified to apply:[1]

(a)   A relative or, in certain circumstances,[2] a step-parent with whom the child has had his home for the three months preceding the making of the application, provided there is the requisite consent to the application. 'Relative' has the same broad meaning as it has for adoption.[3] It covers a grandparent, brother, sister, uncle or aunt, whether of the full blood or half blood or by affinity. Although the definition also includes the unmarried father of a child, he is disqualified from applying for a custodianship order.[3a]

(b)   Any other person[4] with whom the child has had his home for a period or periods of at least 12 months before the making of the application, including the three preceding it, but subject to the same consent.

(c)   Any person with whom the child has had his home for a period or periods of at least three years before the application is made, including the three months preceding that date.

Paragraph (c) will thus include a relative or step-parent applying without consent, but, that apart, paragraphs (b) and (c) relate to foster parents, whether the child has been placed with them privately by the natural parents or by a local authority or voluntary organisation.

1   CA 1975, s. 33(3).
2   See post, para 6.12.
3   Adoption Act 1976, s 72(1).
3a See post, para 6.13.
4   Section 33(3)(b) refers to 'any person', but, since the qualifications imposed by para (b) are stricter than those of para (a), relatives and step-parents will obviously always fall within the latter. For the purposes of custodianship (Part II of CA 1975) references to any relationship between two persons are (when the relevant provisions are brought into force) to be construed in accordance with s 1 of FLRA 1987; see ibid s 2(1)(e) and Sch 2, para 60, adding a new sub-s (9A) to s 33 of CA 1975.

6.03   The qualifications differ from those required of applicants for an adoption order in two important respects. No minimum age is imposed and joint applications are not restricted to married couples.[1] An application for a custodianship order may be made by 'one or more persons' who are qualified under the above rules.[2] Thus, an order could be made in favour of a brother and sister of a much younger child where they continue to live together in the family home on the death of their parents. However, where there is more than one applicant, the court may choose to appoint only one (or some) of them as custodian.[3] Although there is no statutory minimum, the age of an applicant will be a relevant factor. In applying the principle of the paramountcy of the child's welfare, as it is obliged to do,[4] the court will be as reluctant to make anyone under the age of 21 a custodian as the local authority in its report will be so to recommend.[5] Equally, where there are joint applicants, of whatever age, the stability of their relationship will be highly relevant in applying the paramountcy principle, for example, where the applicants are a childless, unmarried couple living as husband and wife.

1   Cf AA 1976, ss 14(1) and 15(1); ante, para 5.52.

2 Section 33(1).
3 Ibid. The person in whom legal custody is vested under a custodianship order may be referred to as custodian of the child (s 33(2)), a cold and unattractive term.
4 Section 33(9).
5 It is highly unlikely that persons so young will be foster parents. In particular, local authority fostering policy will probably exclude them from so acting. Occasionally it will be relatives under that age who may be suitable applicants.

1 The time limits

6.04 The period for which a child needs to have his home with someone[1] before the court can effectively reach a decision on whether or not to make an order can vary according to the individual. For some children three years can be a very long time. It is therefore arguable that it would have been better if the legislation had left each application to the operation of the paramountcy principle rather than to the crude arbitrariness of minimum time limits. There is no consistent rationale underlying those prescribed. They represent a conglomeration of views and produce a compromise between the child's welfare and the rights of the natural parent. Some would see them as a safeguard against frivolous and premature applications that will protect the natural parent from the anxiety of being involved in proceedings after only a short time.[2] While relevant to applications under paragraph (c), the point seems scarcely valid where an application is made with the consent of the parent either under paragraph (a) or (b), except to the extent that the consent may too easily be given. But the safeguards against that risk lie in the court's power to withhold an order and in the local authority practice of providing parents with explanatory leaflets. The difference between the respective periods under paragraphs (a) and (b) is justified on the ground that a longer period is needed to assess the suitability of foster parents than that required for relatives. Generally that is so, but three months may be too short for relatives if they have had little previous contact with the child. In such a case, however, the court may prefer to make an interim custodianship order until the child has spent a longer period with the relatives.[3]

1 In calculating the respective periods account can be taken of the first six weeks of the child's life (cf AA 1976, s 13(1) re adoption, ante, para 5.61) and of any time during which the child is in hospital or at boarding school or otherwise temporarily absent from the applicant's home (see ante, para 1.65).
2 Houghton Committee Report, Cmnd 5107, para 122.
3 For the power to make interim orders see post, para 6.77.

6.05 The twelve-month period is further defended on the ground that it gives a local authority, in whose care the child is, sufficient but not excessive time to decide whether it wants a particular fostering relationship to continue without allowing things to drift. If the legal custody is still vested in the natural parent, because the child has only been received into care under section 2 of the Child Care Act 1980, the authority will have to decide whether or not to withdraw the child from the foster parents before the completion of the statutory period in order to avoid an application being made with the consent of the natural parent.[1] On the other hand, there has been criticism that 12 months is too short a period, because some unsuccessful placements do not manifest themselves until the second year after placement and there is the risk that meanwhile the natural parent will too readily give his consent. Such differing views serve to emphasise the vital role of the court and the importance of the report which the local authority will have to prepare for it.[2]

1 However, if the local authority were to take this step, it would be open to the parent to recover the child and then again place him with the foster parents, as private foster parents, with a view eventually to allowing them to apply for custodianship.
2 See post, paras 6.23 to 6.28.

6.06 The period of three years required by paragraph (c),[1] which is to be read in conjunction with the restriction on removing the child from the applicant while the custodianship application is pending,[2] may be defended on the ground that it is sufficiently long to avoid any serious risk of parents being discouraged from allowing their children to be temporarily fostered. Causes for temporary fostering, such as parental illness, are likely to have disappeared before the foster parents are in a position to apply for custodianship and the parents will be able to recover the child.[3] On the other hand, to make it any longer could unduly delay vital decisions concerning the child's future. The operation of the paragraph in respect of children in local authority care is likely to depend to a marked degree on the advice and information given to natural parents by the local authority about its own powers and duties and those of foster parents.[4] Whenever possible parents and foster parents should be involved 'in planning and decision making' and there should be 'a clear understanding by all concerned of the nature of the child's continuing relationship with his parents. Observance of these principles should help to minimise the risk of difficulties and disappointments arising because foster parents build up unrealistic hopes and expectations which conflict with the parent's expectations or with the local authority's plans for the child or both; and which may lead foster parents to seek custody in opposition to the local authority'.[5] If there is planning with co-operation, some parents, while opposed to adoption, may be willing to consent to a custodianship application without the foster parents having to rely on paragraph (c), and, if during the fostering period there has been access between parent and child, an unopposed access order may readily be made at the same time as the custodianship order.[6] However, if planning and co-operation break down and there is a likelihood of a custodianship application, which the local authority does not support, the authority may anticipate the application by withdrawing the child from the foster parents' home before the effluxion of the three years.

1 The Act recognises that the paragraph is likely to give rise to problems since it empowers the Secretary of State to substitute, in the light of experience, a different period for that of three years (s 33(7)). An order is subject to affirmative resolution by each House of Parliament.
2 Section 41, post, para 6.29.
3 On the possibility of the foster parents relying on wardship see post, para 8.51a.
4 The Department of Health and Social Security has stressed the need for this publicity. See LAC (85)13, para 14, and the Code of Practice on Access to Children in Care (HMSO 1983).
5 LAC (85)13, para 13.
6 For the power to make access orders see post, para 6.62.

2   Consent

6.07   Usually the person with legal custody whose consent will be necessary where application is made under paragraph (a) or (b), will be the natural parent or a local authority. Less frequently it may be a guardian or a voluntary organisation in whom the parental rights and duties are vested. The possibility of a custodian giving consent is closely connected with revocation of a custodianship order and is considered under that topic.[1]

(i) *A parent.*   This covers both a natural and adoptive parent, subject to the qualification that where the parents have never been married the father is eligible to give consent (a) where, until the coming into force of the Family Law Reform Act 1987, he has been granted legal custody under section 9 of the GMA 1971 and that order is still operative or (b) where, after the relevant provisions of the 1987 Act have come into force, he has been granted all the parental rights and duties under section 4 of that Act or (only) legal custody under an order made under section 9 of the 1971 Act.

(ii) *A guardian.*   This means a guardian in the strict sense of one so appointed by deed or will or by the court. His consent would not, however, be appropriate where the court has granted legal custody to someone else.[2]

(iii) *A local authority.*[3]   A local authority occupies a special position in relation to consent. If the child is the subject of a resolution under section 3 of the Child Care Act 1980[4] or of a care order under the Children and Young Persons Act 1969,[5] then, of course, it is the local authority and not the parent whose consent is required, since the parental rights and duties and therefore the legal custody are vested in it. It is, however, questionable whether in such cases it is proper that the Children Act 1975 should automatically exclude the need for the parent's consent. A section 3 resolution, for example, is more often than not based on the neglect or ill-treatment of the child by the parent or on some other inadequacy of conduct. In cases of that kind the exclusion of any parental veto is justifiable, but there are cases where the rights and duties have been vested in the local authority and no blame can be laid at the door of the parent, for example, a section 3 resolution based on some permanent disability from which the parent suffers. Yet, the Act fails to distinguish between the two kinds of cases. Instead it leaves it to the parent to make any representations through the local authority report which has to be presented to the court and through personal hearing as a defendant at the application. This legislative defect makes it all the more desirable that the local authority should, if the whereabouts of the parents are known, discuss the proposed application with them and take their views into account before deciding whether or not to consent to it. It should then let the parents know its decision through a social worker. Prior discussion will also assist the local authority in preparing its report, since it must deal with the views of the parents and the extent to which they understand the nature and effect of a custodianship order.[6]

If the child is in care under section 2 of the Child Care Act,[7] the consent of the parent, and not of the local authority, will be needed, since the former will have retained legal custody; but the authority can make its representations through its report to the court and as a defendant to the custodianship application. Where a child has been committed to the care of a local authority by an order made under various enactments,[8] because it is impracticable or undesirable for the child to be entrusted to a parent or other individual, he is to be treated as if he had been received into care under section 2. Although the precise effect of such an order is uncertain,[9] the legal custody remains in the parent, even though he cannot remove the child from the local authority. So, as in the case of reception into care under section 2, it is the parent's consent to the application that would be required. However, unlike the case of voluntary care, the local authority should seek the guidance of the court which placed the child in care on how to proceed, since the proposed custodianship would be a major decision affecting the child.[10] If that court is opposed to the proposed custodianship, even though the parent consents to the application,[11] the appropriate procedure, it seems, would be to convey its view through the local authority report to the court hearing the custodianship application. It would be unlikely that the latter court would take a different view.

(iv) *A Voluntary Organisation.* Where a voluntary organisation holds the parental rights and duties by virtue of a resolution passed by a local authority,[12] the consent of the organisation to the custodianship application will be needed.[13] If that is given but the local authority does not approve of the applicant, it can oppose the application through its report or, if the opportunity is still open, rescind its resolution and thus vest the parental rights and duties in itself,[14] before the application is made. Where the child is in the care of the organisation but without the parental rights and duties being vested in it, the organisation's own views on a custodianship application should be conveyed to the court through the local authority report.

1 Post, para 6.55.
2 Under GMA 1971, s 10(1)(a) or 11(a) (prospectively substituted as s 10(1)(a) or (2)(a) by FLRA 1987, s 11), s 11 ante, paras 4.20-4.21, where the likelihood of a person other than the guardian being granted legal custody is questioned.
3 See Freeman, *Law and Practice of Custodianship* (1986) pp 23-27.
4 See post, paras 15.14 et seq.
5 See post, paras 15.47 et seq.
6 See LAC (85)13, para 15.
7 See post, paras 15.08 et seq.
8 Namely, an order under the Matrimonial Causes Act 1973 (ante, para 3.57); the Domestic Proceedings and Magistrates' Courts Act 1978, s 10(1) or its predecessor, the Matrimonial Proceedings (Magistrates' Court) Act 1960, s 2(1) ante, para 3.38; the Guardianship of Minors Act 1971, s 9, as extended by the Guardianship Act 1973, s 2(2)(b) (in turn prospectively substituted by FLRA 1987, Sch 2, para 54(2)), ante, para 3.22; Children Act 1975, s 17(1)(b) (care order on refusal to make an adoption order), ante, para 5.101; Children Act 1975, s. 34(5) and s 36(3)(a) (care order on refusal to make a custodianship order or a revocation of a custodianship order), post, para 6.75 and para 6.55 respectively. A care order can also be made in wardship proceedings under the Family Law Reform Act 1969, s 7, but in such a case any later application for custodianship would in itself constitute contempt of the High Court.
9 See post, para 15.57.
10 Ibid, and see *Turney v Turney and Devon County Council* (1981) 4 FLR 199.
11 For example, while one parent so consents, the court may have it in mind that the child should eventually be returned to the other parent.
12 Under s 64 of the Child Care Act 1980, post, para 15.114.
13 The organisation will be a defendant to the application; see post, para 6.20.
14 Under s 65 of CCA 1980.

6.08   The requirement of consent is irrelevant (1) where no person has legal custody, for example, in the case of an orphan with no guardian, no one to whom custody has been granted by an order of a court and no custodian; or (2) where the applicant for custodianship already has legal custody, as, for example, where he jointly shares legal custody and wants to become sole custodian; or (3) where the person with legal custody cannot be found. In each of these circumstances the period for which the child must have his home with the applicant is three months if the latter is a relative, 12 months if he is not.[1] It seems clear that the rule relating to a person who cannot be found is to be interpreted in the same way as the corresponding provision which enables the court to dispense with agreement to the making of an adoption order,[2] and therefore it will be necessary to ensure that every reasonable step has been taken to trace a person having legal custody. The onus will lie on the applicant to do this, but because of its obligations relating to the submission of a report[3] the local authority will necessarily be involved in the investigation and should pursue its enquiries into the person's whereabouts with the same standard of thoroughness. Paragraphs (a) and (b) require the consent of 'a person',[4] and not each person, having legal custody. Thus, where the married parents of a child are living apart, but, there being no order of a court granting one of them custody, both are entitled to the legal custody, it will be sufficient for the applicant to rely on the consent of one of them to his application, without having to take all reasonable steps to seek out the other and satisfy the court that he cannot be found.[5] However, the local authority is not, it is submitted, relieved of the duty to take those steps in view of its obligation,[6] 'so far as the information can reasonably be obtained', to provide the court with details relating to each parent of the child, including, inter alia, the wishes and feelings of each parent in relation to the application. Although the consent of, for example, one parent is sufficient, it seems that if the other parent has previously signified his disapproval of an application, the consent of the first is a nullity.[7]

1   CA 1975, s 33(6).
2   See ante, para 5.24.
3   See post, para 6.23.
4   See ante, para 6.02.
5   Another instance would be where a local authority and a parent are jointly entitled to legal custody, a resolution under s 3 of CCA 1980 having vested only the parental rights and duties of the other parent in the local authority. In those circumstances the custodianship applicant need rely only on the consent of the local authority.
6   Under the Custodianship (Reports) Regulations 1985.
7   See Freeman, op cit, p 30.

6.09   In the terms of section 33(3) the requisite consent relates to the application, and not to the order, being made. In practice the distinction will usually be academic. Indeed, the Rules[1] on custodianship proceedings expressly state in their respective Forms of Consent that consent is being given to the making of an order:

'I understand that the court cannot make a custodianship order without my consent.'

and the Rules governing the High Court and county courts add:

'I consent to the making of a custodianship order.'[2]

In exceptional circumstances, however, the difference in wording between section 33(3) and the Rules could be crucial. The Form of Consent accompanies the application, and a parent who has given his consent may have changed his mind by the time of the hearing. It is submitted that the terms of section 33(3) are overriding. On that premise any change will be too late to affect the validity of the application, but the court will be able to take account of it in applying the principle of the paramountcy of the child's welfare when deciding whether or not to make a custodianship order. No question arises, however, of having to dispense with the parent's consent on any specific grounds, as in adoption. Nevertheless, the wording in the Form of Consent is wholly misleading, if section 33(3) prevails. It clearly suggests to the parent that his consent is a sine qua non to the making of an order. It should be amended in the light of the subsection. If it is allowed to stand, it should be amended so as to make it clear that his consent to an order, given when he signs the Form, is irrevocable.[3]

1 See post, para 6.17.
2 Disconcertingly those relating to magistrates' courts state: 'I consent to the application . . . for a custodianship order . . .'
3 Ie so far as the making of an order; but see post, paras 6.51 et seq for the right later to apply for revocation of an order.

6.10 The Custodianship (Reports) Regulations 1985[1] fill a gap in section 33(3) since they require the local authority in its report to state whether the consent has been freely given. That imports understanding of what is involved. It follows, therefore, that a foster parent caring for a child whose parent, for example, is incapable of giving consent because of his mental condition will have to wait until three years have passed before being eligible to apply for custodianship, unless there is some other person with legal custody who can provide the requisite consent.

1 SI 1985/792, as amended by SI 1985/1494.

3 The step-parent[1]

6.11 The position of a step-parent as an applicant calls for special comment. It has already been seen[2] that, where the spouse, say the wife, of the step-parent was previously married and that marriage was dissolved or annulled, the court may refuse to allow them to adopt the child and leave them to seek a remedy in the divorce court under section 42 of the Matrimonial Causes Act 1973. Yet, with the court having a discretion in the matter the step-father can at least try to obtain adoption, if he is so determined. In similar circumstances he is, however, normally disqualified from seeking a custodianship order, and, if he wishes to establish a legal relationship with the step-child, he is obliged to turn to the divorce court. Section 33(5) of the Children Act provides:

'A step-parent of the child is not qualified under any paragraph of subsection (3) if in proceedings for divorce or nullity of marriage the child was named in an order made under paragraph (b) or (c) of section 41(1) (arrangements for welfare of children of family) of the Matrimonial Causes Act 1973.'

An order will have been made under paragraph (b) if the divorce court was satisfied either (1) that the arrangements for the welfare of the child were satisfactory or the best that could be devised in the circumstances or (2) that it was impracticable for the parties appearing before the court to make such arrangements. An order under paragraph (c) will have been made where the circumstances made it desirable that the decree should be made absolute without delay notwithstanding that there were or might be children of the family and the court was unable to make a declaration in accordance with paragraph (b).[3]

1   For the meaning of step-parent see ante, para 5.58.
2   Ante, para 5.58.
3   For s 41 see ante, paras 3.48 et seq.

6.12   The most likely circumstance to arise is where the divorce court declared its satisfaction with the arrangements concerning the step-child and granted custody to the wife and access to her former husband. Application can then be made[1] to that court for variation of the custody order in favour of the wife and step-father jointly. The application can be made by the wife alone or, as is more likely, by her and the step-father jointly, or even by him alone.[2] The step-father is, however, likely to be a sole applicant only where the mother is dead. In that event it will still be necessary to proceed in the divorce court, since he remains ineligible for custodianship. Nor could he apply for guardianship so long as the other parent remains alive.[3] But the disqualification as an applicant for custodianship is lifted if that other parent is dead or cannot be found,[4] whether or not the parent whom the step-parent married is still alive.[5] The disqualification is also removed if the order made under the Matrimonial Causes Act 1973, section 41(1), was based on paragraph (c) of that subsection and it has since been determined that the child was not a child of the family to whom section 41 applied. Moreover, if the natural parents were never married, and a step-father marries the mother, no restriction would arise under section 33(5), at least so long as their marriage continues. If it should be dissolved or annulled and an order made under section 41(b) or (c), then the step-father would have to invoke the divorce court's jurisdiction in any claim concerning custody of the child of the family and would be disqualified from applying for a custodianship order[6] — not that this is really a disqualification, because the rights acquired through a custody order are wider.

1   In accordance with s 42(7) of the Matrimonial Causes Act 1973.
2   He may apply without any need for leave to intervene; Matrimonial Causes Rules 1977, r 92(3).
3   See GMA 1971, s 5 (prospectively amended by FLRA 1987, s 6(3) and Sch 2, para 29).
4   Ie after every reasonable step has been taken to trace him; see ante, para 6.08 and para 5.24.
5   CA 1975, s 33(8)(a). If that parent is dead, the alternative possibility of guardianship is available; see note 3 supra.
6   The terms of s 33(5) cover this type of case.

4   The mother and father

6.13   The mother and father of a child are not qualified applicants for a custodianship order.[1] The reason for the exclusion is that, if either of them wishes to seek legal custody, the appropriate jurisdiction is conferred by section 9 of the Guardianship of Minors Act 1971, and duplication of custody and custodianship proceedings is to be avoided. The disqualification operates whether or not the mother and father are or have been married to each other.[2]

1 CA 1975, s 33(4).
2 See CA 1975 s 33(9A) (as prospectively inserted by FLRA 1987, Sch 2, para 60).

6.14 It has already been noted[1] that, where there are proceedings between the mother and father under section 9 but the court is minded to grant the legal custody to a third person, it can direct that the application by the mother or father be treated as if it had been a custodianship application by the third person under section 33 of the 1975 Act.[2]

1 Ante, para 3.20.
2 See similarly proceedings under the Domestic Proceedings and Magistrates' Courts Act 1978, s 8(3), ante, para 3.36.

III   THE APPLICATION

1   Jurisdiction

6.15 Jurisdiction over custodianship substantially corresponds to that over custody and guardianship under the Guardianship of Minors Act 1971. Thus, the High Court, county courts and magistrates' courts are all authorised to hear custodianship applications,[1] with power to transfer proceedings between the High Court and a county court, the details of which have already been examined.[2] Under the Family Law Act 1986 a custodianship order, including an interim custodianship order, is a 'custody order' for the purposes of that Act and jurisdiction therefore depends on the child[3] either (a) being habitually resident in England and Wales or (b) being present in England and Wales and not habitually resident in any part of the United Kingdom on the relevant date and in either case the jurisdiction of the court is not excluded.[4] Jurisdiction is excluded if on the relevant date proceedings for divorce, nullity or judicial separation are continuing in Scotland or Northern Ireland in respect of the child's parents,[5] except if that court has made an order either waiving jurisdiction[6] or sisting or staying custody proceedings so as to enable proceedings with respect to the custody of the child to be taken in England and Wales.[7]

A court which has jurisdiction to make a custody order has a discretion under section 5 of the 1986 Act to refuse an application or to stay proceedings.[8]

A custody order does not include an order which varies or revokes a custodianship order. The powers of variation remain exercisable notwithstanding that the original basis of jurisdiction has ceased.[9]

1 CA 1975, s 100(2) and (7), as respectively amended and substituted by FLA 1986, Sch 1, para 20(2) and (3). As in adoption cases, magistrates' courts should not (normally at least) deal with contested cases, since most justices will probably not be available to sit for the requisite number of days in continual session; see Sheldon J in *Re RP (a minor) (Application to free for Adoption)* [1985] FLR 394 at 396.
2 See MFPA 1984, ss 32, 38 and 39; *Practice Direction* [1988] 2 All ER 103, [1988] 1 WLR 558; and ante, para 3.17.

3 Ie a person under 18; see FLA 1986, s 7.
4 See s 1(1)(a)(iv), s 2(1) and s 3(1). For habitual residence after removal of the child without consent see s 41.
   In the case of an application for a custodianship order, the 'relevant' date is the date of the application, or first application if two or more are determined together, for example, if there are cross applications (see FLA 1986, s 3(5)). Otherwise, the relevant date is the date of commencement of the proceedings in which the order is made (s 3(4)); for example, where there is no application for custodianship but a court exercising its powers under the CA 1975, s 37 or the DPMCA 1978 directs some other application to be treated as if it were an application for custodianship.
5 FLA 1986, s 3(2); see also s 42(2)–(4).
6 Under FLA 1986, ss 13(6) (except s 13(6)(a), 21(5), 14(2) or 22(2)).
7 Provided any such order is in force (s 3(3)).
8 Section 5 is discussed in the context of wardship, post, Chapter 8. See also ante, para 3.15, note 11.
9 FLA 1986, s 1(2)(a). See also ante, para 3.15A, note 2.

6.16 The appropriate county courts and magistrates' courts to hear applications relating to custodianship are, in accordance with the jurisdictional rules prescribed by the Family Law Act 1986,[1] as follows:

(a) The county court

    (1) The county court for the district in which the child to whom the application relates has his habitual residence, or

    (2) where the child has no habitual residence in any district, the county court for the district in which he is present at the date when the proceedings are commenced, or

    (3) where the child, having been habitually resident in a district, leaves or remains outside, or is removed from or retained outside, that district either without the permission of the person or all the persons having the right to determine where he is to reside or in contravention of an order made by a court in any part of the United Kingdom, the county court for that district, for the period of one year beginning with the date of leaving, remaining, removal or retention.[2]

(b) a magistrates' court for the commission area in which a child has his habitual residence or, where the child has no habitual residence, for the commission area in which the child is present at the time when proceedings are commenced.[3]

1 See ante, para 6.15.
2 CCR Ord 47, r 7(2A), as inserted by the County Court (Amendment) Rules 1988, SI 1988/278 (L 1), r 23.
3 Magistrates' Courts (Family Law Act 1986) Rules 1988, SI 1988/329 (L 4), r 5(1). For an equivalent rule to that referred to in (a)(3) above see ibid, r 5(2).

2   Procedure[1]

6.17 The rules governing procedure and allied matters are contained in Rules of the Supreme Court, Ord 90, Part III, rr 13–27;[2] County Court Rules 1981, Ord 47, r 7;[3] and the Magistrates' Courts (Custodianship Orders) Rules 1985.[4] Unlike their counterparts those relating to county courts are not set out *in extenso*, but are instead to be found by way of untidy cross reference to the High Court provisions, which are to apply with the necessary modifications, substitutions and omissions.

1 See Rutherford, *Custodianship - The Procedure*, [1986] Fam Law 180; Pearce, *Custodianship - The Law and Practice* (1986).
2 As inserted by RSC (Amendment No 2) 1985, SI 1985/846.
3 As amended by the County Court (Amendment No 2) Rules 1985, SI 1985/1269 and the County Court (Forms) (Amendment No 2) Rules 1985, SI 1985/1503.
4 SI 1985/1695. See also Home Office Circular 86/1985.

6.18 An application for a custodianship order is made by originating summons in the High Court, by originating application in a county court[1] and by way of complaint in a magistrates' court in accordance with the appropriate form prescribed by the respective Rules.[2] Proceedings in the High Court or a county court must be dealt with in chambers, unless the court otherwise directs, as, for example, when there is some point of law of significance for the future.[3] Those in a magistrates' court must be dealt with by a domestic court sitting in accordance with the restrictions regulating domestic proceedings.[4] Unlike adoption proceedings,[5] representatives of newspapers and news agencies may be present.[6] Although this rarely happens, there is the express protection given for proceedings under the Guardianship of Minors Act 1971 that a magistrates' court can hear the application in camera.[7] Surprisingly and illogically there is no corresponding provision made for custodianship proceedings by the Magistrates' Courts (Custodianship Orders) Rules 1985.[8]

1 In the High Court and a county court where proceedings for a custodianship order are pending or have been determined by the making of a custodianship order, any application under Part II of CA 1975 must be made by summons or application respectively in those proceedings; RSC Ord 90, r 14(2)(a); CCR Ord 47, r 7(3). Proceedings in the High Court must be begun in the Principal Registry; see RSC Ord 90, r 2, as amended by the Rules of the Supreme Court (Amendment No 2) 1986, SI 1986/1187, r 11.
2 RSC Ord 90, rr 14(1) and 20(1); CCR Ord 47, r 7(3) and MC (Custodianship Orders) Rules, r 4(1) and (2). The High Court or a county court may dispense with service of any summons; RSC Ord 90, r 22; CCR Ord 47, r 7(3).
3 RSC Ord 90, r 19; CCR Ord 47, r 7(3).
4 See Magistrates' Courts Act 1980, ss 65, 66, 69 and 71; MC (Custodianship Orders) Rules, r 18 amending MC Rules 1981, rr 36 and 51.
5 See ante, para 5.77.
6 MCA 1980, s 69(2).
7 Magistrates' Courts (Guardianship of Minors) Rules 1974, r 6.
8 Quaere whether protection is given by MCA 1980, s 69(5).

3 Defendants[1]

6.19 The mother and father or (if he is not the plaintiff/complainant) the guardian must be made defendants to the proceedings. Only the Rules governing proceedings in magistrates' courts make clear the position of the father where he and the mother are not and never have been married to each other.[2] In a complaint for an order under Part II of the Children Act 1975 to which the mother or father can be made defendants, he can only be a defendant if he has been adjudged by a court to be the father of the child or if he was a party to proceedings for an order which it is sought to vary or revoke.[3] It is submitted that in the absence of express provision the same rule should be followed in the High Court or a county court. With the passing of the Family Law Reform Act 1987 the opportunity may be taken to amend the Rules

1 See RSC Ord 90, r 16(1); CCR Ord 47, r 7(3); MC (Custodianship Orders) Rules, r 5(1).
2 See MC (Custodianship Orders) Rules, r 5.
3 Ibid, r 5(17)(b).

6.20 Depending on the circumstances, a number of other persons or bodies must also be made defendants. The most frequent will be a local authority,[1] and it will be the local authority:

(i)   to whose care the child has been committed by a care order under the Children and Young Persons Act 1969; or
(ii)   in whom the parental rights and duties are vested, whether jointly or not, by virtue of a section 3 resolution under the Child Care Act 1980; or
(iii) which received the child into its care under section 2 of the 1980 Act; or
(iv)   which has the child in its care under any other enactment; or
(v)   in whose area the child resides and which would be the appropriate authority, for example, where the applicants are relatives or private foster parents.

A voluntary organisation must be made a defendant if the parental rights and duties are vested in it, whether jointly or not. So must anyone who is liable by virtue of a court order, or an agreement, to contribute to the child's maintenance, and so must anyone else (not being a plaintiff complainant) who has actual or legal custody of the child, for example, a person who is jointly sharing the parental rights and duties with a local authority or voluntary organisation. Because the child must have had his home with the applicant for at least the three months immediately preceding the application, the chances of someone else having actual custody are very unlikely, but it would, for example, include a person who is living with the applicant and the child but who is not himself an applicant.

1 A local authority may be represented in any proceedings under Part II of CA 1975 by its director of social services or other officer employed by it for the purposes of its social services functions; RSC Ord 90, r 25; CCR Ord 47, r 7(3); MC (Custodianship Orders) Rules, r 16.

6.21 So, in practice, there will be at least three defendants — the parents and the local authority[1] but sometimes there may be as many as four or five. There is no power to make the child a defendant to county court or magistrates' court proceedings,[2] but the High Court may, if it considers a child should be represented, appoint a guardian ad litem and, if it does so, must make the child a party to the proceedings.[3] The most that can be said in favour of this grave deficiency is that it is consistent with the absence of separate representation of the child in proceedings in a county court under the Guardianship of Minors Act 1971 or in those proceedings or proceedings under the Domestic Proceedings Magistrates' Courts Act 1978 in a magistrates' court. Subject to that power of the High Court, the custodianship rules, unlike those relating to adoption,[4] do not give a court a residual power to direct that anyone else may be made a defendant, but the Custodianship (Reports) Regulations 1985[5] do enable a local authority to state in its report to the court whether in its opinion 'any other person should be made a respondent to the applicant'. *Semble*, this oblique reference does give a residual power.

1 Exceptionally there may be two local authorities, e.g., where the child is in the care of one of them but residing in the area of another.
2 But he can be made a defendant to certain proceedings relating to orders for periodical payments; see MC (Custodianship Orders) Rules, r 5(16).
3 RSC Ord 90, r 18, which authorises the application of the Matrimonial Causes Rules 1977, r 115(1) to (4).
4 See ante, para 5.70
5 See infra, para 6.24.

4 The application and accompanying documents and information

6.22 The application must provide particulars relating to the applicant, the child, the parents or guardian, the local authority or voluntary organisation (if any) in whose care the child is, any person or body paying maintenance for the child under a court order or agreement, the period(s) for which the child has lived with the applicant, information about any earlier proceedings and orders concerning the child and the name(s) of referees.[1] The applicant must also submit medical certificates in respect of himself, unless he is a step-parent, and of the child, and these must have been made not more than three months before the date of the application.[2] The exemption of the step-parent is difficult to reconcile with the court's duty to treat the child's welfare as paramount when deciding whether or not to make a custodianship order. A child could be as much at risk from a step-parent's illness, disability or abnormality as from that of anyone else. If the applicant is relying on the consent of a person having legal custody, he must also submit a Form of consent signed by that person and witnessed by an authorised officer of a county court, a justice of the peace or a justices' clerk.[3] The prescribed Form notifies him of the effects of a custodianship order, and advises him before signing it to obtain legal advice if in doubt about his rights.

1 There is no need to name a referee where the applicant or one of them is a relative or step-parent.
2 RSC Ord 90, r 20(2); CCR Ord 47, r 7(6); MC (Custodianship Orders) Rules, r 4(3).
3 See previous note and RSC Ord 90, r 23; MC (Custodianship Orders) Rules, r 14. A document so witnessed is admissible in evidence without further proof of the signature of the person by whom it was executed; see CA 1975, s 102.

6.22A As already noted,[1] a custodianship order is a custody order within the meaning of the Family Law Act 1986. Where there are proceedings for or relating to a custody order under that Act and the court does not have available to it adequate information about the child's whereabouts, it may order any person who it has reason to believe may have relevant information to disclose the information to the court.[2] A person is not excused from supplying information by reason that to do so might incriminate him or his spouse of an offence, but any statement or admission made in compliance with an order for disclosure is not admissible in evidence against either of them in proceedings for an offence other than perjury.[3]

1 See ante, para 3.15.
2 FLA 1986, s 33(1).
3 Ibid, sub-s (2).

5   Reports

6.23   A custodianship order cannot be made unless the applicant for it has given written notice of his application to the local authority in whose area the child resides.[1] This must be done within the seven days following the making of the application unless the court or local authority extends the period. An applicant who has to seek extension will probably find it administratively more convenient to look to the local authority, relying on the court only if the authority is not amenable. The notice is essential to enable the local authority to discharge its duty, under section 40 of the Children Act 1975, of providing the court with a report.[2] For that reason also the plaintiff in High Court or county court proceedings must, when notifying the local authority, also serve it with a copy of the originating summons or originating application, as the case may be, together with the medical certificates and any Form of consent.[3] In magistrates' court proceedings the clerk to the justices will send a copy of the complaint and the certificates and Form to the local authority.[4] The local authority must report to the particular court before the hearing and in any event within six weeks of receipt of the documents.[5]

1   CA 1975, ss 40(1) and 107(1). In magistrates' court proceedings the complainant *must* make use of the Form of Notice provided (MC (Custodianship Orders) Rules, r 4(4)).
2   Section 40(2). When it reports it must confirm that the notice was given; see the Custodianship (Reports) Regulations 1985, infra.
3   RSC Ord 90, r 24(1); CCR Ord 47, r 7(3).
4   MC (Custodianship Orders) Rules, r 15(1). He will also notify the local authority of the date and time of the hearing of the complaint.
5   RSC Ord 90, r 24(2); CCR Ord 47, r 7(3); MC (Custodianship Orders) Rules, r 15(2). In High Court and county court (but not magistrates' court) proceedings the court officer must notify the parties that they may inspect and take copies of the report; RSC Ord 90, r 24(5); CCR Ord 47, r 7(3).

6.24   This duty to report lies at the heart of custodianship proceedings, and is a vital factor in safeguarding the interests of the child. However, given the conflicting interests that may be present in custodianship proceedings, it must be seriously doubted whether the local authority report is an adequate substitute for a right of separate representation, which the child is denied. The Custodianship (Reports) Regulations 1985[1] do give some flesh to the skeletal provisions of section 40(3) by prescribing the matters to be covered, so far as reasonably practicable, in the report. The Regulations follow closely the provisions in the Adoption Rules 1984 governing reports in adoption proceedings, but take account, in points of detail, of the different objects and consequences of custodianship and adoption. The lists of matters are comprehensive in respect of the child, each parent, any guardian and the applicant. Apart from obvious factual matters, such as age, residence and status, there are some on which it may not be so easy to report; for example, the child's 'personality and social development'; the extent of access and contact by parents and relatives with him and 'the nature of the relationship enjoyed'; any special needs regarding his health;[2] his emotional and behavioural development; his wishes and feelings about the application, having regard to his age and understanding; the hopes and expectations of the applicant for the child's future and his suitability to continue to bring up the child. As for the

wishes of the mother and father of the child, in some cases both will already
have indicated them when they consented to the application, unless only
one of them has given consent, or unless neither has because some other
person has legal custody (for example, a local authority). Even if they have
consented and even though they will be able further to express their wishes
as defendants at the hearing, the reporting officer is obliged to deal with
the matters in his report. Here again there is uncertainty about the position
of the father where he and the mother are not and never have been married[3]
but, if he has all the parental rights and duties vested in him by an order
under section 4 of the Family Law Reform Act 1987 (when that section
is brought into force) or has legal custody or is maintaining the child,
he will be a defendant and the reporting officer will have to ascertain his
wishes. Otherwise it would seem that there is no duty to seek him out,
but, if the officer does come to learn of his whereabouts, he ought to
consult him and report his wishes.

1   As amended by the Custodianship (Reports) (Amendment) Regulations 1985.
2   The reporting officer will have the medical certificates before him. If, in the light of them,
    he needs professional advice, he should obtain it from the appropriate medical advisers
    in the District Health Authority; see LAC (85)13 para 86. Local authorities should ensure
    that medical certificates are treated as confidential; see ibid.
3   See ante, para 6.19 with regard to the father as a defendant.

6.25   The final part of the report must express an opinion on (1) the
implications of an order for the child's health,[1] (2) whether a custodianship
order would be in the child's best interests, (3) the effect of making the
order on the natural parents or other person who has the legal custody,
and (4) how well the child is integrated into the household, family and
community of the applicant. It must then state its final conclusions on
whether a custodianship order should be made and, if not, alternative
proposals, including any for a supervision order or care order. Thus, unlike
other reports, such as welfare reports or social inquiry reports, it does
not leave the reporting officer with a discretion whether or not to include
recommendations.

1   There is no such duty to comment where the applicant is a step-parent; cf supra, para
    6.22 with regard to medical certificates.

6.26   Although the Regulations prescribe matters to be covered, they do
not prescribe a particular Form of report. It is left to each local authority
to prepare its own, if it so wishes, or leave it to the individual reporting
officer. But, whatever the form, this statutory guidance has the double
advantage of assisting the social worker in preparing the report and assisting
the court when it comes to applying the paramountcy principle in accordance
with section 1 of the Guardianship of Minors Act 1971. It is, indeed, an
advantage which could profitably be extended to welfare reports presented
in custody disputes and to social inquiry reports in the juvenile court.[1]
There is no risk of inhibiting the social worker or the court, because the
matters to be prescribed are not exclusive. In fact, the Regulations expressly
state that the report shall include any relevant information which might
assist the court and any relevant to the operation of the paramountcy
principle under section 1 of the 1971 Act.

1   The Law Commission has recommended that there should be a statutory 'checklist' to assist the court; see Law Com No 172, paras 3.17–3.18.

6.27   Clearly, the demands made by section 40 on the reporting officer are heavy. Where the child is in the care of a local authority a social worker who has been directly involved with him may be the appropriate person, but as a matter of general policy local authorities are likely to draw upon experienced officers and, in view of the complementary relationship between adoption and custodianship, will find members of guardian ad litem panels particularly suitable. Experience will also be needed because time for preparation of the report is limited. It must be submitted to the court at the latest within six weeks after the local authority has been served with a copy of the originating summons, originating application or complaint (as the case may be), and to prepare it the social worker has to interview the applicant and his referees, any guardian, the child and, 'wherever that is possible',[1] the natural parents.

1   LAC(85)13, para 80.

6.28   In the light of the report the court may exercise the general discretion it has under section 39(1) of the Children Act to request from a local authority or a probation officer a further report on any specified matters arising from it.[1] Where the child is in the care of the local authority which reported under section 40, the court is likely to ask a probation officer or a different local authority to do so.[2]

1   The request may be of the court's own volition or as the result of representations made by a party to the proceedings or of a suggestion in the s 40 report that a further opinion be sought.
2   See LAC (85) 13, para 85.

6   Restrictions on removal of child pending hearing

6.29   The special protection by way of criminal sanctions, which section 41 of the Children Act gives to an applicant for custodianship who has provided a home for the child for at least three years, follows very closely the lines of the protection afforded to the applicant for adoption who has similarly provided a home for five years,[1] and the same penalties for wrongful removal apply, namely imprisonment for up to three months or a fine not exceeding level 5 on the standard scale (currently £2,000) or both. There is, however, the distinction that, whereas under the adoption rule the relevant period is the five years preceding the application, for the purpose of section 41 the three-year minimum need not be a continuous period, although, in accordance with section 33(3)(c), it will have to include at least the three months preceding the application.[2] The effect of section 41 is that once the custodianship application is made the position is frozen, and the child cannot lawfully be removed from the applicant's actual custody against his will, except with the leave of the court[3] or under the authority conferred by any enactment (for example, those relating to place of safety orders[4]) or on the arrest of the child. The kinds of circumstances which would allow removal have already been considered.[5]

1 Adoption Act 1976, s 28; see ante, para 5.81.
2 Like its counterpart of five years, the three-year period is intended to be experimental and subject to possible amendment (s 41(4)). Any substitution would correspond to any new period substituted for the purpose of s 33(3)(c). See s 41(1) as amended by HASSASSAA 1983, Sch 2, para 60. It is suggested that the shorter protective period of three years should apply to adoption as it does to custodianship.
3 It is expressly provided that, where the custodianship application has been made to a magistrates' court, that court must hear any application to remove the child; MC (Custodianship Orders) Rules, r 7(1). There is no corresponding provision where the custodianship proceedings have been commenced in the High Court or a county court, but in practice it will be the same court that would hear an application to remove.
4 For these orders see post, para 14.34 et seq.
5 See ante, para 5.82.

6.30 Where the child was already in the care of a local authority before he was placed with the applicant and is still in the care of a local authority, the latter authority cannot remove him from the applicant's actual custody except with the applicant's consent or the leave of a court.[1] Thus, the authority cannot rely on its power under a care order or a resolution under section 3 of the Child Care Act 1980 to remove the child. If the child has in an emergency to be removed from the home of the applicant and the latter is not in a position to give consent, reliance should, it is suggested, be placed on the power of the police to remove until an application can be made by the local authority to the court.

1 Section 41(2). In the vast majority of cases the authority will be the same throughout, but s 41(2) recognises the exceptional possibility of a child being in the care of one authority when placed and boarded out, and then in the care of a different authority by the time the custodianship application has been made, for example, where the foster parents and the child have moved to another authority's area.

6.31 Where an application for leave to remove is made, the defendants to those proceedings must be (1) the plaintiff/complainant who has applied for custodianship under section 33 and (2) the defendants (other than the applicant under section 41) to the section 33 proceedings.[1] If the application for leave to remove is granted, the court may, if it sees fit, then treat the hearing of it as the hearing of the section 33 application and refuse a custodianship order,[2] thus avoiding a further hearing where it is clear that the applicant for that order is unsuitable.

1 RSC Ord 90, r 16(11); CCR Ord 47, r 7(3); MC (Custodianship Orders) Rules, r 5(11).
2 RSC Ord 90, r 21(1); CCR Ord 47, r 7(3); MC (Custodianship Orders) Rules, r 7(2).

7 Application for order for return etc of a child

6.32 Apart from the preventative sanctions of the criminal law, measures are provided to enable the person whose custodianship application is pending to seek the return of the child who, in breach of section 41, has been wrongfully removed from his actual custody or to prevent wrongful removal where he has reasonable grounds for believing that a person is intending such action.[1] The application for an order to return the child or to forbid removal must be made to 'an authorised court'[2] and the defendants to the proceedings must be not only the person who has allegedly removed the child or who is believed to be intending to do so, but also the defendants to the custodianship application.[3] In exercising its discretion whether or

not to make an order the court must act in accordance with section 1
of the Guardianship of Minors Act 1971.[4]

1   Section 42(1) and (2).
2   See ante, paras 6.15–6.16 and CA 1975, s 100, as amended by FLA 1986, Sch 1, para
    20, and Sch 2.
3   RSC Ord 90, r 16(12) and (13); CCR Ord 47, r 7(3); MC (Custodianship Orders) Rules,
    r 5(12) and (13).
4   See CA 1975, s 33(9).

6.33   These measures run parallel with those which aid the applicant or
prospective applicant for adoption of a child who has had his home with
him for at least five years.[1] Thus, if an order for the return of a child
is not complied with and the court making the order is the High Court
or a county court, it can further order one of its officers to search specified
premises, and, if he finds the child, to return him to the applicant.[2] If
the order for return was made by a magistrates' court, and also as an
alternative to the above procedure where the order was made by the High
Court or a county court, a justice of the peace can authorise search and
return, if he is satisfied by information on oath that there are reasonable
grounds for believing the child is in specified premises.[3]

1   See ante, para 5.85.
2   Section 42(3). The order to the officer may be enforced in the same manner as a warrant
    for committal (s 42(5)).
3   Ibid, sub-s (4). The search warrant must be in Form 10 of the Magistrates' Courts (Children
    and Young Persons) Rules 1970 or to like effect; see MC (Custodianship Orders) Rules,
    r 17(3).

6.34   Where an application under section 42(1) or (2) is refused, the court
may treat the hearing of the application as the hearing of the application
for a custodianship order and proceed to refuse that order.[1]

1   RSC Ord 90, r 21(1); CCR Ord 47, r 7(3); MC (Custodianship Orders) Rules, r 8.

IV   THE CUSTODIANSHIP ORDER

1   The effects of a custodianship order

6.35   The general effect of a custodianship order was noted in the
Introduction to this chapter, and its specific effects are to be found in
the analysis of legal custody in Chapter 1.[1] The exercise of the parental
powers and responsibilities which pass to the custodian are subject to the
principle enunciated by the House of Lords in the *Gillick* case,[2] that the
law does not recognise that there is any rule of absolute parental authority
until the child reaches the age of majority.

1   See ante, paras 1.59, et seq.
2   [1986] AC 112, [1985] 3 All ER 402; see ante, para 1.13.

6.36   The express inclusion within legal custody of the power to determine
the place and manner in which the child's time is spent[1] means that the
custodian can take most of the important decisions about the child's day
to day care and control and upbringing. In this regard there are, however,

restrictions imposed by the Child Abduction Act 1984. It is an offence for a custodian to take or send a child out of the United Kingdom, for example, for holiday or study, unless the custodian obtains the consent of *either* each parent, guardian or joint custodian[2] *or* of the court which made the custodianship order.[3] Where an application for an order is pending, the leave of the court to which the application was made is required.[4] It has been suggested[5] that, when a custodianship order is made, the custodian should ask the court officer to inform him of the arrangements for obtaining the court's consent for the child to take trips abroad.

1   CA 1975, s 86.
2   There is no liability if he acts in the belief that any such person had consented or would consent if aware of all the relevant circumstances or if he has taken all reasonable steps, though unsuccessfully, to communicate with that person (s 1(5)).
3   Section 1(1)-(3). On the 1984 Act see further ante, paras 3.92 et seq.
4   Para 3 to Schedule.
5   LAC (85) 13, para 104.

6.37   In addition to the powers and responsibilities to be inferred from the definition of legal custody, the custodian is expressly given the powers to consent to the child's marriage[1] and to challenge a parental rights resolution under the Child Care Act 1980.[2] On the other hand, by reason of that definition the following powers do not vest in a custodian:

(i)   to administer the child's property;
(ii)   to change his nationality or domicile;
(iii)   to arrange for his emigration from the United Kingdom;
(iv)   to give or withhold agreement to his adoption;
(v)   to appoint a testamentary guardian for him.

Instead, all these remain with the parent. If there were no parent but a guardian, those relating to property, adoption and (apparently) emigration would still be vested in the guardian. Questions of determining the child's religion and of changing his surname call for special comment.

1   See the Marriage Act 1949, s3(1), as amended by CA 1975, Sch 3, para 7. Where a custodian is a spouse of a parent of the child that parent's consent is also required; see ibid.
2   Section 5(4).

(a)   Religion

6.38   There is some uncertainty about the custodian's role with regard to the religious upbringing of the child, due partly to doubts whether the parental power to choose the child's religion relates to the person of the child.[1] Even if it does, the custodian's role may be restricted. The local authority report to the court must specify the religion of the child, the parents and the applicant, and it must state whether the custodian is willing to follow any wishes of the child or his parents in respect of the child's religious and cultural upbringing.[2] If he is not, the court in applying the principle of the paramountcy of the child's welfare, may refuse to make a custodianship order. If he is and an order is made but he ignores those wishes, there is the possibility of revocation of the order.[3]

1   See ante, para 1.61, note 1.
2   Custodianship (Reports) Regs 1985.
3   For revocation see infra, para 6.51.

(b)   Surname

6.39   It has already been suggested[1] that the power to change a child's surname does not fall within the definition of legal custody, and so custodians cannot exercise it. The name can be changed with the consent of the parents, and, if they have consented to the custodianship application, they may feel that it is in their child's best interest to allow the change. A divorce court exercising its matrimonial jurisdiction has express power to change a child's name.[2] So, too, it is submitted, has the court power in wardship jurisdiction, since custody in the wide sense is vested in it, and the exercise of the power to change the surname is an incident of it.[3] But it is more doubtful whether a court when making a custodianship order can order a change. It has neither express statutory power nor custody vested in it.

1   See ante, para 1.64.
2   MCR 1977, r 92(8).
3   But an order to change is less likely than it is in divorce proceedings, if the marriage of the child's parents is still subsisting.

6.40   A number of other consequences of a custodianship order need to be noted.
(1) So long as the order is operative the right of any person other than the custodian to legal custody of the child is suspended, but, subject to any further order made by any court, revives on the revocation of the custodianship order.[1] The person who normally will be affected by this rule is the parent of the child, for example the mother; but the rule will not apply where she already has custody and the person who becomes custodian is her husband. In such a case they have the legal custody jointly.[2] Nevertheless, additionally she will still have vested in her alone, as parent, all the other parental rights and duties which legal custody does not carry.

1   CA 1975, s 44(1). For revocation and revival see post, para 6.55.
2   Ibid, sub-s (2).

6.41   This kind of division is not limited to the case of the step-parent who shares legal custody. Whenever anyone is appointed custodian the residual parental powers and responsibilities remain with the person or persons in whom they were vested before the making of the custodianship order, be it a parent, a guardian, a local authority or a voluntary organisation. Thus, where at the date of the custodianship order a resolution under section 3 of the Child Care Act 1980 is in force, it does not wholly cease to have effect.[1] But some of the residual powers and responsibilities remain with the local authority, for example, to administer the child's property,[2] while others, (ie agreeing to the making of an adoption order or a provisional adoption order (under section 55 of the Adoption Act 1976) or consenting to an application for a freeing for adoption order (under section 18 of that Act)), are still vested in the parents.[3] Similar consequences result where the custodianship order relates to a child who is the subject of a care order, for the former does not bring to an end the latter.[4] On the other hand, where the child was received into care under section 2 of the Child Care Act without a section 3 resolution subsequently being passed, there is no transfer of parental powers and responsibilities from the local authority to the custodian since none as such were vested in it. Nevertheless, the effect of the custodianship order will be to relieve the authority of the responsibilities it has under Part III of the Child Care Act to children in its care, most notably those of providing accommodation and maintenance.[5]

1 Compare s 5(2), which provides for the termination of a resolution when an adoption order or a freeing for adoption order or an order with a view to a foreign adoption is made or when a guardian is appointed under s 5 of GMA 1971.
2 In theory the power to arrange for the child's emigration could still be exercised by the local authority, subject to the limits imposed by s 24 of the Child Care Act. However, in practice, so long as there is a custodian the Secretary of State would never, it is suggested, give his consent to the emigration. The authority would first have to obtain revocation of the custodianship order.
3 CCA 1980, s 3(10).
4 CYPA 1969, s 21A, as amended, provides for care orders to cease to have effect when certain other orders are made, notably adoption orders, freeing for adoption orders and provisional adoption orders.
5 But see post, para 6.96 for the discretion of the local authority to continue to provide financial aid.

6.42 (2) The power of the court to appoint a guardian under section 5(1) of the Guardianship of Minors Act 1971 depends on the minor's having no parent, guardian or other person having 'parental rights' with respect to him. It follows, therefore, that once a person has been appointed a custodian under a custodianship order, he is not eligible for appointment as a guardian under that section,[1] unless his custodianship order is first revoked. Nor, as we have seen,[2] will he be able to appoint a testamentary guardian. These points can be particularly relevant when a child's parents die and his custodian is a relative.

1 That would not, however, prevent the parent from appointing him a testamentary guardian in accordance with s 4 of the 1971 Act.
2 Ante, para 6.37.

6.43 (3) Where, prior to the making of a custodianship order, the natural parents had disagreed on a matter affecting the child's welfare and consequently the court, in accordance with the Guardianship Act 1973,[1] made an order regarding the matter, the custodian is eligible to apply, as a person 'having the legal custody of the minor',[2] for the order to be varied or discharged; for example, where an order vetoed the issuing of a separate passport to the child but the custodian considers the child is now sufficiently mature to be issued with it. Such orders are rare, and it may long remain an unresolved question whether or not the subject matter must fall within the province of the custodian's powers and responsibilities as relating to the person of the child.[3] The point could be significant if the order was concerned with the religious upbringing of the child and the custodian found it was proving disturbing to the child.[4]

1   Section 1(3); see ante, para 1.67.
2   Sub-s (5), as amended by the Domestic Proceedings and Magistrates' Courts Act 1978, s 36(2).
3   Cf an order relating to administration of the child's property.
4   See ante, para 6.38 for the uncertainty of classifying the parental right to determine the child's religion.

6.44   (4) What is the effect of a custodianship order made in favour of an apparent step-parent when it is subsequently found that his marriage to the natural parent is void? The order might, for example, have been made on the basis that a person qualified as a step-father under section 33(3)(a)[1] of the Children Act, the child having had his home with him for the requisite three months but for less than 12 months. In *Re F*[2] it was held that an adoption order granted to joint adopters whose marriage turned out to be void was itself voidable and not void. It is submitted that analogously a custodianship order would have the same effect.

1   Read with s 33(8).
2   [1977] Fam 165, [1977] 2 All ER 777.

6.45   It remains to add a comment on the consequence of *not* making a custodianship order. It has already been frequently pointed out that the court hearing a custodianship application must apply the principle of the paramountcy of the child's welfare. Where the reason is not a technical one (for example, failure to satisfy the rules governing qualification to apply) but, in accordance with that principle, relates to the merits of the case, the child is not likely to be left with the applicant. So, if the order was refused because of opposition by the local authority, it may well be that the authority will recover the child from the applicant, if he is already in care. If he is not, then it may decide that care proceedings under section 1 of the Children and Young Persons Act 1969 are appropriate.

6.46   If a custodianship order is sought in respect of a ward of court, leave of the wardship court must be obtained in accordance with the principle established in relation to adoption proceedings by *F v S (adoption: ward)*.[1] The court must consider whether or not it is appropriate to divest itself of its control, and decide that issue in accordance with the paramountcy of the ward's welfare. If, for example, the applicants for custodianship are Jehovah's Witnesses who would in no circumstances permit the child to have a blood transfusion, the court may regard the matter of sufficient concern for it to be in the child's interest to remain a ward of court and thus for a custodianship order to be refused.[2]

1   [1973] Fam 203, [1973] 1 All ER 722, CA; see *Practice Direction* (23 July 1987, unreported) at Supreme Court Practice 1988, 2nd Supplement, p 61).
    An application for leave to commence custodianship proceedings in respect of a ward of court may be made ex parte to a registrar; see RSC Ord 90, r 4A(1)(b), as substituted by RSC (Amendment) 1988, SI 1988/298, r 8.
    Where a local authority has been granted leave to place a ward with foster parents with a view to adoption, it is not necessary for an application to be made for leave to commence proceedings for a custodianship order unless the court otherwise directs; see RSC Ord 90, r 4A(1) and (2), as substituted by RSC (Amendment) 1988, r 8.
2   *Re J (a minor) (wardship: adoption custodianship)* [1987] 1 FLR 455, [1987] Fam Law 88.

For a close examination of the relationship between custodianship and wardship see Lowe and White, *Wards of Court*, (2nd edn), Chapter 15.

2 Termination of a custodianship order

(a) Termination otherwise than by revocation

(i) Age of child

6.47 A custodianship order may be made in respect of any child who is under 18,[1] but, especially since it can relate only to the person of the child, it will rarely be sought or made once he has attained the age of 16.[2] Courts will follow the practice in other custody proceedings and recognise the unreality of an order once a child has reached that age of discretion. However, once an order is made, whatever the child's age at that time, it will continue in force until he attains majority.[3]

1 See CA 1975, s 107(1).
2 Exceptionally an order may be desirable where the child is continuing his education beyond that age.
3 CA 1975 s 35(6). Quaere such an order is suspended if he is serving in the armed forces before reaching 18; cf ante, para 1.72.

(ii) Marriage of child

6.48 Whereas the Adoption Act 1976 expressly forbids an adoption order being made in relation to a child who is or has been married,[1] the Children Act 1975 is silent on the effect of marriage upon custodianship orders. For the reason just stated the making of such an order in respect of a married child, even if permissible, is in any event highly unlikely, since compliance with English matrimonial law will require him to be at least 16.[2] However, the point could be relevant where the child, though under that age, is validly married by the spouses' foreign personal law(s). It is arguable that, in view of the Act's silence, a custodianship order could be made in those circumstances, for example, where the child is widowed. Indeed, custodianship would be most appropriate to help meet his or her needs.[3] There is, however, judicial support for the view that marriage ends parental custody over a minor daughter and apparently the same consequence attaches to marriage of a son.[4] If so, it would be anomalous if marriage did not have the same effect on legal custody under a custodianship order. Otherwise, it would mean that those residual powers and responsibilities which remain vested in the parent when the order is made would cease so to remain on the child's marriage, whereas those of the custodian would still be operative. Assuming that marriage does impliedly terminate a custodianship order, it would be inconsistent if it did not equally preclude the making of such an order.

1 Adoption Act 1976, s 12(5).
2 Marriage Act 1949, s 2.
3 There would be power to make a care order under CYPA 1969, s 1; see *Alhaji Mohamed v Knott* [1969] 1 QB 1, [1968] 2 All ER 563, *Aliter* if he or she were at least 16; see s 1(5)(c).
4 See ante, para 1.71.

(iii)   Death of custodian

6.49   The Children Act 1975 is also silent about the effect of the death of a custodian on the order. Where he was one of joint custodians the legal custody will remain vested in the survivor(s). This is by analogy with the rule that on the death of one parent custody resides solely in the other, in the absence of any testamentary guardian. What if he was the sole custodian? It will be seen[1] that, on the revocation of a custodianship order, the legal custody is automatically restored to the person in whom it was previously vested, unless the court otherwise orders. It seems that on death there is implied restoration to that person. It would, it is submitted, have been better if, as with revocation, the court had been given the power to review the circumstances.

1   Post, para 6.55.

(iv)   Child Abduction and Custody Act 1985

6.50   Where an order is made for a child's return under Part I of the Child Abduction and Custody Act 1985[1] or a decision, other than a decision relating to rights of access, is registered under section 16 of that Act, any custodianship order relating to him ceases to have effect,[2] as does any order committing the care of the child to a local authority or any interim order granting legal custody, which was made under Part II of the Children Act 1975.[3]

1   See ante, paras 3.108 et seq for the Act.
2   Child Abduction and Custody Act 1985, ss 25(1) and (2), 27(1) and Sch 3 para 1(1)(g).
3   Ie under CA 1975 ss 36(2), 36(3)(a) or GA 1973, s 2(2)(b) or (4) (as prospectively amended by FLRA 1987, Sch 2, para 54).

(b)   Revocation

6.51   An authorised court[1] may revoke a custodianship order,[2] but its power is subject to the restriction that it cannot proceed to hear an application for revocation if the applicant was previously refused it, unless (a) when so refusing the court then directed that this restriction should not apply, or (b) the court hearing the later application considers that because of a change in circumstances or for any other reason it is proper to proceed with the application.[3] In exercising its power to revoke or, as the case may be, to entertain a further application, the court is governed by the paramountcy of the child's welfare.[4] The fact that that principle was applied when the custodianship order was made suggests that there will have to be a pronounced change of circumstances to justify revocation.

1   See post, para 6.53 for jurisdiction.
2   CA 1975, s 35(1).
3   Section 35(2). Compare a similar restriction on a further application for an adoption order (Adoption Act 1976, s 24(1) ante, para 5.75) and a further application for revocation of a freeing for adoption order (s 20(4) and (5), ante, para 5.48).
4   See s 33(9).

(i)   The applicant

6.52   Any of the following may apply for revocation.[1]

(i)   The custodian. A likely circumstance is where he is a joint custodian and seeks sole custodianship.[2]

(ii)   The mother or father (whether or not they are or have been married to each other[3]) or a guardian of the child.

(iii) Any local authority. It is not necessary that the child should, prior to the custodianship order, have been in the care of a local authority, nor that he should have been received into care under section 2 of the Child Care Act 1980 by the date of the local authority's application for revocation. Nevertheless, it is in the latter circumstances that an application is most likely. The local authority may take the view that a custodianship order is no longer in the child's best interests. In deciding whether to apply it should bear in mind the options open to the court if the order is revoked.[4]

1   Section 35(1). Note that the child himself cannot.
2   See post, para 6.58.
3   See CA 1975, s 33(9A) (as prospectively inserted by FLRA 1987, s 33(1) and Sch 2, para 60).
4   See LAC (85) 13, paras 45 and 46, and infra.

(ii)   Jurisdiction

6.53   Although an order for revocation of a custodianship order is not a 'custody' order within the meaning of the Family Law Act 1986,[1] it seems clear from the amendments which that Act[2] makes to section 100 of the Children Act 1975 that the appropriate county courts and magistrates' courts to hear applications for revocation are those which hear applications for custodianship orders.[3] Additionally, of course, the High Court has jurisdiction.

1   See s 1(2)(a), ante, para 6.15.
2   See Sch 1, para 20 (2) and (3).
3   As to which see ante, para 6.16.

(iii)   Defendants

6.54   The following must be made defendants to the proceedings:[1]

(i)   any person or body (not being the applicant) who would be a defendant to a custodianship application;[2]

(ii)   the person who would have legal custody of the child if the custodianship order were revoked, where he is not the applicant; and

(iii) the custodian, where he is not the applicant.

Here, again, the child is not a party and is not represented, subject to the exceptional power of the High Court to appoint a guardian ad litem, already noted.[3]

1   RSC Ord 90, r 16(5); CCR Ord 47, r 7(3); MC (Custodianship Orders) Rules, r 5(5).
2   See ante, paras 6.19 to 6.21.
3   Ante, para 6.21.

(iv)   Effect of revocation and the options open

6.55   While a custodianship order is in force the right of anyone[1] other than the custodian to legal custody of the child is suspended, but when the order is revoked the right of that other will revive, subject to any further order by the court. Obviously, therefore, it is vital for the court to know what is going to happen to the child on revocation. Section 36(1) of the Children Act 1975 consequently imposes on it the duty of ascertaining who would have legal custody, if on revocation no further order were made.[2] This may be the mother or father or both of them jointly or a guardian or some other person to whom a court granted legal custody in matrimonial proceedings or under the Guardianship of Minors Act 1971.[3] It will be a local authority in those cases where, prior to the custodianship order, it held the parental rights and duties by virtue of a care order or parental rights resolution. If there is no person who would have legal custody (for example, in the case of an orphan with no guardian) and the court decides to revoke the order (for example, on the application of a local authority that the custodian is unsatisfactory), then it must commit the care of the child to a specified local authority.[4] On the other hand, if there is such a person, the court must decide whether to do nothing other than revoke the order, and allow the rule of revival to operate. This action may be followed where legal custody revives in a local authority. In that kind of case the court may decide to leave it to the local authority or a parent or guardian subsequently to apply to the juvenile court for discharge of the care order or rescission of the parental rights resolution. Alternatively, in addition to revoking the custodianship order the court may either (1) allow that person to reassume legal custody, but make a supervision order placing the child under the supervision of a specified local authority or of a probation officer, or (2) commit the care of the child to a specified local authority.[5] In deciding whether to exercise either power the court must consider what 'is desirable in the interests of the welfare of the child', and in so doing it must remember that all applications under Part II of the Children Act are subject to the paramountcy of the child's welfare.[6] Desirability is to be understood within that principle. This provision is much more enlightened than those found in other enactments, for example those relating to matrimonial proceedings, which allow the courts to order supervision or to commit to local authority care only in exceptional circumstances. Where the court chooses the alternative of committing to local authority care it can order either parent to pay maintenance to the local authority or to the child.[7]

1　Except a parent with custody whose spouse is the custodian; they have joint legal custody (CA 1975, s 44(2)); see post, para 6.58.
2　For the power of the court to call for a report see post, para 6.60.
3　For the position of joint custodians see post, para 6.58.
4　Section 36(2). For the right of the local authority to make representations under this subsection and sub-s (3), post, see post, para 6.83.
5　Ibid, sub-s (3). Sub-s (6) further provides that ss 3 and 4 of the Guardianship Act 1973 (which contain supplementary provisions relating to children who are subject to supervision or in local authority care by virtue of orders made under s 2 of that Act) shall apply in relation to an order made under s 36. For these provisions see also post, paras 6.73–6.76.
6　Section 33(9).
7　Section 36(5). There is no such power where it commits to care under s 36(2), supra.

6.56　The rule of revival on revocation may create problems of jurisdiction where the person in whom legal custody revives had been granted it by an order of a court. Supposing, for example, that F, the father of C was granted legal custody by a county court order made under section 9 of the Guardianship of Minors Act 1971. Later he consented to a custodianship application by X and Y in whose favour a custodianship order was made by a magistrates' court. That court now revokes the custodianship order with the result that under section 36 F's right to legal custody revives, unless the court otherwise decides. But has a magistrates' court power to direct otherwise in the face of the county court's section 9 order? Can it 'attach' an order of supervision or ignore the section 9 order by committing the care of the child to a local authority? And what if the section 9 order had been made by the High Court? Such questions of concurrent jurisdiction are ignored by the Children Act 1975.[1] It is submitted that section 39 of the Family Law Act 1986 now provides means for avoiding such conflicts by its requirement that parties to proceedings for or relating to a custody order must give particulars of other proceedings known to them which relate to the child. Thus, in the above example F will have to inform X and Y of the county court custody order and X and Y should then apply for a custodianship order in a county court and not a magistrates' court.

1   See also infra, para 6.58, for problems over concurrent jurisdiction where joint custodians are in dispute.

6.57   The power to revoke is also particularly relevant to the question of a custodian's giving consent to a later custodianship application under section 33. For example, A is the custodian of her nephew B, an orphan. Through failing health A cannot cope with B, who has consequently gone to live with another aunt, C. A and C agree that C should be a custodian in place of A. Presumably, A can give her consent to C's application, and the appropriate procedure would be that, when the new custodianship order is made in favour of C, the court should there and then revoke the first custodianship order.[1]

1   Momentarily A and C would be joint custodians, and the revocation would leave C as sole custodian. A would have to be the applicant for the revocation order (as custodian under it) and C the defendant (as a person having legal or actual custody).

(v)   Joint custodians
6.58   Where joint custodians have been appointed or where a natural parent is sharing legal custody with a step-parent who has been appointed a custodian[1] and they cannot agree on the exercise or performance of a parental power or responsibility, either of them may apply to an authorised court,[2] which may make such order regarding the exercise or performance as it thinks fit.[3] Like its counterpart which governs disputes between a mother and father[4] this provision will rarely be relied on. In practice the dispute over the child's upbringing will be general and not particular. If so, it will not be open to one of them to surrender his or her legal custody to the other.[5] In the absence of matrimonial proceedings, the appropriate step will be for one of the spouses who are joint custodians to seek revocation of the joint custodianship order and the making of a new order giving the applicant sole custodianship.[6] This would avoid any revival of the powers and responsibilities of those who originally had legal custody. In the case of legal custody being jointly shared by the natural parent and step-parent, the natural parent, say the mother, could seek revocation of the custodianship order granted to the step-father, thereby leaving her with sole legal custody, together with the residual parental powers and responsibilities which she

never lost. What the Children Act fails to do is to provide a converse remedy for the step-father. He will have to rely on wardship or matrimonial proceedings. The existence of the custodianship order in his favour will not, it is submitted, oust the court's inherent wardship jurisdiction. Wardship may be invoked on the ground that the relief sought is outside the jurisdiction of the court which made the custodianship order.[7] He will, therefore, be able to apply for the child to be made a ward of court with a view to his obtaining sole care and control. As for matrimonial proceedings, the divorce court can make a custody order notwithstanding the existence of a similar order made by a magistrates' court under its matrimonial jurisdiction. That being so, there seems to be no reason why it could not equally make a custody order under section 42 of the Matrimonial Causes Act 1973 granting the step-father sole custody, if there were divorce proceedings between him and the mother. Similarly, a magistrates' court in exercise of its matrimonial jurisdiction over them could grant the step-parent sole legal custody.[8] If these conclusions are correct where the matrimonial proceedings are between the natural parent and the step-parent, they would apply *mutatis mutandis* to such proceedings between joint custodians. The court would not be prevented from making a custody order[9] in favour of either.

1   See CA 1975, s 44(2).
2   Ie the High Court or the appropriate county court or magistrates' court; see ante, para 6.16
3   CA 1975, s 38.
4   Guardianship Act 1973, s 1(3).
5   See CA 1975, s 85(2), as prospectively amended by FLRA 1987, s 33(4) and Sch 4.
6   There is no power to vary the original order. Section 36 refers only to revocation of custodianship orders. Compare the power to revoke or vary orders made under s 34, *infra* para 6.69.
7   Cf *Re H(GJ) (an infant)* [1966] 1 All ER 952, [1966] 1 WLR 706; *Re P (infants)* [1967] 2 All ER 229, [1967] 1 WLR 818.
8   Sed quaere, if the custodianship order has been made by the High Court.
9   Ie custody in a divorce court, legal custody in a magistrates' court. As already pointed out, ante, para 6.56, where there are matrimonial proceedings between joint custodians, the court should be informed of the existence of the custodianship order in accordance with s 39 of FLA 1986.

6.59   Problems of this kind not only reflect some of the uncertainties to which custodianship is likely to give rise; they are also part of the wider problems of concurrent jurisdiction to make orders affecting children, which persist in the absence of a system of family courts.

(vi)   Reports in revocation proceedings
6.60   The duty of a local authority under section 40 to provide the court with a report does not extend to an application for revocation of a custodianship order, but in such a case a duty is initially imposed on the court to request a report. Unless it already has sufficient information, it must not exercise its functions under section 36 without a written or oral report from a local authority or probation officer about the desirablility of the child's returning to the legal custody of any individual if revocation were ordered.[1] Apart from this duty, the court has a general discretion when dealing with any application concerned with custodianship to request a written or oral report from a local authority or probation officer on

any specified, relevant matter.[2] Any report made under the above provisions should, like a report made under section 40, state clearly the child's wishes and feelings on the particular application and on related matters, such as access.[3]

1 Section 36(4). The local authority need not be the local authority in whose area the child resides; cf s 40. It may be preferable to rely on the authority for the area in which the individual resides.
2 CA 1975, s 39(1). Any request by the appropriate court officer for a report under s 36 or s 39 must be accompanied by a copy of all documents filed with the application. The local authority or probation officer must report within six weeks of the request, and in High Court and county court (but *not* magistrates' court) proceedings the court officer must notify the parties that they may inspect and take copies of any written report. See RSC Ord 90, r 24(3)-(5); CCR Ord 47, r 7(3); MC (Custodianship Orders) Rules, r 15(3) and (4).
3 See LAC (85) 13, para 84. For the procedure for admitting reports in magistrates' courts see ante, para 3.73. The procedure is extended to proceedings relating to custodianship by CA 1975, ss 36(7), 39(2) and 40(4).

V   OTHER ORDERS

6.61   When a custodianship order is made, or while it is in force, the court[1] will be able under section 34 to make certain orders relating to access and maintenance, especially affecting the child's mother or father.[2] There is also jurisdiction parallel with that exercised in custody cases under the Guardianship of Minors Acts 1971 and 1973 which enables the court to make a supervision order or to commit the child to the care of the local authority.[3]

1 Ie the High Court or the appropriate county court or magistrates' court, as to which see ante, para 6.16.
2 Section 34 (as substituted by the Domestic Proceedings and Magistrates' Courts Act 1978, s 64 and prospectively amended by FLRA 1987, Sch 2, para 61(2)) is to be read in conjunction with ss 34A, 34B and 35A (which were added to the Children Act by the 1978 Act, ss 65 and 67).
3 See ante, para 6.18 note 1 for the form of commencement of proceedings in the High Court or a county court where an application is made under Part II of CA 1975 and proceedings for the grant of a custodianship order are pending or have been determined by the making of a custodianship order. Where an application under Part II is made in pending proceedings a party to the application who is not a party to the pending proceedings shall not, unless the court otherwise directs, be joined as a party to those proceedings.

1   Access

6.62   The court may order access by and on the application of any of the following.[1]

(i)   The child's mother or father.
(ii)   A grandparent of the child.[2] The right of grandparents to apply corresponds to the right given to them in custody proceedings under section 9 of the Guardianship of Minors Act 1971[3] and under the Domestic Proceedings and Magistrates' Courts Act 1978.[4]
(iii)   Any other person in relation to whom the child was treated as a child of the family, as that term is defined in the Matrimonial Causes Act 1973.[5] The following are examples of persons who fall into this category.

(a) After several years living together S separated from his wife, W, and his step-daughter, D. W died and her relatives, with whom D has since been living, have applied for a custodianship order. S had regularly been seeing D both before and since W's death. S may apply for access.

(b) A and his wife, B, brought up their nephew, C, an orphan. B has died, and A has placed C with other relatives, who have applied for a custodianship order. A may apply for access.

1   Section 34(1)(a) and (2). The defendant to the application will be the person seeking a custodianship order if proceedings under s 33 are pending, and the custodian if a custodianship order is in force; RSC Ord 90, r 16(2); CCR Ord 47, r 7(3); MC (Custodianship Orders) Rules, r 5(2).
2   Where the grandparent applies to a magistrates' court and a custodianship order made by that court is already in force, the grandparent must be notified of the particulars of that order by the clerk; MC (Custodianship Orders) Rules, r 12.
3   Section 14A, ante, para 3.88.
4   Section 14, ante para 3.88.
5   Section 52(1), ante, paras 3.16 and 3.47, and see RSC Ord 90, r 13(b); CCR Ord 47, r 7(3); MC (Custodianship Orders) Rules, r 5(17)(a).

6.63   Since one of the purposes of custodianship is to make it easier for the natural parents to retain a relationship with their children, applications by the mother or father for access are likely to be sympathetically entertained, but an order will be refused if the paramountcy of the child's welfare so requires.[1] The fact that the mother or father has been making financial provision or that the court when making a custodianship order also orders maintenance will strengthen the case for access, but will not carry an automatic right to it, any more than it does in custody proceedings between the mother and father. If there is going to be a real chance of access and custodianship working together, it is of the utmost importance that the question of access be agreed or decided at the outset when the custodianship order is made. Where there is an access order, local authorities should see that it is observed,[2] and custodians who are intending to change their address should notify the court.[3]

1   If the parents are refused access, it is pertinent to ask why the custodians did not apply for adoption instead of custodianship; see Bromley, p 369, note 15.
2   See LAC (85) 13, para 17.
3   As to the enforcement of access orders see ante, para 3.87.

2   Maintenance

6.64   Since a custodianship order vests in the custodian the parental rights and duties which by law the mother and father have in relation to the person of their legitimate child,[1] one necessary implication, it is submitted, is that the statutory duty to maintain, imposed by section 26(3) of the Social Security Act 1986 on the mother and father, is transferred to the custodian. He is, however, eligible to claim child benefit, and is also able to look to the natural parents for possible financial assistance by applying for an order for periodical payments and/or a lump sum to be made by either or both of them.[2] The same orders can also be sought against any other person in relation to whom the child was treated as a child of the family, but in line with the Matrimonial Causes Act 1973[3] the court, in determining whether that person should be ordered to pay, must have regard (among the circumstances of the case) to the extent, if any, to which he assumed responsibility for the child's maintenance, the basis of it, the length of time for which he discharged it, whether in so doing he knew that the child was not his own child, and the liability of anyone else to maintain the child.[4] Thus, in the two illustrations above, if the relatives were appointed custodians, the step-father S and the child's uncle A respectively could within these limits be ordered to make payments.[5] This extension of the family maintenance provisions outside matrimonial proceedings has not escaped criticism, mainly on the ground that it is inconsistent with the principle that neither a step-parent nor any other non-parent is liable at common law or under section 26(3) of the Social Security Act 1986 to maintain the child. There is in particular a risk that, since a local authority cannot recover from a non-parent contributions in respect of a child in its care,[6] it may prompt a local authority to encourage its foster parents to apply for custodianship and an accompanying order for maintenance and thereby save itself the cost of maintaining the child.[7]

1   CA 1975, ss 85(1) and 86.
2   CA 1975, s 34(1)(b) and (c); RSC Ord 90, r 16(3); CCR Ord 47, r 7(3); MC (Custodianship Orders) Rules, r 5(3). Unlike the provisions on which they are modelled, s 34(1)(b) and (c) do not expressly provide for both periodical payments *and* a lump sum to be payable, but the conclusion in favour is not open to serious doubt; see Law Commission Report No 77, paras 7.10 and 7.14 and p 307.
3   Section 25(4), as substituted by the Matrimonial and Family Proceedings Act 1984, s 3.
4   CA 1975, s 34A(2).
5   Section 52(1) of MCA 1973 refers to the child who 'has been treated': s 34(2) of CA 1975 to the child who 'was treated'. Presumably the difference is deliberate and is intended to allow for the fact that the marriage of the natural parent and the step-parent, or of two non-parents, may, as in the two illustrations, have come to an end by the time of the custodianship application.
6   See Child Care Act 1980, s 45.
7   See Snow, (1985) 135 NLJ 1170.

6.65   In deciding whether to order payments the court must have regard to all the circumstances of the case, but the matters which it has specifically to take into account follow very closely those to be considered in proceedings under sections 11B and 11C of the Guardianship of Minors Act 1971.[1] These cover the means and obligations of the parents[2] and the custodian; and the means, if any, and the needs of the child, including needs arising from any physical or mental disability. As with sections 11B and 11C proceedings, one notable omission is any reference to the manner in which the child is being educated and to parental expectations about his education. Nevertheless, it is a matter to which the court should be alert. The court can order periodical payments and/or a lump sum to be paid either to the custodian for the benefit of the child or to the child himself.[3] One particular purpose for which a lump sum may be ordered is to meet liabilities or expenses reasonably incurred in maintaining the child before the date of the order.[4] There is no limit on the amount of periodical payments, but the maximum lump sum that a magistrates' court can order is now £1,000.[5] A lump sum may be ordered to be paid by instalments.[6] Periodical payments may be ordered from the date of the application for an order or any later date, but an order must not in the first instance normally extend beyond the child's seventeenth birthday.[7] It can be extended to his eighteenth birthday and even beyond that age (a) where he is or will be receiving further education or training (whether or not in gainful employment) or (b) where there are special circumstances, such as severe physical or mental handicap, justifying extension.[8] An order for payments under section 34 is enforceable as a magistrates' court maintenance order[9] and may be made the subject of an attachment of earnings order.[10] If the section 34 order is made in the High Court or a county court it may be registered, and thereby enforced and varied, in a magistrates' court: if made in a magistrates' court, it may be registered in the High Court.[11]

1 CA 1975, s 34A(1) and (3); GMA 1971, s 12A, as inserted by DPMCA 1978, s 43. See post, para 16.08. Is there any reason why there should not be uniformity of presentation of these respective provisions?
2 Including any person in relation to whom the child was treated as a child of the family; CA 1975, s 34A(3)(a).
3 CA 1975, s 34(1)(b) and (c). For the tax implications of payments see post, para 16.54. Further information may be obtained from the Inland Revenue, Policy Division, Somerset House, London WC2R 1LB.
4 CA 1975, s 35A(1).
5 Section 35A(2); Magistrates' Courts (Increase of Lump Sums) Order 1988, SI 1988/1069.
6 Section 35A(5).
7 Ie 'the date of the birthday of the child next following his attaining the upper limit of the compulsory school age', which is currently 16; s 34B(1).
8 Section 34B(1) and (2).
9 Section 43(3), as prospectively inserted by FLRA 1987, Sch 2, para 65.
10 Attachment of Earnings Act 1971, Sch 1, para 12, as added by CA 1975, Sch 3, para 76(b).
11 Maintenance Orders Act 1958, Part I, as prospectively amended by FLRA 1987, Sch 2, para 18; Administration of Justice Act 1970, Sch 8, para 12, as added by CA 1975, Sch 3, para 73(2)(b).

6.66 A custodian cannot rely on section 34 to seek maintenance from the unmarried father of a child, but is obliged to rely on affiliation proceedings. The Family Law Reform Act 1987 will remove the disability.[1]

1 See s 33(4) and Sch 4, prospectively repealing s 34(3) of CA 1975.

6.67 In preparing its report under section 40 the local authority is expressly directed to report on the means of the mother and father and the custodian.[1] The court needs this information in order to assist it in deciding whether or not to order either or both of the parents to pay maintenance.[2] How far the social worker will be able to obtain information about means is, however, another matter. It is more likely that this will require the energies of the court at the hearing of the custodianship application, that is, if an application is made. The fact that inquiry can be made into the means of a prospective custodian may deter him from applying.

1 CA 1975, s 40(3)(d); Custodianship (Reports) Regulations 1985.
2 If the custodian seeks maintenance at a date subsequent to the making of the custodianship order, the court can call for a report under s 39 (ante, para 6.60).

3   Revocation and variation of access and maintenance orders

(a)   Maintenance order made otherwise than under section 34

6.68 Apart from its power to order maintenance, the court[1] may, under section 34, revoke or vary orders requiring the mother or father[2] to contribute towards the child's maintenance which another court has made.[3] Revocation is possible on the application of the mother or father.[2] The defendant to the application will be the person seeking a custodianship order if section 33 proceedings are pending, and the custodian if a custodianship order is in force.[4] Variation is possible on the application of the mother or father[2] or of the custodian or the person applying for a custodianship order. Where the applicant to vary is the mother or father the defendant is the applicant for custodianship or, as the case may be, the custodian. Conversely, where the applicant for custodianship or the custodian is applying to vary, the defendant is the mother or father.[5] The power to vary extends to altering the amount of the contributions and to substituting the custodian for the person to whom the contributions were ordered to be made. The kinds of orders subject to these powers are those made in exercise of matrimonial jurisdiction or of jurisdiction under the Guardianship of Minors Act 1971 and 1973, and those requiring the mother or father to contribute towards the maintenance of their children who are in care.[6] A remarkable feature of these powers is that no guidance is given by the Children Act or the Rules of Court on the extent to which a court can exercise its powers of revocation and variation in respect of an order made by a court of different jurisdiction, and no system of registration of orders between the courts for the purpose of those powers has been introduced.

1 Ie the High Court or the appropriate county court or magistrates' court, as to which see ante, para 6.16.
2 Including any person in relation to whom the child was treated as a child of the family (s 34(2)).
3 Section 34(1)(d) and (e).
4 RSC Ord 90, r 16(2); CCR Ord 47, r 7(3); MC (Custodianship Orders) Rules, r 5(2).
5 RSC Ord 90, r 16(4); CCR Ord 47, r 7(3); MC (Custodianship Orders) Rules, r 5(4).
6 See post, Chapter 15. A contribution order in favour of a local authority could, for example, be varied in favour of the custodian.

(b) Access and maintenance orders made under section 34

6.69 Section 35 provides for the revocation or variation of any order made under section 34, except a lump sum order — although section 35A provides supplementary rules relating to the latter order. Application can be made by the custodian[1] or by any other person on whose application the order was made.[2] Thus, the application could relate to an order granting access to the mother and/or father or grandparent (for example, where the access is not working satisfactorily) or an order requiring the mother or father or both of them or a person in relation to whom the child was treated as a child of the family to contribute towards the child's maintenance (otherwise than by the payment of a lump sum). The person so liable to contribute can also apply for revocation or variation of that order.[3] If the child has attained the age of 16, he can himself apply for variation of an order for periodical payments.[4] A number of rules apply to that kind of order. The court can suspend and subsequently revive the operation of any provision in the order,[5] a power which, for example, may be particularly useful where the payer is temporarily off work and unable to meet his commitments under the order. Where the maintenance order ceases to have effect not earlier than the child's sixteenth birthday but not later than his eighteenth, he may apply himself for the order to be revived.[6] If he is over 18 he will have to satisfy one of the conditions that enable the court to extend an order beyond that age.[7] If the order is revived, then it can be varied or revoked on the application of the child or the person named in the order.[8] Where the court decides to vary the payments, it can fix a date of commencement for the new payments as early as the making of the application for variation or revocation.[9] In varying or revoking an order it can order the mother or father to pay a lump sum.[10] If the court is a magistrates' court the sum must not exceed the statutory limit of £1,000, but that court can make a lump sum order even though the mother or father was ordered to pay a lump sum by a previous order.[11] In deciding whether or not to revoke or vary a maintenance order the court must consider all the circumstances of the case, including any change in any of the matters which the court was required to consider when making the order.[12] It may find it necessary to call for a report.[13] Where there is a lump sum order and it is payable by instalments, the court may vary the number and amount of the instalments (but not the total sum) and the date on which they are to be paid.[14] Application may be made by the person liable to pay or the person entitled to payment.

1 Section 35(3). The defendant will be the parent or grandparent against whom or in favour of whom the order sought to be varied or revoked was made; RSC Ord 90, r 16(6); CCR, Ord 47, r 7(3); MC (Custodianship Orders) Rules, r 5(6).
2 Section 35(4). The defendant will be the custodian; RSC Ord 90, r 16(7); CCR Ord 47, r 7(3); MC (Custodianship Orders) Rules, r 5(7).
3 Section 35(4) and for the defendant see previous footnote.
4 Section 35(4A). The defendant will be the mother or father against whom the order sought to be varied was made; RSC Ord 90, r 16(8); CCR Ord 47, r 7(3); MC (Custodianship Orders) Rules, r 5.
5 Section 35(7).
6 Section 35(10) (as prospectively substituted by FLRA 1987, s 33(1) and Sch 2, para 62). The defendant to the application is the mother or father against whom the maintenance order was made; RSC Ord 90, r 16(9); CCR Ord 47, r 7(3); MC (Custodianship Orders) Rules, r 5(9).
7 For these conditions see s 34B(2), ante, para 6.65.
8 The defendant to the application is the person in whose favour the order was made. Any order made by a magistrates' court under s 34(1)(b) for financial provision for the child which is revived by an order under s 35(10) shall for the purposes of the enforcement of the order be treated as an order made by the magistrates' court by which the order was originally made; see s 35(10A) (as prospectively added by FLRA 1987, Sch 2, para 62).
9 Section 35(9).
10 Section 35A(3). It should be remembered that this includes any person who has treated the child as a child of the family (s 35A(6)).
11 Section 35A(4).
12 Section 35(8); see s 34A, supra, para 6.65.
13 See s 39, supra, paras 6.60 and 6.67.
14 Section 35A(5).

6.70 An access order, like a custodianship order itself, ceases to have effect when the child attains 18;[1] a maintenance order ceases on the death of the person liable to make the periodical payments under the order;[2] and an access order and/or maintenance order automatically end on the revocation of the custodianship order.[3]

1 Section 35(6).
2 Section 34B(3).
3 Section 35(5).

6.71 This rule of automatic cessation also extends to an order which varied a maintenance order made by another court,[1] for example, by requiring the father, who was liable under the original order to pay maintenance for the child to the mother to whom legal custody was granted, instead to make the payments to the custodian. In such a case the custodian would no longer be entitled to payments when the custodianship order is revoked. But does the revocation revive the original order so that the mother is once again entitled to the payments? The Children Act 1975 is silent on the point. It is arguable that, if the court allows the legal custody in the mother to revive by operation of the Act, the maintenance order in its original form also revives in her favour, but not where the court chooses instead to commit the child to the care of the local authority. However, it is doubtful whether such rule of partial revival will operate. There is much to be said for a clean break. The financial position of the parents may have changed substantially since the date of the original order, and it would, it is submitted, be preferable for a fresh application to be made by the mother. Where the court commits the child to the care of the local authority, it may order the parent to make payments to the authority towards the child's maintenance.[2] It would be highly artificial to regard the former order in favour of the parent as having been revived yet lying dormant so long as the child is in care and payments are made to the authority.

1 See s 34(1)(e), supra, para 6.68.
2 Section 36(5), ante, para 6.55. The power to order will extend to the unmarried father of a child; see FLRA 1987, Sch 2, para 63 and Sch 4, prospectively repealing CA 1975, s 36(5A).

6.72 These uncertainties can be avoided where, as usually happens, the maintenance order directs, for taxation reasons, that payments be made to the child. There would be no need to vary the original order in favour of the custodian when the custodianship order was made. But the basic problem considered in the previous paragraph would still be relevant to any order made under section 34(1)(e) which altered the amount of the contributions to the child. Supposing the variation had been upwards in the amount payable, would the effect of revocation of the custodianship order be to entitle the child only to the amount under the original order? It is suggested that equally here the 'clean break' principle is the best solution, so that fresh application can be made by the person in whom legal custody revives.

4 Orders for supervision, local authority care, etc

6.73 Following the pattern of similar enactments and in particular the Guardianship of Minors Acts 1971 and 1973, the court can make a supervision order to accompany a custodianship order or, instead of making the latter order, commit the care of the child to a local authority.[1] These orders can, however, only be made in exceptional circumstances.

1 CA 1975, s 34(5) (as substituted by DPMCA 1978, s 64 and prospectively amended by FLRA 1987, Sch 2, para 61(3)), extending to custodianship applications, with modifications, ss 2(2), (3), (3A), (3B), (4), (4A), (5A), (5B), (5C), (5D), and (5E), and 3 and 4 of the Guardianship Act 1973.

(a) Supervision orders

6.74 If a child is in local authority care and living with foster parents, the authority is not likely to recommend in its report the making of a custodianship order supported by a supervision order. Where foster parents continue to need supervision it will normally be better for the child to remain in care.[1] But, where the exceptional circumstances make a supervision order desirable, the child will be placed under the supervision of a specified local authority or of a probation officer,[2] and will remain so until he reaches 18[3] or until the order is discharged. The persons qualified to apply for discharge or variation of the order are either parent or the custodian or (after the death of either parent) a guardian or the supervising probation officer or local authority.[4] In practice only the custodian or the supervising authority or probation officer will be applicants. Neither parent is very likely to be content with seeking revocation only of the supervision order, but will want revocation of the custodianship order itself.

1 See LAC (85) 13, para 11.
2 GA 1973, s 2(2)(a) (as prospectively substituted by FLRA 1987, Sch 2, para 54). The local authority will in practice be that within whose area the child and custodian reside. For appointment of a probation officer see s 3(1) and (4).
3 Section 3(2).
4 GA 1973, s 3(3) as amended by CA 1975, s 34(5), s 108(1)(b) and Sch 4. The defendants must be also those persons other than the one who is the applicant; see MC (Custodianship Orders) Rules, r 10(2). Where proceedings under Part II of CA 1975 are pending, any application under s 3(3) of GA 1973 must be made in those proceedings; RSC Ord 90, r 5(2) (as substituted); CCR Ord 47, r 6(1A) (as inserted).

(b) Local authority care

6.75 Where there are exceptional circumstances making it impracticable or undesirable for the child to be entrusted to either of the parents or to any other individual, ie to the applicant for custodianship or the person (other than a parent) who would retain custody if a custodianship order is refused, the court can commit the child to the care of the local authority in whose area he is residing, provided he is under 17.[1] Before it does so it must inform the local authority of its intention to make the care order and hear any representations from the authority on that matter and about making an order for maintenance in the authority's favour.[2] So long as the care order is in force the child remains in the care of the local authority notwithstanding any claim by a parent or other person,[3] and the effect of the order is that, subject to a number of exceptions, Parts III and V of the Child Care Act 1980 (which relate to the treatment of children in local authority care and contributions towards their maintenance) apply.[4] The details of these consequences are explained elsewhere.[5]

1 CA 1975, s 34(5) (as substituted by DPMCA 1978 s 64, and prospectively amended by FLRA 1987, Sch 2, para 61(3)), extending to custodianship applications with modifications, ss 2(2), (3), (3A), (3B), (4), (4A), (5A), (5B), (5C), (5D) and (5E) and 3 and 4 of the Guardianship Act 1973.

2   GA 1973, s 4(2). There is no need to inform the local authority if it has already recommended a care order in its report (made under s 40 or, if applicable, s 39 of CA 1975); see CA 1975, s 34(5)(c).
3   GA 1973, s 4(5).
4   GA 1973, s 4(4).
5   See post, Chapter 15.

(c)   Parental contributions towards maintenance

6.76   Each parent or guardian of a child in care must notify the local authority of any change of address.[1] This duty is particularly relevant where there is an order to pay maintenance to the local authority or to the child. When the court makes a care order it can further order periodical payments, but not a lump sum, to be paid by either parent.[2] An order for payment must not in the first instance extend beyond the child's seventeenth birthday. It can be extended to his eighteenth birthday and even beyond (a) where he is or will be receiving further education or training, or (b) where there are special circumstances justifying extension.[3] However, an order in favour of the local authority is payable only as long as the child is in care.[4] An order comes to an end on the death of the parent liable to make payments under it. In deciding whether to order payments the court must consider all the circumstances, including the means and obligations of the parent and the means, if any, of the child and his needs, including needs arising from any physical or mental disability.[5] Any change in those circumstances must be taken into account if there should be an application to vary or discharge the order.[6] An application to vary or discharge an order for periodical payments or a care order[7] may be made by either parent or, after the death of either parent, by a guardian or by the local authority to whose care the child was committed,[8] and an application to *vary* a periodical payments order may be made by the child himself, if he has attained the age of 16.[9] Where the court decides to vary the payments on any application to vary or discharge, it can fix a date of commencement for the new payments as early as the making of the application.[10]

1   GA 1973, s 4(6). Failure to do so without reasonable cause carries a penalty not exceeding level 2 on the standard scale (currently £100).
2   GA 1973, s 2(3).
3   Section 2(3B), applying the provisions of s 12 of GMA 1971 (as prospectively amended by FLRA 1987, Sch 2, para 31); cf orders made under ss 34 and 34B of CA 1975, ante, para 6.65.
4   GA 1973, s 2(3).
5   Section 2(3A), applying the provisions of s 12A of GMA 1971 (as prospectively amended by FLRA 1987, Sch 2, para 32).
6   Section 4(3B).
7   An application relating to a care order will be for discharge. It is difficult to visualise a case of application to vary it.
8   All those persons other than the one who is the applicant must be made defendants to an application relating to a care order, and the persons by whom payment is required to be made and the local authority (other than the one who is the applicant) must be the defendants to an application relating to an order for periodical payments; see MC (Custodianship Orders) Rules, r 10(3) and (4).
9   GA 1973, s 4(3A), as inserted by CA 1975, s 108(1)(a) and Sch 3, para 80.
10   Section 4(3C).

5   Miscellaneous provisions relating to jurisdiction and orders

(a)   Interim orders

6.77   Section 2 of the Guardianship Act 1973, as applied to a custodianship application,[1] enables the court to make an interim order for a specified period not exceeding three months, which may be extended for a further period of not more than three months.[2] This extension by cross reference does not lend itself to clarity of application, but the effects appear as follows. Firstly, where 'by reason of special circumstances the court thinks it proper' it can make an order providing for legal custody and access.[3] Thus, for example, it may wish the local authority to conduct further investigations but during the adjournment allow the applicant for custodianship legal custody and meantime grant the parent access.[4] Secondly, it can make an interim order requiring 'either parent to make periodical payments to the other or to the child'.[5] For this purpose reference to a parent includes a reference 'to any other individual'.[6] Thus, for example, an interim order for payments may be made in favour of the applicant for custodianship;[7] while a person in respect of whom the child was treated as a child of the family may be ordered to make payments.

There is also power to make interim orders relating to legal custody, access and periodical payments where the court dismisses the custodianship application on the ground that the matter is one that would more conveniently be dealt with by the High Court.[8]

1   By CA 1975, s 34(5) (as amended by FLRA 1987, Sch 2, para 61(3)).
2   GA 1973, s 2(5C), (5D) and (5E).
3   GA 1973, s 2(4) (as prospectively substituted by FLRA 1987, Sch 2, para 54). The court can postpone the operation of any order regarding the legal custody (s 2(5A)).
4   Semble, from the wording of s 2(4) the parent would have to apply for access.
5   GA 1973, s 2(4A) (as prospectively substituted by FLRA 1987, Sch 2, para 54).
6   CA 1975, s 34(5)(a), as prospectively amended by FLRA 1987, Sch 2, para 61(3).
7   Here, too, in view of the wording of s 2(4A) there would have to be an application for periodical payments.
8   GA 1973, s 2(5) (as prospectively substituted by FLRA 1987, Sch 2, para 54).

(b)   Restrictions on removal of child out of the jurisdiction

6.78   Reference has already been made to the restrictions imposed by the Child Abduction Act 1984 on taking or sending a child abroad and to the rule that the custodian has no power to arrange for the child's emigration.[1] Quite apart from them, the court, when making a custodianship order or an interim order that contains provision regarding legal custody or while either such order is in force, may order that no-one shall take the child out of the United Kingdom or out of any part of the United Kingdom specified in the order except with the leave of the court.[2] An application for that order or later for its variation or discharge may be made by (1) the mother or father, in which case the defendant is the custodian or the person with legal custody under the interim order or (2) the custodian, in which case the defendants are the mother *and* father *and* any guardian.[3]

As already noted,[4] an order restricting removal of a child under 16 out of the United Kingdom or any specified part of it has effect in other parts of the United Kingdom as if it had been made in that other part.[5] Moreover, there is power to require surrender of United Kingdom passports.[6]

1   Ante, paras 6.36 and 6.37.
2   CA 1975, s 43A(1) and (1A). Section 43A was inserted by DPMCA 1978, s 70 and amended by HASSASSAA 1983, Sch 2, para 24 and by FLA 1986, s 35(1)(b).
3   Section 43A(2) and (3); RSC Ord 90, r 16(14); CCR Ord 47, r 7(3); MC (Custodianship Orders) Rules, r 5(14).

4 See ante, para 3.22 for further details.
5 FLA 1986, s 36.
6 Ibid, s 37.

(c) *Enforcement of orders*

6.79 The Children Act[1] includes additional methods of enforcement of custodianship orders and maintenance orders which are made by magistrates' courts. They run parallel with similar provisions in the Guardianship of Minors Act 1971[2] for the enforcement of orders for custody and maintenance. The custodian may, without prejudice to any other remedy, enforce his custodianship order by service and enforcement of a copy of the order under section 63 of the Magistrates' Courts Act 1980, and recover the child from anyone who has actual custody of him, for example, from someone who has taken the child away or who refuses to return him after a period of staying access.[3] A maintenance order made under section 34 of the Children Act 1975 may be enforced in the same manner as an affiliation order or, when the relevant change is brought into effect, as a magistrates' court maintenance order.[4] The person ordered to contribute must notify any change of address to the person specified in the order, usually the justices' clerk.[5]

Where a person is required by a custody order, as defined by the Family Law Act 1986, or an order for the enforcement of a custody order, to give up a child to another person, and the court which made the order is satisfied that the child has not been given up, it may make an order authorising an officer of the court or a constable to take charge of the child and deliver the child to that other person. The authorisation includes authority to enter and search any premises and to use such force as may be necessary.[6]

1 Section 43.
2 See s 13, and ante, para 3.28.
3 CA 1975, s 43(1).
4 Section 43(3), as prospectively substituted by the Family Law Reform Act 1987, s 33(1) and Sch 2, para 65. For magistrates' court maintenance orders see the Magistrates' Courts Act 1980, s 150(1).
5 Section 43(2). Failure to comply without reasonable excuse is an offence punishable by a fine not exceeding level 2 on the standard scale (currently £100).
6 See FLA 1986, s 34.

(d) *Magistrates' courts*

6.80 A magistrates' court has jurisdiction even though the proceedings are brought by or against a person residing outside England and Wales.[1] However, an application for a custodianship order by such a resident is very unlikely, since, as has been pointed out,[2] he has to give notice to the local authority in whose area the child resides and the child must have his home with him. The court cannot make an order requiring a person to make periodical payments or pay a lump sum or vary an order to increase periodical payments unless he has been served with a summons,[3] but otherwise it can entertain an application for any order, notwithstanding that the defendant has not been served with a summons.[4] Where there are two or more defendants, the power of the court under section 64(1) of the Magistrates' Courts Act 1980 to award costs includes a power, whatever adjudication the court makes, to order any of the parties to pay the whole or part of the costs of all or any of the parties.[5]

1   CA 1975, s 46(1).
2   Bromley, *Family Law*, 6th edn, p 384, note 4.
3   Section 46(3).
4   Ibid, s 46(2).
5   Ibid, s 46(4).

6.81   The powers of a magistrates' court under section 60 of the Magistrates' Courts Act 1980 to revoke, revive or vary an order for periodical payments and to suspend the operation of any provision of such order and to revive the operation of any provision so suspended do not apply to a custodianship order or an order under section 34 of the Children Act.[1]

1   CA 1975, s 35(11).

(e)   Jurisdiction of registrar

6.82   A registrar of the High Court or a county court has jurisdiction over the following applications:[1]

(a)   an application for an order under section 34(1) of the Children Act relating to maintenance of a child or to access, where the only question is the extent of the access;

(b)   an application for revocation or variation of an order relating to access or periodical payments made under section 34(1);

(c)   an application by the child for variation of an order for periodical payments;

(d)   an application by the child for revival of an order for periodical payments;

(e)   an application under section 43A for an order restricting the removal of the child from England and Wales, or for variation or revocation of such an order, where the application is unopposed, or where the application is for the temporary removal of the child, unless it is opposed on the ground that the child may not be returned.

1   RSC Ord 90, r 15; CCR Ord 47, r 7(3).

(f)   Care order – local authority representations

6.83   Before the court may make an order, whether on hearing an application for a custodianship order or on revoking such an order, committing the care of the child to a local authority,[1] the authority, whether or not it is a party, may make representations either (a) when the court indicates that it proposes to make such an order or (b) at a date fixed by the appropriate court officer.[2] It seems that representations may be made at the hearing even if the authority has already in a report to the court recommended that the child be placed in care. If the proceedings are in the High Court or a county court and the local authority wishes to represent that, in the event of a care order being made,[3] the Court should order periodical payments in favour of the child, the authority must (within seven days after being notified by the appropriate court officer) file an affidavit setting out such facts as are known to it which are relevant to the property and income of the person against whom the periodical payments order is sought and at the same time serve a copy of the affidavit on him. That person within 14 days after service must in turn file an affidavit giving full particulars of those matters and serve a copy of it on the local authority.[4]

1 Ie under GA 1973, s 2(2)(b), as applied by CA 1975, s 34(5) or under CA 1975, s 36(2) or (3)(a).
2 RSC Ord 90, r 26(1); CCR Ord 47, r 7(3); MC (Custodianship Orders) Rules, r 9. Not less than 14 days' notice of the date must be given.
3 Under GA 1973, s 2(2)(b) or CA 1975, s 36(3)(a).
4 RSC Ord 90, r 26(2) and (3); CCR Ord 47, r 7(3).

(g) Effects of Family Law Act 1986 on orders

6.83A The Family Law Act 1986[1] provides that if a custody order (or a variation of a custody order) made in Scotland or Northern Ireland comes into force while a custodianship order (including an interim order)[2] is in effect, the Scottish or Northern Ireland order will prevail over the English order in so far as they overlap. Thereafter, the English court does not have power to vary its own order so as to make provision for the matters covered by the later order.[3] Any supervision order which is dependent upon the custodianship order ceases to have effect.[4]

The court does not have jurisdiction to vary a custodianship order if at the relevant date[5] proceedings for divorce, nullity or judicial separation are continuing[6] in Scotland or Northern Ireland in respect of the marriage of the child's parents,[7] unless the court in Scotland or Northern Ireland waives its jurisdiction to make an order or decides to sist or stay custody proceedings before it in favour of the English court.[8]

1 Section 6(1).
2 Ibid, s 1(1)(a)(iv).
3 Ibid, s 6(2).
4 S 6(6)(d).
5 Ie the date of the application (or first application, if two or more are determined together) and where no application is made, the date of the variation (s 6(7)).
6 In Northern Ireland proceedings, unless they have been dismissed, are treated as continuing until the child attains the age of 18, whether or not a decree has been granted or made absolute (s 42(2)). In Scotland proceedings are treated as continuing until the child attains 16, unless they have been dismissed or a decree of absolvitor granted (s 42(3)).
7 S 6(3).
8 S 6(4).

(h) Appeals and transfer of cases

6.84 The powers of the High Court and county courts to order the transfer of cases between those courts have already been examined, and apply to custodianship proceedings in those courts.[1] Additionally, any order made by the High Court on an appeal[2] from a decision of a magistrates' court, made on an application (under Part II of the Act) relating to custodianship (other than a High Court order directing that an application shall be re-heard by a magistrates' court), shall for the purposes of the enforcement of the order and of sections 35, 35A and 36[3] be treated as if it were an order of the magistrates' court from which the appeal was brought and not of the High Court.[4]

1 See ante, para 3.17 and the Matrimonial and Family Proceedings Act 1984, ss 32, 38, 39 and (repealing CA 1975, s 101(1)) 46(3) and Sch 3.
2 Under s 101(2).

3   Which deal respectively with revocation and variation of orders, provisions relating to lump sums and committing the child to local authority care on revocation of a custodianship order.
4   CA 1975, s 101(4), as inserted by DPMCA 1978, s 71.

6   Adoption or custodianship order?[1]

6.85   Section 37 is one of the main provisions in the Children Act 1975 that was thought to be designed to discourage and restrict adoptions.[2] It seeks to do this by empowering the court on hearing an application for an adoption order or a Convention adoption order to make instead a custodianship order. The scope of the court's discretion depends on the kind of applicant, but a positive duty is imposed to consider the suitability of custodianship.[3]

The court may exercise this power only if the requirements of section 16 of the Adoption Act 1976, are satisfied, namely, that the child is free for adoption or that the parents agree to adoption or that their agreement is dispensed with, or, where the application is for a Convention adoption order, that the requirements of section 17(6) of that Act are satisfied, namely, that, where the child is not a UK national, the requisite foreign rules relating to consent are observed. So, a prerequisite of applying section 37 is that the option of adoption is available. Consequently, the section cannot be invoked if the court has already decided that it will not dispense with the parent's agreement to adoption.[4] The disappointed prospective adopters will therefore have to make a fresh application, namely, for a custodianship order,[5] but they may find themselves at a disadvantage, because they will have to prove that they are eligible to apply in accordance with section 33 of the 1975 Act, whereas the power under section 37 to direct that an adoption application be treated as a custodianship application arises even if the applicant is not qualified under section 33.[6]

Section 37 does not preclude the possibility of a custodianship order being made, even though the applicants for adoption do not wish it; but it is unlikely that in those circumstances a custodianship order will be in the child's interests.[7]

The mere fact that the natural parent is prepared to agree to the making of a custodianship order but is opposed to an adoption order does not necessarily mean that it is not unreasonable for him to oppose adoption. It is a question of fact in each case,[8] but the onus is on the parent as objector to adoption to persuade the court that custodianship is more appropriate.

1   On the wider implications of this question see post, para 6.95.
2   Cf ss 14(3) and 15(4) of AA 1976, ante, para 5.58.
3   Where an applicant seeks adoption but there is a report favouring custodianship, it is highly desirable and may be essential, in order for the court to carry out the delicate task imposed upon it by s 37, that the reporting authority should either appear in order to argue for its view or at least authorise a member or employee to attend and address the court. The court should also consider whether or not it can discharge its duty without appointing a guardian ad litem; see Sir Roualeyn Cumming-Bruce in *Re S (a minor) (adoption or custodianship)* [1987] Fam 98 at 106, [1987] 2 All ER 99 at 104.
4   *Re M (a minor) (custodianship : jurisdiction)* [1987] 2 All ER 88, [1987] 1 WLR 162, CA; *Re J (a minor) (wardship : adoption : custodianship)* [1987] 1 FLR 455, [1987] Fam Law 88.
5   *Quaere* such an application under s 33 would necessitate separate proceedings. In *Re J,* supra, note 4, as the applicants were qualified to apply under that section had they wished

to do so, Sheldon J would have given them leave to make such an application without service and treated the adoption proceedings as its hearing.
6 See post, para 6.91.
7 See Glidewell LJ in *Re M, supra*, [1987] 2 All ER 88 at 95, [1987] 1 WLR 162 at 172.
8 *Re A (a minor) (adoption : parental consent)* [1987] 2 All ER 81, [1987] 1 WLR 153, CA; *Re B (a minor) (adoption)* [1988] Fam Law 172.

(a) Relative or step-parent

6.86 Where an applicant is a relative or step-parent and the court is satisfied that (a) the child's welfare would not be better safeguarded and promoted by granting the applicant an adoption order than it would by granting him a custodianship order, and (b) a custodianship order in his favour would be appropriate, then it must treat the application as if it were an application under section 33 for a custodianship order.[1] Presumably, in satisfying itself on these matters the court is governed by section 1 of the Guardianship of Minors Act 1971 and not section 6 of the Adoption Act 1976.[2] One might have thought on the wording of section 37(1) that its effect was to place on the court the onus of being satisfied that adoption would offer the child greater benefit than custodianship and that otherwise a custodianship order would be made. Surprisingly, the Court of Appeal has reached the reverse conclusion,[3] a conclusion which, with respect, does much to subvert the purpose of the subsection, especially in regard to a relative, in respect of whom the subsection was introduced in order to avoid distortions in relationships which adoption can create.

1 Section 37(1). In this and in all other cases under s 37 where the court can treat an adoption application as a custodianship application, it may order any person who is not a party to the adoption proceedings but who would have been a defendant to a custodianship application (see ante, paras 6.19-6.21) to be added as a defendant; (RSC Ord 90, r 21(3); CCR Ord 47, r 7(3) and (8)); MC (Custodianship Orders) Rules, r 6(1) and (4)-(6).
2 Compare the Houghton Committee (HCR, Rec 20): '. . . where a relative (including a step-parent applying jointly with his spouse) applies to adopt a child the law should require the court first to consider whether guardianship would be more appropriate in all the circumstances of the case, first consideration being given to the long-term welfare of the child.' Without referring expressly to s 1 of the 1971 Act the Court of Appeal in *Re S (a minor) (adoption or custodianship)* [1987] Fam 98, [1987] 2 All ER 99, CA, seems to have accepted the paramountcy principle.
3 *Re S (a minor)*, supra.

(i) The relative

6.87 In *Re S* the applicants for adoption were the paternal grandfather and his second wife. His daughter, the natural mother, agreed to the proposed adoption of her child, who had been brought up by the applicants as their son ever since he was six months old (being at the date of the proceedings about four years old). The Court of Appeal took the view that, in considering whether the child's welfare would not be better safeguarded or promoted by an adoption order than by a custodianship order, if the balance of advantage is even and the court cannot decide which course is preferable, the application must be treated as one for adoption without further consideration of custodianship. The paramount factor affecting the child's future welfare was to make an order that would secure the child in his de facto relationships in such a way as to minimise the risk of the natural mother or anyone else seeking to disrupt them. Applying the subsection in the way above indicated, the court held that an adoption order could achieve that result with greater prospect of success than a custodianship order. It is submitted that the conclusion underestimates the stability of a custodianship order, which cannot be disturbed by a side wind, but can only be revoked if revocation accords with the paramountcy of the child's welfare. Given the circumstances and the mother's ready and continued acceptance of them, the likelihood of revocation would be remote. It is difficult to predict the long-term effects of the decision, but a similar approach was adopted by the Court of Appeal in *Re W (a minor) (adoption: custodianship: access)*,[1] where not only was adoption granted to the child's grandfather and his second wife but also the unusual step was taken of granting access to the natural parents. Both decisions are likely to be welcomed by those who have found little enthusiasm for custodianship.[2]

1   [1988] 1 FLR 175, [1988] Fam Law 92, CA.
2   The reasoning in *Re S* is defended, for example, by Rutherford, *Adoption or Custodianship* (1987) 84 Law Soc Gaz 1031.

(ii)   Step-parent

6.88   As already noted,[1] desire to avoid breaking the link between the child and one of his natural parents and concurrently converting the natural relationship with the other into an artificial one of adoption mainly accounts for the restrictions imposed on the step-parent to apply for adoption. A secondary factor is the requirement that the step-parent should seek a remedy by way of custody order from the divorce court, if there have been earlier divorce or nullity proceedings involving the natural parent whom he later married. As has also been noted,[2] this factor restricts the step-parent's right to apply for a custodianship order. Both factors are relevant in operating section 37(1) in relation to the step-parent and their combined effect is that the subsection applies to the following cases:

(i)   where there have not been divorce or nullity proceedings between the natural parents because either they were never married to one another or, if they were, their marriage was terminated by the death of that natural parent who did not marry the step-parent;

(ii)   where there were such proceedings, but the parent other than the one the step-parent married is dead or cannot be found.[3]

1   Ante, para 5.58.
2   Ante, para 6.11.
3   See s 33(8)(a).

(b)   Persons other than a relative or step-parent

6.89   In the case of an application for adoption by anyone who is neither a relative nor a step-parent or of a joint application by a married couple who fall into neither category, the court is empowered to make a custodianship order instead of an adoption order if it is of opinion that the former is more appropriate.[1] The court does not have to be satisfied that the child's welfare would not be better safeguarded by adoption than it would by custodianship, as it must in cases under section 37(1). This omission takes account of the fact that considerations of distortion of natural relationships and their conversion into artificial ones are here irrelevant and that the desirability of maintaining links with the natural parents carries much less weight. Accordingly, the legislative intention seems to be that a presumption in favour of custodianship is not nearly so strong, and it is unlikely that the court will make a custodianship order against the wishes of the applicant, even though section 37 envisages that possibility, since that would not be in the child's interests.[2]

1 Section 37(2). There is, it is submitted, neither substantive nor semantic justification for the distinction between having to be 'satisfied' under sub-s (1) and having to be 'of opinion' under sub-s (2). In prescribing the qualifications of applicants for adoption ss 14 and 15 of the Adoption Act 1976 state that they are to be read subject to s 37(1). Why not also s 37(2)? This seems to be a drafting oversight.
2 See Glidewell LJ in *Re M (a minor)*, supra, para 6.85, note 7.

6.90   The implications of section 37(2) are particularly important for the long-term foster parent with whom the child has had his home for at least three years. He will need to weigh carefully whether to seek custodianship or adoption. If the parent will not agree to adoption, a custodianship application is prima facie attractive, for not even parental consent to the application will be needed. If he does proceed with an adoption application, he has the double hurdle of persuading the court to dispense with parental agreement and of effectively satisfying it that it would not be more appropriate to make a custodianship order, if the court is minded to make that order. Nevertheless, the advantage to the foster parent of going for adoption is that it does in the first instance put the onus on the court to decide whether the alternative may be appropriate: it is not a matter that he has to raise. The present inclination of the courts to favour adoption rather than custodianship is a further reason for seeking the former.

6.91   The duty and power of the court under section 37(1) and (2) respectively to direct that the adoption application be treated as a custodianship application arise even though the applicant could not have qualified as an applicant for custodianship had he been proceeding under section 33.[1] For example, the child may not have had his home with the applicant for the minimum period of 12 months or three years prescribed by that section.[2] Where a direction is given under section 37, Part II of the Act then operates, just as if there had been an application under section 33. Thus, the court could, for example, make accompanying orders relating to access and maintenance. The only exception to the rule is that section 40 does not apply. For obvious reasons the applicant is relieved of the duty imposed by section 40 to notify the local authority of his application, and the authority of any duty to present a report to the court. The court will already have before it the report of the adoption agency in those cases where the child was placed by an adoption agency with the applicant for adoption and, in all other cases, the report which the local authority has to present in accordance with section 22 of the Adoption Act 1976.[3] This does not, however, preclude the court from calling for a further report on any specified matter.[4]

1 Section 37(4).
2 But he will have had his home with the applicant for at least three months, otherwise (except where he is a joint applicant) the requirements of s 13 of AA 1976 could not have been satisfied. For s 13 see ante, para 5.61.
3 See ante, para 5.66.
4 Under s 39(1).

6.92   The restriction imposed on the mother or father alone to apply for adoption has already been noted.[1] Even where such an application is permitted, section 37(1) and (2) cannot apply,[2] for a custodianship order cannot be made in favour of the mother or father.[3] Nor does the Act allow the court as an alternative to adoption to make a custody order. Thus, where the applicant for adoption is the father and the court regards custody as more appropriate, there will have to be a separate application made under section 9 of the Guardianship of Minors Act 1971. The ineligibility of the mother or father to be made a custodian under section 33 also accounts for the rule that where the application for adoption is made jointly by the parent and step-parent and the latter is eligible to fall within section 37(1),[4] the application will be treated for the purpose of that subsection as if it were an application by the step-parent alone.

1   See AA 1976, s 15(3), ante, para 5.56.
2   Section 37(6).
3   Section 33(4).
4   See ante, para 6.88.

6.93   One effect of section 37(1) and (2) is that the parent may have agreed to the making of an adoption order, intending to surrender and be relieved of all parental rights and duties, only to find that because a custodianship order has been made some of those rights and duties remain vested in him or her, coupled with the possibility of being ordered to maintain the child. It is therefore important that any explanatory leaflet issued to parents should clearly explain section 37 and these possible consequences. Similarly, where the child has been freed for adoption, with the result that the parental rights and duties vest in the adoption agency,[1] and then custodianship is ordered instead of adoption, the residuary rights and duties which do not pass with legal custody remain vested in the agency. Because of these consequences the court should have cogent reasons for finding custodianship more appropriate than adoption.

1   AA 1976, s 18(5); see ante, para 5.33.

7   Conclusion

6.94   Waiting for something for over a decade may diminish one's enthusiasm for it, and doubt must be expressed about whether custodianship will have the impact it might have expected had Part II of the Children Act 1975 been implemented much earlier,[1] or whether it would have been framed in the way it is.[2] Four closely integrated factors will determine its future: its attractiveness as an alternative to adoption and to wardship; the crucial role of the local authority; judicial attitudes; and the availability of advice and resources.[3,4]

1   For healthy scepticism about its future role see Adcock and White, *Adoption, Custodianship or Fostering?* (1985) 9 Adoption and Fostering 14; Maidment, *Custodianship – the New Law* [1986] Fam Law 5. The Court of Appeal does not appear to be too enamoured with it; see *Re S (a minor)* [1987] Fam 98, [1987] 2 All ER 99, CA. See also Montgomery, *Custodianship – Twelve Months on*, [1987] Fam Law 214.

2   For example would there be more emphasis on the responsibilities of the custodian and more on the child's wishes and feelings? See Freeman, op cit, p 7.
3   For a careful assessment of the comparative advantages of custodianship and adoption, especially in the light of recent case law, see Bromley, op cit, pp 377-378. See also Williams, *Custodianship and Adoption,* [1988] JSWL 250.
4   On wardship see generally Lowe and White, op cit, Chapter 15 and see the comment of Maidment [1986] Fam Law 173.

6.95   The position of foster parents of children in local authority care is likely to differ from that of relatives and friends who are caring for the child. As already indicated,[1] many of the former will see section 37 as a means of putting the onus on the court to decide between the alternatives of adoption and custodianship, and will continue to prefer the permanent nature of adoption to the revocable nature of custodianship, especially in view of the additional disadvantage that custodians probably cannot legally change the child's name.[2] That preference may well be supported by the local authority. Greater readiness on the part of the court to dispense with parental agreement to adoption, increased access to subsidised adoption and the introduction of freeing for adoption have led not only to more children in care being adopted but also to a more positive attitude by local authorities in favour of adoption than was the case ten years ago. Nevertheless, custodianship does provide a new option for planning for children in care, and its possibility will have to be considered in review procedures.[3] It may, for example, be the better alternative where an older foster child still has his ties with his natural family which ought to be maintained, for example, by granting access when the custodianship order is made. Much will depend on the relationship existing between the foster parent and the natural parent. Again, there may be cases where foster parents are willing to 'make a commitment for their lifetimes to a severely handicapped child but reluctant to accept future responsibility on behalf of their own children or relatives', which adoption implies.[4] For relatives and private foster parents, on the other hand, custodianship is likely to be the preferred alternative in many cases, and even where it is not and they seek adoption, some courts at least, relying on section 37, may see it as the better solution. Before the implementation of Part II of the Act dicta in adoption cases, where there was still some contact between the foster child and natural parent, suggested that that might have been the course of action had custodianship been available,[5] and there was some evidence of courts adjourning adoption hearings until the new provisions were in force. But it may well be that there will be variations in judicial attitudes as there have been with regard to step-parent adoption applications,[6] and there are distinct indications that some courts are favouring adoption. Some concern has also been understandably expressed that custodianship may be seen both by foster parents and the courts as a 'soft option' to adoption,[7] especially where parents may be willing to agree to the former but not to adoption. Moreover, there may be the temptation to order custodianship in the knowledge that adoption is open as a later alternative. As cases like *Re H (a minor) and Re W (a minor)*[8] forcibly demonstrate, the need for thorough investigation, for example on such matters as the nature and extent of access and contact between child and natural parent, is crucial and should be reflected in the local authority's section 40 report.

1   Supra, para 6.90.
2   See Rowe, Cain, Hundleby and Keane, *Long term fostering and the Children Act* (1984)
    pp 31-32; Adcock, *Alternatives to Adoption*, (1984) 8 Adoption and Fostering 12.
3   For the duty to review the case of every child in care see post, para 15.107.
4   See LAC (85) 13, para 10.
5   See, for example, *Re H (a minor) (adoption)* [1985] FLR 519, [1985] Fam Law 133, CA,
    'which cried out for a consideration of the custodianship provisions of the Children Act'
    (p 526); *Re M (minors) (adoption : parent's agreement)* [1985] FLR 921 at 926.
6   See ante, para 5.59.
7   See, for example, Maidment 135 New LJ 1227 at p 1228.
8   (1983) 13 Fam Law 144, CA; see ante, para 5.27, note 2.

6.96   Availability of advice and resources may prove a bigger obstacle
for relatives and private foster parents than for foster parents of children
in local authority care. A local authority has a discretion to make
contributions to a custodian towards the cost of the accommodation and
maintenance of the child, except where the custodian is the husband or
wife of a parent of the child.[1] In some cases without financial assistance
custodianship would not be practicable, for example, because of the limited
means of the applicant or the expensive special needs of the child.
Contributions may take the form of a regular allowance, payments at
irregular intervals or a single lump sum.[2] Payments cannot continue beyond
the child's eighteenth birthday, when the custodianship order ceases to have
effect. If the child continues his education thereafter, the local authority
will not be able to use its power under section 27 of the Child Care Act
1980[3] to give further assistance to him, unless he has been in care for
some time after he ceased to be of compulsory school age. This is a matter
which the local authority and the foster parent should have in mind when
considering whether a custodianship order would be in the child's best
interest.[4] Indeed, the question of possible financial contribution has to be
considered in all cases where there is a custodianship application, since
the local authority is required in its section 40 report to the court to state
whether or not a contribution is to be paid.[5] Where the local authority
foster parent has been receiving financial assistance and the authority
supports his application for custodianship, continued assistance will be
forthcoming. But the story may be different for the relative or private foster
parent who is thinking of custodianship. Assuming that he is fully informed
about his right to apply, the consequences of a custodianship order and
the possibility of local authority financial assistance,[6] he may find it more
difficult to negotiate payments than the local authority foster parent who
is already in receipt of assistance.[7] Moreover, in view of the current intense
economic pressures on local authorities, there is the risk that, as a matter
of policy, an authority will be reluctant, if not unwilling, to provide
allowances for children who have not been in their care.

1   CA 1975, s 34(6), as substituted by DPMCA 1978, s 64.
2   The local authority must state in its report (under s 40) whether it proposes to pay a
    custodianship allowance, if an order is made.
3   See post, para 15.109.
4   See LAC (85) 13, para 41.
5   This does not prevent the authority from subsequently deciding to make payments. It
    can do so at any time while the custodianship order is in force.
6   It may be a large assumption. Local authorities are advised by the DHSS (see LAC (85)
    13, para 14) to see that leaflets are provided advising parents and prospective custodians
    on custodianship and its effects. Such information is likely to be readily available for

local authority foster parents, but it may also need other agencies (eg Citizens Advice Bureaux) to publicise such information to relatives and private foster parents. See also *Payments to Custodians* [1986] Fam Law 320.

7 In all cases local authorities are advised to take legal advice before agreeing to make payment; see LAC (85) 13, para 40.

6.97 The delay in bringing into operation Part II of the Children Act has been explained on the ground of lack of resources, both staffing and financial, with the latter including the cost of providing for Legal Aid.[1] With its implementation, however, the DHSS has expressed the view that 'any costs that arise are likely to be offset by savings in expenditure on children in care and in connection with adoption proceedings and should be met by adjustments within the [local] authorities' budgets as necessary'.[2] In view of the central role of local authorities and the demands which Part II makes on them, it remains to be seen whether this is an optimistic and sanguine estimation.

1 *The Cost of Operating the Unimplemented Provisions of the Children Act 1975* (DHSS 1980); and see Cretney, op cit, p 409, note 7.
2 LAC (85) 13, para 107.

CHAPTER 7

Foster parenthood, boarding out and day care

I INTRODUCTION

7.01 In general terms, a foster parent may be described as any person other than a legal guardian or custodian who stands in loco parentis to a child, ie one who takes upon himself the duty of the parent to make provision for the child and assumes the responsibility for his care and control.[1] This broad definition[2] will include, for example, the relative who assumes that duty and responsibility on the death or protracted absence (for example, in employment abroad) of the child's natural parent. Because of the assumption of responsibility the foster parent is under the common law duty to protect the child from physical harm, and similarly certain duties arise under the Children and Young Persons Act 1933.[3] In the terms of the Children Act 1975, he has the actual custody of the child and therefore the duties, but not the rights, of a custodian.[4] These obligations are incurred whatever may be the reason for assuming responsibility, but other rules are applicable only if the foster child falls within one of two categories, namely (1) those protected by the Foster Children Act 1980, and (2) those who are in the care of a local authority or a voluntary organisation and are boarded out. Strictly, in the latter case the persons with whom the child is boarded out are not foster parents, because it is not they but the local authority or voluntary organisation which stands in loco parentis.[5] Nevertheless, this is commonly described as a fostering relationship, and it is examined here rather than in Chapter 15, because juxtaposition of the two categories may emphasise the inadequate recognition and protection given to the privately fostered child.

---

1   See Jessel MR in *Bennet v Bennet* (1879) 10 Ch D 474, citing with approval the definition given by Lord Eldon in *Ex p Pye* (1811) 18 Ves 140 and approved and elaborated by Lord Cottenham in *Powys v Mansfield* (1837) 3 My & Cr 359.
2   Cf Cretney p 289, note 13, who uses the term 'foster parent' to mean '(unless otherwise indicated) a person who looks after the child of another on other than a purely transient basis, and foster child has a corresponding meaning'.
3   See post, paras 9.02 and 9.33. For the duty to see that the child receives full-time education see post, paras 11.18 et seq.
4   Section 87.
5   Cf Law Com No 25, para 31.

II   FOSTER CHILDREN ACT 1980

1   Introduction

7.02   In 1870 two notable events occurred in the history of child fostering. The Local Government Board began to issue directions for boarding out children who were subject to the Poor Law, and the House of Commons set up a Select Committee on the Protection of Infant Life to investigate baby farming, a pernicious system whereby a person undertook for reward the care and maintenance of children, usually illegitimate, whose parents were anxious to abdicate their responsibilities. The absence of any supervision and the failure to relate the amount of the fee realistically to the child's needs resulted in a high incidence of child neglect and mortality. To combat these evils the Infant Life Protection Act 1872 required anyone who received two or more children under a year old for hire or reward to register with the local authority. Subsequent legislation[1] gradually raised the maximum age and enlarged the powers of control over foster parents, but it only partially succeeded in removing the earlier evils. Indeed, the large number of casual, unsatisfactory placements with foster parents was one of the main reasons for setting up the Curtis Committee in 1946. Yet, neither the Children Act 1948 which amended the earlier law nor the Children Act 1958 solved the problem. Potentially significant amendments to the latter Act were made by the Children and Young Persons Act 1969 and the Children Act 1975 which were aimed at strengthening the powers of local authorities, especially with regard to visiting, inspecting and controlling the use of premises, widening the class of children to be supervised, strengthening the duty to notify local authorities of fostering arrangements and further restricting the advertisement of private fostering. However, most of these changes were to turn on the making of Regulations. The provisions in the Acts of 1958, 1969 and 1975 have been consolidated in the Foster Children Act 1980, but Regulations are still awaited, their appearance apparently depending on the availability of resources. The private foster child may no longer be the Cinderella of English family law, but remains its poor relation.

1   Infant Life Protection Act 1897; Children Act 1908; CYPA 1932; Public Health Act 1936.

(a)   Foster children protected by the Act[1]

(i)   Definition
7.03   For the purpose of the 1980 Act a foster child is basically defined in wide terms as a child below the upper limit of the compulsory school age (ie under 16) whose care and maintenance are undertaken by a person who is not a relative, guardian or custodian.[2] The care and maintenance need not be, and very often are not, undertaken for reward.[3] 'Relative' has the same wide meaning[4] as it has for the purposes of adoption and custodianship,[5] but the term 'guardian' is not defined. It is submitted that it has the same meaning as it has in the Child Care Act 1980,[6] namely, a person appointed by deed, will or order of the court to be the guardian of a child.[7]

1   See B Hoggett, *Parents and Children,* 3rd edn (1981) pp 24–30; R Holman, *Trading in Children—A Study of Private Fostering* (1973). In its White Paper, *The Law on Child Care and Family Services,* (1987) Cd 62, the Government has indicated (in para 80) that it intends to simplify the definition of private foster parents and foster children, and reduce substantially the present number of exclusions from the definition.
2   Section 1.
3   But the element of reward is relevant for the purpose of the Life Assurance Act 1774. A policy taken out by a foster parent on the life of a child whom he fosters for reward is void under that Act; see FCA 1980, s 19.
4   Section 22.
5   AA 1976, s 72(1); CA 1975, s 107(1).
6   CCA 1980, s 87(1).
7   See ante, Chapter 4. Reference in s 5(5)(b) of FCA 1980, infra, para 7.11, note 3, to every person who is a parent or guardian or 'acts as a guardian' tends to support this interpretation. See also s 12(6).

(ii)   Specific categories of children excluded from the definition
7.04   Having laid down the broad limits of the definition of a foster child, section 2 proceeds to exclude the following categories of children below the upper limit of compulsory school age who would otherwise come within it, the reason being either that they are considered otherwise adequately supervised and protected or that the care and maintenance are for a strictly limited period.

(1)   A child who is in the care of a local authority or voluntary organisation or is boarded out by a local authority or local education authority.[1]
(2)   A child who is in the care of a person in certain specified premises:
    (a)   In premises in which a parent,[2] adult relative or guardian is for the time being residing.[3] It is submitted that the appropriate test is whether there is residence in the same household and not merely under the same roof.
    (b)   In a voluntary home.[4]
    (c)   In a school where he is receiving full-time education.[5] A child who is living away from home at a boarding school where he is being educated is not, therefore, a foster child.[6] But if he resides in a school, which is not maintained by a local education authority, for more than two weeks during school holidays he is, subject to certain modifications, to be treated as a foster child.[7]
    (d)   In a hospital or nursing home.[8]
    (e)   In any other home or institution maintained by a public or local authority.[9]
(3)   A child is not a foster child for the purpose of the Act if the person undertaking his care and maintenance:
    (a)   is not a regular foster parent and does not intend to, and does not in fact, do so for a continuous period[10] of more than 27 days; or
    (b)   is a regular foster parent and does not intend to, and does not in fact, do so for a continuous period of more than six days.

For these purposes a regular foster parent means a person who, during the period of 12 months immediately preceding the date on which he begins to undertake the care and maintenance of a child and otherwise than as a relative or guardian had the care and maintenance of one or more children either for a period of not less than three months (or periods amounting in all to not less than three months) or for at least three continuous periods, each of which was for more than six days.[11] The reason for the rule in sub-paragraph (b) is that the child is in those circumstances protected by the Nurseries and Child-Minders Regulation Act 1948,[12] and for that in sub-paragraph (a) that it exempts from supervision the casual fostering arrangement of less than a month, for example, where a person occasionally looks after a child while the parent is absent on holiday or in hospital.

(4) A child who is in the care of a person in compliance with a supervision order.[13]

(5) A child who is liable to be detained or subject to guardianship under the Mental Health Act 1983 or who is resident in a residential care home for the disabled and mentally disordered.[14]

(6) A child who is in the care and possession of a person who proposes to adopt him under arrangements made by an adoption agency or who is a protected child within the meaning of Part III of the Adoption Act 1976.[15]

1   Section 2(1).
2   This has its usual meaning of the mother and father of a legitimate child and the mother of an illegitimate, the father of the latter falling within the definition of relative. The meaning has not been altered by the Family Law Reform Act 1987.
3   Section 2(2)(a).
4   Section 2(2)(b). For voluntary homes see post, paras 15.74 et seq.
5   Section 2(2)(c).
6   *Aliter* if he were residing at the school but was being educated at another.
7   Section 17.
8   Section 2(2)(d), The nursing home must be registered or exempted from registration under the Nursing Homes Act 1975.
9   Section 2(2)(e).
10   Continuity is not broken by allowing the child to spend a week-end at the home of his parent; *Surrey County Council v Battersby* [1965] 2 QB 194, [1965] 1 All ER 273. To hold otherwise would allow for easy evasion of the supervisory purposes of the Act.
11   Section 2(3).
12   See post, paras 7.32 et seq.
13   Section 2(4). The exception also applies to a child who is subject to a supervision requirement under the Social Work (Scotland) Act 1968.
14   FCA 1980, s 2(5), as amended by HASSASSAA 1983, Sch 9, para 26. For residential care homes see Part I of Sch 4 of the latter Act.
15   FCA 1980 s 2(6), and see ante, para 5.67.
     For an admirable comparative summary of the functions of local authorities with regard to foster children and protected children see Leeding, *Child Care Manual for Social Workers*, 4th edn.

(iii)   Children above compulsory school age
7.05   The protection given by the 1980 Act does not come to an end when the foster child attains the upper limit of the compulsory school age. It continues until he would, apart from that limit, have ceased to be a foster child or until he becomes 18 or until he lives elsewhere than with the person with whom he was living when he attained the limit, whichever of those events first occurs.[1]

1   FCA 1980, s 18.

(b)   The duty and powers of a local authority

(i)   Visits and inspections

7.06   The responsibility for ensuring the well being of foster children, as defined by the 1980 Act, falls upon the local authority within whose area the children are.[1] They must discharge their duty through visits to foster homes by their officers,[2] which are to be made 'so far as appears to the authority to be appropriate'.[3] They are therefore left with a wide discretion,[4] and are thus able, if so minded, to concentrate their resources on those cases which most need supervision, for example, where the foster parents have no previous experience of fostering or the children are young or handicapped. The 1980 Act enables the Secretary of State to make regulations requiring visits to be made on specified occasions or within specified periods of time.[5] The signs are not propitious. Already the Act with this new power has been in operation for over seven years,[6] and no regulations have been enacted. If and when they are, the frequency of the visits which will be laid down will doubtless depend on the provision of resources.

1   Section 3(3). Ie are living. The Act avoids any reference to residence.
2   Normally a social services department allocates responsibility for supervising private foster homes to a social worker of some experience and seniority.
3   Section 3(1) and (3).
4   This consequence is further emphasised by the fact that they must 'satisfy themselves' as to the child's well-being. No objective standard is imposed.
5   Section 3(2).
6   The power was in fact conferred by CA 1975, s 95.

7.07   An authorised officer of a local authority may inspect the whole of premises where foster children are kept.[1] If admission is refused or is expected to be refused or if the occupier is temporarily absent, a justice of the peace may issue a warrant authorising an officer to enter and inspect the premises at any reasonable time within 48 hours of the issue.[2] Refusal to allow a visit or inspection of premises or the wilful obstruction of an officer acting under a justice's warrant is an offence, carrying a penalty on summary conviction of imprisonment for up to six months or a fine not exceeding level 5 on the standard scale (currently £2,000) or both.[3] Refusal to allow a visit or inspection may also be automatically treated as giving reasonable cause for suspecting that a foster child is through ill-treatment the victim of unnecessary suffering or that an offence within the first Schedule to the Children and Young Persons Act 1933[4] has been committed against him, thereby enabling a justice of the peace to issue a warrant under section 40 of that Act, authorising a constable to search for and remove the child to a place of safety until he can be brought before a juvenile court.[5] In view of the wide incidence of child abuse, local authority officers who are refused visits or inspections should, it is suggested, make it the invariable practice of notifying the police so that concurrent applications can be made for warrants under the 1980 Act and the 1933 Act. Then, if on visit or inspection there is evidence of ill-treatment, removal of the child can be immediately effected.

1   FCA 1980, s 8. He can be required to produce written authority to visit. See also Child Care Act 1980, ss 74 and 75 for the power of the Secretary of State to authorise inspection.
2   Section 13(1). Compare the similar power made under the Nurseries and Child-Minders Regulation Act 1948, s 7(2), post, para 7.39.

3   FCA 1980, s 16(1)(b) and (f) and (3), as amended by CJA 1982, ss 37, 38 and 46.
4   For those offences see post, Chapter 9, Part III.
5   FCA 1980, s 13(2).

(ii)   Requirements and prohibitions
7.08   In addition to visits and inspection, the local authority may impose on a foster parent requirements with regard to any one or more of a variety of matters. These relate to the number, age and sex of the foster children; particulars concerning a particular child and of any change in the number or identity of the children; the accommodation and equipment provided for them (for example, to ensure the children's safety); fire precautions; medical arrangements; the giving of particulars of the person in charge; the number, qualifications or experience of those employed in looking after the children; and the keeping of records. The power may be exercised even though the home is not used wholly or mainly for keeping foster children, and a requirement may be limited to a particular class of foster children or made applicable only if the number kept in the premises exceeds a specified figure.[1]

1   FCA 1980, s 9(1)–(3).

7.09   A local authority also has power to prohibit the keeping of foster children.[1] The extent of the prohibition will depend on the ground on which it is made. If the premises in which a prospective foster parent intends to keep a foster child are not suitable, the authority may prohibit him from keeping any foster child there. If it is the person and not the premises which are unsuitable, they may prohibit him from keeping any foster child in any premises in their area. Thirdly, where, however, they consider that it would be detrimental only to the particular child to be kept in specified premises by the particular person they may limit the prohibition accordingly. The authority may cancel a prohibition either of their own volition or on the application of the person against whom it is made on the ground of a change in circumstances in which a foster child would be kept by him.

1   FCA 1980, s 10(1)–(3).

7.10   A requirement or prohibition[1] must be imposed by written notice, which must inform the 'person aggrieved' by the decision of his right to appeal against it to a juvenile court within 14 days.[2] A requirement does, whereas a prohibition does not, take effect while an appeal is pending.[3] There is also a right to appeal against the local authority's refusal to cancel a prohibition. If it allows the appeal, the court may, instead of cancelling a requirement, vary it or allow more time for compliance.[4] Similarly, instead of cancelling an absolute prohibition, it may substitute a prohibition to use the premises after such time as it may specify, unless such specified requirements as the local authority could have imposed are complied with.[5] The restrictions on the time and place at which a juvenile court may sit and on the persons who may be present[6] do not apply to sittings in these appeals or to any other proceedings under the 1980 Act,[7] the reason being that an adult and a local authority, and not the child, are the parties to the proceedings. Nor are the proceedings of such a nature as to call for provision for his being made a party, with separate legal representation. A further appeal by either party, the aggrieved person or the local authority, lies to the Crown Court.[8] Appeals against requirements or prohibitions are rare, but there is no firm evidence to indicate the extent to which this fact is attributable to the efficacy, moderation and/or insistence with which local authority officers exercise their powers or to the reluctance of aggrieved persons to challenge their decisions.

1   Where a requirement is imposed on a person with regard to any premises, he may also be prohibited from keeping foster children there after the time specified for compliance with the requirement unless it is complied with. (FCA 1980, s 10(4)).
2   Ibid, ss 9(4) and 10(5).
3   Ibid, s 11(1).
4   Ibid, s 11(2)(a).
5   Ibid, s 11(2)(b).
6   See post, paras 12.78 and 12.81 et seq.
7   FCA 1980, s 14(1).
8   Ibid, s 14(2).

(c)   Notification to the local authority

7.11   If a local authority are to exercise their powers effectively, it is obviously essential that they know which homes are being used for private fostering. Consequently, a person is required to give notice when he becomes, and when he ceases to be, a foster parent of a particular child.[1] The notice to become a foster parent must state the date on which it is intended that the child should be received or that on which he has already been received or become a foster child, and the premises where he is being kept.[2] But that is all that is required. Remarkably, no details concerning the child have to be provided. If the local authority want them, it is up to them to call for them.[3] Nor does Central Government show any inclination to insist on them. Power is given to the Secretary of State to make regulations requiring parents whose children are, or are going to be, maintained as foster children to provide the local authority with such information about the fostering as the regulations may specify. There are none. It might, for example, be a vitally important matter for the local authority to know that the child is so physically handicapped as to require special equipment to be provided in the foster home. The present rules about giving of notice unjustifiably assume that there will be an automatic visit by a local authority officer to the foster home, whereas there is no obligation so to do. A further defect is that no infallible method exists for ensuring that notice is given, and the likelihood of this not happening may be high where the fostering arrangements are informal and without reward. The foster parent may well be ignorant of the requirement of giving notice or avoid giving it by design.[4] One possibility which would partly meet the difficulty would be an administrative arrangement whereby local authorities are informed of child benefit paid to persons other than a parent. This is a matter which could be covered by Regulation. Certainly, the present practice of publicising the law through local authority notices in post offices, other public places and in the press has not been enough to ensure compliance.

1   FCA 1980, ss 5(1) and (2) and 6(1) and (2).
2   Ibid, s 5(3). For notice of change of address see sub-s (4).
3   See s 9(1)(h) and supra, para 7.08. Additionally, when a prospective foster parent gives

notice, the local authority may request him to provide particulars of (a) the child's name, sex and date and place of birth, and (b) the name and address of his parents, guardians, persons who have been acting as guardians or from whom the child is received (s 5(5)).

4 The fact that failure to notify is an offence (s 16(1)(a)) has apparently not proved an effective sanction. For penalties see supra, para 7.07.

7.12 Normally notice must be given not less than two, but not more than four, weeks before the intending foster parent receives the child.[1] The purpose of fixing a maximum period is to dissuade persons from notification where they have only a general intention to begin private fostering at some date in the future if the opportunity should arise but are not immediately committed to the responsibility. However, in the exceptional cases where a person receives the child in an emergency, or the latter becomes a foster child while in his care,[2] the period is only 48 hours from the date of those respective events.[3] This enables the local authority to intervene promptly in case the placement is unsuitable. The fact that a 48 hour notice is given should in itself put the local authority on inquiry and prompt an immediate visit.

1 Section 5(1).
2 For example, where the natural parent has also been living in the premises but has now left there or died.
3 Section 5(2); 48 hours is also the period within which a foster parent must notify the local authority that he has ceased to maintain the child or that the child has died, (s 6(1)–(4)).

(d) Advertising

7.13 An advertisement that a person will undertake, or will arrange for, the care and maintenance of a child must not be published unless it truly states the name and address of that person.[1] This is a modest restriction compared with those concerning adoption. They forbid the publication of any advertisement which indicates that the parent or guardian of a minor wishes to have his child adopted or that a person desires to adopt a child or that anyone except an adoption agency is willing to make arrangements for adoption.[2] Admittedly, the Foster Children Act allows for regulations to be made,[3] *pari passu* the adoption provisions, which would forbid a parent or guardian from seeking a foster parent through advertisement or, unless specifically exempted, any other person from advertising that he is willing to make arrangements for fostering; but none have been made, and the anomaly between the two present sets of rules has been perpetuated. Paradoxically, though the rules relating to fostering are more restricted, the penalties for breach are more severe than those for breach under the Adoption Act.[4]

1 FCA 1980, s 15(1).
2 AA 1976, s 58(1); see ante, para 5.65.
3 Section 15(2)–(4).
4 For the penalties under the Foster Children Act see ante, para 7.07. Under the Adoption Act the penalty is a fine not exceeding level 5 on the standard scale (currently £2,000); see s 58(2).

(e) Disqualification from keeping foster children

7.14   A person against whom any of the following orders or decisions has been made is disqualified from keeping foster children unless he discloses that fact to the local authority and obtains their written consent.[1] Contravention of this rule is an offence.[2] As has been pointed out,[3] a serious omission from the list of disqualifications are those persons who have applied unsuccessfully to become local authority foster parents.

(1)   an order under the 1980 Act, or its predecessor Part I of the Children Act 1958, removing a child from his care;[4]

(2)   an order under the Children and Young Persons Acts 1933 or 1969 resulting in removal, which in practice means a care order made under the latter Act.[5]

(3)   his conviction of an offence specified in the First Schedule to the Children and Young Persons Act 1933 or his being placed on probation or discharged absolutely or conditionally for any such offence;[6]

(4)   a resolution of a local authority under section 3 of the Child Care Act 1980, or its predecessor section 2 of the Children Act 1948 vesting in them his rights and powers with respect to a child;

(5)   an order under the Nurseries and Child-Minders Regulation Act 1948 refusing, or cancelling, the registration of premises occupied by him or his registration;[7]

(6)   an order under the Adoption Act 1958 removing a protected child who was being kept or was about to be received by him.[8]

---

1   FCA 1980, s 7(1).
2   Section 16(1)(c). For penalties see supra, para 7.07.
3   Hoggett, op cit, p 26.
4   See infra, para 7.16.
5   For care orders see post, para 15.47.
6   The reference to probation and discharge is required since a conviction followed by a probation order or order for discharge is normally a conviction only for the purposes of those proceedings in which the order was made (Powers of Criminal Courts Act 1973, s 13.)
7   Sections 1(3) and (4) and 5.
8   Section 43 (or prospectively under the Adoption Act 1976, s 34).

7.15   The disqualification attaches not only to the person in respect of whom an order is made but also to anyone else living in the same premises as he does or in premises at which he is employed.[1] So, if that other person knows of his disqualification, he, too, must disclose it and obtain the consent of the local authority before he may act as a foster parent. On the other hand, anyone who keeps a foster child without knowing or reasonably believing that there is a disqualified person living or employed in the same premises is not guilty of an offence.[2] This is more likely to happen where the disqualified person is a lodger or employee rather than a member of the same family.

---

1   FCA 1980, s 7(2).
2   Section 16(2). The onus is on the person to prove lack of knowledge and belief.

(f)   Removal of foster children kept in unsuitable surroundings

7.16   An order may be made removing a child from a foster home and taking him to a place of safety[1] on the ground that the foster parent is unfit to have care or that he is disqualified from keeping foster children or that the local authority have imposed a prohibition on his doing so or that the child is being kept in premises or an environment detrimental to him.[2] Apparently, unfitness is to be determined according to the criteria which would justify disqualification.[3] The order will be made by a juvenile court on the complaint of a local authority, but, where there is proof of imminent danger to the health or well-being of the child, a justice of the peace may do so on the application of a person authorised to visit foster children.[4] The order must specify a period, not exceeding 28 days, beyond which the child must not be detained in a place of safety.[5] Within the period he can be restored to a parent, relative or guardian or other arrangements can be made with respect to him.[6] One possibility is that he be received into the care of a local authority under section 2 of the Child Care Act 1980, and this may be done even though he appears to be over 17.[7] If he still remains in the place of safety at the end of the specified period, he must be brought before a juvenile court, which must then release him or make an interim order[8] committing him to the care of a local authority. Such an order will afford further opportunity to make arrangements for him, the most likely outcome being that he will be received permanently into care under section 2 of the Child Care Act.

1   This has the same meaning as for the purposes of the CYP Acts; see CYPA 1933, s 107(1) and FCA 1980, s 22.
2   FCA 1980, s 12(1) and (3).
3   Clarke Hall and Morrison, op cit, para A[587].
4   Section 12(2). Appeal from an order of the juvenile court or a justice lies to the Crown Court (s 14(2)).
5   CYPA 1963, s 23(1). For place of safety orders see post, paras 14.34 et seq.
6   FCA 1980, s 12(1). Where a child is removed to a place of safety the local authority must, if practicable, inform a parent or guardian of his or anyone who acts as his guardian (s 12(6)).
7   Section 12(5).
8   For interim orders see post, paras 14.94 et seq.

(g)   Conclusion

7.17   Comparatively little sustained research has been undertaken into private fostering. For reasons already stated,[1] the extent of use of this form of care cannot be fully ascertained, but it is known that there are at least 10,000 children privately fostered. Holman's valuable study,[2] albeit of a limited sample, in the early 1970s revealed that the fostering is mainly of children under five who are of one parent families or whose parents have come from overseas, especially married student couples, seeking temporary foster parents. Often many of these placements have been made casually, without preparation and without the assistance of a social worker. One of the main, depressing, conclusions is the variation in the degree of supervision exercised by local authorities, a conclusion confirmed by a survey by the Social Work Service.[3] The main consequences therefore are that the special needs of some children, the unsuitability of some foster parents and the possibility that support in rehabilitating the child with his natural parents is the desirable solution are all matters that may be unknown to the local authority. In the light of this picture the delay in providing Regulations for more effective control is, frankly, inexcusable, even when due allowance has been made for restrictions on resources. The picture must not, however, obscure that of good fostering found in many families. The work, for example, of the National Foster Care Association and of local groups in advising and helping foster parents in the upbringing of the children has made a substantial contribution in this regard.[4] The 'reward', if that be the term, is the knowledge that those are the parents who are most likely to be successfully in applications for adoption or custodianship.

1   Supra, para 7.11.
2   Supra, para 7.03, note 1.
3   *Private Fostering* (1977) Circular DSWS 77(1).
4   Their work equally extends to local authority foster parents.

III   BOARDING OUT

1   Introduction

7.18   The system of boarding out deprived children is a product of the Poor Law. It first appears in the sixteenth century when orphans and children abandoned by their parents were apprenticed out from workhouses, but it acquired most of its modern characteristics in the second half of the nineteenth century,[1] when Boards of Guardians began to board out with private individuals children for whom they remained legally responsible. From 1870 onwards the Local Government Board issued Orders with regard to the fostering of Poor Law children. Initially, a distinction was drawn between Guardians boarding out children within their own union and boarding them out with foster parents outside their union, but the distinction virtually disappeared in 1911 and thereafter the system remained essentially unaltered.

1   See further J S Heywood, *Children in Care: The Development of the Service for the Deprived Child,* 3rd edn (1978); V George, *Foster Care: Theory and Practice* (1970) Chapter 1; B Hoggett and D Pearl, *The Family, Law and Society,* 2nd edn (1987) Chapter 14.

7.19   One of the main recommendations of the Curtis Committee[1] was that a child deprived of home life should be brought up in a private household rather than in the more impersonal atmosphere of an institutional home. As originally enacted, the Children Act 1948[2] sought to give effect to this recommendation by requiring a local authority to board out privately a child in their care, and it was only where it was not practicable or desirable for the time being to make such arrangements that he was to be accommodated in a local authority home or a voluntary home. However, the high failure rate in long-term placements,[3] the unsuitability of foster care for many juvenile offenders in care[4] and the decline in the number of persons willing to offer themselves for fostering compelled the Legislature, through the Children and Young Persons Act 1969,[5] to remove this statutory requirement to give priority to boarding out. The Child Care Act 1980 preserves the complete discretion of the local authority in the choice of accommodation for children in their care,[6] and the preference is still for boarding out,[7] in spite of many unsatisfactory placements.[8] One of the advantages of boarding out is that it is less costly than institutional care. The amount of boarding out allowance made to foster parents varies at the discretion of the particular local authority. Some provide special rates to encourage fostering of difficult or handicapped children. A foster parent cannot claim child benefit,[9] but once the child is placed with him for adoption he is no longer boarded out,[10] and the foster parent in his new capacity of a prospective adopter is entitled to claim that benefit.[11]

1   Report of the Care of Children Committee (1946) Cmd 6922.
2   Section 13. For the changes in policy on boarding out since 1948 see Packman, *The Child's Generation: Child Care Policy in Britain,* 2nd edn (1981).
3   Packman, supra; Adcock, *The Right of a Child to Permanent Placement* in *Rights of Children* (BAAF, 1981) p 22.
4   Hoggett, op cit, p 143.
5   By substituting a new s 13 in the 1948 Act.
6   Section 21(1). For other forms of accommodation see post, paras 15.00 et seq.
7   See Cretney, pp 574–576.
8   See Adcock and White, *The Use of Section 3 Resolutions* (1981) Adoption and Fostering 9.
9   Child Benefit (General) Regulations 1976, reg 16(8).
10 Boarding-out of Children Regulations 1955, reg 1(2).
11 *Department of Health and Social Security v Simpson* [1985] FLR 552. *Semble,* the local authority may continue to make an allowance after placement for adoption; see Clark Hall and Morrison, para A[280].

2   Children covered

7.20   The 1980 Act[1] leaves regulations to prescribe the duties imposed on local authorities and voluntary organisations. These are contained in the Boarding-Out of Children Regulations 1955,[2] which attempt to ensure the welfare of children under 18 who are boarded out. They apply to children in the care of a local authority[3] and to those in the charge of a voluntary organisation,[4] both those received directly into care by a voluntary organisation and those who, being already in care under the 1980 Act, are placed by the local authority in the charge of a voluntary organisation who then arrange the boarding out.[5] In all cases, however, it is an essential requirement that the child is boarded out as *a member of the family.*[6] They do not, however, extend to those who are boarded out for a short holiday not exceeding 21 days,[7] nor to those who are placed with persons who propose to adopt them. In the latter case the children are protected by the Adoption Act 1976.[8] It is submitted that similarly, if a child is boarded out with foster parents without adoption in mind but later they give notice of intention to apply for an adoption order, the Regulations by implication cease to apply, since the child becomes a protected child under the 1976 Act.[9]

1   Section 22.
2   SI 1955/1377, as amended by the Boarding Out of Children (Amendment) Regulations 1982, SI 1982/447.
3   Section 21(1)(a).
4   Section 61(1); reg 1.
5   Hence, apparently, the use of the term 'charge' in reg 1; see also reg 11(3).
6   Compare a 16-year-old who is put into lodgings or a hostel or is in residential employment.

7   The period could be usefully extended to 27 days to correspond with the rule governing short-term arrangements and private fostering, ante, para 7.04.
8   Section 32, ante, para 5.67.
9   See s 32(1). Clarke Hall and Morrison, para A [1051], seem to imply otherwise.

3   Restrictions on boarding out

7.21   Some of the restrictions on boarding out are of general application; others depend on whether it is expected to continue for more than eight weeks. There is, however, no statutory limit on the number of children who may be placed in a foster home, and the local authority has a complete discretion in its policy of finding persons who are willing to act as foster parents, whether short-term or long-term, and in its choice for a particular child. However, only where the special circumstances of the case make it desirable should a foster home be found outside England and Wales (for example, with a relative), and then steps should be taken to ensure that the child's welfare is safeguarded by visits and supervision as it would be if he were boarded out in England or Wales.[1] Except in an emergency, a child must have been medically examined within the last three months and a written report on his health provided before he can be placed with foster parents.[2]

1   Reg 3. This provision may occasionally be useful where the child is to be fostered in Scotland.
2   Reg 6. This requirement does not apply to short-term placements of school children who were with the same foster parents within the previous four months (reg 29).

4   Requirements before placement

7.22   Apart from this last mentioned requirement, before a child may be boarded out a social worker must, on behalf of the local authority or voluntary organisation, visit the foster parents and their home and report thereon. But the extent of his inquiry depends on whether the boarding out is likely to be long term. If it is, a visitor personally acquainted with the child and his needs or fully informed about them before his visit must report on the suitability of the accommodation and domestic conditions of the proposed foster home. He, or another social worker, must also report on the reputation and religious persuasion of the foster parents and their suitability in age, character, temperament and health to have the charge of the child; whether any member of the foster parents' household is believed to be suffering from any illness which might affect the child or to have been convicted of any offence rendering it undesirable that the child should associate with him; and on the number, sex and age of the members of the household. The foster parents should, where possible, be of the same religious persuasion as the child or give an undertaking that he will be brought up in that persuasion.[1] The placement in that household must not be made unless the child's antecedents and the relevant reports indicate that it would be in his best interests.[2] If the investigations have been thoroughly conducted, the chances of successful matching of child and foster parents are obviously enhanced.

1   Regs 19 and 20.
2   Reg 17. If the foster home is in the area of a local authority other than that having care of the child, the latter must inquire of the former whether they know of any reason

why boarding out would be detrimental. A voluntary organisation must similarly inquire of the area authority.

7.23 These requirements of detailed inquiry do not apply where the boarding out is likely to be for a period not exceeding eight weeks.[1] Under Regulation 25 all that is necessary to justify such a short-term placement is a report that the placement would be suitable to the needs of the child for that period. That may be sufficient where the foster parents have already had experience of fostering, and the local authority have had the opportunity of assessing them, or where members of the child's family will maintain close and regular contact with the child during the placement. But a lot can happen to a child in eight weeks, and it is submitted that at least in other circumstances the same requirements should apply to the choice of short-term foster parents as apply to long-term, with the possible exclusion of that relating to religious persuasion.[2] Certainly, a local authority would be ill-advised to rely solely on Regulation 25. They would, for example, not escape criticism if, having so relied, the child was the victim of sexual abuse by a short-term foster father whose criminal record a careful inquiry would have disclosed.

1   If it extends beyond that period, the stricter requirements of investigation must then be observed, unless the extension is for not more than four weeks; see reg 30.
2   Short-term foster parents must either give the same undertaking as long-term foster parents, namely, to bring him up in his own religion or be notified by letter of the child's religion and the obligations they would have under the undertaking (reg 27).

7.24 Sometimes a child may have had his home with the foster parents, for example relatives, before being received into the care of the local authority. If so, he does not have to be removed from the home while the above enquiries are being carried out.[1] This kind of case may arise where the foster parents realise that by the child's being received into care they may be granted boarding out allowances for the child. Local authorities should be alert to this notice. As has been pointed out,[2] if finance is the only problem, that can be solved by reference to State benefits, without having to rely on the hammer of the Boarding Out Regulations. However, it is suggested that the local authority should first conduct its preliminary enquiry so as to be satisfied that the home provided for the child is satisfactory.

1   Reg 1(4).
2   Leeding, *Child Care Manual for Social Workers,* 4th edn, pp 159–160.

5   Visits, supervision and removal

7.25 The Regulations provide for regular seeing of the long-term foster child and visits to his foster home.[1] These must be made within one month after the commencement of the boarding out;[2] within one month after any change of address of the foster parents; and forthwith after a complaint is made by or concerning the child, unless it appears (presumably to the visiting social worker) unnecessary. The regularity of other interviews and visits depends on the period of boarding out. If the child has been with the foster parents less than two years and he is under five, they must take place once every six weeks, and, if he has attained that age, once in every two months.[3] It is questionable whether this distinction should be drawn and whether it would not be preferable to have a uniform rule for all children under the upper limit of compulsory school age. Once the child has been with the foster parents for two years subsequent interviews and visits are at three monthly intervals. When he reaches 16 the duty to visit comes to an end, but the social worker must still *see* the child within three months after attaining that age and thereafter at least once in every three months, whether he does so by visiting the foster home or otherwise.[4] The Regulations lay down the minimum frequency of interviews and visits. The child's welfare may require more, but there may not be the resources to meet the need.

1   Reg 21. For the occasions on which visits must be made where the boarding out is not expected to exceed eight weeks see reg 28. If the period is exceeded, reg 21 then applies. See also reg 29 for visiting of children who, receiving full-time education, are boarded out at intervals with the same foster parents.
2   Twice, if there is only one foster parent—once in the first two weeks, once in the next two; reg 21(1)(a).
3   If there is only one foster parent, visits in the first two years must be every six weeks, whether the child is under or over the age of five; see reg 21(1).
4   Reg 23(3)(a) and (b); and see regs 23(2) and 28(2) for the rules relating to children who are already 16 when they are boarded out.

7.26   On each occasion that he sees a child the visitor must, after considering his welfare, health, conduct and progress, report about him to the local authority or voluntary organisation, who must review those matters in the light of the reports. The first review must be held within three months after placement and thereafter as often as considered expedient, but not less than once in every six months.[1] The authority or organisation must also see that the child undergoes regular medical examination,[2] and receives medical and dental treatment as required.[3] Local authorities and voluntary organisations need carefully to note that reviews must, so far as is practicable, be conducted by persons who do not usually act as visitors, and a note of the review must be entered in the child's case record together with particulars of any recommended action.[4]

1   Regs 9 and 22(1).
2   Reg 7. There must be an examination within one month after placement, except that the child who is over two and was examined before placement is exempted. Subsequent examinations are at six-monthly intervals for children under two and annually for those over that age.
3   Reg 8.
4   Reg 22(2).

7.27   It is in the light of the visitor's reports that the local authority or voluntary organisation are able to exercise their powers of terminating the boarding out where it no longer appears to be in the child's best interests,[1] but, until they receive adverse reports, they are usually willing to leave to the foster parents a wide discretion as to how the child should be brought up. The delegation is consistent with the written undertaking by the foster parents that they will care for the child and bring him up as their own,[2] but, as has been pointed out,[3] the undertaking conflicts with that which allows the child to be removed from the foster parents when the authority or the organisation so request. The ultimate decision on removal lies with the authority or organisation, and may occasionally turn on policy rather than the record of the foster parents. For example, one local authority may be ready to allow foster parents to educate the child in a private school, provided that the foster parents meet the cost, whereas another authority may, as a matter of general policy, insist on State education for all foster children in their care.

1   Reg 4.
2   Reg 20. Foster parents are not the agents of the local authority. Therefore the authority is not vicariously liable for their negligent acts which result in injury to the foster child; *S v Walsall Metropolitan Borough Council* [1985] 3 All ER 294, [1985] 1 WLR 1150, CA.
3   Hoggett, op cit, p 145.

7.28   The functions of the visitor are not confined to visiting, supervising and reporting. Where he considers that the conditions in which the child is boarded out endanger his health, safety or morals, he may remove him from the foster parents forthwith.[1]

1   Reg 5.

6   Records and registers

7.29   A local authority must keep up-to-date records of every child boarded out by them or whom they are supervising on behalf of another authority,[1] and a similar obligation is imposed on a voluntary organisation which is boarding out a child.[2] These records are confidential and privileged,[3] but may be disclosed by the authority or organisation at their discretion. They must be kept for at least three years after the child reaches 18 or dies earlier, and are open to inspection by an authorised person of the DHSS.[4] A local authority must also keep a register containing particulars of every child boarded out in their area, whether by them or by another authority or by a voluntary organisation. The register must be kept for at least five years after the child has or would have attained the age of 18 and similarly be open to inspection by DHSS.[5]

1   Ie in accordance with reg 13. Compare the more limited requirements to notify the local authority imposed in private fostering, ante, para 7.11.
2   Reg 10(1) and (2). The authority or organisation is allowed to microfilm its records (reg 10A, added by SI 1982/447, reg 3).
3   On confidentiality of records see post, para 15.107.
4   Reg 10(3).
5   Reg 11.

IV   DAY CARE

1   Introduction

7.30   The need for preventive and supportive social work is likely to be most acute in the family with pre-school children. Deprivation and disadvantage in a child's earliest formative years may well lead to behavioural and educational problems in later childhood. More than one Committee has drawn attention to the dangers,[1] and the needs of families with young children have been increasingly recognised by the expanding range of family support and day care related services provided for them by statutory and voluntary agencies and private individuals (for example, in the form of self-help groups). Another relevant factor has been the establishment of joint consultative committees of representatives of health authorities and local authorities to plan, operate and monitor services[2] which are of common concern to them,[3] as part of the general duty of the authorities to co-operate with one another 'in order to secure and advance the health and welfare of the people of England and Wales'.[4] If fully utilised, they have a valuable function in relation to young children. Nevertheless, as the Seebohm Commitee noted,[5] there is still 'no direct statutory responsibility on local authorities to provide for the general social care of children [under five]'. There is their general duty to promote the welfare of children so as to diminish the need to receive them into, or to keep them in, care under the Child Care Act 1980,[6] but this relates to anyone under 18 and no special obligations in that respect are imposed with regard to younger children. There are, however, some services particularly provided for the latter. Thus, in addition to the general national health schemes available to persons of all ages and the child care provisions for all under 18,[7] there are special health, welfare and educational services provided for their benefit. As will be seen,[8] nursery schools and nursery classes provided by a local education authority under the Education Act 1944 are two examples. Others are local authority day nurseries and private nurseries and child-minders.

1   See the Plowden Report on *Children and their Primary Schools* HMSO (1966), paras 296–304; the Yudkin Report on *The Care of Pre-School Children* (1967); the Seebohm Report on *Local Authority and Allied Personal Social Services*, Cmnd 3703, paras 191–212 and 447–450.
2   Although services have considerably expanded since their dates of publication (March 1976 and January 1978), useful reference can still be made to the Joint Circular Letters issued by DES and DHSS (LASSL (76)5 and LASSL (78) 1) on *Co-ordination of Services for Children under 5.*
3   National Health Service Act 1977, s 22.
4   Sub-s (1).
5   Para 193.
6   Section 1. See post, para 15.05.
7   Principally in the Child Care Act 1980 and the Children and Young Persons Act 1969.
8   Post, paras 11.42 et seq.

2   Local authority day nurseries

7.31   A general function entrusted to a local authority, through its social services department, is the making of arrangements for the care of expectant and nursing mothers and for children under five who are not attending primary schools.[1] As part of this function,[2] the authority may provide day nurseries and may make reasonable charges.[3] The local education authority may make available to a day nursery the services of teachers of its own nursery schools or nursery classes.[4] In recent years there has been a significant increase in the use of teachers in day nurseries.

1   National Health Service Act 1977, s 21(1) and Sch 8. Another responsibility thereunder is the provision of home help, including such help where the household includes a child under the upper limit of compulsory school age.
2   Note also in this context particularly the function of health visitors to visit homes and give advice concerning the care of young children.
3   HASSASSA 1983, s 17.

4   Education Act 1980, s 26.

3   Private nurseries and child minders

(a)   Introduction

7.32 Employment of women during World War II popularised the use of private nurseries and child-minders, but the abuse to which the system lent itself led to its being controlled (initially by local health authorities) through the Nurseries and Child-Minders Regulation Act 1948. The Act did not diminish the popularity of private care. On the contrary, apart from the increase in the employment of mothers, other factors increasingly contributed to its popularity, such as the recognition of the incapacity of many parents to cope with a young family, especially where it is large or badly housed or where the child creates acute behavourial problems or where there are special difficulties for ethnic minority groups. Over the last decade, ironically, it is unemployment which has proved a popularising factor, causing as it does additional strains on the young family. Moreover, the rise in unemployment of women has led to more of them undertaking day care, especially as child-minders.[1] The 1948 Act did not, however, provide an effective system for ensuring registration of nurseries and child-minders, and the number of cases of neglect and lack of proper facilities was reminiscent of Victorian baby-farming.[2] The Health Services and Public Health Act 1968,[3] amending the earlier Act, removed some of its defects, but many remain, including the problem of effective registration. The long-term solution may lie in the creation of a sufficient number of local authority nursery schools and nursery classes, as the Plowden Committee urged,[4] and in the provision by local authorities of community care facilities for children under five when not attending nursery schools, as the Seebohm Committee recommended.[5] Although there has been a significant response to both recommendations, especially to the latter, the present and foreseeable financial restrictions on local authority spending make the long-term solution as far off as ever. Indeed, the preponderance of day care facilities are being provided by voluntary organisations. The immediate and foreseeable solution is therefore likely to lie in reform of the present legislation relating to private nurseries, child-minders and other day care, which may be linked to the wider statutory changes planned for child care.[6]

1   See the Consultative Paper issued by the Department of Health and Social Security (September 1985) on Revision of the 1948 Act, para 5. This paper is subsequently referred to as CP with the appropriate paragraph number.
2   See Sonia Jackson, *The Illegal Child Minders*.
3   Section 60.
4   Para 314. See M Hughes et al, *Nurseries Now: A Fair Deal for Parents and Children*, arguing for a comprehensive system of local authority nursery education; P Newell and P Potts, *Under 5's with Special Needs* (Advisory Centre for Education), p 11.
5   Cmnd 3703, para 204.
6   See Consultative Document of the DHSS on Review of Child Care Law, paras 5.12–5.15, followed by the White Paper, *The Law on Child Care and Family Services*, (1987) Cd 62, Chapter 6.

(b)   Registration

7.33 The 1948 Act firmly distinguishes between the registration of premises and the registration of persons. Premises must be registered as nurseries where children under the upper limit of compulsory school age[1] are received, whether or not for reward, to be looked after for the day or for at least two hours as part or parts of a day or for a longer period of not more than six days. Persons must be registered as child-minders when they receive children into their homes for any of the same periods, but registration is necessary only if the children are under five and are received for reward.[2] Where the period of care extends beyond six days the Foster Children Act 1980 will normally operate, but, as already noted, not where a person who is not a regular foster parent cares for and maintains a child for more than six but less than 28 days.[3] Thus, a residential holiday scheme which is for a longer period than six continuous days does not require registration.

1   See s 13(2).
2   Section 1, as amended by the Health Services and Public Health Act 1968, s 60(2).
3   See ante, para 7.04; FCA 1980, s 2(3)(a).
     The Government intends a single system of registration, together with closer regulation of private schemes for organised play or leisure activities outside school hours or during school holidays; see supra para 7.32, note 6.

7.34   *Premises* do not have to be registered if they are wholly or mainly used as private dwellings, but the person receiving children into them will have to register as a child-minder if the relevant conditions are present. Hospitals, schools, nursery schools or play centres maintained or assisted by a local education authority or any institution mentioned in section 2 of the Foster Children Act 1980[1] are exempted from registration.[2] For example, if school premises are used by a parents' association to provide recreational facilities for children during school holidays, no registration is required. Thus, a holiday play centre run by a voluntary organisation in a school does not require registration. It is questionable whether certain categories of institutions should be automatically excluded.[3]

1   See ante, para 7.04.
2   N & CMRA 1948, s 8.
3   Another question is whether holiday day care organised by a voluntary body in parks, centres and adventure playgrounds should be included; see CP paras 16 and 31.

7.35   The responsibility for registration and inspection rests with the social services department of the local authority,[1] who may refuse registration or allow it subject to conditions. Registration of premises may be refused on the ground that a person employed there is not fit to look after children or that the premises are not suitable as a nursery because of their condition, situation, construction or size or because of defects in the equipment used.[2] Registration of a child-minder may be refused on similar grounds.[3] Moreover, an application for registration of premises is of no effect unless it contains a statement with respect to each person employed in looking after children at the premises and every other person who has attained the age of 16 and is normally resident there. The statement must declare[4] whether or not (1) the person has been disqualified from keeping foster children,[5] (2) he has been convicted of an offence specified in the First Schedule to the Children and Young Persons Act 1933,[6] (3) his rights and powers with respect to a child have been vested in a local authority under section 3 of the Child Care Act 1980 (or its predecessor, section 2 of the Children Act 1948),[7] and (4) an order has been made removing a 'protected child' from his care and maintenance in accordance with section 43 of the Adoption Act 1958 or section 34 of the Adoption Act 1976.[8] A similar statement has to be made in an application for registration as a child-minder. Knowingly or recklessly making a false statement is an offence punishable on summary conviction with a fine not exceeding level 3 on the standard scale (currently £400) or imprisonment for up to six months or both.[9] A weakness in the present rules is the lack of verification made by the local authority of the contents of a statement. Another improvement would be a requirement that registration is subject to prior satisfactory inspection of the premises or home.

1 Local Authority Social Services Act 1970, s 2 and Sch 1.
2 N & CMRA 1948, s 1(3).
3 Ibid, s 1(4).
4 Health Services and Public Health Act 1968, s 60(7).
5 See ante, paras 7.14 and 7.15.
6 For reference to the First Schedule see post, Chapter 9. Should not this requirement be extended to include every person living in the home of a child-minder? A local authority would surely want to know, for example, of a history of child abuse by a child-minder's spouse?
7 Post, paras 15.14 et seq.
8 Ante, para 5.68.
9 The local authority may prosecute (N & CMRA 1948, s 11).

7.36 On, or at any time after, the registration of a nursery or a child-minder the local authority may impose conditions with regard to the number of children that may be received; the precautions to be taken against the exposure of the children to infectious diseases; the number and the qualifications or experience of the persons employed; the safety and maintenance of the premises and equipment; the feeding and diet arrangements; and the records to be kept. For nurseries requirements may also be imposed concerning the qualifications of the person in charge and the medical supervision of the children.[1] There does not seem to be any cogent reason for not allowing the latter requirement to be imposed where the registration relates to child-minding. The certificate which the local authority has to issue on registration must specify the requirements imposed.[2] No statutory time limits for compliance are laid down,[3] but a reasonable time should be allowed.

1 N & CMRA 1948, s 2; HS & PHA 1968, s 60(9). An order imposing a condition may be varied or revoked (N & CMRA 1948, s 2(6)).
2 N & CMRA 1948, s 3.
3 See Clarke Hall and Morrison, op cit, para A[70].

7.37 There is no power to limit registration to a fixed period or to impose a condition that it is reviewed at specified dates or intervals. However, registration may be cancelled for breach of any requirement imposed or on any ground which would have justified refusing the registration initially,[1] but before a local authority may refuse an application or cancel a registration or impose a requirement it must give to the person affected[2] at least 14 days' notice of their intention to do so and allow him or his representative[3] an opportunity to show cause why the particular order should not be made. There is, therefore, no power of immediate suspension of registration.[4] If an order is made, there is a right of appeal within 21 days to a magistrates' court with a further right to a Crown Court.[5] It is suggested that, unless and until family courts are created, the appellate system should follow the same lines as those adopted by the Foster Children Act 1980[6] in that the appeal from the order of the local authority should lie to a juvenile court and not an adult magistrates' court.[7]

1   N & CMRA 1948, s 5.
2   Ie to the applicant for registration, the occupier of the premises to which the registration relates or to the person registered as a child-minder, as the case may be.
3   Not necessarily a lawyer but any nominated person.
4   For proposed rectification of the omission see CP para 28.
5   See N & CMRA 1948, s 6; Public Health Act 1936, ss 300–302; Courts Act 1971, s 8 and Sch 1.
6   See ante, para 7.10.
7   Another possibility, suggested in the Consultative Paper, para 30, is an appeal to a tribunal along the same lines as an appeal in connection with registration of voluntary homes.

7.38   A basic defect of the Nurseries and Child-Minders Regulation Act 1948 is that it fails to guarantee the registration of nurseries and child-minders.[1] Indeed, section 1 appears to make the application for registration of premises or persons discretionary.[2] The fact that failure to register leads to criminal liability[3] might suggest that the distinction is academic, but that conclusion is only valid on the assumption that the person who should apply for registration is the one who is liable if there is failure to register. With regard to registration of nurseries there is some doubt as to whether this is necessarily so. The penalty for failure to register attaches to the occupier of the premises.[4] The person who should register is he who receives or proposes to receive children.[5] If the term 'occupier' is intended in this context to mean the person in actual occupation there is no point in the argument, but the better opinion would seem to be[6] that occupation refers to legal occupation, so that the persons may not be the same. As for registration of child-minders, it is clear that exceptionally they may be different persons. On a strict interpretation of section 1 anyone, including a relative, who receives children into care should apply for registration, but the provisions in section 4 relating to criminal liability do not extend to a person receiving a child of whom he is a relative.[7] These are untidy and unnecessary discrepancies, which a proper correlation between sections 1 and 4 would remove. More widely, it may be questioned whether local authorities do enough to publicise the requirements of registration and the criteria to be met.

1   One improvement with regard to registration of child-minders which was proposed but not incorporated into the HS & PHA 1968 was that, before accepting advertisements from persons offering child-minding services, newspapers and newsagents should ask for proof of registration.
2   Section 1(2) provides: 'Any person receiving or proposing to receive children . . . may make application . . . for registration . . .'
3   On summary conviction to a fine not exceeding level 3 on the standard scale (currently £400) or to imprisonment for up to three months or both (s 4(4)). Note the heavier maximum term of imprisonment for making a false statement in an application for registration, supra, para 7.35. The local authority may prosecute (s 11)..
4   Section 4(1).
5   Section 1(2).
6   See Clarke Hall and Morrison, op cit, para A[78].

7   See sub-s (2). 'Relative' has the same wide meaning as it has for the purposes of adoption
     and custodianship; see N & CMRA 1948, s 13(2), as amended by CA 1975, Sch 4, Part
     I.

(c) Inspection

7.39 The powers of inspection are similar to those conferred on local
authorities with regard to foster children. A person so authorised by the
local authority may enter without a warrant a registered nursery or the
home of a registered child-minder and inspect the premises and the children
who are being kept there, the arrangements for their welfare and the records
relating to them. Where he has reasonable cause to believe that children
are being kept in premises or by persons which or, as the case may be,
who have not but ought to have been registered, he may apply to a justice
of the peace for a warrant authorising entry and inspection.[1] Obviously,
if there is any doubt about whether premises or persons are registered
a warrant should be obtained. It is an offence, which the local authority
may prosecute,[2] to obstruct the exercise of these powers, and it carries
on summary conviction a fine not exceeding level 2 on the standard scale
(currently £100). The leniency of the penalty compares unfavourably with
those available for the obstruction of the exercise of corresponding powers
in respect of foster children.[3]

1   N & CMRA 1948, s 7, as amended by HS & PHA 1968, s 60(11).
2   Ibid, s 11.
3   See ante, para 7.07.

7.40 Sometimes premises are simultaneously used for the care of foster
children in accordance with the Foster Children Act 1980 and for the day
care of children under the 1948 Act. Dual supervision under the Acts is
avoided by providing that the powers of entry and inspection under the
one or the other are to be invoked according to whether the premises are
being mainly used for the one purpose or the other.[1] Thus, if the premises
mainly accommodate foster children, the occupier is exempted from the
penal consequences of non-registration, and the premises from inspection,
under the 1948 Act. A child-minder and his home are similarly exempted,
if in addition to day care he is looking after at least one foster child or
a child boarded out with him under a particular enactment. In such a
case the powers of entry and inspection under the Foster Children Act
1980 are applicable.

1   N & CMRA 1948, ss 9 and 10.

CHAPTER 8

Wardship[1]

1 INTRODUCTION

8.01 Wardship of court is the oldest institution connected with English child law. It has also proved the most adaptable. As an incident of feudal military tenure wardship entitled the lord to manage for his own profit the land of his deceased tenant during the minority of the tenant's heir.[2] As liege-lord it was the King who most benefited from wardship on the death of his tenants-in-chief, and, though it was also to be seen as an obligation to protect the property and, incidentally, the person of the minor, wardship was a rich source of revenue which mainly accounted for the Crown setting up in 1540 the Court of Wards and Liveries to administer it.[3] With the abolition of that Court in 1660[4] the responsibility was assumed by the Court of Chancery. Thereafter the feudal associations were still pronounced in that wardship of court was in practice only sought where the minor had large property interests to protect. Nevertheless, even in those cases his personal interests were not overlooked, for example, through the guardian's duty to educate the ward according to the latter's station or through his control over the marriage of a female ward so as to prevent her property falling into the hands of fortune hunters. However, it is not until the nineteenth century[5] that it came to be accepted that the origins of wardship of court lay in the Sovereign's duty as parens patriae to protect his subjects, especially minors, who were incapable of looking after themselves;[6] and even then it was only in the last decade of that century, by which time jurisdiction had passed (in 1875) to the Chancery Division of the High Court, that emphasis was being placed on the protection of the person of the ward, and the prerogative jurisdiction was being increasingly invoked to settle disputes over custody, care and control between the parents or between a parent and a stranger. That has remained one of its main uses, but, as will be seen, it serves several other purposes.

1   See generally Lowe and White, *Wards of Court* (2nd edn, 1986); Parry, Butterworths Family Law Service, Division E, Chapters 3 and 4; Cross, *Wards of Court*, (1967) 83 LQR 200; Pearce, *Wardship: The Law and Practice* (1986); Law Com Working Paper No 101 on Wards of Court.

2   Littleton's *Tenures* 103. For the early history of wardship see Holdsworth, *A History of English Law* (7th edn, 1956), Vol III, pp 61–66; Plucknett, *A Concise History of Common Law* (4th edn 1948) pp 504 and 514; Milsom, *Historical Foundations of the Common Law* (2nd edn 1981) pp 107–110; Baker, *An Introduction to English Legal History* (2nd edn 1979) pp 106–207; and Lowe and White, paras 1.1–1.2.

3   Previously it had been the responsibility of the Chancellor; see Holdsworth, (7th edn) Vol 6, p 648.

4   By the Tenures Abolition Act 1660, s 1.

5   For judicial references see Lowe and White, paras 1.3–1.6.

6   But the Crown's protective jurisdiction in respect of adults who are unable, because

of mental disorder, to look after themselves has been entirely superseded by statute. So it was held by Wood J in *T v T* [1988] 1 All ER 613, [1988] 2 WLR 189, relying on a statement in Halsbury's Laws of England (1974) Vol 8, para 901. But the conclusion is questionable, since there is no express statutory exclusion of the common law perogative jurisdiction; and see Brahams (1987) 84 Law Soc Gaz 867 and Bennion, ibid, at p 2327,

II   JURISDICTION

1   The court

8.02   Since the Administration of Justice Act 1970[1] wardship jurisdiction has been exercised by the Family Division of the High Court. Only that Court can make a minor a ward of court or order that a ward of court cease to be a ward of court.[2] Otherwise, as with other Family business,[3] the Court may either of its own motion or on the application of any party to the proceedings, order the transfer of the whole or a part of the proceedings to a county court,[4] for example, for that court to determine who shall have care and control of, or access to, the child. The High Court must not order transfer unless the parties have either had an opportunity of being heard on the issue or consented to the order.[5] Moreover, proceedings must be dealt with in the High Court (a) where it appears to the Court that by reason of the complexity, difficulty or gravity of the issues they ought to be tried in that Court; (b) where an application is opposed on the ground of want of jurisdiction, unless in the latter circumstance the nature of the issues of fact or law raised in the case makes them more suitable for trial in a county court;[6] or (c) where a local authority is or becomes a party to the proceedings, unless similarly the issues are such as to make a county court trial more suitable.[7]

Where the case has been transferred to a county court, that court (through the judge or the registrar) may similarly order the whole or part of the proceedings back to the High Court either (a) of its own motion after considering any representations which the judge or registrar must give the parties an opportunity of making; or (b) on the application of any party on notice to all other parties.[8]

These rules of transfer and re-transfer between the High Court and a county court are complicated, and it has already been questioned[9] whether much use will be made of them. They are more likely to be invoked where the High Court judge or deputy judge has made the initial order warding the child in the provinces, leaving secondary issues, such as access, to a county court judge at the local registry.[10]

1   Section 1(2) and Sch I. See now the Supreme Court Act 1981, s 6(1) and Sch I, para 3(b)(ii).
2   SCA 1981, s 41; Matrimonial and Family Proceedings Act 1984, s 38(2)(b).
3   See ante, para 3.17.
4   MFPA 1984, ss 32 and 38.
5   RSC Ord 90, r 2B(1), as inserted by Rules of the Supreme Court (Amendment) 1986, r 27, SI 1986/632.
6   See *Practice Direction* [1988] 2 All ER 103, [1988] 1 WLR 558.
7   See ibid. For other circumstances where the High Court must exercise jurisdiction, unless county court trial is more suitable see post, para 8.24.
8   MFPA 1984, s 39; County Court Rules Ord 16, r 12, as added by the County Court (Amendment) Rules 1986, SI 1986/636, r 26.
9   Lowe and White, para 4.22.
10   See ibid, para 4.23.

2 The inherent jurisdiction to ward a child and make orders

8.03 In the vast majority of cases the child is a British subject, ordinarily resident and actually present in England and Wales at the date of the institution of proceedings.[1] However, by invoking the principle that the duty of the Crown to protect the child arises from the duty of allegiance owed by the child, the court has been ready to assume jurisdiction if the child satisfies any one of those three conditions of nationality, ordinary residence or physical presence, although whether it will be willing to order wardship may be another matter. The earliest recognition of British nationality as a separate ground for jurisdiction[2] co-incided with the Nationalist movements in mid-nineteenth century Europe.[3] The ground is now firmly established,[4] although not frequently invoked. Jurisdiction based solely on the child's presence has been very largely assumed in response to the increasing incidence of 'kidnapping' of children abroad who have then been brought to England in defiance of the wishes of those who have had custody, care and control of the child abroad, whether or not under a foreign order. But this ground of jurisdiction may also extend to cases where there is no kidnapping.[5] The court has had no difficulty in holding that the child's presence gives rise to allegiance and thereby to protection, but it will be reluctant to assume jurisdiction where the presence is transitory unless it considers that its intervention is needed in an emergency (especially where the child's well-being is at risk) or to support a foreign order or proceedings.[6] Nor will wardship usually be ordered if enforcement is impracticable[7] or if proceedings are pending abroad and are considered more appropriate.[8] The English court will take into account not only such matters as the physical convenience of the parties and witnesses and questions of expense, but also the system of law which the foreign court would apply.[9] If that should be English law, that might well persuade the English court to assume jurisdiction. But the overriding principle to be applied in deciding whether or not to accept jurisdiction and to hear the case on its merits is the paramountcy of the child's welfare.

1   It has been suggested that where jurisdiction is based on the child's presence, see infra, presence by the time the court comes to make the order might suffice; see Lowe and White, para 2.8. If jurisdiction on that basis would facilitate protection of the child, the court should assume it. Compare the rules where jurisdiction is assumed under the Family Law Act 1986; see the meaning of 'relevant date', post, para 8.06.
2   See *Hope v Hope* (1854) 4 De GM & G 328, per Lord Cranworth at 344–345; *Re Willoughby* (1885) 30 Ch D 324, per Cotton LJ at 331.
3   Compare the influence of those movements on the emergence of domicile in English law.
4   *Re Liddell's Settlement Trusts* [1936] Ch 365, [1936] 1 All ER 239; *Harben v Harben* [1957] 1 All ER 379, [1957] 1 WLR 261. For criticism and the suggestion that this basis of jurisdiction should be narrower and rest on Citizenship of the United Kingdom see Lowe and White, paras 2.6–2.7.
5   *Re D* [1943] Ch 305, [1943] 2 All ER 411, where a German refugee, whose parents were believed to be in a concentration camp, was made a ward of court.
6   See Pearson LJ in *Re P(GE) (an infant)* [1965] Ch 568 at 588, [1964] 3 All ER 977 at 984. In *Re C (an infant)* (1956) Times, 14 December, an illegitimate child, born in the United States, was passing through England with his putative father who was taking him to Russia. On the application of the mother, who wished to take him back to the United States, he was made a ward of court, but this was subject to the condition that he cease to be so as soon as he arrived back in the United States with her.
7   Aliter if, for example, sequestration of property is available to secure obedience. In *Re Chrysanthou* [1957] CLY 1748, the child was made a ward of court but the order

did not include a direction to the parent to bring him back from abroad, since there was no evidence that the direction would be obeyed.

8 *Re S(M) (an infant)* [1971] Ch 621, [1971] 1 All ER 459.
9 See *Re Kernot (an infant), Kernot v Kernot* [1965] Ch 217, [1964] 3 All ER 339.

8.04 It was the same reasons of protection and allegiance that led the Court of Appeal in *Re P(GE) (an infant)*[1] to hold that wardship jurisdiction could be exercised over a minor who is ordinarily resident in England but who is not actually present here at the time of institution of the proceedings. The parents in that case had come to England in 1957 as stateless persons and refugees from Egypt. Eventually they separated and the boy then spent most of each week with his mother and the weekends with his father, until one weekend in 1962 when, without the mother's knowledge or consent, the father flew with him to Israel, where by the date of the present wardship proceedings instituted by the mother they had been living for almost three months and where the father had acquired for himself and the boy Israeli nationality. It was held that where a child's parents are living apart and by arrangement between them he is living most of the time with one of them he is ordinarily resident with that parent, even though the other may have the child to stay with him. The boy was therefore ordinarily resident with his mother in England when he was spirited away to Israel, and that residence could not be terminated by the unilateral action of the father, especially as the child was still entitled to return to England under a British travel document which had enabled him and the father to leave England.[2] The assumption of jurisdiction on the basis of ordinary residence was essential in such a case as the present one where the minor had been kidnapped and removed from the jurisdiction by force, deception or secrecy,[3] and there seems to be no justification for limiting the jurisdiction to cases where the parties are stateless.[4]

1 [1965] Ch 568, [1964] 3 All ER 977. For a close analysis of the case see Lowe and White, paras 2.9–2.11.
2 See Lord Denning MR at 586 and 982 respectively. Pearson and Russell LJJ took the view that the father had not yet abandoned his ordinary residence in England, and therefore there could not be any question of depriving his son of ordinary residence.
3 See further PRH Webb (1965) 14 ICLQ 663.
4 See Lowe and White, para 2.11.

8.05 In accepting ordinary residence as a basis the Court of Appeal decisively rejected domicile, on the ground that it is an archaic, artificial and unrealistic concept which may be wholly unconnected with allegiance. It is also firmly recognised that property owned by the child within the jurisdiction is not a sufficient basis,[1] notwithstanding the strong historical association which wardship had with the protection of his proprietary interests.

1 *Brown v Collins* (1883) 25 Ch D 56.

3 Orders under the Family Law Act 1986

8.06 The above jurisdictional rules have been substantially affected by the Family Law Act 1986. An order, made in wardship proceedings, which gives care and control of the ward to a person or provides for education or access is a 'custody order' within the meaning of the Act, but that term does not include an order committing a ward to the care or care and control of a local authority.[1] Nor does it include an order which varies or revokes a previous custody order made in the exercise of wardship jurisdiction;[2] for example, an order varying an order giving care and control to a person. Subject to cases where the Act specifically restricts the jurisdiction to vary,[3] a court in England and Wales retains its inherent jurisdiction to vary or revoke an order made by it, even though it would not have jurisdiction under the 1986 Act to make the order which is varied or revoked.[4]

Jurisdiction may be assumed where the child:

(a) is habitually resident in England and Wales, or
(b) is present in England and Wales and is not habitually resident in any part of the United Kingdom, ie not in England and Wales, Scotland or Northern Ireland.[5]

But jurisdiction on neither basis may be assumed if proceedings for divorce, nullity or judicial separation are continuing in a court in Scotland or Northern Ireland in respect of the marriage of the child's parents,[6] except if the court in which proceedings are continuing has made an order either waiving its jurisdiction[7] or staying custody proceedings so as to enable proceedings with respect to the custody of the child to be taken in England and Wales.[8]

However, the Act preserves the emergency jurisdiction in wardship by allowing the court to rely on the child's presence in England and Wales where it considers that the immediate exercise of its powers is necessary for the child's protection, even if he is habitually resident in a part of the United Kingdom or even if divorce, nullity or judicial separation proceedings are continuing in a Scottish or Northern Ireland court.[9] Any order made is, however, liable to be suspended by an order of the court having jurisdiction other than emergency jurisdiction.

The relevant date for determining jurisdiction is the date of the application for a custody order (or first application if two or more are determined together) and, where no such application is made, the date of the order.[10] The latter alternative is intended for the case where a custody order was not contemplated when the wardship proceedings were instituted;[11] for example, where the court of its own motion makes an order for care and control.

1   See s 1(1)(d).
2   Section 1(2)(c).
3   See post.
4   See Law Com No 138, para 4.30 and p 137, para 13.
5   Sections 2(2)(a), 3(1) and 42(1). For habitual residence after removal without consent, see s 41.
6   Section 3(2). For circumstances in which proceedings are treated as continuity, see s 42(2), and (3).
7   Under ss 13(6) (except s 13(6)(a)), 21(5), 14(2) or 22(2).
8   Provided that any such order is in force; see s 3(3).
9   See s 2(2)(b).
10   Section 3(6).
11   See Law Com No 138, para 4.28.

8.06A   A court which has jurisdiction to make a custody order under the Family Law Act 1986 has a discretion to refuse an application or to stay proceedings.[1] It may do the former where the matter to which the application refers has already been determined in proceedings outside England and Wales.[2] Refusal is most likely where the issue has already been fully explored and there has been no change of circumstances to justify the issue being reopened; but it is difficult to see how the court could properly exercise its discretion without some evidence about the earlier determination.

It may stay proceedings where it appears to the court that proceedings relating to custody are continuing outside England and Wales or that, although such proceedings have been commenced, it would be more appropriate for the custody matters to be determined in proceedings taken outside England and Wales.[3] There is power to revoke such a stay if it appears to the court that there has been an unreasonable delay in the taking of those proceedings or that those proceedings have been stayed, sisted or concluded.[4]

1   This statutory power does not affect any other power the court has to refuse an application or to grant or remove a stay; see FLA 1986, s 5(4).
2   Ibid, s 5(1). Such proceedings include proceedings before a tribunal or other authority having power to determine questions relating to the custody of children; see s 42(7). A party to proceedings for or relating to custody who knows of other proceedings (including proceedings out of the jurisdiction and concluded proceedings) relating to the child must file an affidavit giving particulars of the other proceedings; see s 39 and RSC Ord 90, r 55 as inserted by SI 1988/298 (L3); CCR Ord 47, r 11(9), as inserted by SI 1988/278 (L1).
3   FLA 1986, s 5(2).
4   Ibid, s 5(3).

4   Who can be warded

8.07   Subject to the above jurisdictional rules[1] wardship can extend to any child who is under 18,[2] but an unborn child cannot be made a ward of court, since a fetus does not have rights of its own.[3] This refusal to protect is justified on the ground that otherwise the mother would be subjected to unacceptable restrictions during her pregnancy, for example, so as to prevent harm to the fetus;[4] but, since protection can begin from birth, there is considerable force in the argument that wardship proceedings may legally be instituted during pregnancy and an order obtained that the child will become a ward on birth.[5] If this is legally possible, it would be an appropriate procedure where the mother's conduct during pregnancy, such as persistent taking of drugs, was likely to prove harmful to the child, and it would provide a local authority with a method of removing the child at birth without having to rely, as it did in *D (a minor) v Berkshire Council Council*[6] on care proceedings. Its appropriateness was also recently (November 1987) highlighted by the intention of Tameside local authority to commence wardship proceedings as soon as a baby was born of parents three of whose children had died when they were very young. In the event the baby was still-born, but if, as in that case, a local authority allegedly has evidence which, if substantiated, might justify removal at birth, it would, it is submitted, be in the interests of all parties concerned that the issue be determined before that event.

1   See ante, paras 8.04 to 8.06.
2   See FLRA 1969, s 1.
3   See *Re F (in utero)* [1988] 2 All ER 193, [1988] 2 WLR 1288, CA.
4   See Lowe (1980) 96 LQR 29 and (1981) 131 NLJ 561; Radevsky, (1980) 130 NLJ 813.

For the contrary view that a fetus may be warded see Phillips (1979) 95 LQR 332 and Lyon and Bennett (1979) 9 Fam Law 35 at p 36.

5   Lowe and White, para 2.3, who also argue that exceptionally wardship of the fetus ought legally to be permitted, for example, so that the court could decide whether a life support system should continue to keep the fetus alive in the womb of the mother after she becomes clinically dead. It is clear since *Re F*, supra, that no such exception is permissible. Any change in the law is a matter for Parliament.

6   [1987] 1 All ER 20, HL; see post, para 14.07.

8.08   Given the long history of wardship it is surprising that there is no firm authority on the question whether a married minor may be warded,[1] but the ruling that the marriage of a minor who is already a ward of court does not terminate wardship[2] supports an affirmative answer. The possibility of making a married minor, who under English law must be at least 16 years old,[3] a ward of court is very unlikely, especially in view of the *Gillick* principle and the limited number of under majority marriages.[4] It may, however, occasionally be useful where the minor is much younger and validly married under his or her personal law. The circumstances may be such that he or she needs protection from the spouse and wardship may be appropriate where care proceedings are not.[5]

1   Compare the uncertainty about the effect of the marriage of a ward on guardianship; see ante, para 4.45.
2   *Re Elwes (No 2)* [1958] CLY 1620, (1958) Times, 30 July.
3   Marriage Act 1949, s 2.
4   One possibility, for example, is where an immature minor is being influenced by his or her spouse into becoming a drug addict.
5   Compare *Alhaji Mohamed v Knott* [1969] 1 QB 1, [1968] 2 All ER 563, DC; see post, para 14.14.

Exceptions

8.09   Where a child is the subject of wardship proceedings a person who is entitled to diplomatic immunity is immune from wardship proceedings, but the position of the child whose parent is so immune is not entirely clear. In *Re C (an infant)*[1] Harman J, applying a dictum of Lord Phillimore in *Engelke v Musmann*,[2] held that immunity extended to the child, provided he was a member of the parent's family, which for this purpose meant that he must be ordinarily resident with, or under the control of, the parent. In *Re C* the child was living with his English stepmother and not with his Greek father, who was entitled to diplomatic immunity, but the matter in issue, on which the stepmother initiated wardship proceedings, was the child's education and the court liberally extended immunity to the child on the ground that the father still retained control over him in regard to that matter. The decision must, however, now be seen in the light of the Diplomatic Privileges Act 1964, which extends immunity to a member of the household of the parent entitled to immunity, provided the member is not a national of, or permanently resident in, the receiving State. Some uncertainty exists about the meaning to be given to 'household' in this context.[3] Notwithstanding *Re C*, it is unlikely that the test is now one of parental control. The 'preferable test in all cases is to equate the notion of "household" with that of "home"'.[4]

1   [1959] Ch 363, [1958] 2 All ER 656.
2   [1928] AC 433 at 450.

3   Compare the wide meaning given for the purpose of care proceedings under CYPA
     1969; see *R v Birmingham Juvenile Court, ex p N* [1984] 2 All ER 688, [1984] Fam
     Law 277, post, para 14.10.
4   Lowe and White, para 2.14.

8.10   Another uncertainty is the extent to which the criterion of presence
entitles the court to assume jurisdiction over a child who is actually in
England but subject to an order to leave made by the immigration authorities.
It is clear that the wardship proceedings will not be allowed to challenge
the decision of the authorities to order the child's removal so long at least
as they have exercised their powers fairly and honestly.[1] However,
exceptionally the wardship jurisdiction might be necessary for the child's
welfare until the final decision (by the Secretary of State) that the child
be not permitted to enter the United Kingdom.[2]

1   *Re Mohamed Arif (an infant); Re Nirbai Singh (an infant)* [1968] Ch 643, [1968] 2 All
     ER 145. See also *Re S (minors)* (1980) 11 Fam Law 55, CA, where a mother who was
     subject to a deportation order made two of her children wards of court, but the Court
     of Appeal upheld the dismissal of her originating summons.
2   See *Re F (a minor)* (1988) Times, 2 July, CA.

III   PROCEDURE

8.11   When the jurisdiction of the Court of Chancery was mainly being
invoked to protect the ward's property, it came to be accepted that any
action to administer the trusts of a settlement of property on him or any
payment into court of money or securities in which he had interests
automatically rendered him a ward of court. When it came to be recognised
that protection of the person was at least as important, a petition to appoint
a guardian for a child had the same result. Notwithstanding the shift of
emphasis towards the protection of the person, the older methods were
still mainly relied on for instituting wardship proceedings, even though
there were no substantial property interests to protect. The use of the device
of settling a small sum (usually £50) on a child and then bringing an action
for administration of the trust[1] so as to make him a ward of court was
often unreal and sometimes vexatious.[2] Yet, it was not until the Law Reform
(Miscellaneous) Provisions Act 1949[3] that a new procedure was introduced.
It is now to be found in section 41 of the Supreme Court Act 1981.

1   As, for example, in *Re Liddell's Settlement Trusts* [1936] Ch 365, [1936] 1 All ER 239,
     CA; *Re X's Settlement* [1945] Ch 44, [1945] 1 All ER 100.
2   See the Report of the Denning Committee, Cmnd 7024, para 32.
3   Section 9.

1   The application

(a)   The originating summons

8.12   The section enacts that a child can only be made a ward of court
pursuant to an order under that section.[1] Even when occasionally a divorce
court in proceedings for divorce, nullity of marriage or judicial separation
exercises its power of directing that proceedings be taken to have a child
of the family made a ward of court,[2] the provisions of section 41 must
be strictly observed.[3]

Application for the child to be warded is by way of originating summons[4] issued out of the Principal Registry or a district registry. The summons must include a statement of the child's whereabouts or that they are unknown to the applicant,[5] and must warn the defendant that it is a contempt of court to take the child out of England and Wales. In addition to seeking an order that the child be made a ward of court during minority or until further order the applicant's statement of claim[6] must set out any other orders sought, which is usually an order that care and control of the child be entrusted to him, and sometimes accompanied by an application for an injunction or for directions on such matters as access or education.[7]

1   See SCA 1981, s 41(1).
2   MCA 1973, s 42(1). The Court is likely to direct the Official Solicitor to institute proceedings. It seems that other courts when exercising jurisdiction (for example, under the Child Care Act 1980) may direct that the child be made a ward of court; see *Re H (a minor)* [1978] Fam 65 at 76, [1978] 2 All ER 903 at 909–910; *O'Dare Ai v South Glamorgan County Council* (1980) 3 FLR 1.
3   The Mental Health Act 1983, s 96(1)(i) confers a similar power on the Court of Protection when it exercises its general powers.
4   See RSC Ord 90, rr 1, 2 and 3(1), as amended by Rules of the Supreme Court (Amendment) 1986, rr 26, 27 and 28, SI 1986/632.
5   RSC Ord 90, r 3(4); see also *Practice Direction* [1973] 1 All ER 144, [1973] 1 WLR 60.
6   See RSC Ord 7, r 3.
7   There should also be a claim for costs.

(b)   The parties

(i)   The plaintiff

8.13   The applicant must state in the originating summons each party's interest in, or relationship to, the child.[1] Often the applicant is a parent of the child, seeking an order for care and control; and, where the child is in the care of a local authority, it is sometimes that authority.[2] It is too early to assess the impact which the introduction of the custodianship provisions[3] is having as a substitute for the care and control order which may be sought by persons, such as relatives and foster parents, who might be eligible to apply for a custodianship order; but any person wishing to rely on wardship must show that he has a proper interest[4] in having the child made a ward of court. This is to avoid frivolous or improper applications, and, if the registrar considers the application is an abuse of the process of the court,[5] he may dismiss the summons forthwith or refer the point to the judge.[6] However, abuse of process rarely occurs.[7]

The child may himself apply to be made a ward of court, but the originating summons will have to be filed by a next friend.[8] Such an application is unlikely, but in view of the *Gillick* principle may eventually become more frequent, if older children are minded to test the validity and enforceability of their rights, for example, to be sterilised or to donate an organ or tissue for transplant. Where the application is directed against the child's own parents (who would normally be his next friend), it will require some other person with a 'proper interest'[9] to act in that capacity.[10] If a child is seeking to enforce a right, an appropriate person is likely to be a member of the staff of the Children's Legal Centre.

1   RSC Ord 90, r 3(3B).
2   See post, Chapter 15. Where a local authority is a party the proceedings must be dealt

with in the High Court unless the nature of the issues of fact or law raised makes them more suitable for county court trial and unless to do so would cause undue delay or hardship; see *Practice Direction* [1988] 2 All ER 103, [1988] 1 WLR 558.

3   See ante, Chapter 6.
4   For a clear illustration see *Re D (a minor) (wardship: sterilisation)* [1976] Fam 185, [1976] 1 All ER 326, where an educational psychologist was allowed by means of wardship to intervene and prevent sterilisation of the child; see ante, para 1.32. Occasionally the 'interested person' may be the Official Solicitor as in *Re B (a minor) (sterilisation)* [1988] AC 199, [1987] 2 All ER 206, HL (ibid para 1.33) or other guardian ad litem as in *Re JT (a minor) (wardship : sterilisation)* [1986] 2 FLR 107, [1986] Fam Law 213.
5   As in *Re Dunhill* (1967) 111 Sol Jo 113, where a night-club owner made a female model (just under the age of majority) a ward of court for publicity purposes.
6   See *Practice Direction* [1967] 1 All ER 828, [1967] 1 WLR 623. The applicant is almost certain to be liable for costs and possibly for contempt of court.
7   Law Com Working Paper No 101, para 2.5.
8   RSC Ord 80, r 2.
9   See supra.
10 See Parry, op cit, para E [125].

(ii)   Defendants

8.14   Where the plaintiff is a parent and the wardship relates to a dispute between the parents, the other parent is the proper defendant[1] and, where the child is, or has recently been, in the care of a local authority, the authority is the appropriate defendant.[2] In those cases where the applicants are parents seeking to terminate an association between their teenage child (usually a daughter) and another person, that person should not be made a party to the originating summons, but should be made a defendant in a summons within the wardship proceedings for injunction or committal and should not be allowed to see any documents other than those relating to the summons. Time should be allowed for any such person to obtain representation and any order for injunction should in the first instance extend over a few days only.[3]

1   If the plaintiff is a stranger bringing proceedings against a parent, he should carefully consider whether other persons having a close interest, such as a step-parent or cohabitee, should also be made a defendant; see Lowe and White, para 3.6.
2   But not its officer; see *Re L (an infant) (practice note)* [1963] 1 All ER 176, [1963] 1 WLR 97.
3   See *Practice Direction* [1983] 2 All ER 672, [1983] 1 WLR 790.

8.15   A case of 'teenage' wardship may be an appropriate one in which to make the child a defendant,[1] but only in special circumstances should a child ever be joined and rarely if not old enough to express a view as to his future.[2] The parties should not seek to join the child even by consent unless special reasons are shown. In most cases his interest will be sufficiently protected by a welfare report.[3] Where leave is given to make him a defendant,[4] the judge or registrar must indicate the special reasons, together with any special directions for enquiries. A copy should be sent to the Official Solicitor and he should be the first person to be asked to represent the child.

1   For other possibilities see Clarke Hall and Morrison, para C [84].
2   His role in wardship contrasts sharply with that in care proceedings where not only is he a party but also his interests are usually protected by a guardian ad litem and a solicitor; see post, Chapter 14.
3   See *Practice Direction* [1982] 1 All ER 319, [1982] 1 WLR 118; *Re C (a minor) (wardship proceedings)* [1984] FLR 419, [1984] Fam Law 273, CA.
4   RSC Ord 90, r 3(2).

2   Commencement of proceedings

8.16   Where the originating summons is issued out of a district registry, the registrar must send the particulars of the summons to the Principal Registry for recording in the Register of Wards.[1] With the originating summons (whether issued out of the Principal Registry or a district registry) the plaintiff must file a copy of (1) the child's birth certificate or entry in the Adopted Children Register,[2] (2) a Certificate as to Other Proceedings, which must certify whether or not there are any matrimonial or other proceedings in which the child is involved and, if so, details thereof and (3) a Legal Aid Certificate, if any.

1   RSC Ord 90, r 3(3).
2   Ibid, r 3(3A). The originating summons must include the date of the child's birth. If the plaintiff fails to lodge a copy, he must apply at the first hearing of the summons for directions as to an alternative method of proof of birth.

8.17   With a copy of the originating summons there must also be served on the defendant a copy of the Notice of Wardship giving notice of the date on which the minor became a ward of court; that he may not marry or go outside the jurisdiction without the court's leave; that there should be no material change in the arrangements for his welfare, care and control or education without such leave; that where necessary a guardian will be appointed to present the ward's views to the court; and that the ward may approach the Official Solicitor for advice pending the formal appointment of a guardian. A copy of the notice should also be served on anyone who should be made aware of the wardship and on the minor, if his age and situation are such that he may be in need of advice or assistance.

8.18   The summons must be served no later than 12 calendar months after the date of issue, unless renewed by the court, and must not be served out of the jurisdiction except with its leave.[1] The defendant must within 14 days of service (inclusive of the day of service) acknowledge service.[2] If he fails to do so, the court may give such judgment or make such order against the defendant as it thinks just and expedient. After the acknowledgement of service or the defendant's failure to acknowledge within the time limit, the plaintiff must within 21 days of the issue of the summons apply for an appointment for attendance of the parties before the court.

1   An application for leave must be supported by affidavit; RSC Ord 11, r 4(1)(2) and r 9.
2   Ord 12, r 9.

3   Effect of issuing summons

8.19   This 21-day period is crucial in relation to the protection of the child. Protection begins from the time the originating summons is issued, but, if at the expiration of that period no application for an appointment for a hearing has been made, the child ceases to be a ward of court.[1] If such application has properly been made, wardship continues until on final determination of the summons the court decides whether or not to make an order confirming the wardship. But these rules do not affect the court's powers at any time to order that a ward of court shall cease to be so.[2] Nevertheless, the effect of immediate protection is that no 'material step' can be taken without the leave of the court. The procedure therefore runs the risk of being used as a device for delaying final determination of the dispute.[3]

1   Supreme Court Act 1981, s 41(2); RSC Ord 90, r 4(1). The failure to make the application within the period does not terminate the originating summons, so that an ordinary summons may later be issued reviving the wardship. However, a notice stating whether the applicant intends to proceed with the application must be left at the registry immediately after the expiration of the 21-day period; r 4(3).
2   Ord 90, r 4(2).
3   See Law Com Working Paper No 101, para 4.13.

4   Emergency injunction

8.20 Although the procedure provides for immediate protection once the originating summons is issued, urgent action may exceptionally be necessary before the issue, for example, to prevent the child being removed from a parent[1] or out of the jurisdiction.[2] The appropriate step is an application for an injunction which may, because of the emergency,[3] be made ex parte on affidavit.[4] This may be done by contacting the Clerk of the Rules at the Royal Courts of Justice or the district registry. A duty judge is available for out of hours emergencies, and can be contacted through the High Court at any time.[5] If an injunction is granted, it may and is likely to be on the terms that the intended plaintiff give an undertaking that an originating summons will be issued forthwith. Any delay on his part in doing so is a contempt of court and the failure of his solicitor, knowing of the undertaking, to implement it constitutes a grave breach of his duty to the court and may amount to aiding or abetting the contempt.[6]

1   Cf *L v L* [1969] P 25, [1969] 1 All ER 852.
2   *Re N (infants)* [1967] Ch 512, [1967] 1 All ER 161.
3   See *Re H (a minor)* [1985] 3 All ER 1, [1985] 1 WLR 1164, CA.
4   RSC Ord 29, r 1(1)–(3). It has been pointed out that the deponent should attend the hearing of the application in case difficulties arise or to give evidence on any matters arising since swearing the affidavit; see Clarke Hall and Morrison, para C [83].
5   On 01–936–6000.
6   *Refson (PS) & Co Ltd v Saggers* [1984] 3 All ER 111, [1983] 1 WLR 1025.

5   The hearing

(a)   The first appointment

8.21 This is very largely in the hands of the registrar. At the first appointment he gives directions concerning the filing and giving of evidence, the addition of other parties and the appointment of the Official Solicitor or a court welfare officer. He usually calls for a welfare report and adjourns the application for hearing before himself[1] or before the judge. In cases proceeding in the Principal Registry, except where exceptional circumstances are shown, the registrar should order that a child ceases to be a ward within three months of the first appointment, unless the case is brought before the judge within that period or application is made for extension.[2]

In dealing with custody cases attention was drawn[3] to the in-court conciliation scheme available in the Principal Registry in contested cases. The scheme also extends to contested care and control and access in wardship proceedings.[4] The power of a registrar in proceedings in the Principal Registry to direct that duly authorised circuit judges sit as Deputy High Court judges to hear cases was also there noted. This power equally extends to wardship cases, subject to the same exceptions as apply to custody cases.[5]

In a divorce court a registrar has no jurisdiction to make orders relating to custody, care and control except with the consent of the parties.[6] His powers in wardship are not expressly so limited, since he may 'transact all such business and exercise all such authority and jurisdiction as may be transacted and exercised by a judge in chambers'.[7] Nevertheless, he should not make an order for care and control or any other except with the consent of the parties.[8] Instead he should refer the making of a final order to the judge. When a case is referred to the judge, either party can then apply for a hearing, but the registrar should ensure that the case is brought before a judge within a reasonable time of the issuing of the originating summons, even if the parties are not ready.[9]

1   In proceedings in the Principal Registry the wardship application is reserved to a particular registrar.
2   See *Practice Direction* (16 July 1982, unreported) (noted in Supreme Court Practice Ord 90/3/13).
3   Ante, para 3.49, note 5.
4   See *Practice Direction* [1982] 3 All ER 988. [1982] 1 WLR 1420; and *Practice Direction* [1984] 3 All ER 800, [1984] 1 WLR 1326.
5   See *Practice Direction* [1985] FLR 536.
6   MCR 1977, r 92; *Practice Direction* [1977] 3 All ER 944, [1977] 1 WLR 1226.
7   RSC Ord 90, r 12(1).
8   See Ormrod LJ in *Re L (a minor) (wardship proceedings)* [1978] 2 All ER 318 at 320, [1978] 1 WLR 181 at 182; *Practice Direction* [1980] 1 All ER 813, [1980] 1 WLR 321.
9   *Stockport Metropolitan Borough Council v B; Stockport Metropolitan Borough Council v L* [1986] 2 FLR 80, [1986] Fam Law 187.

(b)   Final hearing

8.22   The final hearing may not take place until some months after the first appointment. The case will be heard in chambers unless exceptionally it is adjourned into open court,[1] for example, because it raises a matter of principle or because the court wishes to give it publicity.[2]

1   Under RSC Ord 32, r 13.
2   As in *Re Wolfe* [1958] CLY 1619, (1958) Times, 15 November (assistance of press sought to help trace missing child).

6   Evidence and reports

8.23   These matters have already been examined in relation to custody cases,[1] except for the report of the Official Solicitor.

1   See ante, paras 3.66–3.74.

7   The Official Solicitor[1]

(a)   Appointment as guardian ad litem

8.24   In the great majority of cases the child's interests will be sufficiently protected by a welfare officer's report,[2] and only where there are special reasons should the child be joined as a party.[3] Where he is, the Official

Solicitor should be the first person to be approached and asked whether he consents to be appointed guardian ad litem.[4] The appointment may be made by a judge or registrar, either of the court's own motion or on the application of a party. The kinds of cases in which he is usually appointed have been categorised[5] into:

(1) Cases where the ward is old enough to express an independent view.[6]
(2) 'Teenage wardships' where the parents are in dispute with the ward over his or her association with an allegedly undesirable person.
(3) Cases where the court requires a specific task or enquiry to be carried out, the most likely being a psychiatric examination of the ward.[7]
(4) Cases which involve a foreign element, as in abduction cases,[8] or a difficult point of law or other difficult questions, such as medico-legal problems over sterilisation,[9] life-saving operations,[10] or surrogacy arrangements.[11]

If the Official Solicitor accepts appointment[12] he acts both as guardian ad litem and as his own solicitor instead of requesting a solicitor in private practice to conduct proceedings on the child's behalf. This is the normal procedure in disputed wardship and custody cases, where the child's welfare is the central issue. If the Official Solicitor should already be acting for a party in the proceedings, for example, a parent who is a minor,[13] the ward's guardian ad litem should be a suitable near relative or a divorce court welfare officer from an area outside the area of the court making the order[14] or a guardian chosen from a panel set up under the Guardians Ad Litem and Reporting Officers (Panel) Regulations 1983, who would then instruct a solicitor.[15] Where the Official Solicitor is or becomes the guardian ad litem of the ward or of a party to the proceedings, the case must be dealt with in the High Court unless the nature of the issues of fact or law raised in the case makes it more suitable for trial in a county court.[16]

1 See generally Lowe and White, Chapter 9; Clarke Hall and Morrison, paras C [120]–[124]; Parry, Butterworths Family Law Service, paras E[134]–[137]; and for the comments of past and present holders of the office see Evans, *The Office of the Official Solicitor to the Supreme Court* (1966) 63 Law Soc Gaz 270–2, 335–7; Turner, *Wardship: the Official Solicitor's Role* (1977) 2 Adoption and Fostering 30; and Venables, *The Official Solicitor: Recent Developments* (1982) 3 Adoption and Fostering 45.
2 It is undesirable for the ward's views to be presented by persons who are officers of one of the parties to the proceedings, even if those officers are social workers; see *Re A (minors) (wardship: children in care)* (1979) 1 FLR 100. Moreover, if a party is proposing to appoint an independent social worker, the court's prior leave should be obtained, otherwise the social worker might be in breach of the general confidentiality of wardship proceedings; see *Re C (wardship: independent social workers)* [1985] FLR 56, [1985] Fam Law 56. See further on independent social workers ante, para 3.70, note 5.
3 See *Practice Direction* [1982] 1 All ER 319, [1982] 1 WLR 118; *Re C (a minor) (wardship proceedings)* [1984] FLR 419, [1984] Fam Law 273, CA.
4 *Re JD (wardship: guardian ad litem)* [1984] FLR 359, [1984] Fam Law 119; *Re C, supra,* note 3. If he consents but a party represents that some other person should be appointed, the registrar must refer the representation to a judge; see ibid.
5 See Venables, op cit; Lowe and White, paras 9–12 to 9–16.
6 But usually his view can equally effectively be communicated to the court through a welfare officer's report after the welfare officer has interviewed him.
7 See ante, para 3.69.
8 See ante, paras 3.105 et seq.
9 *Re D (a minor) (wardship: sterilisation)* [1976] Fam 185, [1976] 1 All ER 326, ante, para 1.32.

10   *Re B (a minor) (wardship: medical treatment)* [1981] 1 WLR 1421, ante para 1.37.
11   *Re C (a minor) (wardship: surrogacy)* [1985] FLR 846, [1985] Fam Law 191, ante, para 2.16.
12   Should he refuse on the ground that he considers the case is not suitable for appointment of a guardian ad litem, but the registrar considers it is, the matter should be referred to a judge; *Re JD (wardship: guardian ad litem)* [1984] FLR 359, [1984] Fam Law 119; *Re C (a minor) (wardship proceedings)* [1984] FLR 419, [1984] Fam Law 273, CA.
13   See *A v B and Hereford and Worcester County Council* [1986] 1 FLR 289, [1986] Fam Law 133.
14   See *Practice Direction* [1984] 1 All ER 69, [1984] 1 WLR 34.
15   For possible increased use of such guardians see Lowe and White, paras 9.18–9.20.
16   See *Practice Direction* [1986] 2 All ER 703, [1986] 1 WLR 1139, and ante, para 8.02.

(b)   Functions of Official Solicitor

8.25   As guardian ad litem the Official Solicitor investigates the case on behalf of the ward and represents his interests in the conduct of the proceedings,[1] but his discretion in so doing is not unfettered,[2] and on major decisions he will need to seek the court's approval or authority. This is most likely to happen where he considers it in the ward's interests that the latter undergo a psychiatric examination or be blood tested. As part of his investigations he must interview the ward, if old enough, the other parties and anyone else involved in the case. In the light of his investigations and interviews he must present before the court the evidence which he considers to be material.[3] Usually this is in the form of a written report, which sets out the details of his inquiries, the issues involved and the options available to the court. He has the option of making written submissions in the report or oral submissions at the hearing or both. He may also, if he wishes, make specific recommendations,[4] having regard to the child's best wishes.[5] Only in exceptional circumstances, where he considers disclosure of information might be harmful to the child, should he submit a confidential report. In those circumstances the court will exercise its discretion to refuse to disclose the contents, but it may as a compromise be willing, if the parties so agree, to disclose only to their counsel.[6]

1   See Goff J in *Re R(PM) (an infant)* [1968] 1 All ER 691, [1968] 1 WLR 385 at 692 and 387 respectively.
2   See *Re L (an infant)* [1968] P 119, [1968] 1 All ER 20 at 160 and 26 respectively.
3   He may, if he wishes, instruct counsel.
4   *Re W and W (minors)* (1975) 5 Fam Law 157, CA; *Re JD (wardship: guardian ad litem)* [1984] FLR 359, [1984] Fam Law 119.
5   But he is not to be seen as a welfare officer (*Re W and W (minors)*, supra, note 4) and his office does not generally offer a direct welfare service.
6   See *Re K (infants)* [1965] AC 201, [1963] 3 All ER 191, HL.

8.26   The responsibilities of the Official Solicitor do not necessarily end with the hearing of the application. He may be involved in implementation of the order or he may serve as a means of communication between the parties or of allowing a watch to be maintained over the ward.[1] Moreover, having acted as a guardian ad litem he remains an interested party, and therefore should be informed of any application in subsequent proceedings to obtain the confidential wardship papers and be given an opportunity to be heard on the application.[2]

1   See *Re JD (wardship: guardian ad litem)* [1984] FLR 359, [1984] Fam Law 119.
2   *Re H (a minor)* [1985] 3 All ER 1, [1985] 1 WLR 1164, CA.

8   Costs

8.27   The court has an unfettered discretion over costs.[1] Where it has of its own motion appointed the Official Solicitor as guardian ad litem, it may feel it appropriate to make no order as to costs or because, for example, of a party's conduct, to make that party pay the costs of the Official Solicitor.[2] In the case of a court appointment it is unusual to seek from a party any undertaking or security as to costs. Where, however, the Official Solicitor was appointed on the application of one or more of the parties, the court may decide that the party seeking his appointment should give a personal undertaking or security, and at the end of the hearing it might decide that he should bear all or a proportion of the Official Solicitor's costs[3] or that the parties jointly and severally should be responsible in such proportions as the court considers reasonable.

Where the proceedings are between the parents and both are acting in the ward's interest, it is unusual to make an order as to costs between the parties or an order for security for costs. A parent is entitled to put his case with regard to the welfare of the child and ought not to be prevented from doing so by means of an order for security for costs.[4]

1   *Re G (a minor) (wardship: costs)* [1982] 2 All ER 32, [1982] 1 WLR 438.
2   See ibid. Whenever parties are legally aided the Official Solicitor will not seek costs.
3   *Re PC (an infant)* [1961] Ch 312, [1961] 2 All ER 308.
4   *Re B (infants)* [1965] 2 All ER 651 at 652, [1965] 1 WLR 946 at 948. The court will want to hear the parties involved; see *H v H and C* [1969] 1 All ER 262, [1969] 1 WLR 208, CA.

9   Legal aid

8.28   Legal aid is available for wardship proceedings in the High Court or a county court, but there are two serious limitations for a prospective party. Firstly, legal aid must not be given unless the applicant has 'reasonable grounds for taking, defending or being a party to proceedings, and it may also be refused if it appears unreasonable that he should receive it in the particular circumstances of the case'.[1] Not only does this limitation leave the court with a wide discretion, but it also fails to indicate the matters to which reasonableness is to be related. It ought to be considered in relation to the question whether wardship is the most appropriate remedy for securing the child's best interests.[2] Secondly, the current qualifications of income and capital on which availability of legal aid is assessed are so low as to exclude many suitable parties. Because of the high cost of proceedings they may well feel unable to risk a wardship application, especially if they know that, even though successful in their application, they can be awarded costs out of the legal aid fund only in exceptional circumstances where it is just and equitable and the court is satisfied that the unassisted party will suffere severe financial hardship unless the order is made.[3]

When the work for which the legal aid certificate was granted has been completed the certificate should be discharged even though the wardship continues. If there is any need to take further steps, advice and assistance can be given under the Green Form Scheme, and if necessary a fresh application for legal aid should be submitted, including, where urgent action is demanded, an application for the issue of an emergency certificate.[4]

1 · Legal Aid Act 1974, s 7 and Sch 1.
2   See Lowe and White, para 4.48.
3   Legal Aid Act 1974, s 13. See also Lowe and White, paras 4.50–4.51.
4   See *Practice Note (Wardship Proceedings)* (1982) 13 Fam Law 161.

10   Appeals

8.29   Appeal from the registrar lies to a judge in chambers by way of rehearing.[1] Appeal from the judge lies to the Court of Appeal without leave[2] and thence, with leave, to the House of Lords. The power of an appellate court to set aside the decision of the court below has already been examined.[3]

1   RSC Ord 58, rr 1, 3(1).
2   See Supreme Court Act 1981, s 18(1)(h)(i), RSC Ord 58, r 6(2) and Ord 59.
3   See ante, para 3.81.

IV   THE LEGAL EFFECTS OF WARDSHIP

1   Introduction

8.30   The general effect of wardship is that all the parental powers and responsibilities in respect of the child vest in the court. In current legal terms it is said[1] that the court has custody,[2] but formerly it was seen as being guardian of the ward.[3] The change reflects the change in emphasis from protection of property to protection of the person of the ward. The guardianship operates from the moment the child becomes a ward of court, ie from the date of issuing the originating summons,[4] and from that moment no important step can be taken in his life without the court's consent[5], and decisions relating to his future are to be made by the court and not by orders.[6] This automatic protection, which is a unique feature of wardship, leaves the court with the ultimate responsibility for the child.[7] Although there is no precise test for determining what are 'important steps', the following will require the court's consent.

1   *Re W (JC) (infant)* [1964] Ch 202 at 210, [1963] 3 All ER 459 at 462, CA; *Re CB (a minor)* [1981] 1 All ER 16 at 24, [1981] 1 WLR 379 at 388.
2   In the wide sense, see ante, para 1.58.
3   *R v Gyngall* [1893] 2 QB 232 at 239, CA.
4   Ante, para 8.19.
5   *Re S (infants)* [1967] 1 All ER 202 at 209, [1967] 1 WLR 396 at 407, per Cross J.
6   *Stockport Metropolitan Borough Council v B; Stockport Metropolitan Borough Council v L* [1986] 2 FLR 80, [1986] Fam Law 187.
7   See Lord Scarman in *Re E (SA) (a minor)* [1984] 1 All ER 289 at 290, [1984] 1 WLR 156 at 159.

2   Acts requiring the court's consent

(a)   Marriage

8.31   One of the oldest rules of wardship, now given statutory effect, is that which forbids a ward of court marrying without the court's consent.[1] Where a marriage or attempted marriage[2] takes place without that consent, even though the parents consent,[3] either party to it[4] and any other person who has helped bring it about commits a contempt of court.[5] On present authority[6] liability is strict in that the restriction operates even if the participant is ignorant of the wardship, but the rule has understandably been strongly criticised,[7] and Lord Denning MR's suggestion (obiter),[8] that knowledge or intent should be required, may well commend itself to the court, if the point should directly arise.[9]

1   *Eyre v Countess of Shaftesbury* (1725) 2 P Wms 102; Marriage Act 1949, s 3(6).
2   *Warter v Yorke* (1815) 19 Ves 451.
3   *Wellesley v Duke of Beaufort* (1827) 2 Russ 1.
4   Ie including the ward, *Re Leigh, Leigh v Leigh* (1888) 40 Ch D 290, CA; *Re H's Settlement, H v H* [1909] 2 Ch 260.
5   *Re Crump (an infant)* (1963) 107 Sol Jo 682. A warning about this effect should be included in the Notice of Wardship; see ante, para 8.17.
6   *Herbert's Case* (1731) 3 P Wms 116, affd by *Re H's Settlement, H v H,* supra, note 4.
7   Miller, *Contempt of Court,* p 224; Munro (1977) 40 MLR 343.
8   *Re F (otherwise A) (a minor) (publication of information)* [1977] Fam 58 at 88, [1977] 1 All ER 114 at 122.
9   It seems already to be accepted that a clergyman or anyone else actively involved in celebrating the marriage will not be regarded as having contrived the marriage, provided that he has carried out all the necessary preliminary enquiries; *Re H's Settlement H v H* [1909] 2 Ch 260 at 264.

(b)   Removal from the jurisdiction

8.32   To take a ward out of England and Wales without the consent of the court, even though the parents consent, is similarly a contempt of court,[1] since it deprives the court of exercising its protective and supervisory powers over the ward. Here, too, ignorance of the wardship does not exclude contempt. Nor does the fact that removal was at the ward's instigation,[2] though both circumstances will be relevant to the exercise of the court's powers for contempt.

This restriction on removal is modified by the Family Law Act 1986, which enables a ward to be removed to another part of the United Kingdom, ie Scotland or Northern Ireland,[3] if either (1) divorce, nullity or judicial separation proceedings relating to the marriage of the ward's parents are continuing there[4] or (2) the ward is habitually resident there.[5] But in either case, if that other part is Scotland the ward must be under 16 in order to be lawfully removed.[6] Additionally, removal to any other place is permitted if made either with the consent of the appropriate court[7] in the other part of the United Kingdom or by the court before which divorce, nullity or judicial separation proceedings are continuing.[8]

1   A warning about this effect should be endorsed on the originating summons and included in the Notice of Wardship; see ante, paras 8.12 and 8.17. Semble, an attempt to remove is also contempt (cf *Warter v Yorke* supra, para 8.31, note 2); but there may be difficulty in deciding at what point preparation to remove the child amounts to attempt—see *Balogh v St. Albans Crown Court* [1975] QB 73, [1974] 2 All ER 283, and Lowe and White, para 8.4.
2   *Re J (an infant)* (1913) 108 LT 554.
3   See FLA 1986, s 42(1).
4   See also ibid, s 42(4).
5   Section 38(1) and (2).
6   Ibid.
7   Ie in Northern Ireland the High Court and in Scotland the Court of Session; see ibid, ss 40 and 32.
8   See s 38(3)(b)

8.32A It has already been pointed out[1] that an order restricting removal of a child under 16 out of the United Kingdom or any specified part of it has effect in other parts as if it had been made by the appropriate court[2] in that other part.[3] Moreover, if the order prohibits removal from England and Wales without leave of the court but the child has, for example, been taken to Scotland, it automatically has effect in Scotland as if including a provision prohibiting further removal except back to England.[4]

Where an order prohibiting removal of a child is in force, the court which made the order or by which, in accordance with the above rule, the order is treated as having been made, may require any person to surrender any United Kingdom passport which has been issued to the child or contains particulars of the child.[5]

1   Ante, para 3.22.
2   Ie in England and Wales or Northern Ireland, the High Court and in Scotland, the Court of Session; see FLA 1986, ss 40 and 32.
3   FLA 1986, s 36(1), (2)(a) and (4).
4   Ibid, s 36(2)(b).
5   Ibid, s 37.

(c) Adoption, guardianship and custodianship

8.33 The consent of the court is necessary before proceedings may be commenced to adopt, or to free for adoption, or to obtain a custodianship order in respect of, a ward of court.[1] The fact that parental agreement to proposed adoption is forthcoming does not relieve the applicants of the duty to obtain the court's consent. On the other hand, that consent does not remove the need for parental agreement to adoption. If leave is given, the court in suitable cases may direct that the adoption or freeing for adoption or custodianship proceedings may be commenced in the appropriate county court, for example, where adoption or freeing for adoption will not be contested by a natural parent. Such an order should also include a direction that, in the event of the making of an adoption order or custodianship order, the wardship be discontinued.[2]

1   *F v S (adoption: ward)* [1973] Fam 203, [1973] 1 All ER 722, CA; *Re F (wardship: adoption)* [1984] FLR 60, 13 Fam Law 259, CA. On applications for leave see RSC Ord 90, rule 4A, as substituted by RSC (Amendment) 1988, SI 1988/298, r 8. The application must be made by summons in the relevant wardship proceedings; see *Practice Direction* [1985] 2 All ER 832, [1985] 1 WLR 924.
2   *Practice Direction* [1986] 2 All ER 832, [1986] 1 WLR 933, as extended by *Practice Direction* (23 July 1987 unreported) at Supreme Court Practice 1988, 2nd Supplement, p 61.

8.34 The court's consent for the marriage or adoption of a ward of court is, it is submitted, based on the premiss that, since they involve a change of the child's status, ex hypothesi each constitutes an important step in his life. On the same basis consent, it is submitted, is needed for an application to be made for a person to be appointed a guardian or a custodian of the ward.[1] An application for guardianship, it will be remembered,[2] is only possible where there is no parent, no guardian and no other person having parental rights with respect to him.[3] Such an application might, therefore, for example, be appropriate by relatives of a ward of court on the death of the ward's surviving parent who was given care and control of his child under an order made in the wardship proceedings. Where leave is given to apply for guardianship there should be a direction that, if a guardianship order is made, the wardship is discontinued.[4]

1   A similar view is taken by Lowe and White, para 5.7.
2   Ante, para 4.13.
3   GMA 1971, s 5.
4   Compare adoption supra, para 8.33.

8.35   An application for a custodianship order will only be feasible where the applicant already has care and control, since otherwise he will not be able to meet the requirements of section 33 of the Children Act 1975 with regard to the child already having his home with him for one of the requisite periods imposed by the section.[1] Even if leave to apply is given and a custodianship order is made, the residual parental powers and responsibilities of wardship which are not embodied within the concept of legal custody will remain vested in the court, so that a direction, when leave is given, that wardship be discontinued would not be appropriate. It seems very unlikely that a person entitled to care and control under wardship will want to 'convert' his care and control into legal custody.

1   See ante, paras 6.04–6.06.

(d)   Change of caretaker[1]

8.36   If a local authority wishes to place a ward of court with long-term foster parents with a view to adoption, leave of the court to do so must be obtained before the placement,[2] but it is not necessary that the foster parents should already have been selected.[3] Where such leave has been granted, it is not necessary for an application to be made for leave to commence adoption proceedings or freeing for adoption proceedings or custodianship proceedings unless the court otherwise directs.[4]

If there is evidence that the ward will never be rehabilitated with his parents and it is in his best interests to be placed with long-term foster parents with a view to adoption, access should not be granted to the natural parents.[5]

1   This term is used by Clarke Hall and Morrison, para C [89], and Lowe and White, para 5.7.
2   *Re F (wardship: adoption)* [1984] FLR 60, [1984] Fam Law 259, CA; *Practice Direction* [1985] 2 All ER 832, [1985] 1 WLR 294. The summons by which leave is sought must be served on every other party not less than two clear days before the day specified in the summons for the hearing in accordance with RSC Ord 32, r 3; see *Re P, Lincolnshire County Council v P* (1987) Times, 10 August, CA.
3   *Practice Direction* [1986] 1 All ER 652, [1986] 1 WLR 286. Where a local authority in wardship proceedings intends to ask the court for directions for the placement of the ward with long-term foster parents with a view to adoption and the originating summons has not been amended to show that intention, notice should be given in good time to the natural parent's solicitors; *Re W (a minor) (wardship: adoption)* (1982) 3 FLR 356, 12 Fam Law 147, CA.
4   RSC Ord 90, r 4A(2), as substituted by RSC (Amendment) 1988 SI 1988/298, r 8.
5   *Re K (minors) (access)* [1988] Fam Law 340, CA.

(e)   Change of whereabouts

8.37   A party to wardship proceedings must inform the registry of any change in the ward's whereabouts.[1] Whether it is necessary after the hearing for any interested person, in practice the person who has the care and control of the ward, to obtain the prior consent of the court to any change of residence would seem to depend on its nature and the extent to which it will affect the present wardship arrangements.[2] For example, a move within the neighbourhood may not significantly affect access arrangements; a move to another part of the country clearly would, in which case prior consent would be necessary. It is suggested that, as with wardship generally, wherever there is doubt it is wiser to err on the side of caution and seek consent. The Notice of Wardship,[3] it should be remembered, warns that there should be no material change in the care and control of the ward without the court's leave.

1   RSC Ord 90, r 3(6).
2   See Lowe and White, para 5.14.
3   Ante, para 8.17.

(f)   Education and career

8.38   The same warning is given with regard to education. Most changes, however, will not be seen as 'material', for example, moving from a primary to a secondary school, and will require no more than a note of information to the registry. Aliter, where there is a significant difference in the kind of education provided, for example,[1] transfer to a school providing for special educational needs under the Education Act 1981, when the court's prior consent will be necessary.

It seems that a 16 year-old ward who has left school and is about to embark on a particular career does not require the court's consent before he may do so, but apparently, if that career, for example in the armed forces, is likely to take him out of the jurisdiction, he will require the court's approval before he leaves.[2] If it be the law that a ward may choose his career without leave of the court, it accords with the *Gillick* principle. Nevertheless, where the intended occupation is intrinsically dangerous to life, limb or health, any person who has been given care and control of the ward should be advised to notify the court in advance of the ward's intention. That will put the onus on the court to decide whether it can and should intervene.

1   See Lowe and White, para 5.15.
2   Lowe and White, paras 5.4 and 5.5.

(g)   Medical matters

8.39   It has already been noted[1] that the leave of the Court is a prerequisite to sterilisation of a minor child, at least if he is under 16 and possibly even if he has reached that age,[2] as semble it is in respect of other seriously important medical matters, whether the child is or is not already a ward of court. Subject to that rule, where persons are in dispute over whether a child should receive medical treatment, the onus can be placed on the Court to resolve the problem by making the child a ward of court. Subject to the same rule, more difficult to determine is the need to obtain the court's prior consent to medical examination and treatment of a child who is already a ward of court and those who have been granted care and control of him are not in dispute over the matter. Examination and treatment need separate consideration.

1   Ante, para 1.35.
2   Paragraph 1.43.

(i) Examination

8.40   *(i)   Physical*   It is at least clear that leave of the court is not required to subject the ward to a physical examination where neither psychiatric nor psychological examination is involved.[1] Thus, the caretaker, whose ward shows symptoms of physical illness, can take him to the family doctor, and can consent to school medical and dental examinations.

1   *Practice Direction* [1985] 3 All ER 576, [1985] 1 WLR 1289. See also *Barnes v Tyrrell* (1981) 3 FLR 240, CA.

8.41   *(ii)   Psychiatric*   It has already been pointed out[1] that any psychiatric or psychological examination of the child with a view to a report being submitted in evidence is subject to the leave of the court.[2] The court should normally make such an order only if the child is separately represented and the application is supported by his representative or if the application is supported by a local authority having the care or supervision of the child. An order should not normally be made unless there is, or is suspected to be, a specific and identifiable problem or potential problem on which the court needs assistance which can only or most conveniently be provided by a qualified psychiatrist or psychologist.[3] Where leave is given, the costs of the examination and report will normally be allowed on taxation, but where it has not been obtained the court may refuse to admit the report in evidence, and may direct that the costs of obtaining any examination or report should be disallowed.[4]

Apparently this requirement to obtain leave is not limited to examinations connected with court proceedings, but is also applicable where a ward of court is psychologically or neurologically ill and his caretaker wishes him to be examined.[5] Where there are proceedings and the Official Solicitor, having been appointed to act on behalf of the ward, has instructed medical experts to advise him, it is vital that they should not be impeded in their investigations. On the contrary, any member of the medical profession who has been instructed by a party to the proceedings should actively consult with the Official Solicitor and his experts.[6]

1   Ante, para 3.69.
2   See *Re S (infants)* [1967] 1 All ER 202, [1967] 1 WLR 396; *Re R (PM) (an infant)* [1968] 1 All ER 691 n, [1968] 1 WLR 385; *B (M) v B(R)* [1968] 3 All ER 170, [1968] 1 WLR 1182, CA; *Re A-W (minors)* (1974) 5 Fam Law 95. The rule is now embodied in a *Practice Direction* [1985] 1 All ER 832, [1985] 1 WLR 360; and see infra.
3   *Practice Direction* [1985] 3 All ER 576, [1985] 1 WLR 1289.
4   *Practice Direction* [1985] 1 All ER 832, [1985] 1 WLR 360. There is also the possibility of contempt of court.
5   The relevant *Practice Direction* (see previous note) states: 'It is a firmly established principle in wardship cases that the minor should not be subjected to psychiatric examination without leave of the court'. For comment see Lowe and White, para 5.19.

6   See the guidance given by Butler-Sloss J to the medical profession in *Re C (minors) (wardship: medical evidence)* [1987] 1 FLR 418, [1987] Fam Law 162, where the father's consultant had advised the father to make a tape recording of access visits and had himself engaged in a series of independent investigations without reference to the Official Solicitor and his medical adviser.

(ii) Treatment

8.42   The difficulty for the person who has the care and control of a ward of court is determining when he may authorise treatment without reference to the court.[1] The principle to be borne in mind is that 'no important step in the life of [the] child can be taken without the consent of the court',[2] but its application to medical treatment creates problems over the importance to be given to particular treatment. In this regard it is to be noted that application can be made to a judge at very short notice.[3] Therefore, it is submitted, the rule that emergency treatment may be given without consent should be narrowly construed. On the one hand, treatment for minor ailments or chronic conditions, such as asthma, do not require reference. On the other hand, treatment for such serious non-therapeutic purposes as abortion,[4] sterilisation and organ transplants[5] obviously do, and from what has already been stated[6] reliance should not be placed on the *Gillick* principle, even if the ward has the intellectual understanding to give his own consent to any of those kinds of treatment, nor, possibly, on the fact that he has attained the age of 16. The same considerations should apply to the giving of contraceptive treatment.[7] But between these limits of minor clinical treatment and serious non-therapeutic treatment lies a grey area of uncertainty. Would, for example, the leave of the court be necessary to perform a tonsillectomy or for an operation for cosmetic purposes?

1   It has been urged that a Practice Direction should be issued giving detailed guidance on the kind of treatment requiring prior court sanction; see Lowe and White, para 5.23.
2   Per Heilbron J in *Re D (a minor) (wardship: sterilisation)* [1976] Fam 185, [1976] 1 All ER 326.
3   See Balcombe J in *Re G-U (a minor) (wardship)* [1984] FLR 811, [1984] Fam Law 248.
4   *Re G-U.* See Radevesky, *Wardship and Abortion* (1980) 130 NLJ 813; Lowe, *Wardship and Abortion—A Reply* (1981) 131 NLJ 561.
5   See ante, paras 1.31–1.40.
6   Paragraph 1.36.
7   For support for this view see White, *The Court's Responsibility in Wardship* (1984) 14 Fam Law 250 at 251. Lowe and White (op cit para 5.17) suggest that leave is not necessary to give medical *advice* to a ward, but admit as an exception to the principle advice to a female ward about contraception.

8.43   One firm rule is that no application for compulsory admission of a ward to hospital under Part II of the Mental Health Act 1983 can be made without leave of the court.[1] Nor can the powers of the nearest relative under the Act be exercised except with the court's leave.[2] Moreover, the Act does not authorise the making of a guardianship application[3] in respect of a ward of court and a ward may not be transferred into guardianship,[4] a veto which apparently recognises that the guardianship already vested in the court is not to be disturbed.[5]

1   Section 33(1).
2   Section 33(2).
3   Under s 7.

4   See s 33(3).
5   Cf Hoggett, *Mental Health Law*, 2nd edn, p 79.

(iii) Blood tests

8.44   It seems clear that to take a blood test of a ward of court in order
to establish paternity is an important step and therefore it will require
the leave of the court. From what has been said with regard to consent
to medical treatment,[1] the consent of the person having care and control
of a child under 16[2] does not govern, and arguably the court's consent
is equally required where the *Gillick* principle applies and possibly even
where the ward has reached the age of 16.[3] In accordance with the principle
already noted,[4] the court[5] will refuse leave if satisfied that it is against
the ward's interests to be blood tested.[6] The same principle, it is submitted,
applies to the use of DNA fingerprinting of the child.

1   See ante, paras 1.26 et seq.
2   FLRA 1969, s 21(3).
3   Ante, para 1.43.
4   Ante, para 2.37.
5   An application for blood tests in wardship proceedings must be dealt with in the High
     Court unless the nature of the issues of fact or law raised in the case makes them
     more suitable for trial in a county court and unless to do so would cause undue delay
     or hardship to any party or other person involved; see *Practice Direction* [1988] 2 All
     ER 103, [1988] 1 WLR 558.
6   *S v S: W v Official Solicitor* [1972] AC 24, [1970] 3 All ER 107, HL.

(h) Publicity

8.45   Wardship proceedings are held in the privacy of chambers, and it
is a contempt of court knowingly[1] to publish, whether in written or oral
form,[2] any information relating to them, unless it is with the leave of the
court, which, for example, is sometimes given in order to help trace a
missing ward,[3] or unless judgment is delivered in open court, which is usually
done where the wardship is concerned with a matter of major importance.[4]
The prohibition, which is contained in section 12(1)(a) of the Administration
Act 1960, extends not only to the proceedings before the judge or registrar[5]
but also to matters prior to and consequent upon the hearing, such as
pleadings, documentary evidence, reports of the Official Solicitor or a welfare
officer and documents in the possession of a local authority.[6] Leave must
be obtained to disclose evidential documents to every person who is not
a party, for example, to psychiatrists, psychologists and medical experts
or to any other person.[7] Disclosure without prior leave may be a contempt
of court, and this is none the less the case where the purpose of the disclosure
is only to obtain advice from the expert concerned whether relevant expert
evidence would be forthcoming or would be helpful to the court.[8] The
prohibition does not, however, impose a total ban on publication. It relates
to the wardship proceedings not to the state of wardship,[9] so that statements
about a ward's achievements or other information unconnected with the
proceedings are permissible.

A publication is punishable as contempt only if it would be so punishable
otherwise than by virtue of the Administration of Justice Act 1960.[10] This
means that it must amount to contempt at common law. That requires
mens rea,[11] but it is not certain whether knowledge of the wardship
proceedings suffices or whether it must also be known that publication

of such proceedings is prohibited by law.[12] Even if there is this additional requirement, it should not normally be difficult to establish knowledge of prohibition now that it is the practice, following that relating to welfare officers' reports,[13] to endorse the Official Solicitor's report with a clear warning that it be treated as confidential. It is, however, now clear that a person who in good faith publishes information about a ward which has been prohibited by an order of the court but who does not know of the order does not commit contempt of court.[14] Moreover, an order prohibiting publication of information by a newspaper is a prohibitory injunction and it requires personal service of the order unless the court has dispensed with personal service on the grounds that it was just to do so,[15] or unless it is impracticable to serve the injunction and the newspaper subscribes to the Press Association, in which case the inference *may* be drawn that there was sufficient knowledge of the restriction on publication.[16]

Usually the court will give leave to publish only where publication is in the ward's interests, and those interests may demand restrictions on the information published, for example, that the ward's identity should not be disclosed, which may mean prohibiting publication of the identity of the parents or other persons connected with the ward.[17] Exceptionally, the court may give consent to publication where it is in the public interest, but then only if publication will not harm the ward's interests.[18]

1   For the requisite knowledge see infra.
2   See Lowe and White, op cit, pp 169–170.
3   See, for example, *Re Wolfe* [1958] CLY 1619, (1958) Times, 15 November. Leave is given by way of an invitation to the media to assist with publicity, but there is no power to order publication. Nor, on the other hand, should the media approach the judge direct, save in very exceptional circumstances.
4   For example, surrogacy; see ante, para 2.16. The court may impose restrictions on publication in relation to a judgment given in open court; see *Re T (AJJ) (an infant)* [1970] Ch 688 at 689.
5   Administration of Justice Act 1960, s 12(3).
6   Thus, a distinction is to be drawn between a local authority's records which have been prepared for the wardship proceedings and those which have not. Publication of the former requires leave of the court; of the latter does not, and thus the local authority in its discretion may make them available, for example, to the police; *Re S (minors) (wardship: police investigation)* [1987] Fam 199, [1987] 3 All ER 1076.
7   For example, an independent social worker. See *Re C (Wardship: Independent Social Worker)* [1985] FLR 56, [1985] Fam Law 56. See also *Practice Direction (minor: independent reporter)* [1983] 1 All ER 1097, [1983] 1 WLR 416, which forbids an independent social worker seeing a welfare report.
8   See *Practice Direction*, [1987] 3 All ER 640, [1987] 1 WLR 1421.
9   *Re F (otherwise A) (a minor) (publication of information)* [1977] Fam 58, [1977] 1 All ER 114, CA.
10   See s 12(4).
11   See *Re F (otherwise A), supra. See also Re L (a minor) (wardship: freedom of publication)* [1988] 1 All ER 418 at 422.
12   See ibid; Lowe and White, op cit, pp 171–173; and Lowe, *Wardship Contempt and Freedom of Speech* (1977) 93 LQR 180.
13   See *Practice Direction* [1984] 1 All ER 827, [1984] 1 WLR 446.
14   *X County Council v A* [1985] 1 All ER 53, [1984] 1 WLR 1422. It must be established that the alleged contemnor has knowledge of the material term of the order; *Re L (a minor) (wardship: freedom of publication)* [1988] 1 All ER 418. Any order restricting publication must be clear and precise in its terms, the boundaries of restriction must be defined and the persons against whom the order is intended to be effective must be identified; see ibid.
15   See *Re L* [1988] 1 All ER 418 at p 421.
16   *Re W (minor)* (1988) Times, 30 April.

17   *X County Council v A*, supra; *A v C* [1985] FLR 445, CA; *Re C (a minor) (wardship: surrogacy)* [1985] FLR 846, [1985] Fam Law 191; *Re P (minors) (wardships: surrogacy)* [1987] 2 FLR 421, [1987] Fam Law 414; *Re W (minors)*, supra, note 16.
18   *Re R (MJ) (a minor) (publication of transcript)* [1975] Fam 89, [1975] 2 All ER 749; *Re F (minors)* (1988) Times, 23 July, CA. Compare *Re J (a minor) (wardship)* [1984] FLR 535, [1984] Fam Law 308, where to have allowed a psychiatrists report on the ward, which had been given in wardship proceedings, to be used by the mother in criminal proceedings would not have been in the ward's interests.

8.46   Parties to wardship procedings may obtain transcripts of the proceedings without the leave of the court, but those who are not parties may do so only in special circumstances, and by leave of the judge, who has an unfettered discretion in what may be disclosed.[1] Any application to obtain confidential papers filed in wardship for use in subsequent proceedings, if made at all, should not be made ex parte or without informing the Official Solicitor, if he acted as guardian at litem, because all interested parties should have an opportunity to be heard. If the subsequent proceedings are criminal proceedings, it is preferable that such an application is made by the Director of Public Prosecutions, once he has ascertained that there is a proper case.[2] Where there are subsequent criminal investigations the court must balance the interest of the ward against the public interest that requires that no obstacle should be placed to hamper the police in the course of their investigations. The protection afforded to the ward by the exercise of the wardship jurisdiction should not be extended so as to give protection to a criminal offender. The court must consider as a matter of public policy the need to safeguard the ward and other children against any harm which they might suffer as a result of recurring crimes by undetected criminals.[3] Thus, where the wardship court is involved at an early stage in the criminal process before the child has been interviewed by the police, the court must decide whether or not to grant leave for him to be interviewed and in so deciding must perform a balancing exercise, weighing the potential damage to the child against the public interest as a responsible parent would do; and in reaching a decision the best interests of the child might not be the first and paramount consideration. However, if the child has been interviewed before being warded, the court should decline to exercise jurisdiction. There is then no need for the Crown Prosecution Service to seek the leave of the wardship court to call the ward as a witness and it would be contrary to public policy to involve the wardship jurisdiction.[4]

1   *Practice Direction* [1972] 1 All ER 1056, [1972] 1 WLR 443; *Re F (minors)* (1988) Times, 23 July, CA.
2   *Re H (a minor)* [1985] 3 All ER 1, [1985] 1 WLR 1164, CA.
3   See *Re S (minors) (wardship: police investigation)* [1987] Fam 199, [1987] 3 All ER 1076, where the court in wardship proceedings granted leave for the disclosure of medical records and video recordings of diagnostic interviews at a special clinic for sexually abused children, and for leave for the police to interview the children and to subject them to medical examination.
4   See *Re K (minors) (wardship: criminal proceedings)* [1988] Fam 1, [1988] 1 All ER 214.

8.46A   Recent Practice Directions concerning leave to interview wards of court who are the alleged victims of child abuse reflect the increasing importance which is being attached to achieving a delicate balance between the interest of the ward and those of the public.

Where leave is given, the order should, unless there is some special reason which requires the contrary, give leave for any number of interviews which may be required by the prosecution or the police.[1] If it is desired to conduct any interview beyond what is permitted by the order, further application should be made for this purpose. No evidence or documents in the wardship proceedings or information about those proceedings should be disclosed in the criminal proceedings without the prior leave of the wardship court.[2]

All applications must be made to a judge on summons on notice to all parties,[3] except that application for leave may be made ex parte without notice to a party where he may become the subject of a criminal investigation and it is considered necessary for the ward to be able to be interviewed without that party knowing that the police are making enquiries. Notice should, however, where practicable, be given to the guardian ad litem.[4]

Sometimes the police need to deal with complaints or alleged offences concerning wards in circumstances where it is appropriate for action to be taken straight away without the prior leave of the wardship court. In such circumstances[5] the police should notify the parent or foster parent with whom the ward is living or other 'appropriate adult',[6] so that that adult has the opportunity of being present when the police interview the ward. If practicable, any guardian ad litem should also be notified and invited to attend or nominate a third party to do so. The guardian should be supplied with a record of the interview or any statement made by the ward. Where the ward has been interviewed without the guardian's knowledge he should be informed at the earliest opportunity and notified that the police wish to conduct further interviews, if such is the case. The wardship court should be appraised of the situation at the earliest opportunity by the guardian ad litem, the parent, foster parent (through the local authority) or other responsible adult.[7]

Where a party proposes that a ward be (a) medically examined to establish whether sexual abuse has taken place; or (b) subjected to questioning by police officers; or (c) subjected to questioning involving the use of anatomically correct dolls, an application for leave should be brought inter partes, save in exceptional circumstances, and heard by a judge of the Family Division.[8]

1 See *Practice Direction* [1988] 1 All ER 223, [1987] 1 WLR 1739. A special reason for not allowing a series of interviews without leave could, for example, be the ward's state of health.
2 See ibid.
3 See ibid.
4 See *Practice Direction* [1988] 2 All ER 1015, [1988] 1 WLR 989.
5 For examples, see ibid.
6 Ie within the Home Office Code of Practice for the Detention, Treatment and Questioning of Persons issued under the Police and Criminal Evidence Act 1984; see post, paras 12.54 et seq.
7 See *Practice Direction* [1988] 2 All ER 1015.
8 *KSM v CG and MCC* [1988] Fam Law 173.

8.46B A Practice Direction also governs disclosure where the ward has a right to make a claim for compensation to the Criminal Injuries Compensation Board.[1] Application must be made by the guardian ad litem for leave to apply and to disclose to the Board such documents on the wardship proceedings file as are considered necessary to establish eligibility and quantum. If leave has not been given by the judge at the wardship hearing, application may be made ex parte to a registrar by the guardian or, if no guardian has been appointed, by the Director of Social Services of the local authority having the care of the child, or by the person(s) having care and control. Any order giving leave should state that any award made by the Board be paid into court immediately on receipt, and application made forthwith thereafter to the court as to its management and administration unless the judge or registrar otherwise directs.

1   See [1988] 1 All ER 182.

V   ORDERS

1   The welfare of the ward

8.47   The effect of wardship is to vest in the court custody in the wide sense.[1] Its essence is that the court remains in control of, and has ultimate responsibility for, the child,[2] but the court can delegate and can exercise a wide range of powers relating to the person and property of the ward. The weight to be attached to his welfare and interests depends on whether the court is exercising its custodial or protective jurisdiction.

1   See ante, para 1.58.
2   See Ormrod LJ in *Re CB (a minor) (wardship: local authority)* [1981] 1 All ER 16 at 24, [1981] 1 WLR 379 at 380; Lord Scarman in *Re E (SA) (a minor: wardship)* [1984] 1 All ER 289 at 290, [1984] 1 WLR 156 at 159.

(a)   Custodial jurisdiction

8.48   Where the wardship proceedings relate to the custody or upbringing of the ward or the administration of his property, the exercise of jurisdiction is governed by the principle in section 1 of the Guardianship of Minors Act 1971 that the ward's welfare is the first and paramount consideration.[1] The section is explicit: the principle applies to 'proceedings before any court', unless excluded by statute.[2] However, it is now established that the section applies only where the child's legal custody or upbringing or the administration of his property is *directly* in issue.[3] The main factors that in practice are taken into account in applying the section have been considered in Chapter 3.[4]

1   Where a wardship application and an application under the Matrimonial Homes Act 1983 are heard together, it is quite proper for the wardship application to be decided first on the basis of the paramountcy of the child's welfare and for the decision to be taken into account as one of the considerations relevant to the MHA 1983 application; see *Re T (a minor) (wardship) T v T (ouster order)* [1987] FLR 181, [1986] Fam Law 298, CA.
2   As it is in respect of adoption proceedings and care proceedings see ante, para 3.03.
3   *Richards v Richards* [1984] AC 174, [1983] 2 All ER 807; see ante, para 3.04.
4   See paras 3.05 to 3.13.

(b)   The protective jurisdiction

8.49   Although protection of the ward lies at the heart of wardship, the distinction between the court's custodial and protective jurisdiction was not judicially recognised until the decision of the House of Lords in *S* *v S: W v Official Solicitor*,[1] and, as has been pointed out,[2] there is still no express reference by the courts to this protective jurisdiction in wardship cases.[3] Nevertheless, there is now a body of case law which recognises that section 1 of the GMA 1971 is not applicable to all matters raised in wardship proceedings and that, where it is not, the weight to be attached to the interests of the ward is variable. If there are no competing interests, the court will apply the paramountcy principle. This will operate, for example, where the question is whether the ward should receive non-therapeutic treatment. It was on this basis that the House of Lords held in *Re B (a minor) (wardship: sterilisation)*[4] that as a last resort it was in her best interests that a girl should be sterilised. On the other hand, the paramountcy principle may be excluded in order to protect wider interests, such as freedom of publication[5] or control of immigration of children[6], even though the effect may be harmful to the child. The question is the degree of harm that the court is prepared to allow. In *Re X (a minor) (wardship: jurisdiction)*[7] the step-father of a 14-year-old girl made her a ward of court in order to restrain the publication of a book which contained in one chapter descriptions of the ward's deceased father's alleged depraved sexual malpractices. There was evidence that the girl was psychologically fragile and highly strung, and the applicant feared that publication was likely to be psychologically grossly damaging to the ward. The Court of Appeal held that, although wardship jurisdiction is unrestricted in protecting the ward, it should be exercised within limits and with due regard to the rights of others, which the court also has a duty to protect. In the circumstances the jurisdiction should not have been invoked to interfere with the right of freedom of publication, which was already sufficiently circumscribed at common law and by statute.[8] That does not mean that that freedom must always prevail over the interests of a ward. Thus, in *X County Council v A*,[9] the court prohibited any publication by the media at large of any information which could identify the ward or her whereabouts. It has been pointed out[10] that 'the key difference' between those two cases is that in the former the kind of information, if published, could only have indirectly harmed the ward, whereas in the latter it would have directly done so. It follows that, if there is no harm, direct or indirect, there is no justification for invoking the protective jurisdiction. So, in *Re R (MJ) (a minor) (publication of transcript)*,[11] the court allowed a copy to be obtained of a transcript of wardship proceedings for use in a subsequent bankruptcy hearing, since no legitimate interest of the ward would thereby be harmed. On the other hand, in *Re J (a minor) (wardship)*,[12] it refused a mother who was charged with inflicting grievous bodily harm on her 13-year-old daughter leave to use in her defence in the criminal proceedings a psychiatrist's report on the girl which had been given when the girl was earlier made a ward of court. The girl was the main prosecution witness and the purpose of disclosure of the report was to show that she was mentally disturbed and that her evidence was pure fabrication. Leave was refused on the grounds that availability of the report would harm the ward's interests.[13]

---

1   [1972] AC 24, [1970] 3 All ER 107. See Lord MacDermott at 47–51 and 113–118 and Lord Hodson at 59 and 124 respectively.
2   Lowe and White, op cit, p 147.
3   *S v S: W v Official Solicitor* was concerned with an issue of paternity arising in divorce proceedings and whether to order a blood test of a child. It was held that a court

should order a blood test unless it was shown to be against the child's interests. It is submitted that, if similarly the issue were to arise in wardship proceedings in respect of a ward of court, the same rule would be applied and would fall within the scope of the court's protective jurisdiction as described hereunder.

4   [1988] AC 199, [1987] 2 All ER 206. See ante, para 1.33. The Court of Appeal recognised that s 1 of GMA 1971 was not relevant. The House of Lords did not advert to that point, but without reference to protective jurisdiction took it for granted that the paramount consideration for the exercise of jurisdiction was the welfare and best interests of the ward.

5   *Re X (a minor) (wardship: jurisdiction)* [1975] Fam 47, [1975] 1 All ER 697, CA.

6   *Re Mohamed Arif* [1968] Ch 643, sub nom *Re A* [1968] 2 All ER 145, CA; see also *Re S (minors)* (1980) 11 Fam Law 55, CA. Any relief for impropriety on the part of the immigration authorities must be sought by way of judicial review.

7   See supra note 5.

8   This conclusion exaggerates the importance of freedom of publication in the particular case. As has been pointed out (Markesinis, [1985] CLJ 209 at 210), the book contained only eight pages of offending material which could have been removed at very small cost for which the parents of the ward were willing to pay.

9   [1985] 1 All ER 53, [1984] 1 WLR 1422.

10   Lowe and White, op cit, p 139. For qualified approval of the later decision see Markesinis (supra, note 8).

11   [1975] Fam 89, [1975] 2 All ER 749.

12   [1984] FLR 535, [1984] Fam Law 308.

13   The mother also wanted her daughter to be examined by a psychiatrist. This was refused for the same reason.

8.50   In exercising its wardship jurisdiction, whether custodial or protective, the court is not necessarily confined to deciding the issues raised by the parties as in a normal adversarial dispute. Exceptionally it may decide on a course of action not advocated by any party to the proceedings. In *Re E (SA) (a minor) (wardship)*,[1] a local authority had sought an order that a ward be committed to its care with a view to adoption. The ward's father strongly opposed this proposal and had sought an order that care and control of the ward be committed to him. The father succeeded before the trial judge, and the local authority successfully appealed to the Court of Appeal. The House of Lords in the course of the father's appeal considered a third option, namely, committing the ward to the care and control of the local authority but granting access to the father under the supervision of the court welfare officer, in order to see whether father and son could develop a sound relationship, and it remitted the case back to the trial judge with directions, inter alia, to that effect.

1   [1984] 1 All ER 289, [1984] 1 WLR 156, HL.

2   Kinds of orders

(a)   Care and control[1]

8.51   The most frequent order is that granting care and control of the ward, usually to a party to the wardship proceedings, but sometimes to some other person or persons, for example, grandparents or foster parents or a local authority.[2] The effect is to leave that person with the power and responsibility for the day-to-day upbringing of the ward, but subject to any specific directions which the court may make when granting the order or at any time thereafter. Thus, it may impose a restriction as to where the ward should reside,[3] and in giving care and control to one of the parties it may direct that the other party be given access or additionally specified powers and responsibilities, for example, with regard to the ward's education. Where there is no dispute between the parties, the appropriate order may be joint care and control.

Where care and control is vested in third parties, for example, foster parents, the court can grant leave for the ward to be known by their surname. Such is likely to be appropriate, however, only where the ward's rehabilitation with his natural family is unlikely and, if the ward is of sufficient age and understanding, the change is in accordance with his wishes.[4]

Where a local authority has care and control but the court has ordered the initiation of rehabilitation of the ward with a parent, it is important that the order is complied with. Otherwise, if the parent delays in seeking compliance with the order the ward's bonds with his foster parents may develop to such an extent that the court will feel unable, in the child's interests, to direct compliance with its order.[5]

1   For the meaning of this term see ante, para 1.65.
2   For committal to care to a local authority under the inherent jurisdiction see *Re CB (a minor)* [1981] 1 All ER 16, [1981] 1 WLR 379, CA; *Salford City Council v C* (1981) 3 FLR 153; *Re SW (a minor) (wardship: jurisdiction)* [1986] 1 FLR 24, [1985] Fam Law 322 and under the statutory jurisdiction see FLRA 1969, s 7(2) and post, paras 8.60 et seq.
3   *Re H (GJ) (an infant)* [1966] 1 All ER 952, [1966] 1 WLR 706.
4   See *Re J (a minor)* [1987] 1 FLR 455, [1987] Fam Law 88.
5   *Re D (a minor)* (1987) Times, 17 February, CA.

(i)   Wardship, custodianship, custody and guardianship
8.52   This power to grant care and control raises questions concerning the relationship between wardship and custodianship, custody and guardianship.

8.53   *Custodianship*   Before the introduction of the custodianship order an order for care and control obtained in wardship proceedings was the only means whereby persons other than parents could seek an order for care and control of a child.[1] In principle, the custodianship order has distinct advantages. It confers the wider powers and responsibilities of legal custody, including actual custody; it leaves the custodian free from the direct supervision and control which is exercisable by the courts in wardship proceedings; and, being available in the county courts and magistrates' courts, it is less expensive to obtain, though the extent to which this advantage is diminished by the recently conferred power of the High Court to order the transfer of wardship proceedings to a county court remains to be seen. However, for reasons already considered,[2] these advantages have so far not been enough to popularise the custodianship order. Moreover, there will be circumstances where a person is unable to meet the qualifications imposed by section 33(3) of the Children Act 1975 on applicants for custodianship orders, for example, where the child does not have his home with that person or has not done so for the particular requisite period. In such circumstances only the alternative possibility of a care and control order under wardship is available.

1   Except that in matrimonial proceedings under the MCA 1973 or the DPMCA 1978 a step-parent who is a party may be granted such an order if the child is a child of

the family. In the case of proceedings under the 1978 Act the order would be one for
legal custody including actual custody, see ante, para 3.36.
2   See ante, paras 6.94 et seq.

8.54 *Custody*   Where parents wish to recover care and control of their
child from some third person they will invoke wardship, but where the
dispute is between themselves they are likely to rely on the various statutory
jurisdictions. Most frequently their dispute over custody will arise in
connection with matrimonial proceedings, and where it does not the
advantages which a custodianship order has over a care and control order
made in wardship[1] correspondingly apply to an order for legal custody
made in proceedings between them under section 9 of the Guardianship
of Minors Act 1971. Moreover, although the unmarried father of a child
has sometimes preferred wardship to section 9 proceedings, the new option
of an order under section 4 of the Family Law Reform Act 1987, which
will enable him to be granted all the parental powers and responsibilities,
albeit jointly with the mother,[2] is likely in the long run further to reduce
reliance on wardship. Nevertheless, there can exceptionally be circumstances
where wardship, because of its more effective methods of enforcing orders,
is to be preferred to an application for custody, for example, where a parent
is threatening to remove the child from the jurisdiction or where the child's
whereabouts are unknown.[3]

There is nothing to prevent wardship proceedings being instituted even
though the child is already the subject of custody proceedings, and conversely
a wardship application may later be joined by an application under the
Guardianship of Minors Act 1971.[4] If both sets of proceedings are in the
Family Division they should be heard together. If the custody proceedings
are in the magistrates' court or a county court they should be adjourned
to the High Court.[5] However, where only custody proceedings have been
commenced and a custody order has been made, wardship should
subsequently be invoked only where either the relief sought is outside the
jurisdiction of the court which made the custody order[6] or where there
are exceptional circumstances.[7] Wardship should certainly not be used as
a means of appeal or variation of a custody order.[8]

1   See supra, para 8.53.
2   See ante, para 2.47.
3   See Lowe and White, paras 11.8 and 11.9.
4   RSC Ord 90 r 5.
5   See, for example, *Re K (minors) (children: care and control)* [1977] Fam 179, [1977]
      1 All ER 647, CA.
6   *Re H (GJ) (an infant)* [1966] 1 All ER 952, [1966] 1 WLR 706; *Re P (infants)* [1967]
      2 All ER 229, [1967] 1 WLR 818.
7   *Re D (minors) (wardship: jurisdiction)* [1973] Fam 179, [1973] 2 All ER 993.
8   *Re K (KJS) (an infant)* [1966] 3 All ER 154, [1966] 1 WLR 1241; *Re P (AJ) (an infant)*
      [1968] 1 WLR 1976; *Re S (minors)* (1983) Times, 30 July.

8.55 *Guardianship*   Wardship has a special relevance to guardianship
where there are competing claimants for appointment as a guardian under
section 5 of the Guardianship of Minors Act 1971.[1] A guardian so appointed
is entitled to care and control of the child, but that Act does not confer
on him any right to enforce the powers of a guardian.[2] Anyone contemplating
seeking appointment, who expects his care of the child to be challenged,
should therefore consider the possibility of wardship with a consequent

care and control order, either as an alternative, or as a supplement, to appointment as guardian.

1   Ie appointment where there is no parent, no guardian of the person and no other person having parental rights with respect to the child; see ante, para 4.13.
2   See *Re N (minors) (parental rights)* [1974] Fam 40, [1974] 1 All ER 126, DC; and see [1974] CLJ 74.

(b)   Access

8.56   The power to award access has already been examined in Chapter 3.[1]

1   See paras 3.84 to 3.88.

(c)   Removal out of jurisdiction

8.57   Leave of the court is necessary to take the ward out of the jurisdiction.[1] If the court is not minded to allow it and there is a risk of unlawful removal, it can make a restraining order, not only against the parties but also third persons.[2] In deciding whether to grant leave to take the ward out of the jurisdiction, whether permanently or temporarily, the court is governed by the principle of the paramountcy of his welfare, and in applying it will take account of his long-term interests. If it decides to allow permanent removal, it is likely to deward the child either immediately[3] or on his leaving the jurisdiction;[4] but sometimes it may retain wardship in order to try to protect the continued relationship between the ward and the non-custodial parent, for example, by requiring the custodial parent to give an undertaking to arrange access visits by the ward to the non-custodial parent in this country.[5] Usually, a decision to allow permanent removal will have been reached after full investigation of the merits of the case, but alternatively the court may make a summary order without such investigation. The latter approach is likely where the ward has been 'kidnapped' from a foreign jurisdiction and brought to this country, and the court orders his immediate return.[6]

In considering whether to allow temporary removal out of the jurisdiction a major factor will be the likelihood of the ward being returned. The court will require some security that any future order will be obeyed, and an undertaking and/or a financial bond may be required as to compliance with any future order.[7] If the proposed removal is temporary and the court is satisfied that the ward should be able to leave for temporary visits abroad, without the necessity for special leave (which is always required in cases of permanent removal), it may make an order giving general leave for such visits.[8] The party in whose favour the order is made must lodge, at the registry in which the matter is proceeding, at least seven days before each proposed departure (1) an unqualified written consent by the other party to the proposed visit, (2) a written statement giving the date of departure, the period of absence and the whereabouts of the minor during such absence, and (3) unless otherwise directed, a written undertaking to return the ward at the end of the proposed visit. On compliance with these requirements a certificate for production to the immigration authorities, stating there has been compliance, may be obtained from the registry.

1   See ante, para 8.32.

2   *Re Harris (an infant)* (1960) Times, 21 May (order restraining airlines from carrying
     ward on their aircraft). If the ward has been removed without leave, the court can
     order his return; *Re O (a minor) (wardship: adopted child)* [1978] Fam 196.
3   *Re G (a minor) (wardship: jurisdiction)* [1984] FLR 268, [1984] Fam Law 244.
4   *Re L (minors)* [1974] 1 All ER 913, [1974] 1 WLR 250, CA.
5   *Bates v Morley* (1981) 3 FLR 244.
6   *Re L (minors)*, supra, note 4.
7   *Re O (infants)* [1962] 2 All ER 10, [1962] 1 WLR 724, CA; *Re A (a minor)* (1978) 8
     Fam Law 201, CA.
         For guidance to practitioners and an appropriate form of bond see [1987] Law Soc
     Gaz 661, ante, para 3.60.
8   *Practice Direction* [1973] 2 All ER 512; sub nom *Practice Note* [1973] 1 WLR 690.

8.58   Application for leave to remove a ward from the jurisdiction is made
by summons supported by affidavit.[1] Application must be made to a judge,
except in the following cases when it may be made to the registrar, namely
(a) where it is unopposed, or (b) is for the temporary removal of the ward
unless it is opposed on the ground that the ward may not be duly returned.
The registrar may make such order as he thinks fit or may refer the
application or any question arising thereon to a judge.[2] Where there is
an opposed application for leave to take a ward permanently out of the
jurisdiction or where there is an application for temporary removal which
is opposed on the ground that the ward may not be duly returned, the
proceedings must be dealt with in the High Court unless the nature of
the issues of fact or law raised in the case makes them more suitable for
trial in a county court and unless to do so would cause undue delay or
hardship to any party or other person involved.[3]

1   Application should not be made ex parte; *Re C (a minor)* (1976) 6 Fam Law 211, CA.
2   *Practice Direction* [1984] 2 All ER 407, [1984] 1 WLR 855.
3   *Practice Direction* [1988] 2 All ER 103, [1988] 1 WLR 558.

(d)   Maintenance

8.59   The power to order a parent to pay maintenance in respect of a
ward is examined in Chapter 16.[1]

1   See para 16.11.

(e)   Committal to the care of a local authority

8.60   The court may commit the ward to the care of a local authority
either under its statutory jurisdiction or its inherent jurisdiction.

(i)   Statutory jurisdiction

8.61   Section 7(2) of the Family Law Reform Act 1969 gives the court
a power similar to that given under custody, domestic, matrimonial, adoption
or custodianship jurisdictions.[1] The court may commit to local authority
care where it appears to it that 'there are exceptional circumstances making
it impracticable or undesirable for a ward of court to be, or continue to
be, under the care of either of his parents or any other individual'.[2] As
with orders under the other jurisdictions, the effect is that the child is
to be treated as if he had been received into care under section 2 of the
CCA 1980. A number of provisions which apply to orders made under
section 43 of the MCA 1973 are expressly made to apply to orders made

in wardship proceedings.[3] Thus, an order cannot be made if the ward has reached the age of 17, but an order made in respect of a ward continues until 18, unless it is earlier discharged. So long as the care order is in force neither a parent nor anyone else may claim the child,[4] except by means of an application to discharge the order.[5] The exercise of the powers of the local authority relating primarily to the accommodation and welfare of the child under the 1980 Act[6] are subject to any directions given by the court.[7] These include directions as to access.[8] It can give any proper direction which is for the child's benefit, although if the local authority has acted bona fide in reaching its own decision (for example, refusing a parent access), the court should take that fact into account in reaching its own decision.[9] However, whether or not directions have been issued, the local authority, in accordance with the general principle in wardship, must consult the court about any major decision,[10] such as consent to an abortion[11] or fostering the ward or attempting to reunite him with his parents.[12] The court may then give directions, but should do so in a broad way.[13]

It has already been noted[14] that in making a committal to care order under section 43 of the MCA 1973 it may exceptionally be appropriate to make a care order even though it is the intention of the local authority, if an order is made, to leave the child in the actual care of one of the parents. In those circumstances, if the experiment of rehabilitation should fail, the local authority will be able to remove the child promptly from the parent without the expense and delay of further recourse to the court.[15] Whether the same power·exists where an order is made under section 7(2) of the FLRA 1969 has yet to be unequivocally established, but in principle there seems to be no objection to the court making an order in similar terms in wardship proceedings.[16] Such an order would not relieve the local authority of its obligation to consult the court in any major decision. For example, if after removing the ward from his parent the local authority wishes to place him with long-term foster parents, it ought, it is submitted, to consult the court.

The court can make an order under section 7(2) committing the care of a ward to a local authority if it is in his best interests to do so,[17] notwithstanding that the ward is already the subject of a care order made by a juvenile court in the exercise of its criminal jurisdiction.[18] Such an order would be appropriate where the child is in the care of one local authority under the care order and it is considered best in his interests that he be committed to the care of another local authority under a section 7(2) order.[19]

1   GA 1973, s 2(2)(b), as prospectively amended by FLRA 1987, Sch 2, para 49 (ante, para 3.22); DPMCA 1978, s 10(1) (ante, para 3.38); MCA 1973, s 43(1) (ante, para 3.57); Adoption Act 1976, s 26(1)(b) (ante, para 5.101); and Children Act 1975, s 34(5) (ante, para 6.75).
2   See post, para 15.64 for the general effect of such an order in relation to the paramountcy of the ward's welfare.
3   See s 43(2)–(6), as extended by FLRA 1969, s 7(3).
4   Any parent must keep the local authority informed of his address; see MCA 1973, s 43(6).
5   For discharge see infra, para 8.62.
6   Ie under ss 18, 21, 22 and 22A.
7   MCA 1973, s 43(5)(a).
8   *Re Y (a minor) (Child in care: access)* [1976] Fam 125, [1975] 3 All ER 348, CA. See also *Lewisham Borough Council v M* [1981] 3 All ER 307, [1981] 1 WLR 1248.

9   *Re R (a minor)* [1983] 2 All ER 929, [1983] 1 WLR 991, CA. In *Re B (wards) (local authority: directions)* [1988] 1 FLR 484 it was held that, whilst the court has jurisdiction to intervene in a local authority's decision whether or not to allocate a social worker to a ward in care, it would not in the circumstances exercise the jurisdiction, as there was no evidence that the authority had declined on some malicious or improper ground. It was not possible for the court in wardship to reopen the local authority's decision and investigate the priorities of social worker allocation.

10   *Re CB (a minor)* [1981] 1 All ER 16, [1981] 1 WLR 379, CA; *Re El-G (minors) (wardship and adoption)* (1982) 4 FLR 421, 12 Fam Law 251.

11   *Re G-U (a minor) (wardship)* [1984] FLR 812, [1984] Fam Law 248.

12   It is expressly provided that the local authority cannot arrange for the child's emigration; MCA 1973, s 43(5)(b) as extended by FLRA 1969, s 7(3). But it can guarantee apprenticeship deeds or articles of clerkship in accordance with CCA 1980, s 23; see FLRA 1969, s 7(3).

13   *Surrey County Council v W* (1982) 3 FLR 167, 12 Fam Law 91, CA; *Cf Re AL* [1983] 7 No 4 Adoption and Fostering 60.

14   See ante, para 3.57.

15   *R v G (Surrey County Council intervening)* [1984] Fam 100, [1984] 3 All ER 460, CA.

16   For discussion of the matter see Lowe and White, pp 102–103.

17   Semble it can similarly do so under its inherent jurisdiction.

18   *Re C (a minor) (wardship: care order)* [1983] 1 All ER 219, [1982] 1 WLR 1462.

19   As in *Re C*.

8.62 Any interested party may apply for the variation or discharge of a section 7(2) order.[1] Variation is most likely to be sought with regard to access, either where the local authority has refused it to a parent[2] or where the parent seeks more generous access. This is a particularly important right for the parent where there has been total denial of access, since the provisions which allow him to apply under CCA 1980[3] to a juvenile court for an order for access do not extend to children committed to local authority care by a High Court order.[4] Moreover, application under section 7 of the 1969 Act enables access to be varied, a power denied to juvenile courts under the 1980 Act where there has not been total refusal. However, any power under section 7 is subject to the caveat that the court may be unwilling to intervene if the local authority has acted in good faith in the interests of the child.

Discharge of a section 7(2) order is most likely where there has been a change in the circumstances of the parent which justifies his now being given care and control of the ward. For example, the order may have been made on the ground of his deplorable living conditions,[5] but he is now able to provide a suitable home for his child. In those circumstances his application for discharge is likely to be accompanied by one for care and control of the child. Instead, there might be an accompanying application to deward the child, but the court is more likely to give care and control in the first instance in order to review the ward's rehabilitation with his parent.

A section 7(2) order ceases to have effect when an order is made for the ward's return under Part I of the Child Abduction and Custody Act 1985 or a decision, other than a decision relating to rights of access, is registered under section 16 of that Act.[6]

1   See FLRA 1969, s 7(5). Where the applicant is a local authority, it may, in case of urgency or where the application is unlikely to be opposed, apply by way of a letter addressed to the court; see MCR 1977, r 93(4) as extended by RSC Ord 90, r 11(1) to wardship.

2   *Re R (a minor) (child in care: access)* [1983] 2 All ER 929, [1983] 1 WLR 991.

3   See ss 12A–12G.
4   See CCA 1980, s 12A(2).
5   See *F v F* [1959] 3 All ER 180n, [1959] 1 WLR 863.
6   See ss 25(1), (2), 27(1) and Sch 3, para 1(1)(a); and for the Act generally see ante, paras 3.108 et seq.

(ii)   Inherent jurisdiction

8.63   In *Re CB (a minor)*[1] the Court of Appeal recognised that the court could rely on its inherent jurisdiction, and, if the paramount interests of the ward so required, entrust care and control of him to a local authority. Subsequent cases have confirmed this recognition. The jurisdiction is useful to fill gaps in the statutory jurisdiction. It was so invoked in *Re SW (a minor) (wardship: jurisdiction)*[2] to place a 17-year-old girl in the care and control of a local authority. Until recently it was thought[3] that the jurisdiction might also be appropriate so as to make an interim care and control order, on the ground that an interim care order made in pursuance of section 7(2) of the 1969 Act was not possible, but it has now been recognised that the latter order is possible.[4] It is submitted that the inherent jurisdiction should be limited to this gap filling process. For this reason reliance on it in *Salford City Council v C*[5] in order to grant more generous access to the parents is open to criticism. The same result could have been achieved by a section 7(2) order, given the wide powers of the court thereunder to issue directions on access. Doubt exists as to whether there is another gap which the inherent jurisdiction is needed to fill. In *Re CB (a minor)*, Ormrod LJ took the view that, if a local authority wished itself to apply in wardship proceedings for an order committing a child to its care, it would have to rely on the inherent jurisdiction, since 'section 7(2) was passed to give the court power, in proceedings between a parent and a third party, to make an order committing the child to the care of the local authority, or to make it clear that the court, in wardship proceedings, had the same power as it had under the Matrimonial Causes Act 1973'. However, Hollings J in *London Borough of Lewisham v M*[6] regarded that conclusion to be obiter and himself held that by its terms the power in section 7(2) was unrestricted, so that a local authority could be an applicant.[7]

1   [1981] 1 All ER 16, [1981] 1 WLR 379.
2   [1986] 1 FLR 24, [1985] Fam Law 322.
3   See DHSS *Review of Child Care Law* (1985), para 8.23.
4   *Re G (a minor) (role of the appellate court)* [1987] 1 FLR 164, [1987] Fam Law 52, CA.
5   (1981) 3 FLR 153.
6   [1981] 3 All ER 307, [1981] 1 WLR 1248.
7   For comment see Morgan, *Care Orders in Wardship Cases* [1984] JSWL 66 at pp 67–78; Lowe and White, op cit, pp 103–104.

8.64   A major distinction between the two jurisdictions is that an order under the statutory brings into operation the powers conferred on the local authority under Part III of the CCA 1980 so that, inter alia, the local authority has power to maintain the ward. Moreover, Part V of that Act is also operative in so far as the ward may be required once he has attained the age of 16 to make contributions towards his maintenance. Those provisions are not activated where a care and control order is made under the inherent jurisdiction. Arguably, the inherent jurisdiction does enable the court to give the power to maintain to the local authority. Support for this conclusion[1] can be derived from the decision in *W v Avon County Council*[2] that under its inherent jurisdiction the court may order a local authority to pay maintenance to foster parents who, in wardship proceedings, have been granted care and control of a child in the local authority's care. However, it is much more doubtful whether the inherent jurisdiction enables the court to order a 16-year-old who is in the care and control of a local authority to contribute towards his maintenance, especially if, as has been suggested,[3] the concept of custody in the wide sense does not include a parental power to enforce against the child an obligation to contribute to his maintenance.

Another relevant distinction between the two jurisdictions relates to the power to place the ward in secure accommodation. Under the inherent jurisdiction the local authority may seek directions thereon direct from the court,[4] whereas, if the ward has been committed to care under a section 7(2) order, the authority is hampered by the provisions of section 21A of the CCA 1980 and the Secure Accommodation (No 2) Regulations 1983, which, as will be seen,[5] require prior resort to the juvenile court.

1   The conclusion was, however, doubted by Hollings J in *London Borough of Lewisham v M* [1981] 3 All ER 307, [1981] 1 WLR 1248.
2   (1979) 9 Fam Law 33.
3   Ante, para 1.54.
4   *Re SW (a minor) (wardship: jurisdiction)* [1986] 1 FLR 24, [1985] Fam Law 322.
5   See post, para 15.78.

(iii)   The application
8.65   An application to commit the ward to local authority care may be made by any party to the proceedings. Where it is for an order under section 7(2) of the 1969 Act the proceedings are governed by those Matrimonial Causes Rules which relate to proceedings for a committal to care order under section 43 of the MCA 1973.[1] It is usually made to the judge, but where it is unopposed or its terms are agreed it may be made to a registrar.[2] Before an order can be made the court must hear representations from the local authority, including any as to the making of a financial provision order in favour of the ward.[3] The registrar must fix a date, time and place for the hearing of those representations. Fourteen days prior notice must be given to the local authority,[4] and, if it wishes to make representations relating to financial provision for the ward, it must within seven days of receipt of the notice file an affidavit, setting out the facts it knows about the property and income of the person against whom the order is sought. The local authority must serve a copy of the affidavit on that person who, within four days after service, must file an affidavit in answer and serve a copy on the authority.[5]

Where the application is made under the inherent jurisdiction for an order for care and control it should be by way of summons in the wardship proceedings. The Matrimonial Causes Rules do not apply, but it is submitted that the court should follow similar procedures with regard to local authority representations.

1   See RSC Ord 90, r 11(1); MCR 1977, rr 92 and 93.
2   Rule 92(2), as amended by SI 1984/1511.
3   MCA 1973, s 43(2), as extended by FLRA 1969, s 7(3).

4   By way of Form 18 of MCR 1977. A care order made without first hearing representations
     is void; *M v M (divorce: care order)* (1980) 1 FLR 327, CA.
5   See MCR 1977, r 93(2)–(3).

(f)   Supervision order

8.66   Where a ward is not in local authority care under section 7(2) of
the Family Law Reform Act 1969, section 7(4) gives the court a power,
similar to that given under custody, domestic, matrimonial, adoption or
custodianship jurisdictions.[1] Where it appears to it that there are exceptional
circumstances making it desirable that the ward should be under the
supervision of an independent person, the court may order that he be under
the supervision of a welfare officer or of a local authority. Although section
7(4) does not expressly so provide, a supervision order will in practice
be associated with an order granting care and control. The power to order
supervision is additional to the court's general duty of supervision of wards,
and is appropriate where the general duty is unlikely to provide the close
day-to-day supervision which the circumstances may require[2] or where,
because of the special difficulties facing the person having care and control,
there is an experienced person readily available to whom he can turn for
advice if and when needed.[3]

1   See GA 1973, s 2(2)(a), as prospectively amended by FLRA 1987, Sch 2 and para 49
     (ante, para 3.22); DPMCA 1978, s 9(1) (ante, para 3.38); MCA 1973, s 44(1) (ante, para
     3.56); Adoption Act 1976, s 26(1)(a) (ante, para 5.101); and Children Act 1975 s 34(5)
     (ante, para 6.74).
2   See Parry, Butterworths Family Law Service, para E[172].
3   See, as examples, *Re C (minors) (wardship: jurisdiction)* [1978] Fam 105, [1978] 2 All
     ER 230, CA; *A v C* [1985] FLR 445, [1984] Fam Law 241, CA; *Re CB* [1981] 1 All
     ER 16, [1981] 1 WLR 379, CA; *Re J* [1987] 1 FLR 455, [1987] Fam Law 88.

8.67   An application for a supervision order may be made by any party
to the proceedings, and, similar to an application for an order under section
7(2) of the 1969 Act, the proceedings are governed by those Matrimonial
Causes Rules which relate to proceedings for a supervision order under
section 44 of the MCA 1973.[1] Thus, application is made to a judge, but
where unopposed or its terms are agreed it may be made to a registrar.[2]

The court can in its discretion fix the period of supervision[3] and has
power to vary[4] or discharge the order.[5]

1   See RSC Ord 90, r 11(1); MCR 1977, rr 92 and 93.
2   Rule 92(2).
3   FLRA 1969, s 7(4).
4   For example, where the ward moves to a new area. Where there is a supervision order,
     the person with care and control must notify the supervising officer of any change of
     address.
5   FLRA 1969, s 7(5).

(g)   Religious and secular education

8.68   The court may make orders with regard to the religious upbringing
and secular education of the ward. With regard to the latter, the court
must limit the exercise of its prerogative jurisdiction so as to avoid conflict,
or a risk of conflict, with the exercise by the local authority of its statutory
powers; but the court can intervene when it is desirable to do so in order

to assist the local authority to perform its statutory duties, and should intervene when invited to do so by the local authority. Subject to the above restriction, the court will apply the principle of the paramountcy of the ward's welfare. The relevant factors that will be taken into account have already been briefly mentioned in relation to secular education[2] and will subsequently be examined concerning religious upbringing.[3]

1   *Re D (a minor)* [1987] 3 All ER 717, [1987] 1 WLR 1400, CA, applying the principle established by *A v Liverpool City Council* [1982] AC 363, [1981] 2 All ER 385, HL (as to which see post, para 15.124).
2   See ante, para 3.13.
3   See post, paras 11.04 et seq.

(h)   Miscellaneous protective orders

8.69   The court may make a variety of orders in exercise of its protective jurisdiction. For example, the powers to restrict publicity of wardship proceedings and to authorise or restrain medical treatment of a child have already been examined.[1] The following are further examples.

1   See respectively ante, para 8.45 and paras 1.26 et seq.

(i)   Restriction on the ward's undesirable activities

8.70   Changing social attitudes, the reduction of the age of majority to 18 and the emergence of the *Gillick* principle have combined to reduce markedly the use of the court's power to restrict the ward's activities. This is reflected in the declining importance of the so-called 'teenage wardship' case,[1] in which, at the instance of the parents, a person is by order restrained from continuing an association with their child. When it does arise it is likely to be an association between a daughter and a man whom she intends to marry or with whom she intends to cohabit. The practical problem for the court is whether termination of the association would be in the ward's interests and, if so, whether the continuance of wardship and the making of such an order would be effective.[2]

Future use of wardship in this context is likely to be more in relation to association with 'bizarre or fanatical quasi-religious sects or groups (or individuals) suspected of drug abuse'.[3] An order can be made against a group.[4]

1   For this kind of case see Cross, *Wards of Court* (1967) 83 LQR 201 at pp 209–211.
2   The order is usually made against the man, but he should not be made a party to the originating summons; see *Practice Direction* [1983] 2 All ER 672, [1983] 1 WLR 790. If the association continues, not only is the man in contempt but also the girl for aiding and abetting the breach of the order.
3   Lowe and White, op cit, p 127; and see post, para 11.08.
4   *Iredell v Iredell* (1885) 1 TLR 260 (order against a group who had tried to persuade a girl to become a member of the Roman Catholic Church, contrary to her father's wishes).

(ii)   Non molestation

8.71   The court may make a non-molestation order to protect the ward,[1] if that is in his interests, but it cannot, under its wardship jurisdiction, attach to the order a power of arrest.[2] Instead it must rely on its powers of contempt for breach of the non-molestation order.

1   *Re V (a minor) (wardship)* (1979) 123 Sol Jo 201.
2   *Re G (wardship) (jurisdiction: power of arrest)* (1982) 4 FLR 538, 13 Fam Law 50, CA.
    Quaere whether it may do so under its inherent jurisdiction; see Lowe and White, p 128,
    note 6, citing *Lewis (AH) v Lewis (RWF)* [1978] Fam 60, [1978] 1 All ER 729.

VI   CONTEMPT[1]

8.72   Contempt by way of publication of information relating to wardship
proceedings has already been considered.[2] Reference has also incidentally
been made to failure to obtain the consent of the court where it is required
(which is further considered below) and to non-compliance with an order
of the court or with any direction it issues relating to the ward. Contempt
for non-compliance with a court order is only committed if the order is
clear and unambiguous and the alleged contemnor has adequate notice
of it. Such notice requires service of a copy of the order with an endorsement
thereon warning of the effect of non-compliance.[3] The procedure must be
strictly observed, especially since breach of the order must be proved beyond
reasonable doubt,[4] a burden of proof which apparently reflects the rule
that, though disobedience of an order constitutes civil contempt[5] whereas
other forms of contempt are criminal,[6] the court's powers to punish it
are penal.

A party who fails to comply with an order is liable to arrest by the
Tipstaff, who is also responsible, if so required by the court, for securing
compliance with any direction relating to a ward,[7] for example of requiring
a party with care and control of the child to deliver him up to the person
named by the court or to return the child to another jurisdiction.[8] There
is also the possibility of sequestration of the contemnor's property, a remedy
which is particularly useful where he is resident abroad but has property
in England and Wales.[9]

1   See Lowe and White, Chapter 8; Borrie and Lowe, *Law of Contempt* (2nd edn, N Lowe
    (1983)); Miller, *Contempt of Court* (1976); Arlidge and Eady, *The Law of Contempt* (1982).
2   See ante, para 8.45.
3   See RSC Ord 45, r 7.
4   See *Re Bramblevale Ltd* [1970] Ch 128, [1969] 3 All ER 1062, CA.
5   As does breach of an undertaking to the court.
6   On this classification see Lowe and White, pp 181–183.
7   RSC Ord 90, r 3A.
8   *G v L* [1891] 2 Ch 126.
9   *Re Liddell's Settlement Trust* [1936] Ch 365, [1936] 1 All ER 239, CA.

8.73   The other main kind of contempt is interference with the court's
special protection over its wards. Its precise scope has never been determined,
but it may take many forms of which the most common are those where
there is a failure to obtain the consent of the court where it is required.
A number of them have already been considered. Marriage of a ward,[1]
referral of a ward for psychiatric examination,[2] major medical treatment
for the ward,[3] taking a blood test of the ward to establish paternity,[4] removal
of a ward from the jurisdiction,[5] all require the prior leave of the court.
Other kinds of wrongful interference are interference with the evidence
relating to wardship proceedings, such as threatening witnesses[6] or the
parties, and concealing the ward's whereabouts.[7] The latter is becoming
increasingly frequent, and its seriousness is reflected in a number of rules

designed to curb it. The parties to the wardship proceedings must state the whereabouts of the child,[8] and the court can compel attendance of anyone who might know of the ward's whereabouts.[9] Moreover, a solicitor cannot claim client's privilege, but must give the court any information, obtained in the course of his employment as a solicitor, which may lead to the discovery of the ward's whereabouts.[10] Mention has already been made of the court's power to lift reporting restrictions in order to trace a missing ward,[11] and leave should be sought to publish as much information as is necessary to attract publicity. Where the judge considers that press publicity may assist, he should adjourn for about ten minutes to enable the press to attend, so that the widest publicity may be given.[12]

Frequently the Tipstaff is used to help missing wards, and he liaises with the Police and Port Authorities. On request for their assistance a description of the child and brief details are included in the Police Gazette by the force from whose area the child has been taken, and enquiries should be made by the police in the area where the child is thought to be.[13] If the child is traced the Tipstaff should be informed immediately so that he can enforce the High Court order. There are also formal arrangements with Government Departments for tracing a missing ward.[14] Application may be made to the Department of Health and Social Security requesting the address of a missing ward or of the person with whom a missing ward is said to be, but this must be done officially through the court, and it is the responsibility of the applicant or his solicitor to supply the registrar with as much relevant information as possible.[15] If enquiries fail to reveal an address, or if there are strong grounds for believing that the person sought may have made a recent application for a passport, the applicant's solicitor may make enquiries of the Passport Office, but accompanied by an undertaking that any information provided by the Office will be used solely to assist in tracing a missing ward.[16] Where the person sought is known to be serving or to have recently served in the armed forces, the applicant's solicitor may obtain the address for service of the wardship proceedings direct from the appropriate service department, subject to an undertaking that the address will be used solely for the service of process and that so far as possible he will disclose the address only to the court and not to the applicant or any other person, except in the normal course of proceedings.[17] Should the circumstances suggest that some other government department may know the address, the registrar may apply to it for the information.

1   Ante, para 8.31.
2   Paragraph 8.41.
3   Paragraph 8.42.
4   Paragraph 8.44.
5   Paragraph 8.32.
6   *Re B(JA)* [1965] Ch 1112, [1965] 2 All ER 168.
7   *Mustafa v Mustafa* (1967) Times, 11 and 13 September.
8   RSC Ord 90, r 3(4)–(8). See also FLA 1986, s 33 for the power to order disclosure of a child's whereabouts in proceedings relating to a custody order (as defined by FLA 1986, s 1(1)(d), ante, para 8.06) made in wardship proceedings.
9   *Rosenberg v Lindo* (1883) 48 LT 478. The practice is to proceed by summary order and not by subpoena.
10 *Ramsbottom v Senior* (1869) LR 8 Eq 575.
11 Ante, para 8.45.
12 *Practice Note* [1980] 2 All ER 806.

13   For further details see Home Office Circular No 174/1973.
14   See Lowe and White, p 315.
15   For details see *Practice Direction* [1988] 2 All ER 573, [1988] 1 WLR 648.
16   See the *Practice Direction,* supra, for the information to be provided by the solicitor.
17   Where the applicant is acting in person, the service department will disclose his address or that of his commanding officer to the registrar on the assurance that the applicant has given an undertaking that the information will be used solely for the purpose of serving process.

Proceedings

8.74 Contempt proceedings are commenced by way of an application for a committal order. Where the original wardship proceedings have been heard solely in the High Court, application is by motion to a judge of the Family Division,[1] specifying precisely the alleged contempt[2] and supported by affidavit evidence.[3] A copy of the motion and the affidavit must be served personally on the alleged contemnor, who is entitled to give oral evidence.[4] However, the recently conferred power to order transfer of proceedings from the High Court to a county court[5] has raised some uncertainty about when an application for a committal order should be made to a county court. It has been suggested[6] that, where proceedings have been so transferred and the contempt is by way of a breach of an order of the county court, that court should hear the application,[7] except where a sequestration order is sought when proceedings would have to be transferred to the High Court, since the county court has no power in that regard.

Where, however, there has been wrongful interference with the court's protective jurisdiction, then it is suggested[6] that the appropriate court to hear the application is the High Court.

Where the contempt relates to the rights of a particular person, he, as the prejudiced party, usually has to institute the proceedings. Although the Attorney General[8] and the Official Solicitor[9] are empowered to do so, they rarely do so except in cases of criminal contempt, such as removal of the ward from the jurisdiction[10] or interference with the course of justice. Where the contempt is committed in the face of the court, for example refusal to attend, or to answer questions at, the hearing, the court may act of its own motion.[11]

1   RSC Ord 52, rr 1(3) and 4(1).
2   *Re C (a minor) (contempt)* [1986] 1 FLR 578, [1986] Fam Law 187, CA; *Dorrell v Dorrell* [1985] FLR 1089, [1986] Fam Law 15, CA; *Harmsworth v Harmsworth* [1987] 3 All ER 816, [1987] 1 WLR 676, CA.
3   RSC Ord 52, r 4(1). See also *Re B(JA) (an infant)* [1965] Ch 1112, [1965] 2 All ER 168.
4   RSC Ord 52, r 6(4).
5   See ante, para 8.02.
6   Lowe and White, p 189.
7   The relevant procedure would then be governed by the County Court Rules 1981, Ord 29. See Fricker, *Committal for Contempt in the County Court* [1988] Fam Law 232.
8   See *Re Crump (an infant)* (1963) 107 Sol Jo 682.
9   See *Re F (a minor) (publication of information)* [1977] Fam 58, [1977] 1 All ER 114, CA.
10   *R v D* [1984] AC 778, [1984] 2 All ER 449, HL.
11   RSC Ord 52, r 5.

8.75 The application for a committal order may be heard in private,[1] but, if the court decides to make an order, the judge must state in open court the name of the contemnor, the precise nature of the contempt, and the length of the period for which he is being committed.[2] However, a committal order should be 'the very last resort',[3] and the real purpose of committal procedure is to bring the matter back to court to secure future compliance with the order. Consequently, even the imposition of a fine or the making of a sequestration order, as alternatives to committal, are exceptional. Where a committal order is made, its operation may be suspended[4] conditional upon future compliance with the terms of the order. But, even if there is a breach of the suspended order, the court has a discretion whether or not to activate the order, depending upon what is just in all the circumstances.[5]

There is a right of appeal against an order to the Court of Appeal.[6] It is essential that the order states the precise particulars of the contempt,[7] so that the Court of Appeal can assess the appropriateness of the sentence passed. Where there has been a failure to observe meticulously the required formalities in contempt proceedings the Court of Appeal may discharge the order or, if there has been no unfairness and no material irregularity, exercise its discretion[8] by remedying the irregularity and substituting a lawful penal order, either custodial or pecuniary.[9]

1　RSC Ord 52, r 6(1)(a); *Re an Infant* [1965] 2 All ER 254, [1965] 1 WLR 754.
2　RSC Ord 52, r 6(2), as amended by RSC (Amendment) 1986, r 18. See also *Re C (a minor) (contempt)* [1986] 1 FLR 578, [1986] Fam Law 187, CA.
3　*Per* Ormrod LJ in *Ansah v Ansah* [1977] Fam 138 at 144, [1977] 2 All ER 638 at 643. Where an order is made it is usually for about a month. The maximum permitted period of imprisonment is two years; see Contempt of Court Act 1981, s 14(1).
4　RSC Ord 52, r 7.
5　*Re W(B) (an infant)* [1969] 2 Ch 50, [1969] 1 All ER 594, CA.
6　Administration of Justice Act 1960, s 13.
7　The order should be in Form 85 in RSC Appendix A.
8　Under the Administration of Justice Act 1960, s 13(3).
9　*Linnett v Coles* [1987] QB 555, [1986] 3 All ER 652, CA; *Wright v Jess* [1987] 2 FLR 373, [1987] Fam Law 380, CA.

VII TERMINATION OF WARDSHIP

8.76 On the ward's attaining majority not only does the wardship come to an end but also any undertakings or restrictions connected with it,[1] for example not to associate with or marry the ward. Wardship also automatically ceases if an application for an appointment for the hearing of the summons is not made within 21 days of the issue of the summons.[2] If the High Court on hearing the summons confirms the wardship, it has power at any time thereafter, either upon an application by a party or at its own motion, to order that the minor shall cease to be a ward of court.[3] Only the High Court may entertain an application to 'deward', even though it may have transferred all or part of the wardship proceedings to a county court.[4] In deciding whether or not to terminate the wardship, the court is governed by the principle of the paramountcy of the ward's welfare and will apply it in the light of the change of circumstances since its original order.

A wardship order giving the care and control of a child to any person ceases to have effect where an order is made for the child's return under

Part I of the Child Abduction and Custody Act 1985 or a decision, other than one relating to access, is registered under section 16 of that Act.[5] Where that occurs, it may lead to an application to deward the child.

It seems[6] that, if a care order or supervision order was made in the wardship proceedings, it automatically comes to an end on the termination of the wardship.[7] Moreover, the power to make either of these orders in wardship proceedings, is not available on an application to deward.[6]

Where the court decides to terminate wardship it may find it appropriate to make a custody order in favour, for example, of the parent who is applying for the termination. It is uncertain whether it can do so in exercise of its inherent jurisdiction. It is arguable that on dewarding the child the court has thereby divested itself of its jurisdiction to make orders in respect of him.[8] The alternative open to the parent is to couple his application to deward with an application for legal custody under section 9 of the Guardianship of Minors Act 1971. Because of the present uncertainty it would be wiser to include a section 9 application.

1   *Bolton v Bolton* [1891] 3 Ch 270, CA.
2   Supreme Court Act 1981, s 41(2), ante, para 8.19.
3   A person who was not a party to the wardship proceedings and who wishes to apply for termination of the wardship should first apply to be joined as a party.
4   MFPA 1984, s 38(2)(b).
5   See ss 25(1) and (2), 27(1) and Sch 3, para 2.
6   See Parry, Butterworth Family Law Service, para E[148].
7   See FLRA 1969, s 7(5); MCA 1973, s 43(3)(5)(a).
8   But see *Re P (minors) (wardship: surrogacy)* [1987] 2 FLR 421, [1987] Fam Law 414, where an order forbidding publicity was made notwithstanding the termination of wardship.

8.76A   Under the Family Law Act 1986,[1] if a custody order (or a variation of a custody order made in Scotland or Northern Ireland comes into force with respect to a ward at a time when a custody order in wardship[2] made in England and Wales is in effect, the Scottish or Northern Ireland order will prevail over the English order insofar as they overlap. Thereafter the English court does not have power to vary its own order so as to make provision for the matters covered by the later order.[3] Any supervision order made in the wardship jurisdiction[4] ceases to have effect.[5]

The court does not have jurisdiction to vary a custody order in wardship if at the relevant date[6] proceedings for divorce, nullity or judicial separation are continuing in Scotland or Northern Ireland in respect of the marriage of the ward's parents,[7] unless either:

(1) the court in Scotland or Northern Ireland waives its jurisdiction to make a custody order or decides to sist or stay custody proceedings before it in favour of the English court; or
(2) the ward is present in England and Wales on the relevant date and the court considers that the immediate exercise of its powers is necessary for the ward's protection.[8]

1   Section 6(1).
2   As defined in FLA 1986, s 1(1)(d); see ante, para 8.06.
3   Section 6(2).
4   Under FLRA 1969, s 7(4), ante, para 8.66.
5   FLA 1986, s 6(6)(a).

6   Ie at the date of the application (or first application if two or more are determined
    together) and where no application is made, the date of the variation; see FLA 1986,
    s 6(7).
7   Ibid, s 6(3).
8   Ibid, s 6(4) and (5).

VIII   REFORM

8.77   The Law Commission's Working Paper on Wards of Court has formed
part of its review of the private law relating to the upbringing of children,
and one of the principal questions which the Commission has addressed
is whether wardship will be further needed or justified as a separate
jurisdiction once the statutory codes relating to the custody and care of
children have been comprehensively re-examined. The Commission offered
three main approaches to reform,[3] namely: (i) to retain wardship as a separate
jurisdiction, perhaps with some specific reforms; (ii) to make wardship a
residuary jurisdiction; and (iii) to incorporate some features of wardship
within the statutory codes. The respective arguments for and against these
options were closely analysed,[4] but it was implicit in their presentation
that the reform of wardship should form part of the general review and
not await final determination of the revised statutory codes. In the event
the Commission has decided to postpone making substantial
recommendations for the court's inherent powers in wardship proceedings.
Instead it has incorporated the most valuable features into its proposed
new statutory system for guardianship and custody which 'should reduce
the need to resort to wardship proceedings save in the most unusual and
complex cases'.[5] If there is any area of law where it is unlikely that statute
law, however wide its compass, will cover every circumstance and eventuality
and properly provide for them, it is child law. Recent developments in
the field of human assisted reproduction demonstrate this.[6] Indeed, such
are the rapid scientific and technological changes in this as in other fields[7]
that the need for a 'safety net' in the form of wardship is greater than
it has ever been.

1   Law Com Working Paper No 101.
2   See Law Com Working Paper Nos 91 and 96.
3   See para 4.6. The Commission recognises that 'many combinations and variations of
    these broad options could be devised'.
4   See paras 4.7–4.25.
5   See Law Com No 172, para 1.4.
6   See ante, paras 2.02 et seq.
7   See especially medical matters, ante, paras 1.26 et seq.

The child and the state

CHAPTER 9

The protection of children from harm — I Physical harm

1 INTRODUCTION

9.01 Protection of children from physical and moral harm is, to some extent, secured by the sanctions of the criminal law.[1] Its provisions dealing with offences against the person apply generally to children as they do to adults, but some of them have special application where the victim is a child. In addition there are certain offences specifically created to protect children. Most are concerned with protection from physical harm, some from moral harm and others from both. They are dealt with in this and the next chapter under the broad classification of Physical Protection and Moral Protection, with 'mixed' offences being placed into the one or other category according to whether their emphasis is on the one form of protection or the other. Sexual offences are, however, separately treated, as, in a later chapter,[2] are those relating to the employment of children.

1 See Linda M Pollock, *Forgotten Children: Parent-Child Relations from 1500 to 1900* (1983), especially at pp 92–95.
2 Chapter 11.

9.02 A parent may render himself criminally liable by inflicting upon his child physical injury which exceeds the bounds of reasonable chastisement[1] or by failing to fulfil his duty to protect the child from physical harm, especially by failing to provide the necessities of life. This duty to protect, a natural incident of parenthood, is not, however, restricted to the parent-child relationship. At common law it arises whenever anyone old enough to be held legally responsible assumes the care of someone who, because of immaturity or disability, is unable to look after himself. Thus, for example, it is imposed on the step-parent or the foster parent[2] or on the spouse who nurses his or her sick partner.[3] Moreoever, as the last illustration indicates, the duty does not depend on the age of the person to be protected. Obviously, it exists in relation to very young children,[4] but it does not apply to those who, though still minors, are sufficiently equipped to look after themselves.[5] On the other hand, exceptionally, children who have attained majority may need protection.[6]

1 For the parental power to administer corporal punishment see ante, paras 1.21–1.23.
2 *R v Bubb* (1850) 4 Cox CC 455; *R v Gibbins and Proctor* (1918) 13 Cr App Rep 134, CCA.
3 *R v Bonnyman* (1942) 28 Cr App Rep 131, CCA.

4 Apart from the parent-child relationship, historically the duty was most apparent in connection with apprentices and servants; see, for example, *R v Friend* (1802) Russ & Ry 20 (neglect of master to provide for 13-year-old girl apprentice).

5 *R v Shepherd* (1862) Le & Ca 147 (mother of 18-year-old pregnant girl under no duty to send for a midwife).

6 *R v Chattaway* (1922) 17 Cr App Rep 7, CCA.

9.03   The common law duty has been immensely reinforced by statute. The need for this was due to the inability or unwillingness to enforce the duty rigorously. Even where the failure to protect had caused the death of the child, juries were either ready to acquit[1] or, at least, inclined to convict for manslaughter rather than murder. The reluctance to hold the parent liable is demonstrated by *R v Renshaw*[2]. In that case a ten-day-old illegitimate baby had been left by the mother in a large piece of flannel at the bottom of a dry ditch in a field, but was found alive soon after it had been left. The mother was acquitted of attempted murder because of lack of evidence of the necessary intent, an understandable verdict in the circumstances. She was, however, also acquitted of common assault, for a reason which the court expressed in the following terms:[3]

> 'There were no marks of violence on the child and it does not appear in the result that the child actually experienced any injury or inconvenience, and it was providentially found soon after it was exposed; and therefore, although it is said in some of the books that an exposure to the inclemency of the weather may amount to an assault, yet if that be so at all, it can only be when the person exposed suffers a hurt or injury of some kind or other from the exposure.'

Moreover, the common law insisted that the injury suffered was serious.[4]

1 This was particularly common where the death of a newly born child was caused by the mother's post-natal neglect.

2 (1847) 3 Cox CC 285.

3 Ibid at p 287. See also *R v Friend* (1802) Russ & Ry 20.

4 *R v Phillpot* (1853) Dears CC 179.

9.04   The inadequacy of a rule which was prepared to punish neglect of children only if there was proof of actual, serious harm was eventually acknowledged. A series of statutes creating offences relating to cruelty to children has successively embodied the principle that neglect in itself[1] is punishable provided that there is a likelihood of resultant harm. The first notable step was taken by the Poor Law Amendment Act 1868, section 37 of which made it an offence for a parent wilfully to neglect to provide adequate food, clothing, medical aid or lodging for his children, who were under 14 years of age and in his custody, so that their health 'shall have been or shall be likely to be seriously injured'.[2] This enactment was repealed and replaced by the more comprehensive provisions of the Prevention of Cruelty to, and Protection of, Children Act 1889, which not only made the ill-treatment and neglect of children a statutory offence, but also made provision for children who were ill-treated and neglected to be removed from the parent, or anyone else having custody or control, and entrusted to a fit person. This Act was amended,[3] but was at once replaced by the Prevention of Cruelty to Children Act 1894. The effect of the changes was to extend the legislation to cases of assault as well as ill-treatment and neglect. It was also specifically provided that a parent would be neglecting his child if, being without means to maintain him, he failed to provide for his maintenance under the Poor Law,[4] and the power to deal with the child and commit him to the charge of a fit person was no longer limited to cases of assault, ill-treatment and neglect under the 1894 Act, but also applied where various offences under the Offences against the Person Act 1861 had been committed in respect of the child.[5] The Act of 1894 was in turn replaced in 1904 by an Act of the same name and this remained the principal Act[6] until the Children and Young Persons Act 1933 placed the law on its present footing.[7] This will be considered later.[8]

1 Subject to its being 'wilful'; for the requisite mental element see post, para 9.37.
2 Even before this enactment it was an offence for anyone unlawfully to abandon or expose a child under two years of age so that his life was endangered or his health was or was likely to be permanently injured; Offences against the Person Act 1861, s 27. See post, para 9.46.
3 By the Prevention of Cruelty to Children (Amendment) Act 1894.
4 Cf *R v Hogan* (1851) 2 Den 277, where it had been held that to be liable the parent must have had the means of supporting the child.
5 For example, an offence under s 27, supra, note 2. Other sections dealt with assault (s 34), sexual offences (s 52) and unlawful removal of children (ss 55 and 56).
6 It was amended by the Children Act 1908 and the CYPA 1932.
7 A useful summary of the earlier legislation is to be found in *R v Sheppard* [1981] AC 394, [1980] 3 All ER 899.
8 Post paras 9.34 et seq.

II HOMICIDE OF CHILDREN

9.05 The law of homicide has special application to children in two ways: in relation to childbirth and to the breach of the duty to protect, although the two are sometimes interrelated.

1 Homicide and childbirth[1]

(a) Murder and manslaughter

9.06 The law of murder and manslaughter in its application to the newly-born child has been narrowly construed and reluctantly enforced.[2] These offences are only possible if the child is completely born alive. The conditions necessary for live-birth are that the child must be alive after complete extrusion from the mother,[3] but it is not necessary that there should have been expulsion of the after-birth or that the umbilical cord should have been severed.[4] On the basis of nineteenth century authorities the legal test for determining whether the child has been born alive has been one of independent existence. Has the child carried on its/his/her being without the help of the mother's circulation[5] and has it/he/she breathed after birth?[6] There are intrinsic objections to the test. While on the one hand a child may be born alive without yet having breathed, on the other hand it/he/she may have breathed at some stage in the process of birth and yet not be born alive.[7] More fundamentally, however, the test is based on 'a biological misconception' in that it ignores the fact that for several months before birth there has been an independent circulation, since there are separate fetal and maternal bloodstreams during the pregnancy.[8] Instead, therefore, the appropriate test suggested for determining whether the child is alive is the functioning of the heart,[9] but there is no direct judicial authority for the proposition.

1 See generally, Williams, *Textbook of Criminal Law*, 2nd edn, Chapter 13; Atkinson, *Life, Birth and Live-Birth* (1904) 20 LQR 134; Davies, *Child-Killing in English Law* in *Modern Approach to Criminal Law*, p 301.
2 In addition to the above references see Williams, *The Sanctity of Life and the Criminal Law* pp 19–23.
3 *R v Poulton* (1832) 5 C & P 329; *R v Brain* (1834) 6 C & P 349; *R v Sellis* (1837) 7 C & P 850.
4 *R v Reeves* (1839) 9 C & P 25; *R v Trilloe* (1842) 2 Mood CC 260.
5 Per Wright J in *R v Pritchard* (1901) 17 TLR 310.
6 See *R v Handley* (1874) 13 Cox CC 79 at 81.
7 *R v Brain* supra, note 3.
8 Williams, *Textbook on Criminal Law*, p 290 note 7; and supra note 2.
9 Ibid.

9.07   Although live-birth is a prerequisite to murder or manslaughter, the act causing death may have been committed while the child was en ventre sa mere or may occur in the process of being born, as happened in *R v Senior*,[1] where a man who practised midwifery was convicted for the manslaughter of a child who had died immediately after birth because his skull had, through gross negligence, been broken and compressed by the accused during the birth. Moreover, a person who causes a pre-natal injury will, depending upon the mental element, be guilty of murder or manslaughter if the injury results in a premature birth which thereby renders the child much less capable of surviving and he in fact dies soon afterwards.[2] The courts have declined, however, to extend these principles to the case where the death after birth has been caused by gross pre-natal neglect by the mother, so as to render her liable for the manslaughter of her child.[3] Legally it can be explained, or explained away, by imposing on her a duty of care only from the date of the child's birth; it may be merciful to her;[4] and it may accord with the feminist principle that her body is her own; but, by withholding penal sanctions, it totally ignores the interests of the child. The mother who persists, for example, in taking hard drugs during pregnancy knowing of its potentially harmful effects to her child should, it is suggested, be held accountable if the consequence of that conduct is the death of her child soon after birth.[5] This refusal to hold the mother liable for pre-natal neglect[6] has been paralleled by the unwillingness of juries to convict her for manslaughter of her new-born child where there has been post-natal neglect. Such deficiencies in the law and its administration have emphasised the need for other offences concerning childbirth.

1 (1832) 1 Mood CC 346.
2 *R v West* (1848) 2 Car & Kir 784.
3 *R v Knights* (1860) 2 F & F 46; *R v Izod* (1904) 20 Cox CC 690.
4 Williams, *Textbook of Criminal Law*, p 289.
5 She can be held accountable for the purpose of care proceedings under s 1 of CYPA 1969; *Re D (a minor)* [1987] AC 317, sub nom *D v Berkshire County Council* [1987] 1 All ER 20, HL, post, para 14.07.
6 For abortive nineteenth century attempts to fill this gap in the law of manslaughter see Davies, op cit, p 309. But any imposition of legal liability for pre-natal neglect is bound to be controversial and it may be impracticable to define realistic limits. See the *Independent*, 22 December 1987, for the controversy surrounding the conviction and imprisonment

of a Californian mother, Pamela Stewart, for pre-natal neglect that led to the death of her six-week-old baby.

(b)   Abortion[1]

(i)   Introduction

9.08   Although the common law insisted on live-birth for the purposes of murder and manslaughter, it did apparently recognise that it was a misdemeanour to destroy a child when it was quick[2] in the mother's womb.[3] An Act of 1803[4] made it an offence to administer a poison to a woman with intent to procure her miscarriage, and the offence was made punishable by death if she was in fact quick with the child and by transportation or imprisonment if she was not. In 1828 the offence was extended to any means of procurement,[5] but the distinction between the quick and the non-quick woman was retained until the Offences against the Person Act 1837,[6] recognising the difficulty of sometimes drawing the distinction, abandoned it. The present governing statutes are the Offences against the Person Act 1861 and the Abortion Act 1967.

1 See Williams, *The Sanctity of Life and the Criminal Law*, pp 139—223; Report of the Committee on the Working of the Abortion Act (Hon Mrs Justice Lane) (1974) Cmnd 5579 (referred to herein as the 'Lane Report').
2 Ie from the time when the movement of the fetus is felt.
3 For the history of abortion see Davies, *The Law of Abortion and Necessity* (1938–39) 2 MLR at pp 130–135.
4 43 Geo 3, c58.
5 By the Offences against the Person Act 1828 (9 Geo 4, c31), which replaced the earlier Act.
6 1 Vic, c85.

(ii)   The offence

9.09   Section 58 of the 1861 Act does not use the term abortion, but refers to an intent to procure (ie cause) a miscarriage.[1] It may be committed by the woman herself, provided that she is in fact 'with child',[2] or by a third person whether the woman is pregnant or not.[3] Even where she is not pregnant, she herself may be guilty of conspiring to procure her own miscarriage[4] or of aiding and abetting in the commission of abortion.[5] The offence is punishable with imprisonment for life, but sentences are in practice substantially less, sometimes no more than fines,[6] and prosecution of the woman herself is rare.

1 For the uncertainty of meaning of this word see Keown, *Miscarriage: A Medico-Legal Analysis,* [1984] Crim LR 604.
2 For the significance of these words see infra.
3 Where a third person is charged, the woman is in the position of an accomplice and the jury should be warned about the danger of convicting in reliance on the uncorroborated evidence of an accomplice; *R v Price* [1969] 1 QB 541, [1968] 2 All ER 282, CA.
4 *R v Whitchurch* (1890) 24 QBD 420, CCR.
5 *R v Sockett* 1 Cr App Rep 101, CCA.
6 But in *R v Scrimaglie* and *Young* (1971) 55 Cr App Rep 280 it was said that, now that legal abortions are available under the 1967 Act, insanitary, backdoor abortions call for custodial sentences.

9.10   The offence may be committed by unlawfully administering a 'poison or other noxious thing' or by unlawfully using any instrument or 'other means whatsoever' to procure the miscarriage. The fact that the method used could not produce a miscarriage is not material, provided that there is the necessary intent.[1] Moreover, under section 59 of the 1861 Act, it is an offence[2] for anyone to supply or procure[3] any poison, noxious thing, instrument or other thing knowing that it is intended to be unlawfully used with intent to procure a miscarriage. This offence has been too widely construed,[4] for it is sufficient to show that the accused intended that the particular thing should be used to abort, even if the person supplied did not intend so to use it[5] or even if the woman for whom it was intended was not in fact pregnant.[6] The term 'noxious thing' means a thing other than a recognised poison, but it is not limited to a thing which is an abortifacient.[7] However, a sufficient amount of the thing must be administered so as to be harmful,[8] and logically the same should be true of a poison.[9] The reference in section 58 to 'any other means whatsoever' has acquired special significance with the appearance of modern anti-pregnancy techniques. If it is still the law, as it certainly appears to be, that a woman is 'with child' from the date of fertilisation of the ovum, several of those techniques, if used, must be unlawful, and, even if the date of conception is legally postponed until the date of implantation[10] (some ten days after fertilisation), so that some of these techniques[11] become lawful, there are still others[12] which are caught by the terms of section 58 so as to render them unlawful unless protected by the Abortion Act 1967.

1 *R v Spicer* (1955) 39 Cr App Rep 189 (manual interference such as not to be able to cause a miscarriage).
2 Punishable with imprisonment for not more than five years.
3 The word 'procure' has been narrowly construed to mean getting possession from someone else and does not include making use of something already in one's possession; *R v Mills* [1963] 1 QB 522, [1963] 1 All ER 202, CCA.
4 See Smith and Hogan, *Criminal Law*, 6th edn, pp 368–369.
5 *R v Hillman* (1863) 9 Cox CC 386, CCCR.
6 *R v Titley* (1880) 14 Cox CC 502.
7 *R v Marlow* (1964) 49 Cr App Rep 49.
8 *R v Cramp* (1880) 5 QBD 307 (harmless quantities of oil of juniper) and see *R v Weatherall* [1968] Crim LR 115 (sleeping pill not noxious).
9 Smith and Hogan, op cit p 367.
10 As argued by Williams, *Textbook of Criminal Law*, pp 294–295, but there is no judicial authority in support, and compare Keown, op cit.
11 Notably the intrauterine device (IUD) and the post-coital contraceptive pill.
12 Viz, the biochemical technique of expulsion of the fetus, known as prostaglandin, and the mechanical device of suction, known as vacuum cannula. For discussion of the legality of abortion by prostaglandin see Wright [1984] Crim LR 347 and [1985] Crim LR 140; Tunkel, [1985] Crim LR 133; and Norrie [1985] Crim LR 475, especially at pp 478–479.

(iii) Medical termination of pregnancy: the Abortion Act 1967
9.11 Section 58 excludes from its provisions lawful acts to terminate pregnancy but the exemption was limited to therapeutic abortion undertaken by the medical profession. The exemption, based on the doctrine of necessity, was not judicially recognised until 1938 in the well-known case of *R v Bourne*.[1] As a test case the facts could hardly have been stronger. A 14-year-old girl was the victim of a brutal and horrifying rape which left her pregnant. A distinguished gynaecologist openly performed an operation in a hospital to terminate the pregnancy because he was of the opinion that otherwise the girl would probably become a physical and a mental

wreck. He was acquitted of an offence under section 58, but the precise effects of the case were uncertain.[2] It was made abundantly clear by Macnaghten J that if an operation was performed in good faith in order to preserve the mother's life it was lawful. Whether it was enough to show that the object was protection of her health was left open to doubt, although subsequent cases supported this wider principle.[3] The Abortion Act 1967 has in this respect clarified the law, but, being a compromise between the pro-abortion and the anti-abortion lobbies, has in others created uncertainties.

1 [1939] 1 KB 687, [1938] 3 All ER 615.
2 See Lord Diplock in *Royal College of Nursing of the United Kingdom v Department of Health and Social Security* [1981] AC 800 at 826, [1981] 1 All ER 545 at 567–568.
3 *R v Bergmann and Ferguson* (1948) unreported; see Williams, *The Sanctity of Life*, p 154; *R v Newton and Stungo* [1958] Crim LR 469. Medical textbooks had long taken the view that acts done to preserve either the life or health of the pregnant woman were lawful. Yet, after *Bourne* doctors were still reluctant to operate.

9.12 Section 1 of the Act provides:[1]

'*1 Medical termination of pregnancy* – (1) Subject to the provisions of this section, a person shall not be guilty of an offence under the law relating to abortion when a pregnancy is terminated by a registered medical practitioner if two registered medical practitioners are of the opinion, formed in good faith –
(a) that the continuance of the pregnancy would involve risk to the life of the pregnant woman, or of injury to the physical or mental health of the pregnant woman or any existing children of her family, greater than if the pregnancy were terminated; or
(b) that there is a substantial risk that if the child were born it would suffer from such physical or mental abnormalities as to be seriously handicapped.
(2) In determining whether the continuance of a pregnancy would involve such risk of injury to health as is mentioned in paragraph (a) of subsection (1) of this section, account may be taken of the pregnant woman's actual or reasonably foreseeable environment.
(3) Except as provided by subsection (4) of this section, any treatment for the termination of pregnancy must be carried out in a hospital vested in the Minister of Health or the Secretary of State under the National Health Service Acts, or in a place for the time being approved for the purposes of this section by the said Minister or the Secretary of State.
(4) Subsection (3) of this section, and so much of subsection (1) as relates to the opinion of two registered medical practitioners, shall not apply to the termination of a pregnancy by a registered medical practitioner in a case where he is of the opinion, formed in good faith, that the termination is immediately necessary to save the life or to prevent grave permanent injury to the physical or mental health of the pregnant woman.'

Section 1(1)(a) embodies two distinct grounds, one relating to risk to the woman and one relating to risk to her children. In examining them and that contained in section 1(1)(b) it must be remembered that none is a defence to the killing of a viable child, ie one who is capable of being born alive, and 28 weeks or more of pregnancy is prima facie proof of viability.[2] Section 5(2) of the Act expressly provides that the three grounds are the only ones on which termination of pregnancy is allowed, and it is generally accepted that they supersede the common law.[3] However, it has been persuasively argued that the provision does not entirely eliminate the operation of general defences to crime.[4]

1 For detailed analyses see Hoggett, *The Abortion Act 1967*, [1968] Crim LR 247 and Williams, *Textbook of Criminal Law*, pp 297–304.
2 See post, para 9.25.
3 For example, see Scarman LJ in *R v Smith* [1974] 1 All ER 376 at 378.
4 Smith and Hogan, op cit, p 372, and with regard specifically to the defence of necessity see post, para 9.20.

(iv)   Risk to life or health of the woman
9.13   Section 1(1)(a) allows termination of pregnancy whenever medical opinion[1] considers that its continuance would involve a greater risk to the woman's life or health than its termination would.[2] Literally construed the test would normally allow abortion in the first three months of pregnancy – the earlier the safer – since during that trimester the risk attendant on an abortion operation is significantly less than that involved in child bearing. Certainly this is so as far as concerns the risk of mortality, so that even if it is more difficult to assess the relative risks of injury to the health of the woman, especially the risk to mental health, logically it does not matter because the alternative condition of risk to life is satisfied.[3] Twenty years without this construction having been judicially tested have left the individual doctor with a wide safety net within which to operate. Moreover, the Act does not restrict the kind of mental health which has to be at risk.[4] This is particularly relevant in cases of rape, for, while this is not a ground for termination, there should be little difficulty, in practice, establishing that the victim is likely to suffer some degree of depression if the pregnancy is not terminated.

1 See infra, para 9.19.
2 The Lane Committee found that this is by far the most common ground (para 200).
3 But the Lane Committee stressed the need for doctors to treat each case on its merits rather than rely on statistics which show that continued pregnancy is always a higher risk (para 201).
4 In a large number of cases it is mental distress and not physical injury which is the key factor (ibid, para 204).

(v)   Risk to health of existing children of the family
9.14   Similarly the test here is whether the continuance of the pregnancy would result in a greater risk of injury to the health of any existing children of the woman's family. It seems clear that what this means is that if the pregnancy is not terminated the additional responsibility of bringing up the newly born child will be likely to affect the health of the mother's other children. This additional ground introduced into the law of abortion a novel aspect of child protection. Both it and the third ground cut deep inroads into the long established principle that protection which the law gives to human life extends to the unborn child. It may be difficult for a doctor to decide whether the continuance of the pregnancy would involve greater risk to an existing child. It would be easier to assess if the increase

had to be substantial. Although it is clear that something more will have to be shown than a mere reduction in the standard of living of the family which an addition to it would entail, it is suggested that in most cases the question for consideration is whether the addition would seriously handicap the woman's ability to take care of her children. This may more readily be proved if any existing child is suffering from a serious physical or mental disability. It would be much more difficult to prove that a child will be put at greater risk of being subjected to physical abuse by the mother because of the additional pressure put on her through her having to bring up another child; but a history of abuse in the family may justify that conclusion.

9.15   Another uncertainty arises from the failure of the Act to define the term 'any existing children of the family'. It should be widely construed. It does, it is submitted, include not only any natural or adopted child but also one who is in fact a member of the woman's family, even though not a natural or adopted child of her or her husband.[1] Nor should the term necessarily be restricted to children under the age of majority: the true test, it is suggested, is the child's dependence on the woman, not his age.

1 Ie the same meaning as for matrimonial causes; see ante, para 3.34.

9.16   In calculating the risk of injury to the health of the woman or of an existing child of the family, account may be taken of her 'actual or reasonably foreseeable environment'. This is a remarkably vague and inapt determinant.[1] It would have been preferable if the Act had listed the main matters to be considered. 'Environment' would seem to include the woman's place and mode of living, the persons with whom she is living, their financial resources and, arguably, their views about the proposed abortion. This last matter is of special importance in relation to the husband. It may well be that, if he is consulted, he will be able to satisfy the doctors that, contrary to what the mother may say, no great strain will be imposed on her health or that of existing children, if there is an addition to the family. But consultation is wholly a matter for the discretion of the doctors.[2] The Act does not require the husband to consent to abortion or even to be consulted, and he has no civil remedy, through an injunction, to stop his wife having, or a doctor from performing, a legal abortion.[3] The unmarried father is similarly not entitled to an injunction.[4] This is probably so even though the doctors have not acted in good faith in reaching their opinion that one of the legal grounds for abortion exists, so that the proposed abortion would be unlawful.[5] The Act is concerned only with the criminal law, so that those matters are better left to the Crown Prosecution Service to consider for possible prosecution.

1 Surprisingly, the Lane Committee could not suggest 'any alternative which would make the meaning plainer' (para 203).
2 It is submitted that where one of the certifying doctors is the mother's own doctor, his statutory duty in respect of certifying his opinion on abortion overrides his duty of confidentiality to his patient, and he is therefore entitled to consult others if that will enable him the better to discharge his statutory duty.
3 *Paton v British Pregnancy Advisory Services Trustees* [1979] QB 276, [1978] 2 All ER 987.
4 *C v S* [1988] QB 135, [1987] 1 All ER 1230, CA; and see Bromley, op cit, p 262.

5 See Sir George Baker P (obiter), [1979] QB at 282, [1978] 2 All ER at 988 and 991.

9.17   Such is the indeterminate nature of 'environment' that there is a risk, fully recognised by the Lane Committee,[1] that it becomes in itself a 'social' ground justifying abortion, without the need for proof of risk to health – a ground of convenience to the woman in which her future career[2] or way of life looms large. This is not far short of abortion on demand or on request, which the Committee rejected and which Parliament in 1967 never intended.

1 Paragraph 207.
2 In *Re P (a minor)* [1986] 1 FLR 272, one matter taken into 'environmental' account was the fact that a 15-year-old girl's O level study would be ruined if her pregnancy was not terminated.

(vi)   Substantial risk of child being seriously handicapped
9.18   The introduction of this ground met a demand of the medical profession,[1] but the rationale underlying it is that parents should be saved from the substantial risk of bringing up such a child.[2] The ground imposes a heavier test for the certifying doctors than do the health grounds, but the technique of amniocentesis for screening pregnancy provides for reasonably accurate calculation of the chances of a baby being born with serious congenital abnormality or physical defects resulting from damage in the womb. The new screening test of chorionic villus sampling (CVS), which is at its early stages of medical trial, should eventually improve that accuracy. One of its advantages over amniocentesis is that it can be completed within the first three months of pregnancy, so that termination of the pregnancy, if needed, can be performed earlier.

1 See Havard, *Therapeutic Abortion* [1958] Crim LR 600 at p 606.
2 Williams, *Textbook of Criminal Law* p 297.

(vii)   The role of the doctor
9.19   To come within the 1967 Act the pregnancy must be terminated by a registered medical practitioner. However, the increasing reliance on medical methods of induction, such as prostaglandin, as opposed to surgical intervention, led the House of Lords by a majority of three to two in *Royal College of Nursing of the United Kingdom v Department of Health and Social Security*[1] to hold that a pregnancy may be lawfully terminated by a registered medical practitioner even though nursing staff play a large part in the process. The test is whether the doctor remains in charge and accepts responsibility throughout, and the treatment is carried out in accordance with his directions. Normally, a prerequisite to termination is a certified opinion by two registered medical practitioners that one of the three grounds exists. The opinion must be formed in good faith. That is a question for the jury and not for the evidence of medical expert witnesses, but proving lack of good faith may be difficult. Evidence of medical practice is usually needed, but conviction is still possible without it.[2] Normally, too, treatment for termination must be carried out in a National Health Service hospital or in a place approved by the Secretary of State for Health. However, where a medical practitioner is of the opinion that the termination is immediately necessary to save the woman's life or to prevent grave

permanent injury to her health, it may be carried out in another place and without a second concurring opinion.[3]

1 [1981] AC 800, [1981] 1 All ER 545.
2 *R v Smith* [1974] 1 All ER 376, [1973] 1 WLR 1510, CA.
3 Section 1(3) and (4).

9.20   No-one is compelled to participate in treatment authorised by the Act if he has conscientious objections to it,[1] but this does not affect any duty to participate which is necessary to save the life or to prevent grave permanent injury to the health of the woman,[2] and it has been argued that there may be a common law duty on a doctor to act in such circumstances, notwithstanding his conscientious objections.[3]

1 Section 4(1). A nurse who types letters of referral of patients to specialists does not participate in treatment; see *R v Salford Health Authority, ex p Janaway* [1988] 1 FLR 17, [1987] Fam Law 345.
2 Section 4(2).
3 Smith and Hogan, op cit, pp 373–374. Compare the position in Canada, where there is no equivalent to s 1(4) of the Abortion Act 1967, and so the Supreme Court has relied on the common law defence of necessity. See Leigh, *Necessity and the Case of Dr. Morgentaler*, [1978] Crim LR 151.

(viii)   Multiple transfers of embryos
9.21   The process of *in vitro* fertilisation (IVF)[1] has given rise to dispute over whether there should be restrictions imposed on the number of embryos to be transferred to the woman. The problem is likely to be a major factor in expediting legislation on IVF. Multiple transfers are made in order to improve the chances of pregnancy. The Voluntary Licensing Authority[2] has recommended to the 30 IVF clinics that no more than three or, in exceptional circumstances, four embryos should be transferred.[3] If more are transferred the risk of too many implanting is increased. There can, it is submitted, be no doubt that to make a selective reduction and remove some of the fetuses prima facie constitutes the offence of abortion,[4] ie unless the doctor can rely on any of the defences provided by the Abortion Act 1967. As already mentioned,[5] the risk to the life of the mother has left the doctor with a wide safety net to terminate within the first three months of pregnancy, and doctors who do engage in selective reduction are likely to be protected by the Act. Selective reduction may be necessary not to save the mother's life, but to prevent risking the loss of the whole pregnancy. That possibility is not specifically covered by the Act, but in such a case removal of some fetuses may be covered on the ground that to lose the whole pregnancy would cause mental distress to the mother. What may well have to be determined eventually is whether selective reduction can be justified in the particular case on the ground of risk to the health of existing children of the family. From what has already been said[6] the possibility of multiple births could well affect the mother's ability to take care of her existing children. The matter clearly raises large moral and social issues.

1 See ante, para 2.06 et seq.
2 Set up by the Medical Research Council and the Royal College of Obstetricians and Gynaecologists as an interim measure to monitor IVF treatment.

3 The refusal of one clinic to observe this restriction has led to the Voluntary Licensing Authority withdrawing its approval of the clinic.
4 The fact that termination is by way of injection of a drug which enables the fetus to be reabsorbed into the woman's body and not by any expulsion from the body does not make it anything less than abortion; see ante, para 9.10.
5 Ante, para 9.13.
6 Ante, para 9.14.

(ix) Consent of the woman
9.22 Normally, the consent of the woman to terminating her pregnancy is necessary as it would be if she were undergoing any other surgical operation or other medical treatment. Indeed, it is not simply a matter of consent but also of consultation.[1] '. . . obviously the mother is going to be right at the heart of the matter consulting with the doctors if they are to arrive at a decision in good faith, unless, of course, she is mentally incapacitated or physically incapacitated (unable to make any decision or give any help) as, for example, in consequence of an accident'.[2] Nevertheless, in a case of emergency where her life is in danger termination of pregnancy without her consent would be justified, provided there is compliance with the conditions of the Abortion Act 1967.[3] The position in respect of the consent of a girl under 16 who is pregnant has already been examined.[4]

1 For a striking illustration see *Re P (a minor)* [1986] 1 FLR 272, where a 15-year-old girl was closely consulted. See ante, para 1.28.
2 Per Sir George Baker P in *Paton v British Pregnancy Advisory Service Trustees* [1979] QB 276, [1978] 2 All ER 987 at 281 and 991 respectively.
3 But see also para 9.20, note 3.
4 See ante, para 1.28.

(x) Conclusion
9.23 The Abortion Act 1967 leaves a wide discretion to the medical profession, and it is uncommon to establish in the courts breach of its provisions. Soon after its implementation there were clear indications of marked divergence in operating it within the National Health Service, while abuse of the powers conferred made it necessary to tighten up on Ministerial approval of private clinics. Some of the concern and doubts about its early years of operation, especially in the private sector,[1] were confirmed by the Lane Committee. Between the date of that Report, in 1974, and the next major survey, completed ten years later, there were no less than six unsuccessful attempts in Parliament to tighten up the Act,[2] for example, by amendment of section 1(1)(a) so that the continuance of the pregnancy would involve 'serious' risk to life or health which would be 'substantially' greater than if the pregnancy were terminated. It was the controversy over one of these Bills,[3] which, inter alia, would have set an upper time limit on abortion, that prompted an inquiry by the Royal College of Obstetricians and Gynaecologists. Its Report[4] is the first national survey to look at the confidential abortion notification which doctors must send to the Chief Medical Officer at the Department of Health. Among its many findings and conclusions the following are particularly noteworthy:
(1) Except where performed primarily because of the risk of congenital deformity, the great majority of abortions during the second trimester (13–27 weeks) of women resident in England and Wales were performed in the private rather than the NHS sector. Indeed, for abortions between 20th and 27th week the ratio was six (private) to one (NHS).

(2) Women under 20 were the largest group to seek abortion during the second trimester (40%) and in the later period, after the 19th week, they were as high as 50% of the total.

(3) Delay in seeking an abortion was sometimes due to failure to recognise the pregnancy, but more important were 'human factors', such as indecision or extended discussion with the father. Another 'substantial contribution' was delay in hospital services, especially those under the NHS.

(4) Unusually for British medicine generally, over 50% of abortions outside the NHS were self-referrals by the women rather than referrals through the family doctor.

(5) NHS hospitals generally relied on medical and thus lengthier methods of abortion rather than surgical intervention.

(6) The methods of detecting fetal defects were improving, but most abortions have to be delayed to the second trimester and often beyond the 20th week.

(7) Less than 50% of fetal defects were based on a very high risk or certainty of abnormality. The majority related largely to previous family history, anxiety of patient or doctor, or problems diagnosing rubella in the first trimester.

(8) A large number of second trimester abortions were carried out on foreign women, and a large number were performed by a relatively small number of doctors.

The Report recommends[5] that there is an 'urgent need' to provide more education[6] for young women about the recognition of pregnancy and to seek advice and help when it is recognised. In this regard the provision of youth advisory centres would be advantageous.[7] The study shows that, so far as concerns hazards to life or health, late abortions 'appear to be relatively safe',[8] and that continued research will help diagnose abnormalities earlier and thus increase the number of first trimester abortions.

1 See Cmnd 5579, Section N.
2 In addition to Bills in 1975, 1977, 1978, 1979, 1980 and 1982, there had been two others in 1969 and 1970; and there was a debate on a Private Member's motion in 1985. In 1986 another Bill was introduced by the then Bishop of Birmingham. Although it fell with the dissolution of Parliament in June 1987, a House of Lords Select Committee on the Infant Life (Preservation) Bill produced a Special Report on the subject. Its investigations revealed 'a gentleman's agreement' between Government and private abortion clinics to deter doctors from carrying out late abortions. The most recent unsuccessful Bill was that introduced in November 1987 by Mr David Alton, which proposed an upper time limit of 18 weeks on abortion. Compare the Report of the House of Lords Select Committee, which, though it calls for stiffer conditions before allowing abortion between 24 and 28 weeks, warns of the dangers of reducing the time limit.
3 Introduced in 1979 by Mr John Corrie.
4 *Late Abortions in England and Wales* – Report of a National Confidential Study.
5 See pp 106–107.
6 It is doubtful and controversial how far school authorities would provide it.
7 The Lane Committee (Section K) recommended more counselling before, and more care after, abortion.
8 Out of 172,000 terminations in England and Wales in 1986, 5,665 were performed after 18 weeks, including 2,723 after 20 weeks and 29 later than 25 weeks. See the Guardian Newspaper (1987) 26 September.

9.24 There are few subjects that arouse greater passion but achieve less legal change than abortion. However, the following statistics show that its increasing significance as a social matter will eventually compel legislative change or additional resources or, most probably, both.

The details, monitored by the Office of Population and Censuses, are based on notifications in England and Wales under the Abortion Act 1967.

Year	Total Number of Abortions of Residents in England and Wales	Single Women	Married Women	Total Number of Abortions, including Non-Residents[1]
1980	128,927	68,756	44,253	—
1981	128,955	70,021	42,427	162,454
1982	128,553	71,836	40,510	162,797
1983	127,375	73,259	38,431	162,161
1984[2]	136,388	81,097	38,651	169,993
1985	141,101	87,213	37,698	171,873
1986	147,619[3]	93,041	38,203	172,286

1 The non-residents are mainly Spanish (circa 18,000 per annum), French (3,500–4,000); Irish (circa 3,500).

2 The number of abortions of girls under 16 recorded for the years 1985 and 1986 were 4427 and 4240 respectively; see HC Debs (WA) 15 May 1987, col 423.

3 Figures for 1987 show an increase of 5.5 per cent to over 156,000.

(c)   Child destruction

9.25   Closely related to, and overlapping with, abortion is the offence of child destruction, created by the Infant Life (Preservation) Act 1929 because of the restrictive rule that murder is only possible if the child is born alive.[1] Under section 1 it is an offence, punishable with imprisonment for life, to cause a child, capable of being born alive, to die before it has an existence independent of its mother; and evidence that the mother has been pregnant for 28 weeks or more is prima facie proof that the child is capable of being born alive. On the other hand, it has been held[2] that a fetus of a gestational age of 18 to 21 weeks cannot be described as being capable of being born alive. Although it could demonstrate real and discernible signs of life, namely a primitive circulation and movement of its limbs, it would be incapable of breathing either naturally or with the aid of a ventilator. It follows that unlawfully procuring a miscarriage while the fetus is non-viable can only be the offence of abortion, whereas procuring a miscarriage once it becomes viable may be abortion or child destruction. Unlawfully killing the child while being delivered can only be child destruction.[3]

1 See ante, para 9.06.
2 C v S [1988] QB 135, [1987] 1 All ER 1230, CA.

3 In *R v Bourne* [1939] 1 KB 687, [1938] 3 All ER 615 Mcnaghten J stated obiter that child destruction was concerned only with killing in that situation, but there is nothing in the Act so limiting it. Because it may be difficult to determine whether the child was killed before or after birth, the indictment will include counts of murder and of child destruction.

9.26 The Abortion Act 1967 expressly provides[1] that that Act does not affect the 1929 Act. One of the consequences therefore is that the legal grounds which permit abortion do not extend as defences to child destruction. Instead the 1929 Act provides its own defence, namely, that a person cannot be convicted of the offence unless it is proved that the act which caused the child's death was not done in good faith for the purpose of preserving the life of the mother. A question on which there is still uncertainty is whether the defence is to be narrowly construed and restricted to preservation of life or whether in the light of *R v Bourne* and later cases,[2] albeit cases on abortion decided before the Abortion Act 1967, the defence is established by proof that the destruction was done to protect the mother's health.[3] The combined effect of the overlapping of the two offences is that destroying a viable fetus will only be lawful if both one of the legal grounds and other conditions of the 1967 Act are satisfied and the destruction is done only in order to preserve the mother's life.

1 Section 5(1).
2 See ante, para 9.11, note 3.
3 See further Smith and Hogan, op cit, pp 365–366.

The twenty-eight week presumption
9.27 As indicated above, one of the effects of the statutory presumption of viability after 28 weeks of pregnancy has been the practice of restricting abortion to the first 28 weeks. The Lane Committee, taking account of modern scientific methods which enable earlier survival of the fetus, considered that upper limit to be too high. It proposed[1] instead a limit of 24 weeks, but added that 'thereafter every effort should be made to preserve the life of the child' – one of those few instances in official publications and in commentaries of positive reference to the protection of the child. On the other hand, the Committee did not recommend a right of the woman to choose to have an abortion during the first trimester. That right was endorsed by the United States Supreme Court in *Roe v Wade*,[2] but the fixing of any upper limit has been left to individual States, and there has been similar pressure to reduce from 28 to 25 weeks.[3]

1 Cmnd 5579, para 283. Two years earlier an advisory body recommended to the Secretary of State for Social Services that a fetus should be viable at 20 weeks – *The Use of Fetus and Fetal Material for Research* (HMSO 1972).
2 410 US 113 (1973).
3 *Akron v Akron Center for Reproductive Health* 462 US 416 S Ct (1983).

(d) Infanticide[1]

9.28 This offence owes its origins to the notorious unwillingness to apply the full rigour of the law of murder to cases of killing by mothers of their very young children. Even if in such cases juries could be persuaded to convict of murder the death sentence was invariably commuted.

1 See Davies, *Child-Killing in English Law*, Modern Approach to Criminal Law, p 301; Williams, *The Sanctity of Life*, pp 25–45; O'Donovan, *The Medicalisation of Infanticide*, [1984] Crim LR 259 (which includes a neat summary of the history of the offence).

9.29   Section 1(1) of the Infanticide Act 1938, which replaced an Act of 1922, provides that, where a woman wilfully causes the death of her child who is under the age of 12 months and, but for that section, the circumstances would have amounted to murder, she will be guilty of infanticide if at the time of her act or omission the balance of her mind was disturbed because she had not fully recovered from the effect of giving birth to the child or because of the effect of lactation consequent upon the birth.[1] She may then be dealt with as if she had been guilty of manslaughter of the child. Theoretically, therefore, she may be sentenced to life imprisonment, but imprisonment for even a short period is uncommon as is a suspended sentence. More likely is a hospital order or probation order or even a discharge. The readiness to treat the offence as a minor one gives added force to the view that it 'is an illogical compromise between the law of murder and humane feelings'.[2]

1 Where she is indicted for murder she may instead be convicted of infanticide if s 1 is satisfied (s 1(2)). An indictment for attempted infanticide is possible; *R v KA Smith* [1983] Crim LR 739. In its Report on Offences against the Person the Criminal Law Revision Committee had expressed the view that the wording of the 1938 Act did not permit a charge of attempt (Cmnd 7844, para 113).
2 Williams, op cit, p 37. An Infanticide Bill, in 1970, would have made the offence a summary one.

9.30   As with other offences relating to child-killing, this is long overdue for reform, preferably as part of a comprehensive scheme of reform relating to homicide and childbirth; but there is the same reluctance to effect it, in spite of two influential Reports recommending it. The Committee on Mentally Abnormal Offenders recommended its abolition on the ground that there is now the general defence of diminished responsibility.[1] The Criminal Law Revision Committee preferred retention,[2] but would have broadened the scope of the offence to take account of the fact that the woman's disturbed balance of mind may sometimes be due not to the effect of giving birth but to the social stresses consequent upon the birth.[3] There is, it is submitted, something artificial about this conclusion. These stresses may persist long beyond the 12 month period and may equally affect the father.[4]

1 (1975) Cmnd 6244, paras 19-23–19.24.
2 Fourteenth Report, *Offences Against the Person*, (1980) Cmnd 7844, paras 100–106.
3 Compare the 'environmental' factor in abortion cases, ante, para 9.16.
4 See also the strong dissenting views of Sir David Napley, Cmnd 7844, at p 145; and for the clash between medical and socio-economic justifications for retaining the offence see O'Donovan, op cit.

(e)   Concealment of birth

9.31   'The offence most pressed into service to fill part of the gap later to be largely closed by the creation of Child Destruction and Infanticide was that of concealment of birth.'[1]

But the gap-filling was a gradual process. The offence originated in an

Act of 1623,[2] passed because of the difficulty of proving live-birth in a charge of murder of a new-born child. In practice the person who for that reason most commonly escaped liability was the mother who killed her illegitimate child and tried to conceal the death by secretly disposing of the body, and it was against her alone that the Act was aimed. Although it required the child to have been born alive, all that was needed to be proved was the secret disposition of the body, because then the onus was put on the mother to prove that the child was born dead. Eventually the offence acquired its modern features[3] and under the present provisions[4] it relates to all children whether or not the parents are married, it may be committed by the mother or by anyone else and it applies whether the child died before, at or after birth. It is, however, necessary that the fetus shall have become a child but the legal test for determining this is uncertain. It seems that it is not sufficient for the fetus to have the outward appearance of a child,[5] but that the child must have 'arrived at that stage of maturity at the time of birth that it might have been a living child'.[6]

1 Davies, op cit at p 312.
2 21 Jac 1, c 27. See Radzinowicz, *History of English Criminal Law*, Vol I, pp 430 et seq.
3 For its subsequent history see 43 Geo 3, c 58, s 2 and 9 Geo 4, c 31, s 14, as amended by 10 Geo 4, c 34, s 17(1).
4 Offences against the Person Act 1861, s 60. The offence is punishable with two years' imprisonment.
5 *R v Colmer* (1864) 9 Cox CC 506 to the contrary is a doubtful authority; see *Russell on Crime*, p 611.
6 Per Erle J in *R v Berriman* (1854) 6 Cox CC 388 at 390.

2   Breach of the duty to protect

9.32   If a parent fails to fulfil his duty of protecting his child, who consequently dies, he may be guilty of murder or manslaughter.[1] As already noted,[2] the duty at common law has been largely replaced by statute. The breach of the duty may take various forms.[3] Often it is neglect by the parent, or whoever else has the charge or care of the child, to provide the child with the necessities of life, for example, adequate food or medical aid. If his neglect is wilful,[4] he is guilty of an offence under section 1 of the Children and Young Persons Act 1933. If the neglect results in the child's death and the parent intended to kill or cause serious injury to the child, he is guilty of murder. In the absence of that alternative intention he may for the following reasons be guilty of manslaughter.

1 A detailed analysis of the mental element in homicide is outside the scope of this book. The reader is referred to textbooks on the criminal law. See especially Williams, *Textbook of Criminal Law*, 2nd edn and Smith and Hogan, *Criminal Law*, 6th edn. But particular reference now needs to be made to *R v Moloney* [1985] AC 905, [1985] 1 All ER 1025, HL; *R v Hancock* [1986] AC 455, [1986] 1 All ER 641, HL; *R v Nedrick* [1986] 3 All ER 1, [1986] 1 WLR 1025, CA.
2 Ante, para 9.03.
3 See further paras 9.34 et seq.
4 For the meaning see post, para 9.37.

9.33   Although its exact scope was disputed, it was a long accepted principle that the commission of an unlawful act resulting in death in itself constituted manslaughter and neither motive nor state of mind was material. That general principle has been qualified by *R v Church*[1] in that, where an unlawful act causes death, to constitute manslaughter it 'must be such as all sober and reasonable people would inevitably recognise must subject the other person to, at least, the risk of some harm resulting therefrom, albeit not serious harm'. But this objective test requires only a recognition of the risk of some harm; there is no need to prove risk of death or of grievous bodily harm. However, in relation to a case of neglect of a child there is a further limitation, imposed by the Court of Appeal in *R v Lowe*,[2] where a distinction was drawn between an act and an omission:

> '. . . if I strike a child in a manner likely to cause harm it is right that if the child dies I may be charged with manslaughter. If, however, I omit to do something with the result that it suffers injury to its health which results in its death, we think that a charge of manslaughter should not be an inevitable consequence even if the omission is deliberate.'

The effect seems to be[3] that neglect, such as the failure to call for medical aid, which is due to negligence, is not an unlawful act. To amount to manslaughter the omission must be deliberate, knowing that the aid is needed, or there must be gross negligence in that a reasonable man would have foreseen that the failure to provide aid would result in death or at least grievous bodily harm. It is suggested that refusal to provide food, clothing or shelter is almost certain to be deliberate, but refusal to seek medical aid may sometimes be due to gross negligence – or may even be 'only negligent' so that there would then be no liability for manslaughter.

1 [1966] 1 QB 59, [1965] 2 All ER 72, CCA.
2 [1973] QB 702, [1973] 1 All ER 805. The case was also concerned with wilful neglect under s 1 of CYPA 1933. On that point the House of Lords in *R v Sheppard* [1981] AC 394, [1980] 3 All ER 899 overruled *Lowe* (see post, para 9.37) but on the present point *Lowe* was not affected.
3 See Smith and Hogan, op cit, p 350.

III   PHYSICAL HARM NOT CAUSING DEATH

1   Cruelty to children under 16

9.34   It has already been explained[1] how the weakness of the common law in protecting children led in the second half of the nineteenth century to a series of statutes which dealt with neglect and ill-treatment of children and also with other aspects of protection from physical and moral danger. The relevant law is now to be found in Part I of the Children and Young Persons Act 1933, of which section 1 is undoubtedly the most far-reaching provision. Subsection (1) provides:[2]

> If any person who has attained the age of 16 years and has the custody, charge or care of any child or young person under that age, wilfully assaults, ill-treats, neglects, abandons or exposes him or causes or procures him to be assaulted, ill-treated, neglected, abandoned or exposed, in a manner likely to cause him unnecessary suffering or injury to health (including injury to or loss of sight, or hearing, or limb or organ of the body and any mental derangement) that person shall be guilty of [an offence] . . .

This provision is doubly comprehensive: in the nature of the conduct which may give rise to liability and in the kinds of persons who may be held liable for it.

1 Ante, para 9.04.
2 As amended by CYPA 1963, Sch 3, para 1 and Sch 5; CA 1975, Sch 4, Pt III; and MCA 1980, s 32(2).

(a) Nature of the conduct

9.35 Subsection (1) shows that the cruel conduct may take one of five forms, but these are not five mutually exclusive offences. In *R v Hayles*[1] the three-year-old son of the defendant fell and sustained serious head, neck and facial injuries. The defendant put him to bed, but did not obtain medical aid. The child died. The Court of Appeal held that, although the defendant's conduct was essentially neglect, the neglect was such that it could properly be described as ill-treatment, and that therefore he could be convicted of the offence of wilfully ill-treating the child, with which he was charged in the indictment.[2]

1 [1969] 1 QB 364, [1969] 1 All ER 34, CA. See also *R v Holmes* [1979] Crim LR 52, (assault) and post, para 9.44.
2 An alternative count for manslaughter based on the allegation that the defendant had occasioned the son's injury was withdrawn. But, given the seriousness of the injuries, could not manslaughter have been alternatively based on his wilful neglect to seek medical aid? Cf supra, para 9.32.
   Although there are not five distinct offences, the prosecution in charging the defendant should use the word in the subsection that most appropriately describes the allegations made; see *R v Beard* (1987) 85 Cr App Rep 395, CA. Quaere whether this ruling is limited to drafting indictments so as not to present a judge with a difficult sentencing problem when faced with a conviction by a jury on an uncertain basis and that 'different considerations may apply to the trial of an information before the magistrates who are judges of fact and who also pass sentence'. See Clarke Hall and Morrison, op cit, para B [206].

(i) Unnecessary suffering or injury to health

9.36 Whichever form the conduct may take it must be such as is likely to cause unnecessary suffering or injury to health. This is a flexible term, but the words which elaborate it are redolent of a bygone age. The specific reference to injury to or loss of sight, hearing, limb or organ of the body is superfluous, while the mention of mental derangement has tended to imply the need for proof of severe mental cruelty. The Ingleby Committee[1] recommended an amendment to make it clear that subsection (1) covers mental suffering falling short of mental derangement. Surely, the solution is a straightforward reference to 'suffering or injury to health, whether physical or mental'.

1 Report on Children and Young Persons, Cmnd 1191, para 535.

(ii) Neglect

9.37 This form of conduct is the one first examined not only because most charges are based on it but also because it is the one in which the mental element required by section 1(1) has been judicially considered. The question whether a parent has 'wilfully' neglected his child has been specifically analysed in relation to the failure to seek medical treatment.

For some 80 years the accepted principle, formulated in *R v Senior*,[1] was that section 1(1) and its predecessors[2] created an offence of strict liability. Thus, all that had to be proved was that the child needed medical aid, a fact to be determined objectively by reference to the reasonable parent, that the particular parent had not obtained it and that there was the consequent likelihood of unnecessary suffering or injury to health. The state of mind of the parent was irrelevant: it mattered not whether he knew, ought to have known or was justifiably ignorant of the need for medical aid. Thus, the emphasis was entirely on the protection of the child and not on the limitation of the parent's liability. In *R v Sheppard*[3] the basic issue for the House of Lords was whether to allow a shift in favour of the parent. By a majority of 3 to 2 it gave an affirmative answer by deciding that for neglect to be wilful there must be imported an element of foresight or recklessness as to the consequences of the neglect. It must be shown either that the parent, having directed his mind to the matter, knew that his child's health might be at risk but consciously decided not to arrange for medical treatment or that he omitted so to arrange because he had not cared whether the child might or might not need it. The practical effect of the change is that the parent who genuinely fails to appreciate that his child needs medical care is no longer guilty of wilful neglect. For some[4] the change removes an injustice to that kind of parent but without increasing the risk to his child, since juries and magistrates will be alert to false claims by parents that they did not realise that their child's condition required medical care; for others,[5] who see the protection of the child as overriding, a rule of strict liability can still sometimes serve as a deterrent,[6] and the difficulty of proving foresight or recklessness against stupid or feckless parents may show that confidence in the acumen of jury and magistracy can be too optimistic. However, on either view the significance of the change must not be overstated. *Sheppard* does not exculpate, any more than *Senior* did, the parent who deliberately refuses to seek medical aid because of a religious conviction that it is sinful and that his child's well being would best be served by spiritual healing.

1 [1899] 1 QB 283, CCCR.
2 For the history see ante, para 9.04.
3 [1981] AC 394, [1980] 3 All ER 899.
4 Eg the majority of the House of Lords in *Sheppard* (Lords Diplock, Edmund Davies and Keith).
   See also Glanville Williams, *Textbook of Criminal Law*, (1978) p 88 and (2nd edn) 1983, p 208 note 4.
5 Eg the minority of the House of Lords in *Sheppard* (Lords Fraser and Scarman).
6 But hardly against those whose stupidity or ignorance genuinely prevents them from seeing the harm their neglect would cause.

9.38 Apart from religious objections, another difficulty concerning medical aid is where the parent, though agreeable to some such aid being given, refuses to allow an operation on the juvenile. In such a case the test of wilful neglect depends on the nature of the operation and the reasonableness of the refusal to allow it. Thus, in *Oakey v Jackson* it was held to be wilful neglect to refuse to let a 13-year-old daughter have her adenoids removed.[1] At the other end of the scale, refusal to allow a life-saving operation (for example, a kidney transplant) may, it is submitted, similarly amount to wilful neglect, but, where there is a risk of attendant danger without that degree of urgency, refusal may be reasonable. In such cases prosecutions are unlikely. Much more important for the child is an application in wardship by an interested party with a view to the court's consenting to the operation.

1 [1914] 1 KB 216, DC. See also *R v De Crespigny, ex p Carter* (1912) Times, 21 May, DC (refusal to allow operation for a cleft palate).

9.39 Section 1(2)(a) of the 1933 Act prescribes some of the steps expected of a parent or whoever else is legally liable to maintain the juvenile by providing that he is deemed to have neglected him in a manner likely to cause injury to his health[1] if he has failed to provide adequate food, clothing, medical aid or lodging or has failed to seek State aid to meet any of those needs.[2] Apart from the House of Lords in *Sheppard*[3] referring to it in its analysis of wilfulness, this deeming provision has escaped judicial attention. That is not surprising, because examination shows that it is much ado about largely nothing. Before the deeming can operate the court will have to determine whether or not the provision, if any, made for the child is adequate. If it is not, because, for example, I do not provide adequate food for my child, then *ex hypothesi* it is likely that he will suffer injury to his health. There is no need to 'deem' that result. Moreover, even if deeming is in any circumstance to have significance, its reference to legal liability to maintain creates, as will be seen,[4] both uncertainty and anomaly.

1 Silence on the alternative effect of unnecessary suffering seems to be a legislative oversight.
2 Apart from liability under s 1 of the 1933 Act, a parent is liable under s 26 of the Social Security Act 1986 (formerly s 25 of the Supplementary Benefits Act 1976) if social security benefits have to be provided for his child because of persistent refusal or neglect to maintain him. But the penalties for that offence are not so severe as those for neglect under the 1933 Act, being imprisonment for up to three months or a fine not exceeding level 4 on the standard scale or both.
3 [1981] AC 394, [1980] 3 All ER 899.
4 Post, para 9.54.

9.40 One kind of neglect singled out by the Act is where a child under three years of age dies as the result of suffocation[1] while he is in bed with a person over the age of 16, and it is shown that that person was under the influence of drink when he went to bed. He is in those circumstances deemed to have neglected the child in a manner likely to cause injury to his health.[2] Surprisingly, this rule has yet to be extended to a person under the influence of drugs. The neglect must, however, be wilful in the sense laid down in *R v Sheppard*. In the light of the decision of the House of Lords in *DPP v Majewski* relating to drunkenness as a possible defence,[3] it seems clear that an offence under section 1 of the 1933 Act is one of 'basic intent' and not of 'specific intent', as vaguely categorised in that case. On that basis it would be no defence if the drunkenness was self-induced, especially if the parent knew that later he was going to share the bed with a child. But in such circumstances he would equally be liable for manslaughter.[4] It is therefore difficult to see what practical value section 1(2)(b) of the 1933 Act now has.

1 But not suffocation caused by disease or the presence of a foreign body in the child's throat.
2 Section 1(2)(b). Whereas the other provisions in s 1 and other sections of the Act refer

to 'child or young person', this anomalously refers to 'infant'. Section 1(3)(b) expressly provides that the death of a juvenile does not prevent conviction under s 1. Nevertheless, to describe, as s 1(2)(b) does, conduct resulting in death as being likely to cause injury to health is not the most felicitous use of language.

3 [1977] AC 443, [1976] 2 All ER 142. For the scope and complexity of this defence see especially Williams, op cit, chapter 21; Smith and Hogan, *Criminal Law*, 6th edn pp 209–222.

4 Cf *R v Lipman* [1970] 1 QB 152, [1969] 3 All ER 410, CA.

9.41   Apart from the Act, it is also wilful neglect to omit to pay part of one's earnings towards the support of one's child,[1] but in view of *Sheppard*[2] it will have to be proved that the parent knew that the child needed support. Moreover, a person is equally guilty of neglect if, not having the means for providing those necessities, he fails to take steps to procure their provision under the appropriate legislation; for example, not claiming benefits under the National Insurance or Social Security legislation. A question yet to be unequivocally answered is whether a parent can ever be liable under section 1 if he deliberately refuses to accept or continue suitable employment and relies on State benefits provided for children. It is now clear that he certainly can not if, in custody proceedings, a court has held that he was justified in remaining unemployed so that he could bring up his children.[3] But a more difficult question could arguably arise where his refusal to work or continue to work has meant a drastic drop in the standard of living of the children. Could he, nevertheless, successfully plead that he was adequately providing for them, since it must be taken that the Legislature has enacted what is to be regarded as the minimum financial provision needed to provide adequately the necessities of life so as to prevent unnecessary suffering or injury to health? There are two possible answers. Firstly, it is a rule that a person may still be liable under section 1 even though actual or likely suffering or injury was obviated by the action of another person,[4] and arguably this could apply where intervention is by way of State-provided financial benefits. Secondly, it is arguable that for the purpose of section 1 adequacy is to be given a relative meaning, depending upon the standard of living to which the juvenile has hitherto been accustomed, so that if there is a sharp drop in that standard he may well be said to suffer thereby and, since this is due to conduct which the parent could have avoided, the suffering may be said to be unnecessary.

1 *Cole v Pendleton* (1896) 60 JP 359, DC; *R v Connor* [1908] 2 KB 26, CCCR.
2 [1981] AC 394, [1980] 3 All ER 899, HL, supra, para 9.37.
3 *B v B (custody of children)* [1985] FLR 166, [1985] Fam Law 29, CA; *B v B (custody of child)* [1985] FLR 462, [1985] Fam Law 119, CA.
4 Section 1(3)(a). The rule applies to any kind of conduct and not only to neglect. See, for example, *R v Falkingham* (1870) 11 Cox CC 475, CCCR, (intervention of relieving officer); *R v White* (1871) 12 Cox CC 83, CCCR (police constable).

(iii)   Assault
9.42   Prior to *R v Sheppard*[1] it was held on the authority of *R v Senior*[2] that it was only necessary to prove that the act was done 'deliberately and intentionally, not by accident or inadvertence, but so that the mind of the person doing the act goes with it', ie that it was voluntary. Although *Sheppard* was directed to neglect, it is, it is submitted, implicit in the majority decision of the House of Lords that, where the alleged cruelty takes the positive form of assault, ill-treatment, abandonment or exposure, there must

also be either foresight of the consequences, namely, the likelihood of unnecessary injury or suffering, or recklessness as to whether those consequences may ensue.

1 [1981] AC 394, [1980] 3 All ER 899, HL.
2 [1899] 1 QB 283, CCCR.

9.43 Where the conduct is in the form of assault it usually involves the use of personal violence to a degree that proof of unnecessary suffering or injury to health or both will not be difficult.[1] But under section 1 it is not necessary to show actual suffering or injury: it is enough that the juvenile was treated 'in a manner likely to cause' either result. So, where there is an assault without an accompanying battery, it will still be possible to prosecute under section 1 if the likelihood of unnecessary suffering can be proved. Proof of the likelihood may, however, be difficult, because, although it is an essential element of assault that the victim should fear that personal violence is about to be used against him, his fear may be too superficial or transient to produce the consequences which section 1 requires.[2] An assault without battery is most likely to be by way of confinement of the juvenile or threatening him with some instrument or by means of words (for the better opinion is that threatening language may amount to an assault).[3] In deciding whether the particular assault comes within the section much will depend on the age of the juvenile and also on his peculiar sensibilities, because, although the wording of section 1 suggests that the likelihood of suffering or injury is to be determined objectively, that standard must, it is submitted, be related to the particular individual. For example, to keep a three-year-old child locked in a dark room for an hour is a traumatic experience likely to cause him unnecessary suffering and possibly also affect his health.[4] On the other hand, neither effect is normally likely if he is a 12-year-old;[5] but it would be otherwise if he were of an abnormally nervous disposition. On the same principle an act involving minimum violence in relation to most children may, because of the particular child's physical condition, cause unnecessary suffering or injury, for example, because of a brittle bone disease.[6] But, in these cases of abnormality, for the parent to be liable he must be aware of the child's condition, otherwise the requirements of wilfulness as imposed by *Sheppard* would not be met.

1 Cf *R v Hatton* [1925] 2 KB 322, CCA (and preferably) 19 Cr App Rep 29, where only slight force was used in that the accused, the step-father of a 15-year-old girl, put his hand over her mouth to stop her screaming after he had committed an indecent act, not against her, but in her presence. It was held that, although his conduct prior to the act of force was 'likely to cause, if not suffering, at any rate no little agitation of mind and astonishment and disgust', the only assault was his act of putting his hand on her mouth and the question for the jury was whether that constituted a wilful act likely to cause unnecessary suffering.
2 For this reason it has been suggested that the parent should also alternatively be charged with common assault under s 42 of the Offences against the Person Act 1861; See Clarke Hall and Morrison, on *Children*, 10th edn, para B[207].
3 See Smith and Hogan, op cit, pp 377–378, and references therein.
4 Arguably, it is also the offence of false imprisonment. Certainly a protracted period of detention of a child would become an unlawful restraint and no longer the exercise of the parental power of reasonable chastisement. See *R v Rahman* (1985) 81 Cr App Rep 349, [1985] Crim LR 596, CA.

5 Assuming that he is still responsive to such form of correction, which may be a large assumption.
6 The court may order tests to be carried out; *R v Cottee* [1984] CLY 603, CA.

(iv)   Ill-treatment

9.44   In the absence of abnormality an assault without, or with only slight, violence may, therefore, be outside the scope of section 1, but if the conduct is repeated over a period of time the point may be reached where it is likely to cause unnecessary suffering or injury to health; for example, repeated threats of violence or repeated confinements alone in a room or constant nagging. If so, it would constitute ill-treatment; but continuity is not an essential element of this form of conduct, one act may be enough.[1]

1 *R v Holmes* [1979] Crim LR 52 (one slap of face of mentally ill patient held to be ill treatment); and see *R v Hayles* [1969] 1 QB 364, [1969] 1 All ER 34, CA, ante, para 9.35.

(v)   Abandonment or exposure

9.45   For the purpose of section 1, to abandon a child means to leave him to his fate, and the fact that a parent takes some measures to avoid this result may not be enough to escape liability. This principle, which was affirmed in *R v Boulden*[1] is illustrated by a comparison of that case with *R v Whibley*.[2] In the latter case a father, who took his five children with him when he had to attend a juvenile court and then in a moment of passion left them there, was held not to have abandoned them, since he had not left them in a place which would expose them to injury. They could have immediately been put into the care of a society or, today, received into the care of a local authority under the Child Care Act 1980.[3] On the other hand, in *Boulden*, after the mother had left the matrimonial home one afternoon to return to her parents in Scotland to seek assistance for her children, the father about 9 pm that evening telephoned to the headquarters of the NSPCC to inform them that the children were alone in the house and asked them to send someone to look after them. When asked why he could not look after them he gave a false excuse. Shortly afterwards a policewoman arrived and found the house in darkness and the children alone there, with only a small quantity of food. The following night the father followed the mother to Scotland. It was held that there was evidence on which the jury were entitled to find abandonment and neglect of the children. It would seem in the light of these cases that the test is whether the parent has taken all reasonable steps to ensure that the child has been received into care.[4]

1 (1957) 41 Cr App Rep 105, CCA.
2 [1938] 3 All ER 777, CCA.
3 The Ingleby Committee rejected a proposal which would have widened the meaning of abandonment so as to empower a local authority to prosecute a person who had abandoned his child in such circumstances that the authority had to receive the child into their care under (then) s 1 of the Children Act 1948, even though as in *Whibley* it cannot be said that the parent left the child to his fate. It was felt that to extend criminal liability to such and similar cases must cause parents, through fear of prosecution, to keep in unsatisfactory conditions children who should have been received into care – see Cmnd 1191, paras 538–540.
4 In *Boulden* the father said that he watched the arrival of the policewoman from the other side of the street and that, had he not seen her take the children away, he would have

returned to the house himself. It is submitted that if the jury believed that statement he could not have been found guilty of abandonment.

9.46 Often the abandonment is accompanied by exposure of the child, a typical illustration being the mother who leaves her young baby on the doorstep of a house.[1] But a parent may sometimes expose a child to suffering or injury without ever having abandoned him; for example, by depriving him of shelter which has been made available to them both.[2] It must, however, be exposure to suffering or injury: section 1 does not apply to exposure to risk.[3]

1 If she should leave the child outside the father's house and he will have nothing to do with the child, he, too, is guilty of abandonment and exposure; *R v White* (1871) LR 1 CCR 311, CCR. For another illustration see *R v Falkingham* (1870) LR 1 CCR 222, CCR (mother sending baby by rail in hamper to father). Both these cases were concerned with an offence under s 27 of the Offences against the Person 1861, infra, but the principles therein would apply equally for the purpose of s 1 of CYPA 1933.
2 *R v Williams* (1910) 4 Cr App Rep 89, CCA.
3 *R v Gibbins* [1977] Crim LR 741 (father not liable for taking eight-year-old son and other boys on a baulk of timber punting in deep water in London docks).

9.47 Apart from section 1, a person may be convicted of abandoning or exposing a child under section 27 of the Offences against the Person Act 1861. This section, however, is limited to children under two years of age, and it must be shown that the abandonment or exposure is such that the life of the child is endangered or his health has been or is likely to be permanently injured. This imposes a heavier burden of proof than does section 1 of the 1933 Act, and probably accounts for the fact that section 1 has virtually superseded it,[1] even though conviction on indictment for an offence under section 27 carries a heavier maximum penalty.[2]

1 The Criminal Law Revision Committee has recommended the repeal of s 27; (Fourteenth Report, para 206).
2 In imprisonment for not more than five years, compared with two under s 1.

(b) Persons who may be liable

9.48 Anyone aged at least 16 who has the custody, charge or care of the child may be liable for an offence under section 1. As elsewhere in child law, these terms are not defined, and certain rules in the 1933 Act tend to confuse rather than clarify them. Section 17 lists three presumptions, one in respect of each of the concepts of custody, charge and care. It is to be noted that they are not conclusive.

'Any person who is the parent or legal guardian of a child or young person or who is legally liable to maintain him shall be presumed to have the custody of him, and as between father and mother the father shall not be deemed to have ceased to have the custody of him by reason only that he has deserted, or otherwise does not reside with, the mother and the child or young person;
Any person to whose charge a child or young person is committed by any person who has the custody of him shall be presumed to have charge of the child or young person;

Any other person having actual possession or control of a child or young person shall be presumed to have the care of him.'

An additional and unnecessary complication is the distinction drawn by the Act[1] between a 'legal guardian' which means a person appointed to be guardian by deed or will or order of a court (which is the normal meaning of a guardian)[2] and a 'guardian' who, for the purpose of the Act, includes anyone who in the opinion of the court has for the time being the 'charge of or control over' the juvenile.

1 Section 107(1).
2 See ante, Chapter 4.

(i)   Custody

9.49   It seems clear from the wording of the presumption relating to custody that the concept has its wide meaning of the bundle of parental powers and responsibilities[1] and in the light of that and case law the following conclusions may be drawn.

1 See ante, para 1.52.

9.50   *(1) Parents who were married at date of their child's birth*   Where the parents are living together, both obviously have custody. In those circumstances it has been held[1] that, if the child has been the victim of cruel conduct which could have been committed by one or other or both of them, but there is no explanation from either of them and no evidence pointing to the one rather than the other, the court may properly draw the inference that they are jointly responsible. The ruling is a concession to the practical difficulty of proving what happens within the privacy of the home, but it has been argued[2] that the rule needs elaboration and that to justify the conviction of both parents it must be proved in respect of each that 'if he did not himself inflict the harm, he assisted or encouraged the other to do so, either actively or by failing to intervene when, as he knew, he could by taking reasonable steps prevent the harm from occurring'. There must be some evidence of acting in concert.[3] The alternative reference to non-intervention recognises the parental duty to intervene and that failure to do so can amount to encouragement and authority to the other parent to commit the offence.[4] It is submitted that this duty to intervene and its consequences are not limited to parents, but that, by virtue of the common law duty to protect anyone for whom one assumes control,[5] the effect of non-intervention and the ruling in *Gibson* extend to others jointly caring for the child, for example, natural parent and step-parent, cohabitees, joint custodians and foster parents.

1 *R v Gibson and Gibson* [1984] Crim LR 615, CA (where there were charges of inflicting grievous bodily harm and of cruelty under s 1 of the 1933 Act); *R V Russell and Russell* (1987) 85 Cr App Rep 388, CA. See also *Marsh v Hodgson* (1973) 137 JP 266.
2 [1984] Crim LR at 616 (in comment by Professor JC Smith).
3 Cf *R v Lane (L) and Lane (J)* [1985] Crim LR 789, CA and comment by Professor Smith at p 791.
4 Ibid, citing *R v Russell* [1933] VLR 59, a Victoria State case where a husband who stood by and watched his wife drown their children was guilty of abetting the homicide.
5 See ante, para 9.02.

9.51 Where the parents are living apart,[1] then, in the absence of an order of a court, both still have custody. Consequently, if the mother is wilfully neglecting her child who is living with her, the father will himself be guilty of wilful neglect if he knows of her neglect but does nothing himself about it.[2] Moreover, even if he sends the mother an adequate amount for the child's support, but he learns that she is neglecting him, he is still liable.[3] The rule has been based on the doubtful premise that she is acting as his agent, but the better explanation, especially for contemporary society, is that under section 17 the father is deemed still to have custody. In those circumstances he should take the children away or, if this is opposed, seek an order of legal custody. If he cannot himself provide accommodation and there are no possible private foster parents, he should take steps to ensure that the child is received into local authority care.[4] Section 17 makes it clear that the presumption, and thus the above consequences, operate where the father is living apart from the mother and child, whatever be the cause of the separation. The corresponding situation, where mother is living apart from father and child was apparently not contemplated by the 1933 Act, but, given now the parity between the spouses with regard to legal custody,[5] the presumption by implication correspondingly applies to that situation.

1 Section 17 refers to residence, but the test of separate households, as in matrimonial causes, is, it is submitted, the appropriate one.
2 See *R v Bubb, R v Hook* (1850) 4 Cox CC 455 (both cases of homicide).
3 *Poole v Stokes* (1914) 110 LT 1020, DC.
4 In *Poole v Stokes*, supra, the father went to the NSPCC and drew their attention to the facts, but it was held that this did not relieve him of the duty of protecting his children and seeing that they were properly clothed and fed. There was nothing, so far as the court could see, to prevent him from taking his children away from his wife. But, supposing that he could not have accommodated them, what more could he have reasonably been expected to do?
5 See Guardianship Act 1973, s 1(1).

9.52 It is not possible for one parent by his own act, for example by a purported agreement surrendering sole custody to the other parent,[1] to get rid of the presumption in respect of custody; he must be deprived of custody by an order of a court.[2] Where an order has been made under the Domestic Proceedings and Magistrates' Courts Act 1978 or the Guardianship of Minors Act 1971, the mother will have been given legal custody (including actual custody) but not, as in divorce court proceedings, custody in the fullest sense. It is submitted that, nevertheless, the fact that the father shares with the mother the residual custodial rights (for example, to administer the child's property) and that he still has certain rights as natural guardian (for example, to give or withhold his agreement to adoption) or that the court has reserved to him and the mother jointly specific rights are not enough to prevent the presumption in respect of custody from ceasing to apply to him.

1 Such an agreement is normally unenforceable; see GA 1973, s 1(2).
2 *Brooks v Blount* [1923] 1 KB 257. See also *R v Connor* [1908] 2 KB 26, CCCR.

9.53 *(2) Persons legally liable to maintain the child* The presumption concerning custody operates in relation not only to the parent, a term which includes in addition to the mother and father who were married at the time of their child's birth, the mother who was not so married,[1] or to the legal guardian but also to any person who is legally liable to maintain the child. There is nothing in the Act to suggest that these words are to be interpreted restrictively, and their effect, it is submitted, is to give 'custody' an even wider meaning than the one already stated.[2] For example, a step-parent who has entered into an agreement with his wife to maintain her child will be presumed to have custody even though at common law he is not accorded custody. Another example is the step-parent ordered by a court in exercise of its matrimonial jurisdiction to maintain a child of the family. But it is in respect of the father who was not married to the mother at the date of their child's birth[3] that the test of legal liability to maintain is specifically relevant. In *Butler v Gregory*[4] it was held that the father of an illegitimate daughter whose mother was dead and who was not living with him could not be presumed to have custody of her, since no affiliation order had been made against him. The decision has been firmly accepted as establishing that in the absence of such an order the presumption of custody cannot operate,[5] and this conclusion is not altered by the Family Law Reform Act 1987, except that the test will be whether, in place of the affiliation order, there is an order for financial provision by the father under section 11B of the Guardianship of Minors Act 1971.[6] In *Butler v Gregory* Lord Alverstone CJ urged a statutory amendment 'to throw the obligation on parents who were in fact fathers', a reform which is still awaited, notwithstanding the changes prospectively made by the FLRA 1987. It must be stressed, however, that it is only where the father and child are not living together that the presumption of custody cannot arise unless a financial provision order is in existence. If he has actual custody, charge or care he may be liable under section 1 of the 1933 Act.[7]

1 For the meaning of these terms see FLRA 1987, s 1(2)–(4), ante, para 2.20. The father who was not married to the mother at the time of the child's birth does not have custody unless granted it by a court or unless, a fortiori, an order under s 4 of that Act (when it comes into force) has given him all the parental rights and duties.
2 Supra, para 9.49.
3 See note 1, supra.
4 (1912) 18 TLR 370, DC.
5 But this would not prevent him from being liable where there was an agreement by him to maintain; cf the step-parent, supra.
6 As prospectively inserted by FLRA 1987, s 12.
7 *Liverpool Society for The Prevention of Cruelty to Children v Jones* [1914] 3 KB 813.

9.54   To revert to the deeming provisions of section 1(2)(a) of the 1933 Act, there is nothing to indicate that the words 'legally liable to maintain' therein have a meaning different from that in section 17. So, any of the persons mentioned in the previous paragraph will be deemed to have neglected the child in a manner likely to cause injury to his health if they have failed to provide adequate food, clothing, medical aid or lodging for him. That creates an anomaly in relation to the legal guardian. Whereas he is presumed to have custody of the child for the purpose of section 1, unlike all other persons who fall within the presumption he is not deemed to have neglected the child by failing to provide those necessities, since he is not under a legal liability personally to maintain the ward.

1 See ante, para 4.25.

(ii)   Charge and care

9.55   It is very difficult to know exactly what these terms mean. Possibly 'charge' is intended to emphasise the power of the adult to control the child's conduct in the latter's interests;[1] 'care' to emphasise the responsibility of the adult to protect the child from harm. Whatever the distinction may be, it is better to treat them as going hand in hand and to recognise that they may be simultaneously entrusted to more than one person, either generally or specifically. For example, a parent may during his absence abroad generally commit his child to the charge and care of a relative, who in turn for a limited period may delegate the charge and care to another, for example, a baby sitter.

1 But the matter is further complicated by the fact that s 1(7) of the 1933 Act apparently treats control and charge as distinct concepts.

(c)   Prosecutions and penalties

9.56   Prosecutions of an offence under section 1 or of any other offence under Part I of the 1933 Act are usually brought by the Crown Prosecution Service and much less often by the National Society for the Prevention of Cruelty to Children; but a local authority may also do so, either as the local education authority or through its social services committee.[1] The express power given to a local education authority is justified since it emphasises the vital part schools have to play in protecting children from parental harm.[2]

1 See CYPA 1933, s 98 and CYPA 1963, s 56. These provisions also empower an authority to prosecute for an offence, under Part II of those two Acts, relating to employment of children, as to which see post, paras 11.69 et seq.
2 The dangers so amply illustrated by Clegg and Megson in *Children in distress* (1968) should still serve as a warning.

9.57   An offence under section 1 is triable on indictment or summarily. For conviction on indictment the penalties are a fine or up to ten years' imprisonment or both;[1] on summary conviction they are a fine not exceeding the prescribed sum[2] or imprisonment for up to six months or both.[3] Penalties should be related to the varying degrees of seriousness of cruel conduct, in the light not only of the actual injuries to the child but also the circumstances in which they are caused – from the case of extreme wickedness to those which 'can really be described as disasters . . . cases in which the parents or the parent concerned are or is completely out of his or her depth',[4] for example, because of poverty, unemployment or bad housing. These judicial comments are, of course, not to be confined to cases under section 1 of the 1933 Act, but should apply to all other offences against the person of a child. However, variety in sentencing does not in practice relate only to such matters. Where mother and father or step-father are both prosecuted, there is a notable tendency to impose more lenient sentences on the former and/or to charge her with a less serious offence than the father or step father.[5]

1 CYPA 1933, s 1(1)(a), as amended by CA 1975, s 108(1)(b) and Sch 4, and CJA 1988,

s 45(1). The Criminal Justice Bill presently before Parliament provides for a maximum of ten years' imprisonment.
2 Ie prescribed under the Magistrates' Court Act 1980 and, by virtue of the Criminal Penalties etc (Increase) Order 1984, SI 1984/447, currently £2,000.
3 CYPA 1933 s 1(1)(b), as amended by CA 1975, s 108(1)(a) and Sch 3, para 1.
4 Per May J in *R v Dennis Smith* (1984) 6 Cr App Rep(S) 174 at 175.
5 As in the Jasmine Beckford Case, where the step father was sentenced to ten years' imprisonment for manslaughter and concurrently to eight years for cruelty, and the mother to 18 months' imprisonment for wilful neglect.

2   Assaults under the Offences against the Person Act 1861

9.58   This Act may be invoked to deal with more or less serious cases of assault than those contemplated by section 1 of the Children and Young Persons Act 1933. Moreover, only the 1861 Act is available if the accused did not have custody, charge or care of the child. Of the more serious cases the most likely to arise are offences under sections 18, 20 and 47 of the Act:[1] ie unlawfully and maliciously wounding or causing grievous bodily harm to the child with the intention of doing such harm to him;[2] the lesser offence under section 20[3] of unlawfully and maliciously wounding or inflicting grievous bodily harm upon the child; and, under section 47, assault occasioning actual bodily harm.[4] Where any of these offences are charged there may be an additional charge of an offence under section 1 of the 1933 Act.[5]

1 Other offences which on rare occasions may be charged are attempts to choke, suffocate or strangle a child in order to commit an indictable offence (ss 21 and 22), and unlawfully and maliciously administering poison to him (ss 23 and 24).
2 Section 18, as amended by the Criminal Law Act 1967, s 10(2) and Sch III, Part III. The offence is punishable with imprisonment for life.
3 Punishable with five years' imprisonment.
4 See, for example, *R v Frank Beanland* (1970) 54 Cr App Rep 289, CA. This offence is also punishable with five years' imprisonment.
5 If a person is charged with an offence under s 1 and elects trial by jury, the facts disclosed at the preliminary examination may justify other counts being added in the indictment charging, for example, offences under ss 18 and 20 of the 1861 Act; see *R v Roe* [1967] 1 All ER 492, [1967] 1 WLR 634, CA.

9.59   Where, on the other hand, the assault is not sufficiently serious to be likely to produce the unnecessary suffering or injury which section 1 of the 1933 Act requires, proceedings for the summary offence of common assault may be brought.[1] They must be brought by the victim,[2] but it has been held that where, because of age or infirmity, he is incapable of doing so, the information may be laid by a third person.[3]

1 Common assault is now classified as a summary offence, punishable with a fine not exceeding level 5 on the standard scale (currently £2,000) or with imprisonment for up to six months or with both; see Criminal Justice Act 1988, s 39.
   It is also now classified as a special offence within Schedule 1 to CYPA 1933 to which special provisions of that Act apply; see CJA 1988, Sch 15, para 8.
2 *Nicholson v Booth and Naylor* (1888) 16 Cox CC 373, DC.
3 *Pickering v Willoughby* [1907] 2 KB 296, DC.

3   Exposing children under 12 to risk of burning

9.60   This offence[1] is concerned with children under the age of 12, an age limit higher than is generally realised. As with section 1 of the 1933

Act, the duty is imposed on a person who, being 16 or over, has the custody, charge or care of the child, and the offence is committed if the child is allowed to be in a room containing an open fire grate or any heating appliance liable to cause injury by contact with it and the grate or appliance is not sufficiently protected to guard against the risk of his being burnt or scalded, with the result that the child is killed or seriously injured. Notwithstanding the need to prove such serious consequences, the offence is only a summary one with a maximum penalty of a fine not exceeding level 1 on the standard scale,[2] but this does not prevent prosecution for any appropriate indictable offence, eg manslaughter if there has been gross negligence. It may not be generally realised that, for the purposes of this offence, heating appliances include central heating systems, so that parents must ensure that their young children keep away from unprotected radiators and hot water pipes.[3] This is, indeed, an illustration of the general responsibility of parents to take all reasonable steps to protect their children from harm in the home. Another is safeguarding the child against access to poisonous medicines and other dangerous materials.[4]

1 See CYPA 1933, s 11, as amended by CYP (Amendment) Act 1952, s 8 and Sch I, and CJA 1982, ss 37 and 46.
2 Currently £50.
3 Cf *Ryan v London Borough of Camden* (1983) 13 Fam Law 81, CA (neither Landlord local authority nor parents civilly liable in negligence for injury sustained by child being trapped between bed and very hot piping system provided by the authority).
4 In *Jauffur v Akhbar* (1984) Times, 10 February it was held that a parent is negligent if, knowing that there are candles in the home, he fails adequately to instruct and supervise his children about them with a view to preventing danger arising from their use.

4 Consumer safety

9.61 Several Regulations under the Consumer Protection Acts 1961 and 1971 and the Consumer Safety Act 1978 aim at securing the safety of products which either particularly or exclusively affect children, especially the young.[1] The following list illustrates the variety:[2] Stands for Carry-cots (Safety) Regulations 1966; Toys (Safety) Regulations 1974; Children's Clothing (Hood Cords) Regulations 1976; Babies Dummies (Safety) Regulations 1978; Children's Furniture (Safety) Order 1982; Pushchairs (Safety) Regulations 1985; Nightwear (Safety) Regulations 1985; Child Resistant Packaging (Safety) Regulations 1986.[3] Regulations are now made under the Consumer Protection Act 1987.[4]

1 The Regulations are now continued under the Consumer Protection Act 1987.
2 See further Miller, *Product Liability and Safety Encyclopaedia*, Division IV.
3 See also the Medicines (Child Safety) Regulations 1975 and 1976, SI 1975/2000 and SI 1976/1643 made under the Medicines Act 1968, which require children's aspirin and paracetamol to be contained in standard resistant containers. The Regulations were made after taking into account the advice of the Medicines Commission and after consulting various organisations.
4 Section 11. The Benzene in Toys (Safety) Regulations 1987, made under that section, prohibit the supply of toys which contain benzene in excess of a specified concentration.

5 Providing for safety of children at entertainments and on the road

9.62 Anyone who provides in a building an entertainment for children[1] under 14 at which more than 100 of them are present must post there a sufficient number of adult attendants in order to prevent more persons being admitted than the building can accommodate, to control the movement of the children and others admitted while they enter and leave, and generally to take all other reasonable precautions for the children's safety.[2] The occupier of the building, who for hire or reward permits the building to be used for entertainment, must take all reasonable steps to see that the above precautions are observed.[3] The offence is a summary one punishable with a fine,[4] but, in addition, if the building is licensed as a cinema, theatre or place for music or dancing, the licence is liable to be revoked.

1 Or an entertainment at which the majority of those attending are children.
2 CYPA 1933, s 12(1); see also the Cinematograph (Children) (No 2) Regulations 1955, SI 1955/1909, reg 4.
3 Section 12(2).
4 Not exceeding level 3 on the standard scale (currently £400); s 11(3), as amended by CJA 1982, ss 35, 37, 38 and 46.

9.63 Further control is exerted through the Cinematograph Act 1952,[1] which requires the licensing authority to give its consent to the holding of any cinematograph exhibition organised wholly or mainly as an exhibition for children under 16. In so doing the authority may impose conditions.

1 Section 4. See also the Cinematograph (Children) (No 2) Regulations 1955, regs 2 and 3 which require a child under 12 to be accompanied by a person aged at least 16.

9.64 Two statutory provisions relating to children and road safety may be noted here. First is that which empowers, though not compels, local authorities to provide school crossing patrols to control road traffic at places where children cross roads on their way to and from school. But, if an authority does arrange patrolling, it must ensure that adequately qualified and trained persons are appointed, although they may also arrange for the police to patrol an area.[1] Secondly, special provision is made for ensuring that children under 14 wear seat belts when travelling in motor vehicles.[2]

1 See Road Traffic Regulations Act 1984, ss 26–28.
2 Motor Vehicles (Wearing of Seat Belts by Children) Regulations 1982, SI 1982/1203 (made under the Road Traffic Act 1972, ss 33B(1)(3) and 199(2)).

6   Supplying intoxicating liquor and tobacco to children and cognate offences

9.65 Most of the offences relating to this subject are primarily designed to protect the child from physical harm, but some are also concerned with moral protection. The big question mark to be placed against them is the extent to which they are observed and enforced.[1]

1 See Tildesley, *Children and Young Persons and Licensed Premises* (1986) 150 JPN 644 and 662.

(a)   *Intoxicating liquor*

9.66 The most widely known provisions are to be found in section 169 of the Licensing Act 1964, which makes it an offence (a) for a licensee knowingly to sell intoxicating liquor, or allow it to be sold, in licensed premises to a person under 18[1] or knowingly to allow such a person to consume liquor[2] in a bar, (b) for anyone to buy liquor for consumption in a bar by such a person, and (c) for such a person to buy or consume liquor in those circumstances.[3] An exception is allowed enabling the sale of beer, porter, cider or perry to a person who has attained 16 for consumption at a table meal. For the licensee to be liable he must know[4] that the person has not attained 18, so that an honest belief that he has done so is a good defence.[5] It seems certain that anyone who buys liquor for consumption in a bar by a person under 18 must also have the knowledge, even though section 169 does not expressly say so.[6]

1 Evidence of age should be given, but the court may be able to act on its own visual evidence of the person; see *Wallworth v Balmer* [1965] 3 All ER 721, [1966] 1 WLR 16, DC.
2 Since shandy is partly composed of beer, the sale or consumption of it may be contrary to s 169; see *Hall v Hyder* [1966] 1 All ER 661, [1966] 1 WLR 410, DC.
3 An offence is not committed under s 169(2) if an adult purchases drink for a person under 18 who is waiting outside the licensed premises, even though the latter is the real purchaser and has provided the money. The purchase must be for consumption in the premises; *Woby v B and O* [1986] Crim LR 183, DC. But see infra, para 9.67. An offence under (a) and (b) is subject to a fine not exceeding level 2 on the standard scale (currently £100) on a first conviction and not exceeding level 3 (currently £400) on any further conviction, provided that for this purpose a conviction that took place more than five years previously is to be disregarded (s 194(2)). In the latter event, if the defendant is the licensee his licence may be forfeited. For an offence under (c) the fine must not exceed level 3.
4 The knowledge of another person, eg a servant, will not be imputed to the licensee (*Emary v Nolloth* [1903] 2 KB 264, [1900–3] All ER Rep 606, DC, provided the licensee exercised all due diligence to avoid the commission of an offence (s 169(10), as inserted by Criminal Law Act 1977, s 65 and Sch 12).
5 *Groom v Grimes* (1903) 20 Cox CC 515, DC.
6 Compare sub-ss (1) and (2) of s 169 with sub-paras (a) and (b) of s 178 with the reference in sub-s (1) and para (a) to knowledge and with no such reference in sub-s (2) and para (b). In *Sherras v De Rutzen* [1895] 1 QB 918, DC, which was concerned with interpreting provisions which para (b) re-enacts, it was held that, notwithstanding the absence of express mention of knowledge, that was an essential element. But the further conclusion of Day, J that the effect of the omission was to shift the legal burden of proof on to the defendant to show that he did not have knowledge has been doubted; see Devlin J in *Roper v Taylor's Central Garages (Exeter) Ltd* [1951] 2 TLR 284. It would seem that the first principle, though probably not the second, enunciated in that case would apply to s 169(2).

9.67 Similar provisions forbid the delivery to a person under 18 of intoxicants to be consumed off the licensed premises, except where the delivery is made at the residence or, oddly, the working place of the purchaser, and forbid anyone to send such a person to obtain intoxicants for consumption off the premises. These provisions do not apply where the person under 18 is a member of the licensee's family or is his servant or apprentice and is employed as a messenger to deliver intoxicants.[1]

1 Licensing Act 1964, s 169(5)–(7).

9.68 The Licensing Act 1964 also imposes restrictions on the employment and presence of children in a bar. A person under 18 cannot be employed there even if he receives no wages for his work[1] and a child under 14 is not allowed to be there during the permitted hours of sale and consumption, unless he is the licensee's child or resides in the premises but is not employed there or uses the bar merely as a means of transit to other parts of the premises.[2] Proof of the child's presence renders the licensee liable unless he shows that he used due diligence to prevent the child's admission or that the child had apparently attained 14.

1 Section 170. The maximum penalty is a fine not exceeding level 1 on the standard scale (currently £50).
2 Section 168. The maximum fine must not exceed level 1. Apart from any other person a local education authority may institute proceedings under this section.

9.69   Other relevant offences affecting children are: to give intoxicating liquor to a child under five unless ordered by a doctor or in a case of sickness, apprehended sickness or other urgent cause;[1] to sell intoxicating liquor in confectionery to a person under 16, knowing him to be so;[2] to be drunk in any highway or other public place or on any licensed premises while in charge of a child under seven.[3]

1 CYPA 1933, s 5, as amended by the Criminal Justice Act 1967, s 92 and Sch III, Part I. The maximum penalty is a fine not exceeding level 1.
2 Licensing Act 1964, s 167(2). The maximum penalty is a fine not exceeding level 2.
3 Licensing Act 1902, s 2, as amended by the Penalties for Drunkenness Act 1962, s 1, which imposes a maximum penalty of a fine not exceeding level 2 or one month's imprisonment.

(b)   Tobacco

9.70   Wide concern over the high incidence of smoking by schoolchildren and ineffectual enforcement of the law led to the Protection of Children (Tobacco) Act 1986, which seeks to strengthen the provisions in the main enactment, section 7 of the Children and Young Persons Act 1933,[1] by widening the definition of tobacco, extending strict liability and tightening up on the use of tobacco vending machines.

1 As amended by CYPA 1963, s 32 and CJA 1982, ss 35, 37, 38 and 46.

9.71   It is an offence to sell tobacco or cigarette papers to a person who is apparently under the age of 16. Tobacco includes cigarettes, any product containing tobacco and intended for oral or nasal use, and smoking mixtures intended as a substitute for tobacco.[1] Where tobacco in any of these forms is so sold, the liability is strict in that it makes no difference whether they were for the buyer's use or not and whether or not the seller knew by whom they were to be used.[2]

1 CYPA 1933, s 7(5). The term 'cigarette' covers cut tobacco rolled up in such form as to be capable of immediate use for smoking.
2 The maximum penalty is a fine not exceeding level 3 on the standard scale (currently £400).

9.72   In order to counter as far as possible the evasive effect which the widespread use of automatic vending machines has on the enactment, a magistrates' court, in a case where a machine is being extensively used by persons apparently under 16, must order the owner of the machine or the person on whose premises it is kept to take precautions to prevent it being used or, if necessary, to remove it within a specified time.[1]

1 Section 7(2). The maximum penalty is a fine not exceeding level 3 on the standard scale and a further fine of £10 each day during which the offence continues. Given the objects of the 1986 Act one might have expected a substantial increase in the per diem tariff.

9.73 Another power[1] conferred is that on a constable or uniformed park-keeper to seize any tobacco or cigarette papers in the possession of anyone apparently under 16 whom he finds smoking in any street or public place. It seems rarely to be exercised. Will the spirit of the amending 1986 Act excite positive action? One wonders.

1 Section 7(3). None of the provisions in s 7 applies to persons apparently under 16 who are employed by a manufacturer or dealer in tobacco.

(c) Drugs and noxious substances

9.74 It is remarkable that, while elaborate provisions are enacted with regard to consumption of alcohol and tobacco, there is nothing in the Misuse of Drugs Act 1971 which imposes stiffer sanctions and penalties on those who supply drugs to children, in spite of the increasing incidence of drug addiction among persons under 16 and as low as the age of 12. A cognate problem is the supply to children of glue-sniffing kit. Addiction to glue-sniffing may be a ground for bringing care proceedings under section 1 of the Children and Young Persons Act 1969,[1] especially as it is often associated with truancy from school. As for those who supply the kit, it has been argued[2] that they may be held liable under section 24 of the Offences against the Person Act 1861 of 'unlawfully and maliciously administering to or causing to be administered to or taken by any other person any poison or other destructive or noxious thing with intent to injure, aggrieve or annoy such person . . .'. Support for the conclusion has been drawn from *R v Marcus*,[3] where the Court of Appeal held that a substance which might be harmless in small quantities could be 'noxious' if the quantity administered was sufficient to injure, aggrieve or annoy. Accordingly, the defendant was convicted of an offence under section 24 for having put eight sedative and sleeping tablets into her neighbour's bottle of milk. The consequences of consumption were sedation and possibly sleep and were therefore a potential danger to someone who drank the milk, for example, if he carried out a potentially hazardous operation, such as driving a car, while his faculties were impaired. Arguably, therefore, the supplier of a glue-sniffing kit may be held liable under section 24. By providing it he may be held to have 'caused [the glue] to be taken' and 'with all the current publicity . . . must be said to intend harm to the glue sniffer or at the very least be reckless with regard to it'.[4] If the section can apply, it would still be difficult to prove the offence against a retail shopkeeper who sells glue to a juvenile. Nevertheless, it is surprising that there is no reported case of its having been tested.

1 Post, Chapter 14.
2 Crosta, *Glue Sniffing* (1984) 148 JPN 198; cf Williams, *Can glue sniffing be controlled under the present law?* 148 JPN 387.
3 [1981] 2 All ER 833, [1981] 1 WLR 774. See also *R v Hill* (1986) 83 Crim App Rep 386, [1986] Crim LR 815, where the House of Lords held that an intention to injure may include administering drugs with the intention of keeping someone awake for an unnatural period of time.
4 See Crosta, supra, note 2.

7   Restrictions on possession and handling of dangerous weapons and explosives by juveniles

(a)   Firearms

9.75   The main object of these restrictions, imposed by the Firearms Act 1968, is to protect others from the juvenile's inexperience in the use of firearms, but they also serve to protect him from possible harm to himself and may therefore be conveniently noted here.

The Act distinguishes shot guns and air weapons (ie an air rifle, air gun or air pistol not of a type declared to be specially dangerous) from all other firearms,[1] and the restrictions imposed on the acquisition, handling and possession of firearms by a juvenile depend partly on this classification and partly on the juvenile's age.[2] Thus:

(i) no-one under 17 may purchase or hire any firearm or ammunition;

(ii) subject to certain exceptions, no-one under 14 may have in his possession any firearm or ammunition. This restriction does not apply to a shot gun or air weapon; but

(iii) no-one under 15 may have with him an assembled shot gun except while under the supervision of a person aged 21 or over or while the gun is so covered that it cannot be fired; and

(iv) no-one under 14 may have with him an air weapon (or ammunition for it) except while under supervision or while using it at a rifle club or shooting gallery; and, subject to similar exceptions, this restriction extends to persons under 17 so far as having such a weapon in a public place.

1 For this classification see s 1, which, along with s 2, makes the lawful possession of a firearm other than an air weapon normally depend on the holding of a firearm or shotgun certificate. The Firearms Act 1982 extends the provisions of the 1968 Act to imitation firearms which are readily convertible into firearms.
2 See ss 22 and 23.

9.76   The remarkable feature of these provisions is that they carry with them penalties imposable by magistrates' courts which conflict with basic rules relating to methods of dealing with juvenile offenders. As will be seen,[1] no imprisonment may be imposed by such (or any court) on any person under 21 and the maximum fine imposable by those courts is £100 on a child and £400 on a young person. Yet, offences under sub-paragraphs (i) and (ii) above are punishable with six months' imprisonment or a fine not exceeding level 5 on the standard scale (currently £2,000) or both, and under (iii) and (iv) with a fine not exceeding level 3 (currently £400). With regard to (i) and (ii) the court can, however, exercise any of its sentencing powers (for example, pass a sentence of detention in a young offender institution[2]) which are available in respect of offences that are punishable with imprisonment in the case of offenders aged 21 or over. There are also provisions essentially corresponding with the above which create various offences for supplying firearms to juveniles, but they are subject to the general defence that the supplier reasonably believed that the juvenile was not under the age prescribed.[3]

1 Post, paras 13.76 and 13.15 respectively.
2 Under s 1(3A) of CJA, 1982, as inserted by CJA 1988, s 123; see post, Chapter 13.

3 Firearms Act 1968, s 24.

(b)   Crossbows

9.77   The Crossbows Act 1987 similarly aims at the double object of protecting both others and the juvenile himself from his inexperience in the use of crossbows. Thus, in provisions similar to those relating to firearms, the Act makes it an offence[1] for a person under 17 to purchase or hire a crossbow; and he may lawfully have one in his possession only if he is under the supervision of a person aged 21 or over.[2] The penalty for either offence is a fine not exceeding level 3 on the standard scale, and the court may order forfeiture of the weapon.[3] It is also an offence for anyone to sell or let on hire a crossbow to someone under 17, but this is subject to the defence that the supplier reasonably believed that the juvenile was not under the age of 17.[4] This offence carries a maximum penalty of six months' imprisonment or a fine not exceeding level 5 or both.[5]

1 Section 2.
2 Section 3. The police have powers of search and seizure where there is reasonable cause to suspect an offence under s 3. These include entry on land other than a dwelling house.
3 Section 6(2) and (3).
4 Section 1.
5 Section (1). Forfeiture can also be ordered (s 6(3)).

(c)   Explosives

9.78   No explosive substance including fireworks, may be sold to any child apparently under the age of 16.[1] The offence carries a maximum penalty of a fine not exceeding level 4.[2]

1 Explosives Act 1875, s 31(1) as amended by the Explosives (Age of Purchase &c.) Act 1976, s 1.
2 Section 31(2), as amended by CJA 1982.

8   Tattooing of children

9.79   Many people, women as well as men, have grown up to regret the tattooist's needle. Its ultimate effects are surprisingly varied.[1] It may lead to social ostracism; it may cause difficulties over obtaining employment; it may impede the rehabilitation of prisoners; it may even create matrimonial problems; and, with the demand for operations, under the National Health Service, to remove tattoos, it can be an additional charge on the taxpayer.

1 See Post, *Relationship of Tattoos to Personality Disorders*, 59 J Crim L, Criminal & PS 516.

9.80   Until the Tattooing of Minors Act 1969, the tattooing of a consenting child was an offence[1] only if he was unable to appreciate the nature of the Act, in which case his consent was held to be ineffectual,[2] but the Act imposes a general prohibition on the tattooing of any person who is under 18, unless performed for medical reasons by a qualified medical practitioner or a person working under his direction. It is, however, a defence that the person charged had reasonable cause to believe and did believe that the person tattooed was of or over that age.[3] Even in those circumstances further protection against the risk of harm is provided by the Local Government (Miscellaneous Provisions) Act 1982, which empowers a local authority to control tattooing by bringing into operation within its area Part VIII of the Act enabling the authority to require persons who practise tattooing to register themselves as practitioners and their premises. The authority may also make bye-laws to secure cleanliness of the practitioner, his premises and equipment. These provisions, it may be added, also extend to those who practise acupuncture, ear-piercing and electrolysis.

1 Ie assault or assault causing actual bodily harm.
2 *Burrell v Harmer* [1967] Crim LR 169.
3 The penalty on summary conviction is a fine not exceeding level 3 on the standard scale.

9   Circumcision of girls[1]

9.81   Given the firm medical evidence of the harmful short-term and long-term effects of female circumcision, it seems clear that, if the matter had been tested in the courts, the conclusion would have been that circumcision of a girl under 16 would have constituted an offence under section 1 of the Children and Young Persons Act 1933. There is no longer any need to pursue that possibility. The Prohibition of Female Circumcision Act 1985 makes it an offence[2] for anyone to perform any form of circumcision on a female, whatever her age,[3] and a parent who consents to the act is liable as aider and abetter. Strictly, the female may aid and abet her own circumcision. Consequently, it would seem in the light of the *Gillick* principle that a girl under 16 could consent and render herself liable, but, as in cases of abortion, it is very unlikely that the patient/victim would be prosecuted. As with abortion, it is a defence to perform circumcision on the grounds (1) that it is necessary for the physical or mental health of the female,[4] provided it is performed by a registered medical practitioner, or (2) that it is performed during the labour or birth of a child by a registered medical practitioner or registered midwife or a trainee for either of those professions.[5]

1 For an informative article on this practice and its legal implications see Hayter, *Female Circumcision – Is there a Legal Solution?* [1984] JSWL 323.
2 Punishable on conviction on indictment with a fine or up to five years' imprisonment or both and on summary conviction to a fine not exceeding the statutory maximum (currently £2,000) or to imprisonment not exceeding six months or both (s 1(2)).
3 In this country female circumcision is very largely performed on persons over the age of 16.
4 In deciding whether the operation is necessary for the female's mental health the court must not take account of any belief by her or anyone else (for example, her parent) that the operation is required as a matter of custom or ritual (s 2(2)).
5 Section 2(1).

10   Children born disabled

9.82   Although an unborn fetus has no right of action,[1] the Congenital Disabilities (Civil Liability) Act 1976[2] does, within limits, confer such a right on a child who is born disabled as the result of personal injuries caused before his birth.[3] The Act, which implements the recommendations of the Law Commission,[4] enables the child to sue the person responsible for an occurrence affecting the child's parent which caused the child to be born disabled, if that person would have been liable in tort to the parent affected,[5] whether as the result of an intentional act or negligence or breach of statutory duty. The injury may have been to either parent before conception, for example, where the father was subjected to irradiation which affected his progenitive capacity,[6] or to the mother only during her pregnancy or in the course of giving birth to the child. But in either circumstance the practical difficulty may be proof of causation, especially in those cases where the injury which is alleged occurred long before conception or where it is due to administration of drugs to the mother.[7] The Act makes the defendant 'answerable to the child', and action lies even though the parent suffered no actionable injury.[8] But there are a number of defences available to the defendant. He is not answerable for an occurrence preceding the time of conception if at that time either of the parents knew the risk of their child being born disabled as a result of the occurrence.[9] If he is a professional person, for example a doctor, he is not liable for treatment or advice given to the parent in accordance with the prevailing standards of care of his profession.[10] Liability to the child may also be excluded, limited or reduced by a contract made by the defendant with the parent[11] or by the contributory negligence of the parent.[12]

1 See Baker P in *Paton v British Pregnancy Advisory Services Trustees* [1979] QB 276, [1978] 2 All ER 987; and Heilbron J in *C v S* [1987] 1 All ER 1230 at 1234–1235. The point was not pursued by the Court of Appeal in the latter case. See also *Re F (in utero)* [1988] 2 All ER 193, [1988] 2 WLR 1288, CA.
2 See Eekelaar and Dingwall, *Some Legal Issues in Obstetric Practice*, [1984] JSWL 258, for critical comments on the restrictive effects of the Act and for an examination of wider issues relating to questions of the legal rights of mother and baby during pregnancy, labour and childbirth.
3 The Act removes any doubts which existed at common law and which were not resolved by the Thalidomide cases, since the parties there settled without the issue being determined; see *S v Distillers Co (Biochemicals) Ltd* [1969] 3 All ER 1412, [1970] 1 WLR 114.
4 See the *Report on Injuries to Unborn Children* (1974) (Cmnd 5709).
5 Section 1.
6 But see s 3, infra, for compensation payable under the Nuclear Installations Act 1965.
7 See Lovell and Griffith-Jones, *'The Sins of the Fathers' – Tort Liability for Pre-natal Injuries* (1974) 90 LQR 531.
8 Section 1(3).
9 Section 1(4). Ie volenti non fit injuria binds the child. But see infra, where the father is the defendant.
10 Section 1(5).
11 Section 1(6).
12 Section 1(7).

9.83 The parents occupy a special position vis-à-vis the child. In the case of the mother she is liable to the child when the latter's disability arises from the mother's negligent driving of a motor vehicle when she knows, or ought reasonably to know, that she is pregnant.[1] Otherwise no action lies against her under the Act, although in the light of *Re D (a minor)*[2] it is arguable that the matter should be reconsidered. Her exemption cannot be justified on the ground that an action against her would be divisive of the family unit, since the child's father is not exempted from liability to his child.[3] He, for example, is liable if the child's disability is the result of his having assaulted the mother during her pregnancy; and if the 'occurrence'[4] affecting the mother (for example, his transmitting a disease to her) had preceded conception, his knowledge of the risk of consequent disability will not exempt him from liability.[5] On the contrary, his knowledge all the more justifies liability. But there is the practical limitation. The child has to sue through his 'next friend'. Usually, that will be a parent, who may be ready to institute proceedings against a wealthy defendant such as a drugs company or insurance company, but much more reluctant or even unwilling to do so where the defendant is the father.

1 Section 2.
2 [1987] AC 317, sub nom *D v Berkshire County Council*, [1987] 1 All ER 20, HL; see post, para 14.07.
3 Cf Eekelaar and Dingwall, op cit pp 266–267.
4 See s 1(1) and (2).
5 See s 1(4).

9.84   Where the disability of the child results from an injury caused to either of his parents which was in breach of the duties under the Nuclear Installations Act 1965 to secure that nuclear incidents do not cause injury to persons, the child's disabilities are to be regarded as injuries caused on the same occasion and by the same breach of duty as was the injury to the parent.[1] The child is then entitled to compensation under the 1965 Act, which provides a code for compensation.

1 See Congenital Disabilities (Civil Liability) Act 1976, s 3. As under the general provisions of the 1976 Act, compensation is not payable where the injury to the parent preceded the child's conception and one or both parents knew the risk of their child being born disabled; see s 3(5).

9.85   It is clear that the Congenital Disabilities (Civil Liability) Act is based on the fault principle, and so long as that principle remains the Act must be recognised as a welcome relief for a particular category of children born disabled.[1] But a preponderant section of our disabled children remain financially unprotected. Their needs and the stresses imposed on their families will not be alleviated until the possibility, long since canvassed, of a Family Fund to provide financial aid to them is realised.[2]

1 But see Eekelaar and Dingwall, op cit.
2 For the problems those children and families have to face see S Baldwin, *The Costs of Caring: Families with Disabled Children* (1985).

11   Protection from violence within the home

9.86   The most drastic protection is the removal of the child from his parents and his placement in the care of a local authority. This remedy is considered in Chapter 14. The present section deals with the situation where one parent is abusing the other and/or the child and the objective is to stop that conduct but to leave the child within the home.

(a)   Complaint to the police

9.87   The first and most obvious recourse lies with a complaint to the police. They possess wide powers of entry and arrest and, where violence has been used or threatened against a child, they are likely to arrest the perpetrator and can also remove the child to a place of safety.[1] The 'innocent' parent can be compelled to give evidence for the Crown in any proceedings for assault, injury or sexual offence against a person under 16.[2] The more difficult situation is where the violence is currently directed against a parent (usually the woman) and the child is not in immediate danger. The woman may well be reluctant to lodge a complaint and the police have been loath to interfere in what they regard as domestic situations. Attitudes are changing, and Parliament has helped by making the wife a compellable witness against her husband in any prosecution for violence committed by him on her.[3] That said, prosecution may be an excessive response from the child's point of view. The violence may have been directed at or threatened against the mother; it may be the symptom of problems (such as overcrowded accommodation or unemployment) which can be remedied in other ways. Even if a prosecution is proposed the civil remedies considered below may still be relevant, especially if the accused is granted bail and threatens to return to the family home.

1 CYPA 1969, s 28(2); see further *post*, paras 14.34 et seq.
2 Police and Criminal Evidence Act 1984, s 80.
3 Ibid. See also the decision by the Metropolitan Police to issue new guidelines to its officers instructing them to treat cases of domestic violence as criminal offences and to respond accordingly, (National Press, 25 June 1987).

(b) Alternative accommodation

9.88 The most natural relief is for the mother and child to flee the home and head for relatives, friends, one of the all too few refuges, housing charities or the local authority's housing department.[1] As for the last possibility, if they are driven out of the home and cannot find suitable accommodation, they will often qualify as 'homeless'[2] and a 'priority need'[3] under Part III of the Housing Act 1985 and the local authority will be under a duty to rehouse them.[4] The authority could try to avoid this duty by regarding the family as being intentionally homeless because of the mother's failure to use her civil legal remedies (below) against the man who has evicted her. However, the Code of Guidance which accompanies the Act discourages such an approach and advises that 'a battered woman who has fled the marital home should never be regarded as having become homeless intentionally because it would clearly not be reasonable for her to remain'.[5] The more difficult problem can arise in convincing the local authority that violence has been used or threatened. Again the Code helps. 'Authorities are asked to respond sympathetically to applications from women who are in fear of violence; the fact that violence has not yet occurred does not, on its own, suggest that it is not likely to occur.'[6] On the other hand, the woman must produce some evidence of probable violence (such as an attempt to re-enter the house) in order to satisfy the authority.[7] Indications of violence threatened against a child are likely to satisfy it more easily. Finally, if sufficient evidence of violence can be produced, the duty to house can attach to a local authority other than the one in whose area the family normally resides,[8] and this can be useful for a family which wishes to put many miles between it and the violent husband.

1 See further Pah (ed), *Private Violence and Public Policy* (1985), Chapter 6.
2 A person is homeless if, inter alia, he has accommodation but 'it is possible that occupation of it will lead to violence from some other person residing in it or to threats of violence . . .', Housing Act 1985, s 58(3)(b).
3 Defined as a 'person with whom dependent children reside or might reasonably be expected to reside', (s 59(1)(b)). The children need not be related to the applicant. The Code of

Guidance (below) suggests that all children under 16 and those under 19 in education or who are unable to look after themselves qualify as 'dependent'.

4 Staying at a refuge centre or temporarily with friends will rarely amount to suitable alternative accommodation; see *R v Ealing London Borough Council, ex p Sidhu* (1982) 3 FLR 438 (which dealt with the similar, earlier provisions of the Housing (Homeless Persons) Act 1977).

5 Paragraph 2.16.

6 Paragraph 2.10(a).

7 See *R v Wandsworth London Borough, ex p Nimako-Boateng* [1984] FLR 192; *R v Purbeck District Council, ex p Cadney* [1986] 2 FLR 158; *R v Eastleigh Borough Council, ex p Evans* [1986] 2 FLR 195. The chances of successfully challenging an authority's decision by way of judicial review are slim, if the reticence in *Pulhofer v Hillingdon London Borough Council* [1986] AC 484, [1986] 1 All ER 467, HL is maintained.

8 HA 1985, s 67.

9.89 Rehousing will be an unsatisfactory solution for most children, and so other remedies designed to exclude the violent parent from the home and to prohibit further acts of violence must be considered. Various jurisdictions offer protection to children from violence by their parents, but for most the protection is indirect, being the consequence of a court order obtained by one parent against the other.

(c)   Exclusion of a parent from the home[1]

9.90 Under the Matrimonial Homes Act 1983 a spouse, but not a child, can obtain from the High Court or a county court an order excluding the other spouse from the matrimonial home. It is the appropriate Act to be used when matrimonial proceedings are pending. One advantage of the jurisdiction is that the court may additionally[2] order the resident spouse to pay an occupation rent to the other and can order either spouse to pay or contribute to the repair, maintenance and upkeep of the home. An ouster injunction can also be obtained under the Domestic Violence and Matrimonial Proceedings Act 1976. This jurisdiction extends both to married couples and cohabitees[3] and enables a county court to exclude a person not merely from the home but also from a specified area surrounding it. This last provision can be useful, if, for example, the man threatens to pester his child en route to school. Whichever Act is used, the criteria to be applied before making an order are those set out in section 1(3) of the 1983 Act.[4] One of them[5] is 'the needs of any children' and in *Richards v Richards* a majority in the House of Lords tried to halt the trend by the courts, including the Court of Appeal in *Richards*, of treating the needs of the children as the paramount consideration.[6] Instead, the 'needs of the children' are an important and specified, but not in every case first and paramount, consideration to be applied.[7] This is emphasised by the requirement in section 1(3) that, after considering the various criteria, the court should make an order which is 'just and reasonable'. But, as Lord Hailsham recognised, 'this is not, of course, to say that if, on consideration, the "needs of the children" are so clamant as in the circumstances of the case require them to be given paramountcy the court should not in the proper exercise of its discretion give effect to precisely that'.[8] Indeed, in most cases involving children, their need for secure and familiar accommodation remains the crucial factor.[9] However, what *Richards v Richards* has done is to alert the courts against the automatic granting of orders, to the drastic effect which an order can have on the respondent, and against insubstantial efforts by a custodial parent to evict a partner from the home.[10] On the other hand, the applicant does not have to prove violence by the respondent. As Lord Scarman has said, 'Homelessness can be as great a threat as physical violence to the security of a woman (or man) and her children. Eviction, actual, attempted or threatened, is therefore within the mischief [of the 1976 Act], likewise conduct which makes it impossible or intolerable . . . for the other partner, or the children, to remain at home.'[11]

1 For fuller treatment of the subject generally, see C M Lyon, Butterworths, Family Law Service, Division B; Freeman MDA, *Dealing with Domestic Violence* (1987). For wider background material see Select Committee on Violence in Marriage, Report HC 553-i and Evidence HC 533-ii (1974–75); Eekelaar J M and Katz S N (eds.), *Family Violence – an International and Interdisciplinary Study* (1978); Johnson N (ed.) *Marital Violence* (1985); Martin J P (ed), *Violence and the Family* (1978); Pah LJ (ed) *Private Violence and Public Policy* (1985) and see the bibliography therein; Borkowski M, Murch M and Walker V, *Marital Violence: The Community Response* (1983).
2 Section 1(3).
3 Section 1(2).
4 *Richards v Richards* [1984] AC 174, [1983] 2 All ER 807, HL; *Lee v Lee* [1984] FLR 243, CA.
5 The others are the conduct of the spouses, their needs and resources, and all the circumstances of the case.
6 For cases where a party was excluded from the matrimonial home for the benefit of children, see *Gurasz v Gurasz* [1970] P 11, [1969] 3 All ER 822, CA; *Hall v Hall* [1971] 1 All ER 762, [1971] 1 WLR 404, CA; *Bassett v Bassett* [1975] Fam 76, [1975] 1 All ER 513, CA; *Walker v Walker* [1978] 3 All ER 141, [1978] 1 WLR 533, CA; *Rennick v Rennick* [1978] 1 All ER 817, [1977] 1 WLR 1455, CA; *Wood v Wood* (1978) 9 Fam Law 254; *Smith v Smith* (1979) 10 Fam Law 50; *Beard v Beard* [1981] 1 All ER 783, [1981] 1 WLR 369, CA.
7 Per Lord Hailsham, at 203 and 815.
8 Ibid at 204 and 816.
9 See *Lee v Lee*, supra and *Anderson v Anderson* [1984] FLR 566, [1984] Fam Law 183, CA; although the legacy of *Richards* is such that the courts are still sometimes concerned about the drastic effect which an ouster order can have on the respondent; see *Summers v Summers* [1986] 1 FLR 343, [1986] Fam Law 56, CA; *Robson v Robson* (1985) 135 NLJ Rep 84, CA; *Wiseman v Simpson* [1988] 1 All ER 245, [1988] 1 WLR 35, CA; but cf *Thurley v Smith* [1984] FLR 875, [1985] Fam Law 31, CA. Note also *Summers v Summers* (1987) Times, 19 May, where the Court of Appeal warned against the practice of granting orders as a 'routine stepping-stone' on the road to divorce.
10 For example, an unmarried woman could threaten to put her children in care unless the father (whose rights over children in care are very limited) leaves the house.
11 *Davis v Johnson* [1979] AC 264 at 348, [1978] 1 All ER 1132 at 1156.

9.91   It should be noted that section 1(3) of the 1983 Act refers to the needs of 'any children' so that if, for example, a wife and the children are driven out of the home and replaced by the husband's girlfriend and her children, the girlfriend's needs must also be considered,[1] as must the future needs of a wife pregnant with her husband's child.[2] Correspondingly, the court is restricted to the criteria in section 1(3) and cannot exercise its power for other motives (for example, by granting an ouster order to 'allow the dust to settle' and promote a reconciliation between the parties).[3]

1 See *Eade v Eade* (1983) 4 FLR 573, 13 Fam Law 142.
2 *Anderson v Anderson* [1984] FLR 566, [1984] Fam Law 183, CA.
3 *Summers v Summers* [1986] 1 FLR 343, [1986] Fam Law 56, CA.

9.92   An ouster injunction issued under the 1976 Act is normally of a 'first aid' nature and, where the applicant has other, longer term remedies available, such as a petition for divorce or an application for an order under section 9 of the 1983 Act (to solve a dispute over rights of occupation), it should not extend beyond three months.[1] But in those rare cases where other remedies are unobtainable, an injunction can be directed to last 'until further order of the court'.[2] The 1976 Act extends to 'a man and woman who are living with each other in the same household as husband and wife'.[3] In spite of the use of the present tense, the parties need not be cohabiting at the time of the application.[4] Indeed, a woman with young children, for example, may need several weeks to find alternative accommodation and to pluck up courage before seeking an ouster order. However, the matter is one of degree, and relief should be sought at the first realistic opportunity, otherwise the fact of cohabitation will dissipate.

1 *Practice Note* [1978] 2 All ER 1056; sub nom *Practice Direction* [1978] 1 WLR 1123. This can put cohabitees in a precarious position.
2 *Galan v Galan* [1985] FLR 905, [1985] Fam Law 256, CA; *Spencer v Camacho* (1983) 4 FLR 662, 13 Fam Law 114, CA.
3 Section 1(2).
4 *McLean v Nugent* (1980) 1 FLR 26, CA; *McLean v Burke* (1982) 3 FLR 70, CA; *O'Neill v Williams* [1984] FLR 1, [1984] Fam Law 85, CA.

9.93   An application for an order to exclude a spouse (but not a cohabitee) from the home can also be made by the other spouse (but again not by anyone else) under section 16 of the Domestic Proceedings and Magistrates' Court Act 1978.[1] A magistrates' court may well be a more convenient venue than the county court,[2] but there are two serious disadvantages. Firstly, an order can be made in respect of a 'child of the family'[3] but not any other child living with the applicant. Secondly and more importantly, the applicant must satisfy the detailed requirements of section 16(3), to the effect that violence has in fact been used against a member of the family or some other person and the applicant or child is in danger of being physically injured.[4] In contrast the powers of the High Court and county courts under the 1983 and 1976 Acts can be exercised on proof of non-physical violence (such as emotional harm) or of molestation short of violence.[5] If therefore an application under the DPMCA is rejected, the spouse can still try the 1976 and 1983 Acts and the county court judge is not bound by the magistrates' decision.[6]

1 See Wilton, *Summary Justice and the Violent Spouse* (1985) 135 NLJ 574.
2 And it may be the only one for which legal aid will be granted.
3 Ie, a child of both parties or one treated by both as a child of the family, s 88(1); cf MHA 1983 s 1(3), ante, para 9.91; and Domestic Protection Act 1982 (New Zealand) where child means a child of the spouses, or cohabitees, and a child who is or has been a member of the family or household, s 2.
4 Though the danger of violence need not be immediate; see *McCartney v McCartney* [1981] Fam 59, [1981] 1 All ER 597.
5 *Horner v Horner* [1982] Fam 90, [1982] 2 All ER 495, CA; *Galan v Galan* [1985] FLR 905, [1985] Fam Law 256, CA.
6 *O'Brien v O'Brien* [1985] FLR 801, [1985] Fam Law 191, CA.

Age limit for children
9.94   The 1976, 1978 and 1983 Acts speak of orders relating to 'children' but do not specify an age limit. It is suggested that 18 is at the very least

an appropriate limit but that the spirit behind the legislation justifies the inclusion of older children who are still living with and are dependent on the applicant, for example, because of continuing education, or because of physical or mental handicap.

(d) Protection of the child from violence within the home

9.95 In some cases it may be sufficient to prohibit a parent from using or threatening violence rather than exclude him from the home. Thus, under the DVMPA 1976 a non-molestation order[1] can be brought by a spouse or cohabitee to protect 'a child living with the applicant'.[2] This broad definition enables a mother to seek protection for a child against, for example, his putative or step-father.[3] Moreover, 'molestation' though not defined by the 1976 Act, has been construed broadly. Thus, 'Violence is a form of molestation, but molestation may take place without the threat or use of violence and still be serious and inimical to mental and physical health'.[4] Indeed, 'molest' can mean to annoy, cause trouble or even pester.[5] So, an injunction may be obtained to prevent a father from, for example, loitering around school gates or from writing to his children.

1 In 1987 11,081 non-molestation only orders were granted by county courts; Judicial Statistics, Cm 428, Table 5.17.
2 Section 1(1)(b).
3 But 'living with' would not on a strict construction extend to a child who is currently in hospital or in voluntary care under the Child Care Act 1980.
4 Per Viscount Dilhorne in *Davis v Johnson* [1979] AC 264 at 334, [1978] 1 All ER 1132 at 1144. See also *Galan v Galan* [1985] FLR 905, [1985] Fam Law 256, CA.
5 *Vaughan v Vaughan* [1973] 3 All ER 449, [1973] 1 WLR 1159, CA; *Spindlow v Spindlow* [1979] Fam 52, [1979] 1 All ER 169, CA.

9.96 A non-molestation injunction can also be granted as ancillary relief in matrimonial proceedings where the court is satisfied that molestation has occurred and an injunction is needed. It is also available after the parties have obtained the matrimonial relief,[1] and is therefore a useful device to protect a family from visits by the former spouse. In the magistrates' jurisdiction, what is commonly known as a personal protection order can be made in favour of 'a child of the family',[2] but only on proof that the respondent spouse has used, or threatened to use, violence[3] and that an order is necessary to protect the child. Again the necessity to prove violence could defeat an application, but resort to the DVMPA 1976 would still be possible.[4] The 1978 Act does not, however, extend to cohabitees and their children.[5]

1 *Stewart v Stewart* [1973] Fam 21, [1973] 1 All ER 31, CA; *Phillips v Phillips* [1973] 2 All ER 423, [1973] 1 WLR 615, CA; *Webb v Webb* [1986] 1 FLR 541, CA.
2 DPMCA 1978, s 88(1).
3 Ibid, s 16(2). If there is imminent danger of physical injury, an expedited order can be made, s 16(6).
4 *Horner v Horner* [1982] Fam 90, [1982] 2 All ER 495, CA.
5 An attempt to include them (by an amendment in the Family Law Reform Bill 1987) was unsuccessful; HC Debs 12 May 1987, col 215.

(e) Emergency applications

9.97 Applications for orders can be made ex parte, but the courts have stressed the need for clear evidence that there is a real and immediate danger of serious injury before an order is granted;[1] and, since an ouster order may render the respondent homeless, an ex parte order should be strictly limited in time.[2] On the other hand, an applicant is far more likely to persuade a court to grant an ex parte injunction if there is evidence of injury or danger to a child.

1 *Practice Note* [1978] 2 All ER 919; sub nom *Practice Direction* [1978] 1 WLR 925.
2 *Ansah v Ansah* [1977] Fam 138, [1977] 2 All ER 638, CA.

(f)   Enforcement

9.98   A power of arrest can be attached to an order[1] made under the 1976 and 1978 Acts, but should not be a routine addition.[2] However, there is a high likelihood of it being granted if the violence has been directed against a child rather than his parent.[3] Breach of an order can be punished by committal to prison, provided that the proper procedures are observed.[4] But committal is 'the very last resort'[5] and only appropriate when every other effort has failed, such as use of warnings, adjournment for a cooling off period, inquiries by the court welfare officer, attaching a power of arrest to an order and suspension of the committal order.

1 Exceptionally this can include an order made ex parte; see *Latif v Latif* (1986) 136 NLJ 517.
2 *Lewis v Lewis* [1978] Fam 60, [1978] 1 All ER 729, CA; *Horner v Horner* [1982] Fam 90, [1982] 2 All ER 495, CA. If no arrest power is attached but the parent commits an act of violence, the police have wide powers to arrest him under the Police and Criminal Evidence Act 1984, s 25(3)(d)(i) and (e) and at common law for breach of the peace; see *R v Howell* [1982] QB 416, [1981] 3 All ER 383, CA.
3 *Re H (a minor)* [1986] 1 FLR 558, [1986] Fam Law 139 (nine months, reduced to three on appeal); *Wright v Jess* [1987] 2 All ER 1067, CA (two years following a history of non-compliance). See further, Butterworths Family Law Service, Division B, paras 191–200.
4 *Re C* [1986] 1 FLR 578, [1986] Fam Law 187; *Tabone v Seguna* [1986] 1 FLR 591, [1986] Fam Law 188. If the respondent assaults a child in breach of an injunction, he should be punished for contempt even though the police intend to prosecute him; *Caprice v Boswell* [1986] Fam Law 52, CA; *Szczepanski v Szczepanski* [1985] FLR 468, [1985] Fam Law 120, CA.
5 *Ansah v Ansah*, ante, para 9.97, note 2.

(g)   Other jurisdictions

9.99   Section 37 of the Supreme Court Act 1981 (and its equivalent in section 38 of the County Courts Act 1984) expresses the High Court's inherent jurisdiction to grant an injunction if it is needed to support the legal right claimed in an action. *Richards v Richards*[1] has decided that this jurisdiction should not be used by spouses to obtain ouster orders ancillary to matrimonial relief such as divorce.[2] It could still be used by other persons such as a mother who is pursuing a proprietary claim over the family home or, of course, a child (if he has someone to act for him). Indeed, even between spouses, this jurisdiction can still be invoked in appropriate cases, such as molestation, 'for the protection of minors'.[3] It can even be used after the parties have divorced if the child's protection requires it;[4] for example, if the former husband returns to the home and makes a nuisance of himself to the detriment of the child. Injunctions are also available from the High Court in wardship proceedings,[5] and this jurisdiction is not only open to a much larger category of applicants (such as cohabitees or relatives who fear for a child's safety) but is also guided by the paramountcy of the child's welfare. The expense of High Court proceedings and the availability of legal aid mean that the other jurisdictions are normally more appropriate, along with (in the case of relatives) a complaint to the local authority. As far as the Guardianship of Minors Act 1971 is concerned, the position is unclear. A *non-molestation order* can be made if the effective custody of the child demands it and logically an ouster order should also be available so that, for example, the court can grant custody to the mother, restrain the father from molesting the child and entering the home and even evict him from the home, at least where the mother already has a proprietary interest in it.[6] This last qualification is important,[7] for otherwise the GMA 1971 would enable a parent to circumvent the hurdles of the DVMPA, MHA and DPMCA, by applying for a custody order and tacking on an application for an ouster order, the issue being decided on the paramountcy principle in the GMA rather than the criteria in section 1(3) of the MHA.[8] It is submitted that as far as *ouster orders* are concerned *Re W*[9] is incompatible with *Richards v Richards* and that the GMA 1971 should not be used to grant them against spouses or cohabitees.

1 Supra; and see *Baggott v Baggott* [1986] 1 FLR 377, [1986] Fam Law 129, CA.
2 MHA 1983 or DVMPA 1976 should be used instead.
3 Per Lord Hailsham in *Richards v Richards* [1984] AC 174 at 202, [1983] 2 All ER 807 at 814.
4 *Phillips v Phillips* [1973] 2 All ER 423, [1973] 1 WLR 615, CA; *Quinn v Quinn* (1982) 4 FLR 394, CA. (The jurisdiction may be available in the absence of children; see *Webb v Webb* [1986] 1 FLR 541, CA, but cf the more authoritative view in *O'Malley v O'Malley* [1982] 2 All ER 112, [1982] 1 WLR 244, CA, which was not cited in *Webb*.)
5 See *Re V* (1979) 123 Sol Jo 201.
6 *Re W* [1981] 3 All ER 401, 11 Fam Law 207, CA.
7 See *Ainsbury v Millington* [1986] 1 All ER 73, [1986] 1 FLR 331, CA.
8 Ante, para 9.90.
9 Supra, note 6.

9.100 The GMA 1971 clearly does have a role to play in resolving custody of the child and, more practically, access to him and maintenance of him by the non-custodial parent during the period of an ouster or exclusion order. It is thus good practice to add an application under the Act to any proceedings for injunctive or other domestic violence relief. This practice poses a dilemma, for under the GMA 1971 the paramountcy of the child's welfare is the test, whereas welfare is only one of the relevant factors for injunctions. In *Re T*[1] May LJ could 'see no difficulty in first deciding what is best for the children under the guardianship proceedings and then, having so decided, to take that decision into account as one of the four criteria under the Matrimonial Homes Act, without in any way elevating the children criterion above all the others'. Whilst it is possible to agree with His Lordship that 'any other approach would be illogical', the result of his analysis is that in reality the child's welfare is very likely to dictate the outcome of the proceedings. The decision clearly encourages applicants for injunctions to join an application for custody to the proceedings.

The more straightforward use of the GMA in this context is where the proceedings solely concern custody and/or access and the court is persuaded of the need to grant an injunction against violence. For example, the child's guardian may want an injunction to prevent the father from disrupting the child's life.

1 [1987] 1 FLR 181, [1986] Fam Law 298, CA.

(h) Conclusion

9.101   If there is evidence of harm only to a child and not also to a parent, the civil remedies examined in this Section of the chapter are very unlikely to be used. Care proceedings and the criminal law will normally be employed, especially in the emotive climate of public opinion generated by child abuse. Where the remedies can be useful from the child's point of view are firstly, in enabling a mother to bolster her claim for an order, for example, by showing the psychological and behavioural effect which the father's violence on her is having on the child.[1] Secondly, they can deter further violence which is currently directed at the parent but which may sooner or later be targetted at the child. However, the protection which they offer to the child rests firmly on the determination and willingness of the custodial parent to pursue them.

1 See *Phillips v Phillips* [1973] 2 All ER 423, [1973] 1 WLR 615, CA; *Walker v Walker* [1978] 3 All ER 141, [1978] 1 WLR 533, CA; *D v D* (1983) 4 FLR 82, 12 Fam Law 150, CA.

CHAPTER 10

The protection of children from harm — II Moral and emotional harm[1]

1 OFFENCES OTHER THAN SEXUAL OFFENCES

10.01 Under this heading are grouped various statutory provisions, most of which are aimed at protecting the child from influences and pressures which may harm his character and moral upbringing but a few of which are designed to save him from emotional strain and embarrassment. One or other object is to be found in the first group to be mentioned.

1 See *Children in Danger*, published by the National Children's Home.

1 Protection of juveniles in relation to judicial proceedings

10.02 This protection is given by a number of provisions in Part III of the Children and Young Persons Act 1933 (as extended by the CYPA 1963).

(a) Separation of juveniles from adults

10.03 In order to minimise the risk of contact with hardened criminals, arrangements must normally be made for keeping juveniles apart from adult defendants both while they are at a police station and during the course of attending any criminal court.[1] Moreover, during such times a girl must be under the care of a woman,[2] and, if the juvenile is attending as a witness, he should have a trusted adult close at hand at all times, especially when giving evidence.[3]

1 CYPA 1933, s 31. See further post, paras 12.67 and 12.79.
2 Ibid.
3 Home Office Circular No 208/1964.

(b) Provisions relating to the attendance of juveniles at court

10.04 No child[1] (other than an infant in arms) is allowed to be present in court during the trial of any other person who is charged with an offence or during any proceedings preliminary thereto, except during such time as his presence is required as a witness or otherwise for the purpose of justice.[2]

1 The rule does not apply to a young person.
2 CYPA 1933, s 36.
There is a remarkable proviso that the rule does not apply to messengers and the like who are required to attend court for purposes connected with their employment, but it is very doubtful whether children are ever so employed. In any event they would have

to be at least 13 years old (see post, para 11.77). There ought to be an absolute prohibition on such employment.

10.05 There are also provisions designed to minimise tension and embarrassment when a juvenile has to give evidence in adult courts. This topic is considered within the wider subject of Children and Evidence, which forms a separate section of this chapter.[1]

1   Paras 10.42 et seq.

(c)   Protection against publicity

10.06   Restrictions are imposed by the Children and Young Persons Act 1933 on newspaper and broadcast reports of proceedings in, or on appeal from, magistrates' courts[1] or of proceedings in any court in which a juvenile has been concerned, whether as a party or a witness.[2] These are designed to protect the anonymity of the juvenile. They are examined in Chapter 12.[3] Similarly, as we have seen,[4] restrictions are imposed in wardship proceedings in the interests of the child.

1   Section 49 (as amended by CYPA 1969, s 10).
2   Ibid, s 39.
3   Paragraph 12.83 to 12.85.
4   Ante, para 8.45.

2   Protection from harmful publications

10.07   The law of obscenity to some extent protects juveniles and adolescents from the corrupting influences of certain kinds of publications, but no more than it protects the public at large. The test of obscenity is whether the article is such as to tend to deprave and corrupt persons who are likely to read, see or hear it.[1] In applying this test the possible effect of the work on young people is an important factor,[2] but it is not overriding, unless the work is primarily intended for them, because as Stable J, put it:[3]

> 'A mass of literature, great literature, from many angles is wholly unsuitable for reading by the adolescent, but that does not mean that a publisher is guilty of a criminal offence for making those works available to the general public.'

Even if the work is mainly intended for the young, it may still be doubtful whether it is obscene, and it has been necessary to provide other protective legislation.

1   Obscene Publications Act 1959, s 1.
2   *R v Reiter* [1954] 2 QB 16, [1954] 1 All ER 741, CCA.
3   In *R v Martin Secker and Warburg Ltd* [1954] 2 All ER 683 at 686.

10.08   The Children and Young Persons (Harmful Publications) Act 1955 was enacted in order to put a stop to the widespread publication of 'horror comics', ghoulish pictorial publications which were calculated to stimulate brutish emotions in young people. The Act accordingly applies to any 'book, magazine or other work' having the following characteristics.[1]

(i)　It is of a kind likely to fall into the hands of a juvenile.
(ii)　It consists wholly or mainly of stories told in pictures whether with or without written matter: the picture tells the story.
(iii)　The story portrays the commission of crimes, acts of violence or cruelty or incidents of a repulsive or horrible nature.
(iv)　The portrayal is in such a way that the work as a whole would tend to corrupt a juvenile into whose hands it might fall.

Happily, the Act never needs to be mentioned. Its efficacy is shown by the fact that horror comics are now unknown.[2] Indeed, even while the Bill was before Parliament there was a decline in circulation.

1　Section 1.
2　See Zellick, [1972] Crim LR 192.

10.09　The 1955 Act was a necessary response to a known, widespread evil. When enacted the same could not be said of the Protection of Children Act 1978, which seeks to protect children from being used for purposes of pornographic photography. There was no evidence that the practice was widely prevalent,[1] and where it did exist there were and are other statutory provisons available to deal with it. Thus, the Customs Authorities are empowered to seize indecent photographs imported from abroad,[2] and the sending of 'indecent or obscene' material through the post is covered by the Post Office Act 1953.[3] Nevertheless, there were in 1978 gaps in the law. In particular it is doubtful whether the taking of indecent photographs falls within the provisions of the Indecency with Children Act 1960,[4] and such indecency does not necessarily amount to obscenity so as to be caught by the Obscene Publications Act 1959.

The 1978 Act extends to children under 16. It makes it an offence to take[5] or permit to be taken, or to distribute or show, or to have in one's possession with a view to distributing or showing or to publish an advertisement likely to be understood as conveying that the advertiser distributes or shows, any indecent photographs of a child.[6] There are two defences to distributing or showing photographs, the onus of proof in each case being on the defendant.[7] First, that there was a legitimate reason for doing so. This will rarely arise but will, for example, apply to the use of photographs by the police for training purposes. Second, that the defendant did not see the photographs and did not know, nor had any cause to suspect, them to be indecent.[8] Indecency is not defined by the Act and is a question of fact to be decided apparently in the light of 'the recognised standards of propriety',[9] but subject to provisional determination by the Director of Public Prosecutions in that his consent to a prosecution is necessary, whether proceedings are brought in the Crown Court or in a magistrates' court.[10]

In deciding whether a photograph of a child is indecent, his age is not to be ignored: the photograph is not to be judged intrinsically.[11] On the other hand, the motive of the photographer and the circumstances in which he took the photograph are irrelevant.[12]

The Criminal Justice Act 1988[13] takes the law further by making it a summary offence for a person merely to have in his possession an indecent photograph[14] of a child who is under 16.[15] Two of the defences available are similar to the defences to a charge of an offence under the Protection of Children Act 1978, namely: (a) that the defendant had a legitimate reason for having the photograph in his possession, for example, a police officer carrying it on him in the course of his investigations; or (b) that he had not himself seen the photograph and did not know nor had any cause to suspect it to be indecent.[16] But additionally there is the defence that he was sent the photograph without any prior request for it and that he did not keep it for an unreasonable time.[17]

A justice of the peace has power to issue a warrant authorising entry and search of premises in order to remove indecent photographs,[18] and a court which finds an offence proved under the 1978 Act or the 1988 Act must order forfeiture of the indecent photographs.[19]

1 See HL Debs, Vol 391, cols 574–579.
2 Customs Consolidation Act 1876, s 42; and Customs and Excise Act 1952, ss 44 and 277.
3 Section 11.
4 For this Act see post, para 10.42.
5 Thus it applies to a person who takes indecent photographs of children for his own private satisfaction, even though he does not show or distribute them to other persons.
6 Section 1(1) and (2). 'Photograph' includes a film and any video recording (s 7).
7 Section 1(4).
8 Thus, it is no defence if he saw them, even though he did not think they were indecent.
9 Per Parker LJ in *R v Stanley* [1965] 2 QB 327, [1965] 1 All ER 1035, CCA, explaining the words 'indecent or obscene' in s 11 of the Post Office Act 1953, supra.
10 The penalties for conviction on indictment are a maximum of three years' imprisonment or a fine or both, and on summary conviction a maximum of six months' imprisonment or a fine on level 5 of the standard scale or both, (s 6).
11 *R v Owen (Charles)* [1988] 1 WLR 134, CA.
12 *R v Graham-Kerr* [1988] 1 WLR 1098.
13 Section 160(1).
14 For the meaning, see supra, note 6.
15 The penalty for conviction is a fine not exceeding level 5 on the standard scale (s 160(3)).
      The Director of Public Prosecutions must consent to a prosecution; see CJA 1988, s 160(4), read with PCA 1978, s 1(3).
16 CJA 1988, s 160(2)(a) and (b). The latter defence is highly unlikely.
17 Ibid, s 160(2)(c).
18 PCA 1978, s 4, as amended by CJA 1988, Sch 15, para 61.
19 PCA 1978, s 5, as amended by CJA 1988, Sch 15, para 62.

10.10 The Indecent Displays (Control) Act 1981 makes it an offence to make, cause or permit the display of indecent matter in, or so as to be visible from, a public place. The Act is aimed at indecent displays in such places as bookshops or sex shop windows, which the public cannot avoid seeing. An offence is not committed if the display occurs in a place to which the public are permitted to have access only on payment for the display or in a shop or part of a shop to which the public can only gain access by passing beyond an adequate warning notice. But these exclusions only apply where persons under 18 are not permitted while the display is continuing, and the warning notice must expressly warn that there is no admittance allowed to persons under that age.

3   Protection from gambling

10.11 Certain provisions in the Betting, Gaming and Lotteries Act 1963 are specifically aimed at protecting the young from the temptations of gambling. Thus, the Act[1] makes it an offence for anyone to effect with or through a young person any betting transaction[2] or to employ him in

Penny against wall

Private betting

a licensed betting office. A young person here means one who either (a) is under 18 and whom the other person knows or ought to know is under that age, or (b) is apparently under 18. No betting circulars may be sent to anyone known to be under 18 and, if such a circular is sent to a person at a place of education and he is under that age, the sender is deemed to have known that the addressee is under age, unless he proves that he has reasonable grounds for believing the contrary.[3]

The Gaming Act 1968 forbids anyone under 18 taking part in certain forms of gaming in public houses in which adults are allowed to participate,[4] and no one under that age is allowed in a room in licensed premises, clubs or institutes while gaming takes place.[5] A licensing authority must refuse to register, or to renew registration of a club or institute for the use of gaming machines if the premises are frequented wholly or mainly by persons under 19.[6]

As with drinking by juveniles on licensed premises, there is considerable doubt about effective enforcement of these restrictions. In particular there is considerable concern about the playing of gaming machines in amusement arcades by juveniles who are truanting from school, and there is strong evidence of addiction to gambling.[7]

1   Section 21.
2   Using a young person to effect such a transaction by post is, however, permitted.
3   Section 22, as amended by FLRA 1969, s 1(3) and Sch 1.
4   Section 7.
5   Section 17. They may, however, attend bingo clubs provided they do not participate (ss 20(6) and 21(4)).
6   Section 30 and Sch 7, para 7.
7   A report in 1988 by the National Housing and Town Planning Council indicated that 607,000 juveniles had borrowed money to play the machines; 289,000 spend their school dinner money on machines; and 108,000 missed lessons in order to play them. A report from the Chairman of the National Council on Gambling and evidence from Gamblers Anonymous support the view that addiction is widespread, but this conclusion is doubted by the Home Office whose survey, carried out by its Research Unit and the Gaming Board, found that only 2 per cent of a sample of 2,000 juveniles played every day and not all of them were addicted. Nevertheless, increasing pessure to ban under 18-year-olds from playing gaming machines may well lead to legislation.

4   Miscellaneous forms of protection from moral harm

10.12   There are a few enactments contained, or originating, in the Children and Young Persons Act 1933 which offer special protection to juveniles. They are not directly inter-related but may be grouped together on the basis that they all seek to prevent juveniles from participating in undesirable dealings.

Thus, it is an offence[1] for anyone to cause or procure a juvenile under 16 to be in a street, premises or place for the purpose of begging. This is also committed by anyone who, having custody, charge or care of the juvenile, allows him to be in such places and it is proved that the juvenile was there for the purpose of begging. The onus is on the defendant to prove that he did not allow the juvenile to be there for that purpose. Apart from criminal liability, in such circumstances it may be appropriate to bring care proceedings in the juvenile court.

A person is forbidden to take an article in pawn from anyone whom he knows to be, or who appears to be and is, a minor,[2] and scrap metal dealers must not acquire scrap metal from those apparently under 16.[3]

1 CYPA 1933, s 4, as amended by CYPA 1963, s 64(1) and Sch III, para 3.
2 Consumer Credit Act 1974, s 114(2). Note also s 50, which makes it an offence for a person, with a view to financial gain, to send to a minor a circular inviting him to borrow money or obtain goods on credit or hire services on hire or apply for information about any of those matters. It is, however, a defence for the sender to prove that he did not know and had no reasonable cause to suspect that the addressee was a minor.
3 Scrap Metal Dealers Act 1964, s 5(1), replacing CYPA 1933, s 9.

II SEXUAL OFFENCES

1 Introduction

10.13 Further protection of children is provided by the sanctions in respect of sexual offences, almost all of which are to be found enacted in the Sexual Offences Acts 1956 and 1967. Most of these relate to adults and children alike, but others are concerned only with children. They are dealt with on that basis and also according to whether the victim is a girl or boy.

10.14 This discrimination between the sexes, both children and adults, and both as victims and offenders, is one of the criticisms of an area of law that has come under close scrutiny over the past decade. The main examinations have been conducted under Home Office Research;[1] by two official Committees reporting to the Home Secretary, namely, the Criminal Law Revision Committee[2] (CLRC) and the Policy Advisory Committee[3] (PAC); and, more recently, by a Working Party of the Howard League for Penal Reform (WPHL).[4] Although there is a substantial measure of agreement for reform on some matters in an area where opinions, not always rational, sharply contrast and conflict, early legislative implementation does not seem likely. The fact that there are over 40 statutory offences relating to the control of sexual conduct[5] gives some indication of the size of the problem to be faced, but it conceals the further fact that some of the statutory provisions each include within them two or more offences, a point strikingly illustrated by *R v Courtie,*[6] a case of buggery, in which the House of Lord pointed out that the effect of the amending Sexual Offences Act 1967 had been so to complicate the law as to hasten the need for reform. As a result of that Act[7] there are no less than four different offences, depending upon age and consent, carrying different maximum penalties.[8] But complaint does not stop with the number of offences. There is also considerable overlapping, as will be seen, for example, in respect of sexual conduct involving a girl under 16; many of the offences are anomalous, for example, with regard to abduction of girls; and many carry unrealistic or anomalous maximum penalties, reflected in the fact that they are not often imposed. The defects are not, however, to be exaggerated, because less than one per cent of all recorded offences are sexual.[9] Nevertheless, it is of considerable significance that in a high proportion of sexual offences the victims are under 16, particularly cases involving indecent assaults of girls.[10]

1 Walmsley and White, *Sexual Offences, Consent and Sentencing* Research Study No 54, (HMSO 1979).
2 Fifteenth Report, *Sexual Offences* (1984) Cmnd 9213 (preceded by a Working Paper (1980)). The Report took eight years to complete.

3 Report on the *Age of Consent in relation to Sexual Offences* (1981) Cmnd 8216.
4 *Unlawful Sex: Offences, Victims and Offenders in the Criminal Justice of England and Wales.*
5 See WPHL Report, Appendix I, listing some 43.
6 [1984] AC 463, [1984] 1 All ER 740.
7 Sections 1 and 3, read with the main provision, s 12(1) of the 1956 Act.
8 (i) Buggery of a boy under 16 — life imprisonment;
   (ii) buggery of a boy over 16 without his consent — ten years' imprisonment;
   (iii) buggery of a boy between 16 and 20 with his consent — five years' imprisonment;
   (iv) buggery of a boy between 16 and 20 with his consent but accused is not an adult — two years' imprisonment.
9 Home Office Statistical Bulletin 16/87.
10 See HOSB 5/84.

2   Protection of girls

(a)   General protection

10.15   Many of the provisions of the Act of 1956 apply whatever the age of the female victim may be.[1] They include those dealing with rape and kindred offences involving unlawful sexual intercourse by force, intimidation or fraud (sections 1–4), or with mental defectives (sections 7 and 9),[2] incest (section 10), indecent assault (section 14), abduction (sections 17 and 21) and offences relating to prostitution (sections 22, 24, 27 and 29).[3] But even some of these may have special application if the victim is a girl.

1   References in the Act to a woman may extend to a girl and references to a man may extend to a boy (s 46).
2   See also the Mental Health Act 1959, s 128 (member of hospital staff having unlawful sexual intercourse with a mentally disordered female patient or a man having intercourse with such a patient when she is subject to his guardianship, custody or care under the the Act). Note that this provision is not repealed by MHA 1983. The section is a striking illustration of how amending legislation can run amok. Sub-s (1)(b), dealing with the point on guardianship, is amended by:
   (1) National Health Service Reorganisation Act 1973, ss 57, 58, Sch 4, para 92;
   (2) National Health Service Act 1977, s 129, Sch 15, para 29;
   (3) Residential Homes Act 1980, s 11(4), Sch 1, para 2(2);
   (4) Mental Health Act 1983, s 148, Sch 4, para 15;
   (5) Health and Social Services and Social Security Adjudications Act 1983, s 29, Sch 9, Part I, para 6;
   (6) Registered Homes Act 1984, s 57(1), Sch 1, para 2.
3   See also ss 30–31 (living on earnings of prostitution and exercising control over prostitutes) and ss 33–36 (relating to brothels).

(b)   Rape

10.16   Thus, while every successful prosecution of rape[1] requires proof of absence of consent to sexual intercourse,[2] in the case of a girl under 16 who is not proved to have physically resisted the act it will be enough to show that her understanding and knowledge were such that she was not in a position to decide whether to consent or resist,[3] and for this purpose she may be so young that little, if any, evidence other than her age will be required,[4] although there is not a prescribed age limit below which rape must be held to have been committed.[5] It is a defence to rape that the defendant honestly believed that the victim consented,[6] but, as with the question of her consent, her age will be highly relevant and so will her understanding and knowledge as they evinced themselves by her conduct. It will be rare to establish the defence where the victim is a child.

1   The maximum penalty for both rape and attempted rape is imprisonment for life (SOA 1956, s 1, Sch 2 as amended by SOA 1985, s 3(2)).
2   For the difficulty of distinguishing between reluctant compliance and lack of consent see *R v Olugboja* [1982] QB 320, [1981] 3 All ER 443.
3   *R v Howard* [1965] 3 All ER 684, [1966] 1 WLR 13, CCA.
4   *R v Harling* [1938] 1 All ER 307, CA. The genuine consent of a girl under 16 is recognised by the law to a limited extent, viz, to negative a charge of rape, but the accused in such a case may be guilty of other offences, post, para 10.20.
5   At one time if the girl was at least ten years old, proof that the act was against her will was necessary, but if she was under that age the offence was committed whether it was with or against her will; see infra.
6   Sexual Offences (Amendment) Act 1976, s 1(2). The provision is declaratory of the rule laid down by the House of Lords in *DPP v Morgan*, [1976] AC 182, [1975] 2 All ER 347. The Criminal Law Revision Committee, Cmnd 9213, para 2.40 recommended extending the provision to all sexual offences, so that magistrates or a jury should have regard to the presence or absence of reasonable grounds for such a belief, together with other relevant matters, in considering whether the defendant did have the belief. For a critical comment on the Committee's recommendations concerning rape, see Leng [1985] Crim LR 416.

(c) Incest[1]

10.17   There has been a significant increase in the number of rapes recorded by the police — over the decade 1973–83 a recorded increase of one-third,[2] and almost one-third of the victims are girls under 16. That is a worrying figure, but equally disturbing, though not surprising, is the finding that in 1982 70 per cent of the victims of recorded incest were also girls under that age.[3] Figures about the latter offence must be treated with particular caution, especially since so many cases remain unreported;[4] but the main incidence of incest is between fathers and daughters aged 13–16, usually repeated over months or years. The offence carries a heavier maximum penalty, imprisonment for life instead of seven years, if it is committed with a girl under 13,[5] and a person so convicted is most likely to receive a custodial sentence, though rarely in practice is it more than seven years. Where the girl is over 13 most custodial sentences range from six months to five years.[6] About three-quarters of the fathers are given custodial sentences.

1   See generally Batten, *Incest—A Review of the Literature* (1983) 23 Med, Sci & Law 245.
2   WPHL, para 3.15.
3   Ibid, para 3.11.
4   For a rare survey see that conducted by Beezley-Mrazek, Lynch and Bentovim, referred to by CLRC Cmnd 9213, para 8.6.
5   SOA 1956, s 37 and Sch II, para 14. For attempted incest with a girl under 13 the penalty is also heavier, namely seven years instead of two; see Indecency with Children Act 1960, s 2.
6   WPHL, para 6.40; Walmsley and White.

10.18   Ever since incest was made a crime in 1908 there have been different views about the extent to which the offence is based on eugenic factors.[1] The Criminal Law Revision Committee recognised that there are eugenic risks, especially for the child born to parties who are related in the first degree, ie the parent-child or brother-sister relationship,[2] but regarded these as a secondary reason for retaining incest as a crime. For the Committee the primary reasons for retention were social and psychological. In their view, which was in line with that of the Policy Advisory Committee, the criminal law still had a role to play, albeit a limited one. The social worker could, for example, still sometimes find the threat of sanctions of the law a back-up in his or her work with the particular family. But the most important reason was 'the potentially harmful with possible long-term psychological consequences [of incest] for those involved and their families'.[3] Having committed itself to these reasons the Committee, logically it is submitted, proposed a widening of the offence to include adoptive parent and child,[4] but stopped short of extending it to the step-parent/step-child relationship, instead proposing a separate offence for unlawful sexual intercourse with a step-child under 21. They declined, however, to extend that new offence to the foster parent/foster child relationship on the ground of the difficulties of defining who is in a position of trust or authority. That is a difficulty which the Scottish Law Commission has not found insurmountable.[5] A basic problem facing the Committee was the fact that they felt on the one hand the need to retain incest as a crime because its abolition would be 'unacceptable and incomprehensible to the vast majority of people in this country',[6] but on the other hand that the nature of the offence did not permit its extension to protect the wider family unit. This dilemma has prompted other informed opinion[7] to grasp the nettle and propose the abolition of the offence. It has frequently been pointed out that the criminal law, in so far as it can fulfil a protective function, adequately covers the child under 16 without the need for incest. The real need is two-fold, to extend protection to members of the family over 16 and to widen the class of children protected so as to impose liability for sexual abuse on the natural and the adoptive parent, the step-parent, the guardian, the custodian and the foster parent.[8] More controversial is whether liability should end when the child reaches 18. It has been asked:

'But once a person has attained majority, which is now attained at 18, is it really good enough for the rest of us to say that their sexual conduct[9] should remain criminal because the thought of it makes us sick?'[10]

Not, perhaps, for most of the rest of us; but the rest of the family might so say, especially those of its members still under 18 who themselves might still be at risk.

1 Compare, for example, Bailey and Blackburn, The *Punishment of Incest Act 1908: A Case Study of Law Creation* [1979] Crim LR 708, with Wolfram, [1983] Crim LR 308.
2 Incestuous relationships can exist between a man and his grand-daughter, daughter, sister or mother (SOA 1956, s 10(1)) and, if proceedings are against her, between a woman, provided she is 16 or over, and her grandfather, father, brother or son (s 11(1)). Half blood and illegitimate relationships are included (ss 10(2) and 11(2)).
3 CLRC Report, para 8.8, referring to the views of the PAC.
4 The change would not affect the present proscription on natural relations.
5 'If any person over the age of 16 years is in a position of trust or authority in relation to a child under the age of 16 years and is a member of the same household, it should be a criminal offence for that person to have sexual intercourse with the child.' *The Law of Incest in Scotland,* (1981) Cmnd 8422. The Report is a more detailed analysis than that of CLRC and many of its recommendations receive the latter's approval.
6 The words of the PAC Report.
7 See especially, Honore, *Sex Law* (1978); Card, *Sexual Relations with Minors* [1975] Crim LR 371; Bailey and McCabe, *Reforming the Law of Incest,* [1979] Crim LR 749; Hogan [1985] Crim LR 425 at pp 429–430.
8 Some would extend liability beyond the home, for example, to the schoolteacher.
9 Ie sexual intercourse between parent and child who has reached 18.
10 Hogan, [1985] Crim LR 425 at p 430.

10.19   A power available to the trial court enables it to divest the man convicted of incest or attempted incest with a girl under 18 of 'all authority' which he has over her.[1] If he is her guardian the court may also order him to be removed from the guardianship and may appoint someone else a guardian during the girl's minority or for any lesser period.[2] The term 'guardian' is normally understood to mean a person other than the parent who is appointed to the office by deed, will or order of the court.[3] Because of the definition of incest[4] the only persons who could qualify would be the girl's grandfather or brother. It seems clear, however, that the present provision also applies to the father who, stricto sensu, is by law her guardian, at least if she is legitimate. In practice, however, section 38 is rarely invoked, and the likely method of divesting the father of authority is through a care order made in care proceedings. Those proceedings, including particular reference to cases of incest, are later considered in Chapter 14.

1   SOA 1956, s 38(1). Section 38 was substituted by GA 1973, ss 1(8), 15(3) and Sch 1.
2   Section 38(2) and (3). Any order under s 38 may be varied from time to time or rescinded by the High Court. Moreover, if the girl is defective, the order may, so far as it has effect for the purposes of the Mental Health Act 1983, be rescinded before or after the girl has attained 18; s 38(4), as amended by MHA 1983, s 148 and Sch 4, para 12.
3   Cf the distinction drawn by CYPA 1933, s 107(1) between 'guardian' and 'legal guardian'.
4   Supra, para 10.18, note 2.

(d)   Indecent assault

10.20   The offence of indecent assault of a woman[1] also has special application if the victim is a girl under 16, because, if she is, she cannot give any consent which, in the case of a person over that age, would be a defence. A consequence of the rule is that, although a man may be acquitted of the rape of a girl under 16 because of her consent, he may still be convicted of indecent assault.[2] To the rule there is one qualification. If the girl has married — which necessarily means that her marriage is void for lack of age,[3] unless both parties have a foreign personal law which recognises the marriage as valid[4] — the man cannot be guilty of the offence because of her incapacity to consent, if he believes her to be his wife and has reasonable cause for this belief.[5] The case of a girl under 16 who is polygamously married will be considered later.[6]

1   SOA 1956, s 14.
2   *R v Hodgson* [1973] QB 565, [1973] 2 All ER 552, CA.
3   Marriage Act 1949, s 2; Matrimonial Causes Act 1973, s 11(a)(ii).
4   See further post, para 10.24.
5   SOA 1956, s 14(3).
6   Post, para 10.24.

10.21   'Assault' has both its strict meaning, namely, an act which causes another person an apprehension of immediate and unlawful personal violence and also an act which includes battery, but to be liable for indecent assault there must be an intention to commit not just an assault but an assault which right-minded persons would think was indecent, and evidence to establish that intention may include an admission by the defendant of a sexual motive.[1] Clearly the degree of assault and indecency can vary enormously, and this has recently been recognised by increasing the maximum penalty to ten years to meet the worst cases.[2]

1 See *R v Court* [1988] 2 All ER 221, [1988] 2 WLR 1071, HL (Lord Goff dissenting).
2 SOA 1985, s 3(3), amending SOA 1956, Sch 2, para 17. The substantial increase from two years or, where the victim was a girl under 13, from five years, to ten years gives effect to a recommendation of CLRC, Cmnd 9213, para 4.8.

(e) Special protection

(i) Unlawful sexual intercourse with girls under 16

10.22 Legislation dealing with the corruption of girls has a long history. It began[1] with the Statute of Westminster I, 1275, which made it an offence, punishable by two years' imprisonment and fine and at the King's pleasure, to ravish 'any maiden without age', whether she gave her consent or not. The Statute of Wesminster II, 1285, made it a felony punishable by death. The history of these two enactments is not wholly clear. It seems that initially the term 'within age' was understood to mean 'under 12 years', that being then the age of discretion,[2] but gradually it became established that if the girl was between 10 and 12 it was not the felony of rape if she consented. However, it seems that in the latter case the earlier Statute was invoked and the case was treated as a misdemeanour to which the lesser penalty attached.[3] If this be so, the effect of an Act of 1575,[4] which made carnal knowledge of a girl under ten a felony without benefit of clergy, whether she consented or not, was merely to restate the law with regard to girls under that age without affecting those between ten and 12. This early legislation was repealed by an Act of 1828[5] which clarified the law by distinguishing between the felony of carnal knowledge of a girl under ten and the misdemeanour of carnal knowledge of a girl over ten but under 12. Subsequent legislation,[6] though eventually raising the ages to under 13 and over 13 but under 16 respectively, has preserved the distinction, which is now to be found in sections 5 and 6 of the Sexual Offences Act 1956. These provisions were, however, amended by the Criminal Law Act 1967, not only by its abolition of the division of indictable offences into felonies and misdemeanours, but also by amending section 6 so that the lesser offence applies to any girl under 16, instead of, as formerly, to a girl over 13 but under 16.[7] This latter change is a minor one, for a man who has unlawful sexual intercourse with a girl under 13 will in practice still be charged with the more serious offence under section 5, but the amendment enables an alternative verdict to be given[8] on the lesser offence under section 6, for example, where from the evidence there is doubt as to whether the girl is under 13.[9]

1 Anglo-Saxon law does not seem to have dealt separately with defilement of girls. One of Alfred's Laws (Cap 11) was concerned with sexual offences against 'young women', but these were not defined, and, although another (Cap 29) referred to a rape of a girl 'not of age' (also not defined), the compensation payable was no greater than if she was of age.
2 See 1 Hale PC 261.
3 4 Bl Comm 212. See also Russell, *Crime* 12th edn p 715 note 63.
4 18 Eliz I, c 7.
5 9 Geo 4, c 31.
6 See successively the Offences against the Person Act 1861; Offences against the Person Act 1875; Criminal Law Amendment Act 1885; Sexual Offences Act 1956. The legislation was aimed against parents who sold their children to brothel keepers; see WPHL, para 2.14 referring to Stafford, *The Age of Consent* (1964).
7 Criminal Law Act 1967, s 10(1) and Sch II, para 14.
8 In accordance with the Criminal Law Act 1967, s 6(3).

9   The maximum penalty for an offence under s 5 is imprisonment for life (SOA 1956, Second Sch) and for an attempt seven years (Indecency with Children Act 1960, s 2(1), as amended by SOA 1985, s 5(2)), and for an offence under s 6 is two years' imprisonment (SOA 1956, Second Sch).

10.23   The policy of protection which underlies much of the Sexual Offences Act 1956 and its predecessors accounts for the rule that the girl's consent is not material to either of the offences under sections 5 and 6.[1] Nor can it render the girl herself liable for aiding and abetting, or inciting to commit either offence,[2] the underlying reason for the decision being that the legislation is aimed not only at protecting her from the man who seeks to take advantage of her but also at protecting her against herself. Notwithstanding criticism of the rule, the Criminal Law Revision Committee and the Policy Advisory Committee have come down in favour of its retention.[3] The same reason of protection explains the undoubted acceptance of the view that the defendant's belief that the girl was not under age (ie not under 13 or not under 16, as the case may be) is no defence. This conclusion is inevitable in view of the fact that such a defence has been firmly rejected in relation to the offences of abduction of a girl under 16[4] and indecent assault of a girl under that age.[5] The Act admits an exception if the offence is under section 6 and the defendant is under 24, has not previously been charged with a like offence[6] and with reasonable cause believes the girl is over 16.[7] This arbitrary defence, passed as a political compromise during the enactment of the Criminal Law Amendment Act 1922, produces the 'grotesque state of affairs'[8] that the man's belief is a defence to a charge of unlawful sexual intercourse, and of rape[9] but not to the lesser charge of indecent assault. The Criminal Law Revision Committee has recommended its abolition and the substitution of a general defence to an offence under section 6, namely, that the accused, whatever his age, genuinely believed that the girl was aged 16 or over. Similarly there should be a defence to an offence under section 5 that he genuinely believed that the girl was aged 16 or over.[10] The Committee further recommended that, unlike the present law which imposes on the defence the burden of proving on a balance or rather preponderance of probabilities any expressed exception,[11] the burden on it should be evidential only, leaving the general burden on the prosecution in the usual way.[12] Given that in cases of this kind there must be corroboration or at least a warning of the risks of acting without it, this shift of the burden would substantially strengthen the hand of the defence and correspondingly weaken the protective purposes of the legislation, a risk to which the Committee did not advert.

1   See similarly s 14(2), ante, para 10.20.
2   *R v Tyrrell* [1894] 1 QB 710, [1891–4] All ER Rep 1215. See similarly the rule that a girl under 16 who permits incestuous intercourse does not aid or abet or incite incest, although since the Criminal Law Act 1977 it is an offence for a man to incite a girl under that age to have incestuous intercourse with him (s 54).
3   See Cmnd 9213, Appendix B.
4   *R v Prince* (1875) LR 2 CCR 154.
5   *R v Maughan* (1934) 24 Cr App Rep 130.
6   Ie an offence under s 6 or an attempt to commit one.
7   Reasonable cause is not enough: the defendant must in fact have believed; *R v Banks* [1916] 2 KB 621. Therefore it follows that the defendant who wishes to rely on this defence must have directed his mind to the question of age. If he was indifferent to it, the defence

is not available to him; *R v Harrison* [1938] 3 All ER 134, CCA. Indeed, s 6(3) of the Act expressly requires belief.
8 See *R v Laws* (1928) 21 Cr App Rep 45 at 46.
9 See *DPP v Morgan* [1976] AC 182, [1975] 2 All ER 347 and SO(A)A 1976, s 1(2), ante, para 10.16.
10 See Cmnd 9213, paras 5.11–5.14 and 5.17. Note the recommendation in relation to s 5 that the belief should be 16 or over not 13 or over, otherwise the man would have as a defence the belief that he was committing another offence, ie under s 6.
11 See SOA 1956, s 47.
12 Paragraph 5.18.

10.24 Where the defendant is married to the girl but the marriage is invalid under section 2 of the Marriage Act 1949 because of her non-age, it is still a defence to a charge under section 6 of the 1956 Act that he believed on reasonable grounds that she was his wife and accordingly had sexual intercourse with her.[1] Section 2 of the Marriage Act applies whether both parties, or only one of them, are domiciled in England, and in the latter case whether it is the party under 16 or the one over 16[2] who has the English domicile. Thus, for example, a man domiciled in England who has married abroad a 14-year-old girl whose ante-nuptial domiciliary law permits her to marry will be able to rely on the above defence if charged under section 6 of the 1956 Act. If both parties are domiciled abroad and their marriage is invalid because the 14-year-old is under age by her ante-nuptial personal law, and if the parties then come to this country, the defence provided in section 6 would not, it is submitted, be available, since the marriage would not be invalid under s 2 of the Marriage Act, but under the foreign law.[3] Nevertheless, it is suggested that, if in such a case the defendant did believe his marriage was valid, a defence by analogy to that in section 6 should be admitted. Where, on the other hand, the marriage is valid by the parties foreign personal law, there cannot be any liability under section 6, because the sexual intercourse, taking place within the bonds of marriage, would be lawful.[4] In *Alhaji Mohamed v Knott*[5] the Divisional Court expressed the view that this principle would also apply if the parties marriage were polygamous, providing that it is valid by the foreign law. Nor in this latter kind of case would it make any difference if the man acquired an English domicile while the wife was still under 16. Their union would still be a marriage and there would, it is submitted, be no reason to inquire whether the change of domicile has converted it into a monogamous relationship.[6] A question still to be settled is whether the validity of a foreign marriage of a girl under 13 could also be invoked as a defence to a charge under section 5 of the 1956 Act on the ground that any sexual intercourse would be lawful. The answer must depend on how far as a matter of public policy the English court would be prepared to go in recognising the incidents of such a marriage. Would it, for example, apply the factual test of whether the particular girl had attained puberty, or would it prescribe a minimum age below which it would refuse recognition.[7]

1 Section 6(2). Cf s 14(3), ante, para 10.20.
2 *Pugh v Pugh* [1951] P 482, [1951] 2 All ER 680.
3 It is, however, noteworthy that, although the long title to the Marriage Act refers to consolidation of 'certain enactments relating to the solemnization and registration of marriages in England', this did not prevent the court in *Pugh v Pugh*, (supra) from applying s 2 to a marriage celebrated abroad.

4   Cf *R v Chapman* [1958] 3 All ER 143, CCA post, para 10.30, note 1.
5   [1969] 1 QB 1, [1968] 2 All ER 563. For the main point of this case see post, para 14.00.
6   Cf *Ali v Ali* [1968] P 564, [1966] 1 All ER 664, where conversion was necessary to enable the English court to assume divorce jurisdiction. See now the Matrimonial Causes Act 1973, s 47.
7   Cf Dicey and Morris, *Conflict of Laws*, 11th edn, p 642; Karsten 32 MLR 212. The extent to which an English court will take account of foreign ways of life may also be relevant in cases of unlawful sexual intercourse with girls under 16 where the accused and the victim are not married, in that the foreign background may mitigate the gravity of the offence and affect sentence; see *R v Byfield* [1967] Crim LR 378, where the accused and the girl, aged 14, were both Jamaicans and the Court of Appeal reduced sentence because 'it was important to bear in mind that the girl came from a place where girls of her age reached maturity, and perhaps greater maturity than English girls of 17 or 18'.

10.25   The modern permissive attitude towards teenage sexuality has raised doubts about the extent to which sexual intercourse with a girl between 13 and 16 should remain an offence, particularly as the Crown Prosecution Service exercise considerable discretion in deciding whether to prosecute. As long ago as 1968 it was questioned by the then Chairman of the Law Commission[1] whether it was right that young men should be prosecuted for this offence. 'If a child is born to such a girl, it gives the three young people a pretty poor start in life if the police prosecute the father.' However, both the Policy Advisory Committee[2] and the Criminal Law Revision Committee[3] have supported the retention of 16 as the age of consent and 13 as that where the line should still be drawn for the more serious offence. In so recommending both Committees were fully aware of the wide discretion exercised both in prosecuting offences under section 6 and in sentencing.[4] Police cautioning is now very frequent, especially with defendants under 17, and the majority of defendants who are convicted are dealt with by non-custodial sentences. However, the older the defendant is and the younger the girl the more likely a custodial sentence, especially where the man is acting in a supervisory capacity to the girl and abuses his position of trust. On the other hand where sexual intercourse is the eventual outcome of a virtuous friendship between teenagers a punitive sentence would normally be inappropriate.[5] Where there is a custodial sentence it is likely to be for a period of 3 to 12 months where the victim is a 15-year-old and for 6 to 18 months where she is 13 or 14 years of age, but this is no more than general guidance. A man who abuses his trust can expect about the maximum penalty of two years for a section 6 offence.

1   Scarman J, as he then was, addressing the Golden Jubilee Conference of the (then) National Council for the Unmarried Mother and her Child.
2   Cmnd 8216, paras 11–21 and see generally Part I of the Report.
3   Cmnd 9213, paras 5.6 and 5.19–5.21.
4   See Walmsley and White.
5   See the guidelines provided for lower courts by the Court of Appeal in *R v Taylor* [1977] 3 All ER 527, [1977] 1 WLR 612, CA.

(ii)   Miscellaneous sexual offences involving girls
10.26   Closely connected with sections 5 and 6 are sections 25 and 26 of the 1956 Act,[1] which make it offences for the owner, occupier or anyone involved in the management or control of premises to induce or knowingly suffer a girl under 13 or under 16 to use the premises for the purpose of having unlawful sexual intercourse with men or with a particular man.[2] Either offence may be committed by, apart from anyone else, the girl's

parent,[3] except where the girl has already had intercourse with the man and the parent allows him to be brought to the home to have further sexual intercourse so that he may be trapped into committing an offence under section 5 or section 6.[4] It seems that, in accordance with the principle established in the well-known case of *R v Prince*[5] on abduction of girls under 16, a belief that the girl has attained the specified age is no defence.[6] Such a belief that the relevant age has been reached would apparently also not be available where there is a charge of procuring a girl under 21 to have unlawful sexual intercourse with a third person,[7] or a charge of causing or encouraging the prostitution of, or the commission of unlawful sexual intercourse with, or of an indecent assault on, a girl under 16.[8] This last offence[9] may be committed by anyone who is 'responsible' for the girl, ie any of the following:[10]

(a)   Her parent or legal guardian. For the purpose of this provision the term 'parent' includes the parent of an adopted child and, in the case of an illegitimate girl, her mother and the adjudged putative father; but it does not include a person deprived of the girl's custody by order of a court. 'Legal guardian' has its common meaning of one appointed by deed, will or court order to be guardian.

(b)   Any person who has actual possession or control of the girl, or to whose charge she has been committed by her parent or legal guardian or by a person having the custody of her; for example, a relative looking after the girl while her parents are abroad.

(c)   Any other person who has the custody, charge or care of her; for example, a custodian under a custodianship order. It has already been noted that even this wide category does not extend to the doctor of a clinic whom a girl consults for contraceptive advice or treatment.[11]

This classification is unnecessarily complicated and the purposes of section 28 could easily be met by imposing liability on anyone who has the custody/legal custody or care or control/actual custody of the girl.

1 Section 26 is amended by the Criminal Law Act 1967, s 10 and Sch II, para 14.
2 As with ss 5 and 6 the maximum penalties under ss 25 and 26 are respectively imprisonment for life and two years.
3 *R v Webster* (1885) 16 QBD 134.
4 *R v Merthyr Tydfil Justices* (1894) 10 TLR 375.
5 (1875) LR 2 CCR 154; see post, para 10.36.
6 Cf s 27 of the 1956 Act, which deals with the offence of permitting a woman who is a defective to use premises for unlawful sexual intercourse, where it is expressly provided that it is a defence to show that the accused did not know or have reason to suspect her to be a defective.
7 For this offence see s 23; (maximum penalty is two years' imprisonment). The age of 21 is anomalous now that 18 is the age of majority. Cf s 38, ante, para 10.19, which was expressly amended by the Family Law Reform Act 1969 so as to reduce the age to 18.
8 Section 28; (maximum penalty of two years' imprisonment).
9 Where a girl has become a prostitute or has had unlawful sexual intercourse or has been indecently assaulted, a person shall be deemed to have caused or encouraged it, if he knowingly allowed her to consort with, or enter or continue in the employment of, any prostitute or person of known immoral character (s 28(2)). For the purpose of s 28, a girl who appears to the court to have been under 16 at the time of the offence charged shall be presumed to have been so, unless the contrary is proved (sub-s (5)).
10 Section 28(3) and (4).
11 *Gillick v West Norfolk and Wisbech Area Health Authority* [1986] AC 112, [1985] 3 All ER 402, HL.

(iii) Abduction
10.27 Like the former offence of child-stealing,[1] abduction of girls has been primarily regarded as a wrongful interference with parental possession, but it also usually involves some harm to the girl, and that is likely to be in the form of having unlawful sexual intercourse with her. For this latter reason, if the girl is under 16, proceedings under section 6 of the Sexual Offences Act 1956 are far more likely than a prosecution for abduction and that will probably remain so even since the creation of the new offence of child abduction under section 2 of the Child Abduction Act 1984,[2] although it is to be noted that the maximum penalty is heavier for the latter offence, seven years instead of two.

1 See ante, para 3.91.
2 Ante, paras 3.92 et seq.

10.28 As with kidnapping,[1] the common law does not appear to have developed effective rules of criminal liability for dealing with the abduction of women and girls,[2] but this inadequacy was gradually met by legislation. Indeed, the provision in the Statute of Westminster I, noted earlier,[3] was wide enough to cover not only rape but also abduction by force,[4] although doubtless the two invariably went together. An Act of 1487[5] created the distinct offence of abduction of heiresses of property against their will and its policy was extended in 1557 by an Act[6] which made it an offence to take an unmarried child below 16 out of the possession and against the will of her father or mother or the person who at the time lawfully had the order, keeping, education or governance of the child.[7] This and subsequent legislation was repealed but re-enacted and extended during the nineteenth century[8] and then finally consolidated in the Sexual Offences Act 1956, which contains four[9] offences for abduction. Two of these concern girls of different maximum ages, but there is considerable overlapping.

1 See ante, para 3.89.
2 For an isolated reported instance see *R v Lord Grey* (1682) St Tr 127. But even on this case there is a dispute about whether it is an authority on abduction or criminal conspiracy; see Russell, *Crime*, 12th edn p 1479, note 86.
3 Paragraph 10.22.
4 'The King prohibiteth that none do ravish, nor take away by force, any maiden within age (neither by her own consent nor without) nor any wife or maiden of full age nor any other women against her will.'
5 3 Hen 7, c 2.
6 4 and 5 Phil and Mar, c 8.
7 For a comparison of this provision with the term 'guardian' in the present context see infra.
8 First by an Act of 1828 (9 Geo 4, c 31) and then by the Offences against the Person Act 1861 and the Criminal Law Amendment Act 1885.
9 Apart from those under s 19 and s 20, infra, there are abduction of a woman by force or for the sake of her property (s 17) and abduction of a woman who is a defective out of the possession of her parent or guardian (s 21).

(iv) Abduction of girls under 16 (section 20)
10.29 It is an offence for a person acting without lawful authority or excuse to take an unmarried girl under 16 out of the possession of her parent or guardian against his will. No sexual motive is required. A comparison between this provision and section 2 of the Child Abduction Act 1984[1] shows that section 20 can be repealed since its terms are impliedly

within those of section 2. Until that happens it must be compared to and related with section 19 of the 1956 Act.

1 See ante, paras 3.93–3.94.

(v) Abduction of girls under 18 (section 19)
10.30 This is the offence of taking an unmarried girl under 18 out of the possession of her parent or guardian against his will with the intention that she shall have unlawful sexual intercourse[1] with men or with a particular man.

1 Ie sexual intercourse outside the bonds of marriage; *R v Chapman* [1959] 1 QB 100, [1958] 3 All ER 143, CCA.

10.31 Certain rules apply to both sections, others to one or other of them.[1] Both require the girl to have been *taken* out of possession, but it makes no difference whether this was the result of force, fraud or mere persuasion with the girl's consent.[2] The defendant must, however, have taken some active step.[3] His acquiescence is not enough,[4] unless it is shown that he had previously induced the girl to leave,[5] in which case he is liable even if when it comes to her leaving he disapproves of it.[6]

1 Both carry a maximum penalty of two years' imprisonment.
2 *R v Manktelow* (1853) 6 Cox CC 143, CCCR.
3 *R v Robins* (1844) 1 Car & Kir 456 (bringing ladder to a girl's window).
4 *R v Jarvis* (1903) 20 Cox CC 249; *R v Colville-Hyde* [1956] Crim LR 117.
5 *R v Manktelow*, supra.
6 *R v Olifier* (1866) 10 Cox CC 402.

10.32 The taking must be out of the *possession*[1] of the parent or guardian. The test of possession here seems to be whether the parent or guardian still has the care and control of the girl.[2] A clear case where he has not is where she is living away from home, even if from time to time she spends periods at the parent's home.[3] So, too, she ceases to be in his possession once she leaves home intending permanently or at least indefinitely not to return; but not if her absence is temporary for some specific purpose.[4] It would be absurd if a father were to be held to lose possession of his daughter every time she went out of the house, with the result that if she were later picked up in the street that could never constitute abduction. There is no need, however, for the taking to be permanent. In *R v Timmins*[5] a man who, without the father's consent, took the girl away for three days, during that period slept with her at night and then told her to go back home, was guilty. The question is whether the act of taking is 'quite inconsistent with the existence of the relation of father and daughter',[6] as it was in *R v Baillie*[7] where, though absent for only a couple of hours from her home, the girl was during that time induced by the defendant to marry him. But there must be a substantial interference with parental possession.[8]

1 Compare the preferable term 'lawful control' in s 2 of the Child Abduction Act 1984, ante, para 3.94.
2 Cf Jervis CJ in *R v Manktelow* (1853) 6 Cox CC 143 at 147: does the girl continue to be 'under the care, charge and control of the parent'?

3   *R v Miller* (1876) 13 Cox CC 179; *R v Henkers* (1886) 16 Cox CC 257.
4   *R v Mycock* (1871) 12 Cox CC 28.
5   (1860) 8 Cox CC 401.
6   Ibid at 404.
7   (1859) 8 Cox CC 238.
8   *R v Jones* [1973] Crim LR 621 (attempt to take ten-year-old girl for walk with intention of indecently assaulting her held not to be sufficient interference).

10.33   The taking must be against the will of the parent or guardian, but positive proof of dissent is not needed. It is sufficient to show that, had he been asked, he would have refused his consent.[1] On the other hand, his past failure to take reasonable care of his daughter, for example, by allowing her to lead a lax way of life may be evidence of his consent.[2]

1   Per Wightman J in *R v Handley* (1859) F & F 648 at 649.
2   *R v Frazer* (1861) 8 Cox CC 446; *R v Primelt* (1858) 1 F & F 50.

10.34   The particular offence is committed if either a parent or guardian is deprived of possession. The latter is defined as the person having the 'lawful care or charge of the girl'.[1] It thus is not limited to a legal guardian, stricto sensu, ie a person so appointed by deed, will or order of the court. It includes anyone in whom the parental powers and responsibilities have been vested by operation of law or to whom care or charge has been entrusted by the parent himself.[2] It is submitted that the term is to be construed as widely as that of 'unlawful control' in relation to the offence of child abduction.[3] There may, however, be a distinction to be drawn in respect of the unmarried father of a child. In *R v Cornforth*[4] it was held under the old Act of 1557[5] that an illegitimate girl may be wrongly taken out of the possession of her putative father, a remarkably mature decision for the time. But does the principle of *Cornforth* apply to sections 19 and 20? Since the term parent is not defined by those sections, the common law meaning applies and the putative father is excluded.[6] When, then, is he to be regarded as 'guardian'? Certainly where he has been granted legal custody by an order of a court,[7] or where the mother has entrusted the child to him and, it is submitted, where he assumes possession on her death or where she has abandoned the child. In all those circumstances, if a third person were to remove the child from the father, that person could be liable under section 19 or section 20. It is, however, submitted that, even if the father had removed his daughter from the mother against the mother's wishes, he, nevertheless has, in accordance with *Cornforth*, 'lawful care or charge' so far as concerns the liability of a third person who takes the child away. That, however, does not exculpate the father from liability vis-à-vis the girl's mother where he is charged with an offence under section 20.[8]

1   Compare the wording of the former offence of child-stealing in s 56 of the Offences against the Person Act 1861, ante para 3.91, which referred to the 'parent, guardian or other person having lawful care or charge of the child'.
2   Compare the wide meaning given by s 107 (1) of CYPA 1933 to a guardian so as to include anyone who 'has for the time being the charge of or control over the child or young person'.
3   CAA 1984, s 2, ante, para 3.94.
4   (1742) 11 East 10 n.
5   Ante, para 10.28.

6 The 1557 Act referred to the 'father or mother' and not to the 'parent', but *Cornforth* was decided on the basis not that the putative father was a father but that he had lawfully the order, keeping, education or governance of the child.

7 Under GMA 1971, s 9, or an order under FLRA 1987, s 4, giving him all the parental rights and duties, when s 4 comes into effect.

8 *R v Tegerdine* (1982) 75 Cr App Rep 298, [1983] Crim LR 163, CA. Compare the special defence available under the Child Abduction Act 1984, ante, para 3.96.

10.35 Section 20, unlike section 19, does not need a specific wrongful intent, but it does require the defendant to have acted without lawful authority or excuse. A welfare officer acting in pursuance of an order of the court would be a case of lawful authority. An honest but mistaken belief, for example, on the part of a relative that he has a right to the custody of the girl would be a lawful excuse.[1] But intervention based on religious or philanthropic motives is not excusable.[2] So, a belief by a putative father that the child is not being properly looked after is not a valid defence.[3]

1 *R v Tinkler* (1859) 1 F & F 513.
2 *R v Booth* (1872) 12 Cox CC 231.
3 *R v Tegerdine* (1982) 75 Cr App Rep 298, [1983] Crim LR 163, CA.

10.36 Under section 19 the defendant may prove that he reasonably believed that the girl was over 18,[1] but a belief that the girl is of the specified age is never a defence under section 20.[2] This strict view has not, however, been adopted where the defendant mistakenly believes that the girl is not in the possession of her parent or guardian. On the contrary, in the case of both sections the onus is on the prosecution to prove that the accused knew or had reason to know or believed that the parent or guardian had possession.[3]

1 Sub-s (2).
2 *R v Prince* (1875) LR 2 CCR 154. The Criminal Law Revision Committee, Cmnd 9123, para 13.9, recommended that belief should be a defence.
3 *R v Green* (1862) 3 F & F 274; *R v Hibbert* (1869) LR 1 CCR 184.

10.37 It has already been suggested[1] that, since section 2 of the Child Abduction Act 1984 effectively covers the circumstances for which section 20 of the 1956 Act was designed, the latter could be repealed. It would also seem that in any future reform of the law relating to sexual offences section 19, which additionally[2] gives protection for 16 and 17 year-olds, is not likely to survive in the light of the *Gillick* principle.[3] Meanwhile the number of prosecutions under that section is likely to remain very small.[4]

1 Ante, para 10.29.
2 Section 2 of the 1984 Act is wide enough to cover the case of a person who removes a girl under 16 with intention that she shall have sexual intercourse.
3 The Criminal Law Revision Committee, para 13.8, recommended a maximum age of 16.
4 Over the period 1974–1984 the number of abduction offences in all (s 19 not separately recorded) recorded by the police averaged between 90–95 and less than one third led to convictions or cautions; see Criminal Statistics, England Wales, 1984, Cmnd 9621, Tables 2.9 and 5.13.

(vi)   Power to search for and remove girls detained for immoral purposes.
10.38   Where there is reasonable cause to suspect that a woman is being detained at some place in order that she may have unlawful sexual intercourse and that she is being detained against her will or is under 16 or is a defective or is under 18 and is detained against the will of her parent or guardian, a warrant may be issued to search for her and remove her to a place of safety until she can be brought before a justice of the peace.[1] He may then order her to be handed over to her parent or guardian, who for this purpose is defined as the person having lawful care or charge of her.[2] In strict law this is possible so long as she is a minor, since prima facie the parent, at least, has the right of custody up to that age, but this is not likely to happen if the girl is 16 or over.[3] Alternatively she may be 'dealt with as circumstances may permit and require'.[4] The most likely outcome is that she will be brought before the juvenile court as being in need of care or control.

1   Sexual Offences Act 1956, s 43, as amended by the Police and Criminal Evidence Act 1984, s 119(2) and Sch 7, Part I. These powers are additional to those conferred by s 40 of the CYPA 1933. A 'place of safety' is not defined, but has, it is submitted, the same meaning as it has in the Act of 1933, s 107(1), (as amended by CYPA 1969, s 72(3) and Sch 5, para 12(2)), namely, a community home provided by a local authority or a controlled home, any police station or any hospital, surgery or any other suitable place, the occupier of which is willing temporarily to receive a child or young person.
2   Cf definition of 'guardian' in s 107(1) of 1933 Act.
3   *R v Lord Grey* (1682) 9 State Tr 127.
4   Sexual Offences Act 1956, s 43(2).

3   Protection of boys

10.39   There are no sexual offences concerned exclusively with boy victims, but those dealing with males generally afford special protection to boys by imposing heavier sanctions and by restricting their ability to consent to sexual acts. Thus, if the offence of gross indecency[1] is committed by a man of or over the age of 21 with a male under that age the maximum penalty is five years' imprisonment instead of the normal two.[2] Where an indecent assault is committed on a boy under 16 his consent to the act is no defence,[3] and the general exemption from criminal liability of homosexual acts between consenting males in private does not apply if one or both parties is under 21.[4]

1   Sexual Offences Act 1956, s 13.
2   Sexual Offences Act 1967, s 3(2). So, too, where a person of or over 21 years of age is a party to or procures or attempts to procure the commission of gross indecency by a male under that age with another man. These age limits are not affected by the Family Law Reform Act 1969. For heavier penalties where buggery is committed with a boy under 16 see infra under *Protection of Girls and Boys*.
3   Sexual Offences Act 1956, s 15 (2). A woman, as well as a man, may commit the offence; *R v Hare* [1934] 1 KB 354, CCA; cf *R v Mason* (1968) 53 Cr App Rep 12, infra.
4   Sexual Offences Act 1967, s 1(1). The exemption relates to the offences of buggery and gross indecency (s 1(7)).

10.40   A surprising statutory omission is that which fails to empower a court convicting a woman of incest, or attempted incest,[1] with a boy to divest her of all authority which she had over him.[2] So, if she is his guardian, that court will not be able to remove her from office and appoint someone else. Separate guardianship or wardship proceedings will have to be instituted. Of course, as with a girl who is the victim of incest, the boy could be brought before the court under care or control proceedings.

1 If the boy is under 14, semble the presumption that he is incapable of sexual intercourse will apply, but the woman may be convicted of the attempt. So it has been held in South Africa; see *The State v A* 1962 (4) SA 679.
2 For incest by a woman see s 11 of the Sexual Offences Act 1956, and for the divesting power where a man commits incest see s 38 and ante, para 10.19.

4 Protection of boys and girls[1]

10.41 The offence of indecent assault requires some act to be directed towards another person, whether or not it involves a battery. It has, therefore, been held that for a man to invite a child to touch his person is not enough to constitute the offence.[2] But where there is an act and it is against a boy or girl who is under 16 it makes no difference to the defendant's liability that the child willingly participated since, as already noted, his or her consent is no defence to a charge of indecent assault;[3] but the assault must be indecent.[4]

1 See Williams, *Textbook of Criminal Law*, 2nd edn, pp 234–236.
2 *Fairclough v Whipp* [1951] 2 All ER 834, DC; *R v Burrows* [1952] 1 All ER 58n. A woman cannot be guilty of indecent assault on a boy merely by allowing him to have sexual intercourse with her; *R v Mason* (1968) 53 Cr App Rep 12.
3 SOA 1956, s 14(2), ante 10.19, and s 15(2) supra; *R v McCormack* [1969] 2 QB 442, [1969] 3 All ER 371, CA. This decision must be regarded as overruling earlier cases which held that the act against the child had to be 'hostile', ie against his will; see *Burrows*, supra; *DPP v Rogers* [1953] 2 All ER 644, [1953] 1 WLR 1017, DC; *Williams v Gibbs* [1958] Crim LR 127, DC, and for a criticism thereof see Smith and Hogan, op cit, pp 448–449.
4 Cf *R v Sutton* [1977] 3 All ER 476, [1977] 1 WLR 1086, CA.

10.42 The gap in the law left by the case where there is only an invitation and not an act is largely filled by the Indecency with Children Act 1960,[1] because in such circumstances, if the child is under 14, the invitor, whether male or female, is guilty of the offence of gross indecency with the child under section 1 of the Act.[2] This offence is also committed by anyone who incites a child under that age to commit such an act with him or her or with some third person and even if the child does not respond to the incitement. It seems that the general principle established by *R v Prince*[3] applies, so that it is no defence that the accused reasonably and honestly believed that the child had attained the age of 14.[4] Where both parties to the act are male, proceedings may alternatively be taken, subject to the consent of the Director of Public Prosecutions,[5] for an offence of gross indecency under section 13 of the Sexual Offences Act 1956. Where there is no assault that section is particularly useful if the boy is between 14 and 16. The Criminal Law Revision Committee, indeed, recommended[6] that the protection of the 1960 Act should be extended to boys and girls under 16, but that the offence should carry a heavier penalty where the child is under 13,[7] namely five years' imprisonment as opposed to two years for an offence with a 14 or 15 year-old. Belief by the defendant that the child was aged 16 or over or that the defendant was validly married to the child should, it was recommended, both be allowed as defences. Neither section 1 of the 1960 Act nor section 13 of the 1956 Act, it should be added, defines gross indecency, but it has been held that actual physical contact is not necessary.[8]

1 Passed as a result of the First Report of the Criminal Law Revision Committee, Cmnd 835.
2 The defendant's initial inactivity may amount to an invitation if he allows the child to continue the conduct; *R v Speck* [1977] 2 All ER 859; and for criticism see Williams, op cit, p 233.
3 (1875) LR 2 CCR 154.
4 The maximum penalty for an offence under s 1 is, on conviction on indictment, two years' imprisonment and, on summary conviction, six months or a fine of £2,000 or both.
5 Sexual Offences Act 1967, s 8. Proceedings under s 1 of the 1960 Act do not now require such consent; see Criminal Justice Act 1972, s 48.
6 Cmnd 9213; see generally Part VII, *Indecency with the Young.*
7 The distinction would be consistent with that drawn for the purpose of offences of unlawful sexual intercourse with girls under 16.
8 *R v Hunt* [1950] 2 All ER 291.

10.43   The Sexual Offences Act 1967 also requires the consent of the Director of Public Prosecutions before a man can be prosecuted for buggery with another man if either of them is under 21, but consent is, it is suggested, not likely to be withheld if the patient is a boy under 16. No such restriction is imposed where the patient is a female. The Act also imposes the heavier maximum penalties of imprisonment for life and for 10 years where buggery and attempted buggery respectively are committed with a boy under 16 or with a female.[1]

1 Section 4. See CLRC Report, Cmnd 9213, paras 6.7–6.19 for recommended changes in the law relating to buggery.

10.44   One other offence relating to boys and girls alike is to be found in section 3 of the Children and Young Persons Act 1933, which forbids anyone having the custody, charge or care of a juvenile who is at least four years old but under 16 to allow him to reside in or to frequent a brothel.

1II   CHILDREN AND EVIDENCE

10.45   Cases involving children raise several issues for the law of evidence. Some are common to the civil and criminal jurisdictions: others are distinctive to each. It is convenient to deal with them in one section,[1] and this chapter seems as appropriate as any.

1 But see also Chapter 14, paras 14.80–14.85 for the application of certain rules to care proceedings.

1   Standard of proof

10.46   In civil proceedings (with which this book is predominantly concerned) it is misleading to state that the standard of proof is always 'proof on a balance of probabilities'. In many child-related proceedings, such as custody disputes, it will be so, but the courts have come to recognise that the degree of probability can fluctuate according to the gravity of the issue before a civil court,[1] and where, for example, allegations of misconduct are levelled against parents or guardians a high degree of probability may be required. This is comforting from the adult's point of view but less so from the child's. The dilemma was neatly illustrated in *Re G*.[2] There wardship proceedings supplanted a place of safety order following allegations of sexual abuse levelled against a father. There was insufficient evidence to satisfy the criminal standard of proof beyond a reasonable doubt. As to the civil standard, that had to be higher than a mere balance of probabilities before the court could properly conclude that a father had sexually abused his child,[3] and it had to be a higher degree of probability than was required to justify the conclusion that the child had been a victim of sexual misbehaviour. With the child's welfare as the paramount consideration in wardship proceedings, any tilt in the balance suggesting that a child had been the victim of sexual abuse was sufficient to justify a finding to that effect, and there might be circumstances where the suspicion of sexual abuse or other wrongdoing, although incapable of formal proof, was such as to lead to the conclusion that to leave the child in his present environment would be an unacceptable risk. Contrast the position in care proceedings where paramountcy of the child's welfare does not apply in deciding whether the conditions in section 1 of the Children and Young Persons Act 1969 are satisfied.[4] It is surely arguable that the specific grounds of misconduct etc have to be proved to a very high degree of probability. If this is accepted, local authorities can face severe difficulties in trying to convince magistrates not simply that on balance a child was sexually abused[5] but further that he almost certainly was.[6] It will be interesting to see whether a consequence of the *Report of the Inquiry into Child Abuse in Cleveland 1987*[7] will be an insistence on that higher standard of proof.

1 See for example, *Khawaja v Secretary of State for the Home Department* [1984] AC 74, [1983] 1 All ER 765 (detection of illegal immigrants) and its effect in *Ali v Secretary of State for the Home Department* [1984] 1 All ER 1009, [1984] 1 WLR 663; *Winans v A-G* [1904] AC 287; *IRC v Bullock* [1976] 3 All ER 353, [1976] 1 WLR 1178 (loss of domicile of origin); *R v Milk Marketing Board, ex p Austin* (1983) Times, 21 March (loss of man's livelihood); *New South Wales Bar Association v Livesey* [1982] 2 NSWLR 231 (disciplinary proceedings against a barrister).
2 [1987] 1 WLR 1461, [1988] 1 FLR 314.
3 This standard was, on the facts, satisfied in *Re G*.
4 Aliter when deciding how to deal with the child if those conditions are satisfied; see post, para 14.106.
5 Eg by use of an anal dilatation test and evidence of some behavioural problems.
6 Cf *Department of Social Welfare v SN* (1985) 3 NZFLR 472, where the normal civil standard was applied to answer the question whether the child had been abused, but a higher standard was used in order to discover the culprit.
7 Cm 412.

2 A child giving evidence

(a) Competence

10.47 Under the general rules of evidence, a child's testimony is admissible if he is a competent witness. In determining whether he has the ability to give sworn evidence, it is not necessary to show that he has an appreciation of theology.[1] Instead he must be asked by the court[2] (1) whether he has sufficient appreciation of the solemnity of the occasion and (2) whether he understands that taking the oath means more than the duty to tell the truth which arises in day-to-day life.[3] There is no fixed age for determining this competency,[4] but five years is clearly too young.[5] The watershed may lie between eight and ten,[6] although the Court of Appeal in *R v Khan*[7] more recently has suggested that in criminal proceedings a court should be put on alert with any child under the age of 14. For those unable to appreciate the gravity of an oath, section 38(1) of the CYPA 1933 permits children of tender years to give unsworn evidence in criminal proceedings provided that they have 'sufficient intelligence to justify the reception of the evidence' and understand the duty of speaking the truth. The difference between the tests for sworn and unsworn evidence is narrow and their application may be unrealistic.[8] Hitherto their legal consequences have been crucial because a child giving unsworn evidence has had to be corroborated.[9] So, for example, three children giving unsworn evidence of sexual abuse could not corroborate each other (though an unsworn child could corroborate a sworn child[10].) Indeed, it is the recent public outcry over cases of sexual abuse of children that has led to changes incorporated in the Criminal Justice Act 1988.[11] This enables children of tender years[12] to give unsworn evidence in criminal proceedings without it having to be corroborated.[13] This amendment is likely to lead to further blurring of the difference between the above tests for sworn and unsworn evidence.

1 For the earlier practice, see *R v Brasier* (1779) 1 Leach 199.
2 If necessary, the court should call upon expert witnesses, such as child psychiatrists, to assist in assessing the child.
3 See *R v Hayes* [1977] 2 All ER 288, [1977] 1 WLR 234, CA; and *R v Campbell* [1983] Crim LR 174, CA.
4 Cf Criminal Law Revision Committee's Eleventh Report On Evidence (1972) paras 204–8 which recommended that children over 14 give sworn evidence and those under 14 unsworn; a simple but arbitrary conclusion.
5 *R v Wallwork* (1958) 42 Cr App Rep 153.
6 Suggested in *Hayes*, supra.
7 (1981) 73 Cr App Rep 190, [1981] Crim LR 330.
8 See the criticisms of CLRC, supra.
9 See the proviso to s 38(1).
10 *DPP v Hester* [1973] AC 296, [1972] 3 All ER 1056, HL.
11 Section 34(1), repealing the proviso to s 38(1) of the 1933 Act.
   For criticism and reform of the former law see, for example, Spencer, *Child Witnesses, Corroboration and Expert Evidence* 1984 Crim LR 239; Williams, *The Corroboration Question* (1987) 137 NLJ 131; Dennis, *Corroboration Requirements Reconsidered* [1987] Crim LR 316 at 325–336.
12 Possibly as young as five. For a striking example (a Colorado case) of the reliability of a very young child as a witness, see Jones, *The Evidence of a Three-Year-Old Child* [1987] Crim LR 677; and for a review of the research findings on the reliability of children as witnesses, see Hedderman, *Children's Evidence: The Need for Corroboration* (1987) (Home Office). See also Spencer, *Reforming the Competency Requirement* (1988) 138 NLJ 147–148.
13 Unsworn evidence of a child may corroborate evidence, sworn or unsworn given by any other person; CJA 1988, s 34(3).

10.48   In civil proceedings the same requirements for the giving of sworn evidence apply. There is no statutory equivalent for unsworn evidence but, when a child is sufficiently mature for his views to be given consideration, the court may hear them and, following the *Gillick* decision,[1] may be more prepared to do so. His evidence may be relevant in a wide range of matters, such as his views on his own custody, access by a non-custodial parent, and a proposed adoption or custodianship order. The court may need to consider three matters; first, whether the rest of the evidence in the case is inconclusive, so that the child's views might make a contribution to the decision-making; second, whether the child is mature enough to express a coherent opinion; and, third, if the child is heard, what weight should be given to the evidence, bearing in mind the danger that he may have been 'coached' in its preparation?

1   See ante, para 1.13.

(b)   Corroboration warning

10.49   Under the former law, in criminal proceedings if a child was deemed mature enough to give sworn evidence the jury had to be warned of the danger of convicting the accused without evidence corroborating the child; and, as just noted, if the child gave unsworn evidence, then corroboration had to be produced. Those rigid rules often proved a fatal stumbling block to a prosecution. They were compounded by the rule that a corroboration warning had to be given for the evidence of the victim of a sexual offence. Thus, it could happen that two warnings had to be given for one witness— in his capacity as a child and as a sex offence victim. Section 34(2) of the Criminal Justice Act 1988 has removed the need for the first of those warnings but not for the second. It could be argued that the latter should be extended to civil proceedings involving a child who is a sex offence victim,[1] for example, in applications under section 1 of the CYPA 1969. The point has not been decided, but it is doubtful whether any lay bench is ever called upon to consider the matter, and it is suggested that such rules or even emasculated versions of them are out of place in proceedings where the interests and future of the child should predominate over the guilt of a third person. Instead, the court should simply weigh the child's testimony as part of the totality of the evidence. Certainly, this is the approach adopted by the High Court in wardship proceedings. The difficulty with this reasoning is that in care proceedings where obligations of misconduct are levelled by or on behalf of the child against the parents, in effect they are put 'on trial' and their legal adviser may well consider it his duty to call for strong supporting evidence (corroboration by any other name) before those allegations can justify a care order. Insistence on such evidence may well be an outcome of the Cleveland Report of Inquiry.[2]

1   See a similar approach formerly adopted in relation to proof of matrimonial offences; *Alli v Alli* [1965] 3 All ER 480; and see Hayes and Bevan, *Child-care Law* 2nd edn, pp 11–12.
2   Cf ante, para 10.46.

(c)   Presentation of the child's evidence

10.50   With regard to the giving of the child's testimony, civil proceedings are heard in camera, the participants are fewer than at a criminal trial and the atmosphere is usually less tense. Moreover, the judge may choose to speak to the child in chambers,[1] though, as already noted,[2] he should never make any promises to the child about the outcome of the case. In criminal proceedings the ordeal for the child is likely to be far more disturbing. The frequently more exalted surroundings of a Crown Court

— a jury, robes, police officers and the presence of the accused — are likely to be intimidating. Simple steps of reducing formality can be taken; for example, showing the courtroom to the child in advance of the hearing, the removal of wigs and robes and the non-wearing of uniforms, the judge sitting beside the child in the well of the court when testimony is given,[3] and the provision of a screen to separate the child from the accused. There are also statutory provisions designed to minimise tension and embarrassment when a child or young person has to give evidence in adult courts.

1 For the power of the magistrates in care proceedings to hear the juvenile while his parents are removed from the court see post, para 14.88.
2 See ante, para 3.11.
3 Mr Justice McNeill proposed these steps in Cardiff Crown Court ((1986) Times, 25 November).

10.51   If the proceedings relate to an offence against, or conduct contrary to, decency or morality, which seems here to mean sexual decency or morality, the court is empowered, though not compelled, to hear his or her evidence in camera, with only those directly concerned in the case and newspaper representatives being present.[1] It is advisable that the court be cleared before the juvenile enters. This protection extends to anyone who, in the court's opinion, is a child or young person. It is suggested that this procedure should be made compulsory and not left to the court's discretion. The interests of the juvenile will always be best served by it, without those of the parties to the case being prejudiced.

1 CYPA 1933, s 37(1).

10.52   The following rules[1] apply to committal proceedings relating to: (1) an offence involving an assault, or injury or a threat of injury[2] to a person; (2) an offence under section 1 of the Children and Young Persons Act 1933 (cruelty to persons under 16); (3) an offence under the Sexual Offences Act 1956, the Indecency with Children Act 1960, the Sexual Offences Act 1967, section 54 of the Criminal Law Act 1977 or the Protection of Children Act 1978; and (4) an offence which consists of attempting or conspiring to commit or of aiding, abetting, counselling, procuring or inciting the commission of, an offence falling within categories (1), (2) or (3). A child[3] who is to be called as a witness for the prosecution must not normally be called to give oral evidence at the committal proceedings. Instead, at that stage a written statement by him is admitted,[4] in so far as it complies with the rules of admissibility of evidence. This leaves him to give oral evidence at the trial itself,[5] and saves him a double appearance in court.[6] The procedure is not, however, permitted if the defence objects to it, or the prosecution requires the child's attendance in order to identify a person, or the court is satisfied that it has not been possible to obtain a statement from the child, or the inquiry into the offence takes place after the court has discontinued to try it summarily and the child has given evidence in the summary trial.

1 Magistrates' Courts Act 1980, s 103, as substituted by CJA 1988, s 33.
2 Semble, thus means a threat made otherwise than in the victim's presence, eg, a threat over the telephone.
3 Ie a person under 14, as opposed to a young person.
4 The officer who took the statement should be called to produce it and prove that it was made by or taken from the child; see HO Circular No 17/1964.
5 See Magistrates' Courts Act 1980, s 103.
6 But the child must give oral evidence on at least one occasion. Hence the provision in s 103(4) that s 28 of the Act shall not apply to any statement admitted under s 103. Section 28 provides that, in a case where an inquiry into an offence is followed by summary trial, evidence given for the purpose of the inquiry is treated as having been given for the purposes of the trial.

10.53 Other provisions, in the CYPA 1933, relieve a juvenile of the duty of giving oral evidence where he has been the victim of any of the offences listed in Schedule I to that Act. In such a case the court may wholly dispense with the child's attendance if satisfied that it is not essential to the just hearing of the case,[1] but its discretion should be exercised cautiously, since it is more likely than not that the juvenile's evidence will be essential for a just hearing, especially as otherwise the accused is deprived of the opportunity of cross-examination. Special powers also exist concerning the use of depositions where his attendance 'would involve serious danger to his life or health'. Section 42 of the Act empowers a justice, who is satisfied on medical evidence that there would be such a danger, to take a deposition of the juvenile, which, under section 43, is then admissible in evidence without further proof if the court of trial is similarly satisfied of the danger. However, the deposition is not admissible *against* the accused unless he had reasonable notice of the intention to take the deposition and he or his legal representative had an opportunity to cross-examine the juvenile.

1 CYPA 1933, s 41. See *R v Hale* [1905] 1 KB 126, CCR.

10.54 There is room for further protecting the juvenile who has to give evidence. The Home Office has recommended,[1] at least in a sexual case, that the hearing should be on a fixed date, as early as possible in the day's list, with the juvenile giving his evidence early in the proceedings and then being released from attendance. But these admirable arrangements ought not to be left to the discretion and goodwill of those who arrange the court's business: they should be the subject of a statutory duty in all cases. Another defect in the present rules is that they do not place on the prosecution a duty to draw the court's special attention to them. Again, sections 42 and 43 are too restrictive and ought, as the Ingleby Committee recommended,[2] to be amended so that the powers thereunder may be invoked where the juvenile's attendance 'would involve injury to his health'. Improvements of this kind can be made without disturbing the balance between the welfare of the juvenile witness and the right of the accused to receive a fair trial.[3] The problem of cross-examination is, however, a different matter and may give rise to a sharp conflict between the respective interests of the juvenile and the accused. To deny any cross-examination would clearly favour the one but prejudice the other. On the other hand to allow it to proceed too far may place an unbearable strain on the juvenile, particularly if he is a young child. The court should, therefore, be ready to impose limits.

1   HO Circular No 208/1964.
2   Cmnd 1191, para 261.
3   See, as illustrations of the protection given to the accused, his right to object to a written statement under s 103 of MCA 1980, supra, and the rule that depositions are not admissible against him under ss 42 and 43 of the 1933 Act, supra, if he has not had the chance to cross-examine.

10.55   Such problems over cross-examination and the limits of the protection given by statutory provisions and informal procedures have led to a growing demand for reform. At the heart of this reform lies the use of video cameras to record and transmit the child's testimony from outside the courtroom. Section 32 of the Criminal Justice Act 1988 is a tentative step down this path of reform. A witness under the age of 14 appearing in a trial on indictment[1] involving assault, injury, cruelty to a person under 16, or a sexual offence[2] may with leave of the court give his evidence through a live video link.[3] Detailed rules are to be drafted before implementation,[4] but some limitations are readily apparent and stem from Parliament's concern to preserve the rights of the accused.[5] The testimony is to be given 'live' rather than in prerecorded form, the child will be subject to cross-examination by the accused's counsel and not through an intermediary, and apparently the equipment and facilities will have to be such that all persons concerned in the case can see and hear the child and he them.[6]

1   Or on appeal to the criminal division of the Court of Appeal or the hearing of a reference under s 17 of the Criminal Appeal Act 1968; see CJA 1988, s 32(1).
2   The categories of offences covered are the same as those to which s 103 of MCA 1980 applies; see ante, para 10.52.
3   Fourteen court centres are to be established providing live video links.
4   See CJA 1988, s 32(4) and (5).
5   See the discussion of possible rules raised in the Home Office paper, *The Use of Video Technology at Trials of Alleged Child Abuse*; (May, 1987).
6   Arguably 'see' means the ability to detect subtle variations in the witness' appearance and hence the need for close-up pictures of him. Will the rules so allow?

10.56   A more ambitious proposal is to allow the court to view a videotape of the child telling his story to an interviewer specially trained for the task.[1] The tape would be prerecorded and could be made available to the defence in advance of the trial, giving the defence time to study it, raise objections to its admissibility and, if necessary, to ask that the child be called to repeat the story before the court. A clear advantage of this prerecording would be that the child would relate the incident whilst it is fresh in his mind.[2] A major obstacle lies in the method of interviewing. Research into and experience of this type of interviewing are in their infancy. One controversial technique is the use of anatomically correct dolls to assist the child in telling his story.[3] Videotapes of such interviews have been viewed by the High Court in wardship proceedings,[4] and this has highlighted, inter alia, the following difficulty. The interviewer is usually a health care or social work professional who is motivated towards treatment of the child and not the prosecution of a child abuser. Pursuit of that goal can lead to suggestive questioning and persistent pressure which, if practised against a suspected offender, would lead to exclusion of the conversation from the trial.[5] In contrast, in wardship proceedings the High Court is prepared to relax the rules of evidence (for example, in relation to hearsay) and to receive any relevant evidence which can help it to decide what is the best decision for the child. In this way videotapes can be readily admitted, but their forensic value can then be weighed against the totality of the circumstances. However, in other civil, and in criminal, proceedings, the successful reception of these tapes will necessitate relaxation in the laws of evidence as regards the competence of child witnesses, the rule of corroboration warning where the child is a sex offence victim and the rule against hearsay.[6] Needless to say, these are thorny issues and they are not going to be resolved by the Criminal Justice Act 1988. Thus, for the immediate future, the use of prerecorded videotapes is confined to wardship proceedings.[7]

1   For elaboration see Spencer, *Child Witnesses, Video-Technology and the Law of Evidence* [1987] Crim LR 76, and the series of articles by Williams (1987) 137 NLJ 108, 351 and 369, and Morton, ibid, 216.
2   Moreover, it may be that the child will only be persuaded to speak of the matter once, hence the value of having it on tape.
3   See further Vizard, Bentovin and Tranter, *Interviewing Sexually Abused Children* (1987) 11 Ad and Fostering 20; Vizard, *Interviewing Young, Sexually Abused Children* [1987] Fam Law 28; and for interviewing in the criminal context, see the Final Report of the Bexley experiments *Child Sexual Abuse* (1987) HMSO.
4   See the cases reported at [1987] 1 FLR 269 to 346. For a detailed analysis of these cases see Hayes, *Child Sexual Abuse and the Civil Courts* (1988) 7 Civil Justice Quarterly 9. See also Douglas and Willmore, *Diagnostic Interviews on Evidence in Cases of Child Sexual Abuse* [1987] Fam Law 151; Enright, *Refuting Allegations of Child Sexual Abuse* (1987) 137 NLJ 633, 672.
5   Because of 'oppression'; see s 76(2)(a) and (b) of the Police and Criminal Evidence Act 1984.
6   See Spencer, op cit [1987] Crim LR at pp 80–82.
7   But there may be wider use following the current inquiry by a Home Office appointed advisory group headed by Judge Pigot, QC. This inquiry, related to but one aspect of child evidence, compares unfavourably with the Discussion Paper produced by The Scottish Law Commission, which tackles the whole question of the evidence of children. See further thereon Spencer, *How Not to Reform the Law* (1988) 138 NLJ 497.

(d)   Hearsay

10.57   The rule against hearsay is riddled with exceptions[1] and, even when applicable, its observance in child law varies considerably. However, when applied it can cause considerable difficulty, especially in care proceedings. For the purpose of exposition the following distinctions need to be drawn, though it should be noted that there is a regrettable dearth of authorities.

1   For general and detailed consideration of hearsay, see textbooks on evidence, for example, Phipson on *Evidence* (13th edn) Chapters 16–24 and Cross on *Evidence* (6th edn) Chapters 15–19.

(i)   High court and wardship

10.58   In this jurisdiction the High Court adopts a healthy scepticism towards the rule against hearsay. Thus, the Court should not exclude hearsay but instead 'carefully assess the weight to be attached to such indirect evidence'.[1] Where the hearsay consists of allegations of serious misconduct by a person, particular caution is needed. That said, the more relaxed attitude of the High Court could encourage local authorities to seek care orders in wardship proceedings rather than under the child care legislation where, as will be seen, the rule against hearsay is more readily observed.

1   Per Anthony Lincoln J in *Re N* [1987] 1 FLR 65.

(ii)   Superior courts and civil proceedings
10.59   In many of these proceedings the court is governed by the
'paramountcy principle' in section 1 of the GMA 1971 and objections to
hearsay are regarded as inappropriate.[1] As in wardship, if the testimony
amounts to a serious allegation it should be carefully weighed. In other
civil proceedings such as under the DVMPA 1976 and the MCA 1973,
where 'paramountcy' does not govern, the rule against hearsay should apply.
Some relief is offered by the provisions of the Civil Evidence Act 1968,[2]
whereby certain kinds of hearsay are admissible subject to various procedural
requirements.[3] Moreover, the court may grant leave to admit the evidence
even if the procedures of the Act have not been followed;[4] the parties can
always agree to admit the hearsay; and the court may still frown upon
'technical objections' to hearsay. The evidence may also fall within one
of the exceptions (preserved by the Act[5]) to the rule — the most likely
being hearsay evidence as to pedigree, the existence of a marriage and
admissions by a party. This last exception can be most useful, encompassing,
for example, a husband's admission that he has beaten his wife when the
latter is bringing ouster proceedings against him.

1   *Hurwitt v Hurwitt* (1979) 3 FLR 194, 10 Fam Law 183, CA; see also *Foote v Foote* [1986]
    6 WWR 474.
2   Usefully amended in 1972 so as to admit expert opinion evidence.
3   Section 8 and RSC Ord 38, rr 20–44.
4   Section 8(3)(a).
5   Section 9.

(iii)   Civil proceedings in a magistrates' court
10.60   Again, where section 1 of the GMA 1971 operates, the court should
not object to hearsay.[1] Elsewhere, the Civil Evidence Act 1968 does not
extend to magistrates' courts and so the admissibility of hearsay will depend
upon the availability of an exception to the rule, the forbearance of the
parties and the indulgence of the court.[2]

1   In proceedings under s 9 of GMA 1971 a magistrates' court is specifically instructed to
    take account of any relevant statement included in a report by a social worker or probation
    officer, notwithstanding any rule of law to the contrary, and this includes a rule of evidence;
    see GA 1973, s 6(3A).
2   For the subtleties of identifying hearsay, which can tax the best of legal minds, see *Myers
    v DPP* [1965] AC 1001, [1964] 2 All ER 881, HL.

(iv)   Care proceedings in magistrates' courts[1]
10.61   It is here that problems of hearsay can be difficult.[2] For example,
the applicant may wish to introduce a child's statement made to a social
worker or health visitor, or the allegation of a neighbour; a doctor may
want to refer to information passed to him from his colleagues, or a guardian
ad litem to repeat stories which he has heard about the family; and, most
commonly, a social worker's file will contain information compiled by a
predecessor. Unfortunately the law here is unclear and practice varies. On
the one hand, counsel may not endear himself to a court by taking every
objection to hearsay, especially if the Bench encourages a 'non-adversary'[3]
atmosphere to its proceedings. On the other hand, it is clear that the rule

against hearsay does apply in juvenile courts[4] and the events in Cleveland and other areas in 1987 may provoke parents into adopting a more combative attitude and counsel into using every opportunity to exclude prejudicial testimony. The rule can be avoided in the following ways:

(1) *Admissions* Since the child is a party to care proceedings (he is the respondent), a statement by him contrary to his interest can amount to an admission which in turn is a well recognised exception to the rule against hearsay. For example, a complaint by a child to his mother to the effect that his father or stepfather has abused him would be admissible. The weight of such evidence would then be for the court to assess. The same rule now applies to a parent or guardian where he is a party to the proceedings.[5]

(2) *Agreement* The parties may simply agree to tender the hearsay or they may even be persuaded to do so by the court.

(3) *Evidence Act 1938* Under this Act[6] a document containing the statement of someone with personal knowledge of the events (eg a police officer's account of a child's behaviour) or of someone who was under a duty to record information supplied by another person who had the knowledge (eg a medical record compiled by hospital staff) may be admitted even if the maker of the statement is not called as a witness. It is also possible that an expression of opinion by an expert witness is included within the Act.[7] However, it cannot embrace a statement 'made by a person interested at a time when proceedings were pending or anticipated',[8] and this can clearly exclude the evidence of a social worker who was involved in the particular case.[9]

1   See further para 14.80.
2   See *R v Wood Green Crown Court, ex p P* (1983) 4 FLR 206.
3   Per Lord Widgery CC in *Humberside County Council v DPR* [1977] 3 All ER 964 at 967, [1977] 1 WLR 1251 at 1255.
4   See the striking case of *Re S* (1980) 1 FLR 301 (a mother's allegation against her husband could not be recounted by others who heard them, the mother having refused to repeat them in court).
5   For the circumstances in which a parent will be a party, see CYPA 1969, s 32A, as amended by CYP(A)A 1986, s 3, and post, Chapter 14.
6   It would be repealed if the CEA 1968 were to be extended to magistrates' court.
7   Opinion on the point was divided in *Dass v Masih* [1968] 2 All ER 226, [1968] 1 WLR 756, CA.
8   Section 1(3).
9   This was the preliminary view expressed in *R v Wood Green Crown Court, ex p P*, supra, at 216, and is surely correct. The phrase 'person interested' is to be interpreted in the light of the particular circumstances; *Bermans Ltd v Metropolitan Police District Receiver* [1961] 1 All ER 384, [1961] 1 WLR 634, CA.

(v)   Criminal proceedings

10.62   Here the common law rule against hearsay is more strictly observed and *Sparks v R*[1] is a striking illustration. There a white man accused of indecent assault of a three-year-old was not able to use the child's statement to her mother to the effect that her assailant was a coloured boy. In addition to the common law exceptions, Parliament has recently relaxed certain aspects of the rule against documentary hearsay,[2] but of more pertinence to the present context are sections 42 and 43 of the CYPA 1933, which have already been noted,[3] under which a magistrate may take a deposition from a child or young person whose attendance at court would otherwise pose a serious danger to his life or health.[4] However, the defence has a right to cross-examine the child when the deposition is taken.[5]

1 [1964] AC 964, [1964] 1 All ER 727, PC.
2 See Part VII, Police and Criminal Evidence Act 1984 and Part II, Criminal Justice Act 1988.
3 Ante, para 10.53.
4 For detailed comment see Spencer and Tucker, *The Evidence of Absent Children* (1987) 137 NLJ 816.
5 Section 43.

CHAPTER 11

Education and employment of children — education

I INTRODUCTION

11.01 In so far as it exists, the right of a parent to determine his child's education is no longer simply a constituent part of the right to custody: it is for several purposes recognised as distinct from it.[1] Nevertheless, in practice the two are often inextricably involved in the same dispute. Where education is in issue it is normally the child's religious upbringing which is involved, although the same principles apply to secular education. If there is a dispute over the latter, it will often be associated with a dispute over religion,[2] since a parent will want the child to attend a school where he will receive instruction in a particular faith. Occasionally, however, the issue may relate solely to secular matters,[3] and such instances are likely to increase, since Parliament has recently conceded to parents a greater influence over the kind of education which their children receive. Moreover, the question of a child's schooling can prove a significant factor in those cases where a parent is seeking to take the child out of the jurisdiction. In such cases his welfare may best be served by his continuing to be educated in England,[4] especially if removal to a foreign country would create immediate language problems for him.[5]

As part of their statutory jurisdiction to make custody orders, courts may make orders concerning education and for those purposes the power extends to religious and secular education.[6] On the other hand, other provisions under the Children and Young Persons Acts, the Child Care Act 1980, the Education Act 1944 and the Children Act 1975 relate only to religious upbringing. It is therefore convenient to deal with religious and secular education separately.

1　This is recognised by s 4 of the Custody of Children Act 1891, post, para 11.06.
2　For example, as in *J v C* [1970] AC 668, [1969] 1 All ER 788, HL.
3　See, for example, *R v S (an infant)* [1967] 1 All ER 202, [1967] 1 WLR 396; *B v B (parental rights : dispute)* (1978) 1 FLR 87, CA.
4　See, for example, *Re S; J v C; Bevan v Bevan* (1973) 4 Fam Law 126, CA.
5　For example, as in *Dyter (now Kandler) v Dyter* (1973) 4 Fam Law 52, CA.
6　Post, para 11.11.

II   RELIGIOUS EDUCATION

1   History of parental right

(a)   The legitimate child

11.02   At common law and equity the right of the father concerning the religious education of his legitimate child was even stronger than his right to custody. Only rarely, where there was grave misconduct on his part, did he forfeit his right, and it prevailed even in those cases where the child was living with the mother, so that the effect of bringing him up in the father's religion was likely to affect adversely her relationship with the child,[1] and even where the father was dead.[2] As ready indicated,[3] under the influence of statutory changes, which gave to the mother rights to claim custody of her legitimate child, greater attention began to be paid to the child's welfare in custody disputes and this change was becoming more pronounced by the close of the nineteenth century. It was not, however, accompanied by the same emphasis on the child's welfare vis-à-vis the father's right regarding religious education, although there were indications of some undermining of that right following the enactment of the Guardianship of Infants Act 1886.[4] If there is still a conflict of opinion on whether section 1 of the Guardianship of Infants Act 1925 further diminished the father's right of custody or merely declared the existing law in making the child's welfare paramount, it was recognised by the Court of Appeal in *Re Collins (infant)*[5] that the section materially affected his right concerning religious upbringing, and the paramountcy of his right has been firmly replaced by that of the child's welfare.

1   *Hawksworth v Hawksworth* (1871) 6 Ch App 539, where, per James LJ, the court was enjoined to have 'sacred regard to the religion of the father'.
2   *Andrews v Salt* (1873) 8 Ch App 622.
3   Ante, para 1.10.
4   See *Re McGrath (infants)* [1893] 1 Ch 143, CA; *Re Nevin (infant)* [1891] 2 Ch 299, CA, which should be compared with such cases as *Re Austin, Austin v Austin* (1865) 4 De G J & Sm 716; *Re Newberry* (1866) 1 Ch App 263. See also Viscount Cave in *Ward v Laverty* [1925] AC 101 at 108.
5   [1950] Ch 498, [1950] 1 All ER 1057.

(b)   The illegitimate child

11.03   The recognition of the legal right of the mother to custody of her illegitimate child was delayed until the last decade of the last century,[1] but, once accorded, recognition of her right to determine his religion soon followed,[2] and for some time after section 1 of the Guardianship of Infants Act 1925 had been enacted the right remained as strong as ever it had been. Indeed, in *Re Carroll*[3] the majority of the Court of Appeal held that the section did not affect the mother's right so as to make the child's welfare paramount, since it was confined to cases where the dispute was between the mother and father of a legitimate child. This narrow construction of the section having been rejected in *Re Collins*,[4] the way was open for the Court of Appeal in *Re A (an infant)*[5] (where the dispute was between the mother and the father) to hold that the section applied to the illegitimate child as to the legitimate and therefore that it was the child's welfare and not the mother's right which was the paramount consideration. The same reasoning prevailed in *Re E (an infant)*,[6] where the dispute was between the mother and a third person. Finally, in *J v C*[7] the House of Lords disapproved of *Re Carroll*.

1 Ante, para 2.40.
2 *R v New* (1904) 20 TLR 583, CA, where the mother's religion played a large part in awarding her custody, although the child had lived for ten years with a married couple as if they were her parents.
3 [1931] 1 KB 317, [1930] All ER Rep 192.
4 Supra, para 11.02, note 5.
5 [1955] 2 All ER 202, [1955] 1 WLR 465.
6 [1963] 3 All ER 874, [1964] 1 WLR 51.
7 [1970] AC 668, [1969] 1 All ER 788.

2   Principles on which the court acts when determining disputes over religion

11.04   Although the child's welfare is paramount, the court should still pay 'serious heed to the religious wishes of the parents';[1] but they do not generally carry much weight today, especially on the one hand where the child is so young that influences have not yet made their mark and on the other hand where, in accordance with the *Gillick* principle, he is old enought to have views of his own.[2] In taking into account parental wishes the court must remember that the Guardianship Act 1973 gives the parents equal and separate rights,[3] and, in accordance with section 1 of the Guardianship of Minors Act 1971, it must disregard, from every point of view other than the child's welfare, whether the father's claim in respect of religious upbringing is superior to the mother's or vice versa. This is a particularly important point to remember when the court is dealing with a religious culture in which the father is traditionally given pre-eminence. Moreover, the principle of the paramountcy of the child's welfare operates not only where there is a dispute between living parents over religion but equally where the issue of custody involves their respective religious views and one or both of them are dead.

1 Per Ungoed-Thomas J in *J v C* [1969] 1 All ER 788 at 801.
2 See infra.
3 Section 1(1).

11.05   In considering parental wishes a relevant factor is the parent's past conduct. For example, he may have agreed to his child being brought up in a particular religion. Such an agreement is unenforceable,[1] except where it is made between the mother and father during any period when they are not living with each other in the same household: even then it will not be enforced if that is not for the child's benefit.[2] Nevertheless, the fact that the parent entered into the agreement is evidence of lack of interest shown in the religious upbringing of the child.[3] The same conclusion may be drawn where, though there has not been an agreement, the parent over a period of time has acquiesced in the child's being brought up in a particular faith.[4]

1 CA 1975, s 85(2), as amended by FLRA 1987, Sch 4.
2 GA 1973; s 1(2), as prospectively substituted by FLRA 1987, s 3.
3 *Lyons v Blenkin* (1821) Jac 245; *Andrews v Salt* (1873) 8 Ch App 622 at 637.
4 *Hill v Hill* (1862) 31 LJ Ch 505.

11.06   It would seem, in the light of the *Gillick* principle,[1] that a person can acquire the right to choose his own religion while still a minor. Indeed, already before *Gillick* there was some statutory authority to support that conclusion. Section 4 of the Custody of Children Act 1891, though never invoked, is still on the statute book. This enables a court to give effect to the parent's 'legal right to require' that the child be brought up in the parent's religion where custody is granted to some other person; but the court's power is subject to the limitation that 'nothing in this Act . . . shall diminish the right which any child now possesses to the exercise of its own free choice'. Since the Act is apparently concerned only with children who are minors, it impliedly recognises a choice at some time (whatever that might be) below that age.[2] Section 4 seems not to have been invoked in modern law because the court has relied on the principle of the paramountcy of the child's welfare. Now, in accordance with the *Gillick* principle, the parent's wishes over religious upbringing yield to the child's right to make his own decision once he has reached sufficient intellect and understanding to be capable of doing so; but a point which *Gillick* does not cover is the extent, if any, to which the child's right to choose must yield to the paramountcy of his welfare, as the court sees it. Supposing, for example, in divorce proceedings that a 14-year-old of mature intellect and understanding for his age wants to live with his father because they share the same religious faith, whereas his mother does not, and assuming that there is nothing to choose between the material advantages and care that the parents can respectively provide. In those circumstances the court will be very likely, arguably obliged, to give care and control to the father. However, if the particular religion is intrinsically harmful to the child, then his wishes will not prevail and the court in his interests would grant care and control to the mother. In order to determine in any case the strength of a child's religious convictions the court may interview him. There is no minimum age but, unless the child is exceptionally mature, he is not likely to be interviewed if he is under 11 or 12 years of age and almost certainly not if he is under eight.[3] Another example of a court overruling the child's wishes would be where the wardship jurisdiction is invoked by a parent to rescue the child from a sect which has harmfully indoctrinated him.[4]

1   Ante, para 1.13.
2   *Re May, Eggar v May* [1917] 2 Ch 126 is irreconcilable with s 4. There it was held that the child could not determine what his religion could be 'until he has reached years of discretion', which the court fixed at 21.
3   The courts have not over the years changed their attitude. See Viscount Cave in *Ward v Laverty* [1925] AC 101 at 109; *Ingham v Ingham* [1976] LS Gaz R 486.
4   See infra, para 11.08.

11.07   In seeking to ensure the child's welfare it is very unlikely that the factor of religious upbringing will prevail over that which attaches so much importance to the need for young children normally to be with their mother, especially if she is a caring mother[1] and they are happy with her.[2] Consequently, the court will need a great deal of persuading that the children will suffer such spiritual and emotional harm if allowed to share a home with their mother and the man with whom she is living in adultery that they need to be removed and entrusted to their father, so that in their best interests he may actively bring them up in a particular faith.[3] However, the court may be willing to attach more importance to the effects which any change of religion would be likely to have on the child. Much will depend on his age and maturity. The mere fact that he was baptized into a particular faith is of little moment.[4] Far more significant are the facts that he has embarked on a course of religious education and the consequent strength of his existing convictions. Where they are firmly held, to disturb them could create a high risk of emotional harm,[5] and the court will almost certainly not make any order which is likely to cause him to abandon all religious belief, unless there are exceptional, overriding considerations of material welfare or, equally exceptionally, the tenets and practices of his faith are intrinsically harmful to him.

1 *Haleem v Haleem* (1975) 5 Fam Law 184, CA.
2 *Roughley v Roughley* (1973) 4 Fam Law 91, CA.
3 *Re K (minors) (Children : care and control)* [1977] Fam 179, [1977] 1 All ER 647, CA.
4 *Re C(MA) (an infant)* [1966] 1 All ER 838, [1966] 1 WLR 646.
5 *Re M (infants)* [1967] 3 All ER 1071, [1967] 1 WLR 1479, CA.

11.08 On this latter point, while the courts have consistently declined to discriminate between one faith and another[1] and *semble* no longer do so between one and none,[2] they may occasionally hold that a particular form of religious upbringing is intrinsically harmful to the child, for example, because it unduly isolates him both socially and educationally. This view has been taken of the rules of the sect of Exclusive Brethren,[3] but much stronger opposition has been shown to the cult of scientology, which has been judicially described as immoral, socially obnoxious, corrupt, sinister and dangerous, and its profession to be a religion has been denied.[4] However, generally where the courts have reservations about the practices of a sect they are much more inclined to seek from the parent, who is bringing the children up in the faith, undertakings which will prevent potentially harmful consequences from the practice of faith. This has been the approach to Jehovah's Witnesses, and in *Re T (minors) (custody : religious upbringing)*[5] the Court of Appeal has laid down the following principles:

(a) It is not for the court to pass any judgment on the beliefs of a parent where they are socially acceptable and consistent with a decent and respectable life.

(b) There is no reason why a parent should not espouse the beliefs and practices of the Jehovah's Witnesses, since there is nothing immoral or socially obnoxious in them.

(c) It is not necessarily wrong or contrary to the welfare of children that they should be brought up in a narrower sphere of life and subject to a stricter religious discipline than that enjoyed by most other people. Thus, indoctrination with the beliefs and tenets of the Jehovah's Witnesses is not of itself indicative that harm will come to a child so indoctrinated, provided that there is a level-headed parent in charge of the child.[6]

(d) The court can impose undertakings designed to protect the welfare of the child; eg by obtaining an assurance from the parent that he or she will allow the child to have blood transfusions, if these were necessary for his life and health,[7] or by requiring an undertaking which enables the child to enjoy with the parent, who is not a Jehovah's Witness, the benefits of such occasions as Christmas holidays and birthdays of which he would otherwise be deprived;[8] or by an undertaking that the custodial parent will not take the child on proselytising missions. However, the efficacy of such undertakings is another matter and can cause extreme frustration to the non-custodial parent.

1   See eg *Re Carroll* [1931] 1 KB 317, [1930] All ER Rep 192.
2   *Haleem v Haleem*, ante, para 11.07, note 1. They have certainly abandoned the positive antipathy shown towards atheism; *Shelley v Westbrooke* (1817) Jac 266n; *Re Besant* (1879) 11 Ch D 508, CA.
3   *Hewison v Hewison* (1977) 7 Fam Law 207, CA; *Re C (an infant)* (1964) Times, 1 August. See Bradney '*Religious Questions and Custody Disputes*' (1979) 9 Fam Law 139.
4   Per Latey J in *Re B and G (minors) (custody)* [1985] FLR 134, [1985] Fam Law 58; affd [1985] FLR 493, [1985] Fam Law 127, CA where it was held that the harmful effects of the cult necessitated transferring the care of the children from father to mother, even though they had lived with him for some five and one-half years in a stable relationship.
5   (1981) 2 FLR 239, CA. See also *Re H (a minor) (Custody : Religious Upbringing)* (1980) 2 FLR 253, 10 Fam Law 248, DC, and the judgment of Stamp LJ in *T v T* (1974) 4 Fam Law 190.
6   *T v T* (1974) 4 Fam Law 190.
7   This can be best achieved by the parent's signing a certificate consenting to such transfusions. If the parent is not prepared to give the appropriate assurance, the court may be able to protect the child by a split order giving that parent care and control but the other parent custody, so that the latter will be able to give the requisite consent to a transfusion; *Jane v Jane* (1983) 4 FLR 712, 13 Fam Law 209, CA. Of course, in an emergency the doctor can proceed, regardless of consent.
8   See also *Re C (minors) (wardship : jurisdiction)* [1978] Fam 105, [1978] 2 All ER 230, CA. Quaere, in the light of *Re T*, the courts will continue to take such a strict view of the rules of the sect of Exclusive Brethren. Although *Re T* was decided before *Hewison v Hewison* (n 3), it was not reported until some time later.

11.09   Difficulties sometimes arise where the person seeking custody or care and control has no faith or belongs to a religion different from that in which the child has been brought up. Considerations of material welfare may result in the court allowing the person custody or care and control but subject to his undertaking that he will bring up the child in the religion to which the latter is already committed. Such a solution may not, however, be in the child's long-term interests in that it may give rise to conflict within the family.[1] The court will have to weigh the risks carefully.[2]

1   The danger was emphasised by the Court of Appeal in *B (M) v B (R)* [1968] 3 All ER 170, [1968] 1 WLR 1182.
2   See *J v C* [1970] AC 668, [1969] 1 All ER 788, HL, where English foster parents who were Protestants were ordered to continue to bring up the son of Roman Catholic Spanish parents as a Roman Catholic; and *Re E (an infant)* [1963] 3 All ER 874, [1964] 1 WLR 51, where a Jewish couple were similarly required to bring up a ward of court as a Roman Catholic.

3   Jurisdiction to make orders relating to religious education

(a)   Wardship[1]

11.10   As part of its inherent jurisdiction, the Family Division may make orders relating to the religious and secular education of a ward of court. Where the minor is already a ward of court and later an order relating to his education is being sought, the High Court may, either of its own motion or on application by a party to the proceedings, order the transfer of the proceedings to a county court,[2] but must not do so unless a party has had an opportunity to be heard on the issue or has consented to the order.[3] The county court can order the transfer of the proceedings back to the High Court.[4]

1 This and the next two paragraphs also apply to secular education.
2 Matrimonial and Family Proceedings Act 1984, ss 32 and 38(2)(b).
3 RSC Ord 90, r 2B(1), as inserted by RSC (Amendment) 1986, r 27, SI 1986/632.
4 MFPA 1984, s 39(2)(b). See *Practice Direction* [1988] 2 All ER 103, [1988] 1 WLR 558.

(b) Matrimonial proceedings

11.11 In proceedings for nullity, divorce or judicial separation the High Court or a divorce county court has power to make orders for 'custody and education'.[1] Although this provision is apparently to be construed disjunctively, orders dealing only with education are rarely made. Occasionally the custody order may expressly include a provision relating to education, but usually it does not. However, as already noted, the party who is not given custody must, on the authority of *Dipper v Dipper*,[2] be consulted on the child's education, thereby enabling him to bring the matter before the court if he disagrees with the action proposed by the custodial parent. These rules equally apply where a custody order is made in proceedings for neglect to maintain, but, apparently through legislative oversight, there is no power thereunder to make an order dealing only with education.[3] Different rules apply to proceedings under the Domestic Proceedings and Magistrates' Courts Act 1978, where the power of the court to grant one party legal custody is in such terms that the court must expressly reserve to the other party a joint right in order that he may be involved in the child's education.[4]

One difficulty facing the non-custodial parent who retains a right over education is keeping in touch with the child's educational progress. Reports will be routinely sent to the child's residence as it appears on the school register. It is not clear as a result of *Dipper* whether the onus is on the custodial parent or the non-custodial parent to arrange with the school for copies of the reports to be sent to the latter. The non-custodial parent is advised to ensure arrangements.[5]

1 MCA 1973, s 42(1). For the transfer of proceedings from the one court to the other see MFPA 1984, ss 32, 38 and 39, ante, para 3.17.
2 [1981] Fam 31, [1980] 2 All ER 722, CA, ante para 3.53. See ibid for the scope of a custody order. See also paras 3.48 for the protective provisions of MCA 1973, s 41 relating to arrangements for the child's welfare which includes his education and training (ss 41(1)(b) and 52(1)).
3 MCA 1973, s 42(2).
4 Section 8(4); see ante, para 3.37.
5 Quaere, if the school knows of the terms of the custody order, it must take the initiative in keeping him informed.

(c) Guardianship of Minors Acts 1971 and 1973

11.12 Those rules in the 1978 Act similarly apply to proceedings under the Guardianship of Minors Act 1971, so that where legal custody is given to a person, whether a parent or guardian or anyone else, any parent not given it can be given a joint right in respect of education.[1] In the case of a dispute between the mother and the father over education there is also the right of either to apply under the Guardianship Act 1973 for the court's discretion on the matter.[2] A person against whom an order for maintenance is made under the 1971 Act can be required to contribute towards the expense of his child's education, since maintenance includes education.[3] Thus (1) if the mother is given legal custody, the father may be required to contribute; (2) if a person is appointed sole guardian to the exclusion of the parent, the parent may have to contribute; and (3) if there is a dispute between joint guardians, one of whom is a parent, the parent may equally be ordered to contribute.[4]

1   See ss 9(1)(a), 10(1)(a) and 11A(1), as prospectively amended by FLRA 1987, ss 10 and 11 and Sch 2, para 30.
2   Section 1(3) ante, para 1.67.
3   Section 20(2), as prospectively substituted by FLRA Sch 2, para 43.
4   Sections 11B and 11C, as prospectively inserted by FLRA 1987, ss 12 and 13 respectively.

(d)   Guardianship, adoption, custodianship and religious education

(i)   Guardianship

11.13   The inherent jurisdiction of the Family Division and the statutory jurisdiction of a court under the Guardianship of Minors Act 1971 have special relevance to religious education. A guardian is not entitled to choose the ward's religion,[1] but prima facie is obliged to bring him up in that in which the parents would have brought him up, unless the ward has acquired strong convictions of his own, in which case the guardian should see, *pace* the *Gillick* principle, that those convictions are protected. To impose his own choice of religion on the ward is a ground for removing him from office.[2] Moreover, although the guardian may be ready to see that the child continues his past education, a subsequent change of his own faith may also be a ground for removal.[3] If he is uncertain about the parental intentions concerning the education of their child or if the parents were in dispute over it or if he is doubtful about the strength of the child's convictions or considers the particular religious upbringing harmful, he should apply to have the child made a ward of court and seek the directions of the court,[4] which should act in accordance with the principles already considered.[5] These principles will also operate where there is a dispute between a guardian and a surviving parent[6] or between two guardians.[7]

1   For his duties with regard to secular education see post, para 11.20.
2   *Re Savini, Savini v Lousada* (1870) 22 LT 61, 18 WR 425.
3   *F v F* [1902] 1 Ch 688.
4   The need to apply is especially important where the child is approaching an age where the court may uphold a right to choose his own religion, in accordance with the *Gillick* principle.
5   Ante, paras 11.04 to 11.09.
6   In such a case the parent's wishes may carry great weight; see Eekelaar, *What are Parental Rights?* 89 LQR 210 at 234.
7   See GMA 1971, s 7.

(ii)   Adoption

11.14   Obligations in relation to adoption have already been mentioned.[1] In the process of placement of a child, the adoption agency must inquire into the wishes of the parent in respect of the child's religious upbringing and the adoption panel in making its recommendation to the agency must take acount of them, but the parent cannot impose conditions when agreeing to the adoption. The duty of the agency and its panel to consider also the wishes of the child has, if he is old enough to have views, added significance since *Gillick*. In deciding to make an adoption order, the court could give effect to a parent's wishes by including a condition regarding the child's religious upbringing, but this would be a most exceptional step to take.[2]

1 Ante, para 5.15.
2 Ante, para 5.94.

(iii) Custodianship

11.15 Assuming that the right of a parent to determine the religion of his child falls within the definition of legal custody, as a matter referring to the person of the child,[1] the custodians would have the right to change it. There is no power, corresponding to that in adoption, which enables the court to include a condition in a custodianship order, but the intentions of the prospective custodians would be relevant in determining whether the order was in the child's interest in accordance with section 1 of the Guardianship of Minors Act 1971. If an order were made and then a decision taken by the custodians to change the child's religion, that step could be challenged by the parent or the local authority through revocation proceedings or through wardship. A parent who, in the custodianship proceedings, has been granted access should be in a position to keep an eye on the custodians.

1 See ante, para 1.61.

4 Religious upbringing of children in care of persons other than parents, guardians or custodians

11.16 A feature of much of the legislation relating to children is the responsibility it imposes on persons looking after them to take account of their religious persuasion. Thus, a local authority who have received a child into their care under section 2 of the Child Care Act 1980 and are willing to allow a relative or friend to take over the care must try to see that the person is of the same religious persuasion as the child or undertakes to bring him up in that persuasion.[1] A similar obligation is imposed on an authority who intend to board out a child with foster parents.[2] These obligations must, it is submitted, be discharged subject to the qualification that, in accordance with the *Gillick* principle, the local authority should comply with the request of the child to be placed with a person of the *child's* religious persuasion, if that should differ from his parent's and if he is considered mature enough by the authority to decide that matter for himself. Moreover, when a child in care is placed in a community home or a voluntary home the local authority or other person responsible for carrying on the home must see that facilities for religious instruction appropriate to his persuasion are provided.[3] Where a local authority have assumed parental rights under a resolution passed in accordance with section 3 of the Child Care Act 1980 or as a result of a care order, they must not cause the child in their care to be brought up in any religious creed other than that in which he would have been brought up but for the resolution or the order.[4] Usually the religion will be that of his parents, but by the date of the resolution or order he may have acquired his own, especially where he has been living apart from his parents. Furthermore, if at a later date a child while still in care decides to adopt a particular religion the local authority must, it is submitted, comply with his wishes. If they consider the religion harmful, they should take out wardship proceedings and obtain the directions of the court.

1   Section 2(3).
2   Boarding-Out of Children Regulations 1955, reg 19.
3   Community Homes Regulations 1972, reg 8; Administration of Children's Homes Regulations 1951, reg 4.
4   CCA 1980, ss 4(3) and 10(3). In the context of the law of trusts the essential elements of 'religion' have been described as 'faith in a god and worship of that god', per Dillon J in *Barralet v A-G*, [1980] 3 All ER 918, [1980] 1 WLR 1565.

III   SECULAR EDUCATION[1]

1   The parental duties/responsibilities

(a)   Historical introduction

11.17   Given that the common law was not prepared to impose on a parent a direct duty to maintain his child,[2] it would have been surprising if it had imposed a duty to educate him.[3] Moreover, it would have been unrealistic to have done so as long as a comprehensive system of education did not exist. The consequence was that education depended upon the whim of parents who could afford to pay for it.[4] If they could, their children were sent to Charity Schools, most of which appeared, with varying standards of education, in the 18th and 19th centuries. As with so many other spheres of activity affecting children, the advancement of education owed much to individual philanthropists and reformers.[5] Yet, it was not until 1870 that a system of public education was introduced. The main cause of the delay was religious dissension. This, for example, was still apparent when the State began in 1833 to assist in the endowment of schools: Treasury grants were carefully divided between the rival National Society (representing the Church of England) and the British and Foreign Schools Society (a non-conformist organisation). Had they been able to agree on the religious tests to be imposed on teachers, legislation might have been enacted earlier than it was. Some impetus to the movement for reform was, however, given by the creation from 1857 onwards of Industrial Schools.[6]

One of the main objects of the Elementary Education Act 1870 was to make education more readily available by enabling schools to be established in districts where there was serious deficiency, but it was the Elementary Education Act 1876 that introduced a compulsory system throughout the country and imposed on the parent the duty to ensure that his child received elementary instruction in reading, writing and arithmetic. A major step forward was the Education Act 1902, which instructed local councils to act as education authorities and charged them with, inter alia, the powers and duties of school boards and the duties to maintain efficiently all public elementary schools and to aid the provision of higher education. The Board of Education, created in 1899,[7] was the Department of Government responsible for superintending all matters relating to education. The superintendence proved to be inadequate and was finally swept away by the Education Act 1944. That Act made a fresh start in the provision of education, created a Minister of Education and gave considerable power to central government. Despite numerous amendments,[8] the Act remains the primary text. Under its provisions a two fold system of administration is provided. In essence, it is the overall responsibility of the Secretary of State for Education and Science to promote the education of all persons and to ensure that local education authorities fulfil their functions of providing a varied and comprehensive educational service. Such are his statutory powers of intervention, and especially his power over the purse strings, that the Secretary of State wields considerable control.[9]

1 See generally *The Law of Education* (9th edn) (1984), edited by Peter Liell and John B Saunders. Subsequent references to it herein are by 'LE' and its appropriate paragraph number.
2 See post, para 16.02.
3 In *Hodges v Hodges* (1796) Peake Add Cas 79 it was recognised that no duty existed.
4 While the common law did not enforce a parental duty, it did recognise and enforce a parental power to educate the child; see *Tremain's Case* (1719) 1 Stra 167; *Hall v Hall* (1749) 3 Atk 721.
5 Bentham, for example, was a strong advocate of a system of public education. So was Colquhoun, who published a Tract on *A New and Appropriate System of Education for the Labouring People* (1806). Such individual interests probably influenced Henry Brougham in 1816 to introduce, though unsuccessfully, a Bill to provide a general education to be financed by local rates.
6 See post, para 14.01.
7 Board of Education Act 1899.
8 Twenty three at the last count. The need for a consolidating statute is long overdue. The Education Reform Act 1988 is to be construed as one with the 1944 Act; see ERA 1988, s 235(7).
9 For a list of the duties and powers of the Secretary see LE paras A [3] to [10] and for those of a local education authority A [11] to [17]. To these must be added the duties imposed and powers conferred by the Education Reform Act 1988.

(b) Duty to secure education of children

11.18 Under section 36 of the Education Act 1944[1] the present parental duty is to see that his child, being of compulsory school age, receives, either by regular attendance at school or otherwise, efficient full-time education suitable to his age, ability and aptitude and to any special educational needs he may have.[2] Compulsory school age extends from 5 to 16 years.[3] The parent is relieved of the duty during any period in which it is not practicable for him to arrange for his child to become a registered pupil at a school because the proprietors have refused to admit children during the currency of a school term.[4] Thus, if they refuse to admit a child who reaches the age of five during a school term, he must attend from the beginning of the following term.[5] For the child who attains 16 there are two school leaving dates. If he attains that age during the period 1 September to 31 January the date is the end of the Spring Term following the date when he attains that age; otherwise it is the Friday before the last Monday in May.[6]

1 As amended by EA 1981, s 17.
2 For children requiring special educational needs see post, paras 11.44 et seq.

3   EA 1944, s 35; Raising of School Leaving Age Order 1972. Once the child attains 16 he ceases to be of compulsory school age.
4   Education (Miscellaneous Provisions) Act 1948, s 4(2). For the scope of the duty see Dutchman-Smith, (1970) 114 Sol Jo 921.
5   If his fifth birthday falls on the day on which term begins he must be admitted for that term.
6   EA 1962, s 9, as amended by the Education (School-leaving Dates) Act 1976, s 1.

11.19   The duty extends not only to a parent[1] but also to a guardian and every person having actual custody[2] of the child. Where the child is living with both parents either or both may be held responsible.[3] Where he is living with only one of them and there is no order of a court relating to custody of him, it would seem, in the light of *London School Board v Jackson*,[4] that the parent who is not living with him may nevertheless be held liable, since it was there held that where another person has actual custody the parent is not exempted from liability. But what is the position where in divorce proceedings custody, care and control have been given to one of the parents. Is the other relieved of liability under section 36 if his child has not received full-time education? A logical affirmative answer must be doubted in view of the decision and dicta of the Court of Appeal in *Dipper v Dipper*.[5] If in those circumstances the non-custodial parent is 'entitled to know and be consulted' on such an important issue as education, as the court there ruled, it is arguable that he should correspondingly take all reasonable steps to ensure that his child is being fully educated and that neglect to do so renders him liable under section 36. Such a conclusion demonstrates the dubiety of *Dipper*.

1   See the definition in EA 1944, s 114(1).
2   This was a rare statutory use of this term prior to its general adoption in the Children Act 1975, s 87; see ante para 1.65.
3   *Plunkett v Alker* [1954] 1 QB 420, [1954] 1 All ER 396, where in such circumstances the mother was alone charged and held liable under s 54(6) of EA 1944 for her neglect in allowing her son once more to be in a verminous condition after he had already been cleansed under a compulsory cleaning order.
4   (1881) 7 QBD 502.
5   [1981] Fam 31, [1980] 2 All ER 722; see ante, para 3.53.

11.20   Apparently the term guardian in section 36 is to be given its normal meaning, namely, a person so appointed by deed or will or by an order of the court,[1] but doubt surrounds his responsibilities with regard to educating the ward. Equity insisted that he saw that the ward received an education that accorded with the latter's position in life and expectations,[2] but that obligation was laid down in a bygone age when there was no compulsory education, and its survival in the face of the statutory duty now imposed by section 36 must be questioned. It is submitted that there would be no breach of his duties if the guardian insisted that the interests of his wealthy ward were best served by attendance at a State school and not at a private school. Whether, in the light of the *Gillick* case,[3] the child, if old enough, should have the right to insist otherwise is another matter. Supposing a mature 16-year-old feels that preparation for entry into a University would be improved by moving from a secondary school to a sixth form private school. Would the guardian be justified in not consenting on the ground that the school fees were disproportionately high in relation to the ward's property? Would his consent in those circumstances relieve him of his fiduciary responsibilities? Would it make any difference if the fees were not disproportionately high? Because of the present uncertainties which *Gillick* raises,[4] the wisest precaution for the guardian in those circumstances, it is suggested, would be an application for wardship of court, seeking the court's directions.

1   There is no express definition in the Education Acts. Compare the CYP legislation, ante, para 9.48.
2   *Powel v Cleaver* (1789) 2 Bro CC 499.
3   [1986] AC 112, [1985] 3 All ER 402, HL.
4   See also Grenville, *Compulsory School Attendance and the Child's Wishes* [1988] JSWL 4.

(c)   Breach of the duty: school attendance order

11.21   The responsibility for seeing that the parent fulfils his duty lies with the local education authority. Where the parent is educating his child otherwise than by sending him to school the authority will examine closely the facilities provided. They may, for example, find that the accommodation or the standard of teaching provided is inadequate or that the child is not receiving lessons in prescribed courses of study, as was the case in *Baker v Earl*,[1] where the mother, who had no educational qualifications, merely encouraged her four children, aged between 10 and 14, to follow at home any subject which interested them. Whenever it appears to the authority that there is a failure to perform the duty they must serve a notice on the parent requiring him to satisfy them to the contrary.[2] In order so to proceed it is not necessary that the authority should have positive evidence that the parent is in breach of his duty. If they know that the child is not a registered pupil with them and the parent gives no information about his child's education or merely states that he is discharging his duty without giving any details, the authority may be justified in serving the notice.[3] That does not preclude the parent from challenging the validity of the notice by adducing evidence that it could not have 'appeared' to a reasonable local education authority that he was in breach of his duty, although it might well be better for him to reserve his defence until a school attendance order is made.[4]

1   [1960] Crim LR 363. See also *Re B (infants)* [1962] Ch 201, [1961] 3 All ER 276, CA. For relevant cases under the earlier law see *R v Walton Justices, ex p Dutton* (1911) 75 JP 558; *R v West Riding of Yorkshire Justices, ex p Broadbent* [1910] 2 KB 192; *Osborne v Martin* (1927) 91 JP 197.
2   EA 1944, s 37(1), as amended by EA 1981 s 21 and Sch 3, para 2. He must be given at least 14 days in which to comply. But the obligations of natural justice on the authority are limited; see *R v Gwent County Council, ex p Perry* (1985) 129 Sol Jo 737, CA.
3   *Phillips v Brown* (1980) Lexis, Enggen Library Cases, File, DC, noted in LE, para F[82]. It was said in that case that the local education authority has a 'duty to be alert' to ensure that s 36 is obeyed by parents and 'the most obvious step to take is to ask the parents for information'. The first indication of regular non-attendance will often appear from the school register.
4   Ibid, and see infra.

11.22   If the parent fails to satisfy the authority that the child is receiving efficient full-time education,[1] and the authority is of the opinion that it is expedient[2] that he should attend school, they will have to serve on the parent a school attendance order requiring him to cause the child to become a registered pupil at the school named in the order.[3] However, before doing so they must give the parent the opportunity to name a school of his preference.[4] They must, therefore, first serve a written notice of their intention to serve the order, specifying the school they intend to name in it and possibly also suitable alternatives. The parent then has the opportunity to select one of those schools and, if he does, it will be named in the order.[5] Alternatively, he may apply for a place at some other school maintained by that or another local authority or for education to be provided by the authority at their expense at a non-maintained school.[6] The authority must comply with the parent's preference, unless they have justifiable grounds for not doing so.[7] If they decline, the parent has a right of appeal.[8] If the parent is offered a place at the school of his choice, that will be named in the order. Another possibility is for the parent to apply for and be given a place at a non-maintained school but at his and not the authority's expense.[9] These several possibilities must be pursued by the parent within 14 days of service of the notice, otherwise the authority will name in the order the school originally specified in the notice.[10]

1 See, for example, *R v Surrey Quarter Sessions Appeals Committee, ex p Tweedie* (1963) 107 Sol Jo 555, where the authority was not so satisfied by reports of the work done by the children and would not have been without an inspection.
2 Ie 'advantageous, fit, proper or suitable'; per Donaldson LJ in *Phillips v Brown*, ante, para 11.21, note 3.
3 EA 1944, s 37(2), as amended by EA 1981, s 21 and Sch 3, para 2 and Sch 4.
4 For an authority's obligations with regard to parental preference see post, para 11.38.
5 EA 1980, s 10(1) and (2).
6 Sub-s (3)(a) and (b).
7 See EA 1980, s 6, post, para 11.38.
8 See s 7 for the duty imposed on local education authorities or school governors to make arrangements for appeals; and Sch 2 for the composition and procedure of appeal committees.
9 Section 10(4).
10 These procedures under s 10 are modified in the case of a child with special educational needs (post, paras 11.44 to 11.55); see EA 1981, s 15.

11.23   Where an attendance order has been served[1] the parent may later apply to the authority for the order to be revoked on the ground that arrangements have been made for the child to receive efficient full-time education otherwise than at school. Unless they consider that no satisfactory arrangements have been made, they must revoke the order. A parent whose request is not met by the authority may apply to the Secretary of State for a direction on the matter.[2]

1   For the Form of an order see the School Attendance Order Regulations 1944 (SR & O 1944/1470).
2   EA 1944, s 37(4), as amended by EA 1981, s 21 and Sch 3, para 2.

11.24   Failure to comply with an attendance order renders a parent criminally liable,[1] unless he proves that he is causing the child to receive efficient full-time education otherwise than at school.[2] The court may find the education provided is efficient without deciding that it is as efficient as he would receive at a primary or secondary school.[3] In the event of acquittal the court *may* direct that the order ceases to operate, but a change of circumstances might require the authority to take further action under section 37.[4] Apart from such a direction an order remains in force so long as the child is of compulsory school age,[5] unless revoked by the authority.[6] Apart from its power to revoke, the authority may amend an order, for example, where the child moves from a primary to a secondary school or where a parent applies for a change of school.[7]

1　For the penalties see EA 1944, s 40(1), infra, para 11.26, note 3.
2　Ibid, s 37(5), as amended by EA 1981, s 21 and Sch 3, para 2.
3　*Bevan v Shears* [1911] 2 KB 936, DC.
4　See sub-s (6).
5　For the purpose of prosecutions under s 37 or s 39 (infra) a child is presumed to be of compulsory school age at a material time, unless the parent proves otherwise; Education (Miscellaneous Provisions) Act 1948, s 9(1).
6　EA 1944, s 37(7).
7　See EA 1980, s 11. For amendment and revocation of orders made in respect of children with special educational needs see EA 1981, s 16.

11.25　However there are three important limitations to the use of school attendance orders. First, the offence under section 37(5) is not a continuing one.[1] Thus, once a parent is prosecuted for breach of the order or as soon as he has satisfied the order's requirement by registering the child as pupil, the order is *spent* even though the parent continues to ignore the duty to register or the child ceases to be a registered pupil at the named school. If the authority wish to prosecute again, they must embark on the procedure of notice[2] afresh. Second, as will be seen, the penalties under section 37 for non-compliance with an order are modest. Third, in practice as the child approaches school leaving age, education authorities are reluctant to embark on prosecutions.

1　*Enfield London Borough Council v F and F* [1987] 2 FLR 126, [1987] Fam Law 163, DC.
2　Ante, para 11.21. An alternative to prosecution would be the threat of, or the taking of, care proceedings.

(d)   Duty to secure regular attendance at school

11.26　Distinct from the above duty is that which requires the parent[1] to see that his child regularly attends the school at which he is a registered pupil.[2] If the child fails to attend regularly, the parent is guilty of an offence,[3] whether or not a school attendance order has been served on him and whether or not the parent is aware of the child's absences.[4] It is, therefore, an offence of strict liability, and the tendency has been to construe its terms narrowly.[5] Nevertheless, there are specific grounds of defence. The first two listed apply in respect of children who are day pupils and those who are boarders at school, the remainder only to the former.[6]

1　Including a guardian or any person having actual custody; ante, para 11.19, note 2.
2　EA 1944, s 39.
3　The penalties on summary conviction are a fine not exceeding level 3 on the standard scale (currently £400) or imprisonment up to one month or both (s 40(1), as amended by CJA 1982, ss 35, 37 and 46).
4　*Crump v Gilmore* (1969) 113 Sol Jo 998, 68 LGR 56, DC, and for critical comment see Cretney, [1987] Fam Law at 164.
5　Thus, regular attendance means regular attendance for the times prescribed by the local education authority, and a pupil who regularly arrives after the attendance register has been closed fails to attend regularly; *Hinchley v Rankin* [1961] 1 All ER 692, [1961] 1 WLR 421, DC.
6　See s 39(2) and (4).

(i)   Leave to be absent was granted by a person (usually the head teacher) authorised by the governors or proprietor of the school[1]

11.27   There are strict limits on granting leave to enable a child to undertake employment during school hours[2] or to take an annual holiday during term time.[3] A child who is suspended from school is not on leave of absence,[4] but the question whether the parent can be held liable under section 39 must, it is submitted, depend upon whether conditions are attached to the suspension. If the child is unconditionally suspended for the remainder of the school term because of his misbehaviour, it would not be open to hold the parent liable.[5] In such a case it would be a refusal to admit not a failure to attend. *Aliter*, if suspension were subject to the condition that, if the child gives assurances of future good behaviour, he may return to school, and the parent will not agree to that and keeps the child at home.[6] A controversial example of this was the decision in *Happe v Lay*. There a boy of 14 ran away from school because he was to receive two strokes of the cane for misbehaviour. The father refused to return him to school unless some other punishment was given, but the acting headmaster would not re-admit him unless he received the caning, and suspended him from school. The boy stayed at home for the rest of the term, and the father was held liable under section 39. In view of the absolute nature of the offence it is difficult to see how the court could have reached a different decision. The result of such a case today would be different, since refusal to submit to corporal punishment would not constitute a reasonable ground for suspending the child.[7]

---

1   Section 39(5), as amended by EA 1980, s 1(3) and Sch 1, para 10.
2   See post, para 11.77.
3   Education (Schools and Further Education) Regulations 1981 (SI 1981/1086) regs 11 and 12 respectively. Save in exceptional circumstances, no more than two weeks' leave in a year are to be granted for holidays.
4   *Happe v Lay* (1977) 76 LGR 313, DC.
5   There must, however, be reasonable grounds for suspending.
6   Because of the absolute nature of the offence, the parent will equally be liable where the child refuses to agree and stays at home.
7   For the current position on corporal punishment see post, para 11.61.

(ii)   The child was prevented from attending because of sickness or any unavoidable cause

11.28   As with sickness, the cause must be one that affects the child himself and not anyone else,[1] and it must be unavoidable. A reasonable cause is not enough to exclude liability. Mrs Jarman[2] was made to realise this. She objected to corporal punishment being administered to her children, and wrote to the headmaster to tell him so. His response was to refuse her children admission to the school so long as she persisted in that attitude. Their subsequent non-attendance was held to be a failure to attend regularly.[3] Nor will a parent have a defence if he disagrees with the educational or political opinions of the headmaster and boycotts the school.[4] Similarly, if a child's parents are ill, cannot therefore accompany him to school and keep him at home, the reasonableness of their action is no defence,[5] though it would be a formidable factor in favour of mitigation[6] and against prosecution in the first place.

1 Cf *Jenkins v Howells* [1949] 1 All ER 942, DC, where the child had been kept at home to look after the home and younger brothers and sisters because of the mother's illness.
2 *Jarman v Mid-Glamorgan Education Authority* (1985) Times, 11 February, DC.
3 On the particular facts this case would be decided differently now in view of the abolition of corporal punishment.
4 But compare the controversy which surrounded Mr Ray Honeyford at Drummond Middle School in Bradford. The attitude of the parents who boycotted the school was supported by the education authority, and no prosecutions were brought under s 39.
5 Lord Ackner's suggestion to the contrary in *Essex County Council v Rogers* [1987] AC 66 at 78, [1986] 3 All ER 321 at 326 was clearly obiter, and neither the *Jenkins* nor the *Jarman* case was cited.
6 Cf the penalty imposed in *Rogers* (substitution of conditional discharge by absolute discharge on appeal).

(iii)   His absence was on a day exclusively set apart for religious observance by the religious body to which his parent[1] belongs.

11.29   It is difficult to see why this ground should be included. Absence for this purpose will only occur on occasional days, and that can hardly amount to failure to attend school regularly. That objection apart, the ground has its inherent objections. Difficulties could arise over its interpretation where a person other than a parent has actual custody and the religion of that person and that of the parent differ.[2] Moreover, the exemption from liability depends on the religious faith of the parent, guardian or person having actual custody; but, in the light of the *Gillick* principle,[3] can the child any longer be ignored? Supposing, for example, that an independently minded 15-year-old is living with parents who are atheists but he has become a confirmed Anglican and absents himself on Ascension Day.[4] It would be absurd to hold the parents liable, yet the wording of section 39(2)(b) so allows. For all these reasons this statutory ground is best abolished.

1 Including a guardian or any person having actual custody; supra, para 11.19 note 2.
2 Although a person with actual (but not legal) custody has duties, he normally has no rights in respect of a child (Children Act 1975, s 87(3)), but his religion is relevant for present purposes.
3 See ante, para 1.13.
4 Ascension Day is a day for religious observance; *Marshall v Graham, Bell v Graham* [1907] 2 KB 112.

(iv)   The school at which the child is a registered pupil is not within walking distance of his home and no suitable arrangements have been made by the local education authority for transport to and from, or boarding accommodation at or near, the school or for enabling him to attend a school nearer to his home.

11.30   'Walking distance' means, in relation to a child under eight, two miles and in the case of any other child three miles, 'measured by the nearest available route'. In *Shaxted v Ward*[1] this definition was narrowly construed: the test of nearest availability was one of distance — the shortest route — not of the child's safety. This approach was confirmed by the House of Lords in *Essex County Council v Rogers*,[2] where it was held that a route which the interests of children demand that they should not use, such as an isolated track which was unlighted and generally considered by parents and others to be dangerous, was still to be regarded as the shortest walking distance. In the words of Lord Ackner, available route 'must be a route along which a child accompanied as necessary can walk and walk with reasonable safety to school. It does not fail to qualify as "available" because of dangers which would arise if the child is unaccompanied'.[3] On the other hand, it has been held that a local education authority must provide arrangements for transport for the full distance between the child's home and school and vice versa.[4] When deciding whether or not it is under a duty to provide transport, the authority must in particular pay regard to the child's age and the nature of the route, or alternative routes, which he could reasonably be expected to take.[5] Then the following questions must sequentially be answered. (1) Should the child be accompanied on the route or alternative routes? If the answer is 'No', then normally there will be no case for free transport. If the answer is 'Yes', then: (2) the question is whether the nature of the route or alternative routes is dangerous for the child if accompanied. If the answer is 'Yes', then normally there is a case for free transport. If the answer is 'No', then: (3) the question is whether it is reasonably practical for the child to be accompanied. If the answer is 'No', then normally there is a case for free transport.[6]

1   [1954] 1 All ER 336, [1954] 1 WLR 306, DC.
2   [1986] 3 All ER 321, [1986] 3 WLR 689. The Divisional Court offered a brief contrary view; see [1985] 2 All ER 39, [1985] 1 WLR 700.
3   [1986] 3 All ER 321 at 326, [1986] 3 WLR 689 at 696.
4   *Surrey County Council v Ministry of Education* [1953] 1 All ER 705, [1953] 1 WLR 516. Where the authority in accordance with its obligations makes arrangements for transport (for example, by providing a bus pass) but later finds that the distance is less than three miles, it may withdraw the arrangements; *Rootkin v Kent County Council* [1981] 2 All ER 227, [1981] 1 WLR 1186, CA.
5   EA 1944, s 55(3), as inserted by E(No 2) A 1986, s 53.
6   *R v Devon County Council, ex p G* [1988] 3 WLR 49, CA.

11.31   The present ground obviously has no application where the child has no fixed abode, but, if proceedings are taken under section 39 against a parent who is engaged in a trade or business which requires him to travel from place to place, he is not guilty of an offence if the child has attended a school as regularly as the parent's occupation permits.[1] This defence similarly operates where a person is charged under section 10 of the Children and Young Persons Act 1933 as a vagrant who takes a child from place to place with him and so prevents the child from receiving efficient full-time education.[2]

1   Sub-s (3). In the case of a child aged six or over there must, however, have been at least 200 attendances during the 12 months ending on the date on which the proceedings were instituted. The Children's Legal Centre has estimated that there are 'probably between 12,000 and 15,000 travellers' children of school age in the UK' (Education *Rights Handbook*, p 5).
2   But note the maximum penalty for this offence is only a fine not exceeding level 1 on the standard scale (currently £50); s 10(1), as amended by CJA 1982, ss 35, 37 and 46.

11.32   In addition to the above grounds, a parent is protected from liability under section 39 where his child, being suspected of being verminous, has been excluded from attending school pending his examination or cleansing.[1] Otherwise the list of grounds set out in the section is exhaustive. Thus, in *Spiers v Warrington Corp*[2] a 14-year-old girl who had had rheumatic fever on two occasions was sent to school dressed in trousers to keep her warm. This form of dress was contrary to a school rule, but the headmistress told the parents that she would waive it if a medical certificate were produced stating that trousers were necessary. No certificate was produced, and so whenever the girl appeared at school in trousers she was sent home. It was held that a headmaster had the right and power to prescribe discipline for his or her school, that to send one's child to school knowing that he would not be admitted amounted to failure to see that he attended regularly and that the father of the girl was therefore guilty of an offence under section 39.[3]

1   EA 1944, s 54(7).
2   [1954] 1 QB 61, [1953] 2 All ER 1052.
3   Quaere the disciplinary power of the headteacher to forbid girls wearing trousers is impliedly abrogated by the Sex Discrimination Act 1975. The point has still to be judicially tested. For possible problems in schools over discrimination relating to sex, race, disability, language or religion see the *Education Rights Handbook* (pp 22–29) of the Children's Legal Centre. In *Mandla v Dowell Lee* [1983] 2 AC 548, [1983] 1 All ER 1062 the House of Lords held as unlawful discrimination under the Race Relations Act 1976 a headteacher's refusal to admit an orthodox Sikh boy to a school unless he removed his turban and cut his hair.

11.33   The effect of the section, therefore, is that the reasonableness of the parent's attitude is irrelevant and the teacher's authority must override his wishes. Not surprisingly it has occasioned sharp criticism in some quarters. Its implications are not confined to questions of whether parents shall have the right to choose the mode of dress that their children shall wear. As already noted, it can equally apply where the child's absence is the result of the parent's objection to the views of the headteacher.[1] Similarly, a parent would not, for example, be legally justified in keeping his child away from school on the ground that he considers that specific contents of a sex-education book used in the school are exposing his child to moral danger. In such a case the general duty of the local education authority to educate a child in accordance with the parent's wishes is unlikely to be of any avail.[2] Nor could sections 44 (dealing with political indoctrination), 45 (balanced treatment of political issues), and 46 (sex education) be pleaded, since the task of enforcing them rests with the local education authority, the school's governing body and the headteacher. So, a dissatisfied parent's remedy is to press those bodies into action (if necessary by judicial review), and not to withhold his child from school attendance. Illustrations such as those above argue for a reversion to the former rule where it was open to the parent to put forward any 'reasonable excuse' as a valid defence.[3] A further advantage in that rule would be that in considering reasonableness account would be taken, *pace* the *Gillick* principle, of the right of the child to make his own decisions when he reached sufficient understanding and intelligence to be capable of making up his own mind. If, for example, a 15-year-old considers, contrary to the parent's views, that the contents of a sex-education book are not exposing him to moral danger, it is arguable that parental objection would not be reasonable. More difficult would be the situation where the pupil objects to the school's actions. It is basically a matter of how far the courts want to take the *Gillick* principle.

1   Or, under the former law, because of objection to corporal punishment. See *Happe v Lay* and *Jarman v Mid-Glamorgan Education Authority*, ante, paras 11.27 and 11.28.
2   See EA 1944, s 76, post, para 11.36.
3   See EA 1921, s 49; *LCC v Maher* [1929] 2 KB 97, DC.

(e)   Care proceedings concerning juveniles not receiving proper education

11.34   Proceedings against a parent for an offence under section 37 or section 39 of the Education Act 1944 or under section 10 of the Children and Young Persons Act 1933 may be instituted only by a local education authority;[1] but, as will be seen,[2] before doing so the authority must consider whether it would be appropriate instead of or as well as instituting those proceedings to bring the juvenile before a juvenile court under section 1 of the Children and Young Persons Act 1969.[3] Apart from the discretion of the authority, the court which convicts the parent of an offence under section 37 or before which he is charged with an offence against section 39 may direct the authority to proceed under section 1 of the 1969 Act.[4] Where the juvenile is brought before the juvenile court and a school attendance order has been made in respect of him, but the relevant condition in section 1(2)(e) of the 1969 Act is not satisfied, the juvenile court may direct that the school attendance order shall cease to be in force.[5]

1   *Semble*, the appropriate court is that in whose area the school is situate or the child resides or the school attendance order was made; see Clarke Hall and Morrison, op cit, para B [466].
2   Post, para 14.17.
3   See EA 1944, s 40(2), as substituted by CYPA 1969, Sch 5, para 13; CYPA 1933, s 10 (1A), as inserted by CYPA 1969, Sch 5, para 2.
4   EA 1944, s 40(3), as substituted by CYPA 1969, Sch 5, para 13. There is no corresponding power conferred on a court before whom a person is brought under s 10 of CYPA 1933. Note that in the case of proceedings under s 39 a direction may be given whether or not the parent is convicted of an offence.
5   EA 1944, s 40(4), as substituted by CYPA 1969, Sch 5, para 13.

2   The parental rights and powers

11.35   In examining the parental duties concerning secular education oblique reference has been made to certain parental rights. Thus, the parent has the basic right to secure his child's education otherwise than by sending him regularly to a school, although the right is rarely exercised. Moreover, when a local education authority are compelled to take steps to make a school attendance order the parent has the right, subject to overriding considerations, to choose a particular school. But over and above these is imposed on the Secretary of State and on local education authorities a general duty to have regard to the wishes of the parent.[1] Quite frequently the duty has had to be measured against the background of the expansion of comprehensive education and what has been seen by some parents as a consequent restriction on their wishes and choice of school.[2] As will be seen Parliament has responded recently by giving parents a greater role in the management of schools.

1   There is also a duty to consult before deciding whether or not to close or amalgamate schools; *R v Brent London Borough Council, ex p Gunning* (1985) 84 LGR 168. See post, para 11.41.
2   See especially *Secretary of State for Education and Science v Metropolitan Borough of Tameside* [1977] AC 1014, [1976] 3 All ER 665, HL.

(a)   Parental wishes

11.36   Section 76 of the Education Act 1944 states:

'In the exercise and performance of all powers and duties conferred and imposed on them by this Act the Secretary of State and local education authorities shall have regard to the general principle that, so far as is compatible with the provision of efficient instruction and training and the avoidance of unreasonable public expenditure, pupils are to be educated in accordance with the wishes of their parents.'

The obligation relates to the wishes of parents with regard to such educational matters as the school curriculum, religious instruction, co-education and the like, but not about the size of a school or conditions of entry; and the duty is to consult particular parents about their children and not parents generally.[1]

1   *Wood v Ealing London Borough Council* [1967] Ch 364, [1966] 3 All ER 514.

11.37   Clearly the provisos concerning compatibility with efficient instruction and the avoidance of unreasonable public expenditure are themselves marked restrictions on the general principle, but there is the further limitation that the local education authority is not precluded by the section from taking into account other matters. This point has been considered in connection with the duty of an authority to make sufficient schools available,[1] either by providing them themselves[2] or by making arrangements with the proprietors of independent schools.[3] In *Watt v Kesteven County Council*[4] it was held, inter alia, that provided they fulfil this general duty,[5] as by paying tuition fees at an independent school with which they have made arrangements, they are not obliged to pay fees at some other independent school chosen by the parent; and in *Cumings v Birkenhead Corp*[6] the authority were held entitled to insist for good educational reasons, namely the pressure on places in their comprehensive schools, that children leaving Roman Catholic primary schools should attend Roman Catholic, and not other, secondary schools, even though the parents objected to this restriction. Moreover, no obligation arises under section 76 when the school chosen by the parents is unsuitable,[7] since it is not part of the authority's general duty under section 8 to keep a child at a school which is unsuitable for him.[8]

1   Under EA 1944, s 8, as amended by E(MP)A 1948, s 3, EA 1980 s 38(6) and Sch 7, EA 1981, s 2(1), and (prospectively) ERA 1988, Sch 13, Part II. The duty of the authority under s 8 of the 1944 Act is to provide a suitable education, not the most suitable; *R v Mid-Glamorgan County Council, ex p Greig* (1988) Independent, 1 June.
2   EA 1944, s 9(1), as amended by EA 1980, s 38(6) and Sch 7.
3   E(MP)A 1953, s 6, as amended by EA 1980, s 38(6) and Sch 7 and EA 1981, s 21 and Sch 3, para 8(2).
4   [1955] 1 QB 408, [1955] 1 All ER 473, CA.
5   If they have not, the duty can be enforced by the Secretary of State (under s 99 of the 1944 Act), but this remedy does not exclude an action for damages or an injunction by a parent who has suffered damage when there has been a breach of the duty under s 8 and that was due to a decision taken ultra vires or to an act of malfeasance or (per Lord Denning MR) even of nonfeasance; *Meade v London Borough of Haringey* [1979] 2 All ER 1016, [1979] 1 WLR 637, CA. Section 8 does not, however, impose an absolute duty on local authorities: there can be reasonable grounds for closing schools; see ibid at pp 1027, 1031 and 650, 654 respectively. Where the local education authority has properly

carried out its statutory requirements with regard to school closure, the court has no jurisdiction to prevent closure; *R v Gwent County Council, ex p Bryant* (1988) Times, 18 April. Moreover, where the Secretary of State has heard argument and representations from all interested parties, he is in an excellent position to make a decision on the proposals of the authority to close a school and may do so as speedily as possible; *R v Secretary of State for Wales, ex p South Glamorgan County Council* (1988) Times, 25 June.

6 [1972] Ch 12, [1971] 2 All ER 881, CA.
7 *Winward v Cheshire County Council* (1978) 77 LGR 172.
8 *Gateshead Union v Durham County Council* [1918] 1 Ch 146, CA.

(b) Parental preferences[1]

11.38 Closely related to the obligation under section 76, though their precise relationship has yet to be determined by the courts, is the more closely defined one under section 6 of the Education Act 1980, which requires a local education authority to make arrangements for enabling the parent of any child in their area who is under 19 to express a preference as to the school at which he wishes his child to be educated and to give reasons for his preference.[2] The authority, or the governors where they are responsible for admission to the school, must then comply with the parental preference.[3] The duty extends to preferences expressed both for maintained schools and for non-maintained with which the authority might make arrangements for education of the child, but the authority[4] are relieved of their duty[5] where admitting the child to the school selected by the parent:

(a) would prejudice the provision of efficient education or the efficient use of resources, or
(b) if the preference is for an aided school or a special agreement school,[6] would be incompatible with the school's admission arrangements, or
(c) if the preferred school's admission arrangements are based on selection by reference to ability or aptitude, would be incompatible with selection under those arrangements, as, for example, where there is an entrance examination which the child fails to pass.

1 See Marson, *Parental Choice in State Education*, [1980] JSWL 193; Lee, *Parental Choice of School* (1980) 10 Fam Law 44.
2 It has been argued that s 6 'does little to change the effect of s 76'; Marson ibid at p 196.
3 Section 6(1) and (2) and s 38(4).
4 Or, as the case may be, the governors.
5 By s 6(3).
6 For these two classifications of voluntary schools (ie schools maintained but not established by a local education authority) see EA 1944, s 15(2) and Sch 3.

11.39 With regard to the first of these exemptions from compliance, the burden is on the authority to prove that there is 'prejudice' and that it outweighs the parental considerations and reasons for preference such as geographical factors, denominational grounds, the school curriculum,[1] exceptional medical or social factors or the fact that the child has older brothers or sisters in the preferred school.[2] Each of these may be cogent considerations for giving effect to the parental preference in the particular case. Nevertheless, the terms of the exemption are wide, and in some cases the burden of proof should not prove onerous. It would seem, for example, that the *Cumings* parents[3] would be as disappointed under section 6 as they were under section 76. Similarly, an authority would be justified in refusing admission to a school that was full, but unequivocal evidence of that fact would be essential and difficult in the individual case to sustain.[4] Again, it would be prejudicial to the efficient education of a child if the journey he had to make to the parent's preferred school would be a physical strain on him. Clearly, there can be no proper and effective exercise of a parental preference unless, before expressing it, the parent is fully informed about the authority's or governors' admission arrangements to their schools, the education provided, examination policies and such matters as the arrangements provided for transport to schools and whether it is free or subsidised. Accordingly, a statutory duty is imposed to publish the relevant information.[5] The parent has a right of appeal to an Appeal Committee against any admission decision;[6] and, although the appellate procedure has its defects,[7] it is more likely to be invoked than resort to complaint[8] by the parent to the Secretary of State on the ground that the local education authority has acted unreasonably.

1 Or in Wales the linguistic character of the instruction.
2 See *R v South Glamorgan Appeal Committee, ex p Evans* (10 May 1984, unreported) but noted in LE para F[43], and commented on by Maidment in (1987) 137 NLJ 607. See generally on parental preference LE paras A [49] – [59].
3 See para 11.37.
4 *R v South Glamorgan Appeal Committee ex p Evans,* ante.
5 EA 1980, s 8; the Education (School Information) Regulations 1981 (SI 1981/630).
6 EA 1980, s 7 and Sch 2. For a detailed examination of the Parliamentary history of those provisions and the conflicting political stances which lay behind them see Bull, *Schools Admission: A New Appeals Procedure*, [1980] JSWL 209.
7 See Bull, ibid.
8 Under EA 1944, s 68.

(c) Religious worship and instruction

11.40 The one matter on which the wishes of parents are, without exceptions, effectively protected is religious instruction. A parent may not only request that his child be excused from attendance at the daily act of collective worship[1] and at classes of religious instruction which schools are obliged to provide,[2] but also, if he wishes him to receive a particular kind of denominational instruction which cannot be provided in the school which the child attends or by his being transferred to another school, he can require the local education authority to make arrangements for the child to receive the instruction elsewhere during school hours, provided that the authority are satisfied that the arrangements will interfere only with his attendance at school at the beginning or end of the daily school session.[3]

This is another area where *Gillick* may eventually raise its head. A local education authority may find itself in difficulty where a parent requests that his child be excused attendance at classes of religious instruction or, on the contrary, that he be given particular denominational instruction and the child, being old enough to express an opinion, takes a diametrically opposed view to that of his parent. The matter could be brought before the court by an application for mandamus against the local education authority, but the most satisfactory jurisdiction would be wardship within the Family Division.

It should be noted that parental wishes will not be respected to the extent that the education provided is too narrow, and hence unsuitable, for the child. The Secretary of State is fully entitled to lay down minimum requirements for curricula, whatever the teachings of the parent's religion may say.[4]

1   For the general duty of pupils at maintained schools to attend an act of collective worship, see now the Education Reform Act 1988, s 6 (which replaces EA 1944, s 25). Maintained schools are defined (by ERA 1988, s 25) as: (a) any county or voluntary school; (b) any maintained special school which is not established in a hospital; and (c) except in relation to a local education authority, any grant-maintained school. (For the new kind of school, 'the grant-maintained school' created by the 1988 Act see Chapter IV of the Act).
   The collective worship at county schools must be 'wholly or mainly of a broadly Christian character [reflecting] the broad traditions of Christian belief without being distinctive of any particular Christian denomination'; see ERA 1988, s 7(1) and (2), but the section does allow for some modification of those requirements; see sub-ss (4)–(6): Section 7 is not yet in force.
2   For the religious education which maintained schools are obliged to provide in the basic curriculum see ERA 1988, ss 2(1)(a), 8, 84–86 and EA 1944, ss 26–28. Any agreed syllabus must reflect the fact that the religious traditions are in the main Christian while taking account of the teaching and practices of the other principal religions represented in Great Britain.
3   ERA 1988, s 9(3)–(8).
4   R v Secretary of State for Education and Science, ex p Talmud Torah Machzikei Haddass School Trust (1985) Times, 12 April; LEXIS, Enggen Library, Cases' file (concerning an orthodox Hasidic School).

(d)   Rights over the management of a school

11.41   Apart from a parent's right to stand for election as a parent governor and thereby influence the management of a school,[1] all parents have the following rights:

(a)   to make representations to the governing body as to the content of the school's curriculum;[2]

(b)   to be supplied by the governing body with information about the running of the school, including information on the syllabuses offered;[3]

(c)   to receive, whenever practicable, an annual report from the governing body free of charge;[4]

(d)   to attend the annual parents' meeting;[5]

(e)   to be consulted prior to the closure of a school[6] insofar as fairness requires consultation.[7]

1   For the appointment and functions of a governing body see Part II of the Education (No 2) Act 1986 and LE, paras A[18] to [63], and for comment see Harris, Regulation of Schools under the Education (No 2) Act 1986, [1987] Fam Law 287. For the appointment and functions of a governing body of grant-maintained schools see ERA 1988, ss 53–71. As for pupil governors, the Government's initial view was that 'a school or college governor holds an office of public and pecuniary trust. Such an office may not properly be held by a minor.' Baroness Young, HL Debs 10 March 1986, col 469. This was a doubtful approach in the light of the Gillick case, and so the possibility of pupil governors is specifically prohibited by s 15(14) of the 1986 Act. Pupils can of course be invited to attend governors' meetings.
2   Ibid, s 18(3).
3   Under ERA 1988, s 22, which relates to maintained schools, regulations may be made by the Secretary of State specifying the information which the local education authority, the governing body or the head teacher is to make available either generally or to prescribed persons (which doubtless will include parents). For the power to make regulations requiring the governing body of a grant-maintained school to publish information and reports see ERA 1988, s 103. The Secretary of State may similarly make regulations for information

on meetings of governors of both maintained and grant-maintained schools; see E (No 2)
A 196, s 62, as amended by ERA 1988, Sch 12, para 37.
4   Section 30.
5   Section 31. Resolutions can be passed at the meeting which must then be 'considered'
    by the headteacher and/or local education authority.
6   Under EA 1980, ss 12–14 and 16.
7   The right is not 'absolute' — see *R v Sutton London Borough Council, ex p Hamlet* (1986)
    LEXIS, Enngen Library, Cases' File (cf *R v Brent London Borough Council, ex p Gunning*
    (1986) 84 LGR 168); and derives from a series of circulars setting out the Secretary of
    State's policy in favour of consultation.

3   Education of special categories of children

(a)   Children under five years of age

11.42   The educational needs of children under the age of five were
recognised by the Education Act 1921, which conferred power on local
education authorities to provide nursery education. The Education Act 1944
substituted a duty, but it was a qualified one because it was imposed in
the terms that, in fulfilling its general duty under the latter Act[1] to provide
primary schools, an authority was required to have regard to the need
for the provision of nursery schools or nursery classes for children under
five. It thus left the authority with a discretion as to the priority it would
give to nursery education. Notwithstanding the importance which several
influential committees have attached to nursery education,[2] the Legislature
has reverted to a mere power to provide it, thus further emphasising the
need for alternative forms of day care.[3]

1   Section 8.
2   See especially the Plowden Report on *Children and their Primary Schools* HMSO (1966),
    para 314; the Seebohm Report on *Local Authority and Allied Personal Social Services*
    (1968), Cmnd 3704, paras 196, 202–210; and the Warnock Report on *Special Educational
    Needs* (1978) Cmnd 7212, para 5.51. A White Paper, *Education: A Framework for Expansion*
    (1972) recommended free, part-time provision be made available for children between
    three and five whose parents wanted it.
3   See ante, Chapter 7. An Under Fives Initiative was launched by the Government in 1983
    and ended in March 1987. Its future funding would appear to be precarious; see HC
    Debs, 12 December 1986, col 284 (WA) for the provision of temporary Government grants
    to assist schemes started under the Initiative. The trend between 1981 and 1986 was for
    local authorities to reduce the availability of full time nursery facilities, HC Debs, 18
    February 1987, col 655 (WA). For a depressing picture of the inadequate provision of
    nursery education, see Cohen *Caring for Children* (1988). Separate surveys conducted
    respectively by the National Children's Bureau and the National Child Care Campaign
    confirm the inadequacy and the fragmented provision of facilities.

11.43   The power of the local education authority is to provide nursery
education either (1) by establishing and maintaining nursery schools or
financially assisting any nursery school not maintained by it, or (2) by
providing for nursery classes in other schools.[1] A nursery school is defined
as a primary school used mainly for the purpose of providing education
for those who have attained the age of two but not five.[2] A nursery class
is defined by the Schools Regulations 1959 as a class mainly for children
aged at least three but under five.[3] Those Regulations restricted admissions
to nursery schools to those over two and to nursery classes to those over
three, save in exceptional circumstances,[4] and stated that children must
not be kept in any nursery school or class after the end of the term in
which they become five. The Education (Schools and Further Education)

Regulations 1981 have removed the restrictions. A notable distinction between nursery education provided by a local education authority and that in the form of day nurseries provided by a local social services authority is that the former may not, but the latter may, make charges for the teaching and facilities they provide.

1   EA 1980, s 24.
2   EA 1944, s 9(4).
3   Reg 3(1).
4   Reg 7(2).

(b)   Children with special educational needs

(i)   Introduction

11.44   In discharging their basic duty under the Education Act 1944[1] to secure the provision of sufficient primary and secondary schools, local education authorities had to have regard to the need for providing 'special educational treatment' for children suffering from mental or physical disability. An essential feature of the system was that the child had to fall within one of eleven categories of handicap.[2] The Warnock Committee drew attention to the stigmatising and discriminatory effects of this categorisation and recommended its abolition and the substitution of the wider concept of 'special educational needs'.[3] This and many of the Committee's recommendations appear in the Education Act 1981.[4]

1   Section 8.
2   As specified by the Handicapped Pupils and Special Schools Regulations 1959 (as amended).
3   Cmnd 7212, paras 3.21–3.33.
4   See generally Cox, *The Law of Special Educational Needs* (1985); Galloway, *Schools, Pupils and Special Educational Needs* (1985); Nice, *Education and the Law*; Milman, *Educational Conflict and the Law* (1986) pp 54–57 and *The Education Act 1981 in the courts* [1987] JSWL 208; Goulty, *The Education Act 1981 in practice* (1984) 81 Law Soc Gaz 2928.

(ii)   Definitions

11.45   The new concept is itself based on the concept of 'a learning difficulty which calls for special educational provision'.[1] A child has a learning difficulty if:

(a)   he has a significantly greater difficulty in learning than the majority of children of his age; or

(b)   he has a disability which either prevents or hinders him from making use of educational facilities of a kind generally provided in schools, within the area of the local authority concerned, for children of his age; or

(c)   he is under five years of age and is likely to fall within category (a) or (b) when he is over that age or is likely to do so if special educational provision is not made for him.[2]

The definition does not, however, include a learning difficulty due to the fact that the language or form of language used for instruction in school is different from that spoken at home.[3] Problems in that regard should be met by the local education authority securing that there are sufficient schools and teachers to meet the needs of linguistic minorities.[4] Similarly, speech therapy to assist a child's learning does not qualify as special educational provision.[5]

For children under the age of two special educational provision means any kind of educational provision.[6] Otherwise it means educational provision which is additional to or otherwise different from the educational provision made generally for children of his age in schools maintained by the local education authority.[7]

1 EA 1981, s 1(1).
2 Section 1(2).
3 Section 1(4). But it may be difficult, particularly in a younger child, to determine whether there are linguistic and cultural problems or a need for special education. See further DES Circular 1/83, para 70.
4 Ie in accordance with their duty under EA 1944, s 8.
5 *R v Oxfordshire Education Authority, ex p W* (1986) Times, 22 November, DC.
6 See post, para 11.54.
7 EA 1981, s 1(3).

(c) Provision of special education

(i) In ordinary schools

11.46 In discharging its general duty to secure the provision of sufficient primary and secondary schools a local education authority must have regard to the need for securing that educational provision is made for pupils with special educational needs.[1] That requirement must be seen against the background of one of the major changes in the law made by the Education Act 1981, namely the shift from primarily providing for the education of children with special needs in separate, special schools to provision normally in ordinary schools. This emphasis on integration with children without such needs is, however, modified by the conditions that account must be taken of the views of the parent and that educating the child in an ordinary school is compatible with his receiving the special educational provision that he requires, the provision of efficient education for other children in the school and the efficient use of resources by the local education authority.[2] If these conditions are met and provided it is reasonably practicable, those concerned with making special educational provision available must secure that the child engages in the school activities together with children who do not have special educational needs.[3] Equally the authority must keep under review its arrangements for special educational provision.[4] So far progress towards integration has been slow.[5]

1 EA 1944, s 8(2)(c), as substituted by EA 1981, s 2(1).
2 Section 2(2) and (3).
3 Section 2(5) and (6).
4 Section 2(4).
5 In 1987 the Inner London Education Authority was reported as being the first authority to adopt integration as an 'overriding objective' (Times, 4 March 1987). For the number of pupils in special schools see HC Debs, 25 February 1987, col 246 (WA).

(ii) In special schools

11.47 These are schools specially organised to make special educational provision for children with special educational needs, and must be so approved by the Secretary of State.[1] Approval may also be given to an independent school to provide for pupils with special educational needs.[2] A parent cannot exercise a preference as to which special school his child shall attend,[3] and cannot withdraw him from such a school without the consent of the local authority.[4] These restrictions make it all the more

particular child is available in an ordinary school. That, however, may
be a view with which the parents disagree.[5] Their chances of persuading
an authority to opt for a special school are limited not only by the 1981
Act's policy of integration,[6] but also by the observation[7] that 'there is no
question of Parliament having placed the local authority under an obligation
to provide a child with the best possible education. There is no duty on
the authority to provide such a Utopian system, or to educate him or her
to his or her maximum potential'.

1   See EA 1944, s 9(5), as substituted by EA 1981, s 11(1); and for approval and discontinuance
    of special schools see ss 12 and 14 of the latter Act, the Education (Approval of Special
    Schools) Regulations 1983 and DES Circular 8/81, paras 26–34.
2   EA 1981, s 13. If there is no such general approval, the Secretary of State may still authorise
    individual placements at an independent school (s 11(3)(b)). The local authority may be
    obliged to pay the fees. It also has a discretion to do so, which should not be unlawfully
    fettered; see *R v Hampshire Education Authority, ex p J* (1986) 84 LGR 547.
3   See EA 1980, s 9(2).
4   EA 1981, s 11(2). But the parent may refer the matter to the Secretary of State for his
    direction.
5   See [1984] Fam Law 195–196 for an unreported case where a parents' claim that the
    local education authority should have provided education for their dyslexic children in
    a special school was rejected. But see also *R v Hampshire Education Authority ex p J*,
    supra, where it is made clear that dyslexia can amount to a learning difficulty necessitating
    special educational provision.
6   Supra, para 11.46.
7   Per Slade LJ in *R v Surrey County Council Education Committee, ex p H* (1985) 83 LGR
    219 at 235.

(iii)   Provision otherwise than in schools

11.48   Under section 3 of the Education Act 1981 where a local education
authority is satisfied that it would be inappropriate for special educational
provision to be made in a school, for example, because the child is in
hospital or convalescing at home, it may, after consulting his parent, arrange
for provision to be made for his full-time or part-time education otherwise
than in school. This power is wider than but does not replace that under
section 56 of the Education Act 1944 which enables an authority to arrange
for a pupil to receive primary or secondary education otherwise than at
school. That power may only be invoked in 'extraordinary circumstances'.
Moreover, while its exercise requires the approval of the Secretary of State,
it does not require the authority to consult the parent, although it is arguable
that failure to do so would be unreasonable so as to justify a complaint[1]
by the parent to the Secretary of State with a view to his rescinding his
approval. It would be better if a comprehensive enactment were substituted
for sections 3 and 56.[2]

1   Under EA 1944, s 68.
2   Note also the right of the parent to arrange for his child to receive education otherwise
    than at a school (ante, para 11.21).

(d)   Identification and assessment

(i)   Children over the age of two

11.49   *(1) Identification*   In complicated terms section 4 of the Education
Act 1981 requires a local education authority to exercise its powers with
a view to ensuring that it identifies among the children for whom it is

responsible those who have special educational needs which are such that the authority must determine the special educational provision that should be made for them. The responsibility of an authority in effect extends to all children who either are registered at a school in its area[1] or are aged between two and 16 and have been brought to the attention of the authority as having special educational needs. Children most likely to fall into this second category are those aged between two and five who are not attending nursery schools or nursery classes.

1   This includes any pupil under the age of 19; see EA 1981, s 20(1).

11.50   *(2) Assessment*   Another key feature of the 1981 Act is the importance it attaches to the involvement of the parent throughout the process of assessment.[1] Thus, before the local education authority proceeds to make an assessment of a child whom it considers has, or probably has, special needs calling for special provision, it must notify the parent of its proposed intention to assess;[2] the procedure relating to assessment; a named officer from whom to obtain further information; and the right to make representations and submit written evidence within a period of not less than 29 days from the date the notice is served.[3] It may also serve notice on the parent requiring the child's attendance for examination, and the parent is entitled to be present if he so wishes.[4] Any representations and written evidence must be taken into account in any assessment.[5] If the authority decides to make an assessment, it must notify the parent of its decision and the reasons for it.[6] Should it decide after making the assessment that it is not required to determine the special educational provision that should be made for him, the parent has a right of written appeal to the Secretary of State, who may, if he thinks fit, direct the authority to reconsider its decision.[7] These are the formal procedures to be observed, but local education authorities have been encouraged to develop 'a co-operative relationship with parents which will be in the best interest of the child concerned,'[8] and before the first notice is issued 'every possible effort should be made to effect initial contacts between the teacher, or any other professional making the referral, and the child's parent.'[9]

1   In accordance with the recommendation of the Warnock Committee. 'Parent', it will be remembered (see ante, para 11.19) includes a guardian and any person having actual custody of the child. So, if the child is in the care of a local authority, it will be for the Director of Social Services to involve the natural parent where appropriate; see DES Circular 1/83, para 19.
2   It should be noted that an assessment can alternatively be made at the request of the parent; see EA 1981, s 9(1),
3   EA 1981, s 5(1)–(3).
4   Ibid, Sch I, Part I, paras 2(1) and (2). Failure without reasonable excuse to present one's child for examination is an offence carrying a fine not exceeding £50; (reg 2(4)).
5   Section 5(4); Education (Special Educational Needs) Regulations 1983, reg 8(a) and (b). The representations may be written or oral; see reg 2(1).
6   EA 1981, s 5(5). Equally a parent must be informed of a decision not to assess (s 5(10)).
7   Ibid, s 5(6)–(8).
8   DES Circular 8/81, para 13.
9   DES Circular 1/83, para 17.

11.51   The assessment procedure involves not only the parent. The local education authority must also send copies of its notification of proposed assessment to the social services authority and the district health authority, and must take account of any information relating to the child's health or welfare which those authorities may provide.[1] For the purpose of making an assessment the local education authority must also seek and take account of educational, medical and psychological advice from prescribed persons and any other advice the authority considers desirable.[2]

1   See E (SEN) Regs 1983, regs 3 and 8(d)
2   Regs 4–7 and 8(c).

11.52   If, having made an assessment,[1] the authority considers that it should determine the special educational provision for the child, it must make and maintain a statement of his special educational needs, but before doing so must serve a draft of the proposed statement together with an explanation of the following consequences.[2] If the parent disagrees with any part of the statement, he may, within 15 days of service of the draft, make representations to the authority and require it to arrange an interview with one of its officers,[3] and, if he is still dissatisfied, he can require further meetings to discuss the relevant advice on assessment with the person who gave it or with any other appropriate person.[4] The authority must take into account the parental representations before finally deciding whether to make its statement.[5] If parents have been fully involved from the earliest stages of assessment, such interviews and representations should be exceptional, as should any appeal against the special educational provisions specified in the statement. Where the right of appeal is exercised, the appeal lies to an appeal committee[6] with a further right of written appeal to the Secretary of State.[7] Once a statement has been made it must not be disclosed without the parent's consent except for specified reasons such as disclosure for the purpose of an appeal or where it is in the child's educational interests.[8]

1   The authority can decide whether itself to determine the special educational provision for a child or to leave the decision to others, eg to the child's school. If it delegates the decision, it need not make and maintain a statement of the child's special educational needs; see *R v Secretary of State for Education and Science, ex p Lashford* [1988] 1 FLR 72, [1988] Fam Law 59, CA.
      Where the High Court in wardship proceedings has decided what educational provision should be made for a child, the local education authority is entitled, in its discretion, to conclude that there is no need to determine and state the child's educational needs; see *Re D (a minor)* [1987] 3 All ER 717, [1987] 1 WLR 1400.
2   EA 1981, s 7(1) and (3).
3   Ibid, s 7(4) and (7)(a) and (c).
4   Ibid, s 7(5) and (6).
5   Ibid, s 7(8). DES Circular 1/83, para 49 advises that 'wherever possible, the parent should be given the opportunity to visit the school being considered for the child before the statement is finally made'.
6   For details see EA 1981, s 8 and EA 1980, Sch 2.
7   EA 1981, s 8(6) and (7). Such an appeal does not oust the jurisdiction of the court; see Waller LJ in *R v Surrey County Council Education Committee, ex p H* (1984) 83 LGR 219 at 229.
8   E (SEN) Regs 1983, reg 11.

11.53   Statements must be reviewed at least annually by the local education authority,[1] who should consider, in the light of reports from the school and from others who work with the child, whether different arrangements for educational provision should be made. The review may well call for a re-assessment of the child's educational needs. Alternatively, the parent may request re-assessment whenever six months have elapsed since the previous assessment, and the authority must comply with it, unless they are satisfied that assessment would be inappropriate.[2] When a child in respect of whom a statement is maintained attains the age of 13 years and six months and his educational needs have not been assessed since before he attained the age of 12 years and six months, those needs must be re-assessed during the next following year.[3]

The local education authority are now specifically required to seek an assessment during the child's 15th year of age as to whether he is or is not a disabled person. If he is assessed as disabled, the authority must arrange for the social services department to carry out an assessment of his needs, so that they may make plans for the child from the time when he ceases to receive full-time education.[4]

1   EA 1981, Sch I, Part II, para 5.
2   Ibid, s 9(2).
3   E (SEN) Regs 1983, reg 9.
4   Disabled Persons (Services, Consultation and Representation) Act 1986, ss 5 and 6.

(ii)   Children under the age of two
11.54   A child under two may be assessed by the local education authority if it considers he has, or probably has, special educational needs that call for special educational provision and the parent consents, and it must assess if the parent requests it.[1] The above rules relating to assessment and the making of a statement of the child's needs do not apply. Instead assessment may take whatever form the local education authority considers appropriate, as may any consequent statement of needs that may be made,[2] and there is no parental right of appeal.[3] As already noted,[4] special educational provision means any kind of educational provision. This may include such forms of provision by social services and voluntary bodies as opportunity groups and mother and toddler groups, but it should especially cover support and advice to help the parents help their child. As the Departmental Circular has urged, 'maximum flexibility will be required in order to meet the needs of the child in a way which also provides support for his family'.[5] Moreover, as the Warnock Committee emphasised,[6] 'in the earliest years parents rather than teachers should be regarded, wherever possible, as the main educators of their children'.

1   EA 1981, s 6(1).
2   Ibid, s 6(2).
3   Ibid, s 8 is restricted to statements made under s 7.
4   Ante, para 11.45.
5   DES Circular 1/83, para 66.
6   Cmnd 7212, para 5.3.

(iii)   Early warning of needs of under fives
11.55   The 1981 Act recognises the importance of early identification by local education authorities of children with special educational needs. Thus,

when a district health authority 'in the course of exercising any of its functions' in relation to a child who is under five forms the opinion that he has, or is likely to have, such needs, it must inform the parent and after discussion with him bring its opinion to the attention of the local education authority.[1] A likely way in which this might happen is where a health visitor has been put on inquiry when visiting the family. Health authorities are, however, the only bodies on whom this statutory duty to report is imposed, being the bodies most closely involved with very young children. It is submitted that the duty should be extended at least to the local authority social services department where it is already involved with the family. Against the objection of intrusion into the privacy of the family must be set the long-term risk to the child's welfare if his special needs are not discovered early. If the health authority considers that the child would be helped by a particular voluntary body it must so inform the parent.[2] It is then a matter for the parent whether he seeks that help, but voluntary bodies who have a special role in counselling the parents of children with special educational needs have been encouraged to provide full information about their services to education and health authorities.[3] If they offer special help, should they not, again in the interest of children, be statutorily obliged to provide the authorities with that information? Such a requirement would not militate against the voluntary nature of their work.

1   EA 1981, s 10(1). Here, again, a sympathetic relationship with the parent needs to be established, and the health authority should guard against premature prognosis of the child's special needs.
2   Ibid, s 10(2).
3   See DES Circular 1/83, para 69.

4   The teacher and pupil relationship

(a)   Powers over discipline

11.56   'A parent, when he places his child with a schoolmaster, delegates to him all his own authority, so far as it is necessary for the welfare of the child.'[1] This statement of the law has been questioned[2] on the ground that the view it embodies was formulated before the introduction of compulsory education,[3] in cases where a contractual relationship existed between the parent and the school authority and there could fairly be said to be delegation,[4] but that to rely on that principle now is unrealistic in view of the modern parental duty to secure the child's education. Nevertheless, it has to be admitted that the above statement is still widely recognised as the proper basis of the law.

As will be seen, the teacher's common law authority, be it delegated or independent, has recently been supplemented by statute. One aspect of that authority is the power to discipline the child. The primary responsibility for discipline and the promotion of good behaviour lies with the head teacher. Indeed, in the maintained sector articles of government of each school will make that clear.[5] However, he must comply with any general principles which the governing body has set down, and he must have regard to any of its guidance in relation to particular matters.[6] Of the many disciplinary measures which a head teacher may want to take,[7] two call for special attention because of the recent intervention of Parliament and one because of the courts.

1 Per Cockburn CJ in *Fitzgerald v Northcote* (1865) 4 F & F 656 at 689, 176 ER 734 at 749.
2 See the first edition of this book at p 211, and Street, *Torts*, 7th edn, pp 79–80.
3 By the Elementary Education Acts 1870 and 1876, ante, para 11.17.
4 But see the footnote to *Fitzgerald v Northcote*, where it is pointed out that Hawkins (PC 150) seems to place the parent, master and schoolmaster 'on the same footing' with regard to the right to punish. This suggests an early willingness to treat the teacher independently. Cf the same tendency in s 1(7) of CYPA 1933, which expressly refers to the teacher: 'Nothing in this section shall be construed as affecting the right of any parent, teacher or other person having the lawful control or charge of a child or young person to administer punishment to him'.
5 Education (No 2) Act 1986, s 22(a).
6 Ibid, s 22(b).
7 For a list see *Education and the Law* (ed D Nice) at pp 172–173.

(i) Suspension and exclusion of pupils

11.57 The power to suspend or expel a pupil is exercisable only by the head teacher and must be on reasonable grounds.[1] However, in the maintained sector, once he exercises it a complex system of appeals and checks and balances can operate.[2]

1 *Gateshead Union v Durham County Council* [1918] 1 Ch 146.
2 The relevant provisions (ss 22 to 27) of E (No 2) A 1986 are to be fully operative in all maintained schools by 1 September 1989.

11.58 *(1) Notification* The head teacher must without delay try to inform the parent of his decision to exclude the pupil, his reason for doing so and the right of the parent to make representations to the governing body and the local education authority. If the exclusion exceeds five days (in aggregate) in a term or causes the pupil to miss a public examination or if a temporary exclusion is made permanent, the head teacher must also inform the governing body and the education authority.[1]

1 E (No 2) A 1986, s 23(b).

11.59 *(2) Reinstatement*[1] In a particularly cumbersome fashion section 24 provides that, where a local education authority has been told of a pupil's exclusion for a fixed, indefinite or permanent period, it must consult the school's governing body and then consider whether, and if so when, the pupil should be reinstated. If it so decides, it will direct the head teacher accordingly. Similarly, the governing body has the power to direct reinstatement. Both the governing body and the authority must keep each other informed as to their proposed action and, if they send conflicting directions to the head teacher, he must comply with that which will lead to the earlier reinstatement of the pupil.

1 The following discussion concerns county, controlled and maintained special schools. Similar provisions for aided and special agreement schools are set out in s 25.

11.60 *(3) Appeal* There are two rights of appeal, which apply only if a pupil has been permanently excluded from the school. First, if the governing body and education authority decide to endorse the head teacher's decision, a parent (or pupil if aged 18 or over) can appeal. Second, if the authority has overruled the head teacher and ordered reinstatement, the governing body can appeal[1] against the authority's direction. The appeal lies to the Appeal Committee set up by the Education Act 1980.[2]

These are the minimum guarantees, and it is quite permissible for a school's articles of government to grant parents additional rights of appeal against decisions of lesser severity.[3]

1   It has seven days in which to appeal, (Sch 3, para 3(1)).
2   See EA 1980, Sch 2, as amended by E (No 2) A 1986, Sch 3.
3   E (No 2) A 1986, s 27.

(ii)   Corporal punishment

11.61   At common law a schoolteacher may inflict 'moderate and reasonable corporal punishment'[1] for disciplinary purposes. The practice faced increasing criticism in the 1970s and was out of step with the United Kingdom's European neighbours. Indeed, the strongest stimulus for abolition came in 1982 when the European Court of Human Rights ruled that a parent's objection to corporal punishment, or, in the words of Protocol No. 1 to the European Convention for the Protection of Human Rights, 'philosophical convictions', had to be respected.[2] The Government eventually responded with the Education (Corporal Punishment) Bill 1985, which would have allowed parents to give notice to education authorities refusing permission for corporal punishment. After a stormy passage the Bill was withdrawn. As originally drafted the Education Bill 1986 made no provision for the matter, but an opposition amendment moved in the House of Lords and aimed at abolishing corporal punishment was carried by a majority of two votes and successfully negotiated the House of Commons by a majority of one.

1   Per Cockburn CJ in *R v Hopley* (1860) 2 F & F 202 at 206, 175 ER 1024 at 1026.
2   *Campbell and Cosans v UK* (1982) (Judgment, Series A 48). Further cases are in the process of being considered and some have been settled out of court, for example, *Townend v UK* (No 9119/80), January, 1987, where a man who six years earlier had been suspended from school after refusing to be caned was awarded £3,000 compensation by the European Commission on Human Rights.

11.62   Section 47 of the Education (No 2) Act 1986 abolished corporal punishment[1] in all maintained schools, special schools, independent schools which are maintained or assisted by public funds[2] and wherever any education is otherwise provided by a local education authority, for example, in pre-school nurseries, hospitals or children's homes.[3] It also extends to pupils who attend independent schools and who are supported by public funds.[4] This could lead to the invidious spectacle of two categories of pupils in independent schools — those who can be beaten because their parents agree to it and those who cannot, either because of section 47 or because their parents exercise the right acknowledged in *Campbell and Cosans v UK* and instruct the school not to inflict corporal punishment. For those few independent schools where corporal punishment is retained and is applicable, the common law governs. Thus, the punishment must be moderate and reasonable,[5] for otherwise criminal and tortious liability will arise. An assistant master can administer it,[6] and it can be used to discipline conduct arising outside the school premises.[7] It is highly likely that the power of caning in these schools will be tested in the European Court of Human Rights.

1   Operative since 15 August 1987. Apart from beating, the throwing of articles is covered. Action taken to avert personal injury or immediate danger to property is permitted, (s 47(3)); for example, self-defence by the teacher, separating fighting pupils, stopping a child running in a dangerous manner. The Education Reform Act 1988, Sch 12, para 35, extends s 47 of the 1986 Act to grant-maintained schools.
2   The Education (Abolition of Corporal Punishment) (Independent Schools) Regulations 1987, SI 1987/1183 prescribe existing direct grant schools and Ministry of Defence schools as the classes of independent schools where corporal punishment may not be lawfully administered.
3   The prohibition extends to community homes, voluntary and private children's homes and youth treatment centres; see HC Debs 9 March 1987, cols 64–5, WA.
4   Section 47(6).
5   *R v Hopley* (1860) 2 F & F 202, 175 ER 1024, ante para 11.61 note 1.
6   *Mansell v Griffin* [1908] 1 KB 160.
7   *Cleary v Booth* [1893] 1 QB 465 (fighting outside school); *R v Newport (Salop) Justices, ex p Wright* [1929] 2 KB 416 (smoking in the street).

(iii)   Detention

11.63   The headmaster may permit detention of pupils (individually or collectively) as a method of promoting discipline.[1] What happens if a parent objects and forbids the school to detain his child? Any detention thereafter is unlikely to breach the European Convention for the Protection of Human Rights, since the parent's objection hardly amounts to a 'philosophical conviction' which, under the Convention, the law must respect.[2] As for a civil action of false imprisonment, lawful authority is a defence and this could be found in (a) the headmaster's approval of detention, and (b) its proper application, ie that it was justified in the circumstances and was reasonable in length.[3] If on the other hand the pupil refuses to stay in detention, forcible detention[4] would not, it is suggested, be a defence to an action for false imprisonment. Resort should be had to suspension or other disciplinary powers.

1   In *Hunter v Johnson* (1884) 13 QBD 225 it was held that detention after school hours for not doing home lessons was not permitted, since there was no power to set them. The decision has not been challenged, and it is noteworthy that the EA 1944 does not expressly authorise the setting of such lessons by any school administered by a local authority under the Act. Nevertheless, it has been pointed out by the Children's Legal Centre (*Education Rights Handbook*, p 14) that schools 'may make completion of homework a condition of taking some courses or examinations' though the 'legality of this has never been tested'.
2   Art 2, Protocol 1. Cf *Cambell and Cosans v UK* (1982) (Judgment, Series A 48), where a parent's objection to caning was held to constitute a philosophical conviction, ie 'such convictions as are worthy of respect in a "democratic society"' (para 36, judgment).
3   In practice, advance warning should be given to the parents and as part of a teacher's duty of care to the pupil (see post) the detention should not end too late and expose the child to a dangerous return to his home. In a county court case, *Terrington v Lancashire Education Authority* (cited in LE para A [78]), it was held just and reasonable for a teacher to keep a class of 25 pupils, including the plaintiff's son, in detention for ten minutes after continuous disruption to his lesson, but blanket punishment of a whole class should be used only as a last resort.
4   By locking the classroom door. Quaere physical restraint would amount to corporal punishment and thereby infringe s 47 of E (No 2) A 1986.

(b)   The teacher's duty of care[1]

11.64   A teacher owes a duty of care to his pupils and the standard imposed is that of the careful parent.[2] The most important aspect of it is the adequate supervision of pupils so as to prevent them injuring themselves, each other or third parties.[3] It is unclear to what extent a teacher should go in detecting injuries done or about to be done to the child. Morally he may well feel obliged to report his suspicions of child abuse to the social services department or the police. Legally he is under no duty to report a suspected crime nor does his contract of employment impose one.[4] It is hard to imagine that a child, suing by his next friend (for example, a foster parent), could successfully establish negligence on the part of a teacher who had earlier seen bruises on the child but had allowed the child to return home to his parents where he was then battered. The answer is the same where the child has told the teacher of the abuse. For the teacher's action is one of omission, in failing to alert others, and the law of negligence is loath to impose liability for omissions.[5] Desirable though intervention by teachers is,[6] it is fraught with danger. First, if training to detect child abuse becomes standard practice, does detection of it become an implied duty in the teacher's contract, and does failure not then entail civil liability? Second, must a teacher report (to the social services) every suspicion he has? If it proves unfounded, would the local authority be able to conceal the source of their information from an aggrieved parent intent on pursuing defamation or other civil proceedings.[7] More generally, there is the harmful effect on the local authority/parent relationship and sometimes, too, on that between the parent and the child, which may well follow from the fruitless investigation of a teacher's suspicions.

1　For a summary of relevant cases on this topic see LE paras F [112] to [180].
2　See Lord Esher MR in *Williams v Eady* (1893) 10 TLR 41, CA.
3　For example, by dashing out of a school playground into the path of traffic; *Carmarthenshire County Council v Lewis* [1955] AC 549, [1955] 1 All ER 565, HL.
4　Moreover, teachers are not trained to become child abuse detectives.
5　See further Winfield and Jolowicz, *Tort* (12th edn) pp 80–82.
6　The 1987 Conference of the Assistant Masters and Mistresses Association called for training in the matter.
7　Cf *D v NSPCC* [1978] AC 171, [1977] 1 All ER 589, HL.

(c)　Access to information

11.65　A head teacher must make generally known within the school any measures which are taken with regard to discipline and behaviour[1] and must arrange for school rules to be brought to the attention of pupils and parents. Under the Data Protection Act 1984[2] a pupil has the right, subject to payment of a fee, to be informed, and obtain a copy, of any computerised records about him which are kept by the school or the local education authority.

1　E (No 2) A 1986, s 22.
2　Sections 21–24.

(d)　Conclusions

11.66　Since 1980 Parliament has been extensively active in the field of education. Many of the changes have concerned the uneasy and shifting relationship between parent and school and between the internal management of a school and the local education authority, the financing and governing of schools and the provision of a national curriculum. During this period there has also been a significant increase in litigation, particularly at the instance of parents. Yet, in all these changes only indirectly and marginally has the child acquired a voice in the conduct of his education.

IV EMPLOYMENT OF CHILDREN

1 Introduction

11.67 The history of employment of children has been so frequently and graphically examined that there is little room for fresh comment on it,[1] but one aspect which has largely escaped attention is the influence of parental rights on it. This was exerted in two ways. Firstly, the virtual absoluteness of the father's right of custody[2] was relied on to justify both child slavery, ie the right of the father to sell his children to an employer,[3] and 'free' child labour, ie his right to arrange with an employer for his children to attend for work daily. Secondly, his right to the services of his child indirectly contributed to the wretched conditions which prevailed under the system of apprenticeship. To enable the father to enforce the right against anyone who unlawfully interfered with it, it was essential to impute to him and his child a master/servant relationship, since actions for loss of service could only be founded on that relationship. The temptation to equate the relationships — father/child, master/servant — for other purposes could hardly have been resisted. Not until the nineteenth century was it firmly laid down that the father's powers of punishment were limited to those of reasonable chastisement,[4] and it seems that earlier law countenanced excessive powers of paternal control.[5] If, therefore, the father could invoke those powers in relation to his child of whom he could demand the performance of services, why should the master not insist on the same powers in controlling and punishing his apprentice? The analogy was able to give to the barbaric conditions of apprenticeship an aura of respectability.[6]

1 A comprehensive account is given by W Clarke Hall, *The Queen's Reign for Children.*
2 See ante, para 1.08.
3 The common law rule that an agreement to surrender custody of one's child is contrary to public policy and void (ante, para 1.68) seems to have been ignored.
4 *R v Hopley* (1860) 2 F & F 202.
5 See ante, para 1.21.
6 Ironically, in the seventeenth century reliance was placed on the master/servant relationship to presume a parent's right to his child's services and the presumed relationship was then invoked to justify a master's wide powers of control.

11.68 Attempts to mitigate the severities of child labour appeared from the beginning of the nineteenth century. Broadly, the relevant legislation of the century regulated the hours and conditions of employment of children employed in the textile industry, as chimney-sweeps, in the mines, in non-textile industries, in agriculture and in the entertainment industry — in that chronological order;[1] but its efficacy was variable partly because of 'restrictive and hostile judicial interpretations'.[2] A notable feature of the first Factory Act in 1802, which was concerned, inter alia, with children employed in textile mills, was a provision that they were to receive instruction in 'reading, writing and arithmetic', but this, like the remainder of the Act, was blatantly ignored by employers. Moreover, the Act only applied to apprentices and this led to increased use of 'free' child labour in the industry. The next principal Act, the Factory and Workshops Act 1844, was more far-reaching. It extended to a number of classes of child labour;[3] it raised the minimum age of employment and reduced the hours of employment; it introduced the principle of factory inspection, including safety precautions for children and it insisted on proper school attendance for them. It remained the principal Act until superseded by the Factory and Workshop Act 1878, which set the pattern for modern factory legislation.

The complexity of the modern law governing the employment of minors is partly explained by overlapping classifications of the persons affected, partly by the variety of sources of specific restrictions (many of which have complicated exceptions) and partly by the general restrictions which override them.

1   Efforts were also made to regulate the apprenticeship of pauper children. The apprenticeship statutes of Elizabeth I were repealed in 1814 (54 Geo III, c 96) and replaced by an Act of 1816 (56 Geo III, c 139); see Holdsworth, *History of English Law*, Vol XIII, p 313.
2   Hepple and O'Higgins, (4th edn) para 390.
3   A major omission was child employment in brickfields a defect cured by the Factory and Workshop Act 1871.

2   Employment of children under school-leaving age

11.69   For purposes of employment law minors are basically classified into children and young persons, the former being those not over compulsory school age, ie under 16, and the latter those over 16 but under 18.[1] The classification does not, therefore, identically correspond with that which normally applies for the purposes of the Children and Young Persons Acts.[2] It is the employment classification which applies to the employment provisions in those Acts, but the law is complicated by the fact that for certain kinds of employment, a distinction has been drawn between young persons under 16 and those over 16 but under 18.

1   EA 1944, ss 58 and 114.
2   See CYPA 1933, s 107(1).

(a)   Specific restrictions according to nature of employment

11.70   No child under the upper limit of compulsory school age can be employed in any industrial undertaking (except in those cases where only members of the same family are employed),[1] or below ground in a mine, or quarry,[2] or in a factory,[3] or in a shop,[4] or a United Kingdom registered ship.[5] The Children and Young Persons Acts 1933 and 1963 prohibit the employment of children in street-trading, except in so far as local authority bye-laws may permit,[6] and only allow children to take part in entertainment performances subject to strict safeguards relating to their health, welfare and education.

1   Employment of Women, Young Persons and Children Act 1920, s 1(1). An industrial undertaking includes the transport of passengers and goods by road or rail (Sch, Part II) but the Act has not been amended to take account of air transport. However, employment of, say, a 14-year-old at an airport would be likely to be caught by the general restrictions on employment of children, post, para 11.77.
2   Mines and Quarries Act 1954, s 124.
3   Factories Act 1961, s 167.
4   Shops Act 1950, Part II and s 74(1); but see CYPA 1933, s 18, post, para 11.77.
5   Merchant Shipping Act 1970, s 51. Regulations may, however, permit employment.

6 See further street-trading in relation to young persons, post, para 11.81.

(i) Performances by children

11.71 *(1) CYPA 1963* Part II of the 1963 Act and Regulations[1] provide a comprehensive code.[2] In replacing certain provisions in the 1933 Act,[3] they allow children under 12 to engage in public performances, and they take account of the expansion of the film, broadcasting and television industries. The essence of the system is that performances by children under the upper limit of compulsory school age normally depend on the granting of a licence by the local authority.[4] This rule applies to any performance[5] in connection with which a charge is made, any performance in licensed premises or a registered club, any broadcast, any performance in a cable programme service and any performance recorded with a view to use in a broadcast or a cable programme service or a film intended for public exhibition.[6] No licence is required,[7] however, when the child has not performed in any of the above circumstances on more than three days in any period of six months or his performance is given under arrangements made by a school or by a body approved by the Secretary of State or by the local authority and no payment for his performance is made to him or anyone else.[8]

1 The Children (Performances) Regulations 1968, SI 1968/1728.
2 There is a Home Office Guide to the law (*The Law on Performances by Children*, HMSO (1968)).
3 The changes were largely the result of a Departmental Committee (Cmnd 8005). Part II of the 1963 Act operates as if it were included in Part II of the 1933 Act; see CYPA 1963, s 44(1).
4 CYPA 1963, s 37(1).
5 This includes the case of a child who is a 'stand-in'.
6 CYPA 1963, s 37(2), as amended by the Cable and Broadcasting Act 1984, Sch 5.
7 Section 37(3).
8 The most likely example of the exemption would be a child performing in an amateur production of a play on more than four days.

11.72 No licence may be granted[1] unless the local authority is satisfied that the child is fit to perform, that proper provision has been made to secure his health and kind treatment and that his education will not suffer.[2] The grant is also subject to restrictions imposed by the Regulations. These include a general limit on the number of performing days in any period of 12 months to 80 days for children aged 13 or over and to 40 for those under that age[3] and there are further limitations on the number of weekly and daily performances, depending upon whether they are broadcast or recorded performances or other performances.[4] The local authority must approve arrangements for the child's education during the period when he is engaged for performances, for example, the approval of private tuition;[5] and they may also safeguard his financial interests, for example, by requiring the whole or part of his earnings to be set aside and a trust fund created.[6] During the period of operation of a licence the child must at all times be in charge of a 'matron', who may be a man or a woman.[7] The local authority must approve the choice of a matron. They must be satisfied that he or she is suitable and competent to exercise proper care and control, having particular regard to the age and sex of the child. The maximum number of children who at any time may be in the care of a matron is 12.

1   The application for it must be made in writing by the person responsible for the production of the performance and should be made at least 21 days before the first performance (reg 1 and Sch 1). For the form of licence see reg 3 and Sch 2.
2   CYPA 1963, s 37(4). The authority may make such inquiries as they consider necessary, including calling for a school report and a medical examination, and they may interview interested parties, including the applicant, the child and his parent; see reg 2 and, for medical examinations, reg 8.
3   Reg 6. Although rehearsals are not performances, they can be taken into account in deciding whether to grant a licence, and, if so, the number of days for which it is granted; see reg 6(4)(a).
4   See Parts IV and V of the Regulations. Similarly there are limitations on the number and duration of performances for which a local authority licence is not required (Part VI).
5   Reg 10. A licence must specify the times when a child may be absent from school (s 37(7)).
6   Reg 11.
7   Reg 12.

11.73   A licence in respect of a child cannot be granted unless (a) the licence is for acting and the application for it is accompanied by a declaration that the part cannot be taken except by a child of about his age; or (b) it is for dancing in a ballet and there is a similar declaration that only a child of his age can dance the part; or (c) the nature of his part in the performance is also wholly or mainly musical or the performance consists only of opera and ballet.[1] The restriction extends to children under 14.[2]

1   CYPA 1963, s 38(1).
2   Ibid, s 38(2).

11.74   Subject to giving notice to the holder of the licence, the local authority may vary or revoke it for breach of any condition on which it was granted or because they are not satisfied about the child's health, treatment or education. Appeals against refusal, variation or revocation of a licence or against any condition which the authority is not entitled to impose lie to a magistrates' court.[1]

1   CYPA 1963, s 39.

11.75   *(2) CYPA 1933*   In addition to the above control through local authority licences, there are overriding restrictions on performances. No one under 16 is allowed to take part in a public performance in which his life or limbs are endangered, and anyone who causes or procures, or, being his parent or guardian,[1] allows the juvenile to participate is guilty of an offence.[2] Children under 12 must not be trained to take part in any performance of a dangerous nature,[3] and those who have reached that age but are under 16 may be so trained only if a local authority grants a licence, which may be made subject to conditions but which cannot be refused if the authority is satisfied that the juvenile is fit and willing to be trained and that proper provision has been made to secure his health and kind treatment.[4] There is power to vary or revoke such a licence and a right of appeal against refusal, variation or revocation similar to that relating to licences granted under section 37 of the 1963 Act.[5] Finally, persons under 18 may only be employed outside the United Kingdom and the Irish Republic in singing, playing, performing or being exhibited for profit (including performing for broadcasts or recordings) if a licence is granted for the purpose,[6] and this can only be granted in respect of a child under 14 within the same limits as apply to licences granted to children under 14 to perform within the United Kingdom.[7] The maximum period for which a licence may be granted is three months, but it is subject to renewal, revocation or variation. Where there is reasonable cause to believe that a child or young person is about to leave the United Kingdom in breach of these rules, an application can be made for a place of safety order.[8]

1 Guardian includes anyone having the charge of or control over the child (CYPA 1933, s 107(1)).
2 CYPA 1933, s 23, as amended by CYPA 1963, Sch 3, para 5, and CJA 1982, ss 35, 37, 38 and 46.
3 Including performances as an acrobat or contortionist (CYPA 1933, s 30). See also s 3 of the Hypnotism Act 1952 (as amended by the Family Law Reform Act 1969) which forbids hypnotism of a person under 18 at a public entertainment (penalty is maximum fine of level 3 on the standard scale (currently £400)).
4 CYPA 1933, s 24, as supplemented by CYPA 1963, s 41.
5 See CYPA 1963, s 41(2) and (3).
6 CYPA 1933, s 25, as supplemented by CYPA 1963, s 42. See also the Appendix to Home Office Circular No 155/1968. The prohibition extends to all children except those who are temporarily resident in the United Kingdom.
7 Ante, para 11.72.
8 CYPA 1969, s 28(1)(c). For place of safety orders see post, paras 14.34 et seq.

(ii) Penalties and enforcement
11.76 There is considerable variation in the maximum penalties that may be imposed for offences relating to the restrictions imposed on employment of children. Some of them can hardly be said to be commensurate with the dangers attendant upon the activities which it is sought to restrict. A parent, for example, who allows his child to be employed in an industrial undertaking or underground or in a factory can be fined no more than level 1 on the standard scale.[1] One who allows him to participate in a performance endangering his life or limbs or to train for performances of a dangerous nature without a licence can be fined up to level 3,[2] whereas consenting to participation in a performance without a licence contrary to section 37 of the Children and Young Persons Act 1963, which may be a much less dangerous activity, carries a fine not exceeding level 3 or imprisonment for up to three months or both.[3] So, too, does contravention of the restrictions on a child going abroad to perform.[4] These heavier, alternative penalties are, it is submitted, more realistic and should be made generally applicable to all the above offences. However, prosecutions for any of the offences are uncommon, and there is no firm evidence about the incidence of contravention. In respect of offences under the Children and Young Persons Acts 1933 and 1963 a local authority or a constable may be given the power, by an order of a justice of the peace, to enter premises and make enquiries where there is reasonable cause to believe there is a contravention,[5] but it is rarely invoked, and there has been no pressure to confer on local authorities closer supervisory functions.

1 See Mines and Quarries Act 1954, s 160 (as amended by CJA 1982, ss 37, 38 and 46) and s 166; Factories Act 1961, s 158 (amended by CJA 1982, ss 37, 38 and 46) and s 167.
2 CYPA 1933, ss 23 and 24(1) (as amended by CJA 1982, ss 35, 37, 38 and 46).
3 CYPA 1963, s 40(2) (as amended by CJA 1982, ss 37, 38 and 46), and see generally s 40 for the various offences for breach of s 37.

4   CYPA 1933, s 26(1) (as amended by CJA 1982, ss 37, 38 and 46). However, a person procuring the child to go abroad by means of false pretence or false representation is liable on conviction on indictment to imprisonment for up to two years.
5   CYPA 1933, s 28. The power is not affected by the provisions of the Police and Criminal Evidence Act 1984 relating to search and entry.

(b)   General restrictions

11.77   No child below the upper limit of compulsory school age may be employed until he has attained the age of 13 years.[1] Those who are outside this prohibition (ie those between 13 and 16) are subject to the following restrictions. They must not be employed before the close of school hours on a school day (except in those circumstances where leave to be absent can be given[2]); before 7 am or after 7 pm on any day; for more than two hours on a school day;[3] or for more than two hours on a Sunday. They cannot, moreover, be employed to lift or carry anything so heavy as to be likely to cause them injury.[4] These restrictions are all subject to any local authority bye-laws affecting employment of children,[5] which may add further restrictions or even prohibit absolutely employment in a specified occupation; or, on the other hand, may allow employment of children under 13 in limited circumstances. The system lends itself to variation in operation, and so the Employment of Children Act 1973, if and when it is brought into force, will replace these powers of local authorities to make bye-laws with increased powers of the Secretary of State to make uniform regulations governing the employment of children.[6] It should be added that none of the above general restrictions applies[7] so as to prevent a child taking part in a performance under a local authority licence or in a case where no such licence is required.[8]

1   CYPA 1933, s 18(1)(a); EA 1944, s 58; Children Act 1972, s 1.
2   See infra, para 11.80.
3   See the previous note.
4   CYPA 1933, s 18(1)(b)–(f) (as amended by CYPA 1963, Sch III).
5   See CYPA 1933, s 18(2); EA 1944, s 120(5).
6   Section 1(2) and (5). Apparently, the failure to implement the Act is due to the opposition of local authorities on the ground that they do not have the necessary resources to enforce it.
7   See CYPA 1933, s 18(3).
8   See ante, para 11.71.

11.78   The maximum penalty for a breach of any of those restrictions is a fine not exceeding level 3 on the standard scale,[1] but it is open to an employer to prove that the contravention was due to the act or default of some other person and that he himself used all due diligence to secure compliance with the rules.[2] Apart from this statutory defence,[3] a person is not liable if he does not knowingly permit the employment of the child.[4]

1   CYPA 1933, s 21(1) (as amended by CJA 1982, ss 35, 37, 38 and 46). The power of entry, conferred by s 28 (ante para 11.76) applies also in respect of these restrictions.
2   Section 21(1) and (2). The other person must be made a party to the proceedings and convicted of the offence.
3   The defence, it is submitted, is mainly relevant to those cases where there has been a breach of one or more of the conditions set out in s 18(1)(b)–(f) of the 1933 Act.
4   *Robinson v Hill* [1910] 1 KB 94, DC; *Portsea Island Mutual Co-operative Society Ltd v Leyland* [1978] Crim LR 554, [1978] ICR 1195, CA, (without knowledge and authority of his employer a milk roundsman employed a ten-year-old boy to help him).

(c)   The role of the local education authorities

11.79   Local education authorities are expressly empowered to discharge the following functions relating to the employment of children who are under the upper limit of compulsory school age.
(1) They may institute proceedings for any of the above offences arising under Part II of the Children and Young Persons Act 1933 (including those incorporated by Part II of the Children and Young Persons Act 1963).[1]
(2) They have power to prohibit or restrict the employment of children when they are being employed in a manner prejudicial to their health or rendering them unfit to obtain the full benefit of the education they are receiving, and they may require the parent or employer to provide them with any necessary information.[2] Breach of the rules is an offence carrying a maximum penalty of a fine not exceeding level 1 or imprisonment for not more than one month or both.[3] A power of entry is conferred.[4] When it comes into force the Employment of Children Act 1973[5] will substitute wider but not specific powers, the main change being that the authority will be able to intervene before the child is even employed and prevent his entering into unsuitable employment. This will mean calling in advance for information from his parents and prospective employer about the intended employment.
(3) In the following circumstances leave may be given for a pupil to be absent from school during school hours to enable him to undertake employment (paid or unpaid):[6]

(i)   to participate in a performance on the authority of a licence granted under section 37 of the Children and Young Persons Act 1963;
(ii)   to take up employment abroad under a licence granted by virtue of section 25 of the Children and Young Persons Act 1933;[7]
(iii)   to take up employment in accordance with the Education (Work Experience) Act 1973.

---

1   CYPA 1933, s 98. They may also institute proceedings in respect of an offence under Part II which relates to a young person who is still a pupil at school.
2   EA 1944, s 59(1) and (2).
3   Ibid, s 59(3) (as amended by CJA 1982, ss 35, 38(4) and 46). Yet another variation on the penalty theme; see ante, para 11.76.
4   EA 1944, s 59(4); and see ante, para 11.76.
5   Section 2.
6   Education (Schools and Further Education) Regulations 1981, reg 11.
7   Leave would similarly be needed for a young person to be absent.

11.80   The Education (Work Experience) Act 1973 enables local education authorities to arrange for children in their last year of compulsory schooling to have work experience as part of their education.[1] The statutory provisions prohibiting and regulating the employment of children do not apply during this last year if the education authority has made the necessary arrangements, but no arrangements can be made for employment of the child which would be contrary to (1) any enactment which applies to the employment of persons under a specified age, (2) to the provisions regulating the employment of children on ships,[2] or (3) to any provision prohibiting or regulating the employment of young persons.[3]

1   See s 1.
2   See ante, para 11.70.
3   The child is to be treated as if he were a young person.

V   EMPLOYMENT OF YOUNG PERSONS

11.81   A mass of varied legislation governs the employment of young persons, especially the maximum number of hours they may work. The protection is given to those over compulsory school age but under 18. The Employment of Women, Young Persons and Children Act 1920 markedly restricts the employment of young persons in industrial undertakings at night and the Young Persons (Employment) Acts 1938 and 1964 limit the number of hours they may work in a number of specified occupations, most of which relate to delivery of goods and running of errands.[1] The latter Acts confusingly distinguish between young persons under 16 and those over that age — confusingly because of the meaning of children in relation to employment.[2] The same distinction is made by the Factories Act 1961 (Part VI) and by the Shops Act 1950 for the purpose of controlling hours of employment in factories and shops. Thus, as already noted,[3] persons under 16 are prohibited from working below ground in a mine or quarry, and there are restrictions on employment of all young persons above ground.[4] Those under 17 may not engage or be employed in street trading,[5] except that bye-laws may permit a young person under that age to be employed by his parents.[6] Bye-laws may also be made regulating or prohibiting street trading by persons under 18, which, by virtue of the previously stated rule, means that to engage or be employed (otherwise than by a parent under a bye-law) in street trading a person must be at least 17.[7] However, these provisions do not affect the right to employ young persons or children under the maximum school age limit at established places where it is customary to carry on a retail trade or business, for example, in an open air market.[8]

1   The provisions in the list relating to young persons employed on board ship are replaced by the Merchant Shipping Act 1970, s 57.
2   See ante, para 11.69.
3   Ante, para 11.70.
4   Mines and Quarries Act 1954, Part VIII.
5   See *Morgan v Parr* [1921] 2 KB 379, [1921] All ER Rep 579, DC (selling newspapers in street); *Sweet v Williams* (1922) 128 LT 379, DC; *Newman v Lipman* [1951] 1 KB 333, [1950] 2 All ER 832, DC.
6   CYPA 1933, s 20(1), as amended by CYPA 1963, s 35. The maximum penalty for unlawful employment is a fine not exceeding level 3 (s 21(1)); but see ante, para 11.78 for the defence available to an employer.
7   CYPA 1933, s 20(2) and the maximum penalty is a fine not exceeding level 1 (s 21(3)).
8   CYPA 1963, s 35(2); but compare *Vann v Eatough* [1935] All ER Rep 911, 154 LT 109, DC.

Conclusion

11.82   The preceding paragraphs have done no more than outline, or refer to, the main enactments regulating the employment of minors. Many of them are still to be found in outdated legislation, and, as in so many other areas, this aspect of child law has appeared piecemeal and with spasmodic amendments, some of which have yet to be implemented. An overhaul is long overdue.[1] As a prelude to consolidating legislation there is need to remove many anomalies, particularly in relation to the age of children and young persons now that the compulsory school leaving age is 16, and to rationalise and provide a greater degree of conformity in the penalties for offences. Most immediate, however, is the need to strengthen enforcement of the present laws, for example, by a more effective system of factory inspection. There is firm evidence of blatant breaches of the law.[2]

1 A comprehensive survey, has not proved attractive to the authors of leading treatises on employment law.
2 A Sunday Times newspaper investigation (April 1987) revealed abuse of employment of children under 13 in makeshift shoe factories, and an Observer newspaper investigation (August 1987) disclosed widespread illegalities in employment during summer holidays, with an estimated million under-age children involved.

CHAPTER 12
Juvenile offenders

I ORIGIN AND DEVELOPMENT OF SEPARATE JURISDICTION[1]

12.01   In spite of the centuries-old jurisdiction of justices of the peace over juvenile offenders, a system of separate courts exercising that jurisdiction dates only from 1908. This comparative modernity of the juvenile court is partly explained by the fact that individual philanthropists and voluntary organisations of the eighteenth and nineteenth centuries were, rightly, directing their main energies to securing reform of the substantive law relating to the care and protection of children and to the treatment of convicted juvenile offenders. For them the establishment of a distinctly constituted tribunal to deal with the young was not a priority, although some recognised the moral dangers arising from juvenile offenders having to associate with hardened criminals while they were awaiting trial.

1 See Parsloe, *Juvenile Justice in Britain and the United States*, Chapter 5.

12.02   However, the main reason for the late appearance of the court was the persistent belief that the improvement of the administration of the criminal law with respect to juvenile offenders lay, not in the establishment of a separate process of trial, but merely in the enlargement of the summary jurisdiction of the justices. Some expansion of that jurisdiction, over adult and juvenile offenders alike, had taken place in the eighteenth century, but in 1800 there were still many offences which were triable only on indictment even though they were of a minor nature, petty larceny being the most common. Henry Fielding, who had been Chief Magistrate of Bow Street (1748–54) had advocated a simpler process of trial in cases of petty theft, and in 1819 the Select Committee on Criminal Laws made a similar recommendation, a proposal which 'doubtless . . . had juvenile offenders particularly in mind'.[1] But it was the Commissioners on the Criminal Law, who, in 1836, came down firmly against the idea of a distinction being drawn in the mode of trial of adult and of juvenile offenders, and were content to see the summary jurisdiction over juvenile offenders extended.[2] This opinion prevailed. Following the recommendations of a Select Committee of the House of Lords, an Act of 1847 provided that offenders under the age of 14 years who were charged with petty larceny could be tried summarily by two justices, who could discharge the accused if they thought it expedient not to inflict any punishment.[3] The Act was replaced by the much wider provisions of the Summary Jurisdiction Act 1879, which distinguished between children, ie persons under 12 years, and young persons, ie those who were at least 12 but under 16.[4] It provided that the former could be dealt with summarily when charged with any indictable offence other than homicide if the court thought it expedient and providing that the parent or guardian did not object. Young persons charged with certain indictable offences (mainly stealing or receiving stolen goods) could be tried summarily if they consented and the court thought it expedient.[5] This distinction was later widened and to some extent remains a feature of the present law.[6]

1 Radzinowicz, *A History of English Criminal Law*, Vol I, p 551, note 85; and on the history of juvenile offenders generally see Radzinowicz and Hood, *A History of English Criminal Law*, Vol 5, Chapters 6, 7 and 19.
2 Third Report from the Commissioners on Criminal Law, British Sessional Papers (1836) [79] xxxi, p 1.
3 10 and 11 Vict, c 82, s 1.
4 42 and 43 Vict, c 49, s 49.
5 Ibid, ss 10 and 11.
6 See post, para 12.14.

12.03 It was only when this extended jurisdiction was well established that attention was really turned to the problem of minimising contact between juvenile and adult criminals pending trial by the establishment of separate courts for dealing with the former. The suggestion that there should be separate courts seems to have been first put forward much earlier by Sir Eardley Wilmot, a Warwickshire justice of the peace,[1] when Sir Robert Peel was preparing his programme of reform of the criminal law and penal administration. His proposal was that there should be special courts each consisting of two justices to deal with young offenders. It is noteworthy that just about the same time, in 1828, Joseph Parkes, a leading advocate of reform of the Court of Chancery, published his *History of the Court of Chancery* in which he recommended[2] a separate court to exercise wardship and guardianship over infants. But these were lone voices, and it seems that it was not until some fifty years later that the idea of separate courts was again seriously canvassed, when Benjamin Waugh in his book, *The Gaol Cradle*, published in 1873, advocated it. Eventually at the turn of the century courts in some cities, probably influenced by the practice which had already obtained for some years in some of the States of America,[3] began to arrange special sittings to hear juvenile cases, and this procedure soon received legislative approval when the Children Act 1908[4] provided that a court of summary jurisdiction, when dealing with persons under 16, must sit in a different building or room or on a different day or at a different time from the ordinary sittings of that court.

1 In *A Letter to the Magistrates of England on the Increase of Crime: and An Efficient Remedy Suggested for their Consideration* (2nd edn, 1827); see Radzinowicz, op cit, Vol 1, p 571, note 12, who describes this and other proposals of Wilmot as 'remarkably progressive suggestions'.
2 At pp 402–404.
3 Orphan courts had long existed in some States; Parkes, supra, referred to them. Still, it was not until 1898, in Illinois, that the first specialised court to deal with juvenile offenders was established.
4 Section 111(1).

12.04 Significant though this provision was in establishing a separate court to deal with juveniles, it simply provided for the separate venue of the court, and nothing was done to prescribe rules for its constitution. The Royal Commission on the Selection of Justices of the Peace, which reported in 1910,[1] was silent on the matter, partly, it would seem, because there must have been some doubt about whether the composition of juvenile courts was within its terms of reference,[2] and partly because the new system had been in existence for too short a time to evoke criticism. It is likely that some juvenile courts followed the practice which had been adopted in the experimental courts[3] existing at the date of the Act, notably in the court in Birmingham. The practice was to call on particular justices to sit in rotation in the court. The first step to lay down statutory rules was taken with regard to the metropolitan area of London when the Juvenile Courts (Metropolis) Act 1920 required each juvenile court in the area to consist of a metropolitan stipendiary magistrate, who was to preside, and two lay justices, one of whom was to be a woman and both of whom were to be chosen from a panel of justices nominated by the Home Secretary. Nothing was done about the rest of the country until the Children and Young Persons Act 1933, accepting the recommendations of the Departmental Committee on the Treatment of Young Offenders,[4] introduced a system of selecting for juvenile court work those justices who were specially qualified for it. The system remains basically unaltered.

1 Cmnd 5250.
2 The Commission was asked 'to consider and report whether any and what steps should be taken to facilitate the selection of the most suitable persons to be Justices of the Peace, irrespective of creed and political opinion'.
3 Supra.
4 (1927) Cmnd 2831, pp 26–28.

II   CRIMINAL JURISDICTION

1   The criminal responsibility of children

(a)   Minimum age

12.05 From the fourteenth century, if not earlier, the common law gradually accepted the principle that children of tender years should not be the subject of criminal liability. Initially no minimum age was prescribed, but eventually it was established at seven years. The precise origin of this fixed rule has not been traced, but Hale stated it to be the law,[1] and it was not subsequently questioned. It remained unaltered until the Children and Young Persons Act 1933[2] raised the age to eight, and then the Children and Young Persons Act 1963[3] to its present minimum of ten. Though a rule of substantive law, it is one of those which are unhappily described in the form of irrebuttable presumptions.[4] One of its consequences is that a child under ten who commits an act which in an older person would constitute an offence can be brought before the juvenile court only by way of care proceedings.[5] If criminal proceedings are mistakenly instituted, any order therein is invalid. Another consequence is that anyone who arrests a child under ten for what in a person over that age would be an alleged arrestable offence (as defined by the Police and Criminal Evidence Act 1984, section 24) may render himself liable to an action by the child for false imprisonment.[6] On the other hand, anyone who receives goods from a child under that age, knowing that he took them in circumstances which would have amounted to theft by an older person, cannot himself be convicted of receiving stolen goods.[7]

1 1 PC, 27–28.
2 Section 50.
3 Section 16(1).
4 Section 50, as amended by s 16, states: 'It shall be conclusively presumed that no child under the age of ten years can be guilty of any offence.'
5 For care proceedings see post, Chapter 14.
6 *Marsh v Loader* (1863) 14 CBNS 535. Damages are not likely to be more than nominal, but this is not necessarily so. In *March v Loader* the court declined to upset a jury's award of £20 damages.
7 *Walters v Lunt* [1951] 2 All ER 645.

(b) Presumption of innocence or incapacity

12.06 It was also accepted by the common law that a rebuttable presumption of innocence or (as it is sometimes described) incapacity applied in respect of children aged between 7 and 14.[1] Subject to the statutory increase of the minimum age this presumption still operates. A child over ten but under 14 is in law not capable of committing a crime unless it is proved that at the time of the act he knew that it was wrong.[2] But, in addition to proof of that knowledge, it must, of course, be shown that the child had the necessary mental element for the crime in question.[3] The point tends to be overlooked when stating the presumption, but is particularly relevant in cases of homicide, where, in a charge of murder, it may be difficult because of the child's age to prove an intention to kill or to cause serious bodily harm. He may, for example, know that it is wrong to use violence on another, but he may not be expected, in the absence of further evidence, to appreciate that for all practical purposes his actions would inevitably result in death or serious injury.[4]

1 Here, too, the upper age limit was not firmly laid down until the seventeenth century when Hale (1 PC, 22 et seq) following Coke (Littleton, 405, para 247 b) accepted 14 as the 'age of discretion'.
2 The presumption has been stated in this form since the first half of the nineteenth century (*R v Owen* (1830) 4 C & P 236; *R v Manley* (1844) 1 Cox CC 104; *R v Smith* (1845) 5 LTOS 393); but it is also commonly described in the terms that the child is presumed to be *doli incapax*. This latter form of stating it has been criticised on the ground that the child may act with a mental state involving *dolus* (fraud or intention) without necessarily knowing that his act is wrong; see Williams, *Criminal Law: The General Part*, 2nd edn, p 815, note 8, where other ways of expressing the rule are criticised because they do not necessarily import the need for knowledge of wrongness.
3 If the offence is one of strict liability, it is still apparently necessary in the case of a child to prove that he knew his act was wrong; see Howard, *Strict Responsibility*, p 192.
4 For the mental element in homicide the reader is referred to textbooks on the criminal law. See especially Williams, *Textbook of Criminal law*, 2nd edn, and Smith and Hogan, *Criminal Law* 6th edn. But particular reference now needs to be made to *R v Moloney* [1985] AC 905, [1985] 1 All ER 1025, HL; *R v Hancock* [1986] 1 All ER 641, [1986] 2 WLR 357, HL; and *R v Nedrick* [1986] 3 All ER 1, [1986] 1 WLR 1025, CA.

12.07 The presumption is undoubtedly anachronistic,[1] its scope uncertain and its application variable.[2] In the juvenile courts it is often given little attention; indeed, probably in the majority of courts. Its operation is, however, usually significant in the case of the child who, because he is charged with homicide or because he has been committed for trial jointly with an adult charged with an indictable offence,[3] is being tried by a jury.

Doubts still exist about the nature of the knowledge needed to rebut the presumption, and the pronouncements of the Divisional Court in *J M H v Runeckles*[4] have increased rather than settled them. There it was established that it must be shown that the child appreciated that what he was doing was something 'seriously wrong', 'something beyond mere naughtiness or childish mischief', and that what was morally wrong was merely a species of what was seriously wrong.[5] The decision offers no guidance on the relevance of the test of serious wrongness to cases of knowledge of legal wrongness,[6] but the widely held view among commentators, particularly since the decision in *R v Windle*,[7] has been that the child's knowledge that his act was legally wrong, that it would excite the attention of a policeman is a sufficient rebuttal, even though there was no knowledge that the act was morally wrong. So, a ten-year-old-boy who takes food from a store while looking over his shoulder for any store detective, but who does so because he believes that he is morally justified in so acting in order to provide the necessities of life for his widowed mother, will be held to be guilty. The motive for his conduct would, however, be highly relevant in considering the appropriate order to make in respect of him.[8] Leaving aside legal wrongness, it is the reference in *J M H v Runeckles* to moral wrongness being only one type of serious wrongness that is most perplexing, for it is difficult to visualise in the present context any kind of wrongness other than moral, in the sense of a child's ability to 'discern between good and evil'.[9] The test of serious wrongness should go to the extent of wrongness required not to its nature. Being naughty or mischievous is strictly morally wrong, but it falls far short of satisfying the test. That, it is submitted, is how *Runeckles* should be understood.

1 '. . . in these days of universal education from the age of five it seems ridiculous that evidence of some mischievous discretion should be required if a case of malicious damage is committed . . .' per Forbes J in *J B H and J H (Minors) v O'Connell* [1981] Crim LR 632, DC.

2 For its history see Kean, 53 LQR 364. Stephen, *History of the Criminal Law of England*, ii, 98, did not take kindly to it: 'the rule is practically inoperative, or at all events operates seldom and capriciously'. One of its main modern critics has been Glanville Williams; see *Criminal Law: The General Part*, 2nd edn, pp 814–821; [1954] Crim LR 493; *Textbook of Criminal Law*, 2nd edn, p 639.

3 See post, para 12.15.

4 (1984) 79 Cr App Rep 255.

5 Ibid, per Mann J at 259 and 499 respectively. The principle was applied in *IPH v Chief Constable of South Wales* [1987] Crim LR 42, DC. In *R v Gorrie* (1918) 83 JP 136 Salter J had formulated a similar test of 'gravely wrong, seriously wrong'.

6 Williams would deny the relevance on the ground that a child can scarcely be expected to distinguish crimes according to their seriousness. 'The most he knows of the law is whether the policeman will or will not take him to court for it.' See [1954] Crim LR 493 at 494.

7 [1952] 2 QB 826, [1952] 2 All ER 1, CCA. The case established the rule that, for the purpose of the M'Naghten rules as a defence to a criminal charge, 'wrong' means legal wrong.

8 A police caution would be likely to be the more appropriate step in these circumstances, or possibly care proceedings based on the offence condition; see post, para 14.19.

9 Hale, 1 PC 26. Similarly, Plowden, I 19n (f) and Blackstone, *Commentaries*, iv, 23.

12.08   The onus is on the prosecution to rebut the presumption, and the ordinary criminal burden of proof applies.[1] If the defence is properly alert to the presumption, the onus can be a heavy one, and it has justifiably been suggested that the burden should be on the defence to prove lack of 'mischievous discretion'.[2] As the law stands, mere proof that the child committed the act is obviously not enough.[3] Evidence must be adduced to establish (1) the requisite knowledge of wrongness, and (2) that the child was of normal mental capacity.[4] Nevertheless, in practice there is considerable variation in the kind and amount of evidence needed to establish the requisite knowledge.[5] A plea of guilty by the child may be, and often is, held to be sufficient to rebut the presumption.[6] So, too, may be the evidence of a police officer that the child admitted the offence under interrogation.[7] The child's conduct immediately before and after the alleged act may also be highly relevant. Some of these aspects are well illustrated by *J M H v Runeckles*.[8] D, aged 13, stabbed another girl, X, with a broken bottle, and was charged with assault occasioning actual bodily harm. It was held that the presumption was rebutted by (1) D's coherent statement, which was made under caution and in her mother's presence shortly after her arrest and which was remarkably similar to X's account; (2) D's handwriting, which was commensurate with the ability of an average girl of her age; (3) D's actions, including following X home, knocking on and threatening to break the door, taunting and hitting X several times before the stabbing and then running away; and (4) her running away from police officers and admitting that she thought they were looking for her. Clearly, there was strong evidence of knowledge of both moral wrongness and legal wrongness.

1 *J M H v Runeckles*, supra.
2 *JBH and JH (Minors) v O'Connell* [1981] Crim LR 632, DC, and comment thereon.
3 *R v Kershaw* (1902) 18 TLR 357.
4 *JBH and JH (Minors) v O'Connell*, supra. Quaere the extent to which this second requirement is strictly observed.
5 On the practical difficulty of attributing to a child knowledge of wrongness see Cavenagh, *Juvenile Courts, the Child and the Law*, pp 149–152. Obviously, the younger he is the greater the difficulty.
6 *R v Thomas* (1947) 111 JP 669.
7 *W (an infant) v Simpson* [1967] Crim LR 360.
8 Supra.

12.09 Another form of evidence, though controversial, which the court is ready to admit is that of the child's home background. In *B v R*[1] evidence that a boy, aged just under nine, came from a respectable family, had been properly brought up and was well behaved was held sufficient to prove that he knew that house-breaking and theft were wrong. In *F v Padwick*[2] the Divisional Court went further by emphasising the general desirability of admitting evidence of the child's home background 'and all his circumstances',[3] even at the risk of disclosing information highly prejudicial to him; and in *R v B, R v A*[4] the Court of Appeal applied and extended this principle so as to allow in evidence of the child's previous findings of guilt. Wide though this discretion is, it does not, it is submitted, allow the admission of every previous finding of guilt. Even though the test is whether such evidence is relevant to the issue of the child's capacity to know good from evil, it would have to be shown that the earlier finding was in respect of the same or similar kind of conduct as that now alleged, and even then the evidence would have to comply with the general rules concerning the admissibility of similar fact evidence.[5] It is arguable that similar principles may be extended to previous police cautions. These considerations are relevant when the question of admissibility of evidence of family and other circumstances relates to the rebuttal of the presumption of innocence, but they do not affect the admissibility of such evidence in care proceedings to prove the need for care or control[6] or in those proceedings or criminal proceedings to assist the court in deciding how it is going to deal with the juvenile.

1 (1958) 123 JP 61, 44 Cr App Rep 1, sub nom *X v X* [1958] Crim LR 805. This case was, of course, decided when the minimum age of criminal responsibility was eight.
2 [1959] Crim LR 439.
3 But the demeanour of the child and his parent in court, if it is a matter of evidence, which is doubtful, is of very little weight in rebutting the presumption; see *ex p N* [1959] Crim LR 523.
4 [1979] 3 All ER 460, [1979] 1 WLR 1185, CA.
5 For those rules see treatises on the law of evidence.
6 See post, para 14.22.

(c)   Sexual offences

12.10   A boy under the age of 14 cannot be found guilty of committing rape[1] or of offences involving sexual intercourse.[2] In spite of the fact that this rule rests on the principle of physical impossibility, no evidence is admissible to prove that the particular boy had attained puberty before the age of 14[3] and that the act did take place.[4] This irrebuttable rule is in marked contrast to that of the civil law where, in proceedings relating to paternity, a boy under that age can be found to be the father of a child.[5] Small wonder that the Criminal Law Revision Committee has recommended the abolition of the common law rule.[6] Its intrinsic artificiality also makes it uncertain whether a boy under 14 can be held guilty of an attempt to commit any of the above offences.[7] It seems that the Criminal Attempts Act 1981, even as interpreted in *R v Shivpuri*,[8] does not render him liable. Section 1(1) only applies to an offence which, if completed, would be triable as an indictable offence. Since as a matter of law rape by a boy under 14 would not be so triable, attempted rape by him is not within the section. However, the boy can be convicted of indecent assault[9] or common assault,[10] and, while these two offences are less serious than some of the above from the point of view of punishment of an adult offender, the distinction is of minimal significance in relation to the boy under 14. It may be relevant to any future record of his previous convictions,[11] but otherwise it would not matter whether he was charged with, for example, rape, if that were possible, or with indecent assault. If he could be charged with the former, it would still be the juvenile court who heard the case and their powers of dealing with him would be the same as if he were found guilty of assault.

1 *R v Groombridge* (1836) 7 C&P 582; *R v Brimilow* (1840) 2 Mood CC 122.
2 For example, unlawful sexual intercourse with a girl under 13; *R v Jordan and Cowmeadow* (1839) 9 C&P 118; *R v Waite* [1892] 2 QB 600, CCR. So far as it concerns rape the rule is an old one; see Hale 1 PC 630.
3 *R v Jordan and Cowmeadow*, supra; *R v Philips* (1839) 8 C&P 736.
4 Cf *R v Brimlow*, supra, where the report speaks of the 'commission of the act [being] proved'.
5 *L v K* [1985] Fam 144, [1985] 1 All ER 961, DC, (affiliation proceedings).
6 *Report on Sexual Offences* Cmnd 9213, para 2.48.
7 See the conflicting dicta in *R v Williams* [1893] 1 QB 320, CCR.

8 [1987] AC 1, [1986] 2 All ER 334, HL. But see Smith and Hogan, op cit, p 438.
9 *R v Williams*, supra.
10 *R v Philips*, supra; *R v Brimilow*, supra.
11 Even in this respect its importance is much diminished by CYPA 1963, s 16(2), which
provides that, in any criminal proceedings against a person over the age of 21, any offence
of which he was found guilty while under 14 is to be disregarded for the purposes of
any evidence relating to his previous convictions, and he cannot be asked or compelled
to answer any question relating to such an offence. The finding of guilt of that offence
should be included in the proof of evidence of the police officer when in the later proceedings
he gives evidence of the offender's antecedents; but the finding must not be included
in the factual statement of previous convictions and findings of guilt which is attached
to the proof of evidence; see *Practice Direction* [1966] 2 All ER 929, [1966] 1 WLR 1184
CCA.

12.11   There is, however, nothing in the above rules to prevent a boy
under 14 from being found guilty as an aider and abetter if he assists
another to commit rape[1] or, semble, any of the other offences which he
himself cannot in law commit.

[1]   *R v Eldershaw* (1828) 3 C&P 396 [obiter]; cf *R v Ram and Ram* (1893) 17 Cox CC 609,
[a woman can be convicted of abetting rape].

12.12   How far he can be liable for buggery is by no means clear. It is
commonly stated that he cannot, either as agent or patient. There is no
direct authority for the view that he cannot be liable as an agent, but
his exemption is usually said to rest on the same conclusive presumption
of physical incapacity as exempts him from liability for rape and other
offences involving unlawful sexual intercourse.[1] As for non-liability where
he is the patient, the Court of Criminal Appeal in *R v Tatam*[2] had no
doubt that 'he was unable at law to commit [the] offence', but offered
no reason for its conclusion. There is a conflict of authority and opinion[3]
as to whether he can abet buggery. The point arose in *Tatam* and in *R
v Cratchley*[4] in relation to the question of the need for corroboration of
the boy's evidence. In *Cratchley* a ten-year-old boy was told to keep a
look-out while the accused, an adult, committed buggery upon a 13-year-
old boy. The Court of Criminal Appeal held that he was not an accomplice
but this was on the ground that there was no evidence of his having guilty
knowledge, and it is clear that it recognised that, with such evidence, he
could have been liable. But in *Tatam* the Court held that three boys under
14 were not accomplices to buggery committed upon themselves. These
cases must either be regarded as in conflict or distinguishable on the ground
that in the one the patient was a third person and in the other the boys
themselves.[5] It can at least be said in favour of *Cratchley* that it is logically
consistent with the rule relating to rape that a boy under 14 can abet that
offence even though he cannot in law himself commit it. On the other
hand, although current opinion increasingly recognises that protection of
the child should be a basic feature of the law, it is not possible to explain
Tatam on the ground that, in relation to the young boy, the sole object
of the law relating to buggery is to protect him and not to render him
criminally liable for offences commited upon himself.[6] There is no such
suggestion in the judgment, which was based simply on the principle that
since the boy cannot commit the offence he cannot be an accomplice. It
seems that his total exemption from liability as a patient has arisen from
a misinterpretation of what was written by Coke, Hale and East on the

subject.[7] All that they seem to have said is that there was no liability without proof of mischievous discretion: in other words, that the normal presumption of innocence should operate if the boy was between the minimum age of criminal responsibility and 14.

But the question arises: even as the law stands, need the juvenile court really concern itself with these uncertainties and niceties of distinction? It clearly need not, because, as will be seen,[8] its care jurisdiction, apart from that part of it which is based on the offence condition, is sufficiently comprehensive to include all cases where a child has been a party to an act of buggery, whether as agent or patient or look-out.

1 But if he in fact performs the act and the pathic is an adult, the latter can be convicted; *R v Allen* (1849) 1 Den 364.
2 (1921) 15 Crim App Rep 132.
3 Cf Hogan, [1962] Crim LR 683, and Glanville Williams, [1964] Crim LR 686.
4 (1913) 9 Crim App Rep 232.
5 But the distinction is tenable only if it is assumed that in *Tatam* none of the boys abetted the buggery of another; see Smith and Hogan, op cit, p 473 note 8.
6 Cf the rule which prevents a girl under 16 who consents to a male having unlawful sexual intercourse with her from being liable for abetting or inciting the particular sexual offence because the statute (formerly the Criminal Law Amendment Act 1885, s 5, now the Sexual Offences Act 1956, s 6) is designed to protect her from such conduct; see *R v Tyrrell* [1894] 1 QB 710 (CCR), [1891–4] All ER Rep 1215.
7 See respectively 3 Inst 59; 1 PC 670 and 1 PC 480, and see Smith and Hogan, op cit, pp 472–473.
8 Post, Chapter 14.

2   The scope of the criminal jurisdiction

(a)   Introduction

12.13 Since the creation of the juvenile court it has, with two slight qualifications,[1] been consistently recognised that adult[2] offenders are to be excluded from its jurisdiction;[3] but the principle that that court alone should deal with juveniles has required some modification, mainly in order to meet the case where a juvenile and adult are jointly involved in the commission of an offence but, at one time, partly because of an unwillingness to abolish the young person's right of election to trial by jury. In practice that right was seldom exercised; when it was, it was usually on the advice of a parent or solicitor. It was therefore represented to the Ingleby Committee that the right should be abolished as it had been in respect of children by the Children and Young Person Act 1933,[4] but the Committee, while acknowledging that abolition would not cause great hardship, thought it would have little effect.[5] The principal argument in favour of abolition was that by retaining the right the young person would be deprived of the specially qualified experience which the juvenile court had in dealing with persons of that age, but against that it was argued that the principle of exclusive jurisdiction over young persons had in any event been qualified where there were joint charges and there seemed no overriding reason why a fundamental right like that of election for jury trial should not also be a recognised exception, particularly in view of the power of an adult court which finds a juvenile guilty to remit him to the juvenile court to be dealt with by that court.[6] The former view finally prevailed in the Children and Young Persons Act 1969.

1 CYPA 1933, s 48(1) and (2), post, paras 12.30 and 13.11.
2 For the purpose of the juvenile court the term 'adult' is here used to mean a person who has attained the age of 17 years.
3 While generally approving this exclusion, the Ingleby Committee was prepared to allow an exception to enable the court to deal with an adult who failed to secure his child's attendance at school; see Cmnd 1191, para 181.
4 Following the recommendations of the Departmental Committee on the Treatment of Young Offenders, Cmnd 2831, pp 30–31.
5 Cmnd 1191, para 239.
6 See post, para 12.20 and note there the effect of CJA 1982 on the power to remit.

(b)   The general rule

12.14   Leaving aside for the moment cases of joint charges, every child must be tried summarily by the juvenile court for all offences, summary and indictable,[1] other than homicide for which he must always be committed for trial. Jurisdiction over summary offences rests on the fact that that court is by definition a court of summary jurisdiction.[2] That over indictable offences is conferred by the Magistrates' Courts Act 1980.[3] The same rules apply to a young person,[4] except that, if he is charged with a grave indictable offence of the kind which, if he were convicted of it, would render him liable to be sentenced to be detained for a long period,[5] he must be committed for trial, provided that the juvenile court considers (1) that, if he is found guilty, it ought to be possible so to sentence him, and (2) that either there is sufficient evidence, under section 1 of the 1980 Act, to put him on trial or the court has power, under section 6(2), to commit him without consideration of the evidence.[6] The second proviso is a preliminary matter, where the court is deciding whether summary trial or committal for trial on indictment is appropriate. That preliminary stage does not oblige the court to consider all the evidence in the sense that it would have to when deciding whether or not there is sufficient evidence to put the accused on trial. It must, however, at that stage consider all the circumstances[7] and listen to representations by the prosecutor and the juvenile or his representative, including representations that he is of good character. If the court decides that committal for trial is appropriate the juvenile then has the option of either consenting to committal under section 6(2) or placing the onus on the prosecution of adducing the requisite evidence under section 6(1). If he chooses the latter, he will then have the opportunity[8] to make submissions to the justices reviewing in effect their preliminary decision to send the matter for trial and inviting them to retain it in the juvenile court.[9] Should the court, however, decide that summary trial and not committal is appropriate[10] but adjourn the hearing before a plea has been taken, it is not open to a differently constituted court at the adjourned hearing to review the mode of trial, unless there has been a change of circumstances (for example, the commission of further offences while on bail) *and* those circumstances are taken into account at the adjourned hearing.[11] If a plea has been taken, there is no possibility of such a review.[12]

1 In an offence which, if committed by an adult, is triable on indictment, whether exclusively so triable or triable either way; see Interpretation Act 1978, s 5 and Sch 1.
2 CYPA 1933, s 45; and see s 46(1), infra.
3 Section 24(1), replacing CYPA 1969, s 6(1).
4 Ibid.
5 Under CYPA 1933, s 53(2); see post, para 13.98.
6 Ie where all the evidence tendered consists of written statements.

7 See MCA 1980, s 19(3).
8 In accordance with MCA 1980, s 25(7).
9 *R v South Hackney Juvenile Court, ex p RB (a minor) and CB (a minor)* (1983) 77 Crim
  App Rep 294.
10 See note 3, supra.
11 *R v Newham Juvenile Court, ex p F* [1986] 3 All ER 17, [1986] 1 WLR 939, DC.
12 *R v Hammersmith Juvenile Court, ex p O* [1987] Crim LR 639, DC.

(c)   Joint charges

12.15   Where a juvenile is charged jointly with an adult[1] and the offence
charged is an indictable one, other than homicide, the magistrates' court
must, if it considers (1) that it is necessary in the interests of justice,[2] and
(2) that either there is sufficient evidence to commit the juvenile for trial
or it has power to commit him for trial without consideration of the evidence,[3]
commit them both for trial.[4] In practice it is often the case that the adult
is no more than 17 years of age, for example, where an offence is committed
by a gang of youths, some of whom are still in school, the others recent
school leavers.

1 In *R v Newham Justices, ex p Knight* [1976] Crim LR 323 the rule was liberally construed
  to cover the case of a mother and child who had been involved in the same incident
  of stealing but who had in fact been separately charged with theft. For the meaning of
  adult in the present context see ante, para 12.13, note 2.
2 In considering this necessity the court should take account of the juvenile's age and that
  trial by jury may be an ordeal for him; see *R v Newham Justices, ex p Knight*, supra.
3 Ie under MCA 1980, s 6(2), supra.
4 MCA 1980, s 24(1). Where the offence is homicide both must be committed if there is
  prima facie evidence. When deciding whether to commit a juvenile for trial to the Crown
  Court jointly with an adult both juvenile and adult must appear at the same time. However,
  that decision having been made, it is not necessary for both to appear at the same time
  when considering the adequacy of the evidence against each; see *R v Doncaster Crown
  Court, ex p Crown Prosecution Service* (1986) 151 JP 167, 85 Cr App Rep 1.

12.16   A juvenile who is jointly so charged and committed may also be
committed for trial for any other indictable offence with which he is charged
at the same time (whether jointly with the adult or not), if the other offence
arises out of circumstances which are the same as or connected with those
giving rise to the joint offence.[1] However, the Magistrates' Courts Act 1980
does not cover the case of a child who allegedly commits with a young
person a grave offence of the kind which, if the young person had alone
committed it, would have led to his being committed for trial.[2] Apparently,
in such a case there cannot be a joint charge, and the child will have to
be dealt with separately in the juvenile court. It seems strange that a child
may be jointly committed for trial with a 17-year-old, but not with a 16-
year-old, even though the offence committed in the latter case may be
very much more serious than the one committed with the adult.

1 MCA 1980, s 24(2).
2 See supra, para 12.14.

12.17   Section 46(1) of the Children and Young Persons Act 1933 establishes
the general principle that the criminal jurisdiction over juvenile offenders
is to be exercised by a juvenile court and not by any other magistrates'
court, but the following exceptions to this principle are admitted so as

to enable an adult court to hear the charge. These exceptions[1] occur where the juvenile is involved with an adult in the same or an allied offence. They are designed to keep the adult offender out of the juvenile court, but at the same time normally to avoid separate trials.

1 For two further exceptions to the general principle of s 46(1) see post, paras 12.21 and 12.33.

12.18 First, there is the apparently mandatory rule that a charge made jointly against a juvenile and an adult must be heard by an adult court;[1] but even this is subject to a discretion to remit to the juvenile court. Should the adult plead guilty and the juvenile not guilty, the latter may be remitted for trial to a juvenile court acting for the same place as the remitting adult court or for the place where he habitually resides.[2] An order for remission may similarly be made where the adult court, proceeding as examining justices, commits the adult for trial or discharges him and proceeds to the summary trial of the juvenile, who is pleading not guilty.[3] The juvenile has no right to appeal against the order of remission, and the remitting court can remand him in custody or release him on bail until he is brought before the juvenile court.[4]

1 Paragraph (a) of the proviso to s 46(1).
2 MCA 1980, s 29(1)–(3). These rules re-enact former provisions in the Criminal Law Act 1977, s 34, which implemented a recommendation of the Interdepartmental Committee on the Distribution of Criminal Business between the Crown Court and Magistrates' Courts, (1975) Cmnd 6323.
3 MCA 1980, s 29(2).
4 Ibid, s 29(4). These rules equally apply in the rare case where a juvenile is charged with a corporation (sub-s (5)).

12.19 In each of the following circumstances the adult court has a discretion to hear a charge against a juvenile: (1) if an adult is charged at the same time with aiding or abetting the offence with which the juvenile is charged;[1] or (2) if, conversely, the charge against the juvenile is one of aiding or abetting an offence with which an adult is charged at the same time,[2] or (3) where the offence with which he is charged arises out of circumstances which are the same as or connected with those giving rise to an offence with which an adult is charged at the same time,[3] for example, in a case where there are cross summonses for assault. In these cases where there is a discretion for the adult court, instead of the juvenile court, to hear the charge against the juvenile the prosecutor should seek the court's directions through the clerk.[4]

1 Paragraph (b) of proviso to s 46(1) of CYPA 1933.
2 CYPA 1963, s 18(a).
3 Ibid, s 18(b).
4 Clarke Hall & Morrison, para B [360]

3 The power to remit juvenile offenders to juvenile courts

12.20 While the effect of these exceptions is to confer on adult courts jurisdiction over juvenile offenders,[1] the Children and Young Persons legislation does seek to ensure that normally such offenders are not deprived of the benefit of the special experience which juvenile courts have in dealing with persons like them. Apart from the discretion, just noted,[2] to remit in certain circumstances a juvenile to the juvenile court for trial where he has been jointly charged with an adult, there is the general rule[3] that, once an adult court has found a juvenile guilty of an offence,[4] it must remit him to a juvenile court 'unless satisfied that it would be undesirable to do so'. The proviso adopts a recommendation of the Ingleby Committee,[5] but gives no indication of what is to be regarded as undesirable. It must, however, now be considered against the background of the Criminal Justice Act 1982. That Act aligned the powers of the Crown Court and the juvenile courts, so that the concept of the juvenile court as the only proper forum in which juveniles could be dealt with is now out of place. In *R v Lewis*[6] the Court of Appeal listed a number of reasons why it might be undesirable for the Crown Court to remit: the trial judge might be better informed as to the facts and circumstances; where there were co-defendants there might be an unacceptable risk of disparity if they were sentenced in different courts on different occasions; remission might lead to delay, duplication of proceedings and fruitless expense; account should be taken of the differing provisions for appeals (which from the Crown Court lies to the Court of Appeal and from the juvenile court to the Crown Court). To this list might be added the possible limited experience which the appropriate juvenile court (for example, in a rural area) has in dealing with the particular type of offender. It might, on the other hand, be desirable to remit a juvenile where a report has to be obtained and the judge would be unable to sit when the report would be available, but even this situation can and should be avoided where possible by the committing justices giving direction for the preparation of reports before the trial.[7] These are all cogent reasons for not remitting, and it is suggested that, so far as concerns the Crown Court, for the present rule with its emphasis on remission there should be substituted a general discretion in that Court to remit or not remit.

1 See also Part D, post, paras 12.25 et seq.
2 Ante, para 12.18.
3 CYPA 1933, s 56(1), as amended by CYPA 1963, s 64 and Sch 3, para 14(1) and by CYPA 1969, s 72(3) and Sch 5, para 6.
4 This, of course, excludes homicide, which is entirely outside the jurisdiction of the juvenile court.
5 Cmnd 1191, para 176.
6 (1984) 79 Cr App Rep 94, [1984] Crim LR 303.
7 Ibid.

12.21   Different considerations apply to adult magistrates' courts, where those reasons are very largely irrelevant.[1] Indeed, the Children and Young Persons Act 1969 imposes a specific obligation on an adult magistrates' court to remit to a juvenile court an offender who is a juvenile or was a juvenile when the proceedings were begun.[2] The court must remit unless it considers that the case can be properly dealt with by means of an order for absolute or conditional discharge, or for payment of a fine, or for a recognisance to be entered into by the parent or guardian to take proper care of, and exercise proper control over, the juvenile.[3] Unless the offence is a minor one justifying any of these orders, the adult court should not, it is submitted, proceed to the making of any of them without the benefit of full information on the juvenile and his background and antecedents.

1 Though not wholly so. For example, there could be the risk of disparity in sentences, and, up to a point, there is duplication of proceedings.
2 Cf *R v Billericay Justices, ex p Johnson* (1979) 143 JP 697, [1979] Crim LR 315, DC, where the decision of the justices to remit was quashed because the defendant was already aged 17 when the summons was issued. For the time factor see post, paras 12.25 et seq.
3 CYPA 1969, s 7(8), as amended by the Criminal Justice Act 1972, Sch 5. Section 7(8) refers only to young persons, but the rule also applies to children aged 10 or over so long as they remain liable to criminal prosecution; see CYPA 1969 (Transitional Modifications of Part I) Order 1970, SI 1970/1882.

12.22 The case will be remitted by the Crown Court to a juvenile court acting for the place where the offender was committed for trial, or, if he was not committed, by the adult magistrates' court to a juvenile court acting either for the same place as the remitting court or for the place where he habitually resides.[1] The remitting court may remand him in custody or on bail until he is brought before the juvenile court.[2] There is no right of appeal against the order of remission,[3] but before remitting the case the court must inform the juvenile and his parent or guardian (if present) or anyone assisting him in his defence of how it proposes to deal with the case, and allow them to make representations.[4] If he is remitted, the juvenile court may then deal with him in any way in which it might have dealt with him if he had been tried and found guilty by that court, but apparently it may allow him to change an earlier plea of guilty before the remitting court to one of not guilty.[5]

1 CYPA 1933, s 56(1).
2 Section 56(3). For remands in custody see post, para 12.122.
3 CYPA 1933, s 56(2)(a), as substituted by CYPA 1969, s 64 and Sch 3, para 14(2).
4 Magistrates' Courts (Children and Young Persons) Rules 1988, r 11(1). The court need not inform the juvenile if it considers it undesirable.
5 This seems to follow from *S (an infant) v Manchester City Recorder* [1971] AC 481, [1969] 3 All ER 1230, HL, where it was held that in summary cases, as in those tried on indictment, the accused may at any time before sentence apply to change his plea and the court may allow this. The fact that two different courts are involved should not affect this principle.

12.23 The remitting court must send to the juvenile court a certificate stating the nature of the offence, the fact that the offender has been found guilty and that an order for remission has been made. That is evidence on which the juvenile court can act,[1] and there is no need to call witnesses to prove the offence, although their appearance may sometimes be desirable to assist the court in deciding how best to deal with the particular offender.

1 CYPA 1933, s 106(2)(a).

12.24 Remission from one juvenile court to another juvenile court is also permissible, but is entirely discretionary.[1] It is exceptional, but may be suitable where it is administratively convenient for the purpose of obtaining background information about the offender.

1 Section 56(1) of the 1933 Act states: 'Any court . . . may and, if it is not a juvenile court shall, unless satisfied that it would be undesirable to do so, remit the case . . . .'

4   The application of the upper age limit

(a)   The relevant date

12.25   Since the jurisdiction of the juvenile court depends upon the person, who is the subject of criminal proceedings, being below the age of 17, problems may arise where he attains the age before or during the course of the proceedings. Various provisions in the Children and Young Persons Acts and the Magistrates' Courts Act 1980 deal with this matter, and these show that no uniform date has been fixed to which attainment of that age is to relate. It has, however, been established by the House of Lords in *R v Islington North Juvenile Court, ex p Daley*[1] that, where an accused person is charged with an offence which is triable either way, summarily or on indictment,[2] the crucial date is that when he appears or is brought before the court and the court decides the mode of trial. If at that date he has attained the age of 17, then he has the right to elect trial by jury, notwithstanding the fact that he was under that age when he allegedly committed the offence and was still so when he first appeared or was brought before the juvenile court to answer the information, on which occasion the court did no more than adjourn the hearing and remand him.[3] Nor would the right to elect be lost if on that first occasion the case was listed for plea only and the accused then pleaded not guilty.[4] It would be a different matter if on that occasion the juvenile court there and then decided, in pursuance of section 24(1) of the Magistrates' Courts Act 1980,[5] to try the case summarily, but adjourned the trial date. It would not be open to the accused, who by that later date had attained the age of 17, then to elect the jury trial,[6] nor the court to commit him for trial at the Crown Court.[7] Where the *Daley* principle applies, and the accused instead of electing trial by jury consents to summary trial,[8] the justices would have to cease sitting as a juvenile court and proceed to hear the information as an adult court.

1 [1983] 1 AC 347, [1982] 2 All ER 974. The house approved the decision of the Divisional Court in *R v St Albans Juvenile Court, ex p Godman* [1981] QB 964, [1981] 2 All ER 311.
2 Such offences are listed in Sch 1 to the Magistrates' Courts Act 1980, but certain of them in the Criminal Damage Act 1971 are to be tried summarily if the damage caused is below a specified sum (MCA 1980, s 2 and Sch 2).
3 There may, of course, be further adjournments before the decision as to the mode of trial.
4 As occurred in the *St Albans* case, supra.
5 See ante, para 12.14.
6 *R v Lewes Juvenile Court, ex p Turner* (1984) 149 JP 186. In the circumstances described above the juvenile court, when deciding on summary trial at the first appearance, should record in its register 'remanded for summary trial'; see ibid McNeill J.
7 *R v Hammersmith Juvenile Court, ex p O (a minor)* (1987) 151 JP 740, [1987] Crim LR 639.
8 In accordance with MCA 1980, s 20(3).

12.26   *Daley* gives the widest protection to the right to elect jury trial by postponing the relevant date for determining jurisdiction, but it does not indicate what that date is where the offence is one triable only by way of indictment or only summarily. The problem may be considered by assuming the following facts. D is charged with an indictable offence. As a 16-year-old he appears or is brought before the juvenile court, which adjourns the hearing. When he next appears, and the court is ready to proceed, determine the mode of trial and hear the evidence, he is 17. If, *pace Daley*, the later appearance determines jurisdiction, the justices will have to proceed as examining justices and decide whether he is to be committed for trial[1]. If, on the other hand, the relevant date is the first appearance, the justices will continue to sit as a juvenile court at the second appearance and proceed to hear the case summarily, unless, in accordance with section 24(1) of the 1980 Act, they consider that the offence is a grave one which would justify a sentence under section 53(2) of the Children and Young Persons Act 1933,[2] in which case they would proceed as examining justices. Should the offence be triable only summarily, the difference between the two dates has the following consequences. If the relevant date is the later appearance, the justices would have to sit as an adult court with the powers which that court has in respect of young offenders (ie persons between 17–20), whereas, if the appropriate date is the first appearance, the court would still sit as a juvenile court at the later hearing, with its powers in respect of juvenile offenders, even though the defendant was 17.

1 Support for this view is now provided by *R v Vale of Glamorgan Juvenile Justices, ex p Beattie* (1985) 82 Cr App Rep 1, DC, (a case of robbery) where it was held that the material date for determining the mode of trial is when the defendant appears and the charge is put to him and the proceedings are ready to commence.
2 See ante, para 12.14 and post, para 13.98.

12.27 Support for the conclusion that the correct date for determining jurisdiction, other than where the offence is triable either way, should be that of first appearance may possibly be derived from section 29(1) of the Children and Young Persons Act 1963.[1] This states:

'Where proceedings in respect of a young person are begun under section 1 of the Children and Young Persons Act 1969 or for an offence and he attains the age of seventeen before the conclusion of the proceedings, the court may deal with the case and make any order which it could have made if he had not attained that age.'

In the *St Albans* case this provision was construed[2] as applying 'only to questions of disposal and not to questions of trial'. Certainly it covers the case of the offender who is still under 17 when he is found guilty but who reaches that age during a period of adjournment ordered for reports. At the resumed hearing the juvenile court would, for example, have the power to make a care order or a supervision order, notwithstanding his age. However, as the Divisional Court made clear in *R v Amersham Juvenile Court, ex p Wilson*,[3] there are persuasive reasons for not limiting its scope to questions of disposal. Its view was thus summarised:[4]

'This section is wholly consistent with the statutory approach of classifying offenders as adult or juvenile by reference to their age when they first appear or are brought before a magistrates' court, provided that on the true construction of the section proceedings are "begun" at that time and not at the earlier time when an information is laid or a charge preferred. We have no doubt that it should be so construed, particularly bearing in mind the manner in which care proceedings are begun . . .'

The history of this section is relevant. It originally applied only to care proceedings, and these begin when the juvenile is first brought before a juvenile court.[5] The original form of words read, 'the court may continue to deal', but, when the Children and Young Persons Act 1969 extended the section to criminal proceedings,[6] the words 'continue to' were omitted. In the view of the Divisional Court that amendment suggests that the section similarly extends to criminal proceedings ab initio, ie when the juvenile first appears or is brought before the court, a conclusion strengthened by the separate reference to the power to 'deal with the case' in contradistinction to the later power to 'make any order'.

1 As amended by CYPA 1969, s 72(3) and (4) and Sch 5, para 49 and Sch 6.
2 Per Skinner J [1981] QB 964 at 969, [1981] 2 All ER 311 at 315.
3 [1981] QB 969, [1981] 2 All ER 315.
4 Per Donaldson LJ at 974 and 318 respectively.
5 See CYPA 1969, s 2(14).
6 By the addition of the words 'or for an offence'.

12.28   Relying on this construction, the Divisional Court in the *Amersham* case expressed the view obiter[1] that the date of the first appearance determined jurisdiction even if the offence was triable either way. Although the House of Lords in *Daley* rejected this approach in favour of that adopted by the Divisional Court in the *St Albans* case, it did not attempt to construe section 29.[2] Nevertheless, persuasive though the arguments may be in favour of the date of first appearance,[3] it seems in the light of the most recent decision of the Divisional Court[4] that even where the offence is not one triable either way the relevant date is that when the defendant appears and the charge is put to him and the proceedings are ready to commence.

1 Obiter, because it was in fact concerned with an offence triable only by way of indictment.
2 Lord Diplock [1983] 1 AC 347 at 361, [1982] 2 All ER 974 at 977 said: '. . . although in the *Amersham* case the Divisional Court relied on [s 29] as being consistent with the construction it placed on what is now s 24 of the Magistrates' Courts Act 1980, the Children and Young Persons Act 1969 is not the Act that your Lordships have to construe and does not, in my view, assist on its construction'. With respect, this comment overlooks the fact that s 24(1) is substantially a re-enactment of s 6(1) of the 1969 Act see ante, para 12.14, note 3.
3 See also infra, para 12.29.
4 *R v Vale of Glamorgan Juvenile Justices, ex p Beattie*, supra, para 12.26, note 1.

12.29   Further support for the date of first appearance may be derived from section 99(1) of the Children and Young Persons Act 1933, for, in laying down for both criminal and care proceedings the rules for presuming or determining whether a person is within the statutory age of a child or young person, it requires the court to presume or determine what his age is at the time when he is brought before the court. The age presumed or declared by the court is deemed to be the true age, and any order or judgment of the court is not invalidated if it is subsequently proved to be otherwise.[1]

1 In trying to decide the age the court may admit the evidence of a welfare officer; see

R v Cox [1898] 1 QB 179, [1885–9] All ER Rep 1285, CCR, where evidence of an officer of the NSPCC, a police constable and a schoolmistress was admitted and held sufficient.

(b)   Court's mistake as to age of defendant

12.30   The question of fixing the time of commencement of jurisdiction is particularly relevant in interpreting the rather vague provisions of section 48(1) of the Children and Young Persons Act 1933. This, as amended, reads:

> A juvenile court sitting for the purpose of hearing a charge against a person who is believed to be a child or young person may, if it thinks fit to do so, proceed with the hearing and determination of the charge, notwithstanding that it is discovered that the person in question is not a child or young person.

The situation apparently contemplated by this provision is one where the person has in fact attained the age of 17 when jurisdiction is first assumed but because of some mistake or misrepresentation the court initially believes that he has not and only in the course of the proceedings finds out his actual age. The effect of the subsection seems to be that on discovery of the age the court may either refer the case to an adult court of summary jurisdiction or, at its discretion, continue to hear the charge. In the latter event it seems that it must proceed as if it were now itself an adult court. It could not, therefore, make an order which is within the exclusive jurisdiction of a juvenile court, for example, a supervision order or care order. If, however, the discovery is not made until after the juvenile court has made an order, the validity of the order is expressly preserved by section 99(1) of the 1933 Act.

12.31   If this is the scope of section 48(1) and if the date of first appearance before the court is the date of commencement of jurisdiction, the court would not be entitled to proceed with the hearing of a charge against a person who was already 17 when the charge was preferred and whose true age is discovered by the time when he first comes before the court, even though when the charge was preferred he was believed by those preferring it to be still a young person.[1]

1 In *R v Chelsea Justices, ex p DPP* [1963] 3 All ER 657 at 658 Roskill J said: 'Further s 48(1) . . . does not, in my view, apply to a case where a defendant appears before the court on a charge preferred for the first time after his 17th birthday and which *the court then* knows to have been so preferred.' (Italics supplied). 'Then' refers to the moment of appearance and not, as the headnote to the report suggests, 'when the charge was first preferred'. Because of the special circumstances of that case the court happened to know of the age at the latter date, but in the normal case how could it possibly know of the matter at that date when it had not yet itself been convened?

12.32   The 1933 Act provides a corollary to section 48(1). Where an adult court of summary jurisdiction is dealing with a person and in the course of the proceedings it appears that he is a child or young person, the court may, nevertheless, continue the hearing instead of transferring the case to a juvenile court.[1] Its object is thus to provide for the situation where the adult court was mistaken about the person's age when it assumed jurisdiction.

1 Paragraph (c) of the proviso to s 46(1). The prosecutor should seek the court's directions
   through its clerk; see Clarke Hall & Morrison, para B [360].

12.33   In addition to those cases where there are joint charges,[1] the Children
and Young Persons Act 1969 admits a further exception to the principle
in section 46(1) of the 1933 Act that criminal jurisdiction over juveniles
must be exercised by a juvenile court. It arises where an adult court of
summary jurisdiction, mistakenly assuming that a young person is 17 years
of age or over, summons him to appear before the court and he pleads
guilty by post under the Magistrates' Court Act 1980. Any consequent
order is valid and will not be invalidated on discovery of the true age.[2]

1 Ante, paras 12.15 to 12.19.
2 CYPA 1933, s 46 (1A), as added by CYPA 1969, s 72(3) and Sch 5, para 4, and MCA
   1980, Sch 7, para 6.

III   THE INSTITUTION OF CRIMINAL PROCEEDINGS

1   The decision to institute proceedings

(a)   Persons who may bring proceedings

12.34   Any person may lay an information against a juvenile, but, if he
decides to do so, he must give notice of his decision to the appropriate
local authority, unless that authority itself is laying the information.[1] The
appropriate authority is that for the area in which the juvenile appears
to reside or, if he appears not to reside in a local authority's area, that
within whose area it is alleged that the offence was committed.[2] Moreover,
if the juvenile is aged 13 or over, the prosecutor must give notice to a
probation officer.[3]

1 CYPA 1969, s 5(8). Unless and until criminal proceedings in respect of children are abolished
   the rule applies to children aged 10 or over as to young persons; CYPA 1969 (Transitional
   Modifications of Part I) Order 1970, SI 1970/1882.
2 Section 5(9).
3 Section 34(2). The subsection requires 'the person proposing to begin the proceedings'
   to notify the probation officer. The Prosecution of Offences Act 1985 does not amend
   s 34(2), and this leaves it open whether the police who intend referring the file to the
   Crown Prosecution Service so notify or whether the Crown Prosecution should do so
   after the decision is made to prosecute.

(b)   Consultation

12.35   Co-operation on a voluntary basis resulting from close consultation
between the parents, the local authority, the police, the probation service
and the school authorities lies behind the Children and Young Persons
Act 1969, both in respect of criminal proceedings and care proceedings,
but the Act is very largely silent on how the policy is to be carried out.
The above statutory requirement that a person other than a local authority
who decides to prosecute, nearly always the police and Crown Prosecution
Service, must notify the authority of that decision ought to result in
consultation with the local authority before the decision is reached;[1] but
there is no statutory duty to consult among the agencies, especially between

the police and local authorities.[2] Instead the Home Office issued detailed guidance which it recommended agencies to follow.[3] During the 1970s the response was variable. Some of the police juvenile liaison schemes that were already operating before the 1969 Act[4] were strengthened, and in some other areas new ones created. Their success or failure has partly depended on the policy of the agencies, partly on whether or not there are sufficient personnel (both in the police and social services department) to staff them and partly on the personalities of those running them. Increase in juvenile crime has led to a growing recognition of the value of diverting offenders from the juvenile justice system at an early stage in their offending, since the available evidence suggests that they are less likely to re-offend than if they are prosecuted.[5] This recognition has in recent years given fresh impetus to the practice of consultation,[6] especially in relation to police cautioning.

1 But it does not always happen; for example, there are some police cautioning schemes where the police may inform that they intend to caution but do not first invite the social agencies to consult.
2 There will be a duty if ever s 5 of the 1969 Act should be brought into operation. For that section (which restricts the bringing of criminal proceedings) see post, para 14.02.
3 See the Guide to Part I of the CYPA 1969, paras 83–107.
4 For these early schemes see the Ingleby Committee, Cmnd 1191, paras 138–149; Cavenagh, *Juvenile Courts, The Child and the Law*, Chapter 7. For a post-1969 study, see Shone and Christie, *Police, Social Workers and Children in Trouble — A Study in Liaison* [1979] JSWL 147.
5 See the Government White Paper, *Young Offenders*, HMSO, (1980).
6 Examples of a most successful scheme are the Juvenile Liaison Bureaux set up under the auspices of Northamptonshire County Council; see *Diversion – Corporate Action with Juveniles* (1984) published by the Council.

(c) Cautioning of offenders

12.36 Both the White Paper on Young Offenders and a document of the All Party Penal Affairs Group in 1980 recommended expansion of the use of police cautioning as an alternative to prosecution of juvenile offenders. The Home Office has added its influence by a Circular[1] which, in setting out guidelines, aims at promoting more effective and consistent cautioning practices on a national basis since there were wide disparities both in cautioning rates among police forces and in practices of consultation between the police and other agencies.[2]

1 HOC No 14/1985.
2 For an account of earlier schemes see Watson and Austin *The Modern Juvenile Court*, Chapter 7; for more recent examination and on the topic of cautioning generally see Tutt in Chapter 3 of *Diversion – Corporate Action with Juveniles, supra.*

12.37 As a general principle prosecution of a first-time juvenile offender where the offence is not serious is not justifiable. It is in those circumstances a matter for discretion whether instead a formal caution is issued or whether informal advice or warning is given. If the former alternative is chosen, a formal procedure must be followed in which the following criteria must be met.

(a) There must be sufficient evidence to support a prosecution; the caution must not be used as a substitute for a weak prosecution.

(b) The juvenile must admit the offence.

(c) His parents or guardian must consent to the caution being issued.

The significance of a caution and the possibility of future reliance on it if the juvenile should re-offend must be explained to him and his parents. If these criteria are met, the decision whether to caution will depend on the offence not being serious and the offender's record not being serious. Normally, unless the offence is serious (for example, arson, rape), first offenders will be cautioned, and so, too, a caution is likely to be appropriate for a second or subsequent offence where there has been a reasonable lapse of time since the earlier caution or where the offence is trivial or different in character from the first. Generally account should be taken of the views of the aggrieved party, especially since a caution deprives the victim of redress through a compensation order, unless he were to institute private proceedings.

A caution should normally be administered in a police station by a police officer in uniform in the presence of the parent.

2   The institution of the proceedings

12.38   The statutory provisions for securing the attendance of a juvenile offender before the court, and, where necessary, for his prior temporary detention are complicated and derived from several sources, but those regulating arrest and detention are very largely to be found in the Police and Criminal Evidence Act 1984. What follows is an outline of the powers and procedures, but with particular reference to juveniles.[1]

---

1 For the complex details readers are referred to works on the Act. See especially Bevan and Lidstone, *A Guide to the Police and Criminal Evidence Act 1984*; Zander, *The Police and Criminal Evidence Act 1984*.

(a)   Summons, warrant or arrest without warrant

12.39   A juvenile offender, like an adult, comes before the court as the result of a summons requiring his attendance at a particular court on a stated date and time or of a warrant for his arrest or after his being arrested without a warrant[1] and charged with an offence. Summonses are far more common than warrants,[2] but the choice between proceeding by way of a summons and arresting and charging the juvenile is wholly within the discretion of the police, subject to any restrictions imposed by the Police and Criminal Evidence Act. The Ingleby Committee rejected the suggestion that 'a child ought never to be arrested unless a breach of the peace is threatened or the offence is so grave that the child charged with it ought never to be left-at-large', and felt that 'it would be neither practicable nor desirable to restrict by statute the manner in which proceedings should be started'.[3] This unfettered discretion may be questioned. A justice of the peace when considering whether to issue a summons or warrant is expected to apply the principle that the latter should not be issued where a summons will be equally effective, except where the charge is of a serious nature.[4] It is not unrealistic to impute to a police officer equally an ability to assess the gravity of an offence,[5] so that a similar principle should operate when he has to decide whether proceedings be set in motion by the issue of a summons or by arrest and charge. Moreover, where the juvenile is a child, as opposed to a young person, there should be a particularly strong presumption that a summons will suffice to secure attendance. After all, it has been laid down that he shall be tried summarily for all offences except homicide. Since the summons is the normal method of instituting proceedings against adults in respect of summary offences, it ought to be the normal method for ensuring the child's appearance in respect of all offences other than homicide. Its one disadvantage compared with the method of proceeding by way of arrest without warrant is that it can sometimes lead to delay in bringing the juvenile before the court, especially if the prosecutor does not promptly apply for a summons;[6] whereas the juvenile who is arrested without warrant and charged with an offence must, if he is not released, be brought before a magistrates' court as soon as practicable, which normally must be the day on which he is charged or the next day,[7] or, if he is released on police bail, will be ordered to appear at an early sitting of the court, subject to the power of the court to appoint a later time for appearance.[8]

The risk of reliance on arrest without warrant rather than on the summons as the method of instituting proceedings has been substantially increased by the Police and Criminal Evidence Act 1984, since the Act enlarges the powers of the police to arrest and detain a suspect for questioning.[9] Indeed, there is now 'potentially a power of arrest for every criminal offence'.[10]

---

1 The purpose of arrest is to take a person before a justice of the peace or the police. It is therefore unlawful to use it in order to take a juvenile to his parent for him to deal with him; *R v Brewin* [1976] Crim LR 742.
2 For warrants see post, para 12.43.
3 Cmnd 1191, para 117.
4 *O'Brien v Brabner* (1885) 49 JP Jo 227.
5 Compare the more difficult matters he has to consider under s 28(2) of CYPA 1969 when deciding whether to release a juvenile or arrange for him to be kept in a place of safety; see post, para 14.41.
6 The need to avoid delay in bringing the juvenile before the court prompted the Ingleby Committee (Cmnd 1191, para 118) to recommend that normally criminal proceedings should be instituted not more than 28 days after the identity of the offender first becomes known to the prosecutor, but this proposal has not been adopted. On the other hand, the Committee saw no justification for altering, in its application to juveniles, the general rule (now contained in s 127(1) of the Magistrates' Courts Act 1980) that, unless a particular enactment otherwise provides, an information alleging a non-indictable offence must be laid within six months from the time when the offence was committed. It rejected a suggested limit of three months.
7 See PCEA 1984, s 46.
8 Magistrates' Court Act 1980, s 43(1), as substituted by PCEA, s 47(8)(a). If the court so acts, it may enlarge the recognisances of any sureties.
9 This shift of emphasis in the use of the law of arrest for questioning before charging began with the Criminal Law Act 1967. For a succinct history of the law see Bevan & Lidstone, op cit, paras 5.01–5.04.
10 Ibid, para 5.06. The common law power to arrest for breach of the peace is not affected by the Act.

12.40   First, there is a power of summary arrest (ie without formalities) where a person is reasonably suspected of having committed an arrestable offence. All serious offences, both statutory and common law, fall within this category, since it covers offences for which the sentence is fixed by law and those which are punishable by five years' imprisonment.[1] It therefore includes the serious offences against the person, all offences under the

Criminal Damage Act 1971 and nearly all those under the Theft Act 1968
– in other words, the kinds of offences for which juveniles most frequently
appear before the court. The remaining arrestable offences are a
miscellaneous group, included in the 1984 Act[2] so that they may attract
the additional investigative powers which attach to arrestable offences, for
example, the power without a warrant to enter and search the premises
of the person under arrest.[3] In the context of juvenile offending the most
relevant of these offences are taking a motor vehicle without authority[4]
and, to a lesser extent, going equipped for stealing[5] and indecent assault
on a woman.[6] For completeness it should be added that any conspiracy
or attempt to commit an arrestable offence or aiding and abetting the
commission of it is also itself an arrestable offence.[7]

1 PCEA 1984, s 24(1)(a) and (b).
2 See s 24(2), as amended by the Criminal Justice Act 1988, Sch 16.
3 Section 18.
4 Theft Act 1968, s 12(1).
5 Ibid, s 25(1).
6 Sexual Offences Act 1956, s 14.
7 This is the cumulative effect of the Criminal Law Act 1977, s 3; Criminal Attempts Act
  1981, s 4; the Accessories and Abettors Act, 1861, s 8 (as amended by the Criminal Law
  Act 1977, Sch 12); and the Police and Criminal Evidence Act 1984, s 24(3) (as amended
  by the Criminal Justice Act 1988, Sch 15, para 98).

12.41   Second, the 1984 Act confers on a constable a power of arrest without
warrant in respect of a number of listed offences,[1] even though they are
not serious enough to be classed as arrestable. With the possible exception
of certain Road Traffic offences[2] (for example, driving whilst under the
influence of drink or drugs or with excess alcohol in the blood), none
of those offences is likely to be the subject of criminal proceedings against
a juvenile. More importantly, however, this power of arrest is also available
in circumstances where, inter alios, a juvenile is unlawfully at large, namely,
where he is in breach of bail conditions[3] or where, being a child in the
care of a local authority, is absent from the premises in which he is required
by the authority to live[4] or where a juvenile needs to be detained in a
place of safety because he is in need of care or control[5] or where he has
absented himself from a place of safety.[6]

1 Section 26 and Sch 2.
2 Road Traffic Act 1972, ss 5 and 7 (as amended by the Transport Act 1981, s 25(2) and
  Sch 8) and s 100.
3 Bail Act 1976, s 7.
4 Child Care Act 1980, s 16; see post, para 15.105.
5 CYPA 1969, s 28(2); see post, para 14.41.
6 Ibid, s 32.

12.42   Third, where the offence is one not covered by either of the above
powers of arrest,[1] a constable has power to arrest without warrant a person
reasonably suspected of having committed it if, but only if, it appears to
him that a summons cannot be served or is inappropriate because any
of the 'general arrest conditions' is satisfied.[2] The prescribed conditions
are such that the power may be invoked (1) where the name or address[3]
of the suspect is unknown or that provided is doubted, or (2) where arrest
is reasonably believed to be necessary to prevent the suspect from, inter

alia, causing physical injury to himself or another person or suffering physical injury or causing loss of or damage to property, or (3) where arrest is reasonably believed to be necessary to protect a child or other vulnerable person from the suspect. For the purpose of this last condition the term child is not defined, but means, it is submitted, anyone under 18 and not, as defined by the Children and Young Persons legislation, one under 14.[4] The power of arrest under this last condition may sometimes be closely associated with care proceedings in respect of the child or relief under the Domestic Violence legislation,[5] although it must be remembered that the power relates to less serious offences (eg minor assaults) and not to arrestable offences.

1 Thus, by definition all summary offences fall into this category.
2 PCEA 1984, s 25.
3 Ie a satisfactory address for service of a summons (s 25(3)(c) and (4)).
4 Compare s 52 of PCEA 1984, which expressly provides that the narrower meaning applies for the purpose of Part IV of that Act (detention). Even if for present purposes that meaning applies, it may well in the circumstances of the case not be difficult to show that a young person is a 'vulnerable person'.
5 See ante, para 9.98.

Warrants of arrest
12.43 A warrant of arrest issued by a justice of the peace remains in force until executed or withdrawn.[1] It may be executed by a constable notwithstanding that he does not have it in his possession at the time of arrest, provided that it is shown to the arrested juvenile, if he demands to see it, as soon as practicable.[2] Where a juvenile has been arrested in pursuance of a warrant he can be released by the custody officer[3] at the police station where he is detained to attend the hearing of the charge, but according to section 29 of the CYPA 1969[4] release can be ordered only on a recognisance being entered into in his own name or in that of his parent or guardian[5] and either with or without sureties.[6] The custody officer will fix the amount of the recognisance, and he may and normally should impose a condition that the parent or guardian also attend the hearing. However, it has been pointed out[7] that the section overlooks the fact that the Bail Act 1976 abolished recognisances, and therefore the police have been advised to ignore it.

1 Magistrates' Courts Act 1980, s 125(1).
2 Ibid, s 125(3), as amended by PCEA 1984, s 33, which extends the rule to other warrants, such as warrants of commitment or distress.
3 See infra, para 12.45.
4 As substituted by PCEA 1984, s 119 and Sch 6, Part I, para 19(b).
5 For the meaning of guardian see CYPA 1933, s 107(1).
6 The Criminal Justice Act 1988, Sch 15, para 36 (prospectively amending s 29 of CYPA 1969) will abolish the right of the juvenile to enter into a recognisance in his own name.
7 Clarke Hall and Morrison, para B [802].

12.44 In issuing the warrant the justice of the peace may, however, have endorsed it for bail, in the terms that the juvenile is to be released on bail subject to a duty to appear before the juvenile court at the time specified in the endorsement. If the terms are that he is to be released on his entering into a recognisance without sureties and he agrees to it, it is not necessary to take him to a police station. If the endorsement provides for bail with sureties, he must be taken there, but the custody officer, subject to approving any surety, must then release the juvenile from custody.[1]

1 Magistrates' Courts Act 1980, s 117(3) as substituted by PCEA 1984, s 47(8)(b).

(b)   Release or detention of arrested juveniles[1]

12.45   The essential features of the powers and procedures relating to police detention under the Police and Criminal Evidence Act are that investigation of serious offences and detention for that purpose must normally take place at a designated police station,[2] and that, in the interests of both the suspect and the police, there should be a designated police officer, known as a custody officer,[3] to ensure the observance of the statutory safeguards and accompanying Code of Practice.[4] In order properly to fulfil that role he must not concurrently act as an officer investigating the case.[5] His basic duty is to see that the juvenile is released from detention once he becomes aware that the grounds for it have ceased to apply and provided that he is not aware of any other grounds that justify continuing the detention.[6] The grounds depend upon whether the juvenile is being detained before being charged with an offence or after being charged.

1 For the purpose of the rules relating to police detention under PCEA 1984, the term 'arrested juvenile' means a person appearing to be under the age of 17 and aged not less than ten who is arrested with or without warrant for any offence and also a child under ten arrested without warrant for homicide; see ss 37(15) and 52.
2 Ie a station designated by the Chief officer of police for each police area to be used for the purpose of detaining arrested persons. He must designate a sufficient number for that purpose (PCEA 1984, s 35(1) and (2)).
3 Section 36. The custody officer must be of at least the rank of sergeant, and there must be at least one appointed for each designated police station. If, however, a custody officer is not readily available a police officer of any rank may perform his functions, but this should be permitted only in an emergency.
4 Code of Practice for the Detention, Treatment and Questioning of Persons by the Police.
5 Section 36(5).
6 Section 34(2).

(i)   Detention before charge[1]

12.46   If the juvenile (a) has been arrested without warrant or under a warrant not endorsed for bail and then detained at a police station, or (b) returns to a police station to answer to bail, the custody officer must as soon as practicable after the juvenile arrives there or, if arrested at the police station, as soon as practicable after arrest, determine whether or not he has sufficient evidence to charge the juvenile with the offence for which he was arrested. If he has insufficient, he must release the juvenile, either on bail to return (or further return) to a police station or without bail, unless he has reasonable grounds for believing that detention without being charged is necessary for evidentiary reasons, namely to secure (ie obtain) evidence relating to the offence for which the juvenile was arrested, for example, articles believed to be in the juvenile's home, or to preserve such evidence, for example, by preventing him getting his hands on them to destroy them, or to obtain such evidence by questioning him.[2] If he decides that there is sufficient evidence, there are two options open to him.

1 See s 37.

2 Section 37(2).

12.47 (i) He may release the juvenile without charging him, either on bail or without bail.[1] There may be various reasons for this course of action. The police may have decided not to take steps to prosecute, but only to caution the juvenile or, exceptionally, to do neither; or they may not yet have made up their mind which of those steps to take, in which event the custody officer must notify him that a decision whether to prosecute has not yet been taken.[2] Where there is the possibility that proceedings may still be taken against him, he must be released on bail (to return to a police station) and not without bail.[3] (ii) He may charge the juvenile.[4]

1 Section 37(7)(b).
2 Section 37(8).
3 See s 34(2) and (5).
4 Section 37(7)(a).

(ii) Detention after charge
12.48 If he does, he must release him on bail or without bail, unless any of the following conditions is satisfied, in which case the custody officer may authorise the juvenile to be kept in police detention:[1]

(a) the juvenile's name or address cannot be ascertained or the custody officer has reasonable grounds for doubting whether a name or address furnished by him is his real name or address;

(b) the custody officer has reasonable grounds for believing that the detention of the juvenile is necessary for his own protection[2] or to prevent him from causing physical injury to anyone else or from causing loss of, or damage to, property;

(c) the custody officer has reasonable grounds for believing that the juvenile will fail to appear in court to answer to bail or that his detention is necessary to prevent him from interfering with the administration of justice or with the investigation of offences or of a particular offence;

(d) the custody officer has reasonable grounds for believing that the juvenile ought to be detained in his own interests.

This last condition clearly overlaps with that in condition (b) relating to detention for the juvenile's own protection, but apparently is intended to cover wider circumstances than threat from specific harm, for example, where he would not on release be able immediately to return home because of the temporary absence of his parents.[3]

1 Section 38(1)(a) and (b).
2 Eg to remove him from undesirable associations.
3 For another illustration see Bevan and Lidstone, op cit, para 6.31.

12.49 The custody officer must make arrangements for a juvenile who is kept in police detention for any of the above reasons to be taken into the care of, and detained by, a local authority, unless he certifies that such a step is impracticable, as, for example, where the local authority is unable to provide accommodation suitable for the particular juvenile.[1] If the juvenile is transferred to local authority care, the custody officer's duties in regard to a person subject to police detention come to an end,[2] and the local authority are then obliged to provide the juvenile with such advice and assistance as may be appropriate in the circumstances.[3] This, it is submitted, should extend to communication and co-operation with the juvenile's parents, and include advising on the desirability of legal representation, if this has not already been arranged.

1 See s 38(6). A certificate under the sub-section must be produced to the court before which the juvenile is ultimately brought (s 38(7)).
2 Section 39(4).
3 Section 39(5).

(iii) Limits on the period of detention without charge

12.50 Police detention begins either from the time the juvenile arrives at the police station after being arrested for an offence or, if he is arrested at the police station after attending there voluntarily or accompanying a constable to it, at the time of his arrest.[1] Ordinarily it is from the one or other of those times, 'the relevant time',[2] that the maximum periods of permitted detention without charge are calculated. Normally the maximum is 24 hours,[3] and, if the juvenile is not charged by the end of that period, he must then be released on bail or without bail;[4] but detention beyond that period is allowed, subject to the following conditions and limits.

1 Section 118(2).
2 For other relevant times which instead operate in a minority of cases see s 41(2)–(5).
3 Section 41(1).
4 Section 41(7).

12.51 *(1) Authorisation by a police officer* Section 42 of the Act empowers a police officer of at least the rank of superintendent to authorise detention for up to 36 hours from the relevant time, if he has reasonable grounds for believing that:

(a) the detention of the juvenile without charge is necessary to secure or preserve evidence relating to an offence for which he is under arrest or to obtain such evidence by questioning him;[1]

(b) an offence for which he is under arrest is a serious arrestable offence; and

(c) the investigation is being conducted diligently and expeditiously.

Because of their intrinsic seriousness certain arrestable offences are automatically defined as serious but otherwise the definition[2] extends to any other arrestable offence if its commission leads to such serious consequences as serious harm to State security or public order, serious interference with the administration of justice or with the investigation of offences, death of or serious injury to any person, substantial financial gain or serious financial loss.

Before determining whether to authorise continued detention under section 42 the officer must give the juvenile or, if available at the time, any solicitor representing him or any appropriate adult[3] an opportunity to make representations about the detention.[4]

1 Ie his duties in this regard are the same as those of a custody officer; see s 37(2), supra.
2 See s 116 and Sch 5.

12.52   *(2) Warrants of further detention*   The effect, therefore, of the above rule is that, where the conditions exist, the police may authorise detention for up to 36 hours, although the authorisation for extension beyond the normal 24 hour period must be made within that period but after the second review of the juvenile's detention has been carried out, which means after the first 15 hours of detention.[1] Any further extension requires the authorisation of a magistrates' court,[2] which is given under section 43 by way of a warrant of further detention. The same three conditions must be satisfied as under section 42. Application to the court for a warrant may be made at any time before the expiry of 36 hours after the relevant time, but if it is not practicable for the court to sit at the expiry of that period but it will sit during the subsequent six hours the application can be made before the expiry of the six hours. The juvenile must be brought before the court for the hearing and is entitled to be legally represented. The information submitted in support of the application must state the nature of the offence and of the evidence on which the juvenile was arrested, the inquiries already made and the further inquiries proposed by the police and the reasons for believing the continued detention without charge to be necessary. If the court allows the application, it can authorise further detention for a period not exceeding 36 hours, but, if it refuses, the juvenile must either be forthwith charged or, not later than the end of the normal 24 hours period or the expiry of any longer period authorised under section 42, be released on bail or without bail. Where a warrant has been issued the court may, on application, later extend the detention for a further period, which must not exceed 36 hours and which, in any event, must end not later than 96 hours after the relevant time. Again, the juvenile must be present at the later hearing and has the right to be legally represented.[3]

1 For reviews see infra.
2 Ie a court consisting of two or more justices sitting otherwise than in open court (s 45(1)).
3 Section 44.

(iv)   Reviews of detention

12.53   The above rules prescribe maximum periods of police detention, but they are subject to the duty of the police to conduct periodic reviews to see whether continued detention is justified.[1] If the juvenile has not yet been charged, the reviewing officer must be a police officer of at least the rank of inspector who has not been directly involved in the investigation. In conducting the review he must determine whether there continue to be the grounds for detention prescribed by section 37(2).[2] If the juvenile has been charged, the reviewing officer is the custody officer and he must similarly be satisfied that the grounds prescribed by section 38(1)[3] still obtain. Before reaching a decision the reviewing officer must give the juvenile or, if available at the time of review, his solicitor, or an appropriate adult[4] an opportunity to make representations about the detention. Normally the first review must be not later than six hours after the detention was first authorised, and subsequent reviews must be at intervals of not more than nine hours, but there is power to postpone a particular review.[5]

1 See s 40.
2 See ante, para, 12.46.
3 Ante, para, 12.48.
4 See infra, para, 12.54.
5 See s 40(4).

(v)   Detention and the role of the parent or guardian or other
appropriate adult

12.54   Such is the complexity of the rules governing police detention that few juveniles are likely to understand the rights which the Act gives to them and thus to be able to insist on their observance, for example, the right to be told of the grounds for detention or continued detention.[1] Accordingly, section 57 of the Police and Criminal Evidence Act substitutes new provisions in section 34 of the Children and Young Persons Act 1933,[2] which impose on the police a duty to take all practicable steps to identify a person responsible for the juvenile's welfare and then to notify him[3] as soon as practicable of the fact of the juvenile's arrest, the reason for it and the place where he is being detained. The person who may be so responsible, referred to in the Code of Practice as 'the appropriate adult', is:[4]

(i)   his parent or guardian (or, if he is in care, the care authority or organisation);
(ii)   a social worker; or
(iii)   failing either of the above, another responsible adult who is not a police officer or employed by the police.

1 Under ss 37(5), 38(4) and 42(5).
2 Section 34(2)–(9). These provisions also apply where a juvenile is detained by the police under the provisions of the Prevention of Terrorism (Temporary Provisions) Act 1984; sec CYPA 1933, s 34(10) and (11).
3 This duty of the police to notify is quite distinct from the right of the juvenile to have a relative or friend notified of his arrest (PCEA 1984, s 56), which he might wish to exercise where he and his parents are at arms' length. But that right can be suspended for up to 36 hours in certain circumstances, for example, where communication would impede the arrest of other persons.
4 Code of Practice for the Detention, Treatment and Questioning of Persons by the Police, para 1.7(a).

12.55   These categories call for comment.
(1) Guardian   Since the rules of detention in relation to juveniles are incorporated into the Children and Young Persons Act 1933, the term 'guardian' has the meaning given to it by that Act,[1] and is thus not limited to a person appointed by law to be a guardian, but includes anyone who for the time being has the charge of or control over the juvenile. That is a wide definition and would, for example, include a relative who is temporarily looking after the juvenile while his parents are holidaying abroad. For that reason it reduces the need to rely on the residuary category of 'another responsible adult'.
(2) The local authority or voluntary organisation   The rule in the Code is to be read subject to the express definition which section 57 of the 1984 Act includes in section 34 of the 1933 Act. For the purpose of the present obligation, as indeed for any purpose connected with the 1984 Act,[2] the term 'parent or guardian' means (i) a local authority, if the juvenile is

in its care, and (ii) a voluntary organisation if the juvenile is in its care by virtue of the parental rights and duties being vested in it.[3] The distinction makes it clear that a local authority will be a 'parent or guardian' whether or not it has assumed the parental rights and duties; but a voluntary organisation is not an appropriate adult in respect of a child in its voluntary care, unless it falls within the residuary category of 'another responsible adult'. Where the juvenile is in the care of a local authority or a voluntary organisation but is living with his parents, the Code of Practice advises that they, too, should normally be contacted, unless suspected of involvement in the offence concerned, although there is no legal obligation to inform. Even if the juvenile is not living with the parents, consideration should be given to informing them as well.[4] Where the parental rights and duties are still vested in them, this procedure should be regarded as essential.

(3) A social worker This term, it is suggested, should be construed generically, so as to include, for example, a probation officer, and not be restricted to a person employed by the local authority social services department. It seems that a social worker with whom the juvenile and his family are in contact under voluntary supervision falls within this category, although it is questionable whether in those circumstances the social worker can be strictly said to have assumed responsibility for the juvenile's welfare. Certainly, if the juvenile is the subject of a supervision order,[5] reasonable steps must be taken to notify the supervisor.[6]

(4) Some other responsible adult If there is no-one 'appropriate' under one or other of the above categories, some other responsible adult may be chosen as the appropriate adult to alert to the fact of the juvenile's arrest and detention. This is most likely to occur where the parents are unwilling or unavailable to attend the police station[7] or where they or guardians are suspected of involvement in the offence or are victims of it (for example, of assault or theft).[8] Where, however, the guardian is the local authority and also the victim, for example, theft from the community home where the suspected juvenile lives, it should not be necessary to alert a person other than the authority, but the authority should itself choose a social worker unconnected with the circumstances to be the adult.[9]

---

1 Section 107(1).
2 There is the same definition in the 1984 Act itself; see s 118.
3 Ie through a resolution being passed under s 64(1) of the Child Care Act 1980; see post, para 15.114.
4 Notes of Guidance, para 3A.
5 For supervision orders see post, paras 13.37 et seq, and paras 14.110 et seq.
6 Code of Practice, para 3.8.
7 See the Research Study No 4 for the Royal Commission on Criminal Procedure which found that a third of parents failed to attend the interviewing of juveniles.
8 See Code of Practice, Notes for Guidance, para 13A.
9 See Bevan & Lidstone, op cit p 227, para 7.07.

12.56 There are several reasons for this duty to inform an appropriate adult, coupled with a request to attend the police station, as is made apparent in the Code of Practice. Most importantly, the juvenile must not be interviewed in the absence of the adult unless delay in doing so will involve an immediate risk of harm to persons or serious loss of, or damage to, property.[1] If the adult is present at the interview and is still at the police station when a written record of it is made, he must be given the opportunity to read it and sign it or indicate in which respects he considers it inaccurate. Failure to do either must itself be recorded. In order that the adult may understand what is happening at the interview, he must on arrival at the police station be provided with the information that will already have been given to the juvenile when the custody officer authorised his detention, namely, the grounds for it, his right to have someone informed of it,[2] his right to legal advice and his right to consult the Codes of Practice, a copy of which must be readily available.[3] Before the arrival of the adult the juvenile is highly unlikely to have taken action over legal advice, so that it will in practice be a matter for the adult to consider.[4] It is an important matter, because, if the adult considers that advice should be taken, then the juvenile may not be interviewed until he has received it, unless (1) the offence is a serious arrestable offence and the police reasonably believe that the exercise of the right to advice will interfere with or harm relevant evidence or interfere with or physically harm other persons or alert other suspects or hinder the recovery of property, or (2) the police reasonably believe there is a risk of harm to others or serious loss of or damage to property or that awaiting the arrival of a solicitor would cause unreasonable delay in the investigation.[5] The protection afforded to the juvenile by the Act and Code could be seriously undermined if interviewing were to take place outside the police station.[6] The Code of Practice therefore directs that a juvenile should not be interviewed at school, unless it is unavoidable and then the head teacher or nominee must agree and be present.[7] Nor, unless unavoidable, should he be arrested there: if he is, that person should be informed.[8]

1 Paragraph 13.1 and Annex C.
2 See infra.
3 Paragraphs 3.1–3.3 and 3.6.
4 Paragraph 13.2.
5 See PCEA 1984, s 58 and Code of Practice, para 6 and Annex B.
6 See the definition of police detention; PCEA 1984, s 118(2).
7 Paragraph 13.3.
8 Ibid, Note of Guidance 13D.

12.57   Once the investigating officer believes that a prosecution should be brought against the juvenile he must bring him before the custody officer, who will then determine whether to charge him or inform him that he may be prosecuted. This must be done in the presence of the appropriate adult.[1] If the juvenile is charged, the adult must be given a written notice showing particulars of the offence.[2] As already noted, it may well be that before the point for determining whether to charge the juvenile has been reached the appropriate police officer may have authorised further detention of the juvenile.[3] Before deciding whether or not to do so he must give not only the juvenile or any solicitor representing him but also the appropriate adult an opportunity to make representations. Other persons having an interest in the juvenile's welfare (for example, a social worker) may, at the discretion of the police, also be allowed to do so.[4]

1 Paragraph 17.1.
2 Paragraph 17.3.
3 Under s 40(12) or s 42(6), ante, para 12.53 and para 12.51 respectively.
4 Code of Practice, paras 16.1 and 16.2.

(vi)   Identification of a suspected juvenile

12.58   Other important functions of an appropriate adult relate to the identification of a suspected juvenile. The relevant procedures are partly enacted by the Police and Criminal Evidence Act and partly regulated by Codes of Practice.[1] Any procedure requiring information to be given to a suspected juvenile[2] and any involving his participation must be given in the appropriate adult's presence.[3] Many of the procedures require the 'appropriate consent'. Where the juvenile is aged between 14 and 17 both his consent and that of the appropriate adult are required; where he is under 14 only that of the adult.[4] Thus, in accordance with these general requirements, information about the procedures to be adopted at an identification parade or group identification must be given orally and in writing to the juvenile in the adult's presence, and the appropriate consent(s) to a parade requested by the investigating police officer must be obtained.[5]

1 Code of Practice for the Detention, Treatment and Questioning of Persons (DTQ) and Code of Practice for the Identification of Persons by Police Officers (IP), replacing Home Office Circular 109/1978.
2 For the purpose of the Codes anyone who appears to be under 17 must be treated as a juvenile; Code DTQ, para 1.5; Code 1P, para 1.4.
3 Code IP, paras. 1.11 and 1.12.
4 PCEA 1984, s 65.
5 Code IP, paras, 2.1, 2.7 and 2.8. Alternatively the juvenile may ask for a parade, but this is unlikely unless the appropriate adult has advised it.

(vii)   Searches and samples of a detained juvenile

12.59   The 1984 Act abolished all statutory and common law powers[1] to search a person arrested and detained at a police station,[2] and provided new rules which are supplemented by the Code. These distinguish between non-intimate searches and intimate searches and between non-intimate and intimate samples.

1 Except those relating to offences of terrorism under the Prevention of Terrorism (Temporary Provisions) Act 1984.
2 PCEA 1984, s 53.

12.60   When a juvenile is arrested and brought to a police station or is arrested there or detained there (under section 47(5) of the 1984 Act), the custody officer[1] must ascertain what the juvenile has with him and, if necessary, can authorise a constable of the same sex as the juvenile to search the suspect.[2] If the juvenile does not consent, reasonable force may be used,[3] but a strip search (ie one involving the removal of more than outer clothing) may take place only if the custody officer considers it necessary to remove an article which the juvenile is not allowed to keep[4] because it may cause injury to a person (including himself) or damage to property or it may interfere with evidence or assist him to escape or because it may be evidence relating to an offence.[5] Stricter rules[6] govern intimate search.[7] The search must be authorised by an officer of at least superintendent rank and he must have reasonable grounds to believe that the juvenile may have concealed either articles which could be used to injure himself or others or Class A drugs with the intention of supplying them to others or of exporting them.[8] An intimate search of a juvenile

will be very exceptional. Where it is authorised, it requires the presence
of an appropriate adult of the same sex.[9]

1 See ante, para 12.45.
2 Section 54, as amended by CJA 1988, s 147.
3 Section 117.
4 Code DTQ, Annex A.
5 Section 54(4).
6 Section 55.
7 Defined as 'the physical examination of a person's body orifices' (s 118(1)).
8 Section 55(1).
9 Code DTQ, Annex A.

12.61   A distinction is drawn between the procedures for taking intimate
samples, such as blood or urine,[1] and non-intimate samples,[2] such as hair
(other than pubic hair) or nail cuttings. The taking of the former requires
two conditions to be satisfied, namely, (1) the giving of the appropriate
consent(s), which must be in writing, and (2) authorisation of the search
by an officer of at least superintendent rank, who must have reasonable
grounds to believe that the taking of a sample will tend to confirm or
disprove the juvenile's involvement in a serious arrestable offence.[3] The
taking of non-intimate samples requires the fulfilment of one or other of
those conditions, but, even if consent is given, an inspector or officer of
higher rank must reasonably believe that the sample will tend to confirm
or disprove the juvenile's involvement in the particular offence, which,
however, need not be a serious arrestable offence.[4]

1 See s 65.
2 Ibid.
3 Section 62.
4 See s 63; Code IP, para 5.4.

(viii)   Fingerprints and photographs
12.62   The rules relating to non-intimate samples also apply to body
impressions, such as footprints, but there are separate rules for fingerprints.

12.63   Under the former law a magistrates' court could order the taking
of the fingerprints of a person not less than 14.[1] An order could be made
where he was summoned to appear before the court for any offence which,
if the offender were 21 or over, would have been punishable with
imprisonment, or where he was arrested and brought before the court
charged with any offence. No order could therefore be made in respect
of children between 10 and 14, but apparently the view taken by the police
was that their fingerprints could lawfully be taken with the consent of
the parent on the basis that the giving of consent was incidental to the
parental right of custody. Whether parental consent was also sufficient
where the juvenile was a young person or whether his consent was also
required was never put to the judicial test.

1 Magistrates' Courts Act 1980, s 49.

12.64   That point has been clarified by the Police and Criminal Evidence
Act; but, in providing new rules[1] for the taking of fingerprints (including

palm prints[2]), a wide and powerful discretion is given to the police. Prints may be taken in the following circumstances:

(i) Where a person consents. In the case of a juvenile this means the appropriate consent, as already defined,[3] ie of the juvenile and of the appropriate adult or only of the latter if the juvenile is under 14. The consent must be in writing if given when the juvenile is at a police station.

(ii) Where a juvenile is arrested and detained at a police station but has not been charged or reported for *an* offence, an officer of at least superintendent rank can authorise[4] the taking of fingerprints if he reasonably suspects the juvenile is involved in an offence and reasonably believes the prints will tend to confirm or disprove his involvement.

(iii) Where a juvenile has been charged with a *recordable* offence[5] or informed he will be reported for it, and is still detained at a police station, his prints can be taken.

The combined effect of these powers in (ii) and (iii) is 'the routine taking of fingerprints for all those detained at a police station and who are due to be prosecuted'.[6]

(iv) Where a juvenile has been convicted of a *recordable* offence, he may not later than one month after the date of the conviction be required to attend a police station in order that his fingerprints may be taken. This power will be particularly relevant to the juvenile who was prosecuted for the offence by way of a summons and was not held in detention at a police station.

In any of the above circumstances an appropriate adult must be present[7] when the fingerprints are taken.

1 See s 61 and Code IP, para 3.
2 Section 65. The palm includes the 'leading edge' of the hand; see *R v Tottenham Justices, ex p ML* (1986) 82 Cr App Rep 277, CA.
3 Ante, para 12.58.
4 In writing or, if orally, confirmed in writing.
5 Ie an offence listed in Regulations made by the Secretary of State (s 27(4)).
6 Bevan & Lidstone, op cit, p 262, para 7.69.
7 Code IP para 1.12.

12.65 Similar procedures are provided[1] for the taking of photographs. These may be taken (i) with the appropriate consent in writing; or (ii) where the juvenile and others were arrested at the same time and a photograph is necessary to show who was arrested, at what time and at what place, for example, in an incident after a football match; or (iii) where the juvenile has been charged or reported for a recordable offence and has not yet been released or brought before court; and (iv) where he has been convicted of a recordable offence and his photograph has not already been taken.

1 Not by PCEA but by the Code IP, para 4.

(ix) Destruction of samples, fingerprints and photographs[1]
12.66 Samples, fingerprints (including all copies) and photographs (including negatives) taken by the police during the investigation of an offence must be destroyed if (i) the juvenile is cleared of the offence, or (ii) he has not been prosecuted or cautioned for it, or (iii) the records

were taken to eliminate suspects and he is thereby eliminated. The juvenile and an appropriate adult are entitled to witness the destruction. Moreover, any computer data relating to fingerprints must be made inaccessible once the fingerprints are destroyed, and the juvenile is entitled on request to a certificate stating that that has occurred.[2]

1 See s 64.
2 Section 64(5), as substituted, and (6A) and (6B) as inserted by CJA 1988, s 148.

(x)   Separation of juveniles from adult defendants
12.67   Whenever a juvenile is arrested and detained in a police station the police must make sure that he or she is not able to associate with adult defendants (ie over 17), and, if the juvenile is a girl, she must, while detained, be placed under the care of a woman.[1] Separation is not, however, obligatory where the adult and the juvenile are related nor where they are jointly charged, although in both cases it may be desirable.

1 CYPA 1933, s 31. For the application of this section when the juvenile is attending a court, see post, para 12.79.

IV   THE HEARING

1   Introduction

12.68   There is no distinct code of procedure exclusively applicable to the trial of a juvenile offender. The rules governing criminal proceedings in a juvenile court are an adaptation of those followed in an adult court exercising summary jurisdiction. The provisions of the Magistrates' Courts Act 1980 which are applicable to the adult magistrates' court operate, therefore, in the juvenile court, except in so far as they are modified or excluded by special enactments.[1] These are to be found mainly in the Children and Young Persons Acts 1933 to 1969 and the Magistrates' Courts (Children and Young Persons) Rules 1988.[2] As will be seen, they seek to modify the formalities that have to be observed in the hearing of an adult case and to provide a greater degree of simplicity in the juvenile court proceedings. But they can only provide the framework within which the juvenile court must work. The extent to which formality and complexity give way to informality and simplicity depends very much on the experience and practice of the particular court and on the age and character of the juvenile before it.

1 Section 152 of the Act states that its provisions 'relating to the constitution, place of sitting and procedure of magistrates' courts, shall, in their application to juvenile courts, have effect subject to any provision contained in the rules or any enactment regulating the constitution, place of sitting or procedure of juvenile courts'.
2 SI 1988/913 (L12).

2   Constitution and organisation of juvenile courts

12.69   Different rules still govern the organisation of juvenile courts in the Inner London Area[1] from those elsewhere. Those in London are split up into a number of divisions with juvenile courts sitting in these divisions but 'without prejudice . . . to their jurisdiction with respect to the whole area'.[2] The members of the courts are chosen from a panel nominated by the Lord Chancellor from the lay justices of the Inner London area. The Lord Chancellor also nominates the chairman of each court, who must be either a stipendiary magistrates or one of the lay justices on the panel.

1 The main rules are contained in CYPA 1933, s 45 and Sch 2; Administration of Justice Act 1964, s 12; and the Juvenile Courts (London) Order 1975, SI 1975/1385, as amended.
2 CYPA 1933, Sch 2, Part II, para 14.

12.70   Similarly, outside the Inner London area[1] a justice is not eligible to sit unless he is a member of a juvenile court panel. Normally there is a panel for each petty sessions areas, but the Home Secretary can create a combined panel for two or more areas,[2] and Magistrates' Courts Committees can make recommendations in that regard. Members of a panel are chosen by the justices from among their own number. They serve for three years, but are eligible for re-appointment, and that usually happens. There are two restrictions on qualification for appointment to a panel. A justice must be under 65 and automatically ceases membership on that age;[3] and he must be specially qualified to deal with juvenile cases.

1 The rules are to be found in CYPA 1933, s 45 and Sch 2, Part I, and the Juvenile Courts (Constitution) Rules 1954, SI 1954/1711, as amended.
2 He can also correspondingly dissolve a combined panel.
3 Exceptionally if there is a shortage of members on the panel the Lord Chancellor may extend the period of service of a justice.

3 Qualifications

12.71   The rules provided no criteria for determining what are special qualifications, but the Home Office[1] 'suggests that these should include some direct practical experience of dealing with young persons (eg through working with youth organisations, teaching or welfare or similar work) and a real appreciation of the surroundings and way of life of the children who are likely to come before the courts'. The Royal Commission on Justices of the Peace 1946–48[2] and the Ingleby Committee[3] both stressed the desirability of justices being normally between 30 and 40 years of age when first appointed to the juvenile panel, although it was recognised that there could not and should not be an inflexible rule. The Royal Commission also saw practical objections to the appointment of teachers on the ground that there is a distinct danger of a conflict of interest arising, since most teachers are employees of a local authority. They are not, however, subject to any general disqualification, but may be disqualified from sitting in a particular case involving their employing authority.[4]

1 See HOC No 138/1979.
2 Cmnd 7463, paras 184–190.
3 Cmnd 1191, paras 154–162.
4 See post, para 12.76.

12.72   Since the members of the juvenile court panel are drawn from the justices of the particular area, it is essential that when advisory committees are submitting to the Lord Chancellor nominations for appointment as justices they include in their list a sufficient number of persons who will be specially qualified to sit in the juvenile court. At the same time it is undesirable that persons should be appointed solely for that purpose. Certainly the demands of the juvenile court are heavy, with its special jurisdiction and, to some extent, distinctive procedure and methods of treatment, and justices appointed to the panel should, it is suggested, devote much of their time to the work of that court; but some experience in adult courts, particularly in adjudicating in matrimonial cases, will give justices insight into the various causes of the break up of the matrimonial home, which often accounts for juvenile delinquency and the need for children to be given care or control.

4   Composition of the court

12.73   The main rules regulating the composition of a juvenile court outside the Inner London area are contained in the Juvenile Courts (Constitution) Rules 1954. Except where there is statutory authority for a single justice to act,[1] a juvenile court must consist of at least two justices, but not more than three.[2] Usually and preferably [3] three sit. Normally, the court must include a man and a woman 'on the analogy that it requires a parent of either sex to bring up a child properly',[4] and one of the justices must be the chairman or a deputy chairman of the juvenile court panel, who will preside.[5] Exceptions are allowed to these normal requirements.[6] Thus, the chairman or a deputy chairman may nominate one of the other justices to act as chairman at the sitting. If at a particular sitting the chairman or a deputy chairman is not available 'owing to circumstances unforeseen when the justices to sit were chosen', or he cannot properly sit as a member of the court (for example, because the juvenile is personally known to him),[7] the members of the court can choose one of their number to preside. If, for the same reasons, no man or no woman is available or properly entitled to sit, the other members may proceed to sit if they think it inexpedient in the interests of justice to adjourn the case. Moreover, where a stipendiary magistrate finds that he is the only member present at a sitting, he may sit alone, if he considers adjournment inexpedient.[8] Exceptions will only be allowed on the ground of 'unforeseen' circumstances if at the time of arranging the composition of the court the panel took steps to 'ensure'[9] that the court would be fully composed in accordance with the normal requirements. Merely giving notice to a woman justice to attend without inquiring whether she can do so is not ensuring her attendance, so that proceedings held by two male justices in her absence are void.[10] It cannot be said that they are entitled to proceed because the circumstances of her absence are unforeseen when they have no evidence as to what those circumstances are.

1   As, for example, as an examining justice; Magistrates' Courts Act 1980, s 4(1).
2   MCA 1980, s 121(1); JC(C) Rules, r 12(1) and (4). Section 45 of CYPA 1933 defines a juvenile court as a court of summary jurisdiction, which must now be regarded as synonymous with a magistrates' court; see Clarke Hall and Morrison, paras B [357] – [358].
3   *R v Hertfordshire Justices, ex p Larsen* [1926] 1 KB 191; *Barnsley v Marsh* [1947] KB 672, [1947] 1 All ER 874.
4   John Watson, *The Child and the Magistrate*, 3rd edn, p 55.
5   JC(C) Rules, rr 12(1) and 13(1).
6   Rr 12(3) and 13(1A) and (2).
7   See also infra for disqualifications.

8 JC(C) Rules, r 12(2).
9 Rule 11.
10 *Re JS (an infant)* [1959] 3 All ER 856, [1959] 1 WLR 1218.

12.74 A comparison of these exceptions with those applicable in juvenile courts in the Inner London area shows that while there are basic differences there are also some unjustifiable distinctions which might have been removed by the Children and Young Persons Act 1963 when it amended the rules of composition of courts in that area.[1] It is difficult to see why the power to choose a temporary chairman should depend in that area on the chairman's not being available because of 'illness or other emergency',[2] whereas elsewhere it depends on his absence being due to unforeseen circumstances.[3] These respective provisions are almost certainly intended to cover the same contingencies. They should be expressed in the same terms. To the rules governing the Inner London juvenile courts there ought expressly to be added a provision that the power to appoint a temporary chairman is exercisable where the chairman 'cannot properly sit as a member of the court'.[4]

1 See Sch 2 of CYPA 1933, as substituted by CYPA 1963, Sch 2.
2 Ibid, para 16.
3 JC(C) Rules, r 13(2).
4 As in JC(C) Rules, r 13(2). As another example of discrepancy compare the following: Rule 12(1) of the JC(C) Rules states: 'Each juvenile court shall be constituted of not more than three justices and subject to the following provisions of this Rule, shall include a man and a woman.' But para 15 of Sch 2 of CYPA 1933 provides: 'Subject to the following provisions of this Schedule – (a) each juvenile court shall consist of a chairman and two other members and shall have both a man and a woman among its members.' In the Inner London area the chairman may be a metropolitan stipendiary magistrate.

12.75 An opportunity to achieve greater uniformity in the rules is afforded by section 146 of the Magistrates' Courts Act 1980. This enables rules to be made with regard to (a) the formation and revision of juvenile court panels and the eligibility of justices to be members; (b) the appointment of chairmen of juvenile courts; and (c) the composition of those courts. They may confer on the Lord Chancellor powers with respect to any of those matters and may, in particular, provide for the appointment of panels by him instead of by the justices themselves. It is likely that in exercising his powers he will be guided by the advice of local committees of justices. Different provisions may be made for different areas, but the section does not affect the present system concerning the areas for which panels are formed and juvenile courts constituted or the formation of combined panels.[1] The power to make rules was given as long ago as the Children and Young Persons Act 1969, but their appearance seems as far off as ever. Indeed, the whole question of the need for a duality of systems, within and without the Inner London area, is open to challenge.

1 Ante, para 12.70.

12.76 Because of the extent to which a local authority is involved in the work of the juvenile court, both in criminal proceedings through its social inquiry report and in care proceedings as one of the parties, a question which not infrequently arises is whether a member of the authority may be disqualified from sitting in the court. First, there is the general disqualification, imposed by section 64 of the Justices of the Peace Act 1979, that the member cannot be a member of a magistrates' court (adult or juvenile) in any proceedings to which the local authority or any of its committees or officers is a party. Second, the Lord Chancellor has directed that membership of a local authority social services committee is incompatible with membership of a juvenile court panel.[1] Third, a member of a local authority should not adjudicate in a case in which the authority has a direct interest, as where the offence relates to property belonging to the authority, for example, damage to a school. In a case of that kind a justice who is a co-opted member of a local authority committee (for example education)[2] or a governor or teacher of the school should similarly disqualify himself or at the least draw his connection with the authority and school to the attention of the parties.[3]

1 See The Magistrate, (1978) vol 34 p 50.
2 *R v Altrincham Justices, ex p Pennington* [1975] QB 549, [1975] 2 All ER 78, DC.
3 See The Magistrate (1981) vol 37, p 21.

5   Sittings of the court

(a)   Frequency

12.77   Juvenile courts must sit as often as necessary to exercise jurisdiction,[1] and may sit on any day to hear an indictable charge.[2] Indeed, being magistrates' courts, they may sit on any day of the year to exercise any of their jurisdiction.[3] The demands made upon the courts over the past decade through the increase in juvenile delinquency and the need in many cases to adjourn hearings for further inquiries[4] have meant more frequent sittings, especially in London and the large cities and towns, where regular sittings are held weekly on several days, with concurrent sittings of two or more courts a common occurrence. Elsewhere, practice varies considerably according to the amount of business of the courts. It is obviously desirable that delay in bringing the juvenile before the court should be avoided,[5] so that even in rural areas the periods between sittings should not be too long. Moreover, there should be a readiness to convene the court ad hoc, if this would avoid delay.

1 CYPA 1933, s 47(1).
2 Ibid, s 48(4).
3 Magistrates' Courts Act 1980, s 153.
4 Another major factor has been the expansion of care jurisdiction; see post, Chapter 14.
5 Otherwise 'the memory of the occurrence that occasions [the proceedings] may often have little connection in the child's mind with the steps that are being taken' (Home Office Circular No 19/1955). There may be other reasons for delay, such as hesitation over whether to caution the juvenile or prosecute or where there are lengthy adjournments and remand on bail.

(b)   Place

12.78   The Children Act 1908[1] gave juvenile courts considerable latitude in the choice of place and time of their sittings. It enabled them to sit in a different building or room or on different days or at different times from the sittings of other courts. The Children and Young Persons Act 1933[2] abolished the right to sit merely 'at different times', but otherwise preserved the earlier rule. Now[3] there is simply a general prohibition that juvenile courts 'shall not sit in a room in which sittings of a court other than juvenile court are held if a sitting of that other court has been or will be held there within an hour before or after the sitting of the juvenile court'.[4] It makes no difference whether the court is a criminal or civil court.[5] The reason for this change was to overcome the problem of shortage of court accommodation that exists in many areas, but that point could have been met by a simple amendment which restored the words 'at different times'[6] and returned to the original rule laid down in 1908. That method would, it is suggested, have been preferable because it might have emphasised that it is still desirable whenever practicable that the juvenile court should sit in a different building or a different room or on different days from any other court.

1 Section 111(1).
2 Section 47(2).
3 Ie since CYPA 1963, s 17(2) amended CYPA 1933, s 47(2).
4 This restriction does not apply to (1) proceedings in a juvenile court in respect of a protected child under s 34 of the Adoption Act 1976 (see ante, para 5.68), or (2) proceedings in a juvenile court in respect of a foster child under ss 11 or 12 of the Foster Children Act 1980 (see s 14(1) of that Act, ante, para 7.10). The reasons for this are that the parties are a local authority and an adult and the proceedings are in open court.
5 Cf CYPA 1933, s 31, infra, para 12.79.
6 With the addition that there should be a minimum interval between the sitting of a juvenile court and that of any other court.

(c) Accommodation

12.79 Of those three possibilities the ideal solution is clearly the first, provided that there are suitable buildings. But the number of these is limited, and there are still courts in many areas being held in unsatisfactory conditions. The accommodation provided for juvenile courts should be such as to meet the following requirements.[1] Even where existing facilities are wholly inadequate there should be adaptation to secure as far as possible these objectives.

(1) The court room should be so arranged and furnished as to create an atmosphere of dignity but simplicity. This effect is more likely to be produced if the 'trappings' of an adult court room such as the raised bench and the dock are excluded.[2]

(2) There should be adequate ancillary accommodation in the forms of:

(i) waiting and interviewing rooms which should be so arranged that juveniles remanded in custody are kept separate from those who have been summoned or remanded on bail and that boys are kept separate from girls;

(ii) separate rooms for each of the following, namely, the magistrates, their clerk, witnesses, probation officers and officers of the local authority and the police;

(iii) lavatory facilities.

(3) The whole of the accommodation should be so arranged as to provide a separate entrance to the court and a separate exit, so that the juvenile who has appeared before the court should not encounter those still to be called. This can be an important consideration where the juvenile or parent is leaving it in a distressed condition.[3]

(4) The arrangements must be such as to ensure compliance with the rule

that juveniles must, while being conveyed to the court and while waiting before or after attendance in court, be kept apart from adult defendants. This restriction applies to attendance in any criminal court and therefore includes a juvenile court when exercising its criminal jurisdiction.[4] It extends to juvenile witnesses and not only juvenile offenders.[5]

1 For a further examination see Watson, *The Child and the Magistrate*, 2nd edn, pp 62–69. The Home Office has issued guidance on factors to be taken into account in designing new court accommodation; see HOC No 112/1977.
2 Hence the desirability of avoiding, if possible, the use of an adult court room. If it has to be used, it should be re-arranged so as to make it as informal as possible. Opinion on the use of a raised bench and a witness box is divided. The retention of the latter is defended by some justices on the ground that it can help to impress on the juvenile witness the seriousness of the oath.
3 See Watson, op cit, p 64.
4 CYPA 1933, s 31, which also requires girls to be under the care of women; and see ante, para, 12.67.
5 Where a juvenile is a witness in proceedings in respect of a sexual offence it is desirable that he or she be able to wait in privacy and comfort – if possible, in a separate room; see Home Office Circular No 208/1964, para 4.

12.80 Save for this last mentioned restriction, there are no statutory provisions imposing a minimum standard of suitable accommodation, and the subject continues to hold low priority in the expenditure on legal and social services. There has in particular been no serious effort to pursue the realistic suggestion of the Ingleby Committee that juvenile courts should form part of a 'multi-purpose' centre, used also for other local authority services.[1]

1 Cmnd 1191, para 193.

6　Persons present

12.81 The Children and Young Persons Act 1933 restricts the classes of persons allowed to attend juvenile court proceedings to the following.[1]

(a)　*Members and officers of the court*

The clerk to the justices, officers of the social services department of a local authority (usually acting as liaison officer between the court and the authority), probation officers, a court usher and police officers are allowed to be present. It is desirable, if practicable, that a woman officer should be there where the court list includes any female defendant.[2]

1 Section 47(2). The restriction does not apply to certain proceedings in respect of protected children and foster children; see ante, para 12.78 note 4.
2 It is a matter for the Bench whether the police are allowed to appear in uniform. This is another matter on which opinion is divided, but the increase in the number of young persons appearing before the courts for serious offences has strengthened the views of those supporting the wearing of uniforms; and see Watson, op cit, p 68; Ingleby Committee, para 85.

(b)　*The parties to the case before the court, their solicitors and counsel, and witnesses and other persons directly concerned[1] in the case*

12.82 A social worker who is supervising the juvenile because he is in care is a person 'directly concerned', but the Divisional Court has taken the narrow view that the consequent right to attend is directory and not mandatory, so that a refusal to allow him or her to attend does not in itself invalidate the proceedings.[2] Nevertheless, in the particular circumstances of a case by excluding him or her justice may not be seen to be done, and for that reason certiorari may lie.[3]

1 For the attendance of parents see post, para, 12.87.
2 *R v Southwark Juvenile Court, ex p NJ* [1973] 3 All ER 383.
3 See ibid, where that was the consequence of not allowing the social worker to be present to advise the juvenile to ask for an adjournment so that he could obtain legal advice.

(c) Bona fide representatives of newspapers or newsagencies

12.83 Although the press can be present in a juvenile court, the right to publish reports of the proceedings is subject to certain restrictions, imposed primarily by section 49 of the Children and Young Persons Act 1933. These restrictions also apply to radio and television broadcasts.[1] Unless the court itself or the Home Secretary gives express permission to do so, a newspaper report or broadcast must not reveal the name, address or school of a juvenile or any other details which are likely[2] to lead to his identification, and a newspaper must not carry a picture of him.[3] If there is publication, it is no defence to show that there were irregularities in the conduct of the proceedings.[4] Even these restrictions may not always guarantee complete protection from publicity; enough may be published for the juvenile to be identified by those living in the immediate neighbourhood.[5] Permission to disclose is uncommon and may only be given where it is 'appropriate to do so for the purpose of avoiding injustice to a child or young person'.[6] Its object is to exculpate a juvenile who, but for the disclosure of the details of the offender, might himself be wrongly identified as the offender.[7]

1 CYPA 1933, s 49, as amended by CYPA 1963, s 57 and CYPA 1969, s 10 and Sch 5, para 53. The provisions extend to the publication in England of reports and broadcasts of proceedings in Scottish juvenile courts and vice versa.
2 Section 49(1) of the 1933 Act speaks of the disclosure of particulars which are 'calculated' to lead to identification. It has been pointed out that 'calculated' apparently means 'likely' rather than 'intended'; see Clarke Hall and Morrison, op cit, para B [384].
3 Wrongful disclosure is a summary offence carrying a penalty of a fine not exceeding level 5 on the standard scale (currently £2,000); CYPA 1933 s 49(2) as amended by the Criminal Justice Act 1982, ss 35 and 75. It is also a matter which may well be brought to the attention of the Press Council.
4 *Roberts v Dolby* (1935) 80 Sol Jo 32. (Juvenile court was held in an ordinary court room but not on a different day from sitting of the adult magistrates' courts, so that the hearing was contrary to s 47(2) of CYPA 1933, as it then stood. *Held*, that this did not excuse disclosure of name of juvenile's school in a newspaper report.
5 See Cavenagh, *Juvenile Courts, The Child and the Law*, pp 220–221.
6 CYPA 1933, s 49(1) as amended by CYPA 1969, s 10(1)(c).
7 It may be advisable for the details of the order granting permission to be drawn up in writing; see Clarke Hall and Morrison, op cit, para B [385].

12.84 These provisions relate to criminal and civil proceedings alike, and they apply to persons who are witnesses as well as to those against or in respect of whom the proceedings have been taken. Moreover, they are not limited to juveniles but also apply to (1) persons aged 17 but under 18 who may be the subject of proceedings in a juvenile court, and (2) persons of any age in respect of whom proceedings under Part I of the 1969 Act are brought in that court. These extensions are particularly relevant to the variation and discharge of supervision orders and care orders.[1] Indeed, for that reason section 49 of the 1933 Act also extends to proceedings in an adult magistrates' court to vary or discharge a supervision order where the supervised person has attained the age of 18. Since this jurisdiction is essentially a continuation of the juvenile court jurisdiction, the extension is logical and desirable, but the court must announce in the course of the proceedings that the section is applicable, otherwise no liability under it will arise for any disclosure.[2]

1 See post, Chapter 13.
2 CYPA 1969, s 10(1)(b) and (2).

12.85 The section further applies to proceedings on appeal (whether to the Crown Court or by case stated) as it does to those at first instance,[1] and, in the case of committal proceedings in respect of a juvenile, the publication of the notice of the result of those proceedings must not disclose the name and address of *any* juvenile,[2] unless the examining justices are of the opinion that disclosure would avoid injustice to him.[3] But section 49 does not apply to the trial of a juvenile who has been committed for trial. There is, however, a general power, conferred by section 39 of the 1933 Act,[4] for *any* court to direct that the matters stated above shall not be disclosed in a newspaper report or broadcast of its proceedings, civil as well as criminal, in which a juvenile has been concerned whether as the party by or against or in respect of whom the proceedings were taken or as a witness.[5] Where the court is a magistrates' court the clerk should remind it of its powers,[6] and where there are committal proceedings in which a juvenile is concerned, whether as defendant or witness, the clerk must send to the trial court a statement of whether the examining justices gave a direction under section 39.[7] Both that section and section 49[8] rest on the principle that publicity may not be in the interests of the juvenile,[9] but there is a difference of emphasis. Under section 49 the publication of details of identification is intended to be exceptional, whereas under section 39 it is the restriction on publication that is the exception: if the court does not prohibit, the details are freely publishable, subject, however, to the general law relating to the publication of judicial proceedings.[10] It is suggested that section 49 should be extended to all criminal proceedings in any court[11] on the ground that it is inherent in their nature that there is real risk of harm to the juvenile offender by identification. The onus should, therefore, in such proceedings always be placed on the court to decide whether in the exceptional case to allow publication. With a uniform rule of this kind there would also be less chance of the court's overlooking the question of publicity.[12] As for civil proceedings outside the juvenile court, identification is not likely to be harmful and section 39 should continue to apply thereto.

1 CYPA 1963, s 57(2); CYPA 1969, s 10 (1)(b).
2 Ie not only the juvenile charged with the offence.
3 Magistrates' Courts Act 1980, s 6(5) and (6).
4 As amended by CYPA 1963, s 57.
5 Until it was amended s 39 was limited to proceedings arising 'out of any offence against, or any conduct contrary to decency and morality', and was probably intended to relate

mainly, if not wholly, to proceedings concerning sexual offences. This is the kind of case in which it is still most likely to be invoked.

6 Home Office Circular 17/1964.

7 Magistrates' Courts Rules 1981, r 11(2).

8 Section 39 carries the same penalty for breach of it as s 49, and the relevant provisions extend to publication in England of reports and broadcasts of proceedings in Scottish reports and vice versa.

9 For the merits of the principle see Cavenagh, op cit pp 146–147.

10 For example, photographs, portraits and sketches of persons involved in judicial proceedings cannot be taken in a court; (Criminal Justice Act 1925, s 41).

11 The Ingleby Committee (Cmnd 1191, para 260) saw no reason for extending even s 39 to all criminal proceedings; see supra, note 5 for the original scope of the section.

12 Cf s 10(2) of CYPA 1969, supra, which allows for oversight.

(d) Other persons specially authorised by the juvenile court to be present[1]

12.86 This power is particularly useful to enable new justices on the juvenile court panel to observe proceedings and for students of social welfare and researchers into the working of juvenile courts to attend. The discretion should, however, be carefully exercised and the number present restricted to one or two specific individuals at any one sitting.

1 CYPA 1933, s 47(2)(d).

(e) Attendance at court of parents of juvenile

12.87 Under section 34(1) of the Children and Young Persons Act 1933 any court before whom a juvenile is brought, whether as an alleged offender or for any other reasons, can insist that 'any person who is a parent or guardian' attends the proceedings. For the purpose of the Children and Young Persons legislation a guardian includes not only a legal guardian appointed by deed or will or order of a court but also one who in the opinion of the court 'has for the time being the charge of or control over' the juvenile.[1] The court can compel attendance at either all the stages of the proceedings or, where it considers it desirable, a particular stage. Thus, for example, where the juvenile has admitted the offence and the court proceeds to inquire into his antecedents and family background,[2] it may, in the light of that information, adjourn the hearing for a parent to be present. Courts vary in exercising their power to compel. Indeed, it is not unknown (though regrettable) for a court to proceed to a decision without adjourning and requiring at least one parent to attend, especially if the juvenile offender is legally represented.[3] Many courts are usually content with the presence of only one parent and only exceptionally insist on both. Others are more insistent that both attend. This is especially so where they are living together and are jointly responsible for bringing up the juvenile. But, even where they are living apart, the court may not be able to have proper regard to the juvenile's welfare, as it is statutorily directed to do,[4] without seeing and hearing both of them. Much will depend on the circumstances. If the parent who does not have care and control (actual custody) has totally abdicated his parental responsibilities, it is most unlikely that the court will want to see him. It may, and should, be a different matter if a court has granted him access and he is seeing the juvenile regularly; a fortiori if he has also been jointly entrusted with some of the parental powers and responsibilities by a court. Where the parent with whom the juvenile is living has remarried, the attendance of the step parent may also be most desirable. In some cases he may prove to be a supportive figure; in others an underlying cause of the juvenile's being before the court.

1 CYPA 133, s 107(1). Subsequent references within the present topic to a parent include, unless the context otherwise requires, references to a guardian.
2 Such an inquiry is a distinct stage in the proceedings; see *R v Wheeler* [1917] 1 KB 283, [1916–17] All ER Rep 1111, CCA.
3 This approach tends to be adopted where it is known that the parents have rejected the juvenile. In a case of that kind the court may allow another relative (eg an elder brother or sister) to be present – not as a guardian (since he or she will not usually have charge of or control over the juvenile), but as a person specially authorised to be present (supra).
4 CYPA 1933, s 44(1); see post, para 13.117.

12.88 The attendance of the parents can be important for various reasons. There is, firstly, the obvious one that appearance before the court, particularly if it is a first appearance, is for many juveniles an ordeal which is likely to be more resolutely faced if there is accompanying parental support and comfort. Secondly, unless the juvenile is legally represented, his parents ought to be there to help him conduct his case. But there is the further advantage that attendance often enables the court to bring home to the parents their own responsibilities concerning the upbringing of their child and to point to their past failures in this respect. Consequently, the court's discretion under section 34 not to require attendance if that is unreasonable should be exercised sparingly.

12.89 The importance of parental attendance under the section is reflected in the measures which can be taken to ensure it. It can be enforced by summons or warrant, and the former can be included in a summons to the juvenile to attend.[1] Moreover, as already noted,[2] where the juvenile is in police detention, the police must, if it is practicable, notify the 'appropriate adult' responsible for the juvenile's welfare of his arrest,[3] and in most cases this will be a parent. It has also been noted[4] that when a juvenile is arrested in pursuance of a warrant and is released on his or his parent entering into a recognisance, the attendance of the parent as well as the juvenile may be a condition.[5]

1 Magistrates' Courts (Children and Young Persons) Rules 1988, r 40. The police are not obliged to summon the local authority having care of the juvenile; *R v Southwark Juvenile Court, ex p NJ* [1973] 3 All ER 383, [1973] 1 WLR 1300.
2 Ante, para 12.54.
3 CYPA 1933, s 34(2)–(11), as substituted by PCEA 1984, s 57.
4 Ante, para 12.43.
5 CYPA 1969, s 29, as substituted by PCEA 1984, s 119 and Sch 6, Part I, para 19(b). The terms of the Magistrates' Courts Act 1980, s 120 are such that the juvenile court can itself enforce the recognisance against the parent.

12.90 The above provisions are concerned with the power of a court to compel attendance. Whether a parent has a general *right* in all cases to attend the *juvenile* court is another question,[1] and the answer depends upon whether he can claim to be a person 'directly concerned' in the case within the meaning of section 47(2) of the Children and Young Persons Act 1933. It may be difficult to sustain that claim in criminal proceedings, but different considerations apply to care proceedings.[2]

1 For his right to be heard before the court imposes on him a fine, costs or an order for compensation see post, para 13.24.
2 See post, para 14.69.

7 Legal representation and legal aid

12.91 Usually, where a juvenile appears for very minor offences, for example, certain road traffic offences, he will not be legally represented, and sometimes in more serious ones he and his parents will prefer him not to be represented in the hope, sometimes mistaken, that the court will dispose of the case quickly and without adjournment. Nevertheless, there has in recent years been a marked increase in the number of cases where juveniles are legally represented. This is due partly to a rise in the number of serious offences committed,[1] especially by 15 and 16 year olds; partly to the restrictions imposed by the Criminal Justice Act 1982 on the making of custodial orders[2] or care orders,[3] if a juvenile is unrepresented; and partly to the need for legal aid normally to be available for breach of certain orders, namely, in respect of juveniles, breach of an order for conditional discharge[4] and, in the case of a 16-year-old, breach of a community service order.[5]

1 Legal aid is also available where a juvenile has been charged before an adult court and remitted to a juvenile court to be sentenced in accordance with the CYPA 1933, s 56(1), ante, para 12.20.
2 Post, para 13.77.
3 Post, para 13.70.
4 Post, para 13.11.
5 Post, para 13.36.

12.92 Most juveniles legally represented are legally aided.[1] The application may be made by the juvenile himself, but it is usually by the parent on his behalf and should be made to the clerk to the justices as early as possible before the date of the hearing. In certain circumstances the court is obliged to grant legal aid in respect of a juvenile,[2] namely, (i) where he is committed for trial on a charge of murder; (ii) where, having been remanded in custody, he is brought before the court again to be remanded in custody, was not on the previous occasion legally represented, is not on the present but wishes to be represented; but in those circumstances there is no obligation to grant legal aid if he has already been found guilty of the offence charged; (iii) where he is to be sentenced or dealt with for an offence and is being kept in custody to enable inquiries or a report to be made to assist the court in dealing with him. Otherwise, the making of a legal aid order depends on whether the court considers it desirable in the interests of justice.[3] Guidance is given by the so called 'Widgery Criteria'.[4] One of these is the inability of the accused to follow the proceedings and state his own case because of his inadequate knowledge of English or his mental illness or other mental or physical disability. There is no mention here of immaturity because of age. Nevertheless, courts in practice are generally disposed to granting legal aid to juvenile offenders because of this factor, even where there is no real likelihood of a custodial order. The court may not grant a person legal aid unless it appears that his disposable income and disposable capital are such that he requires assistance.[5] In the case of a juvenile under the age of 16, the court may, but is not obliged to, require him and his parent or guardian to furnish a statement of their means.[6] Resources are assessed in accordance with the Legal Aid in Criminal Proceedings (Assessment of Resources) Regulations 1978, as amended. These expressly allow the assessor to take into account the resources of (a) any person liable under the Social Security Act 1986[7] to maintain the juvenile and (b) any person having the care and control or actual custody of him, otherwise than by reason of a contract or for some temporary purpose.

1 For the detailed provisions see the Legal Aid Act 1974, Part II, as amended, and the Legal Aid in Criminal Proceedings (General) Regulations 1968 (LACPR).
2 See LAA 1974, s 29(1) and (1A).
3 LAA 1974, s 29(1).
4 Ie as stated by the Departmental Committee on Legal Aid in Criminal Proceedings (Widgery Committee) in its Report of 1966.
5 LAA 1974, s 29(2).
6 Ibid, s 29(4) and (5). For the prescribed forms of application for legal aid and of statement of means see Schs to the LACP Regs 1968.
7 Section 26. See post, Chapter 16. For this purpose it involves a juvenile who has attained the age of 16.

8   The conduct and order of the proceedings

12.93   It is highly desirable that the juvenile and his parents should have a clear understanding about what is going to happen at the hearing, whether or not he is being legally represented. The Ingleby Committee suggested that it is well worth explaining to them beforehand what they can expect,[1] and some courts try to do this, useful methods being the poster displayed in waiting rooms and the explanatory leaflet outlining the order and conduct of proceedings.[2] A good solicitor or counsel will similarly inform. Nevertheless, the onus of making clear by means of the simplest language what is going on rests mainly on the chairman of the court throughout the proceedings.

> 'Special qualities are called for in the chairman of a juvenile court. He is in charge of the proceedings, not the clerk, and the chairman should be the court's mouthpiece. He should be sympathetic but not complacent; patient but not easy-going; firm but not unkind. He will always try to carry his colleagues with him, and consult them in advance on the line he should take whenever he can reasonably do so. A good chairman is sensitive to their feelings and quick to detect a divergence of view. In the retiring room he will make a point of asking the opinions of his colleagues before expressing his own.'[3]

1 Cmnd 1191, para 186.
2 See ibid, Appendix v. Following the recommendation of the Eleventh Report of the House of Commons Expenditure Committee (HMSO) para 158 and the White Paper (Cmnd 6494) commenting on the Report, the Home Office has provided for the use of courts, if they so wish, a draft pamphlet for the guidance of parents (HOC No 125/1978 (CS26/1978)).
3 See Watson and Austin, *The Modern Juvenile Court*, p 22. This paragraph briefly but essentially summarises the views expressed more fully by Watson, a chairman with considerable experience of the office, in his *The Child and the Magistrate*.

12.94   The hearing[1] begins with the court, through its clerk, explaining to the juvenile in simple language suitable to his age and understanding the substance of the charge and then asking him whether he admits it.[2]

This duty to explain does not mean that in all cases the court must go into complicated details about the essential features of the offence,[3] but it must make sure that he sufficiently understands the charge.

1 For a practical account of criminal proceedings in a juvenile court see especially Watson and Austin, Chapter 6, and for rules of procedure see the Magistrates' Courts (Children and Young Persons) Rules 1988. Within the present topic subsequent citations of rules refer to those rules. They do not apply to a juvenile brought before the court with a view to being bound over. For that the procedure is by way of complaint under the MCA 1980, ss 51–57 and MC Rules 1981, r 14.
2 Rules 6 and 7.
3 *R v Blandford Justices, ex p G (infant)* [1967] 1 QB 82, [1966] 1 All ER 1021.

9   Plea of guilty

12.95   If he pleads guilty, the prosecutor then relates the facts of the case, but, unlike the trial of an adult, the magistrates should at this stage hear what the juvenile has to say about the events, even though he has so pleaded. This is desirable for two reasons. First, because his statement may show that he did not understand the nature of the charge and that, if the statement is true, there would be no criminal intent; in which case the court should enter a plea of not guilty.[1] Second, because it will help the Bench to assess the character and background of the juvenile and, where there is more than one alleged offender, the extent of his participation in the commission of the offence. One of the major practical problems, however, is to persuade the juvenile to be forthcoming: it requires skill and tact to elicit relevant information.[2]

1 *R v Durham Quarter Sessions, ex p Virgo* [1952] 2 QB 1, [1952] 1 All ER 466.
2 See Watson and Austin, op cit pp 64–67. It is helpful to tell the juvenile before the prosecution opens that the court will afterwards want to hear his account of what happened.

12.96   The rule which allows a person charged with a summary offence, not being one for which a sentence of more than three months imprisonment may be imposed, to plead guilty in his absence does not apply to juvenile courts.[1] After careful consideration the Ingleby Committee came down against extending it to those courts.[2] One of the main arguments in support of this view is that when the court is dealing with a juvenile offender it must have regard to his welfare,[3] and this it may not be able properly to do without first having the benefit of seeing him and questioning him. Furthermore, the commission of a minor offence is sometimes indicative of deeper troubles, which a personal appearance might reveal.

1 MCA 1980, s 12. But see ante, para 12.33, that, if an adult court mistakenly proceeds on the assumption that a juvenile is over 17, any finding and order is valid (CYPA 1933, 46 (1A)).
2 Cmnd 1191, paras 140–246.
3 CYPA 1933, s 44(1), post, para 13.117.

10   Plea of not guilty

12.97   Apart from the court of its own volition directing a plea of not guilty to be entered,[1] a defendant may, at any time before the court makes its final order, apply to change a plea of guilty to one of not guilty, and the court may in its discretion allow it where that is in the interests of justice.[2] Those are exceptional possibilities. Normally, of course, if the juvenile is not admitting the charge he so pleads at the beginning of the hearing. After the prosecution has made its opening statement the court will hear the evidence of the witnesses for the prosecution and each of them may be cross-examined by or on behalf of the juvenile.[3] Where he is not legally represented the court *must* allow his parent or guardian to assist him in cross-examining and in generally conducting his defence, and, if the parent or guardian cannot be found or cannot in the court's opinion reasonably be required to attend (for example, because of ill-health) the court *may* allow his place to be taken by any relative or other responsible person.[4]

1 Supra, para 12.95.
2 *S (an infant) v Manchester City Recorder* [1971] AC 481, [1969] 3 All ER 1230, HL.
3 Rule 8(1). The order of evidence and speeches is the same as in criminal proceedings against an adult; see Magistrates' Courts Rules 1981, r 13.
4 Rule 5. This rule equally applies where the juvenile court is acting as examining justices; see r 4.

(a)   Parent

12.98   The meaning of 'parent' for the purpose of the Children and Young Persons legislation has already been considered.[1] If a person has that status, the court is under a duty to allow him to assist. It has been argued that he should qualify even though he has been deprived of legal custody by order of a court or is a parent of a juvenile in care.[2] Against that it is arguable that, if he has been so deprived or if there has been a parental rights' resolution passed in respect of him,[3] he has lost the parental right to assist which rule 5 confers on him.[4] It is submitted that the latter argument is to be preferred on the ground that it accords with the general tenor of the Rule, namely, that the person assisting the juvenile should be a responsible person.

1 Ante, paras 9.50 et seq.
2 See Clarke Hall & Morrison, op cit, para B [3098]. Some indirect support for that view may be derived from s 34(1) of CYPA 1933, ante, para 12.87, requiring attendance at court of parents of a juvenile. As originally enacted, a parent's attendance could not be required where the juvenile had, before the institution of the proceedings, been removed from the custody or charge of the parent by an order of the court. By its terms this rule was applicable even though the parent had been deprived only temporarily of his parental rights and duties and might still have some concern at least for the juvenile's welfare (for example, where he was already the subject of what was then a fit person order or an approved school order). Since amendment by CYPA 1963 the general power to compel attendance entitles the court to require even a parent deprived of custody to attend, although that possibility is unlikely. If it can require such a parent to attend, can it deny him the right to do so to assist his child?
3 Clarke Hall & Morrison do not draw a distinction between a child in care under s 2 of the Child Care Act 1980 and one the subject of a s 3 resolution.
4 In the case of being deprived of legal custody, this conclusion rests on the assumption that the right to assist relates to the person of the juvenile; see ante, para 1.59 for the definition of legal custody.

(b)   Guardian

12.99   There is some doubt about whether, for the purpose of Rule 5, the term 'guardian' has its wider meaning to include anyone for the time being having the charge or control of the juvenile[1] or its narrower one of a person so appointed guardian by deed or will. It is expressly provided by the Magistrates' Courts (Children and Young Persons) Rules 1988[2] that it has the former for the purpose of care proceedings but there is no corresponding provision for criminal proceedings. Even if the term is to be narrowly construed, it is submitted that anyone having charge or control, provided it is not transient, would qualify as a 'responsible person'.

1 See CYPA 1933, s 107(1).
2 See r 13(2).

(c) Relative or other responsible person

12.100 The term relative is not defined for the purpose of the Children and Young Persons legislation. Nor does section 1 of the Family Law Reform Act 1987 assist so as to extend it to 'relatives' of all children, whether or not at the time of birth their parents were married to each other.[1] The principle embodied in that section only applies to existing legislation so far as the section expressly so provides,[2] and it does not provide for the Children and Young Persons legislation. Nevertheless, taken in conjunction with the term 'other responsible person' (also not defined), 'relative' ought to be construed liberally so as to include not only, as it prima facie means,[3] legitimate relatives but also illegitimate.

The position of the father who was not married to the mother at the time of the child's birth also remains undefined so far as concerns the Children and Young Persons legislation. If he has been granted all the parental 'rights and duties' by an order made under section 4 of the Family Law Reform Act 1987[4] or by virtue of an order has custody, legal or actual custody or care and control or, without any order has the charge of or control of the juvenile (so as to qualify as a 'guardian'), he should be legally *entitled* to represent the juvenile.[5] If he has none of those rights, he ought to be allowed to represent. Even if he does not qualify as a relative he should be treated as a 'responsible person' in view of his interest in the child.

The latter term would also, it is suggested, include a social worker who is, under voluntary arrangements, supervising the juvenile and his family.[6]

1 Compare the detailed definition of 'relative' for the purpose of adoption or custodianship; see ante, para 6.02.
2 See ante, para 2.20.
3 *Seale – Hayne v Jodrell* [1891] AC 304, [1891–4] All ER Rep 477, HL.
4 See ante, para 2.47.
5 See ante, para 12.97. The above principles will operate when the relevant provisions of the 1987 Act are brought into force. Meantime, the court can grant the father legal custody under s 9 of GMA 1971.
6 But the employing authority may have a policy which forbids its social workers being used for this purpose. Compare the possible use of a social worker as an 'appropriate adult' for the purpose of PCEA 1984; see ante, para 12.55.

12.101 When a juvenile is not legally represented and not assisted in his defence the chairman is often hard put to it to control him in conducting his cross-examination. Invariably, when the juvenile does ask questions they will include irrelevant ones, as is readily to be expected in view of the difficulties in the art of cross-examination; but it frequently happens that he asks few or no questions, preferring at this point to give his own version of the story and then not always coherently. Should this happen, the court must on his behalf put to the witness such questions as it deems necessary, and in order to do this it can question the juvenile so as to clarify any point arising from the assertions he has made.[1]

1 Rule 8(2). The rule also applies where the juvenile court is acting as examining justice.

12.102   If at the conclusion of the case for the prosecution the court decides that there is a case to answer, it must tell the juvenile, if he is not legally represented, that he may either give evidence or address the court.[1] It should explain to him that if he chooses the first alternative his evidence must be given on oath[2] and that he may be cross-examined on it. Subsequent stages in the hearing of the case for the defence follow the same lines as in the summary trial of an adult. Witnesses for the defence are heard,[3] and the juvenile or the parent or other person assisting him in his defence or, where he is legally represented, his advocate may address the court on the evidence. The court then decides whether the juvenile is guilty of the offence.[4]

1 Rule 9. The rule amends its predecessor (MC (C & YP) Rules 1970, r 9) so as to accord with the Criminal Justice Act 1982, s 72(1) which, in abolishing the right of an accused to make an unsworn statement, preserved his right, if he is not legally represented, to address the court on any matter on which, if he were so represented, his counsel or solicitor could address the court.
2 For the form of oath to be used by juveniles see CYPA 1963, s 28, as amended by the Oaths Act 1978, s 2. A juvenile, like an adult, may, however, be allowed to affirm.
3 Rule 9.
4 Exceptionally the court may exercise its power in the interests of justice to direct within 28 days of a finding of guilt that the case be heard again by different justices (MCA 1980, s 142(2)–(4)).

12.103   Where the juvenile is found guilty, whether after a plea of guilty or a plea of not guilty, he and, if present, his parent or guardian must be given the opportunity to make a statement,[1] and the court must take into consideration various reports before making its order.[2] This may mean adjournment and remand of the juvenile.[3]

1 Rule 10(1)(a). The rule does not allow any relative or other responsible person who has assisted him in his defence to make a statement – a strange omission.
2 Rule 10(1)(b). In practice the court will examine the reports before the statement is made, so that the juvenile, parent or guardian in their statement may comment on them. Although the Rules allow them later an opportunity to make representations on the way in which the court proposes to deal with the juvenile (post, para 13.04), some courts merge the two rules so that only one statement is made.
3 See post, paras 12.117 to 12.127.

V   INQUIRIES AND REPORTS

12.104   In deciding how to deal with the juvenile after he has been found guilty of an offence,[1] the court must not only have regard to his welfare but also, where the circumstances so warrant, see that he is removed from undesirable surroundings and that proper provision is made for his education and training.[2] The court cannot properly discharge these duties unless it is fully informed about such matters and about his background and antecedents.

1 The terms 'conviction' and 'sentence' are not strictly to be used in relation to juveniles dealt with summarily, but instead 'finding of guilt' and 'order' (CYPA 1933, s 59(1)).
2 CYPA 1933, s 44(1), as amended by CYPA 1969, Sch 6; see further post, para 13.117.

1 Preparation and presentation of reports

12.105 The responsibility for providing the necessary information falls upon the local authority who have been notified that proceedings are being brought.[1] They must investigate, and report on, the home surroundings, school record, health and medical history, and character and general conduct of the juvenile, unless they consider it unnecessary,[2] for example, where the offence is trivial such as a minor traffic offence. They are also relieved of the obligation where the juvenile has reached the age of 13[3] and, by a direction of justices or a probation and after-care committee, local arrangements are in force for information with respect to his home surroundings to be furnished to the court by a probation officer.[4] Apart from the normal duty of the local authority to investigate, the court may request it to make inquiries, whether it has already done so or not.[5] The court can also call for post-conviction reports from a probation officer.[6]

1 For the duty to notify see CYPA 1969, s 5(8).
2 CYPA 1969, s 9(1), as supplemented by MC(C & YP) Rules 1988, r 10(1)(b). Section 9(1) refers only to a young person, but for this purpose includes a child of ten or over, of prosecutable age, see CYPA 1969 (Transitional Modifications of Part I) Order 1970, Art 4, SI 1970/1882.
3 Ibid, Art 5.
4 CYPA 1969, s 34(3). It should be noted that this provision is expressly limited to 'home surroundings', and does not include the other matters listed in s 9(1), supra; and see Art 5, supra, note 3, which speaks ambiguously of 'the *modification* of a local authority's duty under s 9 to make investigations and provide the court with information'. Nevertheless, in practice those other matters are also generally investigated and reported on by the probation officer.
5 CYPA 1969, s 9(2). For example, the authority may be directed to obtain a psychiatrist's report.
6 Powers of Criminal Courts Act 1973, Sch III, para 8(1).

12.106 All information presented must be considered by the court, and, if it is thought desirable, the juvenile may be remanded for further inquiries to be made,[1] for example, for a medical report on him or for the author of the social inquiry report, not being present, to attend an adjourned hearing. In most cases, however, remand will not be necessary, if there have been pre-trial inquiries. Evidence of background and antecedents is, of course, not admissible until proof of the offence, except where it is necessary to rebut the presumption of innocence.[2] In principle, therefore, there are objections to inquiries being made on the assumption that the juvenile will be found guilty, especially where he intends not to admit the offence.[3] For example, the calling for a school report will draw to the attention of the school authorities his appearance before a juvenile court, notwithstanding the fact that he may be 'acquitted' of the offence. On balance, however, pre-trial inquiries seem desirable, especially where the juvenile admits the offence, since they enable an early decision on the juvenile to be reached, a consequence which is more likely than not to be in his interests.[4]

1 MC (C & YP) Rules, r 10(1)(c).
2 See ante, para 12.09.
3 For a cogent criticism of pre-trial inquiries in relation to adult offenders and the Home Office advice on the subject (HOC 28/1971) see Mitra, *The Pre-Trial Social Inquiry Report*, 148 JPN 22.
4 See Ingleby Committee, Cmnd 1191, paras 219–220; Williams, *Criminal Law: The General Part*, pp 823–824.

(a)   The social inquiry report

12.107   The social inquiry report presented by the local authority or by a probation officer is the most comprehensive that the court receives. Prepared after interviews with interested parties, it should deal with inter alia, (1) the juvenile's antecedents, especially any record of illnesses and of offences of which he has previously been found guilty, together with the orders then made; (2) his family, particularly its composition and income, the home and the relationship between him and the other members; (3) his general activities or lack of them. Both courts and reporting officers vary in their views on whether it is part of the functions of a reporting officer to recommend the kind of order that the court might appropriately make.[1] Certainly there is no obligation to do so, but many courts find recommendations helpful, even if they do not always adopt them. Opinions also differ on whether statutory guidance should be given on the matters to be covered by a social inquiry report, as, indeed, is given by the relevant Rules in adoption and custodianship proceedings.[2] The overriding advantage of a guide is that it reduces the risk of the author of the report and the court overlooking matters which are practically important. The experience of school reports warns, however, against a restrictive format.

1 It is a difference of opinion of long standing; see the Report of the (Streatfeild) Interdepartmental Committee on the Business of the Criminal Courts (1961) Cmnd 1289, paras 343–346.
2 See respectively ante, para 5.42 and ante, para 6.24.

(b)   The school report

12.108   The report of the juvenile's school record ought to include a record of his attendance over a period of some two months with reasons for any absences, his conduct in relation to his teachers and to other children, his state of health, his ability and aptitude to deal with school work and the attitude of him and his parents to his education. These matters should be dealt with fully, but the stereotyped form in which reports are usually given and the concern of some teachers that their reports may be shown, or read out, to the juvenile and the parents militate against frankness.[1]

1 For a criticism see Kirk, *School Reports to the Juvenile Courts* 132 JPN 27, and see further, post, para 12.115.

(c)   Record of previous findings of guilt and of formal cautions

12.109   The prosecution should provide the court with a report on the juvenile's antecedents, together with a report of any previous findings of guilt, the nature of the offence(s) and the order(s) made. It should also report any formal cautions which have been given,[1] but this should be done separately as part of the statement of antecedents and only the fact of the caution and the offence should be mentioned.[2] Both previous findings of guilt and formal cautions should be put to the juvenile and his legal representative or his parents or guardian, so that they have the opportunity, if necessary, to challenge the accuracy.

1 Seen ante, paras 12.36 and 12.37.
2 See the guidance given by the Home Office in Circular No 49/1978. The Circular recommends that, compared with previous findings of guilt, 'if anything, the juvenile court should be more disposed towards the disregard of cautions in deciding what weight to attach to particular incidents, having in mind the lapse of time, the relevance of the caution to the offence currently being considered, and the juvenile's best interests'.

(d)   The medical report

12.110   The court may consider it necessary to call for a medical report on the juvenile's physical or mental condition or the defence may wish to present such a report. If the court decides that a psychiatrist's report should be obtained, it will remand[1] the juvenile for psychiatric examination at a child guidance clinic. These clinics exist to deal with a wide class of children who are delinquent, maladjusted or educationally disabled or who have serious psychological difficulties in relation to their own family. Like many other social and welfare services they owe their origin to the efforts of voluntary organisations, the first independent clinic being set up in 1927 in the East End of London by the Jewish Health Organisation of Great Britain. But their value was soon recognised by local education authorities. Since 1946 a number have been established under the National Health Service, each of these forming a psychiatric unit within a particular hospital. Of the local authority clinics some are run entirely by local authorities, but the remainder are joint clinics with medical staff provided by health authorities.

1 See post, para 12.124 for the power to remand for medical examination.

12.111   The juvenile court may remand a juvenile for psychiatric examination either on bail or to a community home. A juvenile remanded on bail or in a home without its own clinic will have to attend for examination at an outside clinic provided by a local authority or at a hospital unit or at a clinic attached to some other community home. This may well mean delay in the examination.

12.112   Besides an examination of physical health, there is an assessment of the juvenile's intelligence, character and emotions and an inquiry into his home environment, with particular reference to the relationship between him and his parents who, unless unwilling to co-operate, are almost always interviewed. To assist in the examination the court should ensure that copies of social inquiry reports, which the local authority or the probation officer have submitted, are provided. The subsequent report of the psychiatrist ought to refer to the causal connection, if any, between the juvenile's health and his delinquency and proceed to make recommendations as to the most suitable treatment.

2 Disclosure of contents of reports

12.113 The procedure governing disclosure of reports in a juvenile court is contained in rule 10 of the Magistrates' Courts (Children and Young Persons) Rules 1988. That court may consider any written report of a probation officer, local authority, local education authority, educational establishment or registered medical practitioner without having it read aloud.[1] The court must arrange for copies of any written report before the court to be made available to the legal representative of the juvenile, any parent or guardian who is present at the hearing and the juvenile himself, except where the court otherwise directs on the ground that it appears impracticable to disclose the report to him having regard to his age and understanding, or appears undesirable to do so having regard to the serious harm which he might thereby suffer.[2] These rules follow closely, but are an improvement on, those governing disclosure of reports on a juvenile offender in an adult court. There, he or his legal representative must be given a copy of the report, but, if he is not legally represented, a copy need not be given to him but must be given to his parent or guardian, if present in court.[3] Rule 10 does not, however, prescribe the procedure for providing copies, but the Home Office[4] and the Department of Social Security[5] have expressed the hope that, when a case is adjourned for reports after a finding of guilt, wherever practicable they will be available and copies distributed by the court (which means, in effect, by the clerk to the justices) well in advance — preferably at least seven days before — the resumed hearing.

1 Rule 10(1)(d). The rule prior to 1988 did not extend to school reports.
2 R 10(2). For these exceptional grounds see infra, para 12.114.
3 Powers of Criminal Courts Act 1973, s 46.
4 See Home Office Circular No 33/1988 (CS4/88). See also Welsh Office Circular 10/88.
5 See local authority circular LAC (88)9.

12.114 The emphasis which Rule 10, unlike its predecessor in the Magistrates' Courts (Children and Young Persons) Rules 1970, places on making written reports available to the interested parties, especially the juvenile, will remove much of the former criticism of variety in methods and extent of disclosure of reports.[1] Certainly, the availability of reports should obviate the need for reports to be read aloud. But in the following circumstances it is still necessary to disclose the substance of parts of the report. Rule 10(3) provides that in any case in which the juvenile is not legally represented and where a report, which has not been made available to him in view of his age and understanding or because disclosure could seriously harm him,[2] has been considered without being read aloud or where the juvenile, his parent or guardian has been required to withdraw from the court in the interests of the juvenile,[3] then the juvenile must be told the substance of any part of the report concerning his character or conduct which the court considers to be material to the manner in which the case should be dealt with, unless it is impracticable to tell him because of his age and understanding. So, too, the parent or guardian must, if present, be informed of the substance of any part of the report which refers to his own character or conduct or to the character, conduct, home surroundings or health of the juvenile, insofar as these matters are similarly considered material. The juvenile or the parent or guardian must be allowed to produce rebutting evidence concerning the matters so disclosed to him, if the court thinks it would be material, and for this purpose the proceedings will be adjourned and the court can require the person who made the report to attend the adjourned hearing, when (although the rules do not expressly so provide) the juvenile and the parent or guardian will have the opportunity to cross-examine him.

1 See the Report of the Ingleby Committee, Cmnd 1191, paras 207–217; and on school reports, see Ball, *'Secret Justice': The Use Made of School Reports in the Juvenile Court* 13 British Journal of Social Work (No 2) 197; and at 147 JPN 808, 810.
2 Supra, para 12.113.
3 MC (C & YP) Rules 1988, r 10(1)(e). Thus, delicate matters in a report which could distress him (for example, that his parent has previous convictions) could be mentioned and discussed with the parent in his absence.

VI   ADJOURNMENTS AND REMAND

1   Powers of juvenile court to adjourn and remand

12.115   In criminal cases the juvenile court may at any time before or during the trial adjourn it, and may remand and further remand the juvenile either in custody or on bail.[1] Adjournments and remands are most likely to occur in juvenile courts after the court has found the offence proved and it wants further information about the juvenile before deciding on the method of dealing with him;[2] but sometimes, for example when the facts are complicated, the court may have to adjourn before it has reached the stage where it can determine whether or not the juvenile is guilty.

1 MCA 1980, ss 10(1), (3) and (4) and 128. The power may be exercised by a single justice. Moreover, an adult court may hear an application to adjourn and remand, even though a juvenile court is to hear the case (CYPA 1933, s 46(2)).
  When the court sits as examining justices it *must* on adjourning remand the juvenile; see s 5(1).
2 If, when so adjourning, the court should indicate to the defendant that it has in mind a certain course of action (for example, making a community service order) should there be a favourable report on him, any subsequent custodial sentence made in the face of such a report is liable to be quashed; see *R v Rennes* [1986] Crim LR 193. It should therefore consider carefully what it tells him when adjourning.

12.116   Where the adjournment is without a remand, the court need not, but in practice does, fix the time and place at which the trial is to be resumed,[1] but, whether it does so or not, there should be no avoidable delay in resuming. Where, however, a remand is ordered, the time and place of resumption must be fixed when adjourning.[2] If there is an adjournment before the offence is proved, the remand must not be for more than eight clear days,[3] unless it is on bail and the juvenile and the prosecutor consent to a longer period.[4] An adjournment after proof of the offence may be for up to four weeks, unless there is a remand in custody when the maximum period allowed is three weeks.[5] This latter distinction seems unjustified in view of the power in care proceedings to detain for up to 28 days under an interim care order.[6]

1 MCA 1980, s 10(2).
2 See ibid.

3 Ie not including the day of remand and the day on which the juvenile is again to appear before the court.
4 MCA 1980, s 128(6), proviso (a). Where a person is remanded on bail for such longer period but is initially committed in custody because the recognisances of his sureties have not yet been taken, he must be brought before the court at the end of eight clear days or at such earlier time as may be specified in the warrant of commitment, unless in the meantime the sureties have entered into their recognisances; see MCR 1981, r 23.
5 MCA 1980, s 10(3).
6 Compare the view of the Ingleby Committee (Cmnd 1191, paras 226–227) who regarded a period of three weeks as normally reasonable for completing inquiries and reports and opposed any extension, since the courts and reporting agents would tend unnecessarily to work to the new maximum. On that argument an interim care order should correspondingly be reduced to a maximum of three weeks.

12.117 Where there is a remand for obtaining information with respect to a juvenile, the court may extend the period of remand in the juvenile's absence, providing that he appears before the court or a justice at least once in every 21 days.[1] It seems that this provision is limited to a remand after the case has been proved. There are other similar powers to order further remands in the juvenile's absence, but apparently these may be exercised before or after the case is proved. Thus, if illness or accident prevent his appearance when the period of remand has expired, he can be further remanded in his absence and (where it is before he has been found guilty) for more than eight clear days, if the court wishes.[2] Moreover, a juvenile who has been remanded on bail and who fails to appear before the court, whether because of illness, accident or any other reason, may in his absence have his recognisance and those of his sureties enlarged to a later time.[3] There is one further exceptional situation which allows further remand in the juvenile's absence, namely, where the Secretary of State has made a transfer direction under the Mental Health Act 1983 in respect of a juvenile who has been remanded in custody, ie a direction that, because he is mentally ill, he be removed to, and detained in, a hospital.[4]

1 CYPA 1933, s 48(3)(a). Notice must be given to him and his sureties (if any) of the date when he is to appear; see MC (C & YP) Rules 1988, r 12.
2 MCA 1980, s 129(1).
3 Ibid, s 129(2) and (3). Where the absence is not due to illness or accident (so that s 129(1) does not apply) the enlargement is deemed to be a further remand.
4 Mental Health Act 1983, ss 48 and 52.

2 Bail or custody

12.118 Subject to a rare exception,[1] the court has a complete discretion to remand on bail or in custody, provided the discretion is exercised judicially. The proviso does not, therefore, permit the power to remand in custody for inquiries and reports after the juvenile has been found guilty to be used as a means of punishing the offender.[2] In deciding whether to remand on bail or in custody the court should take account of the same factors as it would when considering the remand of adult offenders.

1 If the adjournment is due to the non-appearance of the prosecutor, the remand must not be in custody, unless the juvenile has been brought to the court from custody or cannot be remanded on bail because of his failure to find sureties (MCA 1980, s 15(2)).
2 *R v Toynbee Hall Juvenile Court Justices, ex p Joseph* [1939] 3 All ER 16; *R v Brentford Justices, ex p Muirhead* (1941) 166 LT 57.

(a) Bail

12.119 Unless the general right to bail is excluded,[1] bail must be granted unless one of the grounds specified in the Bail Act 1976 applies.[2] Unconditional bail is the more likely, but conditions may be imposed; for example, residence at home or at a specified address, regular reporting to the police, and observance of a curfew. Where the offence is an imprisonable offence the court may refuse bail if there are substantial grounds for believing that the juvenile will not surrender to custody or will commit an offence or interfere with witnesses or obstruct the court of justice. In deciding whether any such grounds for belief exist, the court has to take into account several factors; for example, the nature and seriousness of the offence, the juvenile's character and antecedents and his associations and whether there is a history of non-compliance with bail. A juvenile may also be refused bail for his own protection or his welfare, as where there is a risk of moral danger.

1 For example, where the juvenile has been arrested for breach of bail or where he is appealing to the Crown Court against a finding of guilt and/or consequent order.
2 See s 4 and Sch 1.

(b) Custody

12.120 If the remand is in custody but for a period not exceeding 24 hours, the juvenile may be committed to the custody of a constable,[1] but otherwise it must be to the care of the local authority for the area where he or she resides or where the offence was committed,[2] unless the offender is a male aged 15[3] or over and the court certifies that he is so unruly that he cannot safely be committed to its care, in which case he will be sent to a remand centre or, if that is not available, to a prison.[4] Either the police or a local authority may apply for a certificate. An unruly young person, as so defined, who is already remanded to the care of a local authority, may, on its application, similarly be committed to a remand centre or prison for the remaining period of remand.[5] Until criminal proceedings against children are abolished,[6] the power to commit to the care of a local authority applies to all juveniles charged with or found guilty of an offence or committed for trial or 'sentence',[7] except that a young person aged not less than 15 but under 17 who is committed in custody to the Crown Court with a view to a sentence of detention in a young offender institution in excess of the juvenile court's powers *must* be committed to a remand centre, if available, or otherwise to a prison.[8]

1 See MCA 1980, s 128(7) and Sch 7, para 83, and CYPA 1969, s 23(5). A magistrates' court that has power to commit to prison a person convicted of an offence can order his detention in a court house or at a police station up to 8 pm of the day on which the order is made (MCA 1980, s 135(1)) but, since the court cannot impose imprisonment on a juvenile, this power cannot be exercised in respect of a juvenile and reliance must instead be placed on s 128(7).
2 CYPA 1969, s 23(1). The Home Office has issued a Circular (No 242/1970) advising on procedures to be followed when conveying to and from courts juveniles who have been committed and remanded to the care of local authorities.
3 See CYPA 1969 (Transitional Modifications of Part I) Order 1981, SI 1981/81. There is power to raise the age (CYPA 1969, s 34(1)(e)), which, in effect, now means up to 16. The proviso does not apply to any female young person; CYPA 1969 (Transitional Modifications of Part I) Order 1979 SI 1979/125.

4 CYPA 1969, s 23(2). Concern has been expressed, for example by the National Association
  of Probation Officers, about excessive use of prisons for remanding 15 and 16-year-olds.
  Their use for that purpose should be limited to serious charges such as murder or rape.
5 Ibid, s 23(3).
6 See CYPA 1969, s 4.
7 If and when s 4 comes into operation, the power will apply to a child (as opposed to
  a young person) only if convicted of homicide or committed for trial for that offence.
8 MCA 1980, s 37, as prospectively amended by CJA 1988, Sch 15, para 67.

3   Certificates of unruliness

12.121   Both section 69 of the Children Act 1975 and the Certificate of
Unruly Character (Conditions) Order 1977[1] state that the court must not
certify a person as unruly unless one or more of the following conditions
is satisfied:

(a) That he is charged with an offence punishable in the case of an adult
     with imprisonment of 14 years or more; or
(b) that he is charged with an offence of violence or has been found guilty
     on a previous occasion of an offence of violence; or
(c) that he has persistently absconded from or seriously disrupted the
     running of a community home whilst resident there.

According to the Order, in cases (a) and (b) the court may issue a certificate
only if satisfied on the basis of a written report from the appropriate local
authority[2] that there is no suitable accommodation in a community home
where he may be placed without substantial risk to himself or others, except
that, where it is remanding him for the first time in the proceedings, it
must be satisfied that there has not been time to obtain such a report.
In case (c) it has to be satisfied from the local authority report that
accommodation cannot be found in a suitable community home where
he could be accommodated without risk of his absconding or seriously
disrupting the running of the home. Notwithstanding the apparently
mandatory terms of section 69 and the Order, it has been held[3] that the
court has a complete discretion in the matter, and so, even if the local
authority report states that there is suitable accommodation or semble even
without any report (written or oral),[4] the court may decide otherwise, and
issue a certificate. However, in those kinds of cases as in all others, the
court must be satisfied that the juvenile's unruliness is of such degree as
to justify committing him to a remand centre or prison. Neither section
23 of the Children and Young Persons Act 1969 nor the 1977 Order gives
guidance, but, in addition to the local authority report, the court may
call for other evidence of previous violence or disruptive behaviour or
absconding, as the case may be, and it should give the juvenile, his legal
representative or his parent or guardian the opportunity to address it before
deciding whether to issue the certificate. If it does not do so and the juvenile
is remanded to the care of the local authority, there is, if needed, the right
of the authority to seek a secure accommodation order.[5]

1 SI 1977/1037.
2 Ie the local authority in whose area the court is sitting or the young person resides.
3 *R v Leicester City Juvenile Justices, ex p Capenhurst* (1984) 149 JP 409, DC.
4 See Wilkinson, *Custodial Remands of Juveniles* 83 Law Soc Gaz 91.
5 For these orders see post, paras 15.77–15.85.

4   Remand for medical examination

12.122   When the court considers a medical examination is needed it will adjourn the case and *must* then remand the juvenile.[1] The maximum period of adjournment is four weeks at a time where there is a remand on bail, three weeks if a remand in custody.[2] The duty to adjourn and remand is imposed by section 30 of the Magistrates' Courts Act 1980 on every magistrates' court which is trying an offence punishable on summary conviction with imprisonment;[3] but, if the offence is not punishable by imprisonment, the court can exercise its powers under section 10(3) of the Act.[4]

1 Compare MCA 1980, s 10(4), ante, para 12.117, where on adjournment remand is discretionary.
2 Further remands may be necessary.
3 Although no court can impose imprisonment on a person under 21 (Criminal Justice Act 1982, s 1(1)), the application of s 30 of MCA 1980 to a juvenile court is preserved by s 150(6) of that Act, which provides that 'references in this Act to an offence punishable with imprisonment shall be construed without regard to any prohibition or restriction imposed by or under this or any other Act on imprisonment of young offenders'.
4 Ante, para 12.117; *Boaks v Reece* [1957] 1 QB 219, [1956] 3 All ER 986, CA; affd [1957] 1 WLR 454, HL.

12.123   When the juvenile is remanded on bail under section 30 it must be subject to the conditions that he will undergo medical examination by a duly qualified medical practitioner or, if it relates to his mental condition and the court so directs, two practitioners; that he will attend at a particular place for the examination; and, where the inquiry is into his mental condition, that he will comply with any other directions concerning the examination that are given by a person specified by the court.[1] In addition to its general power alternatively to remand in custody to the care of a local authority,[2] the court may remand the juvenile to a specified hospital for a report on his mental condition, provided the offence is one punishable on summary conviction with imprisonment.[3] The maximum period of remand is 28 days[4] with the possibility of further remands up to 12 weeks in all.[5] Before it can exercise this power the court must be satisfied on medical evidence that (1) there is reason to suspect that the juvenile is suffering from mental illness, psychopathic disorder, severe mental impairment or mental impairment, that (2) a remand on bail for a medical report would be impracticable, and that (3) arrangements have been made for his admission to a hospital within the next seven days.[6]

1 Section 30(2).
2 Supra, para 12.122.
3 Mental Health Act 1983, s 35(1) and (2).
4 Compare the maximum of three weeks under MCA 1980, s 10(3), supra, para 12.118.
5 Mental Health Act 1983, s 35(5)–(7).
6 Ibid, s 35(3)–(4). Meantime he can be detained in a place of safety, as defined in Mental Health Act 1983, s 55(1).

12.124   A court proceeding under section 30 must send to those responsible for the examination a statement of its reasons for the examination together with information about the juvenile's physical and mental condition.[1]

Magistrates Courts Rules 1981, r 24, and for advice and Forms see Home Office Circulars 113/1973 and 1/1975.

5   Constitution of court at resumed hearing

12.125   When there has been an adjournment, whether before or after the court has found the case proved, there is the possibility that at the date of the resumed hearing one or more of the justices cannot attend. The Juvenile Courts (Constitution) Rules 1954 go far to meet this situation, because those[1] which allow exceptions to the general requirement that the court shall consist of not more than three justices and shall include a man and a woman, apply to 'any sitting of a juvenile court' and, therefore, it is submitted, include a sitting at a resumed hearing of a criminal case or care case. These exceptions, it will be remembered,[2] allow the court to be constituted without a man or without a woman or allow a stipendiary magistrate to sit alone, in each case if it is inexpedient in the interests of justice for there to be an adjournment.

In criminal proceedings, as an alternative it may be possible to rely on section 48(3) of the Children and Young Persons Acts 1933. This allows, inter alia, a juvenile court other than that which remanded the juvenile finally to deal with him. Its term show[3] that it is intended primarily to apply where there has been adjournment and remand under section 10 of the Magistrates' Courts Act 1980 for inquiries after a finding of guilt,[4] but it is submitted that it can also be invoked where there has been a remand for medical examination under section 30 of that Act.

Whether or not it has this additional scope, it must be read in conjunction with section 121(7) of the 1980 Act. The latter permits a magistrates' court, which has adjourned the trial of an information after the accused has been convicted, to be differently constituted when it comes to sentence or deal with him, but it does require the court, firstly, to inquire into the facts and circumstances of the case so as to enable the justices who were not sitting when the offender was convicted to be fully acquainted with them.

Every effort is made to see that the court as originally constituted finally deals with the juvenile, because the justices who have already had the opportunity of making some assessment of the juvenile and his background during the course of the trial are likely to be best suited to determine the final order. For that reason and in view of the additional requirement imposed by section 121(7), if all members of the court cannot be present at the resumed hearing, reliance should, when possible, be placed on the Juvenile Courts (Constitution) Rules 1954 rather than on the provisions of the Acts of 1933 and 1980.

---

1 Rule 12(2) and (3).
2 See ante, para 12.73.
3 'When a juvenile court has remanded a child or young person for information to be obtained with respect to him, any juvenile court acting for the same petty sessional division or place . . . (b) when the information has been obtained, may deal with him finally;'.
4 It does not apply to any adjournment before such finding.

CHAPTER 13
Orders in criminal proceedings

I HISTORICAL INTRODUCTION

13.01 Whatever view earlier law or practice may have adopted concerning the punishment of juveniles—and there are indications of some mitigation in their favour[1]—certainly by the seventeenth century the principle of equality was firmly established, with no distinction being drawn between juvenile and adult offenders in the forms of punishment that could be inflicted. Depending upon the penalties attaching to the particular offence committed, juveniles, like adults, could be hanged, transported, imprisoned, subjected to various forms of corporal punishment[2] or fined.

1 As early as the tenth century Aethelstan decreed that an offender under 15 should not be slain for any offence unless he chose to defend himself or tried to escape and refused to give himself up; Ordinance VI cap 12 1 and 2; see Attenborough, *The Laws of the Earliest English Kings*, p 169. The various ways in which the child could be dealt with if he did surrender show that this enactment was one of the more sophisticated of the Anglo-Saxon laws. The child on giving himself up must be imprisoned, but, if no prison is available, his relatives must stand surety for him to the full amount of his wergeld (the price to be paid for the offence) for his future good behaviour. If they would neither redeem him nor stand surety, he had to 'swear, as the bishop directs him, that he will desist from every form of crime, and he shall remain in bondage until his wergeld is paid. If he is guilty of theft after that, he shall be slain or hanged as older offenders have been.' There were also other enactments of Aethelstan the effect of which was that thieves not over the age of 12 were spared from capital punishment; see Ord II, cap 1, VI cap II (Attenborough, pp 127 and 157). The Report of the Departmental Committee on the Treatment of Young Offenders (1927) Cmnd 2381, p 7, cites a case in the Year Books (YB 32 Ed I, rot 13) where judgment for burglary was spared to a boy of 12. The significance of this isolated reference to medieval leniency is uncertain, but it suggests a willingness to distinguish between juvenile and adult offenders.
2 'The records show that in the seventeenth century the pillory was one of the milder ways in which the country sought to deal with some of its juvenile delinquents . . .' (Eddy, *Justice of the Peace* p 45, referring to an entry in Pepys diary).

13.02 In the eighteenth century cases of juveniles being sentenced to death were quite common and sometimes the sentence was carried out.[1] Nevertheless, there was a distinct reluctance to execute children, save for a period at the beginning of the nineteenth century when there was apparently some readiness to do so in order to try to check the practice of parents ordering their children to steal on the assumption that the latter would escape the penalty because of their age.[2] This stricter attitude seems to have been short lived. Yet, it was only with the passing of the Children Act 1908 that sentence of death was abolished in respect of persons under the age of 16.[3]

1 The youngest recorded instance seems to be that of a seven-year-old boy who was hanged in 1708; see Kenny, *Outlines of Criminal Law*, 19th edn, p 80, note 4.

2   See Radzinowicz, A History of English Criminal Law, Vol I, p 523, note 4.
3   Subsequent legislation raised the age to under 18. See now CYPA 1933, s 53(1), as substituted by the Murder (Abolition of Death Penalty) Act 1965, s 1(5), and post, para 13.97.

13.03   The steep rise in the number of juvenile offenders from 1800 onwards is, however, only partly explained by parental pressures. The main cause lay in the new social conditions created by the Industrial Revolution. Overpopulated urban areas soon became fertile breeding grounds for juvenile offenders, many of whom, especially in London, frequented the notorious 'flash houses', which served as social centres for debauchery and the organisation of criminal activities.[1] That juvenile delinquency was one of the main social problems is evidenced by the formation in quick succession of two reforming bodies both of which devoted much of their work to inquiries into the reasons for its widespread existence. These were the Society to Inquire into Causes of Juvenile Delinquency, founded in 1815, and the Society for the Improvement of Prison Discipline and for the Reformation of Juvenile Offenders, founded in 1818. But the solutions to the problem would not be found merely in inquiries of this kind. Reformers recognised also the need for mitigation of the severity of the criminal law and the introduction of separate methods for dealing with juvenile offenders. The immediate response of the Legislature was modest. As already noted,[2] its relevant contribution to the substantive law was essentially to extend summary jurisdiction over young offenders, but gradually much more began to be done with regard to the treatment of young offenders. Indeed, some of the orders which a court may make today owe their origin to nineteenth century legislation; but most are the product of three major enactments: the Criminal Justice Act 1948, the Children and Young Persons Act 1969 and the Criminal Justice Act 1982.

1   For an account of these dens of vice see Radzinowicz, op cit, Vol II, pp 297–306. A glimpse at contemporary social life of young people is shown by the Third Report of the Commissioners on Criminal Law (1836) (British Sessional Papers, 79, xxxi, p 11). 'We are persuaded that it is desirable that increased powers should be given to the police to withdraw young persons from public houses, beer-shops, penny theatres and other notorious places of meeting for the idle and dissolute. Much advantage also might be derived from giving to the police a more distinct authority than they now possess to disperse or apprehend as vagrants boys wandering in companies in the streets or loitering around theatres and other places of public amusement without any ostensible employment.'
2   Ante, para 12.02.

II   THE DUTY TO EXPLAIN PROPOSED ORDER AND ITS EFFECTS

13.04   After inquiries and reports have been completed the court must tell the juvenile and his parent or guardian (if present) or anyone assisting him in his defence of the way in which it proposes to deal with the case, except that it must not so inform the juvenile where it considers disclosure undesirable.[1] Those informed are then allowed to make representations.[2]

1   The exception is rarely relied on. It might apply where it is obvious to the court that the juvenile's emotional or psychological condition is so highly charged that disclosure would unnecessarily exacerbate his condition.

2   MC (C & YP) Rules 1988, r 11(1). A duty to disclose also arises if the case is to be
     remitted to another court; for remittal see ante, paras 12.20 to 12.24.

13.05 On making an order the court must normally explain to the juvenile
its general nature and effect;[1] but the rules do not expressly require
information to be given about the right to apply for discharge or variation
of supervision orders or care orders. This is a serious omission in view
of the wide powers of local authorities under those orders, and courts ought
always to refer to the matter. Where the order is one requiring the parent
or guardian to enter into a recognisance there is no obligation to explain
this to the juvenile, if it is considered undesirable.

1   Rule 11(2).

III ORDERS

1 Non-custodial orders

(a) Discharge

13.06 The Larceny Act 1987 empowered a justice of the peace to discharge
a first offender who was summarily convicted for an offence under the
Act upon his making to the aggrieved party satisfactory payment for damages
and costs. Although not confined to the young offender, this enactment
seems to have been mainly intended for him.[1] An Act of 1847[2] went further.
When a juvenile who was not more than 14[3] was found guilty of simple
larceny, the justices could discharge him, if they thought it expedient not
to inflict any punishment. Subsequently, under the Summary Jurisdiction
Act 1879,[4] discharge became bound up with orders for release during good
behaviour and then, under the Probation of Offenders Act 1907, with the
new system of probation. So it remained until the Criminal Justice Act
1948 firmly distinguished between discharge and probation.

1   The Act was part of Peel's programme of reform, none of which, however, was exclusively
     directed to the young offender.
2   10 and 11 Vict, c 82, s 1.
3   An Act of 1850 (13 and 14 Vict, c 37) raised the age to 16.
4   Section 16.

13.07 An order for absolute or conditional discharge may be made when
the court is 'of opinion, having regard to the circumstances including the
nature of the offence and the character of the offender that it is inexpedient
to inflict punishment and that a probation order is not appropriate'.[1] Since
the supervision order has replaced the probation order in respect of juvenile
offenders, the above enactment must be construed accordingly. The court
has complete discretion whether to make the discharge absolute or
conditional. It can additionally order the payment of compensation and/
or costs,[2] but not a fine since that is a form of punishment;[3] and it can,
if it thinks it expedient for the reformation of the juvenile, allow any person
who so consents to give security for the good behaviour of the offender.[4]
Discharge cannot be ordered where the offence is one the sentence for
which is fixed by law.[5] So, it cannot be made in a case where the court
must detain the juvenile during Her Majesty's Pleasure.[6]

1   PCCA 1973, s 7(1).
2   Ibid, s 12(4).
3   *R v McClelland* [1951] 1 All ER 557.
4   PCCA 1973, s 12(1).
5   Section 7(1).
6   See CYPA 1933, s 53(1), post, para 13.97.

13.08   A conviction of an offence for which an order for absolute or conditional discharge is made is deemed not to be a conviction for any purposes other than (i) the proceedings in which the order is made, including restoration of any property in consequence of the conviction, (ii) the rules covering breach of an order for conditional discharge, (infra), (iii) care proceedings based on section 1(2)(bb) of the Children and Young Persons Act 1969 (post, para 14.11),[1] and (iv) reliance on the rule of autrefois convict.

1   PCCA 1973, s 13(1) and (4).

(i)   Absolute discharge

13.09   This is a dismissal after proof of guilt. Unless the offence is trivial or special circumstances provide powerful mitigation, the court will rarely order it. Even in trivial cases some courts are reluctant to make use of it because of a feeling that more harm than good may be done if the juvenile and his parents are left with the mistaken idea that he has 'got away with it'; but this wrong impression may sometimes be corrected if the court explains the reason for its leniency. It is a correction which should also sometimes be made where the order is for conditional discharge.

(ii)   Conditional discharge

13.10   This means that the offender is discharged subject to the condition that he commits no offence during a specified period not exceeding three years from the date of the order.[1] The order is commonly used for first offenders, especially where the imposition of a fine would cause unjustified hardship to the parents. The majority of orders are for 12 months, sometimes for two years, especially where the court feels it desirable to hold a sanction over the juvenile until he is due to leave school, and less frequently for three years. Before making the order the court must in ordinary language explain to him that if he does commit another offence during the period he will be liable to be dealt with for the original offence, quite apart from his liability for the later offence.[2] However, in dealing with the juvenile for any breach of an order for conditional discharge, a court is not obliged to take action on it, in which event the order remains operative; but that should be the exception and not the rule.

1   PCCA 1973, s 7(1) and (2).
2   Section 7(3).

(iii)   Breach of order

13.11   The appropriate court for dealing with him for the original offence is normally that which made the order for conditional discharge,[1] but complicated provisions recognise other possibilities.[2] The rules apply to juvenile cases as follows:

(a) Where the original order was made by the Crown Court that Court has exclusive jurisdiction to deal with the original offence. So, where the juvenile is found guilty by a juvenile court in respect of the later offence, that court commits him in custody or on bail to the Crown Court to be dealt with for the original offence.[3]

(b) Where the original order was made by a juvenile court that court normally deals with the original offence, but, if the court which finds him guilty of the later offence is another juvenile court, the latter may, with the consent of the first court or the justices' clerk deal with him for the original offence.[4] A juvenile court may deal with him for that offence as if he had just been found guilty of it,[5] and it still has jurisdiction even though he has attained the age of 17 since the original order.[6]

Where the juvenile is found guilty of the further offence by the Crown Court the latter may deal with him for the original offence instead of the juvenile court, but the orders which it can make are limited to those available to the juvenile court.[7]

If an offender is sentenced for breach of conditional discharge, his conviction for the original offence then counts as a conviction, for example, for the purpose of his criminal record.

1 If the order was made on appeal it is deemed to have been made by the court from which the appeal was brought; PCCA 1973, s 12(2).
2 PCCA 1973, s 8. The juvenile's appearance at a court is secured through summons or warrant for arrest; see sub-ss (1), (3) and (4).
3 Section 8(1), (2)(a), and (6).
4 Section 8(9); Justices' Clerks Rules 1970.
5 Section 8(7) and (9).
6 CYPA 1933, s 48(2).
7 PCCA 1973, s 8(8).

(b) Binding over

(i) The juvenile

13.12 The juvenile court may rely on the ancient powers of justices and order a juvenile to enter into a recognisance with or without sureties to keep the peace and/or to be of good behaviour. The exact scope of the powers is uncertain, as are the sources,[1] but they may be invoked where it is apprehended that a person may commit a breach of the peace or some other offence or may incite others to do so.[2] It may occasionally be useful in respect of a juvenile, for example, in a case of obstructing the police, but juvenile courts rarely rely on it,[3] partly because of its inappropriateness but partly because of its inefficacy. The court can bind over a juvenile if he consents,[4] but the power of a court, where there is non-compliance with an order, to commit the offender to custody for up to six months or until he sooner complies with it[5] does not extend to a juvenile.[6] Nor apparently can an attendance order be made.[7]

1 It is not clear how far the powers are derived from the common law, from the commission of peace held by justices or from the Justices of the Peace Act 1361.
2 *R v Sandbach, ex p Williams* [1935] 2 KB 192, [1935] All ER Rep 680.
3 The power of the Crown Court to release an offender to come up for judgment if called upon is also very rarely exercised in respect of a juvenile.
4 *Conlan v Oxford* (1984) 79 Cr App Rep 157, DC.
5 Ie under MCA 1980, s 115(2). For its application to persons aged 17–20 see *Howley*

v Oxford (1985) 81 Cr App Rep 246, [1985] Crim LR 724, DC; and *Chief Constable of the Surrey Constabulary v Ridley and Steel* [1985] Crim LR 725, DC.

6   *Veater v G* [1981] 2 All ER 304, [1981] Crim LR 563, DC.

7   See Clarke Hall and Morrison, op cit, para B[113] and compare comments at 147 JPN 721 and 148 JPN 230.

(ii)   Parent or guardian

13.13   The court may require the parent or guardian of the offender to enter into a recognisance to take proper care of the juvenile and exercise proper control over him, but the order is subject to the consent of the parent or guardian.[1] The recognisance must not exceed £1,000 and its maximum duration is either three years or until the juvenile attains 18, whichever is the shorter period.[2]

1   CYPA 1969, s 7(7).
2   Section 2(13). The forfeiture of a recognisance is on the same conditions as forfeiture to keep the peace under s 120 of the Magistrates' Courts Act 1980.

(c)   Fines, compensation and costs

13.14   A juvenile may be ordered to pay a fine, damages for injury, compensation for loss and costs, but the powers of a court in respect of him differ in two respects from its corresponding powers in relation to an adult. First, if the court is a magistrates' court (usually a juvenile court) there are limits on the amounts of the payment that can be ordered. Second, whatever kind of court makes such orders the parent or guardian can be, and usually is, ordered to make the payment instead of the juvenile.

(i)   Fines

13.15   Lack of data precludes any firm conclusion about the extent to which the fine was used historically as a method of dealing with juveniles. It seems that, whatever the age of the offender, Assizes and Quarter Sessions made little use of it. The position in courts of summary jurisdiction was even more uncertain until the Summary Jurisdiction Act 1879 restricted the power of those courts to impose fines on juveniles.[1] The maximum fines permitted were £10 in respect of a young person and 40 shillings in respect of a child. The present limits for magistrates courts are £400 and £100 respectively for any one offence, whether it is summary or indictable, unless the statutory maximum prescribed for the particular offence is less.[2] So, a juvenile court cannot fine a young person more than £400, even though the maximum amount for an adult offender in respect of the offence is £2,000.[3] In fixing the amount a juvenile court must take into account 'the means of the person on whom the fine is imposed so far as they appear or are known to the court'.[4] Two points call for comment. First, in view of the obligation of the parent or guardian normally to pay the fine,[5] this provision must, it is submitted, be read subject to the additional requirement that account is also taken of his means. Second, the rule does not require the court to *investigate* the means of the juvenile or parent or guardian.

1   Sections 10(1), 11(1) and 15. When in 1847 juveniles were allowed to be tried summarily for simple larceny, the court was given power to fine the offender up to £3; see ante, para 12.02.
2   MCA 1980, s 36. See also s 24(3) and (4).

3   That is the current maximum that a magistrates' court can impose on an adult for an indictable offence (MCA 1980, s 32, as amended), and for a summary offence if level 5 of the standard scale of fines applies to the offence; for the standard scale see Criminal Justice Act 1982, s 37, as amended.

4   MCA 1980, s 35.

5   See post, para 13.20.

13.16   Although the fine is much less frequently used to deal with juveniles than with adults, it is a likely order to be made by a juvenile court, especially in cases of first offences of theft and also of those which spring from mischievous behaviour rather than from more deeply seated causes. Its exclusively punitive nature renders it of limited value, and even the punitive effect may be lost on the juvenile if, as most often happens, the parent is required to pay the fine.[1] But, where he is personally required to pay, his means are generally such that he is ordered to pay by way of instalments,[2] and the penalty is likely to have a more salutary effect where he has to pay it over a period of time from his wages. There is a further advantage in that a juvenile court can then also order him to be supervised (usually by a probation officer or social worker) until completion of payment.[3] This supervision is a modest but useful substitute for supervision under a supervision order, especially, for example, where the juvenile is estranged from his parents and needs someone to help organise his resources.[4] It can also be ordered where there is an order to pay compensation or costs. Instead of being made initially, a supervision order may later be made if the juvenile defaults in payment, ie before the court proceeds otherwise to enforce payment.

1   See post, para 13.20.

2   The power to do this is conferred on magistrates' courts by MCA 1980, s 75, and on the Crown Court by PCCA 1973, s 31.

3   MCA 1980, s 88.

4   The supervisor must advise and befriend the juvenile with a view to inducing him to pay the fine and thereby avoid committal to custody, and, if required, must inform the court about the juvenile's conduct and means (MCR 1981, r 56(2)).

(ii) Compensation order

13.17   Instead of, or in addition to, dealing with the juvenile in any other way the court may, on application or otherwise,[1] order him to pay compensation for personal injury, loss or damage resulting from the offence of which he has been found guilty or from any which is being taken into consideration in deciding how to deal with him.[2] The court must give reasons for not making a compensation order where it has power to do so.[3] This requirement ensures that the court addresses its mind to the question of compensation. Where property has been stolen an order for restitution may be made.[4] Compensation can be given for any damage done to it before it is restored to its owner.[5] This rule has particular relevance, for example, to the case of damage to a car caused while the juvenile, who had taken it without the owner's consent was driving it.[6] In respect of traffic accident cases the court also has power[7] to make a compensation order in any case where injury, loss or damage results from an offence involving a motor vehicle in the control of the offender, provided that he is uninsured in respect of the vehicle and that compensation is not payable under any arrangements to which the Secretary of State is a party.[8] The power to make a compensation order without making any other order may have a greater impact on a juvenile than the imposition of a fine. Where the court considers both are appropriate but the means of the offender and his parent are insufficient to pay both, the court must give preference to the compensation order, although this does not prevent it also imposing a fine.[9] One notable omission is that the court cannot make an order in respect of an offence for which the juvenile received a police caution and which is reported to the court as part of the juvenile's antecedents.[10]

1   So, the court of its own motion may make an order.
2   PCCA 1973, s 35(1), as substituted by CJA 1982, s 67, and amended by CJA 1988, s 104(1), which enables a court to order payments for funeral expenses or bereavement if the offence resulted in the victim's death.
3   PCCA 1973, s 35(1), as amended by CJA 1988, s 104(1).
4   Theft Act 1968, s 28.
5   PCCA 1973, s 35(2).
6   See ibid s 35(2) and (3), as amended by CJA 1988, s 104(2).
7   See ibid s 35(3)–(3D) as amended and inserted by CJA 1988, s 104(2).
8   Ie under the Motor Insurers' Bureau arrangements.
9   PCCA 1973, s 35(4A), as inserted by CJA 1982, s 67. The subsection refers only to the offender, but must, it is submitted, impliedly include the parent or guardian given the duty normally imposed on him to make payments; see post, para 13.20.
10 For criticism see Walker, *Sentencing: Theory, Law and Practice,* para 16.52.

13.18   The maximum amount of compensation that a juvenile court can order is £2,000 for each offence of which he is found guilty, and where other offences are taken into consideration the total amount for which compensation can be ordered for them is the difference (if any) between £2,000 and the amount awarded in respect of the offence of which he is found guilty.[1] Awards of the maximum are exceedingly rare. In deciding whether to make an order and, if so, the amount, the court must take account of the means of the juvenile and his parent or guardian[2] so far as they appear or are known to the court,[3] and in fixing the amount regard must also be had to any evidence and to any representations made by the juvenile or by the parent or guardian[4] or the prosecutor.[5] The power to make an order should only be used for dealing with claims in straightforward cases,[6] since there is alternatively a civil remedy. The amount ordered should be realistic and payment of instalments over a long period avoided.[7] However, whereas courts have taken the view that payments of instalments of a fine should normally be completed within about 12 months,[8] periods of up to two and even three years have been ordered for compensation.[9]

1   MCA 1980, s 40(1). If the juvenile is found guilty of two offences and compensation in respect of each is say £800, £2,400 would be available to compensate for those offences taken into consideration.
2   See supra, para 13.15, note 4.
3   PCCA 1973, s 35(4).
4   Representations may, it is submitted, be made either on his own behalf or on behalf of the juvenile or both of them.
5   PCCA 1973, s 35(1A) as inserted by CJA 1982, s 67. There is power to discharge the order or reduce the amount to be paid; see PCCA 1973, s 37.
6   *R v Daly* [1974] 1 All ER 290, [1974] 1 WLR 133, CA.
7   *R v Miller* [1976] Crim LR 694, CA.
8   *R v Knight* (1980) 2 Cr App Rep (S) 82, [1980] Crim LR 446, CA.
9   *R v Daly,* supra note 6; *R v Makin* (1982) 4 Cr App Rep (S) 180.

(iii) Costs

13.19 The Prosecution of Offences Act 1985, Part II, applies to juveniles as to adults, subject to the statutory limit that, where a fine is imposed on a juvenile by a magistrates' court and is to be paid by him personally, the amount of the costs to be paid to the prosecutor must not exceed the amount of the fine.[1]

---

1   Section 18(5).

(iv) Ordering parent or guardian to pay fine, compensation or costs

13.20 The power of a court to order the parent or guardian instead of the juvenile to pay a fine, compensation or costs first appeared in the Youthful Offenders Act 1901. It was introduced mainly because it was recognised that juveniles almost always lacked the means to pay the fines themselves, but it was also seen as a way of making the parent aware of his parental responsibilities and ensuring he exercised proper control over his child. Consistent with these objects, section 55 of the Children and Young Persons Act 1933,[1] as originally enacted, enabled the court, if the offender was a young person, and obliged it, if he was a child, to make an order against the parent or guardian, unless it was satisfied (a) that the latter could not be found, or (b) that he had not conduced to the commission of the offence by neglecting to exercise due care or control of the juvenile. Parents and guardians, probably because they have no right of legal representation in criminal proceedings in the juvenile court, were either unaware or reluctant to invoke the second proviso, even though they might be seriously concerned about the juvenile's behaviour, had sought to control it and could not be said to have conduced to the commission of the offence. Section 55, as substituted by the Criminal Justice Act 1982[2] makes two substantial changes. First, no distinction is drawn between a child and a young person and in all cases, subject to two provisos, the court must order that the payment of a fine, compensation or costs be paid by the parent or guardian instead of by the juvenile himself. Second, while proviso (a) above is re-enacted, a new one is substituted for proviso (b), namely, that it would be unreasonable to make an order for payment, having regard to the circumstances of the case. This gives the court a wide discretion, and in all cases it should direct its mind to the matter, since by the terms of section 55 it can invoke the proviso without the parent or guardian having first to raise it. As under the former law, the parent's neglect to control his child will be a relevant factor.[3] Another will be the respective means of the juvenile and of his parent or guardian. If the juvenile, usually a young person and not a child, has the means to pay, then, it is submitted, it is prima facie unreasonable to make the parent or guardian pay. The section does not, however, permit division of responsibility. For example, if a fine and compensation are ordered against a 16-year-old earning a living, it is not permissible for the court to order him to pay the fine and his parent the compensation. Except where the parent or guardian has failed to comply with a request to attend the court, no order is to be made without giving him an opportunity of being heard.[4] He has a right of appeal to the Crown Court against any order made against him.[5]

---

1   Re-enacting provisions in s 99 of the Children Act 1908.
2   Section 26.

3   In assessing the parent's responsibility the court should not make use of the contents
    of a social inquiry report; *Lenihan v West Yorkshire Metropolitan Police* (1981) 3 Cr
    App Rep (S) 42.
4   Section 55(2).
5   Sections (3) and (4).

13.21   *The meaning of guardian*   The term 'guardian' in the present context
has its usual meaning in the Children and Young Persons legislation so
as to include any person having 'for the time being the charge of or control
over' the juvenile.[1] The scope of the definition and its origin were fully
considered by the House of Lords in *Leeds City Council v West Yorkshire
Metropolitan Police*.[2] Both on historical grounds and as a matter of public
policy the definition does not extend to a local authority which has a juvenile
in its care by virtue of a care order or because of having received him
into care under (now) the Child Care Act 1980.[3] Section 55 of the 1933
Act, like its predecessor, is aimed at the 'de facto' guardian, ie an individual
human person who has assumed the charge and control of the juvenile.
But, even in that sense, it excludes not only the local authority itself but
also the foster parents with whom the juvenile is boarded out or the persons
who manage the community home or voluntary home where he resides.
The test is whether the local authority has transferred the charge and control.
That depends on the arrangements it makes with the individual. In the
above cases by retaining supervision it has not transferred charge or control
to the foster parents or managers of the home.[4] Nor does the fact that
the local authority allows the juvenile to visit a parent or other person
on holiday or for a weekend in itself constitute a transfer. On the other
hand it may, without terminating its care, arrange with a parent or a guardian
(in the strict legal sense) or a relative or friend to transfer charge and
control to him, in which event he willingly assumes or, if a parent, reassumes
the role of a 'parent or guardian' within the meaning of section 55.[5] That
consequence is likely, for example, where the local authority has placed
the juvenile with the parent in confident expectation of a successful
rehabilitation. It follows in these cases of juveniles in local authority care
who offend and of whom charge and control has not been transferred
to an individual that the victim of the offence must seek his remedies for
compensation against the local authority, if it is at fault, for breach of
statutory duty and at common law where it fails to take reasonable care
to prevent a juvenile in its care from causing damage to others.[6]

1   CYPA 1933, s 107(1).
2   [1983] 1 AC 29, [1982] 1 All ER 274.
3   The case was decided under the Children Act 1948. Within the present context of criminal
    proceedings the term juvenile is being used in the text, but for the purpose of local
    authority care the correct term is 'child', ie a person under 18.
4   As Lord Diplock pointed out (at 36 and 276 respectively), if the foster parents had
    charge and control and were thereby liable for payment of fines etc, that would be
    'a disincentive to act as foster parents to children as to whom there was some risk
    of their reverting to delinquency'.
5   See Lord Scarman at 45 and 283 respectively.
6   See *Home Office v Dorset Yacht Co Ltd* [1970] AC 1004, [1970] 2 All ER 294, HL.

13.22   The House of Lords' decision does, in relation to section 55, raise
a query about the position of a parent whose offending child is not in
local authority care. Can such a parent only be liable if he has charge

or control or may his status of parent in itself render him liable unless the proviso of unreasonableness applies? Referring to the section, Lord Scarman stated[1] that its object 'was and is to provide a sanction against the parent or other person who, having the charge and control of the child *at the time of the offence*,[2] failed to exercise proper control . . . The section imposes a penalty on parents or other individuals who assume the *de facto* guardianship of a child, if they fail to exercise proper control of the child in their charge . . .' However, the section is not in those restrictive terms,[3] and it is suggested that the court should be able to order payment by a parent who is not living with the juvenile, unless this is unreasonable. It would, it is submitted, be reasonable to hold him liable, if, prior to leaving the matrimonial home, the parent through his neglect to control the child had contributed to his delinquent behaviour.

1　*Leeds City Council v West Yorkshire Metropolitan Police* [1983] 1 AC 29 at 39–40, [1982] 1 All ER 274 at 279.
2　Italics supplied.
3　Especially in its re-enacted form.

(v)　Enforcement of fines and orders for compensation and costs

13.23　*(1) Against the juvenile*　The possibilities of enforcing payment[1] against a defaulting juvenile by issuing a distress warrant[2] or by civil proceedings in the High Court or a county court[3] are in practice unheard of, and the method of an attachment of earnings order[4] is uncommon, being limited by its nature to the young person who is working. The Children and Young Persons Act 1969 deprived the courts of the powers to impose sanctions for non-payments until the defaulting offender reached the age of 17,[5] but the value of the attendance centre order for this purpose was recognised by the House of Commons Expenditure Committee, which recommended its re-introduction.[6] The Criminal Justice Act 1982 gives effect to this.[7] Indeed, the order is the only realistic measure for dealing with the juvenile in default, although it cannot be made unless since he was found guilty the court has inquired into his means in his presence on at least one occasion.[8] However, once a young person reaches the age of 17 it is possible to commit him for default in payment of a fine or any other sum imposed when he was under that age, provided the court considers that no other method of dealing with him is appropriate.[9]

1　Instead of enforcement of a fine the court may remit the whole or part of it. The power is not, however, often used and it does not extend to any other sums adjudged to be paid on conviction; MCA 1980, s 85.
2　Under MCA 1980, s 76.
3　Ibid, s 87.
4　Attachment of Earnings Act 1971, s 1.
5　The powers were, to commit the juvenile to a remand home, to require him to attend an attendance centre or, if he was a young person, to commit him to a detention centre.
6　Eleventh Report, para 38.
7　Section 17(1). See infra for attendance centre orders. The order ceases to have effect on payment of the outstanding sum or, if part of it is paid, the number of hours of attendance are proportionately reduced (sub-s (13); and MC (C & YP) Rules 1988, r 41).
8　MCA 1980, s 81(3).
9　CJA 1982, s 9.

13.24   *(2) Against the parent or guardian—where the juvenile is the defaulter*   Where a juvenile, having the means to pay, has defaulted and, were it not for the rule which prevents a sentence of imprisonment being imposed on anyone under 21,[1] a juvenile court would have power to commit him to prison for the default or for want of sufficient distress to satisfy the sum due, that court may make one of two orders. It may require his parent or guardian, provided he consents, to enter into a recognisance to ensure that the juvenile pays the sum outstanding. Alternatively it can direct that the outstanding amount be paid by the parent or guardian instead of by the juvenile, if in all the circumstances such an order is reasonable and provided he is given an opportunity to be heard or, having been required to attend, has failed to do so.[2] The parent or guardian has a right of appeal against the latter order.[3] Whereas the court has no duty to inquire into means before imposing a fine or ordering compensation or costs, it must after the conviction do so at least once and in the defaulting juvenile's presence before it can make either of the above orders.[4] If the parent or guardian is ordered to pay, the amount may then be recovered from him as if the order had been made on his being convicted of an offence.[5]

1   CJA 1982, s 1(1).
2   MCA 1980, s 81(1), (2), (4), (5) and (8). 'Guardian' here has its strictly legal meaning; see ante, Chapter 4.
3   Ibid, s 81(6).
4   Ibid, s 81(3). The same prerequisite applies to the making of an attendance centre order for default; see the previous paragraph.
5   Ibid, s 81(7).

13.25   *Where the parent or guardian is the defaulter*   Similarly, if the parent or guardian has been ordered to pay the fine, compensation or costs and defaults, the amount may be recovered on the basis that he was convicted of the offence with which the juvenile was charged.[1]

1   Administration of Justice Act 1970, s 41 and Sch 9.

(d)   Attendance centre orders

(i)   Introduction

13.26   The Departmental Committee on Corporal Punishment in its Report in 1938[1] drew attention to the need for juvenile courts to be given further powers enabling them to deal with juvenile offenders whose behaviour did not warrant institutional treatment but rather some form of short and sharp punishment which would act as a deterrent. Implementation was delayed by the War, but appeared in the Criminal Justice Act 1948 in the form of the attendance centre order.[2] The need for it was made greater by the abolition of corporal punishment of juveniles, for which the Act also provided, although it would be wrong to think that the order was created simply as a substitute for such punishment: it was designed to serve a distinct purpose of its own.[3] Twenty years later the Children and Young Persons Act 1969[4] planned for its eventual abolition as and when schemes for intermediate treatment under supervision orders were developed, but the House of Commons Expenditure Committee acknowledged the useful function attendance centres could perform and recommended their retention.[5] Confidence in them is reflected in the substantial increase in their number since 1978 and the Criminal Justice Act 1982 has, with some amendments (mainly affecting the Crown Court), re-enacted the provisions of the 1948 Act.

1 Cmnd 5684, para 31.
2 Section 19. The minimum age of 12 was reduced to ten by the Criminal Justice Act 1961.
3 See McClintock in the *Report of the Cambridge Institute of Criminology on Attendance Centres* (1961) p 25.
4 Section 7(3), Sch 4, para 6, and Sch 5, para 23.
5 Eleventh Report (1975), para 49.

(ii) The nature, scope and purpose of the order
13.27 An order may be made by the Crown Court[1] or by any magistrates' court in respect of an offender under the age of 21.[2] Attention is here directed to juveniles. The order has two basic uses:

1 It can be made whenever the court would have power, but for the restrictions upon the imprisonment of persons under 21,[3] to impose imprisonment.[4] Thus, it is available as a method of dealing not only with a juvenile found guilty of an offence punishable with imprisonment but also with one who defaults in complying with an order of the court, especially default in paying a fine, compensation or costs.[5]
2 It can be used to deal with a supervised person who fails to comply with requirements in a supervision order, which was made in criminal procedings.[6] This is considered later.[7]

1 Whether as the court of trial or in exercise of its appellate jurisdiction or when an offender is committed to it for sentence.
2 CJA 1982, s 16(2)(a).
3 Ibid, s 1.
4 Section 17(1)(a).
5 See ante, para 13.23.
6 CJA 1982, ss 16(2)(b) and 17(1)(b), and CYPA 1969, ss 15(2A) and (4) and 16(10).
7 Paragraph 13.67.

13.28 Because the times of attendance must be such as to avoid, so far as practicable, interference with the offender's school, or working hours,[1] Saturday attendance is usually ordered.[2] This is preferred to evening attendance on other days because it is felt to be more punitive; for example, in respect of the hooligan at football matches. The aggregate number of hours for which attendance of a juvenile may be ordered must (a) be not less than 12 except where he is under 14 and the court considers that period is excessive, and (b) must not exceed 12 unless the court considers that that is inadequate, in which case it may be for up to 24 hours.[3] The first date and time of attendance is fixed by the court, but all subsequent attendances by the officer in charge of the centre.[4] The juvenile cannot be required to attend on more than one occasion on any day or for more than three hours on any occasion.[5] On the other hand, so far as practicable an attendance must not be for less than one hour.[6] Within these limits the officer has an unfettered discretion and as a method of punishment may increase the number of attendances by reducing each to one hour. The court may make a new attendance centre order while an earlier one is still in force, and in fixing the number of hours may disregard the number specified in the previous order and the fact that that order still exists,[7] but it is not empowered to make attendance centre orders on the same occasion to run consecutively.

1   CJA 1982, s 17(8).
2   So the order might not be appropriate for the juvenile who works on Saturdays.
3   Section 17(4) and (5). For young persons either the maximum or a period of 18 hours is frequently ordered.
4   Section 17(9) and (10).
5   Section 17(11).
6   Attendance Centre Rules 1958, r 4(2), (SI 1958/1990) as amended by Attendance Centre Rules 1978 (SI 1978/1919).
7   Section 17(6).

13.29   The Home Secretary is responsible for seeing that centres are provided, and does this by arranging with local authorities or police authorities for them to be established,[1] for example, in school buildings or police premises.[2] Because of central government responsibility the cost of running centres is borne by the Exchequer and therefore the Home Office conducts regular inspections. In deciding whether to establish a centre the Home Office consults the local juvenile court panel, the social services department of the local authority and the probation service.

1   CJA 1982, s 16(1) and (4).
2   Most centres are run by the local police authority with an inspector or person of higher rank or a retired police officer in charge. There are well over 100 Junior Centres (ie for persons under 17) mostly for boys, but some 10% are mixed, and very limited provisions for girls under 17 in girl centres. See the list published by the Home Office (August 1984) in its Note on Attendance Centres.

13.30   The use of the order is considerably restricted by the rule that it can only be made if the court has been notified by the Home Secretary that a centre is available for the reception of persons of the offender's description[1] and that it is 'reasonably accessible . . . having regard to his age, the means of access available to him and any other circumstances'.[2] The Home Office has suggested as guidance[3] that ten miles or travelling time of 45 minutes for children[4] and 15 miles or 90 minutes for young persons is a reasonable maximum to travel. It is mainly for this reason that centres are in practice confined to urban areas. However, this is no more than guidance, and the question of accessibility is for the court; for example, it should take account of any hardship to the juvenile and his parent that the cost of travel would cause. Moreover, it is possible for a court in one area to make an order for the juvenile to attend a centre in another area (provided the court has checked that there is a place available). This can be particularly useful when dealing with a juvenile, for example, a football supporter who lives in another area.[5]

1   CJA 1982, s 17(1). No guidance is given on the meaning of 'description', but in practice the relevant question is whether the offender is a juvenile or a young offender (17–20). Formerly s 19(1) of the CJA 1948 indelicately referred to 'class or description'.
2   Section 17(7).
3   See Home Office Note, supra, para 13.29, note 2.
4   The Ingleby Committee (Cmnd 1191), para 291, thought that for 10 and 11 year olds the distance and time should be less.
5   See Home Office Circulars No 136/77 (CS22 1977) and No 64/1983.

13.31   The purposes of the order have never been clarified. A recent study of six local juvenile justice systems[1] has shown the varied but uncertain use made of it. Some courts see it as an early alternative to the fine or supervision order. Sometimes that may be appropriate where the imposition of a fine would cause hardship to the parent and the family or where 'ongoing contact with a supervisor is not thought necessary or has not proved effective'.[2] But the risk is that the first or inexperienced offender may be too readily deprived of other non-custodial orders. This applies particularly to the supervision order, in view of the policy of the Criminal Justice Act 1982 to strengthen it through more effective arrangements for intermediate treatment.[3] Some courts, however (properly it is suggested), see the attendance centre order as an alternative to a custodial order for the experienced offender. Nevertheless, that it is not designed for the recidivist is clear from the rule[4] which prevents an order being made in the case of a juvenile previously sentenced to youth custody or detention in a detention centre or (in future) in a young offender institution,[5] unless the court considers there are special circumstances (relating to the offence or the offender) which warrant such an order. Careful consideration should also be given before relying on the order as a means of dealing with violent offenders for 'if unruly or recidivist offenders are sent to [attendance centres] they could adversely affect the established regime of a centre and place the system in jeopardy'.[6] For this reason the Home Office has advised caution in using the order in relation to football hooligans. The aims of the order are partly punitive, by imposing loss of leisure, and partly reformative, by providing occupation and instruction at a centre 'such as to occupy the persons attending there . . . in a manner conducive to health of mind and body'.[7] Since 1977 the Home Office has given guidance on both these aspects in an effort to provide greater uniformity in the treatment of offenders in centres,[8] but much still depends on the attitudes of those who run them, with some insisting more on the strictness of the discipline, especially in physical training,[9] and others more concerned with providing constructive forms of occupation that will encourage better use of leisure hours.

1   Gelsthorpe and Nutt, *The Attendance Centre Order* [1986] Crim LR 146.
2   Cavenagh, *The Juvenile Court* (1976) p 18.
3   See post, paras 13.47 et seq.
4   Section 17(3).
5   Other restrictions, by their nature uncommon, are where the juvenile has previously been sentenced to custody for life or detention for murder or other grave offences under s 53 of CYPA 1933, post.
6   Home Office Circular No 95/1978.
7   Attendance Centre Rules 1958, r 2(1).
8   Moreover, the occupation and instruction at a centre must be in accordance with a scheme approved by the Home Secretary; r 2(2).
9   Thus, the juvenile's medical condition may sometimes be a factor in deciding whether an order is appropriate. Those representing juveniles should be alert to this.

(iii)   Breach of rules relating to attendance
13.32   Whenever an offender has failed without reasonable excuse to attend the centre as required or has while attending committed a breach of the Attendance Centre Rules 1958 (as amended), for which under those Rules he cannot adequately be dealt with, a magistrates' court may revoke the order and deal with him in any way in which the court making the original

order could have dealt with him had it not made the order.[1] There is a right of appeal to the Crown Court against sentence.[2] Where the attendance centre order was made by the Crown Court, the magistrates' court may remand him in custody or on bail to appear before the Crown Court.[3] It is, however, very uncommon to bring an offender back before the court for a breach of the Rules. Instead, the officer in charge may exercise various disciplinary powers; for example by separating the offender from others and giving him less pleasant tasks, or by requiring him to leave the centre and discounting his attendance on that occasion, or by reducing the duration of each period of attendance and correspondingly increasing the number of attendances.

1   CJA 1982, s 19(1)–(3)(a). The juvenile's appearance is compelled by summons or warrant issued by a justice.
2   Section 19(6) and (7).
3   Section 19(3)(b), (5) and (7).

(iv) Reports
13.33   Although an attendance centre must keep certain records (for example, of attendance and breach of rules),[1] there is no statutory duty to provide the centre with reports on the offender before his first appearance. Nor is there a duty for the centre to report on him when his attendance ends. The need to provide the officer in charge with records relating to previous appearance in court, a social inquiry report and a school record was stressed in the Cambridge Report.[2] In most cases these documents are forwarded and correspondingly many officers in charge report to the court; but the importance of these measures is self-evident and they ought to be made compulsory.

1   Attendance Centre Rules 1958, r 3(1).
2   Pages 41–42; see ante, para 13.26, note 3.

(v) Discharge and variation of orders
13.34   The offender or the officer in charge may apply for the order to be discharged or varied,[1] but the only variations permissible are the day or hour specified for the offender's first attendance at the centre or a change to a more accessible centre because of the offender's change of residence.[2] Either a magistrates' court acting for the area in which the centre is situated or the magistrates' court which made the order may discharge or vary it.[3]

1   CJA 1982, s 18(1) and (5).
2   Section 18(6).
3   Section 18(3). But, if the Crown Court made the order, either that court may discharge it or, unless the Crown Court reserved the power to discharge to itself, a magistrates' court for the area where the centre is situated. The latter court is the appropriate one to *vary* a Crown Court order. See s 18(3), (4) and (5).

(e) Community service orders

13.35   This is another order which is only available in respect of an offence punishable with imprisonment but for the restrictions upon the imprisonment of persons under 21.[1] However, unlike the attendance centre order,[2] it cannot be used as a method of dealing with a defaulter[3] or with a breach of a supervision order. Primarily intended as a substitute for a custodial sentence, it has tended to be used as an alternative to a fine or a probation order.[4]

1 The relevant law is to be found in the PCCA 1973, ss 14–17C, as amended and added by the CJA 1982, s 68 and Schs 12 and 13.
2 See ante, para 13.27.
3 CJA 1972, s 49 provides for this but has not been brought into operation.
4 See Walker, op cit, para 18.19, and generally paras 18.16–18.27.

13.36   The Criminal Justice Act 1982 reduced from 17 to 16 years the minimum age of offenders for whom the order is available, but the maximum number of hours of service that can be ordered in the case of 16-year-olds is 120, half of that applicable to older defendants,[1] and an order cannot be made unless the court has been notified by the Secretary of State that arrangements for community service by juveniles of that age exist in the area in which the juvenile resides and is satisfied that provision can be made for him to perform work.[2] Regrettably, the extension of the system by local probation committees was delayed in several areas because of lack of resources and of availability of unpaid work, and there is unfortunately no statutory obligation imposed on committees to give priority to juveniles in the provision of arrangements. Before the court can make an order it must obtain the juvenile's consent, and it must be satisfied, in the light of a social inquiry report from a probation officer or a local authority social worker (and an oral report if necessary), that the juvenile is suitable for community service.[3] Where a social worker reports, it is essential that he or she first consults the community service organiser before recommending an order, since the court will want to be satisfied on that point.[4] The court must also explain to the juvenile the purpose and effect of the order, the power to review it and the consequences of non-compliance.[5] Those consequences are that he will be brought before a magistrates' court,[6] which may impose a fine not exceeding £400 or deal with him in a manner in which he could have originally been dealt with for the offence.[7] The latter power may similarly be exercised where a court, on application, revokes a community service order.[8] Where it is exercised, credit should be given for hours already completed under the order.[9] There is also power to vary an order where the juvenile changes his residence from one area to another.[10] Where there is a breach of an order and the order was made by a magistrates' court there is no power to commit the offender to the Crown Court for sentence: the magistrates' court must itself deal with him.[11]

1 PCCA 1973, s 14(1A). The minimum is 40 hours in all cases. Normally the work must be performed within 12 months from the date of the order (s 15(2)), but the court may extend the period (s 17(1)).
2 Section 14(2A)(b).
3 Section 14(2).
4 See Home Office Circular No 43/1983, para 9.
5 For his obligations see s 15.
6 Ie a court acting for the area specified in the order. If the breach occurs after the offender reaches the age of 17, it seems clear that an adult magistrates' court will have to deal with him; see Clarke Hall and Morrison, para B[880.1].
7 See s 16. If the order was made by the Crown Court, the magistrates' court must remand him in custody or on bail to that court. The CJA 1988, s 127 (adding sub-s (1A) to s 55 of CYPA 1933) puts the onus on the parent or guardian to pay the fine instead of the juvenile, unless the court is satisfied that the parent or guardian cannot be found

or that it would be unreasonable to make an order for payment, having regard to the circumstances of the case.

8   Section 17(2). For jurisdiction and power to revoke where the offender is later convicted of another offence see s 17(3), (4A) and (4B).
9   *R v Whittingham* [1986] Crim LR 572.
10   Section 17(5A), (5B) and (6).
11   *R v Worcester Crown Court, ex p Lamb* (1985) 7 Cr App Rep (S) 44, DC; *R v Daniels* (1986) 8 Cr App Rep (S) 257, [1986] Crim LR 824, CA.

(f)   Supervision orders

(i)   Introduction

13.37   The supervisory system has a long history. It is widely acknowledged that it originated in the practice of Warwickshire justices passing a sentence of one day's imprisonment upon a young offender on condition that he returned to the care of his parent or master, by whom he was to be carefully supervised. The practice dates from about 1820, and commended itself to Matthew Davenport Hill, Recorder of Birmingham, who, some 20 years later, strengthened it by ordering inquiries concerning the offender to be made before deciding whether to order his release, by requiring the parent or master to acknowledge his obligation to supervise the juvenile and by requesting the police to follow up cases to see how the juvenile was behaving and whether the parent was fulfilling his obligation. The next stage of development was when the duty of supervision was undertaken by religious workers, known as 'court missionaries', who became increasingly active from 1890 onwards. So much so that some courts, with Home Office encouragement, made use of them to advise and befriend offenders who had been bound over under the Summary Jurisdiction Act 1879 or the Probation of First Offenders Act 1887.

13.38   The Probation of Offenders Act 1907 gave statutory recognition to this long established voluntary practice of supervision of offenders, and the system was immediately extended to juveniles who were not offenders but who were for various reasons in need of care or control.[1] One of the additional powers conferred by the Children Act 1908 in relation to them was that which enabled the court to make an order under the former Act placing under the supervision of a probation officer a juvenile who was being committed to the care of a relative or other fit person.[2] The Children and Young Persons Act 1933[3] went further by enabling the court to make a supervision order not only in addition to a fit person order but also without the latter order being made, and the Children and Young Persons Act 1963[4] brought supervision orders very largely into line with probation orders. The Children and Young Persons Act 1969 completed the unifying process by abolishing the probation order in relation to juvenile offenders[5] and making the supervision order available both for them[6] and for juveniles who are the subject of care proceedings.[7] However, in several respects the distinction between the offender and the juvenile found to be in need of care and control is still relevant, and the Criminal Justice Act 1982 widened the distinction.

1   See post, paras 14.110–14.111
2   Children Act 1908, s 60. A child (ie a person under 14) beyond parental control could also be placed under supervision (s 58(4)).
3   Section 62.

4   Section 5 and Sch 1.
5   Section 7(2).
6   Section 7(7)(b).
7   Section 1(3)(b).

(ii)   The choice of supervisor

13.39   Under the 1933 Act the supervisor could be either a probation officer or 'some other person appointed by the court',[1] but the 1963 Act recognised the rapid expansion of the child care service after 1948 by expressly providing that a local authority could be so appointed.[2] The 1969 Act showed a further shift towards local authorities, and the legislative policy is to make them very largely responsible for the supervision of children, as opposed to young persons. Thus, while a supervisor of a juvenile may be either a local authority or a probation officer,[3] the latter may only be appointed in respect of a child under 13,[4] if the authority whose area is to be named in the order[5] so requests and a probation officer is, or has been, concerned with supervising[6] another member of the same household.[7] When the resources of the social services so permit, this limitation will extend to those under 14. The continued use of the probation service for the supervision of children in such circumstances recognises that it is normally undesirable and unnecessary to have two social workers involved with the same family. In any event, the local authority will wish to consult the probation officer who is already working with the family before deciding whether to recommend to the court that, if a supervision order is made, a probation officer be appointed as supervisor.[8] There are no precise data showing the extent to which juvenile courts favour choosing a probation officer rather than a local authority as supervisor of a juvenile offender where there is no legal restriction on the appointment of a probation officer.[9]

1   Section 62.
2   Section 5(3).
3   Section 11.
4   CYPA 1969, s 34(1)(a); CYPA 1969 (Transitional Modifications of Part I) Order 1970 (SI 1970/1882) as amended by SI 1974/1083.
5   A supervision order must name the area of the local authority and the petty sessions area in which it appears that the supervised person resides or will reside (s 18(2)(a)); residence means habitual residence (s 70(1)).
6   Ie by virtue of para 8 of Sch 3 of the Powers of Criminal Courts Act 1973.
7   For the meaning of household see post, para 14.10. *Semble*, the member need not be a juvenile; for example, a probation officer may be supervising an adult member under a probation order.
8   See Home Office Guide to Part I of the 1969 Act, para 112.
9   The House of Commons Expenditure Committee in its Eleventh Report, para 39, recommended that the transfer of responsibilities from the probation service to the local authority social services departments be halted until the latter had adequate staff for supervisory functions. It further recommended, para 97, that some social workers be encouraged to specialise in the field of juvenile delinquency, an important proposal in view of the fact that juvenile courts spend most of their time exercising their criminal jurisdiction.

13.40   Normally the appropriate authority to act as supervisor is that within whose area the supervised person resides or will reside, but exceptionally it may be another if it agrees to be designated.[1] The probation officer must be one who is assigned to the petty sessions area which is named in the supervision order.[2] The order does not have to name him but the juvenile should be told his name, if the court knows it.

1   CYPA 1969, s 13(1).
2   Sections 13(3) and 18(2)(a).

(iii)   Duration of orders
13.41   A court must not make a supervision order unless satisfied that
the supervised person resides or will reside in the area of a local authority.[1]
An order operates for three years or for any shorter period it specifies,
unless it is earlier discharged.[2] Terms of one year or two are the most
common. Whereas a supervision order made in care proceedings or on
the discharge of a care order[3] automatically ceases when the supervised
person becomes 18,[4] when it is made in criminal proceedings it may continue
beyond that age. Thus, an order for two years, made when the juvenile
was $16\frac{1}{2}$-years-old will continue until he is $18\frac{1}{2}$, unless it is earlier
discharged.[5]

1   CYPA 1969, s 18(1)
2   If a supervision order, made in criminal proceedings, is in force, a court in later criminal
     proceedings may make a new supervision order and discharge the earlier one (s 7(7)).
3   See post, para 14.110.
4   CYPA 1969, s 17.
5   For discharge and variation see post, paras 13.59 et seq.

(iv)   Contents of orders
13.42   Unlike a probation order, a supervision order may be made without
the supervised person's consent, but his consent is a prerequisite to the
inclusion of certain requirements in the order, if he has attained the age
of 14.[1]

1   See post, para 13.45 and para 13.55.

13.43   *(1)   Contact and visits*   So long as an order is in force the supervisor
must 'advise, assist and befriend' the juvenile.[1] These are his basic functions,
and to facilitate the performance of them the order may and should include
a provision (1) that the juvenile inform his supervisor of any change of
residence or employment, and (2) that he keep in touch with his supervisor
as the latter so instructs and, in particular, that he receive visits from the
supervisor at his home.[2] In all cases regular contact is essential, especially
during the early part of the period of supervision, and, given the wide
powers which the Children and Young Persons Act 1969 entrusts to a
supervisor where the order authorises 'intermediate treatment',[3] the need
to establish an early personal relationship in those circumstances is all the
greater. Frequency of meetings will depend partly on the behaviour and
progress of the juvenile,[4] but unfortunately, largely because of lack of
resources and because of pressures on the individual social worker, the
supervisor quite often is unable to insist on regular attendance or to make
home visits. It is, for example, not uncommon for a supervisor to be unaware
of the juvenile's truancy and to learn of it only shortly before preparing
his social inquiry report when the juvenile is due to appear before the
court for re-offending. Indeed, it is not unknown for that report and the
school report to be contradictory about the juvenile's school attendance.

1   CYPA 1969, s 14.
2   Section 18(2)(b) and MC (C & YP) Rules 1988, r 43(2).

3   See infra, para 13.47.
4   But sometimes partly on the influence and co-operation of the parent. On the possibility
    of imposing requirements on parents see post, para 14.111.

13.44 *(2) Residence with an individual*   Section 12 of the 1969 Act, which
was substantially amended by the Criminal Justice Act 1982, confers on
the court wide powers to include requirements relating to residence and
treatment.[1] Under subsection (1) an order may require the juvenile to reside,
either for the whole or part of the period of supervision,[2] with a named
individual, such as a relative or friend, subject obviously to the latter's
consent. Its purpose is to allow residence in the household of a private
person, but the juvenile remains subject to the general control of the
supervisor[3] and to any specific requirements imposed by the order. It does
not authorise residence at a specified place, and, therefore, if the court
considers residence at an institution is desirable, it may give the supervisor
a discretion to direct residence in such a place[4] or make a care order,
the advantages of that order being that it is not subject to limitations on
the period of residence and it allows for flexibility in moving the juvenile
from one institution to another,[5] although whether that is desirable may
be another matter. A requirement relating to mental treatment or to
intermediate treatment or one directly imposed by the court overrides a
residence requirement in so far as they conflict.

1   Section 12 and the amending provisions of the 1982 Act are, along with further
    amendments, consolidated by the Criminal Justice Act 1988, Sch 10, Part I, and appear
    as ss 12, 12A, 12B, 12C and 12D of the 1969 Act.
2   There is no statutory restriction in this regard.
3   Compare the former fit person order whereby the juvenile was placed in the care of
    an individual.
4   See infra, para 13.51.
5   See Home Office Guide to Part I of CYPA 1969, para 119, and for care orders post,
    paras 15.47 et seq.

13.45 *(3) Treatment for a mental condition*   Where the court has medical
evidence[1] that the mental condition of the juvenile needs treatment (for
example, because of drug addiction) but does not warrant the making of
a hospital order,[2] it may include in the supervision order a requirement
that for a specified period he submit to treatment by a named doctor or
at a hospital or nursing home as a resident or out-patient.[3] No maximum
period is prescribed, but the requirement is automatically terminated when
the supervised person becomes 18,[4] even though a supervision order made
in criminal proceedings may continue beyond that age,[5] an illogical
consequence. The requirement is subject to two further restrictions, namely,
that before including it the court must be satisfied that arrangements for
treatment can be made and, where the juvenile is a young person, that
he consents to the inclusion.[6]

1   Clarke Hall and Morrison, op cit, para B[722], point out that a written statement under
    CJA 1967, s 9 may be submitted. The clerk to the justices should be consulted about
    calling medical evidence; see Cavenagh, op cit, p 24.
2   For hospital orders see post, para 13.105.
3   CYPA 1969, s 12B(1).
4   s 12B(2).
5   See supra, para 13.41.
6   The Review of Child Care Law, undertaken by the Department of Health and Social

Security, (1985) recommends (para 18.21) that the requirement of consent should extend to conditions requiring medical treatment generally.

13.46 A juvenile who is a resident patient has no right to have his case periodically reviewed,[1] the reason being that in theory at least he is free at any time to leave the hospital. There is also the possibility of his seeking variation or cancellation of the requirement.[2] But it is essential that when the requirement is inserted these matters should be made clear to him, as should the fact that, if he leaves, the supervisor may bring him back before the court, with the possible result of a care order being substituted.

1   See Holden, *Child Legislation*, pp 141–142.
2   See post, para 13.60.

13.47 *(4) Intermediate treatment—(a) Origin* One of the major changes proposed by the White Paper, *Children in Trouble*, was that there should be 'new forms of treatment, intermediate between supervision in the home and committal to care'[1] which would enable the juvenile to be brought under different environmental influences. The proposal was not entirely novel. The Advisory Council on the Treatment of Young Offenders had been asked to consider the possibility of introducing a system of training centres where juvenile offenders, especially those who might otherwise be the subject of a custodial order, could receive intensive and constructive training without being removed from their homes. For various reasons the Council came down firmly against such a system,[2] preferring increased efficiency in the use of the existing methods of treatment coupled with experimentation 'within the framework of the existing services that are designed to provide for the general and social education of young people in the community as a whole'.[3] Eventually, giving effect to the general recommendation of the White Paper, sections 12 and 19 of the Children and Young Persons Act 1969, as originally enacted, provided for a system which would:

> 'make available to supervisors additional resources, sufficient finance for the use of these resources, and compulsory powers for use where necessary. The aim [would be] to take action which is constructive and remedial, not punitive, by extending the preventive approach, by making the maximum possible use of the existing resources of each local community and by spending relatively small sums for this purpose so as to avoid, where possible, the need for more expensive measures later on.'[4]

That remains partly the aim of intermediate treatment, (IT), but, as will be seen,[5] new powers relating to supervision have meant new purposes and heavier expenditure.

1   Cmnd 3601, para 21.
2   See the Report on *Non-Residential Treatment of Offenders Under 21* (1962).
3   There is a duty under s 41 of the Education Act 1944 to provide leisure-time occupation for persons over compulsory school age as part of the wider duty of every local education authority to provide further education, but the forms of occupation provided are limited and largely out of date; see Liell and Saunders, *The Law of Education*, 9th edn, para B[40].

4   Home Office Guide to Part I of the 1969 Act, para 121; and see Local Authority Circular,
     (LAC 77(1)).
5   Infra, para 13.48.

13.48 Responsibility for providing facilities was entrusted to the twelve regional planning committees which the Act established. Each regional scheme provided both residential centres (for example, for adventure holidays and field courses) and local non-residential facilities such as youth centres and youth clubs, run by various public and private organisations. But the picture to emerge in the early years was generally unfavourable,[1] with some local authorities failing to make any provision for IT. Consequently, the House of Commons Expenditure Committee urged that 'more should be done to encourage RPCs and local authorities to produce more imaginative plans and to stimulate the development of intermediate treatment in those areas where it is inadequate.'[2] Further impetus came from the White Paper on Young Offenders,[3] which recommended more effective powers being entrusted to the courts in the making of supervision orders. The eventual outcome was the substantial amendment of sections 12 and 19 of the 1969 Act by the Criminal Justice Act 1982.[4]

1   See Watson and Austin, op cit, pp 114–116 and 151. For a wider survey see LAC 77(1).
2   Eleventh Report, para 117, and see generally paras 105–116 for a summary of the aims,
     hopes and doubts concerning intermediate treatment.
3   (1980) Cmnd 8045.
4   Sections 20 and 21.

13.49 *(b) Present facilities for IT*   Responsibility for providing IT facilities now lies with each local authority, acting either individually or in association with other local authorities.[1] Every local authority had to provide a new scheme of facilities by 30 September 1983,[2] but from time to time it may make further schemes.[3] In deciding what facilities should be listed in a scheme the authority should satisfy itself about the standard and support provided, the relevance of the activities offered and their cost effectiveness.[4] The facilities must be approved, or of a kind approved, by the Secretary of State.[5] There is a lengthy list of approved activities of a 'recreational, educational or cultural nature or of a social value', the last mentioned including 'training designed to establish better links with members of the community and with community groups and clubs'.[6] A notable feature of the statutory duties of a local authority is the authority's obligation to consult all probation committees in its area before arranging IT facilities.[7] A probation committee may itself provide facilities.[8] If so, they may be incorporated into the local authority scheme.[9] The local authority must also keep the courts informed of details of facilities by sending copies of schemes to the clerks to the justices.[10] But beyond the duty to inform is the desirability to co-operate with the courts and agencies involved in IT in the planning, operation and monitoring of facilities.[11]

1   CYPA 1969, s 19(1).
2   The date finally fixed by the Secretary of State under s 19(15); see Local Authority
     Circular LAC (83)6.
3   Section 19(7). By March 1983 there were 90 approved schemes, involving 52 local
     authorities and voluntary groups, providing almost 3,000 places for juvenile offenders
     (NACRO, Annual Report 1984/85, p 12).
4   See LAC (83)6.

5 Section 19(11).
6 See Annex to LAC (83)6.
7 Section 19(2) and (9).
8 Powers of Criminal Courts Act 1973, Sch 3, para 3(2A), inserted by CJA 1982, Sch 11, para 6.
9 See Home Office Circular No 42/1983, para 54.
10 Section 19(5) and (10). Copies must also be available to the public (s 19(6)).
11 See LAC (83)6 and see post, para 13.55, note 3.

13.50 The duty to provide IT facilities is to be discharged so that certain powers conferred by section 12 of the 1969 Act can be exercised effectively.[1] The section provides for delegated IT, ie directions for IT are delegated by the court to the supervisor, and stipulated IT, ie the court itself imposes requirements relating to IT. Delegated IT is available in respect of juveniles both in care and criminal proceedings, and when a supervision order is substituted for a care order made in either proceedings. Stipulated IT, as an alternative to delegated IT, may only be ordered in criminal proceedings or when a supervision order is substituted for a care order made in those proceedings.[2]

1 Section 19(1).
2 See s 12A(1) and (2), as substituted by CJA 1988, Sch 10, Part I.

13.51 *(c) Delegated IT* The decision whether a supervision order should include a provision relating to IT is solely a matter for the court. Under section 12(2) of the 1969 Act[1] the order may authorise the supervisor to give to the juvenile from time to time directions on all or any of the following, but the decision whether they should be given and, if so, their precise form and date of commencement is one for the supervisor:

(i) to live at a place or places specified in the directions for a period or periods so specified;
(ii) to present himself to a person or persons specified in the directions at a place or places and on a day or days so specified;
(iii) to participate in activities specified in the directions on a day or days so specified.

The total number of days in respect of which the juvenile may be required to comply with the directions is 90 days or such lesser number as the court may specify. Any day on which there was non-compliance may be disregarded.[2] The fact that the supervisor may give directions from time to time indicates that he may vary any already given, for example, by shortening the period for which he directed the juvenile to live at an establishment.

1 As substituted by CJA 1982, s 20(1).
2 Section 12(3), as substituted. Section 12(2) and (3) are re-enacted by CJA 1988, Sch 10, Part I.

13.52 The discretion which may be conferred on a supervisor is limited by three factors. It depends upon the terms of the requirement of IT laid down in the supervision order. The supervisor may direct the juvenile to participate only in activities provided at facilities listed in a current IT scheme.[1] If there is also included in the order a requirement relating to mental treatment,[2] that takes precedence.[3]

1   Section 19(12), as substituted by CJA 1982, s 21.
2   Supra, para 13.49.
3   Section 12(2).

13.53 *(d) Stipulated IT*   Most of the changes made to section 12 of the 1969 Act by the Criminal Justice Acts 1982 and 1988 are designed to enable the court to make more effective use of the supervision order as an alternative to custodial orders for juvenile offenders and to 'restore confidence in the supervision order'.[1] Under section 12A(3) the court may include in the order any one or more of three kinds of requirements:[2] a positive requirement, corresponding to any or all of the above directions given by a supervisor under delegated IT, that the juvenile does certain things; a night restriction requirement; and a negative requirement that the juvenile does not participate in specified activities. By their nature they introduce into the supervision order a punitive element, strengthened by the rule that breach of any of them may lead to penal consequences.[3]

The Criminal Justice Act 1988[4] has conferred an additional power on the court to require an offender who is of compulsory school age to comply with such arrangements for his education as may from time to time be made by his parent, provided the arrangements are approved by the local education authority.

1   *Young Offenders*, Cmnd 8045. Many juvenile courts had been critical of the 'leniency' of the old systems of IT.
2   Former requirements (introduced by the Criminal Law Act 1977) that could be ordered were (1) to be of good behaviour, (2) to comply with such specified requirements as the court considered appropriate for preventing commission of further offences by the juvenile, and (3) to comply with directions for school attendance.
3   See post, para 13.67
4   By adding a new s 12C to CYPA 1969.

13.54   The first of these requirements[1] directly relates to IT, for the court is empowered[2] to require a supervised person:

> 'to do anything that by virtue of subsection (2) of this section a supervisor has power, or would but for section 19(12) of this Act have power, to direct a supervised person to do.'

It can, therefore, require the juvenile to participate in specified activities which are provided by an IT scheme. However, and the point needs to be stressed, it can instead arrange a programme of activities outside such a scheme, but not if those activities involve spending more than two consecutive nights or more than two nights in any week away from home or, not being facilities arranged by his local education authority, if they require the juvenile's participation during normal school hours.[3] In any of those circumstances they must be IT facilities. As with a supervisor's directions, the maximum number of days that the juvenile may be subject to the court's requirements is 90 days.[4]

The Criminal Justice Act 1988[5] provides that where the court would have imposed a custodial sentence if it had not made a supervision order including a requirement that the juvenile participate in specified activities, it must state in open court (i) that it is making the order instead of a custodial sentence; and (ii) that it is satisfied that (a) the offender has a history of failure to respond to non-custodial penalty and is unable or unwilling to respond to any non-custodial penalty other than a supervision order including such a requirement, or (b) only such an order with such a requirement or a custodial sentence could be adequate to protect the public from serious harm from him, or (c) the offence was so serious that a non-custodial sentence other than a supervision order including such a requirement could not be justified; and (iii) why it is so satisfied.

1   For the other two see infra, paras 13.57 and 13.58.
2   By CYPA 1969, s 12A(3)(a), as substituted by CJA 1988, Sch 10, Part I.
3   Section 19(13) and (14).
4   Section 12A(5), as substituted by CJA 1988, Sch 10, Part I.
5   By adding a new s 12D to CYPA 1969.

13.55   The court's power to include requirements under section 12A(3)(a) is subject to the following limitations.[1] They also apply to night restriction requirements and requirements prohibiting specified activities. Their purpose is to ensure that a requirement is not included where inappropriate.

1   As already noted,[2] co-operation between various agencies is essential. This applies to the court and the supervisor. Thus, the court must not include any of the above requirements unless it has first consulted the supervisor about the offender's circumstances and the feasibility of securing compliance with the requirements.[3] This will usually be done through the social inquiry report and, if necessary, supplementary oral evidence. The report should cover such matters as the offender's special needs, the facilities available and their suitability in the particular case. In this way the supervision order can be flexibly used to fit the individual offender in a way that a custodial order can not. Only if it is satisfied on the feasibility of compliance should the court include a requirement.

2   The requirement must be necessary for securing the good conduct of the supervised person and for preventing further offending.

3   The supervised person or, if he is under 14, the parent or guardian must consent to the inclusion of the requirement.

4   So must any person (other than the supervisor or the supervised person) on whose co-operation the requirement depends.

5   Non requirement may be included which requires the supervised person to reside with a specified individual.

6   Nor can a requirement be included which requires the supervised person to submit to medical treatment. If the court has that in mind it must proceed in accordance with section 12B(1).[4]

1   See s 12A(6) and (7), as substituted by CJA 1988, Sch 10, Part I).
2   Ante, para 13.49.
3   Apart from consultation in the individual case, the Home Office recommends local discussions between the courts and supervising services about the various kinds of requirements that might not be suitable in certain circumstances; see HOC No 59/1983.
4   As substituted by CJA 1988, Sch 10, Part I.

13.56   *(e) Expenditure on IT*   The local authority in whose area the supervised person resides or will reside is responsible for any expenditure incurred by the supervisor in using the facilities of an IT scheme, when giving directions under section 12(2) of the 1969 Act or when carrying out requirements under section 12A.[1] Even where a probation committee provides IT facilities[2] for the purpose of those statutory provisions, it seems clear that the local authority is liable for the cost of using them in each case. Consequently, where a probation officer is appointed supervisor, the consent of the local authority to the inclusion of a section 12(3C) requirement is necessary as a person whose co-operation is involved. Where, however, the facilities used are not listed in an IT scheme the cost falls on the supervisor, and that could be either the local authority or a probation officer.

1 Section 18(4) as substituted by CJA 1982, s 20(2), and amended by CJA 1988, Sch 10, Part II.
2 See ante, para 13.49.

13.57 *(5) Night restriction requirement* The supervision order may require the juvenile to remain in a specified place or places during specified periods between 6 pm and 6 am.[1] There is no breach of this requirement if the juvenile leaves the place accompanied by his parent, guardian, supervisor or other person specified in the order.[2] Of the several limitations on inclusion of this night restriction requirement which have already been mentioned,[3] the need to consult the supervisor is particularly important, because the court will want to weigh the chances of effective compliance. Moreover, the co operation of the parents will be vital, so that even where the supervised person is at least 14 years of age the consent of the parent as one involved in co-operation will in practice be necessary. There are other limitations which relate only to the night restriction requirement. The place or one of the places specified must be the place where the juvenile lives.[4] He cannot be required to remain at a place for longer than ten hours in any one night.[5] The restriction must operate within the first three months of the date of the supervision order, and must not be imposed in respect of more than 30 days in all,[6] but within those temporal limits the court may spread the restriction over a period of time, for example, Fridays, Saturdays and Sundays.[7]

1 Section 12A(3)(b). This and all other statutory references in the footnotes to this paragraph have been substituted by CJA 1988, Sch 10, Part I.
2 Section 12A(12).
3 Supra, para 13.55.
4 Section 12A(8).
5 Section 12A(9).
6 Section 12A(10) and (11).
7 A restriction imposed in respect of a period beginning in the evening and ending in the morning is treated as imposed on the first day only, (s 12A(13)).

13.58 *(6) Requirement of non-participation* The supervision order may require the juvenile to refrain from participating in activities specified in the order, for example, not to attend week-end social functions at a particular youth club. The restriction may be imposed for a specified day or days during the period the supervision order is in force or for the whole or a specified portion of that period.[1] The limitations on inclusion of this requirement in the order have already been noted.[2] Early indications have been that neither it nor the night restriction requirement is often imposed.[3]

1 Section 12A(3)(c), as substituted by CJA 1988, Sch 10, Part I.
2 Supra, para 13.55.
3 See Home Office Statistical Bulletin 12/85.

(v) Variation and discharge of supervision orders

13.59 *(1) Appearance of juvenile before juvenile court* The supervisor or the juvenile or his parent or guardian on his behalf may apply for the supervision order to be discharged or varied.[1] If the supervisor does so, he may bring the juvenile before the juvenile court and, if necessary, may apply for a summons or warrant to secure his attendance.[2] A warrant should be issued only if a summons cannot be served or was served within a reasonable time before the hearing.[3] If the juvenile is arrested in pursuance of a warrant and cannot immediately be brought before the court, he may be detained in a place of safety for up to 72 hours, by which time he must be brought before a justice who must release him forthwith or make an interim order committing him to the care of a local authority.[4] However, if the supervised person has attained the age of 18, then instead of making an interim order as alternative to release, the court must remand him on bail or in custody.[5]

1 CYPA 1969, s 15(1), as amended by CLA 1977, Sch 12 and 13, by CJA 1982, Sch 14, para 25, and by CJA 1988, Sch 10, Part II. Proceedings are regulated by Part III of MC (C & YP) Rules 1988, of which only some are relevant to the variation and discharge of supervision orders made in criminal proceedings. Guardian has its usual meaning in the CYP legislation, namely a person having charge or control, but for the present purpose it also includes a person who was guardian when the order was originally made, (s 70(2)).
2 Section 16(1) and (2).
3 MCA 1980, s 55(3), as applied by CYPA 1969, s 16(2). Should the juvenile fail to appear at an adjourned hearing, the court must not issue a warrant unless satisfied that he has had adequate notice of that hearing; MCA 1980, s 55(4), as similarly applied.
4 CYPA 1969, s 16(3). Compare the similar rule in s 2(4) and (5) of the Act, post, para 14.34. The court may make a further interim order, if needed; s 16(4)(a).
5 Section 16(3). This rule applies only to criminal proceedings, since only in them can a supervision order continue beyond the age of 18.

13.60 *(2) The powers to vary or discharge* The court[1] may vary the order by cancelling any requirement included under sections 12, 12A, 12B, 12C or 18(2)(b) or by inserting any provision which could have been included in the order if the court had then had the power to make it and were exercising the power. But there is no power to insert after the expiration of three months from the date of the order a requirement relating to treatment for a mental condition unless it is in substitution for such a requirement already included in the order. Nor can a night restriction requirement be varied by imposing a restriction on any day which falls outside that three-month period.[2] If the court discharges the order, it may make a care order, other than an interim order.[3] In the event of dismissal of an application for discharge, no such further application may be made by any person (whether the original applicant or not) for at least three months from the date of dismissal, unless the court otherwise consents.[4]

1   The appropriate juvenile court is one acting for the petty sessions area named in the
     supervision order (under s 18(2)(a)); see s 16(11).
2   Section 15(1).
3   Ibid, except that it may make an interim order both on discharge and variation where
     it wants further information before coming to a decision (s 16(4)(b)).
4   Section 16(9).

13.61   Normally the juvenile must be present before the court but orders
concerned only with the following matters may be made in his absence:[1]

a   discharging the supervision order;
b   cancelling a provision included by virtue of sections 12, 12A, 12B,
     12C or 18(2)(b);
c   reducing the duration of the order or any provision made under sections
     12, 12A, 12B or 12C;
d   altering the name of any area;
e   changing the supervisor.

1   Section 16(5), as amended by CJA 1988, Sch 10, Part II.

13.62   The power to order variation or discharge is subject to the same
basic principle as applies to care proceedings under section 1 of the 1969
Act,[1] namely, that the court's decision must be governed by the juvenile's
need for care or control. Thus, it must not substitute a care order, discharge
a supervision order or insert, vary or cancel a requirement authorised by
sections 12, 12A, 12B or 12C unless it is satisfied that the juvenile either
is unlikely to receive the care or control he needs unless the court makes
the order or is likely to receive it notwithstanding the order.[2] By its terms
this rule allows for several permutations of application, but there is at
least one kind of case which neither of its provisos covers. An independent
17-year-old, having no parents or guardians or being estranged from them,
who is in a self-supporting job may not need care or control, so that the
provisos are irrelevant. Yet, that could be a most suitable case for discharge
of the order. Indeed, those circumstances are not unknown, and,
notwithstanding the mandatory terms of the statutory provision, courts
do, rightly, order discharge.

1   Post, paras 14.22–14.24.
2   Section 16(6)(a), as amended by CJA 1988, Sch 10, Part II.

13.63   There are special limitations on the variation of a mental treatment
requirement. If the doctor responsible for the treatment is unwilling to
continue it or is of opinion that (a) it should be continued beyond the
period specified in the order, or (b) that different treatment is needed,
or (c) that the juvenile is not susceptible to treatment, or (d) does not
further require it, he must so report to the supervisor who must then refer
the matter to the court, which in turn may cancel or vary the requirement,[1]
subject to (1) the above principle that an order is needed in the interests
of the juvenile's proper care or control,[2] and (2) the juvenile's consent
if he is a young person and if the order is to alter the mental treatment
requirement otherwise than by removing it or reducing its duration.[3] Consent
is similarly needed to insert into the order by way of variation a mental
treatment requirement.[4]

1   Section 15(5), as amended by CJA 1988, Sch 10, Part II. Compare the power of a doctor
     under PCCA 1973, s 3(4) and (5) to change arrangements for the treatment of a probationer
     without the court's approval.
2   Section 16(6)(b).
3   Section 16(7), as amended by CJA 1988, Sch 10, Part II.
4   Ibid. The same medical evidence is required as would be necessary to include the
     requirement in an order in the first instance (s 16(6)(c), as amended by CJA 1988, Sch 10,
     Part II).

13.64 *(3) Attaining the age of 18* Where the supervised person is still
under the age of 18 the jurisdiction to discharge or vary resides exclusively
with the juvenile court.[1] Once he attains that age jurisdiction passes to
an adult magistrates' court,[2] but the powers conferred on it[3] are not as
wide as those of a juvenile court in that (1) if the order is discharged,
a care order cannot be substituted, since the latter is appropriate only to
persons under 18, and (2) for the same reason no requirement in pursuance
of sections 12, 12A, 12B or 12C[4] may be added to the order. There is,
therefore, no practical advantage to be derived from the rule[5] that, if the
supervised person is between the ages of 17 and 18 or becomes 18 while
the application is pending, the juvenile court can, as an alternative to its
own powers,[6] exercise the above powers which an adult magistrates' court
has over a person who is 18. As will be seen,[7] different considerations
apply where the juvenile court is concerned with a breach of a supervision
order by a person between those ages.

1   For the special powers of that court where the supervised person becomes 17 see infra,
     para 13.67.
2   Ie a court acting for the petty sessions area named in the order (s 16(11)).
3   By s 15(3), as amended by CJA 1988, Sch 10, Part III.
4   See ante paras 13.44, 13.45, 13.51 and 13.53 respectively.
5   Sections 15(2) and 16(11).
6   Under s 15(1).
7   Infra, para 13.67.

13.65 *(4) Appeals* A supervised person has the right of appeal to the
Crown Court against an order for variation, except one which could have
been made in his absence or one relating to a mental treatment and he
consented to the variation. He also has a right of appeal against the dismissal
of an application to discharge the order.[1]

1   Section 16(8).

(vi) Breach of supervision
13.66 Sanctions are imposed for breach of a supervision order made either
in criminal proceedings or in substitution of a care order which had earlier
been made in such proceedings. If there is non-compliance with any of
the requirements included under section 12A(3) relating to stipulated IT,
night restriction or non-participation in specified activities or under section
18(2)(b)[1] to prescribed matters such as contact and visits, the court may,
additionally or alternatively to its powers to discharge or vary, exercise
the following powers, depending upon the age of the supervised person.
Illogically, these sanctions do not extend to breach of an order providing
for delegated IT under section 12(2), but this may be due to legislative

oversight.[2] There is, however, no firm evidence that the omission has encouraged courts to use stipulated IT.

1 And the Rules thereunder; see ante, para 13.43.
2 See Gibson, *Intermediate Treatment*, (1985) 82 Law Soc Gaz 1241.

13.67 The application to invoke the following powers must be made by the supervisor.

(i) Under 17[1]

A juvenile court may impose a fine on the juvenile not exceeding £100 or make an attendance centre order.[2] It may do either whether or not it also makes an order under section 15(1) of the CYPA 1969 cancelling any requirement included in the original supervision order or inserting any provision which could have been included in that order.[3] If an attendance centre order is made, the rules relating to discharge and variation of such an order under section 18[4] of the CJA 1982 and to breach of that order under section 19[5] of that Act will then apply.[6]

(ii) Age of 18

An adult magistrates' court has the same powers, and it is immaterial whether the breach of the order occurred before or after the supervised person reached that age.[7] But, if the court *discharges* the order, it can impose 'any punishment', other than a sentence of detention in a young offender institution, which it could have imposed had it just been convicting him as an 18-year-old of the offence for which the order was made.[8] The terms in which this power is conferred, with the reference to punishment, raise doubts about whether the court can discharge him absolutely or conditionally, as it can where there is a breach of a probation order. It is equally doubtful whether it can make a probation order. It is expressly provided that, where the offence for which the supervision order was made is of a kind which the magistrates' court has no power to try or no power to try without appropriate consents, the punishment cannot exceed that which any court having power to try such an offence could have imposed in respect of it, and, if the punishment imposed is a fine, it must not exceed £2,000.[9] Should there be a reasonable chance that the supervised person may still respond to supervision, the court should vary rather than discharge the order and rely on its additional power of imposing a fine or making an attendance centre order.

(iii) 17 but under 18[10]

Jurisdiction resides with the juvenile court, but it has the alternative of proceeding as it would in the case of a person under 17 or of exercising the above wider powers which an adult court has over a person who has attained the age of 18.[11]

1 Including a person who attains that age pending the application (s 16(11)).
2 CYPA 1969, s 15(2A), as substituted by CJA 1988, Sch 10, Part III.
   The CJA 1988, s 127 puts the onus on the parent or guardian to pay the fine instead of the juvenile, unless the court is satisfied that the parent or guardian cannot be found or that it would be unreasonable to make an order for payment having regard to the circumstances of the case.
3 For s 15(1) see ante, para 13.60.

4   See ante, para 13.34.
5   See ante, para 13.32.
6   See CJA 1982, s 16A, as inserted by CJA 1988, Sch 3, Part IV.
7   CYPA 1969, s 15(4), as substituted by CJA 1988, Sch 3, Part III.
8   Ibid.
9   Ibid. For a court's powers where it discharges a supervision order which requires the juvenile to participate in specified activities (ante, para 13.54) and he fails to comply, see CYPA 1969, s 15(4A)–(4D), as inserted by CJA 1988, Sch 3, Part III.
10   Including a person who attains that age pending the application (CYPA 1969, s 16(11)).
11   CYPA 1969, s 15(2).

13.68   It should be noted that a juvenile who commits a further offence during the period of supervision can only be dealt with for that offence, and the special powers which the juvenile court has where a juvenile commits a further offence during the period of an order for his conditional discharge do not apply to the supervised juvenile.[1]

1   See ante, para 13.10.

(g)   Care orders

13.69   The nature, scope and effects of a care order are fully examined in Chapter 15. So, too, is the power to discharge an order; except that it is more convenient to note here that, if a court makes a care order in criminal proceedings while another such order, also made in criminal proceedings, is in force, it may discharge the earlier order.[1]

1   CYPA 1969, s 7(7).

(i)   Power to make care order

13.70   The order may be made where the juvenile is found guilty of an offence punishable in the case of an adult with imprisonment[1] but only if the court is of opinion[2] that (a) the order is appropriate because of the seriousness of the offence, and (b) the juvenile is in need of care or control which he is otherwise unlikely to receive.[3] No statutory guidance is given on what may constitute seriousness of an offence, but it must, it seems, be determined on its intrinsic nature and not in the light of previous similar offences. However, previous offences will be highly relevant to the question of need of care or control. There is the further restriction[4] that an order cannot be made in respect of a juvenile who is not legally represented, unless he has been refused legal aid on the ground of means[5] or, having been informed of his right to apply for it, refused or failed to do so. If, therefore, a court is prima facie minded to make a care order and the juvenile is unrepresented, it should adjourn the hearing so that an application can be made. As will be seen, this rule relating to legal representation applies to other orders made in criminal proceedings.

1   Section 7(7)(a).
2   Section 7(7A) as inserted by CJA 1982, s 23.
3   There is an irony in the addition of this requirement; see post, para 14.19. The court should not make an order under s 7(7)(a) if a matrimonial care order is already in force; see *W v Heywood* [1985] FLR 1064, [1985] Fam Law 282.
4   Section 7A, as inserted by CJA 1982, s 24.
5   For the relevance of the means of a parent or guardian and for assessment see ante, para 12.92.

13.71 These statutory restrictions should be seen against the background of the concurrent changes affecting supervision orders that were made by the Criminal Justice Act 1982. Previously courts were too readily using the care order as a means of dealing with the offender because of lack of confidence in the effectiveness of the supervision order. The underlying strategy of the changes is, therefore, to strengthen the sanctions of the latter order[1] and to limit the availability of the care order, which is to be seen more as 'a substantial intervention comparable to a custodial sentence'.[2] These are matters which should be borne in mind in the preparation of social inquiry reports and any recommendations that are made.

1   See ante, para 13.67.
2   HOC No 42/1983, para 63.

(ii)   Condition as to charge and control
13.72 A local authority may allow a child in its care to be under the charge and control of a parent, guardian, relative or friend, either for a fixed period or until the authority otherwise determines.[1] When a juvenile commits an imprisonable offence and at the time he was already the subject of a care order made (1) in care proceedings based on his having committed *an* offence[2] or (2) in criminal proceedings[3] or (3) in substitution for a supervision order which itself had been made in criminal proceedings in respect of an imprisonable offence, then the court can add to the care order a condition that the local authority shall not exercise that power or shall exercise it only in relation to a specified parent etc.[4] The restriction can be imposed for up to six months. Should the juvenile during the specified period commit a further imprisonable offence, the court may substitute a new condition for the old. The power to include this condition is subject to the rule relating to legal representation, just noted,[5] and to the rule that the court is of opinion that it is appropriate to exercise the power because of the seriousness of the offence and that no other method of dealing with the juvenile is appropriate. The court must seek information on this last matter. The social inquiry report may not have covered it, in which case adjournment for further inquiries will be necessary. Before the condition is included its purposes and effect must be explained to the juvenile.[6] He, his parent or guardian on his behalf[7] or the local authority may apply to a juvenile court to revoke or vary the condition, in practice by reducing the period of its operation or by removing it in relation to a specified person.

1   Child Care Act 1980, s 2(2); see further post, para 15.13.
2   See post, para 14.19 for the 'offence condition'.
3   And, therefore, for having committed an imprisonable offence, supra, para 13.70.
4   CYPA 1969, s 20A, as inserted by CJA 1982, s 22.
5   Supra, para 13.70.
6   The juvenile may appeal against the imposition of the condition to the Crown Court in accordance with his general right of appeal under MCA 1980, s 108. The local authority also has a right of appeal to that court under CYPA 1969, s 20A(7), but not from that court where *it* has imposed the condition.
7   But not on the parent's own behalf, even though he may be affected by the condition.

13.73 The general effect of this provision is that the court can, within the statutory time limit, prevent the juvenile being sent home without having to impose a custodial sentence. That might be a preferable alternative if he is in some respects favourably responding to the local authority care. Where a condition is included,[1] apparently it does not prevent the local authority from allowing the juvenile to make short home visits to the parent, provided the authority retains charge and control.[2] Nevertheless, the authority should be cautious about allowing visits, especially where the parent had influenced, or himself been involved in, the further offence during a time when the juvenile was at home.

1　Its significance has yet to be established. In the first year of its operation, it was included in less than 20 of the 1,800 care orders made during that year; see Home Office Statistical Bulletin 12/85.
2　On retention of charge and control see *Leeds City Council v West Yorkshire Metropolitan Police* [1983] 1 AC 29, [1982] 1 All ER 274, HL.

2　Custodial orders

(a)　Introduction

13.74　In spite of the barbaric conditions which prevailed in English prisons throughout the eighteenth century, Parliament refused to do anything to provide for the separate detention of juvenile and adult offenders. Even when the influence of Howard and Bentham began to be felt soon after 1800 the early reforms of the prison system did not include special provisions for young offenders.[1] It was only as the result of the persistent efforts of voluntary organisations that Parliament finally accepted what had come to be known as the reformatory movement. Under the legislation relating to reformatory schools and industrial schools[2] young offenders could be sent to those schools, but an initial defect in the legislation was that a school order could only be made if the offender first served a term of imprisonment, and not until 1899 was it enacted that an order was to be a substitute for, and not an addition to, imprisonment. The process of restricting the imprisonment of juveniles was carried much further by the Children Act 1908, which abolished imprisonment of children and only allowed it with regard to young persons (14–16) in exceptional cases of unruliness or depravity.[3] The total abolition of imprisonment was finally achieved by the Criminal Justice Acts 1948 and 1961.[4]

1　As late as 1849 more than 10,000 juveniles were imprisoned or transported during that year; see the Report of the Committee on the Treatment of Young Offenders (Cmnd 2831 at pp 7–8).
2　The first Reformatory Schools Act was in 1854 and the first Industrial Schools Act in 1857; see post, para 14.01.
3　Children Act 1908, s 102. The Act also abolished penal servitude in relation to juveniles.
4　Under the 1948 Act magistrates' courts were not to impose imprisonment on anyone under 17 and courts of assize and quarter sessions on anyone under 15. The later Act brought the latter courts into line with magistrates' courts.

13.75　The effect of the above provisions of the Act of 1908 was that, unless some other form of detention was introduced, the reformatory or industrial school order would be the only method of detaining juveniles; but such an order must, as the law then stood, be for a training period of three to five years, so that there was no power to detain for a short period of strict discipline even though that might be the most appropriate way of dealing with the juvenile. To fill this gap the Act created the remand home and, inter alia, provided for the punitive detention of juvenile offenders there for a maximum period of one month. As a substitute for imprisonment these homes proved, however, to be of limited value, and the Criminal Justice Act 1948 sought partly to meet the deficiency by providing for the establishment of a new type of institution which would permit a somewhat longer period of detention. That appeared in the form of the detention centre. The Children and Young Persons Act 1969 abolished the approved school order, the order committing to a remand home and the fit person order.[1] It also provided for the eventual abolition of the detention centre order and the sentence to borstal training in so far as they applied to juveniles.[2] The system of borstal institutions had been established by the Prevention of Crime Act 1908, and, like that of the reformatory schools, was inspired by the need to separate young offenders from adults and give them specialised treatment. Indeed, basically it started as an extension of the reformatory principle to young offenders, ie persons no longer juveniles but still under 21. Subsequent legislation extended it to young persons who had attained the age of 15.[3]

1 Section 7(5) and (6).
2 Section 7(3) and (1) respectively.
3 CJA 1948, s 20, as amended by CJA 1961, s 1.

13.76 The Criminal Justice Act 1982 made several changes with regard to custodial sentences for persons under 21. It abolished imprisonment in respect of them[1] and borstal training,[2] replacing both with sentences of youth custody and custody for life, and it made significant changes with regard to detention in detention centres. Essential features of the Act are its emphasis on making non-custodial orders—hence, for example, the attempt to strengthen supervision orders—and its restrictions on imposing custodial sentences. In its earliest years the Act is apparently not uniformly achieving that purpose. That may be partly due to the fact that the courts are not paying sufficient attention to the restrictions on passing custodial sentences.[3] Whether the amendments made by the Criminal Justice Act 1988 will encourage readjustment remains to be seen, but one of the major changes introduced by this Act, within the present context, is the replacement of detention centre orders and youth custody sentences by a unified sentence of detention in a young offender institution.

1 Section 1(1). But a person under that age can be committed to prison when remanded in custody or committed for trial or sentence (s 1(2)).
2 Section 1(3).
3 See Allen, *The Criminal Justice Act—Its Lack of Appeal*, (1985) 82 Law Soc Gaz 1846; Gibson, *Abolition of Custody for Juvenile Offenders* (1986) 150 JPN 739 and 755. Research for the Home Office by the Department of Social Studies at Liverpool University has disclosed wide discrepancies in sentencing (see the Times Newspaper, 19 January 1987, p 4); and the Parliamentary All-Party Penal Affairs Group has expressed its concern.

(b) General restrictions on custodial sentences

13.77 There are certain general restrictions imposed on passing a sentence of detention in a young offender institution or a sentence of custody for life.[1] First, the circumstances, including the nature and gravity of the offence must be such that if the offender were aged 21 or over the court would pass a sentence of imprisonment. Second, the offender must qualify for a custodial sentence. This he may do for any one or more of three reasons:

(a) he has a history of failure to respond to non-custodial penalties, and he is unable or unwilling to respond to them;
(b) only a custodial sentence would be adequate to protect the public from serious harm from him. The major consideration here may be the nature of the offence (but see (c) below), but another important factor will be the risk of reoffending. Offending may be 'so frequent or troublesome that the public should be shielded from [it] by a period of custody'.[2]
(c) the offence of which he has been convicted or found guilty was so serious that a non-custodial sentence for it cannot be justified. To satisfy this 'qualification' it seems that it is not necessary to show a risk of reoffending.[3] A custodial sentence would, therefore, be justified where a juvenile's commission of arson of the school he attends was motivated solely by hostility to his teachers and there is no real likelihood of repetition. Nevertheless, in most cases the second and third reasons may be closely inter-related, for example, where the offence is sexual assault.[4]

1   CJA 1982, s 1(4) and (4A), as substituted by CJA 1988, s 123(3).
2   Walker, op cit, para 20.10.
3   See ibid.
4   But the offence may be so serious (for example, rape) as to justify detention under s 53(2) of CYPA 1933; see post, para 13.97.

13.78   In order to determine whether there is any appropriate non-custodial method of dealing with the juvenile the court must obtain and consider information about the circumstances and must take into account any information before the court which is relevant to his character and his physical and mental condition.[1] Evidence of character and previous offences is particularly relevant to satisfying grounds (a) and (b) above. Apart from information which has emerged during the trial, including any given by the juvenile's solicitor or counsel, the court will very largely rely on the social inquiry report. Indeed, it is obliged to obtain that report, unless, in the circumstances of the case, it considers it unnecessary,[2] and, if it proceeds to impose a custodial sentence without one, it must state in open court the reason for regarding it as unnecessary.[3] Although a sentence is not invalidated by failure to obtain a report,[4] it will be exceptional for a juvenile court to act without one.

1   CJA 1982, s 2(1).
2   Section 2(2), (3) and (10). A solicitor representing the juvenile should himself discuss with the social worker the desirability and feasibility of a non-custodial sentence; see 83 Law Soc Gaz at p 1847.
3   Section 2(6). This duty falls on any magistrates' court, but not on the Crown Court, when imposing a custodial sentence.
4   Section 2(8). Where the court of trial, whether a juvenile court or other magistrates' court or the Crown Court, acts without a social inquiry report, the appellate court must obtain one unless it considers it unnecessary; see ibid. In making its own decision the appellate court must consider any report it obtains or any obtained by the court below (s 2(9)).

13.79   A juvenile court or any other magistrates' court or the Crown Court which passes a sentence of detention in a young offender institution must state in open court that it is satisfied that he qualifies for a custodial sentence for one or more of the statutory reasons,[1] the reason or reasons in question and why it is so satisfied.[2] With regard to the last point, it seems clear that there must be a full, reasoned explanation.[3] The court must also explain to the offender in open court and in ordinary language why it is passing a custodial sentence on him.[4]

1   See ante, para 13.77.
2   See CJA 1982, s 2(4), or substituted by CJA 1988, s 123(5).
3   The reason(s) given by a magistrates' court must be stated in the warrant of commitment and entered in the register, as must the reason for not obtaining a social inquiry report; see CJA 1982, s 2(7) and s 2(6) respectively.
4   CJA 1982, s 2(4).

13.80   (4) As in the case of making a care order,[1] the rule relating to legal representation applies.[2] Any custodial sentence passed in breach of it is invalid.[3]

1   See ante, para 13.70.
2   CJA 1982, s 3.
3   *R v McGinlay and Ballantyne* (1975) 62 Cr App Rep 156, [1976] Crim LR 78, CA.

(c) Sentence of detention in a young offender institution

(i) Scope and duration of sentence
13.81 This new sentence, which replaces the detention centre order and the youth custody sentence, may, subject to the general restrictions already noted,[1] be passed in respect of male offenders aged not less than 14, but under 21 and female offenders aged not less than 15 but under 21.[2] The rules governing the duration of sentences are complicated,[3] and are a merger of the former rules relating to detention centre orders and youth custody sentences. The basic rule is that the maximum term of detention that the court may impose is the maximum term of imprisonment it could impose for the particular offence.[4] Where the offender is a boy under 15, that basic rule will apply if the maximum term of imprisonment that the offence can carry is less than four months. Where it is more, the maximum period of detention that can be ordered for the 14-year-old boy is four months.[5] For the 15 and 16-year-old offender, male or female, the maximum term of detention is whichever is the lesser of (a) the maximum term of imprisonment that is imposable for the offence and (b) 12 months.[6] Where the court is dealing with two or more offences it may pass sentences to run concurrently or consecutively,[7] but on the latter alternative the aggregate terms must not exceed the above maxima of four months in the case of a 14-year-old boy or 12 months in the case of a 15 or 16-year-old offender.[8] The same restriction applies if, while one sentence is in force, a different court later passes another to commence on the expiration of the first.[9] If the aggregate terms are erroneously made in excess of the maximum of four months or of 12 months, as the case may be, the excess is remitted.[10]

The normal minimum period of detention is 21 days,[11] but for the 15 and 16-year-old female offender it is four months.[12] Also, where there is a breach of supervision after release from detention, then the period of detention for the breach may be anything from one to 30 days.[13]

1   See ante, para 13.77.
2   See CJA 1982, s 1A, as inserted by CJA 1988, s 123(4).
3   Ibid and s 1B, as inserted by CJA 1988, s 123(4).
4   Section 1A(2).
5   Section 1B(1).
6   Section 1B(2).
7   Section 1A(5).
8   Section 1B(4) and (6).
9   Ibid.
10 Section 1B(5).
11 Section 1A(3).
12 Section 1B(3).
>   This discrimination between male and female offenders and between the minimum
>   age at which they are liable to detention in a young offender institution (ie 14 for boys
>   and 15 for girls, supra) is apparently explained on the ground that the number of girls
>   under 17 who would be subject to short-term detention would be too small to justify
>   a separate institution for them, a doubtful conclusion in view of increasing criminality
>   among girls of that age group. Compare the comment of McEwan on *The Criminal
>   Justice Act 1982* in (1983) 46 MLR 178 at 184.
13 CJA 1982, s 1A(4) and s 15(11), as amended by CJA 1988, Sch 15, para 90.

(ii)   Remission

13.82   Time on remand in custody to a remand centre or prison, time
spent on remand in the care of the local authority in accommodation
provided for restricting liberty and time spent in police detention count
towards time to be served.[1] The practical effect is that, apart from allowance
for police detention, with full remission the time spent in a young offender
institution for a sentence of detention for 21 days is two weeks and for
a period of four months is 11 weeks. A short sentence could therefore
mean immediate release. However, in view of the fact that a juvenile can
only be remanded to a remand centre or prison if he is of unruly character,[2]
in those cases where he is so remanded it is unlikely that a court would
have in mind a short period of detention. Nevertheless, what ought to
be resisted is the temptation to make the period of detention longer than
it would have been had the juvenile not been kept in police detention and/
or remanded in custody or kept in local authority secure accommodation,[3]
in order to ensure that he does have some experience of the treatment
in a young offender institution.

1   CJA 1967, s 67, as amended by CJA 1982, s 10, by PCEA 1984, s 49 and prospectively
    by CJA 1988, s 130.
2   See CYPA 1969, s 23(2), ante, para 12.122.
3   This amendment by the CJA 1988 is not yet in force.

(iii)   Young offender institutions

13.83   Subject to section 22(2)(b) of the Prison Act 1952 (which provides
for the removal of a prisoner to hospital), an offender who is sentenced
to detention in a young offender institution will be detained in such an
institution unless the Secretary of State directs that he be detained in a
prison or remand centre. This, however, may only be done for a temporary
purpose if he is under 17.[1]

The effect of section 123 of the Criminal Justice Act 1988 is to redesignate
the former detention centres and youth custody centres as young offender
institutions. The Home Office has explained the new arrangements.[2] There
are separate establishments for (a) all male juveniles (ie 14- to 16-year-
olds); (b) male young adults (ie 17- to 20-year-olds) sentenced to four months'

or less detention; and (c) male young adults sentenced to more than four months' detention. Those in categories (a) and (b) are committed direct from court, whereas those in category (c) are normally taken to an allocation unit for assessment and allocation to other appropriate young offender institutions, except that, if, because of remission for time spent in custody on remand,[3] they have only a relatively short part of their sentence left to serve, they may be allocated to institutions catering for those in category (b). The arrangements for allocation and accommodation of females are continuing as they were for those who were formerly sentenced to youth custody.

1   CJA 1982, s 1C, as inserted by CJA 1988, s 123(4).
2   See HOC 78/1988 and HOC 79/1988 (CS 5/88).
3   Supra, para 13.82.

13.84   What's in a name? The time-honoured question may fairly be asked with regard to young offender institutions. How will they differ from detention centres and youth custody centres? The Home Office has provided the barest of indications of their nature.[1]

> 'The distinctive needs of juveniles and young adults serving short terms in custody require a regime which will differ in important respects from that provided in longer-term institutions. In juvenile and shorter-term institutions there will be a busy, brisk regime. Its distinctive features will include a full and structured daily routine and an emphasis on education (including physical education). Young adult offenders serving longer terms will receive a regime building on that in youth custody centres.'

A clearer picture may emerge from an examination of the centres which they replace.

1   HOC 79/1988, para 2. See also post, para 13.87.

Nature of detention centres
13.85   Although increasing use had been made of the detention centre order, it remained a controversial method of treatment of offenders, and changes in the 1980s in the regime at centres excited further dissatisfaction.[1] Rule 4 of the Detention Centre Rules 1980 set out the aims of centres, namely:

> '. . . to provide a disciplined daily routine: to provide work, education and other activities of a kind that will assist offenders to acquire or develop personal resources and aptitudes: to encourage offenders to accept responsibility, and to help them with their return to the community in co-operation with the services responsible for supervision.'

Introduced as a punitive and deterrent measure, the detention centre order retained those primary purposes. The discipline at centres had always been severe and, some claimed, too military in outlook. The emphasis was on manual work, physical training and strict supervision. Gradually its reformative aims received limited recognition.[2] Some educational and vocational training facilities had to be made available, especially for young persons of compulsory school age, for whom at least 15 hours weekly had to be allocated.[3] However, earlier critics doubted whether those functions were consistently and positively discharged.

1　See Kuper, *Should young people be sentenced to a 'short sharp shock'?* (1986) 150 JPN 792.
2　Particularly as the result of the Report of the Advisory Council on the Penal System with regard to Detention Centres, HMSO 1970.
3　DC Rules 1983, r 36.

13.86　In 1980 a pilot project was introduced in a junior and senior centre (and later extended to two others) in order to determine whether with a more rigorous regime the detention centre order could be made a more effective deterrent against re-offending. Emphasis was to be placed on harder work and more demanding physical education, drills, parades and inspections. The experiment was not a success. The Prison Department's own Young Offender Psychology Unit in a report in 1984 found that trainees did not regard the new regime as more rigorous and demanding and thus less acceptable. On the contrary, trainees' attitudes to staff were more positive. In particular, emphasis on drill and physical education had in fact led to a more co-operative and pleasanter relationship between them. Disappointing, though not surprising, was the finding that the reconviction rates of trainees who had experienced the 'short, sharp shock' treatment were not significantly different from those of trainees who, over roughly the same period, had been at other centres. The response of the Government was to modify the experimental regime, particularly by removing formal drill sessions and extra physical education (which trainees had found acceptable) and thereby allowing more time for hard work. Furthermore, under the new regime, which was extended to all centres, the initial two weeks of training was very intensive with the emphasis on physical training and unskilled work, but thereafter more time was devoted to skilled occupations and education and vocational training.[1] Nevertheless, doubts about the efficacy of the detention centre order remained as strong as they were almost 40 years ago, and there was concern about 'the prospect of [offenders] going through the range of penal measures faster than before.'[2]

1　The Home Office summarised the essential features of the present regime in HOC 9/ 1985.
2　See McEwan *The Criminal Justice Act 1982* (1983) 46 MLR 178, at p 186, and for a general criticism of the Act, based on an empirical study of 12 courts, see Burney, *Sentencing Young People: What went wrong with the Criminal Justice Act 1982?*

Youth custody centres

13.87　Youth custody centres were places where offenders were 'given training, instruction and work and prepared for their release.'[1] Most centres were the former borstal institutions, and, like their predecessors, provided for the juvenile offender a form of medium term custodial training. Their nature was described as follows:[2]

'They will aim to lay emphasis on individual assessment and personal development in work, training, education and positive preparation for release to life in the community, and to offer a range of activities including employment, employment training courses, a group personal officer scheme (in which trainees come under the oversight of and are advised by particular officers) and a physical education programme. So far as possible the aim will be to prepare a programme suitable for the individual offender which takes account of the length of his sentence, bearing in mind that youth custody sentences, unlike sentences of borstal training, will be determinate. A youth custody sentence should not be regarded primarily as a means of securing that the offender receives training. The regime for young women and girls will generally operate on similar lines to those in the male youth custody centres.'

Like the Detention Centre Rules 1983, the Youth Custody Centre Rules 1983[3] contained detailed provisions concerning the treatment, employment, discipline and control of inmates, but facilities and training varied widely from the open establishments to those with a regime of strict security, including a few providing for psychiatric needs. Presumably, this variety will continue in young offender institutions.[4]

1   Prison Act 1952, s 43(1)(c), as substituted by CJA 1982, s 11; see also the Youth Custody Centre Rules 1983, r 3.
2   Home Office Circular No 42/1983, para 29.
3   SI 1983/570.
4   See the Young Offender Institution Rules 1988, SI 1988/1422. Rule 3 states that the aim of such an institution will be to help offenders to prepare for their return to the outside community, and this is to be achieved, in particular, by—
     '(a) providing a programme of activities, including education, training and work designed to assist offenders to acquire or develop personal responsibility, self-discipline, physical fitness, interests and skills and to obtain suitable employment after release;
     (b) fostering links between the offender and the outside community;
     (c) cooperating with the services responsible for the offender's supervision after release.'

(iv)   No power to suspend sentence
13.88—13.93   There is no power to suspend the operation of a sentence of detention in a young offender institution, as there is a sentence of imprisonment.[1] Where a court would have partly suspended the sentence had the defendant been an adult, the proper approach is to pass an immediate sentence on the juvenile of the sort of length (within, of course, the statutory maximum limits[2]) that would have been the non-suspended part of a partly suspended sentence.[3]

1   For the respective arguments for and against the rule see Walker, op cit, para 20.6. The National Association for the Care and Resettlement of Offenders (NACRO), in a paper to the Home Office (March 1986) is firmly opposed to the suspended sentence for offenders under 21, mainly because it has led courts to impose such sentences on offenders they would not normally have sent to prison and to make the sentences longer than they would have been had they sent the offenders directly to prison.
2   See ante, para 13.81.
3   *R v Dobbs and Hitchings* (1983) 5 Cr App Rep (S) 378; *R v Trew* [1985] Crim LR 168.

(v)   Supervision after release from a detention centre or youth custody centre

13.94   An offender who is released from a detention centre or youth custody centre is subject to supervision by a probation officer or local authority social worker.[1] Normally the period is for three months from the date of his release, but, where he has been granted remission or is on parole, it may be up to 12 months. In the case of the juvenile supervision may occasionally be longer than the normal period, namely, where he was granted remission and the period between the date of his release and that on which his sentence would have ended exceeds three months.[2] For example, if the Crown Court imposes a sentence of nine months detention in a young offender institution on 1 March and the juvenile was released on 31 July, the period of supervision continues for four months to 30 November.

1   CJA 1982, s 15(1).
2   Section 15(3) and (7).

13.95   The supervised juvenile must comply with any requirements specified in a notice by the Secretary of State, and breach of any of them is an offence carrying a penalty of either a fine not exceeding level 3 on the standard scale[1] or a sentence of detention in a young offender institution for a period not exceeding 30 days.[2] He will not be liable to further supervision for the breach, but the original supervision period will continue to run and may, indeed, end while he is in detention for the breach.

1   Currently £400.
2   Section 15(10)–(12), s 11 being amended by CJA 1988, Sch 8, Part I, para 1.

13.96   A period under supervision is an integral part of the sentence, and the court should inform the juvenile of this when sentencing him.[1] Nevertheless, it is questionable whether a period of three months is long enough for supervision of juveniles.[2] They are at a critical age where guidance and control may still have beneficial effects, especially where it is the offender's first custodial sentence. For this reason, too, the sanctions for breach of supervision are, it is suggested, inadequate.

1   The Home Office so advises; see HOC No 42/1983, para 34.
2   It contrasts sharply with what was at one time a period of 12 months' supervision after a detention centre order and two years after release from borstal training.

(d)   Detention for very serious offences

(i)   Murder
13.97   Section 53(1) of the Children and Young Persons Act 1933 (as amended) provides that a person found guilty of murder committed when he was under 18 must be sentenced to detention during Her Majesty's pleasure[1] in such place and under such directions as the Home Secretary may direct.[2]

1   For a person aged 18–20 the sentence is custody for life, CJA 1982, s 8(1). That is also the sentence to be imposed on anyone under 21, *including a juvenile*, for any other offence which, in respect of a person aged 21 or over, carries a fixed sentence of imprisonment for life (s 8(1)).
2   For appropriate places of detention see infra.

(ii)   Other very serious offences
13.98   Under section 53(2) of that Act[1] a young person who is found guilty of an offence which, in the case of an adult,[2] would be punishable with imprisonment for 14 years or more (the sentence not being a fixed one)

may be sentenced to be detained for a specified period at such place and on such conditions as the Home Secretary may direct.[3] The subsection now extends only to children (ie under 14) who are convicted of manslaughter. If the juvenile court considers that, if a young person is found guilty of the offence, it ought to be possible to exercise the power under the subsection, it must commit him for trial,[4] and then, if he is convicted, the Crown Court will, at its discretion, exercise it. The application of this latter rule may be straightforward in most cases, given the seriousness of the offence charged, for example, rape;[5] but the rule is defective in that in others the juvenile court will not have the requisite information (for example, the previous convictions and custodial sentences of the juvenile) which might have led it to commit him for trial instead of proceeding summarily. The extended use of the subsection has paradoxically highlighted the defect.[6]

1   As amended by CJA 1961, s 2(1) and Sch 4, and by CJA 1988, s 126. For a succinct history of the subsection see [1984] Crim LR 187–188.
2   Ie a person aged 21 or over.
3   If the offender is aged 17–20, the offence is one for which a person aged 21 or over would be liable to imprisonment for life and the court considers a sentence for life would be appropriate, it must sentence him to custody for life, CJA 1982, s 8(2).
4   MCA 1980, s 24(1)(a); see ante, para 12.14. Detention under section 53(2) is only available following committal for trial, not a committal for sentence under MCA 1980, s 37; *R v Corcoran* (1986) 8 Cr App Rep (S) 118, [1986] Crim LR 568, CA; *R v McKenna* [1986] Crim LR 195, CA.
5   A magistrates' court dealing with rape should never accept jurisdiction to deal with the case itself but should invariably commit for trial to ensure that the power is available; *R v Billam* [1986] 1 All ER 985, [1986] 1 WLR 349, CA.
6   See infra.

(iii)   The specified period
13.99   The period of detention must not exceed the maximum term of imprisonment which could be imposed on a person aged 21 or over in respect of the particular offence.[1] It must be a determinate period,[2] but that includes detention for life.[3] In fixing the period the court has the difficult task of balancing the protection of the public from the risk of further harm by the offender and, a factor which some recent cases have emphasised, the deterrence of the sentence against the long-term interests of the juvenile. In view of the inherent seriousness of the offence it should err, if it has to, on the side of the public interest. Although the sentencer should not take into account the ultimate power of the Home Secretary to release the offender on licence,[4] the sentence should be such that the offender can see the light at the end of the tunnel, and, in the case of a juvenile, his long-term interests may sometimes justify a shorter period of detention than would be so in an older offender.[5] Certainly it should not be longer than would be passed on an older offender.[6]

1   Section 53(2). It may be a common law offence; *R v Bosomworth* (1973) 57 Cr App Rep 708, CA, (affray, but for which see now the Public Order Act 1986).
2   Thus, a sentence 'for such period not exceeding 14 years as the Secretary might direct' is not a specified period; *R v McCauliffe* (1970) 54 Cr App Rep 515, CA.
3   *R v Abbott* [1964] 1 QB 489, [1963] 1 All ER 738, CCA.
4   *R v Burrowes* (1985) 7 Cr App Rep (S) 106, [1985] Crim LR 606, CA. For release on licence see infra, para 13.104.
5   *R v Storey* 6 Cr App Rep (S) 104, [1984] Crim LR 438, CA.

But the gravity of the defendant's conduct may not justify making allowance for his youth: *R v Cummins* [1986] Crim LR 569, CA.

6   *R v Burrowes*, supra.

(iv)   No other suitable method

13.100   The making of an order is subject to the general restriction relating to legal representation[1] and to the court being of opinion that none of the other methods of dealing with the juvenile is considered suitable.[2] But the reasons for considering them unsuitable are not statutorily laid down, as they are[3] for justifying the passing of a sentence of detention in a young offender institution or sentence of custody for life. Nor is the court obliged to obtain a social inquiry report before making an order, as it normally must before it can make either of the other custodial sentences.[4] Desirable though it be to correct what seems legislative oversight, the practical consequences of the anomalies are not significant. Because of the serious implications of the order and the problem of fixing its duration it is highly unlikely that the court will proceed without the guidance of a report. As for the statutory reasons relevant to the other custodial sentences, in practice at least one of them *ex hypothesi* will always be present when the court is considering the possibility of a section 53(2) order, namely, the seriousness of the offence. What is more regrettable is the fact that the court is not obliged to state in open court its reasons why it considers that no other method of dealing with the juvenile is appropriate.[5] The omission has had added significance in the light of the readiness in recent cases to extend the scope of section 53(2). That readiness has been inspired by the limited powers of the Crown Court to deal with young persons. The substitution, by the Criminal Justice Act 1982, of a maximum period of 12 months' youth custody for young persons in place of the indeterminate sentence of borstal training led to a relaxation in the degree of gravity necessary to justify an order under section 53(2). After some uncertainty the Court of Appeal seems to have eased its way to a solution. Its earlier view in *R v Oakes*[6] that the subsection was available only in exceptionally serious cases was not followed in *R v Butler*,[7] where the court took the view that the crucial question was whether 12 months' youth custody adequately reflected the seriousness of the offence: if it did not, the court should take advantage of the subsection and pass the appropriate term of detention.[8] But in *R v Fairhurst*[9] the Lord Chief Justice, Lord Lane, regarded those decisions as having possibly gone too far, in opposite directions, and, adopting a *media via*, laid down the following guidelines for applying the subsection:

1   In order to invoke it, the offence does not have to be one of exceptional gravity, such as attempted murder, manslaughter, wounding with intent, armed robbery or the like.

2   On the other hand, it is not good sentencing practice to pass a sentence of detention under section 53(2) simply because a 12 months' youth custody sentence (now a sentence of detention in a young offender institution) seems to be on the low side for the particular offence committed.

3   Where the offence plainly calls for a greater sentence than 12 months' detention in a young offender institution and is sufficiently serious to call for a sentence of 2 years' detention or more, had the offender

been at least 17 years old, then it would be proper to sentence to a similar term of detention under section 53(2). If the offence merits a sentence of less than 2 years but more than 12 months for an offender aged 17 or over, then the sentence should normally be one of detention in a young offender institution and not of section 53(2) detention.[10]

Matters become much more complicated where two or more offences are involved, as the further guidelines provided in *Fairhurst* demonstrate.

4   (i) Where two or more offences are involved, only one of which deserves detention, it is appropriate to give detention for it and either consecutive or concurrent sentences of detention for the other(s).[11]

(ii) Where a 15 or 16-year-old commits two offences, one of which (A) carries a minimum sentence of 14 years and the other (B) a lower maximum, then generally it is not proper to sentence under section 53(2) for A (which would not otherwise merit it) in order to compensate for the inadequacy of a maximum sentence of 12 months detention in a young offender institution for B. However, such a sentence may properly be passed where the same course of conduct gave rise to both A and B.

(iii) It is undesirable for a section 53(2) sentence to run consecutively or concurrently with a sentence of detention in a young offender institution,[12] especially since there are large procedural differences applicable to the two types of sentence.[13] Where, however, there is no alternative, the solution may be to impose no separate penalty for the offence(s) for which section 53(2) detention is not available. If that is done and there is a successful appeal against conviction for the section 53(2) offence, the court's hands are not tied, since it is enabled by section 4 of the Criminal Appeal Act 1968 to sentence for the offences for which no separate sentences have been passed.[14]

5   Although time spent in custody awaiting sentence is allowed off sentences of detention in a young offender institution, it does not count towards section 53(2) sentences. This anomaly should therefore be borne in mind when fixing the length of a section 53(2) sentence. Similarly, allowance should be made for time spent on remand in care where the offender is held under a regime comparable to a remand in custody, for example, where he is placed in secure accommodation[15] or held under highly structured and closely supervised conditions.

1   CJA 1982, s 3(1)(d); see ante, para 13.70. This restriction does not apply to proceedings under s 53(1), ante, para 13.97, presumably because the court has no discretion as to the order it can make. Nevertheless, in practice legal aid and legal representation are provided at the outset in those proceedings.
2   CYPA 1933, s 53(2).
3   By CJA 1982, s 1(4), ante, para 13.77.
4   See CJA 1982, s 2, ante, para 13.78.
5   Compare the duty of a court under CJA 1982, s 2(4), ante, para 13.79, when passing a sentence of detention in a young offender institution, to state reasons.
6   (1983) 5 Cr App Rep (S) 389, [1984] Crim LR 186, CA.
7   [1985] Crim LR 56.
8   As it did in *R v Nightingale* (1984) 6 Cr App Rep (S) 65, [1984] Crim LR 373, CA, where there was 'a wicked attack on two old people in their own home', and three years' detention of a 16-year-old was upheld by the Court of Appeal on charges of assault with intent to rob.
9   [1987] 1 All ER 46, [1986] 1 WLR 1374, CA.
10   See, for example, *R v Horrocks* (1986) 8 Cr App Rep (S) 23, [1986] Crim LR 412, CA; *R v Davis (Jason Michael)* (1986) 8 Cr App Rep (S) 35, CA.

11   See *R v Gaskin* (1985) 7 Cr App Rep (S) 28, CA.
12   See *R v Gaskin*, supra; *R v McKenna* [1986] Crim LR 195, CA.
13   See also remission, infra.
14   See *R v Dolan* (1975) 62 Cr App Rep 36 at 39, CA.
15   See *R v Murphy and Duke* (1986) 8 Cr App Rep (S) 72, [1986] Crim LR 571, CA.

(v)   Limits of section 53(2)

13.101   Welcome though this extension is, it does highlight the limits of section 53(2) and the inadequacy of the sentence of detention in a young offender institution in relation to juveniles.[1] There are two fundamental defects.

1   The requirement that the offence must be punishable with imprisonment for 14 years or more excludes from the operation of the subsection several serious offences which carry a lesser penalty, and many of which are being committed by young persons; for example, serious thefts, malicious wounding, assault occasioning actual bodily harm, indecent assault, public order offences. Consequently, in such cases the court is left to rely on a maximum 12 months' sentence of detention in a young offender institution, which itself may be subject to discount if there is a plea of guilty.[2]

2   As already indicated, the juvenile court may not initially have sufficient information to lead it to commit the juvenile for trial with a view to a section 53(2) order being made.[3] If it proceeds summarily and then decides that its own power of imposing a sentence of six months' detention in a young offender institution is inadequate it may commit the offender for sentence,[4] but the powers of the Crown Court are limited to imposing the maximum 12 months' term of youth custody or dealing with him in any manner in which the juvenile court might have dealt with him. It cannot invoke the powers of section 53(2),[5] whereas, if the offender were aged 17 or over, it could.[6] Moreover, if the juvenile court is dealing with two indictable offences, it can itself impose a six months' term of detention for each to run consecutively, so that the 'aid' of the Crown Court will not be necessary.

1   See His Honour Judge JMA Barker, *Some Problems in Sentencing Juveniles*, [1985] Crim LR 759.
2   *R v Stewart* (1983) 5 Cr App Rep (S) 320; [1983] Crim LR 830.
3   For example, it is only after it has accepted jurisdiction and proceeded on summary trial that it will be made aware of any offences to be taken into consideration.
4   Under MCA 1980, s 37(1), as substituted by CJA 1982, Sch 14, para 49.
5   PCCA 1973, s 42(2), as inserted by CJA 1982, Sch 14, para 34. For illustrations of the practical problems that can thereby arise see [1985] Crim LR at pp 762–763, and see *R v McKenna* [1986] Crim LR 195, CA.
6   PCCA 1973, s 42(1). On the power to commit for sentence see Carlin, *Sentencing Problems in Juvenile Courts: Committal to the Crown Court* 84 L S Gaz 1529.

13.102   The changes made by the Criminal Justice Act 1982 were generally designed to create for offenders under 21 a continuum in custodial sentences from the 21 days to four months of the detention centre order upwards through the sentence of youth custody, a continuum maintained by the provisions regulating detention in a young offender institution. The Court of Appeal has extended the continuum in respect of juveniles by the enlarged use of section 53(2). However, it is a contrived extension, and the better solution, it is suggested, is through increasing the maximum period of detention in a young offender institution that can be ordered for juveniles from 12 months to, say, three years, restoring section 53(2) to its original purpose of dealing as an exceptional order with grave crimes, but at the same time enabling the Crown Court to invoke it in respect of those under 17 as of those over that age when the offender is committed for sentence.[1]

1   See supra, PCCA 1973, s 42(1) and (2).

(vi) Places of detention

13.103   Many of those sentenced under section 53(1) and (2) have been detained in youth treatment centres or youth custody centres or, in future, young offender institutions but the Home Secretary has power[1] to direct detention by a local authority in a community home provided by the authority or in a controlled community home,[2] although in such cases the person cannot be detained there after attaining the age of 19.[3] He may also be able to arrange with the managers detention in an assisted community home.[2]

1   CYPA 1969, s 30.
2   For community homes see post, para 15.67.
3   Section 30(1). The local authority is entitled to be reimbursed by the Home Office for any expenses reasonably incurred (sub-s (2)).

(vii) Release on licence

13.104   The Home Secretary may on the recommendation of the Parole Board release on licence a person detained under section 53, but, in the case of detention during Her Majesty's pleasure or for life, he must also first consult the Lord Chief Justice and the trial judge if available.[1] The release may be made subject to conditions and the Home Secretary may revoke the licence and recall the person to detention.[2]

1   CJA 1967, s 61. For the review procedure see Walker, op cit, paras 22.62–22.63.
2   Ibid, s 62.

(f)   Hospital and guardianship orders

13.105   Because of his mental disorder a juvenile offender may be ordered to be detained in a specified hospital or, occasionally, placed under the guardianship of a local social services authority or a person approved by the authority. The Crown Court may make either order where the offence is punishable with imprisonment,[1] other than one the sentence for which is fixed by law.[2] So, the order can be made where the offence is manslaughter, but not murder. A juvenile or other magistrates' court may make the orders where the offence is one punishable on summary conviction with imprisonment.[3] If either order is made, the court cannot impose a fine or make a supervision order or an order that the parent enter into a recognisance to take proper care of him and exercise proper control over him or any order for his detention. But a care order may be combined with either a hospital order or guardianship order.[4]

1   Given that these orders can be made in care proceedings (post, para 14.113) they ought to be available where an offence is non-imprisonable. For criticism of this limitation

see Walker and McCabe, *Crime and Insanity in England Vol II: New Solutions and New Problems* (1973) p 103.
2　Mental Health Act 1983, s 37(1).
3　Ibid. Where the mental disorder is in the form of mental illness or severe mental impairment (see infra), a magistrates' court, if satisfied that the accused did the act or made the omission charged, may make an order without proceeding to a finding of guilt; see sub-s (3), and for appeals post, para 13.115.
4　Section 37(8).

(i)　Restrictions on making orders

13.106　There are three restrictions on making these orders.

(1)　Nature and degree of mental disorder　There must be the evidence of two doctors that the juvenile is suffering from a particular kind of mental disorder[1] and that it is such that either (i) it is appropriate[2] to detain him in a hospital and, in the case of psychopathic disorder or mental impairment, the medical treatment is likely to alleviate or prevent deterioration of his condition, or (ii) provided he is at least 16, it warrants his reception into guardianship.[3] The evidence may be oral or written,[4] but the doctors must be agreed about the kind of disorder from which the juvenile is suffering.[5] Where a written report is submitted (otherwise than on the juvenile's behalf) and the juvenile is legally represented, a copy of the report must be given to his counsel or solicitor.[6] If the 'person who is the subject of the report' is not legally represented, the substance of it 'shall be disclosed to him *or*, where he is a child or young person, to his parent or guardian if present in court'.[7] On the face of it this means either that a juvenile is never entitled to be told even where his parent or guardian is not in court or (less likely) that he is only so entitled if the parent or guardian is not present. On either construction the rule compares sharply with the general rules relating to disclosure in criminal proceedings in a juvenile court,[8] where he is entitled, as is the parent or guardian, if present. The rules under the 1983 Act do not make it clear whether the legal representative has the right or duty to show the report or disclose its substance, to the juvenile and/or his parent or guardian. In any event, the juvenile may require the doctor to be called to give oral evidence,[9] which may result in the whole of the written report in effect coming to the knowledge of the juvenile. The precise relationship between the rules in the 1983 Act and the general rules is uncertain. For example, is that contained in the latter, which enables the court to require the juvenile to withdraw,[10] overriding even though the 1983 Act is silent on the point?

1　The different kinds are mental illness, psychopathic disorder, severe mental impairment or mental impairment. Each of these except the first is defined by MHA 1983, s 1. In *W v L* [1974] QB 711, [1973] 3 All ER 884, CA, Lawton LJ took the view that in the absence of a statutory definition 'the words [mental illness] should be given their ordinary meaning and should be construed in the way ordinary sensible people would construe them'.
2　This seems to mean primarily, if not exclusively, appropriate for medical reasons; see Walker, *Sentencing: Theory, Law and Practice* (1982) para 21.39.
3　Section 37(2)(a).
4　For requirements as to medical evidence see s 54.
5　Section 37(7).
6　MHA 1983, s 54(3)(a).
7　Section 54(3)(b); italics supplied.

8   Magistrates' Courts (Children and Young Persons) Rules 1988, r 10(1)(d) (2) and (3), ante, para 12.113.
9   MHA 1983, s 54(3)(c).
10 MC (C & YP) Rules 1988, r 10(1)(e).

13.107 *(2) Suitability of either order* The court must be satisfied that a hospital order or guardianship order is 'the most suitable method of disposing of the case'.[1] In determining this it is directed to have regard to all the circumstances of the case including the nature of the offence and the character and antecedents of the offender and the other methods of dealing with him. So far as concerns juveniles this statutory direction might be said to be superfluous, since they are all matters of which a juvenile court should always take cognisance, if it is to discharge its general duty[2] of having regard to the juvenile's welfare when deciding how to deal with him.

1   MHA 1983, s 37(2)(b).
2   Under CYPA 1933, s 44(1), post, para 13.117.

13.108 *(3) Arrangements for admission or reception* No hospital order can be made unless the court is satisfied that arrangements have been made for the juvenile's admission to a hospital within 28 days of the order.[1] It is obviously preferable to place the juvenile in a hospital near to his residence so that relatives may visit him, but it is not necessary that there should be a vacancy in a hospital in a particular region. The court can request the Regional Health Authority for the region in which the juvenile resides, or any other RHA that appears appropriate, to provide it with information about hospitals at which arrangements can be made for the juvenile's admission,[2] but only the Secretary of State can compel a hospital to admit the juvenile. A guardianship order may only be made if the court is satisfied that the local social services authority or other person is willing to receive the juvenile into guardianship.[3]

1   MHA 1983, s 37(4). If an order is made, the court may give directions for the juvenile to be kept in a place of safety pending his admission to the specified hospital within the 28-day period.
2   Section 39.
3   Section 37(6).

(ii) Duration of orders
13.109 The effect of an order is that the juvenile is very largely treated as if he had been compulsorily admitted to hospital or guardianship, as the case may be, under Part II of the Mental Health Act 1983.[1] The order is for an indefinite period, but lapses after six months unless renewed for a further period of six months and, if necessary, thereafter for yearly periods.[2] A hospital order may, however, be discharged at any time by the responsible medical officer or the hospital managers, and a guardianship order by the medical officer or local social services authority.[3] But there is no power, as there is in cases under Part II, for the nearest relative to order discharge.[4] Instead, he may apply to a Mental Health Review Tribunal for discharge of a hospital order or guardianship order.[5] The juvenile may himself apply for discharge of a guardianship order during the first six months of the order.[6]

1   Section 40(2) and (4).
2   Section 20.
3   Section 23(2).
4   Ibid.
5   Section 69(1)(a) and (b)(ii).
6   Section 69(1)(b)(i).

(iii)   Restriction orders
13.110   When a hospital order is made by the Crown Court, an order restricting the discharge of the offender may also be made, if this is considered 'necessary for the protection of the public from serious harm'.[1] In deciding whether it should make the order the Court should have regard to the nature of the offence, the juvenile's antecedents and the risk of his committing further offences if set at large. Normally no time limit is fixed, and this should only be done where the doctors are confident of recovery within a fixed period.[2] The main effects of a restriction order are that none of the above rules relating to the duration and expiration of the authority for the detention of patients applies,[3] no application for discharge can be made to a Mental Health Tribunal and the juvenile cannot be discharged by the responsible medical officer without the consent of the Home Secretary.[4]

1   MHA 1983, s 41(1).
2   *R v Gardiner* [1967] 1 All ER 895, [1967] 1 WLR 464.
3   Supra, para 13.109.
4   Section 41(3).

13.111   A juvenile court cannot make a restriction order. If it considers such an order should be made, it may instead of making a hospital order or otherwise dealing with the juvenile, commit him to the Crown Court to be dealt with, provided he has attained the age of 14.[1] The Crown Court may then make a hospital order with or without a restriction order or deal with him in any other way in which the juvenile court could have dealt with him;[2] but the latter court may also commit him for sentence[3] with a view to greater punishment than it has power to inflict, and then those 'greater' powers may be exercised by the Crown Court if it decides not to make a hospital order.[4] A juvenile who is so committed can be ordered to be detained in a specified hospital.[5]

1   Section 43(1).
2   Sub-s (2).
3   Under MCA 1980, s 38.
4   MHA 1983, s 43(4).
5   Section 44.

(iv)   Interim hospital orders
13.112   Both the Crown Court and a juvenile or other magistrates' court[1] may make interim hospital orders. The conditions on which such an order can be made follow closely those that apply to full hospital orders.[2] An interim order may be made for any period up to 12 weeks, renewable for further periods up to 28 days at a time with a maximum of six months in all, unless the court earlier makes a hospital order or deals with the offender in some other way.[3] Where an interim order is in force a hospital order or further interim order may be made without the juvenile being

brought to court, if he is legally represented.[4] Should the juvenile abscond from the hospital, he may be arrested without warrant by a constable, and the court may terminate the interim order and deal with him as if the order had not been made.[5]

1   But only on convicting the offender; cf ante, para 13.105, note 3.
2   MHA 1983, s 38(1) and (4).
3   Ibid, s 38(5).
4   Ibid, s 38(2) and (6).
5   Ibid, s 38(7). The power to arrest without warrant is preserved by the Police and Criminal Evidence Act 1984, s 26 and Sch 2.

3   Deferring, altering and appealing against sentence

(a)   Deferment of sentence

13.113   A court may defer sentence for a specified period up to six months.[1] It is a power which is not frequently exercised, but juvenile courts are tending to make greater use of it, usually for a maximum period of about four months.[2] The object of deferment is to enable the court to take into account the juvenile's conduct after conviction or any later change in his circumstances, and, in deciding whether to defer, it must have regard to the nature of the offence and to his character and present circumstances.[3] Deferment may, for example, be appropriate where he has been on remand on bail for some time before conviction and there is evidence that during that period he is beginning to act more responsibly, especially if he is making genuine efforts to find work or undergo training. The juvenile must consent to deferment, and, if the court decides on it, it must not remand him.[4] When he later appears before the court for sentence, it must determine whether he has 'substantially conformed or attempted to conform with the proper expectations of the deferring court . . .. If he has, then [he] may legitimately expect that an immediate custodial sentence will not be imposed. If he has not, the court should be careful to state with precision in what respects he has failed.'[5] In practice the court will rarely impose a custodial sentence where no further offence has been committed during deferment, even though the juvenile has not otherwise met the court's expectations.[6] If he has committed a further offence, the court may then deal with him both for that offence and the earlier one.[7] For obvious reasons he should come back for sentence before the same justices, or at least one of them, who deferred sentence. Regrettably there are many cases where this does not happen. Moreover, there is all too often insufficient information about the expectations of the Bench who deferred sentence.[8]

1   PCCA 1973, s 1, as amended by CJA 1982, s 63.
2   See Nott and Corden, *Deferring Sentence* (1984) for a study of the use of the power in West Yorkshire Courts.
3   See the guidelines indicated by the Court of Appeal in *R v George* (1984) 79 Cr App Rep 26, 6 Cr App Rep (S) 211.
4   PCCA 1973, s 1(3) and (6A).
5   *R v George*, supra; *R v Fletcher* (1982) 4 Cr App Rep (S) 118, CA.
6   See Nott and Corden, op cit, Chapter IV.
7   PCCA 1973 s 1(4) and (4A).
8   Nott and Corden, Chapter III.

(b)   Alteration of sentence

13.114   A juvenile court, like any other court, may vary or rescind any
sentence or other order it imposed, but it must do so within 28 days and
it must be composed of the same, or two of the three, justices who passed
the sentence.[1] It can substitute a different[2] and/or more severe[3] sentence.
If that is a custodial sentence, the general restrictions on imposing custodial
sentences apply.[4] Indeed, in all cases of altering sentence the juvenile should
be present, and he or his legal representative or parent or guardian should
be allowed to address the court.[5]

1   MCA 1980, s 142.
2   *R v Sodhi* (1978) 67 Cr App Rep 260.
3   *R v Tuart* (1973) unreported.
4   See ante, para 13.77.
5   *R v Rowe* (1974) unreported.

(c)   Appeals

13.115   A juvenile may, in the same way as an adult who has been convicted
and sentenced by a magistrates' court, appeal against his conviction or
sentence or both, or, where he pleaded guilty, against his sentence.[1] Legal
aid may be granted by the magistrates' court or the Crown Court.[2] The
right to appeal includes cases where the juvenile has been granted an order
for conditional or absolute discharge,[3] but does not apply to an order for
payment of costs. Appeal also lies against a hospital order or guardianship
order including where it is made without a conviction, and it may be brought
by the juvenile or his parent on his behalf.[4] Once notice of appeal has
been given, then, if the juvenile 'is in custody', the juvenile court may
grant him bail.[5] The Crown Court has similar powers.[6] However,
notwithstanding the fact that appeal lies against a care order made in criminal
proceedings, since it is a sentence,[7] there is a conflict of authorities on
whether a juvenile appealing against that order can be granted bail. The
answer turns on whether he is considered to be 'in custody'. In *R v K*[8]
it was held that he was not—he was in care—but the contrary view was
taken in *R v P*.[9] Indirect support for the former view may be drawn from
the rule that time spent in custody on remand counts towards remission,
whereas remand to the care of a local authority does not, unless he is
in secure accommodation.[10]

1   Magistrates' Courts Act 1980, s 108, as amended by CJA 1982, s 66(2) and Sch 16.
   Where the juvenile has been sentenced for several offences but only appeals against
   sentence on one offence, the Crown Court may deal with the sentences on the other
   offences, if necessary; see *Dutta v Westcott* [1987] QB 291, [1986] 3 All ER 381.
2   Legal Aid Act 1974, s 28(5).
3   Section 108(1A).
4   Mental Health Act 1983, s 45.
5   MCA 1980, s 113(1), but not where he has been committed to the Crown Court for
   sentence (see sub-s (3)).
6   Courts Act 1971, s 13(4).
7   *R v Crown Court at Snaresbrook, ex p S* [1982] Crim LR 682.
8   [1978] 1 All ER 180, [1978] 1 WLR 139.
9   (1979) 144 JP 39. For an analysis of the conflicting views see 142 JPN 52, 58 and
   83 and 143 JPN 662.
10 See ante, para 13.82.

13.116 Apart from a right of appeal, the juvenile may apply for the justices to state a case for the opinion of the High Court on the ground of error in law or excess of jurisdiction.[1] There is also the possibility of judicial review, a remedy more likely to be invoked in connection with care proceedings.

1   MCA 1980, s 111. The court may release him on bail; see s 113, supra.

IV   CONCLUSION

13.117 Section 44(1) of the Children and Young Persons Act 1933[1] provides:

> 'Every court in dealing with a child or young person who is brought before it, either as an offender or otherwise, shall have regard to the welfare of the child or young person and shall in a proper case take steps for removing him from undesirable surroundings and for securing that proper provision is made for his education and training.'

Although this principle is not limited to the jurisdiction of the juvenile court, the fact that it applies both to criminal proceedings and to care and certain other civil proceedings is explained by the close historical association between those respective proceedings in the juvenile court.[2] The enactment has never been subjected to close judicial scrutiny, and its operation in criminal proceedings is variable owing to the differing opinions held on the extent to which criminality should involve the interests of the public as well as those of the juvenile.[3] 'Welfare' in the sense of the individual juvenile's needs, especially but not exclusively in the light of his criminal behaviour, is not made the paramount consideration, much less the sole,[4] but those who would argue for that may derive some support from the rule that after the juvenile is found guilty of the offence 'the court shall take into consideration such information as to the general conduct, home surroundings, school record and medical history of the child and young person as may be necessary to enable it to deal with the case *in his best interests* . . . .'[5] This rule, too, has yet to be tested by higher authority, but those who represent juveniles seem either to ignore or to overlook it.

1   As amended by CYPA 1969, Sch 6.
2   See post, para 14.02.
3   For a survey of the views of the members of the juvenile court panels of four different Benches see McEwan, *The Sentencing of Children and Young Persons,* [1981] JSWL 270.
4   The lack of a coherent policy and philosophy towards juvenile offenders and equivocation over the weight to be given to their welfare have aroused considerable criticism in various quarters. For the highly critical views of two leading critics see Morris A and Giller H, *Justice for Children* (1980); *Providing Criminal Justice for Children* (1983); *Understanding Juvenile Justice* (1986). See also Adler RM, *Taking Juvenile Justice Seriously* (1985); Parsloe P, *Juvenile Justice in Britain and the United States. The Balance of Rights and Needs* (1978); Preistley P, Fears D and Fuller R, *Justice for Juveniles. The 1969 Children and Young Persons Act: A Case for Reform* (1978); Morris A and McIsaac M, *Juvenile Justice? The Practice of Social Welfare* (1978); Parker H, Casburn M and Turnbull D, *Receiving Juvenile Justice: Adolescents and State Care and Control* (1981); McCabe S and Treitel P, *Juvenile Justice in the United Kingdom: Comparisons and Suggestions for Change* (1984); Allen N, *The Reform of Children's Jurisdictions* [1984] Fam Law 7; National Association for Care of Offenders and the Prevention of Crime (NACRO), *The Future of the Juvenile*

Court in England and Wales, (1986); Harris R and Webb D, *Welfare, Power and Juvenile Justice* (1987).
5   MC (C & YP) Rules 1988, r 10(1)(b), italics supplied.

13.118   However, the intrinsic nature of most of the sentences which a court is empowered to impose militates against a doctrine of paramountcy of welfare. Their main objects are general deterrence and the protection of the public, with a prominent punitive element. These objects are particularly present in the orders for detention under section 53(1) and (2) of the Children and Young Persons Act 1933, but the welfare of the individual may be relevant in fixing the duration,[1] and the Court of Appeal has pointed out[2] that a sentence under section 53(2):

'is by no means a sentence which will lead to lack of care or to a disregard for the welfare of the young man. Indeed the sentence means that those best qualified to assess the character and to plan the rehabilitation of this young man will make the decision as to when he is to be released . . . the section and the administrative practice that has been developed under it are such that the welfare of the young offender is under constant review.'

That general observation may, in principle at least, be extended to the sentence of detention in young offender institutions if those institutions adopt the proclaimed emphasis on 'individual assessment and personal development in work, training, education and positive preparation for release to life in the community',[3] which were the aims of the youth custody centres. But detention in a young offender institution is seen primarily as a 'tariff' measure, as is the attendance centre order, each aimed at deterrence and/or punishment, and there is nothing of the welfare principle in the fine or order for compensation or costs to be paid by the juvenile himself.[4] At the other end of the scale, the welfare principle underlies the order for discharge, and predominates in the community service order,[5] the order of binding over and the hospital and guardianship orders, although the element of public protection is a secondary factor in binding over and a major one where a restriction order[6] attaches to a hospital order.

1   See ante, para 13.99.
2   *R v Ford* (1976) 62 Cr App Rep 303, at 307–308 (per Scarman LJ).
3   See ante, para 13.87.
4   As for the general rule of payment by the parent, that order is 'incompatible with what purports to be a system of measures for the education and training of [juveniles]' (Report of the Committee on Children and Young Persons, Scotland (Kilbrandon Report) (1964) Cmnd 2306).
5   But see Pease, [1978] Crim LR 269.
6   See ante, para 13.110.

13.119   The supervision order and the care order call for special comment. Even before the changes made by the Criminal Justice Act 1982, there was evidence that ambiguity surrounded these orders, with some magistrates seeing them as being exclusively used for welfare purpose, but others for deterrence or punishment as well as for the juvenile's welfare.[1] Some of the changes made by the 1982 Act with regard to stipulated intermediate treatment, a night restriction requirement and a requirement of non-participation[2] contain punitive and deterrent elements. As for the care order, if it is to be seen as 'a substantial intervention comparable to a custodial sentence',[3] that strongly suggests a tariff as well as its welfare function. The former is certainly present and, it is suggested, predominant where the order is a residential care order.[4]

1   See McEwan, op cit, at pp 275–276.
2   See ante, paras 13.53 et seq.
3   HOC No 42/1983, para 63, ante, para 13.71.1
4   See ante, para 13.72.

13.120   Although the predominance of either the welfare or the tariff purpose is largely determined by the intrinsic nature of the particular sentence, in the final analysis the choice of sentence is a matter for the discretion of the court, and sentencing patterns vary enormously among juvenile courts.[1] In this regard, the welfare purpose has in principle been strengthened by the Criminal Justice Acts 1982 and 1988 through the general restrictions it has imposed on the passing of the sentence of detention in a young offender institution and the youth custody sentence.[2] However, as already indicated,[3] the earliest indications are that the courts are not paying sufficient attention to these safeguards, and the increase in youth custody sentences is in line with the increase in prison sentences for adult offenders aged 21 or over.[4]

1   See Gelsthorpe and Nutt, *The Attendance Centre Order* [1986] Crim LR 146 at 149.
2   See ante, para 13.77.
3   Ante, para 13.76.
4   See NACRO Report, *Non Custodial Sentences* (1985), and for data on juvenile crime and offenders see its Report, *Some Facts About Juvenile Crime* (1987).

CHAPTER 14
Care proceedings[1]

I ORIGIN AND EXPANSION OF CARE JURISDICTION

14.01 The care jurisdiction of the juvenile court is traceable to nineteenth century legislation dealing with juveniles who for various reasons were living in undesirable conditions.[2] The Industrial Schools Acts, first of 1857 and 1861 and then 1866[3] gave to justices of the peace jurisdiction over various kinds of troublesome children, ie children who were vagrants or were found begging or destitute or who, being inmates in a poor law institution were refractory or whose parents were unable to control them or (later) who, under the Elementary Education Act 1876, failed to comply with a school attendance order. Under the legislation such children could be sent to an Industrial School for care, education and training.[4] In establishing the juvenile court,[5] the Children Act 1908 extended the categories of children 'at risk'[6] in respect of whom the jurisdiction could be exercised, and also gave the court additional powers to deal with them. Broadly, the effect was that the court could send to an industrial school, or place into the care of a fit person, a child under 14, (1) who was found begging or, having no parent or no parent or guardian exercising proper guardianship, was a vagrant, or, because his parent was in prison, was destitute; or (2) who was in moral danger because he was in the company of a thief or prostitute or, in the case of a girl, because her father had been convicted of a sexual offence against her;[7] or (3) whose parent because of criminal or drunken habits was unfit to have care of him. A young person in similar circumstances could be the subject of a fit person order.[8] The Act also repeated the earlier provisions of the 1866 Act concerning the child whose parents were unable to control him and the refractory child who was being maintained in a Poor Law institution, and it re-enacted those dealing with the truant whose parent did not comply with a school attendance order made under the Elementary Education Act 1876.[9]

1 The main general references are: Bromley, Chapter 14, pp 448–466; Cretney, Chapter 19, pp 524–556; R Dingwall and J Eekelaar, *Care Proceedings* (1982); Dingwall, Eekelaar and T Murray, *Care or Control?* (1981); and by the same authors *The Protection of Children* (1983); M Hayes and V Bevan, *Child Care Law* (2nd edn, 1988) Chapters 3 and 4; Hoggett and Pearl, Chapter 9, pp 351–370; Graham Hall and Martin, *Child Abuse – Procedure and Evidence in Juvenile Courts* (2nd edn, 1987); Eleventh Report of the House of Commons Expenditure Committee; Observations on the Eleventh Report (1976) Cmnd 6494; House of Commons Social Services Committee (1983–84), *Children in Care*; Report of Working Party of ABAFA on *Care Proceedings* (Ed Rawstron); and see post, para 14.02, note 1.
2 For a general historical survey see Eekelaar, Dingwall and Murray, *Victims or Threats? Children in Care Proceedings*, [1982] JSWL 67; and for certain aspects Lord Scarman in *Leeds City Council v West Yorkshire Metropolitan Police* [1983] 1 AC 29 at 41, [1982] 1 All ER 274 at 281.
3 The 1866 Act replaced the earlier Acts.

4   The Industrial Schools were the counterpart to the Reformatory Schools, to which youthful
    offenders could be committed by virtue of the Reformatory Schools (Scotland) Act 1854
    and Reformatory Schools Act 1857 (replaced by the Reformatory Schools Act 1866).
5   See ante, para 12.03.
6   Section 58.
7   Viz, under s 4 or s 5 of the Criminal Law Amendment Act 1885.
8   CA 1908, s 59.
9   Ibid, s 58(4)–(6).

14.02   Since 1908 there have been three major changes in the legislation,
with the likelihood of a fourth in the near future.[1] These have been in
the Children and Young Persons Acts of 1933, 1963 and 1969.[2] Those of
1933 and 1963 were the direct result of Reports of Departmental
Committees.[3] In both there was still a noticeable association with the earlier
legislation and the juveniles covered fell broadly into two categories: those
whose behaviour was troublesome but not criminal and those who were
the victims of ill-treatment or neglect. Each Act was a variation on the
same basic theme, namely, that State intervention against the wishes of
the juvenile and the parent can be justified only on specified grounds, and
each was a denial of a general guardianship jurisdiction based solely on
the welfare of the juvenile. In all these respects the Act of 1969 followed
its predecessors, but it fundamentally altered the course of care jurisdiction
by introducing a third category of juvenile, the offender. The introduction
was the result of a long campaign to raise the minimum age of criminal
responsibility and bring more juveniles, who would otherwise be offenders,
under the care jurisdiction. The policy commended itself to the Ingleby
Committee, but that later proposed by the Government in its White Paper[4]
was less ambitious in that it did not raise the age of criminal responsibility
but raised that to which juvenile offenders could be the subject of criminal
proceedings. Provision was made in the Act[5] abolishing prosecution of child
offenders, ie those aged between 10 and 14, who instead should be subject
to care proceedings. Young persons were normally to be treated in the
same way, but criminal proceedings could be instituted against them in
certain defined circumstances for serious offences.[6] These changes were to
be phased in as and when sufficient staff and resources in social services
departments became available. However, before any of them were
implemented there was a change of Government which abandoned the policy,
and sections 4 and 5 still remain dead letters.[7] This has had serious
consequences for the so-called 'offence condition', which is one of the
grounds on which care jurisdiction is based,[8] but the more regrettable irony
is that a number of provisions in the 1969 Act, which were enacted primarily
with the proposed changes in mind, for example those relating to care
orders, operate in respect of the other categories of juveniles covered by
the Act, for whom they should never have been designed.[9]

1   See the Interdepartmental Working Party Report on *Review of Child Care Law* (1985)
    HMSO, (subsequent references are to 'RCCL'); the Government White Paper, *The Law
    on Child Care and Family Services* (1987) Cm 62 (subsequent references are to 'CCFS')
    and the Report of the Inquiry into Child Abuse in Cleveland 1987, presented by Lord
    Justice Butler-Sloss, (1988) Cm 412 (subsequent references are to 'the Cleveland Report').
2   See s 61, s 2 and s 1 of the respective Acts. Section 61 re-enacted provisions in CYPA
    1932, but was itself amended by the CYPA (Amendment) Act 1952, s 1, which added
    as a category to be protected those juveniles who were ill-treated or neglected in a manner
    likely to cause them unnecessary suffering or injury to health.

3 The Committee on the Treatment of Young Offenders (1927) Cmnd 2831; the Ingleby
   Committee on Children and Young Persons (1960) Cmnd 1191.
4 *The Child, the Family and the Young Offender* (1965) Cmnd 2742; *Children in Trouble*
   (1968) Cmnd 3601.
5 Section 4.
6 Section 5.
7 Hopefully but unrealistically the Police and Criminal Evidence Act 1984 has prospectively
   amended s 5; see s 37(11)–(13) of that Act.
8 Post, paras 14.19 et seq.
9 See further post, para 14.23.

14.03   Recent publicity concerning the extent of sexual abuse of children,[1]
coupled with the number of inquiries into the tragic deaths of children
who turned out to be victims of various forms of abuse — from Maria
Colwell (1974) to Jasmine Beckford (1985) and, most recently, to Kimberley
Carlile (1987) and Tyra Henry (1987) — may tend to mask the increasing
efforts made over the past two decades to identify and combat a social
evil now known to be so extensive that it can no longer be described as
a phenomenon. The process began[2] before the enactment of the Children
and Young Persons Act 1969. Inspired by the research work of Kempe
and his colleagues in the United States into the 'Battered Baby Syndrome',[3]
the National Society for the Prevention of Cruelty to Children set up a
Battered Child Research unit in 1967 to investigate the incidence of child
abuse in this country. 'The unit's most important function was to publicise
the problem and educate the professionals concerned.'[4] A conference of
experts in various disciplines concerned with child abuse[5] urged the need
for co-ordinating action at local level. The proposal was supported by the
Home Office and DHSS and led to the setting up of area review committees
and case conferences, and the appearance of the non-accidental injury
register.[6] Hard lessons were learnt by the social work and other agencies
from the Maria Colwell and other cases.[7] Not least was the disturbing
difficulty of choosing between removal of the child from a hostile, harmful
environment and support and surveillance of him within his family. Another
was the realisation by local authority social services departments that the
courts should assume a heavier share of responsibility for State intervention
where child abuse is suspected. Where there is some evidence of abuse
a local authority should not be diffident about instituting care proceedings
and placing on the court the responsibility of being satisfied of its existence.
The consequence has been a sharp rise in the number of cases of care
proceedings,[8] which in turn has been affected by new rules relating to separate
representation of the child[9] and the eventual recognition by the legal
profession that his interests should be more effectively represented by
specialist advocates.[10]

1 Vividly highlighted by the BBC Television Programme, *Childline*, (televised on 30 October
   1986). An increasingly important agency in focussing the attention of the public on this,
   as on other forms of abuse of children, is the organisation known as Child Watch. See
   also the Cleveland Report (passim) on the deep controversy concerning the diagnosis of
   sexual abuse of children in the Cleveland area which arose in June 1987, and a relevant
   article by Hobbs and Wynne, *Buggery in Childhood — A Common Syndrome of Child
   Abuse*, The Lancet, 4 October 1986, pp 792–796, where the authors reported a high level
   of abuse in their study of children referred to them in Leeds.
2 For a summary see Chapter 1 of *A Child in Trust*, The Report of the Panel of Inquiry
   into the Circumstances Surrounding the Death of Jasmine Beckford, (1985), and for more
   detailed treatment Parton, *The Politics of Child Abuse* (1985).

3 JAMA (1962), 181, 1 : 17–24.
4 *A Child in Trust*, p 10.
5 Chaired by a paediatrician, the late Dr Alfred White Franklin, and sometimes referred to as the Tunbridge Wells Conference.
6 See further post, para 14.31.
7 See *Child Abuse, A Study of Inquiry Reports 1973–1981*. Written by a professional group in the DHSS (in 1982) it analyses the published reports of inquiries into 18 cases of abuse, 17 of which involved the death of a child.
8 But there are few statistics available. Apparently there were in 1984 about 5,200 applications for care orders and in 1985 approximately 5,600; see HC Debs (WA) col 257 (1 May 1987).
9 See post, paras 14.57 et seq.
10 See post, para 14.75.

II   GROUNDS FOR BRINGING CARE PROCEEDINGS

14.04   Like all its predecessors section 1 of the Children and Young Persons Act 1969 suffers from inherent defects. Some of its provisions are potentially very wide, but there is still only limited guidance from case law on the construction of the section. The court may make an order if of opinion (a) that any one of seven primary conditions is satisfied, and also (b) that the juvenile[1] is in need of care or control which he is unlikely to receive unless the court makes an order under the section.

1   Oddly and incongruously the 1969 Act also refers to the 'relevant infant', see s 1(6). It is a term that should long ago have been abandoned.

1   The primary conditions

(a)   The juvenile's proper development is being avoidably prevented or neglected or his health is being avoidably impaired or neglected or he is being ill-treated (s 1(2)(a))

14.05   This condition is obviously in wide but vague terms, and is the one most frequently relied on.[1] It is a single condition, and the rules of duplicity do not apply. It is therefore not necessary for the applicant local authority[2] to stipulate that they rely specifically on any one or more of the five overlapping possibilities contained in paragraph (a).[3] The term 'proper development' is intrinsically imprecise, both as to its nature and as to the standard against which propriety is to be assessed. The fact that no minimum standard is prescribed, for example that of the 'good' or 'reasonable' parent,[4] leaves the applicant local authority with a wide discretion to intervene in the family and the court to find the condition satisfied. The prevention or neglect of development most often relates to physical abuse or physical neglect or both, but it also covers impairment or neglect of mental health. It includes, too, emotional deprivation.[5] Indeed, quite often behind the screen of physical ill-treatment or neglect lie the more insidious and harmful effects of absence of love and caring affection. However, unless there has already been close supervision of the family by a social worker, proof of emotional deprivation will be difficult,[6] although sometimes it may emerge under close cross-examination of the parent. The recent Cleveland inquiry has demonstrated that in cases of alleged sexual abuse there may be the double difficulty of detection of the physical and the emotional consequences.

1   In over 60% of care cases.
2   For others who may, in practice exceptionally, apply see post, para 14.25.
3   *Wooley v Haines* (1976) 140 JP 16, DC. For criticism of this umbrella effect see Evans (1982) Law Soc Gaz 1240.
4   Section 2 of CYPA 1963 included the test of the good parent, but the introduction of the offence condition into the 1969 Act meant its abandonment.
5   *F v Suffolk County Council* (1981) 2 FLR 208. For comment see [1981] JSWL 245 (BMH).
6   See Dingwall, Eekelaar and Murray, *Care or Control?* p 41.

14.06   Some harm, impairment or neglect must be proved,[1] but no minimum degree is statutorily imposed, for example, that there has been unnecessary suffering or serious harm to the juvenile. Its extent is, however, of strong evidential value, and can be particularly relevant in answering the question whether the juvenile is in need of care or control. Sometimes the ill-treatment or neglect may take the form of failure or refusal to obtain medical treatment for the juvenile.[2] Whichever form it takes, it may be due to, or exacerbated by, the alcoholism or drug addiction or mental or physical condition of the parent,[3] and the better view[4] is that the fact that a parent has no control over his disability does not make any consequent harm to the juvenile unavoidable. Disability is no more a justification for excluding section 1(2)(a) than culpability, and the decision of a magistrates' court in *Salford County Council v C* to the contrary is, it is submitted, unlikely to receive higher approval.[5] That does not mean, however, that the local authority should not first try to invoke its preventive powers under section 1 of the Child Care Act 1980, and provide assistance in the home to help the parent overcome his disability. Section 1 of the 1969 Act should be seen as an unavoidable measure to protect the juvenile.

1   Compare *Re Williams (a minor)* (1976), unreported, where on a balance of probabilities a 16-month-old girl was found to be suffering from *osteogenesis imperfecta* (brittle bones) and not the victim of alleged grievous bodily harm inflicted by the father.
2   For criminal liability see ante, paras 9.37 to 9.38. In the case where the parent refuses consent to a life-saving operation the Ministry of Health and the Home Office have advised that hospital authorities should 'rely on the clinical judgment of the consultants concerned after full discussion with the parents'; see Ministry of Health Circular F/P9/1B dated 14 April 1967 and HOC No 63 (1968). In *Gillick v West Norfolk and Wisbech Area Health Authority* [1986] AC 112, [1985] 3 All ER 402 the House of Lords recognised the power of the doctor to give treatment in an emergency without parental consent (ante, para 1.26), although in practice he will still be likely to discuss it with the parent and seek his consent if possible. What the Circular also advises is that care proceedings should not be instituted with a view to a care order being made and the consent of the local authority being obtained. There is the obvious practical objection to that procedure that an order may not be made in time, but *Gillick* in any event makes it clear that it is wholly unnecessary.
3   Medical evidence of the juvenile or parent may be given in care proceedings by medical certificate; see CYPA 1963, s 26.
4   See Hayes and Bevan, pp 47–48; Bromley, pp 452–453.
5   (1981) 3 FLR 153.

The temporal factor
14.07   By the time the local authority application under paragraph (a) is heard the juvenile will in practice have been in its care for several weeks or more under successive interim orders and being looked after by foster

parents or in a community home. Even when the first interim order is made, it usually follows a place of safety order, so that by that date the juvenile is no longer being neglected or ill-treated. To construe the condition literally, with its reference to the present tense, would therefore render it ineffectual. Instead, it has been applied with reference to the circumstances prevailing at the time when the parent last had the care and control of the juvenile.[1] But 'a child's development is a continuing process. The present must be relevant in the context of what has happened in the past, and it becomes a matter of degree as to how far in the past you go.[2]' In *Re D (a minor)*[3] the Court of Appeal was prepared to go back to the time when the child was in the mother's womb, and decide that development and health had been prevented and impaired by the mother's excessive drug-taking during pregnancy which had caused the child to be born suffering from drug withdrawal symptoms. The decision also illustrates in another way the readiness to construe the condition liberally in favour of the child, because it was held to be satisfied even though the child remained in hospital and the ability of the mother to care for the child had never been put to the test. In this respect the decision is in marked contrast to that in *M v Westminster City Council*,[4] though the outcome was the same. There, after an interim order had been made, the child was allowed to return to live with the parents, who at the date of the final hearing were looking after the child without further harm to him. It was nevertheless held that because of their earlier conduct the condition was satisfied.

1 The point was stressed by the Crown Court in *H v Sheffield City Council* [1981] JSWL 303.
2 Per Butler-Sloss J in *M v Westminster City Council* [1985] FLR 325, [1985] Fam Law 93, DC.
3 [1987] AC 317, [1987] 1 All ER 20, HL. See Maidsment (1987) 137 NLJ 8; Ogbourne, *Care Proceedings: the relevance of conduct during pregnancy,* 151 LG Rev 229.
4 Supra.

14.08 The condition relates to past and usually continuing present circumstances. It cannot be invoked merely on what might happen in the future.[1] So, the fact that the juvenile's development may in the immediate future be adversely affected does not justify care proceedings under paragraph (a), however serious the risk may be; for example, where a severely handicapped mother is unlikely to be able to cope with looking after her new born baby.[2] Protection in such cases is to be sought in wardship.[3] That should have been the step taken by the local authority in *Essex County Council v TLR and KBR*[4] in respect of two children who had been received into its care on their father, a serving soldier, being posted to Hong Kong. Two years later, when he was stationed in Northern Ireland, he informed the local authority foster parents that after visiting Hong Kong to marry a Chinese girl he would be collecting the children to take them with his wife to Northern Ireland. On the basis that the removal would be disturbing to the children the authority instituted care proceedings under section 1(2)(a),[5] but the application was dismissed, since there was no evidence that at the time the children's development was being avoidably neglected. On the contrary they were being well cared for by the foster parents. The point could, indeed, also have been taken that for the same reason the children were not in need of care or control. If effect is given to the recommendations of RCCL and CCFS[6] concerning new grounds for making orders in care proceedings, account will be taken of possible future harm, since an essential element in the grounds will be evidence of harm or likely harm to the child.

1   But, where there is evidence of past and present circumstances, future prospects will be relevant in considering the general condition, ie whether there is need for care or control; see post, paras 14.22–14.24.
2   Hayes and Bevan, op cit, p 49 also cite the example of 'a surrogate mother [who] plans to hand her newborn child to the couple who have used her services'.
3   The undue readiness of local authorities to take babies into care has been sharply criticised. See Freeman, *Removing Babies at Birth: A Questionable Practice* (1980) 10 Fam Law 131.
4   (1978) 143 JP 309, 9 Fam Law 15.
5   None of the grounds for passing a resolution under the then s 2 of CA 1948 was available; see now s 3 of CCA 1980, post, paras 15.14 et seq.
6   See post para 14.25.

(b)   It is probable that the condition set out in paragraph (a) will be satisfied in the juvenile's case, having regard to the fact that the court or another court has found that that condition is or was satisfied in the case of another child or young person who is or was a member of the household to which he belongs.

14.09   By its terms the essential purpose of this condition is preventive, but in one respect it is too narrow, because the earlier finding that condition (a) has been satisfied must be in relation to another juvenile, whereas there could be occasions when neglect or ill-treatment of an older member of the household (for example a 20-year-old son who is mentally infirm), could equally lead to the probability of condition (a) being satisfied in relation to the juvenile who is before the court.[1] That apart, condition (b) provides for a variety of applications, as illustrated by the following examples involving two sisters, A and B. In earlier care proceedings in respect of A, which were based on alleged physical ill-treatment of her by her father, it may have emerged at the hearing that there had been sexual assaults on her by him and that it was on the latter conduct that the court mainly relied in finding that condition (a) was satisfied. That finding might well alert the local authority to the fact that B might be at risk and lead it to institute proceedings relying on condition (b). The circumstances might, however, be such that when investigating them in respect of A the authority then recognised the risk to B. In that event concurrent proceedings may be instituted, with the authority relying on condition (a) in respect of A and condition (b) in respect of B. As was established by the Court of Appeal in *Surrey County Council v S*[2] a further possibility is that the juvenile court can receive evidence about A, who is not the subject of care proceedings, and, if it finds that A has been ill-treated or neglected, it can then proceed to consider whether it is probable that B, who is before the court, will similarly be ill-treated or neglected and, if so, whether she is in need of care or control. Moreover, to satisfy condition (b) it makes no difference that the juvenile in respect of whom condition (a) was satisfied is no longer a juvenile or, as in *Surrey County Council v S*, is now dead. The question is whether condition (a) was satisfied when he or she was a juvenile.

1   The court must consider the probability on the assumption that no order is going to
    be made (CYPA 1969, s 2(7)).
2   [1974] QB 124, [1973] 3 All ER 1074. See also Local Authority Circular, LAC No 18/
    1975, issued by the Department of Health and Social Security.

14.10   The readiness to construe condition (b) widely and thus emphasise
its preventive object is also demonstrated by the extended meaning which
has been been given to the word 'household'. That is a term which appears
in several areas of family law.[1] The primary facts of the case may themselves
dictate a particular result or conclusion, namely, that a person either is
or is not a member of a household. Otherwise the question must be answered
by consideration of all the circumstances as a matter of fact and degree.[2]
In *R v Birmingham Juvenile Court, ex p N (an infant)*[3] it was held that
in the context of section 1(2)(b) of the 1969 Act one of the relevant
circumstances is the care and welfare of the juvenile. Consequently, it is
the membership of the household to which a juvenile belongs, the persons
who comprise it, rather than the place where the household is located as
a matter of residence that is relevant. On this approach it is the mother
who is most likely to be the dominant person regarding the care and welfare
of the child, and therefore her continued presence in a household is highly
relevant in deciding whether there is a continuing household. In the
Birmingham case the child of married parents was made the subject of
a care order in 1978, the condition in paragraph (a) being satisfied because
her development and treatment were unsatisfactory. That child had remained
in care ever since that date. The parents were later divorced, and the mother
gave birth to a child by another man with whom she and her second child
were living when proceedings were brought in respect of this younger child.
The local authority relied for its application on paragraph (b), and the
question therefore was whether the older child was a member of the
household to which the younger belonged. It was held that, although there
had since 1978 been a marked change in the circumstances in which the
mother was living, she had been a member of the household to which
each child belonged and accordingly the elder and the younger child belonged
to the same household. The juvenile court was therefore entitled to make
a care order by virtue of paragraph (b). The decision is a particularly strong
one because the older child had remained in care throughout and not spent
any time with the mother in her second home, not even on weekend visits.[4]
It has been argued that the probable effect of the decision is that 'a new-
born child still in the maternity hospital could be held to have become
a member of the same household as his mother's other children, in which
case this ground could be relied on if there was evidence of ill-treatment
of the parent's other children'.[5] Such consequences should serve as a warning
that the probability of risk should not be too readily assumed. It is, it
is submitted, more common than has been suggested[6] to find cases where
a parent abuses one child but not the other(s), for example, where the
gravamen of allegations made under paragraph (a) in respect of that one
was emotional deprivation. On the other hand, in cases of a father's sexual
abuse of one daughter, the risk to other daughters, depending partly on
age, is high.

1   For example, in determining for various purposes of matrimonial proceedings whether spouses have ceased to live together as one household; for purposes relating to domestic violence (Domestic Violence and Matrimonial Proceedings Act 1976, s 1(2)); and formerly in relation to family income supplement, infra, and now family credit under the Social Security Act 1986.
2   See Woolf J in *England v Secretary of State for Social Services* (1981) 3 FLR 222.
3   [1984] 2 All ER 688, [1984] 3 WLR 387.
4   Compare in this regard *England v Secretary of State for Social Services*, a case relating to family income supplement, where the children were at home at weekends and holidays and the parents maintained as close ties as possible with them when they were away.
5   Cretney, op cit, p 530. On the other hand, it is arguable that in order to be a member of the same household the baby must have *lived* with the mother for a period of time, however short it might have been.
6   By Dingwall and Eekelaar, *Care Proceedings*, at p 53.

(bb)   It is probably that the condition set out in paragraph (a) will be satisfied in the juvenile's case having regard to the fact that a person who has been convicted of an offence mentioned in Schedule 1 to the Children and Young Persons Act 1933 (including a person convicted of such an offence on whose conviction for the offence an order was made under Part I of the Powers of Criminal Courts Act 1973 placing him on probation or discharging him absolutely or conditionally) is, or may become, a member of the same household as the child or young person.[1]

14.11   This paragraph is one of the numerous statutory changes which the Maria Colwell case inspired.[2] Like paragraph (b) its essential purpose is preventive, but it is much less frequently invoked. Given the range and seriousness of the scheduled offences which may be committed against a person under 16, coupled with the wide terms of paragraph (a), there should not be great difficulty in satisfying the court of the probability that the proper development or health of the juvenile before the court will be harmed or that he will be ill-treated. As for proof of the conviction, the Home Office has recommended[3] that chief officers of police should make available to the case conferences held by agencies details of any relevant previous convictions of a person involved in the care of a child, or who is a member of the same household.[4] It is clear that disclosure is permissible in respect of convictions which for other purposes are 'spent' under the Rehabilitation of Offenders Act 1974.[5] Nevertheless, there may still be evidential difficulties where the convicted person is not already a member of the household, but 'may become' so. The court, it is submitted, will want some firm evidence of prospective arrangements for that happening in the near future.[6]

1   This paragraph was inserted by the Children Act 1975, Sch 3, para 67 and in turn replaced by HASSASSAA 1983, Sch 2, para 10.
2   See the Report of the Committee of Inquiry into the Care and Supervision provided in Relation to Maria Colwell (1974) (Chaired by TG Field-Fisher, QC).
3   See Local Authority Social Services Letter, LASSL (76)26, paras 8–14.
4   Details may be given orally at the case conference. If information does not come to light the conviction may be proved by a certified extract from a court register; see Magistrates' Courts Rules 1981, r 68.
5   See s 7(2)(c) and (d).
6   Cf Cretney, op cit, p 531 and Dingwall and Eekelaar, *Care Proceedings*, p 55, who take a less strict view of the evidence requirement.

14.12 It is arguable that, as with paragraph (b), this paragraph is too restrictive in that it limits the condition to an earlier offence committed against a juvenile under 16. A girl who is in the same household as a man who, for example, has been convicted of the offence of unlawful sexual intercourse with an adult woman who is a mental defective[1] may well be at risk. Protection will therefore have to be sought in wardship.

1 Sexual Offences Act 1956, s 7, as amended by the Mental Health Act 1959, s 127(1)(a).

(c) The juvenile is exposed to moral danger

14.13 Any doubt about whether or not 'proper development' in paragraph (a) extends to a juvenile's moral upbringing is obviated by the inclusion of this condition. Instances of its likely operation are where the juvenile is living in a house which is being used for purposes of prostitution[1] or drug trafficking, or where he or she is involved in drug taking or, though not classified as a drug,[2] in sniffing glue or in gambling (for example, on arcade amusement machines) or in a sexual association, including incest,[3] or in criminal activities with older members of the family. His or her age can be particularly relevant. The court is likely to find the condition proved where a 14-year-old boy is associating with an adult woman, but may be more reluctant to intervene if he is 16. Given that he has then reached the minimum marriageable age,[4] much will depend on the nature of the relationship, the age of the woman, the kind of influence she exerts and probably, in the light of the *Gillick* principle, his wishes. On the other hand, where the association is homosexual the court may be as ready to intervene where the juvenile is 16 as where he or she is younger and may well take the view that it has a duty to protect all juveniles who are homosexual from exploitation by adults.

1 Note that it is an offence for anyone having the custody, charge or care of a juvenile aged at least four but under 16 to allow him to reside in or to frequent a brothel; see CYPA 1933, s 3, ante, para 10.44.
2 See *R v Marianchuk* [1977] 5 WWR 444.
3 *Re an infant (Care and Protection)* (1965) 109 Sol Jo 455. In all these illustrations application may alternatively be based on paragraph (a).
4 If he were married, no order in care proceedings could be made; see CYPA 1969, s 1(5)(c), post, para 14.50.

14.14 An increasingly difficult problem for the court is the balancing of recognition of foreign family customs and cultures with English notions of protection of the child.[1] It arose in *Alhaji Mohamed v Knott*[2] under the former provisions in the Children and Young Persons Act 1963 relating to care, protection and control. The parties to a potentially polygamous marriage, celebrated in Nigeria and valid by their personal law, were a girl then aged just over 13 and a man almost twice her age. Soon after the marriage they came to England but within six months a juvenile court made a fit person order in respect of the girl on the ground that she was in moral danger by living with her husband, even though they were happily married. The court found, inter alia, that immediately after the marriage the parties had sexual intercourse when 'almost certainly' the girl had not reached puberty; the husband later contracted venereal disease from a prostitute; he had then abstained from intercourse with his wife, but now that he was cured of the disease he was intending to resume intercourse with her once she was fitted with a contraceptive. In these circumstances, the court concluded, 'a continuance of such an association notwithstanding the marriage, would be repugnant to any decent minded English man or woman. Our decision reflects that repugnance.' The Divisional Court reversed the decision on the ground that the justices had failed to take account of the customs and way of life in which the parties had been brought up, but it recognised that the circumstances of a marriage might be such as to justify intervention and made an appropriate order; for example, if there was evidence of ill-treatment of the wife by the husband or of introducing her to drugs or of similar misconduct; but in such circumstances intervention is more likely to be based on the wider ground of paragraph (a) rather than that of exposure to moral danger, or to be by way of wardship proceedings.

1   It is examined by Dingwall, Eekelaar and Murray, *The Protection of Children*. See also, as a recent illustration of the problem, *Re H (minors)* [1987] 2 FLR 12, [1987] Fam Law 196.
2   [1969] 1 QB 1, [1968] 2 All ER 563, DC. For comment see Karsten, 32 MLR 212; Deech 123 NLJ 110.

(d)   The juvenile is beyond the control of his parent or guardian

14.15   This is a ground which is quite frequently relied on,[1] and a note of caution has been registered about the risk of too readily invoking it. It has been suggested[2] 'that the breakdown in parental control should be serious before compulsory intervention by a court is warranted', since the liberty of the juvenile is involved, and 'a balance must be maintained between allowing a parent to rid himself of the responsibility for a difficult and uncontrollable teenager and the right of the child to remain in his own home'. Accordingly, local authorities should be unwilling either of their own motion or at the request of the parent[3] to proceed under paragraph (d) unless there are complaints of specific misbehaviour. One kind of case which the paragraph covers, as does paragraph (c), is the juvenile who continues a sexual association in spite of every effort by the parent to terminate it. Another is the child under ten who is engaging in activities which would be criminal if he were over that age and the parent cannot curb him;[4] but given his age that should be exceptional and the parents should be thinking in terms of voluntary supervision by the local authority or reception into care under section 2 of the Child Care Act 1980. Yet another example, little researched, is the young teenager who physically attacks his parents, stays out late and dabbles in drink and drugs.

1   About 10% of the orders by reason of which children were in care in March 1980 were made on this ground — see Cretney, op cit, p 533.
2   Hayes and Bevan, op cit, p 52.
3   For the right to request see post, para 14.27.
4   See Hoggett, *Parents and Children*, 2nd edn, pp   100–101. But here, too, Hayes and Bevan counsel caution in the use of the paragraph.

14.16   The wide definition of 'guardian' for the purpose of the Children and Young Persons Acts has already been mentioned.[1] It is not limited to a person appointed guardian by law,[2] but includes anyone who for the time being has the charge of or control over the juvenile, for example, a step-parent or a private foster parent. Those Acts do not define the term 'parent', and the common law presumption excluding the father of an 'illegitimate' child operates,[3] except that, though not married to the mother at the time of their child's birth, he will be included in that term if he has actual custody by virtue of an order of a court, unless there is a contrary intention.[4]

1 Ante, para 9.48. The definition, contained in CYPA 1933, s 107(1) is applied to the CYPA 1969 by s 70(1) of the latter Act.
2 Ante, para 4.02.
3 *Re M (an infant)* [1955] 2 QB 479, [1955] 2 All ER 911.
4 CYPA 1969, s 70(1A) and (1B), as prospectively inserted by FLRA 1987, s 8(1) and Sch 2, para 26.

(e) The juvenile is of compulsory school age within the meaning of the Education Act 1944 and is not receiving efficient full-time education suitable to his age, ability and aptitude and to any special educational needs he may have.[1]

14.17 The duties of a parent to see that his child of compulsory school age receives efficient full-time education and regularly attends school, and the possibility of criminal proceedings being instituted against the parent by the local education authority for breach of those duties have already been examined.[2] It has also been noted that before instituting those proceedings the authority must consider whether it would be appropriate, instead of or as well as taking that step, to bring the juvenile before the court under section 1 of the 1969 Act.[3] Additionally, the court which exercises the criminal jurisdiction may direct the authority to proceed under section 1.[4]

1 CYPA 1969, s 1(2)(e) as amended by the Education Act 1981, Sch 3, para 9.
2 Ante, paras 11.18, et seq.
3 EA 1944, s 40(2).
4 Ibid, s 40(3).

14.18 Care proceedings may be brought under paragraph (e) where the juvenile is not receiving full-time education for any of the reasons covered by sections 37 and 39 of the Education Act 1944 or section 10 of the Children and Young Persons Act 1933, namely, that he is the subject of a school attendance order which has not been complied with, or that he is not regularly attending the school at which he is a registered pupil or that he is with a person who habitually wanders from place to place and takes the juvenile with him. The condition is deemed to be satisfied on proof of any one of these three matters,[1] unless it is proved that the juvenile is in fact receiving full-time education.[2] The exercise of the authority's discretion to bring proceedings will need particularly careful consideration where the juvenile is nearing the upper limit of the compulsory school age. If the only object is to ensure regular attendance at school for the remaining short period of compulsory education, intervention may hardly be justifiable. On the other hand, the truancy might indicate a serious risk of delinquency, and care proceedings would be highly desirable. Should proceedings be brought, then similar considerations should weigh with the court in deciding the kind of order, if any, to make. Where the juvenile is brought before the juvenile court and a school attendance order is in force in respect of him, but the court finds that the condition in subsection (2)(e) is not satisfied, it may direct that the school attendance order shall cease to be in force.[3] The meaning of this provision is not entirely clear. The express reference to paragraph (e) alone suggests that this possibility can only occur where the juvenile is otherwise receiving full-time education or has in fact returned to school but no step has been taken to get the order discharged by the court that made it. The fact that the application under section 1 was dismissed because the secondary condition, namely, that the juvenile is in need of care or control, is not satisfied apparently does not enable the termination of the school attendance order.[4]

1 Evidence of conviction of an offence under any of these provisions may be adduced by way of certificate.
2 See CYPA 1969, s 2(8)(b). A head teacher's certificate relating to attendance is admissible; see EA 1944, s 95(2)(c).
3 EA 1944, s 40(4), as substituted by CYPA 1969, Sch 5, para 13.
4 But the chances of the secondary condition not being satisfied have been considerably reduced. See *Re S (a minor)* [1978] QB 120; sub nom *Re DJMS (minor)* [1977] 3 All ER 582, post, para 14.24

(f)   The juvenile is guilty of an offence, excluding homicide

14.19   The 'offence' condition has proved to be one of the main failures of the 1969 Act. In the first year of operation only 92 cases were based on it, in 1973 only 30 care orders were made, and the annual number then steadily declined to below 20 with the result that statistics no longer distinguish between care orders made under paragraph (f) and those made in criminal proceedings.[1] The reasons for the failure are not hard to find. First, when the 1969 Act was passing through Parliament there was a storm of criticism raised in some quarters, basically on the ground that the condition discriminates against the offender who comes from an unsatisfactory home and in favour of one from a more secure background, since the latter is likely to be able to receive the care or control of which the former may well be deprived.[2] The argument is prima facia attractive, bearing in mind especially the extensive powers of the local authority if a care order is made. But the argument ignores the spirit of the 1969 Act, which was to bring before the courts, and then to help, only those juveniles who are in fact in trouble through lack of care or control. If the powers which the Act confers are too wide, the remedy lies in modifying them and in providing further safeguards against abuse, not in depriving juveniles of their benefits. Instead, from the outset those responsible for juvenile liaison schemes, both police and social workers, seem generally to have set their faces against the condition, and when it became clear that the basis on which the condition was introduced was being eroded by the decision of Government not to phase out prosecution of children and (largely) of young persons, there was every inducement not to rely on it. Whereas criminal proceedings require proof only of the offence, care proceedings, of course, impose the additional test of the need for care or control, albeit on the civil burden of proof on a balance of probabilities. That will usually mean additional evidence, unless exceptionally in the course of the proof of the offence it becomes clear that it was attributable to the parent's lack of control or supervision of the juvenile. Moreover, the criminal jurisdiction offers a much wider range of orders for dealing with the juvenile, and they include all those available under the care jurisdiction. The police are particularly likely to be persuaded by this last consideration, but so, too, increasingly have some social workers who sometimes see the conditional discharge, the fine, the compensation order or the attendance centre order as suitable alternatives to the supervision order or care order. Unfortunately, attitudes have now become so inflexible that, where a juvenile has committed an offence and the decision is made to institute proceedings, prosecution is almost automatic.[3] Even in the most obvious cases, where care proceedings would be beneficial and preferable to criminal proceedings, not only is the offence condition overlooked or rejected but also reliance on paragraph (a) of section 1(2) is ignored. One should not, for example, and the example is not unknown, expect criminal proceedings (even though there has already been a formal police caution for a similar offence) against a diminutive eleven-year-old boy for stealing chocolate from a departmental store when the social inquiry report reveals that, because he was hungry, he has on other occasions been found taking food from the school kitchen including scraps from its refuse bin. If ever a boy needs care it is he. Care proceedings, if not based on paragraph (f) at least on paragraph (a), are more appropriate — if there are going to be proceedings at all. Less dramatically, care proceedings based on one or other of those paragraphs are more appropriate than criminal where the agencies already know the family, know that there are problems between the juvenile and his parents, which may be the underlying cause of his criminal behaviour, and know that the need for the local authority's assistance is immediate. Indeed, in such circumstances the social inquiry report is likely to include a recommendation for a supervision order or care order. Why not seek it through care instead of criminal proceedings?

1 Cretney, p 534, note 22.
2 For the history of the Bill on this test and the arguments advanced for and against it see the summary by Watson and Austin, *The Modern Juvenile Court* (1975) pp 37–42. See also Stone, *Children Without A Satisfactory Home — A Gap Family Law Must Fill* (1970) 33 MLR 649 at p 657.
3 The fact that responsibility for prosecution now lies with the Crown Prosecution Service is not likely to lead to any change of policy, although it should be noted that in the code issued by the Director of Public Prosecutions the CPS is made aware of the alternative possibility of care proceedings.

14.20 Where the offence condition is invoked the rules relating to the age of criminal responsibility apply as they do where there are criminal proceedings, and the general safeguards against liability provided by the criminal law are also extended to the condition.[1] Thus, in accordance with the principles of *autrefois acquit* or *autrefois convict*, no account must be taken of any alleged offence which was the subject of earlier criminal proceedings, and by analogy no reliance can be placed on it if it was alleged in previous care proceedings based on the offence condition.[2] Conversely, a person cannot be charged with an offence which was alleged in care proceedings in order to satisfy that condition.[3] If the offence is a summary one, the time limit of six months on prosecution for such an offence[4] is extended to the care proceedings.[5] The burden of proof of the evidence is that in criminal proceedings[6] and the criminal rules of evidence apply, except that, as has been pointed out,[7] the rules which allow in those proceedings the admission of written statements and formal admissions apparently do not apply.[8] All the above restrictions only operate, however, for the purpose of determining whether the offence condition is satisfied. They do not restrict the admissibility of evidence of an offence, which was the subject of earlier proceedings, for the purpose of proving any other condition in section 1 (for example, that the juvenile is exposed to moral danger) or that there is need for care or control.[9]

1 By s 3(1)–(3) of the CYPA 1969.
2 See s 3(1), paras (c) and (a) respectively. Although the subsection does not expressly so provide, it is submitted that, if the offence had earlier been alleged in order to try to prove a condition other than the offence condition, for example, that the juvenile was exposed to moral danger, it ought similarly not to be admissible in later proceedings to satisfy the offence condition.
3 Section 3(4).
4 MCA 1980, s 127.
5 CYPA 1969, s 3(1)(b).
6 Section 3(3).
7 Clarke Hall and Morrison, op cit, para B[692].
8 See CJA 1967, ss 9 and 10, which expressly refer only to criminal proceedings.
9 CYPA 1969, s 3(2).

14.21   If both the offence condition and the need for care or control are proved, the court can make a care order even though the offence is one which would not, if committed by an adult, be punishable with imprisonment, whereas in criminal proceedings a care order may only be made if the offence is one so punishable.[1]

1 CYPA 1969, s 7(7).

2   The general condition — the need for care or control

14.22   There is a considerable degree of overlapping of the primary conditions, which is not surprising in view of the wide terms in which most of them are expressed. For example, cases of offences of a violent or sexual nature committed against juveniles may fall under one or more of paragraphs (a), (c) and (d), as may cases of sexual behaviour by the juvenile. But, whichever conditions are appropriate, before any order can be made the court must also be satisfied that the juvenile is in need of care or control which he is unlikely to receive unless the court makes an order under section 1 in respect of him.[1] Care includes protection and guidance; control includes discipline.[2]

1 See sub-s (2).
2 CYPA 1969, s 70(1).

14.23   Under the former law it had to be shown that the juvenile was 'not receiving such care, protection and guidance as a good parent may reasonably be expected to give'.[1] It thus 'directed attention solely to the quality of parental care and it meant that proceedings inevitably appeared to cast blame for the child's situation or behaviour directly onto his parents or those looking after him'.[2] Such a test is inappropriate to the offence condition, at least where there is no discernible connection between the juvenile's delinquency and any parental inadequacies, but in introducing that condition the 1969 Act abandoned the former objective test for all categories of juveniles falling within section 1 without substituting another. So, as with the primary condition in section 1(2)(a),[3] the care or control condition leaves local authorities with a wide discretion to intervene in the family and the court to find the condition satisfied.[4]

1   CYPA 1963, s 2.
2   See Home Office Guide on Part I of CYPA 1969, para 25.
3   See ante, para 14.05.
4   See the comment in [1981] JSWL at pp 246–247 (BMH)

14.24   Save for paragraphs (b) and (bb), which by their reference to 'probability' also require assessment of the risk of future harm to the juvenile, all seven primary conditions refer to past or past and continuing present circumstances, but not to future events alone,[1] no matter how imminent they might be. The general condition, on the other hand, is concerned with the present — is the juvenile now in need of care or control? — and the future — will he receive them without an order of the court? Proof of one or more of the primary conditions will be at least presumptive evidence that the juvenile needs care or control, but, since the question of the need for care or control necessarily also involves consideration of the likely course of events, the court must consider all the juvenile's circumstances relevant to that matter, and additional evidence about the home circumstances and the parents' likely ability to look after the juvenile should usually be necessary, especially where proceedings are based on the offence condition.[2] However, the presumptive evidence may be so strong that little, if any, further evidence will be needed or, indeed, be available. For example, where the proceedings are based on paragraph (a), the juvenile may have been so badly ill-treated or neglected that both the need for care and the likelihood of its not being provided, if he returned home, are self-evident. Similarly, where the proceedings are based on paragraph (d), the degree of lack of control by the parent may be shown to be so marked that it would be unrealistic to expect any control in the foreseeable future. But such a conclusion is not inevitable. For example, if the father is temporarily living away from home and the juvenile is meanwhile beyond his mother's control, it might be possible to show that on his father's imminent return he will be likely to 'receive' control without any order having to be made. The need for additional evidence in relation to paragraph (c) will depend on whether the exposure to moral danger arises from the behaviour of the parent or of the juvenile. If the former, then, in the absence of evidence that it has ceased or is immediately to cease, the court will be bound to find that there is need for an order. Where the risk arises from the juvenile's own behaviour the answer will depend on whether, prior to the care proceedings, the parent knew about it.[3] If he did not, he may be able to satisfy the court that now that he knows he can in future control the juvenile; otherwise an order is virtually certain. In proceedings under paragraph (e) proof that a juvenile is not attending school or otherwise being properly educated is sufficient proof to satisfy the general condition, since the juvenile in those circumstances is not being properly cared for, however satisfactory his home background and behaviour in other respects may be. So the Court of Appeal held in *Re S (a minor) (Care order : Education)*,[4] where the parents, without providing suitable alternative arrangements, refused to allow their 11-year-old son to attend school because they were opposed to comprehensive education. The word 'care', it was held, applies not only to the physical well-being of the juvenile — to which should be added his mental, moral or emotional well-being — but also to his proper education. The decision may further encourage courts to blur the distinction between the two stages of proof, that of the primary condition and that of the general condition, and rely entirely on the former,[5] but with far more extensive legal representation in care proceedings there are indications of a contrary trend, with those representing juveniles and the parents calling on the local authority to be more specific about the juvenile's future needs. For this reason it is arguable that the court should be told of the possible effects on the child of making a care order or supervision order, so that it may decide whether the particular order would supply the care or control he needs. However, practice apparently varies and some courts take the view that they can only consider evidence on the kind of order to be made after the primary and general conditions have been proved.[6]

1   See *Essex County Council v TLR and KBR* (1978) 143 JP 309, (1978) 9 Fam Law 15, ante, para 14.08.
2   In such a case it is essential to distinguish between the two stages since the burden of proof differs, the criminal applying to proof of the offence and the civil to proof of the general condition.
3   See *Bowers v Smith* [1953] 1 All ER 320, [1953] 1 WLR 297.
4   [1978] QB 120; sub nom *ReDJMS (minor)* [1977] 3 All ER 582.
5   Cretney, p 535. See also Dingwall, Eekelaar and Murray, *The Protection of Children*, pp 196–197.
6   See (1986) 83 Law Soc Gaz 2452.

3   Reform

14.25   The proposals of the Review of Child Care Law[1] and the subsequent White Paper[2] for reforming the grounds for care proceedings cover not only those proceedings but also (1) the power of local authorities to pass resolutions under section 3 of the Child Care Act 1980[3] vesting parental rights and duties in themselves, and (2) the power of courts in family cases to commit the child in exceptional circumstances to the care of a local authority.[4] The recommendation is that a court should be able to make an order if it is satisfied on each of three essential elements:

(a)   evidence of harm or likely harm to the child; and
(b)   that this is attributable to the absence of a reasonable standard of parental care or the child being beyond parental control; and
(c)   that the order proposed is the most effective means available to the court of safeguarding the child's welfare.

There is no denying that in a formal sense the proposed test would, as the Review suggests,[5] 'simplify the law' and 'avoid the . . . confusion which arises from the existing grounds', but the wide terms in which each element, especially (a), is formulated must raise doubts about whether the test can also avoid 'the arbitrariness' arising from those grounds. As the Review and the White Papter readily recognise, the answer will very largely depend on reforms of procedural rules and evidence. Much of the rest of this Chapter illustrates the serious inadequacies and uncertainties of both of those aspects of care proceedings.

1   Chapter 15.
2   Paragraphs 59 and 60. The Cleveland Report strongly endorsed the White Paper proposals.
3   See post, paras 15.14 et seq.
4   See especially ante, Chapter 3.
5   Paragraph 15.25.

III   THE INSTITUTION OF CARE PROCEEDINGS

1   The decision to institute proceedings

(a)   *Persons who may bring proceedings*

14.26   Except where they are based on the offence condition, care proceedings may be brought by a local authority, a constable[1] or a person authorised to do so.[2] As under the law before the 1969 Act, the only recipient of the specific authorisation is the NSPCC.[3] Proceedings alleging the offence condition must be instituted by a local authority or a constable.[4] In nearly all cases the applicant is a local authority, except that where the proceedings are based on section 1(2)(e) of the 1969 Act, the appropriate body is the local education authority.[5] Occasionally the NSPCC may apply, and this is likely where there is a professional difference of opinion between one of its officers and the local authority social services department over whether care proceedings are approriate and justified.[6] The virtual rejection of the offence condition has meant that in practice the police do not apply.

1   This means a person holding the office of a constable, not the rank of constable in a police force; but usually he is a police officer.
2   CYPA 1969, s 1(1). An 'authorised person' means a person authorised by order of the Secretary of State to bring such proceedings and any officer of a society so authorised (s 1(6)).
3   See CYPA 1969 (Authorisation for the purpose of S 1) Order 1970, SI 1970/1500.
4   CYPA 1969, s 3(2).
5   Section 2(8).
6   RCCL, para 12.25, records that the Society brings proceedings in about 120 cases a year.

14.27   In the case of the juvenile who is beyond parental control the local authority may still feel that care proceedings are not the appropriate method of tackling the problem, but the parent may think otherwise. If he does, he can by written notice request the authority to bring the juvenile before the court, and the former right of the parent himself to commence proceedings[1] has not been wholly superseded in that, if the authority should refuse or fail to do so within 28 days from the date of request,[2] the parent may apply by complaint to a juvenile court for an order directing the authority to do so.[3] When an application is made, the authority must provide the court with full information about the home surroundings, school record, health and character of the juvenile.[4] This will usually mean further investigations having to be made, especially with regard to schooling. A parent who lives apart from the complaining parent (or guardian) must be notified by the latter of the time and place of the hearing, since he is entitled to be heard.[5] The juvenile must not be present at the hearing,[6] and, if the court directs the local authority to institute care proceedings, any justice who was a member of that court is precluded from sitting at the subsequent proceedings.[7]

1   Conflicting views had been expressed to the Ingleby Committee on the desirability of
the parental right. One was that, if a parent took the step of bringing his own child
before the court, this was very likely to lead to an irreparable breach of the parent-child
relationship. On the other hand, it was suggested that such a drastic step sometimes had
the reverse, salutary effect of strengthening that relationship. The former opinion prevailed
(Cmnd 1191, paras 120–134) and has been given effect by CYPA 1963.
2   In reckoning this period the date on which notice was given is to be ignored; *Goldsmith's
Co v West Metropolitan Rly Co* [1904] 1 KB 1, [1900–3] All ER Rep 667, CA.
3   CYPA 1963, s 3(1), as amended by CYPA 1969, Sch 5, para 47. Although there is some
ambiguity in the subsection, the better view is that the parental right only extends to
the ground of 'beyond parental control' and not the other grounds in s 1 of CYPA 1969;
see 140 JPN 619.
4   CYPA 1963, s 3(2).
5   MC(C&YP) Rules 1988, r 36(1).
6   CYPA 1963, s 3(3); but quaere this rule prevents him from being called as a witness
— see Clarke Hall and Morrison, para B [569].
7   MC(C & YP) Rules 1988, r 36(2).

14.28   Either the local authority in whose area the juvenile resides or that
in whose area he is found may commence care proceedings.[1] Usually it
is the former, and, in the case of a juvenile beyond the control of a parent
who insists on his being brought before the court, it must be the 'residential'
authority, since it is only to that authority that the parent can make his
written request.[2]

1   CYPA 1969, s 2(1).
2   CYPA 1963, s 3(1).

14.29   The Review of Child Care Law[1] recommends that the right of the
police or the local education authority to bring care proceedings should
be abolished, subject to the latter having the right to seek a supervision
order in truancy cases. It emphasises that the local authority social services
departments are the focal point in all care cases, especially as the obligations
under a supervision order or a care order fall upon them, and they are
therefore the appropriate applicant. But the Review recognises that the
NSPCC should continue to have power to initiate proceedings, although
the Society should be under a duty to consult the local authority about
which of them, if either, should apply, and, if it is to be the Society, the
authority should be joined as a party. The parental right to seek to compel
the local authority to bring proceedings should be retained but not limited
to cases where the juvenile is alleged to be beyond parental control.

1   Paras 12.20 to 12.23. The recommendation is accepted by CCFS, para 44.

(b)   Consultation

14.30   It is clear that the 1969 Act intends that the main responsibility
for initiating care proceedings shall lie with the local authority. If it receives
information suggesting that there are grounds for bringing care proceedings,
it must see that inquiries are made, unless satisfied that they are unnecessary.[1]
The discretionary proviso should be narrowly construed. The line of tragedies
since Maria Colwell, which have been the subject of public inquiry, and
the frequent, almost weekly, reporting in the media of cases of child abuse
are a constant reminder of the importance of erring on the side of precaution
and, where there is any doubt, of directing inquiries to be made. At this

stage in the process it is not necessary for the local authority to have a reasonable belief that there are grounds for making an order. It is only after, and in the light of, inquiries that such a belief must be held so as to justify the bringing of proceedings.[2] In deciding whether that point has been reached, close consultation will invariably be needed between the authority's social services department and legal department, usually by way of a case conference.[3]

1 Section 2(1).
2 Section 1(1).
3 For the problems facing the social worker in deciding whether or not care proceedings should be instituted see Lawson, *Taking the Decision to Remove the Child from the Family* [1980] JSWL 141; and see generally *Social Work Decisions in Child Care: Recent Research Findings and their Implications* (DHSS 1985).

14.31   That, however, is a matter of internal consultation. Consultation with other agencies should already have taken place,[1] usually in the form of a case conference.[2] In the immediate years following the implementation of the 1969 Act consultation was as variable in care cases as it was in criminal, in spite of the detailed guidance offered by the Home Office in its Guide to Part I of the Act. One of the changes inspired by the Maria Colwell case and encouraged by the Home Office and DHSS[3] was the establishment by social services departments (and in a minority of cases by area health authorities and by the local NSPCC special unit for abused children) of registers of so-called non-accidental injury cases. Compiled after consultation with other agencies, namely the health, education and probation services, the NSPCC and, after initial reluctance to include them, the Police, a register monitors cases of children at risk of being abused by their parents, and thus helps the local authority to decide whether to investigate or investigate further, and, if so, whether to invoke section 1 of the 1969 Act.[4] Central Government Departmental Guidance[5] has provided 'administrative aids' to help ensure standardisation in registration throughout the country. Registration extends not only to physical but also mental or emotional abuse of children who have been or may be the victims of abuse. Diagnosis of abuse normally requires both medical examination and social assessment of the child. The system requires regular monitoring of registered cases, at least once every six months. Any decision to place a child's name on the register, or to remove it, should only be done after a case conference. If a name is removed, the record should still be kept for a further two years or until the child attains the age of five, whichever is the longer. Save in exceptional circumstances, the parents should be told that it has been decided to place the child's name on the register.[6]

In spite of some improvement in inter-agency consultation over the past decade, much more needs to be done. The Cleveland Inquiry has, all too sadly, demonstrated the lack of communication that there may be between the main agencies, and a lack of understanding of each other's functions, especially in relation to child sexual abuse. The Report[7] offers a series of vital recommendations for strengthening consultative and assessment procedures, including that of establishing specialist assessment teams 'to undertake a multi-disciplinary assessment of the child and the family in cases of particular difficulty'. The real question for the future is not whether the recommendations should essentially be implemented, but whether their implementation should be the subject of a voluntary or a statutory framework.

1   The Cleveland inquiry has highlighted the desirability of consultation with the police surgeon in cases of suspected sexual abuse.
2   Legal advice may also have been sought at that stage.
3   See Local Authority Social Services Letter, LASSL (74) 13.
4   In those exceptional cases where the NSPCC or the police decide to institute care proceedings, then, as in criminal proceedings, they must notify the local authority of that decision (CYPA 1969, s 2(3); MC(C & YP) Rules 1988 r 14) and, if the juvenile is aged 13 or over, a probation officer (CYPA 1969, s 34(2); CYPA 1969 (Transitional Modifications of Part I) Order 1981, SI 1981/81).
5   See LASSL (76)2; LASSL (76)27; and LASSL (80)4.
6   For a critical commentary on registration see Geach, *Child abuse registers — a time for a change* in *Providing Civil Justice for Children* (Eds Geach and Szwed) p 40.
7   See pp 248–251.

14.32   Consultation may lead to informed action. The local authority may feel able successfully to invoke its powers under section 1 of the Child Care Act 1980 of providing advice and assistance to the family, particularly in the form of voluntary supervision, or it may with the co-operation of the parents receive the juvenile into its care under section 2 of that Act, if the requisite conditions are satisfied.[1] If neither of those options is considered suitable, the local authority should turn to its duty to bring the juvenile before the court, because, in accordance with section 2(2) of the Children and Young Persons Act 1969, it can no longer be satisfied that bringing care proceedings is neither in the juvenile's nor the public interest or that some other person is about to do so or is to charge him with an offence.

1   For ss 1 and 2 see post, paras 15.04 to 15.07 and 15.08 to 15.13 respectively.

2   The institution of the proceedings

14.33   As with criminal proceedings,[1] the statutory provisions for securing the attendance of a juvenile before the court in care proceedings and, where necessary, for his prior temporary detention are complicated and are derived from several sources, most of them being contained in the Children and Young Persons Acts. The juvenile may be brought before the court either by way of summons or warrant for arrest or as a result of his having been taken to a place of safety.

1   See ante, paras 12.34 et seq.

(a)   Summons or warrant

14.34   In some cases proceedings are commenced by summons, and a warrant may only be issued where a summons cannot be served, or, if it has been served, where the juvenile has failed to answer it or where he has failed to appear at an adjourned hearing after receiving adequate notice of the time and place.[1] If a warrant has to be issued but he cannot immediately on arrest be brought before the court, he must be detained in a place of safety for a maximum period of 72 hours, unless the warrant is endorsed for bail. Within that time he must be brought before the court or, failing that, before a justice.[2] In the latter event the justice must either direct his release or make an interim order committing him to the care of a local authority for a specified period not exceeding 28 days and beginning with the date when he was taken into custody.[3] This 28-day-period is far too long for what is an ex parte application, and normally should be for a much shorter period, so that the parents may have an early opportunity of challenging the order in the juvenile court. The juvenile must be present when the interim order is made, unless the justice is satisfied that he is under the age of five or cannot be present because of illness or accident.[4] On the expiration of the order the local authority must bring him before the court specified in the order, unless that court fixes an earlier hearing.[5]

1   CYPA 1969, s 2(4); MCA 1980, s 55(3) and (4).
2   CYPA 1969, s 2(5).
3   Ibid and s 20(1)(b).
4   Section 22(1).
5   Section 22(2).

(b)   Section 28(1) of the Children and Young Persons Act 1969: the place of safety order

(i) The power to make an order

14.35   Section 28(1) enables a justice to make what is commonly but inadequately described as a 'place of safety order'.[1] It provides what is intended to be a temporary, emergency procedure for the protection of a juvenile who is in actual danger; but over the past decade its emergency purpose has tended to be overlooked with a resulting sharp increase in the number of orders made.[2] The order authorises the detention of a juvenile in a place of safety for a specified period not exceeding 28 days. It may be 'a community home provided by a local authority or a controlled community home, any police station or any hospital, surgery or any other suitable place, the occupier of which is willing temporarily to receive a child or young person'.[3] It is to be noted that an assisted community home is not explicitly included, but may come within the definition as a 'suitable place'. However, those responsible for running that kind of community home[4] are not subject to the statutory duty which is imposed on a local authority[5] with regard to a local authority community home or a controlled community home, namely, to make special provision therein for the reception and maintenance of juveniles who are removed to a place of safety. Where the juvenile is removed to a place of safety which is not a local authority community home or a controlled community home or a National Health Service Hospital, the expenses of maintaining the juvenile are recoverable from the local authority within whose area the juvenile was immediately before his removal.[6] Accordingly, the managers of an assisted community home will be entitled to claim, as will any foster parent in whose home the juvenile has been placed.[7]

1   RCCL proposes the alternative term, 'emergency protection order' (para 13.1), which is accepted by CCFS, para 45, and by the Cleveland Report, p 252.
2   Apparently some 6,300 orders were made in 1982, 2,500 of them relating to children under five (RCCL para 13.3). The increased reporting of alleged sexual abuse of children is leading to a marked increase in the use of orders.
3   So defined by CYPA 1933, s 107(1) as amended by CYPA 1969, s 72(3) and Sch 5, para 12(2).
4   For community homes and their classification see post, paras 15.67 to 15.72.

5   By the Child Care Act 1980, s 73(1).
6   CCA 1980, s 73(2).
7   Local authority short-term foster homes are sometimes used as places of safety.

14.36   The order can be made if the justice is satisfied that the applicant for it has reasonable cause to believe *either* that any of the primary conditions set out in section 1(2)(a) to (e) of the 1969 Act is satisfied in respect of the juvenile[1] *or* that the court would find the condition in section 1(2)(b) relating to the probability of neglect or ill-treatment or that in section 1(2)(bb) relating to the probability of a convicted person being or becoming a member of the same household[2] as the juvenile to be satisfied.[3] This is a difficult duty for a justice to discharge. Not surprisingly, the amount and quality of the evidence vary considerably. Either the applicant should have personal knowledge of the facts, for example, a social worker who has seen bruises on the juvenile, or he should call witnesses who have, for example, a doctor who admitted the juvenile to hospital, or an order may be made on the basis of a medical certificate.[4] There is, however, the risk of improperly relying on hearsay evidence. Much, too, depends on the legal procedures[5] adopted, the experience of the particular justice and the availability of the clerk to the justices or one of his assistants.[6] Some magistrates' courts have procedures which ensure availability,[7] but there appears to be wide variation on whether clerks are consulted.[6] Given the implications of the place of safety order, both for the juvenile and for his parents, and the fact that there is no appeal against it,[8] there should, it is submitted, be a compulsory procedure requiring advice always to be available, save in the most exceptional circumstances. Preferably, a justice should be a member of the juvenile panel, especially as he or she is likely to be familiar with the primary conditions of section 1 of the 1969 Act.[9] There is, indeed, much to be said for assigning to a limited number of justices on the panel the duty of hearing place of safety applications, so that they may gain wider experience in dealing with them,[10] but events in Cleveland show[11] that preferably applications should be heard by a full court. That, indeed, is very likely to be the rule in applying for the proposed 'emergency protection order' which is intended to replace the place of safety order.[12]

1   An emergency arising from a juvenile's truancy is unlikely. Proceedings on that ground are usually commenced by summons.
2   When this primary condition was added to s 1 by the Children Act 1975, s 28(1) of the 1969 Act was not expressly amended to take account of the extension.
3   An order may similarly be made where it is reasonably believed that a juvenile is about to leave the United Kingdom in contravention of the restrictions on juvenile entertainers going abroad; see ante, para 11.75.
4   But events in Cleveland in 1987 revealed the disagreement which can arise between medical experts over the existence and cause of physical signs of injury.
5   Some courts insist on written applications. RCCL recommends (para 13.27) that evidence be given on oath as in ex parte applications to magistrates in matrimonial and criminal cases. For a study of practices see Norris and Parton, *The Administration of Place of Safety Orders* (1987) JSWL 1. See also Ellison, *Place of Safety Orders : The Problem of Emergencies* (1985) 135 NLJ 819.
6   See the conclusions of the Dartington Social Research Unit commissioned by DHSS for its Review of Child Care Law (RCCL, Annex C).
7   Pain, *Minors: The Law and Practice*, (2nd edn, 1987) p 103; Dingwall and Eekelaar, *Care Proceedings*, p 70; and Norris and Parton, *supra*.
8

8 See Sir John Arnold, P, in *Nottinghamshire County Council v Q* [1982] 2 All ER 641 at 644. But the legality of the detention may be challenged by judicial review.
9 Clarke Hall and Morrison para B[798] point out that there seems to be no reason why application should not be made to a court instead of to a single justice, but it is suggested that, if practicable, this ought for the reason stated in the text to be a juvenile court.
10 More cautiously, RCCL, para 13.27, recommends justices who are on the domestic and juvenile panels without limit as to number.
11 See especially paras 10.6–10.9 of the Cleveland Report.
12 See post, para 14.40.

(ii) The applicant

14.37   Usually application for an order is made by a local authority through one of its social workers and, much less frequently, by the NSPCC or the police; but any person may apply for it, and, provided he can show that he reasonably believes that one of the relevant primary conditions in section 1 of the 1969 Act is satisfied, it is not necessary that he should have those proceedings in mind. Thus, it is possible for one parent in an emergency to obtain the order enabling him to remove the juvenile from the other parent's home, bring him to his own and then either seek to persuade the local authority to commence care proceedings or himself institute wardship proceedings. However, where the latter are intended, the parent or anyone else having those proceedings in mind should weigh carefully whether the place of safety order or a preliminary injunction in wardship proceedings is the more effective immediate measure to meet an emergency. A justice may be more readily available than a duty judge or registrar, but in *Re a Baby (Wardship)*[1] Latey J pointed out that the 'High Court in its wardship jurisdiction has very wide powers and resources to call upon, which the juvenile court does not. They include facilities to deal urgently with an urgent case — within hours or sometimes minutes on the telephone, if need be.' Where the juvenile is already a ward of court the same considerations apply. If immediate protection can be better given by a place of safety order, it should be obtained, but before it expires the High Court should be seized of the matter as soon as possible and an application made for directions under the wardship jurisdiction.[2]

1   (1985) Times, 15 January.
2   See *Re B (a minor)* (1980) Times, 19 January.

(iii) Informing the juvenile and parent

14.38   The person who detains a juvenile under section 28(1) is under a duty to inform him as soon as practicable of the reason for his detention.[1] This duty assumes that he is of sufficient age and understanding. Steps must also be taken to inform his parent or guardian of the detention and the reason for it.[2] Delay in doing so should be avoided. For example, evidence of serious physical abuse of a young child may have come to light while he is at nursery school, and he may consequently have immediately been taken to hospital by a teacher or social worker on the authorisation of a place of safety order. Any delay in informing his parents of this action is understandably likely to arouse their ill-feeling and worsen relationships with the local authority in any subsequent care proceedings. The Review of Child Care Law recommends[3] that an application for an order should be in writing, that the justice should give reasons for making the order, and that copies of the application and the justice's reasons should be supplied to the juvenile, his parents and, if it is not the applicant, the local authority. These proposals should not, however, obviate the need for social workers to handle the informing of parents with tact and sensitivity, particularly where the evidence of child abuse is speculative and the social workers may need to work with the family in the future.

1   Section 28(3).
2   Ibid.
3   Paragraph 13.27. The importance of these recommendations has been highlighted by the Cleveland Inquiry.

(iv) The effects of the order
14.39   Apart from the express statutory duty of a local authority to meet the expenses of maintaining the juvenile,[1] the legal effects of a place of safety order are uncertain. The uncertainty is compounded by that over the application of the *Gillick* principle. The effect on the actual custody of the juvenile is far from clear. Strictly the parent no longer has it, since he no longer has 'actual possession' of the juvenile.[2] But it is questionable whether the applicant named in the order has it. Because the juvenile's absence from the parent's home is, at least at this stage under the order, temporary he does not have his home with the applicant,[3] and there must therefore be doubt about the latter having actual custody. However, it has been suggested[4] that, even if a person does not have actual custody, there are some statutory duties corresponding to those attached to custody, especially the duty to protect the juvenile from harm.[5] The applicant has the charge and care of him for the purpose of protective legislation, and these duties would attach not only to him but also to anyone to whom he delegates the actual responsibility of looking after the juvenile, for example, where the applicant is a NSPCC officer and he arranges with the local authority for the child to be placed in one of its community or foster homes. A place of safety order is not, however, a care order and, whether or not the parent still has actual custody, there can be no possibility of his parental powers passing to the applicant. Unless, therefore, it were a matter of emergency, and subject to the possible application of the *Gillick* principle, the consent of the parent to medical *treatment* of the child would, it is submitted, first have to be sought. The position concerning medical *examination* of the child is, it is submitted, a different matter. Where the local authority suspect that he is the victim of sexual abuse they can, for example, authorise a second medical examination, but, if the parents wish for their own doctor to conduct an examination, his access to the child will be at the discretion of the local authority, as will access by him to their medical records and file. The position concerning access is more difficult, especially as section 28(1) does not authorise a justice to attach conditions to a place of safety order. It is submitted that prima facie a parent can exercise his 'right' to access, but it is subject to two qualifications. First, if in the exercise of it there is an immediate risk of harm to the juvenile, for example, by the parent's threatening behaviour when he visits, the applicant, by virtue of his duty to protect the juvenile from harm, can forbid access, at least until wardship can be invoked. Second, in accordance with the *Gillick* principle, if the juvenile is old and mature enough to express a wish not to see the parent, access

can be refused by the applicant; for example, where a 13-year-old girl the
alleged victim of sexual assault by her father, refuses to see him.

1 Supra, para 14.35.
2 Children Act 1975, s 87(1).
3 Section 87(3).
4 Ante, para 1.65.
5 See CA 1975, s 85(1).

14.40 These are some of the uncertainties arising from conceptual
deductions. The Review of Child Care Law, The White Paper and the
Cleveland Report make a number of recommendations.[1] It proposes that
there should be a statutory presumption of reasonable access to the juvenile,
but subject to the power of the justice to refuse access or make it subject
to conditions in his order. Other proposals relate to the applicant. He should
be under the same parental responsibilities as a person with legal custody
of the child, but should not be vested with parental powers, and he should
be subject to the general obligation to safeguard and promote the juvenile's
welfare. It is important that any legislation that follows these and other
proposals should spell out the respective powers and/or responsibilities
of all interested persons — the juvenile, the parent, the applicant, the person,
if any, to whom the applicant delegates his responsibilities and, if it is
not the applicant, the local authority. The place of safety order or, as
proposed, the 'emergency protection order' has serious consequences, as
the Cleveland Inquiry so forcibly illustrated. Those consequences merit
detailed legislative enactment.

1 See RCC paras 13.07–13.28; CCFS, paras 45–47; and the Cleveland Report, pp 228–229
and 252.

(v) Duration of orders
14.41 The uncertainties surrounding the effects of an order are in
themselves reasons for not authorising the maximum 28-day period.
Increasingly justices are fixing much shorter periods of eight to 14 days,[1]
which is now common practice. A shorter period has the further advantage
of concentrating the mind of the applicant, usually the local authority.
The fact that the making of an order depends on proof of reasonable belief
that one of the primary conditions on which care proceedings are based
is satisfied may be seen by the local authority, once an order is granted,
as encouragement to initiate those proceedings. That is a misconception,
and other possibilities, such as persuading the parents to agree to voluntary
supervision or, if the requisite conditions are met, to the juvenile being
received into care under section 2 of the Child Care Act 1980 or instituting
wardship proceedings should be canvassed. If the period authorised by
the place of safety order does not allow sufficient time for consideration
of those possibilities, the local authority should apply for an interim (care)
order,[2] so that the possibilities can be further explored before a final decision
to pursue an order under section 1 of the 1969 Act, or it may institute
care proceedings and apply for an interim order in those proceedings.
Although the matter is not absolutely clear, it seems that an application
for a second place of safety order to follow immediately upon the expiration
of the first is not permitted by section 28(1). Nor can the restriction be

evaded by releasing the juvenile for short periods between successive appllictions under the subsection.[3] On the other hand, it is not an abuse of process for a local authority to apply for an order under the subsection shortly after a care order has been discharged by a juvenile court.[4] It could happen that on returning home the juvenile again became the victim of the kind of abuse, which had been the basis on which the earlier care order had been made.

1   The House of Commons Social Services Committee recommended a week; RCCL proposes eight days (paras 13.21–13.24). CCFS (para 46) accepts the latter proposal but recommends that in exceptional circumstances the local authority should be allowed to apply for a further period of up to seven days, subject to the right of the parents or child to challenge the extension on the ground that there is no risk to the child which justifies such an extension. The Cleveland Report (p 252) goes further and recommends that the seven-day extension should not be restricted to exceptional circumstances but left to the discretion of magistrates. But is that enough? It is suggested that some legislative guidance should be given to magistrates.
2   Under s 28(6). The parent has a right to be heard in those proceedings; *H v London Borough of Southwark* (1982) 12 Fam Law 211. But he is not entitled himself to apply under s 28(6) when his purpose is not to obtain an interim order but to obtain the release of the juvenile. That device, aimed at circumventing the rule that there is no appeal against a place of safety order, is an abuse of the process of the court; *Nottinghamshire County Council v Q* [1982] Fam 94, [1982] 2 All ER 641, DC.
3   See Lord Widgery CJ in *R v Lincoln (Kesteven) County Justices, ex p M (a minor)* [1976] QB 957 at 964–965, [1976] 1 All ER 490 at 495.
4   See ibid.

(c)   Section 28(2) of the Children and Young Persons Act 1969; power of police to detain in a place of safety

14.42   Section 28(2) confers power on a constable to detain a juvenile without the authority of a justice if he has reasonable cause to believe that any of the primary conditions in section 1 (other than the truancy and offence conditions) is satisfied or that a court would find the condition in section 1(2)(b) or 1(2)(bb) satisfied.[1] If he does act under section 28(2), he must ensure that as soon as practicable the custody officer at a police station[2] inquires into the case, and, in the light of the inquiry, the latter must either release the juvenile or, if he considers further detention is in the juvenile's interests, arrange for him to be kept in a place of safety. The maximum period of detention is eight days from the date when the juvenile was first detained by the constable, but the juvenile or his parent or guardian can apply to a justice[3] for earlier release, which must be granted unless further detention is in his interests,[4] a proviso which leaves the justice with a wide discretion. Similar to the procedure governing an application for a place of safety order, the constable who detains a juvenile must inform him of the reason for it and take steps to inform the parent or guardian,[5] and where the juvenile is further detained by a custody officer he and his parent or guardian must be told of the right to apply to a justice for release.[6] At the end of the period of detention of up to eight days the juvenile must be released, unless application is made[7] for an interim order or care proceedings are initiated and an interim order is made in those proceedings.

1 The power is expressly reserved by the Police and Criminal Evidence Act 1984, s 26(2) and Sch 2. The Home Office Guide to Part I of CYPA 1969, para 182, points out that the reason for excluding the truancy condition from the terms of s 28(2) is that truancy does not in itself require the immediate removal of the child. But s 28(2) does apply where a vagrant is guilty of the offence of preventing his child from receiving education; see further ante, para 11.31.

2 For the functions of a custody officer see ante, paras 12.45 et seq.

3 CYPA 1969, ss 28(4) and (5) and 70(2).

4 It seems clear that the justice can only order the detention to continue up to the maximum eight days from the date when the juvenile was first detained. Where there is an application for earlier release, the police should be given notice of the application and an opportunity to be heard and to give evidence; see *R v Bristol Justices, ex p Broome* [1987] 1 All ER 676, [1987] 1 WLR 352.

5 Section 28(3).

6 Section 28(4). RCCL (para 13.34) recommends that the juvenile and the parent or guardian should be told the reason for the detention and their right to legal advice.

7 Under s 28(6).

14.43 This police power to detain can be helpful in urgent cases where no social worker is available and immediate steps to obtain a place of safety order are not practicable. However, the RCCL and CCFS recommend a much shorter period of detention, namely, of 72 hours instead of eight days, with power for a justice or a court to extend it up to eight days and with the possibility of the juvenile and the parent or guardian being given the right to make representations at the hearing.[1] It should be noted that, where either section 28(1) or (2) is invoked, the police may concurrently or soon afterwards exercise their powers to arrest without warrant a parent, guardian or other person for alleged offences against the juvenile.[2] As a consequence he may after he has been charged be detained in custody if the circumstances give rise to a reasonable belief that it is necessary to protect the juvenile from physical harm.[3] In those circumstances it may then be possible to allow the juvenile to return home, although clearly close investigation will first be needed.

1 RCCL, para 13.33, and CCFS, para 48.

2 See Police and Criminal Evidence Act 1984, ss 24 and 25.

3 Section 38(1)(a)(ii). The provision does not, however, extend to protection from moral or psychological harm; see Bevan and Lidstone, *A Guide to the Police and Criminal Evidence Act 1984*, para 5.30.

(d) Section 40 of the Children and Young Persons Act 1933 : search warrants

14.44 There is no power under a place of safety order nor under the powers conferred on a constable by section 28(2) of the 1969 Act to enter premises, search for the juvenile and remove him without the consent of the occupier. If there is immediate danger to the juvenile, a constable has a power of entry without a warrant in order to save life or limb,[1] and may use reasonable force for the purpose.[2] Otherwise section 40 of the 1933 Act[3] must be invoked and a search warrant issued. This can be done at the same time as the granting of a place of safety order.[4] The warrant may be issued if, as a result of an information,[5] the justice reasonably suspects that the juvenile is the victim either (1) of such assault, ill-treatment or neglect as is likely to cause him unnecessary suffering or injury to health, or (2) of one of the offences listed in Schedule I of the 1933 Act.[6] A number of statutory provisions deem certain actions of refusal to give rise to reasonable suspicion:

(i)   refusal to allow a privately fostered child or a 'protected child', as defined by the Adoption Act 1976, to be visited, or premises to be inspected by an officer of the local authority;[7]

(ii) refusal to allow an authorised person to inspect such premises as a local authority community home or a voluntary home[8] or a home or premises registered under the Children's Homes Act 1982;[9]

(iii) refusal to comply with the requirement allowing the supervisor to visit the juvenile or allowing the juvenile to be medically examined, imposed by a supervision order which was made in care proceedings on any of the grounds in paragraph (a), (b), (bb) or (c) of section 1(2) of the 1969 Act.[10]

It is suggested that to this statutory list should be added a persistent refusal by parents to allow a social worker or health visitor to see and examine a child.[11]

1 Police and Criminal Evidence Act 1984, s 17(1)(e).
2 Ibid, s 117. The advantage of the power is that the constable does not have to show reasonable grounds for believing that the juvenile is on the premises, (s 17(2)(a)); see Hayes and Bevan, pp 42–43.
3 As amended by CYPA 1963, Sch III and PCEA 1984, s 119(2) and Sch 7.
4 RCCL, para 13.30, recommends merging the powers to give 'a single power to authorise detention in a place of protection to which a search warrant may be attached'.
5 The information, which must be on oath, may be laid by anyone who in the justice's opinion is acting in the juvenile's interests.
6 For ill-treatment of children see ante, paras 9.34 et seq.
7 Foster Children Act 1980, s 13(2); Adoption Act 1976, s 37(1).
8 Child Care Act 1980, s 75(3).
9 Section 9(5).
10 CYPA 1969, s 14A, as inserted by HASSASSAA 1983, Sch 2, para 11.
11 See the lessons of the Jasmine Beckford and Kimberley Carlile cases, where social workers were at crucial periods refused such access to the children.

14.45 If the justice is of the requisite opinion, he may issue a warrant authorising a constable *either* to search for the juvenile[1] and, if he finds that he is the victim of ill-treatment or neglect or of an offence, to take him to a place of safety *or* to remove him with or without search to such a place.[2] The constable may then enter any premises specified in the warrant.[3] The first alternative apparently leaves the constable with a discretion to remove the juvenile, the second obliges him to do so, and it has been suggested[4] that the second should be followed unless the evidence of ill-treatment or neglect or of an offence is not strong. The warrant may direct that the constable be accompanied by a doctor,[5] and the informant may do so except where the warrant otherwise directs,[6] a direction which might, for example, be appropriate where his presence is thought likely to exacerbate an already difficult situation.

1 There is no need for him to be named in the warrant (CYPA 1933, s 40(5)), but obviously he must be identifiable.
2 The warrant may also authorise the arrest of a person accused of any offence in respect of the juvenile and his being brought before a court of summary jurisdiction (s 40(2)).
3 Section 40(3).
4 Clarke Hall and Morrison, para B[341].
5 Section 40(4).
6 Ibid.

14.46 Where a juvenile is removed to a place of safety he must be brought before a juvenile court within the period specified in the warrant, which must not be more than 28 days, unless he has been released or received into the care of a local authority.[1] As with a place of safety order, the period specified should be as short as possible. If the juvenile is 'not otherwise brought before the court', for example by a constable, the responsibility for doing so lies with the local authority in whose area the place of safety is situated.[2] In such a case the court may order his release or make an interim order committing him to the care of the local authority,[3] which is most likely to be the authority which brought him before the court. If he is under the age of five or cannot be brought before the court because of illness or accident, an application may be made for one or other of those orders to be made without his being present.[4]

1 CYPA 1963, s 3(1), as amended by CYPA 1969, Sch 5, para 48 and Sch 6. The circumstances which would justify the juvenile being received into care must, it is submitted, be those which require a local authority to receive a child into care under s 2 of the Child Care Act 1980, post, paras 15.08 et seq.
2 If the place of safety is not provided by the local authority, the person occupying or in charge must notify the local authority whenever a juvenile is taken there under s 40 of the 1933 Act. The authority will then be alerted to its duty to bring the juvenile before the court; see CYPA 1963, s 23(3).
3 CYPA 1963, s 23(3) and (5), as amended by CYPA 1969, Sch 5, para 48. Sub-s (3) is expressed ambiguously, and is open to the interpretation that the power to make an interim order is not available where the juvenile is 'otherwise brought before the court'.
4 Section 23(4).

(e) Section 43 of the Sexual Offences Act 1956

14.47 Apart from the powers conferred by section 40 of the Children and Young Persons Act 1933, a constable may be authorised by a warrant issued under section 43 of the Sexual Offences Act 1956 to search for and remove to a place of safety a female who is being detained for the purpose of having unlawful sexual intercourse with men. The scope of the power has already been examined,[1] when it was pointed out that a likely outcome of its exercise is the commencement of care proceedings.

1 Ante, paras 10.38.

(f) Notice of proceedings

14.48 If the local authority is proposing to bring proceedings it must send a notice to the clerk of the court, specifying the grounds for the proceedings and the names and addresses of the persons to whom the authority is sending copies of the notice.[1] It must also notify each of those persons of the date, time and place of the hearing[2] unless a summons is issued for securing his attendance.[3] The persons to be notified are (1) the juvenile, unless in view of his age and understanding a notice is inappropriate, (2) the parent or guardian, (3) any grandparent and (4) any foster parent or other person (for example, a relative) with whom the juvenile has had his home for a period of not less than 42 days, ending not more than six months before the date of the local authority's application,[4] provided under categories (2) (3) and (4) the whereabouts of the person are known to the authority or can readily be ascertained by it. The Rule does not expressly require the authority to take all reasonable steps to ascertain the whereabouts, and it is uncertain whether the authority is obliged to make any inquiries. The point is important because it was held in *D v X City Council (No 1)*[5] that a care order made in care proceedings is invalid if there is a failure to give notice to a person entitled to it. Obviously, the matter needs statutory clarification, especially if effect is given to recommendations of the Review on Child Care Law[6] that additional information should be given to addressees. This would include not merely the statutory grounds on which the application is based, but also the reasons why it is alleged they exist, a summary of the facts which are to be proved by the applicant and an indication of the order sought. Moreover, the applicant should, before the hearing, serve its witness statements on the other parties and, if the court so directs, other participants.

1   MC (C&YP) Rules 1988, r 14(1).
2   The authority should therefore arrange the hearing with the clerk before sending these notices.
3   Rule 14(2). A notice must also be sent to the respondent juvenile informing him that he must not later than 14 days after receipt of the notice inform the clerk of the court whether or not he intends to oppose the application; see r 14(4).
4   Rule 14(3). But a child does not have his home with foster parents if his parent is also living in the same house with them and it is the parent who decides where the physical presence of the child shall be; *R v Sittingbourne Juvenile Court, ex p Gilham*, Lexis CO/ 597/87, 10 June 1987.
5   [1985] FLR 275. But the remedy for failure to notify lies now in judicial review and not, as in *D v X CC*, in wardship; see *Re S* [1987] 1 FLR 479, [1987] Fam Law 159, CA.
6   See RCCL paras 16.2 to 16.10. The recommendations are given general approval by CCFS, para 57.

(g)   The upper age limit

14.49   Care jurisdiction extends to juveniles who are below the age of 17, and for the purposes of the jurisdiction the 1969 Act expressly provides that care proceedings are begun when the juvenile is first brought before a juvenile court.[1] The court must presume or determine what his age is at that date,[2] and if it finds he is under 17 it has jurisdiction. Should he attain that age before the proceedings are concluded, the court may nevertheless continue to deal with the case and make any order which it could have made if he had not attained that age.[3]

1   Section 2(14).
2   CYPA 1933, s 99(1).
3   CYPA 1963, s 29(1), as amended by CYPA 1969, s 72(3) and (4) and Sch 5, para 49, and Sch 6.

14.50   This general rule fixing the upper age limit is qualified by that which excludes from the jurisdiction any juvenile who has attained 16 if he is or has been married.[1] A person under 16 who is a party to a valid foreign marriage can be the subject of care proceedings, but, as already noted,[2] the court may be unwilling to find a primary condition proved.

1   CYPA 1969, s 1(5)(c). Jurisdiction also does not extend to a juvenile whose parent is entitled to diplomatic immunity; *R v Hendon Justices, ex p D* (1974) 118 Sol Jo 756.
2   See *Alhaji Mohamed v Knott* [1969] 1 QB 1, [1968] 2 All ER 563, DC, ante para 14.14.

(h) The power to remit a juvenile from one juvenile court to another

14.51 Where a juvenile is brought before a court in care proceedings and it appears that he resides in a petty sessions area other than that for which the court acts, the court must, unless it dismisses the case, direct that he be brought before a juvenile court acting for the area in which he resides. In addition it must either make an interim order and inform the other court of the remission or inform the local authority, in whose area the juvenile lives, of the case, whereupon the authority must bring him before the appropriate court within 21 days.[1] In the rare case where proceedings are based on the offence condition the remitting court may first determine whether the condition is satisfied and any determination is binding on the court to which the case is remitted.[2] In all cases before it the court must inform the juvenile, his representative and, if present, his parent or guardian of the manner in which it proposes to deal with the case and allow them to make representations.[3]

1 CYPA 1969, s 2(11).
2 Section 3(5). The rule saves witnesses of the alleged offence the inconvenience of having to travel to the court of residence; see Clarke Hall and Morrison, para B[693].
3 MC (C&YP) Rules 1988, r 27. For this duty see further post, para 14.104.

14.52 This provision, designed to encourage the almost exclusive jurisdiction of the court of residence, is administratively desirable, since those persons and administrative bodies most familiar with the juvenile and his background are very likely to come from the area in which he lives.[1] Nevertheless, some evidence will have to be adduced before the directing court to enable it to form an opinion that the case should not be dismissed, which means some witnesses, at least, attending both courts to give evidence.

1 Where parent and juvenile are living apart; the court will not constructively assign the juvenile to the parent's residence; his residence is where he eats, drinks and sleeps. See *R v Manchester City Juvenile Court, ex p Bannister* (1983) 4 FLR 717. Compare the readiness of the court to give a constructive meaning to 'household' for the purpose of the primary condition in s 1(2)(b) of the 1969 Act; see ante, para 14.10.

IV THE HEARING

14.53 Neither the Legislature nor the Judiciary has been certain about the nature and purpose of care proceedings.[1] In *Humberside County Council v DPR (an infant)*[2] Lord Widgery CJ described care proceedings as 'essentially non-adversarial' and suggested that they ought to be 'an objective examination of the position of the child'.[3] Yet, as the learned Chief Justice was earlier obliged to recognise, 'in proceedings of this kind the real issue is nearly always between the local authority and the parents',[4] usually involving 'a flavour of fault or guilt'[5] on the part of the parent. The most effective way of securing an objective examination of the condition of the juvenile is an inquisitorial procedure, with the court being able itself to call witnesses and documentary evidence and not being confined, as it presently is, to assessing the evidence adduced by the local authority, the juvenile and the parent and only being able to call for additional information after the case has been proved.[6] Although the Review of Child Care Law wishes to see 'a framework which is less accusatorial and more flexibly structured',[7] it still sees reform within the traditional structures of civil proceedings, making care proceedings 'more like ordinary civil proceedings relating to the custody or upbringing of a child'.

1   Commentators have been much clearer, and thus more critical, about present procedures. See especially Dingwall, Eekelaar and Murray, *Care or Control*, Chapters 11–12; Freeman, *The Rights and The Wrongs of Children*, pp 161–163; Evans, *What's Wrong with Care Proceedings?* (1982) 79 Law Soc Gaz 1240.
2   [1977] 3 All ER 964, [1977] 1 WLR 1251, DC.
3   See pp 966 and 967 and 1254 respectively.
4   *R v Worthing Justices, ex p Stevenson* [1976] 2 All ER 194 at 196.
5   Per Ormrod LJ in *Re C (a minor) (Justices' Decision: Review)* (1979) 2 FLR 62 at 66.
6   CYPA 1969, s 9(2).
7   Paragraph 16.1.

14.54   These comments are pertinent to juveniles who are the subject of care proceedings because they are allegedly the victims of neglect or ill-treatment; but unfortunately some of the rules are designed with the delinquent juvenile in mind, even though the 'offence' condition is rarely invoked.[1] This partly explains the hotchpotch nature of the rules, but, as will be seen, that feature is mainly explained by the ambivalent position occupied by the parent or guardian. The rules are derived from several sources, especially the Children and Young Persons Acts 1933 to 1969 and Part III of the Magistrates' Courts (Children and Young Persons) Rules 1988. Significant amendments were made to Part III of the former Magistrates' Courts (Children and Young Persons) Rules 1970 in 1976 and 1984, which, in conjunction with amendments to the Children and Young Persons Act 1969, provided for more effective representation of the juvenile and of his parents and for limited participation by other interested persons. The Children and Young Persons (Amendment) Act 1986, together with amendments embodied in the 1988 Rules, has extended that process. The Home Office long ago recognised the need for a thorough review of the Rules, intending to institute it 'in due course'.[2] Root and branch reform is needed, and the recommendations of the Review of Child Care Law, if implemented, will go a long way to achieving that object.

1   See ante, para 14.19, and for judicial criticism Ormrod LJ in *Re W (a minor) (Justices' Division: Review)* (1981) 2 FLR 360, and Dunn LJ in *Re E (minors) (Wardships: Jurisdiction)* (1983) 4 FLR 668.
2   HOC No 267/1970.

1   The parties, their representatives, parents (if not parties) and persons entitled to make representations

14.55   Both the Children and Young Persons Acts and the Rules emphasise the tripartite nature of most care proceedings and what may now sometimes be quadripartite. In all cases the applicant (usually the local authority) and the juvenile are parties to the proceedings; in some, indeed most, the parent is now also automatically a party, but in others he is not — a distinction which complicates the procedural rules; and in some, a minority of cases, a grandparent may be made a party.[1] Additionally, there are other persons who are entitled to make representations to the court.

1 See post, para 14.73 for the possibility of a grandparent being a party.

(a) The applicant

14.56 Unless otherwise indicated it is assumed that the applicant is always a local authority and not the NSPCC or the police. Usually the authority is represented at the hearing by one of its solicitors, but sometimes, at least in applications for an interim order or successive interim orders, the court liaison officer, a member of the social services department, appears on behalf of the authority.[1] Exceptionally counsel may be briefed, but that is more likely if there is an appeal to the Crown Court or, for example, where the case involves sharp dispute over medical evidence and necessitates the cross-examination of expert witnesses. The Beckford Inquiry[2] recommended that legal departments of local authorities should arrange for one or more of their solicitors to specialise in juvenile court work, that the Law Society should extend its panel of solicitors to act in child care cases[3] to include local authority solicitors employed by authorities, and that only those local authority solicitors who meet the criteria for membership of the panel should be allowed to represent their authority in care proceedings.

1 A committee representing the Society of County Secretaries, the Association of District Secretaries and the Law Society's Local Government Group has produced guidelines about who should conduct proceedings for the local authority; see (1987) 137 NLJ 629, 84 Law Soc Gaz 1935.
2 See ante, para 14.03, note 2 and Chapters 20 and 28 of the Report.
3 See post, para 14.75.

(b) The juvenile

14.57 Notwithstanding the statutory changes relating to representation of the juvenile, the Rules are still formulated with emphasis on the parent's being entitled to conduct the case on behalf of the juvenile,[1] who is the respondent to the proceedings.[2] The court must allow him to do so unless:

(i)   the juvenile or his parent[3] is legally represented; or

(ii)   the proceedings are brought at the parent's request (or under an order resulting from a request) on the ground that the juvenile is beyond control; or

(iii)   the court has ordered that the parent is not to be treated as representing the juvenile because of an actual or possible conflict of interest;[4] or

(iv)   the juvenile otherwise requests. This is a remote possibility in care proceedings, though it might just arise, for example, where an independently minded 16-year old applies for the discharge of a care order and both the local authority and the parent are opposed to the application. In such rare instances the court could well grant the juvenile legal aid[5] so that he might be represented by a solicitor.

1 MC (C & YP) Rules 1988, r 22(1).
2 Rules 13(2) and 19.
3 References throughout include the alternative of 'guardian', as defined by CYPA 1933, s 107(1), ante, para 9.48. Where, therefore, the juvenile is the subject of a custodianship order, the custodian is the guardian.
4 See infra, s 32A(1) of CYPA 1969.

5 By virtue of the Legal Aid Act 1974, s 28(3)(a), which empowers the court to grant a juvenile legal aid for the purpose of s 1. There is no recourse if aid is refused.

14.58 This emphasis is based on the unreal assumption that the parent will necessarily be acting in the juvenile's interest. In care proceedings the parent's conduct is in most cases inextricably involved, and consequently he often sees the proceedings as a conflict between himself and the local authority, with the need to justify his own conduct. The emphasis as formulated in the Rules no longer reflects the reality. Even before the statutory changes, juvenile courts were increasingly granting the juvenile legal aid so that he could be legally represented. That is an option which a court may still exercise, but the shift now is largely to the new rules, with power to appoint a guardian ad litem. They call for examination.

(c)   Conflict of interest between juvenile and parent[1]

14.59   The powers of the court under section 32A (1) of the 1969 Act[2] to exclude the rule that the parent is to be treated as representing the juvenile or otherwise authorised to act on his behalf and then, under the Rules,[3] to proceed to the appointment of a guardian ad litem are in terms which leave the court with considerable and largely unchallengeable discretion. Firstly, it must appear to the court that there is or may be a conflict between the juvenile's interests and those of the parent on any matter relevant to the proceedings. No statutory guidance is given on how actual or possible conflict is to be determined. However, both in principle and, as is now emerging, in practice, this obstacle to separate representation is not difficult to surmount. In a minority of cases it will not be difficult to conclude that there is no conflict or any risk of it; for example, in proceedings based on truancy (section 1(2)(e)) and the parent is concerned about it and recognises the need for a supervision order or even a care order.[4] However, in the large majority of proceedings there must be a real possibility of conflict. This follows from the very terms of some of the grounds in section 1(2) of the 1969 Act, especially section 1(2)(a), and the fact that the parent is often opposed to the proceedings. The likelihood of conflict is particularly strong where the application is based on alleged parental abuse or neglect of the juvenile, especially if he is already the subject of a place of safety order. Secondly, while the court may well be satisfied that there is an actual or potential conflict, it still has a discretion whether or not to order that the parent is not to be treated as representing the juvenile. Here, too, section 32A(1) offers no guidance on the factors to be taken into account in exercising this part of the discretion, but once the question of conflict is answered affirmatively it is almost certain that the court will order that the parent is not to represent the juvenile.

1 See Lyon, *Safeguarding Children's Interests — Some Problematic Issues surrounding Separate Representation in Care and Associated Proceedings* in *Essays in Family Law* 1985, (Current Legal Problems) (edited by Freeman).
2 As inserted by the Children Act 1975, s 64.
3 MC (C & YP) Rules 1988, r 16.
4 The juvenile himself may be in conflict with his parents, but the question is whether their respective interests are in conflict. The interests of the juvenile presumably mean his best interests, and these must be taken in the context to mean attendance at school, which is the very thing the parents are seeking to promote. The conflict between them is really a conflict of wishes. They wish him to go to school; he wishes not to go.

14.60   Where the court does make such an order, the appointment of a guardian ad litem will not automatically follow, but must be made if it appears to the court that it is in the juvenile's interests to do so.[1] Yet again there is no statutory guidance, but appointment should, it is submitted, be the normal consequence of the decision that there is or may be a conflict of interest. Appointment might be refused if the juvenile is old enough and has the understanding to take part in the proceedings. If so, the court might instead of appointing a guardian grant the juvenile legal aid and enable a solicitor to be appointed to represent him, if that has not already been done. One of the current complaints heard in juvenile courts is that, because of shortage of appointments of guardians ad litem to panels, there is delay in the appointment of a guardian and then in his completing his investigations,[2] with the result that a number of interim orders have to be made before the case is able to proceed to final hearing. Consequently, there is a serious risk that courts might be tempted to use their alternative power of direct appointment of a solicitor, but that would not be likely to be in the juvenile's interests. Those interests require a guardian ad litem to make the necessary investigations and report. Regrettably, present indications are that in some areas at least there are appointments only in a majority of cases where a section 32A(1) order has been made.[3]

1   MC (C & YP) Rules 1988, r 16(1). Notice of appointment must be given not only to the guardian ad litem but also to the applicant and to each person to whom notice of the proceedings has been given (r 16(5)). If considered desirable, the court may replace one guardian ad litem with another (r 16(3)).
2   In practice guardians are usually insistent that they require a minimum of six weeks.
3   See Waterhouse J in *R v Plymouth Juvenile Court, ex p F* [1987] 1 FLR 169.

14.61   An order under section 32A(1) and an order appointing a guardian ad litem may be made by the court before or in the course of the proceedings,[1] or by a single justice[2] or the justices' clerk[3] before the proceedings. Sometimes appointment is made at the first hearing of an application for an interim order.[4] If possible, it should not be delayed beyond that date. Indeed, because of the difficulty of arranging appointments and the time taken by a guardian to investigate and prepare a report, it is from those points of view[5] desirable to make a section 32A(1) order and appoint before any hearing. Where the court appoints, the guardian ad litem must instruct a solicitor to represent the juvenile, unless the court otherwise directs.[6] Where a justice or the justices' clerk appoints, he may direct the guardian to instruct a solicitor.[7] The distinction of emphasis is illogical. Worse is the absence of any prescribed uniform procedure for dealing with 'conflict' cases. The considerable variation in the procedures adopted has thus been summarised.[8]

> 'Courts differ widely on the procedures they adopt. Some hold a formal preliminary hearing before a bench of three justices, allow the parent to be legally represented and determine the issue in a formal judicial manner. Others arrange for a representative of the local authority to speak in private to a single justice who then determines the issue. In some courts the order is made by the justices' clerk, after consultation with the local authority.'

Doubtless, there are variations on these three basic preliminary procedures; for example, it is known that some justices would only act in consultation with, and/or in the presence of, their clerk and his assistant. The first of the three procedures above mentioned is clearly the desirable one, since the parent's point of view is heard. But, if it is not, there can be no objection by way of judicial review on the ground of breach of natural justice, even though the making of a section 32A(1) order is a judicial act. Provided the justice of the clerk acts in the best interest of the juvenile, so far as his powers permit, the order cannot be challenged. So it was held in *R v Plymouth Juvenile Court, ex p F*.[9] Nevertheless, an informal hearing by a justice or the clerk[10] has inherent difficulties. There will be very limited information available to him. As already noted,[11] the notice which the applicant has to send to the clerk merely requires the grounds for bringing the proceedings to be specified. There is no duty to submit any documentary evidence which would support the making of a section 32A(1) order and the appointment of a guardian ad litem. Nor has the justice or the clerk power to call for such evidence, though he should try to elicit as much information as he can from the applicant local authority.

1 Section 32A(1).
2 Section 32A(4); r 16(4).
3 Ibid, and Justices' Clerks Rules 1970, r 3 and Sch, para 13 (as inserted by JC (Amendment) Rules 1976).
4 See post, para 14.62 for a procedure adopted in some courts.
5 But see infra from the parent's point of view.
6 Rule 16(6)(c).
7 Rule 16(4).
8 Hayes and Bevan, op cit, pp 57–58.
9 [1987] 1 FLR 169.
10 In practice the clerk is the more likely to deal with the matter.
11 Ante, para 14.48.

14.62   So long as the present rules operate, probably the best alternative to a formal preliminary hearing is consideration of the 'conflict' matter at the first hearing of the application for an interim order. In some courts it is the practice for the justices' clerk on receipt of the notice of the local authority's application to grant legal aid and appoint a solicitor to represent the juvenile.[1] At the hearing the solicitor will seek a section 32A(1) order and apply for the appointment of a guardian ad litem. The parent, who will have received notice of the hearing, will then be heard on the 'conflict' question. In some courts a solicitor, who has advised the parent under the Green Form scheme,[2] will attend and represent the parent in the expectation that the order will be made so that then the parent can apply for and be granted legal aid.[3] The need for rationalisation of procedures is self-evident.[4]

1 Appointments by the courts are made from the panels of Child Care Solicitors established by the Law Society.
2 Under the Legal Advice and Assistance Regulations (No 2) 1980.
3 See post, para 14.71.
4 RCCL (para 14.12) recommends that the court should be under a duty to appoint a guardian ad litem, unless the child's interests do not require it.

(d) The guardian ad litem[1]

(i) Selection

14.63 A guardian ad litem must be selected from a panel established under the Guardians ad Litem and Reporting Officers (Panels) Regulations 1983,[2] but a member of a panel is disqualified from appointment (a) if he is a member, officer or servant of the applicant local authority[3] or (b) if he is or has been a member, officer or servant of a local authority or voluntary organisation[4] who has been directly concerned in that capacity in arrangements relating to the care, accommodation or welfare of the juvenile or (c) if he is a serving probation officer, except that a part-time probation officer who has not previously been concerned with the juvenile or his family is qualified to act in his own time and not in the course of his official duties.[5] The first two disqualifications seek to ensure the independence of the guardian ad litem. The third 'stems partly from resource considerations and partly from the need to protect the primary work of the probation service'[6]. Other suitable members are independent social workers or workers from voluntary agencies with experience in child care work.

1 See Ludbrook, *Guardians ad Litem in the Juvenile Court* [1984] LAG Bul 89; Swallow, *Guardians ad Litem* [1986] Fam Law 81; Timms, *The Guardian ad Litem — A Practitioner's Perspective* [1986] Fam Law 339.
2 See ante, para 5.94.
3 Or of the NSPCC or the police if either is the applicant.
4 As defined by s 87(1) of the Child Care Act 1980; see post, para 15.112.
5 See MC (C & YP) Rules 1988, r 16(2).
6 HOC No 31/1984 (CS 3/84). Serving probation officers who are on panels are more readily available to act as guardians ad litem in adoption cases.

(ii) Functions

14.64 When the use of guardians ad litem in the juvenile court was partially introduced in 1976 to deal with unopposed applications to discharge supervision orders or care orders, the guardian could conduct the case on behalf of the juvenile. This is still possible, but the emphasis is now very much on legal representation of the child. The later amendments in 1984 recognised the incompatibility generally of the guardian's role of advocate with his other duties, including appearing as a witness. Thus, if arrangements for legal representation have not already been made, before the appointment of the guardian, he must obtain the views of the court on the matter and, unless the court otherwise directs, instruct a solicitor.[1] Nevertheless, though a solicitor may be, and usually is, instructed, the guardian ad litem, like his counterpart in adoption proceedings, is appointed to safeguard the juvenile's interests before the court. The significant difference is that the rules governing his functions do not prescribe as lengthy a list of duties as those in adoption.[2] Apart from his above duty to instruct a solicitor, the following are imposed.[3]

1 MC (C & YP) Rules 1988, r 16(c).
2 Compare ante, para 5.42.
3 Rules 16(6). DHSS has issued a *Guide for Guardians Ad Litem in the Juvenile Court* (1984). Solicitors who appear in care proceedings will find the Guide helpful in discussing their cases with a guardian.

14.65 (a) So far as is reasonably practicable, he must investigate all circumstances relevant to the proceedings and for that purpose interview such persons, inspect such records[1] and obtain such professional assistance (for example, a medical opinion on the juvenile) as he thinks appropriate. Although discharging this duty may involve duplication of inquiries which may already have been made by other agencies, this possibility should not deter the guardian ad litem from undertaking the fullest investigations so as to enable him to come to an independent conclusion on what is best for the juvenile. He is not statutorily required to interview all the persons to whom copy of the notice of the proceeding has to be sent,[2] but invariably he will have to do so if he is to investigate all relevant circumstances. The extent of co-operation which he might receive from the parent will vary considerably, and, where it is not forthcoming, he should, as an officer of the court, report the fact to it and also any other obstruction to the discharge of his duties.

1   For the disclosure of records and claims of privilege, immunity, and confidentiality see post, paras 14.83–14.87. CCFS (para 57) proposes that the guardian ad litem should have a statutory right of access to documents.
2   Ante, para 14.48. Compare the duty of the guardian ad litem in adoption proceedings to interview specified persons.

14.66 (b) He must regard as the first and paramount consideration the need to safeguard and promote the juvenile's best interests until he achieves adulthood. He must take into account the wishes and feelings of the juvenile, having regard to his age and understanding. This may involve several interviews while he gains the juvenile's confidence, and may call for delicacy, especially in cases of alleged sexual abuse. He must make the wishes and feelings known to the court.

14.67 (c) He must consider how the case should be presented on behalf of the juvenile, instructing, and acting in conjunction with, the solicitor who has been instructed (whether by him or otherwise) to represent the juvenile. However, the solicitor is free to consider whether the juvenile wishes and is able, having regard to his age and understanding, to give instructions on his own behalf. If so, he takes instructions from the juvenile and not from the guardian ad litem. It is, nevertheless, a decision which the solicitor should carefully weigh and in so doing he must take account of the views of the guardian. The possibility will arise where the juvenile's wishes conflict with the guardian's views of what are in his best interests. It may be over the question whether the juvenile should go into local authority care. It is more likely that the guardian ad litem will favour that consequence and the juvenile oppose it, but the converse may well be possible, for example, where the juvenile is hostile to a step-parent and does not wish to return to live with him and the natural parent. In the event of the solicitor taking the juvenile's instructions, the guardian ad litem is still free to assist the court by giving evidence, making representations and submitting a report.

14.68 (d) He must seek the views of the court[1] where difficulties arise in performing his duties, for example, where he and the solicitor do not agree or where he has been obstructed in his investigations; and he must perform such others as the court, a single justice or the justices' clerk may direct. Finally, he must make a written report to the court which it can take into account in deciding what order, if any, to make if the local authority proves its case. From all these listed duties it is clear that in care proceedings the guardian ad litem plays a multi-purpose role. He is partly the counterpart to an instructing parent, partly an investigator on behalf of the juvenile and his solicitor, partly, if needs be, an expert witness and partly an adviser to the court. The court is likely to rely heavily on his recommendations.

1   This should be done through the clerk to the justices.

(e)   The parent

14.69   The powers of the court under section 34(1) of the Children and Young Persons Act 1933 to compel the attendance of a parent has been fully examined in relation to criminal proceedings, but it equally applies to care proceedings and the earlier details should be noted.[1] Apart from section 34 there are other provisions which may make the attendance of the parent essential. One of the features of the Children and Young Persons Act 1969 is that it enables care proceedings to be brought in respect of children under five without their presence in court.[2] The procedure is wholly within the court's discretion, but a prior condition is that either notice of the proceedings was served on the parent or he is in fact present before the court. In either event the court may direct that the proceedings continue, subject to the parent (if present) being given an opportunity to be heard. Again, if the court is thinking of making an order requiring the parent to enter into a recognisance to take proper care of the juvenile and exercise proper control over him,[3] the parent must consent, and that means attendance at court to do so.

1   See ante, paras 12.87 to 12.89.
2   Section 2(9). The effect of the direction is that the child is deemed to have been brought before the court under s 1 of the Act.
3   CYPA 1969, s 1(3)(a); see further post, para 14.109.

14.70   The above provisions are concerned with the power to compel or enable attendance. It seems clear that in care proceedings, in those cases where he is not a party, the parent, nevertheless, has the right to attend as a person 'directly concerned' in the case within the meaning of section 47(2) of the Children and Young Persons Act 1933. The requirement in section 1 of the 1969 Act that the juvenile is in need of care or control is a matter with which the parent is directly concerned.

14.71   Where an order is made under section 32A of the Children and Young Persons Act 1969 providing for the separate representation of the juvenile because the court considers that there is or may be a conflict of interest between the parent(s) and the juvenile, the parent(s) (or guardians) who are the subject of the order become full parties to the proceedings.[1] In those cases, albeit a minority, where no such order is made, the parent has a limited right to take part in the proceedings.[2] He is entitled to meet any allegations made in the course of the proceedings, including proceedings for an interim care order,[3] by cross-examining any witness and calling or giving evidence. His evidence must be called at the conclusion of the evidence for the applicant and the respondent juvenile, but before the respondent or the applicant addresses the court.[4] He is additionally entitled to make representations to the court at any such stage after the conclusion of the evidence in the hearing as the court considers appropriate.[5] There is no statutory guidance as to the kinds of matters on which representations may be made. They apparently include objections to the admissibility of evidence, at least if the applicant or respondent first objects,[6] but it is uncertain whether the evidence must relate to allegations made against the parent. They also seem to include representations in favour of or against an adjournment of the hearing of the application. Strictly, a submission that there is no case to answer is a representation, but a court should be slow to allow such a submission, especially by a person who is not a party to the proceedings, since it is preferable in care proceedings to hear all the evidence.[7] There is little doubt that there can be representations with regard to the allegations made against the parent in the course of the proceedings. A skilled advocate making representations on those matters may thereby in effect make a final address, and in so doing insinuate comments on the case presented by the local authority or on behalf of the juvenile. Indeed, some juvenile courts, perhaps most, openly permit such an address. It is unlikely that this permission could be successfully challenged by way of judicial review, since it is highly arguable that it falls within the inherent jurisdiction of a magistrates' court to control its own proceedings and to allow such legal representations as are necessary in the interests of justice.[8]

If a parent is the subject of a section 32A order, the court may grant him legal aid.[9] If he is not, the court in its discretion may allow him to be legally represented, even though he is not a party to the proceedings and even though legal aid is not available.[10] In the latter circumstances the parent is very dependent upon the court's forbearance in allowing him to play a larger part in the proceedings than the Rules formally permit. Thus in *R v Sunderland Juvenile Court, ex p G*[11] an independent social worker appointed by the father was allowed access to the report of the guardian ad litem.

---

1 See CYPA 1969, s 32A(4A), as inserted by CYP(A)A 1986, s 3(1).
   The court must notify the parent(s) (or guardians) concerned and all other parties to the proceedings that a s 32A order has been made and its effect; see MC (C & YP) Rules 1988, r 15.
2 *R v Worthing Justices, ex p Stevenson* [1976] 2 All ER 194; *R v Welwyn Justices, ex p S* (1978) 123 Sol Jo 17.
3 *H v London Borough of Southwark* (1982) 12 Fam Law 211.
4 MC (C & YP) Rules 1988, r 18.
5 Ibid.
6 In *R v Wood Green Crown Court, ex p P* (1983) 4 FLR 206 it was left open whether the parent could object where neither of the parties chose to do so.
7 *M v Westminster City Council* [1985] FLR 325, [1985] Fam Law 93, DC.
8 For this inherent jurisdiction see *M v Westminster City Council*, supra; *R v Milton Keynes Justices, ex p R* [1979] 1 WLR 1062; *R v Gravesham Juvenile Court, ex p B* (1983) 4 FLR 312, (1982) 12 Fam Law 207; *R v Sunderland Juvenile Court, ex p G (a minor)* [1988] 2 All ER 34, [1988] 1 WLR 398, CA.
9 Legal Aid Act 1974, s 28(6A), as amended by CYP(A)A 1986, s 3(3).
10 *R v Gravesham Juvenile Court, ex p B*, supra, note 8.
11 See supra, note 8.

14.72   Where the parent is a party by virtue of a section 32A order, he will automatically have a right of address; but surprisingly the amending 1988 Rules fail to state whether the parent's evidence is to be adduced before that of the juvenile. Indeed, as will be seen,[1] the whole question of the order of evidence and speeches regrettably remains as uncertain as it was before the enactment of those Rules.

---

1   See post, paras 14.79–14.80.

(f)   The grandparent

14.73   Another change made by the Children and Young Persons (Amendment) Act 1986 is that which enables the court to grant leave to a grandparent of the juvenile to be made a party to the proceedings if the court has made a section 32A(1) order.[1] Leave may be granted if the court is satisfied that (a) the grandparent, before the commencement of proceedings, had a substantial involvement in the juvenile's upbringing at any time during the juvenile's lifetime; and (b) making the grandparent a party is likely to be in the interests of the juvenile's welfare.[2] The failure to make the juvenile's welfare the paramount consideration is to be regretted, but the wording of condition (b) may possibly be explained on the ground of the overriding restrictive wording of section 44(1) of CYPA 1933.[3] As for condition (a), it is to be noted that the grandparent's involvement need not be continuing at the date of the proceedings. However, if there has been a substantial period since he or she was involved with the child, that fact will weaken the claim to be made a party. Where leave is given, the court may order legal aid,[4] and as a party the grandparent will be entitled to cross-examine, to give and call evidence and to address the court. The proposed change will not enable the court to make an order entrusting the juvenile to the grandparent (an unsatisfactory omission), but it may decide not to make any order under section 1 of the 1969 Act on being satisfied that the grandparent is able to and willing to have the juvenile live with him or her. In those circumstances the court may well conclude that the general condition of section 1(2) is not satisfied. The juvenile is in need of care or control, but is likely to receive it without the need for a care order or a supervision order. Alternatively, the court might take the view that the latter order would be appropriate to assist the grandparent, at least in the early stages of looking after the juvenile.

The 1986 Act provides a very narrow extension. It would have been far more enlightened if it had enabled any person who can show a real and genuine interest in the child to apply to become a party.

---

1   CYPA 1969, s 32C, as inserted by CYP(A)A 1986, s 3(2).
   It was the absence of a right to be heard in care proceedings that led the grandmother in *TL v Birmingham City Council* [1984] Fam Law 15 to seek, though unsuccessfully, a remedy in wardship. That remedy may still be a possibility for the grandparent who unsuccessfully applies to be made a party to care proceedings.
2   MC (C & YP) Rules 1988, r 17(1). Leave may be granted by the court or a single justice before or during the hearing of the proceedings or by the justices' clerk before the hearing; see CYPA 1969, s 32C(3) and MC(C & Y) Rules 1988, r 17(2).
3   See post, para 14.106.
4   Legal Aid Act 1974, s 28(6A), as amended by CYP(A)A 1986, s 3(3).

(g)   The foster parent, etc

14.74 A foster parent or other person to whom notice of the care proceedings has to be given[1] and who attends the hearing is entitled to make representations to the court.[2] So, too, is any other person (not being a party to the proceedings) who satisfies the court (a) that he has demonstrated an interest in the juvenile's welfare which has been maintained until the commencement of the proceedings *and* (b) that his representations are likely to be of relevance to the proceedings and to the juvenile's welfare.[3] Representations are to be made at such stage after the conclusion of the evidence in the hearing as the court considers appropriate. It should be noted that the right to make representations extends to all care cases and not only to those where a section 32A(1) order has been made, but there is no power to cross-examine or give or call evidence. Instead the matter has to be left to the court's inherent jurisdiction.[4] It is proposed[5] to relax the above rules and to allow anyone whose legal position could be affected by the care proceedings to become a party and to permit anyone who has evidence, opinions or views to offer to participate in the proceedings.

1 See ante, para 14.48. This would include a grandparent whose application to be made a party has been refused.
2 See supra, para 14.71 for uncertainty about the scope of making representations.
3 MC (C & YP) Rules 1988, r 19.
4 See supra, para 14.71.
5 See RCCL, paras 14.6–14.9 and CCFS, paras 55 and 56.

(h)   The solicitor and child – care cases[1]

14.75 One of the more heartening features of care-related proceedings in the juvenile court is the growing recognition by the legal profession of the role it can and should fulfil. Following the full implementation in 1984 of the provisions in the Children Act 1975 relating to separate representation of juveniles,[2] and with legal aid being available in such cases for separate representation of parents, the Law Society set up in March 1985 a panel of solicitors to act in child care cases. In 18 months the number empanelled more than doubled.[3] Regrettably the Government, through the Lord Chancellor's Department and the Department of Health and Social Security, made it clear that no public money would be available to fund the scheme, and the cost of running it falls on the Law Society. The system was generally welcomed by the Beckford Inquiry, but the Report recommended a number of changes, some of which are being pursued by the Law Society, including increasing emphasis on training programmes. One of the Beckford proposals was that a solicitor must see and, if possible, talk to or play with the child whom he represents. The proposal should be treated with some circumspection. As a Working Party of the Law Society has pointed out, solicitors are not trained in child psychology and should be aware of their own limitations when interviewing a child. Where a guardian ad litem has been appointed, the solicitor should first learn as much as he can about the child from the guardian and about the way in which he might approach an interview with the child. Where he is representing the child and there is no guardian ad litem, it is not likely that one meeting with the child will suffice.

1   See Weintroub, *The Solicitor in Care Cases — Who Gives the Instructions?* (1987) 84 Law Soc Gaz 1318.
2   Embodied in the CYPA 1969 in ss 32A and 32B and supplemented by rules in MC (C & YP) Rules 1988.
3   From 450 to 1100. In its Report (published in 1984) the House of Commons Social Services Committee (HC 360–1) recommended the establishment of a list of specialist solicitors.

2   The conduct and order of proceedings

14.76   The following examination of the procedures at the hearing is primarily related to the usual type of case that is now found in care proceedings, namely, where a section 32A(1) order has been made and a guardian ad litem appointed; but, where appropriate, attention is also drawn to procedures where that is not so.

(a)   Informing the juvenile and parent

(i) Procedure
14.77   It is just as important in care proceedings as it is in criminal[1] for the juvenile, if old enough, and his parents to have an outline in advance of what will happen at the hearing. In addition to the issue of an explanatory leaflet,[2] information from their solicitors, if already instructed, will be helpful, especially as care proceedings are more complicated than criminal. Such preliminary steps do not relieve the court of its duty at the outset of the hearing to inform the juvenile of the general nature of the proceedings and of the grounds on which they are brought,[3] and this must be done in terms suitable to his age and understanding. If, because of age and understanding or his absence, this is impracticable, any parent who is present must be informed.[4] It is submitted that this duty to inform (a) must be discharged even though the juvenile and/or the parent are legally represented, and (b) extends also to applications for interim care orders.

1   Compare ante, para 12.94.
2   For the Home Office draft pamphlet see HOC No 125/1978 (CS 26/1978). The need to inform has been further emphasised by HOC No 33/1988 (CS 4/88), para 8.
3   The duty to inform does not arise where he is the applicant (which in effect means where he is applying for variation or discharge of an order) or where the court is allowed to proceed in his absence.
4   MC (C & YP) Rules 1988, r 21(1).

(ii) The applicant's case
14.78   While the Rules are concerned to ensure that the juvenile and the parent know about the procedures to be followed, they do virtually nothing to help them know the substance of the applicant's case. The notice which the local authority as applicant has to serve[1] on the juvenile, the parents and other possible participants merely requires the grounds of the application to be specified. Criticism voiced by the Social Services Committee in its Report[2] has led to the Review of Child Care Law recommending a number of changes[3] designed to give the juvenile, parents and other participants some indication of the case to be answered. In addition to specifying the grounds and the reasons for making the application the notice should contain a short summary of the facts to be proved by the local authority, along the lines of the brief statement which a party has to submit in matrimonial proceedings in a magistrates' court.[4] It should also indicate the order sought and the plans which the local authority have in mind for the juvenile if

an order is made. The Review considers that this 'might lead to agreement or at least diminish the conflict'.[5] It might, as the Review points out, do so where the local authority have in mind a supervision order not a care order, but otherwise it must be questioned whether the proposal is not unduly optimistic. Parents whose conduct is impugned in care proceedings are usually reluctant to co-operate. The Review also recommends that the local authority should before the hearing serve written witness statements[6] on the juvenile, parents and other possible participants, together with copies of documents which it intends to put before the court.

1　Ante, para 14.48.
2　Paragraphs 96–98.
3　See RCCL, chapter 16.
4　See Magistrates' Courts (Matrimonial Proceedings) Rules 1980, r 3 and Forms 1 and 2.
5　Paragraphs 16.7 and 16.8.
6　Apparently this procedure is adopted in some courts in applications for discharge of orders; see RCCL, para 16.6. CFFS, para 57, has accepted the recommendations of RCCL, but with the proviso that where practicable the respondent should disclose the outline of his reasons for contesting the proceedings.

(b)　Order of evidence and speeches

14.79　The order of evidence and speeches is the same as if the proceedings were by way of complaint,[1] but is subject to the special provisions of the CYPA 1969 and the 1988 Rules relating to the parent and grandparent being parties to the proceedings, to other persons making representations and to the guardian ad litem giving evidence. The circumstances in which the parent or guardian[2] is entitled to conduct the case on behalf of the juvenile have already been noted,[3] but with the emergence of the section 32A(1) order those circumstances do not now in practice often arise. The same has to be said of the court's power,[4] where it considers it appropriate, to allow a relative or some other responsible person[5] to do so as the juvenile's friend, unless he otherwise requests. Subject to the inherent power of the court to control its proceedings,[6] the following procedure should be followed where there is a section 32A(1) order and the parent is a party. However, suggested modifications of the procedure where he is not a party are indicated.

1　See MC (C & YP) Rules 1988, r 20(2) and (3) and MC Rules 1981, r 14.
2　'Guardian' here has its wide meaning of a person having charge or control of the juvenile; see MC (C & YP) Rules 1988, r 13(2).
3　Rule 22(1), ante, para 14.57.
4　Rules 22(2). Compare r 5 in relation to criminal proceedings (ante, para 12.97) which is in rather different terms.
5　For the probable meanings of 'relative or other responsible person' see ante, para 12.100. It would not, it is suggested, be appropriate in care proceedings for a social worker who has been voluntarily supervising the juvenile and his family to conduct the case in view of the local authority's deep involvement in the proceedings.
6　See ante, para 14.71.

14.80　(1) The applicant's solicitor or other representative may, and usually does, address the court before calling his evidence. The applicant's witnesses are in the normal way subject to examination-in-chief, cross-examination and re-examination. As the 1988 Rules now recognise, it is important that the parent's solicitor (and the grandparent's where applicable) should cross-examine before the juvenile's solicitor does so, since answers to the former may be elicited which facilitate cross-examination by the juvenile's solicitor. If the parent is not a party and the rules are strictly observed, the parent's solicitor may only cross-examine on matters relating to allegations against the parent.[1]

(2) It is particularly regrettable that the 1988 Rules fail to fix the stage in the procedure when a parent, who is a party to the proceedings, is entitled to address the court and call his evidence. It is submitted that this should precede the presentation of the juvenile's case, as should the address and evidence of a grandparent who is a party. The parent (or grandparent) should have the choice to address before or after calling his evidence. Cross-examination ought first to be by the applicant's solicitor and then by the juvenile's.

(3) Attention has already been drawn to the inappropriateness of a submission of no case to answer.[2]

(4) The juvenile's solicitor has the right to address the court either before or after calling his evidence.[3] It is suggested that witnesses, who may include the guardian ad litem, should be subject first to cross-examination by the parent's solicitor (and the grandparent's solicitor) and then by the applicant's solicitor. Again, strictly the parent's solicitor may only cross-examine on matters relating to allegations against the parent, if the parent is not a party.

(5) The applicant can then adduce evidence in rebuttal of the juvenile's evidence but not to confirm the applicant's own earlier evidence.

(6) Whether or not he has already given evidence, the guardian ad litem may at this point give evidence 'relevant to the applicant's case'.[4] Even where he has already been a witness for the juvenile, there may be matters which he was never asked in examination-in-chief or cross-examination, for example, about the juvenile's emotional development, or which arose in evidence given after his own evidence.

(7) If the parent is not a party, he may then call or give evidence to meet allegations already made against him. The relevant rule[5] does not expressly state that his evidence is subject to cross-examination, but a court should invoke its inherent powers to control its proceedings and allow cross-examination, which ought, it is suggested, to be conducted first by the applicant's solicitor and then by the juvenile's.

(8) A foster parent or other person (for example, a relative) who is entitled to make representations[6] may do so either personally or through a solicitor, but he is not eligible to apply for legal aid.

(9) The parent may then make his representations,[7] if he is not a party.

(10) If the applicant's solicitor and the juvenile's solicitor are both given leave, they may make final speeches, with the former having the final word. It is, indeed, good practice for the applicant's solicitor to state at the commencement of the hearing that he wishes to make a final address to the court.

---

1 On a literal interpretation of r 18 of the 1988 Rules, where the parent is not a party, his solicitor should cross-examine at the conclusion of the evidence for the respondent and applicant — an absurd rule which means recalling the witnesses.

2 *M v Westminster City Council* [1985] FLR 325, [1985] Fam Law 93, ante, para 14.71.

3 Where there is no s 32A(1) order and the juvenile is not legally represented, the court

must tell the juvenile or the parent or other responsible person conducting the case on his behalf that he may give evidence or make a statement and call witnesses; see MC (C & YP) Rules 1988, r 24.
4   Rule 21(3).
5   Rule 18.
6   Rule 14C.
7   Rule 19; see ante, para 14.74.

(c)   Evidence[1]

14.81   Except for proceedings based on the offence condition,[2] the civil rules of evidence and standard of proof govern care proceedings. The parents and any other competent witness are all also compellable witnesses for the local authority or the juvenile. Indeed, where there is alleged abuse of the juvenile by one spouse the local authority may find itself obliged to compel the other spouse to attend[3] to give evidence to support the allegation; but the court should warn the witness that he or she is not obliged to answer any question which puts the other spouse at risk of being prosecuted for any offence against the juvenile. Part I of the Civil Evidence Act 1968, which allows exceptions to the common law rule against the admissibility of hearsay evidence, does not extend to proceedings in a magistrates' court or, apparently, to appeals therefrom to the Crown Court.[4] Thus in *Re S*[5] an out-of-court statement by the mother alleging the father's ill-treatment of the juvenile, which she refused to repeat at the hearing, was held inadmissible. With this decision must be compared that in *Humberside County Council v DPR (an infant)*,[6] where the Divisional Court held admissible a statement by a child's guardian to a probation officer, a social worker, a health visitor and a NSPCC inspector, in which he admitted ill-treating the child. The decision is usually explained as an amelioration of the strict application of the hearsay rule to proceedings involving a juvenile,[7] but it has persuasively been argued[8] that it is 'an amplification' of the common law exception to the rule against hearsay which enables evidence to be given of an admission by a party to the proceedings. A parent or guardian having, or being concerned with, the control of the juvenile is to be treated in the same way as a party. Now, of course, a parent will be a party if a section 32A order has been made.

1   For specific application of various rules of evidence to care proceedings see Hayes and Bevan, Chapter 1; Hall and Mitchell, *Child Abuse — Procedure and Evidence in Juvenile Courts*, Chapters 6–8; Dingwall and Eekelaar, *Care Proceedings*, Chapter 8. For further examination of the topic of Children and Evidence see ante, paras 10.45 et seq.
2   See post, para 14.90.
3   A witness summons can be issued (MCA 1980, s 97; CYPA 1969, s 2(6)), and, if the spouse does not answer to it, a witness warrant can be issued.
4   *R v Wood Green Crown Court, ex p P* (1982) 4 FLR 206. RCCL paras 16.30–16.33 recommends extension.
5   (1980) 1 FLR 301.
6   [1977] 3 All ER 964, [1977] 1 WLR 1251. For a similar approach in Scotland see *W v Kennedy* 1988 SLT 583.
7   See, for example, Clarke Hall and Morrison, para B [61]. See for a similar attitude the willingness to admit hearsay evidence relating to non-contentious matters in custody proceedings; *Thompson v Thompson* [1986] FLR 212, CA.
8   Hayes and Bevan, p 8.

(i) Documentary evidence

14.82   Unlike Part I of the Civil Evidence Act 1968, section 1 of the Evidence Act 1938 does extend to juvenile and other magistrates' courts and the Crown Court. Its effect is that written statements of fact made by persons, such as paediatricians, psychologists, general medical practitioners, school teachers and social workers, who have personal knowledge of the facts,[1] can be submitted and read by the court in advance of any of such persons giving oral evidence at the hearing. However, such a statement is not admissible if made by a person 'interested' in the proceedings.[2] So, a statement of the social worker who instituted the care proceedings or who has been directly involved in investigating the case is excluded.[3] There are certain statutory provisions which allow for documentary evidence without its author having to be called to give evidence. For example, as already noted, a certificate of school attendance signed by the head teacher is admissible as evidence of that attendance,[4] and a certificate of a fully registered medical practitioner, stating a juvenile's physical or mental condition, is evidence of that condition,[5] but not of the cause of the condition.

1   The court should be alert to the possibility of the statement containing hearsay evidence. It then becomes a matter of whether it will adopt a strict attitude and exclude that evidence; see Hayes and Bevan, p 10.
2   Section 1(3).
3   *R v Wood Green Crown Court, ex p P* (1982) 4 FLR 206.
4   Education Act 1944, s 95(2)(c), ante, para 14.18, note 2.
5   CYPA 1963, s 26. A certificate of a medical officer of a local education authority is similarly admissible; Education Act 1944, s 95(2)(d).

(ii) Privilege

14.83   Evidence, whether oral or documentary, may be withheld on any of three well-established grounds.

(a) Legal privilege

Information passing between the juvenile and his legal adviser or between a parent and the parent's legal adviser must not be disclosed unless the client consents. The privilege extends to communications between the legal adviser and a third party made for the purpose of prospective or pending litigation. Because of his diverse functions the guardian *ad litem* should be particularly wary about this privilege. In preparing his report he should be careful that it does not include any information that passed between him and the juvenile's solicitor in the course of preparing the juvenile's case; for example, the juvenile may have told his solicitor about his dislike for his step-father but that he does not want this mentioned in court because of fear of possible repercussions.

14.84   There is no corresponding privilege between a patient and his doctor or a client and his social worker. This may pose serious problems for the professional. In practice, the court has to balance the desirability of protecting confidences against the need to obtain evidence that is highly relevant to the furtherance of the juvenile's best interests. For example, where care proceedings are based on a 14-year-old boy being exposed to moral danger because of an alleged sexual relationship with a woman and the boy has sought advice from his doctor about treatment for venereal disease, disclosure in the boy's interest should prevail. Similarly, a social worker may have obtained vital evidence from the juvenile which he is obliged to disclose in the latter's interests even though disclosure may undermine his professional relationship with the family.

14.85 *(b) Public interest*   Some protection to the social worker is, however, afforded by another privilege, which prevents disclosure of information or of its source on the ground that to allow it would be contrary to the public interest. Its scope is further examined in Chapter 15 where the implications of the decision of the House of Lords in *D v NSPCC* are considered.[1] It means that the local authority or the NSPCC or the police can decline to disclose the identity of an informant; but the protection also extends to records kept by, for example, the local authority.[2] Whether it extends to the probation service and an adoption agency is still an open question,[3] though in principle it should.

1   [1978] AC 171, [1977] 1 All ER 589; see post, paras 15.00 to 15.00.
2   *Re D (infants)* [1970] 1 All ER 1088, [1970] 1 WLR 599 (records kept under the Boarding-Out of Children Regulations 1955); *Gaskin v Liverpool City Council* [1980] 1 WLR 1549 (case notes and records of boy in local authority care); *Re S and W (Minors)* (1982) 12 Fam Law 151 (notes of a case conference).
3   See respectively *Re M (minors)* [1987] 1 FLR 46; *R v Bournemouth Justices, ex p Rodd* [1987] 1 FLR 36.

14.86 *(c) Privilege against self-incrimination*   A party or witness may refuse to answer any question or to produce any document which would tend to expose him or his spouse to any criminal charge or penalty.[1] Its most likely application is where a parent is asked a question about his alleged ill-treatment of his child. If he is legally represented, his advocate is likely to be alert to the possibility. Where he is not represented, the court should be ready to intervene.

1   CEA 1968, s 14.

(iii) Disclosure of contents of reports
14.87   The court must arrange for copies of any written reports of a guardian ad litem, probation officer, local authority, local education authority, educational establishment or registered medical practitioner to be made available to those entitled to receive them and this should be done before the hearing wherever practicable.[1] The persons entitled are the applicant; the appropriate local authority, where it is not the applicant; the juvenile's legal representative; the parent or guardian, whether or not he is a party; any other person who is a party, for example, a grandparent by virtue of a section 32A order; the guardian ad litem; and the juvenile, unless the court directs otherwise on the ground that it appears impracticable to disclose the report to him in view of his age and understanding or undesirable to do so having regard to serious harm which he might suffer by disclosure.[2] In any case in which he is not legally represented and where for either of those reasons there has not been disclosure to the juvenile and the report has been considered without being read aloud or where the juvenile, his parent or guardian has been required to withdraw from the court in the interests of the juvenile,[3] the juvenile must be told the substance of the report concerning his character or conduct which the court considers to be material to the manner in which the case should be dealt

with, unless it is impracticable to tell him because of his age and understanding.[4] This rule is precisely the same as in criminal proceedings.[5]

The court also has a discretion to show written reports to those required to be given notice of the application in care proceedings and to those entitled to make representations to the court.[6] Occasionally, on the order of the court, a report may be disclosed to other persons, such as an independent social worker employed by a parent and whom the parent wishes to call as a witness.[7]

1   MC (C & YP) Rules 1988, r 25(1). The desirability of pre-hearing availability was stressed in *R v West Malling Juvenile Court, ex p K* [1986] 2 FLR 405, and in *R v Epsom Juvenile Court, ex p G* [1988] 1 All ER 329, [1988] 1 WLR 145.
2   Rule 25(1). In deciding whether disclosure would be harmful the court might well want to seek the advice of the guardian ad litem if one has been appointed.
3   See r 25(3)(e).
4   Rule 25(4).
5   See ante, para 12.114–12.116.
6   Rule 25(2).
7   *R v Sunderland Juvenile Court, ex p G* [1988] 2 All ER 34, [1988] 1 WLR 398, CA. But a positive case must be made out that the evidence of such a witness might assist the court to justify authorising disclosure; see ibid.

(d)   Exclusion of juvenile and parent from the court

(i) The juvenile

14.88   Except in the rare instance of a juvenile conducting his own case, the whole or part of the evidence may be given in his absence, if this is thought to be in his interests; but he must be present to hear evidence of his character or conduct.[1] This power to exclude may be necessary, for example, to avoid embarrassment when the parent's conduct is being considered on the question whether the juvenile is in need of care or control or on whether in proceedings based on section 1(2)(b) of the 1969 Act the juvenile is at risk because of the parent's sexual abuse of an elder child in respect of whom care proceedings based on section 1(2)(a) have been, or are concurrently being, brought. The practical difficulty is that the court will not be aware of the possibility of damaging or distressing evidence being adduced. It has therefore been suggested[2] that the solicitor intending to introduce it should alert the court in advance.

1   MC (C & YP) Rules 1988, r 23(1).
2   Hayes and Bevan, p 65.

(ii) The parent

14.89   Conversely, the parent may in special circumstances be required to withdraw while the juvenile is giving evidence or making a statement, although, should the juvenile make any allegations against him, he must be told the substance of them[1] and he is then entitled to meet them by giving or calling evidence.[2] He should therefore be told this in advance. Here, too, it would be wise for the solicitor to inform the court that its power to exclude may be appropriate. Indeed, in care proceedings generally, where there are allegations against the parent — and the principle equally applies to allegations against a juvenile[3] — he must be given sufficient opportunity to prepare his answer to them; otherwise it is a breach of natural justice and judicial review will lie.[4] The local authority and the guardian ad litem have a duty to give advance disclosure of their case either by sending a detailed letter to the parents' solicitors or by sending copies of their witnesses' statements. There should also be early delivery of reports.[5] The power to exclude the parent or a guardian has been extended to a grandparent or any other person entitled to make representations,[6] and the above comments equally apply in respect of them.

1 Rule 23(2).
2 In accordance with r 18.
3 For example where proceedings are based on his being exposed to moral danger because of his conduct.
4 *R v West Malling Juvenile Court, ex p K* [1986] 2 FLR 405 (particulars of allegations against parent only given to him, in the form of reports, on morning of hearing, in spite of earlier request by his solicitors for them. Held: parent should have been allowed an adjournment).
5 See MC (C & YP) Rules r 25(1), ante, para 14.87.
6 See r 23(2).

(e) The offence condition

14.90 When a juvenile is brought before the court under section 1 for an alleged offence, and the nature of the proceedings is explained to him, it must be made clear that a finding of guilt does not mean criminal liability. Nevertheless, the first stage in the procedure then follows the same lines as that in criminal proceedings, depending upon whether there is a plea of guilty or not guilty,[1] with the same burden of proof and rules of evidence applicable.[2] Moreover, there is no power as in other care proceedings to require a parent to withdraw while the juvenile gives evidence or makes a statement,[3] and the juvenile must be present when evidence that the offence condition is satisfied is being adduced.[4] Once it is decided whether or not the offence condition is satisfied the juvenile must be informed of the finding,[5] and, if it is satisfied, the court must then proceed to consider in accordance with the civil burden of proof whether he is in need of care or control, as it would do if the care proceedings were based on one of the other primary conditions.

1 Ante, paras 12.95 et seq, and MC (C & YP) Rules 1988, r 21(2) (a)–(c).
2 CYPA 1969, s 3(1) and (3).
3 See MC (C & YP) Rules 1988, r 21(2)(c).
4 See the proviso to r 23(1).
5 Rule 21(2)(d).

V INQUIRIES AND REPORTS

14.91 In deciding how to deal with the juvenile once it is satisfied that the applicant's case has been proved, the court will proceed to consider reports about him, his background and his antecedents.[1] Where a guardian ad litem has been appointed, his written report will be central to these matters, and he may, if he wishes, supplement it by oral representations to the court. Apart from his report, the main responsibility for providing the necessary information falls upon the local authority[2] who have brought the care proceedings or who, in the case of the applicant being the NSPCC or the police, were notified that proceedings were being brought. As in criminal proceedings, they must investigate, and report on, the home surroundings, school record, health and medical history, and character and general conduct of the juvenile, unless they consider it unnecessary.[3] Rarely, if ever, will it be unnecessary in care proceedings. They are, however, relieved of the obligation where the juvenile has reached the age of 13[4] and, by a direction of justices or a probation and after-care committee, local arrangements are in force for information with respect to his home surroundings to be furnished to the court by a probation officer.[5] Nevertheless, even in areas where such arrangements exist it may instead be arranged that in the case of care proceedings brought by a local authority (as opposed to the NSPCC or the police) the authority will investigate instead of a probation officer, unless the latter is expressly requested to do so by the court. This is a sensible and realistic approach, since the local authority will already have conducted detailed investigation in preparing its case for an application under section 1 of the 1969 Act. Apart from the normal duty of the local authority to investigate, the court may request it to make inquiries, whether it has already done so or not.[6]

1 See MC (C & YP) Rules 1988, r 25; and see ante, para 14.87.
2 Or the local education authority where the proceedings are based on s 1(2)(e) of CYPA 1969.
3 CYPA 1969, s 9(1), as supplemented by MC (C & YP) Rules 1988, r 25(3)(b).
4 CYPA 1969 (Transitional Modifications of Part I) Order 1970, art 5.
5 CYPA 1969, s 34(3); and see ante, para 12.105, note 4.
6 Ibid, s 9(2).

14.92 If it is thought desirable the court may adjourn the case for further inquiries to be made,[1] but in care proceedings this is unlikely, because pre-trial inquiries will have been essential in order that oral evidence may be adduced to prove one of the primary conditions and the need for care or control, and the subsequent information in the local authority report or a medical report (and, if need be, an oral statement in support) which is presented to the court in deciding upon how to deal with the juvenile may be simply a 'follow-up' of that evidence.[2]

1 MC (C & YP) Rules 1988, r 25(3)(c).
2 Watson: *The Juvenile Court — 1970 Onward*, p 39. In the case of the offence condition, evidence of background and antecedents will be necessary to satisfy the condition for need for care or control, but will only be admissible after proof of the offence.

14.93 It has already been noted[1] that the common law excluding hearsay evidence applies, with some qualification, to the first stage in care proceedings, ie until one of the primary conditions and the general condition are proved. But, when the court comes to decide what order, if any, it should make, it usually takes note of hearsay statements contained in a social inquiry report or the report of the guardian ad litem. This tolerance to allow such hearsay must not, however, be construed as a licence to reporters to make use of it indiscriminately, otherwise the reliability of a report may be put into question.

1 Ante, para 14.81.

VI   ADJOURNMENTS AND INTERIM ORDERS

14.94   An adjournment may be ordered before or during the hearing of the application under section 1 of the 1969 Act, and when so ordering the court has the choice either of then fixing the date, time and place for the resumed hearing or leaving those matters to be determined later by the court, except that if it makes an interim order it must then set a date for the resumption.[1] Notice of the adjourned hearing must be given to the parties and those entitled[2] to make representations to the court.

1   MC (C & YP) Rules 1988, r 20(1). RCCL, para 17.19 recommends that the date of resumption should always be fixed when the court adjourns.
2   Under r 19.

1   Interim orders[1]

14.95   Where adjournment is ordered the court may and frequently does make an interim order placing the juvenile in the care of a local authority for a specified period not exceeding 28 days.[2] It may wish to do so after it has found the relevant primary condition and the general condition in section 1 of the 1969 Act proved, in order to obtain a further report from the local authority or the guardian ad litem or occasionally a medical report before deciding what order, if any, to make.[3] It may feel that without that information it would be unwise to allow the juvenile to return home, even though it has that possibility in mind. In such circumstances an interim order would be appropriate, but it is very unlikely that more than one would be needed.

1   See Farmer and Parker, *A Study of Interim Care Orders* (1985), published by the University of Bristol.
2   CYPA 1969, s 20(1).
3   See s 2(10) and MC (C & YP) Rules 1988, r 25(3)(c).

14.96   Different considerations apply before the case is proved. Interim orders are most likely before the hearing in those cases where the juvenile has been the subject of a place of safety order, because either he has been, or is threatened to be, the victim of alleged abuse.[1] When he is brought before the court at the end of the period of the place of safety order, it is in most cases unlikely that the local authority is ready to proceed with the hearing of its application under section 1. Even if it is, the juvenile and/or the parent and their legal representatives may well not be ready to do so, although the application for the interim order will afford them the opportunity to challenge the evidence of the local authority in support of the order, and, where a section 32A(1) order[2] is made and the appointment of a guardian ad litem is ordered, the appointment may take up to six weeks or more and then at least a further six weeks may be needed for the guardian to complete his investigations.[3] So long as the present shortage in the number of guardians ad litem available continues delays seem inevitable. All this means that in section 32A(1) cases it may be necessary to make at least three successive interim orders,[4] each of the 28-day maximum. But the delay is likely to be even longer where criminal proceedings are to be commenced against the person alleged to have abused the child. The Home Office has advised that, where in those circumstances the parent has been committed for trial and the juvenile court has decided to adjourn the care proceedings pending the outcome of the trial, the clerk to the juvenile court should notify the Crown Court so that efforts can be made to expedite the hearing of the case against the parent.[5] It has, however, further advised[6] that the care proceedings should not be adjourned automatically where a parent has been committed for trial. The Circular offers the following alternative advice:

> 'Where there is no reason for believing that the proceedings in the juvenile court are likely to prejudice the trial in the adult court consideration should be given to allowing the care proceedings to proceed. It is not possible to give detailed guidance on all the circumstances in which it would be appropriate to hear an application in care proceedings without awaiting the result of the parent's trial — each case should be considered on its merits — but there would normally for example be no need to delay the hearing in cases where the court is satisfied that the accused intend to pleads guilty and that there will be no issue as to the facts.'

It is suggested that the advice offered by both Circulars is far too cautious. It will not sufficiently influence juvenile courts to avoid delay and continue with the care proceedings: it is exceptional for courts to do so. It pays insufficient attention to the fact that the issues, the parties and the burden of proof are different in criminal and care proceedings, and it largely assumes that the trial of a defendant is more important than the early determination of a juvenile's welfare.[7] The recommendations on expediting the criminal proceedings do not refer to expedition of the committal proceedings, and they leave too much discretion to the Chief Clerks of the Crown Court to arrange the lists in cases where juveniles are the alleged victims. As it is, by the time committal proceedings and the subsequent trial have been completed there may have been at least five interim orders made. Further delay is sometimes caused in cases (for example, alleged incest by a father) where the consent of the Director of Public Prosecutions is required. The problem of rehabilitation of the juvenile with his family if the local authority application should fail or if, even though its case is proved, a care order should not be made, will be made all the more difficult by the protracted period of care. What, therefore, is needed is the provision of Rules and not mere advice to ensure expedition of the criminal proceedings.[8] Committal proceedings should be completed not later than one month after the accused has been charged with the offence, unless the prosecution or the defence can exceptionally show specific good cause for an extension of the period, for example, where there is need for expert medical opinion on the cause of injury to the juvenile; and similarly trial should be listed for a date no more than one month after committal, unless good cause for extension is shown. The increase in the incidence of child abuse and in the consequent number of prosecutions makes reform along these lines all the more urgent.[9] A pre-trial review, which the Review of Child Care Law recommends for all care proceedings, would also help in ironing out interlocking problems arising in care and criminal proceedings. More immediately encouraging is the recent stance of the courts. In *R v Exeter Juvenile Court, ex p H; R v Waltham Forest Juvenile Court, ex p B*[10] Sir Stephen Brown, P, stated that in deciding whether to adjourn the care proceedings the guiding principle is the paramountcy of the juvenile's welfare and delay should be avoided.[11]

If adjournment is granted, it is still open to the local authority to turn to wardship.[12]

1 The power to make an interim order while the juvenile is detained in a place of safety is conferred by s 28(6) of CYPA 1969. Application can be made to a juvenile court or a justice. If the interim order is made by a court, the period begins when the order is made: if made by a justice, with the date when the juvenile was first in legal custody (s 20(1)).
2 Ante, para 14.59.
3 For this reason RCCL, para 17.17 recommends, and CCFS accepts (para 61) that an interim order should be for a period of up to eight weeks, subject to the court fixing the date of the hearing when it makes the order and subject to power to extend the period up to a maximum of 14 days.
4 The power to make more than one interim order is given by CYPA 1969, s 22(3).
5 See HOC No 88/1972.
6 HOC No 84/1982.
7 For similar criticism see Clarke Hall and Morrison, para B [46]. This cautious approach compares sharply with the policy of the Court of Appeal in custody cases to expedite proceedings; see for example, *Ridgeway v Ridgeway* [1986] Fam Law 363, CA.
8 The Jasmine Beckford Report, p 4, recommends that 'in future in all child abuse prosecutions involving children in care of a local authority, where the public is almost certain to express disquiet about the handling of the case by social services and other professional people, the criminal trial should, other than for exceptional reasons, take place within three to four months of the homicidal event, and certainly not beyond six months'. But (a) why limit the rule to such kinds of cases and (b) is the period not too long?
9 Surprisingly, RCCL has little to say on this subject, but does make one helpful suggestion, namely, that the parent's right to refuse to answer questions in care proceedings because his answers might incriminate him should be removed but with corresponding protection given to him in the criminal proceedings (para 17.27). This recommendation could further persuade courts not to adjourn the care proceedings. But it would need careful statutory implementation, especially in relation to information which the parent or any person who is a prospective prosecution witness has given to the guardian ad litem; see Young, (1986) 83 Law Soc Gaz 2091 at p 2093.
10 (1988) Times, 19 February.
11 See *R v Inner London Juvenile Court, ex p G* [1988] 2 FLR 58, where the father, who was the subject of criminal proceedings in respect of the juvenile, was refused an adjournment which otherwise would have meant a further delay of four months in the care proceedings.
12 See *Re P (a minor)* [1987] 2 FLR 467.

14.97   An interim order cannot be made unless the juvenile either (a) is present before the court or justice, or (b) is under five or cannot be present because of illness or accident.[1] The order must require the juvenile to be brought before the court on the expiration of the order[2] or such earlier time as the court requires, except that it may direct that the juvenile is not to be brought before it at the expiration of the order if the juvenile is under five or if legally represented or is incapacitated by illness or accident.[3] Such a direction is likely where it is proposed that a further interim order be made.[4]

1 CYPA 1969, s 22(1).
2 If the order is for 28 days, the juvenile must be brought before the court on the 28th day; *R v Birmingham Juvenile Court, ex p P and S* [1984] 1 All ER 393, [1984] FLR 343.
3 Section 22(2), as amended by HASSASSAA 1983, Sch 2, para 14.
4 As in *Northamptonshire County Council v H* [1988] QB 205, [1988] 1 All ER 598, where such a direction was made in respect of a six-year-old girl who was legally represented.

14.98   Courts vary considerably in the amount of evidence they require in order to be satisfied that the circumstances justify the making of an interim order.[1] Given its consequence, namely, that the juvenile will be in the care of the local authority and almost certainly be separated from his parents and his home, it is surprising that there are no statutory criteria imposed.[2] Publicity, such as that surrounding the alleged sexual abuse cases in Cleveland in 1987, is likely to turn interim order hearings increasingly into more contested proceedings. Most courts in practice will want some evidence that a primary condition in section 1 of the 1969 Act applies, but may be satisfied with that of a social worker who has been involved in the removal of the child to a place of safety or who has seen the child since his removal. It is, however, not unknown for the court to act on hearsay evidence of a social worker, and where the juvenile is legally represented his solicitor will often want an adjournment to prepare his client's case and is therefore unlikely to object to an interim order.[3] Where the application for an interim order is opposed by the parent who wishes to challenge any allegations made against him, the applicant local authority must call evidence. The parent can then cross-examine so as to refute the allegations, call evidence and make representations to the court.[4] Nevertheless, the interlocutory nature of an interim order should be recognised and every effort made to restrict the cross-examination and the evidence to the essential issues and to avoid a dress rehearsal of the hearing.[5] If the application is not opposed, the court is not obliged to receive evidence but must still have sufficient material to enable it to exercise its judicial discretion whether or not to make an interim order.[6]

Where there are successive applications for interim orders the court cannot refuse to hear evidence at the hearing of each application. It must not rubber stamp the first interim order but it should hear the parents and take into account (a) that care proceedings are intended to be dealt with expeditiously, so that generally, if the parents are ready to proceed, the applicant local authority ought also to be ready; (b) that usually it is in the juvenile's interests that a decision about the future be made as soon as possible; (c) that delay may prejudice the parents' as well as the child's interests; and that (d) the only decision the previous juvenile court made[7] was that it was not in a position to decide what order, if any, ought to be made. That is the only reason why an interim order was made.[8]

1   See Jones, *Interim Care Orders*, (1984) 148 JPN 246; Bean, *Interim Care Orders* (1987) 84 Law Soc Gaz 1382.
2   CCFS, para 61 (following RCCL paras 17.8 and 17.9) recommends that the local authority should satisfy the court that there is reasonable cause to believe that there is harm or likely harm to the child attributable to the absence of a reasonable standard of parental care or adequate control but also that the court should be satisfied that detention or removal of the juvenile is necessary in order to safeguard his welfare during the interim period.
3   RCCL, para 17.15, recommends that the court should always examine evidence of the criteria being satisfied and should not be entitled to rely on the parents' agreement to an interim order.
4   *R v Birmingham City Juvenile Court, ex p Birmingham City Council* [1988] 1 All ER 683, [1988] 1 WLR 337, CA, approving *R v Croydon Juvenile Court, ex p N* [1987] 1 FLR 252.
5   Ibid. But see the comment above concerning the risk of increased contested applications for interim orders.
6   *R v Croydon Juvenile Court ex p N*, supra.
7   Ie under s 2(10) of CYPA 1969.

8 Per Ewbank J in *R v Birmingham Juvenile Court, ex p P and S* [1984] 1 All ER 393, [1984] FLR 343.

14.99 The making of an interim order is entirely within the discretion of the juvenile court, and the High Court will not interfere with the exercise of that discretion unless it is shown that the juvenile court has acted mistakenly on the facts or on the basis of some wrong principle,[1] or if the justices were plainly wrong.[2] If it decides to make an order, it cannot impose conditions, for example, that the juvenile should live with a relative during the period of the order.[3] That is a matter for the local authority, but the court may be influenced in the exercise of its discretion if the local authority is willing to give an undertaking about where the juvenile is to live.[4]

1 *Re Jarvis (minors)* [1984] FLR 350.
2 *R v Birmingham Juvenile Court, ex P and S* [1984] 1 All ER 393, [1984] FLR 343.
3 RCCL, paras 17.28–17.30, recommends that as alternatives to an interim care order, the court should be able to make an interim supervision order or an interim custody order granting custody to a parent or spouse. It is submitted that the latter order should also be allowed in favour of other persons.
4 See ibid.

2 Interim hospital order

14.100 Where there is evidence that the juvenile is suffering from mental illness, mental impairment or psychopathic disorder and there is reason to suppose that it may be appropriate for a hospital order to be finally made, the juvenile court may make an interim hospital order instead of an interim care order.[1] The scope of the order has already been examined in relation to criminal proceedings.[2]

1 CYPA 1969, s 2(10)(b).
2 See ante, para 13.112

3 Adjournments, interim orders and truancy cases

14.101–14.102 In what is now widely known as 'the Leeds system' it has long been the practice for juvenile courts in the Leeds area to make extensive use of the court's power to adjourn as a means of trying to get truanting juveniles back to school.[1] How far courts in other areas have adopted the same or a similar system is unknown. Its essence is that the court over a period of some six months repeatedly adjourns the hearing for monthly or shorter periods, and eventually, if there is no satisfactory improvement in attendance, makes an interim or full care order. Attendance for 70 per cent of the time since the last appearance in court is the criterion for determining satisfactory improvement. It is submitted that this procedure is not only irregular but unlawful. It misconceives the purposes of the power to adjourn in care proceedings. The power may be exercised before the case is proved in order to allow the applicant or the juvenile or the parent[2] to complete the preparation of their respective cases or where delay in hearing the application is unavoidable because of, for example, illness of a party or witness. But, when a juvenile is brought before the court by virtue of an application under section 1(2)(e) of the 1969 Act and the court is presented with the evidence that he has been regularly absent from school over a protracted period, clearly paragraph (e) is satisfied in that he is not receiving efficient full-time education,[3] and, in view of *Re S (a minor) (Care order: Education)*,[4] it must be presumed that the general condition that he is in need of care or control is satisfied. With that conclusion the only justification for adjournment will be to obtain a further report on the juvenile to enable the court to decide what order, if any, to make, the choice in reality being between a supervision order and a care order. But no more than one, or at most two, adjournments will be needed for that purpose. Once the case has been proved in accordance with section 1, it does not lie within the jurisdiction of the court to use its power to adjourn even on one occasion, let alone several, for the quite different purpose of encouraging the juvenile to improve his attendance record before it decides how to deal with him. Moreover, once the case is proved, it can only use its power to make an interim order where it adjourns for reports or assessment. In this regard the use of that order under the Leeds system for the purpose of the juvenile's residing for three weeks in a residential observation and assessment centre is in itself proper: it is the reliance on the preceding successive adjournments, with the conditions in section 1 already satisfied, that is unlawful. If the court does not need further reports once those conditions have been proved, it can only make one of the orders permitted by that section,[5] and that expressly excludes an interim order.

1 See I Berg, A Goodwin, R Hullin and R McGuire, *The effect of two varieties of the adjournment procedure on truancy* (1983) 23 Brit J of Criminol 150, and for critical comments thereon see JD Pratt, *Folk lore and fact in truancy research. Some critical comments on recent developments*, ibid, at p 336. See also R Grimshaw and J Pratt, *Delayed Justice in a Juvenile Court: A Research Note*, [1984] JSWL 104 and Pratt and Grimshaw, *An Aspect of 'Welfare Justice': Truancy and the Juvenile Court*, [1985] JSWL 257; Blyth and Milner, *Juvenile Court and non-attendance at school*, 151 JPN 854, and for a Reply see Hullin, 152 JPN 247.
2 Although the parent is not, in the absence of a s 32A order (an order which is unlikely in truancy cases), a party to the proceedings, proper opportunity should be given to him to meet any allegations that are being made against him; see ante, para 14.71.
3 Unless it is provided otherwise than at school.
4 [1978] QB 120; sub nom *Re DJMS* [1977] 3 All ER 582, ante, para 14.24.
5 Sub-s (3).

14.103 Criticism of the Leeds system on these legal grounds does not seek to deny its considerable beneficial results in improving school attendance. What is needed is a new statutory power. It is submitted that, when the juvenile is first brought before the court for non-attendance, the court should immediately direct itself to determining whether the conditions in section 1 have been satisfied, and, if so, should be able to make what might be called an interim education order for a maximum period of 28 days with four as the maximum number of successive orders. Allowing for school holidays, that would in effect enable the local education authority and the court to monitor the juvenile's attendance over a school term. If there is not satisfactory progress over that period, the court should then invoke its power to make a supervision order or a care order.

VII   ORDERS

1   Duty to explain the proposed order and its effect

14.104   After inquiries and reports have been completed the court must in simple language tell the juvenile, anyone conducting the case on his behalf and his parent or guardian (if present) of the way in which it proposes to deal with the case, except that it does not inform the juvenile where it considers disclosure undesirable or, having regard to his age and understanding, impracticable. Those informed are then allowed to make representations.[1]

1   MC (C & YP) Rules 1988, r 27(1). A duty to disclose also arises if the case is to be remitted to another court.

14.105   On making an order the court must explain to the juvenile in simple language its general nature and effect, unless it appears impracticable to do so because of his age and understanding.[1] As with criminal proceedings,[2] there is the serious omission that the rules do not expressly require information to be given about the right to apply for discharge or variation of supervision orders or care orders. The court should always refer to the matter. Where the order is one requiring the parent or guardian to enter into a recognisance there is no obligation to explain this to the juvenile, if it is considered undesirable. In every case, however, the court must give an explanation to the parent or guardian, if present.

1   Rule 27(2).
2   Ante, para 13.05.

2   The welfare of the juvenile

14.106   Section 44(1) of the Children and Young Persons Act 1933 provides:[1]

> Every court in dealing with a child or young person who is brought before it, either as an offender or otherwise, shall have regard to the welfare of the child or young person and shall in a proper case take steps for removing him from undesirable surroundings and for securing that proper provision is made for his education and training.

Whatever the uncertainty may be about the scope of this provision in relation to criminal cases and in particular about the extent to which account should be taken of the public interest,[2] the nature of the care jurisdiction, as defined by section 1 of the Children and Young Persons Act 1969, is such that once the conditions prescribed by the section have been proved the juvenile's welfare should not merely be taken into account but should be the paramount, indeed the exclusive, consideration in deciding what order, if any, should be made in respect of him.[3]

Undoubtedly in practice the court does seek to determine what is in the child's best interest, and there is now strong judicial opinion to support that approach.[4] However, there is still no unequivocal authority that section 1 of the Guardianship of Minors Act 1971, with its principle that the child's welfare is paramount, extends to care proceedings on the basis that they relate to the 'legal custody and upbringing' of a child.[5]

1   As amended by CYPA 1969, s 72(4) and Sch 6.
2   See ante, paras 13.117–13.120.
3   Arguably, where the proceedings are based on the offence condition the public interest may be taken into account; see, for example, infra para 14.108, for the power to order the juvenile to enter into a recognisance to keep the peace or be of good behaviour. On the other hand, one of the purposes of the offence condition was to take the juvenile out of the ambit of the consequences of criminality and treat him as a deprived child, needing care or control.
4   See Lord Wilberforce and Lord Roskill in *A v Liverpool City Council* [1982] AC 363 at 372 and 379, [1981] 2 All ER 385 at 388 and 393, approving a dictum of Ormrod LJ to that effect in *Re H (a minor) (wardship: jurisdiction)* [1978] Fam 65 at 77, [1978] 2 All ER 903 at 910. See Ormrod LJ to similar effect in *Re C* (1979) 2 FLR 62 at 65.
5   RCCL, para 15.7 states: '. . . in care proceedings it appears that section 1 . . . applies.'

14.107   The orders which may be made under section 1 of the Children and Young Persons Act 1969 are:[1]

(a)   an order requiring the parent or guardian to enter into a recognisance to take proper care of the juvenile and exercise proper control over him; or
(b)   a supervision order; or
(c)   a care order (other than an interim order); or
(d)   a hospital order within the meaning of Part III of the Mental Health Act 1983; or
(e)   a guardianship order within the meaning of that Act

The court has the option to make none of them.[2] That may, occasionally at least, be the appropriate decision, for example, where a relative is able and ready to take care of the juvenile and agrees to do so on the basis of voluntary supervision of the juvenile by the local authority. Sometimes parents state that they are ready to accept voluntary supervision. The court should scrutinise their intentions closely before acceding to the request not to make an order, because of the risk that they will later withdraw their agreement. In those circumstances, if the court is not minded to make a care order, it should make a supervision order and not leave the matter to voluntary supervision. If the parents do not then satisfactorily co-operate in the supervision of the juvenile, the local authority can seek the substitution of a care order for the supervision order.

1   Sub-s (3). There is no power to order costs; *R v Salisbury and Tisbury and Mere Combined Juvenile Court, ex p Ball* (1985) 149 JP 346, [1986] 1 FLR 1.
2   'May if it thinks fit make such an order' (s 1(2)).

14.108   Save that a care order and a hospital order may be combined,[1] not more than one of the above may be made; and, if the court makes an order of a kind already in force in respect of the juvenile it may discharge the earlier one, unless it is a hospital or guardianship order.[2] However, in the rare case where the offence condition is invoked and satisfied certain other orders which are similarly available in criminal proceedings may be made. Thus, whether or not the court makes an order under section 1, it can order the payment of compensation. Payment must be made by the parent or guardian, unless, as in criminal cases,[3] the parent or guardian cannot be found or it would be unreasonable to make an order for payment, having regard to the circumstances of the case.[4] Except where the parent or guardian has failed to comply with a request to attend the court, no order is to be made without giving him an opportunity of being heard.[5] He has a right of appeal to the Crown Court against any order made against him.[6] In an 'offence condition' case there is also power to order the juvenile, providing he is a young person and consents, to enter into a recognisance for an amount not exceeding £50 and for a period not exceeding a year to keep the peace or be of good behaviour. But such an order is permissible only if an order under section 1 of the 1969 Act is not made,[7] and that will rarely happen.

1   The combination may be desirable to ensure that the juvenile has someone to visit him in hospital. *Semble*, so far as concerns the place of accommodation, the hospital order prevails over the care order; see Home Office Guide to Part I of the 1969 Act, para 53.
2   CYPA 1969, s 1(4).
3   See ante, para 13.20; and for the amount of compensation see ibid, para 13.18.
4   CYPA 1969, s 3(6) as substituted by CJA 1982, s 27.
5   Section 3(6A) , as inserted by CJA 1982, s 27.
6   Section 3(8).
7   Section 3(7). The order under the sub-section is deemed to be an order under s 1, but without a right of appeal to the Crown Court.

(a)   Recognisance of the parent

14.109   In the same terms as the corresponding order in criminal proceedings,[1] the court may, with his or her consent, require the parent or guardian to enter into a recognisance to take proper care of the juvenile and exercise proper control over him.[2] Since one of the purposes underlying the Children and Young Persons Act 1969 is to encourage the family to assume responsibility for the juvenile rather than to remove him from them, it is disappointing to find that courts are reluctant to invoke the order in less serious cases. Clearly its efficacy depends upon the co-operation of the parents, but courts could be readier to test it, especially in proceedings based under section 1(2)(e) on the truancy of the juvenile. It is also regrettable that the order cannot be combined with a supervision order.

1   See ante, para 13.13.
2   CYPA 1969, ss 1(3)(a) and (5)(a) and 2(13).

(b)   Supervision order

14.110   The supervision order has already been fully examined in relation to criminal proceedings.[1] Most of the provisions applicable to it in those proceedings, including the power to vary or discharge an order, equally apply to the supervision order made in care proceedings[2] or when such an order is made on discharging a care order;[3] but there are important differences. An order in care proceedings cannot extend beyond the juvenile's 18th birthday. It cannot include provision for intermediate treatment (IT) in terms stipulated by the court but only IT in terms which authorise the supervisor to give the juvenile directions.[4] Nor do the statutory provisions relating to night restrictions requirements or a requirement that the supervisee refrain from participating in specified activities apply.[5] For breach of a supervision order made in care proceedings the only possibilities are a variation of the terms of the order or substitution of a care order or even simply discharge of the supervision order. As in criminal proceedings[6] the power to order variation or discharge is governed by the juvenile's need for care or control,[7] but it has been recommended that the test should be solely the best interests of the juvenile.[8]

1 Ante, paras 13.37 et seq.
2 Under CYPA 1969, s 1(3)(b).
3 Section 21(2).
4 For the difference between stipulated IT and delegated IT see ante, paras 13.51 to 13.55; and see Gibson, *Intermediate Treatment* (1985) 82 Law Soc Gaz 1241.
5 Ibid, paras 13.57 and 13.58.
6 Ibid, para 13.62.
7 CYPA 1969, s 16(6)(a).
8 RCCL para 18.19.

14.111 Juvenile courts are much less inclined in care proceedings to make a supervision order than a care order.[1] To encourage use of it the Review of Child Care Law recommends that the order should also extend to the supervision of the parent or other person having actual custody of the child, particularly in circumstances where, if a care order were made, the local authority would be returning the juvenile home on trial. The court should be able to include such requirements as the parent allowing the supervisor access to the juvenile in the home or complying with a direction to attend with the juvenile at clinics, day centres and other places where the parent as well as the juvenile is expected to participate in activities.[2] Welcome though these proposals are, they do not go to the heart of the problem. Courts' disillusionment with the effectiveness of the order will persist until adequate resources, both in personnel and facilities, are provided. Unhappily there are far too many instances of inadequate supervision, and, while some of the proposals, such as allowing access, will facilitate the work of the supervisor, others, for example those requiring the parent to be involved in activities, will increase the supervisor's responsibilities.

1 In 1983 there were over two care orders made for every one supervision order; see RCCL, para 18.5.
2 See paras 18.6 to 18.13.

(c) Care order

14.112 The nature, scope and effects of a care order are fully examined in Chapter 15.

(d) Hospital and guardianship orders

14.113 These orders have already been examined in connection with the juvenile offender.[1] The only point for present note is that, whereas in criminal proceedings a care order may be combined with a hospital order or a guardianship order, in care proceedings it may only be combined with a hospital order. The distinction would appear to be academic. Since the guardian is the local social services authority or a person approved by them, no practical purpose would be served in additionally making a care order.

1 Ante, paras 13.105 to 13.112.

VIII APPEALS[1]

1 Appeal by the juvenile or the parent

14.114 A juvenile may, within 21 days of the decision of the juvenile court,[2] appeal to the Crown Court against an order made in care proceedings.[3] Appeal is by way of a rehearing before a judge and two justices. Where a separate representation order has been made under section 32A of the 1969 Act and a guardian ad litem appointed,[4] the guardian must consider, with the juvenile's solicitor, whether to appeal and, if so, to ensure that notice of appeal is given on behalf of the juvenile.[5] Where there is a section 32A order the parent as a party is entitled to appeal in his own right,[6] but otherwise, including the case where the juvenile was legally represented in the juvenile court but no separate representation order was made,[7] he has the power/responsibility to do so,[8] and where he has it may well be that the appeal is motivated by the parent's own disappointment over the decision. Where the juvenile court finds the offence condition satisfied but makes no order the juvenile can appeal against the finding. This right of appeal equally applies where one court has found that condition proved and has remitted the case to another court which decides not to make an order.[9] A parent who is ordered to pay compensation when the offence condition is proved has himself a right of appeal, as has the juvenile if he is ordered to do so.[10] No appeal lies, either at the instance of the juvenile or of his parent against an order requiring the latter to enter into a recognisance to take proper care and exercise proper control over the juvenile, the reason being that no order could have been made without the consent of the parent. For the same reason there is no right of appeal by a juvenile against an order, made in proceedings based on the offence condition, that he enter into a recognisance to keep the peace or be of good behaviour.[11] As in proceedings under section 1 of the 1969 Act legal aid is available to the juvenile who is appealing against the juvenile court's finding and any order made or only against the order,[12] which in practice means applying for a care order to be substituted by a supervision order. Where there is a separate representation order, the parent is also similarly eligible to apply for legal aid.[13] But neither of them may apply for it in respect of the appeals, mentioned above, which are additionally allowed in connection with the offence condition. Application for legal aid should be made to the juvenile court and then, if refused, to the Crown Court.

---

1 For judicial review and other possibilities see post, paras 15.127.
2 Crown Court Rules 1971, SI 1971/2192, r 7. Notice of appeal must be given in writing to the clerk to the juvenile court. Though not statutorily required, the notice should state the grounds of appeal. The Crown Court may extend the 21-day period, but the grounds for seeking extension must be stated.
3 CYPA 1969, s 2(12).
4 Ante, paras 14.59 to 14.62.
5 MC (C & YP) Rules 1988, r 16(7). The decision to appeal is one for the guardian ad litem to make, unless the solicitor considers, after taking into account the guardian's views, that the juvenile wishes to give instructions which conflict with those of the guardian and that he is able, having regard to his age and understanding, to give such instructions on his own behalf.
6 CYPA 1969, s 2(12), as amended by CYP(A)A 1986, s 2(1). For criticism of the delay in implementing the 1986 Act see Latey J in *R v Newcastle City Juvenile Court, ex p S* (1987) Times, 21 December.

7 *Southwark London Borough Council v C (a minor)* [1982] 2 All ER 636, [1982] 1 WLR 826, DC.

8 *B v Gloucestershire County Council* [1980] 2 All ER 746. The solicitor representing the child must consider whether to serve notice of appeal; see *R v Plymouth Juvenile Court, ex p F* [1987] 1 FLR 169.

9 CYPA 1969, s 3(8).

10 See ibid.

11 Section 3(7).

12 Legal Aid Act 1974, s 28(6).

13 Section 28(6A).

14.115   The Crown Court may confirm or reverse the decision of the juvenile court or substitute another order or, exceptionally, remit the case to the juvenile court with a direction on how that court should dispose of it. There is no right of appeal from the decision of the Crown Court, but the juvenile may apply for it to state a case for the opinion of the High Court on the ground that the decision is wrong in law or in excess of jurisdiction.[1] Instead of appealing to the Crown Court, the juvenile as a party may ask the juvenile court to state a case for the High Court on either of those grounds. This latter right may also be exercised by any person aggrieved by the decision of the juvenile court.[2] That is likely to be a parent or guardian. In accordance with general rules appeal lies from the Divisional Court to the Court of Appeal (Civil Division) and thence to the House of Lords or direct from the Divisional Court on a point of law of general public importance.

1   Courts Act 1971, s 10.

2   MCA 1980, s 111.

2   Appeal, by the local authority

14.116   Where the juvenile court has made a care order (other than an interim order) the local authority to whose care the juvenile is thereby committed may within three months of the date of the order appeal to the Crown Court against it on the ground that at that date the juvenile resided in the area of another local authority and should therefore have been committed to the care of that authority.[1] The appellant authority must give the other authority notice of its intention to appeal. The juvenile is not a party to the appeal and has no right to claim legal aid so as to be represented.

A local authority also has the right, like the child, to ask the juvenile court or the Crown Court on appeal to state a case to the Divisional Court, with the same rights of further appeal to the Court of Appeal and the House of Lords, as already indicated. However, there is no right to appeal against a refusal by the juvenile court to make an order, a defect which has sometimes led local authorities to eschew care proceedings and resort to wardship.

1   CYPA 1969, s 21(5).

CHAPTER 15
Children in the care of local authorities[1]

I INTRODUCTION

15.01 Before 1948 children deprived of a normal home-life were dealt with under a variety of statutes, depending upon the reason for the deprivation.[2] The largest group were the destitute children, cared for either, as part of the Poor Law, by local authorities under the general control of the Ministry of Health or by voluntary organisations who where subject to inspection by that Ministry or, in some cases, the Home Office. Children under the age of nine could be fostered for reward and were then supervised by local authorities, also under the direction of the Ministry. By virtue of the Children and Young Persons Act 1933 juveniles could be committed to the care of a local authority or sent to approved schools, and, finally, children who were physically or mentally handicapped could be placed in local authority or voluntary institutions inspected by the Board of Control or the Ministry of Education.

1 For general reference see Bromley, Chapter 14; Cretney, Chapter 19; Hoggett, Chapter 9; Hoggett and Pearl, Chapter 14; Hayes and Bevan, *Child-Care Law* (2nd edn, 1988); Freeman, *The Rights and Wrongs of Children*, Chapter 4; Slomnicka, *Law of Child Care*; Dingwall, Eekelaar and Murray, *The Protection of Children: State Intervention and Family Life*; Second Report from the Social Services Committee, Session 1984–85, *Children in Care*, Vol I (HC 360–1); Review of Child Care Law, 1985 ('RCCL'); The Law on Child Care and Family Services (1987) ('The White Paper').
2 For a detailed account see the Report of the Care of Children Committee (Curtis Committee) (1946) Cmnd 6922, paras 12–99, and for a learned historical survey of the care of the deprived child see Heywood, *Children in Care* (1965).

15.02 These several methods of providing a substitute for home life involved considerable variation in the degree of responsibility, both at central and local government level, and the Curtis Committee, which was the first thorough inquiry into the care of deprived children, in recommending a large extension of public care stressed the need for concentrating responsibility for it, though not for all aspects of the child's life, in one central department, with immediate responsibility to be undertaken by the local authority, working through a specialised committee. The Committee's recommendations were given effect by the Children Act 1948, which made county councils and county borough councils responsible for the care of deprived children, subject to some central control by the Department of Health and Social Security, and, in Wales, by the Welsh Office. For almost the next 25 years a local authority discharged its functions under the 1948 Act and other statutes[1] through their children's committee, sub-committees and the Children's Officer at the head of what was in effect a separate department of local government. The practice was for the committee to concern itself with issues of general policy, leaving detailed administration and supervision to its sub-committees, with the department being responsible for the day-to-day exercise of the functions of the local authority and the committee.

1 For example, those authorities were the appropriate authorities for dealing with remand homes, approved schools and fit persons under CYP Acts 1933 and 1963; they were responsible for ensuring the well being of foster children (see Chapter 7), of 'protected children' within the meaning of the adoption legislation (Chapter 5), and of mentally disordered children. They were also responsible for supervising nurseries and child-minders (Chapter 7) and supervising children under supervision orders made in matrimonial and other proceedings. Alternatively orders might be made in those proceedings committing a child to the care of a local authority (post, paras 15.56 et seq).

15.03 But the reorganisation of the child care service by the Children Act 1948 still left other departments of the local authority, mainly the health and education departments, to deal with other aspects of child care, and the need for local authorities to co-ordinate those of their services connected with the family gradually became apparent. The problem of co-ordination was examined generally by the Younghusband Working Party on social workers in the local authority health and welfare services (1959) and specifically in relation to child neglect by the Ingleby Committee.[1] The latter recognised the possibility of a long-term solution in a re-organisation of the services into a unified family service,[2] but foresaw formidable difficulties. The Seebohm Committee, to whom the matter was eventually referred,[3] did not find them insurmountable. Admitting that many changes were necessary before an effective family service could be created, it saw as 'the first necessity' the establishment of a new department of local government – a unified social service department within each major local authority, which would merge the existing children's department, welfare department and some sections of the health department. The Local Authority Social Services Act 1970[4] implemented this and some of the other detailed proposals of Seebohm. The social services committee, with its wider functions, replaced the children's committee,[5] and the director of social services replaced the children's officer and the director of welfare services. It was regarded as an essential policy of the reorganisation that social workers should receive generic training which would enable them to discharge any of the committee's functions, so that, for example, their case loads could cover not only children but also the elderly and the mentally ill. In the event, the wheel has turned more than half circle, and with the enormous increase in known child abuse and neglect many social workers find themselves specialising in, and exclusively concerned with, children's cases as their predecessors did before the 1970 Act. On the other hand, there has been complaint that too many social workers 'lack specialist skills',[6] a problem exacerbated by inadequate numbers and inadequate length of training. The Cleveland Inquiry is the most recent public reminder of the need for improved training.[7] But, one sceptically may ask, will Government provide the necessary funding?

1 (1960) Cmnd 1191. The White Paper, *The Child, the Family and the Young Offender* also referred to the matter; see (1965) Cmnd 2742, para 7.

2 Cmnd 1191, para 4.7.
3 The Report of the Committee on Local Authority and Allied Personal Social Services (1968) Cmnd 3703. For changing attitudes towards social policy during this period see Cooper, *The Creation of the British Personal Social Services 1962–74* (1983).
4 See ss 2–6 and Sch 1.
5 Like its predecessor, the social services committee works through sub-committees and can authorise them to exercise any of its functions (s 4(2)). The committee may either be composed exclusively of members of the local authority or include, as a minority, other persons, who in practice are persons specially qualified in matters relating to the committee's functions (s 5). A sub-committee must include at least one member of the local authority. The committee exercises its functions by way of delegation from the local authority, but the duties remain those of the authority; *Birmingham City District Council v O* [1983] AC 578, [1983] 1 All ER 497, HL.
6 See Hazel, *The regulation of family placement* (1982) 6 Adoption and Fostering 19. For a general examination of the role of social workers see the Report of the Barclay Committee, *Social Workers: their role and tasks* (1982).
7 See the Cleveland Report at pp 251–252.

II PREVENTIVE, SUPPORTIVE AND REHABILITATIVE FUNCTIONS OF LOCAL AUTHORITIES

15.04 Although the Children and Young Persons Act 1933 and the Children Act 1948 required a local authority to try to secure the child's return to his family, neither Act gave them power to give positive assistance to the family to rehabilitate the child. Nor were they empowered to help families to prevent the need for children to be received into care. Nevertheless, both objects were pursued by some local authorities 'on the fringe of their statutory responsibility',[1] and preventive work was encouraged by the Home Office. Following the recommendations of the Ingleby Committee, the Children and Young Persons Act 1963[2] provided a legal basis upon which such work could be undertaken. It now rests on section 1 of the Child Care Act 1980.

1 Report of Seebohm Committee, Cmnd 3703, para 182. See also Packman, *The Child's Generation* (1975), Chapter 4.
2 Section 1.

15.05 The section requires a local authority 'to make available such advice, guidance and assistance as may promote the welfare of children[1] by diminishing the need to receive children into or keep them in care under this Act or to bring children before a juvenile court'.[2] It is expressly provided that, at the discretion of the authority, assistance may be given 'in kind or, in exceptional circumstances, in cash', but local authorities vary in their interpretation of 'exceptional circumstances'.

> 'Some local authorities interpret these words broadly as meaning that circumstances in the particular case are exceptional as compared with the rest of the community, therefore justifying regular payments to particular families. Other local authorities treat the words more restrictively as exceptional in the course of the lives of the individuals concerned.'[3]

It must be questioned whether the section was intended to have the broader meaning, but where it has been so applied its relationship to the system of social security has always been uncertain and variable,[4] notwithstanding attempts to clarify it.[5]

1 For the purpose of the section a child means a person under 18 (s 1(5)).
2 Although a duty is imposed (*R v Local Com for Administration for the North and East Area of England, ex p Bradford Metropolitan City Council* [1979] 2 All ER 881 at 902, 903), there is no right of action based on a refusal to give assistance under s 1.
3 RCCL, para 5.19.
4 See Freeman, *Rules and Discretion in Local Authority Social Services Departments: The Children and Young Persons Act 1963 in Operation* [1980] JSWL 84, especially at pp 88–91; Heywood and Allen, *Financial Help in Social Work* (1971); Hill and Laing, *Money Payments, Social Work and Supplementary Benefits* (1978); Lister and Emmett, *Under the Safety Net* (1976) CPAG, Poverty Pamphlet No 25; Murray, *Section 1: A View from the Field* [1980] JSWL 96.
5 *Assistance in Cash*, Association of County Councils, Association of Metropolitan Authorities and SBC, 1976.

15.06 Cash payments are usually made to buy food or pay arrears of rent or (an increasing problem) to pay fuel bills or, less frequently, to pay for bed and breakfast accommodation for the family. Loans instead of grants are sometimes made. They may, for example, be appropriate where the family is in temporary financial difficulty, but, if they are not repaid, they run the risk of harming the relationship between the social worker and the family.[1] Assistance otherwise than in cash may take a variety of forms of provision of services, particularly day nursery care, play groups, day fostering, child-minding, after-school schemes, respite care[2] and home help. Many of these services are particularly relevant for one-parent families.[3] The most effective methods of advice may be through the individual social worker or through advice centres, such as family advice centres or citizens' advice bureaux or the housing department of the local authority, depending upon the circumstances; for example, where a social worker is already known to the family, he or she is likely to be the most suitable person, for example, in advising the family on housekeeping and budgeting.

These illustrations show the wide discretion a local authority have in the kinds of assistance they may provide in order to discharge their duty under section 1, and they cannot adopt any overriding policy which fetters that discretion and prevents them from considering the merits of a particular case for assistance under the section. So the Court of Appeal held in *A–G ex rel Tilley v Wandsworth London Borough Council*,[4] where it declared ultra vires a resolution of a local authority that, where a family with children was intentionally homeless within the meaning of the Housing (Homeless Persons) Act 1977, alternative housing would not be provided under section 1 (of CYPA 1963)[5] but that consideration would be given to receiving the children into care. To implement the inflexible policy[6] would prevent the authority from considering whether housing a particular family would diminish the need to receive the children into care. The fact that the parent has intentionally brought about the homelessness was a matter that could properly be taken into account, not to punish the children, but to decide how the authority's powers under section 1 could best be exercised in the interests of the child. For example, a parent's past irresponsibility by continually changing homes might lead to the conclusion that it was best to take the children into care. On the other hand, it might be in their interests to find accommodation so that they remain with their parents.

1 See Freeman [1980] JSWL at p 91.
2 See post, para 15.09.
3 See Finer Report, paras 8.35–8.50.
4 (1981) 2 FLR 377, 11 Fam Law 119. Compare the view expressed in RCCL, para 5.4 that arguably s 1 imposes a duty to make *general* arrangements for promoting the welfare of children and that in deciding what provision to make for that purpose 'local authorities may be expected to act as a reasonable authority would in the light of their resources and the competing claims upon them'.
5 See now CCA 1980, s 1.
6 Templeman LJ took the view that a policy would be ultra vires even if it allowed specified exceptions, because it would still fetter the authority's discretion under s 1; but the majority of the Court (Lawton and Brandon LJJ) left the point open.

15.07   The Seebohm Committee was 'impressed by the amount of preventive work amongst families accomplished by children's departments since the Children and Young Persons Act 1963',[1] but policies and practice of local authorities continue for several reasons[2] to vary considerably. Clearly, a principal factor is the amount of resources which a local authority is willing to make available for the purposes of section 1 of the 1980 Act. Present control by Central Government of local authority spending is likely to squeeze the availability of resources, especially among those authorities which have been more generous in making provision. In principle, the preventive, supportive and rehabilitative work of local authorities will be strengthened if the proposals of RCCL and the White Paper[3] on the subject are implemented. These recommend that child care law should be unified with the health and welfare legislation which affects children[4] and that family support be strengthened by providing care away from the family home in closer voluntary partnership with the parents. But will these laudable aims be frustrated by inadequate provision of resources? It is at least certain that local authorities will continue to look to voluntary organisations to assist them fulfil their proposed extended functions, as they now do to help them discharge their duty under section 1.[5]

1 Cmnd 3703, para 430.
2 See Freeman, [1980] JSWL pp 92–95.
3 See respectively paras 5.1–5.24 of the Review and Chapter 2 of the White Paper.
4 The Second Report of the Social Services Committee, *Children in Care*, para 27, had similarly proposed closer liaison between the various statutory agencies involved with children.
5 See sub-s (2).

III   RECEPTION INTO CARE

15.08   Although it should be a cardinal aim of a local authority to support the child within his own family in accordance with section 1 of the Child Care Act 1980, the circumstances may be such that the authority will have to receive the child into their care. Section 2(1) of the Act imposes the duty to receive if it appears to the authority:

'(a) that he has neither parent nor guardian or has been and remains abandoned by his parents or guardian or is lost; or
(b) that his parents or guardian are, for the time being or permanently, prevented by reason of mental or bodily disease or infirmity or other

incapacity or any other circumstances from providing for his proper accommodation, maintenance and upbringing; and
(c) in either case, that the intervention of the local authority under this section is necessary in the interests of the welfare of the child.'

This is an ambiguous provision. It is so worded, particularly in its reference to 'either case' in sub-paragraph (c), that it suggests that it would not be open to the local authority to say that one of the conditions in sub-paragraph (a) is satisfied in relation to the one parent and one of those in sub-paragraph (b) to the other. Supposing, for example, that on a decree of divorce the father were granted custody, care and control by the court and the mother, who then remarried, did not maintain contact with the child. The father deserts the child by going abroad and the mother now wants to bring him into her present family but her second husband will not allow her. It is difficult to see how the case can fall wholly within sub-paragraph (a). Accepting that abandonment has the same meaning in that sub-paragraph as it has in section 1 of the Children and Young Persons Act 1933[1] and section 16(2) of the Adoption Act 1976[2] and amounts to leaving the child to his fate in such circumstances as to render the parent criminally liable,[3] the father has abandoned the child, but the mother can hardly be held to have done so, since he was in the father's custody by order of the court. Equally, the circumstances do not wholly fall within sub-paragraph (b) in view of the father's abandonment. But clearly (a) does cover the father and (b) the mother.[4] The narrow construction of mutual exclusion would certainly conflict with the social policy underlying section 2 of the 1980 Act and, in the absence of judicial authority to support that construction, local authorities are likely to intervene in a case of that kind.

1 See ante, para 9.45 for discussion of the term, where, however, it was noted that 'abandonment' probably has a wider meaning for the purposes of s 2 of CCA 1980.
2 Formerly CA 1975, s 12(2); see ante, para 5.29.
3 See as an example for reception into care *Barker v Westmorland County Council* (1958) 56 LGR 267, DC.
4 The 'other circumstances' being the second husband's attitude.

15.09 Apart from this ambiguity the terms of the subsection allow for various possibilities. Sub-paragraph (b) particularly gives it wide scope, for there may be a variety of 'other circumstances' which will justify intervention by the local authority. The child of the homeless family is a common example;[1] the child whose parent is temporarily ill and unable to look after him is another. But there is a risk of the subsection being used for short-term purposes when action under section 1 of the 1980 Act or under other statutory powers is more appropriate. Quite frequently local authorities rely on it to provide 'respite care' for a handicapped child, so that the parent can have a short break away from his child. Only a strained construction of sub-paragraph (b) can justify the conclusion that the parent is *prevented* by 'other circumstances' from providing for the child's upbringing. The authority should instead rely on the powers of short-term placements under the National Health Service Act 1977.[2] Yet, there is a feeling among some social workers that their relationship with the child and with the parent will be more effectively regularised if action is taken under section 2 of the 1980 Act.

1 For an exceptional case see *R v Secretary of State for the Home Department, ex p Hickling and JH (a minor)* [1986] 1 FLR 543, CA, where a child was separated from the mother in prison and received into care.
2 See Schedule 8.

5.10   It is obvious that in many cases a local authority will have to inquire closely into the circumstances of each case to decide whether the conditions laid down by sub-paragraph (a) or (b) are fulfilled, but neither the 1980 Act nor any Regulation imposes any requirements concerning the method or extent of their investigations. Moreover, the question of the necessity for intervention is, under sub-paragraph (c), a matter for the authority to decide and, providing that its officers act with propriety, the wisdom of their decision will not be reviewed by the court.[1] The scope of the duty is thus limited by the discretion, and local authorities have particularly relied on sub-paragraph (c) to justify refusing to receive into care teenagers who are in dispute with their families.[2]

1 For the possibility of judicial review see post, paras 15.127 et seq.
2 See Second Report of the Social Services Committee, *Children in Care*, para 121.

15.11   For the purposes generally of CCA 1980 the term 'parent' refers to the father and mother, if they were married to each other at the time of the birth of their child. If they were not so married at that date only the mother is a parent.[1] In relation to an adopted child the term means the adoptive parents. 'Guardian' is used in the strict sense of one so appointed by deed or will or order of the court.[2] If there is an order of a court in force giving custody to any person, for references in Part I of the 1980 Act to parents or guardian there must be substituted references to that person.[3] This rule can be particularly significant in the case of cohabitees who separate and the father obtains an order for legal custody under section 9 of the Guardianship of Minors Act 1971. He then replaces the mother for the purpose of Part I.[4] When section 4 of the Family Law Reform Act 1987 is brought into force and an order is made under the section in favour of the father, he and the mother will share the actual custody of their child and both of them will be treated as parents for the purpose of Part I.[5]

1 CCA 1980, s 87(1).
2 See ibid.
3 Section 8(2) of FLRA 1987, when it comes into force, will substitute a new s 8(2) in CCA 1980 so that the appropriate reference will then be to a person having the 'actual custody' of the child by virtue of an order of a court.
4 Cf Clarke Hall and Morrison, para A [197], who argue for the alternative construction, namely, that s 8(2) of CCA 1980 *extends* the definition of parents or guardian to include a person having a custody order and does not substitute that person for parents or a guardian. To construe the subsection otherwise 'would prevent a local authority assuming the parental rights of a non-custodial parent, even though he had been missing for many years'.
5 CCA 1980, s 8(3), as prospectively substituted by FLRA 1987, s 8(2).

15.12   Should a local authority receive into care a child who is then ordinarily resident in the area of another authority, the latter may agree, but cannot be compelled, to take over the care of the child.[1] If they do,[2] the first mentioned authority 'may recover', ie are legally entitled at their discretion to recover, from the other the expenses which they incurred in caring for the child. Ordinary residence can be notoriously difficult to determine,[3] and if the authorities cannot agree about it, the Secretary of State must settle the question.

1 CCA 1980, s 2(4). The 'resident' authority cannot be compelled to take the child even though they may know far more about him and his family than the 'receiving' authority does.
2 They must do so not later than three months after the determination of the child's ordinary residence, unless the authorities agree to a later date.
3 In determining it for present purposes no account is to be taken of any period during which the child resided at a school or other institution or at any place in accordance with the requirements of a supervision order or the conditions of a recognisance or while boarded out by a local authority or education authority under the 1980 Act or the CYP (Scotland) Act 1937 or Part II of the Social Work (Scotland) Act 1968.

Rehabilitation

15.13 The duty of the local authority under section 2 extends to any child appearing to them to be under 17,[1] but, once received into care, they must keep him so long as his welfare appears to them to require their care, and this can continue, if necessary, until he is 18.[2] Nevertheless, they must, if they think it consistent with the child's welfare, try to secure that care is taken over either (a) by a parent or guardian,[3] or (b) by a relative[4] or friend, who must, where possible, either be of the same religious persuasion as the child or give an undertaking that the child will be brought up in that persuasion.[5] Although section 2 does not expressly so provide, a local authority in seeking to rehabilitate the child with his family may provide resources, including cash payments,[6] as they may do under section 1 of the Act. Nevertheless, the two sections are still seen as imposing distinct duties on the local authority. As part of the policy of emphasising the relationship between the family and the authority as a voluntary and continuing one, with the authority providing services flexibly within the home or by way of residential facilities, the White Paper proposes[7] the 'amalgamation' of the two sections of the Act.

1 Sub-s (1).
2 Sub-s (2).
3 *Semble a* parent or guardian can take over care by ensuring that someone else accommodates and maintains the child; see Bromley, p 443, note 6, citing *Re AB (an infant)* [1954] 2 QB 385, [1954] 2 All ER 287, DC.
4 By CCA 1980, s 87(1), as amended by FLRA 1987, Sch 2, para 79 and Sch 4, this means a grandparent, brother, sister, uncle or aunt, whether of the full blood, of the half blood or by affinity.
5 CCA 1980, s 2(3).
6 Hayes and Bevan, para 2.1.2.
7 See paras 18 and 19.

IV ASSUMPTION OF PARENTAL RIGHTS AND DUTIES[1]

15.14 Section 2 of the 1980 Act entrusts to the local authority the care of the child. 'Care' is not statutorily defined for this purpose, but it is submitted that it is used comprehensively for care and control, ie, to denote the parental duties to protect the child and regulate his conduct. Section 3 goes much further, because it empowers the local authority on the following specified grounds to pass a resolution vesting in themselves almost all parental rights and duties over a child who has been received into their care. Like section 2 of the 1980 Act, section 3 owes its origins to the Poor Law.[2] The Poor Law Acts of 1889 and 1899 enabled the Poor Law guardians to assume all the powers and rights in respect of a child who was deserted by his parent or whose parent was unfit to have control of the child because of 'mental deficiency or vicious habits or mode of life'.[3] The present grounds for assumption are, however, much wider and leave the local authority a wide discretion in the timing of that assumption.

1 See generally Adcock, White and Rowlands *The Administrative Parent* (1983); Adcock and White, *The Use of Section 3 Resolutions* (1982) 6 Adoption and Fostering 9.
2 See Lord Scarman in *Leeds City Council v West Yorkshire Metropolitan Police* [1983] 1 AC 29 at 41, [1982] 1 All ER 274 at 280.
3 PLA 1899, s 1.

1   Grounds for passing a resolution

15.15   A resolution may be passed on any of the following grounds.

Paragraph (a): The child's parents are dead and he has no guardian or custodian

A resolution on this ground would, for example, be appropriate where the child was received into care under section 1(2)(a) as an orphan and with no guardian, and there is no relative or other person interested in bringing him up under an adoption or custodianship order. In such circumstances a resolution is likely to be passed soon after he has been received into care.

The meanings of parent and guardian have already been noted,[1] where it was pointed out that, if there is an order of a court in force giving custody to any person, for references to parents or guardian there must be substituted references to that person. It has been suggested[2] that this substitution 'appears to have the consequence that, in the case of married or divorced parents, if the custodial parent dies, the child as a matter of law has no parent or guardian'. This conclusion accords with the purpose of section 2, namely, to meet a need of providing care for a child who has no-one else to care for him. The fact that the surviving non-custodial parent has residual powers[3] does not help to meet that need and his parentage can be ignored. Moreover, the conclusion does not lead to an unduly strained construction of section 2(1)(a) – where there is 'neither parent nor guardian'. But the same cannot be said of section 3(1)(a) which speaks of, 'the parents are dead', and it must be doubted whether, in the circumstances envisaged above, there is power to pass a resolution on this ground.

'Custodian' means a person to whom custodianship has been granted under Part II of the Children Act 1975.[4]

1 Ante, para 15.11.
2 Hayes and Bevan, op cit, para 2.3.1.
3 See ante, para 3.53.
4 See ante, Chapter 6.

Paragraph (b): Inability or unfitness of parent[1]

15.16   The following five grounds are based on the parent's inability or unfitness to care for the child.[2]

1 For the purposes of this and the following grounds 'parent' includes a guardian and a custodian (s 3(10)). Where a ground relates to a guardian or custodian, subsequent proceedings to terminate the guardianship or custodianship are likely to be appropriate.
2 Section 3(1)(b).

(i)   A parent has abandoned the child
15.17   Abandonment doubtless has the same meaning as in section 2,[1] but the court will insist on a high degree of culpability. Feckless and irresponsible conduct is not enough, and a mother who leaves her child with a relative and does not know that he is later received into care does not abandon him.[2] Moreover, even where there has been abandonment, that state of affairs must continue up to the date of the passing of the local authority resolution.[3]

For the purpose of section 3 abandonment has a special additional meaning. If the whereabouts of a parent have remained unknown for 12 months, he is deemed to have abandoned the child,[4] and this provision operates whatever may have been the ground for receiving the child into care under section 2. It is therefore important that parents be informed of the provision when the child is received into care, but there is no statutory obligation imposed on the local authority to do so.

1 Supra, para 15.08.
2 *Wheatley v Waltham Forest London Borough Council* [1980] AC 311, [1979] 2 All ER 289. The fact that the relative abandons the child does not justify the making of a resolution in respect of the mother; see *Crosby (a minor) v Northumberland County Council* (1982) 12 Fam Law 92, CA.
3 Cf *Wheatley v Waltham Forest LBC*, supra, where the mother had been visiting her child regularly for at least six months before the purported resolution was passed.
4 Section 3(8).

(ii)   A parent suffers from some permanent disability rendering him incapable of caring for the child
15.18   The disability may be physical or mental. Where the child was received into care under section 2(1)(b) on the ground of the parent's disability, it may well be appropriate to pass a resolution soon after he has been so received, especially in a case of mental disability. Where it is physical, the child's age may be highly relevant in deciding whether the disability prevents the parent caring for the child. The mother who has been rendered a paraplegic by a motor accident may be incapable of physically caring for her 12-month-old child but competent to bring up her 11-year-old daughter, to whose needs as she reaches puberty her mother may best be able to respond.

(iii)   A parent, while not falling within the previous paragraph, suffers from a mental disorder within the meaning of the Mental Health Act 1983, which renders him unfit to have the care of the child
15.19   This ground supplements that in paragraph 15.18, and applies to temporary as well as permanent disorder, but apparently local authorities are reluctant to invoke it,[1] and this is particularly likely where the disorder

is temporary or intermittent. By its nature the ground will usually require medical evidence to support it.

---

[1] See Adcock, White and Rowlands, op cit, pp 52–53.

(iv)   A parent is of such habits or mode of life as to be unfit to have the care of the child

15.20   By its terms this is intrinsically a wide ground. Alcohol or drug addiction, prostitution, persistent gambling or criminal activities are the kinds of behaviour most likely to satisfy the test of unfitness. Evidence of the parent's past mode of life is not merely admissible[1] but usually will be essential to establish the present habits or mode of life. There may be the risk of social workers imposing their subjective values of behaviour when deciding that the ground is established,[2] but opinion varies on the extent of the risk,[3] which, in any event, can be controlled if, as has been held,[4] the court requires a high degree of culpability on the parent's part.

1 *Barker v Westmorland County Council* (1958) 56 LGR 267, DC.
2 Hayes and Bevan, para 2.3.2.
3 See Adcock, White and Rowlands, op cit, pp 50–52; Freeman; *The Rights and Wrongs of Children*, p 159; Maidment in Geach and Swzed (eds) *Providing Civil Justice for Children* (1983) p 77.
4 *Wheatley v Waltham Forest London Borough Council* [1980] AC 311, [1979] 2 All ER 289.

(v)   A parent has so consistently failed without reasonable cause to discharge the obligations of a parent as to be unfit to have the care of the child

15.21   It has already been noted[1] that persistent failure to discharge parental obligations is a ground for dispensing with parental agreement to adoption. Comparative reliance has been placed on it to construe the present ground, because, like an adoption order, a section 3 resolution has the serious consequence of divesting a parent of his rights and duties, albeit without the irrevocable effects of an adoption order. Accordingly, the court requires proof of a high degree of culpability,[2] and the local authority in justifying its resolution has to satisfy the court on several matters, most of which received the attention of the Divisional Court in *M v Wigan Metropolitan Borough Council*.[3]

1 Ante, para 5.28.
2 See *Wheatley v Waltham Forest London Borough Council* [1980] AC 311, [1979] 2 All ER 289.
3 [1980] Fam 36, 1 FLR 45.

15.22   *(1) The parental obligations*   These include not only the common law or statutory duty to maintain but also, *pace* adoption law,[1] the natural and moral duty of a parent to show affection, care and interest towards his child. Indeed, in many, if not most, cases the alleged failure on the part of the parent relates to these 'natural and moral' matters. Moreover, because parental obligations are thus wider than the 'parental rights and duties', which, being 'all rights and duties which by law the mother and father have in relation to a legitimate child and his property',[2] vest in a local authority under a section 3 resolution, there can be a failure to discharge those obligations even when a child is in local authority care,[3] for example,

by the parent showing little or no interest in the child and being unwilling
to have him or her on home visits.[4]

1 See *Re P (infants)* [1962] 3 All ER 789 at 794 [1962] 1 WLR 1296 at 1302.
2 See post, para 15.34.
3 See Sheldon J in *M v Wigan Metropolitan Borough Council* [1980] Fam 36 at 46, 1 FLR
  45 at 50–51.
4 As happened in the *Wigan* case during the six-month period between the adjournment
  and final hearing of the juvenile court proceedings.

15.23 *(2) The nature of the failure to discharge*   The statutory terms of
the ground do not explicitly prescribe standards of parental behaviour,
but, in this regard particularly, the courts have drawn on relevant judicial
authorities in adoption.[1] In order to amount to a failure to discharge his
obligations without reasonable cause, the parent must have behaved with
a callous or self-indulgent indifference for the welfare of his child, as may
be found where he has failed to maintain contact with the child while
in care by refusing to visit him or to have him home for weekends. In
O'Dare Ai v South Glamorgan County Council[2] the requisite standard of
misbehaviour was totally absent. Over a two-year-period from the age of
two months a child was taken into local authority care on a number of
occasions at the request of the mother during times when she was suffering
from anxiety and mild depression and unable to cope with looking after
her child. The Divisional Court held that her recognition of her own
inadequacy as a mother and of the consequent harm or risk of harm to
her child were wholly inconsistent with blameworthy behaviour. On the
contrary, her conduct was held to be reasonable throughout that period.
The appropriate test is the objective test of what a reasonable parent would
do in all the circumstances of the case.[3] A parent who fails to visit his
child because of his own protracted illness obviously has reasonable cause
for not doing so. So has the co-operative parent whose access to his child
is stopped by the local authority because its social workers decide that
contact with the parent is upsetting the child.[4] Indeed, in such cases it
is wholly artificial and unnecessary to separate the nature of the 'failure'
from the cause. The ground cannot be proved because there is not the
requisite blameworthy conduct.

1 See *Re C(L) (an infant)* [1965] 2 QB 449, [1964] 3 All ER 483; *Re D (minors) (adoption
  by parent)* [1973] Fam 209, [1973] 3 All ER 1001.
2 (1982) 3 FLR 1, DC.
3 *M v Wigan Metropolitan Borough Council*, supra.
4 See *W v Nottinghamshire County Council* [1982] 1 All ER 1, CA, where there was co-
  operation with the local authority during a 12-month period between the date of the
  adjournment of the hearing and final decision, Cf the parent's attitude in the *Wigan* case,
  para 15.22, note 4.

15.24 *(3) The failure must be 'consistent'*   Unlike the requirement of
persistent failure for the purpose of adoption law, consistent failure does
not mean that the parent's behaviour, which constitutes the alleged failure,
must have continued over a substantial length of time, but that it has
'constantly adhered to a pattern' over a period of time, the length of which
will depend on the nature of the behaviour.[1]

1 *M v Wigan MBC*, supra; *W v Sunderland Borough Council* [1980] 2 All ER 514, [1980] 1 WLR 1101.

15.25   *(4) Unfitness to have the care of the child*   The consistent failure must have been such as to render the parent unfit to have the care of the child. Whether this consequence has been produced is a question of fact and degree, and is obviously related to the nature and pattern of behaviour. Nevertheless, and notwithstanding the authorities already cited, research suggests[1] that local authorities in practice are influenced more by the impact of the parental behaviour on the welfare of the child than on the intrinsic nature and degree of culpability of the parent's behaviour.

1 See Adcock, White and Rowlands, op cit, pp 44–45.

Paragraph (c): A resolution under paragraph (b) is in force in relation to one parent of the child who is, or is likely to become, a member of the household comprising the child and his other parent

15.26   This is a badly drafted provision.[1] Strictly construed it could only be invoked where the child is already living with the 'other parent', but that would only occur in the very exceptional circumstance where the local authority, in its discretion, had allowed that to happen. Otherwise the strict construction, if applied, defeats the purpose for which paragraph (c) was intended to provide.[2] The kind of case intended to be covered is that where one parent, say the mother, has been deprived of her parental rights and duties because, for example, her alcoholism renders her unfit to have the care of the child,[3] but she is still living with the father and he is likely to take steps to remove the child and bring him to live with them. Because of the uncertainty about whether paragraph (c) can be invoked in order to thwart the proposed removal,[4] the local authority would be well advised to rely instead on wardship.

1 See Bromley, p 445; Cretney, p 511; Adcock, White and Rowlands, op cit, p 56; Eekelaar, *Children in Care and the Children Act 1975*, 40 MLR 121 at 133–134.
2 See the (Houghton) Report of the Departmental Committee on the Adoption of Children (1972), para 157; see also Annex Example Leaflet C in DHSS LA Circular (84) 5.
3 CCA 1980, s 3(1)(b)(iv), ante, para 5.25.
4 This uncertainty apparently accounts largely for the fact that resolutions based on paragraph (c) are very uncommon. Evidence to the House of Commons Social Services Committee 1982–83, HC 26–i, Table 7 shows that of 17.3 thousand children subject to a s 3 resolution in 1981 only 0.1 thousand were based on paragraph (c).

Paragraph (d): Throughout the three years preceding the passing of the resolution the child has been in the care of a local authority under section 2 of CCA 1980 or partly in the care of a local authority and partly in the care of a voluntary organisation

15.27   The paragraph does not exclude the possibility that during part of the three-year-period[1] a resolution made on one of the other grounds was operative. That happened in *W v Nottinghamshire County Council*.[2] The mother objected to a resolution which had been passed on the ground of her consistent failure to discharge her parental obligations. The local authority applied to the juvenile court seeking a determination that the resolution should be confirmed.[3] The matter was adjourned for 12 months and at the resumed hearing the juvenile court ordered that the resolution remain in force on the ground that there was consistent failure both at the date of the resolution and at that of the resumed hearing. Both the Divisional Court and the Court of Appeal found that there was no longer such failure at the resumed hearing,[4] but the Court of Appeal, overruling the Divisional Court, held that, since the child had been in the care of the local authority for at least three years by the time the juvenile court resumed its hearing, the terms of paragraph (d) were satisfied.

Where the child has been partly in the care of a local authority and partly in the care of a voluntary organisation, the parental rights and duties will vest in the body in whose care the child is at the time of the passing of the resolution.[5]

---

1 This statutory period is subject to alteration by an affirmative resolution of both Houses of Parliament; CCA 1980, s 3(9).
2 [1982] Fam 53, [1982] 1 All ER 1, CA.
3 For this jurisdiction see post, para 15.39.
4 See ante, para 15.23, note 4.
5 See CA 1980, s 64(1), post, para 15.114.

2   Removal of child by parent from local authority care[1]

15.28   The highly controversial ground for which paragraph (d) provides, together with the restrictions on removal by the parent imposed where the child has been in care for at least six months[2] and on removal when applications for adoption orders or custodianship orders are made,[3] highlights the importance of the duty imposed on local authorities by section 1 of the Child Care Act 1980[4] to support, help and work with families in order to avoid the need to receive a child into care. The ground also emphasises the need for proper advice and guidance to be given to the parent on the possible consequences of allowing his child to be received into care. There is no statutory right conferred on the parent at the outset to be fully informed of the consequences. Instead, under Departmental Guidance[5] the matter is left to the discretion of the local authority to inform – by sympathetic, personal communication through a social worker, by written information and by way of explanatory leaflets.[6] The three model leaflets prepared by the Department of Health and Social Security (which are intended only as guidance for local authorities in preparing their own) contain respectively the information to be provided when the child is being received into care (Leaflet A), the information to be provided when it seems probable that the child may have to remain in care for more than six months (Leaflet B) and notes on the purposes and consequences of a section 3 resolution (Leaflet C).[7] In spite of the fact that the Department is on record that 'it is envisaged that this power [under paragraph (d)] will be used only where the parents have not been undertaking parental care or have shown little interest in the child's welfare throughout the three years and it has become necessary for the local authority to reach decisions on the child's long-term future',[8] there is evidence that the ground has frequently been invoked when one of the other grounds has been available.[9] It is suggested that, when the local authority are intending so to rely on paragraph (d), they should inform the parents that reliance on it, instead of on an alternative ground, may effectively remove the parental right to challenge the local authority's action.[10] In practice is this information given?

Departmental Guidance certainly urges that in all cases of a decision to recommend a section 3 resolution the reasons for the recommendation are discussed frankly with the parents.[11] Indeed, if there is full discussion, the parents themselves, as has been suggested,[12] may prefer the authority to proceed under paragraph (d) rather than have their conduct impugned if other grounds were invoked.

1 For wrongful removal generally see post, paras 15.102–15.103.
2 See infra, para 15.29.
3 See respectively ante, paras 5.80 and 5.81, and Chapter 6, para 6.29.
4 Ante, paras 15.05–15.07.
5 See DHSS Local Authority Circular LAC (84) 5.
6 LAC (84)5, para 8, emphasises that these 'should not be used as a substitute for either personal explanation or individual letters. There is a danger that parents may be confused or alarmed if leaflets are issued without an explanation of their relevance to individual circumstances'.
7 Leaflet B should be issued no later than four months after the child has been received into care, and it may be appropriate to issue Leaflet C at the same time, 'especially where the prospects of rehabilitation are seriously in doubt'; see LAC(84)5, paras 11 and 12.
8 See DHSS Local Authority Circular No 21/1975, Annex A, Part III.
9 See Adcock, White and Rowlands, op cit, pp 48–50, and Adcock and White, *The Use of Section 3 Resolutions*, (1982) 6 Adoption and Fostering 9.
10 For the parental right to challenge a s 3 resolution see post, para 15.39.
11 LAC (84)5, para 15.
12 Hayes and Bevan, para 2.3.4.

Removal of child after six months in care

15.29 Although it is the duty of a local authority who have received a child into their care under section 2 of the Child Care Act 1980 to keep him in care so long as his welfare requires it,[1] that duty does not authorise them to keep the child if the parent or guardian wishes to take over the care.[2] Indeed, as already noted,[3] they must try to secure that the child is rehabilitated with his family. However, the parent's right to recover his child from local authority care is seriously impaired once the child has been in care for at least six months. Thereafter the parent or guardian must give the authority 28 days' written notice that he intends to take his child away, and, unless the authority consents, it is an offence to remove the child without such notice.[4] The main purpose of the restriction, at least as originally enacted by the Children Act 1975,[5] is to prevent the sudden and impulsive removal of the child without a planned return to the home of the parent.[6] The six-month rule was a statutory comprise between the views that the minimum period of care should be 12 months and that, in all cases, once a child is in care there must be notice of intended removal. It is an uneasy compromise between the child's welfare and the parent's rights. The 1980 Act recognises the arbitrariness of its provisions in that it allows for the possibility of statutory amendment of the six month and 28-day periods.[7] The latter period is intended to allow the local authority some flexibility of action, but whether it is sufficiently long for rehabilitative purposes has been questioned,[8] and, in the light of the *Lewisham* case,[9] it must now be regarded primarily as a 'breathing space'[10] to enable the local authority to take action to keep the child in their care.[11] Occasionally, at least, once notice has been given the authority may consider it appropriate to return the child within a day or so. They may, indeed, have anticipated the notice and waived its requirement; for example, where the child was received into care because of the temporary illness of the parent and the authority is now satisfied that the parent is again fit to look after the child. In some cases, especially where the child has been living with foster parents, the authority may regard as desirable short trial periods of rehabilitation within the 28-day period (for example two or three long weekends in the parental home) in order to assess the child's reaction. However, in most cases the authority are likely to be opposed to returning the child. Their legal position and powers during the 28-day period were considered by the House of Lords in *Lewisham London Borough Council v Lewisham Juvenile Court Justices*.[12] It was held that once a child has been received into care under section 2 he does not cease to be in care when the parent notifies the authority of his desire to resume care: he remains in care until he is actually handed over to, or removed by, the parent. The consequence which their Lordships drew from this principle was that, where section 13(2) applies, the local authority has the 28-day period within which to decide what action to take in the interests of the child.[13] If they are opposed to the return of the child to the parent, there are two effective options available: the institution of wardship proceedings or the passing of a section 3 resolution: but there may be practical temporal difficulties with regard to the latter;[14] for example, being unable to arrange a case conference within the period, and then, if so recommended, to pass the resolution. Moreover, given the popularity of wardship with many local authorities, that option is more likely to be favoured.

1 Sub-s (2).
2 Sub-s (3).
3 Ante, para 15.13.
4 See CCA 1980, s 13(2), as substituted by HASSASSAA 1983, s 9 and Sch 2, para 48. For further consideration of the offence (under s 13(1)) see post, para 15.102. The extended meanings of the terms parent and guardian for the purposes of Part I of the 1980 Act (see ante, para 15.11) also apply for the purposes of s 13; see sub-s (4) (which is prospectively amended by FLRA 1987, s 8(3)). For example, supposing a relative of spouses or parents has been given legal and actual custody as a result of proceedings respectively under DPMCA 1978 or GMA 1971. Because of his protracted illness, the relative arranged for the child to be received into care under s 2. After six months he must give the 28-day notice if he wishes to recover the child.
5 Section 56.
6 Subsequent references to the parent include a guardian etc.
7 Section 13(5). In line with its proposal that there should be a voluntary partnership between a local authority and the parents the White Paper (para 22b) recommends the abolition of the 28-day notice.
8 See Freeman, *Children in Care: The Impact of the Children Act 1975* (1976) 6 Fam Law 136.
9 Infra.
10 Per Waterhouse J in *Wheatley v Waltham Forest London Borough Council* [1980] AC 311 at 315; [1979] 2 All ER 289 at 293.
11 See Cretney, pp 496–497.
12 [1980] AC 273, [1979] 2 All ER 297. For comments see Freeman, supra, note 8, and *The Legal Battlefield of Care* [1982] CLP 117; Hoggett, (1980) 43 MLR 69; Maidment, *The Fragmentation of Parental Rights and Children in Care*, [1981] JSWL 21, 28–30.
13 Ie by giving 'first consideration' to the need to safeguard and promote his welfare throughout his childhood; see CCA 1980, s 18(1), post, para 15.64.
14 Or, though it is less likely, the local authority may not have a ground for passing a resolution.

15.30 The *Lewisham* case leaves a number of matters unsettled. Most of the uncertainty arises over the scope of the rule that a child remains in local authority care until he is actually removed.

(1) If the child has already been in care for at least six months and the parent wrongfully removes him without giving the requisite notice, does the child nevertheless still remain in care so the local authority are empowered to pass a section 3 resolution?[1] If he is and if they do, they will be entitled to seek a search warrant[2] and, if granted, recover the child. If they do have that power and that remedy of recovery, they equally have them in the case where the parent has given notice but removed the child during the 28-day period, provided they invoke them within that period.[3] However, it is arguable[4] that section 13(2) is to be strictly construed. On its wording it does no more than save a parent from criminal liability (under section 13(1)), if he complies with the rule about notice. It does not protect the local authority's 'care' if he does wrongfully remove the child without such compliance. The practical effect of this conclusion, if correct, is that, should the local authority be concerned about the child's welfare, they will have to invoke the wardship jurisdiction or apply for a place of safety order.[5] As has been pointed out,[6] there may well be difficulties over the latter alternative. Since the child will have only just returned home after a lengthy period in care, it will be unlikely that any of the conditions of section 1 of the Children and Young Persons Act 1969 can be satisfied.

(2) Where the child has been in care for less than six months and the parent requests his return, the majority of their Lordships in *Lewisham* took the view that there may still be a brief opportunity to pass a section 3 resolution. But, where the parent turns up, without any notice of intention, at the place where the child is being cared for and demands the immediate return of the child, a resolution is not practicable. In those circumstances it may, however, still be, as Lord Salmon suggested,[7] the moral duty of the local authority to keep the child long enough to make him a ward of court.

(3) Similar conclusions would seem to follow in the case where the child has been in care for more than six months, the 28-day notice has been given and the notice has expired but the parent has not yet come to take away his child. A section 3 resolution could be passed, but, if this had not been done and the parent calls for immediate handing over of the child, wardship proceedings could be instituted.

(4) In *Krishnan v London Borough of Sutton*[8] it was held that, though section 2(3) of the 1980 Act,[9] does not authorise a local authority to keep a child in care if the parent desires to take over the care, the section does not impose a mandatory obligation on the authority to hand over the child, but this apparent inconsistency was explained and narrowed by the Court of Appeal in *Bawden v Bawden*[10] to the case where the handing over would or might involve the authority in taking proceedings against a party, such as a foster parent with whom the child is living. In *Krishnan* itself such proceedings would have been particularly futile, since the child was only a month short of her 18th birthday. But are there other circumstances which would justify refusal to hand over the child? Supposing he is a 15-year-old who has been in care under section 2 and happily living with foster parents for the past two years, and he is adamant that he does not want to return to live with his parents. Will the *Gillick* principle justify refusal to return or is section 2(3) overriding? In such a case the local

authority may well be advised to shift the burden of decision to the court by instituting wardship proceedings.

1 In *Lewisham* Lord Salmon gave an affirmative answer: '. . . if a parent, without having obtained the authority's consent or given the notice required by [s 13(2)] were to come to the authority and take the child away or demand the immediate return of the child, this in my view, would certainly not terminate the authority's care of the child [under s 2 of the Act] nor its right to pass a resolution under [s 3]'; see [1980] AC 273 at 291, [1979] 2 All ER 297 at 307.
2 Under CCA 1980, s 15(3), post, para 15.104.
3 Arguably, provided the resolution is passed within the period, the warrant may be sought outside it.
4 See Cretney, p 500, note 61.
5 Another possibility is a place of safety warrant under CYPA 1933, s 40, ante, para 14.44; see Maidment op cit, p 30.
6 Hayes and Bevan, para 2.1.5.
7 *Lewisham London Borough Council v Lewisham Juvenile Court Justices* [1980] AC 273 at 291, [1979] 2 All ER 297 at 306.
8 [1970] Ch 181, [1969] 3 All ER 1367, CA.
9 *Krishnan* was decided on its predecessor, CA 1948, s 1(3).
10 [1979] QB 419, [1978] 3 All ER 1216, CA.

3 The decision to recommend a resolution[1]

15.31 The decision whether or not to assume parental rights and duties is delegated by the local authority to its Social Services Committee which in some local authorities is further delegated to a sub-committee.[2] This further delegation is encouraged on several grounds:[3] it allows for more frequent meetings, for emergencies and for more attention to individual cases, thus enabling a greater degree of specialisation in child care than is possible in the full committee.

Each case for decision is referred to the sub-committee (or full committee) by a senior officer of the Social Services Department following review and in the light of discussion with those who have been involved with the child, especially the social worker(s), foster parents and/or residential care staff. The social worker should discuss the proposed plans with the child, in so far as he is old and mature enough to understand, and must take account of his wishes and feelings.[4] It is also essential at this stage to involve the parent,[5] by informing him of the legislation, the procedures and his legal rights and by discussing with him the proposed recommendation that there should be a resolution and the reasons for it. At this stage in the process the parent should also be advised to seek 'independent or legal advice' and informed not only of his right to challenge a resolution, if it is passed,[6] but also of the procedures which the particular local authority allows for the parent to make representations to the sub-committee or full committee, as the case may be.[7] They may be allowed to attend part of the meeting at which the proposal for a resolution will be considered or to meet a few of the members, including the Chairman, of the full Committee in advance of the meeting or only to send a written statement. But, whichever procedure is allowed, the parent should be given prior notice of the content of the report which will be presented by the Social Services Department to the members.[8]

1 See Gallagher, *Parental Rights Resolutions, Natural Justice and the Child Care Bill 1982* [1983] 13 Fam Law 54.

2 Delegation to officials instead of to elected members is not unknown, but its legality
   is doubted; see Cretney, p 504 and Adcock, White and Rowlands, *The Administrative Parent*
   pp 34–35.
3 See LAC (84) 5, para 21.
4 LAC (84) 5, para 20; and see infra, para 15.32.
5 See ibid, paras 16–19.
6 For the right to challenge see post, paras 15.38 et seq.
7 See LAC (84) 5, paras 26–28. For the limited but helpful role a solicitor can play in
   advising the parent on the making of representations see Hayes and Bevan, para 2.4.3.
8 See LAC (84) 5, para 29.

15.32   It seems to be accepted that, since the child is 'in care' when the
decision is made whether or not to pass a resolution, that decision must
be governed by the general duty imposed on a local authority by section
18 of the Child Care Act 1980 to give 'first consideration' to the need
to safeguard and promote the child's welfare throughout his childhood,
and in discharging the duty the authority must, so far as is practicable,
ascertain the wishes and feelings of the child and give due consideration
to them, having regard to his age and understanding. That said, the 'first
consideration' as opposed to a paramount consideration, leaves the authority
with a wide discretion in the timing of a resolution once they are satisfied
that a ground exists. The timing is often likely to depend on general policy.
Some authorities are ready to act at an early stage after the child has
been received into care, as part of their policy of arranging long-term
fostering, especially with a view ultimately to adoption or custodianship.
Others see the section 3 resolution as an ultimate solution only where
breakdown in the relationship between child and parent is likely to be
permanent. So long as local authorities continue to have power to assume
parental rights and duties, it is arguable that there should be some restrictions
on their exercise of discretion and that flexibility should be controlled by
statutory guidelines within which the authority would be obliged to act;
for example, that as a normal rule they shall have taken all reasonable
steps to rehabilitate the child with the parent or, at least, to maintain contact
between them.

4   Effects of a resolution[1]

15.33   By passing a resolution the local authority vest in themselves 'the
parental rights and duties' with respect to the child.[2] The precise scope
of this vesting is not entirely certain, but, at least, there are three statutory
qualifications to it, the first two of which are open to criticism.

Firstly, the right of the parent to consent or refuse to consent to the
making of an application for a freeing for adoption order[3] and his right
to agree or refuse to agree to the making of an adoption order or an
order authorising adoption abroad[4] are not transferred to the local authority.
Consequently, if the child is an orphan and has no guardian, no-one's
consent or agreement is necessary, and, if the resolution has been passed
for any of the reasons within section 3(1)(b) of the 1980 Act,[5] it is likely
that the court hearing the adoption application will be able to dispense
with the agreement of the parent or guardian.[6] In any of those circumstances
it seems desirable that the local authority's agreement should be required.
Certainly, the guardian ad litem will have a vital role to play and should
investigate the authority's views on the proposed adoption.

Secondly, the local authority must not cause the child to be brought up in any religious creed other than that in which he would have been brought up but for the resolution,[7] a restriction which can place the authority in difficulties if there has been uncertainty or dispute over religious upbringing; for example, where an Anglican father and Roman Catholic mother of a young child are killed in an accident. However, the restriction would not, it is submitted, bind the authority where, in accordance with the *Gillick* principle, the child is old enough to hold his own religious convictions and decides to change his religion.

Thirdly, the vesting of the parental rights and duties in the local authority does not relieve any person from any liability to maintain, or contribute to the maintenance of, the child.[8] Primarily, this provision ensures the continued duty of the father and mother of the child to provide maintenance under the Child Care Act 1980,[9] but it may have wider effect; for example, the step-father of a child in care will remain liable under an order for maintenance of the child made against him in proceedings under the Domestic Proceedings and Magistrates' Courts Act 1978.

1 See Maidment, *The Fragmentation of Parental Rights and Children in Care* [1981] JSWL 21, at pp 31–34.
2 CCA 1980, s 3(1).
3 Under the Adoption Act 1976, s 18; see para 5.34.
4 See AA 1976, s 55.
5 See ante, paras 15.16–15.25.
6 For the grounds on which this may be done see ante, paras 5.25–5.31. Where, however, a resolution has been made under s 3(1)(c) or (d), ante, paras 15.26 and 15.27, dispensing with parental agreement may be a more difficult matter.
7 CCA 1980, s 4(3).
8 Section 4(2).
9 See Part V.

15.34 Although the Child Care Act 1980 only expressly excludes and qualifies the term 'parental rights and duties' in these three ways, subject thereto that term is to be construed in accordance with section 85 of the Children Act 1975, namely, as '*all* the rights and duties which by law the mother and father have in relation to a legitimate child and his property'.[1] Notwithstanding this expressed totality, it seems that at least one,[2] if not more, of the 'rights and duties' is impliedly excluded from vesting in the local authority.

Although it has been argued that the effect of a resolution is to transfer to the local authority the parent's rights of intestate succession on the death of the child,[3] the predominant view[4] is that, since the intestacy law expressly gives beneficial interests to named persons, ie the father and mother,[5] a local authority is no more entitled to take than any other person who is not a father or mother. On this interpretation the consequence is that the proprietary effect of a resolution is restricted to transfer to the local authority of responsibility for the management of the child's property.

No mention is made in the 1980 Act of the right, or rather power, to consent to the marriage of the child, and it would seem, therefore, that this does pass to the local authority. This could be particularly relevant where both parents are dead and no guardian has been appointed. However, it has been doubted[6] whether the power is transferred to the authority, on the ground that in amending the Marriage Act 1949 in other respects the Children Act 1975 did not provide for the local authority to give consent.[7] Where, one asks, is this implied erosion of the totality of transfer of parental rights and duties to end? Obviously, if local authorities are to continue to have power to pass resolutions, the legal effects need to be clearly defined.

1 Italics supplied. See the Interpretation Act 1978, s 5 and Sch I, read with CA 1975, s 89, the effect of which is that in any Act passed on or after 12 November 1975 the expression 'the parental rights and duties' is to be construed in accordance with s 85 of the 1975 Act.
2 For the position with regard to access by the parent see post, paras 15.86 et seq.
3 See Bevan and Parry, *Children Act 1975*, p 155, para [333], a view from which at least one of those authors now resiles. It is not the only instance of a change of mind; cf Freeman in *The Child Care and Foster Children Acts 1980*, note to s 3(10) and at [1982] CLP 132–133.
4 See Bromley, p 446, note 10; Cretney, pp 513–514; Thompson (1974) 90 LQR 310; Maidment op cit, p 32.
5 Administration of Estates Act 1925, s 46(1).
6 See Bromley, p 446, note 10.
7 But, since the Marriage Act 1949, Sch 2, is ready to give the power to consent to the person to whose custody the child is committed when the parents are deprived of custody, the case for giving the power to a person (ie a local authority) who is expressly stated to acquire all the rights and duties of parents is all the stronger.

15.35   The reception of a child into care under section 2 and the passing of a resolution under section 3 do not affect any supervision order previously made with respect to him,[1] but, and especially where there is a resolution in force, the court is likely, on application, to revoke the order.

1 CCA 1980, s 8(1).

15.36   When a resolution is passed because the parents are dead and there is no guardian or custodian,[1] the local authority acquire the rights and duties which the deceased parents would have had were they still alive. The ground that the child has been in care for at least three years[2] is in such terms as to enable the resolution to relate to both parents, provided, it is submitted, that both are expressly mentioned in the resolution. The five grounds which fall within section 3(1)(b)[3] refer only to 'a parent', but where the parents are living together the circumstances may be such that a resolution in respect of each of them may be made; for example, both of them may have consistently failed to discharge the obligations of a parent.[4] If, however, the resolution is passed only 'on account of' one of them and if the rights and duties were vested in that parent jointly with another person (who is most likely to be the other parent), the effect of the resolution is that thereafter they will be vested in the local authority jointly with that other person.[5] For example, a custody order may have been made in divorce proceedings giving care and control of the child to the mother and joint custody to her and the father, and later a resolution may have been passed in respect of her rights and duties because of her conduct or disability. The husband may at the time have been abroad so that no blame attached to him. In such a case, because he retains joint custody, he shares his parental rights and duties (other than the care and control) with the local authority. But what is the practical effect? It is submitted that, in the light of section 85(3) of the Children Act 1975,[6] the authority are not obliged to consult the father before exercising or performing a parental right or duty, and the onus is on the father to disapprove of the local authority's action.[7] If section 85(3) does not apply, then, it is submitted, the onus is on the local authority to consult with the father before it acts. Consultation on such matters as the child's education or his training for a trade or profession are clear examples; but the local authority are likely to be reluctant to consult on others, such as the choice of foster parents or choice between fostering and residential care, which they may see as functions exclusive to them in implementing their own child care policy. They may well take a hard line where they have reason to believe that the father is unable himself to look after the child. Where he is able to do so, his position is prima facie much stronger. Since a resolution has not been passed on his account, in relation to him the child is only in care under section 2 of the 1980 Act, and therefore he will be entitled to demand the return of the child, subject to giving the 28-day statutory notice if the child has been in care for at least six months. There is hardly any likelihood that he intends to set up home again with his former wife, so that the power to pass a resolution under section 3(1)(c)[8] cannot be exercised and none of the other grounds is likely to be available, except that under section 3(1)(d)[9] if the child has been in care for at least three years. Should the local authority be opposed to handing over the child, they will have to rely on wardship within the short time limit, which, arguably according to the *Lewisham* case, is available to them.[10]

1 Section 3(1)(a), ante, para 15.15.
2 Section 3(1)(d), ante, para 15.27.
3 Ante, paras 15.16–15.25.
4 Cretney, p 516 draws attention to the obscurity of the language of s 3, the effect of which may be to leave it uncertain whether the resolution has vested in the authority the rights and duties of one or both parents. The onus, it is submitted, is on the authority to ensure that both parents are named in the resolution, or separate resolutions be passed, if they are both to be covered.
5 Section 3(1).
6 See ante, para 1.66.
7 Section 85(3) provides: 'Where two or more persons have a parental right or duty jointly, any one of them may exercise or perform it in any manner without the other or others if the other or, as the case may be, one or more of the others have not signified disapproval of its exercise or performance in that manner.' There seems to be no valid reason why 'persons' should not include a local authority.
8 Ante, para 15.26.
9 Ante, para 15.27.
10 See ante, para 15.30.

15.37   But to take the above example further. Suppose there had not been a joint custody order but instead the divorce court had granted the mother the custody, care and control. For the purpose of Part I of the 1980 Act the father is to be ignored: he is not a parent,[1] even though he has residual parental rights, such as the right to appoint a testamentary guardian and to give or withhold agreement to the child's adoption and even though, on the controversial authority of *Dipper v Dipper*,[2] he has the right to be consulted on major matters affecting the child. The most serious consequence for him is that he has no right to remove the child under section 2(3). As has been pointed out,[3] he will have to seek variation of the custody order, whereby he is granted custody or, at least, joint custody. It seems, however, that such an application is now a futile exercise. Since he is not, for the purposes of sections 2 and 3 of the 1980 Act a parent having parental rights and duties, he stands in a position similar to that of the father of a child whose parents were not married at the time of his birth, and in regard to the latter it has recently been held[4] that, though he is not precluded by a section 3 resolution which vests the mother's parental rights and duties in the authority from applying under the Guardianship of Minors Act 1971 for custody or access,[5] once the application is made it should be rejected by the court, since, in accordance with the authority of *A v Liverpool City Council*,[6] the court should not interfere with the wide discretion entrusted to local authorities in the management of children in care.

1 Section 8(2) which provides: 'Where an order of a court is in force giving the custody of a child to any person, the foregoing provisions of this Part of the Act shall have effect in relation to the child as if for references to the parents or guardian of the child or to a parent or guardian of his there were substituted references to that person.'
2 [1981] Fam 31, [1980] 2 All ER 722, CA; see ante, para 3.53.
3 Hayes and Bevan, para 7.2.3.
4 *M v H* [1988] 3 All ER 5, [1988] 3 WLR 485, HL.
5 See *R v Oxford Justices, ex p H* [1975] QB 1, [1974] 2 All ER 356; *R v Oxford Justices, ex p D* [1986] 3 All ER 129, [1986] 3 WLR 447.
6 [1982] AC 363, [1981] 2 All ER 385, HL.

5   Challenging a resolution[1]

15.38   Apart from possible reliance on judicial review, which is considered later,[2] the Child Care Act 1980 confers a right of objection. The local authority must, if they know his whereabouts, forthwith after passing a resolution give to the parent (or guardian or custodian[3]), in respect of whom the resolution is passed, written notice of the fact,[4] and must also inform him of his right to object to the resolution and of the effect of an objection.[5] There is an inherent defect in this duty to inform. In spite of the serious consequences of a resolution to the parent, the local authority is not obliged to take reasonable steps to trace him, if they do not know where he is. The omission contrasts sharply with the duty to take such steps before the court can dispense with a parent's agreement to adoption of his child.[6]

1 See Adcock, White and Rowlands, op cit, Chapter 8.
2 Post, paras 15.127 et seq. Since the passing of a resolution is an administrative procedure (ante, para 15.31), there may also be the possibility of intervention by the local government ombudsman; see post, para 15.132. Hayes and Bevan, para 2.2.2, argue also for revival of the use of habeas corpus proceedings where there is unlawful holding of the child. The fact that wardship is no longer available as an alternative to judicial review (see post paras 15.124–15.125) strengthens the argument for revival.
3 See the definition of 'parent' in CCA 1980, s 3(10), which includes a guardian and custodian.
4 CCA 1980, s 3(2), as substituted by HASSASSAA 1983, Sch 2, para 46. As the subsection expressly recognises, no question of giving notice arises where the resolution was passed on the ground that the child's parents are dead and he has no guardian or custodian.
5 CCA 1980, s 3(3). The notice must be sent by registered post or recorded delivery (s 3(7)). Local authorities have been advised that the notice should be 'as informative and helpful as possible', and should contain a simple tear-off portion which can be returned if the parent objects; see LAC (84)5, para 31.
6 See ante, para 5.24.

15.39   The parent is entitled to object in writing within a month. The initial onus is therefore on him, but, if he objects, it shifts entirely to the local authority, because the resolution will lapse after 14 days from the service of his counter-notice of objection, unless meantime – and the sooner the better[1] – the authority complain to a juvenile court, in which case it remains in force until the court decides whether it should lapse.[2] The court *may* order that it is not to lapse only if three conditions are all satisfied;[3] namely, (a) that the grounds on which the local authority purported to pass the resolution were made out, (b) that at the time of hearing the complaint there continue to be grounds on which a resolution could be founded and (c) that it is in the interests of the child to make such an order. Although in the vast majority of cases the ground on which the resolution was passed will remain the ground for the purpose of condition (b),[4] exceptionally there may be different grounds which will respectively satisfy those paragraphs.[5] Where, however, condition (b) is satisfied but not condition (a) the court must order that the resolution lapse,[6] but the precise effect of lapse is not spelt out by the 1980 Act. The effect, it is submitted, is that the child remains in care under section 2 until, in accordance with the *Lewisham* case,[7] he is returned to, or removed by, the parent. Clearly, the parent will want the child handed back as soon as the court orders that the resolution is to lapse. It seems, however, that the local authority may retain the child long enough to commence wardship proceedings.[8] If they do return the child, it is likely that the authority will place him on their 'at risk' register, in view of the fact that at the time when the juvenile court heard the case there was a ground which would have justified passing a resolution.

1 See LAC(84)5, para 33.
2 CCA 1980, s 3(4) and (5). The local authority must send a notice specifying the time and place fixed for the hearing of the complaint to any other person who is a parent and who lives apart from the parent who is the defendant to the proceedings or who is a foster parent or other person with whom the child has had his home for at least six weeks ending not more than six months before the date of complaint if the whereabouts of such person is known to the local authority; see MC(C&YP) Rules 1988, r 30(1).
3 Section 3(6).
4 It is surprising to find the rules in (a) and (b) expressed in plural terms in s 3(6). In practice there is usually one ground on which a resolution is passed and one ground existing at the time of the hearing.
5 See *W v Nottinghamshire County Council* [1982] Fam 53, [1982] 1 All ER 1, CA, ante, para 15.27.
6 As it did in *Crosby (a minor) v Northumberland County Council* (1982) 12 Fam Law 92.
7 Ante, para 15.30.
8 See ibid.

15.40 The condition contained in (c) is equivocal and fails to make clear the weight to be given to the child's interests.[1] If, as now seems to be the law,[2] the test to be applied by the local authority when deciding whether or not to pass a resolution is that the child's interests are the first consideration, it is difficult to see why a different test should be applied by the court. On the other hand, it is arguable that, once the conditions of paragraphs (a) and (b) above are satisfied, the child's interests should be paramount. That would accord with section 1 of the Guardianship of Minors Acts 1971, and it may be said that, because that section refers to any proceedings in any court and extends to the upbringing of the child, it applies by implication to condition (c). Yet, if that be so why enact condition (c) in its present terms? Although the doubt has still to be judicially settled, it is suggested that in practice courts will and should be guided by what is best for the child.[3]

1 Compare infra, para 15.44, the test for deciding whether the local authority may rescind its resolution, namely, whether rescission would be for the benefit of the child (s 5(3)).
2 See ante, para 15.32.
3 It is noteworthy that, if the court appoints a guardian ad litem for the child (infra), one of his duties is to regard as the first and paramount consideration the need to safeguard and promote the child's best interests (MC(C&YP) Rules 1988, r 31(6)(b)).

15.41 In a procedural respect the interests of the child are partially protected.[1] The juvenile court, or on appeal, the Family Division of the High Court,[2] may, where it considers it necessary in order to safeguard those interests, order the child to be made a party to the proceedings, and, if it does, must order a guardian ad litem to be appointed, unless it is satisfied that appointment is not necessary to safeguard the child's interests.[3] Since there is a serious risk that his interests may conflict with those of the parent or local authority or even of both, the emphasis is in favour of appointment. The rules governing his appointment and his functions and the disclosure of his report to the parties and their representatives follow closely those governing those matters in care proceedings, and these have already been examined.[4] As in care proceedings[5] the whole or part of the evidence may be given in the child's absence, if this is thought to be in his interest, but he must be present to hear evidence of his character and conduct.[6] Conversely, the parent may in special circumstances be required to withdraw while the child is giving evidence or making a statement, although should the child make any allegations against him he must be told the substance of them.[7] Presumably, as a party to the proceedings, the parent is then entitled to meet them by cross-examination and giving and calling evidence.[8] A parent who is not a party to the proceedings but to whom notice has to be given[9] is also entitled to cross-examine, call and give evidence to meet allegations made against him. He may also make representations at the conclusion of the evidence for the complainant and the defence but before the defendant or complainant addresses the court.[10] But the court may, it is suggested, invoke its powers to control its proceedings and allow him wider participation.[11]

1 CCA 1980, s 7(1).
2 Section 6. In accordance with the normal appellate rules there are further rights of appeal to the Court of Appeal and House of Lords. For further details of appeals to the High Court see post, para 15.45.
3 CCA 1980, s 7(2) and MC(C&YP) Rules 1988, r 31(1).
4 See ante, paras 14.63 et seq, and compare rr 31(2)–(7), 32 and 34 with rr 16(2)–(7) and 25 of MC(C&YP) Rules 1988.
5 See para 14.88.
6 Rule 30.
7 Rule 30.
8 Compare care proceedings. Even where he is not a party the Rules (r 18) expressly give him the right to cross examine etc.
9 Under r 21B(1), ante, para 15.39, note 2.
10 See r 21B(2).
11 The same view is taken by Clarke Hall and Morrison, para B[3167].

15.42 Some helpful guidance has been given[1] on the role of the parent's lawyer in presenting the parent's case in section 3 proceedings. They will equally be found helpful to a guardian ad litem and the lawyer instructed to represent the child. The kinds of wide ranging matters which should be explored include the history of social work with the family, especially the degree of contact between it and the social services department since the child was received ito care; any attempts that have been made to rehabilitate the child with his family; whether before and/or since reception into care the local authority have tried, in accordance with their preventive duties under section 1 of the Child Care Act 1980,[2] to offer advice, guidance and assistance to the family; and whether, if such assistance were offered, the parent would favourably respond to it.

1 See Hayes and Bevan, para 2.5.2.
2 Ante, paras 15.04–15.07.

6 Duration of a resolution

15.43   Often the parent, guardian or custodian may agree to the resolution being passed.[1] Where he does or where the court orders that it is not to lapse or where there are no parents, guardian or custodian to give consent or oppose the resolution, it will continue in force until the child attains the age of 18,[2] unless it is earlier rescinded by a further resolution of the local authority[3] or terminated by an order of a juvenile court.[4] It will also cease to have effect[5] where a guardian is appointed under section 5 of the Guardianship of Minors Act 1971, or an order is made for the return of the child under Part I of the Child Abduction and Custody Act 1985 or a foreign custody decision with respect to the child is registered under s 16 of that Act for enforcement, or the parental rights and duties are vested in a person who intends to adopt the child abroad.[6]

1 For the importance of informing parents of the right to make representations before a resolution is passed and of advising them to seek independent or legal advice see ante, para 15.31.
2 CCA 1980, s 5(1).
3 Section 5(3).
4 Section 5(3).
5 See s 5(2), as amended by SI 1986/1049.
6 See Adoption Act 1976, s 55.

(a) Rescission

15.44   The power of the local authority to rescind the original resolution may be exercised if it appears to them that rescission will be for the benefit of the child.[1] Presumably the test is different from that which requires the authority to give 'first consideration to safeguarding and promoting the welfare of the child throughout his childhood' and which it applies when deciding whether to pass a section 3 resolution.[2] In the absence of firm legislative guidance, it is suggested that the local authority should apply the principle that the child's interests are paramount.

1 CCA 1980, s 5(3).
2 Hayes and Bevan, para 2.6, take the view that the same test does apply. That conclusion can be supported on the ground that the child is still in care and so, by virtue of s 18 of CCA 1980, the 'first consideration' test operates. Sed quaere; if it was intended to operate, why does s 5(4) refer to rescission 'for the benefit of the child'?

(b) Termination by order

15.45   A juvenile court may determine a resolution on the complaint of the parent, guardian or custodian in respect of whom the resolution was passed or, where it was passed on the ground that there were no parents and no guardian or custodian, on the complaint of someone claiming to be any of such persons.[1] An order may be made if the court is satisfied either that there was no ground for the making of the resolution or that the resolution should in the interests of the child be determined. As for the former, it may create difficulties for the complainant to prove the negative, especially if it is a lengthy period since the resolution was passed. As for the interests of the child, yet again there is uncertainty about the weight to be given to them, and the absence of clear guidance raises the question[2] whether the court must comply with the test of 'having regard' to the child's welfare, as laid down in section 44(1) of the Children and Young Persons Act 1933 or that of the paramountcy of his welfare as embodied in section 1 of the Guardianship of Minors Act 1971. It is submitted that, as with a local authority rescission of a resolution, the latter test should be applied. Indeed, it is arguable that section 44 relates to juvenile offenders and juveniles otherwise brought before the courts under the Children and Young Persons legislation. It is noteworthy that the test was enacted before the modern child care legislation, which was introduced by the Children Act 1948, and was not, therefore, intended for that kind of legislation. In considering whether, in the light of the child's interests, the resolution should be ended, the court should look not only at what the complainant has to offer the child but also at what those looking after him can and do offer. For example, where he is living happily with foster parents, it may be in his interests that the resolution continue until the foster parents are in a position to apply for an adoption or custodianship order. The longer the child has been living in a happy environment the weaker may be the chances of the complainant obtaining a terminating order.

As with the jurisdiction to challenge the passing of a resolution,[3] the court may order the child to be joined as a party and a guardian ad litem appointed, and the child may be legally represented.[4] The rules which apply in those proceedings to the giving of evidence in the absence of the child or a parent[5] are similarly applicable.

Appeal from an order lies as of right to the Family Division of the High Court.[6] Appeal must be entered, by way of notice of motion within six weeks from the date of the juvenile court's order.[7]

---

1 CCA 1980, s 5(4). The appropriate court is one having jurisdiction where the complainant resides. A parent who is the complainant must send a notice specifying the time and place fixed for the hearing to any other parent who lives apart from him if the whereabouts of such other parent is known to him; see MC(C&YP) Rules 1988, r 30(1).
2 See Cretney, p 518, note 4.
3 See ante, para 15.41.
4 See CCA 1980, s 7(2) and MC(C&YP) Rules 1988, r 31(1).
5 See rr 35 and 30(3).
6 CCA 1980, s 6.
7 For details of the procedure, including the documents to be lodged in the principal registry see RSC Ord 90, rr 9 and 29.

(c)   *Guardianship, adoption, marriage*

15.46   A court may appoint a guardian for a child who has no parent or guardian or anyone else having parental rights with respect to him[1] and this may be done even though a resolution under section 3 is in force. However, such an appointment brings the resolution to an end. So, too does an adoption order, a freeing for adoption order and an order vesting the parental rights and duties in a person who intends to adopt the child abroad.[2] But the 1980 Act is silent on the effect of marriage of the child on a resolution. The absence of any statutory reference apparently means that a marriage does not bring the resolution to an end any more than it causes a child to cease to be in care where he is the subject of a care order or where he has been received into care under section 2. Nevertheless, marriage may well lead to rescission or termination of a resolution[3] or to the local authority entrusting the child to his or her spouse[4] under section 2(3) of the 1980 Act. Such consequences are particularly likely in view of the rule that no order can be made under care proceedings in respect of a juvenile who is or has been married.[5]

1 GMA 1971, s 5, ante, para 4.13.
2 CCA 1980, s 5(2).
3 Or revocation of a care order.
4 Presumably, as 'a friend'!
5 CYPA 1969, s 1(5)(c), ante, para 14.50.

V CARE ORDERS UNDER CHILDREN AND YOUNG PERSONS ACT 1969

15.47 As already noted,[1] one of the orders which the Children and Young Persons Act 1969 enables the juvenile court to make in criminal proceedings and care proceedings is that committing a juvenile to the care of a local authority.[2] It may also be made when a supervision order is discharged.[3]

1 Ante, paras 13.69–13.73 and 14.112.
2 Sections 1(3)(c), 7(7)(a) and 20(1). The appropriate local authority is that in which the juvenile habitually resides or, if he appears not to reside in the area of a local authority, any local authority in whose area the offence was committed or any circumstances arose in consequence of which the order is made (ss 20(2)(a) and 70(1)). In determining the place of residence, any period must be disregarded during which, while in the care of a local authority (whether by virtue of a care order or not) he resided outside the authority's area (s 20(2A), as inserted by HASSASSAA 1983, Sch 2, para 12). Where an interim care order is made (ante, paras 14.95–14.99), the court may choose any of the above authorities, but that of residence is the most likely.
3 CYPA 1969, s 15(1).

1 Effects of a care order

15.48 A care order imposes on the local authority to whose care the juvenile is committed the duty to receive him into their care and keep him in care notwithstanding any claim by his parent or guardian.[1] The general effect of the order is that the authority will have the same powers and duties as the parent or guardian would have had if the order had not been made,[2] but additionally Part III of the Child Care Act 1980[3] provides for further powers and duties in respect of all children in local authority care. The assumption of parental powers and duties is subject to the same qualifications as apply where there is a resolution in force under section 3 of the Child Care Act 1980.[4] So, the right of the parent to consent or refuse to consent to the making of an application for a freeing for adoption order and his right to agree or refuse to agree to the making of an adoption order or an order authorising adoption abroad are not transferred to the local authority.[5] The authority must not cause the child to be brought up in any religious creed other than that in which he would have been brought up but for the order.[6] The father and mother are liable to make contributions to the local authority in respect of their child who is the subject of a care order.[7] Otherwise, as with section 3 resolutions,[8] doubts exist as to the precise legal effects of a care order. The use of the terms 'powers and duties' and not 'rights and duties' further strengthens the conclusion that rights of intestate succession do not pass to the local authority, but here, too, there is need for precise legislation and for adopting uniform terminology for care orders and section 3 resolutions, so long as such resolutions remain part of the law.

1 CCA 1980, s 10(1). A care order is sufficient authority for the detention of the juvenile until he is received into the care of the local authority (s 10(4)).
2 Section 10(2), as amended by HASSASSAA 1983, Sch 10, Part I.
3 Post, paras 15.63 et seq.
4 See ante, para 15.33.
5 CCA 1980, s 10(5), as inserted by HASSASSAA 1983, Sch 2, para 47.
6 Section 10(3).
7 Section 45(1). But compare the wider rule where there is a s 3 resolution. Any person who is liable to maintain the child remains liable after the resolution is passed; see s 4(2), ante, para 15.33.
8 Ante, para 15.34.

2 Duration of care orders

(a) Age

15.49 Unless the care order is earlier terminated or varied, the juvenile remains in care until he is 18 or, if the order was made when he had attained the age of 16,[1] until he is 19;[2] but an order which otherwise would expire at 18 may, on the application of the local authority be extended to 19, if, because of his mental condition or behaviour, this is in his or the public interest.[3] The extension could in exceptional cases be crucial for the juvenile's condition,[4] for example, where he is in the middle of essential medical treatment and the local authority, in his interest, wish to ensure that it is completed.

1 That is most likely where it was made in criminal proceedings.
2 CYPA 1969, s 20(3).
3 Section 21(1). An extension can only be ordered if the juvenile is present before the court, and he must at the time be accommodated in a community home or a home provided by the Secretary of State and not be boarded out or maintained in a voluntary home (other than a community home).
4 See Home Office Guide to Part I of CYPA 1969, para 169.

(b) Adoption

15.50 If an adoption order or a freeing for adoption order or an order vesting the parental rights and duties in a person who intends to adopt the child abroad is made, a care order ceases to have effect.[1] However, the appointment of a guardian by the court under section 5 of the Guardianship of Minors Act 1971 does not terminate a care order, as it does a section 3 resolution,[2] even where the care order was made in care proceedings and not criminal proceedings.[3] As for marriage of the juvenile there is no rule about its effect on a care order, but, in view of the rule that no such order can be made in care proceedings in respect of a juvenile who is or has been married,[4] it is likely that the court will be ready to discharge an order made in those proceedings. It may be less inclined to do so where the order was made in criminal proceedings.

1 CYPA 1969, s 21A, as substituted by HASSASSAA 1983, Sch 2, para 13. Where adoption proceedings have already been instituted in the High Court, a magistrates' court should not proceed to hear an application for discharge of a care order if there would be no power to remove the child without leave of the High Court (under AA 1976, s 28); see *R v Tower Hamlets Juvenile Court, ex p London Borough of Tower Hamlets* [1984] FLR 907, [1984] Fam Law 307. Indeed, as that case indicates, it would generally be desirable not to proceed until the outcome of the adoption hearing, whether, it is submitted, the adoption is being heard by the High Court or a county court or another magistrates' court.
2 See ante, para 15.46.
3 The power to make a s 5 order depends on the child having no parent or guardian and no one else having parental rights. The 'powers' of a local authority under a care order would have to be ignored to enable a s 5 order to be made. Even on that assumption, it is very unlikely that the court would appoint a guardian, knowing that a care order is in operation.
4 CYPA 1969, s 1(5)(c).

(c)   Discharge

15.51   The local authority, to whose care the juvenile has been committed, or the juvenile or, on his behalf, his parent or guardian[1] may apply to a juvenile court[2] for the care order to be discharged.[3] Where the application is opposed, the court may, as in care proceedings, make an order under section 32A(1) of the 1969 Act that the juvenile be not represented by the parent[4] and proceed to appoint a guardian ad litem, if it appears to the court that it is in the juvenile's interests to do so.[5] The parent then becomes a party in his own right. The scope of these powers has already been examined.[6]

Where the application for discharge is unopposed, there is a shift of emphasis. Under section 32A(2), the court *must* order that no parent is to be treated as representing the juvenile or as otherwise authorised to act on his behalf,[7] unless it is satisfied that an order is not necessary for safeguarding his interests. The rule, which owes its origin to the Maria Colwell tragedy, has in mind the case where the parent applies on the juvenile's behalf for discharge and the local authority does not oppose the application, but it can also apply to the converse case where the authority is the applicant. If the court does make an order, it must appoint a guardian ad litem, but this duty is also subject to the discretion not to appoint if the court is satisfied that appointment is not necessary to safeguard the juvenile's interests.[8] The discretion not to appoint is not expressly limited to exceptional circumstances. Nor is the court obliged to give reasons for not appointing. For example, it might feel that, in view of the juvenile's age and ability to instruct a solicitor, it might exercise its own powers to grant legal aid and itself appoint a solicitor. Nevertheless, the normal rule should be a section 32A(2) order and appointment; and the temptation not to appoint because of the heavy pressures currently being imposed on panels of guardians ad litem should be resisted.

As with an order under section 32A(1), an order under section 32A(2) and an order appointing a guardian ad litem may be made before or in the course of the proceedings or by a single justice or the justices' clerk before the proceedings.[9]

1   'Guardian' has its wide meaning under the CYP legislation and this includes not only a legal guardian appointed by deed or will or order of a court but also one who in the opinion of the court has the charge or control of the juvenile (CYPA 1933, s 107(1)). For present purposes it includes anyone who was guardian when the care order was made; see CYPA 1969, s 70(2).
2   Ie a juvenile court acting for any part of the area of the local authority to whose care the child is committed by the care order or for the place where he resides (CYPA 1969, s 21(6)).
3   CYPA 1969, s 21(2). For comment and criticism see RCCL, Chapter 20.
4   Subsequent references to a parent include a guardian.
5   MC(C&YP) Rules 1988, r 16(1).
6   See ante, paras 14.59 et seq.
7   But such an order will not invalidate the application even though it was made by the parent on the juvenile's behalf.
8   Section 32B(1), as inserted by CA 1975, s 64. Appointment can be made by a single justice.
9   See CYPA 1969, s 32A(2) and (4); MC(C&YP) Rules 1988, r 16(4).

15.52   If the court allows the application[1] and discharges the order, it may substitute a supervision order, provided the juvenile is still under 18,[2] but, where he is under that age, it must not discharge the care order if he appears to be in need of care or control, unless it is satisfied that he will received that care or control, whether through the making of a supervision order or 'otherwise, for example, exceptionally by voluntary supervision of the family where the court considers that the parents are more likely to respond to that form of supervision rather than a supervision order'. This restriction relating to care or control is logical, because the care order could not have been made, either in care proceedings[3] or criminal proceedings,[4] unless the court had been satisfied that the juvenile was in need of care or control which he would have been unlikely to receive unless the court made an order.

1   Legal Aid is available to the juvenile (Legal Aid Act 1974, s 28(3)), but, since the application is not by way of complaint, there is no power to order costs; see *R v Salisbury and Tisbury and Mere Combined Juvenile Court, ex p Ball* [1986] 1 FLR 1, [1985] Fam Law 313; see Clarke Hall and Morrison, para B[767].
2   CYPA 1969, s 21(2). There is no power to substitute a supervision order for an interim care order. For the latter order see ante, paras 14.95 et seq.
3   CYPA 1969, s 1(2), ante, paras 14.04 et seq.
4   Section 7(7A)(b), ante, para 13.70.

15.53   In deciding whether to order discharge and whether there is need of care or control, the court should be governed by the welfare principle as stated in section 44(1) of the Children and Young Persons Act 1933,[1] but here yet again no further statutory guidelines or criteria are provided, except for the unhelpful requirement that it 'must be appropriate to discharge the order';[2] and the widely held opinion[3] is that courts tend to be influenced more by considerations of the fitness of the parent to resume care and control than by the need of the juvenile.[4] The discharge of a care order is as serious a matter as the making of the order, and demands the most thorough investigation on the juvenile's behalf, which goes beyond the question of parental fitness, especially where the juvenile has long been separated from the parent in a happy environment. One of the greatest risks is that the substitution of a supervision order may be seen as a means of meeting both the wishes of the parent and the needs of the juvenile, and 'it seems to have led some courts to take an unrealistic view of what is in reality practicable'.[5] There have been more than enough tragedies to illustrate the limitations of effective supervision once the juvenile is returned home, but the risk of harm could be reduced if the court were given power when discharging the care order to impose conditions or make orders regulating the juvenile's return to his home, for example, by allowing it initially for a short trial period and then, if appropriate, planning a phased return. In the absence of such a power it may be necessary to resort to wardship jurisdiction.[6]

1 It has already been suggested, ante, para 14.106 that the paramountcy of the child's welfare should, and in practice does govern in care proceedings, but quaere whether, where the care order was made in criminal proceedings, the question of its discharge should take account also of the public interest; see ante, para 13.117.

2 CYPA 1969, s 21(2). See *R v Chertsey Justices, ex p E* [1987] 2 FLR 415, where it was held that the court is not compelled to discharge the order if the primary condition on which it was made no longer exists.

3 See Adcock and White, *Care Orders or the Assumption of Parental Rights – The Long Term Effects*, [1980] JSWL 257 at p 258; Bromley, p 463; Cretney, pp 542–543; Hayes and Bevan, para 4.9.1.

4 Although the onus is on the parents to show that they are 'now in a position to provide the appropriate degree of care' – per Ormrod LJ in *Re W (a minor) (justices' decision: review)* (1981) 2 FLR 360 at 367.

5 Cretney, p 543.

6 See *Re J (a minor) (wardship: jurisdiction)* [1984] 1 All ER 29, [1984] 1 WLR 81, CA.

15.54 Where the discharge of a care order is refused, no further application can be made for at least three months, unless the juvenile court otherwise consents.[1] The juvenile may appeal to the Crown Court against the dismissal of the application or against any supervision order which is made.[2] Appeal is by way of a rehearing before a judge and two magistrates. A parent can appeal on the juvenile's behalf except where a separate representation order has been made, in which case the parent can appeal in his own right.[3] The local authority has no right of appeal to the Crown Court, but instead will have to rely on wardship. It may, however, appeal on a point of law or want of jurisdiction by way of case stated to the Family Division.[4] For further details on appeals the reader is referred to Chapter 14.[5]

1 CYPA 1969, s 21(3)(b). Where an application to discharge an interim care order is refused, no further application is possible at all, unless the court consents (s 21(3)(a)). It may conveniently be noted here that, apart from a juvenile court, the High Court may also discharge an interim care order on the application of the juvenile or, on his behalf, his parent or guardian (ss 22(4) and 70(2)); but, if discharge is refused, the local authority shall not exercise their powers which enable them to allow a parent or other person to be in charge of the juvenile (under CCA 1980, s 21(2)), except with the consent and in accordance with any directions of the High Court.

2 CYPA 1969, s 21(4).

3 *AR v Avon County Council* [1985] Fam 150, [1985] 2 All ER 981.

4 See MCA 1980, s 111.

5 Paras 14.114 et seq.

(d) Remand to care of local authority

15.55 When a juvenile offender is remanded to the care of a local authority,[1] the authority must, as where a care order is made, receive the juvenile and keep him in their care, notwithstanding any claim by his parent or guardian.[2] This power to remand has already been examined.[3]

1 Under CYPA 1969, s 23(1).
2 CCA 1980, s 10(1). The juvenile then becomes subject to Part III of the Act, as to which see post, paras 15.64 et seq.
3 See ante, para 12.122.

VI COMMITTAL OR REMOVAL TO CARE UNDER OTHER ENACTMENTS

15.56 A number of other statutes provide either for committal or for removal to the care of a local authority. All but one have already been dealt with, but separate treatment does not focus on the lack of uniformity and the uncertain scope of the provisions.

1 Committal to care

15.57 There are six statutes which provide for reception into care 'as if' this has occurred under section 2 of the Child Care Act 1980:

  (i) Guardianship of Minors Act 1971, s 9, as amended by Guardianship Act 1973, ss 2(2)(b) and 4 and prospectively by Family Law Reform Act 1987, s 10 and Sch 2.
 (ii) Domestic Proceedings and Magistrates' Courts Act 1978, s 10.
(iii) Matrimonial Causes Act 1973, s 43.
 (iv) Adoption Act 1976, s 26, (on refusal of adoption order).
  (v) Children Act 1975, s 34(4) (on refusal of custodianship order) and s 36 (on revocation of custodianship order).
 (vi) Family Law Reform Act 1969, s 7 (wards of court).

Reference has already been made[1] to the differing powers of the courts with regard to giving directions to the local authority over the treatment of the child. The other main criticism of the provisions is their failure to state the precise effect of the order. In one respect it is like a care order under the Children and Young Persons Act 1969, because so long as it is in force the child remains in care notwithstanding any claim by a parent, who can only recover the child by obtaining discharge of the order of committal. But the reason for uncertainty of the scope of the order lies in 'the contradiction or perhaps impossibility of fitting a court committal into care into a voluntary scheme whereby parents agree to allow a local authority to care for their children on a temporary basis. These committal to care orders are in fact equivalent to neither a section 2 nor a section 3 care.'[2] The effect seems to be that the child is to be treated as though he has been received into care under section 2 of the 1980 Act, subject to three qualifications; namely (a) his removal by the parent requires discharge of the order, (b) if the order is made by a divorce court or in wardship proceedings or by the High Court in custody cases under section 9 of the Guardianship of Minors Act 1971, the court can issue directions, and (c) *semble*, the local authority are not empowered to pass a section 3 resolution.[3]

1 Ante, para 3.57.
2 Maidment, [1981] JSWL 21 at p 22.
3 This view is preferred by Maidment, ibid at p 23.

2   Removal to care

(a)   Removal from unregistered voluntary home

15.58   As will be seen,[1] provision is made for the compulsory registration of voluntary homes. Where a home, not being a community home under the Child Care Act 1980, is not registered or is removed from the register the Secretary of State for Social Services may require the local authority in whose area the home is situated to remove from the home and receive into their care under section 2 of the 1980 Act all or any of the children accommodated therein. The authority must comply with the request whether or not the circumstances fall within that section and even if the children appear to be over the age of 17.[2] The removal into local authority care may prompt the parents to request the return of the child to them,[3] but it has been pointed out[4] that it is by no means clear whether the parents may remove the child at will. Presumably, the rules applicable to section 2 cases apply, so that, if the child has been in care for at least six months, 28 days' notice of intended removal must be given.[5]

1 Post, para 15.74.
2 See s 57(6) and s 41.
3 See ante, paras 15.28–15.30.
4 See Maidment, op cit at p 24, who also questions whether parental agreement to the reception into care is necessary.
5 See ante, para 15.29.

(b)   Removal of protected child

15.59   On the complaint of a local authority a protected child within the meaning of the Adoption Act 1976[1] may be ordered by a juvenile court or, where there is 'imminent danger' to the child, by a magistrate to be removed from unsuitable surroundings to a place of safety and the local authority *may* then receive him into care under section 2 of the Child Care Act 1980, whether or not the conditions of that section apply and notwithstanding that he may appear to the authority to be over 17.[2] The authority must if practicable inform the parent or guardian of the removal,[3] and it seems[4] that the parent must consent to the child remaining in care, otherwise the local authority may feel it necessary to commence care proceedings.

1 For the meaning see ante, para 5.66.
2 AA 1976, s 34(3).
3 Sub-s (4).
4 Maidment, op cit, p 23.

(c)   Removal of foster child

15.60   The same rules govern the removal of a foster child from unsuitable surroundings under the Foster Children Act 1980.[1]

1 Section 12.

3   Power to make custody orders where child is in care

15.61   There is no legal objection to a custody order being made in divorce proceedings or proceedings under the Domestic Proceedings and Magistrates' Courts Act 1978[1] when a child is in local authority care, but the courts are reluctant to do so, especially if the child is the subject of a care order,[2] and, even if a custody order were made, its operation would in practice be postponed, at least in so far as it would impede the local authority's discretion. Nevertheless, one advantage in obtaining it would be to strengthen the case of the parent to whom it is granted to seek discharge of the care order.[3] That advantage is less likely where the care order was made in criminal proceedings, since the conduct of the juvenile and the public interest will be prominent factors in deciding whether to order discharge. However, even where the care order was made in those proceedings, it may well be convenient for the parents to settle the issue of custody on their divorce, rather than postpone it until the care order comes to an end, even though in the interim the custodial parent will not be able to exercise his powers.

It is expressly provided that a magistrates' court cannot make an order for access in respect of a child who is 'already for the purposes of Part III of the Child Care Act 1980 in the care of a local authority'.[4] The restriction is not, therefore, limited to children who are the subject of care orders. Although there is no corresponding provision in the Matrimonial Causes Act 1973, it is submitted that a divorce court will be as reluctant to make an access order as a custody order, on the ground that to do so would interfere with the local authority's discretion. The fact that a parent may now have a remedy, albeit restricted, for obtaining access under the 1980 Act[5] is a further reason for non-intervention by the divorce court.

1 See *M v Humberside County Council* [1979] Fam 114 at 119, [1979] 2 All ER 744 at 752.
2 See *H v H (Child in Care: Court's Jurisdiction)* [1973] Fam 62, [1973] 1 All ER 801.
3 See Lowe (1980) 43 MLR 586 at p 588; Horsman, *Custody Orders for the Child in Care* (1979) 143 JP 517.
4 DPMCA 1978, s 8(7)(b) as amended by CCA 1980, Sch 5, para 40.
5 See post, para 15.86.

15.62   The Children Act 1975 does not deal with the question of whether or not a custodianship order can be made, and if so its effect, while there is in force an order which has committed the care of a child to a local authority and the authority has then to treat him as if he had been received into care under section 2 of the Child Care Act 1980. In such cases the child continues in local authority care notwithstanding any claim by a parent or other person. It is doubtful whether this restriction will prevent a foster parent, for example, with whom the child was placed by the local authority, from seeking a custodianship order. If he does and a custodianship order is made, it is submitted that the local authority disappears from the picture, as it does when of its own volition it receives a child under section 2 of the 1980 Act without any accompanying order and a custodianship order is later made.

VII TREATMENT OF CHILDREN IN CARE[1]

1 The general duty

15.63 When a child is in local authority care for any of the reasons already considered in this chapter, he must be treated in accordance with Part III of the Child Care Act 1980,[2] which must be read with other provisions in the Act and *either* in conjunction with the general assumption by the local authority of rights/powers and duties where there is a section 3 resolution or a care order under the Children and Young Persons Act 1969, *or* subject to certain directions of the court, where there is a committal to care in divorce or wardship proceedings or in High Court custody cases.[3]

1 See generally, Freeman, *The Rights and Wrongs of Children*, Chapter 5; RCCL, Chapter 9.
2 Sections 17–30.
3 Supra, para 15.57.

15.64 Part III imposes on a local authority a general duty, namely, that in reaching any decision 'relating to' a child in their care they must give first consideration to the need to safeguard and promote the welfare of the child throughout his childhood, and before coming to any decision on any matter they must, so far as practicable, ascertain his wishes and feelings.[1] It is submitted that, even where the parental rights/powers and duties are not vested in the local authority,[2] the *Gillick* principle applies, and the older and more intellectually mature the child is the greater the weight to be given to his wishes and feelings, for example, where there is a choice of schools for him to attend. In providing for him the authority must, where it is reasonable, make use of facilities and services which are available for children who are in the care of their own parents. For example, if the child is living in a community home and it is known that he has special academic or sporting proclivities for which the local neighbourhood provides special facilities the authority must, it is submitted, see that he has the chance to use them. The general duty of the authority is, however, modified to the extent that the 1980 Act[3] enables them and the Secretary of State to act inconsistently with that duty in order to protect members of the public, for example, by restricting the child's liberty in a community home.[4] The powers conferred by that Act and the Children and Young Persons Act 1969 are very wide, but the local authority should always subordinate them to their duty of trying to bring the period of care to an end if the child's welfare is likely to be best served in that way.[5] However, the risk is that shortage of accommodation may lead the authority to return the child to the parents when they are unable or unsuitable to care for him.[6]

1 Section 18(1). For the similar provision in s 6 of the Adoption Act 1976, and for the meaning of 'first consideration' see ante, para 5.12. RCCL, para 2.18 recommends retention of this test rather than the paramountcy test, since there are other relevant considerations.

2 See Maidment, [1981] JSWL 21 at pp 24–26 for the problem of defining the precise legal relationship between the local authority on the one hand and the child and parent on the other where the child is in voluntary care under s 2 of the 1980 Act.
3 Sections 18(3) and 19.
4 For the special provisions relating to secure accommodation see post, paras 15.77 et seq.
5 See ss 2(3) and 21(2) of CCA 1980 (responsibility of trying to have the care of the child taken over by the parent, guardian, relative or friend) and s 1 of that Act (duty of diminishing the need to keep the child in care).
6 For consequent problems arising from such a policy see Hoggett 117 Sol Jo 3 and 27.

15.65   Another closely associated question is the extent to which the general duty under section 18(1) can restrict the power of a local authority to close a children's home. In *A-G v Hammersmith and Fulham London Borough Council*,[1] Dillon J drew a highly artificial distinction between a decision to close a home as one 'affecting' a child in care and a decision what to do with a particular child when the decision to close is implemented as one 'relating to' the child. Only the latter was subject to section 18(1).[2] In *R v Solihull Metropolitan Borough Council, ex p C*[3] McCullough J held that the fixing of the date of closure fell within the subsection, which was to be applied individually in respect of each child in the home, but he found it unnecessary to decide whether it also applied to the decision to close. However, earlier in *Liddle v Sunderland Borough Council*[4] Latey J rejected the distinction drawn by Dillon J and held that a decision to close did 'relate to' each child in the home, so that first consideration must be given to his welfare. There is evidence[5] that courts are following this far more satisfactory approach, and it is suggested that the parents of children in residential care should be alert to any threatened closure so that it may be challenged with a view to ensuring that the local authority comply with their general duty. The application of section 18(1) will entitle them to take account of their resources, or lack of them, and of any competing claims, for example of the elderly, for accommodation, but the need to give 'first consideration' to the welfare of the children should 'weigh the scales down' in their favour.[6] That emphasis may not be enough to meet the views of some critics,[7] but until there is judicial clarification of section 18(1) it would be unrealistic to expect more.

1 (1979) Times, 18 December.
2 For criticism see Freeman (1980) 144 JP 38.
3 [1984] FLR 363, [1984] Fam Law 175.
4 (1982) 13 Fam Law 250.
5 See Freeman, [1984] JSWL 44 at p 45.
6 Per Latey J (1983) 13 Fam Law at pp 252–253.
7 See, for example, Freeman [1984] JSWL 44 at p 46.

2   Accommodation and maintenance

15.66   Section 21(1) of the Child Care Act 1980[1] requires a local authority to provide accommodation and maintenance for children in their care, but gives them a wide discretion in the choice of the kinds of accommodation which the section allows, except that the accommodation must so far as practicable be near the child's home, provided that would be consistent with the authority's general duty under section 18.[2] In many cases encouraging and planning access to the child's family and neighbourhood will be consistent with promoting the child's welfare.[3] The local authority can discharge its duty by (1) boarding out the child,[4] or (2) maintaining him in a community home, or (3) maintaining him in a home provided by the Secretary of State which offers specialised facilities or services, or (4) maintaining him in a voluntary home (other than a community home) whose managers are willing to receive him, or (5) by making such other arrangements for him as seem appropriate to the local authority. When the Children's Home Act 1982 comes into force a local authority will be able to accommodate a child in a children's home registered under that Act.

1 As amended by HASSASSAA 1983, Sch 2, para 49.
2 Supra, para 15.64.
3 See DHSS Circular LAC (83) 13, para 12.
4 See ante, paras 7.18 et seq.

(a) Community homes[1]

15.67 Part IV of the Child Care Act 1980, as amended, has abandoned the comprehensive and integrated system of community homes planned on a regional basis, for which the Children and Young Persons Act 1969 provided. Instead it enables a local authority either alone or jointly with one or more authorities to make such arrangements as they consider appropriate for providing community homes for children, whether in their care or not.[2] In making arrangements the authority must 'have regard to the need for ensuring the availability of accommodation of different descriptions and suitable for different purposes and the requirements of different descriptions of children'.[3] This allows for variety and flexibility in the provision of homes, but does not, it is suggested, give sufficient emphasis to the priority of children's needs, an omission which local authorities may welcome, given the competing needs of others, especially the elderly, for accommodation. It also remains to be seen whether the present powers will effectively replace the regional systems or whether they will lead to a further drain on resources which under the former system might have been borne proportionately on a regional basis.

1 See generally for the neglected topic of residential care, Freeman and Lyon. *The Law of Residential Homes and Day-Care Establishments* (1983), especially Chapter 3.
2 Section 31(1), as substituted by HASSASSAA 1983, s 4(1). A community home may be used as a place of safety to which a child 'at risk' may be taken. Indeed, a local authority is required to make provision in community homes provided by them or in a controlled community home (see infra) for the reception and maintenance of children removed to a place of safety (s 73(1)).
3 Section 31(2). A local authority may provide accommodation in a community home for anyone over compulsory school age (16) but under 21 and the home is conveniently near the place where he is employed or seeking employment or receiving education or training (s 72).

15.68 A community home is either a home provided by a local authority or a voluntary home provided by a voluntary organisation but with a local authority participating in the management of it.[1] The latter kind of community homes are classified into 'controlled' homes and 'assisted' homes, according to the extent of that participation. A home is 'controlled' when the responsibility for its management, equipment and maintenance lies with the local authority[2] and, under its instrument of management,[3] two-thirds of the body of managers are appointed by the authority with the remainder appointed in accordance with the instrument from among those who are managers of the voluntary home. The latter, known as 'foundation managers', represent the interests of the voluntary organisation providing the home and see that, so far as practicable, the character of the home as a voluntary home is preserved and the terms of any trust deed relating to it are observed.[4] When the responsibility is undertaken by the voluntary organisation and the foundation managers constitute two-thirds of the management, with one-third appointed by the local authority, the home is an assisted home.[5] Whether the home is controlled or assisted the premises provided by the voluntary organisation remain vested in it. When an instrument of management is drawn up by the Secretary of State it may include, inter alia, provisions specifying the nature and purpose of the particular home and the number of places in it to be made available to local authorities.[6]

1 Section 31(3).
2 Section 31(4). See also s 37.
3 An instrument is drawn up by the Secretary of State (s 35(1)).
4 See s 35(3)(a) and (4). Should there be any conflict between the terms of the trust deed and those of the instrument of management, the instrument prevails, (s 36(3)). It is up to the voluntary organisation to apply under the law relating to charities to seek amendment of the deed.
5 Sections 31(5) and 35(3)(b) and (4). See also s 38. The Secretary of State is empowered (by s 82) to pay grants to voluntary organisations for the establishment, maintenance and improvement of assisted community homes.
6 Section 36(2).

15.69 The co-operation of local authorities and voluntary organisations is implicit not only in the willingness to make homes available but also in their mutual relationship in the successful running of controlled and assisted homes. The 1980 Act, however, confers on the Secretary of State power to determine disputes whenever they arise[1] (1) in respect of controlled homes, between the local authority specified in the instrument of management and either the voluntary organisation providing the home or any local authority who place a child in their care in the home, and (2) in respect of assisted homes, between the voluntary organisation and a local authority placing a child there.[2] Upon determination of the dispute the Secretary of State can give such directions as he thinks fit to the authority or organisation concerned.

1 The need for his intervention is exceptional.
2 Section 42. Where the trust deed of the home empowers an ecclesiastical authority to decide questions on religious instruction the dispute must not be referred to the Secretary of State (sub-s (5)).

15.70 Community homes, like voluntary homes, come under Central Government inspection,[1] inspection being usually carried out by officers of the Children's Department of the DSS but exceptionally by an officer of a local authority, if the authority consent.[2] Anyone authorised to inspect a home may do so on production of some duly authenticated document showing his authority to do so.[3] Refusal to allow entry is not only an offence, but is deemed to be a reasonable cause to suspect that a child is being neglected in a manner likely to cause him unnecessary suffering or injury to health so as to justify issuing a warrant under section 40 of the Children and Young Persons Act 1933.[4]

If the Secretary of State considers that premises used as a community home are unsuitable or that the home is not being run according to regulations governing them[5] or is otherwise unsatisfactory, he may direct that the premises are not to be used as a community home.[6] A voluntary organisation which wishes to cease to provide a home as a controlled or assisted community home must give at least two years' notice to the Secretary of State before they can do so, and conversely the same period of notice must be given by a local authority to the Secretary of State and the voluntary organisation of their intention to cease to use a home as a controlled or assisted home.[7]

1 Section 74.
2 Sub-s (3).
3 Section 75.
4 For s 40 see ante, para 14.44.
5 Ie the Community Homes Regulations 1972 and the Secure Accommodation Regulations 1983.
6 CCA 1980, s 40.
7 Sections 43 and 43A respectively.

The conduct of community homes
15.71 The conduct of community homes is to some extent regulated by the Community Homes Regulations 1972, which are aimed at securing the well-being of children there. The local authority or the voluntary organisation which is responsible for the home together with the managers must make 'proper provision for the care, treatment and control' of the children whom they accommodate.[1] They must make adequate arrangements for protecting the health of the children, including the appointment of a medical officer;[2] they must ensure adequate precautions against fire and accident;[3] they must ensure that each child has the opportunity to attend religious services and to receive instruction appropriate to his religious persuasion;[4] and they must provide suitable facilities in the home for visits by parents, guardians, relatives or friends.[5] However, the regulations provide only part of the answer, and leave much to the discretion of the local authority or voluntary organisation. They are empowered to approve 'such additional measures as they consider necessary for the maintenance of control in the home',[6] and it seems that this could include measures for the use of corporal punishment,[7] which was expressly allowed when the Administration of Children's Homes Regulations 1951 applied to local authority homes.[8] Regrettably the ban on corporal punishment in state schools[9] has not been expressly extended to children in institutional care. The 1972 Regulations do not prescribe rules about the size of community homes, this being left to discretion. Nor do they lay down conditions about staffing. Nevertheless, these are matters which the local authority cannot ignore if they are to fulfil their general duty of giving first consideration to the need to promote the child's welfare. That duty requires them to run a home as an effective substitute for a normal family home. This, as was pointed out long ago by the Curtis Committee,[10] means giving the child affection and personal attention, stability, the opportunity to make the best of his ability and a share in the common life within a homely environment. Those objectives are partly echoed in the general direction

in the 1972 Regulations that 'the control of a community home shall be maintained on the basis of good personal and professional relationships between the staff and the children';[11] but the objectives may be difficult to achieve.[12]

1 Regulation 3(1).
2 Regulation 5.
3 Regulation 7.
4 Regulation 8. But the regulation does not lay down how and to what extent the opportunity must be provided; see Freeman and Lyon, op cit, p 64.
5 Regulation 9.
6 Regulation 10(2).
7 DHSS Circular No 78/1972, para 13, recognised that 'it would be impracticable at this stage to prohibit the use of all forms of corporal punishment in every home'.
8 They still apply to voluntary homes; see post, para 15.74.
9 Imposed by s 47 of the Education (No 2) Act 1986, ante, para 11.62.
10 Cmnd 6922, para 427.
11 Regulation 10(1).
12 See Freeman and Lyon, p 65. See also DHSS Circular 78/1972, paras 10 and 11.

15.72   To ensure compliance with the Regulations and fulfilment of the general duty imposed by section 18(1) one or more of the managers of a controlled or assisted community home must visit the home at least once a month and a local authority must arrange similar visits for their own community homes.[1]

1 Regulation 2(2). And see supra, para 15.70 for the power of the Secretary of State to order inspection and to direct that a place be no longer used as a home.

(b)   Homes with specialised facilities

15.73   The Children and Young Persons Act 1969[1] recognised the need for new kinds of homes to deal with the special problems of severely disturbed children who are in care and empowered the Secretary of State to provide such establishments. The immediate outcome was the establishment of three Youth Treatment Centres which could 'combine the training and treatment facilities of a school, a children's home and a hospital' and also provide 'substantial provision for psychiatric observation and treatment and an element of secure accommodation'.[2] The Child Care Act 1980[3] re-enacts this provision to accommodate children in homes with special facilities which are unlikely to be readily available in community homes.

1 Section 64.
2 See HC Debs, Vol 779, No 787, col 1183.
3 Sections 21(1)(b) and 80.

(c)   Voluntary homes

15.74   There is nothing in the Child Care Act 1980 to prevent a voluntary organisation from allowing its voluntary home to be used, outside the community home system, to accommodate children who are in local authority care. A local authority may place such a child, if the managers are willing to receive him.[1] A voluntary home is widely defined.[2] It is any home or other institution for the boarding, care and maintenance of poor children which is supported wholly or partly by voluntary contributions or by endowments,[3] but not being a school and not including any mental nursing home within the meaning of the Nursing Homes Act 1975 or a residential care home within the meaning of the Registered Homes Act 1984.[4] Every voluntary home has to be registered with the Secretary of State,[5] and its name may be removed from the register if the home is not conducted in accordance with the Administration of Children's Homes Regulations 1951 or is otherwise unsatisfactory.[6] Those Regulations are more detailed in their directions than are the Community Homes Regulations 1972 but most of them have their counterparts in the latter; for example, with regard to medical care; providing precautions against fire,[7] the religious upbringing of the child,[8] facilities for visits by parents and others; and monthly inspections.[9] There are two notable differences. First, the Secretary of State may give directions limiting the number of children who may be accommodated in a voluntary home.[10] Second, the 1951 Regulations do authorise, albeit within strict limits, the use of corporal punishment. Here, again, it is regrettable that the ban in state schools has not been extended. Ironically, while corporal punishment remains permissible, there are no provisions for restricting the liberty of the child nor for secure accommodation to be available in voluntary homes.

1 CCA 1980, s 21(1)(c).
2 Section 56.
3 For example, the name of Barnardo's Homes readily comes to mind.
4 Defined (by s 1(1)) as an establishment which provides or intends to provide, whether for reward or not, residential accommodation with both board and personal care for persons in need of this by reason of old age, disablement, past or present dependence on alcohol or drugs or past or present mental disorder.
5 Section 57. Application for registration must be made in accordance with the Voluntary Homes (Registration) Regulations 1948. Every year the person in charge of the home must send to the Secretary of State particulars relating to the home as prescribed by the Voluntary Homes (Return of Particulars) Regulations 1949, as amended by CCA 1980, s 59.
6 Section 57(4). Where there is a refusal to register or an approval which is subject to conditions or a removal from the register, there is a right to make representations to the Secretary of State, and, if these are unsuccessful, a right of appeal to a Registered Homes Tribunal; see ss 57A, 57B, 57C and 57D.
7 But the 1951 Regulations do not expressly cover precautions against accidents.
8 But the 1951 Regulations require the body which is responsible for running the home to secure, so far as practicable, that he attends religious services and receives religious instruction, and not merely that he has the opportunity to do so, as the 1972 Regulations require. This anomalous distinction should be statutorily settled one way or the other.
9 Additionally, voluntary homes, like community homes are subject to central government inspection (CCA 1980, s 74).
10 Regulation 12.

(d) Private children's home

15.75 The use of privately owned children's homes to accommodate children who are in local authority care is larger than is generally realised.[1] When the Children's Homes Act 1982[2] comes into force a local authority will only be able to place a child in their care in such a home if it is registered under the Act. The provisions governing registration, annual review and cancellation of registration are similar to those relating to voluntary homes, with rights of representation and appeals in respect of decisions on registration. It is expected that Regulations will be enacted in terms similar to those in the 1951 Regulations.

1 There are about 175 of these homes, with about 2,500 of the children being placed there by local authorities; see Freeman and Lyon, p 20.
2 As amended by HASSASSAA 1983.

(e)   Other arrangements for accommodation

15.76   In enabling a local authority to make such other arrangements as seem appropriate to them for accommodating a child in their care, section 21(1) of the Child Care Act 1980 gives no indication as to what forms these may take. A likely use of this power is in respect of handicapped or physically or mentally ill children who may be accommodated in special schools or long stay hospital wards.[1] Another possibility is placement for adoption. But this power under section 21(1) does not affect that under section 18(2) to make use of any of the facilities and services available for children in the care of their own parents. Thus, the authority may, for example, put the child into lodgings or residential employment. Moreover, under section 21(2) an authority may allow a child in their care to be under the charge and control of a parent, guardian, relative or friend for a fixed period or until the authority otherwise determine, except that where the High Court has refused an application to discharge an interim order the local authority may exercise its powers only with the consent and under the directions of that court.[2] At the end of the fixed period or, where no period is fixed, at any time, it is open to the authority in a case where the child is in care by virtue of a resolution under section 3 of the Child Care Act 1980 to give written notice to the parent etc requiring him to hand back the child to them. If he or anyone else should then harbour or conceal the child or prevent his return, he is guilty of an offence.[3]

1 See further Freeman and Lyon, p 21.
2 CYPA 1969, s 22(4). Note also, ante, para 13.72, the power of the court when making a care order in criminal proceedings, or in care proceedings based on the offence condition, to add a condition that the local authority shall not exercise their power under s 21(2) of CCA.
3 CCA 1980, s 14, post, para 15.103.

(f)   Secure accommodation

15.77   Section 21A of the Child Care Act 1980 and the Secure Accommodation (No 2) Regulations 1983[1] empower a local authority and a juvenile court to restrict the liberty of a child in local authority care by placing and keeping him in 'secure accommodation', but only subject to certain criteria and conditions and within temporal limits. The statutory restrictions are a response to the widespread concern, expressed in various influential quarters,[2] over the former extensive use of secure accommodation in community homes. The Act is not, however, confined to community homes, and most of the Regulations also apply outside the community homes system, for example to secure units in hospitals.[3]

1 SI 1983/1808, as amended by the Secure Accommodation (No 2) (Amendment) Regulations 1986 SI 1986/1591. The Regulations are made under s 21A(2).
2 Notably by the DHSS in *Legal and Professional Aspects of the Use of Secure Accommodation for Children in Care* (1981); a Report of the Parliamentary Penal Affairs Group (1981); and a Report of the Children's Legal Centre (1982).
3 In *R v Northampton Juvenile Court, ex p Borough of Hammersmith and Fulham* [1985]

FLR 13, [1985] Fam Law 124, DC, it was held that a 'behaviour modification unit' in a hospital where the régime was designed to restrict liberty was secure accommodation.

(i) Children to whom section 21A applies
15.78 The section and the 1983 Regulations apply to the following categories of children:

(1) Those in local authority care to whom Part III of the Child Care Act 1980 applies. They are children in care under section 2 of the Act or by virtue of a care order or a warrant under section 23(1) of the Children and Young Persons Act 1969. As will be seen, there are special rules relating to those who are remanded in care under a warrant.

(2) Those specified in the Schedule to the Regulations. The main specified categories are those earlier examined in Section VI.[1] Others who merit express mention are children removed under section 40 of the Children and Young Persons Act 1933[2] and those who are the subject of place of safety orders[3] or interim care orders.[4]

(3) Children committed to local authority care by a judge exercising the inherent wardship jurisdiction.[5] The judge may direct that the ward of court be placed or kept in secure accommodation and it is not necessary, as it formerly was, to apply to the juvenile court for authorisation.[6] In deciding whether to make a direction the judge must consider whether the statutory criteria in section 21A apply.[7] Any direction is not bound by the time limits which operate where an order is made by a juvenile court.[8]

1 See ante, paras 15.56 to 15.60.
2 Ante, para 14.44.
3 Ante, paras 14.35 et seq.
4 Ante, paras 14.95 et seq.
5 Regulation 5. This is distinct from the statutory jurisdiction to commit to care under FLRA 1969, s 7(2), which falls within category (2) above.
6 The law was amended by the Secure Accommodation (No 2) (Amendment) Regulations 1986, r 4, introduced because of a series of conflicting judicial decisions culminating in *M v Lambeth Borough Council (No 3)* [1986] 2 FLR 136, [1986] Fam Law 265, CA. Detailed guidance on the amending Regulations is given in Local Authority Circular LAC (86) 13; and see Maidment (1987) 137 NLJ 92.
7 See infra, para 15.80.
8 Regulation 10(3). For orders by a juvenile court see post, para 15.83.

(ii) Children to whom section 21A does not apply
15.79 The section does not apply[1] to the following children, to whom it would otherwise apply:[2]

(1) Those detained under the Mental Health Act 1983.

(2) Those detained, on conviction for grave crimes, under section 53 of the Children and Young Persons Act 1933.[3]

(3) Those detained in a place of safety under section 25(4) of the Children and Young Persons Act 1969.

(4) Those who are over compulsory school age but under 21 and are accommodated in a convenient community home under section 72 of the Child Care Act 1980.

1 See Regulation 6.

2 Ie because they are in local authority care.
3 See ante, para 13.98 et seq. If a child is not in local authority care and is detained under s 53 a local authority may agree to detain him in secured accommodation. If they do, they will receive detailed instructions and guidance from the DSS; see DHSS Circular LAC (83) 18, para 60.

(iii)   The restrictions
15.80 *(1) Criteria* The criteria which must be met before a child may have his liberty restricted are:

either (a) that (i) he has a history of absconding and is likely to abscond from any accommodation which is not secure accommodation; and

(ii) if he absconds, it is likely that his physical, mental or moral welfare will be at risk;

or (b) that if he is kept in any other accommodation, other than secure accommodation, he is likely to injure himself or other persons.[1]

Moreover, once the criteria of (a) or (b) cease to apply, he can no longer be kept in secure accommodation.

The criteria are modified where the child is remanded into local authority care[2] and is charged with or convicted of an offence which, in the case of a person aged at least 21, is imprisonable for 14 years or more or is charged with or convicted of an offence of violence or has previously been convicted of such an offence. In any of those cases the criteria are that he is likely to abscond or is likely to injure himself or other people.[3]

1 Section 21A(1).
2 Under CYPA 1969, s 23.
3 Regulation 7.

15.81 *(2) Other conditions* No accommodation *in a community home* may be used as secure accommodation without the approval of the Secretary of State, and in giving approval he may impose such terms and conditions as he sees fit.[1] An example of this control is the need for specific approval to be obtained to use single rooms as secure rooms, which, contrary to policy before the present restrictions were introduced, is to be regarded as exceptional.[2] Another restriction is that no child under ten years of age can be kept in secure accommodation *in a community home* without the prior consent of the Secretary of State.[3] This restriction does not apply to a ward of court, but it has been advised[4] that the judge in wardship proceedings may wish to have his attention drawn to the Secretary of State's view in considering an application regarding the placement of a ward of court under the age of ten in secure accommodation.

1 Regulation 3.
2 See DHSS Circular LAC (83) 18, para 6 and Annex B.
3 Regulation 4. Note also the right of the Secretary of State to inspect records of children kept in secure accommodation (post, para 15.83) and his general power under CCA 1980, s 74, to authorise persons to inspect a children's home on his behalf.
4 See LAC (86) 13, para 5.

15.82 *(3) Time limits* A child may not be kept in secure accommodation without the authority of a juvenile court for more than 72 hours, whether consecutively or in aggregate in any period of 28 consecutive days.[1] The maximum period which a juvenile court may initially authorise is three months,[2] but it may authorise a further period not exceeding six months,[3] except that where the child is remanded to local authority care[4] the maximum period is the period of the remand.[5] If the proceedings are adjourned, the court may make an interim order for the child to be kept in secure accommodation for the period of the adjournment.[6]

1 Regulation 10(1). For the purpose of calculation public holidays and Sundays are ignored (Reg 11).
2 Regulation 12.
3 Regulation 13.
4 Under CYPA 1969, s 23.
5 Regulation 14.
6 CCA 1980, s 21A(4).

(iv)   The application for an order
15.83   Application is made by the local authority by way of notice,[1] and, *semble*,[2] may be made to any juvenile court. It is likely to be a court for the area in which the community home, young offender institution or other institution in which the child is being kept is situated. If the child is being kept in secure accommodation *in a community home* the local authority must as soon as possible notify the child's parents or guardian, if practicable, and, where one has been appointed, his visitor[3] of the intention to apply for an order.[4] The child must be legally represented, unless his application for legal aid was refused or, having been given the opportunity to apply, did not do so.[5] But there is no power to appoint a guardian ad litem. Proceedings are governed by the same procedural rules as govern care proceedings and Part III of the Magistrates' Courts (Children and Young Persons) Rules 1988 apply.[6] Where the question of secure accommodation is being considered in exercise of the inherent wardship jurisdiction, the court should, unless the ward is already represented by a guardian ad litem or there are special reasons why the ward should not be so represented, join the ward as a party and appoint a guardian ad litem to protect his interests and ensure that his views are made known to the court.[7]

If the court finds that any of the relevant criteria are satisfied, it must make an order,[8] but the period of authorisation is entirely within its discretion. The local authority are likely to seek an order for the maximum period, arguing that even if it is granted they are still free to and may well release the child before the period expires and while the criteria continue to be satisfied. Courts should be cautious about accepting this argument and should be alert to putting the onus on the local authority to return within a shorter period with a view to seeking extension.

Appeal lies to the Crown Court against a decision of a juvenile court.[9] Where the appeal is being made by the child against an order placing him in secure accommodation, he may continue to be kept in that accommodation until the appeal is heard. In the converse case where the local authority is appealing against a refusal to make an order, the child must not be placed or kept in secure accommodation pending the outcome of the appeal.

1 Regulation 8.
2 See Clarke Hall and Morrison, para B[127].
3 For appointment of a visitor see post, para 15.101.

4   Regulation 15.
5   CCA 1980, s 21A(6).
6   See ante paras 14.76 et seq. Once the court has determined that the relevant criteria are
    satisfied, reports may be considered for determining the maximum period of detention
    in secure accommodation. The rules governing disclosure of reports are the same as those
    applicable in care proceedings. See r 26, and for care proceedings r 25, ante, para 14.87.
7   *Practice Direction* [1986] 3 All ER 320, [1986] 1 WLR 1300. Should the same facility
    not be available to a child in the juvenile court?
8   CCA 1980, s 21A(3).
9   Section 21A(5).

(v)   Reviews

15.84   The local authority must ensure that the case of every child who
is in secure accommodation *in a community home* is reviewed at intervals
not exceeding three months and they must appoint at least two persons
to conduct the review.[1] Those persons must be satisfied that (i) the criteria
for keeping the child in secure accommodation continue to apply, and (ii)
that the placement in it continues to be appropriate. In considering the
latter they must have regard to the child's welfare, and in undertaking
the review must take account of the views of the child, his parent or guardian,
anyone else who has had care of him, his independent visitor (if appointed)
and the authority managing the community home, if different from the
child's care or responsible authority. These parties must, if practicable,
be informed of the outcome of the review.

Where a ward of court has been placed in secure accommodation and
it is considered that the criteria for keeping the ward in it no longer apply,
or that the placement is no longer appropriate, the local authority must
as soon as practicable notify the court exercising wardship jurisdiction in
relation to the child and seek the court's further directions.[2]

1   Regulations 16 and 17.
2   Regulation 17(4).

(vi)   Records

15.85   The local authority responsible for the management of secure
accommodation in a community home must keep a record of each child,
and the record must be available for inspection by the Secretary of State,
who may call for copies.[1] Additional records must be kept about any child
who may be locked on his own in any part of the secure accommodation
apart from normal night arrangements.[2]

1   Regulation 18.
2   See LAC (86) 13, paras 12 and 13.

3   Access to children in care[1]

(a)   Code of practice

15.86   There can be as much resentment and bitterness on the part of
parents if there is a dispute over access between them and the local authority
in whose care their child is as there can be where the dispute is between
themselves in custody proceedings, but an additional consequence of the
former dispute is that it may influence the local authority against efforts
to rehabilitate the child with his family. For that reason in itself the Code

of Practice on Access to Children in Care, published by the DHSS[2] for the guidance of local authorities and voluntary organisations, is to be welcomed. Anticipating one of the major proposals of the Review of Child Care Law and the White Paper, namely, the promotion of a voluntary partnership between parents and local authority wherever possible, the Code is strongly in favour of promoting and sustaining access[3] and, in so doing, of involving the parents, the child's carers and, if he is old enough, the child in planning the access arrangements.[4] The immediate weeks after the child has been received or taken into care can be crucial in the planning. Early visits by the parent to the foster home or residential home are to be encouraged, especially where rehabilitation of the child with his family is seen as the eventual solution;[5] and, as part of planned rehabilitation and in accordance with their duty to secure the return of the child to his family, the local authority will have to decide when it will be advisable to commence staying access at the parental home for weekends or school holidays. On the other hand, should it turn out that access is proving harmful to the child, the local authority will have to decide whether the time has come to terminate it and to look for a permanent substitute family for the child. In some cases it may be necessary to refuse access at the outset. This is more likely where the child has been taken into care under a care order because he has been the victim of gross abuse by the parents. Given the increasing incidence of extreme abuse, it is suggested that the Code is rather too optimistic in its advice[6] that only exceptionally should access be refused from the outset.[7]

1 See generally Bromley, pp 481–486; Hayes and Bevan, Chapter 5; Sachs, [1986] Fam Law 78; Review of Child Care Law, Chapter 21.
2 Made in pursuance of CCA 1980, s 12G, as inserted by HASSASSAA 1983, Sch I.
3 A similar emphasis is made by RCCL which recommends (para 21.13) that there should be a presumption of law in favour of reasonable access.
4 Paragraph 7.
5 The Code (para 8) advises that in considering access the child's wider family should be taken into account so as to include, for example, siblings and grandparents.
6 See para 4.
7 RCCL, para 21.10, recommends that if a local authority intend to deny access at the time a care order is made, they should indicate that intention so that the court may deal with the matter there and then.

15.87 The legal status of the Code is not entirely certain, but the widely held view is that it is not legally binding.[1] Even if it is a 'general guidance of the Secretary of State' under section 7(1) of the Local Authority Social Services Act 1970 so as to oblige the local authority to comply with its terms, it does not give a parent a legal remedy;[2] but breach of its provisions would be of strong evidential value to support an action for judicial review,[3] for example, where the local authority had reduced access arrangements to occasional permitted visits, without entirely terminating them.[4] It is also not entirely clear whether the Code may be used as an aid to statutory interpretation. The Court of Appeal in *Re M (a minor)*[5] so used it, but in the later case, *R v Bolton Metropolitan Borough, ex p B*[6] Wood J held that it could only be referred to after the court has reached its interpretation of the words of the statute to see if that interpretation conflicted with the Code.[7]

1 See Bromley, p 470; Clarke Hall and Morrison, para A[241]. RCCL, para 21.26, recommends that the status should be clarified.
2 Hayes and Bevan, para 5.4.1, point out that 'the general nature of many of the Code's provisions does not easily accord with the precise legal duties which statutes and statutory instruments customarily generate'.
3 For judicial review see post, paras 15.127 et seq.
4 For termination see post, para 15.91.
5 [1985] Fam 60, [1985] 1 All ER 745.
6 [1985] FLR 343 at 351.
7 But it is to be noted that *Re M (a minor)* was not apparently cited to the learned judge.

(b)   Termination or refusal of access

15.88   In addition to setting out basic principles and practical points of guidance for promoting, sustaining, reviewing, terminating or refusing access, the Code requires local authorities to have procedures which will enable parents to pursue complaints about access and ask for decisions to be reviewed.[1] Parents should be able to discuss their anxieties and dissatisfactions with senior social workers and, if agreement cannot be reached, with further reference to the Director of Social Services and, if necessary, to Members.

Where the possibility of termination or refusal of access is being considered, further procedures should be followed by the local authority. A decision to terminate or refuse should always be considered by the Director, and Members may also be involved.[2] The parents should be told in writing that termination or refusal of access is being considered, the legal implications, how they may make their views known and how the decision will be conveyed to them.[3] These are procedures preliminary to the statutory process which follows when a final decision to terminate or refuse is reached. If the parents have been forewarned, it is not likely that the local authority will change their mind, unless they decide to turn to wardship.[4]

1 See paras 28–31. The Code recommends that local authorities should be ready to use these procedures to deal with access complaints from other relatives.
2 See para 32.
3 Paragraph 33.
4 See post, para 15.117.

(i)   Relevant children

15.89   The wider implications of the decision of the House of Lords in *A v Liverpool City Council*[1] are considered later,[2] but the application to issues of access of its ruling that the courts will not generally interfere with the exercise of the local authority's discretionary powers in respect of children in their care focussed further attention on what was already a matter of concern.[3] Part IA of the Child Care Act 1980,[4] supported by the Code of Practice, imposes a partial restriction on that ruling by enabling the parent to challenge in the juvenile court a local authority's decision to terminate access, or to refuse to make arrangements for access, in respect of a child[5] who is the subject of a resolution under section 3 of that Act[6] or of a care order, including an interim order, made under the Children and Young Persons Act 1969, or who has been remanded in care under section 23(1) of that Act or who has been committed to local authority care by an order made by a county court or a magistrates' court (i) in custody proceedings under section 2(2)(b) of the Guardianship Act 1973, (ii) on refusal of an adoption order under section 26(1)(b) of the Adoption Act 1976,[7] or (iii) on revocation of a custodianship order under section 36(2) or (3)(a) of the Children Act 1975, or by an order made by a magistrates' court in proceedings under section 10(1) of the Domestic Proceedings and Magistrates' Courts Act 1978.[8] The scheme for which Part IA provides does not, however, apply to children who have been committed to care (i) in wardship proceedings,[9] or (ii) in proceedings under the Matrimonial Causes Act 1973,[10] or (iii) by the High Court in custody proceedings or when refusing an adoption order or revoking a custodianship order.[11] The reason for these exclusions is that in making orders under any of those jurisdictions the court is empowered to issue directions as to access,[12] which will be binding on the local authority. Nor does the scheme extend to those who are in 'voluntary care' under section 2 of the 1980 Act, the reason for their exclusion being that the parents can request the return of their child.[13]

1 [1982] AC 363, [1981] 2 All ER 385.
2 Paragraph 15.124.
3 The *Liverpool* case was directly concerned with the power of a local authority to control access by the parent of a child who was the subject of a care order.
4 Ie ss 12A–12G, as inserted by HASSASSAA 1983, Sch I.
5 See CCA 1980, s 12A(1).
6 Or its predecessor, s 2 of the Children Act 1948; see *R v Corby Juvenile Court, ex p M* [1987] 1 All ER 992, [1987] 1 WLR 55.
7 Or its predecessor, s 17(1)(b) of the Children Act 1975.
8 Or its predecessor, s 2(1)(e) of the Matrimonial Proceedings (Magistrates' Courts) Act 1960.
9 Under FLRA 1969, s 7(2).
10 Section 43.
11 These are the consequences of s 12A(1) and (2) of CCA 1980, read together.
12 See MCA 1973, s 43(5)(a); FLRA 1969, s 7(3); *Re Y (a minor) (child in care: access)* [1976] Fam 125, [1975] 3 All ER 348, CA.
13 Under s 2(3) ante, para 15.29. Children subject to a place of safety order are also excluded.

(ii)   The decision to terminate or refuse access
15.90   A local authority may not terminate or refuse access to a child, to whom Part IA applies, by his parent, guardian or custodian unless they have first given the parent, guardian or custodian notice of termination or refusal and informed him of his right to apply to a juvenile court for an access order.[1] 'Guardian' has the same meaning throughout the 1980 Act, namely, a person appointed by deed or will or by order of a court to be the guardian of the child,[2] but the meanings of 'parent' and 'custodian' call for closer scrutiny, especially in a comparison of the use of those terms in Part I and Part IA respectively of the Act. The comparison illustrates the present chaotic condition of child law, which will be worsened when amending provisions, made by the Family Law Reform Act 1987, take effect.

For the purpose of Part I a parent means the mother and father of a legitimate child and the mother of an illegitimate child,[3] but the term has a wider meaning in Part I and includes any person who has the custody of the child under a court order.[4] It thus includes, for example, a relative (eg a grandparent) or other person who has been granted custody in divorce proceedings between the child's parents or granted legal custody in custodianship proceedings[5] or in proceedings between the child's parents under the Domestic Proceedings and Magistrates' Courts Act 1978 or in proceedings between the child's mother and father under section 9 of the Guardianship of Minors Act 1971. As for the unmarried father, he will, by virtue of the extended definition be a parent if he has custody by a court order or, when the changes made by the Family Law Reform Act 1987 are implemented, if he has actual custody by an order or has an order under section 4 of that Act giving him parental powers and responsibilities jointly with the mother. Compare Part IA. As the law stands, 'parent' means the mother and father of the legitimate child and the mother of the illegitimate child,[6] but the 1987 Act amends the definition by inserting a new provision, s 87(1A), in the 1980 Act which provides:

> 'In this Act – (a) references to a child whose father and mother were not married to each other at the time of his birth; and (b) except in Part I and sections 13, 24, 64 and 65 references (however expressed) to any relationship between two persons, shall be construed in accordance with section 1 of the Family Law Reform Act 1987.'

So, the unmarried father will, when the amendment comes into force, become a parent for the purposes of Part IA, whether he has a section 4 order or an order giving him actual custody or no order at all, and will be entitled to notice of termination or refusal of access and to seek an access order. This will have particular relevance for cohabiting parents who are not married.

The relative or other person given legal custody in custodianship proceedings qualifies as a custodian for the purposes of section 12B. So, too, it is submitted, is one given legal custody under the Domestic Proceedings and Magistrates' Courts Act 1978 or under section 9 of the Guardianship of Minors Act 1971, since such an order is made on the notional basis that the relative or other person had applied for a custodianship order under the Children Act 1975.[7] But a relative or other person given custody in divorce proceedings between the child's parents cannot qualify, unless an extended meaning is given to 'custodian'. Clearly these discrepancies should be removed and uncertainties clarified.

1 See CCA 1980, s 12B(1) and (2). The notice must be in the form prescribed by the Access (Notice of Termination and of Refusal) Order 1983, SI 1983/1860, and where access is being terminated it must state that it terminates as from the date of service of the notice (s 12B(3)). So the parent etc at least knows where he stands.
2 CCA 1980, s 87(1), ante, para 15.11.
3 Ibid.
4 Section 8(2).
5 For the purpose of s 3 of the Act he is separately recognised as a custodian.
6 Section 87(1).
7 RCCL, para 21.3 states that ss 12A–F cover 'a person granted legal custody in custodianship or *perhaps* other proceedings' (italics supplied).

15.91 The local authority should not prevaricate over their decision whether or not to terminate or refuse access, because in all issues concerning children time is of the essence. Where they are considering terminating access they should make up their mind within 14 days or exceptionally 21 days.[1] There is no termination of access where the authority propose to substitute new for existing arrangements.[2] However, where access is severely reduced to, say, permitted quarterly visits, the question arises whether the reduction is a bona fide exercise of discretion of the statutory powers – as it might be where the local authority see the child's rehabilitation with his parents as impracticable and the reduced access as a gradual, instead of abrupt, withdrawal of contact between him and his parents which is preferable in his interests – or whether the reduction is a device to deny the parent his remedy to seek an access order in accordance with Part IA of the 1980 Act. If the latter is its purpose, it does not constitute termination, but the local authority's decision may be challenged by the parent by way of judicial review on the ground that the decision is irrational or unreasonable.[3]

Where there are no access arrangements and the local authority are considering whether or not to make them, ie are considering whether or not to refuse access as opposed to terminating it,[4] 'a substantial time – certainly weeks and possibly months – may be required before making a decision in the initial stages of care'; for example, it may be necessary to obtain psychiatric advice if the child is seriously disturbed.[5] Under section 12B(5) of the 1980 Act there is no refusal to arrange for access where the local authority postpone access for such reasonable period as appears to them necessary in order to enable them to consider what access arrangements, if any, are to be made. But a 'reasonable period' is 'thinking time' not 'waiting time'.[6] What this seems to mean is that, while the early investigations may be protracted, once they are completed, the local authority must make up their mind quickly. As with terminating access, two or three weeks should be the maximum period needed to do that. Moreover, the fact that adoption or custodianship proceedings are pending does not justify postponing a decision or refusal. If there is a conflict of jurisdiction, that is a matter for the courts to resolve.[7]

1 *R v Bolton Metropolitan Borough, ex p B* [1985] FLR 343, [1985] Fam Law 193.
2 Section 12B(4).
3 See *Re Y (minors) (wardship: access challenge)* [1988] 1 FLR 299, where on the facts the remedy would not have been appropriate. For judicial review see post, para 15.127. RCCL, para 21.22 recommends that the court should be empowered to make and review access arrangements and not only terminate or refuse them.
4 Wood J in *R v Bolton Metropolitan Borough, ex p B* [1985] FLR 343, [1985] Fam Law 193 clearly drew the distinction.
5 See [1985] FLR at 350.
6 See Wood J, ibid.
7 See Wood J ibid and for conflict of jurisdiction post, para 15.96. The Code of Practice (para 9) recommends that the local authority should seek legal advice on postponement.

(iii) The access order
15.92 The parent, guardian or custodian on whom the notice of termination or refusal of access has been served may apply to a juvenile court[1] by way of complaint for an access order.[2] The normal rule applies that complaint must be made within six months from the date of service of the notice;[3] but it is clearly in the interests of the child and the parent that the latter should apply as quickly as possible after service of the notice.[4]

In deciding whether to make an order, and if so on what terms, the court must apply the principle that the child's welfare is the first and paramount consideration,[5] and in so doing must not approach the matter from the point of view that the parent has a right of access or from the fact that there is no evidence that he is not a fit and proper person to come into contact with the child. The crucial question is whether access would be favourable to the child.[6] The longer he has been away from his parents in a settled home with foster parents or prospective adopters, the less likely an order for access, since access is likely to unsettle the child's integration into the family home.[7] *A fortiori* access will be refused if during a lengthy period the parents have not seen their child.[8] On the other hand, if he has been away from the parents for only a short time and there is a reasonable prospect of rehabilitation of the child with his parents, an order may well be appropriate.[9] The application of these guidelines and the scope of the court's powers must now be weighed against the recent ruling of the Court of Appeal in *Re M (a minor) (access application)*.[10] Where the local authority has decided against rehabilitation and is planning the child's future with a permanent substitute family (most probably by way of adoption), the court must fully consider and carefully weigh the authority's reasons for the course that they are advocating when it is deciding whether or not to allow access by the parent.[11] To allow it will effectively scotch or make more difficult the plans for the child that the authority have made in exercise of their statutory discretion. The full impact of this ruling has yet to be felt, but it clearly places firm restrictions on the making of access orders and thereby facilitates long-term planning for children in care.

If the court decides to make an order for access it may specify conditions with regard to commencement, frequency, duration or place of access or to any other matter,[12] for example that a relative should also be present when the parent is visiting the child or that, where there is staying access at the parent's home, the child is not to associate with a particular person. The clear intention is that the court should normally impose conditions and not leave details of access to the discretion of the court.[13] Consequently, in view of the likely tension between the authority and the parent, an order for reasonable access is not likely to be realistic. The court must try to find a *media via* between rigidity and flexibility in the terms of the access allowed. It has been pointed out[14] that in this regard it may be helpful if the parties can suggest specified terms.

1 Bromley, p 484, points out that a parent is unlikely to be denied a right to apply if the local authority mistakenly served a notice of refusal instead of termination or vice versa.
2 CCA 1980, s 12C(1) and (2).
3 Magistrates' Courts Act 1980, s 127(1); *Y v Kirklees Metropolitan Council* [1985] FLR 927, DC.
4 In the unlikely event of his not applying within the six month limit, he may nevertheless, make a fresh application to the local authority for access. If they refuse it, they must serve a new notice and the six month limit will again operate; see *Y v Kirklees Metropolitan Council*, supra.
5 Section 12F(1).
6 See Sir John Arnold P in *Hereford and Worcester County Council v JAH* [1985] FLR 530 at 533–534.
7 See *Devon County Council v Clancy* [1985] FLR 1159, [1986] Fam Law 20, CA.
8 As in *Coventry City Council v T* [1986] 2 FLR 301, [1986] Fam Law 299, CA.
9 In *M v Berkshire County Council* [1985] FLR 257 at 272, Slade LJ stated that the possibility of an access order could not be discounted where the local authority regard rehabilitation as impracticable. Nevertheless, the chances of an order in those circumstances will be slim.
10 [1988] 1 FLR 35.
11 The authority's case will be strengthened if supported by the guardian ad litem, as to whom see infra, para 15.94.

12 Section 12C(3).
13 See *Devon County Council v Clancy*, supra, note 7.
14 Hayes and Bevan, para 5.8.

(iv) Variation, discharge or suspension of access order

15.93 An application to vary or discharge an access order may be made by way of complaint by the parent, guardian or custodian named in the order or by the local authority.[1] Although there is no express statutory provision to that effect, it has been held[2] that the juvenile court when making an access order can ask for further reports from social services or the probation service and thereby keep control over the development of access.[3] Such control is particularly relevant to the power of a justice of the peace, provided he is a member of the juvenile court panel, to make an 'emergency order'[4] suspending the operation of the access order for seven days, where he is satisfied that continued access, in the terms of the access order, will put the child's welfare seriously at risk.[5] During the seven-day-period the local authority will be able to apply for variation or discharge of the order and, if they do so, the suspension will continue until their application is heard.[6]

1 Section 12D(1) and (2). RCCL, para 21.16 recommends that where a local authority wish to vary arrangements under an order, they should be required to serve notice on the parent etc and, unless the latter objects within a specified period (say 28 days), the order should be treated as suspended. If the parent objects, the order should remain in force until the local authority bring the matter to the court. Quaere whether, if an order is discharged, the local authority must serve a further notice of termination or whether the parent can re-apply for access; see Clarke Hall and Morrison, para A[230].
2 *Hereford and Worcester County Council v JAH* [1985] FLR 530.
.3 Hayes and Bevan, para 5.10, suggest that the parent and the local authority could vary informally the terms of an access order 'to accommodate changing circumstances', but they recognise that the time will come when a variation order will be 'prudent'.
4 Section 12E.
5 Application for an emergency order can be made ex parte (s 12E(4)).
6 Section 12E(3).

(v) The child as a party

15.94 Although the child is the central figure in access disputes and the paramountcy of his welfare governs the decision whether or not to make an order for access, he has no right himself to apply for an order or to apply for variation or discharge of an order that has been made. However, where it considers it necessary in order to safeguard his interests, the court may make him a party to the proceedings. If it does, it must then appoint a guardian ad litem unless satisfied that it is not necessary to do so in order to safeguard those interests.[1] It is submitted that, because of the hostility that disputes over access can generate, the views of the parent and the local authority may be too loudly voiced at the expense of those of the child. Separate representation ought therefore readily to be granted.[2] Legal aid and legal representation will be available to the child as it is for parents, but his presence in court is not required.[3]

1 Section 12F(2)–(4). For the duties of the guardian ad litem see MC(C&YP) Rules 1988, r 31 and ante, para 15.41. RCCL, para 21.21, recommends that the child should have an independent right to apply for access.
2 RCCL, para 21.21, similarly emphasises separate representation as the norm.
3 *A v Wigan Metropolitan Borough Council* [1986] 1 FLR 608, [1986] Fam Law 162.

(c)   Appeals

15.95   Appeal from *any* decision[1] of the juvenile court lies as of right to
the Divisional Court of the Family Division[2] by way of notice of motion
within six weeks from the date of the decision;[3] but in access cases (as
in cases of transfer of care and control) the maximum acceptable interval
before the hearing of the appeal is 28 days, and therefore a stay of execution
should seldom exceed 14 days.[4] Appeal can be brought by the parent or,
where he was a party to the proceedings in the juvenile court, by the child
or by the local authority and is by way of a rehearing. The Divisional
Court can therefore admit fresh evidence, and, since the paramouncy of
the child's welfare applies, it is likely to do so. However, the Court of
Appeal has ruled in *Re M (a minor) (access application)*[5] that, where the
local authority have terminated access beause they have decided that no
further rehabilitation of parent with child should be attempted, the powers
of the appellate court are 'strictly circumscribed'. Apart from 'extreme cases
of judicial review', the court has no jurisdiction, without the consent of
the local authority, to interfere in matters entrusted to them by Parliament.
To do so would offend the principle affirmed by the House of Lords in
A v Liverpool City Council.[6]

1   Including, for example, a decision by the court that it would proceed with a hearing
for an access order for which an adjournment was asked; *Southwark London Borough
Council v H* [1985] 2 All ER 657, [1985] 1 WLR 861. *Semble* there is no appeal against
a decision of a single justice to suspend an access order, since it is not a decision of
a juvenile court; see RCCL, para 21.8.
2   CCA 1980, s 12C(5).
3   For details of procedure see RSC Ord 90, rr 9 and 29.
4   *Hereford and Worcester County Council v EH* [1985] FLR 975, [1985] Fam Law 229.
5   [1988] 1 FLR 35, [1988] Fam Law 13, CA.
6   [1982] AC 363, [1981] 2 All ER 385, post, para 15.124.

(d)   Conflict of jurisdictions

15.96   It has already been noted[1] that the fact that adoption or custodianship
proceedings are pending or intended does not justify postponing the local
authority's decision to terminate access, but in practice this will give rise
to a conflict of jurisdiction. By the time notice to terminate is given and
an access order sought by the parent, the local authority may have
commenced adoption or freeing for adoption proceedings. This places the
juvenile court in difficulty in deciding whether or not to proceed with hearing
the access application. In *Southwark London Borough Council v H*,[2] the
Divisional Court held that, where the application for adoption is likely
to raise the issue of dispensing with the parent's agreement to adoption,
the first matter which would have to be decided would be future access
between parent and child. It is therefore 'highly desirable' for that matter
to be heard before the adoption application, and in those circumstances
the only available forum to do so would be the juvenile court. If that
court should decide in favour of access by the parent, it is highly likely
that the adoption court would conclude that the parent is not unreasonably
withholding agreement. Accordingly, the local authority would be best
advised to challenge the decision on access by way of appeal,[3] especially
now that the power of the juvenile court to make access orders has been
significantly curbed by the Court of Appeal.[4] Nevertheless, the *Southwark*

decision does not wholly fetter the discretion of the juvenile court to adjourn its own access proceedings.[5] A vital consideration is expedition of the hearing of the issue of access. If, therefore, the adoption or freeing for adoption proceedings are well advanced, adjournment of the juvenile court proceedings would be appropriate.[6]

The duplication of proceedings which the present system allows could be avoided by giving the juvenile court power to transfer its access proceedings to the court in which the adoption proceedings are pending.[7] This reform would also overcome another disadvantage. It has been pointed out[8] that, if the local authority contest access in the juvenile court, the anonymity of the prospective adopters is threatened, since the power of a juvenile court to hear evidence in the absence of a parent[9] does not extend to them should they be called in support of the local authority's case.

1 Ante, para 15.91.
2 [1985] 2 All ER 657, [1985] 1 WLR 861.
3 See *Re M (minor) (adoption: parent's agreement)* [1985] FLR 921, CA. Hayes and Bevan, para 5.7, point out that the adoption application could then be lodged in the High Court so that there could be consideration of both sets of proceedings.
4 See *Re M (a minor) (access application)* [1988] 1 FLR 35, ante, para 15.92. But there is always the possibility of the local authority turning to wardship; see *Re LH (a minor) (wardship: jurisdiction)* [1986] 2 FLR 306, and post, para 15.117.
5 See *C v Berkshire County Council* [1987] 2 FLR 210.
6 See the Direction for an early hearing of the freeing for adoption application given by the Divisional Court in *R v Slough Justice, ex p B* [1985] FLR 384 at 393, and for the subsequent 'freeing' proceedings see *Re PB (a minor) (application to free for adoption)* [1985] FLR 394.
7 See Bromley, p 486.
8 Hayes and Bevan, para 5.7.
9 Under MC(C&YP) Rules 1988, r 3(2).

4 Miscellaneous powers and duties of a local authority

15.97 Apart from those relating to accommodation and access, there are few specific powers and duties given to a local authority for dealing with children in their care. Instead, within the limit of the general duty[1] to give first consideration to the need to safeguard and promote the child's welfare throughout his childhood, they are left with a wide discretion. As already mentioned[2] they must, where it is reasonable, make use of facilities and services which are available for children who are in the care of their own parents; but, in assisting a child in their care to establish a career, they are also expressly empowered to enter into a guarantee under a deed of apprenticeship or articles of clerkship and may extend the guarantee beyond the period of care.[3]

1 Under CCA 1980, s 18(1), ante, para 15.63.
2 Ante, para 15.64; see s 18(2).
3 CCA 1980, s 23.

15.98 Arranging for the emigration of a child in care is another specific power,[1] but this may only be done with the consent of the Secretary of State, who will only allow it if he is satisfied[2] that emigration would benefit the child, that suitable arrangements for his reception and welfare in the country to which he is going are made and that, where practicable, the parents or guardian have been consulted.[3] The child must also consent, if old enough to express an opinion on the matter. If he is not, the consent of the Secretary of State may still be given, provided that the child is emigrating with a parent, guardian, relative or friend or is to join any one of them abroad.[4] Arrangements may be made even though it is intended that the child be adopted abroad: a provisional adoption order[5] is not needed.[6] The power to allow emigration is exerciseable where a child is in care under section 2 of the Child Care Act 1980 or under a care order, but not where the committal to care is ordered in other proceedings.[7] The decision to allow emigration has obvious immense consequences for the child and, not surprisingly, the Review of Child Care Law recommends[8] that emigration should only take place with the consent of both parents or by leave of the court.

1 CCA 1980, s 24.
2 Because of the seriousness of the decision to allow emigration he will need to be provided with a detailed report by the local authority on the child and the reasons for emigrating. About 10 to 20 cases are considered annually, generally involving children living with parents who obtain employment overseas; see RCCL para 9.18.
3 'Parents' or 'guardian' here refers to all persons who are such (s 24(4)). So, apparently a parent who has been deprived of parental rights will still have to be consulted. The terms have the same meaning as they have for the purpose of Part I of CCA 1980; see ante, para 15.11 and s 24(4A) as prospectively inserted by FLRA 1987, s 8(4).
4 CCA 1980, s 24(3).
5 Ie under s 55 of the Adoption Act 1976.
6 CCA 1980, s 24(5).
7 For these other proceedings see ante, paras 15.56 et seq. The relevant statutory provisions which empower committal expressly exclude the operation of s 24.
8 Paragraph 9.19.

15.99 Running through the legislation relating to children in local authority care is the principle that those who become responsible for looking after the child must take account of his religious persuasion.[1] The principle also underlines the rule which forbids a local authority to order the cremation of a deceased child if this is contrary to his religious persuasion.[2] But has the time not come for express statutory reference to the need to take account also of a child's ethnic and racial background?

1 See CCA 1980, ss 2(3)(b), 4(3) and 10(3), ante, paras 15.13, 15.33 and 15.48 respectively.
2 CCA 1980, s 25(1), which empowers the authority to arrange for the burial or cremation of the child.

(a) Maintaining contact with the family

15.100 We have already seen that the Child Care Act 1980 aims to encourage a local authority to bring the period of care to an end as soon as the child's welfare permits. Hence the duty of the authority to arrange for a child received into their care under section 2 of the Act to be taken over by a parent or guardian, or at least, a relative or friend;[1] and, whether the child is in care under that section or as the result of a care order under CYPA 1969 or other order committing to care, he may be allowed temporarily to be under the charge and control of such a person.[2] If the experiment is successful and the child is the subject of a section 3 resolution or of a care order, the authority may well rescind the resolution or, as the case may be, apply for the discharge of the care order.

In order to facilitate the child's return to his family, whether for a trial period or permanently, access visits by the parent should be encouraged,[3] and the local authority are entitled to make payments to any parent or guardian 'or any other person connected with' the child in respect of travelling, subsistence or other expenses incurred by him in visiting the child, if the authority consider that such visits would otherwise not be possible without undue hardship and that the circumstances warrant the making of the payments.[4] The authority are thus left with a wide discretion whether or not to assist, and there is no procedure for ensuring that the parent is made aware of the local authority's power or for enabling him to make formal application for assistance. Nor is there any specific authorisation for a local authority to make payments for visits made by the child to his family, but it is submitted that this is permitted by virtue either of the authority's general duty[5] to give first consideration to the need to safeguard and promote the child's welfare or that of diminishing the need to keep the child in care.[6] With regard to the visiting of children in voluntary homes, the Secretary of State may from time to time call upon those carrying on the home to inform him of the facilities for visiting.[7]

1 Sub-s (3), ante, para 15.13.
2 CCA 1980, s 21(2), ante, para 15.76.
3 See ante, para 15.86. Maintaining contact also imposes obligations on the parent. He must see to it that the local authority are informed of his address for the time being; see CCA 1980, ss 9 and 12. Failure to inform is an offence punishable on summary conviction with a fine not exceeding level 1 on the standard scale (currently £50).
4 Section 26. The section also enables the authority to meet the expenses of attending the child's funeral.
5 Under s 18(1).
6 Section 1(1).
7 Administration of Children's Homes Regulations 1951, reg 14. The regulation refers, however, only to visits by parents and guardians and does not include anyone else who may be connected with the child.

The visitor
15.101   Contact between the child and his family may be negligible or non-existent. The 1980 Act partly meets the problem by its provision[1] for a 'visitor' in certain circumstances where the child is the subject of a care order. His duties are to advise, assist and befriend the child and, if he considers it appropriate, to apply on his behalf for the discharge of the order. This last mentioned function can be important, since the child's parents may have no interest in him or in whether he ceases to be in care. The Act recognises that both this and the other functions can be properly discharged only if an 'independent person' is appointed visitor, ie, one who is independent of the local authority appointing him and is unconnected with any community home. To secure independence, regulations prescribe the conditions for eligibility for appointment.[2] The local authority is under a duty to appoint only if all the following conditions are satisfied: (1) there is a care order; (2) the juvenile has attained the age of 5; (3) he is accommodated in a community home or other establishment which he has not been allowed to leave during the preceding three months for the purpose of ordinary attendance at an educational institution or at work; and (4) it appears to the local authority that either (a) communication between him and his parent or guardian has been so infrequent that the appointment is appropriate, or (b) he has not lived with a visitor or been visited by

either of his parents or his guardian during the preceding 12 months.[3] Local
authorities are likely to select visitors from volunteers who have experience
of working with children.[4] The number required under the present restrictive
rules will be limited. It is suggested that the visitor should be available
in respect of all children in care who have lost contact with their families.
For example, where the child is the subject of a section 3 resolution, a
visitor may be helpful in persuading the local authority to rescind it.

1 Section 11.
2 Children and Young Persons (Definition of Independent Persons) Regulations 1971.
3 An appointment comes to an end when the care order ceases to operate or it may earlier
   be terminated by the local authority or the visitor (s 11(2)).
4 See DHSS Circular No 2/1971, para 8.

(b)   Absence from care[1]

Removing or harbouring a child in care

15.102   It is an offence if anyone knowingly assists or induces or persistently
attempts to induce a child who is in local authority care and the subject
of a section 3 resolution to run away from the accommodation provided
by the local authority (whether in a home or otherwise) or takes him away
without lawful authority or knowingly harbours or conceals such a child
who has run away or been taken away or prevents him from returning
to the accommodation.[2] As we have already seen,[3] these provisions also
extend to a child who has been in care under section 2 for at least six
months even though there is not a section 3 resolution in respect of him,
and an offence is committed unless (a) the act is done with the consent
of the local authority, or (b) where it is done by a parent or guardian,
he has given the local authority 28 days' written notice of his intention
to do it.[4]

1 For criticism of the present complicated provisions and for proposed simplification of
   the law see RCCL paras 9.28 to 9.38. There is also considerable overlapping with the
   Child Abduction Act 1984, the Sexual Offences Act 1956 and the common law offence
   of kidnapping.
2 CCA 1980, s 13(1) and (3). The maximum penalty is a fine not exceeding level 5 on
   the standard scale or three months' imprisonment or both. The local authority may prosecute
   (s 84).
3 Ante, para 15.29.
4 Section 13(2). The terms 'parent' and 'guardian' have the same extended meanings as
   they have for the purposes of Part I of the 1980 Act; see ante, para 15.11 and (prospectively)
   FLRA 1987, s 8(3).

15.103   Whereas section 13 is concerned with, inter alia harbouring or
concealing a child who has wrongfully left or been removed from local
authority accommodation, section 14 covers the wrongful harbouring or
concealing of a child who has been lawfully removed from local authority
care but has not been returned to the local authority on their written request.
An essential condition is that a section 3 resolution is in force.[1]

1 The offence is not quite so serious as that under s 13. It carries a maximum penalty
   of a fine not exceeding level 3 on the standard scale or two months' imprisonment or
   both.

(c)   Recovery of a child in care

(i)   In care under section 2

15.104   Section 15 of the 1980 Act assists local authorities to recover children who are in their care under section 2 and are the subject of a section 3 resolution and who have run away or unlawfully have been taken away from the place at which they are required by the local authority to live or who, having been allowed by the authority to be in the charge of a parent, guardian, relative or friend, are not returned by that person to the authority after written notice requiring him to do so has been given in accordance with section 14 of the Act.[1] In any of these circumstances a justice of the peace can issue a summons requiring a person to attend and produce the child before a magistrates' court.[2] He may also issue a search warrant authorising search of specified premises where the child is reasonably believed to be.

1 Supra, para 15.103.
2 Apart from any other possible liability, failure to comply with the summons renders the person liable to a fine not exceeding level 5 on the standard scale.

(ii)   In care under a care order

15.105   Similarly, under section 16 of the Act, where a child is the subject of a care order or has been remanded to the local authority by a warrant[1] and he has been absent without permission from the place at which he is required by the local authority to live, a magistrates' court may issue a summons directing a person to produce the child before the court or to issue a search warrant authorising a constable to search for and produce the child before the court.[2] There is also power to arrest without warrant a child who is so absent.[3]

1 Under CYPA 1969, s 23(1).
2 CCA 1980, s 16(2) and (3). Surprisingly, these provisions have not been brought into line with those in s 15, so that the power to issue a summons or search warrant may be issued by a justice of the peace.
3 Section 16(1). RCCL, para 9.38, recommends that the power of arrest should not apply to children committed to care in civil proceedings. Instead reliance should be placed on a place of safety order or, as RCCL proposes (para 13.1), an emergency protection order.

(d)   Reviews and records

(i)   Reviews

15.106   Under section 27(4) of the CYPA 1969 the local authority must review the case of every child who has been in their care throughout the preceding six months, if a review has not been held during that period, and where he is in care as the result of a care order they must in reviewing the case consider applying for discharge of the order. By analogy, where he is the subject of a section 3 resolution, they should at a review consider whether to rescind it, but there is no statutory duty to do so. The 1969 Act imposes only a minimum requirement, and so, if they are properly to discharge their general duty under section 18(1) of the CCA 1980 to safeguard and promote the child's welfare, the authority should be ready to conduct more frequent reviews. The latter Act[1] does in fact substitute a duty to review in accordance with regulations to be made by the Secretary of State. These may make provision as to (a) the manner in which cases are to be reviewed, (b) the considerations to which the local authority are to have regard in reviewing, and (c) the time when a child's case is first to be reviewed and the frequency of subsequent reviews. Regrettably, because this substitution would mean additional demands on the resources of social services departments, its implementation has been postponed. Moreover, even if there were regulations, they would doubtless leave the local authority with a wide discretion, which, in accordance with the principle established in *A v Liverpool City Council*,[2] could not be successfully challenged. Nevertheless, there might still be the possibility of judicial review,[3] and, limited though judicial intervention can be, there could be some rules relating to reviews which could be helpful to the child and the parent; for example, that a person independent of the local authority and other agencies involved in the review be included in the reviewing body and that the child and parent have the right to be legally represented at a review.

1 Section 20. The change was first enacted in CA 1975, Sch 3, para 71.
2 [1982] AC 363, [1981] 2 All ER 385, HL; see post, para 15.124.
3 Post, para 15.127.

(ii)   Personal records

15.107   It has already been briefly mentioned[1] that a local authority can decline to disclose information or its source on the ground that disclosure would be contrary to the public interest. In *D v NSPCC*[2] the House of Lords unequivocally recognised the protection of children 'from neglect or ill-usage'[3] as a specific head of public interest, and held that the identity of a person who informed the NSPCC of an alleged case of child abuse was immune from disclosure, because otherwise persons would be reluctant to come forward with information and the Society's functions of child protection would consequently be frustrated. The application of the immunity principle to the public area of child care and protection had in fact already been recognised in *Re D (infants)*,[4] where records kept under the Boarding-Out of Children Regulations 1955 were held to be confidential and immune from discovery; and it is in relation to the records kept by local authorities and other agencies that the immunity principle is most likely to arise. Thus, in *Gaskin v Liverpool City Council*[5] protection was extended to the case notes and records of a boy who had been in local authority care, and in *Re S and W (minors)*[6] to notes of a case conference. The courts have not attempted to catalogue the kinds of recorded information that may be protected, but, as the House of Lords emphasised in *D v NSPCC*, the test is not merely one of confidentiality. It is, as has been succinctly stated,[7] whether or not 'the information is so sensitive, or given in such sensitive circumstances, that the child-care services could not properly function if it were divulged'. That formulation accords with the ruling in *R v Greenwich Juvenile Court, ex p Greenwich London Borough Council*[8] and with the guidance given by the DHSS.[9] In the former it was held that local authorities cannot claim a blanket immunity for all records and documents relating to the child. Immunity must be sought and justified in respect of each of them. In a revision of Departmental Policy, the DHSS sees non-disclosure to clients (which in the case of children in care extends to parents) as the exception, not the general rule. The general presumption should be that clients or their representatives would be supplied with information about themselves.[10] The kinds of circumstances where exceptionally withholding information is justified are[11] (a) to protect a third party where the client's record contains information which would harm the third party by damaging his reputation or relationships;[12] (b) *pace D v NSPCC*, to protect sources of information; (c) to protect provisional opinions and judgements which social workers may have recorded; (d) to protect the child from disclosure of information to the parent – the child may not want his parent to see the record and, in accordance with its general duty under section 18(1) of the CCA 1980, the local authority must give due consideration to his wishes, having regard to his age and understanding; and (e) to protect the client from damaging revelations, for example, from the fact that his parent has a criminal record or history of mental disorder.[13]

1 Ante, para 14.85
2 [1978] AC 171, [1977] 1 All ER 589.
3 Per Lord Simon of Glaisdale at 240 and 614 respectively.
4 [1970] 1 All ER 1088, [1970] 1 WLR 599.
5 [1980] 1 WLR 1549.
6 (1982) 12 Fam Law 151.
7 Hayes and Bevan, para 1.6.3.
8 (1977) 1 FLR 304, 7 Fam Law 171.
9 In its Circular (LAC (83)14) on *Personal Social Services Records – Disclosure of Information to Clients*.
10 See LAC (83)14, para 11. It is highly desirable that solicitors on the child care panel should be familiar with this Circular and the policy recommended on disclosure.
11 See LAC (83)14, para 5.
12 The Circular gives as an example withholding information about a child's paternity given by the mother. It is submitted that, in the light of present day attitudes to paternity (see especially FLRA 1987, s 1) non-disclosure of the fact of paternity in itself is not justified; *aliter*, if it contained scurrilous allegations about the father.
13 Much will depend on an assessment of the child's likely reaction to such revelations.

5 After-care

15.108 The Child Care Act 1980 enables local authorities to help children who have been in their care but who have ceased to be so after reaching compulsory school age. About 40% of those leaving care are over 16 and about 20% are at the maximum age of 18[1] when they do so.[2] Some of them may return home or may already be living at home as part of the plan of rehabilitation; some may continue to live with their foster parents or in a community home;[3] but there are others who wish as soon as possible to begin an independent life. It is particularly, though certainly not exclusively, for this last class of children that the 1980 Act can be especially helpful in helping them to adapt to new demands. Unfortunately the relevant provisions are complicated and lack coherence. Their defects have been clearly exposed:[4]

'Some of these provisions are in effect aiming at family support, some at helping young people to live independently. Some relate to all children who have been in care, some only to those who have been received into care. Some refer to children of any age, some only to young people between certain ages. Those that do have age limits are not consistent with each other. Some have provisions relating to the transmission of information concerning the young people from one local authority to another, some do not. Some are dependent on the young person requesting assistance, others do not. To some extent the provisions also overlap with each other. Clearly some rationalisation and clarification is needed of what was described by the Select Committee[5] as the "weak and confused state of the law".'

1 Or 19, if the child is in care under a care order which was made after he reached the age of 16 (CYPA 1969, s 20(3)(a)).
2 See RCCL, para 10.1.
3 See especially, infra, s 72 of CCA 1980.
4 RCCL, para 10.3.
5 Ie the House of Commons Social Services Committee.

15.109   The following are the relevant provisions:
(i) A local authority may accommodate in a community home persons over compulsory school age but under 21 who are employed or seeking employment or receiving education or training. They may arrange accommodation whether or not the person has ever been in local authority care,[1] but they may do so only if the community home is near the place where he is employed or receiving education or training.[2]
(ii) A local authority may contribute to the cost of accommodating and maintaining such a person in *any* place near the place of his employment, education or training, if he is, or since ceasing to be of compulsory school age has been, in local authority care, whether by virtue of section 2 of the 1980 Act or as the result of a care order under CYPA 1969 or an order committing him to care under other proceedings.[3]
(iii) A local authority may make grants to persons between 17 and 21 who at or after the time when they attained the age of 17 were in the care of a local authority, (whether by virtue of section 2 or as a result of a care order or otherwise being committed to care[4]), so as to enable them to meet expenses relating to their education or training.[5]
(iv) When it is known to a local authority that there is in their area a child who, when he ceased to be of compulsory school age or subsequently was in the care of a local authority under section 2 of the 1980 Act but is no longer so, they must advise and befriend him until he is 18, unless they are satisfied that his welfare does not require it.[6] They are under the same duty if he is in the care of a voluntary organisation, but if they are satisfied that the organisation have the necessary facilities for advising and befriending they can arrange for them to discharge those functions.[7] Provision is also made to ensure after-care in cases where the child moves to the area of another local authority or ceases to be in the care of a voluntary organisation.[8]
(v) A local authority has the power to visit, advise and befriend and, in exceptional circumstances, to give financial assistance to a person who was formerly in care under section 2 of the 1980 Act up to, or while he was of, the age of 17 and is still under 21; but the onus is on him to request the support of the local authority.[9]

With this array of muddled variety it is small wonder that the Review of Child Care Law proposes radical reforms[10] which would impose on a local authority (1) a duty to advise and assist all children in their care so as to promote their welfare when they leave care, and (2) a duty, when they have left, to advise and befriend them, coupled with power to give assistance, including cash in exceptional circumstances.

1 Preference is likely to be given to those who have been in care.
2 CCA 1980, s 72.
3 See ibid, s 27(1). The provision is complicated, but its effect is that if the child is no longer in care after reaching the age of 17, the section may be invoked: if he is still in care at that age, no assistance can be given until he attains 18.
4 See supra.
5 CCA 1980, s 27(2).
6 Ibid, s 28(1). The duty does not extend to a child who was the subject of a care order, nor, to one committed to care under any other order, as for example, under MCA 1973, s 43(5)(b), as amended by CCA 1980, Sch 5.
7 CCA 1980, s 69(1).
8 See ss 28(2) and (3) and 69(2) and (3).
9 Section 29. Compare the *duty* under s 28(1), supra, to advise and befriend a person up to the age of 18.
10 See paras 10.5 to 10.10.

VIII   CARE AND AFTER-CARE OF MENTALLY DISORDERED CHILDREN

15.110   Section 9 of the Mental Health Act 1959 (as amended) gives to a local social services authority power to accommodate in community homes a child under 18 who is not in their care within the meaning of Part III of the Child Care Act 1980 but who is, or has been, mentally disordered and whose care or after-care is being undertaken by that or any other local authority as a health authority. The power conferred by section 9 does not preclude a local authority as children authority from receiving mentally disordered children into their care under section 2 of the 1980 Act, provided of course the conditions of that section are met.[1]

1 Clarke Hall and Morrison, para A[112], suggest that if the child is to be fostered, he should be received into care under s 2.

15.111   When a local authority assume parental rights and powers over a child as a result of a section 3 resolution under CCA 1980 or a care order under CYPA 1969 and he is a mentally disordered patient, then, if he is admitted to a hospital or nursing home (whether for treatment for mental disorder or for any other reason), the authority must arrange for him to be visited and must take such other steps as would be expected to be taken by his parents; for example the provision of additional comforts and presents.[1]

An authority who have for either of the above reasons assumed parental rights and powers are then deemed to be the juvenile's nearest relative, except for his or her spouse and, where the assumption was by way of a section 3 resolution, except also for a parent whose rights are not affected by the resolution.[2]

1 Mental Health Act 1983, s 116(1).
2 MHA 1983, s 27.

IX   CHILDREN IN THE CARE OF A
VOLUNTARY ORGANISATION[1]

15.112   One of the purposes of the Children Act 1975 was to accord firmer recognition to the work of voluntary organisations involved in child care, to strengthen the protection to be given to the children in the care of such bodies and to bring them closely into line with children in the care of local authorities. The relevant provisions are now to be found in Part VI of the Child Care Act 1980.

1 Ie a body the activities of which are carried on otherwise than for profit, but not including any public or local authority (CCA 1980, s 87(1)).

1   Restrictions on removal

15.113   The restrictions on removing a child who is in the care of a local authority under section 2 of the 1980 Act[1] extend to the child not in care under that section but who is in a voluntary home[2] or is boarded out with foster parents by a voluntary organisation in whose care he is.[3] Thus, it is an offence to remove the child from the home or the foster parents unless the organisation consents or unless the child is removed by a parent or guardian after giving not less than 28 days' written notice of his intention to remove.

In the latter circumstances the voluntary organisation would be given the 'breathing space' to commence wardship proceedings.

1 See ante, para 15.29.
2 For the meaning of 'voluntary home' see ante, para 15.74.
3 See s 63. A child is said to be in the care of a voluntary organisation if (a) the organisation has actual custody of him or (b) having had actual custody of him, the organisation has transferred that custody to an individual who does not have legal custody of him (CA 1975, s 88).

2   Transfer of parental rights and duties to a voluntary organisation

15.114   A local authority may pass a resolution that the parental rights and duties be vested in an incorporated voluntary organisation, but a number of conditions have to be satisfied.[1] A resolution can only be passed if the organisation so requests. The child must be in the care of that organisation at the time when the resolution is passed and not in the care of any local authority, but he must be living in the authority's area. One of the conditions which would entitle a local authority to pass a section 2 resolution must be satisfied,[2] but the authority must also be satisfied that it is necessary in the interests of the child's welfare for the rights and duties to be vested in the organisation. Thus, section 64 expressly refers to the child's interests,[3] unlike section 3, which by implication is to be read in relation to the local authority's general duty, under section 18(1), so that in deciding whether to pass a resolution vesting the parental rights and duties in themselves the local authority must give first consideration to safeguarding and promoting the child's welfare.

The term 'parental rights and duties' has the same meaning as it has for the purpose of section 3, and a resolution has the same effects as a section 3 resolution.[4] Thus, if it is made on account of one parent who has hitherto been sharing the rights and duties with the other parent, the latter will now share them with the organisation.[5] The provisions relating to access[6] apply in relation to a child who is in the care of a voluntary organisation and the subject of a resolution passed by virtue of section 64 as they do in relation to a child in local authority care where there is a section 3 resolution in force.[7] A voluntary organisation may make arrangements for the emigration of children in their care, but only within the limits imposed by section 62 of the 1980 Act and the Emigration of Children (Arrangements by Voluntary Organisations) Regulations 1982,[8] and the Regulations apply even though the parental rights and duties are vested in the voluntary organisation.[9] Moreover, whether or not the rights and duties are so vested, a voluntary organisation are subject to the same general duty as a local authority in respect of children in their care, namely, to give first consideration to the need to safeguard and promote the child's welfare.[10] They are also subject to the duty imposed on a local authority to cause children in a voluntary home to be visited to ensure their well-being.[11]

1 CCA 1980, s 64.
2 This includes the rule that, if the whereabouts of a parent have remained unknown for 12 months, he is deemed to have abandoned his child (s 64(4)).
3 Compare a similar reference to the duty of the juvenile court to be satisfied that it is in the child's interests that a section 3 resolution should not lapse (s 3(6)(c)).
4 See ante, paras 15.33 et seq. Note that s 8 also applies; see s 66(2).
5 Section 64(3).
6 Sections 12A–12G, ante, paras 15.86 et seq.
7 Section 64(8), as inserted by HASSASSAA 1983, Sch I.
8 SI 1982/13. These Regulations follow lines very similar to those relating to children in local authority care (ante para 15.98). Breach of a Regulation is an offence attracting a fine not exceeding level 3 on the standard scale; see s 62(3).
9 Section 64(6). Where they are so vested the consent of the Secretary of State is needed for emigration; reg 3(1)(e).
10 Section 64A, as inserted by HASSASSAA 1983, Sch 2.
11 CCA 1980, s 68. It is an offence (punishable with a fine not exceeding level 2 on the standard scale) to refuse an authorised person entry into the home, but if he is refused entry and the child is believed to be at risk a warrant to search and remove under CYPA 1933, s 40 may be sought or a constable may enter and search under the Police and Criminal Evidence Act 1984, s 17(1)(e) where there is danger to life or limb.

15.115 Unless the aid of the court is sought, only the local authority and not the voluntary organisation can terminate the resolution. This it can do by resolving that the rights and duties are no longer to be vested in the organisation but instead in the authority. In deciding whether to do so it must have regard to the interests of the child.[1] The procedure for objecting to a section 3 resolution extends to a resolution made under section 64,[2] but is not appropriate to one made under section 65.[3] Nor can the parent or guardian apply for rescission of it.[4] However, he is given a right of complaint to the juvenile court by way of an 'appeal', with appeal therefrom to the High Court, with respect to resolutions made under either of those sections. He may do so either because there was no ground for making the resolution or because it should in the child's interests be determined. A guardian ad litem may be appointed in those proceedings.[5]

1 Sections 65(1) and 66(1). Written notice of the new resolution must be given within seven days of passing it not only to the organisation but also to each parent, guardian or custodian whose whereabouts are known (s 65(2)).
2 Section 67(1).

3 Section 66(3).
4 Ibid.
5 See s 67(1)–(4).

X   LOCAL AUTHORITIES AND WARDSHIP[1]

15.116   In summary the wardship jurisdiction of the High Court cannot be used to challenge the actions of a local authority, but it can be used *by* local authorities where their statutory powers are deficient or where the jurisdiction offers advantages over the statutory framework. In fact, local authorities have been encouraged to use the High Court whenever necessary.[2] The reasoning is that because local authorities and wardship are working towards the same goal — the protection of children — the jurisdiction can be properly used to assist the authorities' statutory powers.[3]

1 For further consideration, see Lowe and White, Chapter 16, Bromley, pp 471–477; Parry in Butterworths Family Law Service Division E, Chapter 4; Cretney pp 561–570; Law Commission, Working Paper No 101, pp 47–60; Levy, Chapter 13.
2 See, for example, *Re D (a minor) (justices' decision: review)* [1977] Fam 158, [1977] 3 All ER 481. In 1986, 3,399 summons were issued, of which 1,845 were brought by local authorities (Judicial Statistics 1986, Cm 173 (Table 4.2)).
3 See, for example, Lord Wilberforce in *A v Liverpool City Council* [1982] AC 363 at 373, [1981] 2 All ER 385 at 388.

1   Where the powers of a local authority are deficient

15.117   (a) When a juvenile court refuses to make an order in care proceedings or decides to discharge a care order, the local authority have no right of appeal under CYPA 1969.[1] If they still consider the child to be at risk of harm, they may, and arguably must, invoke the wardship jurisdiction.[2] For, 'if it were otherwise, it would lead to a gross dereliction of duty'.[3] The result is that the authority can appeal the juvenile court's decision by using wardship. It can be similarly used where a parental rights' resolution has been rejected, even though under CCA 1980 the local authority has a right of appeal.[4] Another example is where an access order is granted by a juvenile court and this scuppers the plans which the authority have for the child. Rather than appealing against the access order (the appellate court's powers on appeal being limited to reviewing and if necessary replacing the order), the authority may be tempted to switch to wardship so that much wider issues than access can be decided.[5] A further example is where an authority (as opposed to a parent) wish to organise the 'phased return' of a child in their care to his parents. The juvenile court has no power under CYPA 1969 or CCA 1980 to make such an order.[6] Finally, the jurisdiction can be exercised notwithstanding the existence of a current care order made in criminal proceedings.[7]

1 It does have the right under CCA 1980, s 6.
2 *Re D (a minor) (justices' decision: review)* [1977] Fam 158, [1977] 3 All ER 481; *Re C (a minor) (justices' decision: review)* (1981) 2 FLR 62, 10 Fam Law 84, CA; *Hertfordshire County Council v Dolling* (1981) 3 FLR 423; *Re R (a minor) (discharge of care order: wardship)* [1987] 2 FLR 400, [1988] Fam Law 61, CA. It should be noted that foster parents cannot use wardship in these situations. An application for judicial review or custodianship are the unsatisfactory alternatives. For an example of the parlous position of foster parents, see *Re RM and LM* [1986] 2 FLR 205, [1986] Fam Law 297.

3 Per Stephen Brown LJ, in *Re R* (1987), Lexis, Enggen Library, Cases file.
4 *O'Dare Ai v South Glamorgan County* (1980) 3 FLR 1, 10 Fam Law 215; *Re W (wardship proceedings)* (1982) 3 FLR 129, CA; *Crosby (a minor) v Northumberland County Council* (1982) 12 Fam Law 92.
5 See *Re LH (a minor) (wardship: jurisdiction)* [1986] 2 FLR 306, [1986] Fam Law 271, and *Re M (a minor) (access application)* [1988] 1 FLR 35, [1988] Fam Law 13.
6 Cf *Hertfordshire County Council v A* (1981) Times, 15 December; and *Re J (a minor) (wardship: jurisdiction)* [1984] 1 All ER 29, [1984] 1 WLR 81. (*Parental* applications for a phased return via wardship are clearly now unavailable, see post, para 15.117).
7 *Re C (a minor) (wardship: care order)* [1983] 1 All ER 219, [1982] 1 WLR 1462.

15.118 (b) Often the evidence available to a local authority is insufficient to warrant instituting care proceedings in the first place. For example, the difficulty of proving psychological as opposed to physical harm is well known and an authority may be advised to wait until more visible evidence appears. In such cases wardship may be appropriate.[1] Important considerations are that the rules of evidence are more liberal in the High Court (for example, the Civil Evidence Act 1968 applies in relation to hearsay),[2] the procedure is much simpler than that stipulated for the juvenile court by MC(C&YP) Rules 1988, the evidence is usually in the form of affidavits, and, of course, the High Court is governed by the child's best interests and not by detailed statutory grounds. Wardship may similarly be used where there is insufficient evidence to pass a parental rights' resolution under section 3 of CCA 1980.

1 But the matter should be dealt with expeditiously; *Stockport Metropolitan Borough Council v B, Stockport Metropolitan Borough Council v L* [1986] 2 FLR 80, [1986] Fam Law 187.
2 Indeed the court generally adopts a more relaxed view in relation to evidence; see *Official Solicitor to the Supreme Court v K* [1965] AC 201, [1963] 3 All ER 191, HL.

15.119 (c) Another situation is where the authority does have sufficient evidence of harm to a child but the terms of the statute clearly cannot cover the case. An example is a new-born, first child of a parent who has no history of child abuse but who is unlikely to be able to cope. The present tense drafting of section 1 of CYPA 1969 excludes the possibility of care proceedings.[1] Wardship can fill the gap.[2] There are however limits to wardship and it cannot be used prematurely before the child is born.[3]

1 *Essex County Council v TLR and KBR* (1978) 143 JP 309, 9 Fam Law 15; see ante, para 14.08.
2 See *Re B* (1982) Ad and Fostering 50, CA. Wardship was there preceded, however, by a place of safety order of dubious legality given the preceding footnote; see Bromley, op cit, p 466. On the other hand, a place of safety order is a practical measure which can be used prior to wardship, eg *Re P* (1987) NLJ 406, [1987] FCR 125; and objections to its lawfulness are academic for a parent, given the temporal exigencies. However, the correct procedures must be followed. The child cannot simply be snatched away; see *Havering London Borough Council v S* [1986] 1 FLR 489, [1986] Fam Law 157.
3 *In Re F (in Utero)* [1988] 2 All ER 193, [1988] 2 WLR 1288, CA.

15.120 (d) If a parent demands the immediate return of a child who has been in voluntary care for under six months, the local authority may not have the power to retain the child by passing a 'section 3 resolution' under CCA 1980. In that event an authority might 'well consider it to be their moral duty to keep the child long enough to have it made a ward of court'.[1]

1 Per Lord Salmon in *Lewisham LBC v Lewisham Juvenile Court* [1980] AC 273 at 291, [1979] 2 All ER 297 at 306; see ante, para 15.30. See also *Re CB (a minor) (wardship: jurisdiction)* [1981] 1 All ER 16, [1981] 1 WLR 379, CA.

2   Where wardship offers advantages over the statutory powers

15.121   (a) Cases may be of such difficulty or notoriety that the experience of a High Court judge is desirable.[1] Indeed, in some cases the local authorities will agree to a wardship application brought by someone else and will not contest it on jurisdictional grounds.[2] Examples of this category of cases are requests to the court for guidance on the sterilisation of children,[3] the performing of a life-saving operation[4] or an abortion,[5] on the future of a child born as a result of a surrogacy arrangement[6] or born to a mentally handicapped mother,[7] on the problems posed by the care of a child of a foreign cultural background,[8] on the frequent difficulty of determining whether a child has been sexually abused,[9] and on resolving disputes between two local authorities.[10]

1 See Sheldon J in *Re LH (a minor) (wardship: jurisdiction)* [1986] 2 FLR 306, at 310. For further consideration of the advantages of wardship, see Hershman and Mcfarlane, *Child in Care: Juvenile Court or High Court?* [1988] Fam Law 66.
2 *A v B and Hereford and Worcester County Council* [1986] 1 FLR 289, [1986] Fam Law 133. The court may also recommend to an authority that they consent to wardship, see *R v Newham London Borough Council, ex p MCL* (1987) Lexis, Enggen Library, Cases file.
3 *Re D (wardship: sterilisation)* [1976] Fam 185, [1976] 1 All ER 326; *Re B (a minor) (wardship: sterilisation)* [1987] AC 199, [1987] 2 All ER 206, HL.
4 *Re B (a minor) (wardship: medical treatment)* [1981] 1 WLR 1421, 3 FLR 117, CA.
5 *Re P (a minor)* [1986] 1 FLR 272, (1981) 80 LGR 301.
6 *Re C (a minor) (wardship: surrogacy)* [1985] FLR 846, [1985] Fam Law 191.
7 *Re C (a minor)* (1987) Lexis, Enggen Library, Cases file.
8 *Re H (Minors) (wardship: cultural background)* [1987] 2 FLR 12, [1987] Fam Law 196; *Re JT (a minor) (wardship: committal to care)* [1986] 2 FLR 107, [1986] Fam Law 213; *Re A (a minor) (cultural background)* [1987] 2 FLR 429, [1988] Fam Law 65.
9 In *Re F* [1988] Fam Law 255, CA; and note the many other cases arising in Cleveland since May 1987 which have been heard in wardship proceedings.
10 *Re C (a minor) (wardship: care order)* [1983] 1 All ER 219, [1982] 1 WLR 1462.

15.122   (b) The extra powers available to the High Court may be needed. Principal of these is the injunction, the flexibility of which is such that it can, for example, restrain a person from attempting to contact the ward[1] or restrain publication of information which would identify a ward and his mother[2] or even prevent a ward's mother from leaving the jurisdiction before a paternity test can be conducted.[3] The flexibility of such orders contrasts sharply with the orders available in the juvenile court.[4] A further advantage of wardship is that the case will first come before a registrar who exercises critical control over the preparation of the evidence and the future conduct of the proceedings.[5]

1 Eg *Re B (a minor) (wardship: child in care)* [1975] Fam 36, [1974] 3 All ER 915.
2 *X County Council v A* [1985] 1 All ER 53; sub nom *Re AB* [1984] 1 WLR 1422. Cf *Re X* [1975] Fam 47, [1975] 1 All ER 697.
3 *Re J (a minor) (wardship)* [1988] 1 FLR 65, [1988] Fam Law 91.
4 See further Lowe and White, op cit, Chapter 8; Levy, op cit, Chapter 8.
5 Lowe and White, at pp 54 et seq, and Levy, Chapter 3.

15.123 (c) In wardship the court is able to deal with the whole of the child's future. Thus, in *Re LH (a minor) (wardship jurisdiction)*[1] the local authority planned adoption for a child in their care and terminated parental access. The parents obtained an access order from a juvenile court (on terms 'to be agreed with' the authority). Instead of appealing under CCA 1980,[2] the local authority switched to wardship. This then enabled the High Court to deal with the proposed adoption, access, and other questions concerning the child's future.[3] The disadvantage of wardship from an authority's point of view is that, if wardship is granted, they lose ultimate control over the child.[4] Indeed, many of the applications to court consist of authorities seeking permission from the court to take important decisions about wards, such as adoption, parental access and education. In exercising its jurisdiction the court must do whatever is best for the child and consequently it is not confined to the submissions of the parties.[5]

1 [1986] 2 FLR 306, [1986] Fam Law 271.
2 Section 12C(5); see *Re M (a minor) (access application)* [1988] 1 FLR 35, [1988] Fam Law 13, CA.
3 Pending the wardship hearing, the authority restricted parental access to two hours every six weeks and effectively thwarted the import of the access order. See to similar effect, *Re D (a minor) (wardship: access)* [1987] 2 FLR 365, [1988] Fam Law 63, CA.
4 *Re Y* [1976] Fam 125, [1975] 3 All ER 348, CA; *Re CB (a minor) (wardship: jurisdiction)* [1981] 1 All ER 16, [1981] 1 WLR 379, CA. For example, a ward can only be placed in secure accommodation with the approval of the High Court, *Practice Direction* [1986] 3 All ER 320, [1986] 1 WLR 1300. See also *M v Lambeth Borough Council (No 3)* [1986] 2 FLR 136, [1986] Fam Law 265, CA; his medical records can only be disclosed to the police for their investigation with leave of the court, *Re S (minors) (wardship : disclosure of material)* [1988] 1 FLR 1, and similarly as regards any interview of the ward by the police, *Re K* [1988] 1 All ER 214, [1987] 3 WLR 1233; see *Practice Direction* [1988] 1 All ER 223, [1987] 1 WLR 1739. In an extreme case the court could even order the local authority to appoint a social worker to assist the ward; see *Re B* (1987) Times, 6 October.
5 *Re E (SA)* [1984] 1 All ER 289, [1984] 1 WLR 156, HL.

3 Use of wardship by others against local authorities

15.124 It is a firmly established rule that the wardship jurisdiction of the High Court cannot be used 'to supervise the exercise of discretion within the field committed by statute to the local authority'.[1] This has been broadly interpreted so that parents, other relatives and other persons such as foster parents cannot use wardship to challenge the way in which an authority is performing, or is about to perform, its child care duties. Thus, in the leading case of *A v Liverpool City Council* it was unavailable to review an authority's decision to restrict parental access to a child in its care.[2] Similarly in *Re W (a minor) (wardship : jurisdiction)*[3] an uncle, aunt and grandparent could not repair what they saw as deficiencies in their *locus standi* under the statutory code by resorting to wardship. Local authorities cannot therefore be challenged as to a wide range of decisions relating to children in their care, such as where and with whom the child is to live, or how he is to be educated. This approach has been carried to such an extent that wardship cannot be used where it would anticipate an authority's exercise of statutory powers. Thus in *W v Nottinghamshire County Council*,[4] it was observed that 'where the statutory code provides an appropriate course, then an attempt by a party other than a local authority to pursue an alternative remedy by way of wardship proceedings should not be permitted by the court'.[5] A question left open in that case was whether wardship would be appropriate in circumstances where an authority 'obviously ought to exercise its powers and duties under the statutory code but declines so to do'.[6] It seems clear, in the light of the following paragraph, that judicial review and not wardship would be the permitted (but unsatisfactory) remedy, unless the local authority were to accede to a wardship application. The analogy can be drawn with *Re JT (a minor) (wardship : committal to care)*,[7] where a guardian ad litem objected to an authority's plan to rehabilitate a child with his mother and applied for wardship. The authority could have taken objection on jurisdictional grounds but decided not to do so. Similarly, where an authority hold a child in voluntary care and refuse to hand him back on request to his parents, judicial review (or, arguably, habeas corpus) must be used instead of wardship.

1 Per Lord Wilberforce in *A v Liverpool City Council* [1982] AC 363 at 373, [1981] 2 All ER 385 at 389. The word 'statute' is at large and covers children committed to care under, for example, s 43 of MCA 1973; see *J v Devon County Council* [1986] 1 FLR 597, [1986] Fam Law 162. The basis for the rule in the text was laid in *Re M* [1961] Ch 328, [1961] 1 All ER 788. See also *Re T (AJJ) (an infant)* [1970] Ch 688, [1970] 2 All ER 865. For a forceful endorsement of the rule, see *Re DM (a minor) (wardship : jurisdiction)* [1986] 2 FLR 122, [1986] Fam Law 296. Its rationale extends so as to prevent foster parents from using an adoption application as a means of challenging an authority's decision; see *Re H* [1985] FLR 519, [1985] Fam Law 133; and for a dramatic application of the rule in the context of the Education Act 1981, see *Re D* [1988] 1 FLR 131, [1988] Fam Law 89, CA.
2 See supra, para 15.89.
3 [1980] Fam 60, [1979] 3 All ER 154.
4 [1986] 1 FLR 565, [1986] Fam Law 185, CA.
5 Per Purchas LJ [1986] 1 FLR 565 at 575. See also *W v Shropshire County Council* [1986] 1 FLR 359, [1986] Fam Law 128, CA, where the local authority announced their intention to apply for a care order (which they were virtually certain to obtain) and the court refused to grant wardship on the application of the child's parents.
6 Ibid.
7 [1986] 2 FLR 107, [1986] Fam Law 213.

15.125   Although the point has not been conclusively decided by the House of Lords, the Court of Appeal[1] has interpreted *A v Liverpool City Council*[2] and *Re W*[3] as also excluding wardship as a means of reviewing improper or unlawful action by a local authority. So, for example, if an authority fail to give the required notice of care proceedings to an interested person, his remedy lies in judicial review and not wardship.[4] This is unfortunate, since on review the court is restricted to assessing the legality of an act and, if necessary, remitting the case back to an authority for a proper determination, whereas in wardship the court is able to consider the merits of the case and decide what is best for the particular child. The result is that parents, foster parents and others must hope that the local authority will appreciate the desirability of wardship and accede to the jurisdiction. In some cases where there is an application for leave to apply for judicial review, the judge may assist by putting pressure on the authority and recommending that it institute wardship proceedings.[5]

1 *Re DM (a minor) (wardship : jurisdiction)* [1986] 2 FLR 122, [1986] Fam Law 296; *Re RM and LM (minors) (wardship : jurisdiction)* [1986] 2 FLR 205, [1986] Fam Law 297. See also *Bedfordshire County Council, ex p C, R v Hertfordshire County Council, ex p B* [1987] 1 FLR 239, [1987] Fam Law 55.

2 [1982] AC 363, [1981] 2 All ER 385.
3 [1985] AC 791, [1985] 2 All ER 301.
4 *Re S (a minor) (care proceedings : wardship summons)* [1987] 1 FLR 479, [1987] Fam
  Law 159, CA; cf *D v X City Council (No 1)* [1985] FLR 275, where wardship was available
  and, in a different context, *Re L(AC) (an infant)* [1971] 3 All ER 743.
5 *R v Newham London Borough Council, ex p MCL* (1987) Lexis, Enggen Library, Cases.

XI   MEANS OF CONTROLLING LOCAL AUTHORITIES

15.126   The following section of this chapter deals with the situation where
a person wishes to question the actions of a local authority and there is
no remedy provided in the child care legislation. As will be seen, the available
relief can be cumbersome and often ultimately unproductive.

1   Judicial review

15.127   Now that wardship is unavailable to them, parents, foster parents
and others who wish to challenge in court the actions of a local authority
must turn to judicial review,[1] and that may be possible in three situations.[2]

1 RSC Ord. 53.
2 The classification in the text is based on that proposed by Lord Diplock in *Council of
  Civil Service Unions v Minister for the Civil Service* [1985] AC 374 at 410, [1984] 3 All
  ER 935 at 950.

(a)   Where a local authority have acted unlawfully

15.128   This could happen where the local authority have erred in law
when reaching their decision. Illegality could also occur where the authority
have acted beyond their powers. An example would be the refusal of an
authority to hand a child who is in 'voluntary' care back to his parents
when the authority take no further action to retain the child by passing
a section 3 resolution or seeking wardship. Another would be where a
child is seized without the lawful authority of a warrant, a place of safety
order or wardship.

(b)   Where a local authority have behaved irrationally or unreasonably within the 'Wednesbury Corporation' test

15.129   As Lord Greene MR put the matter in that case:[1]

'Lawyers familiar with the phraseology commonly used in relation
to exercise of statutory discretions often use the word 'unreasonable'
in a rather comprehensive sense. It has frequently been used and is
frequently used as a general description of the things that must not
be done. For instance, a person entrusted with a discretion must,
so to speak, direct himself properly in law. He must call his own
attention to the matters which he is bound to consider. He must exclude
from his consideration matters which are irrelevant to what he has
to consider. If he does not obey those rules, he may truly be said,
and often is said, to be acting "unreasonably". Similarly, there may
be something so absurd that no sensible person could ever dream
that it lay within the powers of the authority.'

Examples in this context could include a local authority removing a child from foster parents solely to prevent the latter from applying for custodianship,[2] or, when deciding upon the child's future, refusing even to consider the representations of a child's grandparents, who have maintained close and regular contact with him.

1 *Associated Provincial Picture Houses Ltd v Wednesbury Corpn* [1948] 1 KB 223 at 229, [1947] 2 All ER 680 at 682, CA. Cf the facts of *Re H (a minor) (adoption)* [1985] FLR 519, [1985] Fam Law 133, CA, and the dicta at 528–9.

(c)   Where a local authority have failed to follow the proper or appropriate procedure

15.130   An example of procedural impropriety would be an authority failing to give notice of pending care proceedings to those persons specified in the MC(C&YP) Rules 1988.[1] 'Appropriate' raises the subject of natural justice or, in its more recent formulation, the duty to act fairly. Thus, for example, an authority should not use the unsubstantiated allegations of sexual misconduct against a father to justify their decision not to send a child in their care home on trial with his parents.[2] The father should be given the opportunity to make representations so as to refute the allegations. It is here that the European Convention for the Protection of Human Rights (see post, para 15.133) may be useful. In its embryonic jurisprudence the European Court has illustrated the need for local authorities to keep in touch with parents when deciding on a child's future. Of particular use to a litigant can be codes of practice and other similar documents which many authorities have adopted. These, for example, encourage close liaison between social services departments and parents and the attendance of parents at case conferences. Failure to observe the standard practice set out in an internally produced circular could well help to found an action in judicial review.

1 See *Re S (a minor) (care proceedings : wardship summons)* [1987] 1 FLR 479, [1987] Fam Law 159, CA.
2 *R v Bedfordshire County Council, ex p C* [1987] 1 FLR 239, [1987] Fam Law 55. However, the case of *R v Hertfordshire County Council, ex p B*, reported at the same reference, indicates that an authority retains a wide discretion in social work decisions.

15.131   Judicial review does, however, pose a number of difficulties in this context. First, leave of the High Court is required before an application for review can proceed,[1] and the applicant may lack sufficient information to clear this first hurdle. Hence the giving of reasons for a decision, the adoption of codes of practice and more openness generally by local authorities can be crucial. However, it should be noted that once this hurdle of leave is cleared the local authority will be required to be more forthcoming and to conduct their case with all the cards face upwards on the table.[2] In addition the process of discovery will then be available. Second, even if the application for judicial review succeeds, the award of a remedy is discretionary and the court may conclude that, for example, the passage of time since an authority's decision makes a remedy inappropriate for the child's interests.[3] A third and related point is that the remedies in this context merely remit the matter to the local authority for a proper reconsideration.[4] Thus, if a care order is quashed on review for failure to give notice of the proceedings, another order may still be made, provided that the proper procedures are on the second occasion observed.[5]

1 RSC Ord 53, r 3.
2 Per Lord Donaldson MR in *R v Lancashire County Council, ex p Huddleston* [1986] 2 All ER 941, CA (a case concerning the award of a student grant). His Lordship's remarks and those of Parker LJ at 946–947, are, arguably, even more pertinent in the context of child care decisions.
3 See *R v Chertsey Justices, ex p E* [1987] 2 FLR 415 (even if the applicant were right, mandamus was unnecessary).
4 Although the court can direct an authority to reach a conclusion in accordance with the court's findings (RSC Ord 53, r 9(4)), this does not assist in the child care field, since the court will not, on judicial review, have reviewed the merits of the particular decision.
5 *Re S (a minor) (care proceedings : wardship summons)* [1987] 1 FLR 479, [1987] Fam Law 159, CA. See also *R v Bedfordshire County Council*, supra, para 15.127, note 6, (certiorari granted to quash an authority's decision and ordering them to give a father the opportunity of making representations before the authority reached a fresh decision).

2 Local Commissioner for Administration[1]

15.132 Social services departments of local authorities fall within the jurisdiction of the local Commissioner or Ombudsman. The Commissioner may investigate complaints made by persons who claim to have suffered injustice as a result of maladministration.[2] The requirement of injustice can be a stumbling block for it is possible for the Commissioner to discover maladministration but to conclude that there has been no injustice since the local authority's decision is likely to have been the same even if it had been taken properly.[3] A further difficulty is the delay attendant upon the Commissioner's report. By the time it is published it will often be too late for an authority to alter their decision on the particular child; alternatively, the delay can postpone a decision on the child's long-term future. The report can, however, have a prospective influence in prompting a local authority to review and change their practices. The Commissioner's experience in the child care field includes the following investigations:

(i) into the way in which an authority received a child into care (maladministration found because the authority failed to use section 1 of CCA 1980 so as to make available advice and assistance and failed to investigate the parents' circumstances adequately);[4]
(ii) into the way in which the authority had passed a section 3 resolution;[5]
(iii) into the failure by an authority to keep a child's parents properly informed of his development;[6]
(iv) into an authority's failure to tell parents of their rights under the Code of Practice on access;[7]
(v) into the ways in which an authority dealt with foster parents,[8] with the selection of prospective adoptive parents,[9] and with the pregnancy and then abortion for a teenage child in their care;[10] and
(vi) into whether an authority's failure to act led to the death of a child.[11]

1 See Local Government Act 1974, Part III. There are three Commissioners for England and one for Wales.
2 Ibid, s 26(1). Fortunately from the complainant's point of view he need not specify the alleged maladministration in any great detail, see *R v Local Com for Administration for*

the North and East Area of England, ex p Bradford Metropolitan City Council [1979] QB
287, [1979] 2 All ER 881, CA.
3 See the facts of *H v UK*, judgment of 8 July 1987, Series A, no 120, para 31.
4 Complaint number 0236/C/86.
5 221/Y/83.
6 See *W v United Kingdom*, Judgment of 8 July 1987, Series A, no 121–A.
7 86/C/0947.
8 543/J/84.
9 777/B/85.
10 807/C/84.
11 1133/C/85.

3   European Convention for the Protection of Human Rights

15.133   The influence of the Convention has begun to appear in the child
care field. Indeed, the leading decisions of the European Court[1] concern
the United Kingdom. The Convention is a time consuming but potentially
useful check on child care legislation and practice. By the time the court
delivers judgment, its ruling cannot assist the particular child in issue, but
the threat or inauguration of proceedings may have already prompted the
Government into taking action. For example, in *W v United Kingdom*[2]
proceedings under the Convention were initiated in January 1982 to
complain about the lack of parental involvement in the decision over a
child's access to his parents. By the time of the court's judgment, Parliament
had responded by including within the Health and Social Services and Social
Security Adjudications Act 1983 provisions for, inter alia, access disputes
to be heard by a juvenile court.[3]

1 *O v UK, H v UK*, judgments of 8 July 1987, Series A, no 120; *W v UK, B v UK, R
v UK*, judgments of 8 July 1987, Series A, no 121,
2 Ibid.
3 See s 12A of CCA 1980 and ante, paras 15.86 et seq.

15.134   The Articles of the Convention which are likely to prove the most
useful are:
Article 6 ('In the determination of his civil rights and obligations . . . everyone is entitled to a fair and public hearing within a
reasonable time by an independent and impartial tribunal . . . ');
Article 8 ('Everyone has the right to respect for his private and family
life . . .'); and
Article 13 ('Everyone whose rights and freedoms as set forth in this
Convention are violated shall have an effective remedy before a national
authority notwithstanding that the violation has been committed by persons
acting in an official capacity').

15.135   The cluster of cases before the European Court involving the United
Kingdom has produced the following noteworthy points.
    First, and controversially,[1] the majority of the judges in *W v UK* and
O v UK have held that Article 6 only covers rights and obligations 'which
can be said, at least on arguable grounds, to be recognised under domestic
law; it does not in itself guarantee any particular content' for the rights
and obligations in the Member State.[2] Given the very few rights and
obligations which still reside in the parent where there is a care order or

section 3 resolution in force, this ruling of the court could severely restrict the relevance of the Convention to the child care field.[3]

Second, the court in *H v UK* stressed the need for speed in reaching important decisions affecting a child. The jurisprudence of the Convention requires that the complexity of the case, the conduct of the parties and of the national courts and the importance of the case from the applicants' point of view must all be weighed. Thus, in *H v UK* a child's adoption was in issue and a delay of two years and seven months in concluding legal proceedings was held not to be a 'reasonable time' for the purposes of Article 6(1). Delay can similarly infringe Article 8, for 'a mere effluxion of time'[4] could in effect terminate a parents' contact with a child and thus lead to a loss of 'family life' within the terms of the Article.

Third, since many decisions taken by a local authority (such as passing a section 3 resolution, or a decision determining parental access) may become irreversible, there is a need to guard against arbitrary action. As part of that need, the local authority's procedures must be fair, so that 'family life' within Article 8 is properly protected. To be 'fair', so the court reasoned,[5] the procedures must take account of parental views and may require parental involvement in the decision making process. This last point could have great influence in the section 3 resolution procedure under CCA 1980 and hastens the call for legislative reform.

1 Six judges disagreed with the majority decision.
2 *W v UK,* judgment para 73; *O v UK*, judgment para 53.
3 In *W v UK* and *O v UK* the court, in spite of its ruling, by a strained reasoning concluded that since the taking of a child into care (or receiving into care and the passing of a resolution) does not extinguish all the rights and responsibilities of the natural parent, arguably a parent could claim a 'right' in regard to access; see *W v UK*, judgment para 77; *O v UK*, judgment para 58.
4 *H v UK*, judgment, para 90. See also *W v UK*, judgment, para 69.
5 *W v UK*; and see also *B v UK* and *R v UK*.

4 Other complaints procedures

15.136 A more practical, effective and certainly cheaper way of dealing with complaints can be an informal or formal grievance procedure set up by a local authority. As the House of Commons Social Services Committee observed,[1] 'the tenuousness of the chain of responsibility and the crucial nature of the decisions made every day by social workers had led to a widely perceived need for a system to provide for the possibility of complaint or appeal against decisions'. Moreover, it is not just parents who need a channel for complaints, but also children in care who are dissatisfied with the way in which the authority are treating them.[2] It would appear that the record of local authorities in devising complaints procedure is patchy[3] and the Review of Child Care Law has called for a more rigorous response:

'Every local authority should have a procedure for handling complaints and resolving disputes on the way it carries out its responsibilities for particular children. In the first place this will amount to reconsideration by social services management. If this does not resolve the complaint, a further channel for challenging decisions or actions should be provided.

Different authorities will have different ways of providing such a channel and we do not recommend that any particular procedure should be laid down by statute. But we recommend all authorities should meet this need in one way or another. This should be a standing procedure rather than ad hoc arrangements, and known and accessible both to parents and children. Sometimes the Social Services Committee of the local authority will act as a forum, sometimes a special panel set up for the purpose by the local authority. Whatever arrangements are made, we would emphasise the importance of involving a person or persons independent of the local authority to satisfy the concern that a decision or action may not be reviewed with a sufficient degree of independence.'[4]

1 Second Report 1983–4, HC 360–1, vol 1, para 360.
2 The Select Committee commented favourably on the practice of some local authorities of issuing guidance to children in their care explaining how complaints can be voiced (para 363).
3 See Lewis, Seneviratne, and Cracknell, *Complaints Procedures in Local Government*, (1987) paras 4 B1.1 – 4B5.
4 Paragraphs 9.11–9.12.

PART III
Financial provision for children

CHAPTER 16

Financial provision for children

I INTRODUCTION

16.01 References to the financial support of children have throughout this book been to this chapter. The following treatment of it recognises that financial provision for children comes from two sources: parents, spouses and guardians (Section II below) and the State (Section III). The former consists of a wide variety of obligations ranging from a father's duty to maintain his child following divorce, to the parents' obligation to contribute towards the upkeep of their child in the care of a local authority, to the liability of a deceased parent's estate to provide for a child. Recent years have seen some legislative attempts to harmonise the various jurisdictions but the area is still characterised by a plethora of statutes sharing similar, but not always identical, provisions. The resulting complexity and overlapping of laws are self-evident. As to the latter (Section III), a reverse trend is seen after 1988 with the move away from rigid, but at least reasonably precise, rules to a larger element of discretion in the distribution of social security. More generally it will be noted that most children's claims for financial provision appear as appendages to parental claims and that relatively few proceedings are solely concerned with child maintenance. This emphasis carries the danger that the child's interests are subsumed within those of the parents and consequently underestimated.

II OBLIGATIONS OF PARENT, SPOUSE OR GUARDIAN[1]

1 At common law

(a) Parent of legitimate child

16.02 A remarkable feature of the common law was that it imposed no direct civil liability on the father to maintain his legitimate child. Consequently he was not liable for any debt incurred by the child, even a debt arising from the supply of necessaries, unless he had given the child authority to incur it or had contracted to pay for it:[2] mere knowledge that his child was being maintained by a third party would not render him liable for necessaries supplied by that party to his child.[3] The severity of this rule which denied the child the benefit of an agency of necessity was partially mitigated by the wife's agency of necessity, because, if she had been deserted by her husband, or for good cause was living apart from him, she was entitled to pledge his credit for necessaries supplied to the child, at least if she had custody under an order of the court.[4] Even that protection disappeared,[5] but, if the common law still has any practical relevance, it may possibly be the rule that a liability to pay for necessaries would be implied if the father has deserted the child.[6]

Initially the exemption from liability related only to the father, since he alone was recognised as having custody, but as the mother acquired rights therein the protection seems impliedly to have been extended to her.

1   For a short historical account, see Eekelaar and Maclean, *Maintenance After Divorce* (1986), Chapter 2.
2   *Mortimore v Wright* (1840) 6 M & M 482; *Shelton v Springett* (1851) 11 CB 452.
3   *A fortiori* if there was no knowledge, *Fluck v Tollemache* (1823) 1 C & P 5.
4   *Bazeley v Forder* (1868) LR 3 QB 559.
5   Matrimonial Proceedings and Property Act 1970, s 41.
6   See *Urmston v Newcomen* (1836) 4 Ad & El 899, especially per Lord Denman, CJ, at 909. But, even if the proposition be valid, it would not apply in respect of a child who has attained majority; see *Coldingham Parish Council v Smith* [1918] 2 KB 90.

(b)   Parent of illegitimate child

16.03   Neither the mother[1] nor the father[2] is liable at common law to maintain the illegitimate child, but, as in the case of the legitimate, either can give the child an authority to incur a debt on her or his behalf or can expressly or impliedly contract to be bound.[3] In *Cameron v Baker*[4] it was held that, though the father:

'is not in the first instance bound to maintain it, unless compelled to do so by an order of magistrates, [yet] if he consents to pay an annual sum for its support he must continue to do so or provide for the child at his own expense or give the most distinct notice of his intention to pay such annual sum no longer';

and shortly after this decision the principle was established that the father can accept liability by contracting with the mother to pay her regular sums for the support of their child.[5] The consideration for his promise to pay may take various forms, such as a promise to have regard to his wishes about the way in which she will bring up their child;[6] it may be a promise not to institute proceedings for maintenance,[7] and possibly even a promise to fulfil her own obligations to maintain the child[8] may be adequate.[9] The agreement is, however, no bar to maintenance proceedings by the mother, because any payment thereby ordered to be made to her is for the maintenance of the child and not for her benefit, with the result that she cannot renounce the right to it.[10] This is so even where the consideration for the father's promise to pay is the mother's promise not to take maintenance proceedings for the child, which is 'probably a unique example of a promise which is valid for one purpose but contrary to public policy for another'.[11] Unless the terms of the agreement are open to a different construction, it seems that it may be terminated by reasonable notice, that it does not end on the father's death but does so on the mother's.[12]

1   *Ruttinger v Temple* (1863) 4 B & S 491.
2   *Seaborne v Maddy* (1840) 9 C & P 497.
3   In the light of *Mortimore v Wright*, supra, it seems clear that the father's mere knowledge that the child is being maintained by someone does not disturb the principle of non-liability and the earlier decision of *Nichole v Allen* (1827) 3 C & P 36 to the contrary cannot be regarded as good law. Nor can that of *Hesketh v Gowing* (1804) 5 Esp 131, where the fact that the father had accepted the child as his own was held enough to render him liable for necessaries supplied to the child.
4   (1824) 1 C & P 268.
5   *Jennings v Brown* (1842) 9 M & W 496.

6 Cf *Ward v Byham* [1956] 2 All ER 318, [1956] 1 WLR 496, CA.
7 *Linnegar v Hodd* (1848) 5 CB 437.
8 Under s 26 of the Social Security Act 1986, see infra, para 16.05.
9 So held by Denning, LJ, in *Ward v Byham*, supra but not adopted by the majority of the Court of Appeal (Morris and Parker LJJ).
10 *Follit v Koetzow* (1860) 2 E & E 730.
11 Bromley, op cit, p 644.
12 Ibid.

(c) Guardian and ward

16.04 The guardian is under a common law duty to maintain his ward out of the latter's property but is not obliged personally to do so. So, in the absence of a contract or an authority to incur a debt on his behalf, he is not civilly liable to a third party for a debt incurred by the ward. However, like a parent or anyone else who has assumed the care of a person, he will be criminally liable at common law as well as under statute if he wilfully neglects to provide the ward with adequate food, clothing, medical aid or lodging.[1]

1 See ante, Chapter 9, especially ss 1 and 17 of CYPA 1933.

2 Social Security

16.05 The inadequacy of the common law led to the creation of a statutory duty on the parent to maintain the child as part of the Poor Law of Elizabeth I.[1] This parental obligation was a cardinal principle of the Poor Law and has been embodied in the modern systems of National Assistance and, more recently, of Social Security. For the purpose of Social Security a man and a woman, whether married or unmarried,[2] are each liable to maintain those of their children who are under the age of 16 (including adopted children[3]). No similar obligation is specifically imposed on a guardian in respect of his ward but he would be included if his contribution to the child's maintenance is such that he can 'reasonably be treated as the father of that child'.[4] Where the parents are unmarried the man's liability may first require proof of paternity through a declaration of parentage.[5] The effect of the duty is that the Department of Social Security may recover from either or both parents the amount which it has had to pay in the form of Social Security in respect of their child.[6]

1 The obligation was first imposed on the parents of an illegitimate child in 1576, 18 Eliz I, c 3, s 2 and then more generally by the Poor Relief Act 1601, 43 Eliz I, c 2, s 7.
2 National Assistance Act 1948, s 42; Ministry of Social Security Act 1966, s 22; Supplementary Benefits Act 1976, s 17; and now Social Security Act 1986, s 26(3) and (4) (as amended by Family Law Reform Act 1987).
3 Adoption Act 1976, s 12 (formerly Children Act 1975, s 8).
4 Income Support (General) Regulations 1987, r 54.
5 See ante, para 2.32.
6 Social Security Act 1986, s 240(1).

3 Guardianship of Minors Act 1971[1]

16.06 This Act has been considerably amended in this context by the Domestic Proceedings and Magistrates' Courts Act 1978 and prospectively by the Family Law Reform Act 1987 so as to bring its provisions more into line with the courts' matrimonial jurisdiction. Its chief beneficiaries will be the unmarried couple for whom affiliation proceedings and its narrow limits have hitherto been available.[2] Importantly, an application can be made whilst the parents are cohabiting. The mother (in the usual case) may wish to do this as a precaution and prior to the Budget of 1988 the father may not have been averse to an order because of the tax advantages.[3] When one parent applies for an order against the other,[4] or when a testamentary guardian is appointed sole guardian of the child to the exclusion of the surviving parent[5] or where there is a dispute between joint guardians,[6] one of whom is a parent, the court may order the parent to provide financial relief for the child.[7] The courts with jurisdiction are the High Court (Family Division), a county court and a magistrates' court.[8] However, their powers are different. All can order periodical payments and/or the payment of a lump sum but only the High Court and a county court can in addition:

(i)   secure periodical payments;
(ii)   order the transfer of property; and
(iii) order the settlement of property.

Furthermore, a magistrates' court cannot deal with any property (or income from it) belonging to, or held in trust for, a child.[9] The orders can be made direct to the child[10] (apart obviously from (iii)) or for the 'benefit'[11] of the child. The former may be desirable for an older child.[12] A lump sum (which is limited to £1,000 in a magistrates' court) can, most usefully, be ordered to pay for expenditure reasonably incurred before the application was made in connection with the birth or maintenance of the child (eg the cost of feeding and clothing the child)[13] and may be ordered to be paid by instalments.[14]

1 Most applications for financial relief will accompany applications for legal custody of the child and the latter aspects are considered in Chapter 3.
2 For affiliation, see post, para 16.69. The provisions of FLRA 1987 which abolish affiliation proceedings have not been bought into operation.
3 See post, para 16.55.
4 Under s 11B
5 Under s 4(4); see ante para 4.09.
6 Under s 7; see ante, para 4.21.
7 Sections 11B, 11C.
8 Section 15(1).
9 Section 15(2)(b).
10 This includes an adopted child (Adoption Act 1976, s 12 (formerly Children Act 1975, s 8)).
11 Benefit is not defined but clearly embraces maintenance and that in turn is defined by s 20(2) as including 'education'.
12 Cf s 12C(4) under which a child, once he has reached the age of 16, can himself apply for a variation of a periodical payments order.
13 Section 12B(1).
14 Section 12B(5).

16.07   In most cases it will be the parent or guardian who will apply for an order, but a child can apply himself, on reaching the age of 18, to the High Court or a county court for a periodical payments order and/or a lump sum to be made against his parent(s).[1] An order will be granted if the applicant is, or wants to be, in education or training or if there are special circumstances. There are two limitations;[2] first, the parents must not be living together in the same household, and second there must have been no periodical payments order in existence just before the child reached the age of 16.

1   Section 11D.
2   Section 11D(3) and (4).

(a)   Assessment

16.08   In its original terms the 1971 Act instructed the court to assess such maintenance as was 'reasonable having regard to the means' of the payer. Reasonableness has now been replaced by a list of factors,[1] similar to those in the courts' matrimonial jurisdiction,[2] and to which the court must have regard. But a notable difference is that the child's welfare is specifically mentioned in the list of factors in the 1973 and 1978 Acts, whereas section 12A of the 1971 Act is silent on the matter.[3] It is possibly arguable that the omission is deliberate because assessment is subject to the overriding principle of the paramountcy of the child's welfare in section 1 of the 1971 Act. But the argument rests on the word 'upbringing' in section 1 including the making of financial provision for the child, a construction which may be doubted. Moreover, even if section 1 does apply, it can only realistically be applied within the limits of the parent's means if there is to be effective enforcement of any order of the court.[4] If it does not apply, the child's welfare should certainly be taken into account as part of 'all the circumstances of the case', and, it is suggested, treated at least as the 'first consideration' consistent with the statutory guidelines of the 1973 and 1978 Acts. Other matters which are included in both those Acts but which the court is not specifically directed to consider under the GMA are any increase in earning capacity which a parent could be reasonably expected to acquire, the standard of living previously enjoyed by the child and the type of education expected of him. These, too, it is submitted, should be considered as part of all the circumstances. Practitioners should ensure that, where relevant, they will be drawn to the attention of the court. It will be interesting to see how liberally the courts exercise their new powers to transfer and settle property,[5] bearing in mind that the GMA extends to unmarried couples. The property rights of a cohabitee are precarious in the absence of a legal title or a clearly evidenced equitable interest.[6] Yet, the new provisions permit an unmarried mother to apply for the transfer or settlement of the home from the father for the benefit of the child. In cases of lengthy cohabitation this is quite likely, but the omission from section 12A of any reference to the child's welfare may count in favour of the property owning father, and the courts, one suspects, will be unwilling to countenance cohabitees using the GMA as a side wind to gain property rights.

1   Section 12A, inserted by DPMCA 1978, s 43.
2   MCA 1973, s 25(2) and (3); DPMCA 1978, s 3(2) and (3).
3   See post, para 16.33 for the factors listed in s 12A.
4   For the methods of enforcing orders see GMA 1971, s 13 and post, paras 16.70 et seq.
5   Prior to FLRA 1987 they were confined to periodical payments and lump sums.
6   Eg *Burns v Burns* [1984] Ch 317, [1984] 1 All ER 244, CA; *Coombes v Smith* [1984] 1 WLR 808, [1987] 1 FLR 351.

(b) *Duration*

16.09 An order for periodical payments can be ordered to run from the date when the application was lodged or any later date. They normally last until the child's first birthday after reaching compulsory school leaving age (ie 17) but may be extended in the first instance to the age of 18 if the court 'thinks it right in the circumstances'.[1] Thereafter they can be extended (and there is *no* time limit) if the child is or will be undergoing education or training or if there are special circumstances. Examples of the latter are physical or mental handicaps which necessitate long-term dependence on the guardian. Payments automatically cease on the death of the payer.[2] An order for periodical payments (but not a lump sum) can be varied or discharged at any time by a further application to court.[3] In appropriate cases a lump sum can be substituted for periodical payments.[4] The original order may also be suspended temporarily and then revived.[5] In the latter category is a provision introduced by the DPMCA 1978 and refined by the FLRA 1987 whereby, if a periodical payments order ceases between the ages of 16 and 18, the child can then apply to revive (and/ or vary) the order if his education or training or special circumstances require.[6] For example, if at the age of 12 the child's prospects are limited, and an order is made to last until 16, but then he takes a poorly paid job to learn a skill or discovers a latent educational aptitude or suffers a debilitating accident, the parent(s) can be called upon again to subsidise the child. After revival the court is empowered to vary the original order and, it is suggested, variation could include a change in the payer so that, for example, where the father alone was required to make payments under the original order but by the time the child reached 17 the mother is in gainful employment, the order could be revived and then varied by adding the mother as a contributor.

1 Section 12(1)(a). Cf DPMCA 1978, s 5.
2 Unless they are secured, for which see the special provisions in s 12D.
3 Sections 11B(1), 11C(1), (2) and 11D(6).
4 Section 12B(3).
5 Section 12C(2).
6 Section 12C(5), (6).

(c) *Maintenance agreements*

16.10 A further step towards equating the financial position of children of married and unmarried couples is achieved by the FLRA 1987 when it permits natural parents to apply for variation of an agreed maintenance order. Thus, where the father and mother have agreed in writing for the making or securing of payments, or the disposition or use of any property, for the maintenance or education of the child and either circumstances have changed or one parent believes that the agreement is unsatisfactory, either parent can apply to the court to vary or revoke its terms.[1] In this case the court is not guided by a list of relevant factors. Instead it must achieve what is 'just having regard to all the circumstances'.[2] A similar application by a surviving parent or personal representative can be made in respect of an agreement which is designed to continue after the death of one of the parents.[3]

1   FLRA 1987, s 15. On application to a magistrates' court, the court's power is confined
    to adding or changing any periodical payments' element in the agreement, s 15(4).
2   Section 15(3); cf the court's duty for agreements under DPMCA 1978; see post, para
    16.17 and MCA 1973, para 16.67.
3   Section 16; though a claim may be overtaken by proceedings under the Inheritance (Provision
    for Family and Dependants) Act 1975, see post, para 16.77.

4   Maintenance for wards of court

16.11   Under section 6 of the Family Law Reform Act 1969 the High
Court (Family Division) can order either or both parents to make periodical
payments to the other parent or to any third party having care and control
of a ward (including a local authority) or directly to the ward. The payments
are intended for the ward's maintenance and education. Assessment of the
amount is based not on a list of factors but on what is reasonable in the
context of the payer's means. The court's power extends to periodical
payments but not to a lump sum. As to the duration of orders, the 1969
Act has been brought into line with the GMA to a certain extent.[1] Thus,
an order normally lasts until the age of 17 unless the court thinks it 'right'
to specify a later date up to the age of 18.[2] The order may be extended
beyond 18 if the ward's education, training or special circumstances require
it. Under section 6(3), as amended, where an order expires between the
child's sixteenth and eighteenth birthdays, he may apply to revive it if he
is still in education or training or if special circumstances justify the revival.
There is no time limit imposed on this revived order. Thus, for example,
an order could be revived to support the ward into graduate training. By
contrast the original section 6(4) allows a former ward aged between 18
and 21 to apply for an order for maintenance *up to the age of 21* and
whether or not such an order previously existed; in other words this is
an application for a new order as opposed to a revival under section 6(3).
Moreover, the power under section 6(4) is not tied to education etc; the
court's discretion is at large and so payments could be ordered where the
applicant is in poorly paid employment. Finally, payments from one parent
to another cannot be ordered where they are living together and, if residence
continues for over six months, an order for maintenance ceases to have
effect.

These provisions are unnecessarily complex and are typical of piecemeal
reform in child law. More generally, it is suggested that section 6 should
be replaced by provisions similar to those which pertain to the courts'
matrimonial jurisdiction under the DPMCA 1978 and MCA 1973. As it
stands the section is out of line in many respects with the financial orders
discussed elsewhere in this chapter.

1   By the FLRA 1987, Sch 2, para 20; and see ante, para 16.09.
2   FLRA 1969, s 6(3), as prospectively substituted by FLRA 1987, Sch 3, para 20(3).

5   Financial remedies before divorce

16.12   A party to a marriage who cannot, or does not wish to, seek a
divorce can apply to the High Court or county court[1] or to a magistrates'
court [2] for financial provision where the other party has failed to provide,
or to make a proper contribution towards, reasonable maintenance for
a child of the family. Similarly, if an order is sought under the DPMCA
1978 that the party cannot reasonably be expected to live with the other

party, or that the other party is in desertion, the magistrates' court can attach an order for financial provision.[3] Most of the provisions under the two Acts coincide. Thus, interim orders can be made, the courts are guided by the same factors as on divorce,[4] a child over 16 can apply in his own right to vary a periodical payments order and, before he reaches the age of 21, he can apply to revive such an order which has expired before he reached 18. Although proceedings before magistrates' courts are cheaper and usually quicker and the number of applications under section 27 of MCA is tiny,[5] the latter does offer the advantages that the court can order secured periodical payments, an unlimited lump sum[6] and a lump sum payable by secured instalments.[7] An order can, under either Act, be made whilst the parties cohabit, but in the case of proceedings in a magistrates' court continued cohabitation for six months brings the order to an end, except in so far as it provides for payments to be made directly to the child. In that event cohabitation will not terminate the order unless the court directs.[8] Rightly, the MCA does not allow continued cohabitation to affect an order, for the sanction of a court order may exceptionally have the salutary effect on, say, the husband of inducing him to discharge the financial responsibilities which he owes to his family with whom he lives.

1   MCA 1973 s 27. For the division of business between the High Court and county court generally, see *Practice Direction* [1987] 1 All ER 1087, [1987] 1 WLR 316.
2   DPMCA 1978 s 1.
3   Ibid, s 1(c) and (d).
4   See post, paras 16.33 et seq for a discussion of these factors.
5   There were 143 applications in 1986, Judicial Statistics, Cm 173, Table 4.8.
6   Magistrates are limited to £1,000; DPMCA 1978, s 2(3), as amended.
7   Section 27(7)(b) of MCA. Under the DPMCA there is no power to order payment by instalments but the court can use its general power to that effect contained in s 75 of Magistrates' Courts Act 1980. Section 22 of DPMCA then permits variation of the instalments.
8   DPMCA 1978, s 25

(a)   Domestic Proceedings and Magistrates' Courts Act 1978

16.13   Under its matrimonial jurisdiction a magistrates' court can order financial provision for a spouse and any child of the family,[1] make a consent order[2] or approve a separation agreement between the parties.[3] It has the power to determine the legal custody of a child and order maintenance for him, even if it rejects the spouse's own application for relief.[4] An interim order (of three months' maximum duration) can also be made.[5]

The term 'child of the family' has been considered in relation to custody orders,[6] but in the present context it is qualified by the provision[7] that, when the court is deciding whether any, and if so what, maintenance is to be paid by a spouse in respect of a child who is not a child of that spouse, it must take into account, inter alia, (a) the extent (including length of time) to which the spouse has assumed responsibility for the child's maintenance and the basis on which he did so; (b) whether in doing so he knew that the child was not his; and (c) the liability of any other person to maintain the child. Factor (a) depends upon the particular facts of each case.[8] However, the simple facts of marriage and the assumption of financial responsibility are not conclusive. The basis of that assumption must be examined to see, it is submitted, whether the spouse also accepted the 'responsibilities and privileges' of parenthood.[9] It follows that factor (a) will not be satisfied in those exceptional cases where the spouse has treated the child as a member of the family but on the strict understanding that he would not at all be responsible for his maintenance. As for factor (c), regard may be had to possible and not only existing liability. So, if the child's natural parents were unmarried and a financial order can be, but in fact has not been, sought against the putative father, the hearing of the maintenance claim between the spouses can be adjourned to allow the mother to seek an order before the final determination of the quantum of maintenance to be ordered in the matrimonial proceedings. Should she refuse to do so, she can be asked for reasons and the putative father can be called to give evidence as a witness in the proceedings.[10] In this way pressure can be brought on the mother to seek a financial order against the biological father and thus relieve the husband of financial liability.

1 Section 2.
2 Section 6, and see post, para 16.17
3 Section 7.
4 Section 11(1).
5 Section 19.
6 See ante para 3.34
7 Sections 3(4), 11(5).
8 See *Bowles v Bowles* [1965] P 450, [1965] 3 All ER 40, CA.
9 Cf the approach in *Re Leach, Leach v Lindeman* [1986] Ch 226. [1985] 2 All ER 754, CA to the Inheritance (Provision for Family and Dependants) Act 1975.
10 *Roberts v Roberts* [1962] P 212, [1962] 2 All ER 967. One practical difficulty remains. A parent who is not the applicant or respondent in the matrimonial proceedings may still be a party to the proceedings; DPMCA, s 12(2) and Magistrates' Courts (Matrimonial Proceedings) Rules 1980, r 9. If he is not present or represented, the court must take steps to give him notice of the proceedings, but it is not obliged to give notice where the child is the issue of an unmarried union and he is the father, unless he has been so adjudged by a court. If therefore the mother does not take proceedings against the father, there will be no obligation to give him notice of the matrimonial proceedings. Arguably the court could do so at its discretion but there would be no power to compel him to attend.

(i) Assessment
16.14 When dealing with an application for financial provision the magistrates' court is guided by the same factors which govern the higher courts' matrimonial jurisdiction.[1] Thus, first consideration must be given to the welfare of any child and section 3(2) then lists a series of matters to which the court must have regard. These are considered below.[2] It can be noted here, however, that the magistrates' courts traditionally deal with many of the poorer litigants, especially in times of unemployment; and, where money is scarce, reference to the statutory list of factors and to the child's welfare as first consideration can be superfluous. It is more a question of how much the payer can spare for maintenance. The court may order periodical payments and/or a lump sum (which must not exceed £1,000). The latter can reimburse the applicant for any reasonable expenditure on the child prior to the hearing (for example, purchase of clothing, a summer holiday). Payment can be made direct to the child and there were formerly sound tax reasons for doing so.[3] In those cases where the child has been committed to the care of the local authority, the court may also order periodical payments in favour of the authority or even directly to the child.[4]

1   MCA 1973, s 25 (save that the divorce court must also consider 'the standard of living enjoyed by the family', s 25(1)(c)).
2   See post, para. 16.33.
3   See post, para 16.55; though actual payment can be made to the person with whom the child has his home, Magistrates' Courts Act 1980, s 62.
4   Section 11(4).

(ii)   Duration

16.15   Where a financial provision order is made under section 2 on the application of one spouse against the other, almost the same rules[1] for duration apply as under the Guardianship of Minors Act 1971, so that, for example, the magistrates can make an order even though the child has reached the age of 18.[2] An order made under section 11 (dealing solely with the child, the spouse's application having failed) on the other hand cannot be made when the child reaches 18.[3] If the parties to the marriage live together for more than six months after the order was made, then any court-ordered payment to one party for the benefit of a child shall cease,[4] whereas payments paid directly to the child do not necessarily terminate on cohabitation of the parties.[5] It will be a matter for the court to decide. But this presupposes that the parties will trouble to bring the matter back before the court for revocation.

1   Section 5, and see ante, para 16.09. The only difference is that, whereas under GMA the order can be extended beyond 17 up to 18 if it is 'right in the circumstances', it is extendable under DPMCA when 'the welfare of the child requires'.
2   Note also that an identical provision, s 20A, for revival of an order has been added by FLRA 1987, Sch 2, para 69; see ante, para 16.09.
3   Section 11(6), (7).
4   Section 25(1).
5   Section 25(2)

16.16   The court has full and complex powers to vary or revoke or suspend and revive an order for periodical payments.[1] For example, periodical payments can be replaced by a lump sum; where a lump sum is payable by instalments, they can be varied;[2] and on reaching the age of 16 the child himself can apply for variation.[3] Unlike the MCA 1973 provisions,[4] a magistrates' court can on variation of a periodical payments order make a lump sum order (to the maximum of £1,000) and even if a lump sum was contained in the original order.[5] On the other hand, the factors which govern the exercise of its variation powers are very similar to those in the MCA,[6] viz first consideration to the welfare of the child and regard to any change in the factors which influenced the making of the original order.[7] Orders are enforced in the same way as magistrates' courts' maintenance orders.[8] It will usually be beneficial to direct payment through the clerk of the bench.[9] Alternatively, the court may direct payment to be made to a third party (for example, the Department of Social Security) on behalf of the recipient.[10] This is a useful procedure whereby, if the payee is in receipt of income support, the maintenance payments are diverted to the Department and the income support is then paid regularly.[11]

1   Section 20.
2   Section 22.
3   Section 20(12).
4   MCA 1973, s 31(5).

5 DPMCA, s 20(7).
6 See post, para 16, s 3.
7 Section 20(11). However, the court must first give effect to any agreement which the parties have reached. Only if it is unjust to do so can the court proceed to consider the aforementioned factors for variation, see *Whitton v Devizes Magistrates Court* (1984) JP 330, [1985] Fam Law 125 and Butterworths Family Law Service, para D160 note 14.
8 Section 32(1) as substituted by FLRA 1987, Sch 2, para 70.
9 MCA 1980, s 59.
10 Section 32(2).
11 This is known as the 'diversion procedure', see Income Support Manual (HMSO, 1988), paras 1015–1019.

(iii) Financial agreements

16.17   Apart from the obvious advantage of consensus between the parties, which may well smooth the path for ultimate divorce proceedings, an agreement which is transformed into a court order is recognised by the Inland Revenue for the purpose of tax concessions to the payer.[1] The DPMCA provides for two situations. In the first, if the parties have agreed terms for financial provision, either can apply to the domestic court for an order embodying those terms.[2] The court must be satisfied that the proposal either provides for the financial needs of each child or makes a proper contribution towards them,[3] and further that it is not contrary to the interests of justice.[4] No guidance is given to the court as to how to apply these prescriptions and there is a danger, particularly if one or both of the parties are unrepresented, that an agreement could 'go through on the nod'. It is suggested that the court should bear in mind the criteria set out in section 3,[5] not simply because they offer a useful checklist but also because, if an agreement satisfies them, a subsequent application for financial provision by one of the parties is likely to be forestalled.[6] If the court is not satisfied with the agreement, it can suggest and approve alternative arrangements provided that the parties agree.[7]

1 See post, para 16.55.
2 Section 6(1). 'Either' was added by MFPA 1984 and enabled the payer to obtain a court order against himself for tax purposes; cf *Sherdley v Sherdley* [1988] AC 213, [1987] 2 All ER 54, HL.
3 Section 6(3).
4 Section 6(5)(a). If payment of a lump sum is involved, the normal limit of £1,000 does not apply.
5 See para 16.14.
6 An active supervisory role by the magistrates is also in line with the instructions of the House of Lords, admittedly given in the context of MCA 1973, but, it is submitted, of wider importance; see *Dinch v Dinch* [1987] 1 All ER 818, [1987] 1 WLR 252, HL.
7 Section 6(5).

16.18   In the second situation, where the spouses have lived apart, though not in desertion, for three months and one has been making payments for the other or for a child of the family, that other spouse can apply for a court order.[1] In most cases the order will reflect the level of payments already made,[2] but the court is not so restricted. It is specifically required to consider the criteria in section 3 and overall it must ensure that the order will 'provide or make a proper contribution towards reasonable maintenance' for the child. If it is not satisfied, the court can treat the application as if it had been made under section 2.[3]

1 Section 7(1). Unlike s 6 the payer cannot apply in his own right.
2 Provided that the proposed aggregate over three months does not exceed the three months' aggregate prior to the application, that the amount does not exceed what the court would have ordered in an application under s 1, and that, if the child is not a child of the respondent, the court would still have made an order for the child's benefit under s 1 (s 7(3)).
3 Section 7(4). For consideration of the factors in s 3 see post, para 16.33.

6   Matrimonial Causes Act 1973

16.19   The powers of the High Court or a divorce county court to make financial orders for the benefit of children are wider than those available to a magistrates' court under the Domestic Proceedings and Magistrates' Courts Act 1978 in respect of the kind of orders that may be made. But, since the 1978 Act and later the Matrimonial and Family Proceedings Act 1984, the powers of higher and lower courts have been significantly harmonised. For example, the factors to be considered in each court are very similar; and all the courts can make orders endorsing an agreement reached between the parties. Consequently much of the following discussion will apply to the magistrates' jurisdiction and differences will be indicated where they arise. Orders can be made in respect of a 'child of the family' and that concept has been considered elsewhere.[1] Where the child is not the child of the respondent, the same qualifications to the latter's liability apply as under the 1978 Act.[2] The usual applicant will be the custodial spouse[3] but leave can be given to others to apply on the child's behalf.[4] Leave can also be given to the child and this can be useful for a teenage child who, for example, needs maintenance so as to pursue higher education.[5] The court may also order that the child be separately represented.[6]

At the outset two types of order have to be distinguished — financial provision orders and property adjustment orders — before proceedings to consider the factors which will influence the court's choice of order.

1 See ante, para 3.34.
2 MCA, s 25(4); DPMCA, ss 3(4) and 11(5); see ante, para 16.13.
3 He can even apply for an order against himself; see *Sherdley v Sherdley* [1988] AC 213, [1987] 2 All ER 54, HL, and post, para 16.60.
4 MCR 1977, r 69 for a complete list of those who can apply.
5 Ibid, r 69(g) and see *Downing v Downing* [1976] Fam 288, [1976] 3 All ER 474 (a 20-year-old student).
6 Rule 72.

(a)   Financial provision orders

16.20   The orders made under the 1973 Act in favour of children may be made in proceedings for divorce, nullity or judicial separation[1] at any stage pending suit[2] or when a decree is granted or at any time thereafter. Moreover, as in the case of proceedings under the 1978 Act, financial provision for the children may be ordered even if the spouse's petition is dismissed.[3] As for duration, orders cannot generally be made in favour of a child over the age of 18.[4] For periodical payments the rules are similar to those in the GMA 1971.[5] Thus, they will usually last until the age of 17 in the first instance but can extend to 18 if the child's welfare so requires. They can extend further if the child is receiving education or training or if there are special circumstances.[6] There is no time limit to this last extension (apart from the death of the payer) and so maintenance can, for example, be ordered for postgraduate study or for the long-term benefit of a handicapped child. In practice a common form of order is 'until the child attains the age of 17 or ceases full-time education or training (whichever is the later)[7] or further order'.

1 For failure to provide reasonable maintenance under s 27, see ante, para 16.12.
2 Section 23(2). Compare the separate rule needed for dealing with maintenance of a *spouse* pending suit, MCA, s 22 and for general consideration see Jackson, op cit Chapter 2, and Butterworth's Family Law Service, paras 601–11.
3 Section 23(2)(b), provided that proceedings are brought forthwith or in a reasonable time after dismissal of the petition. Further provision may be made from time to time, s 23(4). For spouses, an order under s 23 cannot be made until decree nisi, *Board (otherwise Checkland) v Checkland (Board intervening)* [1987] 2 FLR 257, [1987] Fam Law 236, CA.
4 Section 29(1).
5 Ante, para 16.09.
6 Section 29(2), (3).
7 A necessary addition following *Practice Direction* [1987] 2 All ER 1084, [1987] 1 WLR 1165.

Kinds of provision
16.21 A party to the marriage may be required to make to a specified person (usually the other spouse) for the benefit of the child or to the child himself any one or more of the following, namely (1) unsecured periodical payments, (2) secured periodical payments, (3) a lump sum payment. It seems that only one lump sum may be ordered,[1] but it may be made payable by way of instalments, either unsecured or secured, and, in particular, it may be made to the child to meet liabilities reasonably incurred by or for the benefit of the child before the application was made for an order; for example, in connection with his education or, where he suffers from a physical disability, to purchase equipment to overcome it.[2] Although it is clear that either spouse, whether petitioner or respondent, may be ordered to provide for the child, it is not stated whether both may be liable where the custody or care and control has been given to a third person.[3] To interpret section 23 broadly so as to include possible liability of both would accord with the Act's overall concern for the welfare of the child. Like the 1978 Act, section 23 does not prescribe a minimum age limit below which payments cannot be made to the child himself.

1 Compare s 23(1)(c) which, although it expressly allows for the payment of more than one lump sum to a spouse, means no more than that the court can provide for more than one lump sum in one order; *Coleman v Coleman* [1973] Fam 10, [1972] 3 All ER 886.
2 Section 23(3)(b). A lump sum payment may also be made (under s 23(3)(a)) to a party to the marriage for liability reasonably incurred in maintaining a child of the family before an application for an order under that section. The difference between s 23(3)(a) and (b) is that under the latter the child is the recipient.
3 Bromley, op cit p 656, note 12, citing *Freckleton v Freckleton* [1966] CLY 3938, points out that the former law allowed it. Persons other than a spouse who may apply for financial provision for the child are: his guardian; anyone having custody or care and control under a High Court or county court order; a local authority to whom care has been committed under s 43 of the Matrimonial Causes Act 1973; anyone who has obtained leave to intervene to apply for custody; the Official Solicitor if appointed guardian ad litem; anyone else who has care of the child and who has obtained leave to intervene for the purpose of applying for maintenance for him; and finally any child of the family given leave to intervene (Matrimonial Causes Rules 1977, r 69).

(b)   Property adjustment orders

16.22   One of the advantages of a lump sum payment is that it may be used as a method of permanently adjusting the property interests of members of the family on the breakdown of the marriage. Even if awarded to the spouse and not to the children, it may indirectly benefit the latter; for example, where it is given to enable a wife to purchase a new home for herself and them,[1] or to carry out repairs on the existing one.[2] Another advantage is that it may anticipate the risk of a spouse taking his assets out of the jurisdiction in order to defeat the claims of his family.[3] These objects can, however, often be achieved by the use of other, wider powers, conferred by section 24 of the 1973 Act. Orders may be made in proceedings for divorce, nullity or judicial separation for the transfer or settlement of property by one spouse, whether the petitioner or the respondent, to the other or to or for the benefit of a child or for the variation of a marriage settlement or for extinguishing or reducing an interest under such a settlement. Because they are intended as a permanent property adjustment on the breakdown of a marriage,[4] they cannot be made until a decree is granted, and, in the case of divorce or nullity, cannot come into effect until the decree nisi is made absolute.[5] They may also be made at any time thereafter, but only with the leave of the court.[6]

1   *Von Mehren v Von Mehren* [1970] 1 All ER 153, [1970] 1 WLR 56, CA.
2   *Hakluytt v Hakluytt* [1968] 2 All ER 868, 1 WLR 1145, CA.
3   See *Brett v Brett* [1969] 1 All ER 1007, [1969] 1 WLR 487, CA; *Curtis v Curtis* [1969] 2 All ER 207; [1969] 1 WLR 422, CA.
4   The application of s 24 to cases of judicial separation is a concession to those spouses who for conscientious reasons do not seek divorce.
5   Section 24(3). The court may direct that the proper instrument be settled by conveyancing counsel and that the grant of a decree be deferred until that instrument has been executed (s 30). *Dackham v Dackham* [1987] 2 FLR 358, [1987] Fam Law 345, CA.
6   Matrimonial Causes Rules 1977, r 68. For third parties who may apply, see r 69, ante, para 16.21; and note that the child can himself apply.

16.23   As a result of Part III of the Matrimonial and Family Proceedings Act 1984, financial relief under the MCA 1973 may be extended to marriages which have been dissolved or annulled, or to spouses who have been legally separated, by proceedings overseas.[1] This relief can include financial orders for the direct benefit of a child. However, unlike the MCA, he cannot himself apply for it. Only the parties to the marriage can use the provisions of the 1984 Act. Moreover, if the only basis for jurisdiction under that Act is the existence of a matrimonial home in England or Wales, the court is limited to regulating the proprietary interests in that property.[2] On the other hand, relief is available for a party whose marriage was dissolved before the Act came into force.[3]

1   Overseas is defined by s 27 as a country outside the British Islands. Consequently Part III could not be employed to secure financial relief following a divorce in Scotland. For further consideration of the Act see Canton, *The Matrimonial and Family Proceedings Act 1984: Financial Relief after Foreign Divorce* [1985] Fam Law 13; Gordon, *Part III of the MFPA 1984: a panacea for foreign divorces?* [1986] JSWL 329.
2   Section 20.
3   On 16 September 1985; *Chebaro v Chebaro* [1987] Fam 127, [1987] 1 All ER 999, CA.

16.24   Although under the MCA 1973 a property adjustment order can be made in favour of a child, it should be noted that in the normal case the only property of any substance will be the matrimonial home and, as will be seen,[1] that is usually divided in a variety of ways between the spouses without specific provision being made in the order to benefit the child.

1   See post, para 16.44.

Kinds of provision
16.25   (1) *Transfer of property*   A transfer order will usually concern primarily the parties to the marriage and, as with a lump sum payment to a spouse, the children of the family will benefit indirectly. One of the main purposes of the order is to enable the spouse's interest in the matrimonial home to be transferred to the custodial spouse so that he/she may continue to live there with the children. If the property is subject to a mortgage the mortgagee's consent is normally required before the property can be transferred. Consequently a copy of the application for ancillary relief along with the supporting affidavit must be served on the mortgagee.[1]

1   Matrimonial Causes Rules 1977, r 74(4).

16.26   (2) *Settlement of property*   An order for the settlement of property, which must be by one spouse for the benefit of the other and the children of the family or either or any of them, has in theory distinct advantages over a transfer of property. By allowing for a wide variety both in the kinds of interest which may be created and in their duration it enables the court to provide financial assistance for individual members of the family who at any given time will most need it; for example, successive interests for fixed periods may be created to meet the cost of further education of each child as he attains a specific age. As will be seen[1] the outright transfer of property is often either impracticable or undesirable. More fashionable is the limited settlement whereby an interest in the matrimonial home is given to the custodial spouse until the children have reached a certain age and thereafter the property is sold. However, neither a transfer nor a settlement are popular in favour of the children. There would appear to be two reasons; firstly the unfairness, usually to the father, of cutting his interest in the property for ever, and secondly the reluctance to grant a windfall to the children, which, had the marriage survived, might never have arisen.[2]

1   See post, paras 16.46 et seq.
2   See further for the limited parental duty to maintain a child only until the age of majority, post, para 16.48.

16.27   (3) *Variation of a settlement and* (4) *extinguishing or reducing an interest under a settlement*   These orders apply to any ante-nuptial or post-nuptial settlement made on the parties to the marriage. A considerable body of case law has given a wide definition to these 'marriage' settlements.[1] Thus, dispositions to parties to a marriage have been liberally construed as settlements for the purpose of matrimonial proceedings, even though they are not settlements in the usually accepted sense. This has especially been so where the transaction relates to the matrimonial home, as where both spouses have contributed to the purchase price and the property has been conveyed to both[2] or one[3] of them upon trust for sale and to hold the proceeds of sale as joint tenants or tenants in common beneficially. In cases of this kind, so long as the power of sale is postponed, the court has power to vary the settlement, for example by extinguishing the husband's interests. But an order for the transfer of property or order of sale of the property can achieve the same result and the courts usually rely on this rather than an order for variation.[4]

1   The reader is referred to textbooks on matrimonial causes especially Jackson, Chapter 8, and to Bromley, op cit, pp 665 et seq.
2   *Brown v Brown*, [1959] P 86, [1959] 2 All ER 266, CA; *Ulrich v Ulrich and Felton* [1968] 1 All ER 67, [1968] 1 WLR 180, CA.
3   *Cook v Cook* [1962] P 235, [1962] 2 All ER 811, CA.
4   See Ormrod LJ in *Guerrera v Guerrera* [1974] 1 WLR 1542 at 1547.

16.28   Notwithstanding the wide meaning given to a settlement, a disposition must comply with a number of rules if it is to fall under section 24.[1]

(1) It must be made upon a spouse or both spouses in his or her nuptial capacity, and must provide for the financial benefit of one or both of them in that capacity.[2] A settlement made solely on the children of the family is therefore outside the section.[3]

(2) It must have been made in contemplation of, or because of the specific marriage which is the subject of the proceedings for divorce, nullity or judicial separation,[4] but not on the basis that the marriage was soon to be dissolved or annulled or the parties judicially separated.[5]

(3) The settlement must be in existence at the date of decree absolute of divorce or nullity or the decree of judicial separation.[6] Thus, where the settlement is made by will, the testator must already be dead at that date, since it is only on his death that the settlement comes into existence. However, since there is power to make an order for variation at any time after granting a decree,[7] it is possible for a child to seek a variation of a settlement after the death of the testator.[8] He could alternatively consider an application under the Inheritance (Provision for Family and Dependants) Act 1975.[9]

1   See especially *Prinsep v Prinsep* [1929] P 225.
2   An absolute transfer of property is not, however, within the definition, except where the transferor is still obliged to make periodical payments, *Prescott v Fellowes* [1958] P 260, [1958] 3 Al ER 55, CA; but an order for transfer of property could be made under s 24(1)(a) requiring the transferee to return the property to the transferor.
3   But see Bromley, op cit, p 666, where the possibility of the opposite conclusion is canvassed.
4   *Burnett v Burnett* [1936] P 1; *Hargreaves v Hargreaves* [1962] P 42.
5   *Young v Young* [1962] P 27, [1961] 3 All ER 695, CA, (maintenance agreement made between decree nisi and decree absolute).
6   *Dormer v Ward* [1901] P 20, CA. The power to vary can be invoked where the nullity decree relates to a void marriage; see ibid, and *Radziej v Radziej* [1967] 1 All ER 944, [1967] 1 WLR 659; affd [1968] 3 All ER 624, [1968] 1 WLR 1928, CA.
7   Section 24.
8   See *D'Este v D'Este* [1973] Fam 55 at 61, [1973] 1 All ER 349 at 354 and for further points see Passingham and Harmer, *Law and Practice in Matrimonial Causes* (4th edn, 1985) p 93.
9   See post, para 16.77.

16.29 The power in section 24(1)(c) can be traced back to section 5 of the Matrimonial Causes Act 1859 and the courts have taken the view that overall the power must be exercised in such a way as to benefit children interested in the settlement.[1] This objective can even include a restriction on a child's interest (eg by reducing the capital sum of the settlement) if overall and in the long term this will benefit him. For example, a payment of a capital sum to the father may enable him to improve or maintain his standard of living and thereby facilitate a future happy relationship with his children. In return he can be ordered to forfeit any further interest in the settlement with the result that the children are substantially better off.[2]

1 Eg *Purnell v Purnell* [1961] P 141, [1961] 1 All ER 369.
2 See *Garforth-Bles v Garforth-Bles* [1951] P 218, [1951] 1 All ER 308; *Cartwright v Cartwright* (1983) 4 FLR 463.

16.30 Section 24(1)(d) allows the court to extinguish or reduce a spouse's interest under a settlement without necessarily conferring any benefit on the other spouse or a child of the family. But in view of the primacy of the child's welfare,[1] in practice this power will be relevant where there is no child.[2]

1 Section 23(1).
2 For example, where a wife has an interest for life with remainder to the children of the family and, if there be none, to a relative of the wife, her interest could be extinguished, even though there were no children who would thereby benefit.

16.31 When section 24(1)(c) is in issue the court is instructed to order separate representation for the child unless it is satisfied that the 'proposed variation does not adversely affect' his rights and interests.[1] For the exercise of its other powers under section 24(1) the court in contrast 'may' order separate representation. This distinction, it is submitted, is out of keeping with the current law's concern for the child's welfare and the former instruction, in favour of separate representation, should apply throughout.

1 M C Rules, r 72(2). The stakes in the proceedings may be so high between the spouses that the court is well served by spouses' counsel so that the child's interests are adequately protected, see *Cartwright v Cartwright*, supra.

16.32 (4) *Sale of property* In order to implement one of the aforementioned orders, property, principally the matrimonial home, will normally have to be sold. By virtue of section 24A[1] once the court has made an order for secured periodical payments, a lump sum and a property adjustment, it can further direct the sale of property. The court can attach a variety of conditions; for example, it may direct payment of the proceeds of sale to a named person (eg the child or his guardian)[2] or that the proceeds be secured so as to produce an income for the child.[3] Application under the section may be made at any time after decree absolute.

1 Added by s 7 of the Matrimonial Homes and Properties Act 1981. The power is ancillary to another order made under the MCA and for a striking illustration of this point see *R v Rushmoor Borough Council, ex p Barrett* [1987] QB 275, [1987] 1 All ER 353.
2 Section 24A(2)(a).

3 Though the court's discretion to attach conditions to the order is at large, there are limits;
   see *Burton v Burton* [1986] 2 FLR 419, [1986] Fam Law 330.

(c)   Matters relevant to the making of orders

16.33   In exercising its powers to make financial orders for a child of
the family under the Matrimonial Causes Act 1973 and the Domestic
Proceedings and Magistrates' Courts Act 1978, the court is guided by one
principle and is directed to consider a list of factors.[1] The principle is that
first consideration shall be given to the welfare of any child of the family
under the age of 18.[2] The age limitation is significant since, as has been
seen,[3] the courts do have certain powers to extend financial orders beyond
that age. It is thus unfortunate that the statutes do not refer to the 'welfare
of any child of the family in whose favour the court can make an order'.
As for 'welfare', this is not confined to monetary considerations but entitles
the court to assess the quality of the child's life in terms of, for example,
his accommodation and its proximity to his school and friends. 'First' is
clearly not equivalent to 'paramount',[4] but no authoritative guidance as
to the force of the principle has so far emerged. In practice the interests
of the children and above all their need for accommodation will usually
be the paramount consideration and will dictate the form of the order.[5]
Indeed, under the MCA 1973 the court is instructed, inter alia, not to
make absolute a decree of divorce, or nullity or grant a decree of judicial
separation unless arrangements for the children are satisfactory or the best
that can be devised in the circumstances.[6] If the court performs this duty
conscientiously, paramountcy of the child's welfare is all but achieved. It
is again unfortunate that Parliament has refused to recognise this and to
extend the principle of paramountcy into an area of law which has obvious
and fundamental consequences for a child. Three consequences of the 'first
consideration' approach can be noted. The first is that a spouse of limited
means can argue that his first duty is to his children, that his resources
should be channelled primarily to maintain them and that lesser financial
provision is needed for the other spouse. Such an argument fits well with
the other changes in the MFPA 1984 designed to encourage a clean break
between the parties and independence for the custodial spouse. Second,
it can enable a mother to deflect criticism of her conduct and still argue
for a sufficiently high level of maintenance for herself qua mother.[7] Third,
it is the 'child of the family' (ie in relation to the marriage in question)
who will take precedence and not, for example, the father's subsequent
stepchildren or children by later marriage or cohabitation.[8]
   As for the list of factors, it offers a useful checklist for practitioners
and courts and can assist consistency. Rarely will all be relevant in the
same case. Factors (a), (e) and (f) are the most important and some such
as (a) and (d) will overlap. The first four concern the child and the second
four the parties to the marriage.[9] They are as follows:[10]

(a) the financial needs of the child;
(b) the income, earning capacity (if any), property and other financial
     resources of the child;
(c) any physical or mental disability of the child;
(d) the manner in which he was being and in which the parties to the
     marriage expected him to be educated or trained;
(e) the income, earning capacity, property and other financial resources

which each of the parties to the marriage has or is likely to have in the foreseeable future, including in the case of earning capacity any increase in that capacity which it would in the opinion of the court be reasonable to expect a party to the marriage to take steps to acquire;

(f) the financial needs, obligations and responsibilities which each of the parties to the marriage has or is likely to have in the foreseeable future;

(g) the standard of living enjoyed by the family before the breakdown of the marriage;

(h) any physical or mental disability of either of the parties to the marriage.

1 Indeed to the extent that their powers coincide, magistrates' courts are instructed to apply their discretion in the same way as the higher courts; see *Macey v Macey* (1981) 3 FLR 7, 11 Fam Law 248.
2 MCA, s 25(1); DPMCA, s 3(1); both inserted by MFPA 1984, ss 3 and 9(1) respectively. For background, see the Law Commission, *The Financial Consequences of Divorce* (1982, Law Com No 112), and for comment, Cretney, *Money after Divorce*, in Freeman (ed) *Essays in Family Law 1985* (1986).
3 See ante, para 16.20.
4 *Suter v Suter and Jones* [1987] Fam 111, [1987] 2 All ER 336, CA.
5 See, for example, *Tilley v Tilley* (1979) 10 Fam Law 89, CA and *M v M* [1988] 1 FLR 389, CA.
6 Section 41. 'Welfare' in this context includes financial provision, s 41(6). See ante paras 3.48 et seq.
7 An approach approved in *Robinson v Robinson* (1981) 2 FLR 1 (though decided in 1973).
8 Though the interests of such children are clearly an important consideration which the court should not undervalue, *R v R* [1988] 1 FLR 89.
9 The factors are identical under MCA and DPMCA except that strangely factor (h) is not mentioned under the latter Act.
10 MCA 1973, s 25(3); DPMCA 1978, s 3(3).

(a) The financial needs of the child
16.34 Research into the cost of rearing children is in its infancy. There is no agreed yardstick from which the courts should work. The social security rates offer some indication of the minimal costs, though even the standard rates are sometimes supplemented by extra benefits.[1] They have been justly criticised for underestimating the cost of rearing a child.[2] At the other extreme are the National Foster Care Association's recommended charges. These are far more generous[3] but are of limited guidance since they presuppose a family of two parents, whereas in matrimonial proceedings the court is often dealing with a one-parent family.[4] The absence of exhaustive research exacerbates the regional variations in the approach to child maintenance. The research to date does indicate, not surprisingly, that in general children suffer serious financial hardship after their parents separate and that maintenance for them is set at far too low a level.[5] Moreover, the lack of guidance is particularly important if courts are to exercise their jurisdiction properly. Thus, in the context of the DPMCA 1978 the Family Division has said that it is not appropriate for a court 'to pluck from the air a figure', but instead it must 'make detailed findings under a number of heads'.[6] Of course in very many cases the resources of the parents will be insufficient to provide realistic support for the child and only a nominal or small order will be feasible. In those cases where more money is available (especially where the custodial spouse is earning) it behoves practitioners to explore the actual cost of maintaining the child and to produce documentary evidence to the court. The court must have regard to all the

circumstances of each case and is not restricted to those specified in the statute. For example, a notable omission from them is the age of the child,[7] but this is clearly most relevant to his needs and his earning capacity, especially in deciding whether to order financial provision after he has attained the age of 18.

Undoubtedly the greatest need for the child is accommodation with the custodial parent[8] and, as will be seen,[9] the courts have tried various ways of achieving this. Although the needs under (a) must be 'financial', there are many other needs which a child has, such as the need for love and care. These other needs must be considered as part of the totality of the circumstances.[10] As such, a mother can harness the 'need for care' so as to rebuff attempts by the husband to force her into employment.

1 See post, para 16.97.
2 Field, *What Price a Child?* (1985).
3 Eg for a child aged 11 the DHSS weekly rate is £15.30, the NFCA's recommendation is £38.99. The NFCA's recommendations were circulated to local authorities (Home Office Circular 7/1985, Child Maintenance) and then to judges and registrars.
4 See the observations of Eekelaar and Maclean at (1986) New LJ 838.
5 See Eekelaar and Maclean, *Maintenance after Divorce* (1986); Southwell, *A Meal Ticket for Life — Myth or Reality?* [1985] Fam Law 332.
6 Per Waterhouse J in *Osborn v Sparks* (1982) 3 FLR 90 at 93–94; in this case the order of the magistrates' court was reversed because the bench had guessed at a figure of £5 for the child.
7 Cf MCA 1973, s 25(2)(d) and DPMCA 1978, s 3(2)(d), which expressly include the age of the spouses.
8 Eg *Browne v Pritchard* [1975] 3 All ER 721, [1975] 1 WLR 1366, CA.
9 See post, para 16.44.
10 Cf The Republic of Ireland, Family Law (Maintenance of Spouses and Children) Act 1976, s 5(4) which refers to the needs of children 'including the need for care and attention'.

(b) The income, earning capacity (if any), property and other financial resources of the child
16.35   Only actual income,[1] property and other resources are relevant, and allowance for the future receipt of any funds (for example, under the terms of a settlement) should be met by a later variation of the original order.[2] Where the spouse's resources are sufficient to provide reasonable financial provision it is unrealistic to consider the child's modest part-time earnings (eg from a newspaper round) which make up his 'pocket money', but in the many cases where the parental resources are stretched those earnings (eg from a Saturday supermarket job) will play a part since they can relieve a parent of expenditure (eg on the child's clothing) or they may be paid straight into a 'family kitty'. As to earning capacity, this is not as relevant as for spouses.[3] Even for a child approaching, or recently passed, the age of 16, assessment of that capacity may be impossible or his net capacity (eg earnings he could make from an apprenticeship) may be negligible. There will, however, be some cases where the child has given up a part-time job or has refused to take a youth training scheme (for example where the child regards the benefits of a Government training project as illusory) where a court could consider that capacity. Similarly, a court is entitled to consider the earnings or extra earnings which a child in higher education could acquire.[4]

1 This could include income generated from damages awarded to the child; cf the position with regard to spouses, *Daubney v Daubney* [1976] Fam 267, [1976] 2 All ER 453, CA.
2 Cf MCA, s 25(2)(a) and DPMCA, s 3(2)(a), where the income etc which spouses may be expected to earn is taken into account; see post, para 16.39. *Quaere* whether a child's resources include the potential benefit that may arise from trustees exercising their powers of maintenance and advancement.
3 Post, para 16.39.
4 Financial provision for a child over 18 and in education can be ordered even though he is also in gainful employment, MCA 1973, s 29(3)(a); DPMCA 1978, s 5(3)(i); GMA 1971, s 11D(1)(a).

(c) Any physical or mental disability of the child

16.36 This factor may ensure that the child and custodial parent remain in the matrimonial home (especially if it has been adapted to meet his needs) and that financial provision for him will extend beyond the age of 18.

(d) The manner in which the child was being and in which the parties to the marriage expected him to be educated or trained

16.37 This factor can be linked to (a). Payment of school fees can constitute a major part of financial provision. But there are other ancillary payments which may be needed (eg for school uniform, equipment, trips abroad) and which should be incorporated within the total order. The circumstances may not be so grandiose. For example, a father who has secured an apprenticeship for his son in his own trade could be required to supply capital for the training equipment.

After considering these specified matters *and* any others which it regards as relevant to the child, the court must then take into account factors relating directly to the spouses.[1]

1 For a fuller discussion of these factors reference should be made to works on matrimonial causes, eg *Rayden and Jackson on Divorce* (15th edn), ch 20, section IV; *Jackson's Matrimonial Finance and Taxation* (4th edn) pp 67 et seq; Passingham and Harmer, op cit, pp 100–108; and Goldrein and de Haas, *Property Distribution on Divorce* (2nd edn).

(e) The income, earning capacity, property and other financial resources which each of the parties to the marriage has or is likely to have in the foreseeable future, including in the case of earning capacity any increase in that capacity which it would in the opinion of the court be reasonable to expect a party to the marriage to take steps to acquire

16.38 In assessing a spouse's capacity and ability to make financial provision, the court will look at these matters realistically and thus, for example, will put into the reckoning a husband's ability to make money by the use of bank overdrafts,[1] his receipt of a voluntary allowance, whether in money or in kind,[2] his actual and likely resources,[3] and his potential as well as actual earning capacity, including his ability to earn more by overtime[4] or different work shifts. To assist the parties and the court full disclosure of means is required both for contested proceedings and consent orders,[5] and orders can be overturned in the event of material non-disclosure. Even so, the difficulties of accurately assessing the payer's means, especially when self-employed, are well known.

1   *J-PC v J-AF* [1955] P 215, [1955] 2 All ER 85.
2   *Donaldson v Donaldson* [1958] 2 All ER 660, [1958] 1 WLR 827 (husband living rent and board free with girlfriend); similarly *Ette v Ette* [1965] 1 All ER 341, [1964] 1 WLR 1433.
3   Including interests in a settlement, *Calder v Calder* (1975) 6 Fam Law 242, CA; *B v B* (1982) 12 Fam Law 92. If necessary the court can adjourn the proceedings until a time in the 'near future' when resources will become available, *Davies v Davies* [1986] 1 FLR 497, 16 Fam Law 138, CA; *Hardy v Hardy* (1981) 2 FLR 321, 11 Fam Law 153.
4   *Klucinski v Klucinski* [1953] 1 All ER 683, [1953] 1 WLR 522.
5   M C Rules 1977, rr 73, 76A; and see *Livesey v Jenkins* [1985] AC 424, [1985] 1 All ER 106. Questionnaires requesting detailed information from a party can also be used, r 77(4).

16.39   This factor raises the thorny issue of whether a mother, who is capable of earning and who may be professionally qualified, should be required to seek employment. No precise guidance is possible since each case will turn upon its own facts. Thus, if the family is well off and the wife gave up employment to rear the children and they are still young, factor (g), below, can be argued in favour of the status quo.[1] If the wife has worked periodically during the child's life, it may be reasonable to expect her to resume employment so that she will bear some of the cost of maintaining the child.[2] Again, the husband may agree to transfer the matrimonial home to the wife in return for a reduction in his financial provision for the family. A middle course is for the court to set a time limit on the maintenance payments[3] so that the payee knows that at a fixed date she will have to 'fend for herself'. This is particularly useful where the woman requires training or retraining for employment. Above all, the reality of unemployment in the area and the unreality of, for example, a middle-aged woman being able to enter the job market and command a reasonable salary must be borne in mind.[4] Much too depends upon the age, health and education of the child. The older and fitter he is, the higher is the chance of the custodial parent being expected to seek financial independence. However, it should always be borne in mind that the principle of 'clean break' will only apply to the parent/child relationship in very rare cases[5] and that a working mother is far more likely to reduce rather than terminate a father's financial contributions to his children.

1   Cf the rules that a sole parent with a dependent child under 16 need not register as available for employment as a precondition for receiving income support; Income Support General Regulations 1987, r 8 and Sch 1, paras 1 and 2.
2   Note *Mitchell v Mitchell* [1984] FLR 387, [1984] Fam Law 176, CA.
3   Under the powers contained in s 25A (introduced by MFPA 1984).
4   This is especially so in the traditional female preserve of secretarial work where advances in office technology can render earlier training redundant (see *Leadbeater v Leadbeater* [1985] FLR 789, [1985] Fam Law 280, FD). As Sir Roger Ormond has observed, 'it is much easier to talk about married women who have not been working for a good number of years getting back into full-time employment than it is to get the employment. It is to be remembered that 15 years or more of looking after children and not earning is a serious economic handicap.' *Camm v Camm* (1983) 4 FLR 577 at 586. See further *M v M* [1987] 2 FLR 1, [1987] Fam Law 195; *Barrett v Barrett* [1988] Fam Law 475.
5   See post, para 16.47.

(f)   The financial needs, obligations and responsibilities which each of the parties to the marriage has or is likely to have in the foreseeable future
16.40   'Obligations and responsibilities' can include a parent's new dependants, such as his stepchildren or children by a later marriage.[1] Remarriage should not in theory restrict obligations to children but in

practice the limited resources available mean that the payer's new family obligations must inevitably affect the order. This can justify the parent committing himself to a new mortgage even though the effect will be to reduce the amount of money available to support his first family.[2] Moreover, the obligations are not confined to legal ones and therefore a father's moral obligations to a cohabitee can also be considered.[3] This is a good example of how the welfare of the child of the family is the first but not paramount consideration. In other words, it assumes prime importance but does not exclude the interests of other dependants. Remarriage of the custodial parent will terminate financial provision for her,[4] whilst remarriage (or the prospects of it) may well reduce her share of the capital assets from the first marriage. This may then enable the court to order the father to make higher periodical payments to his children. 'Needs' can include payment of school fees for a child where both parents have agreed to that form of education.[5]

1 *Potts v Potts* (1976) 6 Fam Law 217; *Backhouse v Backhouse* [1978] 1 All ER 1158, [1978] 1 WLR 243.
2 *Furniss v Furniss* (1982) 3 FLR 46, 12 Fam Law 30, CA; *Stockford v Stockford* (1982) 3 FLR 58, 12 Fam Law 30, CA. But the expenditure must still be reasonable and necessary, *R v R* [1988] 1 FLR 89.
3 *Blower v Blower* [1986] 1 FLR 292, [1986] Fam Law 56, a case on the identically worded s 3(2)(b) of DPMCA 1978; see also *Roberts v Roberts* [1970] P 1, [1968] 3 All ER 479.
4 MCA 1973, s 28(1) and (2).
5 *Sibley v Sibley* (1981) 2 FLR 121, 10 Fam Law 49, and see also *Williams v Williams* [1965] P 125, [1964] 3 All ER 526, CA.

(g) The standard of living enjoyed by the family before the breakdown of the marriage
16.41 In all but the very rich families, separation of the spouses will inevitably lower the standard of living for the children. But, when allied to the principle that their welfare is the first consideration for the court, this factor can be used to ensure that adequate rather than minimal financial provision is made for them. Moreover, it can be used to ensure that the spouses do not suffer from a marked disparity in comfort,[1] and also that the non-custodial parent has sufficient accommodation to entertain his children on access visits.[2]

1 See *Camm v Camm* (1983) 4 FLR 577, 13 Fam Law 112, CA.
2 *Calderbank v Calderbank* [1976] Fam 93, [1975] 3 All ER 333, CA; *Ibbetson v Ibbetson* [1984] FLR 545, [1984] Fam Law 309.

(h) Any physical or mental disability of either of the parties to the marriage
16.42 This can assist the child where the custodial parent suffers from such a disability and the court orders greater financial support from the other parent so that the child can be properly cared for (eg by the provision of nursing help).

One further factor calls for special comment. The conduct of the parties is not relevant for the purpose of assessing maintenance for the child. Thus, a father, for example, is not entitled to a reduction in maintenance because the mother is denying or restricting his access to the children.[1] Conduct is relevant however vis-à-vis the spouses[2] and there is a danger that by taking it into account in that context the child will suffer indirectly because the custodial spouse will receive less support.

1   *Foot v Foot* [1987] Fam Law 13, FD.
2   Eg *Suter v Suter and Jones* [1987] Fam 111, [1987] 2 All ER 336, CA; *Kyte v Kyte* [1987] 3 All ER 1041, [1987] 3 WLR 1114; *R v R* [1988] 1 FLR 89.

(d)   Application of the factors

16.43   It should be stressed that the foregoing factors are not exclusive. Indeed the court is under a duty to have regard to all the circumstances of the case. It must then exercise its powers with the child's welfare as the first consideration.[1] In divorce proceedings the court should also ensure that the arrangements for each child are satisfactory or are 'the best that can be devised in the circumstances'.[2] Much regional variation exists and, whilst certain generalisations can be made, an understanding of the practice of local registrars and benches is essential for the practitioner. Moreover, in the vast majority of cases the paucity of available resources will both narrow and determine the options for the court. In this context particular attention must be paid to the claim of the Legal Aid Fund. Any money recovered beyond £2,500 is subject to a charge in favour of the Law Society if the party to the proceedings has been in receipt of legal aid.[3] Legal advisers to the spouses should be alert to this, since the court's duty is to consider the child's interests as first consideration and unnecessary prosecution of legal proceedings could call into question the appropriateness of legal aid. Some mitigation is now available since the Law Society's charge can be carried over and attached to a replacement property.[4] But it should be remembered that the charge will at some stage be realised.

1   As originally enacted the MCA instructed the court to place the child as far as was practicable in the financial position in which he would have been if the marriage had not broken down. This objective proved to be unworkable and was removed by MFPA 1984.
2   MCA 1973, s 41(1)(b)(i); for discussion of s 41 see *Yeend v Yeend* [1984] FLR 937, [1984] Fam Law 314, CA, and for reform of procedures, see Report of the Matrimonial Causes Procedure Committee (1985).
3   For warnings as to the disastrous effect of a charge, see *Hanlon v Law Society* [1981] AC 124, [1980] 2 All ER 199, HL; *Mason v Mason* [1986] 2 FLR 212, [1986] Fam Law 217; *Anthony v Anthony* [1986] 2 FLR 353, [1986] Fam Law 294, CA; *Simpson v Law Society* [1987] AC 861, [1987] 2 All ER 481.
4   See Legal Aid (General) (Amendment) (No 2) Regulations 1988, SI 1988/1938.

(i)   Property adjustment

16.44   From the child's point of view the need for secure accommodation will be foremost. Thus, in the typical case of low or modest incomes and small capital this means that the matrimonial home 'has first to be appropriated for the use of the children and whichever parent is going to have the responsibility of bringing them up'.[1] The courts have experimented with and employ a variety of property adjustment orders to achieve this objective. They are frequently caught in the dilemma of the financial sense of transferring the property to the custodial parent, usually the wife, and the need to do justice to the husband by preserving his proprietary interest in the home.

1   Per Cumming-Bruce LJ in *Scott v Scott* [1978] 3 All ER 65 at 68, [1978] 1 WLR 723 at 727.

16.45 Following the decision of *Mesher v Mesher and Hall* in 1973[1] a popular device was an order that the matrimonial home be occupied by, usually, the wife and children and that it be held on trust for sale until the children reach the age of 17 (as in *Mesher*), or 18, or any other age,[2] or finish their education or until further order;[3] and that on sale the proceeds be divided equally or in some other ratio. The proviso of 'further order of the court' retains flexibility in the order, avoids a cumbersome and lengthy list of crystallising events and enables the court to take account of intervening events on the basis of full information.[4] On the facts of *Mesher* (both parties had remarried and their financial positions were 'very evenly balanced'[5]) the solution was ideal; the custodial parent needed temporary security whilst bringing up the children. However, the case 'was not, in any sense of the word, a typical case',[6] and has frequently been criticised.[7] Rarely will the parties to the marriage be equal. Very often postponement of the sale will leave both with an inadequate sum with which to reinvest in property (especially so for a woman in middle age and with slender job and mortgage prospects); and if the children are no longer dependent, the woman will not qualify as a 'priority need' for the purposes of rehousing by the local authority under Part III of the Housing Act 1985; postponement will prolong uncertainty, litigation and any bitterness between the parties and, furthermore, it ignores the fact that children frequently need a family home after they reach majority.[8] Similar criticisms can be levelled against the alternative device of transferring the property to one spouse, usually the wife, on condition that she execute a legal charge to secure to the husband a specified share of the proceeds of sale, the sale being postponed until a certain date, event or order of court.[9] Both types of order can also suffer the defect that the determining date for sale of the property may arise too soon and to the detriment of the child. For example, if the woman remarries or cohabits with an impecunious man, the automatic sale of the home may well not be in the child's interests. It can therefore be argued that such pre-conditions are inconsistent with the court's duties under sections 25(1) and 41 of MCA. On the other hand, it will be recalled that the child's interests are not the paramount consideration for the purposes of MCA[10] and so such preconditions for sale would appear to be permissible. This is a further reason for preferring the adoption of the paramountcy principle. Another and consequential disadvantage of *Mesher* and charge orders is the complex drafting needed in the order to cater for the crystallising event (eg as to what is to happen if the mother dies during the child's minority[11] or, if she wishes to move house but without precipitating the other parent's interest in the proceeds of sale, as to who is to pay the rates, repairs and other maintenance bills on the home). The advantage of leaving sale until 'further order of the court' is obvious, as is the disadvantage of the further litigation. On balance, of the two a deferred charge is the preferable order because the property is vested in one person.[12] It must be repeated, however, that much depends upon the practice of divorce court registrars and for some Mesher orders are still the preferred course.[13]

---

1 [1980] 1 All ER 126.
2 It was 25 in *Mortimer v Mortimer-Griffin* [1986] 2 FLR 315, [1986] Fam Law 305; *Harnett v Harnett* [1973] Fam 156, [1974] 1 All ER 764, CA.
3 *Thompson v Thompson* [1986] Fam 38, [1985] 2 All ER 243, CA. Another popular condition

to trigger sale is if the woman remarries or cohabits with another man for three (or six) months, eg *Chadwick v Chadwick* [1985] FLR 606, [1985] Fam Law 96, CA; *Tinsdale v Tinsdale* (1983) 4 FLR 641, 13 Fam Law 148, CA; *Martin v Martin* [1978] Fam 12, [1977] 3 All ER 762, CA.

4 For a precedent of this type of order see Butterworth's Family Law Service, para K326.1. For detailed consideration of drafting such orders, see Hartley, *Matrimonial Conveyancing — A Draftsman's Handbook* (1985, 2nd ed).

5 [1980] 1 All ER 126, Per Davies LJ at 127.

6 Per Ormrod LJ in *Hanlon v Hanlon* [1978] 2 All ER 889 at 892, [1978] 1 WLR 592 at 596, CA.

7 Eg *Martin v Martin*, supra; *Mortimer v Mortimer-Griffin* supra (a *Mesher* approach should no longer be taken as the 'bible'), and note the observations of Balcombe LJ in *Harman v Glencross* [1986] Fam 81 at 96, [1986] 1 All ER 545 at 556–7, CA. A further difficulty lies in determining the precise share to be given to the occupying spouse, especially so as to compensate her for mortgage and other expenditure on the house, *Scipio v Scipio* (1983) 4 FLR 654, 13 Fam Law 176, CA.

8 Furthermore, if, as seems likely, the order amounts to a settlement under the Settled Land Act 1925, the occupying spouse is a tenant for life with such wide powers over the property (eg power to lease it) as to jeopardise the purpose of the order; see further for a full discussion, Hayes and Battersby [1985] Fam Law 213, [1986] Fam Law 142, (1981) 45 Conveyancer 404.

9 Eg *Dunford v Dunford* [1980] 1 All ER 122, 10 Fam Law 87; *Draskovic v Draskovic* (1981) 11 Fam Law 87.

10 See *Suter v Suter and Jones* [1987] Fam 111, [1987] 2 FLR 232, CA.

11 Note *Leate v Leate* (1982) 12 Fam Law 121, CA, where the charge was made enforceable on the wife's death or remarriage *and* provided the children had reached 18 — the two contingencies had to be concurrent.

12 Who can then, for example, raise money by executing a further charge. Cf the difficulties a *Mesher* order can create if one spouse is uncooperative; see *Harvey v Harvey* [1987] 1 FLR 67, [1987] Fam Law 17, FD. A desirable term in an order is an option for the occupying spouse to purchase the property.

13 For a good example, see *Drinkwater v Drinkwater* [1984] FLR 627, [1984] Fam Law 245, CA.

16.46   Other more appropriate methods of dealing with the property include a transfer of the matrimonial home to the custodial spouse with or without her agreement to forego a claim for periodical payments in her own right,[1] and/or with a reduction in the financial provision for the children; or that the property be held on trust for sale, postponed during the wife's lifetime,[2] but that after the youngest child has reached 18, the mother should pay an occupation rent to her former husband;[3] or the immediate sale of the house and division of the proceeds. The advantage of creating a settlement (eg to the wife for life, remainder to husband) lies in the powers which she holds as a tenant for life (eg power to sell, to raise money for repairs). The complete transfer of the matrimonial home accords with the clean break principle favoured by the courts[4] and MFPA 1984, though much will depend upon the value of the property and its situation. Thus, even a small charge on a house may be extremely valuable to the husband if house prices in the area are rising rapidly and this will militate against a complete transfer. On the other hand, where the house is of modest value transfer to one spouse may be the only practicable solution. Depending on the wife's resources and earning capacity, it may be possible for her, after transfer of the house into her name, to raise funds on it and pay the husband a lump sum.[5] Immediate sale also accords with the clean break objective and is practised widely,[6] but the primacy of the child's welfare requires that sufficient proceeds of sale be available to meet his accommodation needs. Furthermore, if the parent is legally aided, the

proceeds of sale may shrink through the reimbursement of the Law Society.[7]
If the family is housed in local authority accommodation and enjoy a secure
tenancy, the court[8] has the power on decree of divorce (or nullity or judicial
separation) to transfer the tenancy to one spouse[9] under section 24(1)(a)
of MCA or the more specific provisions in Schedule 1 of the Matrimonial
Homes Act 1983. Such an order will deprive the other spouse of his statutory
right to buy the property and this is a factor which the court may take
into account in assessing the other ancillary relief.

1   *Hanlon v Hanlon* [1978] 2 All ER 889, [1978] 1 WLR 592.
2   Or until she remarries or becomes dependent on another man.
3   *Harvey v Harvey* [1982] Fam 83, [1982] 1 All ER 693, CA. For another example of the
    ingenuity of court orders, see *Teschner v Teschner* [1985] FLR 627, [1985] Fam Law 250,
    CA.
4   Eg *Hanlon v Hanlon*, supra.
5   Eg *Scipio v Scipio* (1983) 4 FLR 654, CA.
6   See the research findings of Southwell [1985] Fam Law 184.
7   Before 1989 the Law Society could not postpone enforcement of its charge on the proceeds,
    Simpson v Law Society [1987] AC 861, [1987] 2 All ER 481, but could do so if the home
    was not sold, *Hanlon v Law Society* [1981] AC 124, [1980] 2 All ER 199. This anomaly
    has been removed by allowing postponement in either case.
8   Prior to the Housing Act 1980 (now Housing Act 1985, s 91) the local authority had
    the power to switch tenancies.
9   But not cohabitees.

(ii)   Financial provision

16.47   In strict law a 'clean break' cannot apply to a parent's financial
responsibility for his children.[1] But in some cases a complete severance
is practically possible. Thus, if the children are nearing majority, their
dependence is likely to end soon and, if the non-custodial parent has sufficient
means to pay a lump sum to provide for their maintenance, then for all
practical purposes a clean break can be achieved. Similarly, if there are
very large resources at hand,[2] a lump sum could be ordered which will
in effect secure a clean break; or of course the custodial parent may be
the family's main breadwinner eliminating any need for maintenance from
the other parent.[3] Unfortunately the philosophy of the MFPA 1984 is
contradictory,[4] on the one hand stressing the needs of children, which will
usually necessitate long-term and varying financial provision, and on the
other hand encouraging a clean break between the spouses (eg by setting
a deadline for periodical payments). There is a danger that, in pursuit of
the latter, courts and practitioners will lose sight of the former or give
it insufficient attention.

1   For the parent's statutory duty to maintain the child, see *Hulley v Thompson* [1981] 1
    All ER 1128, [1981] 1 WLR 159. Note also that by s 23(4) of MCA, the court's powers
    in favour of a child are 'exercisable from time to time'; and see *Minton v Minton* [1979]
    AC 593, [1979] 1 All ER 79. In *Moore v Moore* (1981) 11 Fam Law 109, Ormrod LJ
    is reported as saying that it was inappropriate to talk of a clean break where young
    children are involved; and note his Lordship's observations in *Pearce v Pearce* (1980)
    1 FLR 261 at 266, CA; cf the observations in *Suter v Suter and Jones* [1987] Fam 111,
    [1987] 2 All ER 336. The clean break may of course be attainable vis-à-vis the spouses
    (*CB v CB* [1988] Fam Law 471) and that may in fact benefit the child in so far as it
    removes a source of dispute between them, see *S v S* [1986] Fam 189, [1986] 3 All ER
    566.
2   *Preston v Preston* [1982] Fam 17, [1982] 1 All ER 41, CA.
3   Cf *Mortimer v Mortimer-Griffin* [1986] 2 FLR 315, [1986] Fam Law 305, CA.

4   For discussion, see Ingleby, *The Clean Break — Allusions to Illusions and the Welfare of the Child* (1986) JSWL 257.

16.48   Although section 24 of MCA empowers the court to settle property for the benefit of children of the family, it by no means follows that a parent, whose means allow, should be ordered to make a settlement which will benefit the children after they reach majority or complete their education.[1] A parent's obligations are to children qua children and are not open-ended. This approach reflects the ethos that on adulthood the recipient of maintenance must 'stand on his own feet'. Moreover, if a parent is otherwise honouring an order for periodical payments, the child is not entitled to a 'nest egg' in the form of capital or property investment for his long-term future,[2] or a lump sum to set himself up in business or a lump sum to his mother so that she can in turn leave property to the child in her will.[3]

1   *Lilford v Glynn* [1979] 1 All ER 441, [1979] 1 WLR 78, CA.
2   *McKay v Chapman* [1978] 2 All ER 548, [1978] 1 WLR 620, FD.
3   *Page v Page* (1981) Times, 30 January.

16.49   This approach is defended on the basis that (a) an open-ended obligation would create one rule for wealthy parents and another for indigent parents; (b) if the marriage had continued no one can know whether or not the father would have made a settlement for his children.[1] Neither argument is convincing. The first merely acknowledges that parental circumstances vary — a truism that applies across the board of financial provision. The second uses the 'realms of speculation' argument at the expense of the reality that the father would in all probability have devised or bequeathed property to his natural heirs. The more expansive approach, which would warrant the settlement of property on children and payment of maintenance beyond majority, recognises the long-standing nature of family ties and gives real force to the principle that the child's welfare is the first consideration. As it is, 'special circumstances' are needed to justify maintenance for the child after his education is completed.[2] The clearest, if not only, instance of such circumstances would be a child suffering from a physical or mental handicap which requires lifelong support.

1   See *Lilford v Glynn*, supra, and *Kiely v Kiely* [1988] 1 FLR 248, [1988] Fam Law 51, CA.
2   See Scarman LJ in *Chamberlain v Chamberlain* [1974] 1 All ER 33, [1973] 1 WLR 1557, CA.

16.50   As for capital provision for a child, this may be appropriate where the parent has been, or is likely to be, unreliable in fulfilling his periodical payments. Usually he will not have sufficient savings to provide a lump sum, but his share of the proceeds from sale of the matrimonial home does occasionally offer the possibility of ordering a lump sum, preferably secured, which can generate income for the child's maintenance. But again the court will order that the capital revert to the father when the children have reached majority (or some other specified date).[1] If the house has not been sold but the proceeds of sale are subject to a charge in the husband's favour, it is unlikely that he will be ordered to pay a part of these proceeds to the children unless there are special circumstances and there is clear evidence that they will need a lump sum (eg a seriously disabled child).[2]

1   *Griffiths v Griffiths* [1984] Fam 70, [1984] 2 All ER 626, CA.
2   *Kiely v Kiely*, supra. *Sed quaere* if the proceeds are large and the husband can purchase property which will satisfy his needs but still leave him with surplus money.

(iii)   Low earners and non-earners

16.51   When the payer's earnings are low or he is unemployed, the availability of social security becomes relevant. The courts have developed

(a)   *the general rule* that a spouse should not forsake his financial obligations to his family and force them to rely upon state benefits when he is in a position to contribute towards their maintenance;[1] and

(b)   *the aim* that a court order should not depress his financial position below the minimum level prescribed for him under the state benefits' system.[2]

1   *Roberts v Roberts* [1970] P 1, [1968] 3 All ER 479; *Barnes v Barnes* [1972] 3 All ER 872, [1972] 1 WLR 1381, CA.
2   *Shallow v Shallow* [1979] Fam 1, [1978] 2 All ER 483, CA; *Smethurst v Smethurst* [1978] Fam 52, [1977] 3 All ER 1110.

16.52   As for (a), 'the court will not allow a man to absolve himself from his maintenance obligation at the public expense. In assessing a man's maintenance liability one generally excludes from the consideration the fact, as it so often is, that to make him pay maintenance will not improve the financial position of the wife at all, but only reduce the amount of the supplementary benefit being paid to her.'[1] In the typical case of a wife and children left by a working husband, the court will determine what social security the husband (and any new dependants) would be entitled to if he were unemployed and subtract them from his earnings. The remainder is then regarded as being available to pay to his former family. If all of that remainder is paid over, it can be argued that the man has little incentive to remain in work and that therefore it is more realistic to allow him to keep a sum above subsistence level. This more generous approach reflects the liable relative formula adopted by the Department of Social Security as a starting point for assessing a person's liability to pay for relatives. Under this approach the man is often allowed to subtract the social security rates plus one-quarter of his net earnings from his actual earnings before being required to contribute maintenance. The formula was approved in *Smethurst v Smethurst*[2] but hopes for its general adoption were dashed in *Shallow v Shallow*.[3] The Court of Appeal did not reject it out of hand but on the facts its application would have led to the husband enjoying a much healthier financial position than that of his wife and children. Consequently the liable relative formula is 'in essence a ranging shot which suggests a figure which can then be considered in detail in the light of all the circumstances of the particular case. But it must be properly applied if it is not to mislead'.[4] The court was clearly not closing the door against the formula and it is suggested that courts should always bear it in mind. One situation where it would not mislead is if the man's current financial obligations to a second family are high and his income is near to the supplementary benefit level. Indeed, there are indications[5] that courts are prepared to adopt a more realistic position for the payer, admittedly short of the liable relative formula but offering him some room for manoeuvre, by allowing him to keep a part of his earnings over and above the subsistence level. In so far as this will encourage him to continue making the payments it is to the benefit of all and it certainly accords with the primacy of the child's welfare as laid down in the DPMCA and MCA. Another example of realism concerns the relationship between rule (a) above and the 'clean break' provisions introduced by MFPA 1984. It would appear that both must be considered, neither takes priority and, where the payer is likely to continue to make very small contributions to his partner for the foreseeable future, it may be pointless to continue an order and sensible to opt for a clean break. This approach is, however, inappropriate for children since a clean break cannot apply to them.[6]

1   Per Finer J in *Williams v Williams* [1974] Fam 55 at 62, [1974] 3 All ER 377 at 383.
2   Supra.
3   Supra.
4   Per Ormrod LJ, [1979] Fam 1 at 6, [1978] 2 All ER 483 at 487.
5   Eg *Allen v Allen* [1986] 2 FLR 265, [1986] Fam Law 268, CA; *Peacock v Peacock* [1984] 1 All ER 1069, [1984] 1 WLR 532.
6   *Ashley v Blackman* [1988] 2 FLR 278; and see *Seaton v Seaton* [1986] Fam Law 267.

16.53   As for the unemployed, rule (a) is pursued so rigorously that some magistrates' courts will judge for themselves whether the payer is genuinely unemployed; and they may decide that he is not, even though the Department of Social Security is paying him benefits on the basis that he is.[1] At the other extreme, for the earner who is just able to pay his family the equivalent of the social security going rate, it may be to their advantage for the court to order slightly lower periodical payments from him so that the family receives some state benefits and then to use the 'diversion procedure', whereby the man's payments are diverted to the DSS, the Department pays the benefits to the family and the family is thus assured of regular maintenance.

1   Eg *Munt v Munt* (1983) 13 Fam Law 81, *Duncan v Duncan* [1986] 1 FLR 439, [1986] Fam Law 136, and *Williams v Williams*, supra; but note the sharp criticisms of the magistrates' practice by Finer J at 61, 381. If they have doubts as to the man's unemployment, a preferable and more defensible approach is to order maintenance but suspend it so as to allow him time to find work. If he fails, he can then return to court and seek variation to a nominal sum.

16.54   As for the aim (b), this means that the payer's new obligations to his second family can be fully considered.[1] However, in *Tovey v Tovey*, Ormrod LJ asked, 'should he be able literally to off-load the whole of his obligation to his wife and his three children on to the state, simply by taking over another woman with two children?'[2] His Lordship regarded it as a startling proposition that a man in regular employment should make no contribution to his first family's children, who were his primary obligation. This approach was endorsed by the MFPA 1984 which made the welfare of the child of the family the first consideration for courts dealing with maintenance and property claims, and it has been followed by other courts, most notably in *Freeman v Swatridge*.[3] It can even apply if the payer is unemployed, ie he can be ordered to make a contribution to his children out of his state benefits. In *Freeman* the unemployed husband was ordered to pay 50 pence per week for each of his three children. Whatever the morality of this approach may be, its rigorous application is unrealistic.

1   *Blower v Blower* [1986] 1 FLR 292, [1986] Fam Law 56; *Barnes v Barnes* [1972] 3 All ER 872, [1972] 1 WLR 1381, CA; *Winter v Winter* (1976) 140 JPN 597.
2   (1978) 8 Fam Law 80.
3   [1984] FLR 762, [1984] Fam Law 215, CA and see also *R v Cardiff Justices, ex p Salter* [1986] 1 FLR 162 [1986] Fam Law 53; *Billington v Billington* [1974] Fam 24, [1974] 1 All ER 546.

(e)   Relevance of tax

16.55   Prior to the Budget of 1988 a crucial element of any financial provision order was the tax implications, for considerable advantages could be achieved by maximising tax allowances.[1] A child exists for tax purposes from the moment of birth. This means that he is liable to pay tax and able to claim tax allowances in his own right. Normally the child's parent (or guardian or trustee) is assessed to tax on his behalf,[2] but assessment can always be made directly on the child.[3] His residence may even be dealt with separately for tax purposes.[4] The most popular tax-saving device involved the following. The normal rule (aimed at deterring tax evasion) is that, if a parent pays maintenance to his unmarried child under the age of 18, the income remains the payer's for the purpose of his tax bills.[5] However, if the payments were made under a court order and were paid direct to a child under the age of 21 for his own benefit, maintenance or education, the Inland Revenue did not regard them as a 'settlement' for the purpose of section 437 of ICTA 1970. The payer obtained tax relief on them and the child avoided paying tax up to the level of his single person's allowance.[6] The court order was crucial. A voluntary agreement between the parents did not qualify for this concession.[7] The order had to be for the child, though the court did look at the reality of the agreement so that payment to a person *qua* guardian or as agent for the child sufficed.[8] It should be noted that, if there were no tax advantages, then payments direct to the child could not be ordered by a magistrates' court.[9] The foregoing tax advantages were also open to unmarried couples, even if they were still cohabiting.[10] In reality these maintenance payments, though made to the child, had the effect of inflating the family unit's total income. Indeed the artificiality was recognised by the fact that maintenance to a child had to be taken into account when the custodial parent's entitlement to supplementary benefit was assessed.[11] It followed that that parent had to be aware of the future date when the payments would cease (eg as the child reaches majority) because the family's income would consequently drop. Another tax advantage was available in those cases involving two or more children who roughly divided their time between the parents (eg by spending the weekends and school holidays with one). Both parents could claim the additional personal allowances,[12] an allowance designed to assist single parent families, which meant that more of their income was saved from assessment to tax. This advantage was also open to unmarried couples and encouraged the use of affiliation orders.

1   See *Morley-Clarke v Jones* [1986] Ch 311, [1985] 3 All ER 193, CA, for the tax advantages that could have accrued if appropriate provision in favour of the child had been made earlier. For fuller discussion of this tax planning, see Butterworth's Family Law Service,

paras. D 1001 et seq, Jackson op cit, especially Chapters 6 and 18, Passingham and Harmer, op cit, Chapter 15 and Appendix IV. See also for a short guide, Burgess, *Financial Planning in Separation and Divorce* [1986] Fam Law 289.

2 Taxes Management Act 1970, s 72; and the parent is liable to pay tax in default of payment by the child and proceedings may be taken against the former, s 73.

3 *R v Newmarket Income Tax comrs, ex p Huxley* [1916] 1 KB 788.

4 It normally follows that of the custodial parent(s), but note *Miesegaes v IRC* (1957) 37 TC 493 (child at a boarding-school). For the meaning of residence, see *Shah v Barnet London Borough Council* [1983] 2 AC 309, [1983] 1 All ER 226.

5 Income and Corporation Taxes Act 1988, s 663; cf the position for payments to spouses, s 683.

6 If the payments did not exceed £48 per week, they qualified as small maintenance payments and were paid over without deduction of tax, ICTA, s 351. See Schuz [1985] Fam Law 74 for doubts as to the legality of the Revenue's concession.

7 See *IRC v Craw* [1985] STC 512; *Harvey v Sivyer* [1986] Ch 119, [1985] 2 All ER 1054.

8 *Finnie v Finnie* [1984] STC 168: and for school fees see post, para 16.60.

9 *Practice Direction* [1980] 1 All ER 1007, [1980] 1 WLR 354.

10 Provided that an affiliation order had been obtained.

11 *Supplementary Benefits Commission v Jull* [1981] AC 1025, [1980] 3 All ER 65, HL; and for affiliation orders, *Y v Supplementary Benefits Commission* [1981] AC 1025, [1980] 3 All ER 65, HL.

12 Set at £1,490 for 1988–9.

16.56   The Chancellor's budget of 1988 made unheralded and major changes to the taxation of maintenance payments.[1] Briefly, court orders applied for and made before 30 June 1988 (and including those orders which have been varied prior to 5 April 1989) retain the tax advantages mentioned above. However, the tax relief is frozen at the level which was obtained by 5 April 1989. Subsequent increases do not attract relief but fall under the new arrangements. For all new maintenance payments made after 15 March 1988 (Budget day) the following arrangements operate. When a former spouse is paying maintenance to the other spouse[2] and is calculating his income for tax liability, he is allowed to deduct the difference between the married person's allowance and the single person's allowance (£1,490 for 1988–89). The rest of the maintenance he pays must come out of his taxed income. On the other hand, the maintenance is tax free in the hands of the recipient former spouse or child. This regime means that payments made direct to a child do not attract tax relief. Their only advantage is psychological viz, that the spouse is likely to be more willing to pay maintenance for his children than for his former partner. A further change worthy of mention in this context is that after 5 April 1989 only one parent can claim the additional personal allowance in respect of a child. The former practice of unmarried parents each claiming the allowance is abolished.

1 See the Finance Act 1988, ss 36–38 which add these provisions to ICTA 1988.

2 The following provision does not unfortunately apply to an unmarried father paying for his child.

16.57   An alternative to child maintenance payments for tax relief purposes is the settlement of capital, by persons other than a parent, in a trust for the benefit of the child at the age of majority. In this case the income generated is not treated as that of the settlor.[1] A further advantage of a trust is that the transfers of money into it are free from inheritance tax, provided that the donor survives for seven years after the donation. On paying out any accumulated income the child can reclaim tax paid by the trustees up to the limit of his personal allowances. The trust must, however, be irrevocable, for otherwise section 663 of ICTA 1988 will apply and tax on the trust income will be assessed to the settlor.

1 However, the income remains his if he is a parent of the child beneficiary. To avoid this, the parent must create an accumulation settlement, whereby the income earned from the trust is accumulated for the child's future use, ss 664, 665 of ICTA 1988.

16.58 Another, limited tax saving device was the covenant, which was employed by parents and other relatives. If payments were made to a child by a person other than a parent under a deed of covenant, they could be paid after deduction of tax and the child recipient could recoup the tax.[1] When the child reached majority, parents too could take advantage of covenants and this proved a popular method of supporting a child in higher education.[2] The covenant had to be designed to last for at least seven years, but could be drafted to end earlier, the usual contingency being the completion of the child's education. This practice was abruptly halted by the Budget of 1988. Thus, for all covenants (save those for charitable purposes) made on or after 15 March 1988, the covenanted sum cannot be deducted from the payer's taxable income. The payee on the other hand is not taxed on receipt of that sum.

1 See Capital Transfer Tax Act 1984, renamed Inheritance Tax Act 1984 by the Finance Act 1986, Part V.
2 Section 18.

(i) Inheritance tax (formerly capital transfer tax)[1]
16.59 A disposition is not a 'transfer of value' for the purposes of inheritance tax if it is made for the maintenance of a spouse[2] or former spouse,[3] or for the maintenance, education or training of a child of either spouse. Child is widely defined to include a stepchild, adopted child, child of an unmarried couple and, presumably, a child treated as part of the family.[4] This exemption from inheritance tax lasts until the child reaches 18 or ceases full-time education or training. It can be usefully employed to pay for a child's higher education in the form of, for example, lump sum annual payments.

1 See Capital Transfer Tax Act 1984, renamed Inheritance Tax Act 1984 by the Finance Act 1986, Part V.
2 Section 18.
3 Ie a disposition made at dissolution or annulment of the marriage or on variation of a disposition made at that time, ITA 1984, s 11(6).
4 A child over 18 who has previously spent substantial periods of time with the transferor and who is not currently living with his parents, is specifically mentioned, s 11(2).

(ii) Education
16.60 Income from a scholarship fund is exempt from income tax in the hands of the recipient,[1] unless it comes from a fund organised by the parent's employer. Parents cannot take advantage of covenants to fund their children through education once they reach 18,[2] and the general rule is that parents cannot claim tax relief on the payment of school fees. Instead, parents are increasingly being offered a variety of investment plans (similar to life insurance) and for which some tax saving is available (eg a lump sum payment into a charitable educational trust which is free from tax on its

investments). The situation used to be different on the break down of the marriage. Then tax relief was available to parents of means for school fees which were paid out of a court order for periodical payments. The Revenue was satisfied of the genuineness of this arrangement if there was a contract between the school and the child,[3] and the arrangement could be made whether the payer was a custodial or non-custodial[4] parent. A standard form of order, approved by the Revenue, was available which was drafted so as to take account of increases in the school fees.[5] This practice was another casualty of the Finance Act 1988.

1   ICTA 1988, s 331.
2   See ante, para 16.58.
3   For comments on the artificiality of this situation, see the Master of the Rolls in *Sherdley v Sherdley* [1986] 2 All ER 202 at 209, [1986] 1 WLR 732 at 739.
4   *Sherdley v Sherdley* [1987] 2 All ER 54, [1987] 2 WLR 1071, HL; noted by Whitehouse (1987) NLJ 495 and Baigent [1987] Fam Law 391.
5   *Practice Direction* [1983] 2 All ER 679; [1983] 1 WLR 800.

(f)   Variation and discharge of orders under MCA

16.61   The court can vary or discharge certain orders or suspend, then revive, any terms in them.[1] The general principle is that when the marriage is brought to an end there ought to be a final adjustment of property rights. Financial provision orders on the other hand will often need subsequent judicial attention.

1   Section 31.

(i)   Periodical payments

16.62   Secured and unsecured payments are covered. On an application to vary[1] the payments, no property adjustment order can be made, but it may be that a lump sum can be ordered in favour of a party to the marriage.[2] The latter clearly can, however, be ordered for the benefit of a child, for example, to meet his educational needs. Where the order related to secured payments and the payer dies, the application for variation may be sought by the person entitled to the payments or by the payer's personal representatives, but this must be done within six months from the date when representation was taken out, unless the court otherwise directs.[3] If an application is instead made under the Inheritance (Provision for Family Dependants) Act 1975 for an order relating to the deceased's property, then the court dealing with that application will also have the power to vary or discharge the secured periodical payments.[4] Of far greater importance is the general power of the court to treat an application under section 31 regarding secured periodical payments as an application under the 1975 Act, thus attracting that Act's wider powers of dealing with the deceased's property.

1   The rule applies only to variation.
2   Section 31(5) would appear to prevent it, but Waite J, in *S v S* [1986] Fam 189, [1986] 3 All ER 566, used s 31(7) so as to terminate periodical payments on the basis of a capital sum being offered by the payer, *provided* that this arrangement was consistent with the welfare of any children. On appeal this part of the judgment was not argued, [1987] 2 All ER 312, CA.

3   Section 31(6).
4   1975 Act, s 16(1). However, unlike the 1973 Act, the court is not specifically directed
    to regard the child's welfare as the 'first consideration'. The omission is not serious since
    in practice the courts exercise their powers in the child's best interests (see post, para
    16.82).

(ii)   Lump sum
16.63 A lump sum order is final in its effect, so that there can be no
variation in the amount ordered and no question of repayment; but any
provision for payment by instalments is variable, eg by extending the period
of payment of instalments.

(iii)   Transfer order
16.64 Like a lump sum, an order for transfer of property is final and
not subject to variation whether the order was made on a decree of divorce,
nullity or judicial separation.

(iv)   Orders under section 24
16.65 This last rule also applies to orders for settlement of property or
for variation of a settlement or for extinguishing or reducing an interest
under a settlement if made on or after a decree of divorce or nullity, but
if made on or after a decree of judicial separation they may be varied
when there is an application for rescission of the decree or for the dissolution
of the marriage. This exception recognises that in proceedings for judicial
separation a final adjustment of property may be inappropriate because
the parties may later be reconciled or, if divorce does follow, that will
be the moment for final adjustment.

(v)   Order for sale
16.66 When an order has placed the property under a trust for sale[1] or
a charge,[2] a court has the jurisdiction to make an order for sale of the
property under section 24A on a subsequent application by a party.

1   *Thompson v Thompson* [1986] Fam 38, [1985] 2 All ER 243, CA.
2   *Taylor v Taylor* [1987] 1 FLR 142, [1986] Fam Law 366, CA.

(vi)   Agreements
16.67 If the parties agree on terms for financial relief, they can seek a
consent order even if this varies or discharges an earlier court order.[1] They
can also apply to vary a maintenance agreement.[2] In this case the court
can make such order as it considers just with particular reference to ensuring
proper financial provision for the children. Consent orders have virtues,
not least the saving of legal costs, but are attended by some disadvantages,[3]
two of which can be mentioned here. First, there is the difficulty of ensuring
full disclosure by the parties of their resources.[4] Second, concentration on
and speculation about the spouses' future may cause them and their advisers[5]
to underestimate the importance of the children.

1   Section 33A, inserted by MFPA 1984.
2   Section 35. An agreement is widely defined as concerned with 'the making or securing
    of payments or the disposition or use of any property'; s 34(2).
3   See Goldrein and Haas, Chapter 5; Cleary, *Icebergs and Elephant Traps* [1987] Fam Law
    43.

4   Failure to do so can mean that the consent order is set aside; see the leading decision of *Livesey (formerly Jenkins) v Jenkins* [1985] AC 424, [1985] 1 All ER 106, HL.
5   The need for care on the part of lawyers was spelt out by the House of Lords in *Dinch v Dinch* [1987] 1 All ER 818, [1987] 1 WLR 252; and see also *Livesey (formerly Jenkins) v Jenkins*, supra, and *Sandford v Sandford* [1986] 1 FLR 412, CA.

(vii)   Relevant factors

16.68   In exercising its powers of variation the court must consider all the circumstances of the case, including any change in the matters to which it was required to have regard when making the original order (the list of factors set out in section 25).[1] The first consideration, however, must be given to the welfare of any child of the family under 18. In other words the court must act on the same principle as it does when entertaining an original application for an order. This includes the possibility of setting a time limit on the periodical payments to the custodial parent, but not to the child, so that she can adjust to financial independence.[2] Where the payer has died, account must be taken of the changed circumstances resulting from his death. This may be particularly relevant where there is an order for secured periodical payments. If the payer had remarried, it may be desirable in the interests of his second wife and their children to relieve his estate of the security; or the release of capital on his death may justify enlarging the security. Moreover, in the case of an order for periodical payments, where the change of circumstances relates to the person entitled to the payments (eg the child receives a windfall) or to the payer (eg his reduced earning capacity due to ill-health) or where the latter dies, the court may order the recipient or his personal representative to pay to the payer or his personal representative a sum which justly represents the excess payments made since the change of circumstances.[3] It is suggested that there will have to be very compelling reasons before a child recipient will be ordered to make repayment.

1   Section 31(7) and see to like effect ss 20 and 3, DPMCA 1978 – *Riley v Riley* [1988] 1 FLR 273. But there is no general duty lying on a party to inform the other of a material change in circumstances. An undertaking to do so should therefore be sought, see the order made in *Barrett v Barrett* [1988] Fam Law 475.
2   Section 31(7)(a).
3   Section 33. The order may also provide for payment by instalments. There is no equivalent provision in the DPMCA 1978. One significant weakness of s 33 is that there is no duty on the payee to inform the payer of any change in circumstances; see further Butterworths Family Law Service, para D789.

7   Affiliation proceedings

16.69   The principal method by which a mother has been able to obtain financial provision from the father of her illegitimate child is affiliation proceedings, an archaic process bearing the quasi-criminal marks of the early Poor Law.[1] Under that system recognition of the illegitimate child was initially limited to the duty of the mother or father to maintain him and thereby relieve the community wholly or partly of that duty. Even when a right was eventually given[2] to the mother to seek maintenance from the father, it was permitted only within the narrow confines of the Poor Law system. Consequently it was only enforceable under the limited jurisdiction of the justices, with the father's financial liability being severely restricted however wealthy he might be. That glaring injustice was not removed until 1968.[3] Some others were removed by the Domestic Proceedings and Magistrates' Courts Act 1978.[4] The culmination of reform is section 17 of the Family Law Reform Act 1987 which, when operative, will abolish affiliation proceedings. The following comparative statement of the law is based on this prospective repeal of the Affiliation Proceedings Act 1957.[5] Thereafter the unmarried parent will use the Guardianship of Minors Act 1971 to obtain financial relief.[6] Amongst the many changes are the following —

(a) Either parent and not, as formerly, only a 'single woman' will be able to seek relief.[7]

(b) There are no time limits on an application.[8]

(c) The mother's testimony as to paternity need not be corroborated as a matter of law[9] (though in practice supporting evidence will usually be required).

(d) Relief from the magistrates' court will still be limited to periodical payments and a maximum lump sum of £1,000, but will also be available from the High Court or county court and extend to secured periodical payments, an unlimited lump sum, and the transfer or settlement of property.[10]

Affiliation orders survive implementation of the FLRA 1987,[11] but for variation or revocation the parties must use the GMA 1971 and must apply to the High or county court.[12] The court can then either prolong the affiliation order or replace it with an order under the GMA. If prolonged, the affiliation order is still enforceable in the usual way as a magistrates' maintenance order.[13] Alternatively the parents could apply to a magistrates' court for a fresh order under the GMA and the affiliation order will presumably lapse.

1 This originated in a statute of 1576, 18 Eliz I, c 3.
2 By the Poor Law Amendment Act 1844.
3 By the Maintenance Orders Act 1968.
4 Sections 49–53.
5 The changes are not likely to operate before 1989.
6 See ante, para. 16.06.
7 Section 11B of GMA 1971, as opposed to s 1 of Affiliation Proceedings Act 1957.
8 Cf s 2 of APA 1957.
9 Cf s 4(1) of APA 1957.
10 Section 11B(2), of GMA 1971.
11 Schedule 3, paras 6, 7. 'Orders' include those made under National Assistance Act 1948, s 44; Supplementary Benefits Act 1976, s 19; Child Care Act 1980, ss 49, 50; and Social Security Act 1986, s 25.
12 Section 11B.
13 See post, para 16.75.

8 Enforcement of orders[1]

16.70 A general restriction on the enforcement of financial provision orders made under the MCA 1973 is imposed by section 32. The payment of arrears which have been due for over 12 months can only be enforced by leave of the court. It is also a rule of practice that the court will usually remit all arrears which have accrued in the period of over 12 months before the application. Magistrates' courts follow the same practice.[2] Thus, a special reason for the delay in applying will need to be adduced (eg that the payer's whereabouts have been unknown, or that he has a long record of non-payment in spite of apparent ability to pay).[3]

1 See generally the Report of the [Payne] Committee on the Enforcement of Judgments Debts (Cmnd 3909); and for fuller details of the methods of enforcement the reader is referred to Butterworths Family Law Service, paras D187–859; Duckworth, op cit, Chapter 13.
2 *Ross v Pearson* [1976] 1 All ER 790, [1976] 1 WLR 224; *Dickens v Pattison* [1985] FLR 610.
3 See *Russell v Russell* [1986] 1 FLR 465, [19865] Fam Law 156.

16.71 A variety of methods is available to enforce financial provision orders made in the superior courts.[1] Whether the order is made in the High Court or a divorce county court, it can be enforced by a judgment summons; an attachment of earnings order; registration in, and enforcement by, a magistrates' court; a charging order;[2] garnishee proceedings;[3] the appointment of a receiver by way of equitable execution;[4] by a writ of fieri facias in the High Court[5] or a warrant of execution in the county court;[6] and by committal to prison for contempt of court. Additionally, a High Court order is enforceable by writ of sequestration.[7] Arrears due under an order for periodical payments are neither a debt recoverable by action[8] nor provable in bankruptcy;[9] *aliter* a lump sum payment. Orders made in magistrates' courts can be enforced by an attachment of earnings order, registration of the order in and enforcement by the High Court, a warrant of distress and committal to prison.[10]

1 RSC Ord 45, r 1. For consideration of property and lump sums, see Cleary, *Icebergs and Elephant Traps* [1987] Fam Law 46–49.
2 RSC Ord 50. A cumbersome procedure which is inappropriate to enforcement of arrears.
3 RSC Ord 49; a useful method of 'freezing' the payer's funds in a bank or building society provided that the payer has fully revealed his financial resources, that the payer's institution can be identified and that the payer is not forewarned.
4 RSC Ord 51. See *Harvey v Harvey* [1987] 1 FLR 67, [1987] Fam Law 17 (receiver appointed so as to ensure that repairs were carried out on property in the face of an uncompromising husband).
5 RSC Ord 47.
6 CCR Ord 26.
7 RSC Ord 46, r 5.
8 *Robins v Robins* [1907] 2 KB 13.
9 *Re Hedderwick, Morten v Brinsley* [1933] Ch 669.
10 Enforcement can be sought by the child or the person with whom he has his home, Magistrates' Courts Act 1980, s 62.

(a) Judgment summons

16.72 The power to imprison defaulting civil debtors was abolished by the Administration of Justice Act 1970, following the unanimous recommendation of the Payne Committee, but was retained by the Act for the purpose of enforcing maintenance orders.[1] A judgment summons may be issued[2] under the Debtors Act 1869 for payment of arrears or a lump sum. It requires the debtor to appear before the court and be examined as to his means. If the order for payment was made in a divorce county court or in the High Court, the summons may be issued in a divorce county court. If, from an examination of the defaulter's means, it appears that he has the ability to pay, he is normally given the opportunity to do so by way of instalments and, in default thereof, he may be committed to prison for contempt.

1 Its retention divided the Payne Committee, see Cmnd 3909, paras 1008–1108.
2 Where the recipient of the payment is a child, his next friend must issue the summons, *Shelly v Shelly* [1952] P 107, [1952] 1 All ER 70; MCR 1977, r 112(2).

(b) Attachment of earnings

16.73 Where a judgment summons has been issued the court may, instead of ordering committal under the Debtors Act, make an attachment of earnings order, but such an order is usually made as the result of an application for it. The relevant law is consolidated in the Attachment of Earnings Act 1971[1] and extends to, inter alia, orders for payments made under the DPMCA 1978, GMA 1971, GA 1973, and FLRA 1969.[2] The applicant for an attachment of earnings order will usually be the disappointed payee or the clerk of a magistrates' court, but the payer himself can also apply. An order is available against the employed but not self-employed and lapses if the payer leaves employment. An order on the application of the payee cannot be made (1) until the debtor has failed to make one or more payments, and (2) unless the failure is due to his wilful refusal or culpable neglect.[3] The effect of the order is to direct the payer's employer to make periodical deductions from his 'attachable earnings' ie from his earnings[4] which remain after the employer has deducted income tax and certain social security and superannuation contributions.[5] The amounts deducted by the employer must be paid over to the collecting officer of the court at such times as are specified in the order. The scheme for assessing the amount of the deductions is based on the principle of what the payer can reasonably afford, and this is determined by reference to the 'normal deduction rate' and the 'protected earnings rate'.[6] The former is the weekly, monthly or other regular amount which it is reasonable to apply out of the payer's earnings to meet his liability under the original order. However, when the attachment of earnings order is sought to secure payments under a maintenance order (not being a lump sum order), account must also be taken of any right or liability of the payer to deduct income tax when making the payments,[7] and the rate must not exceed that which appears necessary to secure payment of the sums falling due from time to time under the maintenance order and of those already due and unpaid.[8] The protected earnings rate is the weekly, monthly or other regular sum below which, having regard to the payer's resources and needs (including the needs of any person for whom he must, or reasonably may,[9] provide), it is reasonable that the earnings actually paid to him should not be reduced.[10] In most cases and certainly where the payer has acquired new dependants, it would not be reasonable to fix a protected earnings rate below the subsistence level laid down by the social security system, but there may be exceptional circumstances for doing so (eg if the payer is being supported financially by another person).[11] When on any pay-day the attachable earnings exceed the protected earnings, then so far as the excess allows, the normal deduction is made.

1 It partly implements recommendations of the Payne Committee (Cmnd 3909, paras 580–629).
2 AEA 1971, Sch I.
3 Ibid, s 3(3), (5).
4 For the definition of earnings see s 24. It covers (a) wages or salary, together with such emoluments as fees, bonus or commission, or overtime pay, and (b) sums payable by way of pension, including an annuity for past services and periodical payments as compensation for loss of office or employment; but it excludes such items as the pay of servicemen and various social security benefits, including the guaranteed minimum pension. For interpretation of 'pension', see *Miles v Miles* [1979] 1 All ER 865, [1979] 1 WLR 371, CA.
5 Schedule 3, Part 1, para 3.
6 Section 6(5).
7 This has assumed some importance since the abolition of tax relief on small maintenance payments, see ante, para 16.56.
8 Section 6(6).
9 Eg the child of his cohabitee for whom he has assumed financial responsibility.
10 Sections 6(5)(b) and 25(3).
11 See *Billington v Billington* [1974] Fam 24, [1974] 1 All ER 546.

16.74   In order to administer the system a number of obligations are imposed on the debtor and his employer. For example, both can be ordered to furnish statements of the former's earnings and the payer may also be required to give details of his resources and needs. Both must notify the court of changes of employment and earnings.[1] Such provisions do not eliminate the risk of the debtor seeking to evade liability by continual change of employment, but it is a risk that can be overstated particularly in view of the high level of unemployment and especially if the protected earnings rate is set at a realistic level so as not to deter the payer from work. Another risk is that the employer may regard compliance as burdensome and may be tempted to terminate the employment of a person who is the subject of an order. Unfortunately the lack of regular reviews of the 1971 Act means that the incidence of these defects is not properly recorded.

1 Sections 14 and 15; and see s 7 for the employer's duty to comply with the attachment of earnings order.

(c)   *Registration of order in magistrates' court*

16.75   The effect of registering the High Court or county court order in a magistrates' court is that it then becomes enforceable by the magistrates' court in the same way as a maintenance order may be enforced.[1] The magistrates' court also has the power to vary the rate of payments specified by the original court, provided that it acts on the same principles as the High Court or county court;[2] but it may instead remit the application for variation to the original court. The principle of registration and enforcement in another court is not confined to England and Wales. An order made in one part of the United Kingdom or the Commonwealth may be registered and enforced in another part, as may orders made outside the United Kingdom.[3]

1 Maintenance Orders Act 1958, ss 1–5. Correspondingly a magistrates' court maintenance order may be registered and enforced in the High Court. Registration constitutes a significant component of magistrates' business (about 10,000 orders are registered each year, Home Office Statistical Bulletins and annual judicial statistics; and see Gibson (1982) 12 Fam

Law 138). Research indicates that most registered orders are for low sums and that the 'enforcement procedure is largely futile', see Edwards and Halpern [1988] Fam Law 117.
2 *Miller v Miller* [1961] P 1, [1960] 3 All ER 115.
3 See Part II of the Maintenance Orders Act 1950 and the Maintenance Orders (Reciprocal Enforcement) Act 1972; and Dicey and Morris, op cit, pp 770 et seq.

(d) Orders other than money payments

16.76 Orders to transfer or settle property can be enforced by an order for committal in the High Court, or by attachment in a divorce county court, or by the cumbersome procedure of attaching a charge.[1]

1 See Passingham and Harmer, op cit, p 246.

9 Maintenance out of the estate of a deceased parent[1]

16.77 The majority of the population die without making a will and property passes according to the laws of intestacy.[2] Thus, if the deceased is survived by a spouse and children,[3] the surviving spouse will take all personal chattels and, if the resources allow, £75,000[4] plus one-half of the remainder of the estate. In other words, in most cases it will be the spouse and not the children who will succeed to the property. As for succession on testacy, the testator is given considerable latitude in the disposition of his estate. Under many legal systems a deceased's dependants and relatives are automatically entitled to a certain share of the estate regardless of the deceased's intentions. Under others, including the English, a more cautious and uncertain approach has been preferred with a court deciding whether a share should be ordered. Thus, if a deceased has failed to make reasonable financial provision for his dependants, they may seek it by bringing a claim under the Inheritance (Provisions for Family and Dependants) Act 1975. This legislation replaced and improved upon earlier statutes dating back to 1938 and in particular adopted some of the features of the MCA 1973. It can also be used in cases of intestacy, if the rules of intestacy fail to secure adequate provision for dependants. As in the case of financial provision for children where there are matrimonial proceedings, the interests and claims of the children are most commonly bound up with those of the wife. Both she, as the surviving spouse, and they may wish to challenge the will because the whole or substantial part of the testator's estate has been left to a third party, eg a mistress, or the dispute may be between the widow and the children, particularly if the latter are children by a previous marriage of the deceased. This latter dispute may arise either because she or they have benefited under the will at the expense of the other or because the rules of intestacy are operating unfairly against the children. Disputes may also arise between a spouse and a non-dependent child; for example, where the widow is complaining against a will in which the sole beneficiary is a son aged 22.

1 For detailed consideration, see Miller, *Family Property and Financial Provision*, (1983, 2nd edn), Part V; Tyler's *Family Provision* (1984, 2nd edn); Ross Martyn, *Family Provision: Law and Practice* (1985, 2nd edn); Sherrin and Bonehill, *The Law and Practice of Intestate Succession* (1987).
2 As set out in the Administration of Estates Act 1925.
3 If there is no spouse, the children take all.
4 Raised from £40,000 by Family Provision (Intestate Succession) Order 1987, SI 1987/799.

(a) Claimants

16.78 One of the benefits of the 1975 Act was to widen the class of children who can invoke the statutory scheme.[1] Any child[2] of the deceased qualifies and this includes an adopted[3] child and a child *en ventre sa mere* at the date of the deceased's death.[4] Any person who was treated by the deceased[5] as a 'child of the family' also qualifies.[6] This concept appears in other legislation and is considered elsewhere.[7] It is particularly useful for a stepchild, for example, when the deceased took over financial responsibility for his wife's children but died before changing his will. The marital status of a child does not bar a claim under the 1975 Act but can clearly affect the appropriateness and amount of an award. Furthermore, there is no maximum age limit for a claimant and consequently an 'adult child' can seek financial provision. For example, in *Re Callaghan*[8] financial provision was ordered in favour of a 47-year-old plaintiff who had been treated by the deceased as a child of the family long after the child attained majority and up to the date of the deceased's death. In contrast it should be noted that, if it is impossible to assess the long-term financial needs of a young child, the court can decide in principle to award some kind of provision but adjourn its computation until a fixed date or until further application.[9] A general but important limitation on the scope of the 1975 Act is that the deceased must have died domiciled in England and Wales.[10]

1 The previous law (in the Inheritance (Family Provision) Act 1938, as amended) restricted claims to unmarried daughters, sons under 21 and disabled offspring.
2 Even prior to the Family Law Reform Act 1987 (see ante, Chapter 2), an illegitimate child was covered.
3 Children Act 1975, Sch I.
4 I(PFD)A 1975, s 25(1).
5 Not necessarily by both spouses, cf MCA 1973, s 52(1).
6 I(PFD)A 1975, s 1(1)(d).
7 See para 3.34; for discussion in the present context, see *Re Leach* [1985] 2 All ER 754 at 760–762, [1985] FLR 1120 at 1128–1131, CA.
8 [1985] Fam 1, [1984] 3 All ER 790.
9 *Re Franks* [1948] Ch 62, [1947] 2 All ER 638 (adjournment ordered in the case of a one year old).
10 Section 1(1).

(b) Orders

16.79 The court can make a variety of orders very similar to those in matrimonial proceedings under the MCA 1973, viz an order for periodical payments, a lump sum (which can be payable by instalments), a transfer and/or settlement of property, the purchase and then transfer of property, and the variation of a marriage settlement. The order is usually for periodical payments. It may provide for them to be of a specified amount or to be equal to the whole or part of the income of the net estate or of the income of any part of the estate which is to be appropriated for the purpose of the order.[1] It may be made subject to conditions, and this may be particularly desirable to protect the interests of children, for example, where receipt of payments by a widow is to depend on her maintaining the deceased's children during their minority.[2]

1   Section 2(2).
2   *Re Lidington, Lidington v Thomas (No 2)* [1940] Ch 927, [1940] 3 All ER 600; see also
    Re Franks, supra.

16.80   Another useful power is that enabling the court to make an interim
order for one or more payments to meet an immediate need of financial
assistance for an applicant until the making of a final order.[1] At the court's
discretion the latter order may provide that payments made under the interim
order shall be treated as having been paid on account of maintenance due
under the final order. In deciding whether to make an interim order the
same considerations are relevant as for determining a final order.[2] However,
in relation to a child (but not a spouse) the court can only make these
orders for the purpose of the child's maintenance. This raises the question
of how generously 'maintenance' can be construed. In *Re Coventry*[3] it was
held that maintenance is neither synonymous with subsistence level nor
an excuse to pay whatever the claimant regards as desirable. Instead it
is that which is reasonable given the claimant's existing circumstances. A
generous interpretation was adopted in *Re Callaghan*[4] so that the claimant
could use most of the awarded lump sum to purchase a house, and in
Re Leach[5] in order to settle a debt. Strictly speaking such awards exceed
what is required for daily maintenance, but are quite in keeping with the
legitimate goal of satisfying the claimant's overall financial position out
of which, of course, his maintenance is drawn; for example, a lump sum
to a teenage child for the purchase of a house will reduce or relieve him
of the regular expenditure on rent or mortgage.

1   Section 5.
2   The court also has considerable ancillary powers to make its orders effective, see s 2(4).
3   [1980] Ch 461, [1979] 3 All ER 815, CA.
4   Supra.
5   [1986] Ch 226, [1985] 2 All ER 754, CA; cf *Re Dennis* [1981] 2 All ER 140 (order refused
    where payment of a tax bill was the object).

(c)   Assessment

16.81   In determining whether reasonable financial provision has been made
for a child, the court applies an objective test[1] and is directed to consider
the following matters:[2]

(a)   the financial resources and financial needs which the applicant has
      or is likely to have in the foreseeable future;
(b)   the financial resources and financial needs which any other applicant
      for an order under section 2 of the Act has or is likely to have in
      the foreseeable future;
(c)   the financial resources and financial needs which any beneficiary of
      the estate of the deceased has or is likely to have in the foreseeable
      future;
(d)   any obligations and responsibilities which the deceased had towards
      any applicant for an order under the said section 2 or towards any
      beneficiary of the estate of the deceased;
(e)   the size and nature of the net estate of the deceased;
(f)   any physical or mental disability of any applicant for an order under
      the said section 2 or any beneficiary of the estate of the deceased;
(g)   any other matter, including the conduct of the applicant or any other

person, which in the circumstances of the case the court may consider relevant; and

(h)   the manner in which the claimant was being or in which he might expect to be educated or trained.[3]

Further, if the child is not the issue of the deceased, the court must consider the extent, if any, to which he assumed responsibility for the child, whether he did so knowing of the parentage, and the liability of any other person to maintain the child.[4] Thus, if a spouse tricked the deceased into believing that the child was his, the court is unlikely to be persuaded to order a sum beyond that required for the child's minimal maintenance.[5]

1   See *Re Coventry*, supra and *Williams v Johns* [1988] Fam Law 257.
2   I(PFD)A 1975, s 3(1).
3   Section 3(3).
4   Section 3(3). Cf MCA 1973, s 25(3) and DPMCA 1978, s 3(4) and see ante, para 16.13.
5   See Tyler, op cit, pp 61–62.

16.82   The statute gives no guidance as to the weight to be attached to these factors nor as to how competing claims should be treated (eg between the child of an earlier marriage and the widow, or between a housekeeper and a teenage child). However, young dependent children will usually be the most deserving claimants on the estate. Indeed, factor (d) includes the moral obligation of a parent to a child and the court will enforce this obligation against the estate even though the deceased made little if any effort to support the child during his lifetime.[1] 'Needs' in (a) mean 'reasonable requirements'[2] and will in the majority of cases be the critical factor. The court must also take account of the applicant's past, present or future capital or income from any source. The extent to which cognisance will be taken of the receipt of State benefits will, however, be limited. Where the estate is small the court will not make an order if the only effect would be to reduce the amount of State benefits.[3] Where the benefit is in the form of accommodation and maintenance the position is less clear. In *Re Watkins*[4] it was held that a daughter who was insane and detained in a mental hospital, provided under the National Health Service Act 1946, was not entitled to an order against her father's estate even though it was large enough to justify one being made. The same reasoning was applied:

'. . . a man cannot be said to be acting unreasonably in not providing for something for which the State will provide and the provision of which by him would only operate to relieve, not the defendant, but the State.'[5]

But it is difficult to see why a person should not be said to be acting unreasonably if, having the means, he does not make any of them available to enable a dependant to enjoy comforts and facilities over and above those provided by the State. In such circumstances the moral obligation should carry great weight. Moreover, if a comparison is made with the more recent caselaw under the MCA and DPMCA, it will be noted[6] that the courts are quite prepared to order maintenance even if it only serves to reduce the level of State benefits — the payer is not entitled 'to pass the financial buck' to the State. It is suggested that a similar approach is appropriate under the 1975 Act, save where the smallness of the estate is such that any financial provision from it will be negligible.

1 *Re Chatterton* (1978) noted by Tyler, op cit, at pp 360–3, and see *Re Debenham* [1986] 1 FLR 404, [1986] Fam Law 101.
2 Per Dunn LJ in *Harrington v Gill* (1983) 4 FLR 265, CA.
3 *Re E* [1966] 2 All ER 44, [1966] 1 WLR 709.
4 [1949] 1 All ER 695.
5 Per Stamp J, in *Re E*, supra, at 48 and 715 respectively. Similarly factor (h) can justify an award for the payment of fees for private education, but where the resources are limited account will have to be taken of the State system and of State grants.
6 See ante, para 16.51.

16.83 Where there is a dispute between the widow of a third marriage and the deceased's child by a second marriage[1] or between 'a child of the family' and the deceased step-parent's other relatives,[2] the children will be in a stronger position if their other parent had contributed materially to the deceased's estate (for otherwise the 'family fortune' will pass outside the original family unit).

1 *Sivyer v Sivyer* [1967] 3 All ER 429, [1967] 1 WLR 1482.
2 *Re Leach* [1986] Ch 226, [1985] 2 All ER 754, CA; *Re Callaghan* [1985] Fam 1, [1984] 3 All ER 790.

16.84 As to (e), the 'net estate' means all the property of which the deceased had power to dispose by will (otherwise than by virtue of a special power of appointment) less the amount of his funeral, testamentary and administration expenses, debts and liabilities, including any inheritance (formerly capital transfer) tax obligations.[1] Thus, the estate may be too small to be able to provide an amount of provision which would be reasonable;[2] or it may be just sufficient to justify a lump sum payment whereas the income from it could not support an order for periodical payments.

1 Section 29(1). For further scope of the 'net estate', see ss 8 and 9.
2 See *Re E*, supra.

16.85 As to (g), conduct may be relevant in assessing whether the deceased owes a moral obligation to the dependants to maintain them as, for example, where a child has looked after the deceased during a prolonged illness,[1] or whether the child has forfeited any moral claim by his or her conduct, as, for example, where a son has dissipated his life and resources.[2]

1 Note *Re Blanch, Blanch v Honhold* [1967] 2 All ER 468 at 471, [1967] 1 WLR 987 at 991.
2 Cf *Re Dennis* [1981] 2 All ER 140 and see *Williams v Johns* supra.

(d) Procedure[1]

16.86 An application for an order must normally be made within six months from the date when representation was taken out, but the court may permit a late application, for example, where otherwise there is a risk of hardship or injustice.[2] Application is made to the High Court if the estate exceeds £30,000 and to the county court otherwise. If the child's interests are likely to conflict with those of other claimants, most notably a widow of the deceased, he should be made a separate plaintiff. It should be noted that, although a party to a marriage can be ordered on divorce not to bring a subsequent claim under the 1975 Act,[3] a child's right cannot be so curtailed. Thus, for example, if a child was awarded an order for periodical payments on the divorce of his parents, he can later apply for a transfer of property out of his deceased father's estate.[4]

1 See RSC Ord 99.
2 Some guidance as to the court's discretion is set out in *Re Salmon* [1981] Ch 167, [1980] 3 All ER 532.
3 Section 15, as amended.
4 Cf MCA 1973, s 31(5), where a property adjustment order cannot be made on an application for variation.

(e) Duration

16.87 Periodical payments will normally be ordered to cease when the child reaches 18[1], though they can be extended further, for example, if the child is, or is likely to remain, in higher education. The general rule is that an order for financial provision is final. Only an order for periodical payments can be varied. In that event, it can be replaced by a lump sum or transfer of property order.[2] Variation may be made only in respect of that part of the estate which has already been set aside to provide maintenance for the dependant.[3] Since in matrimonial proceedings periodical payments can be secured so as to last beyond the payer's death or the parties can provide for this in a maintenance agreement, the court can treat an application to vary such an order or agreement as an application under the 1975 Act, and similarly any application for financial provision under the 1975 Act can embrace an earlier periodical payments order.[4] For example, on his father's death the child's application to vary a maintenance order can be treated as a request for financial provision so that the court can avail itself of the wide powers in section 2 of the 1975 Act and transfer property to the child or give him a lump sum with which to purchase a house.

1 The statute is silent on the matter, but this age limit reflects the practice in matrimonial proceedings; see the fuller discussion in Tyler, op cit, pp 158–9.
2 Section 6(2).
3 Section 6(6).
4 Sections 16–18.

10 Provision after bankruptcy

16.88 For petitions in bankruptcy lodged after 29 December 1986 the position of a bankrupt's family vis-à-vis the matrimonial home is governed by the Insolvency Act 1986.[1] At first sight the children of the family are placed in a stronger position but on examination this is less apparent and their position is still parlous. If a parent falls into bankruptcy the prospects of his children remaining in the home depend upon the proprietary interest, if any, which the non-bankrupted spouse[2] has in the home, the matrimonial position between the spouses, the attitude of the trustee in bankruptcy and the speed with which he acts, and in part the discretion of the court. If the non-bankrupted spouse (normally the wife) has a share in the ownership of the home under the rules of property law, then only the husband's share passes to the trustee in bankruptcy.[3] If the trustee wishes to force a sale, he must go to court. If the wife has no legal or equitable title, she can claim a right of occupation under the Matrimonial Homes Act 1983. If she qualifies, the trustee in bankruptcy must also go to the court in order to evict the family. If the issue proceeds to litigation, the court is instructed to make such order as it thinks just and reasonable after considering

(a) the interests of the bankrupt's creditors;
(b) the conduct of the spouse or former spouse, so far as contributing to the bankruptcy;
(c) the needs and financial resources of the spouse or former spouse;
(d) the needs of any children; and
(e) all the circumstances of the case other than the needs of the bankrupt.[4]

It is hoped that factor (d) will carry much weight. However, the trustee in bankruptcy has three important advantages. First, if he waits for one year (after the bankrupt's property has vested in him) before applying to the court, then the creditors' interests are assumed to outweigh the family's, unless exceptional circumstances can be established.[5] Experience of the pre-1986 law offers little comfort for children in this 'exceptional' category. In *Re Lowrie*[6] the facts that there were two young children in the house and that the bankrupt husband was unlikely to be able to raise a loan for the purchase of another home did not amount to exceptional circumstances or exceptional hardship so as to justify the court postponing sale. Second, if the spouse and children are to remain in the home, the trustee could seek a court order requiring the spouse to pay him an occupation rent and/or pay for the upkeep of the home.[7] Third, if sale of the home is postponed, the trustee can apply for a charge on a dwelling house which can last beyond the discharge of the bankruptcy.[8]

1 Prior to that date the Bankruptcy Act 1914 applied.
2 A cohabitee's children are not covered by the protection given to spouses. Instead their security will rest on whether the non-bankrupted parent has a proprietary interest in the home which can be utilised against the bankrupt's creditors.
3 If the husband attempts to defeat the trustee by passing his share to his wife, the court may set aside the transaction if made within five years prior to the adjudication of bankruptcy, Insolvency Act 1986, ss 339–342.
4 Ibid, s 336(4).
5 Ibid, s 336(5).
6 [1981] 3 All ER 353.
7 See Bailey and Berry, (1987) NLJ 347, and also p 310 for a discussion of the *Matrimonial Home in Bankruptcy*.
8 IA 1986, s 313.

16.89 If it is the bankrupt who has children living with him[1] (eg after divorce or separation), he is given the right to occupy the home and, if his trustee in bankruptcy wishes to sell it, the trustee must seek leave of the court.[2] The court is then instructed to consider similar factors as on an application under section 336 against a bankrupt's spouse.[3] Again, if the trustee delays for a year, the creditors' interests are assumed to outweigh all others unless exceptional circumstances can be established.[4]

1 Section 337(1)(b) speaks of persons under 18 who 'had their home' with the bankrupt at the commencement of bankruptcy. The children need not therefore be his own. Note also the age limit of 18.
2 Section 337.

3   See ante, para 16.88.
4   Section 337(6).

11   Parental contribution towards maintenance of children in care

16.90   Parents of children in the care of local authorities can be required
to contribute towards, or reimburse in full, the cost of their maintenance.
This simple proposition is achieved by a bewildering array of statutory
provisions which does no credit to child law. The parents of a child[1] who
has been committed to the care of a local authority by a care order (other
than an interim order) or has been received into their care under section
2 of the Child Care Act 1980, are under a duty to contribute to his
maintenance.[2] The duty does not arise if the parent is receiving state benefits
in the form of income support or family credit,[3] and the local authority
have a discretion not to demand a contribution when they consider it would
be unreasonable.[4] The duty to contribute continues until the child attains
the age of 16. Thereafter the child is personally liable to contribute if he
is in employment or, for example, if he receives a benefit under the terms
of a will.[5]

1   For the father of an illegitimate child, prior to FLRA 1987, his liability has depended
    upon there being an affiliation order in force and the local authority may apply for it
    to be varied so that payments be made direct to the authority or, if there was no order,
    the authority may apply for one, CCA 1980, ss 49, 50 (repealed by Sch 2, para 76, FLRA
    1987). These affiliation orders will survive implementation of FLRA; see Sch 3, para 6
    thereto.
2   CCA 1980, s 45. Payments are made to the local authority in whose area the contributing
    parent resides, s 45(2), and it is then for that authority to make over the payments to
    the local authority responsible for the maintenance of the child; s 53.
3   Section 45(1A) as amended by Social Security Act 1986, Sch 10, para 51 (these benefits
    were formerly supplementary benefits or family income supplement).
4   Section 46(4); *R v Essex County Council, ex p Washington* [1987] 1 FLR 148, [1987] Fam
    Law 18.
5   Subsequent references are to the parent but the rules correspondingly apply to the child
    who is liable.

16.91   It is obviously preferable that the local authority and the parent
should reach agreement about the contribution to be made. Section 46
of CCA therefore enables the authority to propose an amount to which
the parent may agree. It is quite in order for the authority to request financial
information from the parents before deciding the matter,[1] and the parent
is usually sent a form to complete. The maximum contribution which may
be proposed must not exceed the amount which the authorities would be
prepared to pay for the boarding out of a child of the same age. In fact
many authorities take advantage of the powers contained in section 46(2)(a)
and fix a standard rate for contribution. Only after a written proposal
has been made but not accepted within one month or, if accepted, after
there has been default in making two or more contributions can the authority
resort to judicial proceedings. Then they may apply to a magistrates' court
for a contribution order, which, if granted, provides for the payment by
the parent of a weekly sum which must not be greater than that already
proposed by the local authority. An order remains in force so long as
the child continues in the care of the local authority unless it is earlier
revoked. It may also be varied,[2] and it is enforceable in the same way
as a maintenance order.[3]

1   *R v Essex County Council*, supra.
2   Where there is a variation, the court cannot order a varied contribution to be greater than that proposed by the local authority, s 48(2).
3   See ante, para 16.75

16.92   Arrears may be recovered not only where they have arisen under a contribution order but also where there is no order and the parent has defaulted in making the agreed contributions. In the latter circumstances the local authority may apply for an 'arrears order', but the aggregate of payments which may be ordered must not exceed the aggregate which would have been payable under a contribution order in respect of the period of default or, if it exceeded three months, the last three months plus any period equal to the time during which the default continued after the application for the arrears order had been lodged.[1]

1   Section 51(1).

16.93   Whether or not there is a contribution order, no contribution is payable during any period when the child is allowed by the local authority to be under the charge and control of a parent, guardian, relative or friend.[1] Similarly if notice is given of intention to apply for adoption of the child, no contribution is payable while he is in the care and possession of the applicants, unless 12 weeks have elapsed since the giving of the notice without the application being made or the application has been refused by the court or withdrawn.[2]

1   Section 45(3). It would appear that 'charge and control' are interpreted by some local authorities to include weekend or similar short stay periods with the parents; see Bazell, *Contribution Orders* [1985] Fam Law 264.
2   Adoption Act 1976, s 31(3) (formerly Adoption Act 1958, s 36(2)).

(a)   Section 3 resolutions

16.94   The transfer of parental rights by a resolution under section 3 of CCA 1980 does not affect the parental duty to maintain, or to contribute to the maintenance of, his child.[1] That duty does not exist at common law but is imposed by the Social Security Act 1986,[2] so that where benefits are paid to support a child the State can be reimbursed by the parent. It is not clear how the duty referred to in the CCA is to be enforced in the context of that Act. Presumably a local authority could initiate a civil action in the county court for recovery of a debt.

1   CCA 1980, s 4(2).
2   Section 26 (formerly Supplementary Benefits Act 1976, s 17 and many earlier statutory provisions).

(b)   MCA 1973, DPMCA 1978 and GA 1973

16.95   In those exceptional cases where a court, exercising its domestic jurisdiction under MCA, DPMCA or GA, has committed a child to the care of a local authority, it may order a spouse to make periodical payments.[1] This power differs from that in Part V of CCA (above) in the following respects:

(i)   Payments can be ordered to the local authority *or* to the child.[2]
(ii)   The court is guided by a list of factors when exercising its jurisdiction.[3]
(iii)   Payments from the parent can be ordered until the child reaches the age of 18.[4] However, once the child reaches 16, he can be ordered to contribute himself in which case the provisions of Part V of CCA *do* apply.[5] Consquently for a child aged 17 and in employment, contributions could, for example, be ordered from him under section 45 of CCA and from his parents under section 11(4) of DPMCA.
(iv)   Under the MCA secured periodical payments and a lump sum can be ordered.[6]

1   MCA 1973, s 23(1), DPMCA 1978, s 11(4), GA 1973, s 3(3). The court must hear any representations from the local authority, s 43(2), s 10(3)(b) and s 4(2) respectively.
2   MCA, s 23(1), GA, s 2(3), but not under the DPMCA.
3   MCA, s 25, DPMCA, s 11(5), GA, s 2(3A).
4   MCA, s 29, DPMCA, s 11(6), GA, s 2(3B).
5   MCA, s 43(1)(b), DPMCA, s 10(4)(b), GA, s 4(4).
6   Section 23(1)(e)(f).

(c)   FLRA 1969

16.96   In wardship proceedings the court can require a parent to make payments to a local authority into whose care a child has been committed. Factors (i), (ii) and (iv) are unavailable. As to (iii), an order for the maintenance of a ward can extend beyond the age of 18.[1] Once he reaches 16, Part V of CCA will apply and he can be ordered to contribute himself.[2]

1   FLRA 1969, s 6(3).
2   Section 7(2)(b).

III   FINANCIAL PROVISION FROM THE STATE

1   Introduction

16.97   The Social Security Act 1986 was the culmination of a review of the social security system[1] and made significant changes to the system. Most of these came into force in April 1988. Briefly, supplementary benefit was replaced by income support, single payments and urgent needs payments by the social fund and family income supplement by family credit. In addition important changes to housing benefit were made. The purpose of this section is to extract some points of relevance for child care and for a wider appreciation of the social security system the reader is referred elsewhere.[2]

1   The Reform of Social Security (Green Paper) Cmnd 9517–9519 (1985), followed by a White Paper, Cmnd 9691 (1985).
2   Eg Butterworths Family Law Service para A21 et seq; Pollard (ed), *Social Welfare Law*; Findlay, *CPAG's Annotated Housing Benefit Legislation;* Mesher, *CPAG's Income Support, the Social Fund and Family Credit: the Legislation; The Law Relating to Social Security* (HMSO).

2   Income support[1]

16.98   As a general proposition a person resident[2] in Great Britain who is over the age of 18, who is not in remunerative work but who is available for work, is entitled to income support in so far as his income falls short of specified sums (known as the *applicable amount*). The SSA 1986 specified a minimum age of 16 for claimants but section 4 of the SSA 1988 requires most young persons between the ages of 16 and 18 to undergo youth training. The result is that the vast majority of that age group will either be in education or in training. Those few who are unable to pursue either or for whom special provision is made will qualify for income support.[3] As for remunerative work, this is defined as an average of 24 hours or more per week[4] and is a reduction from 30 hours which previously governed in the supplementary benefits scheme. Furthermore, if a couple is claiming income support and either partner exceeds the 24 hours limit, the claim will fail. As for the claimant being 'available for work' there are exemptions and in this context the most relevant are a single parent (including foster parent) with a dependent child under 16, a parent looking after a sick or disabled child, and a woman who cannot work because of pregnancy or who has left work within the statutory maternity leave period.[5]

1   The framework is set out in the Social Security Act 1986, ss 20–27, and the detail in the Income Support (General) Regulations 1987, SI 1987/1967, as frequently amended. Reference should also be made to the Income Support Manual (HMSO).
2   SSA, s 20(3).
3   These are the disabled, single parents, young persons caring for others and those who can show that they will suffer severe hardship unless support is given.
4   Regulations, supra, reg 5.
5   For the full list of exemptions, see the Regulations, supra, Sch 1.

Relevant family

16.99   A claimant can qualify for income support for his or her family, and for each family only one claimant is permitted in a particular period. Indeed, the resources and needs of family members are added up and treated as that of the claimant. 'Family' includes a spouse or cohabitee and any child who is a member of the same household as the claimant and for whom the claimant has responsibility.[1] Doubts as to responsibility can be determined by discovering who receives child benefit. A child remains part of the household if he is absent abroad for up to four weeks or is in hospital for up to 12 weeks. Similarly a child in local authority care but who is returned to his parents for a trial period can count as part of the household. The typical family consists of husband, wife and children, but extends to a man and woman who are living together as husband and wife, and most importantly to a single parent and dependent child. Thus, on divorce or separation of partners the custodial parent (typically the mother) can claim income support on behalf of herself and the child.[2]

1   Regulations, regs 14–16.
2   She is not required to be 'available for work' because of her dependent child, Regulations, Sch 1, para 1.

Calculation

16.100   The principle remains the same as that which governed the supplementary benefits scheme but the details of calculation are much simplified. Thus, a person's needs are defined by the state in terms of personal allowances, premiums and housing benefits and these are known generally as the *applicable amount*. The most relevant premiums are 1) the family premium, 2) the lone parent premium, and 3) the disabled child[1] premium. Each one of these premiums can be claimed for the same family. Once the applicable amount is determined, the claimant's income, if any, must be ascertained. Very detailed rules regulate this calculation but in this context the following deserve mention:

(a) a child's earnings are ignored, except where a young person is in remunerative work in which case the claimant can disregard £5 (or £15 if he is receiving a disabled child premium).[2] As for a child's income, this is included up to the amount of the personal allowance (and disabled child premium if relevant) available for that child, but any excess income of the child does not reduce the claimant's right to income support.[3]

(b) As regards capital resources, if a child has capital in excess of £3,000, the claimant cannot receive a personal allowance in respect of that child[4] but the capital is ignored vis-à-vis the claimant's own entitlement to benefit (including the family premium).

(c) Child benefit counts as income but adoption, custodianship and fostering allowances do not.[5]

(d) Also ignored in the calculation is £15 earned by a person who qualifies for a lone parent premium or disability premium, or by a couple who have been receiving income support for a continuous period of two years.[6]

(e) Payments from a liable relative[7] for the support of the claimant and the claimant's family are included in the income support calculation. But there are some financial matters which are treated as capital and not income and which may then qualify for exemption.[8]

Once the claimant's income has been calculated it is compared with the applicable amount. If it exceeds that amount, no payment is made. If it is less, then income support, like supplementary benefit before it, supplies the difference.

---

1   This applies to a child who is registered blind or who is receiving attendance or mobility allowance.
2   Regulations, Sch 8, paras 14 and 15.
3   Reg 44.
4   Reg 21: this is similar to the Supplementary Benefits (Resources) Regulations 1981, reg 8.
5   Sch 9, paras 25 and 26.
6   Sch 8, paras 4–6.
7   As defined in SSA 1986, s 26.
8   Regulations, reg 54 (eg a disposition of property on divorce, a gift of up to £250 in a year, a payment in kind). There are very complex rules for computing the income deemed to be generated from a lump sum, see Regulations, reg 57. For a useful account see Butterworth's Family Law Service, paras A114–116.

3 Social fund

16.101 Before April 1988 single payments and urgent needs payments were available to cope with emergencies and special circumstances not covered by the basic rates of supplementary benefits. They were then replaced by the social fund.[1] The size of this fund is fixed by the Secretary of State and each DSS office is then allocated an annual budget. The fund is available for a) payments or grants (maternity and funeral expenses, and community care grants) and b) loans (budget and crisis loans, which amount to 70% of the fund). The former are distributed by adjudication officers, the latter by social fund officers.

1 Social Security Act 1986, s 32. For the details, see Social Fund Maternity and Funeral Expenses Regulations 1987, SI 1987/481; Social Fund (Application for Review) Regulations 1988, SI 1988/34; Social Fund (Recovery by Deductions from Benefits) Regulations 1988, SI 1988/35; Social Fund (Applications) Regulations 1988, SI 1988/524. See also the Social Fund Manual (HMSO).

(a) Grants

16.102 The grant for maternity expenses is £85 and is available to a woman who is receiving income support or family credit and who is pregnant or who has given birth within three months of the claim or who has adopted a child within the same period. Community care grants are available to those on income support and who (1) need help to adjust to life in the community after leaving institutional or residential care, or (2) need help to avoid entering such care, or (3) belong to a family under stress. The Social Fund Manual identifies certain priority groups and in our context the most relevant are young people leaving local authority care;[1] families with children facing stressful conditions such as a disabled parent or child[2] or parents who have separated;[3] a domestic crisis in which, for example, a child has been sent to live with a relative and the parent needs travel expenses to see him; families who need urgent help (eg on repairs to the home) lest a child be given up to local authority care.

1 Help could include money for travel expenses and essential furniture and clothing.
2 A grant could be made, for example, for a washing machine or a safety barrier on a staircase.
3 A parent may need urgent help to start up a new home with the child. The Social Fund Manual specifically excludes, however, school meals, travel to and from school, and any expenditure on school items (cf to like effect Supplementary Benefit (Single Payments) Regulations 1981, reg 6(2)). A local education authority is obliged to provide facilities for the consumption of meals during school hours and has a power to provide meals and, if they elect the latter, pupils in receipt of income support are not charged (see Education Act 1980, s 22 (as amended by Social Security Act 1986)).

(b) Loans

16.103 These consist of *budget loans* for a person who has been on income support for at least 26 weeks and who needs to meet important intermittent expenses.[1] High priority items include essential furniture, bedclothes and fuel charges. The other type of loan is called a *crisis loan*. It is aimed at helping a person in an emergency or after a disaster, when a loan is the only means of preventing serious damage or serious health risk to the claimant or his family; or when the loan is needed to pay rent in advance for a person who has left institutional or residential care.[2] The loan is available to persons over 16 and could be used, for example, to cover expenses in starting up a job.

These loans are repayable primarily by a deduction from income support, but other social security benefits can be reduced. There is a complaints procedure involving an internal review. The proof of the social fund pudding will lie of course in the size of its annual budget.

1   Social Fund Manual, direction 2.
2   Ibid, direction 3.

Recovery of benefit from a liable relative

16.104   For the purposes of state allowances a man and woman, whether married or living together as husband and wife, are obliged to maintain their children.[1] The duty survives separation of the parents and their divorce, it cannot be waived by agreement between them[2] and it does not lapse simply because the state has intervened and supplied financial support for the child. Thus, where the DSS has had to pay income support for a child, it may seek to recover from the parent (or 'liable relative' as he is known) the cost of benefits already paid and to ensure that the liable relative in future discharges his responsibility. The DSS can apply to a magistrates' court for an order requiring either parent to pay such sum (weekly or otherwise) as the court considers appropriate having regard to all the circumstances and in particular to the income of the liable relative.[3] Payments ordered for the recovery of benefit already paid will be made to the Secretary of State and future payments to the Secretary, the claimant, the dependant or such other person as appears expedient in the interests of the dependant (eg a local authority or other third party who has custody of the child). The DSS may be tempted to exert pressure on the recipient of benefits to take enforcement proceedings against the liable relative. Department guidance[4] makes it clear that the recipient cannot be compelled to do so. Instead the recipient should be asked to take the action. In the face of persistent refusal or neglect to maintain the liable relative can be prosecuted,[5] but the inappropriateness of criminal sanctions in this field is self-evident.

1   Social Security Act 1986, s 26(3) (formerly Supplementary Benefits Act 1976, s 17); amended by FLRA 1987 so as to cover the unmarried father.
2   *Hulley v Thompson* [1981] 1 All ER 1128, [1981] 1 WLR 159.
3   SSA 1986, s 24 (formerly SBA 1976, s 18).
4   Supplementary Benefits Handbook (1982), para 13.11.
5   SSA 1986, s 26.

4   Housing benefit[1]

16.105   A person in receipt of income support qualifies for full housing benefit to meet his rent and 80% of household rates.[2] A person who is not receiving income support and whose earnings are below his appropriate income support level can claim full housing benefit. In so far as they exceed that level, housing benefit is reduced by 65% of the excess for rent and 20% for rates.[3] Benefit is usually available for one property only, but can exceptionally cover two. In this context the most relevant examples are 1) where the claimant has left home through fear of violence and it is reasonable to pay benefit for the former and current home; 2) where the family is so large that the housing authority has had to place them in two dwellings; and 3) where the claimant has not yet moved into a new home but has had to pay rent for it and the move was delayed because the claimant applied to the social fund for a payment to help with the move and the claimant has a child aged five or under, or for whom a disabled child premium can be claimed under the income support scheme (benefit is payable here for a maximum of four weeks).[4] When determining the extent of the claimant's family and a child (under 16) or a young person (16 to 19) is found to be living in two households, the appropriate carer is the one who is receiving child benefit for him or who has primary responsibility for him.[5] A child or young person is not a part of the household if he has been boarded out with the claimant for fostering or adoption or if he is in local authority care. In the latter case if a child returns to his parents for home visits the local housing authority can treat the child as part of the household if it is reasonable to do so in the light of the nature and frequency of the visits.[6] Thus visits with a view to reuniting the family should be so interpreted and that interpretation may of course assist the reunification. If the housing authority considers that the child is living in accommodation which is unreasonably large for his household's needs or is paying unreasonably high rent or rates for the accommodation, it can reduce the housing benefit to a level which it considers appropriate. However, where the household includes a child or young person and the authority[7] is considering what more suitable accommodation would cost the family, some protection is offered. Thus the alternative accommodation must in fact be available, and it must be reasonable to expect the claimant to move into it given the nature and facilities offered, the age and health of the child and finally the effect on the child's education if the move necessitates a change in school. The amount of housing benefit available is very similar to that in income support except that the lone parent premium is higher. The calculation of the claimant's income is similar to that for income support. Points to note are that maintenance paid by a claimant to a former partner or to his children who are not living with him is disregarded in the calculation.[8] A child's or young person's income is included apart from his earnings whilst at school (eg a newspaper round). Where his income equals the applicable amount for him (the child or young person), the entitlement to that amount is lost. Where it exceeds it, that excess will not, however, count so as to reduce the housing benefit due to the claimant in his own right.[9]

1   For background, see Housing Benefit Review: Report of the Review Team Cmnd 9520 (1985). For the detail, see Housing Benefit (General) Regulations 1987, SI 1987/1971; Housing Benefit Guidance Manual (HMSO); and Butterworth's Family Law Service, paras A155–178.
2   SSA 1986, s 21(4), Regulations, supra, reg 61.
3   Regulations, reg 62.
4   Ibid, reg 5(5).
5   Ibid, reg 14(2).
6   Ibid, reg 15(5).
7   Ibid, reg 11.
8   Ibid, Sch 3, para 27.
9   Ibid, reg 36.

5   Family credit

16.106   Family income supplement, a non-contributory benefit, was
adopted in 1971[1] and was aimed at helping a family (including cohabitees
and, importantly, a single parent family) with one or more children on
a low income. It was replaced in April 1988 by family credit.[2] Family credit
is available to a person who is responsible[3] for a child under 16 (or between
16 and 19 and in education) in the same household[4] and who is in full
time remunerative work[5] but whose earnings are so low as to qualify for
state assistance. Family credit consists of an adult and child components
and an award of credit lasts for a period of 26 weeks. If the claimant's
earnings are less than £51.45,[6] maximum family credit is payable. If they
exceed that amount, 70% of the excess is deducted from the family credit.
In calculating the claimant's income a child's or young person's income
(or capital over £3,000) does not count as that of the claimant but the
child or young person will not qualify for his share of the family credit
if his earnings[7] exceed the child component of the credit. Income such
as child benefit, one-parent benefit, and fostering or custodianship or
adoption allowances is ignored, but maintenance paid to the claimant or
a child in the household does count. It remains to be seen whether family
credit will be widely claimed. The experience of its predecessor, family
income supplement, was not encouraging. In spite of that scheme's admirable
simplicity compared to other benefits and of the fact that a recipient was
entitled to a range of other allowances (eg free prescriptions, spectacles)
the take-up rate was low.

1   Family Income Supplements Act 1970. In May 1986 there were 202,000 recipients with
    418,000 dependent children – HC Debs 22 April 1987 col 633.
2   SSA 1986, s 20(5). For the detail see Family Credit (General) Regulations 1987, SI 1987/
    1973.
3   If there is a dispute over this, the person receiving child benefit for the child is the appropriate
    claimant. Only one family credit for a child can be claimed at any one time, Regulations,
    reg 7.
4   'Household' appeared in the earlier legislation and was given a broad interpretation, see
    England v Secretary of State for Social Services (1981) 3 FLR 222. A child placed for
    fostering or adoption does not, however, qualify, Regulations, reg 7.
5   This means an average of at least 24 hours per week, Regulations, reg 4(1).
6   Regulations, reg 47. This is the same as the couple rate for income support.
7   Or capital over £3,000, Regulations, r 46(4).

6   Child benefit and one-parent benefit

16.107   Anyone 'who is responsible in any week' for a child under 16
(or under 19 if the child remains in full-time, non-advanced education[1])
is entitled to a flat rate of child benefit which is tax free.[2] The benefit
can be paid to a mother under the age of 16. It cannot be paid to more
than one person in respect of the same child, and so the Act specifies
the priority which is to operate between two claimants — a recipient of
benefit faced with a rival claim continues to receive it for three weeks,
a person with whom the child is living takes precedence over someone
paying maintenance for the child, a wife (or mother) is entitled over the
husband (or father) and a parent over a non-parent. In other cases the
persons choose who is to receive the benefit and in default the Secretary
of State may elect.[3] An extra payment is available for the first or only

child in a single parent family — 'one-parent benefit'[4] — provided that the claimant has the sole responsibility for bringing up the child.

1   Once a child finishes this education, benefit is payable up to the first Monday in January, the Monday following Easter Monday or the first Monday in September, whichever is earliest, Child Benefit (General) Regulations 1976, SI 1976/965, reg 7.
2   Child Benefit Act 1975, s 1.
3   Ibid, Sch 2.
4   Child Benefit and Social Security (Fixing and Adjustment of Rates) Regulations 1976, SI 1976/1267, reg 2(2).

Conclusion

16.108   The aims of the Social Security Act 1986 are to simplify the system of welfare benefits, to ensure that those most in need receive them and to reduce expenditure wherever possible. The effectiveness of the new scheme in alleviating poverty and hardship for children will depend at the end of the day on the amount of money made available for it. Although families with children and one parent families are given extra premiums, those must be set at a sufficient level to match the previous reliance which these families placed on single payments and the other extras which topped up the supplementary benefit scheme.

Index